Economics

for Siegi
with my love

Economics

A.J.CULYER

Basil Blackwell

First published 1985

Basil Blackwell Ltd
108 Cowley Road, Oxford OX4 1JF, UK

Basil Blackwell Inc.
432 Park Avenue South, Suite 1505,
New York, NY 10016, USA

British Library Cataloguing in Publication Data

Culyer, A.J.
Economics.
1. Economics
I. Title
330 HB171

ISBN 0–631–13799–8
ISBN 0–631–13801–3 Pbk

Library of Congress Cataloging in Publication Data

Culyer, A.J. (Anthony J.)
Economics.

Includes index.
1. Economics. I. Title
HB171.5.C898 1985 330 85–4021
ISBN 0–631–13799–8
ISBN 0–631–13801–3 (pbk.)

Typeset in Baskerville and Futura Book by Katerprint Co. Ltd, Oxford
Printed in Great Britain by Bell and Bain Ltd, Glasgow

Contents

35 Public Sector Borrowing, the Overseas Sector and Macroeconomic Policy 626

types of government securities — financial balance sheets for the main sectors of the economy — functions of the Bank of England — relationships between the public sector borrowing requirement, changes in the money supply, the overseas contribution, bank lending to the private sector and private sector lending to government — government's budget constraint — *PSBR* and the money supply: long term and short term relationships — balance of payments and the money supply under fixed and flexible exchange rates — monetary and fiscal policy under fixed and flexible exchange rates — counterparts to changes in the money supply — problems with controlling the money supply — British policy towards monetary control — money supply, inflation and the exchange rate

36 Controversy, Politics, Economics and Economists 649

interplay between scientific judgements and value judgements — sources of economic controversy — political differences between economists — need for discipline, imagination and judgement

Answers to Self-assessment Questions 659

Index 721

Case Studies

Preface

There is no typical student of economics. Although I have written this book with first year undergraduates primarily in mind, these include students falling into at least the following (not all mutually exclusive) categories:

- people who have done economics before and who will be looking for a book that is different in content and tone from those with which they are familiar
- people who have done no economics before and who will need a book that makes no prior assumptions about their economic knowledge
- people who are unfamiliar with formal languages like maths and who need to be led gently into such material and be given confidence in using it
- people who already have quite advanced maths and who will want to be challenged – or at least not patronized
- people who have come to their undergraduate course direct from school, and who will need briefing on a lot of factual matters and examples of a homely sort to which they can easily relate
- people who are mature students, who bring a wealth of knowledge of the world with them, and who will want to see what economics has to say about things they already know quite a lot about
- people who will do no more than a one year course in economics and who will therefore want a comprehensive account that covers the whole field and uses lots of real world examples
- people whose primary interest lies in political science, economic and social history, social administration or sociology, and who will want therefore to see what economics has to say on topics of interest to them
- people whose main interest in economics is purely intellectual, who will want to see the theory developed from basic axioms and rounded off in a consistent whole
- people whose main interest lies in application and policy, who will want to see lots of examples of economics in action
- people who will buy *only* this book and who will expect to use it as a kind of reference work in the future.

It has not been an easy task to cater for these various needs. I have none the less tried to solve what most teachers of undergraduate first year economics find an almost insoluble problem – with what success only readers can judge.

On occasion I have taken the theory a bit further than is to be found in most introductory texts. This is particularly so in demand theory, which I have used also as a vehicle for posing the issues involved in selecting between rival theories. It is, of course, for the reader and the teacher to decide how far to go in the material I have included, but I have in general tried to go beyond the rather facile approaches that one sometimes comes across. Therefore those who want to dig deep can have an appreciation of what it is that has drawn some of the finest brains in every generation into the discipline of economics, and the impression is not left that elementary ideas are all that economics has to offer. (Lecturers: in microeconomics this implies only an introduction to, say, oligopoly theory and, in macro, that the analysis stops just short of presenting the IS/LM version of the Keynesian model.)

Also, in contrast with other textbooks, this one has it as a fundamental principle that no idea, concept or theory should be presented without early (and repeated) practical examples. These are to be found in the case studies, of which there are almost 100 as well as many direct applications and illustrations in the text itself. The case studies and text illustrations are of various kinds. Some are briefing exercises that describe parts of the economy or aspects of society that it is important to know about (including history), and in respect of which most texts are gravely deficient, or about which misguided views are often held. Others describe experimental techniques for testing theories or revealing information not otherwise easily had. Others are direct empirical tests of theory. Yet others involve policy applications where economics is used to inform decision makers in business, government and so on. Some raise or apply ethical issues and ideas; others are purely scientific. For many I have trawled widely for suitable case material. I have also trawled in a cross-disciplinary fashion and have extracted relevant material from sociology, history, medicine, psychology and politics.

Another distinctive feature is the use of self-assessment questions (SAQs), each of which receives a full answer. The purpose of these is twofold. First, confidence must be built in using economics. Second, you can't read an economics textbook like a novel. Some bits of economics are intrinsically more difficult than others and, for these in particular, one needs lots of practice at manipulating concepts, assessing pros and cons, seeing through the maze of statistics to any messages that may be lurking within, applying one's imagination, and simply checking that one really has understood the material (for which I have provided a fair number of numerical cases to work through).

So integral are both the case studies and the SAQs to the text that I have not hesitated, where it seemed appropriate, to introduce new theoretical material and new concepts in each. This may prove to have been unwise and I shall welcome readers' opinions. One sure way of finding out whether in skipping case studies or SAQs (which, of course, I hope no reader will) you have missed any new material of significance is to use the index at the end of the book in order to find where specific issues and topics are dealt with. The index has been made sufficiently detailed for it to be relied upon in this respect (which, alas, is not always true of indexes).

Useful complementary reading would be the material to be found in the bi-monthly journal for economics students, *The Economic Review*, edited by members of the Southampton University Economics Department and published by Philip Allan. This journal not only adopts an approach and style to economics teaching that is very similar to mine in this book, but it is also able to offer more timely reports and comments on current happenings in the economics world than a textbook can ever hope to achieve.

I do not doubt that despite my efforts – and those of the kind people who have read drafts in whole or part – the finished product only partly succeeds in meeting the needs of the people I have just described. It may also contain some residual slips that I have not spotted. I welcome suggestions for improvements and, if the market is kind to the book, will use them to make it a better book next time. I shall also be happy to acknowledge any help of this sort that anyone – teacher or student – may care to give.

Acknowledgements

I owe a great debt to many who have helped me in writing this book. Michael Hay (then of Martin Robertson) first persuaded me to take the job on and was of inestimable value in the early support and encouragement he gave. René Olivieri subsequently took over Michael's role and deserves scarcely less thanks for seeing the thing through and helping me to overcome countless difficulties. Mary Robinson must be one of the world's best desk editors: her patience, thoroughness and mastery of an immensely complex editorial process can only be marvelled at.

For their quite extraordinary diligence in painstakingly reading the whole of the first draft (and fair chunks of the second), checking arithmetic and SAQ answers, and for providing much valued counsel on style and presentation, my heartfelt thanks to John Black of Exeter University, England, and Rupert Cook of Laurentian University, Canada. It is gratifying to think that they thought the effort worth sustaining and utterly humbling that they sustained it much better than I think I could have, had I been in their shoes.

My immediate colleagues at York – David Gowland, Brian Hillier, John Posnett and Jack Wiseman – commented on individual chapters, which their perceptive and hard-hitting remarks enabled me to improve (I hope!) enormously.

For their willingness to act as guinea pigs and for their devastatingly frank 'consumer reports' on various chapters, I owe a great debt to the following students at York: Paul Bagnall, Noel Collis, Steven Dean, Richard Fearn, Charles Gillespie, Peter Holden, Mark Hutchinson, Maher Masri, Ian Parkes, John Rawsthorne and Andrew Worboys.

I also received extremely helpful comments from Jonathan Brooks (student at LSE), Y. Jao (University of Hong Kong), Robin Johns (Polytechnic of the South Bank), Bernard Kennedy (Market Weighton School), W. Shackley (Queen Elizabeth I Grammar School), T. C. Thompson (Chesterfield School), Nancy Wall (Beacon School) and B. Williams (Rowlinson School). Robert Sugden (University of East Anglia) was kind enough to allow me to adapt a class exercise of his for use as SAQ 19.4.

I have imposed appalling burdens on those who saw their beautiful typing abused by successive annotations and amendments. Some got off more lightly than others, but all have my admiration and thanks: Sally Baker, Tom Culyer,

Sal Cuthbert, Barbara Dodds, Jackie Farnell, Clare Gildener, Mary Grace, Jo Hall, Helen Hawksby, Kath Hunter, Barbara Olive and Gail Shepherd.

Without all these people the job would have taken far longer than four years and the outcome would have been very much worse. I have not always followed the advice given, so no one can share responsibility for the defects of the book. If it has any merit at all, however, the reasons lie in no small measure in the help I have received from the people mentioned here.

A.J.C.

1

Economics and Economists

Economics: Discipline and Topic

Economics as a discipline is about two hundred years old, dating it from Adam Smith's seminal work *The Wealth of Nations* published in 1776. But economics as a topic is as old as the hills. The distinction between the two is important, particularly for the apprentice economist and for those of you who, rather than study economics beyond this book, will specialize in other areas of the social sciences like business studies, economic history, political science, social administration or sociology.

Taking economics *as a topic* first, it refers essentially to **the economy**: to that sphere of social activity that we all commonly see in markets of various kinds; to exchange or trading relations between individuals, groups, firms, nations and so on, that involve priced goods and services; to private and public attempts to monitor, change, control or supersede market relations between people. In short, where there is money – or something used as though it were money – there is also the economy. Economics viewed as a topic is thus descriptive of the productive and trading relationships between people in the private sector, in the public sector and in dealings between these two.

Put like this, you can see that economics as a topic is conventional and contingent. It is *conventional* in the sense that at any time there is a broad consensus in the way ordinary people classify phenomena into the 'economic' and the 'non-economic'. It is *contingent* in the sense that the customs, conventions and institutions adopted in a society to conduct various aspects of its affairs may determine whether or not a particular set of phenomena are regarded as 'economic' or 'non-economic'. For example, in Britain access to education is not usually determined in a market, but in other societies one must purchase education (primary, secondary and tertiary). In Britain it may then seem natural not to regard the consumption of education as a part of the economy, whereas in other countries it will seem perfectly natural to include it.

Now consider economics *as a discipline*. In no way is this to be characterized by *what* is studied. Here the crucial distinguishing feature is *how* it (whatever 'it' may be) is studied – the mode of thinking that is brought to bear upon it. Economics as a discipline, or mode of thought, centres upon the issue of **scarcity** and the consequential necessity for individuals to choose. It starts from the fundamental proposition that resources are too few to satisfy all the wants of mankind, whether they be selfish or unselfish wants, whether they be expressed by individuals or groups, whether they be represented by individuals acting on their own behalf or on the behalf of others. The idea of a **resource** is broad too: it includes not only the naturally provided fruits of nature but those produced by man. It also includes man himself as a resource: his time, natural aptitudes, acquired skills and so on. All economic theory is at root about how people actually choose or ought to choose given the scarcity of resources, which precludes (and will preclude for the foreseeable future) the satisfaction of *all* wants for *all* people.

It should now be rather obvious why economics as a discipline differs from economics as a topic. The crucial implications are two: there are more disciplines than merely economics that can be applied to the topic of economics; and the discipline of economics can be applied to more topics than the merely economic ones. Consider the economic topic of inflation. Everyone agrees that this is indeed a phenomenon of the economy. Obviously economics as a discipline has a good deal to say about this topic. But sociology too has a great deal to say about it. So has political science. Each of these disciplines has its own special insights to offer on inflation: for example, investigating the ways different social classes react to inflationary situations, or investigating the consequences of political attempts to control inflation on the evolution of democratic institutions. Consider the non-economic topic of ill health. Evidently medical science and epidemiology (the study of disease in populations as distinct from individual patients) have a great deal to contribute here. But so has sociology (for example, in analysing why social groups with the same clinical symptoms have a completely different idea of, and attitude to, sickness). And so even has economics (for example, in considering how much of the nation's scarce resources ought to be allocated to a particular patient group rather than to other patients, or to education, or housing, or private consumption, or . . .).

In this book the focus is on economics *as a discipline*, and the analysis will be applied to a very wide range of phenomena, much broader than the topic of economics itself encompasses. For example, it will be applied to topics in social policy as well as to topics in economic policy. It will also be applied to topics in history and to other topics that may superficially seem remote from economics. Some idea of the tremendous range of economics as a discipline can be had by looking through the list of case studies at the beginning of the book.

Economics and other Disciplines

Figure 1.1 contains a list of disciplines (in alphabetical order) and a – rather arbitrarily selected – list of topics. Note that the topics include not only *phenomena* (like inflation) but also *ideas* (like equality) and *procedures* (like majority voting). The lines joining the various disciplines to the various topics show some topics on which the discipline in question has some analytical bearing or, conversely, show some of the disciplines that have a bearing on the

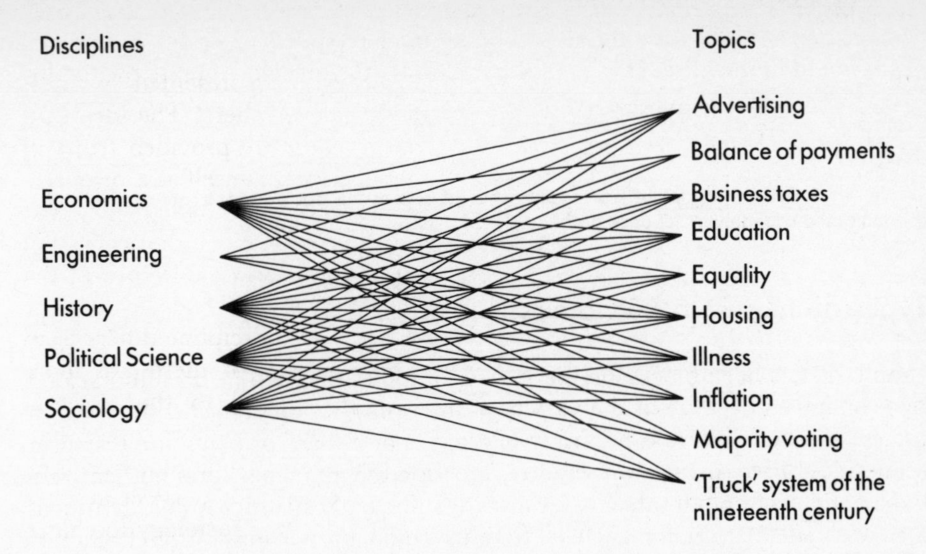

Figure 1.1 Relations between disciplines and topics

topic in question. Note that there are links between the topics (for example between equality, housing and majority voting) that take place through the disciplines (for example these three topics can be linked by any of economic analysis, ethics or political science). But the main point of figure 1.1 is to show the breadth of topic that can be tackled with most disciplines (you may think some have been unfairly treated relative to economics) and how the disciplines will often be *complementary* to one another (though they are not always complimentary about one another!) depending on the topic and the aspects of it being investigated. Thus on the one hand one should never restrict overmuch the topics to which a discipline may be applied (economists hate, for example, a common view of them as glorified cost accountants – people who know the price of everything and the value of nothing); nor, on the other hand, should one suppose that the illumination given by one discipline to a particular problem is *all* the illumination that there is to be given.

SAQ 1.1

Look at figure 1.1. If any of the topics are not reasonably clear to you (e.g. the truck system of the nineteenth century), look them up in the index. Now select any one discipline and try to suggest the ways in which it may relate to the topics with which it is linked. You will, of course, need to know a bit about the theory in each discipline because it is the theory that makes disciplines distinctive and is applied to topics: the discipline in question is the corpus of theory that 'disciplines' the mind to tackle problems in a particular and systematic way.

Figure 1.1 may also have suggested to you that there may be value in multidisciplinary attacks upon some problems. Often that is indeed so, but fruitful multidisciplinary approaches are always based upon a perception of the nature of the problems selected for analysis in a particular topic. There is little value in starting from a multidisciplinary base and then casting around for questions concerning a topic that require contributions from each of the disciplines represented in the base. It is always better to let the question dictate the modes of analysis rather than vice versa.

SAQ 1.2

Do you think that an economist is someone who (a) applies the discipline of economics to topics, (b) studies the economy or (c) does both?

Types of Interest in Economics

Emphasis has been placed on the variety of topics that can be usefully tackled by economists because of the variety of interests that different people have in topics. Similarly, there is a variety of reasons or *motives* for being interested in economics. Five main motives are identified here. They are not entirely independent of one another but they are sufficiently distinct to be identified. I have tried to cater for each in roughly equal proportions throughout this book.

The Political Philosophy Interest

Some seek and often find in economics a means of developing their political interest. It was an accident that the birth of modern economics – if we date it from Smith's *Wealth of Nations* – was the exact year of the American Declaration of Independence (1776), but it was no accident that both events lay close together and that much of the subsequent history of economic ideas was closely linked with the development of liberal political philosophy. Nor is it an accident that the political philosophy of socialism, both liberal and Marxist, in the nineteenth and twentieth centuries is inseparable from the development of economic theory. Although this book will not make any use of Marxist economic theory, a good deal of attention will be paid to many of the traditional questions that have occupied both liberal and socialist political thinkers. For example, the distribution of wealth and arguments for redistribution will be analysed. Arguments will be considered for and against nationalization of the means of production and private property. Economic analysis cannot, of course, tell you what political values you *ought* to hold. But it is of great help in tracing through some at least of the consequences of alternative values that could be held, and thus in making an informed judgement.

The 'We See – Why?' Interest

Others see in the world about them a whole set of puzzles that they seek to understand or 'explain'. In this book dozens of such puzzles will be explained. For example, why is water, which is everywhere obviously more essential to life than diamonds, nearly everywhere so much cheaper than diamonds? Why did IBM, which had a monopoly of punched card machines in the USA but no monopoly in punched cards, charge a monopoly price for the cards and sell the machines at cost? Why do farmers sometimes grow crops and then destroy them? Why are some things in our society done publicly and others privately? Why do people use simple majority voting for some decisions but require more than a majority for others and, for yet others, require no vote at all?

The 'we see – why?' interest seeks *behavioural* explanations of phenomena such as these. It does not ask if the phenomena ought to be so or ought to be changed. The emphasis is on understanding *why* what we observe is the way it is.

The 'What Happens If . . . ?' interest

Others are interested in the consequences of social and economic policies. They seek first a theory to *predict* consequences and then evidence to *test* whether the predictions are reliable enough to be used as the basis for action. You will often meet this kind of issue. For example, if company profits are taxed, what happens to profits, prices, output and investment; if sales of motor cars are taxed, to profits, prices, output and investment; if the rate of increase of public expenditure or the money supply is reduced, to employment and inflation; if road pricing is introduced, to traffic congestion; if minimum wages are introduced, to real wages and unemployment; if the external tariff on imports is raised, to import prices, imported quantities, domestic production, employment and exports?

The 'what happens if . . .?' and 'we see – why?' interests form the bulk of the subject matter of what is often called **positive economics**. The distinctive feature of positivism is that it seeks to make statements about the world as it is, or was, or might be. Economists usually try to present hypotheses about positive matters in such a way that they can be tested *empirically*; that is, in such a way that the predictions about the world based on the hypothesis can be compared with events and facts that can, or could be, actually observed and which could falsify the hypothesis. It is not *always* possible to subject positive theories to empirical testing of this sort, and even when it is there is scope for disagreement about whether the test was a 'fair' one and about what the facts 'really' are. None the less, positive statements are testable in principle even if not always in practice, and that is their distinguishing characteristic.

The Philosophical Interest

For some – and they are a minority – the major fascination of economics is simply as a logical and highly refined edifice of philosophical thought. It is of little concern to them whether the subject matter is relevant to the solution of any of the world's problems (though it usually is!); for them economics is its own justification, like listening to music. Emphasis here is upon the elegance with which a proposition is deduced from assumptions, the generality of economic theorems, parsimony in assumptions and so on. Such minds are naturally drawn to economic theory and, in most cases, towards mathematical economic theory. Needless to say, economic theory has to form a part of *all* economists' interest and many of the greatest theorists have also made major contributions to policy. None the less, for some, the theory is *the* thing. They are the philosophers of the discipline, and at various points in the book some of the issues that have chiefly occupied them will be discussed.

The 'How Can We Do Things Better?' Interest

This focus of interest in economics reflects a concern with reform and improvement. It is clearly related to the political philosophy interest but is usually much more specific and generally concerns the role of government in social and economic problems. The kind of question that reflects this interest is illustrated by the following: should the government spend more on defence; how is monopoly best regulated; should health services be provided free of charge; what pattern of public spending will generate most jobs; should the rate of unemployment be reduced, or should it be the rate of inflation; how should decisions concerning the rate of depletion of natural resources be taken; what information should be gathered in order to decide where to locate a new airport?

These questions always need some positive economics if answers are to be forthcoming, since the expected consequences of a proposed action (or of inaction) will need to be spelled out. However, they also raise what are commonly called **normative questions**: questions, that is, requiring one to make **value judgements** about what is good or bad.

Consider a common economic proposition: a subsidy on the price of a service will lead to an increase in the amount of service demanded. This is plainly a *positive* statement about the expected difference in human behaviour with and without a subsidy. This is also a *testable* proposition: one can examine, for example, what has happened in the past (retrospective testing) when such subsidies have been introduced and, provided that one has allowed in some way for the other changes that may have been going on at the same time, one will find out whether or not the predicted effect actually took place. Alternatively one might look at cross sectional data existing now or in the recent past that include observations of behaviour with and without the subsidy. Or, again, one could perform a prospective test by predicting what will happen subsequent to the introduction of a subsidy, and then studying over a period how future behaviour differs from current or past behaviour. The more frequently such empirical studies turn out to be inconsistent with the predictions of the hypothesis, the less confidence one naturally has in it.

But lying behind this positive statement may be a set of *normative* considerations. After all, why is anyone interested in the behavioural effects of a subsidy? The answer nearly always turns out to be that they have an ethical, moral, political or religious reason for caring about its consequences. For example they may believe that getting people to consume more education is a good thing and so some means of bringing that about (of which a subsidy is only one) may also be a good thing (though it may have some side effects that are not such good things: subsidies *may* involve higher taxation on incomes which *may* deter people from producing valuable output or which *may* bear unfairly on some group of the population). If one takes the view that education of some specified type ought to be subsidized, one is typically making both a value judgement (about the goodness of more education) and a positive judgement (that the subsidy will have the predicted effect on education services consumed). But the fact that people have normative reasons for asking positive questions does not make their positive answers normative: the factual content of a prediction is not to be confused with one's *motives* for drawing attention to the prediction, or for developing the hypothesis in the first place.

Case Study 1.1 Can Economics ever be Value Free?

This excerpt is taken from the 'methodological postscript' to Professor Blaug's (1978) book. This postscript contains a useful interpretation of economics down the ages in terms of modern ideas about scientific method in social science.

> Time and time again it has been claimed that economics is *necessarily* value impregnated and that, in Myrdal's words, 'a "disinterested social science" has never existed and, for logical reasons, cannot exist.' When we sort out the various meanings that such assertions carry, they reduce to one or more of the following propositions: (1) the selection of questions to be investigated by economics may be ideologically biased; (2) the answers that are accepted as true answers to these questions may be likewise biased, particularly since economics abounds in contradictory theories that have not yet been tested; (3) even purely factual statements may have emotive connotations and hence may be used to persuade as well as to describe; (4) economic advice to political authorities may be value loaded because means and ends cannot be neatly separated and hence policy ends cannot be taken as given at the outset of the exercise; and (5) since all practical economic advice involves interpersonal comparisons of (welfare) and these are not testable, practical welfare economics almost certainly involves value judgements. Oddly enough, all of these assertions are perfectly true, but they do not affect the orthodox doctrine of value-free social science in any way whatsoever.
>
> Proposition (1) simply confuses the origins of theories with the question of how they may be validated. Schumpeter's *History of Economic Analysis* continually reminds the reader that all scientific theorizing begins with a 'vision' . . . and in this sense science is ideological at the outset. But that is quite a different argument from the one that contends that for this reason the acceptance or rejection of scientific theory is also ideological. Similarly, both propositions (1) and (2) confuse methodological judgements with normative judgements. Methodological judgements involve criteria for judging the validity of a theory, such as levels of statistical significance, selection of data, assessment of their reliability, and adherence to the canons of formal logic, all of which are indispensable in scientific work. Normative judgements, on the other hand, refer to ethical views about the desirability of certain kinds of behaviour and certain social outcomes. It is the latter which alone are said to be capable of being eliminated in positive science. As for propositions (3) and (4), it may be granted that economists have not always avoided the use of honorific definitions and persuasive classification .... But these are abuses of the

> doctrine of value-free economics and do not suffice to demonstrate that economics is *necessarily* value loaded. ... [As for proposition (5)] welfare economics, whether pure or applied, obviously involves value judgements ... the idea of a value-free welfare economics is simply a contradiction in terms.

Honesty, of course requires us to make as clear as we can the difference between our positive judgements and our normative ones. Moreover, we should not suppose either that value judgements cannot be discussed rationally or that they are not *influenced* by facts. For example, few of those who might subscribe to the value judgement 'planners know best what is good for the rest of us' would deny that in some areas of human choice planners do not know best.

Mark Blaug (1978) *Economic Theory in Retrospect*, 3rd edn, Cambridge, Cambridge University Press, pp. 708–9.

SAQ 1.3

Which of the following statements is positive? (Remember, a positive statement is in principle refutable by factual evidence and contains no value judgement.)

(a) British Conservative governments always reduce the real value of retirement pensions.
(b) The more wine George drinks the greater is his satisfaction.
(c) Australians are less intelligent than New Zealanders.
(d) A zero rate of growth of the money supply will reduce the rate of inflation to zero within weeks rather than years.
(e) If prices rise fewer goods will be sold.
(f) Free health care for the aged is the only way senior citizens in the USA can obtain the care the medical profession thinks they need.
(g) Protecting the British motor industry with tariffs will create fewer jobs in Britain than it destroys in Japan.
(h) Economists make better predictions than sociologists.
(i) Many people thought that Barry Goldwater would make an excellent president of the USA.
(j) If Mary chooses bread rather than cheese, and cheese rather than salami, she will choose bread rather than salami.
(k) If Peter chooses ham rather than steak, and steak rather than peaches, he will choose peaches rather than ham.

The Interplay of Choice, the Environment and Ethics

Economics as a discipline is concerned with human *choices* – how the factors that constrain one's freedom to do all one would like can be changed – and with the consequences of such changes. Nature is the main villain of the piece since it is ultimately the niggardliness of nature that constrains choice and forces human society to formulate rules of conduct that govern how competition for the world's scarce resources shall take place. But nature too has rules – or at least it is convenient to think of it in that way. That is, natural scientists have invented theories about how the physical universe works (which are usually positive theories) and these too constrain us. In production, for example, there may be technical limits on how much output can be obtained from a set of inputs. The extent to which a reduction in one input (e.g. the number of machine-hours) can be compensated for by an increase in the amount of another (e.g. worker-hours) is again largely governed by what one knows about nature or, as one so often says today, by technology.

Place in one category propositions about human choice (these are going to be developed in chapters 5, 6 and 7). Place in another the constraints on human behaviour, both manmade (e.g. property rights) and those set by nature (technology). You might call this second category the *environment*. Now consider a third category of factors that relate to value judgements, and term this *ethics*. You can now see that these three types of consideration relating to human behaviour – choices, the environment and ethics, and in particular the interplay between them – are the stuff from which the discipline of economics is made.

If you imagine three intersecting circles, each of which represents one of these three types of consideration, the interactions can be easily seen. In figure 1.2 they are labelled a, b and c, and the interactions are labelled ab, bc etc.

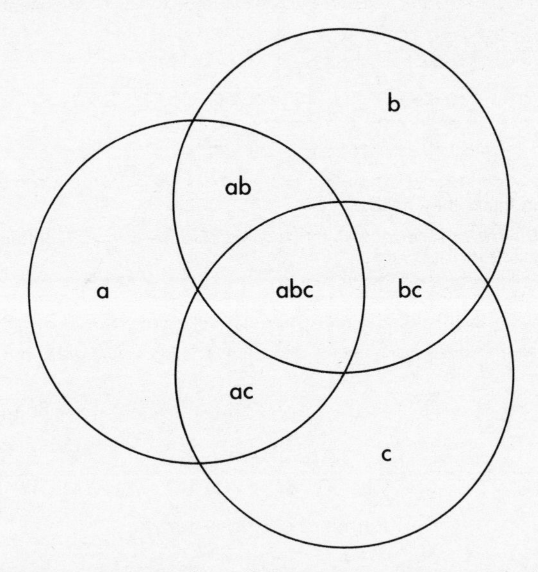

Figure 1.2 Interplay of choice, environment and ethics

Let a stand for the pure theory of human choice, b for the constraining environment and c for ethics. Area ab shows the interaction of the pure theory of human choice with the environment. It is the classic area of positive economics where, for example, propositions about how individuals choose are related to changes in the terms on which they are allowed to choose (by changes in manmade law, in the available technology, in prices and so on). Area ac shows the interaction between the pure theory of choice and ethics.

It is the classic area of normative economic theory where, for example, one considers the moral significance that is to be attached to choice (should the government subsidize education, and how; should firms maximize profits?). Area bc shows the interaction between the environment and ethics and features little in economics. Area abc is where all three interact – where the positive implications of human choices under alternative laws, rules, technologies etc. are considered in conjunction with ethical issues. It is the area of economic policy appraisal, or of **political economy**.

SAQ 1.4

Suppose the technological limitations of a farm's resources enable it to produce under normal conditions (of weather etc.) the amounts of wheat and potatoes shown along or below the line drawn in figure 1.3. That is, given the annual amount of land, seed, machines, fertilizer, etc., production is *constrained* to the attainable area shaded in the diagram. These are the environmental limitations.

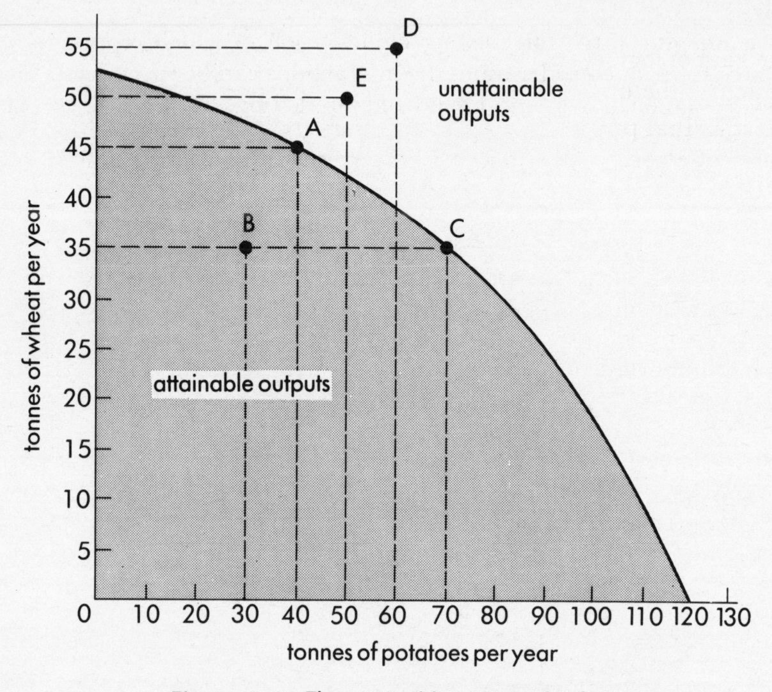

Figure 1.3 The attainable output of a farm

(a) What is the maximum annual amount of wheat that could be produced?
(b) What is the maximum annual amount of potatoes that could be produced?
(c) If 35 tonnes of wheat are planned, what is the maximum crop of potatoes?
(d) What five combinations of potatoes and wheat are represented by the five points A, B, C, D and E?

Now postulate a simple hypothesis of choice: that an individual always chooses more if he or she can (it is hard to think of a simpler hypothesis than this!). Using this hypothesis, the technological constraints, and no more:

(e) Which combination – A, B, C, D or E – will be chosen by the farmer?

Now make the theory a little more sophisticated by adding the following: if an individual chooses one combination rather than a second, and the second rather than a third, then the individual will also choose the first rather than the third. Also add one factual statement: the farmer will choose C rather than E if both are available.

(f) Which combination – A, B, C, D or E – will be chosen by the farmer?
(g) Why did one need the new choice postulate to make this prediction?
(h) Suppose the farmer *actually* chooses another combination from among these five. What has gone wrong?

SAQ 1.4 will have introduced you to a number of common features of economic reasoning:

(a) The use of a graphical technique
(b) The interplay between choice and constraints (in this case technological constraints concerning the outputs of agricultural crops obtainable from given inputs)
(c) The commonly met idea that inputs are substitutable one for another
(d) The kind of logical reasoning that is commonly met in economic theory: in particular the use of *postulates* or *assumptions*
(e) The idea that prediction may go wrong, and where to look for the possible source of error.

Although SAQ 1.4 was rather abstract, you can see that it entailed little more than the ability to apply common sense – but *carefully*. Indeed, economics is little more than carefully applied common sense. The chapters to come will, starting from elementary propositions, show how the corpus of economics is built up step by step and how it can be applied to an immense range of interesting, important and often complex questions. But a caution: do not be too impatient. The chain of an argument is only as good as its weakest link, and if you skip carelessly over such a link it may turn out to be the crucial one in a later argument. As you will see, it is desperately easy to miss a link or two – and eminent economists are not immune from hastiness (I shall cite some examples from time to time).

Disagreements between Economists

Economists are an argumentative lot. You have probably seen enough of them (for example on television) to know that for any one advocating a particular point of view there can always be found another one (or thousand!) arguing another (or various others!). But do not be misled into thinking that, just because different economists have different opinions, economics is simply a matter of opinion. Economists agree on a great deal. For example, all economists would agree that if the government wants to reduce expenditure on a monopolized product and tries to do so by forcing a profit seeking monopolist to sell at a lower price, the result will actually be *increased* expenditure (you will find the reason why this is so in chapter 14).

The most common reason why economists disagree is probably because they hold different value judgements. Thus, every economist may agree that if you make school milk free of charge, more of it will be demanded (this is a proposition in area ab of figure 1.2). But they may disagree as to whether the government might want to provide free milk because they hold different political views about the desirability of raising milk consumption (a proposition in area abc of figure 1.2). This is one reason why it is important to distinguish between positive statements and value judgements: no one expects all economists (or all of any other group) to share exactly the same political views, but it is reasonable to expect economists (and others) to agree about what is logical and what illogical, and about what actually happens and what does not.

Another common reason for disagreement between economists arises, however, because it is not actually always as easy as it may seem to discover what the facts are. In historical analysis the relevant facts may be absent or in dispute. In contemporary analysis the facts may be hard to get hold of quickly enough to settle disputes (for example, official balance of payments figures are subject to amendment years after the accounting period in question as further information comes to hand) or may be too complex to be easily interpreted (for example, the extent to which national income is higher in the UK than it would have been had the UK not joined the European Community). Indeed the last example shows a common problem in many economic issues: one's view depends in part upon a guess about 'what might have been', which is then compared with 'what is'. Even if we can agree on 'what is', the 'what might have been' (sometimes called a **counterfactual**) is not factual but imagined and there is lots of room for disagreement about it, even among people adopting the most stringent scholarly standards.

A third common reason for disagreement is that different economists adopt different conventions about how best to simplify the world. All agree that simplifying assumptions have to be made. There are, however, important areas where the balance of evidence is not yet strong enough to have produced a consensus view. A good example is the assumption that economists make about the way markets behave. Some believe that it is acceptable in practice to presume that markets adjust efficiently and quickly to changing circumstances; others believe that some markets move only slowly and with long adjustment lags. Differences about this issue constitute one of the main reasons why monetarists and Keynesians disagree about policy towards inflation and unemployment. Perhaps one can expect consensus to arrive eventually, but there will always be *some* issues where there is scope for substantial differences in judgement about the best way of stylizing a very complicated world. In such cases it is important to understand the reasons why intelligent men and women can disagree and the kind of information that may eventually settle their differences.

An embarrassing example of economists making public fools of themselves and unnecessarily exposing apparent professional disagreements follows in case study 1.2.

Case Study 1.2 Economists and Britain's Entry into the European Community

On 22 October 1971 two letters appeared in *The Times* signed by members of the Association of University Teachers of Economics. The text of the letters was as follows:

> The undersigned, being full-time teaching officers of economics in British universities, believe that the economic effects of joining the Common Market, taking both short and long term effects into account, are more likely to be unfavourable (favourable) than favourable (unfavourable) to Britain.

There were 154 in favour of entry and 157 against (a small majority against), though those of the rank of reader and professor split 45:29, a rather larger majority in favour. There were 99 undecided.

The letters were organized by Nicholas Kaldor of Cambridge and Harry Johnson of the London School of Economics (both professors, and both against entry).

The foolishness of exposing an apparently muddled and indecisive economics profession was well exposed by Terence Hutchison (Professor of Economics at Birmingham). He wrote (Hutchison, 1977, pp. 140–1):

> To describe this question as 'complex' seems a considerable understatement. It consists of a multidimensional package in which numerous short- and long-range predictions of a most uncertain kind, as well as various kinds of normative value-judgements, were very much mixed up. For example, positive predictions or guesses regarding the effects of joining the Common Market on the rate of growth, or on the distribution of income, or on the power of trade unions, or on other economic phenomena, were likely to vary widely as between one economist and another. At the same time, the normative valuations, or weightings, of these different estimated effects, including the preferred trade-offs between such effects (as, say, more growth and less trade union power, or *vice versa*), might diverge even more widely. Consequently economists making *quite different positive predictions* might, if they also held *quite different valuations or 'weightings' regarding trade-offs,* be found on the *same* side of the crude dichotomy (and *vice versa*). But for whatever purpose this exercise was designed, it was not for that of bringing to bear any kind of refined, expert analysis for the benefit of readers of *The Times.*

My great hope is that readers of this book will value careful analysis, clear specification of goals, lucid distinctions between positive and normative, and candid statements of facts and guesses far above with-it attempts to influence the course of general economic and political events – which in any case (and certainly in this case) help no one, save those to whom these desiderata are anathema and who are the inveterate enemies of economists. For the role of economists is to *elucidate* complex issues by picking them apart and opening up discussion of the (relevant) facts, theories and ethical issues, and thereby to assist those with decision making responsibilities, not to obfuscate the issues let alone supplant those whose job is to make decisions.

Mohsin Khan and Harry Johnson (1972) 'The Common Market questionnaire, October 1971', *Economica*, **39**(155), 316–22.

Terence Hutchison (1977) *Knowledge and Ignorance in Economics*, Oxford, Basil Blackwell.

What You Should Understand Now

The distinction between economics as a topic (the thing studied) and as a discipline (the mode of thinking that is brought to bear).
The complementary nature of economics and other disciplines.
The five various types of interest that people have in studying economics.
The difference between positive and normative economics.
The links between a pure theory of human choice, the environment (natural and manmade) and ethics.
Various reasons why economists disagree and the consequential importance of clarity and need for careful definitions, fine distinctions and thorough factual (empirical) groundwork.

2

Postulates of Economics

Because this and the next few chapters deal with the central core of the economic theory of choice, upon which rests nearly everything else in economics, they are going to have a rather theoretical flavour and will illustrate well the kind of topic in economics that appeals to those of a more philosophical bent. However, the territory you are about to explore is most emphatically *not* the sole preserve of the philosophers, for it contains the central ideas that all economists, whatever their predilections, have in their intellectual toolkits. Indeed the content of the next few chapters underlies everything else that is to come later.

In essence you are here going to be concerned with rational choice and with predicting human behaviour under conditions of scarcity. Each of these ideas can prove a stumbling block to the beginner, so you will have to sort out what is meant by each. But first you should understand why these two basic ideas are needed. Hopefully, having understood the context, the relevance of the concepts will become clear.

Rationality and Predictability

Although it is a commonplace that people's actions are not predictable – they are not machines or automatons, they have **free will** – this commonplace observation is only partly true. It is true that (given the resources they have) people are free to use them as they wish (but subject to socially determined rules that will be discussed in the chapter on property rights). It is also true that it is very hard to predict what tastes individuals have (why some prefer brown to white bread, red to blue cars, Bach to Beethoven, and so on despite all kinds of social conditioning). It is also true that whatever the generalizations you make about human behaviour there will always be some exceptions.

Despite these empirical truths there are also, however, distinct *regularities* about human behaviour. For example, if interest rates rise and all else remains the same, people tend to save more; if the price of a good falls and all else remains the same, people tend to buy more; if the money wage stays the same but inflation occurs, workers will want a higher money wage for the same work and will usually get it. What is common to all these phenomena is that they involve change or, more precisely, *behavioural responses to change*. True, individuals may be free to choose. What seems to happen as a matter of fact, however, is that they choose to respond to certain kinds of change (like a falling or rising price) in common ways that are predictable. One is surprised and puzzled if they respond differently from the ways just suggested, and one tends to regard behaviour like that (for example, buying *less* when price falls) as pathological.

Economists have always tended to focus on *normal* behaviour (as distinct from, say, sociology, where the study of deviance is a central issue) and have also tended to focus on people's normal *responses* to changes in the environment (for example, changes in prices, incomes, inflation rates, wages, interest rates and tax rates).

These responses are regular and are predictable at the *qualitative* level, which says only whether the response is positive (for example, buy more) or negative (buy less), rather than at the *quantitative* level, which says how much more or less.

Given these predictable regularities, it is natural to ask 'why?' Is there some more fundamental aspect of human behaviour that accounts for all of these predictable responses? Can one develop a more *general* theory in which each of the responses (to price changes, income changes and so on) is a *special case*? The quest for this more fundamental or general theory is a fascinating story (which will be told in chapters 5, 6 and 7), and it is in the context of this quest that the economists's special notion of **rationality** has arisen. What rationality means in economics is no more than *behaviour consistent with certain postulates*. The postulates (sometimes called *axioms*) that may produce the results wanted, namely predicted responses to change that are actually observed, are in principle many. One possible approach is described in case study 2.1, which you should now examine.

Case Study 2.1 Random Choice and Predictability

One of the basic requirements of any theory of choice is that it should provide an account of why people characteristically buy more of a good when its price falls relative to others. The economist Gary Becker (1962) has provided an explanation for this phenomenon based on the proposition that individuals choose randomly. Suppose that people have given incomes that can be spent on either Z or X and nothing else. (Imagine, if you like, that Z stands for all goods – including savings – that are not X.) At the prevailing prices for Z and X they could buy a maximum of OZ' of Z or OX' of X, or some combination lying along the line $X'Z'$ in figure 2.1, where Z is measured on the vertical axis and X on the horizontal. (If you do not understand this point, turn immediately to SAQ 2.1 and then return to this case study.) If people choose randomly, they might locate anywhere along the line $Z'X'$ with equal probability. But the *average* combination of X and Z will, of course, be exactly halfway along $Z'X'$, at point a, indicating that the *average* person chooses OZ_a of Z and OX_a of X. Now suppose the price for X falls. The new possibilities for purchase now lie along the line $Z'X''$. If people choose randomly, again the average person will be found at the midpoint of this line, point b, showing that the average person buys, at the new price for X, OX_b and OZ_b. Note that b must lie to the right of a. Hence when the price for X falls, even irrational people (at least if they are irrational in this particular way) will buy more of *X*. Irrationality of this sort is thus consistent with the observed systematic tendency for more to be bought when the price falls. (Incidentally, another implication of this theory which you may be able to see for yourself – that purchases of *Z* remain the same – is not supported by the evidence.)

Gary Becker (1962) 'Irrational behaviour and economic theory', *Journal of Political Economy*, **70**, 1–13.

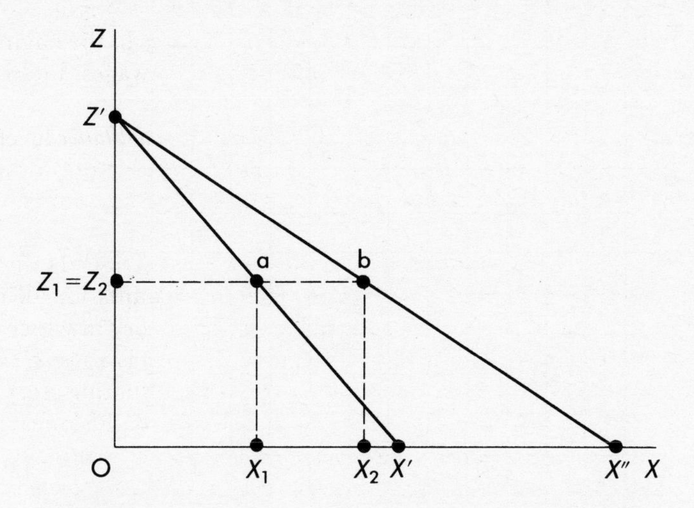

Figure 2.1 Effects of a price change on random choice

If you did not break off from case study 2.1 to look at SAQ 2.1, you should now tackle it.

SAQ 2.1

This SAQ is to reinforce your understanding of the workings of figure 2.1. Figure 2.2 is available for you to plot some points.
You have £180 to spend on either *Z* or *X*.

(a) If the price of *Z* (P_Z) is £18, how many *Z* can you buy?
Label with letter a the point corresponding to this consumption in the graph.

(b) If the price of *X* (P_X) is £22.50, how many can you buy? Label with b the point corresponding to this in the graph.

(c) If you buy 7.5 of *Z*, how much money have you left over for spending on *X*, given the above prices?

(d) How many *X* can you buy, given you are buying 7.5 of *Z* at the above prices?
Label with c the point indicating 7.5 of *Z* and this amount of *X* in the graph.

(e) If you buy 6 of *X*, and spend your entire income on *X* and *Z*, how many *Z* will you buy? Mark with d the point indicating this combination of *X* and *Z* in the graph.

(f) If you buy 5 of *Z* and 4 of *X*, how much will you spend on them? Mark with e this point on the graph.

(g) Connect the points a, c, e, d and b on the graph. Why is this a straight line?

(h) Suppose P_X falls to £15. What is the maximum amount of *X* you can now buy? Mark with f this point on the graph.

(i) If you now choose to buy 3 of Z, how many X would you buy if you spent your entire £180? Mark with g this point on the graph.

(j) Join the points a, g and f with a straight line. What consumption of X and Z is represented by the midpoint (label it h) of af?

(k) What consumption of X and Z is represented by the midpoint of ab?

(l) Is h to the right or the left of e?

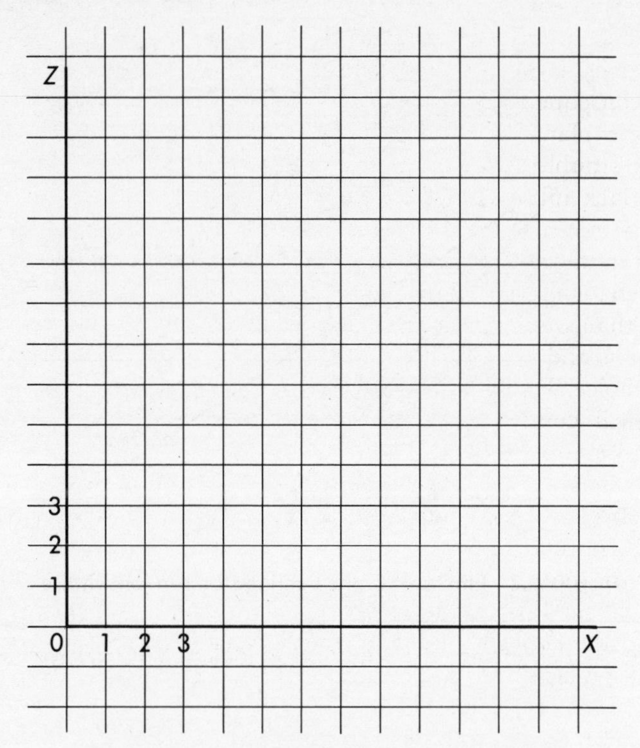

Figure 2.2 Squared graph paper for SAQ 2

Rationality

As has been seen in case study 2.1, it is possible to create a predictive theory of how individuals react to changes in the environment based on the general assumption that they are *irrational* – specifically, that they act in a random fashion. However, that particular idea of irrationality does not really strike a chord of plausibility and, indeed, there is lots of evidence that choices are ordinarily much more purposive than that. Another kind of irrationality to postulate might be that individuals always do what they have previously done and, if this becomes impossible, they do the nearest thing they can to what they have done. This would be to suppose that they are archetypal conservatives in behaviour and, again, is rather implausible.

SAQ 2.2

The text has just asserted that archetypal conservative behaviour is irrational. Do you agree?

The point of all this is that to develop a theory of choice that enables one to make predictions about behaviour requires one to postulate some underlying pattern or motive like randomness or conservatism. This inevitably involves some drastic simplifications in order to focus on the underlying features that capture – so one hopes – the essence of what is going on. This process of theorizing can never tell the *whole truth* about human choice. The question is, does it tell enough relative to alternative possible formulations to be *useful*? Moreover, does it accord sufficiently well with intuitions, and with the observable consequences of choices, for you and others to be ready to rely upon it in making explanations and predictions about the things you see?

The basic troubles with the postulates of randomness or conservatism are three: they lack intuitive appeal, they have some implications that are *not* supported by evidence, and they are likely to cause individuals to be logically inconsistent in their behaviour. That is why they have been dubbed theories of irrational behaviour. Of course, if one or the other of the theories led to better predictions than would otherwise be possible then you would have to swallow your intuitions and simply accept logical inconsistency as an inherent feature of human choice. Fortunately, however, you will soon see that theories that assume logical consistency predict better than those that do not. Hence intuition and empirical validity go hand in hand.

Rational behaviour is usually regarded as behaviour that is consistent with a postulated objective. For example, if your aim is to make a million by the time you are 30 it is probably irrational for you to become a priest. If your aim is to play for a top football club, it is irrational for you to spend all your time listening to music. Rationality, in short, requires a relation between the means adopted and the end postulated. Because economists seek a *general* theory of human choice it is important not to make the end too *specific* (like, for example, making it the maximization of wealth).

In economics the general objective assumed to underlie rational choice is a rather subtle one: *it is assumed that individuals maximize the overall subjective value to them* of the things they choose. Not only is this an extremely general objective, since it includes *all* the things that anyone may value, but it is also not itself directly observable: you can observe the things chosen but you rarely observe their subjective value. Whereas the former aspect of the objective (its generality) is a great virtue, for it means that the theory will be applicable to a wide class of events, the latter aspect is treacherous, and one has to take care not to make it so mysterious that it becomes metaphysical. As it happens, and as you will shortly see, with careful definition and scrupulous attention to logic it is possible sometimes to derive an index of subjective value. But there are also other ways of testing for the rationality of behaviour in the pursuit of an objective that cannot be observed, and this requires the exercise of imagination in inventing *indirect* tests. You will meet several of these when some specific theories of choice are discussed.

The invention of an *unobservable* entity to account for phenomena we *can* observe is very common in science. Case study 2.2 illustrates this with respect to just one example in physics, where the intervals between the collision of particles cannot be observed but the existence and behaviour of particles in the intervals can nonetheless be conjectured.

Case Study 2.2 Are There Atoms?

The following is an extract from Reichenbach (1951):

> As in the world of our daily life, there are observables and unobservables in the world of the atom. What can be observed are collisions between two particles, as between a particle and a light ray; the physicist has devised ingenious instruments that indicate each individual collision. What cannot be observed is what happens during the interval between two collisions, or on the path from the source of radiation to a collision. These recurrences, then, are the unobservables of the quantum world.
>
> But why can they not be observed? Why can we not use a supermicroscope and watch the particles on their path? The trouble is that in order to see a particle we have to illuminate it; and illumination of a particle is something very different from the illumination of a house. A light ray falling on a particle pushes it out of its way; what we observe, therefore, is a collision and not a particle travelling peacefully on its path.
>
> Speaking of particles means attributing to them a definite place and a definite velocity for each time point. For instance, a tennis ball occupies at every moment a certain place on its path and has, at this moment, a determinate velocity. Both place and velocity can be measured, at each moment, by suitable instruments. For small particles, however, the disturbance by the observer, as Heisenberg has shown, makes it impossible to measure both values simultaneously. We can measure either the position or the velocity of the particle, but not both. The question arises whether there do not exist other ways of determining the unmeasured quantity, methods through which the unmeasured quantity is related indirectly to the observed quantities. The analysis of quantum mechanics, however, has given a negative answer.

Hans Reichenbach (1951) *The Rise of Scientific Philosophy*, Berkeley and Los Angeles, University of California Press, pp. 182–3.

Rationality assumes that individuals choose in a logically consistent fashion. What this entails in detail will be seen in the chapters to follow. You will also see why irrational behaviour involves inconsistency. The basic answer to the question of why economics uses a postulate of rational behaviour is, therefore, because it has intuitive appeal and because it appears to be on the whole consistent with the evidence.

This evidence is of two kinds. The first is evidence that *directly* tests the postulates that are shortly to be met and that collectively define rationality. The second kind of evidence is *indirect* and tests the rationality postulates by their indirect implications. The vast majority of the evidence relating to rational behaviour is of the second type.

SAQ 2.3

Which of the following are indicative of irrationality?

(a) A is a doctor who is well aware of the association between smoking and disease but who still smokes.
(b) B says he is going to buy A's house, but then he buys C's.
(c) D gives all his wealth to the poor and enters a monastery.
(d) E makes detailed calculations of the costs and benefits to her of every action she takes.
(e) One society protects children but eats cows, another protects cows and lets unwanted children die.

Predictability

Some behaviour is more predictable than others. Economics usually focuses on a particular kind of behaviour, namely how individuals respond to *changes in the environment* rather than why individuals choose what they choose *given the environment*. The former is more predictable than the latter. For example, some people choose brown bread and others white. Economics has not considered the question why this is so. The kind of question that economics considers is: given that A eats so much wholemeal and so much white bread (for whatever reasons), how will the pattern of bread consumption *change* if the prices of the two kinds of bread alter, or if income changes, or if information about the health consequences of higher roughage content in one kind compared with the other becomes more widespread?

Indeed, the **variability** of basic preferences (whether for bread or anything else) is taken as axiomatic in economics (though it may be an important subject for study in, say, sociology or psychology). Economics focuses on the stimulus–response relationships of a changing or changeable environment. Clearly one's chances of finding that behaviour is predictable in this more restricted set of choices are higher than in the wider set where one would attempt to account for *all* choices. Moreover, from a policy perspective, it is *changes* in behaviour that are the central concern. One does not care so much about why *x* per cent of newly purchased cars are Japanese as about how that percentage will change if domestically produced cars become cheaper or dearer, import quotas on imported cars are imposed etc.

The predictability of individual behaviour becomes even more acceptable as a proposition if it is realized that one is typically concerned with the behaviour of *groups* rather than *individuals*. Invariably one begins with a theory of individual behaviour, but the individual in mind is not a specific named person (who may decide to be as unpredictable as possible just to prove economists wrong!) but a *representative* individual – representative of a whole class of individuals (like car buyers, for example). One may not be able to predict with any reliability that the elderly widow Mrs Freda Jones of 24 Frog Street will go to the chiropodist more frequently if the service is free compared with when she had to pay the chiropodist out of her own pocket. It *is*, however, possible to predict with fair accuracy how much more frequently patients as a whole (or a subset of them like elderly widows) will go to chiropodists as fees are reduced.

It follows that economics does not assume that individual behaviour is **deterministic**: that one can predict with certainty how a named person will respond to a changed environmental stimulus. Instead it is **probabilistic**: one says that a class of people will, on average, behave in such and such a fashion in response to a changed stimulus, or that there is an x per cent chance that Mrs Jones will increase her frequency of consultation by one, two, three etc. visits per year. And that, for many practical purposes, is all that is needed.

Case Study 2.3 Predictable Behaviour in Psychotics

Psychotic patients in mental hospitals usually display erratic and inconsistent performance of routine hospital duties like helping to serve meals, answering the telephone, folding linen and cleaning laboratories. The following experiment by psychologists Ayllon and Azrin (1965) demonstrates, however, that the behaviour of psychotics in response to controlled environmental stimuli is systematic and in accord with what one would normally expect of any individual.

A total of 44 female schizophrenics, psychotics and mental defectives undertook, for a period of 20 days, a variety of jobs in the hospital in return for tokens allowing them certain privileges such as periods of privacy, trips to town (with escort) or private consultations with a social worker. During this period a total of about 45 hours was spent per day on the jobs. For the next 20 days, tokens were given without the obligation to work (a 'paid vacation'). For the next 20 days the award of tokens was again made contingent upon the performance of the tasks. On day 21 the amount of work decreased to 35 hours from 45; on day 23 it fell to 30 hours, and by day 36 it had dropped to 21 hours. On day 41 the time spent on job assignments rose immediately to 45 hours, where it remained until the experiment was terminated on day 60.

T. Ayllon and N. H. Azrin (1965) 'The measurement and reinforcement of the behaviour of psychotics', *Journal of the Experimental Analysis of Behaviour*, **8**, 357–83.

Four Postulates of Choice Theory

There are four postulates that underlie the economic theory of choice. In this chapter they are presented, together with some important definitions, in a general way, and the label **postulates** is reserved for these generalized concepts. Later chapters look at some specific theories of choice where the underlying assumptions, which will be more specific versions of these postulates, will be termed **axioms**. At this stage the emphasis is on the *generality* of the postulates. Later analysis will show how they can be *specifically* used to develop theories of behaviour in response to changing environmental stimuli.

Postulate 1 Each Individual Chooses Many Economic Goods

An individual in this postulate is taken, as you have seen already, to be a normal or representative individual. A good, however, needs definition. It is helpful to consider three definitions:

(a) A **good** is *any* chosen entity or object, material or spiritual, with a money price or without, beautiful or ugly, selfishly motivated or unselfishly. *A good is simply something of which one chooses some rather than none.*
(b) An **economic good** is a *scarce* good: it is an entity or object of which one cannot have as much as one would like. *An economic good is something of which one would choose more if one could.*
(c) A **free good** is a *non-scarce* good: it is an entity or object of which one has as much as one wishes. *A free good is something of which one would not choose more if one could.* A free good in economic parlance is not necessarily one that has no money price: education is free of charge in many countries, but it is for at least some people an economic good, for the resources used in its provision are scarce and many people would like more.

Postulate 1 states that representative individuals choose more than one economic good. It does not assert they always choose more wealth, or that they are selfish in that they always choose entities only for their own benefit. The range of economic goods is immense. For example, all the following are, according to the definition, economic goods: steel, wheat, education, liberty, time and fresh air. It is because of the immense scope of the concept of an economic good that the topics to which the discipline of economics can be applied are so broad.

Postulate 2 For Each Individual Some Goods are Economic Goods

This postulate effectively defines each individual as having to choose, for some of the goods he or she chooses must, according to postulate 2, be scarce. Given the immense scope of the concept of economic goods, and the fact that they need not be chosen for one's own use, this postulate is not very restrictive.

Postulate 3 Economic Goods are Substitutable

This postulate says that an individual will substitute *some* of one economic good to get more of another. What it specifically denies is that an individual will seek *satiation* in one good before beginning to choose more of another, and that there is no absolute need for anything. Even in the poorest communities *some* time is sacrificed that could have been spent gathering food for *some* time spent on cultural activity; *some* hunting is sacrificed for *some* propitiation of the gods; *some* of one's own comforts (mean though they may be) are sacrificed for one's children's comforts. In rich communities, *some* wealth (but not all) is sacrificed to relieve the poverty of others and, in general, *some* of many things is sacrificed for a little more of everything else. People may not sacrifice enough, in your judgement, or may have an order of priority different from that you would choose or that you think right, but these are value judgements. Postulate 3 is a postulate about how people *actually* behave, not how one thinks they ought to.

People often think that there are some areas of activity where choice is not really possible at all, being dictated by, say, technology or 'basic human need'. Case study 2.4 gives an example of how in the highly technical field of medicine this is not so.

Case Study 2.4 The Need for Surgery

Medical care is an area where choice is often made less by the ultimate consumer (the patient) than by the doctor (who can be seen as a kind of agent for the consumer). It is commonly thought that discretion, and hence the possibility of choice, is more limited here than elsewhere and that the need for care is largely technically determined by the diagnosis, prognosis and medical technologies for intervention. But in general this is not so. The following example illustrates this for one of the commonest surgical procedures – surgical removal of tonsils (tonsillectomy).

A total of 389 11-year-old school children with intact tonsils were examined by a group of physicians and 45 per cent (174) were judged in need of tonsillectomy. The remaining 215 were recycled past a second, similar group of physicians and 46 per cent of these (99) were judged in need of tonsillectomy. The remaining 116, who had been given a clean bill of tonsillar health by both the first and the second group of physicians, were then recycled past a third group of physicians and 44 per cent (51) were judged in need of tonsillectomy. Table 2.1 summarizes the results.

Table 2.1 Medical judgements of need for tonsillectomy

	Children examined	*Recommended for tonsillectomy (no.)*	*(%)*	*Cumulative % in need*
Round 1	389	174	45	55
Round 2	215 (389–174)	99	46	70
Round 3	116 (215–99)	51	44	83

Perhaps the most remarkable finding was not so much the inconsistency in diagnosis and therapeutic recommendations as the consistency in the proportion of children recommended for tonsillectomy by the different panels of physicians. This is probably explained by the hypothesis that physicians have prior expectations about what they expect to find in any population of prospective patients.

The 'need' for tonsillectomy appears to vary very much according to the prior expectations of physicians, their place of training, the number of doctors, and the cost of access to care. Nor is tonsillectomy an isolated case.

H. Bakwin (1945) 'Pseudodoxia pediatrics', *New England Journal of Medicine*, **232**, 691–7.

It is now useful to introduce the **marginal rate of substitution**, defined as *the maximum amount of one good an individual will sacrifice to obtain a little more of another.* Typically the *MRS* will vary from person to person, and each individual will have a varying *MRS* depending on the amount or rate of consumption. Such variability will be explored in later chapters.

It is useful to show this postulate graphically. Consider an individual choosing between two economic goods. For maximum generality, term them X and Z. Figure 2.3 shows units of Z on the vertical axis and units of X on the horizontal. Suppose the individual is currently at point a, whose coordinates

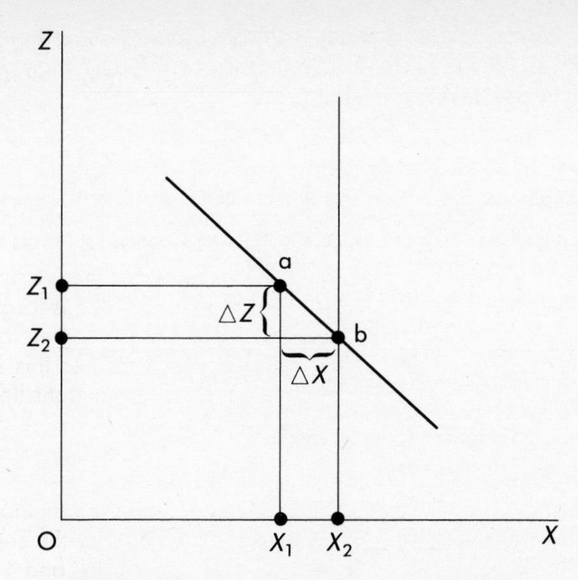

Figure 2.3 The marginal rate of substitution

indicate a rate of consumption or use of OX_a and OZ_a of the two goods. (For the moment you can think of the individual as either having a stock of X and Z or consuming a certain amount per period.) Now consider the amount of X to be OX_b instead of OX_a that is, a small amount X_aX_b *more* of X. The figure has a vertical line down through X_a. What is the *maximum* amount of Z that will be sacrificed by the individual to obtain X_aX_b more of X? The answer cannot be zero, or X would not be an economic good. The answer cannot be all this individual's Z either, or Z would not be an economic good. The answer must therefore be some amount less than OZ_a but larger than zero. Suppose the actual amount to be Z_aZ_b, bringing the individual to point b from point a. The *MRS* between X and Z for this individual is the ratio of this maximum sacrifice of Z for the given increase in X, namely Z_aZ_b/X_aX_b or, where the Greek capital delta Δ signifies the change, $\Delta Z/\Delta X$, which is the slope of the straight line connecting a and b. By conducting an appropriate experiment to find out ΔZ one could say that the *value* to the individual of the ΔX is, in terms of Z, ΔZ.

Postulate 4 Not All Individuals Choose the Same Economic Goods

This postulate is straightforward and merely raises to the status of a postulate what you have seen earlier, namely that one does not seek in economics to explain *all* aspects of choice. It is taken as given that for a variety of reasons individuals have different preferences for different economic goods: some have more cultivated taste than others, some are more selfish than others, some are conditioned by social and cultural backgrounds very different from those of others, and so on.

The four postulates underlie all that is to come. Hopefully they will have intuitive appeal – even seem obvious. If that is the case, so much the better, for the foundations upon which the analysis is to be erected should be relatively uncontroversial and commonsensical.

SAQ 2.4

Which of the following statements violates one or more of the postulates?

(a) In my smoking days, when I offered a cigarette to G (an economics graduate student) he would always accept, even though he was a non-smoker.
(b) Fresh air is abundant and available to all to have as much of as they like. It is therefore a free good.
(c) The economics department chose not to offer a course in business economics.
(d) Everyone needs medical care; therefore it should be free.
(e) Our priorities for public spending should be first defence, then justice and the police, followed by health, education, housing and social security in that order.
(f) In practice only the rich can choose.

What You Should Understand Now

The distinction between rational and irrational choices.
The predictability of human choices.
The possibility of explaining at least one commonly observed phenomenon (a negative behavioural relation between price and consumption rates) by postulating irrational choice.
The role of unobservables in economics and science generally.
The four basic postulates of choice theory.
Some technical terms: good, economic good, free good, marginal rate of substitution.

3

The Law of Demand and Demand Curves

The Law of Demand

A major use to which the postulates of chapter 2 are often put is in providing an explanation of the demand for economic goods. Three such explanations, together with some of the insights they give, are contained in chapters 5, 6 and 7. This chapter and the next, as a preparation for all that, discusses the precise meaning of demand and how it relates to observable behaviour. For the subsequent analysis of social, economic and historical phenomena, economists are not able to do without this central concept.

The basic phenomenon with which this chapter is concerned is an extremely common one characterizing much of human and, indeed, animal behaviour. It may be described in the following law-like form:

> *The greater the relative cost of an economic good, the lower the rate of purchase, acquisition and consumption.*

This is commonly found to be the case with ordinary people. You have already seen in case study 2.3 how the behaviour of psychotics in a psychological experiment conformed with this general rule. The same appears to be true of much animal behaviour (as case study 6.3 illustrates), and so is very widely observed indeed.

The **law of demand** is commonly observed in the market behaviour of individuals. It is then natural to express it in the following form:

> *The higher the relative price, the lower the preferred rate of purchase or consumption.*

Note the emphasis on *relative* price. The law of demand refers always to the price of acquiring a good relative to the prices of acquiring other goods. Thus, if the price of cars rises by 10 per cent and all other prices (including that of labour time) also rise by 10 per cent, the relative price of cars has remained constant and the demand for them will not change (unless, of course, some other non-price determinant of demand has also changed). Uniform inflation across all goods, therefore, will not affect relative demand, but if the price of cars were to rise by 10 per cent and all other prices by an average of 20 per cent, then the relative price of cars would have fallen, and one would expect to see more demanded.

Note also the adjective *preferred*. The law of demand is a behavioural law applicable only when individuals are free to adjust their rate of consumption or purchase. If a law were to be passed placing an absolute maximum on the number of cars that are imported (a **quota** on imports of cars), the fact that individuals *cannot* buy more imported cars even if the price falls is not an exception. In such a circumstance there is said to be an **excess demand** for the good in question.

Note also the emphasis on *rate*. The law of demand is not to be interpreted as an instantaneous phenomenon, for many goods are purchased only occasionally. For example, one may shop only once a week, or go on holiday once a year, or purchase a car once every five years. When the price rises, the law states that one may shop less frequently, purchase less on each occasion, take shorter holidays, buy a smaller car, replace it less frequently, own fewer cars etc., or vice versa for a price fall. Rate, therefore, focuses on purchases or consumption over some relevant period.

Note finally the emphasis on purchase *or* consumption. Purchase and consumption do not normally take place at the same time, and one may consume one's purchases over a much longer period than it takes to purchase them. Indeed some goods, known as **durable goods**, such as domestic appliances and items of capital equipment, are consumed over very long periods. Whether it is purchases or consumption that is being referred to will usually be clear from the context in which the discussion is taking place.

SAQ 3.1

The following phenomena are all explicable by the law of demand. Explain why.

(a) The English drink less French bottled wine per caput than the French, but the average quality is higher.

(b) The average size of apple consumed in the state of Washington (a major fruit growing area of the USA) is smaller and more dried up than Washington grown apples eaten in Indiana.

(c) If the Post Office raises the price of first class mail, letters will be longer and more informative.

(d) Couples with children will go out less frequently than childless couples, but will go to the theatre *relatively* more frequently than to the cinema compared with childless couples.

Although the law of demand has been most frequently observed for human behaviour in the marketplace, it is by no means only there that it can be observed. Case study 3.1 gives an example of how the demand for a recreational resource (Yosemite National Park in California) varied according to the *travel costs* of getting there. Similar results have often been noted in other non-market situations. For example, hospital appointments are most likely to be broken by those living furthest from the facility and by those whose time is the costliest in terms of wages lost.

Case Study 3.1 Demand for a Recreational Resource

The economists Clawson and Knetsch (1966) have analysed the demand for many kinds of outdoor recreation. Figure 3.1 shows the relationship they found by plotting the costs (as comprehensively as they could) of getting to Yosemite National Park in California from 11 different base areas against the frequency of visits in 1953 per 1000 residents of the base area. The various costs were represented in dollars in order that they could be aggregated into a single 'shadow' price.

The line drawn through the points in the diagram is the linear regression line calculated best to fit the scatter of points: its negative slope, revealing the law of demand, is apparent.

Marion Clawson and Jack Knetsch (1966) *Economics of Outdoor Recreation*, Baltimore and London, Johns Hopkins Press.

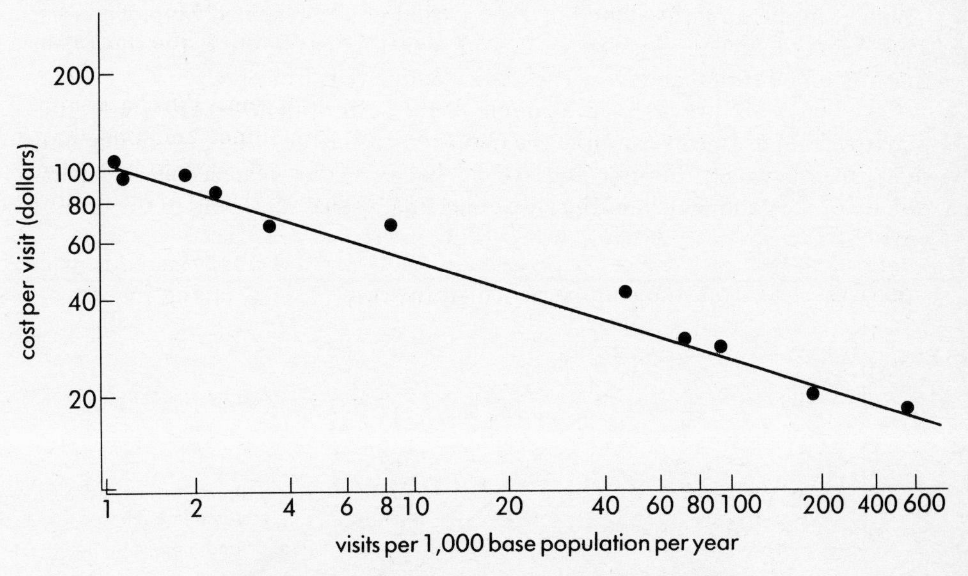

Figure 3.1 Demand for Yosemite National Park

Responses to changes in prices are referred to as *changes in the quantity demanded* as distinct from *changes in demand*. The latter term is used to describe changes in response due to factors *other than* changes in the price of the good in question. (These factors will be examined in a moment.) This gives yet another form of the law of demand:

The higher the relative price, the lower the quantity demanded per period.

It is this relationship that is most frequently depicted in diagrams of the **demand curve** (as in figure 3.1). The curve shows the preferred quantities demanded per period at a variety of prices.

SAQ 3.2

Are the following cases exceptions to the law of demand?

(a) Today's price of apples rises but more are purchased in anticipation of even higher prices next week.

(b) Luxury goods like mink stoles and Rolls Royce cars are bought *because of* their high prices, which bring snob distinction to their owners. The higher the price the more the distinction; therefore the demand curves for such luxury goods have positive, rather than negative, slopes.

(c) Drug addicts are caught up in the problem that the more they have the more they want; therefore an addict's demand for heroin slopes upwards.

(d) The price of a holiday in Spain falls, but I still take only one holiday a year.

Other Determinants of Demand

Changes in the quantity demanded per period are represented by movements *along* demand curves. Changes in the other factors cause the curve to *shift* so that the amount demanded at each price is different from before.

Case study 3.2 provides an example of the shift of demand that may take place over time. In this example the main reason for the difference in demand that exists between the first and second halves of the year seems to be the quality of the good which, in the case of herring, varies according to the time of year.

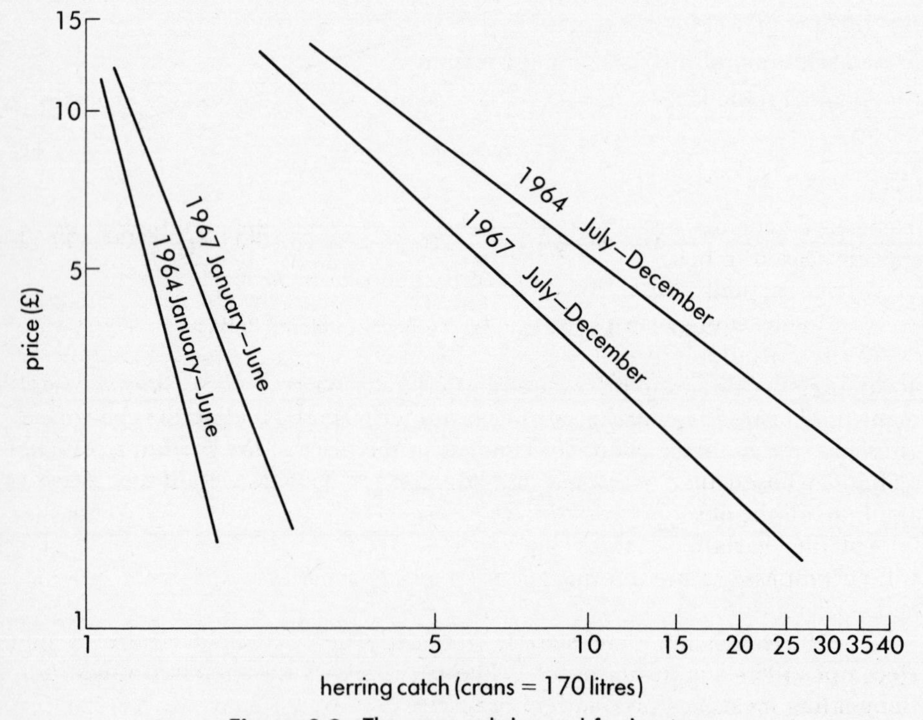

Figure 3.2 The seasonal demand for herring

Case Study 3.2 Demand for Scottish Herring

Allan (1972) has estimated the demand for herring, of which in Britain most is caught by Scottish boats. Herring is a highly perishable good and is bought and sold by auction on the day of landing. Inland prices vary only because of transport costs, and the telecommunications between ports are so good that a single price rapidly becomes established throughout the country (a new landing in one port immediately affects the price of herring at all the others).

Figure 3.2 shows the demand curves for herring in two years (1964 and 1967) each subdivided into two halves. The substantial increase in demand in the second half of the year is very apparent. The main difference between herring in winter and in summer is that summer fish are oily and winter fish rather dry, and the difference in the demand for summer and autumn fish compared with winter and spring is a reflection of the inferior quality of the latter.

C.M. Allan (1972) 'The demand for herring: a single equation model', *Scottish Journal of Political Economy*, **19**, 91–8.

In general, for an economic good that is homogeneous in quality and other attributes, the main factors affecting its demand are the following:

(a) Tastes of consumers
(b) Prices of related goods
(c) Income or wealth of consumers
(d) Distribution of income among consumers
(e) Demographic factors like size of population and its age and sex structure.

Tastes

Tastes are generally assumed to be constant and unchanging unless there is specific reason to believe that, in the period to which the demand data relate, they have actually changed. Changes in taste are, however, notoriously difficult to measure at all precisely. The temptation is to attribute to changes in taste any variation in demand left over when all other factors have been accounted for. But this is not a good procedure. For one thing, the measurement and estimation of the effects of other factors is subject to error and omission, so one may wind up attributing to changes in taste the shifts in demand whose cause really lies elsewhere. For another thing, if one cannot attribute all the observed variation to measurable factors, then to attribute the unexplained variation to taste changes is really no more than guesswork. Taste still encompasses a broad range of factors, such as aesthetics, morals, religion and sense of duty.

None the less, changes in tastes can sometimes be identified. For example, in December 1966 American Roman Catholics were no longer required to abstain from eating meat on Fridays. This led, as case study 3.3 shows, to substantial declines in the demand for fish in America.

Case Study 3.3 American Roman Catholics and Fish on Friday

For over 1000 years the Roman Catholic church required its members to abstain from meat on Friday in the spirit of penance. In February 1966, however, Pope Paul VI relaxed the rules on fasting and abstinence in Lent and local bishops were given discretion regarding the rule of Friday abstinence from meat. The American bishops terminated obligatory meatless Fridays, other than during Lent, as from December 1966.
a monthly basis for ten years prior to the decree and the seven months following it to August 1967 (excluding the months of Lent). The results are given in table 3.1.

Table 3.1 Monthly fish prices 1957–67

Species	*Price change attributed to the decree (%)*
Sea scallops	−17
Yellowtail flounder	−14
Large haddock	−21
Small haddock	−2
Cod	−10
Ocean perch	−10
Whiting	−20

F.W. Bell (1968) 'The Pope and the price of fish', *American Economic Review*, **58**, 1346–50.

Prices of Related Goods

Related goods are divided into substitutes and complements.

In the case of **substitutes**, a rise or fall in the price of one good leads to a fall or rise in demand for it and a rise or fall in demand for some other goods. These other goods will be substituted for it when its price rises, or it will be substituted for these other goods when its price falls. In Bell (1968) (see case study 3.3) meat and poultry were found to be substitutes for fish: a fall in meat and poultry prices led to a rise in the demand for fish, despite the general decline in demand for fish.

In the case of **complements**, the rise or fall in the price of one good leads to a fall or rise in the quantity of that good demanded, and hence also to a fall or rise in the demand for goods consumed in a complementary fashion. Petrol and motor cars are complementary goods; so are cars and recreational sites, and so are bread and butter.

Income and Wealth

The demand for goods *as a whole* always rises with increases in income. For specific goods, however, consumption may fall, rise or remain the same. Those goods whose demand increases with income are said to be **normal** goods, and those whose demand falls with income are termed **inferior** goods. Some goods may be inferior at some income levels and normal at others. Case study 3.4

examines the demand for foodstuffs in Great Britain in 1971 and has examples of normal and inferior goods, as well as some that vary according to income level.

Case Study 3.4 Income and Food Consumption in Britain 1982

Since 1940 there has been a continuous sample survey of domestic food consumption and expenditure in Great Britain. Some of the results for 1982 are contained in table 3.2. These results do not allow for a number of factors (such as the number of children in the household). However, they indicate that butter and coffee are all normal foods, and that vegetables and tea are inferior foods. Cheese is normal and sugar inferior, except at the higher income levels. Margarine is broadly inferior, while meat and fish are rather variable: normal over some income ranges and inferior over others.

Ministry of Agriculture, Fisheries and Food (1984) *Household Food Consumption and Expenditure 1982*, London, HMSO.

Table 3.2 Household food consumption by income group 1982

Weekly earned income of head of household (£)	*Quantity of food per person per week (ounces)*								
	Cheese	*Meat*	*Fish*	*Butter*	*Margarine*	*Vegetables*	*Sugar*	*Tea*	*Coffee*
310+	4.0	36.0	4.4	3.9	2.7	68.8	7.9	1.1	0.8
240–309	4.3	40.1	5.2	3.3	3.3	75.3	7.8	1.5	0.8
127–239	4.0	38.4	4.7	3.1	3.1	81.2	8.7	1.6	0.7
77–126	3.7	39.3	4.7	2.9	4.0	88.4	10.3	2.0	0.6
Under 77[a]	3.2	35.9	4.8	2.7	4.5	91.1	12.5	2.4	0.5

[a] Excludes households without a wage earner and retirement pensioners.
Source: Ministry of Agriculture, Fisheries and Food (1984), table 12.

Even the demand for goods that are often regarded as **necessities** (like health care) can vary systematically with income, though not all such demands do. For example, the demand for salt appears to be rather constant in comparisons between the demands of different income groups. A 'necessity' is presumably necessary *for* something but never make the mistake of supposing that the demand for 'necessities' is not affected by either price or income.

Income Distribution

Although the distribution of income will not affect an *individual's* demand for goods (other than through the level of income), it does affect aggregate demands for entire communities. Thus two societies with identical total incomes may have different degrees of inequality in their income distributions, and this can affect the community demands. How this is so is explained in a later section on individual and group demands.

SAQ 3.3

(a) Which changes in the following could never, ever, cause the demand curve for Scotch WHISKY to move: the price of Scotch, the price of gin, getting divorced, joining a church, getting a rise in salary, having children, becoming an alcoholic, contracting cirrhosis of the liver, the price of dry ginger? Only one is the answer – but which one?

(b) Which of the following do you suppose to be normal goods and which inferior: health care, butter, coffée, margarine, manufactured cakes, tea?

(c) Which of the following are substitutes and which complements: fish and meat, bread and butter, cabbage and broccoli, shoes and shoe polish, theatre shows and television shows, tobacco and matches, Scotch and dry ginger, attendance at university and books.

Demography

Evidently the total demand for a product depends upon how many people there are as potential consumers. Since some products are more demanded by males or females, by children, teenagers, adults or the elderly, by some ethnic groups or others, and so on, the structure of the population can also sometimes represent broad differences in the tastes of different groups when these vary systematically.

Individual and Group Demands

This chapter has illustrated demands by individuals, households and whole communities. Although one begins with individuals in the analysis, much policy interest focuses on the behaviour of groups of people having characteristics in common (for example, living together in a family or household, living in a geographical area, being common purchasers of a particular product), and many of the data used to estimate demand curves and test theories of demand are also available only on a group basis. Consequently one must explore the relationship between the individual and the group demands.

The relationship is perfectly simple: just as the individual demand curve shows the preferred quantity demanded per period at a variety of prices for an individual, so the group demand curve is the relationship between the amounts demanded by all individuals in the relevant group. Figure 3.3 shows how the demands of two individuals for a good X are aggregated to form the group demand curve (the line in the right hand diagram).

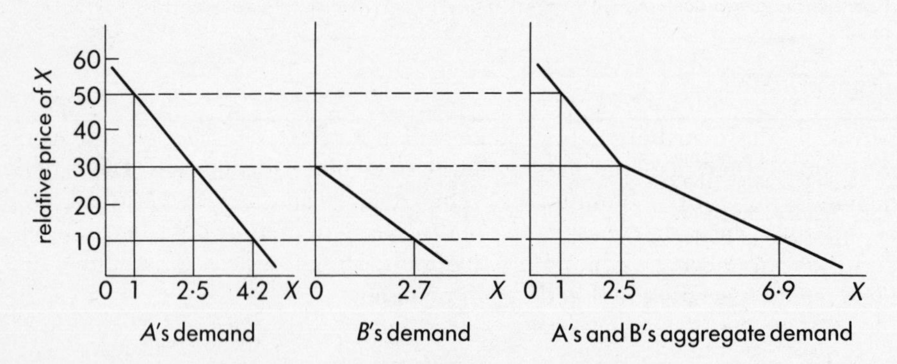

Figure 3.3 Individual and group demands

At a relative price of 50, A demands 1 of X per period and B none, so the group demand curve shows only A's demand (1 of X at price 50). At a price of 30, A demands 2.5 and B is just on the verge of purchasing (but does not), so again the group demand at this price is identical to A's. Below a price of 30, however, B also demands X: for example, at price 10, A demands 4.2 of X and B 2.7 of X, making a group demand of 6.9 of X at that price.

Group demand curves are the horizontal sums of individual demand curves. At each price add the amounts demanded by all the individuals whose demand is to be grouped and plot this total against the relevant price.

One can use this analysis to illustrate the effect of different income distributions on aggregate demand. For simplicity assume that all individuals of type A have an income of £10,000 and all individuals of type B an income of £5000, and that no other differences characterize the As and the Bs. In community 1 there are two As and one B, and it therefore has a total income of £25,000. In community 2 there are one A and three Bs, so it too has a total income of £25,000. If the relative price is 10 in each community, the group quantity demanded in community 1 will be 11.1 of X (4.2 + 4.2 + 2.7) and in community 2 it will be 12.3 of X (4.2 + 2.7 + 2.7 + 2.7). The difference in group demand is due to differences not in group incomes but in the distribution of income within the two communities.

Typically, demand curves are estimated from naturally occurring variations in quantities demanded and the factors affecting demand. A wide range of variation is not always available to determine the whole length of the demand curve in such 'natural experiments'. Since for many purposes one is concerned only with the effects of relatively small changes in the environmental stimuli affecting demand behaviour, this is not a great handicap. Sometimes, however, the estimated relationships may be *extrapolated* into regions where no observations are available. Such extrapolations are simply the best guess one can make about the shape of the demand curve in such regions, and you will meet some cases where this has been necessary in later chapters.

SAQ 3.4

Consider the group demand curve shown in figure 3.4 of a community's weekly demand for sheep meat.

(a) What quantity will be demanded at prices £8, £7, £4 and £1?

(b) What is the total weekly expenditure on sheep meat when 300 kg, 900 kg and 1200 kg are purchased?

(c) What is the maximum amount the community is willing to pay for 300 kg, 900 kg and 1200 kg of sheep meat? (The answers are not the same as those to (b), but can you see why?)

(d) Suppose the sellers of sheep meat to the community required the community to pay £200 for the privilege of buying sheep meat (a kind of licence fee) and then permitted individuals to buy as much as they liked at £7 per kilogram. How much would they buy?

(e) How much would they now be spending on sheep meat per week?

(f) Suppose sheep meat suppliers supply another community whose demand is precisely half that of the previous community at each price. What are the aggregate quantities demanded in the two communities at £7, £5 and £1 per kilogram?

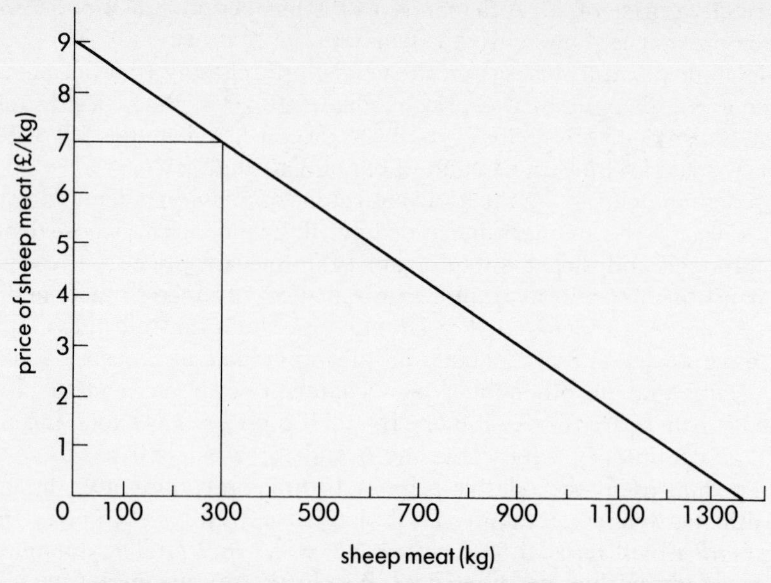

Figure 3.4 A community's weekly demand for sheep meat

What You Should Understand Now

The meaning and interpretation of the law of demand.
The wide variety of behaviour that is observed to be consistent with this behavioural generalization.
The idea of relative price in the law of demand.
The idea of rates of consumption or purchase through time.
Determinants of demand: tastes, prices of related goods, income, the distribution of income and demography.
That the ideas of 'necessity' and 'luxury' do not invalidate the law of demand.
The derivation of group from individual demands.

4

Elasticities of Demand

For many purposes it is not enough to know that there is a negative relationship between price and the rate of consumption or purchase, or a positive (sometimes negative) relationship between the rate of consumption and other determinants of demand. This is, after all, only *qualitative* knowledge, that tells you the *direction* of response to a change in one of the factors affecting demand. It is not *quantitative*, telling you the *size* of the responsiveness. What one often needs is a quantitative measure of the responsiveness of behaviour to these environmental factors. For example you may, with respect to price changes alone, wish to know what effect – but precisely – a 5 per cent increase in value added tax will have on the demand, expenditure and tax revenue of a taxed good; or you may wish to know the precise effect on charitable giving of making charitable donations deductible against income tax; the effect on the price of agricultural goods of a 10 per cent reduction in crops; the effect on the demand for imported cars of a 10 per cent tariff; the effect on food consumption by the poor of a 20 per cent increase in social security benefits; the effect on the demand for home produced goods of an increase of 10 per cent in the price of foreign produced goods; the effect on the demand for places in universities of a 10 per cent increase in fees or reduction in public grants; the effect on the demand for medical care of providing free services; the effect on the demand for owner occupied housing of a 5 per cent increase in interest rates. Similarly the quantification of changes in demand due to other environmental parameters like income, information, other prices and so on is a major policy interest: indeed most practical policy making is crucially dependent upon having some empirical knowledge of these responses.

In economics this responsiveness goes by the name of **elasticity**. This chapter explores the concepts of price elasticity, income elasticity and cross elasticity. You will also meet some of the statistical results that economists have obtained without, however, going into the statistical details of how they were obtained. At this stage the general idea is to introduce you to what can be done rather than explain how to do it, which is a topic in economic statistics and econometrics.

The Importance of Proportionate Changes

In figure 4.1 you can see a demand curve for potatoes (for simplicity taken to be a straight line). You may think that the slope of the demand curve would give a pretty good measure of the responsiveness of the demand for potatoes to price changes. For example, if the price is initially 100p and the rate of consumption is 2.5 kg per week, a fall in price to 25p causes consumption to rise to 5 kg a week. The *change* in quantity is 2.5 kg and the *change* in price is −75 p. The ratio of these two changes is 2.5/−75.0 = −0.03 (that is, bc/−ab on figure 4.1). The **slope** of a curve is, by convention, defined as the ratio of the change in the variable on the vertical axis to the change in the variable on the horizontal axis. Thus the ratio calculated here is the *inverse* of the conventional slope. The ratio of changes is negative because it has been assumed that demand for potatoes increases as their price falls.

The slope measures the steepness of the demand curve. The smaller the (absolute value of the) ratio calculated (or the larger the absolute value of the slope) the steeper the curve and the less responsive consumption is to changes in price. This measure of the responsiveness of demand is, however, fatally flawed by the fact that it is crucially dependent on the *units* used to measure price and quantity. Had one used pounds (sterling) instead of pence, the responsiveness would have worked out at 2.5/−0.75=−3.3. Had one used pence for price but pounds (weight) instead of kilograms, the responsiveness would have worked out at 5.5/−75.0=−0.07.

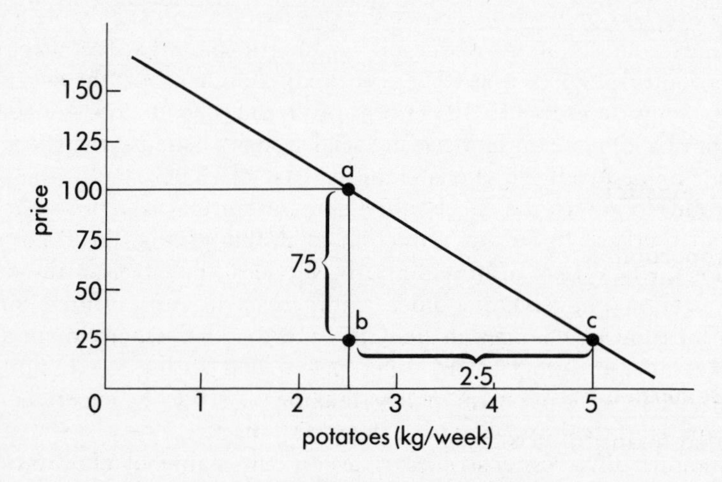

Figure 4.1 Slope of the demand curve as a measure of the responsiveness of demand

How can one arrive at a measure of the responsiveness of behaviour that is independent of the units in which the response (for example consumption rates) and the stimulus (for example price changes) are themselves measured?

The standard procedure is by taking *proportionate* changes in each. Accordingly, the responsiveness of demand to price changes is defined as

$$\text{responsiveness} = \frac{\text{proportionate change in demand}}{\text{proportionate change in price}}$$

Using this measure, the responsiveness of the demand for potatoes as the price falls from 100 pence to 25 is

$$\frac{2.5/2.5}{-\,75/100} = -\,1.33$$

or, using pounds sterling instead of pence:

$$\frac{2.5/2.5}{-0.75/1.00} = -\,1.33$$

or, using pounds (weight) instead of kilograms:

$$\frac{5.5/5.5}{-75/100} = -\,1.33$$

Thus the responsiveness of demand to changes in any measurable part of the environment that affects behaviour – that is, elasticity – is always defined in proportionate terms. This makes it independent of the units in which the variables on the vertical and horizontal axes are measured.

Price Elasticity

The **price elasticity of demand** can be put in more than one way:

the proportionate change in quantity demanded / the proportionate change in price

or

$$\frac{\text{change in quantity demanded}}{\text{original quantity demanded}} \Big/ \frac{\text{change in price}}{\text{original price}}$$

or, using capital Greek delta Δ to signify 'change in', and with X for quantity and P_X for price,

$$\frac{\Delta X}{X} \Big/ \frac{\Delta P_X}{P_X}$$

Let η_X (Greek eta) stand for the price elasticity of demand for a good X. Then, rearranging,

$$\eta_X = \frac{\Delta X}{\Delta P_X} \frac{P_X}{X}$$

Consider figure 4.2. What is the value of Δx for a price fall from £10 to £9? Using the definition,

$$\eta_X = \frac{+10}{-1} \frac{+10}{+20} = -5.0$$

Or consider a fall from £6 to £5:

$$\eta_X = \frac{+10}{-1} \frac{+6}{+60} = -1.0$$

Again, consider a fall from £2 to £1:

$$\eta_X = \frac{+10}{-1} \frac{+2}{+100} = -0.2.$$

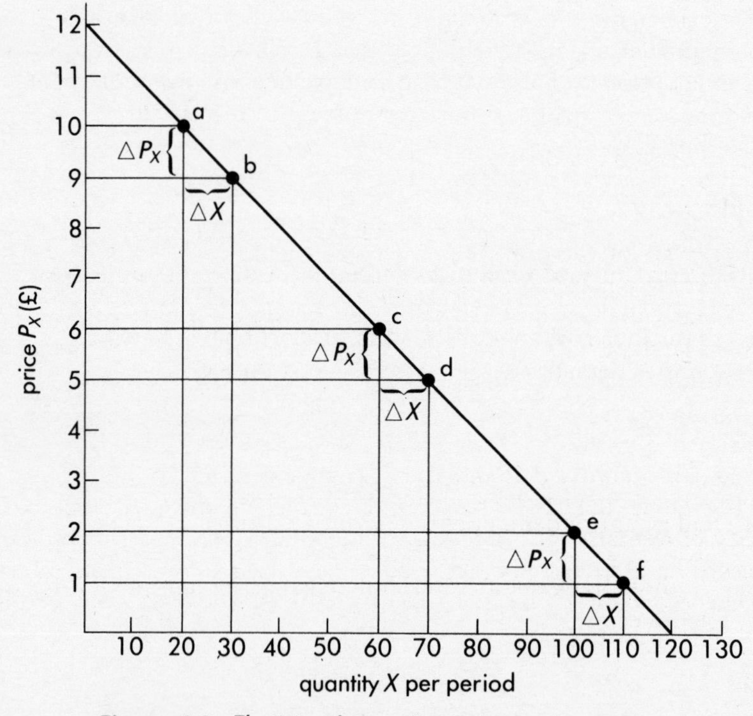

Figure 4.2 Elasticity along a linear demand curve

Two things strike one immediately: the price elasticity is consistently a negative number, and it is not constant along the demand curve. In fact, for a linear (straight line) demand curve such as that in figure 4.2, even though the *slope* of the curve is constant ($\Delta P_X / \Delta X = -0.1$ in the figure) the elasticity approaches zero as we move down the curve. η_X must always be negative for negatively sloped demand curves (whether straight lines or not) because a *fall* in price always induces an *increase* in quantity or a *rise* in price induces a *decrease* in quantity.

The variability of the elasticity along the curve warns one against making comparisons between demands for different goods in terms of one being more or less elastic than the other. Such comparisons should be made only at stated prices.

Instead of considering falls in price, consider some price rises: from £1 to £2, £5 to £6 and £9 to £10. In the case of a rise from £1 to £2,

$$\eta_X = \frac{-10}{+1} \quad \frac{1}{110} = -0.091$$

rather than −0.2 as for the fall in price from £2 to £1. In the case of a rise from £5 to £6,

$$\eta_X = \frac{-10}{+1} \quad \frac{5}{70} = -0.714$$

instead of −1.0 for the price fall. In the case of a rise from £9 to £10,

$$\eta_X = \frac{-10}{+1} \quad \frac{9}{30} = -3.0$$

instead of −5.0 for the price fall.

The differences just observed are often puzzling to beginners. What is their source? Clearly the *slope* of the demand curve is the same for a price rise as for a price fall. The slope is $\Delta P_X / \Delta X$, the inverse of the term in the definition of price elasticity. In figure 4.2, this slope is constant at −0.1. The apparent anomalies must arise therefore from the second part of the elasticity definition, P_X / X. And it is clear that they do: for *discrete* price and quantity changes the elasticity as measured will vary according to whether price rises or falls. Since one is measuring along the arcs ab, cd and ef, this measure is termed the **arc elasticity of demand**. It is a feature of the arc elasticity that the measure will vary according to whether one is looking at price rises or price falls. Because of this, some economists take the average of the two: this is the average arc elasticity.

SAQ 4.1

For the following demand data, calculate the price elasticities (a) for price falls from £9 to £8, £7 to £6, £5 to £4, £3 to £2 and £1 to £0 and (b) for price rises from £0 to £1, £2 to £3 etc.

P_X	10	9	8	7	6	5	4	3	2	1	0
X	10	14	18	22	26	30	34	38	42	46	50

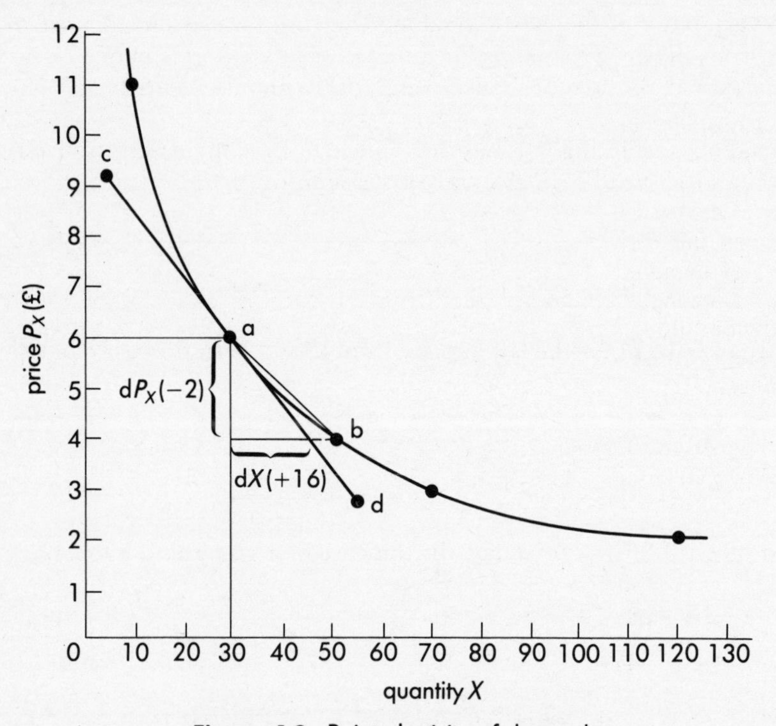

Figure 4.3 Point elasticity of demand

A measure that gives the same answer for both price rises and price falls is the **point elasticity of demand**. This is defined for very small changes in price and is commonly used in theoretical and mathematical economics. Consider figure 4.3. This demand curve is not linear with a constant slope, but has a continuously changing slope.

Suppose that the current price of X is £6 per unit and that the rate of consumption is 30 of X per period. To find the point elasticity of demand, instead of measuring the arc elasticity between points such as a and b, compute dX/dP_X at point a and then multiply by P_X/X as before. The formula for point elasticity is therefore

$$\text{point } \eta_X = \frac{dX}{dP_X}\frac{P_X}{X}$$

where the symbol d denotes a note of change at one particular *point* on the demand curve, compared with Δ which relates to the *arc* connecting *two* points on the curve. At point a,

$$\text{point } \eta_X = \frac{16}{-2}\frac{6}{30} = -1.60$$

The point elasticity is the elasticity usually computed in statistical demand studies.

Case Study 4.1 Energy Demand Price Elasticities in the USA

With the rapidly increasing price of energy sources, particularly oil, much policy interest has focused on ways of conserving its use, partly (in the case of imported and exported energy sources) to estimate effects on balances of payments and partly because of concern over the rate of depletion of naturally occurring energy sources. Clearly one important factor determining the rate of use is price, and the price elasticity of demand becomes an important parameter in assessing the extent to which price changes will reduce quantity demanded.

Joskow and Baughman (1976) have estimated price elasticities of demand in the United States for gas, oil, electricity and coal. Table 4.1 shows their results for two main types of user (residential and commercial on the one hand and industrial on the other). They also distinguished between short run and long run elasticities. (These results are for constant elasticity demand curves (to be discussed later) but for the moment you can imagine them to be the elasticities at the prices of 1968.)

Table 4.1 Energy price elasticities in the USA 1968–72

	Residential and commercial users		*Industrial users*	
	Short run	*Long run*	*Short run*	*Long run*
Gas	−0.15	−1.01	−0.07	−0.81
Oil	−0.18	−1.12	−0.11	−1.32
Electricity	−0.19	−1.00	−0.11	−1.28
Coal	not computed	not computed	−0.10	−1.14

It is striking that the elasticity of demand for all these sources is rather low in the short run – in this case, showing the average reaction within a year of a price change. Thus, in the short term, expenditure rises if price rises. In the longer run, however, as households and firms can adapt their equipment in the light of changing prices, the response is much larger and expenditure generally falls in response to a price rise. This greater responsiveness of quantity demanded in the longer run is sometimes termed the **second law of demand** as it seems to be a general phenomenon – the more time one has to adjust to a price change, the more completely one can adjust. A homely example of the effect can be seen in motoring habits. In response to a higher petrol price you can, in the short run, make fewer trips by car. In the longer run not only can you make fewer trips but you can purchase a car with a smaller engine capacity when the time comes to replace the existing one. Hence your demand for petrol falls by more when you have made the longer term adjustment to higher prices.

P.J. Joskow and M.L. Baughman (1976) 'The future of the US Nuclear energy industry', *Bell Journal of Economics* **7**(1) 3–32.

Elasticity and Expenditure

You saw in chapter 3 that expenditure varies along a linear (straight line) demand curve. It has, in fact, a systematic relationship with the price elasticity of demand. Table 4.2 gives an example of a linear demand relationship. As can readily be seen, the total expenditure per week of this individual (or group) is the product of price and quantity, shown in the third column. The fourth column shows the (point) elasticity of demand. To check your understanding of this, do SAQ 4.2 before going any further.

Table 4.2 Demand elasticity and total expenditure

Price P_X (£)	*X (per week)*	*Total expenditure (£ per week)*	*Point elasticity*
10	0	0	$-\infty$
9	10	90	−9.0
8	20	160	−4.0
7	30	210	−2.3
6	40	240	−1.5
5	50	250	−1.0
4	60	240	−0.67
3	70	210	−0.43
2	80	160	−0.25
1	90	90	−0.11
0	100	0	−0.00

SAQ 4.2

The relationship between price and quantity shown in table 4.2 can be represented by the equation $X = 100 - 10P_X$. By differentiation or from a plot of the data, $dX/dP_X = -10$. Given the data for P_X and X in table 4.2, this enables one readily to calculate η at each price and you may use this result in tackling the following questions.

(a) Given the demand equation $X = 100 - 10P_X$ what is X when $P_X = 9.5$, 8.6, 5.2 and 0.5?

(b) What is the point elasticity when $P_X = 9.0$, 9.5 and 5.5?

Now look at what happens to expenditure as price falls. It rises to a maximum at $P = £5$ when total expenditure is £250. Thereafter it falls to zero as price falls further. Now look at the relationship between expenditure and price elasticity. When the elasticity is high, total expenditure rises as price falls. 'High' elasticity means 'more negative' than −1. When elasticity is equal to −1 (termed **unit elasticity**), total expenditure is constant, neither rising nor falling. When elasticity is 'low' (less negative than −1), total expenditure falls as price falls.

It is common to classify price elasticities in the following fashion:

between $-\infty$ and −1	elastic
equal to −1	unit elasticity
between −1 and 0	inelastic

In the elastic sections of a demand curve, falls in price lead to greater expenditure, so that people respond by spending more. Sellers will receive more, so in this region both expenditure (by consumers) and revenue (of sellers) rise as price falls and fall as price rises. The increase in expenditure or revenue is called **marginal expenditure** or **marginal revenue**. Hence, in this region, marginal expenditure and marginal revenue are positive.

In the inelastic region of the demand curve, price falls lead to lower expenditure and revenue – a *negative* marginal expenditure and a *negative* marginal revenue. When the elasticity is equal to −1, expenditure is constant and so marginal expenditure (revenue) is zero. The relationship between elasticity and marginal expenditure is shown in figure 4.4. Here the demand curve is divided into its elastic and inelastic sections, with a point of unit elasticity where the sections meet (half way along its length). At a price of £7, 30 of X are bought, giving a total expenditure of £210 (or receipts of £210 to sellers). The increase in expenditure as price rises from £7.00 to £7.10 is £210.00 − £205.90 = £4.10, as shown by the *marginal* expenditure curve.

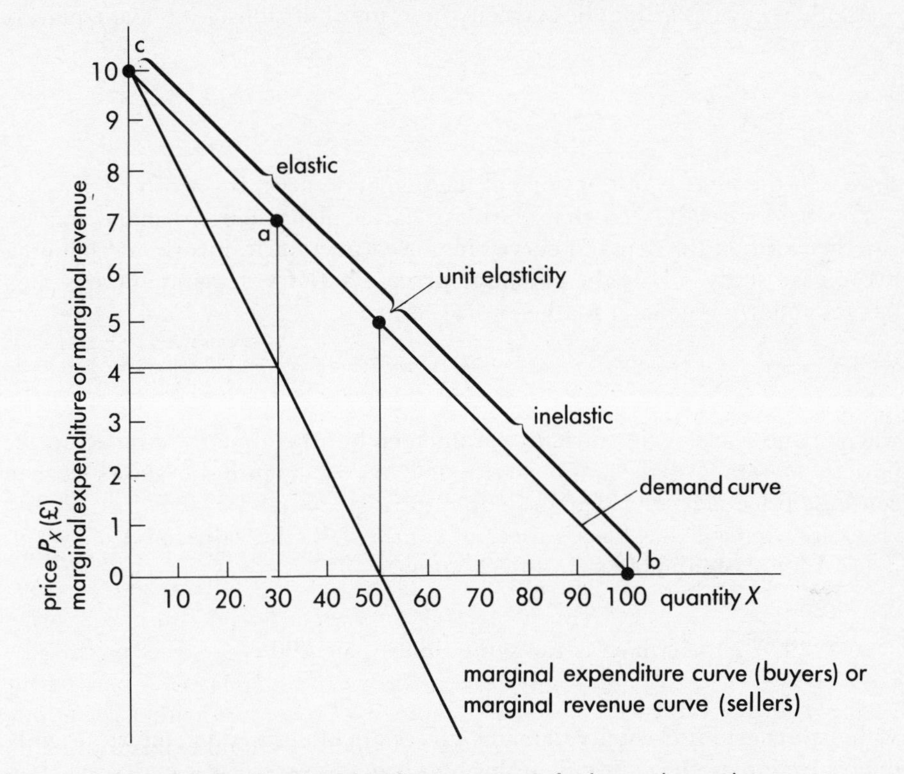

Figure 4.4 Elastic and inelastic sections of a linear demand curve

An easy geometrical method of calculating the point elasticity at any point on a linear demand curve is simply to take the length of the curve to the right of the point and divide it by the length of the curve to its left (and put a minus sign in front of it). Thus in figure 4.4, at $P_X = 7$, if you calulate (−)ab/ac you get −2.3. (Try this for yourself.)

SAQ 4.3

(a) For the linear demand curve $X = 100 - 5P_X$ what is total expenditure at P_X = £20, £10, £5?
(b) For the non-linear demand curve $X = 100/P_X$, what is total expenditure at P_X = £20, £10, £5?
(c) If price falls, total spending on that good must fall and, hence, so must sellers' revenue. Right?

The general mathematical form of linear demand curves appears as

$$X = a - bP_X$$

where X is the dependent variable, P_X is its price, and a and b are constant **parameters** (or given values) corresponding to the intercept of the demand curve on the quantity axis and the inverse of the slope of the curve respectively. For example, the equation corresponding to the demand curve in table 4.2 and figure 4.4 was $X = 100 - 10P_X$.

Another way of writing the elasticity in terms of the linear demand equation is

$$\eta_X = -\frac{P_X}{X}b$$

since $-b$, the inverse of the slope of the demand curve, is $\mathrm{d}X/\mathrm{d}P_X$.

You have already seen that elasticity varies along linear demand curves. Another form of the demand curve often used in empirical work in economics (as in case study 4.1) is the **constant price elasticity** demand curve, which has the following general mathematical form:

$$X = aP_X^{-b}$$

where a and b are again constant parameters, but this time P_X is raised to the power $-b$ rather than simply multiplied by $-b$. Figure 4.5 shows such a constant price elasticity demand curve for $a = 200$ and $b = 2$. You should check for yourself that for a variety of values of P_X the values of X shown in figure 4.5 are obtainable from the equation

$$X = 200\ P_X^{-2} \text{ or (which is the same thing) } X = 200\ \frac{1}{P_X^2}$$

Although constant elasticity demand curves are often used in empirical work, the restriction on the elasticity in this way is not as severe as it may seem. It is usually the case that available data permit estimation of the elasticity only for a relatively small portion of the demand curve – that for which variable price data actually exist. It may therefore be quite possible to obtain a good estimate of elasticity on the assumption that it is constant *in this region*. The danger lies in extrapolating the constant elasticity outside this region: the further outside it one goes, the more arbitrary the restriction will become.

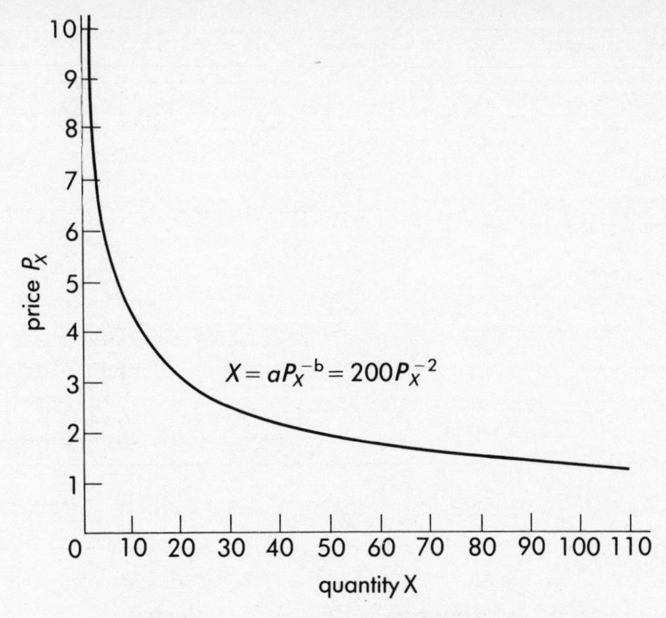

Figure 4.5 Current price elasticity demand curve

SAQ 4.4

Measure the point elasticity of demand by the geometrical method at a variety of prices of your choice on figure 4.5. What do you notice?

To round off this discussion of the price elasticity of demand, case study 4.2 reports some estimates of price elasticities for food in Britain between the two world wars. As you may expect, for broad categories of food (as distinct from particular brands of similar foods) the elasticities are fairly low.

Case Study 4.2 Price Elasticities for Food in Britain 1920–38

Richard Stone (1984 Nobel prize winner for economics) and his colleagues made an extensive study (1954) of the demand for food in Britain between the wars. They made estimates (table 4.3) of the point price elasticities using constant price elasticity formulations of the demand functions, with the price of each good defined relative to the prices of all other consumer goods and services.

Where possible, the results in table 4.3 take account of the presence of substitutes and complements. Of the total number of food commodities studied (36) all save three showed a negative price elasticity, as expected. The remaining three had (contrary to the law of demand) positive price elasticities but they were not statistically reliable. Nearly all the price elasticities lay in the range –1 to 0. In general, the demand for food seems price inelastic.

R. Stone *et al.* (1954) *Measurement of Consumers' Expenditure and Behaviour in the UK 1920–38*, vol. I, Cambridge, Cambridge University Press.

Table 4.3 Price elasticities for food

Commodity	*Price elasticity*
Flour	−0.79
Cakes and biscuits	−0.74
Beef and veal (home produced)	−0.41
Mutton and lamb (home produced)	−1.47
Pork	−0.67
Imported canned meat	−1.05
Fresh fish	−0.57
Butter	−0.43
Potatoes	−0.56
Apples	−1.67
Oranges	−0.97
Sugar	−0.44
Tea	−0.26

Income Elasticity

The **income elasticity of demand** is defined as follows:

the proportionate change in quantity demanded / the proportionate change in income

or, in symbols,

$$\varepsilon_X = \frac{\Delta X}{\Delta Y} \; \frac{Y}{X}$$

where ε_X (Greek epsilon) represents the income elasticity of demand for X, and Y stands for money income of the individual (for individual demand curves) or the group (for group demand curves).

Whereas price elasticity is always negative in statistically reliable studies because demand curves are negatively sloped, ε_X may be positive or negative depending on whether the X in question is normal or inferior. A normal good has a *positive income elasticity* since a change in income will induce a change in demand in the same direction, whereas an inferior good has a *negative income elasticity* since changes in income and demand will move in opposite directions.

Figure 4.6 shows how the consumption of a good X behaves as income varies. For this illustrative good, there are three ranges. In range I, as income rises, so does consumption; so X is normal, having a positive income elasticity. In range II, between points a and b (incomes Y_a and Y_b) on the curve, rising (or falling) income does not affect consumption; so the income elasticity is zero. In range III, rising income implies falling consumption; so the good is inferior in this range. Note that the effects of income *alone* are considered here: implicitly one is taking prices and all other determinants of demand as

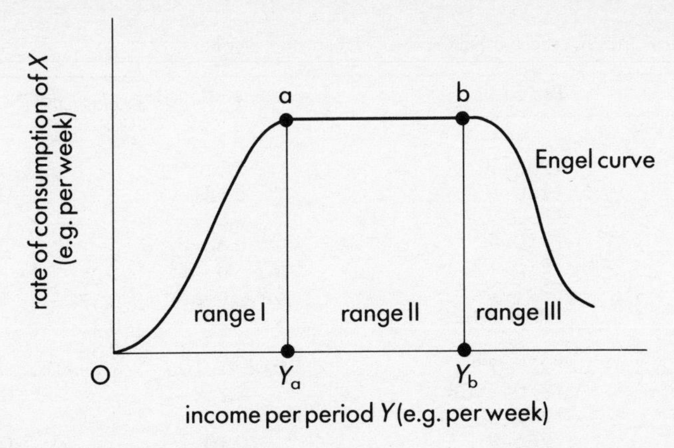

Figure 4.6 Engel curve showing positive, zero and negative income elasticities

constant in order to focus on the effect of income alone. Not all goods will display the same pattern: some generally have negative income elasticities, some zero and some positive. All goods taken together have a positive income elasticity (income has to be spent on *something*, and you can, if you want, treat 'savings' as a good), so the *average* good is normal. However, this does not deny that some goods (like margarine) are generally inferior and others (like salt) have very low income elasticities.

The curve in figure 4.6 is termed an **Engel curve** after Ernst Engel (1821–96), a famous German statistician who made extensive studies of the relationship between income and consumption.

SAQ 4.5

A linear Engel curve is given by the formula $X = -10 + 2Y$, where Y stands for money income.

(a) Make a table of X values for Y = 0, £5, £10, £20, £100.
(b) What is ε_X as income rises from £6 to £7, £10 to £11 and £100 to £110?

Case study 4.3 explores some links between price and income elasticities, showing how the latter can affect the share of taxes paid by different income groups according to their consumption of particular goods.

Case Study 4.3 Sumptuary Taxes on Smokers and Drinkers

Sumptuary taxes are designed to discourage consumption of goods that are regarded as potentially harmful (such as tobacco and alcohol). Unfortunately, such goods often have a low price elasticity, which implies that taxes which raise their prices (*indirect* taxes) will typically lead to an increase in expenditure upon them. This is a useful feature for governments seeking to raise revenue. However, it can lead to injustice if such goods also have a low income elasticity, for the relatively poor will spend proportionately more on such goods and hence bear proportionately more of the tax burden.

Table 4.4 Price and income elasticities for tobacco and alcohol

Country	*Period*	*Income elasticity*	*Price elasticity*
Tobacco			
Austria	1950–9	0.12	−0.95
Finland	1950–9	0.13	−0.41
France	1950–9	0.83	−0.54
Italy	1950–9	0.48	−0.82
UK	1870–1938	0.21 to 0.41	−0.12 to −0.23
UK	1951–67	0.47 to 0.70	−0.60 to −0.83
UK	1957–68	0.30	−1.00
Beer			
Canada	1956–71	0.05 to 0.06	−0.08 to −0.18
UK	1870–1938	0.35	−0.59
USA	1947–60	0.40	−0.50
USA	1956–9	0.40	−0.90
Spirits			
Canada	1956–71	0.03 to 0.31	−0.12 to −0.83
UK	1870–1938	0.69	−0.57
USA	1947–60	1.50	−2.00
Wine			
Canada	1956–71	0.11 to 0.14	−0.12 to −0.23
USA	1947–60	0.6	−1.60
Alcoholic drinks together			
Australia	1956–66	0.81	−0.39

McClure and Thirsk (1978) surveyed available evidence on price and income elasticities of demand for tobacco and liquor (table 4.4).

Although there is substantial variation both between countries and over time, the overwhelming bulk of the evidence clearly indicates relatively low price and income elasticities. The implication is that tax policies will have a substantially less than proportionate 'deterrent' effect and that a useful revenue raiser for the government can be used only at the cost of imposing a burden that falls relatively heavily on the poor compared with the rich, who will spend a smaller proportion of their incomes on these low income elastic goods.

C. E. McClure and W. R. Thirsk (1978) 'The inequity of taxing iniquity: a plea for reduced sumptuary taxes in developing countries', *Economic Development and Cultural Change*, **26**, 487–503.

SAQ 4.6

(a) You have seen that the *average* good must be normal. In other words, the weighted sums of all measure elasticities must seem to unity. Prove this for just two goods X and Z, and assume that all income Y is spent on X and Z.

(b) Let there be two goods, X and Z, representing consumption in general this year (X) and consumption in general next year (Z). Suppose there is zero inflation, so that $P_X = P_Z$ (the prices of goods this year are the same as their prices next year). Suppose individuals save 10 per cent of this year's income in order to be able to consume Z next year and that the income elasticity of demand for X is known to be 0.8. What is the income elasticity of demand for Z (= savings)?

Cross Elasticities

The **cross elasticity of demand** is defined as

the proportionate change in the quantity demanded of one good / the proportionate change in the price of another

or, in symbols,

$$\eta_{XZ} = \frac{\Delta X}{\Delta P_Z} \frac{P_Z}{X}$$

where η_{XZ} is the elasticity of demand for X as the price of Z changes.

Figure 4.7 shows some possible relationships between the quantity demanded of X and the price of Z. Function A shows the demand for X to rise as P_Z rises, implying that X and Z are *substitutes*. Function B shows that the demand for X falls as P_Z rises, implying that X and Y are *complements*. Function C indicates no relationship between the demand for X and P_Z.

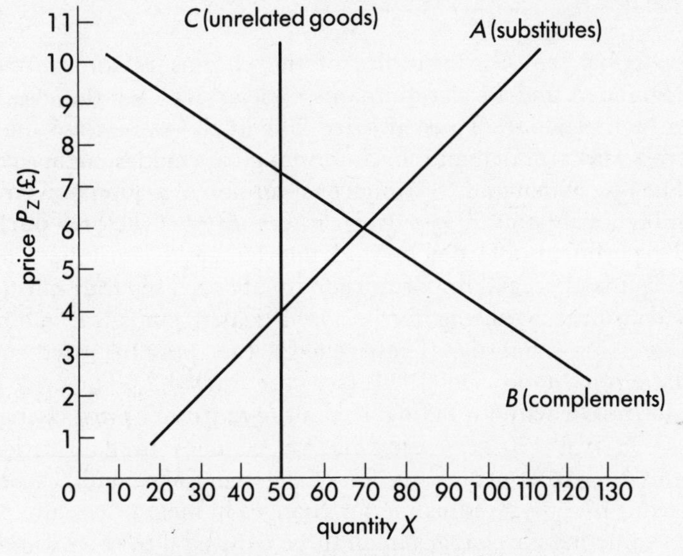

Figure 4.7 Cross elasticities of demand

It should be clear that the cross elasticity of demand for substitutes is *positive*, the cross elasticity of demand for complements is *negative*, and the cross elasticity of demand for unrelated goods is *zero*.

SAQ 4.7

Suppose that the cross elasticity of demand for two goods is minus infinity. What would you infer about the two goods?

Case Study 4.4 Cross Elasticities of Demand for Food in the UK 1920–38

The study by Richard Stone *et al.* (1954) of which part was reported in case study 4.2, examined cross elasticities for several commodities. Those for butter are shown in table 4.5.

Table 4.5 Cross price elasticities of demand for butter

Own price elasticity	*Elasticity with respect to price of flour*	*Elasticity with respect to price of cakes and biscuits*	*Elasticity with respect to price of meat*
−0.43	−0.23	0.59	0.56

These results accord with intuition. The use of butter in home baking is reflected in the negative elasticity of the demand for butter with respect to the price of flour: they are obviously complementary. Home baking is a substitute for buying cakes and biscuits; hence the positive elasticity with respect to cakes and biscuits is also expected. Similarly it turns out that meat and butter are substitute sources of fat.

Ceteris Paribus

So far as possible, empirical studies of the various relationships between quantity demanded and its determinants seek to evaluate the effect of each determinant acting alone. Thus, if price falls at the same time that income rises, the gross effect on demand for a normal good could be either positive or negative. The law of demand, relating consumption of a good to its own price, holds unambiguously only if *other things remain the same* (**ceteris paribus**). In the natural experiments afforded by studying changes in consumption patterns as they occur, it is of crucial importance to isolate each separate effect, holding the others constant, by using fairly sophisticated statistical methods like multiple regression analysis. These effects can be illustrated using the following data from Stone *et al.* (1954) (see case study 4.2). The price elasticity of demand for butter without taking account of any other price changes in the period 1920–38 was −0.37. Adjusting for changes in flour prices alone increased this to −0.32. Adjusting for changes in cakes and biscuits prices alone reduced it to −0.42. Adjusting for changes in meat prices alone reduced it to −0.38. Adjusting for changes in all three reduced it to − 0.41 and, adding the effects of changes in margarine prices, reduced it further to −0.43. This book will not discuss the statistical problems involved in performing these exercises, but their study is, of course, a major part of any complementary statistical course you may be taking.

You saw in chapter 3 that vegetables and tea appeared to be inferior goods (case study 3.5). That study, however, made no adjustment for other features that might have affected demand. For example, Stone found that, when all feasible adjustments had been made, margarine was not significantly inferior and the only other really inferior good seemed to be condensed milk.

Economists and statisticians today rarely make simply tabulations of variables such that a relationship between two factors alone, say income and imports, are examined. There are far too many interdependencies between many variables for that to yield much insight into cause and effect. Case study 4.5 provides an example of the results of a sophisticated study of recent British demand for imports – a controversial topic that has much engaged economic planners in Britain. As before the results are presented without discussion of the technicalities of how they were arrived at.

Case Study 4.5 UK Demand for Imports

In order to make projections of future levels of imports according to a variety of scenarios depicting different assumptions about future inflation, tax rates and so on, Barker (1976) calculated elasticities of demand for UK imports with respect to total demand for a commodity (indicating the level of 'activity', reflecting a hypothesis that as incomes rise greater variety is demanded, which may be largely supplied from overseas), personal after tax income (after allowing for inflation), and the price of imported goods (including tariffs) relative to the price of domestically produced goods. (Barker is a member of the University of Cambridge Growth Project team studying medium term prospects (4–6 years ahead).)

Table 4.6 Elasticities of demand for UK imports

Commodity group	*Elasticity of imports with respect to:*		
	Total demand for the commodity	*Real personal disposable income*	*Relative price*
Food, drink and tobacco	+1.12	+0.74	−0.13
Raw materials	+1.16	+0.43	−0.11
Fuels	+1.91	+0.93	−0.44
Manufactures of which:	+2.00	+0.75	−1.37
Chemicals	+1.49	+0.67	−0.91
Engineering products	+2.40	+0.78	−1.43
Motor vehicles	+2.68	+1.22	−1.44
Metal goods	+1.22	+0.44	−1.31
Textiles	+1.00	+0.62	−2.01
Leather, clothing etc.	+3.44	+1.56	−3.65
Paper and board	+1.41	+0.41	−1.37
Total	+1.64	+0.78	−0.87

Some results are contained in table 4.6. The first column gives the response of import demand when total demand for each good rises by 1 per cent, without taking account of further repercussions on other prices, employment and so on that may also take place. The second colum shows how import demand increases with a 1 per cent increase in after tax income, including estimated feedback effects from changes in other prices, employment and so on. In aggregate a 1 per cent increase in real income increases imports less than proportionately (by 0.78 per cent) but motor vehicles and leather goods more than proportionately (by 1.22 and 1.56 per cent respectively). The third column shows a wide dispersion in import price elasticities which are especially elastic in manufactures and, within these, in engineering goods, cars, textiles and leathers, clothing etc. These elasticities indicate the kind of problem to be faced by UK producers as the UK economy changes. Increasing wealth in the UK will have a more than proportionate effect on imports of cars and clothing; a rising exchange rate, which reduces the price to UK residents of overseas products, will have a more than proportionate effect on most manufactures, especially cars, textiles and leather, clothing etc.

T. S. Barker (1976) 'Imports', in T. S. Barker (ed.) *Economic Structure and Policy with Applications to the British Economy*, London, Chapman and Hall.

Other Demand Elasticities

Elasticities can in principle be defined and sometimes measured empirically between *any* determinant of demand and the rate of consumption. This chapter has focused on those that are central to all demand studies. Which others may be usefully added will depend on the good, the changing circumstances of the period, and the question one is addressing. For example, for advertised products, the elasticity of demand with respect to advertising might be an important statistic: 'advertising' might be measured by, say, minutes of TV commercials broadcast or advertising expenditures.

Even events which affect tastes can be quantified. An interesting study of cigarette consumption in the USA brings this out and is the final case study of this chapter.

Case Study 4.6 Cigarette Advertising and the Demand for Cigarettes

In 1970 radio and TV cigarette advertisements were banned in the USA in the belief that advertising encouraged smoking. This congressional ban also extended to a free broadcast time subsidy previously given to anti-smoking propaganda, since the Federal Communications Commission requires 'fairness' in the balance of broadcasting on controversial issues (which the FCC declared smoking to be). Hamilton (1972) studied the impact of various determinants of the demand for cigarettes, and some of his results are given in table 4.7. The effect of rising income on annual per caput cigarette consumption was +123.8 cigarettes per person per year (shown not as an elasticity here but as an absolute amount). Relative price increases reduced demand by 10.4 cigarettes. Advertising (corporate advertising expenditure) increased it by 95 cigarettes. The remaining 'scare' variables are the first major publicized report of the harmful affects of smoking in 1953, the Surgeon General's report in 1964 leading to printed warnings on all packets of cigarettes, and the 1968 advent of large volume anti-smoking messages on radio and TV.

Table 4.7 Effect of variables on per cent annual cigarette consumption

	Income	*Price*	*Advertising*	*Health scare 1953–70*	*Health scare 1964–70*	*Health scare 1968–70*
Cigarettes consumed per person per year	+123.8	−10.4	+95.0	−47.2	−252.9	−530.7

The first 'scare' had a relatively small impact – probably mainly on doctors. The second was much larger, 2.7 times bigger than advertising (and in the opposite direction). The third was even more powerful in its effect, 5.6 times bigger than advertising. The combined effect of the anti-smoking propaganda was −830.8 cigarettes per person per year, 8.7 times more powerful than (and in the opposite direction to) the cigarette companies' advertisements.

Hamilton concludes that the congressional ban of 1970 was a highly effective substitute for advertising by the tobacco industry, and that it was very much to the industry's advantage since it banned tobacco enemies' propaganda as well as its friends' (less effective) propaganda.

James L. Hamilton (1972) 'The demand for cigarettes: advertising, the health scare, and the cigarette advertising ban', *Review of Economics and Statistics*, **56**, 401–11.

What You Should Understand Now

The distinction between qualitative and quantitative productions.
The importance of proportionate changes.
How to calculate elasticities of demand.
The definitions of price, income and cross elasticities of demand.
How elasticity varies along demand and Engel curves.
The differences between linear and constant elasticity demand curves.
The meaning of complement and substitute.
Some empirical material relating to demand for energy, food, tobacco and alcohol, imports and cigarettes.

5

Choice, Utility and Utilitarianism

Up to this point you have looked in some detail at qualitative and quantitative aspects of demand. This chapter begins the study of the core of economics as a discipline: *utility theory*. This chapter will introduce you to the basic notions, show how they can be usefully applied in the analysis of social problems and indicate the role they have played in the early development of demand theory. The next two chapters will further develop and apply these ideas and introduce you to two other demand theories.

Choosing between rival theories that purport to account for the same phenomenon is a problem in all sciences. Economics is no exception. In these three chapters the basic phenomenon is the empirically observed downward slope of all demand curves (from left to right). The theoretical task is to explain why this is the case: to provide a theory that predicts what is observed. But before turning to theories of demand you must become familiar with the idea of utility and its measurement.

The Meaning of Utility Measurement

Measurement in general means no more than assigning numbers to things according to some rule. The weakest type of measurement is simply to put things, like bundles of goods and services or characteristics of people, in an order according to a rule stipulating that the numbers simply reflect the order. Table 5.1, for example, contains five goods in somebody's order of preference. Any of the numbers in columns (a) to (e) will do as a measure of the order of preference. These numbers are an **ordinal measure** of the listed goods, and show that the person in question would rank the five alternatives in the order shown.

Table 5.1 Measurement of utility on an ordinal scale

	(a)	*(b)*	*(c)*	*(d)*	*(e)*
1 10% less air pollution	5	5	1 million	0	10
2 New Mercedes	4	4.9	672	−1	9.999
3 Holiday in Spain	3	4.8	499	−2	2
4 More obedient children	2	4.7	498	−3	−2
5 Steak on birthday	1	4.6	0	−4	−2 million

Table 5.1 embodies two basic notions. One is the idea that orders of preference, or the orders in which things will be chosen by somebody, can have numbers attached to them. For example, the idea that Freda Jones would rather see 10 per cent less air pollution than have a new Mercedes can be expressed by giving the more preferred thing a higher number than the less preferred. If all that you want to do is to indicate the order of preference then any numbers will do that preserve the order of preference – that is, that give the more preferred things a higher number than the less preferred.

The second basic notion of table 5.1 is that you can attach the label *utility* to these numbers. So utility theory is any theory that uses numbers to represent a person's or a group's order of preference.

This may seem very obvious to you – as indeed it is. Yet numbers (especially utility numbers) can lead one badly astray. One way in which they can do so is by thinking that, in assigning numbers to things, one can leave behind one's critical faculties. Another is to suppose that things with numbers attached to them (especially perhaps money numbers) are more important than things without such numbers. Assigning numbers is often helpful in analysing problems but, if it leads to a worship of what is 'quantified', it can do much mischief. (You will meet some examples of this later; for example, in chapter 23 when the measurement of the standard of living is discussed).

An easy trap to fall into, having said that 10 per cent pollution was preferred to a new Mercedes and that the numbers, say, 5 and 4 represent this preference, is to suppose that the pollution reduction is 25 per cent better than the car: $[(5 - 4)/4] \times 100 = 25\%$. If one's intention in assigning these numbers was to indicate order only, so that 5 and 4, 5 and 4.9, 1 million and 672, 0 and -1, 10 and 9.999 are all equally acceptable numbers for these two goods, then this sort of statement simply cannot be made. An ordinal measure of utility does not enable us to say that good 1 is x times more preferred to good 2. Nor does it enable us to say whether the *increase* in utility as one receives increasingly preferred goods is rising or falling – only that it is positive.

SAQ 5.1

Which of the following statements is correct?

(a) Utility refers to the numbers assigned to objects of choice indicating preferences.
(b) Utility is a measure of the satisfaction to be had from consuming economic goods.
(c) Utility is happiness.
(d) Utility is the usefulness of things as measured by numbers assigned to them according to a rule.
(e) Utility numbers must always be positive.

A second kind of measure is a little stronger than merely ordinal measurement. Look at table 5.2. Column (a) shows an index for measuring the heat state of water indicated on the left hand side. It happens to go under the name of the centigrade or Celsius scale for temperature. Column (b) presents an alternative scale known as Fahrenheit. Each ranks the states on the left in the same order, but neither enables you to make statements like 'boiling is twice as hot

Table 5.2 Measurement of water temperature

	(a) *Centigrade scale*	(b) *Fahrenheit scale*	(c) *Kelvin scale*
Boiling	100	212	373.15
Hot	80	176	353.15
Warm	60	140	333.15
Cool	50	122	323.15
Freezing	0	32	273.15

as cool'. On scale (a) the index score is indeed twice as high for 'boiling' as for 'cool', but this is not true for scale (b), where 'boiling' appears 1.74 times hotter. These scales do, however, have something in common *in addition to* the fact that they put the heat states on the left in the same order. This is that the two scales are linked by a linear equation of the general form $°F = a + b°C$, where a (not equal to zero) and b are constants:

$$°F = 32 + 1.8\ °C$$

or

$$°C = -17.8 + 0.56\ °F$$

where °F and °C stand for degrees Fahrenheit and centigrade. Each is said to be a *linear transformation* of the other. A kelvin (K) scale has also been added, which is related to °C by the linear equation

$$K = 273.15 + °C$$

If measures are linked by linear rules such as these they yield a stronger form of measurement than merely ordinal ranking. The linear rule for assigning numbers to entities enables one to measure *relative increments* in a way impossible with ordinal scales. For example, on the °C scale, the increase from 'hot' to 'boiling' is 20°C, from 'warm' to 'hot' is 20° and from 'cool' to 'warm' it is 10°. The former two increments are the same and the third is half. On the °F scale, the first two increments are again the same, at 36°, and the third is half, at 18°. On the K scale the first two increments are each 20 and the third is half at 10 (exactly the same as the increments of the °C scale).

Measurement 'up to' a linear transformation thus enables one to say whether intervals between the units of measurement are increasing, decreasing or constant, and such scales are commonly termed **interval scales**. Such scales, therefore, can be used in measuring utility when one seeks to do more than just indicate order of preference and when in particular one wants to say something about the rate of increase or decrease in utility – **marginal utility**, as it is termed.

Table 5.3 Measurement of utility on an interval scale

	Scale A	*Scale B*	*Scale C*	*Scale D*	*Scale E*
5 apples	15	40	5	65	1015
4 oranges	13	36	3	55	1013
3 pears	10	30	0	40	1010
2 bananas	6	22	−4	20	1006
10 grapes	1	12	−9	−5	1001

Table 5.3 shows alternative utility numbers for some goods, each of which is a linear transformation of the other and each of which therefore enables increasing or decreasing marginal utility to be identified. The four scales B, C, D and E are related to scale A by the following linear equations:

$$B = 10 + 2A$$
$$C = -10 + A$$
$$D = -10 + 5A$$
$$E = 1000 + A$$

The linear relationships between these scales – or any others similarly related – ensures that if marginal utility is falling according to one then it falls also according to the others. Thus, if you have 10 grapes and I give you 2 bananas instead, your utility rises by 5 on scale A. If I give you 3 pears instead of 2 bananas, your utility rises by 4 on scale A – the increase in utility is smaller. Marginal utility has fallen. The same is true for scale B (marginal utilities are 10 and 8 respectively), scale C (5 and 4 respectively) and scale D (25 and 20 respectively).

SAQ 5.2

(a) Suppose the utility I derive from various rates of potato consumption is as follows:

Utility	15	25	33	40	46	51	55	58
Potatoes per week (kg)	0.5	1.0	1.5	2.0	2.5	3.0	3.5	4.0

1 Is my marginal utility rising, falling or constant?
2 Suppose all the utility numbers to be doubled. Is my marginal utility rising, falling or constant?
3 Add 5 to each utility number. Is my marginal utility rising, falling or constant?

(b) Suppose that I derive the following utilities from seeing some characteristics of an elderly person altered in the ways specified (with utility units called 'utils' for convenience).

	characteristic	*utils*
1	Increased ability to move around house	5
2	Reduced back pain	7
3	Increased ability to feed self	7
4	Improved vision	5
5	Improved hearing	4

What utility would I get if all five changes were made?

Table 5.4 Measurement of utility on a ratio scale

	A	*B*	*C*	*D*
5 apples	15	0.525	8.460	525
4 oranges	13	0.455	7.332	455
3 pears	10	0.350	5.640	350
2 bananas	6	0.210	3.384	210
10 grapes	1	0.035	0.564	35

Utility measurement can take one more form, called a **ratio scale**, when one is measuring utility as one measures weight, height or distance. With this form of measurement it does not matter whether one uses, for example, grams, ounces, pounds, kilograms or tons for weight so long as each scale is transformable into another by a multiplicative term. Table 5.4 has a set of scales for measuring utility on a ratio scale. One can now say, for example, that 5 apples have 1.5 as much utility as 3 pears *whichever scale is used*. One has also preserved the measurability of marginal utility. The relationship between these scales is multiplicative, of the form

$$B = aA$$

where a (in this case) happens to be 0.035. This stronger form of measurement is termed measurement on a ratio scale since, by rearranging, the constant ratio a is obtained:

$$B/A = a$$

Thus the values on each scale are simply ratios of one another. A common mistake is to suppose that *all* numerical measurement is of this type.

These measurement issues may be summarized by defining two broad kinds: **ordinal measurement** and **cardinal measurement**, with the latter subdivided into measurement on interval and ratio scales:

(a) Ordinal measurement
(b) Cardinal measurement
    1 Interval scale.
    2 Ratio scale.

SAQ 5.3

(a) Why was marginal utility falling in (a2) and (a3) of SAQ 5.2?

Suppose the scales in table 5.5 measure the utility I derive from concert visits per year. Are the statements (b) – (g) true or false?

Table 5.5 Utility indexes for SAQ 5.3

	Utility indexes (utils)				
Visits	*A*	*B*	*C*	*D*	*E*
1	50	100	5	51	102
2	90	180	8	91	182
3	120	240	12	121	242
4	135	270	13	136	272
5	147	294	14	148	296
6	158	316	15	159	318
7	168	336	16	169	338

(b) Scales A and B are equally good measures since B = 2A.

(c) Scales A and C are equally good measures since they rank the number of visits in the same order.

(d) Since scales B and D are related by a linear equation, if marginal utility falls according to one it falls according to the other.

(e) Since scale E is twice as large as scale D, utility is twice as great when E is used.

(f) Six visits per year yield three times the utility of one per year.

(g) Cardinal utility involves a contradiction since, according to scale A, one visit yields 50 utils and two visits 90. Therefore three visits should yield the sum of these, 140 utils, not 120 utils.

Applications of Utility Theory

Utility theory has innumerable applications in all the social sciences. A major one in economics is, as you will see, in demand theory. Before this, however, two case studies illustrate how utility numbers have been used in the non-economic topics of measuring handicap and measuring poverty.

Case Study 5.1 Measuring Handicap in Britain

Societies often seek for the noblest of reasons to help the handicapped to overcome their difficulties. A problem that arises in measuring handicap consists in the many different types of restriction of activity that can arise and their severity, which requires one to make an overall judgement bearing in mind these variations. Formally, the problem is to construct an 'index' to measure the degree of handicap (and, hence, need for support).

These problems are in many ways analogous to the problems of utility theory, though instead of goods one has 'bads' – that is, restricted activities of various kinds. Thus, it seems natural to suppose that as handicap increases, so 'disutility' (as measured by the index of handicap) increases. Moreover there is the question of how to 'add up' different types of restriction (disutility) to calculate the general index (level of disutility). So one is involved with somebody's (or some group's) preferences, assigning numbers to them and interpreting them.

Harris and her associates made an extensive survey (1971) of handicapped people in order to measure their need for help. Degrees of handicap for those not in need of 'special care' were coded as in table 5.6.

Table 5.6 Classification of handicap

Code 1	Subject can perform the activity with no difficulty
Code 2	Subject has difficulty performing the activity but can do it on own
Code 3	Subject cannot perform the activity on own, even with difficulty
Code 4	Subject never does the activity because it is too difficult
Code 5	Subject has difficulty in performing the activity but it is not known whether or not can do it on own

The activities, and the scores attached to each code, were as shown in table 5.7. These are plainly *value judgements*, explicitly (and bravely) stated by the researchers. The 'disutils' are not necessarily those of the persons being assessed but of the assessors. This raises another nice value question: whose preferences ought they to be? Each person was thus assigned an index score for each activity and the total score added to produce the classifications in table 5.8.

Table 5.7 Scores for calculating index of handicap

Activity	*Index score for code*				
	0	*2*	*3*	*4*	*6*
Major items					
1 Getting to or using WC	0	4	6	6	5
2 Doing up buttons and zips	0	4	6	6	5
3 Eating and drinking	0	4	6	6	5
Minor items					
4 Getting in/out of bed	0	2	3	3	2
5 Having bath or all-over wash	0	2	3	3	2
6 Washing hands and face	0	2	3	3	2
7 Putting on shoes and socks/stockings	0	2	3	3	2
8 Other dressing	0	2	3	3	2
9 Combing hair (women) or shaving (men)	0	2	3	3	2

Table 5.8 Classification of handicap index scores

Category		*Example*	*Total index score*	*Estimated number of cases in Great Britain*
Very severe	1–3	'special care' needed	27–36	157,000
Severe	4	probably housebound	18–26	103,000
	5	partially paralysed	12–17	254,000
Appreciable	6	arthritic	6–11	616,000
Minor/no	7	lame, angina	1–5	680,000
	8	able to care for self	0	1,262,000
				3,072,000

For present purposes, the interesting methodological aspect of this study is its assumptions that the disutilities (scores attached to the ability to perform activities) are measured on a *ratio scale* and are *mutually independent*. This implies, for example, not merely that two scores of six are considered equally as bad as four scores of three, but also that there is no complementarity or substitutability: for example, inability to comb hair adds 3 to the score regardless of whether or not one is bed bound. One cannot determine theoretically whether this is a correct assumption to have made: one must appeal to one's own intuition, imagination and experience.

Note that utility theory does not have any ideological commitment to a particular source for identifying the utility scales (e.g. consumers or beneficiaries). That is a political question. The social scientific question is whether preferences (whomever they belong to) can be adequately expressed in a utility index.

A. I. Harris with E. Cox and C. R. W. Smith (1971) *Handicapped and Impaired in Great Britain*, part I, London, HMSO.

Case Study 5.2 An Index of Social Deprivation

As part of his major study of poverty in Britain, Townsend (1979) constructed a summary index of deprivation. Individuals in a national sample taken in 1968–9 were assigned 1 (applicable) or 0 (inapplicable) for each of the following twelve 'deprivation' characteristics (the percentages in brackets show the proportion of the population having that characteristic):

1 Has not had a week's holiday away from home in last 12 months (54 per cent)
2 Adults only: has not had a relative or friend home for a meal or snack in the last 4 weeks (33 per cent)
3 Adults only: has not been out in the last 4 weeks to a relative or friend for a meal or snack (45 per cent)
4 Children only (under 15): has not had a friend to play or to tea in the last 4 weeks (36 per cent)
5 Children only: did not have a party last birthday (57 per cent)
6 No afternoon or evening out for entertainment in last 4 weeks (47 per cent)
7 No fresh meat (including meals out) as many as 4 days a week (19 per cent)
8 Has had one or more days in last fortnight without a cooked meal (7 per cent)
9 No cooked breakfast most days of the week (67 per cent)
10 Household has no refrigerator (45 per cent)
11 No Sunday joint three out of four times (26 per cent)
12 No sole household use of four basic amenities (WC, sink and cold water tap, fixed bath or shower, gas or electric cooker) (21 per cent).

The scores on each characteristic were then added up for each individual.

Note that this is a very simple kind of cardinal utilitarian construct. Not only are the scores in each of the 12 characteristics of the index constant and independent of scores on other characteristics (so having no holiday is not regarded as any worse for those who also never visit friends than for those who do), as was the case with the index of handicap (case study 5.1), but in this case they are 'on' or 'off' variables: the worst you can score is 1 and the best 0, with nothing in between.

Again, whether the weights that *ought* to be applied to each characteristic are unitary (as here) or some other (variable) number is a matter of value judgement. (Are vegetarians 'deprived' by virtue of meatless days; is every deprivation equally serious?) So too is the implicit assumption that the researchers' utils are those that should be used rather than someone else's.

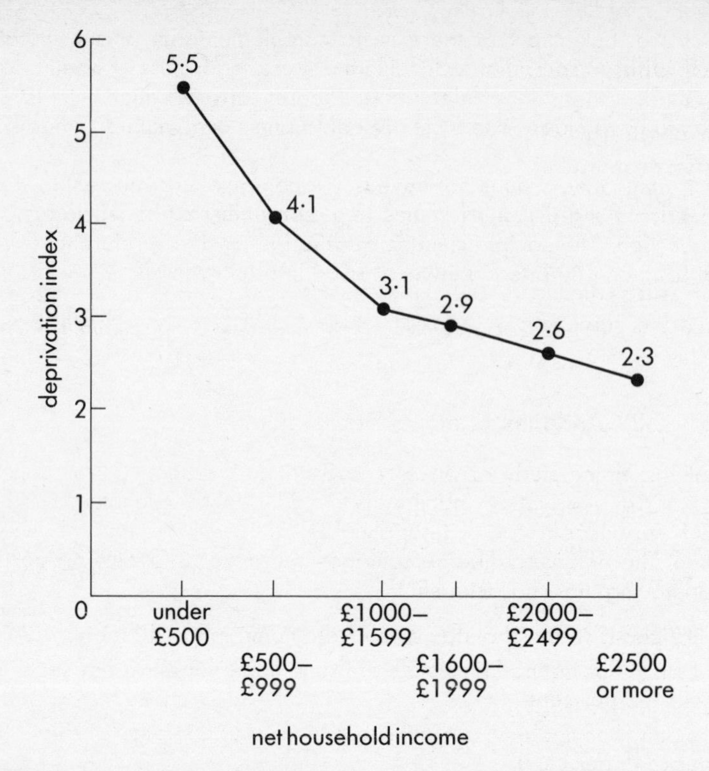

Figure 5.1 Relation between deprivation and household net income

In his sample, Townsend found a mean score on the deprivation index of 3.5 overall, with 3.0 for adults aged 15–44 and 5.1 for adults aged 70 or more. The mean score for children was 3.4. Figure 5.1 shows the relation between the index score and net household income. One would, of course, expect a negative relationship between the two variables since lower incomes imply that less is available to spend on purchasable goods. The gradient, however, depends crucially on the weights placed on the components of the index. For example, if not having a cooked breakfast is thought deserving of a *low* weight, it would cause the gradient to decrease since that characteristic alone is not highly correlated with household income. Conversely, if no fresh meat were regarded as an important characteristic worthy of a relatively *heavy* weight, that would increase the gradient since it is highly correlated with income.

Townsend explores many other relationships in his study: for example, the relationship between the index and family size. The purpose here, however, is to draw attention to the ratio scale assumptions made in the construction of this index. Moreover, the author seems to have become mesmerized by numbers and has failed to note that they entail important value judgements (who should be making them is also a question that ought to have been discussed).

P. Townsend (1979) *Poverty in the United Kingdom*, Harmondsworth, Penguin.

Cardinal Utility and Demand Theory

The first of the three theories of demand to be discussed is due to the great Cambridge economist, Alfred Marshall (1842–1924). In order to be as explicit as possible about the process of theorizing in economics, the assumptions will be laid bare, it will be shown why each is made, and then the logic of the theory itself will be worked through. In the case of Marshall's of theory of demand the notion of utility measurement used is that of the ratio scale. As you will see, other theorists have used other types of measurement.

Axioms of Marshallian Demand Theory

The specific postulates made in each of these theories will be termed *axioms* in order to distinguish them from the general postulates that underlie all economic analysis of behaviour. In the case of Marshall's theory, the essential axioms are five:

(1) An economic good yields utility.
(2) The more of a good an individual consumes the greater his or her utility.
(3) The marginal utility of a good diminishes as more is consumed.
(4) The marginal utility of money income is constant.
(5) Individuals maximize utility subject to their money income.

Since all three theories are being applied to the demand phenomenon, it is assumed that money income is constant in each case, as are the prices of substitutes and complements, tastes, and any other factors that may affect demand. The focus is therefore on the effect of a change in the relative price of one good on its consumption with all else subject to the *ceteris paribus* condition. This is not because anyone believes that other things really do stay constant in the world; it is to enable us to explain why the price–quantity relationship is negative. In an investigation of the impact of another determining factor, price would be held constant.

Marshall's great book *Principles of Economics* first appeared in 1890, and he was naturally very much conditioned by the utilitarian philosophy that had originated with Jeremy Bentham (1748–1832) and dominated much economic and political thought in the nineteenth century. 'Utility' was broadly to be identified with 'satisfaction' or even 'happiness', and it was generally thought not only that individuals sought to maximize utility (= satisfaction = happiness) but that a proper (moral) objective of social organization was to maximize the utility (= satisfaction = happiness) of the greatest number of people possible (the interesting implications of this view for the morally correct income distribution will be discussed in chapter 21).

Marshall's first axiom, then, is straightforward nineteenth century utilitarianism and can be taken as equivalent to the statement that 'individuals derive satisfaction from goods.'

The second axiom says more than this – namely that satisfaction increases the more one has of any good. It is plainly a utilitarian version of the first postulate of economics in chapter 2 (which did not, however, enter into any speculation about the nature of the feelings people have as they choose more or whether those feelings correspond to satisfaction, happiness or anything else).

Marshall's third axiom is sometimes known as the **law of diminishing marginal utility**. In this book, however, the term 'law' in a scientific context is used only for commonly observed phenomena that have a constant, law-like property (like the negative relationship between quantity demanded and price) and not for behaviour postulates. Diagrammatically, the axiom of

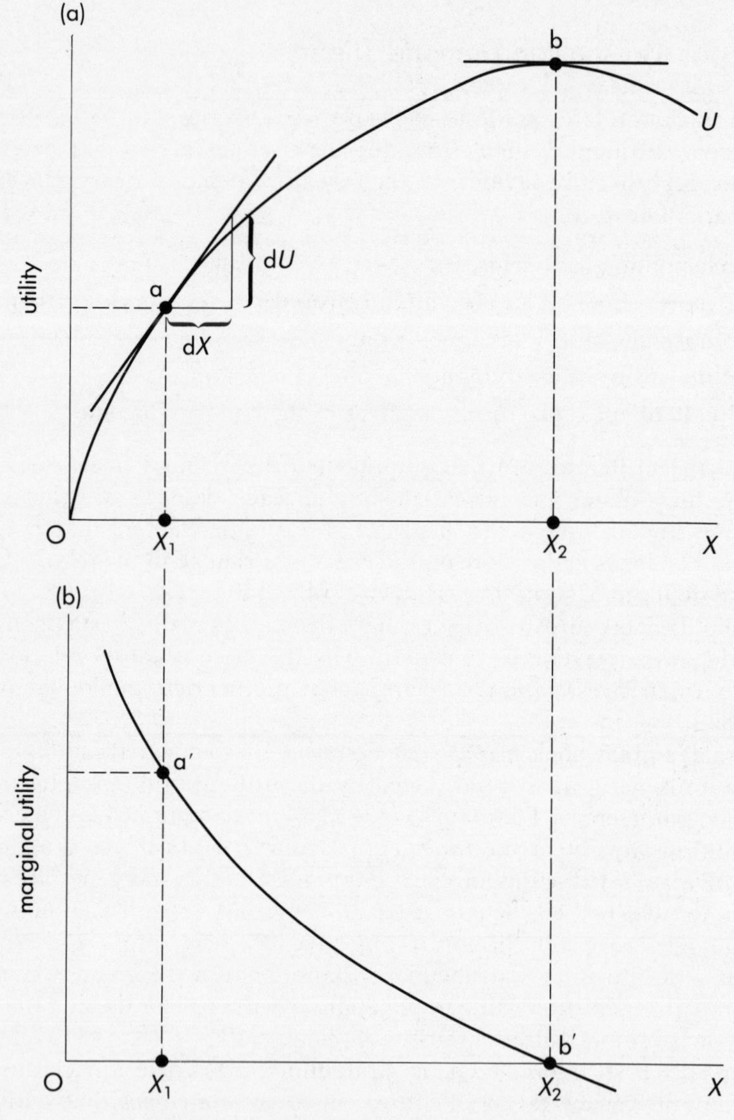

Figure 5.2 Consumption, total and marginal utility

diminishing marginal utility can be portrayed as in figure 5.2. In figure 5.2(a) utility is measured on the vertical axis and is imagined to be measured much as height, weight and distance are measured (that is, on a ratio scale). The horizontal axis measures the quantity of a good X (similarly measured) consumed or purchased per unit of time. The curve U shows how utility increases with X: it increases but at a decreasing rate. Where the curve becomes flat, further increases in X add no further utility (marginal utility is zero). Where it acquires a negative slope, marginal utility is negative: X has ceased being an economic good to the individual in question and has become a 'bad'.

The slope of the U curve is the measure of marginal utility, dU/dX, and is found (as you saw in discussing elasticity) by taking the tangent at the point in question. In figure 5.2(a) the marginal utility of X at X_1 is the slope at point a. The slope at point b is zero, indicating satiation of the individual with X, or zero marginal utility. Figure 5.2(b) plots the marginal utility of X, or the slope of the U curve all along its length, with points a′ and b′ corresponding to a and b in figure 5.2(a).

Marshall's fourth axiom (constant marginal utility of money income) is at first sight puzzling. The reason why it is a necessary axiom will shortly become apparent. Note that Marshall assumed in general that the marginal utility of *all* goods falls the more one has of them. Moreover he assumed that, since income is valued because it enables the purchase and consumption of goods, the marginal utility of income too must fall as income rises, since it can be spent only on goods whose marginal utility falls.

The final axiom is of course the utilitarian one that individuals actually do maximize their utility – but within the constraint imposed by their resources, taken here to be measured accurately by their money income.

The Marshallian Demand Theorem

When one purchases a good one *gains* by the amount of utility the good yields; one also *loses* by virtue of paying a price, hence forgoing other things that one could have bought. The price is, of course, measured in money terms. To determine how an individual will balance the gains and losses from purchases, therefore, it is necessary to reduce both to a common unit of measurement. In Marshallian demand theory this measure is provided by an index of utility. Given that the gain from consumption is already measured in imaginary units called utils, one has therefore also to transform the money measure of expenditure, which is the loss from purchase, into utils.

This is quite easy to do since, if you know the price of the good and the utility of a penny of income (the marginal utility of money income) then multiplying the two together gives the utility forgone by paying the price of one unit. Thus, if MU_Y is the marginal utility of income and P_X is the price of X, the utility forgone is $P_X MU_Y$ – the utility measure of the loss an individual incurs when a unit of X is purchased. With a constant P_X and constant MU_Y, $P_X MU_Y$ is also constant.

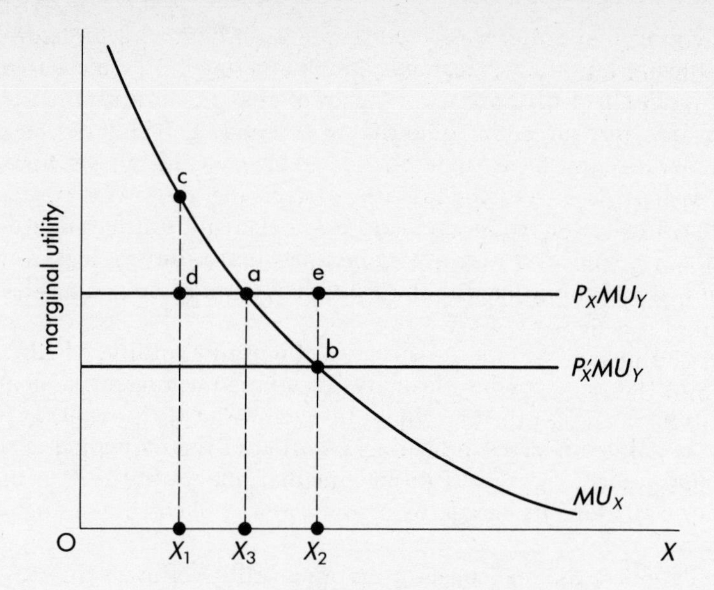

Figure 5.3 Marshall's demand theorem

In figure 5.3 the marginal utility of X is plotted as the downward sloping curve MU_X and, for a given price, the line P_XMU_Y measures the utility sacrificed for each unit of X purchased. These curves embody the first four axioms of Marshall's theory: the first axiom says that X and utility are related; the second requires a positive MU_X; the third causes the MU_X curve to have a negative slope; and the fourth enables one to draw P_XMU_Y as a straight horizontal line.

The fifth axiom says that the individual maximizes utility. At what rate of X purchase or consumption will this be? Suppose an individual consumed X_1 of X. The utility obtained from a little more is given by the height of MU_X above X_1 and is indicated by point c. The marginal utility lost from buying a little more is given by the height of P_XMU_Y above X_1, indicated by point d. Clearly, since the marginal utility gained from the extra rate of purchase exceeds the marginal utility lost, a utility maximizing individual will increase consumption – and continue to do so until the MU_X curve is no longer higher than the P_XMU_Y curve. Conversely, at X_3, the util gain of a small increment in consumption (at b) is less than its util cost (at e); hence a utility maximizing individual will not consume where the MU_X curve lies below the P_XMU_Y curve. Utility maximizing implies that the individual will locate at point a, where consumption is X_2 and

$$P_XMU_Y = MU_X$$

Since it is axiomatic that individuals maximize utility, and you have just seen that utility maximization logically entails the above condition, it follows that the axioms imply the equality. Utility maximizing individuals, therefore, will always maintain this condition.

Now let the price change. Suppose price fell from P_X to P'_X. Since MU_Y is axiomatically constant, and the above equality is always maintained, it follows that MU_X must fall as well. The axioms permit of only one way in which this may occur: axiom 3 has it that marginal utility falls the more X that is taken. Hence X must increase. In short, *a fall in price will lead to an increase in the quantity demanded (and vice versa)*: the axioms generate the required prediction.

Figure 5.3 shows the argument diagrammatically. After the fall in price, $P_X MU_Y$ falls to $P'_X MU_Y$. A new utility maximizing equilibrium is set up at b, entailing a higher rate of X consumption or purchase at the lower price. Note, however, that this figure is *not* a demand diagram – P_X is not measured on the vertical axis. But it is easy to plot the relationship between P_X and X on a diagram, and the resulting curve must clearly take on a negative slope.

It is sometimes useful to cast Marshall's theory in terms of *relative* prices. Suppose there are two goods, X and Z with associated prices P_X and P_Z. Utility maximizing implies

$$P_X MU_Y = MU_X, \text{ so } MU_Y = \frac{MU_X}{P_X}$$

and

$$P_Z MU_Y = MU_Z, \text{ so } MU_Y = \frac{MU_Z}{P_Z}.$$

Rearranging these,

$$\frac{P_X}{P_Z} = \frac{MU_X}{MU_Z}$$

and, in the case of many goods W, X, Z etc.,

$$\frac{MU_W}{P_W} = \frac{MU_X}{P_X} = \frac{MU_Z}{P_Z} = \ldots = MU_Y$$

The first of these alternative formulations says that the ratio of any pair of prices will be set equal to the ratio of the corresponding pair of marginal utilities. The second says that the marginal utility of any good per unit of its price is the same for all goods: income will be spent so that the marginal utility of a penny spent is everywhere the same (and equal to the marginal utility of money income).

SAQ 5.4

This SAQ is a bit tougher but you have been given enough information to tackle it now.

The price of apples is 50p per kilogram and their marginal utility to an individual is 10 utils. That person's price elasticity of demand is −1.5 and consumption is 2 kg per week.

(a) What is the marginal utility of money income?

(b) Suppose all utility numbers are doubled. What happens to apple consumption?

(c) Suppose price doubles. What happens to the marginal utility of apple consumption?
(d) Suppose apple consumption rises by 50 per cent when income doubles. What is the income elasticity of demand?
(e) Suppose the price of apples falls by 5p from 50p. What happens to the rate of consumption and expenditure on apples?
(f) Suppose the individual initially spends 1 per cent of income on apples and their price then falls by half. How much more or less is left over as a percentage of income to spend on other goods?

Marshall's theory is a splendid example of neat logic applied to develop a theoretical explanation of an observed phenomenon. There is a certain lovely quality in an argument that begins apparently remotely from the phenomenon to be explained and then proceeds to show how in logic the fundamental axioms actually imply the phenomenon. What is particularly neat about the Marshallian theory is that although it uses a completely *imaginary* thing called utility, measured in *imaginary* units called utils, these non-observable things drop out of the final result which is entirely in terms of observables: prices and consumption behaviour.

Marshall's theory has sometimes been criticized for being metaphysical and empirically empty. It has been said, for example, that utility theory says no more than that people carry on doing whatever they are doing until they are inclined to stop. If utility theory really did say no more than this then it would indeed be empty. But it *does* do more: it specifies not what will be consumed but *how consumption will change as prices change*. It specifically predicts that, if the relative price of a good falls (rises), all else remaining the same, rates of consumption or purchase will rise (fall). This is an unambiguous *empirical* implication of Marshall's theory that is testable and, moreover, generally upheld by the evidence.

Logical Problems of Marshallian Theory

There are, however, serious difficulties with Marshall's theory. One is that the utility, and hence the marginal utility, of a good depends only upon the amount of that good and is independent of the amount of other goods. The utility of a *bundle* of goods is simply the sum of the utilities of each of its components. This does not really seem very plausible, but is an assumption made not only by utilitarian economists as you saw in case studies 5.1 and 5.2. It is like assuming that the utility from having two shoes without laces can be added to that of two laces in order to arrive at the utility of a pair of shoes with laces. In general, it assumes that goods (or 'bads') are neither complements nor substitutes.

A natural utilitarian thing to say might be that complementary goods (or 'bads' like handicap) would exist when an increase in the amount of one increased the marginal utility (desirability) of whatever amount of the other one had. Conversely, substitutes would exist whenever an increase in the amount of one decreased the marginal utility (disutility) of the other.

Can you see what the consequences for the demand theorem are? In each case changes in the amount of one *shift* the marginal utility curve of the other. If there were substitutes or complements to the good whose demand was being analysed, their marginal utilities would therefore change as the amount of the good in question changed. If that happens, then the marginal utility of the money income one might spend on such goods must also change, since the utility of one's income depends on the utility of what one can get for it. Now that would be all right so long as MU_Y changed *in the same direction* as P_X, for then the equilibrium condition will again be maintained by adjusting MU_X (figure 5.3). But P_X and MU_Y will move in the same direction only if the other goods are *complements* when taken as a whole. Other goods are not, however, complements in general.

A second difficulty arises directly from the constancy of money income. Suppose P_X falls and suppose, moreover, that demand is relatively elastic. As you have seen in chapter 4, this implies that more income will be spent on X. So there is less available for spending on other goods. Consequently the demand for other goods falls – since you also know that on average these goods cannot be inferior – and their marginal utilities therefore must on average rise. But if that is so, then MU_Y must also rise – since it is the marginal utility to be had by spending income on additional goods – and it may rise sufficiently to offset the fall in P_X, destroying the possibility of enunciating the demand theorem.

Or suppose the demand for X was inelastic. A fall in P_X induces *less* expenditure on X, leaving *more* to spend on other goods. Their demand therefore rises on average, leading to a fall in their marginal utilities and a fall in MU_Y. This time the change in MU_Y is in the same direction as the change in P_X, so the demand theorem can still hold – but only for a good in the relatively *inelastic* portion of a demand curve.

These difficulties do not arise if the demand for X always has a unitary elasticity, for in that case expenditure on X stays the same as P_X changes. But to have enunciated a demand theorem only for goods with a unitary price elasticity cannot be counted a tremendous gain!

Marshall was far too insightful an economist to be unaware of these problems. In connection with the problem of substitutes his proposal was, however, not altogether satisfactory: to lump together substitutes (his example was coffee and tea) and treat them as a single commodity. As regards the income effects, he claimed that they belonged to the 'second order of smalls' and could for practical purposes be ignored. This effectively means that Marshall's demand theorem can be applied only for goods on which expenditure constitutes a very small portion of the individual's budget. You might find this an acceptable compromise in examining the demand for matches, but it is scarcely good enough for analysing the demand for housing or food or imports.

As it later turned out many of Marshall's strongest assumptions (e.g. the measurability of utility on a ratio scale; the independent additivity of component utilities to derive the utility of the total) are not actually *necessary* to derive a demand theorem. Consequently the Marshallian theorem is no longer generally accepted as a satisfactory account of the demand phenomenon – it has internal contradictions, it is applicable only to trivial goods, and it makes unnecessarily strong assumptions (or axioms) that alternative starting points avoid. None the less it remains a classic example of an economic theory: an attempt to explain *why* we see what we see in terms of concepts more fundamental than the observations we seek to explain.

SAQ 5.5

(a) The average price of food is £1.00 per kilogram and consumption is 20 kg per week. The price elasticity of an individual's demand is −0.5. If price rises by half, how much is left over to spend on other goods as a proportion of income, given a weekly money income of £100?

(b) The price of *X* is £5 and the average price of all other goods (*Z*) is £2. A household's *X* consumption is 20 units a week and its *Z* consumption 50 units a week. The price of *X* now falls to £2.50. What reduction in money income will leave the household just able to purchase the original combination of *X* and *Z*?

What You Should Understand Now

The meaning of measurement in general.
The distinction between ordinal measurement and cardinal (interval and ratio scales).
What utility is and is not.
The wide variety of applications that is possible using utility theory.
Utility theory as developed by Marshall.
The use of Marshall's five axioms to produce a demand theorem.
The significance of the marginal utility concept.
Some criticisms of the Marshallian theory.

6

Choice, Utility and Revealed Preference

In this chapter and the next a sudden jump is made from the end of the last century, when Marshall developed his theory, to just before the Second World War. At that time two Nobel prize winning economists, one English (John Hicks, born 1904) and the other American (Paul Samuelson, born 1915), developed more general and more satisfactory theories, both of which are still standard parts of every economist's toolkit. Although Samuelson's theory was actually developed after Hicks's you are going to tackle it first, partly because it is in many respects simpler than Hicks's theory and partly because in later chapters you will be making greater use (though not exclusive use) of the Hicksian approach.

Before you can actually tackle Samuelson's demand theorem you will have to do some preparatory work, in the course of which several important concepts of wide applicability will be introduced.

Paul Samuelson gave the name **revealed preference** to his theory of choice, which was first published in 1938 (when he was only 23) and subsequently developed in a series of papers. His aim was to remove from choice theory in general (and demand theory in particular) any vestigial traces of utilitarianism. He sought not only to banish any form of cardinalism but even ordinal utility, to remove any unobservable psychological basis from economics and to use only behavioural and observable elements. The Samuelsonian approach will be set out systematically, beginning with his axioms.

Axioms of Revealed Preference Theory

In these axioms B_1, B_2 and B_3 are bundles of goods having different amounts of, say, goods X and Z in them. The relation **P** stands for 'chosen rather than'. The aim is now to show how from two very reasonable looking axioms you can derive a demand theorem. There seems little doubt that they form a more economical set of axioms than those embodied in the Marshallian demand theorem.

(1) **Comparison axiom** There is a comparability between bundles of goods such that *either* B_1 **P** B_2 *or* B_2 **P** B_1.

(2) **Transitivity axiom** If B_1 **P** B_2 and B_2 **P** B_3, then B_1 **P** B_3.

The *comparison axiom* is simply stating that if one bundle is chosen rather than another when they are each available, then the second will not be chosen rather than the first. The force of the axiom is threefold. First, it is asserting that a comparison can actually be made between any two bundles. This is not self-evident and occasions unquestionably arise when individuals cannot select or compare. For example, let B_1 be an option in which a limited amount of resources are spent in maintaining 50 people with renal failure on kidney machines, without which the 50 would die. Let B_2 be an option in which resources are spent on relief to famine victims in central Africa. You must choose either one or the other. The choice is evidently agonizing and, although such a choice must sometimes actually be made, many individuals may say that they could not, themselves, make it. If that is so, the axiom is not true.

Secondly, the axiom denies the possibility of indifference between two bundles. Samuelson (and others) argue that indifference is not a behaviourally observable phenomenon. Consequently, since only actual choices can be observed, you must choose either one or the other – you are not allowed to wave your hands helplessly when confronted with the option! This property is sometimes termed a **strong ordering**: the bundles are ranked strictly in order one after the other. Orderings where ties are allowed are termed **weak orderings** (see chapter 7).

Thirdly, the axiom is stating implicitly that tastes do not change. One cannot choose B_1 over B_2 this week and B_2 over B_1 next week (other observable things remaining the same) without violating the axiom.

The *transitivity axiom* also seems to be a matter of common sense (which is why it appeals) but, on closer thought, it too is by no means obviously true of all behaviour. Consider the following *intransitive* ordering:

What this is saying is that, if a large apple and a pear are available to a person, the large apple will be chosen rather than the pear. Likewise, in a choice between a pear and a small apple, the pear will be chosen. However, in a choice between a small apple and a large, the individual will choose the small apple (so as not to appear greedy). This is by no means absurd, but it does mean intransitivity, for transitivity requires that the large apple will be chosen rather than the small, since it will be chosen rather than the pear and the pear will be chosen rather than the small apple.

SAQ 6.1

Your ranking of the five bundles B_1, B_2, B_3, B_4 and B_5 is elicited by asking you to compare them in pairs. You reveal the following preferences:

B_1 **P** B_2, B_2 **P** B_3, B_3 **P** B_4, B_5 **P** B_4, B_1 **P** B_3, B_4 **P** B_2, B_3 **P** B_5, B_4 **P** B_1, B_5 **P** B_2, B_5 **P** B_1

Now take any of the ten possible triple comparisons (e.g. B_1, B_2 and B_3) and discover how many (if any) reveal intransitivity.

The sort of intransitivity just described does, however, seem a bit silly. Consider: if I have a pear and you a small apple, you would give me, in exchange for the pear, a small apple and (say) a penny. Suppose I also have a large apple. You will also give me the pear and (say) a penny in exchange for my large apple. But I also have the small apple you originally gave me and, in exchange for this, you will give me the large apple and (say) a penny. If I now offer you the pear you gave me two trades ago in exchange for the small apple you now have, we are back at the beginning and we can do the round again. Each time a cycle is completed I acquire additional pennies from you until your entire wealth has become mine!

This seems unlikely, and lends plausibility to the axiom of transitivity. In a sense, of course, the axiom of transitivity is contained within the comparison axiom, for if your fruity choices are as has just been postulated you implicitly have both

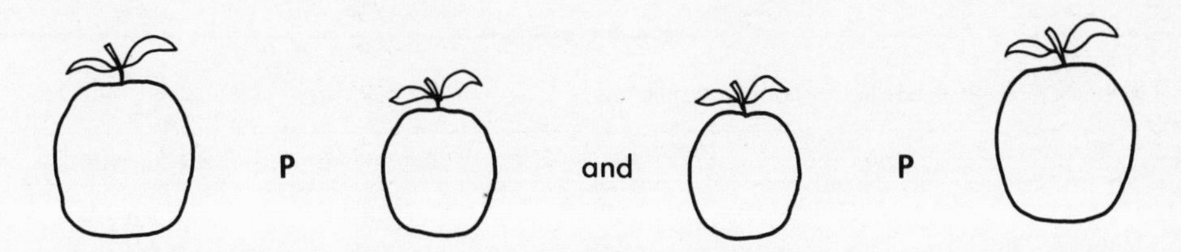

Intransitivity is more likely to be encountered in collective than individual decisions. Suppose there are three individuals 1, 2 and 3 who have to make a choice between three options B_1, B_2 and B_3 by majority voting. (You might imagine that the three relate to alternative ways of spending some additional tax revenue: on more defence (B_1), higher unemployment benefit (B_2) or more school teachers (B_3).) Suppose each individual conforms to the transitivity axiom so that:

for 1 B_1 **P** B_2, B_2 **P** B_3
for 2 B_2 **P** B_3, B_3 **P** B_1
for 3 B_3 **P** B_1, B_1 **P** B_2

In a vote between B_1 and B_2, B_1 wins since 1 and 3 will outvote 2. So, using **C** to denote a collective choice, we have B_1 **C** B_2. In a choice between B_2 and B_3, B_2 wins since 1 and 2 will outvote 3. We therefore also have B_2 **C** B_3. We thus have B_1 **C** B_2, B_2 **C** B_3. Transitivity requires that B_1 **C** B_3. But consider a choice between B_1 and B_3: 2 and 3 will outvote 1 to produce B_3 **C** B_1. This phenomenon has been known since the eighteenth century and is termed the **paradox of (majority) voting**, and it has raised a host of questions concerning the rationality of majority decision making. For present purposes our aim is not, however, to discuss questions of this sort (fascinating and important though they are) but is instead to point out that plausible arguments can be made against the seemingly very reasonable requirements of the Samuelson axioms. Their realism is in the end, of course, an empirical matter, which case study 6.1 addresses.

Case Study 6.1 Choice and Intransitivity

The psychologist Amos Tversky has conducted several experiments in which the aim was to test for intransitivity of preference. In one of these, experimental subjects (undergraduates) were divided into four groups and each group was provided with a set of (imaginary) data about five college applicants (a different five for each group). The data were the scores the applicants were said to have obtained in tests designed to measure intellectual ability, emotional stability and social facility. Each subject was then asked to make comparisons between the applicants, the design of the experiment making it hard for each subject *consciously* to pursue consistency (the pairs for comparison were, for example, put in a random order). The information given was that in table 6.1.

Table 6.1 Characteristics of college applicants

Group	*Applicant*	*Intellectual score*	*Emotional score*	*Social score*
I	a	69	84	75
	b	72	78	65
	c	75	72	55
	d	78	66	45
	e	81	60	35
II	a	66	90	85
	b	72	80	70
	c	78	70	55
	d	84	60	40
	e	90	50	25
III	a	54	90	95
	b	63	78	75
	c	72	66	55
	d	81	54	35
	e	90	42	15
IV	a	42	96	96
	b	54	80	73
	c	66	64	50
	d	78	48	27
	e	90	32	4

There were fifteen subjects in all and the aim was to see if their rankings of applicants a, b, c, d and e in each group were transitive. With five applicants, each subject could make ten triple comparisons as follows: abc, abd, abe, acd, ace, ade, bcd, bce, bde and cde. In fact, however, they were asked only to make pairwise comparisons between the (again, ten) possible pairs: ab, bc, cd, de, ac, bd, ce, ad, be and ae. An intransitivity score π was calculated as the proportion of intransitive triples implied by these pairwise comparisons. The results are set out in table 6.2.

Table 6.2 Frequency of intransitive choices between college applicants

Subject	*Group*	*ab*	*bc*	*cd*	*de*	*ac*	*bd*	*ce*	*ad*	*be*	*ae*	π
1	I	a **P** b	b **P** c	c **P** d	e **P** d	a **P** c	d **P** b	c **P** e	d **P** a	e **P** b	e **P** a	0.4
2	I	a **P** b	c **P** b	c **P** d	d **P** e	a **P** c	d **P** b	c **P** e	d **P** a	e **P** b	e **P** a	0.2
3	I	a **P** b	b **P** c	c **P** d	d **P** e	c **P** a	b **P** d	c **P** e	d **P** a	e **P** b	e **P** a	0.4
4	II	a **P** b	b **P** c	c **P** d	d **P** e	c **P** a	d **P** b	e **P** c	d **P** a	e **P** b	e **P** a	0.3
5	II	b **P** a	c **P** b	d **P** c	e **P** d	c **P** a	d **P** b	e **P** c	d **P** a	e **P** b	e **P** a	0.0
6	II	a **P** b	b **P** c	c **P** d	e **P** d	a **P** c	d **P** b	c **P** e	a **P** d	e **P** b	e **P** a	0.3
7	II	a **P** b	b **P** c	c **P** d	e **P** d	a **P** c	d **P** b	e **P** c	d **P** a	e **P** b	e **P** a	0.2
8	II	a **P** b	b **P** c	c **P** d	e **P** d	a **P** c	d **P** b	e **P** c	d **P** a	e **P** b	e **P** a	0.3
9	II	a **P** b	b **P** c	c **P** d	d **P** e	c **P** a	b **P** d	c **P** e	a **P** d	e **P** b	e **P** a	0.4
10	III	a **P** b	b **P** c	c **P** d	d **P** e	a **P** c	b **P** d	c **P** e	d **P** a	e **P** b	e **P** a	0.5
11	III	a **P** b	b **P** c	c **P** d	d **P** e	a **P** c	b **P** d	c **P** e	d **P** a	b **P** e	e **P** a	0.4
12	III	a **P** b	c **P** b	c **P** d	d **P** e	a **P** c	d **P** b	c **P** e	d **P** a	e **P** b	e **P** a	0.2
13	III	a **P** b	b **P** c	c **P** d	d **P** e	a **P** c	d **P** b	e **P** c	d **P** a	e **P** b	e **P** a	0.3
14	IV	a **P** b	b **P** c	c **P** d	d **P** e	c **P** a	d **P** b	c **P** e	d **P** a	e **P** b	e **P** a	0.3
15	IV	a **P** b	b **P** c	c **P** d	d **P** e	a **P** c	b **P** d	c **P** e	a **P** d	e **P** b	e **P** a	0.4

In the case of subject 1 there are four intransitive triples out of the ten. Specifically, subject I had a **P** c and c **P** d but d **P** a; a **P** c and c **P** e but e **P** a; b **P** c and c **P** d but d **P** b; and b **P** c and c **P** e but e **P** b. The other six triples were all transitive: hence this subject's π score was 0.4. Only one subject was perfectly transitive, and the average proportion of intransitivities was 0.307 – just over 30 per cent.

Does this mean that the axiom of transitivity is unrealistic? It would seem that for some choices involving complex comparisons a rule of thumb is often adopted by choosers (for example, if the difference in scores is 'small', ignore it).

Tversky concludes:

> This approximation may be very good in general, despite the fact that it leads to intransitive choices in some specially constructed situations. The main interest in the present results lies not so much in the fact that transitivity can be violated but rather in what these violations reveal about the choice mechanism and the approximation methods that govern preference between multidimensional alternatives.

If such rules of thumb *typically* gave rise to intransitivity on such a scale, we may conclude that they would cease being used as rules of thumb. Tversky would not wish, therefore, for his results to be taken as showing that people in general often or usually have intransitive preferences.

Amos Tversky (1969) 'Intransitivity of preferences', *Psychological Review*, **76**, 31–48.

Budget Lines

One of the things you may have noticed about these two axioms is that, unlike Marshall's, they refer to *bundles* of goods (and services) rather than specific goods and services. There is a good reason for this, but first you must understand the link between income and consumption.

Suppose that an individual has a given money income Y per period and that it may be spent on either good X or good Z. Given prices of X and Z denoted by P_X and P_Z, the maximum amount of X purchasable per period is Y/P_X and the maximum amount of Z is Y/P_Z (figure 6.1). If the individual buys Z_1 of Z, then the amount of X bought (assuming all income is spent on X and Z) is income net of expenditure on Z divided by the price of X: $(Y-P_Z Z_1)/P_X$. If the individual buys X_1 of X then by the same token the amount of Z is given by $(Y-P_X X_1)/P_Z$. If all such points are connected, we derive the line ab in figure 6.1, where point a corresponds to Y/P_Z and point b to Y/P_X. This line has the technical name **budget line**, and it shows the maximum amounts of X and Z that an individual can purchase given (constant) prices of X and Z and the available income.

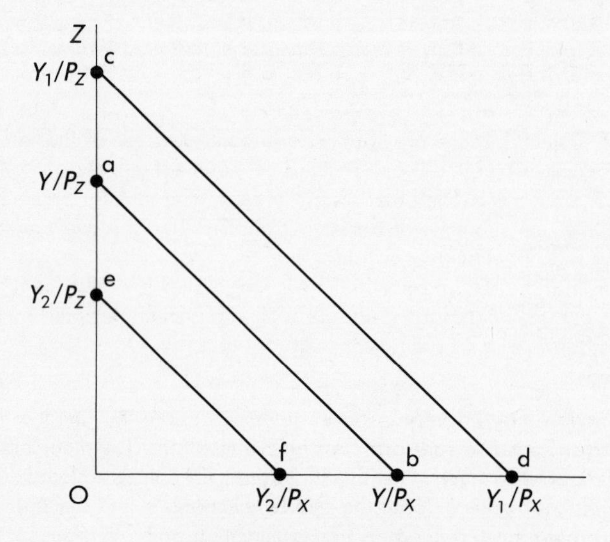

Figure 6.1 Budget lines

The slope of the budget line is given by the ratio of the prices of X and Z. To see this consider the following. The slope of the line viewed from point b is $-\text{Oa}/\text{Ob}$. Since $\text{Oa} = Y/P_Z$ and $\text{Ob} = Y/P_X$, the slope is

$$-\text{Oa}/\text{Ob} = -\frac{Y}{P_Z} \Big/ \frac{Y}{P_X} = -\frac{Y}{P_Z}\,\frac{P_X}{Y} = -\frac{P_X}{P_Z}$$

Since ab has a negative slope from left to right one may therefore say the slope is equal to $-\ P_X/P_Z$.

Line ab is obviously straight so long as the prices of X and Z are not affected as the individual buys more or less of those goods. You are now familiar with the general equation for linear relationships ($A = a \pm bB$) and, in this case, the equation for a linear budget line is

$$Z = \frac{Y}{P_Z} - \frac{P_X}{P_Z} X$$

where Y/P_Z is the intercept on the Z axis and $-\ P_X/P_Z$ is the slope. Thus, if $X = 0$, $Y =$ £100 and $P_Z =$ £5, $Z = 20$. If $P_X =$ £5, $-\ P_X/P_Z = -\ 1$.

Since the budget line is a construct you will often use in later sections, it is worth exploring in some detail. What happens to it, for example, if income rises or falls? Suppose income rose from Y to Y_1 and prices remained the same. The budget line must clearly shift outwards from the origin and take a position such as the budget line cd. If income falls to Y_2 the budget line must shift towards the origin and take a position such as ef. If only income changes and the prices remain constant then *relative* prices also remain the same and the slope of the budget line must also remain unchanged. Consequently the budget lines are always *parallel* when prices remain the same and income alone changes.

SAQ 6.2

Suppose $P_X =$ £10 and $P_Z =$ £20. You have an income of £100.

(a) What is the intercept of the budget line on the X axis?
(b) What is the intercept of the budget line on the Z axis?
(c) If income doubles, what are the intercepts on the X and Z axes?
(d) What is the slope of the budget line?

Budget lines remain parallel even when income is constant but prices *change by the same proportion*, for if they change in the same proportion their ratio remains the same and, therefore, the slope is the same. Thus, if prices rise in the same proportion, the budget line will shift towards the origin parallel to itself; since less X and Z will be purchasable out of a given money income. The converse is obviously the case for a price fall.

Suppose the price of X alone falls. If all income were spent on X then a lower price of X would clearly imply that more X would be bought: Y/P_X moves to the right. Since Y/P_Z is not changed, the budget line *rotates* through point a. This is shown in figure 6.2, where the price of X falls from P_X to P'_X, and the budget line moves from ab to ag. Conversely, a price rise means that less X can be purchased and Y/P_X moves to the left: for a rise in price from P_X to P''_X, the budget line becomes ah.

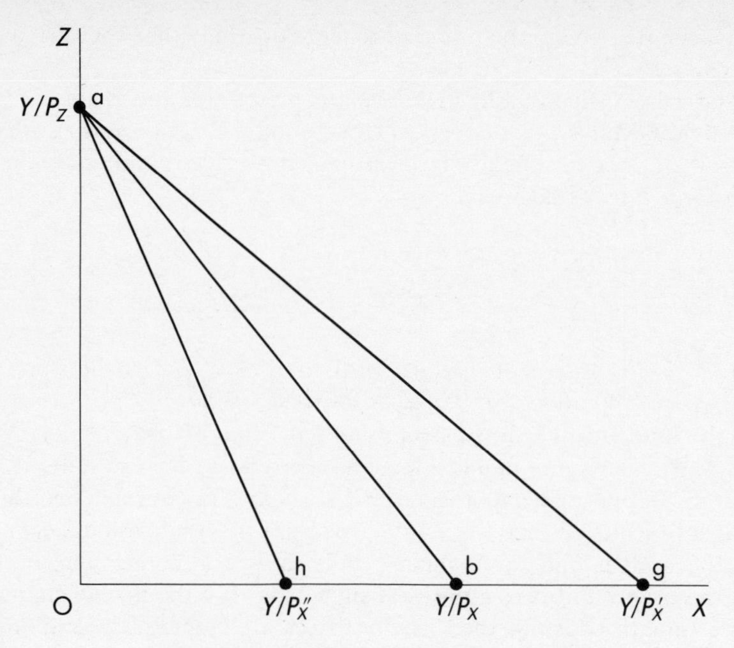

Figure 6.2 Budget lines and price changes

SAQ 6.3

The relative prices of *X* and *Z* are 0.5. If you spent all of your income on *X*, you would be able to buy 20 units.

(a) If the price of *X* is £5, what is your income?
(b) If the price of *X* is £5, what is the price of *Z*?
(c) If the prices of both *X* and *Z* double and income doubles too, what happens to the budget line?

Samuelson's Demand Theorem

Samuelson's demand theorem runs like this:
If the demand for a good increases when income alone rises, then quantity demanded must definitely fall (rise) when price alone rises (falls).
Consider an individual confronted with a choice between *X* (whose demand you are investigating) and *Z* (all other goods). Given income and the price of *X* relative to the average price of all other goods and assuming (as usual) that all income is spent (so *Z* is taken to include savings), the individual will be at some point on a budget line at which a *bundle* of *X* and *Z* will be indicated. Suppose the individual selects bundle B_1 on ab in figure 6.3. Since any point along ab could have been chosen, B_1 is said to have been *revealed preferred* to these other points (hence the name 'revealed preference' given to Samuelson's theory). If, however, you prefer not to assume that an actual choice is to be taken as revealing a preference (which would show a healthy caution), you could simply say that B_1 was *chosen rather than* any other bundle of *X* and *Z* available along ab.

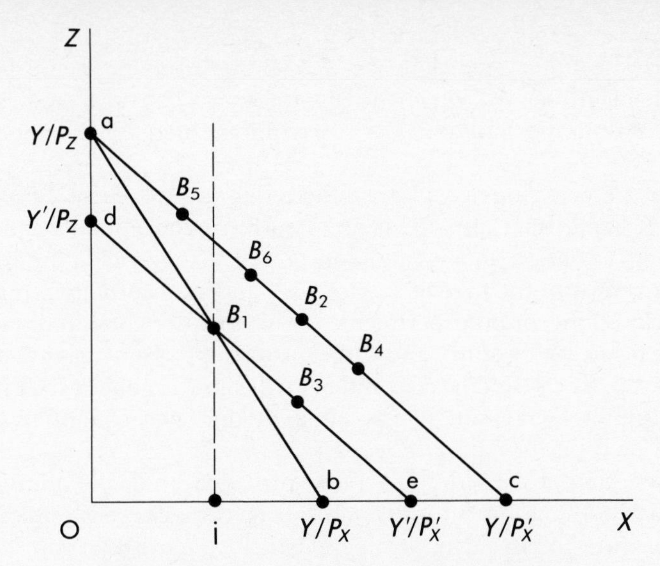

Figure 6.3 The Samuelson demand theorem

Now let the price of X change. Suppose it falls to P'_X. The budget line now rotates through a and takes a new position such as ac. If the Samuelson theorem is to hold, consumption of X must now *increase*: the new bundle chosen along ac must involve an X consumption larger than j (shown by the dotted vertical line), the amount of X assumed in bundle B_1. Can you prove that this must logically be the case?

Proceed as follows. Suppose the fall in P_X has taken place. Immediately reduce the individual's money income so that, at the new price ratio, he or she can still – but only just – purchase the original bundle B_1. This requires a shift of the budget line ac towards the origin (and parallel to itself since the ratio P'_X/P_Z is being held constant) until it passes through B_1. This new budget line is labelled de in figure 6.3, and money income has been reduced to Y' from Y. The individual can still purchase B_1 since it lies on the new budget line de. What can one say about how the individual will now choose given that P_X has fallen and Y too? Clearly a move to any point along de is possible. Will there be a move to a new bundle from B_1 along the section of de to the left of B_1? The answer must be 'no', since these bundles were previously available when the budget line was ab and B_1 was chosen. B_1 was then revealed preferred and, assuming preferences not to change (one is focusing only on the effect of a change in P_X), B_1 must still be preferred.

The section of de to the right of B_1 was, however, not previously available when the budget line was ab. Consequently, B_1 has not been revealed preferred to any bundle along this section. Where will the individual move? Anywhere along this section. However, to make things tough for the theory, let us suppose that the individual remains at the starting point and still prefers B_1 to any point on de to the right of B_1.

Now return the money income previously removed from the individual. The budget line moves from de back to ac. If, as the theorem asserts, the demand for X increases when income alone rises, then a new bundle B_2 must be chosen on ac to the right of B_1, for relative prices are constant and all that is happening is that the individual is receiving an increase in money income equal to $Y-Y'$.

Note that the experiment you are conducting is essentially a cerebral one. That is, it is being done in your head. You have conceptually imagined the compensating variation in income, conceptually removed it from the individual (or given it, in the case of a price rise) and conceptually returned it (or taken it back). Conceptual experiments of this sort are common in economics (as they are in philosophy and other subjects). But they can also be operationalized, as case studies 6.2 and 6.3 will show (in one case at the level of aggregate human behaviour; in the other at the level of individual animal behaviour).

You have now proved the theorem: provided that the individual can compare bundles such as B_1 and B_2, a fall in the price of X must cause its consumption rate to rise if its income elasticity is positive (that is, if it is a normal good). You have even proved this for the difficult case where the change in relative price alone, having subtracted some money income in order to keep purchasing power the same, had no effect on X consumption. If, however, there was some substitution of X for Z when price changed and money income was reduced, the theorem still works. For example, suppose that the individual moved from B_1 to B_3 along de instead of staying put as previously supposed. This is termed the *substitution effect* (see later) of a price change on X consumption. Returning the removed income to the individual must, for normal goods, cause a further rise in demand. Thus the final position B_4 must be to the right of B_3 and, since B_3 is to the right of B_1, B_4 must be to the right of B_1. If B_3 was chosen rather than B_1, and B_4 rather than B_3 then, by the transitivity axiom, B_4 must be chosen rather than B_1. The change from B_3 to B_4 or B_1 to B_2 is termed the *income effect* (see later) of a price change on X consumption.

Case Study 6.2 Income Effects of a Price Change in India

The income effect of a price change in one good is more pronounced (especially on the consumption of other goods) the larger the share in one's total budget that expenditure on the good occupies. In India, food grains represent a major share of total expenditure. In 1964–5, food grain expenditure represented 40 per cent of all consumer expenditure. Since its income elasticity of demand is low, it represents a higher share in the expenditure of the poor than in that of the rich. Price changes therefore have an importance for living standards that is particularly notable for the relatively poor sections of the community.

John Mellor (1978) has studied the impact of the sharp rise in food grain prices during 1964–5 in India. Table 6.3 shows the decline in expenditure on a variety of products due to the income effect of a 10 per cent rise in food grain prices.

In India the top 5 per cent in the income distribution spend more than twice as much per head on food grains as the lowest 20 per cent, but this accounts for only 15 per cent of their spending compared with 54 per cent for the lowest 20 per cent. The income effect of a price change is therefore much greater for the poor than for the rich: a 5.9 per cent decline in spending on food grain, compared with a 2 per cent decline for the very rich and 3 per cent for the middle groups (see table 6.3).

The income effect of the single price change also impacts on consumption of other goods, causing a 17.9 per cent drop in milk and milk product expenditure by the poor, but only 1.3 per cent by the rich. This pattern is shown throughout the table save for 'other foods' and 'house rent'. The explanation for these exceptions is that the very poor scarcely consume any foods other than those in categories 1, 2 and 3 and they typically have a negligible expenditure on housing.

J. W. Mellor (1978) 'Food price policy and income distribution in low-income countries', *Economic Development and Cultural Change*, **27**, 1–26.

Table 6.3 Decline in spending on food grains and other goods owing to the income effect of a 10 per cent rise in food grain price, India 1964–5

	Expenditure group		
Commodity	*Lowest 20%*	*Middle 20%*	*Top 5%*
1 Food grains	5.9	3.0	2.0
2 Milk and milk products	17.9	9.3	1.3
3 Meat, eggs and fish	13.0	7.2	1.4
4 Other foods	0.3	3.7	2.1
5 Tobacco	4.2	3.4	1.1
6 Cotton textiles	9.1	5.2	1.0
7 Fuel and light	7.0	4.3	0.9
8 Housing (rent)	0.0	18.0	3.0

SAQ 6.4

You have a weekly income of £100 which you spend on meat (M) and other goods (G). P_M is £5 per kilogram and P_G is £10 per 'unit'.

(a) Draw your budget line.

(b) Your income rises to £150: draw the new budget line.

(c) The price of meat rises to £10 per kilogram and your income remains at £150: draw the new budget line.

(d) Are you better or worse off as a result of both the price rise and the income rise? (Hint: what if you consumed (1) no meat or (2) no other goods?)

(e) Suppose that your original consumption bundle was at the intersection of the original budget line and the new one incorporating both the price rise and the income rise. Would you be better or worse off?

Substitution and Income Effects

The concepts of substitution and income effects are of central importance in modern economics. The **income effect** shows the increase in purchasing power or *real* income that occurs when price falls (or the fall in real income when price rises) and *money* income is constant. It is measured by removing money income (for a price fall) or adding money income (for a price rise) so as to leave the individual's original purchasing power the same. It is very important both analytically and practically to recognize that real income can change when prices change even though money income remains the same.

The **substitution effect** measures the impact of a price change when the purchasing power of income is held constant. Suppose an individual has the budget line ab in figure 6.4 and chooses to consume at B_1, sacrificing ac of Z consumption per period in exchange for Od of X. Before looking at case study 6.2 you examined income and substitution effects arising from a fall in the price of X. Now consider a rise. Suppose that P_X doubles to produce the new budget line ae, where point e lies half way between O and b. Suppose the individual selects B_2 on the new budget line (obviously B_1 **P** B_2).

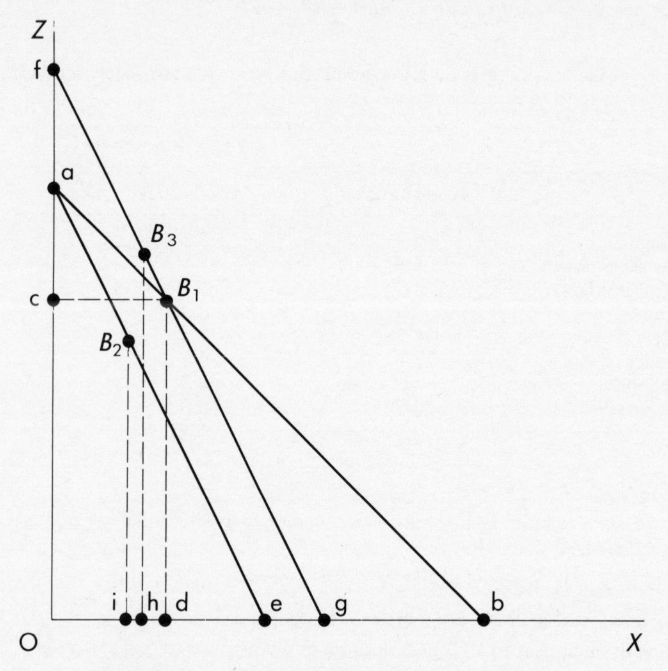

Figure 6.4 Income and substitution effects

To measure the substitution and income effects, first increase income *at the new price for X* so that the original bundle B_1 can still be purchased – but only just. In terms of Z this involves an increase in income of af. Remember, at point a the individual spends all income (say Y_0) on Z. At point f all of a higher income (say Y_1) is spent on Z. The difference between these two incomes (ΔY) is $\Delta Z P_Z$ and, since P_Z has not changed, ΔZ therefore measures ΔY (each is on a ratio scale).

The increase af, in income, produces a new budget line fg passing through B_1. At this new price for X and with the enhanced income, suppose the individual selects bundle B_3 (which must lie to the right of B_2 if X is normal). The substitution effect of the rise in the price of X is the difference in X consumption between B_1 and B_3 (hd) – the effect due to the change in relative price only, keeping purchasing power (that is, the ability to purchase B_1) constant.

Now remove the income supplement so that the budget line returns to ae. The difference in X consumption between B_3 and B_2 (ih) is the income effect of the price rise: it is the reduction in X consumption due to the lower purchasing power of income after the price rise. Consumption hd is measured holding real income constant and letting price change. Consumption ih is measured holding prices constant and letting income change. .

In nearly all empirical studies of demand, prices and *real* income are two crucial variables in the analysis. If, as you saw in chapter 4, the aim is to measure the impact of each variable on demand, holding the others constant, it follows that most empirical studies separate out the substitution and the income effects. The price elasticity is the elasticity with respect to a price change *holding real income constant.* The income elasticity includes the effect of real income changes arising from price changes as well as real income changes arising from any changes in money income that may also have occurred in the period being studied.

SAQ 6.5

Consider the bundles in the diagram contained in the answer to SAQ 6.4. Suppose your order of preference is B_3 **P** B_2 **P** B_5 **P** B_4 **P** B_1.

(a) Which of the following sets of numbers will serve as a utility measure of your choices?

	B_1	B_2	B_3	B_4	B_5
1	6	9	10	7	8
2	7	10	11	8	9
3	0	200	500	2	100
4	−50	0.5	1	−5	0
5	10	50	50	20	30

(b) Is utility being measured on a ratio, an interval or an ordinal scale?

(c) In figure 6.5, with budget lines 1, 2 and 3, the individual chooses bundles B_1, B_2 and B_3 respectively. B_2 is obviously revealed preferred to B_1 since, with budget line 2, the individual chooses B_2 when B_1 is available. However, with budget line 3 bundle B_1 is not available, and with budget line 1 bundle B_3 is not available: is B_3 revealed preferred to B_1?

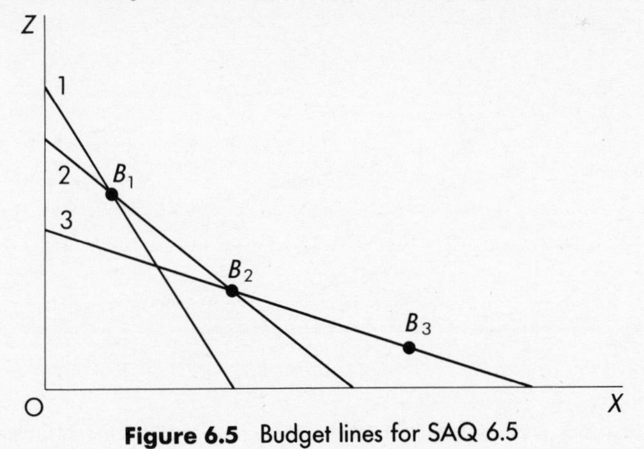

Figure 6.5 Budget lines for SAQ 6.5

Much animal experimentation seems to have little justification in terms of either expected scientific or expected social benefits, particularly when it involves subjecting animals to pain, exposing them to health risks, or subjecting them to emotionally distressing situations. In the following experiment, although there was no social and only modest scientific benefit to be had, at least the animal was not of necessity abused by the experiment in question.

Case Study 6.3 Revealed Preference and Rat Behaviour

A collaborating team of economists and psychologists decided to test rat behaviour for its conformity with the Samuelson theory. A rat was placed in an experimental chamber in which two levers were installed. This, when depressed, delivered a dipper cup of root beer and a dipper cup of Collins mix. Initially, the rat was allocated an 'income' of 300 presses per day which could be distributed in any combination of lever presses. Each press delivered 0.05 ml of each drink. Figure 6.6 shows the budget line for the rat, and its initially chosen combination of root beer and Collins mix is indicated by B_1. The 'price' of root beer was then doubled by halving the size of its dipper cup (so that two presses were required to obtain 0.05 ml) and that of Collins mix was halved by doubling the size of its dipper cup. The total income (number of daily presses permitted) was adjusted so that the new budget line passed through the original consumption bundle. After a transition period, the rat settled at the average daily consumption shown by B_2. The 'price' of root beer was then halved compared with the starting point and that of Collins mix doubled. After a period of adjustment, the rat settled at the average daily consumption shown by B_3.

Using these data it is possible to show the demand for root beer (or Collins mix) in terms of its relative price holding the purchasing power of income constant. This is

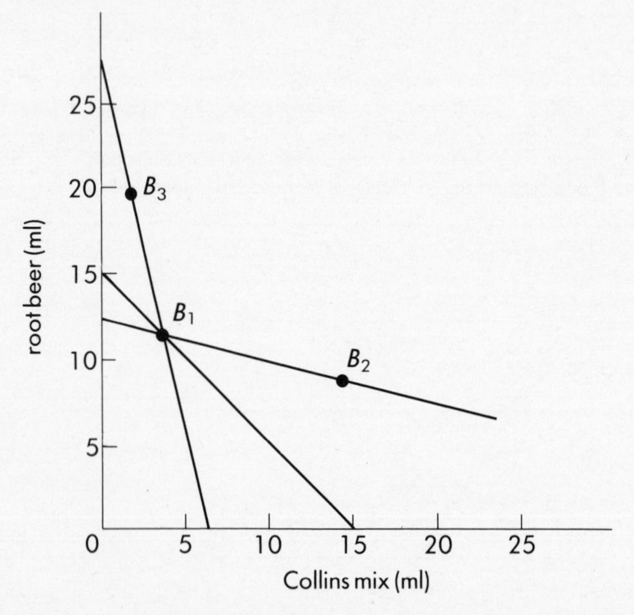

Figure 6.6 Rat's substitution effects between root beer and Collins mix

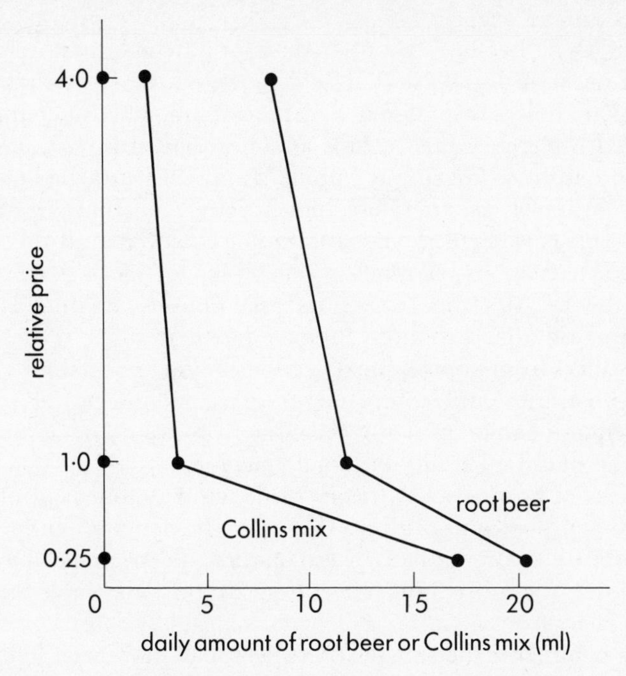

Figure 6.7 Compensated demand curves for rat's consumption of drinks

shown in figure 6.7. These demand curves are termed **compensated demand curves** since compensating variations in income have been made to keep purchasing power constant. They indicate a negative relationship between relative price and daily consumption. Had the demand curves incorporated income effects they would, in this case, have been more elastic because the income elasticity for both root beer and Collins mix turned out to be positive (for this experimental rat).

The purpose of this example is not, of course, to suggest that rat behaviour is useful in explaining human behaviour; rather it shows the wide applicability of the basic psychology of choice theory in economics.

J. H. Kagel *et al.* (1975) 'Experimental studies of consumer demand behaviour using laboratory animals', *Economic Inquiry*, **13**, 22–38.

Evaluation of Revealed Preference Theory

Samuelson's aim was to develop a theory that eliminated any vestigial traces of utilitarianism. Do you think it has succeeded? Clearly it does not use cardinal utility: nothing has been postulated about how the utility of components of bundles can be added up, for the simple reason that this issue does not arise. With this theory one does not have to measure the utility of the components of bundles, which would leave one with the problem of how to add them up to get rankings of bundles: recall the index measures of handicap and poverty.

Instead one enquires directly about the *ranking of bundles* of goods, services, characteristics and so on.

Moreover, nothing has been postulated about how marginal utility behaves as one moves between bundles. It should, however, be clear that the theory does assume that choices or preferences can be *ranked*. This, of course, is *ordinal utility*. Revealed preference theory thus assumes that utility can be measured ordinally, where utilities are simply numbers implicitly attached to bundles to indicate their order. It is, therefore, not strictly true that the theory does without utility measurement. What it does do, however (and this is its great accomplishment), is to use a much weaker kind of measurement than the Marshallian theory. In other words its assumptions are not as strong as Marshall's, and on that ground you may judge it to be a better theory. Moreover, it suffers from none of the objections made to Marshall's theory: the presence of substitutes and complements does not affect the result; price elasticity of demand can take on any (negative) value; and no assumptions are made about the marginal utility of money income.

The weakness of Samuelson's theory of demand is that it applies only to normal goods: it provides us with no theory of the demand curve for inferior goods. Suppose, for example that X were inferior. Then, in figure 6.3, there is the possibility that the substitution effect from B_1 to B_3 may have been followed by an income effect from B_3 to B_5. This entails a *lower* X consumption after the price fall than before. Or the substitution effect may have been followed by an income effect that is still negative in its impact on X consumption, but less strong, taking the individual from B_3 to B_6. Samuelson's demand theorem says nothing about the demand for a good having these characteristics. Thus, if the move is from B_1 to B_6 via B_3, there is still a negatively sloped demand curve for X, but this is not explained by Samuelson's theory since X is an inferior good. Although revealed preference theory is therefore limited in its capacity to generate a general demand theorem (that is, one covering all types of good and not just those with positive income elasticities) its relative simplicity has established the approach as a popular one, and you will frequently meet it in a variety of guises in your study of economics. One lies in the interpretation of standards of living, to which SAQ 6.6 will introduce you and to which chapter 23 will return.

SAQ 6.6

In 1985 you consume the amounts of Z and X at the prices stated compared with the same data for 1984. Assume that these are the *only* goods you consume and that you spend all your income.

1985				1984			
quantity		*price (£)*		*quantity*		*price (£)*	
Z	X	Z	X	Z	X	Z	X
5	5	10	10	2	9	18	6

(a) What is your expenditure on Z and X (taken together) in 1985?

(b) What was your expenditure on Z and X in 1984?

(c) Did your expenditure in total rise or fall?

(d) What has happened to the relative price of *Z* and *X*?

(e) Were you better off in 1984 or 1985? (Treat 'better off' as meaning 'having the consumption bundle that is revealed preferred', and assume that your tastes did not alter.)

What You Should Understand Now

The two axioms of revealed preference theory.
The meaning and relevance of transitivity.
The meaning of a budget line, and how to represent it algebraically and geometrically.
The effects of price and income changes on the budget line.
Samuelson's demand theorem for normal goods.
The difference between income and substitution effects and their empirical significance.
Why revealed preference theory cannot do without utility theory.
Evidence on income effects and the consistency of human and animal behaviour with the axioms of revealed preference theory.

7

Choice, Utility and Indifference Curves

The theory to be discussed in this chapter is the most widely used theory of choice in economics and is due to Sir John Hicks. You will be using it countless times in the rest of the book in both normative and positive versions. For the moment, however, the focus is exclusively on the use of the theory in positive economics. To help you distinguish between indifference curve theory and revealed preference theory, an approach similar to that of chapter 6, and using similar symbols, will be adopted.

Axioms of Indifference Curve Theory

The new symbol here is **I**, which stands for 'indifferent between'.

(1) **Comparison axiom** There is comparability between bundles of goods such that *either* B_1 **P** B_2, B_2 **P** B_1 *or* B_1 **I** B_2 (and B_2 **I** B_1, of course).

(2) **Transitivity axiom** If B_1 **P** B_2 and B_2 **P** B_3, then B_1 **P** B_3; and, if B_1 **I** B_2 and B_2 **I** B_3, then B_1 **I** B_3. Likewise, if B_1 **I** B_2 and B_2 **P** B_3, then B_1 **P** B_3; and, if B_1 **P** B_2 and B_2 **I** B_3, then B_1 **P** B_3.

(3) **Convexity axiom** The marginal rate of substitution of one economic good for another diminishes the more an individual consumes of the one, utility remaining the same.

These are more complicated than the Samuelsonian axioms presented in chapter 6. Before seeing whether the complications are worth while, look at them in more detail.

The addition to the *comparison axiom* makes it possible for an individual to be indifferent between any two bundles. In ordinal utility terms this is precisely equivalent to assigning the same utility number to any bundles between which an individual is indifferent. In behavioural terms, indifference might be revealed by one allowing someone else to select when one is indifferent, or by tossing a coin. In experiments, indifference is most commonly found by adjusting the contents of bundles until the borderline between more preferred and less preferred bundles is located. These bundles on the borderline are neither more nor less preferred: the individual is indifferent between them.

In chapter 6 you saw that the revealed preference comparison axiom commits one to the *strong ordering* of bundles. The comparison axiom in the indifference curve approach is slightly different: it commits one to *weak ordering* since ties are allowed.

The *transitivity axiom* presents no special difficulty apart from those discussed in chapter 6. SAQ 7.1, however, gives a good opportunity to refresh understanding.

SAQ 7.1

(a) An order of preference of five bundles of goods and services is B_1 first, B_2 third equal, B_3 second, B_4 fifth and B_5 third equal. If the utility numbers assigned are $B_1 = 10$, $B_2 = 6$, $B_3 = 8$ and $B_4 = 2$, what utility number must be assigned to B_5?

(b) Suppose the utility numbers were, instead, $B_1 = 100$, $B_2 = 3$, $B_3 = 4$ and $B_4 = -0.3$. What utility number must be assigned to B_5?

In the following comparisons between numbers, identify the preference relation (**I** or **P**) between B_1 and B_3, assuming transitivity:

(c) B_1 **P** B_2 **P** B_3
(d) B_1 **I** B_2 **I** B_3
(e) B_1 **I** B_2 **P** B_3
(f) B_1 **P** B_2 **I** B_3
(g) B_1 **P** B_4 **P** B_2 **I** B_3
(h) B_1 **I** B_4 **P** B_2 **I** B_3
(i) B_1 **P** B_4 **I** B_2 **P** B_3
(j) B_1 **I** B_4 **I** B_2 **I** B_3

The *convexity axiom* is entirely new and obviously needs some explanation. What it states is that if one were to connect together the various bundles of X and Z between which one is indifferent, the resulting curve (the **indifference curve**) will be convex with respect to the axes. Such a curve is drawn in figure 7.1, where three bundles (out of a potentially very large number) B_1, $\dot{B}_2$ and

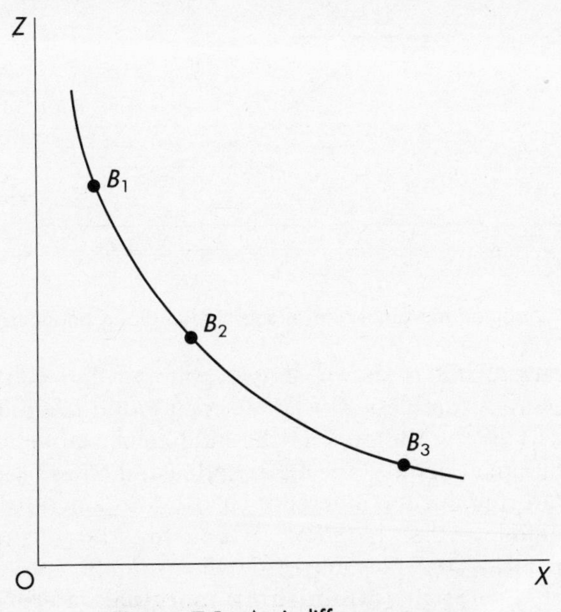

Figure 7.1 An indifference curve

B_3, between which an individual is indifferent, are shown on their indifference curve.

Recall postulate 3 of chapter 2. That postulate asserts that there is *some* amount of one good that an individual will sacrifice to obtain more of another good. The *maximum* amount voluntarily sacrificed for a little more of another good, divided by the extra amount of the other good, is the marginal rate of substitution. Now you should be able to see that if one sacrifices as much as one is willing of one thing to obtain a little more of another, then one must be indifferent between the pre- and post-sacrifice situations. If one preferred the post-sacrifice situation then the sacrifice cannot have been the maximum sacrifice; if one preferred the pre-sacrifice situation then the required sacrifice must exceed the maximum one would voluntarily give up.

This is indeed so, and *the slope of an indifference curve is the marginal rate of substitution (MRS).*

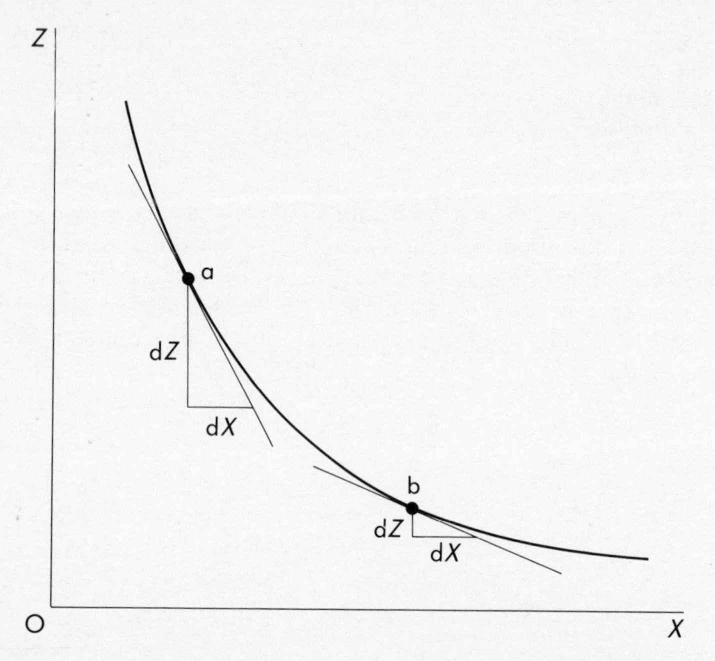

Figure 7.2 Changing marginal rate of substitution along an indifference curve

In figure 7.2 the *MRS* is shown at two points a and b. At point b the individual has more X (and less Z) than at point a, but is indifferent between points a and b. Evidently the slope of the indifference curve, or the *MRS*, is flatter at point b than at point a (the dX at both a and b has been drawn as the same distance to bring out the difference clearly). So long as the indifference curve is convex it follows that the *MRS* of X for Z (dZ/dX) gets smaller as more X is substituted for Z and one moves down an indifference curve. This is sometimes referred to as the **diminishing marginal rate of substitution**.

To have indifference between any two bundles, it is necessary for at least one of the goods in a bundle to be finely divisible, otherwise one might jump sharply from preference for one bundle to preference for another. If you treat all goods that are not X as one 'composite' good, this condition is suitably met, for the composite good will be almost infinitely divisible. Drawing *curves* of indifference, however, requires that *both* goods be divisible. For convenience assume that this is usually the case: recall that X and Z are in units *per period*. Since time can be finely divided, an additional source of divisibility (other than the physical property of the good itself) is the frequency of its consumption. For example, to see half a TV programme may be worse than seeing none of it at all: it cannot be divided without changing the whole character of the good. However, programmes are divisible according to their frequency of viewing: a programme per month, for example, is half as much as a programme per fortnight. Choices under uncertainty also increase the divisibility of options: for example you can have probability 0.01 of getting X, or probability 0.02 etc.

So far the figures have shown only one indifference curve. Normally there will be a great number; these constitute an **indifference map**. Just as the contours of a geographical map join up points of equal height above sea level, so the curves on an indifference map join up points of equal utility. Figure 7.3 shows an indifference map with a selection of indifference curves (a geographical map contains a selection of contour lines). The indifference curves have been labelled U_0, U_1, U_2, U_3 and U_4 in ascending order of preference. Given such a map you can make comparisons between all the bundles in it. For example, how do B_1 and B_3 compare? You know that B_2 **P** B_3, since B_2 has more X *and* Z than B_3 and one assumes both Z and X to be economic goods (for

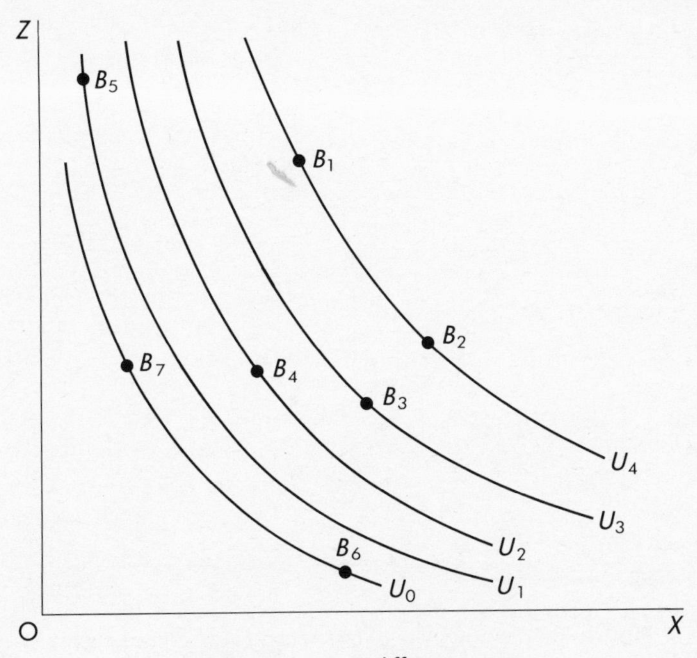

Figure 7.3 An indifference map

example, let Z be one's personal income and X the income of one's favourite charity). Since B_1 and B_2 are on the same indifference curve, B_1 **I** B_2. Hence, by transitivity, B_1 **P** B_3 (in the example, although one likes the thought of one's favourite charity having more, there is some addition to one's own income that one likes *even more*). By a similar argument you may say B_3 **P** B_4 (in this comparison one prefers a drop in one's own income if one is sufficiently compensated by an increase in the charity's). Comparing all the points, you have

$$B_1 \mathbf{I} B_2 \mathbf{P} B_3 \mathbf{P} B_4 \mathbf{P} B_5 \mathbf{P} B_6 \mathbf{I} B_7$$

SAQ 7.2

(a) For the bundles in figure 7.3, state the preference relation between: B_1 and B_2; B_1 and B_7; B_2 and B_5; B_5 and B_6.

(b) If the utility index of B_7 is 10 and that of B_1 is 200, what are the utility indices of B_6 and B_2?

(c) If the utility index of B_7 is 10 and that of B_1 is 200, is it possible for that of B_3 to be 205 and that of B_5 to be 199?

Indifference curves cannot intersect. This can most easily be proved by supposing two curves to cross and by then showing the inconsistency of this with the axioms of the theory. Figure 7.4 shows two curves crossing. The intersection is labelled B_1. B_1 **I** B_2 since they lie on the same indifference curve. Also, B_1 **I** B_3 since they are also on a common indifference curve. By transitivity, therefore, B_2 **I** B_3. But B_2 **P** B_3 since it has more of each good. The axioms are therefore contradicted. Indifference curves *cannot* cross.

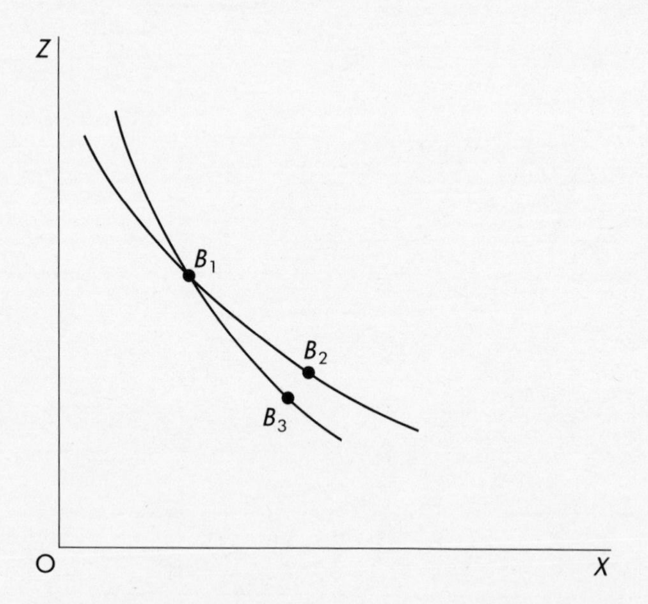

Figure 7.4 Impossibility of intersecting indifference curves

Case Study 7.1 Experimental Estimation of Indifference Curves

MacCrimmon and Toda (1969) conducted an experiment to test the characteristics of indifference curves, namely negative slope (for economic goods), convexity and non-intersection. Using a small sample of students who were familiar with graphical methods (the students were majoring in maths, engineering or economics) they offered choices between money and ballpoint pens in one experiment and money and pastries in another.

Each student was given an initial reference bundle (say $3 and no pens) and then asked to draw an indifference curve passing through this bundle. The method used (for the money versus pens case) was to ask the students to identify bundles which were preferred or less preferred to the reference bundle. Thus in figure 7.5, for the initial starting bundle B_0, points such as B_1 and B_2 could be identified. If B_1 **P** B_0, then all bundles north and east would also be preferred since such bundles had more of both goods (such points are shaded in the figure). Similarly, if B_0 **P** B_2, then all points south and west would also be not preferred (these points are also shaded). By taking a sufficient series of such points (like B_3, B_4 etc.) the boundary between more and less preferred points was identified. This is shown as a dashed line – the indifference curve – in the figure. The experiment was then repeated for another reference bundle (not shown in the figure), and in this way seven indifference curves were drawn by each student.

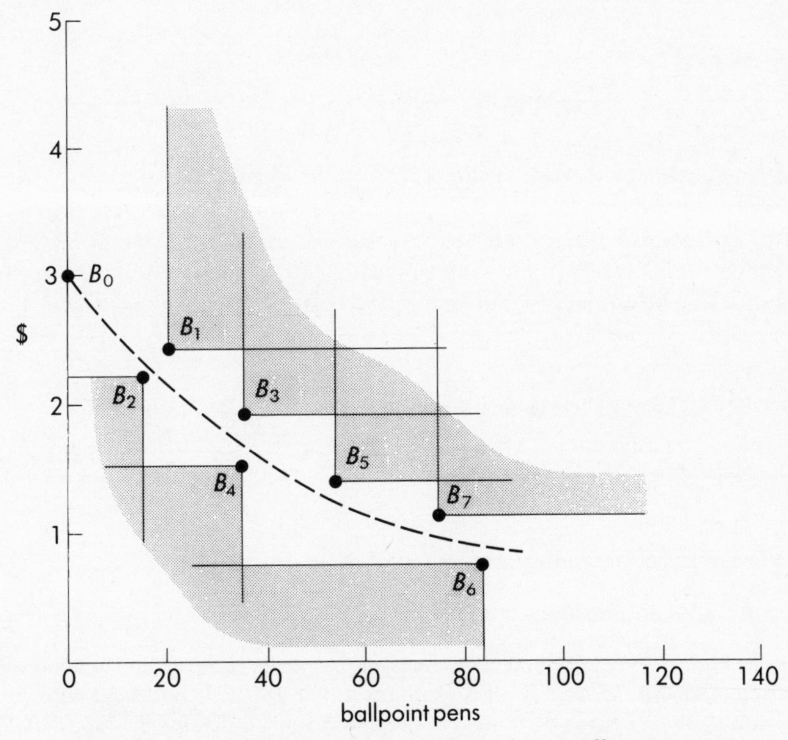

Figure 7.5 Experimental determination of an indifference curve

In general, the axioms of indifference curve theory were upheld. Incidentally, for the men the French pastries ceased to be economic goods after one or two had been chosen, and for the women they were not economic goods right from the beginning!

K. R. MacCrimmon and M. Toda (1969), 'Experimental determination of indifference curves', *Review of Economic Studies*, **36**, 433–51.

The relationship of the *MRS* to marginal utility should be quite easy to grasp by now. Recall that $MRS = \mathrm{d}Z/\mathrm{d}X$, where d$Z$ measures the maximum an individual would sacrifice to obtain the dX. dZ is clearly an objectively revealable *value* of dX; it is its value *in terms of* Z. The marginal value of X in terms of Z is thus given by the *MRS*. We can now make the link with Marshallian theory. dX is the amount of X needed to compensate the individual (exactly) for the loss of dZ. The utility of dX is the marginal utility of X multiplied by dX. The utility of dZ (the sacrifice) is the marginal utility of Z multiplied by dZ. Since the value of the gain exactly compensates for the value of the loss (we are dealing with two points on the same indifference curve) we may write

$$MU_Z \mathrm{d}Z = MU_X \mathrm{d}X$$

where MU_X and MU_Z are the marginal utilities of X and Z. Rearranging,

$$\frac{\mathrm{d}Z}{\mathrm{d}X} = MRS = \frac{MU_X}{MU_Z}$$

Thus the ratio of the marginal utilities is the MRS. The Marshallian theory is a special case, then, of the indifference curve theory. The beauty of the indifference theory, however, is that it needs only an order (a weak order). For purposes of demand theory you do not need to know that MU_X/MU_Z is the *MRS*, though it is always interesting to see how old theories often turn out to be special cases (true under certain restrictive assumptions) of the newer ones.

SAQ 7.3

You are indifferent between the following three bundles:

	X	*Z*
B_1	9	5
B_2	5	25
B_3	1	45

Which axiom of indifference curve theory are you violating?

Case Study 7.2 Indifference and Ill Health

George Torrance (1970) conducted some experiments in order to see whether it was possible to measure the degree of preference that individuals had over two ways of treating tuberculosis: home confinement or sanatorium confinement. The advantages and disadvantages of each were described in terms of pain, discomfort, immobility, restriction of activity and so on. A sample of individuals (Canadian general practitioners) was then asked to consider these two options and two others: perfect health and instant death. There were thus four options in all: perfect health (H), home confinement (HC), sanatorium confinement (SC) and immediate death (D). Subjects were asked first to rank the four, which they did in the order just given: H **P** HC **P** SC **P** D. Arbitrary utility numbers of 1 and 0 were then attached to H and D that preserved their rank order. Using the symbol *U*(1) to indicate the utility of each option, Torrance therefore had *U*(H) = 1, *U*(D) = 0, and the problem was to find *U*(HC) and *U*(SC).

These utility numbers were found by offering the test subjects a series of *standard gambles.* Thus a subject could have either HC for sure *or* a gamble whose outcome would be either perfect health (H) or immediate death (D). By successive adjustments of the probabilities of H and D the point at which the subject became indifferent could be identified.

At the point of indifference:

$$U(\mathrm{HC}) = pU(\mathrm{D}) + (1-p)U(\mathrm{H})$$

where p is the probability, which has to lie between 0 and 1. Torrance found that on average the subjects were indifferent when $p = 0.436$. Putting this in the equation with the arbitrary numbers for *U*(H) and *U*(D) gave:

$$U(\mathrm{HC}) = 0.436(0) + 0.564(1)$$

therefore

$$U(\mathrm{HC}) = 0.564.$$

By a similar procedure, he found *U*(SC) = 0.340.

The utility numbers assigned by this process of identifying points of indifference were thus *U*(H) = 1.0, *U*(HC) = 0.564, *U*(SC) = 0.340, *U*(D) = 0.0. This index of utility is not on a ratio but on an *interval* scale. Although the initial utility numbers of 1 and 0 were arbitrary (save in so far as they correctly placed these two options in order), the resulting scale is precisely analogous to temperature measurement. The selection of a number for death and perfect health is essentially the same as selecting numbers for the freezing and boiling points of water (see chapter 5). Test this for yourself by letting, say, *U*(H) = 5 and *U*(D) = 1.

Torrance went on to show how these results could help health planners in Canada (Ontario) plan their TB mass screening programme (See case study 20.2).

G. W. Torrance (1970) *A Generalized Cost-Effectiveness Model for the Evaluation of Health Programs,* Hamilton, Ontario, McMaster University Faculty of Business.

Closed Indifference Curves

You do not have to assume that preferences are only over *goods*. There may be some entities that are always 'bads', and some that are sometimes goods but beyond a certain rate of consumption become 'bads' (analogous to the pastries in case study 7.1). Instead of having the *open* indifference curves drawn so far, let them be *closed*. Such a case is shown in figure 7.6, where there are two closed indifference curves U_0 and U_1. Implicitly there is again a complete map; it converges on the point labelled 'bliss' where an individual has as much as he or

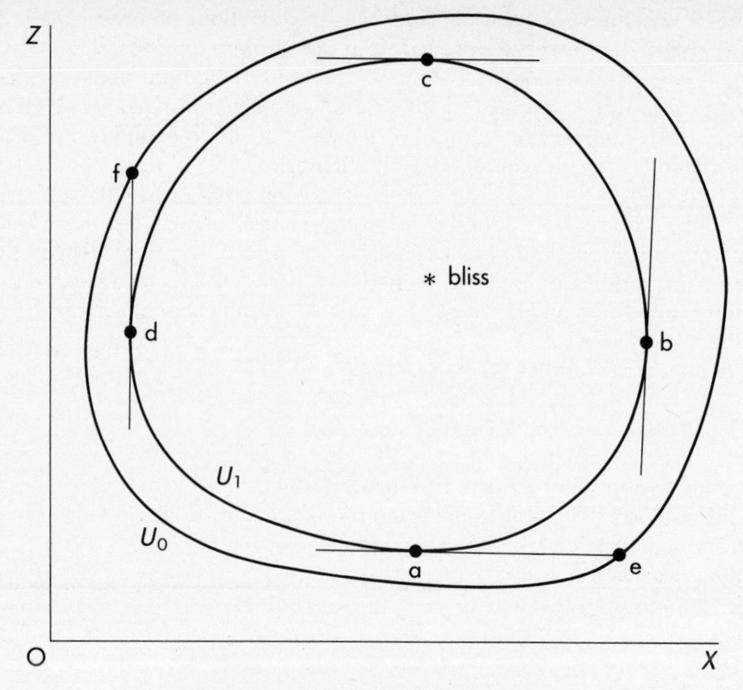

Figure 7.6 Closed indifference curves

she wants of everything. Between points d and a on U_1 both X and Z are goods: more of either increases utility. Note, however, what happens if the individual consumes more X than when at point a, with no less Z. He or she moves to a position such as point e, on a 'lower' (further out) indifference curve which is less preferred. In other words, whenever the indifference curve becomes flat, the individual is *satiated* with the good measured on the X axis; having more reduces the utility index. Note that at point e, although X has become a bad, Z is still a good: more of it adds to the utility index (i.e. more is preferred). Similarly, the individual moves from point d to point f, the opposite is the case: Z has ceased to be an economic good even though X remains one.

In figure 7.6 the points where the indifference curve becomes flat or vertical have been marked a, b, c and d. Between points d and a, both X and Z are goods to the individual. Between points a and b, Z is a good and X a bad. Between points d and c, X is a good and Z a bad. Between points c and b increasing either X or Z will reduce the utility index, so each is a bad.

This analysis shows one of the ways in which indifference curve analysis can be made even more general. For the moment, however (and for most of this book), non-satiation in individual goods and services will be assumed (the most notable exception will be in the discussion of labour supply, where work will be treated as a bad).

The Demand Theorem and Indifference Curves

If you superimpose an indifference map on a diagram showing an individual's budget line, as in figure 7.7, something striking emerges. The budget line is constructed as before and has a slope $-P_X/P_Z$. Assuming that individuals choose the most preferred bundle available to them, the individual will select (note: *will* select, not will *try to* select) the indifference curve with the highest utility number. This requires a move to point a in figure 7.7, where the budget line is tangential to an indifference curve.

At this point
$$MRS = \frac{P_X}{P_Z} = \frac{dZ}{dX}$$
$$(X>0,\ Z>0)$$

That is, the relative price of X to Z is equal to the marginal rate of substitution of X for Z. As long as some of both goods is consumed (i.e. $X>0$ and $Z>0$), this condition is necessary if the individual is to be in *equilibrium*: a state from which there is no reason to move.

SAQ 7.4

(a) In figure 7.7, why is the individual not in equilibrium at point b or c (which are on the budget line)?

(b) What is the link between the Hicksian and the Marshallian equilibrium conditions for a utility maximizing individual?

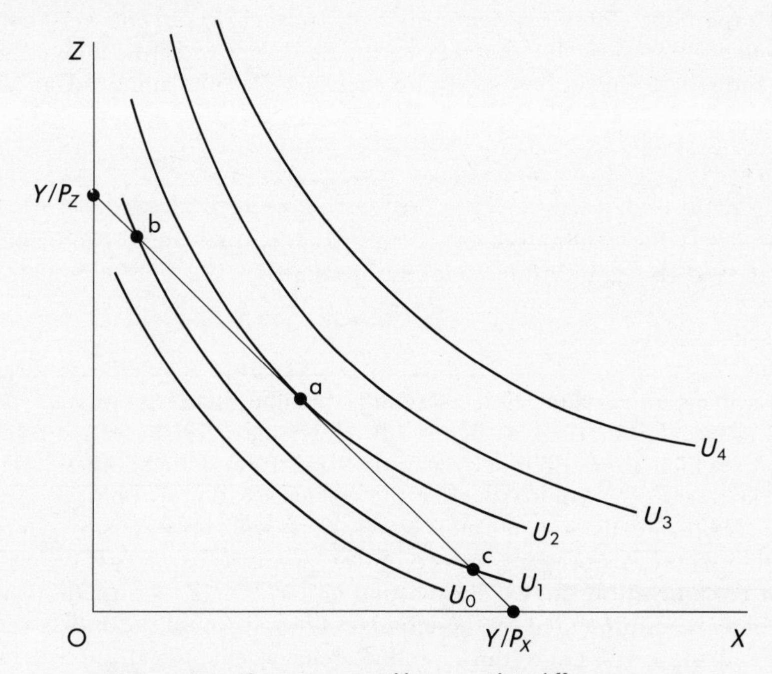

Figure 7.7 Consumer equilibrium with indifference curves

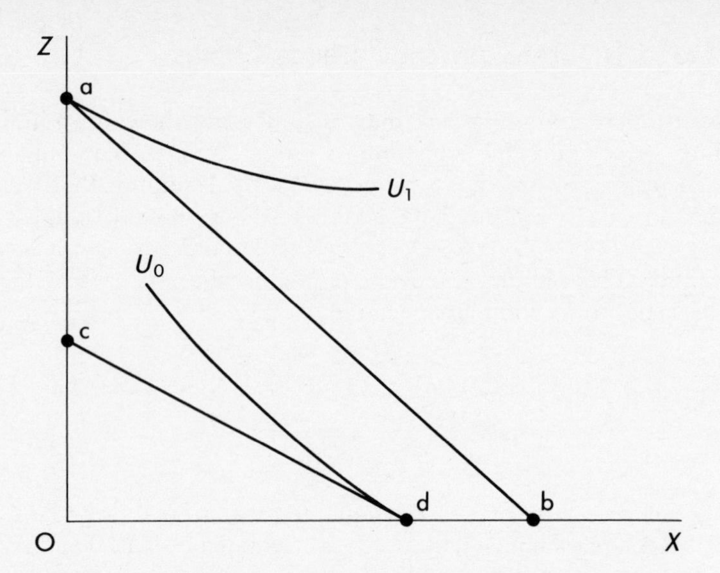

Figure 7.8 Equilibrium of the consumer with corner solutions

Not every point of maximum utility is a tangency point. Postulate 1 of chapter 1 stipulated that individuals choose *many* goods, not that each person consumes *some* of *all* goods. There are some goods (probably the overwhelming majority) that you *never* buy or consume even though you could afford to (in modest amounts, perhaps, for very costly goods). In such cases one gets **corner solutions** such as those illustrated in figure 7.8. Here, when the budget line is ab, the individual maximizes utility by choosing Oa of Z and no X at all, so that

$$P_X/P_Z \geqslant MRS_{XZ}$$

Alternatively, when the budget line is cd, this individual would choose only X (Od of it) and the equilibrium condition becomes

$$P_X/P_Z \leqslant MRS_{XZ}$$

What happens to consumption as money income changes (relative prices remaining the same)? Look at figure 7.9. Here there are successive levels of income at which the individual maximizes utility and therefore selects the appropriate tangency point (save for the corner solution at point a). In the example, both goods are normal goods and will have positive income elasticities. The locus of points traced out by points a, b, c etc. is termed the **income consumption curve**. By plotting either X or Z against the various levels of income represented by these budget lines, it would be an easy matter to trace out the Engel curves for X and Z (refer to chapter 4) implicit in the income consumption curve.

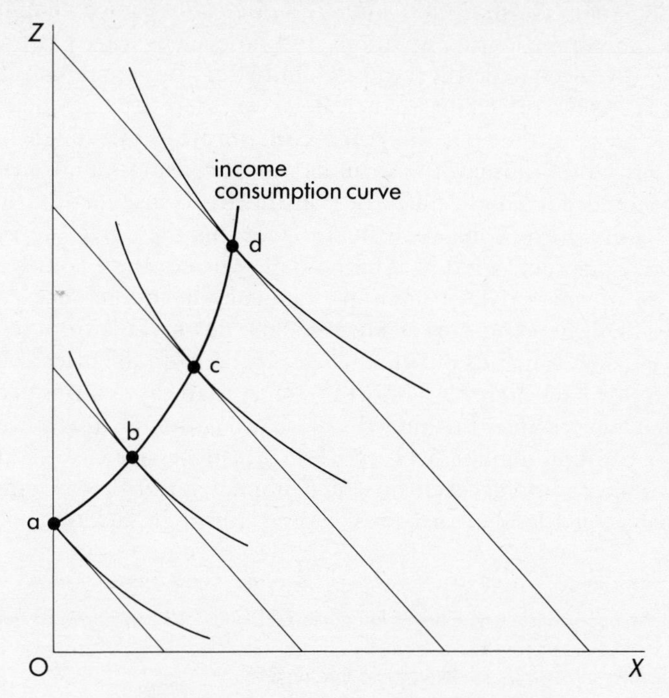

Figure 7.9 An income consumption curve

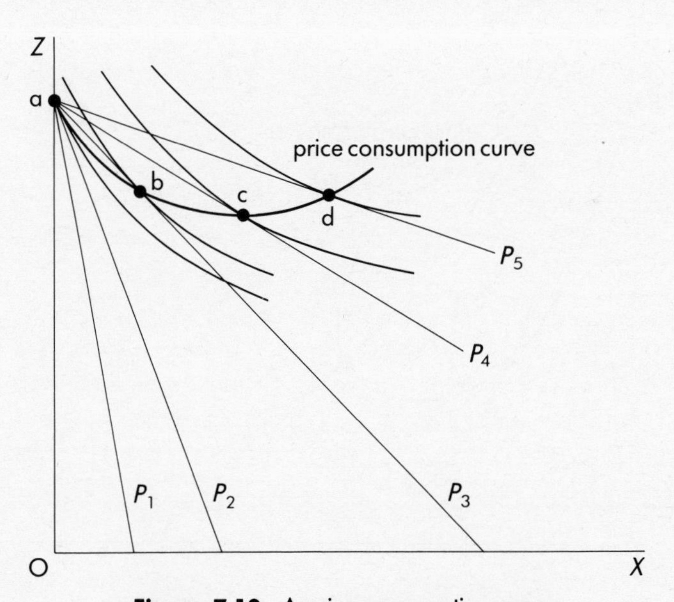

Figure 7.10 A price consumption curve

What happens to consumption when the price of one good changes? Figure 7.10 shows the various corner solutions and tangencies traced out as P_X falls. At P_1 and P_2, X is too expensive and the individual buys none at all (a corner solution at a). As the price falls further, however, there are tangencies at points b, c, d etc. and you trace out the **price consumption curve**. In figure 7.10, falls in the price of X induce *increases* in its rate of consumption (once price has fallen low enough for any at all to be consumed). Consequently the demand curve for X must have a negative slope. Does this then give the indifference curve demand theorem? That is, if individuals who consume some of the good, and have an income, always maintain tangency of indifference curves with budget lines, will demand curves always slope downwards from left to right? The answer clearly depends on whether one can rely on the price consumption curve not to curl back on itself. Unfortunately it is an easy matter to draw price consumption curves that do indeed curl back without violating any of the axioms. For example figures 7.11 and 7.12 illustrate two cases starting from different corner solutions, each of which implies an *upward* sloping demand curve. Have a good look at these two figures and then tackle SAQ 7.5.

SAQ 7.5

(a) Why do the price consumption curves in figures 7.11 and 7.12 imply upward sloping demand curves?

(b) Do the indifference curves in either figure intersect?

(c) Are the indifference curves everywhere negatively sloped?

(d) Does the *MRS* everywhere diminish along indifference curves?

(e) Is transitivity violated?

(f) Is the comparison axiom violated?

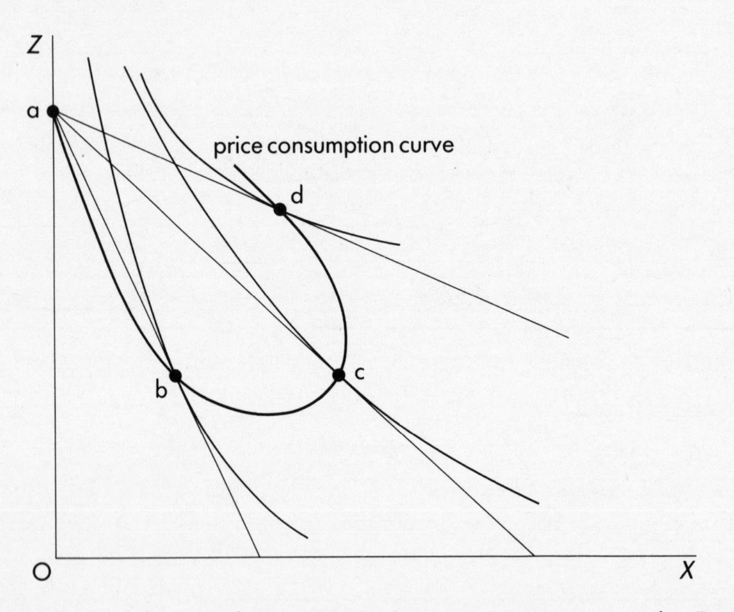

Figure 7.11 A 'perverse' price consumption curve originating on the *Z* axis

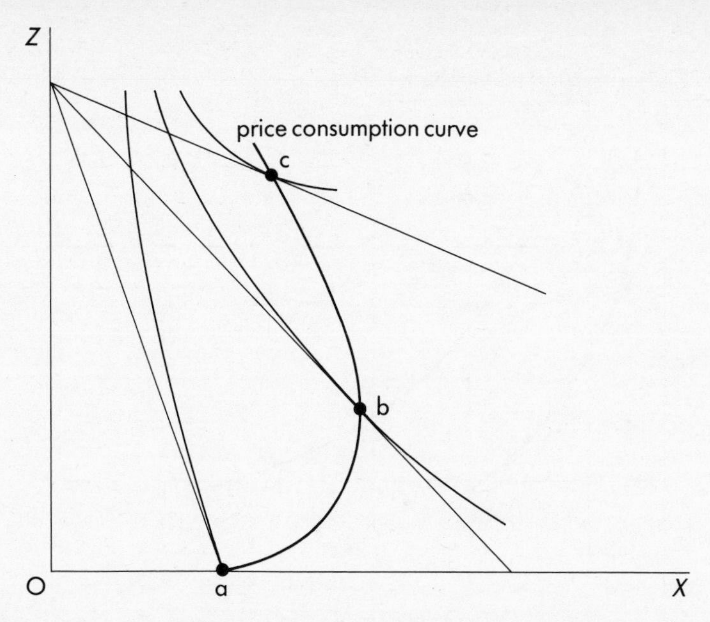

Figure 7.12 A 'perverse' price consumption curve originating on the X axis

Income and Substitution Effects Revisited

Consider figure 7.13. Initially an individual is maximizing utility at point a on an initial budget line, consuming X_1 of X. Now let the price of X fall from P_X to P'_X. The new utility maximizing bundle is at point b where X_2 of X is consumed. In a fashion analogous to that used in the examination of revealed preference theory, the move from point a to point b can be divided into a substitution and an income effect. In indifference curve theory, however, instead of *purchasing power* being held constant (as in revealed preference theory), *utility* is held constant. This is done by removing money income such that, at the *new* price, the individual can just attain the initial level of *utility*. This requires, in figure 7.13, a reduction in income from Y to Y', so the new intercept on the Z axis (where Z represents all goods other than X) of Y'/P_Z is closer to the origin than the initial intercept Y/P_Z. The new utility maximizing point is c, on the same indifference curve as point a, with X_3 of X being consumed. Combining the price fall with the compensating variation in income, the individual will move from point a to point c, and X consumption will increase from X_1 to X_3. This is the *substitution effect* and it shows the effect of the relative change in price *alone* on X consumption (since you have removed any changes in real income and all else is assumed unchanged). For a fall in price this will *always* induce an increase in consumption (other than for corner solutions).

If the individual now has the $Y-Y'$ returned, the budget line moves out parallel to itself and point b is attained. The move from point c to point b is the

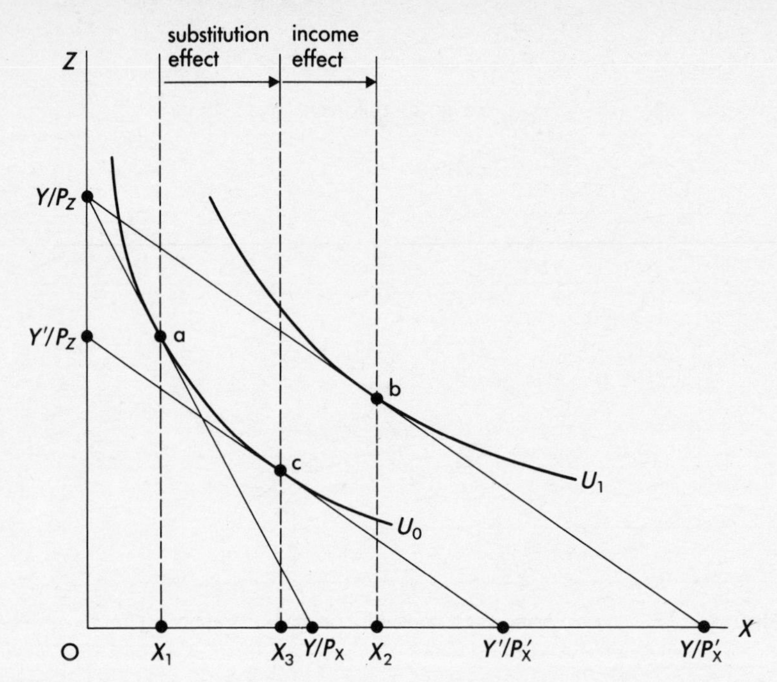

Figure 7.13 Income and substitution effects in indifference curve theory (normal good)

income effect. In this example X is a normal good and an increase in income (alone) increases X consumption (from X_3 to X_2). The income effect reinforces the substitution effect so their combined effect is to increase quantity demanded as price falls: as in the revealed preference theory, if X is a normal good its demand curve must slope down.

But what if X is an inferior good? Figure 7.14 shows a case where X is inferior. As before, the combination of a price fall and a compensating reduction in income is to increase quantity demanded. Returning the income to the individual, enabling a move from point c to point b, now however *reduces* the demand for X: the income effect is negative (which is the same thing as saying X is inferior). In this case, however, the negative income effect on X consumption is quantitatively less than the positive substitution effect, so the final utility maximizing point b is still to the right of the initial point a. Thus, *the demand curve for an inferior good may also slope down*. This proposition could not be made in Samuelson's demand theorem, which is stated only for goods with positive income elasticities.

You will, of course, now be able to see the possibility of the perverse case: what if X is so inferior that the negative income effect outweighs the positive substitution effect? This is shown in figure 7.15. The substitution effect, as before, is positive in its impact on X consumption as the individual moves from point a to point c and changes X consumption from X_1 to X_3. The income effect is, however, now strongly negative as the individual moves from point c to

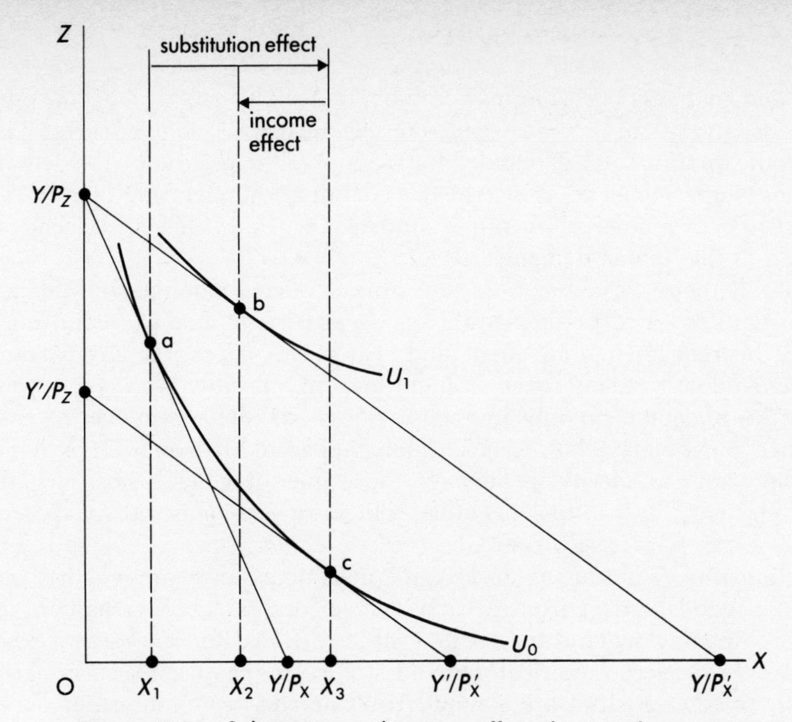

Figure 7.14 Substitution and income effects for an inferior good

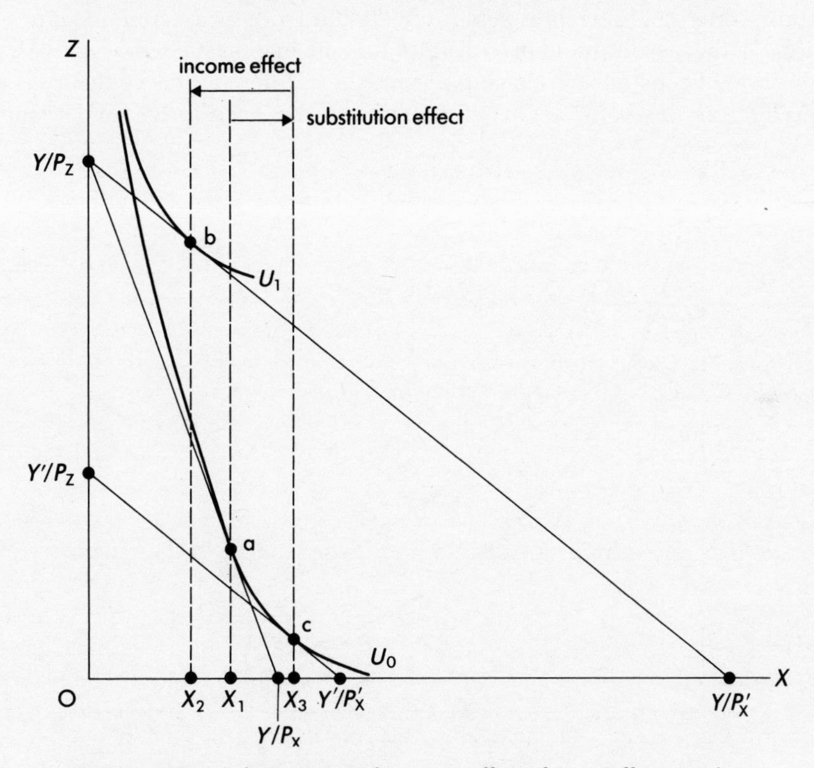

Figure 7.15 Substitution and income effects for a Giffen good

point b and changes X consumption from X_3 to X_2. The negative income effect (X_3-X_2) is larger than the positive income effect (X_3-X_1), so the net result is a *decline* in the quantity of X demanded in response to the price fall – the demand curve slopes up. Such a good is termed a **Giffen good** after Sir Robert Giffen (1837–1910), a nineteenth century statistician who believed he had an exception to the 'law of demand'.

The indifference curve theory is thus able to offer a more general demand theorem than revealed preference theory. In particular, one can enunciate a demand theorem for inferior goods and also specify a possible circumstance when demand curves may (over a range) take on a positive slope (you would look for this phenomenon only among inferior goods). This gain over revealed preference theory may, however, be more apparent than real. It is not in general possible to specify in advance those inferior goods whose negative income elasticity is not 'too' negative, and most economists deny that the Giffen case has ever *actually* been observed.

This difficulty of producing an unambiguous demand theorem (other than for normal goods) arises from a carry-over of one of the Marshallian side conditions defining demand curves: that they are drawn *assuming money income to be constant*. In modern empirical demand studies, as has been seen in earlier chapters, price elasticities are estimated not on this assumption but on the assumption that real income (the purchasing power of income) remains constant, thus enabling one separately to measure price and income elasticities. If the assumption of constant money income is replaced with the assumption of constant purchasing power, the indifference curve theory is able to predict an *unambiguous* negative relation between price and quantity

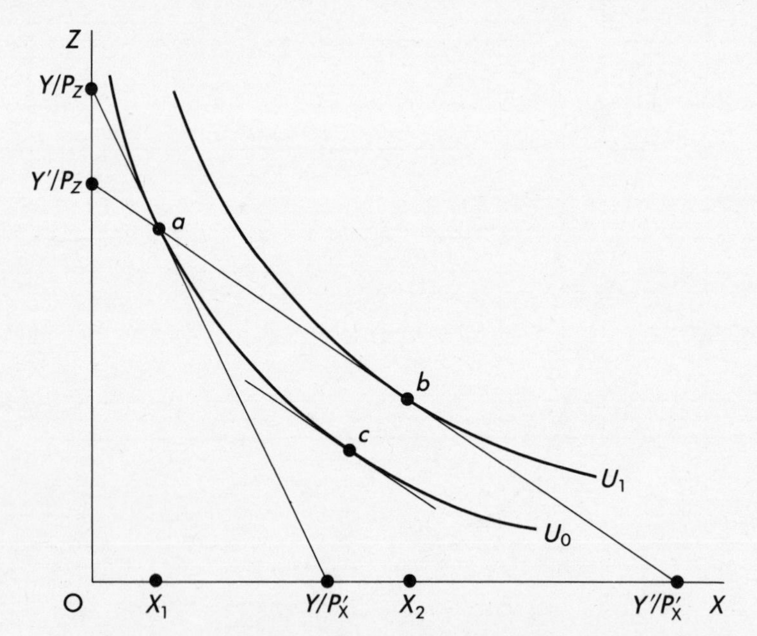

Figure 7.16 Substitution effect keeping purchasing power constant

demanded, whereas all the revealed preference theory can predict is that quantity demanded *will not fall* if price falls.

In figure 7.16 the individual is initially at point a. The price of X falls and at the same time a compensating variation in income is made to keep the individual at the same purchasing power (but not on the same indifference curve). This involves selecting a budget line having a slope given by the new price ratio and passing through point a, so that at the new prices the individual could (just) buy the original bundle at point a (recall the analysis of chapter 6). Now revealed preference theory says that the individual will either stay at point a or move to the right along the new budget line. But it cannot be known which. Indifference curve theory predicts unambiguously that the individual will move to the right to a point such as b, where the new budget line is tangential to an indifference curve. Note that the tangency at point c with the original indifference curve is not the tangency in question; it is not utility that is kept constant but purchasing power (that is, the power to purchase the original bundle at point a). Point b must lie to the right of point a, owing to the convexity axiom) and so *compensated* demand curves must have a negative slope. If the purchasing power of income is kept constant (rather than just money income), demand curves must have a negative slope *even for inferior goods*.

SAQ 7.6

(a) Construct a diagram showing the substitution effect holding purchasing power constant for an inferior good.

(b) The substitution effect for a price reduction measured holding purchasing power constant is always larger than that measured holding utility constant. True or false?

One of the reasons indifference curves have proved a popular method of analysis among economists is that they do produce an unambiguous demand theorem for compensated price changes of the sort discussed (that is, income is adjusted so as to keep purchasing power constant). As will be seen in later chapters, they also have dozens of other applications and their use is by no means confined to the derivation of a demand theorem. They also lend themselves to some interesting *normative* interpretations that you will examine later and that are widely used.

Case study 7.3 illustrates a typical *normative* use of indifference curves and shows the kind of insight you can get into a tricky political issue by using clear analysis. As a final check on your understanding of indifference curves, however, first tackle SAQ 7.7.

Case Study 7.3 Is it Better to Subsidize Consumption or Income?

It is commonly asserted (especially by liberal economists) that individuals are better off with *cash* subsidies than they are with a subsidy *in kind* of the same market value. Indifference curve analysis can help in an examination of the kind of assumptions under which this may be the case. This case study illustrates a quite common way in which economists use indifference curves – for *analytical* purposes, in order to trace out the logical implications of the assumptions or to solve a specific problem like the one posed here.

To begin with it is necessary – since the question is evidently a *normative* question about what is good (or better) – to make the value judgements clear. A common one underlying this assertion is that it is 'better' if an individual can move to a higher indifference curve (so long as no one else moves to a lower one), or can have a more preferred choice, or can have a higher level of utility (you might be willing to take these three statements as being different ways of saying exactly the same thing). Now see what follows from using this value judgement.

Suppose that an individual is initially at point a in figure 7.17 on the budget line, emanating from Z_0, which reflects the market price of *X*. *X* is a specific good or service and *Z* represents all other goods and services. It is decided to subsidize the price of *X*, which falls, and the individual moves to point b on the new budget line. What is the cost of the subsidy?

Measure the cost in terms of *Z*. The individual evidently pays $Z_0 Z_1$ to obtain Z_1b of *X*. The *full* cost of Z_1b is, however, given by the line Z_2b, which has the same slope as Z_0a, indicating that the market cost of this amount of *X* is $Z_2 Z_1$. Since the consumer pays $Z_0 Z_1$, that leaves $Z_2 Z_0$ to be paid by those who finance the subsidy (say taxpayers if the government provides the subsidy). Suppose the individual is not allowed to resell subsidized *X* consumption or that it is a personal service that cannot be resold (say, a visit to the local museum).

Now, instead of the subsidy on the price, suppose one simply gave the individual

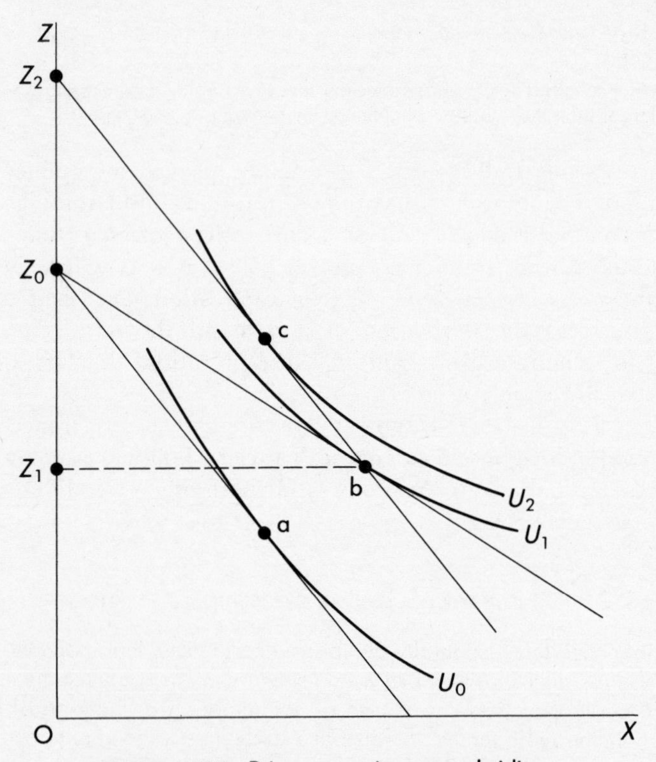

Figure 7.17 Price versus income subsidies

the same subsidy in cash: Z_0Z_2. The budget line is shifted from Z_0a to Z_2b. A point such as c is now chosen which *must*, on the axioms of indifference curve analysis, lie on a higher indifference curve. Therefore, for the same cost (to the taxpayer) the income subsidy enables the individual to reach a higher indifference curve. The income subsidy is therefore – given the normative assumption and given the axioms of indifference curve analysis – unambiguously better.

Note that if the individual can resell X at no extra cost, he or she could, under the price subsidy, move from point b to point c by selling X at the market price. In this case, the two methods of subsidy are equally good.

This is a favourite argument put by liberals for income subsidies and/or freedom to

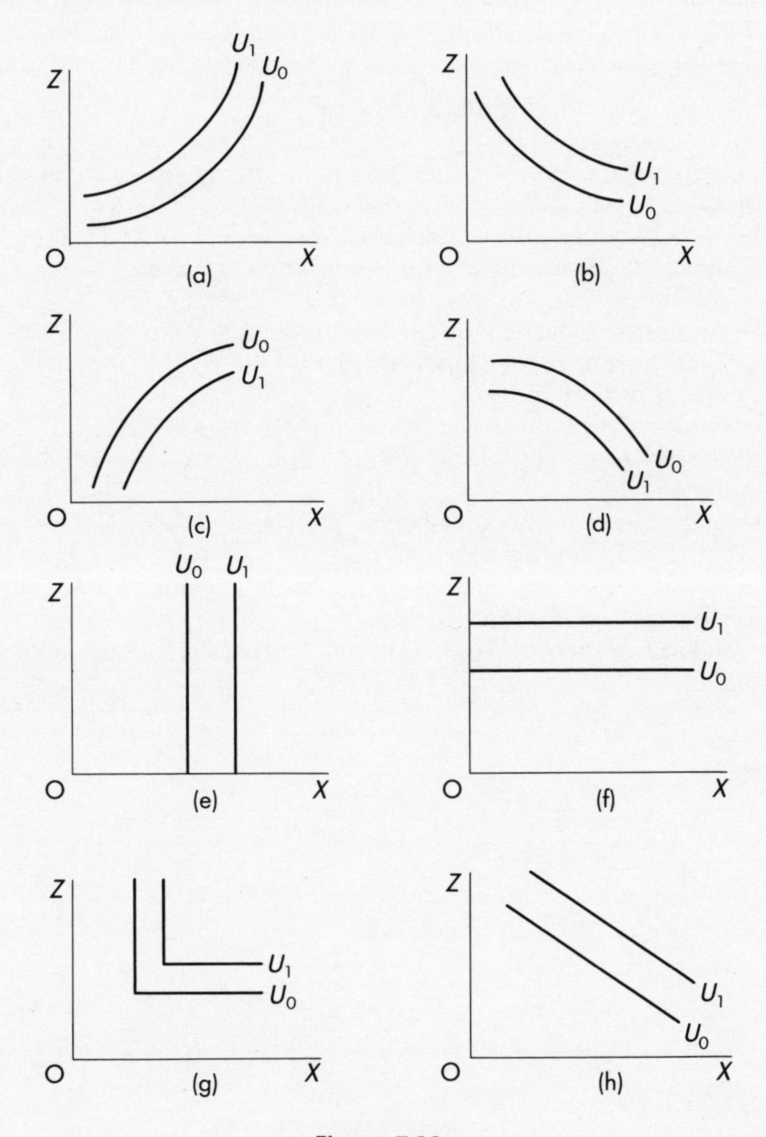

Figure 7.18

resell. Note, however, the assumptions it makes (and ask yourself if you find them – especially the value judgement – acceptable). Note also that at point c the individual consumes less X than at point b (and may consume less even than at point a if X is inferior). Thus, if the purpose of the subsidy was to increase X consumption to the level Z_1b, then the income subsidy may be *not* preferred by those financing it. In that case the subsidized individual may be better off and the subsidizers worse off!

SAQ 7.7

Given the indifference curves in figure 7.18 (a) – (h), where U_1 represents more utility than U_0, comment on the characteristics of goods X and Z in each of the cases (a) – (h).

What You Should Understand Now

The meaning and use of the comparison, transitivity and convexity axioms.
Difference between strong and weak preference orderings.
Marginal rate of substitution and indifference curves.
Why indifference curves cannot cross one another.
How indifference maps may be experimentally derived.
Use of indifference in a standard gamble to develop indices of ill-health (and other things).
Consumer equilibrium as tangency and corner solutions.
Relationship between Marshallian and Hicksian equilibrium conditions.
Difference between the substitution effects in revealed preference theory and indifference curve theory.
Relationships between income and substitution effects needed for negatively sloped demand curves.
Use of indifference curves to discuss normative issues involving subsidies.

8

Demand and Exchange

In previous chapters a lot of attention has been given to the details of demand theory. Although typically this amount of detail is not required in introductory economics, the purpose of going through it there was mainly to show how theories are formulated and rival theories compared. If you were to take a random sample of economics textbooks you would probably find that all three of the main theories of demand you have met were represented in the sample, though not necessarily in each textbook. This shows that different economists have reached different conclusions about the merits of rival theories; choosing unambiguously between them is by no means an easy task. SAQ 8.1 affords an opportunity for you to evaluate the three demand theories discussed. This chapter will take the fundamental rationale for the negative slope of demand curves as given and will explore the idea of demand in exchange or trade.

SAQ 8.1

This is a question for discussion and one that has no 'right' answer. An essay on it might form the basis of a useful seminar.

Which theory of demand (marginal utility, revealed preference or indifference curves) do you judge to be the 'best'? Make the criterion or criteria of 'best' clear at the beginning of your essay.

Two Ways of Looking at Demand Curves

One can look at a demand curve as showing either of two things:

(1) The maximum amount of a good or service purchased per period at a variety of prices

(2) The maximum amount that would be paid for a little more or less of a good or service at a variety of different amounts of a good or service per period.

In either case the word 'maximum' is there for a reason. It is there in the first interpretation because sometimes an individual may be able to purchase less than the amount demanded at a given price (for example, because of rationing). In such a case the individual will be 'off' his or her demand curve. The word 'maximum' is there in the second interpretation because the marginal rate of substitution tells us the *maximum* that will be sacrificed of one

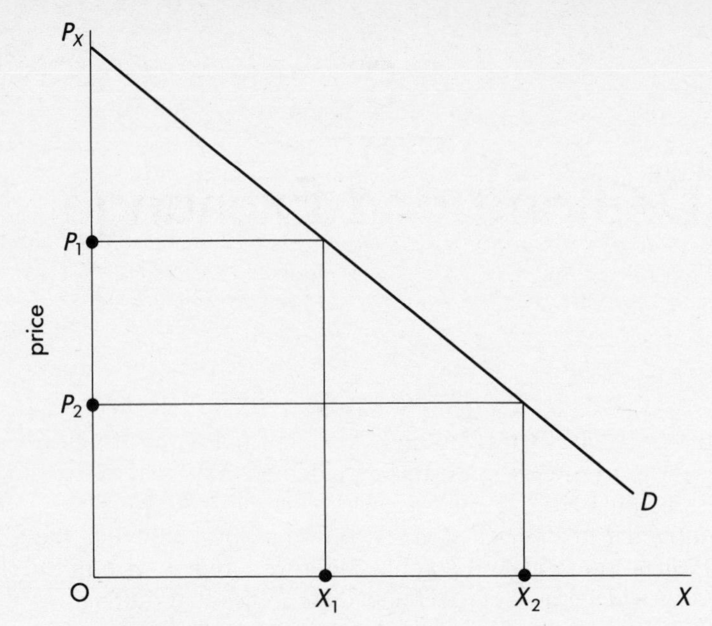

Figure 8.1 Two ways of reading a demand curve

thing for a little more of another and you know that the relative price of a good is equal to the *MRS* in equilibrium.

The first way of looking at the demand curve involves one in reading it *across* (or horizontally, from price to quantity); the second way involves us in reading it *up* (or vertically, from quantity to price).

Consider the demand curve in figure 8.1. According to the first way of reading the curve, the relation between price and quantity runs from left to right: what is the maximum rate of X that will be purchased when price is P_1 or P_2? Answer: X_1 or X_2. According to the second way of looking at it, one asks what is the maximum an individual will pay for a tiny increment in X when he or she already has X_1 or X_2? Answer: P_1 or P_2. According to this way of looking at the curve, you are discovering the **marginal value** placed by the individual on a small increase or decrease in X consumption. For this reason, when the curve is being given this interpretation, it is often referred to as a **marginal valuation curve**. The marginal value is, or course, dependent upon an individual's income, wealth, consumption of other goods etc. If these change, marginal value is likely also to change.

SAQ 8.2

This SAQ is designed to help you explore the link between the idea of marginal value and the *MRS*. You will find it helpful to draw a diagram with X on the horizontal axis and all other goods on the vertical (call this Z), and then to draw an indifference map.

If income rises when an individual is consuming at a rate of X_0 and the demand for X is income elastic, (a) what happens to the marginal value of X at the X_0 rate of consumption, and (b) what happens to it if income falls? (c) If price remains the same, is the marginal valuation of X higher, lower or the same at the new income level?

Value in Use and Value in Exchange

You can now make a distinction between the total value placed on a given rate of consumption of a good and its value as usually revealed in a market. Look at figure 8.2. In this figure, the marginal value of X consumption when X_1 is the rate is indicated by P_1, the height of the demand curve (marginal valuation curve) above X_1. If X is traded in a market at price P_1, the demand curve also says that the total amount spent by an individual on X_1 per unit of time will be P_1X_1 (price times rate of consumption). This is indicated by the rectangle OP_1aX_1. Another term for this is **value in exchange**: the expenditure per period by this individual on X. But this will be *less than* the value placed by the individual on X_1 consumption. To see this, consider the marginal value placed on X consumption when the smallest possible amount is purchased rather than none at all. This is shown by the height of the demand curve at point b. For a further marginal increase in X consumption, the value placed on the increment (the marginal value) is shown by the height of point c above the X axis. The total value placed on two units of consumption is therefore the sum of the two marginal values. A further increment is valued at point d. Further increments are valued at points e, f, g etc. The *total* value of a consumption rate of X_1 is thus the sum of all these increments: the value of one unit rather than none, plus the value of two rather than one, plus the value of three rather than two and so on. This total value is given by $ObaX_1$ – the area between the demand curve and the X axis from the origin to X_1. This is often termed **value in use**. It is clearly larger than value in exchange. The difference between value in use

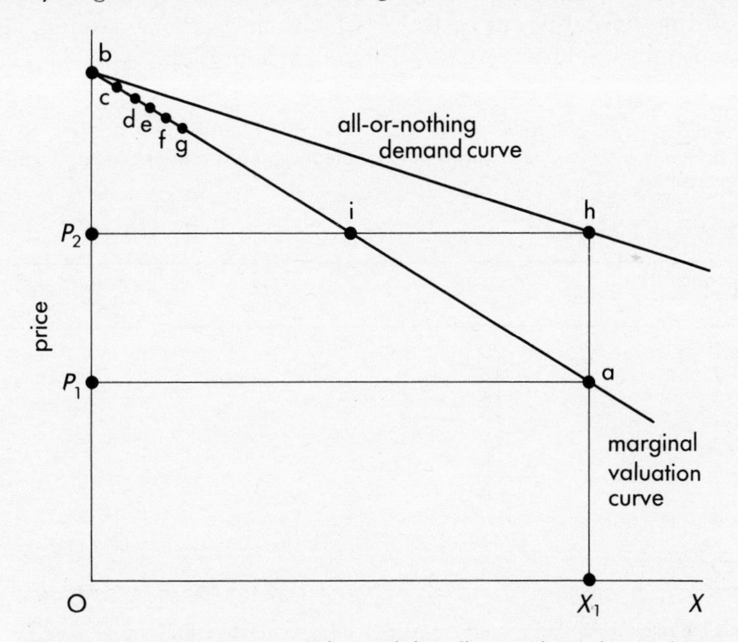

Figure 8.2 Consumer's surplus and the all-or-nothing demand curve

and value in exchange is called **consumer's surplus**: it is the difference between the maximum an individual would pay for X_1 consumption rather than none, and what he or she actually does pay. In figure 8.2 it is equal to area P_1ba.

SAQ 8.3

Draw a straight line demand curve with intercept on the *P* axis at $P = £20$ and intercept on the *X* axis at $X = 40$. Suppose that *P* actually equals £10.

(a) How much *X* will the individual purchase per period?
(b) What is its marginal value if the individual is free to buy as much as he or she likes at the going price?
(c) What is the numerical value of value in exchange?
(d) What is the numerical value of value in use?
(e) What is the numerical value of consumer's surplus?

Market transactions normally reveal value in exchange. They seldom reveal value in use.

It is possible to imagine a situation when market transactions would reveal value in use rather than value in exchange. Suppose there were a sole trader in some good – a *monopolist*. Suppose the monopolist offered the following deal: you may purchase either X_1 of X or none at all at a price of P_2 (in figure 8.2). Would the individual accept the offer? He or she would be indifferent between accepting or rejecting it because, if there were no alternative source of X, P_2X_1 (the rectangle OP_2hX_1) is the maximum amount the individual would pay for X_1 rather than go without it. Its area is equal to $ObaX_1$. The point h lies on the **all-or-nothing demand curve** for X which shows the maximum average amount someone would pay at each rate of consumption.

SAQ 8.4

(a) Table 8.1 gives the marginal value of *X* associated with each rate of consumption. Fill in the missing numbers.

Table 8.1 Values for SAQ 8.4

Rate of consumption of X	*Marginal value*	*Value in use*	*Average value in use or all-or-nothing value*
1	20	—	—
2	18	—	—
3	16	—	—
4	14	—	—
5	12	—	—
6	10	—	—
7	8	—	—
8	6	—	—
9	4	—	—
10	2	—	—

(b) What is the relationship between triangles P_2bi and iha in figure 8.2?

(c) Suppose I have a monopoly of video films for renting and your demand is as described in SAQ 8.3. I offer you the following deal: you may join my video club for £25 per year and then rent as many cassettes per year as you like at £1 per cassette.
1 How many cassettes will you rent a year?
2 How many will you purchase if the membership fee is £50?
3 How many will you purchase if the membership fee is £365?
4 Given your demand curve as stated, which club will you join: one offering cassettes at £1 per rental and an annual membership fee of £25, or one offering cassettes at £2 per rental and free membership?

The idea of value being used is a special one. It does not tell one the *intrinsic* value or the *ethical* value of consumption. It would be possible, for example, to say that the intrinsic value of a concert visit exceeded both its value in use and its value in exchange. One could say that individuals do not perceive the 'true' value of some things, perhaps undervaluing worthy things (like concerts) and overvaluing unworthy things (like pornography). The values embodied in demand curves are those that reflect individuals' preferences. They are also conditional upon their income and wealth. There is, therefore, nothing sacred about marginal value, price, value in use, value in exchange or consumer's surplus. None the less, these concepts are of use in investigating the reason why some phenomena are observed and they also have interesting normative implications, as you will see.

One classic use of the distinction between value in use and value in exchange is in explaining the so-called 'water–diamond paradox'. Why is it that water, which is a necessity of life, should be so much cheaper (appear to be lower in value) than diamonds, which are a luxury and in no way essential for life? At one level the paradox is simply uninteresting since it does not make a great deal of sense to ask if one of two different goods is dearer or cheaper than the other. If, for example, diamond units were taken as one millionth of a carat and water units as cubic metres, the price per unit is likely to be higher for water! More interesting is the question of whether the low value in exchange of water does not, relative to the value in exchange of diamonds, imply that the economic theory of value is wildly unrealistic.

Figure 8.3 helps to account for the paradox. The bottom axis measures the quantities per period of water (in litres per year) and diamonds (in carats per year) and the two demand curves D_W and D_D are the total community demands for the two goods whose prices happen to be, we suppose, P_W and P_D respectively.

Given these prices it is easy to see that the *apparent* higher value of diamonds reflects only their *marginal value*. What of total values in exchange and use? The value in exchange of diamonds may be larger or smaller than the value in exchange of water. It depends on the size of OP_DbD_1 compared with OP_WdW_1. If water were free of charge (as it is in some non-metered areas) then the value in exchange of water would fall to *zero* and consumption rise from W_1 to W_2. But even though the price and the value in exchange of diamonds may be greater than that for water, it is clear that the *value in use* of water is greater

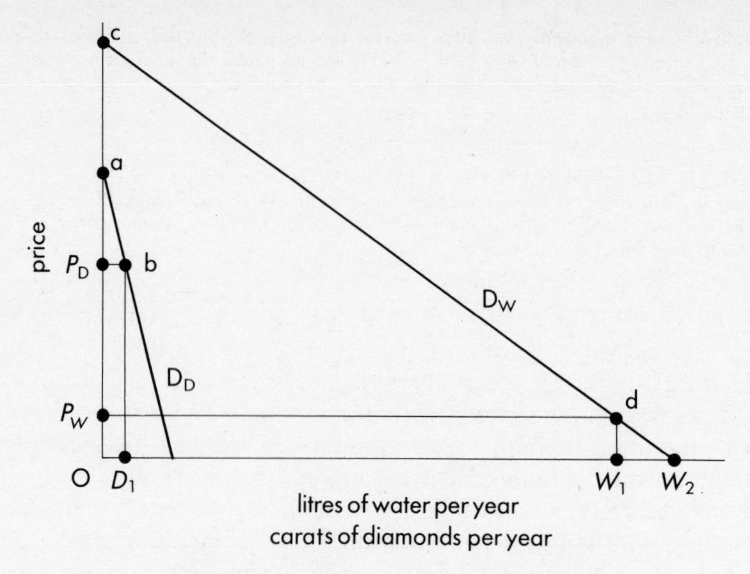

Figure 8.3 The water–diamond paradox

than that of diamonds. At prices P_D and P_W the value in use of diamonds is OabD_1 and that of water OcdW_1, and the latter is many times that of the former. Moreover, consumer's surplus from water consumption greatly exceeds that from diamond consumption ($P_W$cd compared with $P_D$ab). Thus economic analysis tells you that market values reveal only certain aspects of the value attached to goods and services. In particular they may reveal marginal and exchange values quite well while revealing total values in use rather poorly: in the example, value in exchange for diamonds is a closer approximation to their value in use than the value in exchange of water is to its value in use.

Case studies 8.1 and 8.2 provide further samples of positive and normative analyses that utilize the ideas just discussed.

Case Study 8.1 Hiring Films to Cinemas

A common phenomenon in the days when cinemas usually showed a main picture and a B picture was that the owner of the films would hire them in pairs, so that if a theatre wanted to hire the main film it had also to hire the inferior B picture too. Why should this have been?

Consider the following example. There are two films, A and B, and four cinemas, W, X, Y and Z, which place the values in use indicated on each film:

	film A	*film B*
cinema W	£24,000	£7500
cinema X	£21,000	£9000
cinema Y	£18,000	£8000
cinema Z	£10,000	£7000

If the owner of the films knew these values in use then, by charging for each film separately and also each cinema separately, he could obtain a total rental income of

£104,500. The owner does not have this information. In any case, it may be illegal to charge different prices to different customers. None the less, it is possible for an astute owner to have some idea of the *lowest* value placed on the films – cinema Z valuing film B at £7000 (or thereabouts) and cinema Z valuing film A at £10,000 (or thereabouts). If charging different prices to different customers is impossible, it might then make sense to charge every cinema £7000 for the B film and £10,000 for the A film. Total takings will be 4 × £17,000 = £68,000.

The owner could, in fact, do better than this by forgoing the rent received from cinema Z and charging a block rate equal to the combined value in use of the *next* lowest user (if some estimate of that can be made). This is the £26,000 that cinema Y will pay rather than go without the films, and this block booking rate would yield the film owner 3 × £26,000 = £78,000.

Why are takings higher with the block booking requirement than with separate pricing of each film? Because block booking enables the film owner to extract more value in use: cinema W, which values the B film at only £7500, is having implicitly to pay £8000 for it: this it will pay since its surplus on film A is more than enough to compensate it. A high price for the B movie enables the film owner to extract more of the value in use from the A movie, provided the cinemas are required to take a block booking.

G. J. Stigler (1963) 'United States vs Loew's Inc.: a note on block-booking', *Supreme Court Review* (ed. Philip B. Kurland), University of Chicago Press, 152–7.

SAQ 8.5

(a) Before tackling this SAQ it is worth refreshing your memory about the way that a group demand curve is derived from individual demand curves in chapter 3. The data that are most commonly available about prices and quantities nearly always relate to group rather than individual demands. This exercise helps you to see how the interpretation of group demands is very similar to that for individual demands. Suppose there are two individuals, A and B. Their demand curves are

$$X_A = 100 - 5P$$
$$X_B = 50 - 10P$$

1. Plot the two demand curves and the group demand curve using a format similar to that in figure 3.4.
2. At $P = £4$, compute A's consumer's surplus and B's consumer's surplus.
3. Check that the appropriate areas for A, B and A plus B in your diagram measure the same consumer's surpluses as your answer to (a2).

(b) Suppose the aggregate domestic household demand for water is given by the following equation (where X is the quantity of water in litres per year and P is the price per litre in pounds):

$$X = 5{,}000{,}000 - 20{,}000P$$

1. If $P = 0.05$, how much water per year will be demanded?
2. If $P = 0$, how much water per year will be demanded?
3. If water charges take the form of a payment related to the value of one's house rather than to the amount of water used, what effect will this have on water consumption?
4. If water is paid for in the way described in (b3), are people more likely to leave their hot or their cold taps running?

Case Study 8.2 A Problem of Health Insurance in the USA

Most individuals in the USA are insured against the expense of medical treatment. However, they also usually have to make some contribution in the form of a share

(s%) of the hospital and physician fees; the insurance company meets the rest of the expense. The most expensive type of health care is that provided in hospital. Martin Feldstein (economic adviser to President Reagan) has studied (1973) the problem of 'excess' (as he termed it) insurance for hospital care and made estimates of the 'waste' that it entails.

Figure 8.4 shows a community demand curve for days in hospital. It is less than perfectly inelastic since there is discretion as to how long one stays in hospital convalescing etc.

Suppose, initially, that no one was insured and that the price of hospitalization per day is (on average) P. Then the annual number of patient-days in hospital will be X. Now suppose that insurance is available. With the premium paid, the effective price to the patient falls to sP (the patient's share of the price) and patient-days per year rise to X'. In the no insurance situation, total value in exchange (expenditure) is $OPaX$. With insurance, total expenditure rises by $XabX'$ (and patients pay only s of the total, insurance companies paying $100 - s$). The demand curve tells us the value in use of these extra days: $XacX'$. This is less than expenditure by the triangle abc, which is a measure of the waste (the excess of expenditure over value in use).

If one can observe P, s and X' (data that are fairly easily obtained) and one has an estimate of the demand elasticity at point c, one might suppose that the demand curve in the neighbourhood of c is a straight line and thus locate the section ac of the demand curve.

Empirical estimates of demand elasticities varied between -0.4 and -0.8, and s was taken to be about 33% (in 1969). Making various other allowances for the value of avoiding risk through insurance and the reaction of hospitals to changes in utilization rates, Feldstein computed that the reduction in waste by raising s from 33% to 50% would amount to about $3000 million per year. (Can you think of any reasons why this waste may be worth tolerating? Hint: what if individuals' choices about hospitalization are ill informed; what if other (caring) individuals value the health care an individual receives?)

M. S. Feldstein (1973) 'The welfare loss of excess health insurance', *Journal of Political Economy*, **81**, 251–80.

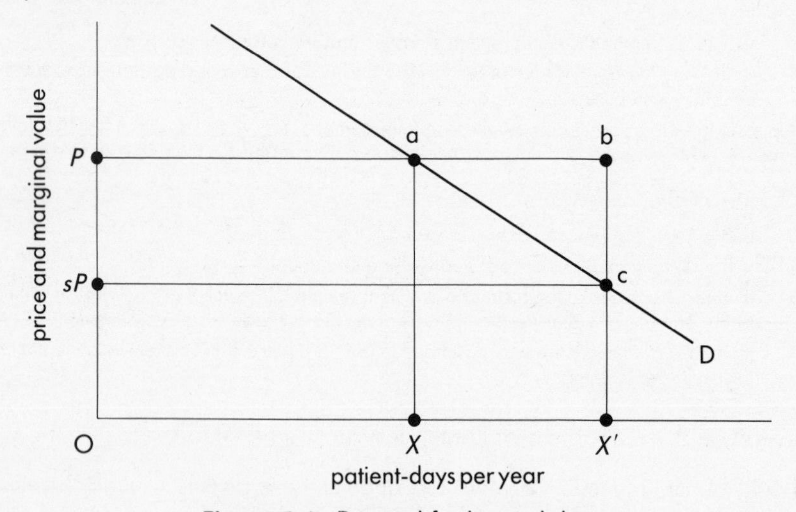

Figure 8.4 Demand for hospital days

Exchange

It can easily be observed that, where a good can be cheaply traded between individuals, a *single price* tends to rule in the market for a specified good of given quantity. This is despite the fact that individuals' demands (marginal valuation curves) may differ substantially owing to differences in tastes, income etc. The theory of exchange helps to explain why this is so.

Suppose there are two individuals, A and B, who between them own X_{AB} (a fixed amount for the purposes of argument) of a good X. A has an initial *endowment* of X_A and B has X_B. Obviously in figure 8.5, $OX_A + OX_B = OX_{AB}$. The vertical line S at X_{AB} indicates this *stock* of X.

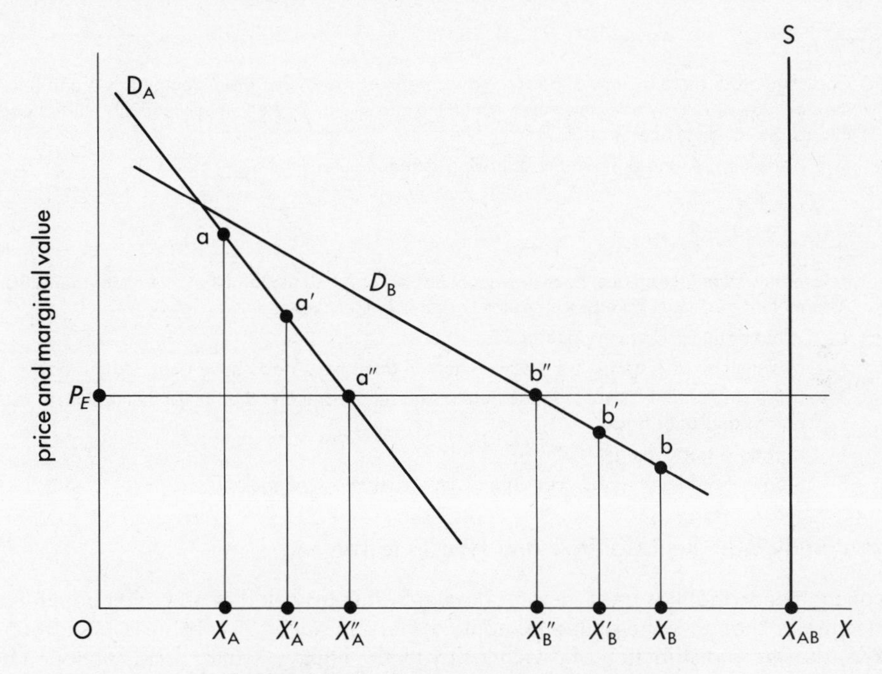

Figure 8.5 Exchange between two persons

In the beginning, with A having an endowment of X_A and B having X_B, the marginal values of the two individuals are clearly different. A's is X_Aa and B's is X_Bb, and $X_A\text{a} > X_B\text{b}$. This implies that the value A places on a little *more* of X (given tastes, income etc.) is higher than the value B places on a little *less* (given tastes, income etc.). There will therefore be some price that lies between these two marginal values that A will pay B that will enable them *both* to be better off by exchange of X. Thus, a price less than X_Aa paid by A for an extra unit of X will seem worth paying from A's point of view, whereas a price less than X_Aa but more than X_Bb will make it worth while for B to sacrifice a unit of X. By a series of such trades, A acquires more X and B sacrifices X until the allocation of X shown by X'_A and X'_B is reached. At this allocation, A's marginal valuation still exceeds B's ($X'_A a' > X'_B b'$) and so further trading can take place to their mutual advantage. No further mutually advantageous gains from trade can be realized when their marginal values are equal. This is when A has X_A'' and B has X_B'', and a″ and b″ are at the same height above the X axis. At this allocation of X between the two, A will have acquired $X_A'' - X_A$ and B will have sacrificed $X_B - X_B''$ ($= X_A'' - X_A$). The ruling price will now be P_E, the **equilibrium price**. This price is that which *clears the market* in the sense that at P_E neither A nor B wants more or less X: there is neither an excess demand nor an excess supply.

Note that this example considers the demands for a given stock of a good rather than for rates of consumption. One is really looking at the way that trade can alter the distribution of ownership of a *stock* of goods.

SAQ 8.6

(a) Copy figure 8.5 on to a piece of paper. Now carefully draw in the *group* demand of A and B for the stock X_{AB} of X. Why does this pass through the intersection of the vertical line S above X_{AB} and the horizontal price line through P_E?

(b) Two individuals, A and B, have the following demand curves for a stock of X:

$$X_A = 100 - 5P$$
$$X_B = 50 - 2P$$

Before any trade takes place, each individual has 40 of X and the total they have together is 80. Assume that trade can take place costlessly and is entirely voluntary.

1 What is the equilibrium price of X?
2 How much will A and B each have when all gains from trade have been exhausted?
3 Calculate A's and B's value in use before and after trade and the sum of their values in use before and after trade.
4 Is trade a good thing?
5 Is equality of consumption consistent with voluntary exchange?

Case Study 8.3 Rent Controls and Houses to Let

A phenomenon that has been very marked in Britain as well as some other countries is the major change in the pattern of home ownership since 1914. Table 8.2 (Stafford, 1975) shows the distribution of dwellings by tenure in the UK since 1914. Although a full analysis of the causes of the changes in the distribution of types of tenure would require a more complete analysis than that offered here, it is clear that a part of the story can be told in terms of the various controls on rents charged by private house owners since the First World War.

Table 8.2 UK tenure distribution

Date	*Owner occupied (%)*	*Rented from public authorities (%)*	*Rented from private owners (%)*
1914	10	0	90
1950	29	18	53
1960	42	26	32
1975	53	31	16

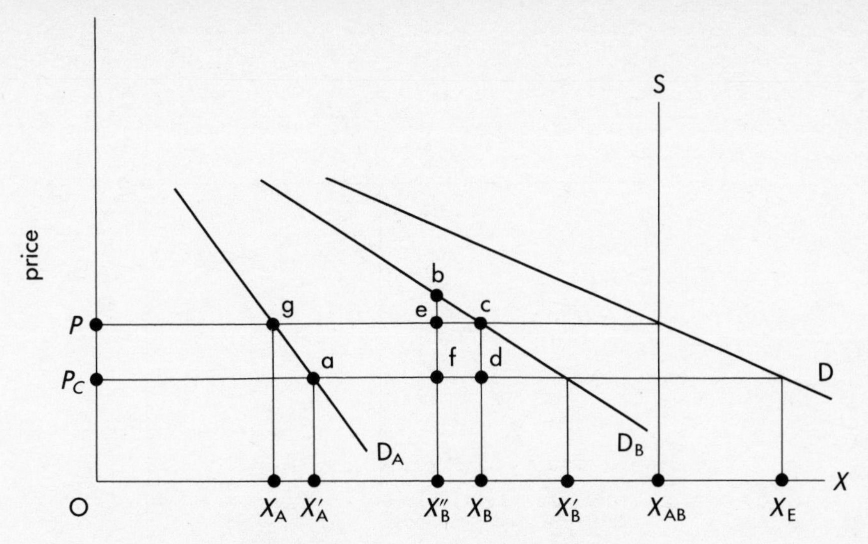

Figure 8.6 Demand for housing units

In figure 8.6 it is assumed that the entire housing stock is owned by the As. For simplicity assume that the stock is homogeneous and that the rent per unit is the same. The As let housing to the Bs. The As demand housing for their own use as shown by D_A, and the demand of the Bs is shown by D_B. Total demand is shown by D. Suppose the initial position is one of equilibrium where the housing stock X_{AB} is allocated with X_A to the As (effectively letting to and renting from themselves) and X_B to the Bs at a weekly rental of *P*. A rent ceiling of P_C is then imposed on the grounds, say, that *P* is unfairly high. What happens? There is an immediate excess demand of $X_E - X_{AB}$, which is equal to the sum of the excess demand of the As ($X'_A - X_A$) and that of the Bs ($X'_B - X_B$). If the law restricts only the rent but permits change of use (for example when a tenant quits or dies) then over time the As will transfer housing from the private rented sector to the owner occupied sector, expanding their own use from X_A to X'_A; the use by the Bs will fall from X_B to X''_B. Although total excess demand remains the same ($X_E - X_{AB}$), excess demand for rented accommodation is exacerbated (rising from $X'_B - X_B$ to $X'_B - X''_B$) and the marginal value of rented housing becomes higher at X''_Bb than that of owner occupied housing (X'_Aa). The housing 'shortage' is intensified, leading to a rise in the price of houses (and increased building of houses for owner occupation) and a demand for public authority housing for renting.

The broad pattern exhibited in table 8.2 is just that implied by this process, though the size of the changes will, of course, depend on demand elasticities, the nature of the law (and its loopholes) and a variety of other factors (e.g. subsidies on home ownership) that a more detailed analysis would have to take into account.

Incidentally, there is also a transfer of wealth from house letters to house renters: house letters lose $P_C P$cd compared with the original position, and renters gain $P_C P$ef (that is, those renters who remain in the rented sector). Letters lose more than renters gain, i.e. ecdf. Note also that the value in use lost by renters is $X_B$cbX''_B and that gained by letters is only $X_A$gaX'_a.

For those who are houseless the prospects become worse unless and until public authority housing comes in to make good the shortage the rent controls have created. Does this imply that rent controls are bad? Not necessarily: it depends among other

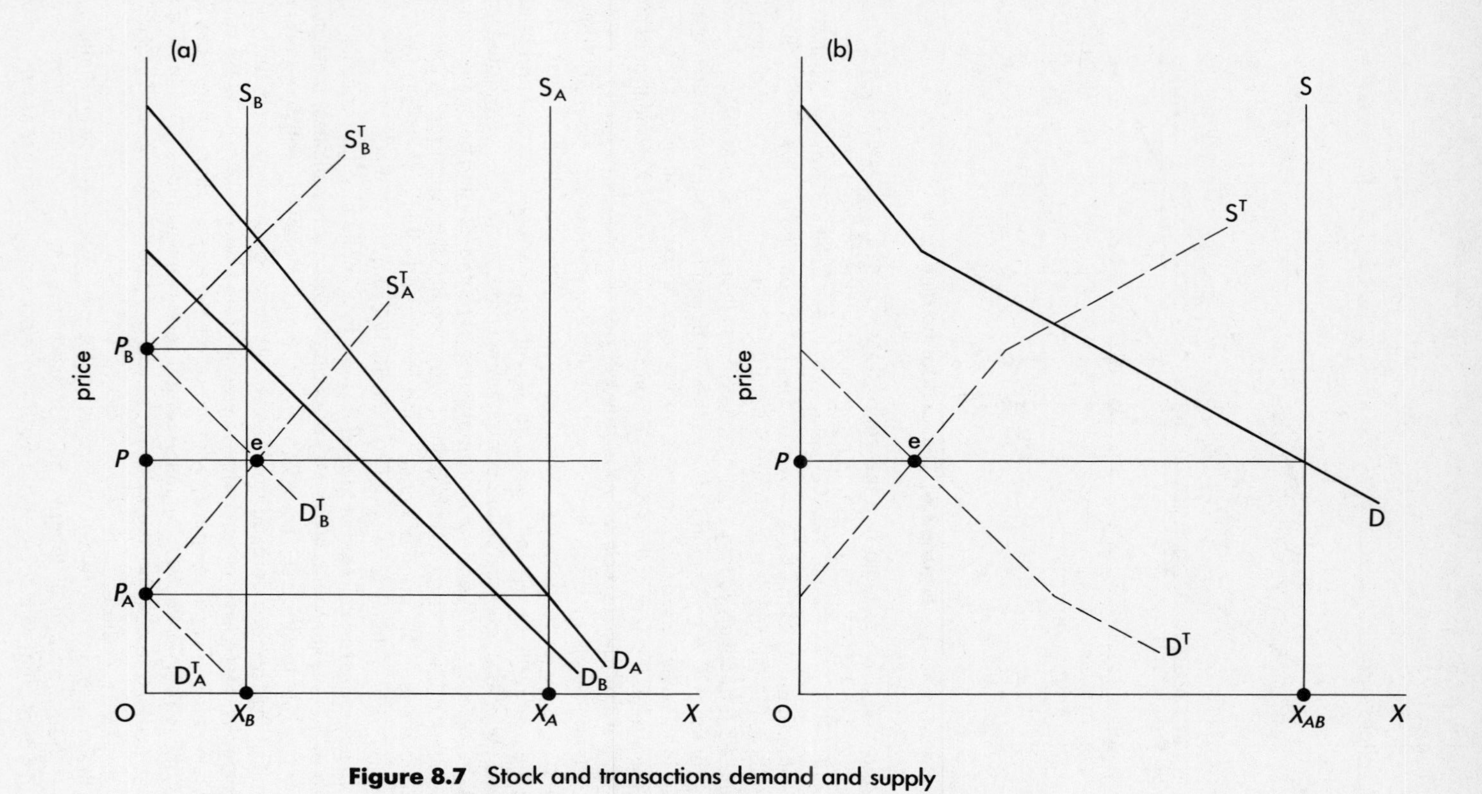

Figure 8.7 Stock and transactions demand and supply

things on how you view the wealth redistribution that the controls imply and how speedily and adequately publicly provided housing fills the gap.

David Stafford (1975) *The Economics of Housing Policy*, London, Croom Helm, p. 49.

Markets, Prices, and Other Ways of Allocating Goods

Human societies have evolved an almost infinite variety of institutions for allocating resources between individuals or groups. One – but just one – of these is the set of markets where goods and services are allocated by price. It is fallacious to suppose either that markets are the only (let alone invariably the *best*) way of allocation or that economics is concerned only with market allocation. Reflect for a moment on how the use of goods and services is allocated within a family. The criteria and rules that determine who gets what and on what terms are clearly not market criteria. Consider alternatively a firm. *Within* a firm goods and services are allocated (e.g. between various departments, along a production line, between subsidiaries) but rarely by price – more normally through a command or hierarchical chain of instructions by those with authority to determine who gets what. Again, consider charity and gifts between individuals and groups. Or consider the immense amount of economic activity that takes place in what we call the 'welfare state'. Here vast quantities of goods and services (health, education and so on) are purchased and allocated – but not usually by price.

Stock Demand and Supply Compared with Transactions Demand and Supply

One sometimes hears it said that in markets 'the tail wags the dog', in the sense that although only a small proportion of the amount of a good in existence at any time is actually traded (e.g. shares in businesses, houses, second hand cars, old masters) it is this tiny proportion that determines the value in exchange of the entire stock. This is a misleading way of looking at the determinants of exchange value, since the fact that some individuals choose *not* to transact itself helps to determine the price: if I choose not to sell stock at the going price it must be (assuming, as before, no costs of making the transactions themselves) because I value my stock higher than the going price.

Look at figure 8.7. Figure 8.7(a) shows the demand curves of two individuals (A and B as usual) for a stock of X (ignore the dashed lines for the moment). It also shows their initial endowments of X_A and X_B. The sum of these endowments, $X_A + X_B$, is shown as X_{AB} in figure 8.7(b). The group's demand for this stock is also shown as the horizontal sum D of the two demand curves D_A and D_B.

The market clearing price P is determined fundamentally by the total demand of the group and the available stock in figure 8.7(b).

Now return to figure 8.7(a). Before exchange, A has X_A. At any price higher than P_A, A is willing to offer X (i.e. run down the stock), and at any price lower than P_A, A demands more. These transactions offers and demands are shown by the dashed lines S_A^T and D_A^T: A's transactions supply and demand. The same thing goes for B: at any price higher than P_B, B will offer X as shown by the dashed line S_B^T and, at any price lower than P_B, B will demand more as shown by the dashed line D_B^T. It is readily seen that A's transactions demand and supply are the difference between A's endowment and stock demand, and B's transactions demand and supply are similarly the difference between B's endowment and stock demand. The S^T curves are sometimes said to show the individuals' **reservation prices** – the prices at which they will begin to supply rather than hold on to their stocks. These transactions supply curves slope upwards from left to right because the demand curves for the stock slope downwards: marginal valuation rises the less one has, and therefore one requires an *increasing* marginal compensation for parting with one's stock.

You can see that A's marginal valuation, with X_A, is lower than B's with X_B. One would expect, therefore, that X will be traded from A to B. If trading can proceed costlessly one can see in figure 8.7(a) that A will offer X along S_A^T and B will demand X along D_B^T. Transactions demand and supply are equal at the equilibrium price P, at which A will have supplied Pe of X and B will have purchased Pe of X.

The group's transaction demand and supply is simply the horizontal addition of the dashed lines in figure 8.7(a), showing how much each supplies out of stocks or demands for addition to stock. This is shown in figure 8.7(b) by the dashed lines S^T and D^T which, again, intersect at point e at the equilibrium price. *Thus, although only Pe of X is actually transacted, the basic determinants of the market clearing price are the demands to hold stock and the total available stock.* If, for example, the initial distribution of the stock was different from X_B and X_A, but the total stock was the same, the market clearing price would still be P. The transaction demand and supply curves would be *different*, and so would the amount traded, but price would be the same.

SAQ 8.7

(a) Suppose, in figure 8.7, that Pe of X were transferred from A to B.
  1. Where in figure 8.7(a) would the new S^A and S^B lines now be located?
  2. Where in figure 8.7(a) would the transaction demand and supply curves for A and B now be located?
  3. Where in figure 8.7(b) would the S^T and D^T curves now be located?
  4. Where in figure 8.7(b) would the S and D curves now be located?

(b) The word *equilibrium* has been used several times in the text. It means no more than the solution to a set of simultaneous equations. Thus, if B's transactions demand is given by the equation

$$X_B^T = 50 - 2P$$

and A's transactions supply is given by the equation

$$X_A^T = 20 + 4P$$

what is the equilibrium price when $X_B^T = X_A^T$?

What may one conclude from this analysis? First, the tail does *not* wag the dog. The amounts transacted are crucially related to the amounts *not* traded; *withholding* goods from the market has impact on the eventual price. Second, note that the eventual price and the eventual distribution of X between the two individuals is *independent* of the initial distribution. A caveat should be entered here to the effect that changing endowments may have income – wealth – effects on D_A and D_B. This subtle point, however, is a matter for more advanced discussion and is, anyway, likely to be of significance only for goods whose value represents a high percentage of total wealth. Third, the analysis here brings out the distinction between the demand *for ownership or consumption* as distinction from the demand for *purchase*. In a given period, A and B may consume or hold in stock an amount that is larger than they purchase. Indeed, transactions could be zero and yet consumption positive, as when individuals have stocks but make no additions to them. Thus one would expect a tax on transactions (e.g. sales) to have a different effect from one on consumption: brewing one's own beer is one way of avoiding the excise duty on transacted beer (the implications for a relationship between taxes and DIY are evident).

However, the analysis of market exchange has so far been based on simplifying assumptions, some of which are for many purposes *too* simplifying. A major one is that we have assumed that transactions are themselves *costless*: no transport costs of transferring X from A to B; no cost of checking the quality or the amount contracted to be bought and sold; no risk of default in payment; no expense of a system of enforcement of contracts; no costs associated with identifying transactors (who will buy more X at what price and who will sell); and no tax. These issues will be examined later.

The presence of such impediments to trade may be one of the reasons why market transactions are not chosen as a means of allocating some goods and services – though not, of course, the only reason. They may also prevent the attainment of equilibrium.

A second major assumption has been that the amount of X available is *given*. Although in the short term there may be given stocks of commodities distributed among consumers and producers (with *both* holding stocks), in the longer term, of course, stocks usually get used up and *production* takes place to augment existing stocks and replace those used up. Production is discussed in the next chapter.

SAQ 8.8

Suppose that those with the relatively high marginal values are also the relatively wealthy.

(a) Will (costless) exchange tend to allocate goods towards their most highly valued uses?

(b) Are uses desired by the rich more valued than uses desired by the poor?

(c) Is an *efficient* allocation also a *fair* one (define your sense of 'efficient' and 'fair')?

What You Should Understand Now

The two ways of interpreting a demand curve.
The meanings of marginal value, value in use, value in exchange and consumer's surplus.
The relationship between the marginal valuation curve and the all-or-nothing demand curve.
The kind of information about value revealed by exchange.
Why exchange or trading takes place.
The conditions under which exchange brings about a single price, and its implications for the marginal values of different individuals.
How to write down a linear demand equation.
The meaning of equilibrium.
The role of price as *just one* way of allocating goods and services.
The distinction between transactions demand and supply and the demand for and availability of a stock.
The use of exchange theory both to explain phenomena and to make recommendations about policy.

9

Production and Production Functions

So far it has been assumed that economic goods are simply 'there' – though scarce – and attention has been focused exclusively on how these goods are demanded and allocated in the community. It is now time to drop this drastic simplification so as to explore the production of goods and services: the processes by which *inputs* like raw materials, labour of various types and capital goods like machinery and buildings are used to produce the *outputs* that constitute the economic wealth of society and that generate, in the process, the incomes that accrue to wage and salary earners (owners of labour) on the one hand and to capitalists (owners of non-labour inputs) on the other. The process is known as *production* and the technical relationship that exists between the resources available as inputs and the maximum output that can be produced is known as the *production function.*

It is conventional to describe the output of an economy in three categories:

(1) **Primary production**, which relates to the extraction of raw materials like ores and minerals from the environment and also to agricultural production
(2) **Secondary production**, which relates to manufacturing industry
(3) **Tertiary production**, which relates to services like hairdressing, education, health and insurance.

Production in the UK

An obvious difficulty confronted in trying to present a summary picture of UK production of goods and services is that they are a very mixed bunch of things that cannot simply be added up as they stand. You might think that the most straightforward way of dealing with this problem would be to take the *value* of output of each firm or industry – its sales. But the trouble with this is that if you then added up the sales of each firm or industry you would be counting some outputs more than once. For example, if rubber is sold to tyre manufacturers and tyres to motor car manufacturers and motor cars to taxi drivers, then the value of rubber will be counted four times, that of tyres three times, that of cars twice and only that of taxi services once. The reason is plain: the cost of rubber is included in the tyre's price, the cost of tyres is included in the car's price and the cost of cars is included (suitably pro rata) in the taxi driver's price. For this reason it is usual to take the outputs of firms and industries to be their **value added** – the value of their sales (at ex-factory prices, before taxes and before deductions for capital depreciation) less the cost of goods and services bought in from other firms.

Output tends to be used in two quite distinct senses in economics. The first sense is in terms of *physical units*: so many 50 horsepower motors, so many loaves of bread and so on, over a period. This is the sense mostly used in this and the next few chapters. The second sense is *value added*, which is what is used when one needs to add outputs together to get an overall picture. The second sense is also that in which 'output' is often used in macroeconomics.

Table 9.1 shows some major categories of output (or value added) in the UK in 1983. You can see that manufacturing industry accounted for only about 23 per cent of the total and that agricultural output was only just over 2 per cent of the total. The smallness of these figures often surprises people who are accustomed to think of the UK as a manufacturing country and who appreciate the enormous land area given over to agriculture. Indeed primary production (the first two items in table 9.1) accounted for only 13 per cent of output.

Table 9.1 Value of output by industry in 1983

	£ million	%
Agriculture, forestry and fishing	5,535	2.04
Energy and water supply	29,645	10.91
Manufacturing	62,258	22.92
Construction	15,319	5.64
Transport	11,543	4.25
Communication	7,092	2.61
Distribution, hotels and catering	35,002	12.88
Banking, finance etc.	31,067	11.43
Ownership of dwellings	15,761	5.80
Education and health services	24,021	8.84
Public administration and defence	18,027	6.64
Other services	16,415	6.04
Total	271,685	100.00

Source: UK National Accounts, 1984, table 2.1

What is very striking is the high share of tertiary or service industries in total output, a share which has been rising continuously. Recently, reductions in secondary industry have become known as **deindustrialization**, a phenomenon usually observed in developed countries. The service industries now account for over half of all output by value.

The output of services that are not sold to the public, especially publicly provided services like health and education, obviously cannot be measured by value in the same way as marketed (priced) outputs are. They are none the less of value, and they appear in table 9.1. The way out of the problem can be seen by recognizing that the value added of an industry producing a marketed output is what is left for that industry to distribute as incomes in the form of wages, salaries, dividends and rents. This then gives us a way of measuring the value added of non-marketed services: it is the sum of all incomes earned in that industry.

Another puzzle may be the category 'ownership of dwellings' in table 9.1. If one supposed that all dwellings were owned by someone other than the occupier, to whom they were rented, this would appear as an annual value of the services of housing during the year in question and net of maintenance. However, many houses are owner occupied and no formal monetary transaction takes place (the owner 'rents', as it were, the house from himself). Consequently estimates have to be made of this rent.

Table 9.2 shows the shares of total output in 1973 and 1983. Energy's share (particularly oil) increased sharply. The share of manufacturing fell – a trend exacerbated by the growth of oil and gas. Construction fell, but the construction industry is notoriously volatile: 1983 was rather a slump. Again, service industries (other than transport) are conspicuous not only for a relatively high share but also for an increasing one.

Table 9.2 Shares of industries in output, 1973 and 1983

	1973	*1983*
Agriculture, forestry and fishing	2.92	2.04
Energy and water supply	4.39	10.91
Manufacturing	30.46	22.92
Construction	7.27	5.64
Transport	4.73	4.25
Communication	2.34	2.61
Distribution, hotels and catering	13.08	12.88
Banking, finance etc.	10.73	11.43
Ownership of dwellings	5.13	5.80
Education and health services	7.68	8.84
Public administration and defence	6.15	6.64
Other services	5.11	6.04

Source: UK National Accounts, 1984, table 2.1

The Index of Industrial Production

The index of output of the production industries is a general measure of changes in the volume of industrial production in the UK. The industries included are energy and water supply and manufacturing. It excludes agriculture, construction and tertiary industries (though indices exist for these too). It is calculated from about 320 industries or parts of industries, where each industry's contribution to the value of output V in the current year is multiplied by its share s in total output in the base year, at present 1980. For example, the share of the oil and gas extraction industry in the total in 1980 was 0.123. The ratio of the sum of all these weighted values added in one year to that in the base year (1980) multiplied by 100 gives the index for the year in question. The formula for an industry in 1985 is thus:

$$\text{index of industrial production} = \frac{s_{1980}\ V_{1985}}{s_{1980}\ V_{1980}} \times 100$$

Figure 9.1 shows how particular industries fared in 1973 and 1982, where 1973 is taken to have index 100. Note that the vertical scale is logarithmic (so that equal distances along the scale represent equal *relative* rather than *absolute* amounts). This has been done so that the spectacular growth in oil and gas can be fitted in. Those industries chosen for inclusion are some that did relatively well (index more than 110 in 1982) and some that did poorly (index less than 90 in 1982). The spectacular growth industries were oil and natural gas, arms, and computers. All the relatively fast growing industries were characterized by their relatively high technological base and were industries that devoted substantial expenditures to research and development (R & D).

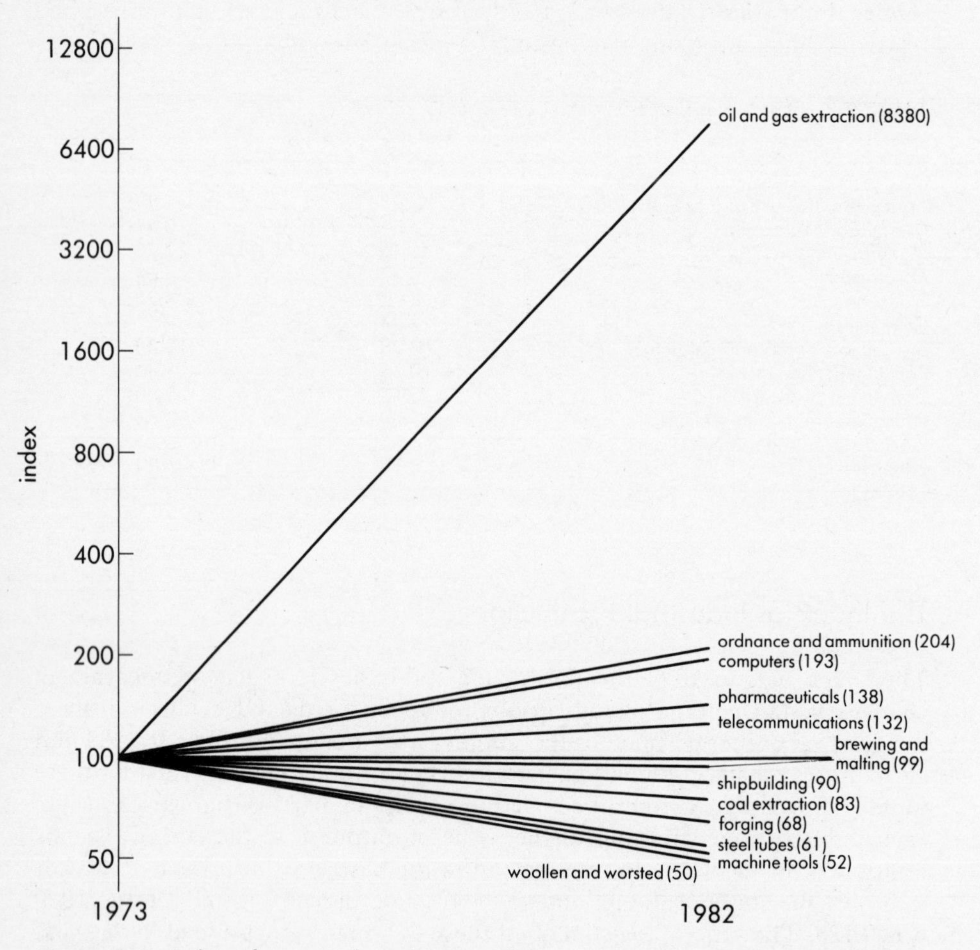

Figure 9.1 Index of output of production industries in selected industries 1973–1982 and 1983

The poor growth performance industries were all 'traditional' industries, most of them having key roles in the pattern of industry that emerged during the industrial revolution. Metal manufacturing in the UK has suffered from a world glut of output of this sort and has faced keen competition from overseas. Shipbuilding and textiles have been in continuous decline for most of the twentieth century. Motor vehicles have declined relatively recently, again with fierce overseas competition. Overall, the index of output for production industries fell from 100 in 1973 to 98.7 in 1982.

The Production Function

The **production function** can be illustrated as in figure 9.2. Inputs (the ellipse on the left) are transformed into outputs (the ellipse on the right) via a set of production processes that constitutes the production function (the rectangle between). Thus, steel plate and a host of other inputs are combined with labour in various combinations to produce motor cars; school rooms, books, teachers and students are combined to produce an elusive output called education. Sometimes an output of one productive process is an input to another (for example, a tyre): such goods are known as **intermediate outputs**.

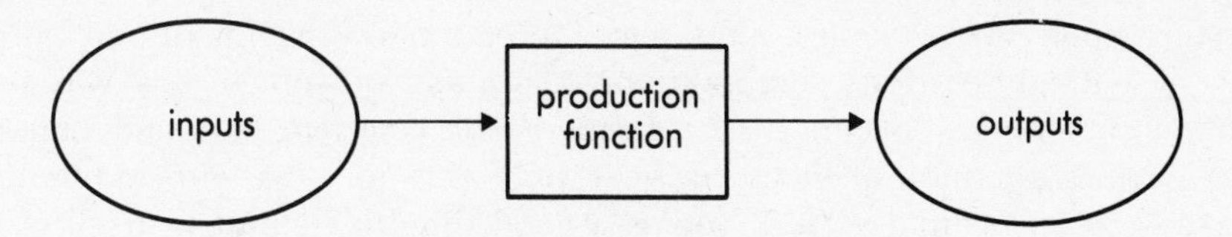

Figure 9.2 The production function

Goods consumed by the ultimate or final consumers are known as **final outputs**. However, the distinction between intermediate and final output is not immutable: it depends both on the nature of the user of the output and the purpose of one's analysis. For example, a motor car is a final output when used by a private motorist but an intermediate output when used by a taxi driver. Scholastic attainment may be a final output from the point of view of a school, or of society in general if it values education for its own sake; but it may be an intermediate output if the flow of people with particular skills is regarded as an input in other productive areas.

There is rarely (if ever) only one way of producing a given flow of goods and services. For example, you can have more or fewer doctors, more or fewer nurses, more or fewer hospital beds in producing 'better health'. In other words *inputs are substitutable* in the production function. Suppose there are just two inputs: machine-hours and labour-hours. These are measured along the axes of figure 9.3. They may be combined in varying proportions so as to produce a given rate of output of X shown by the curve $X = 200$. This curve has the technical name of **isoquant** since the same rate of output or quantity is

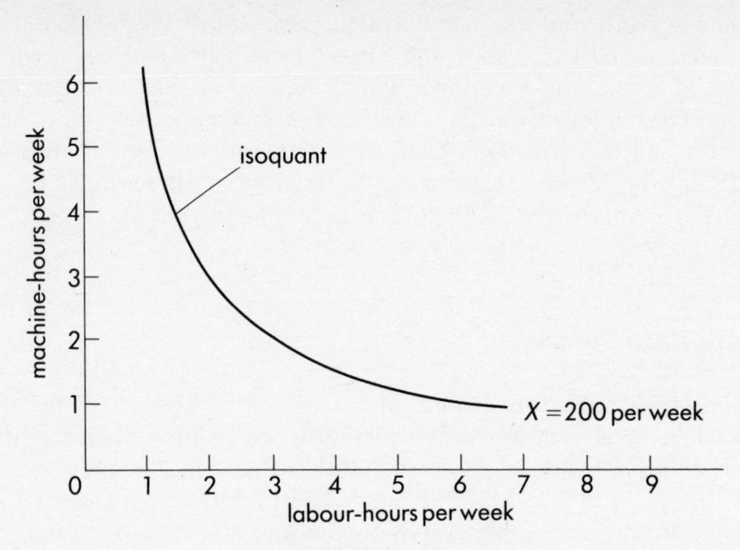

Figure 9.3 An isoquant

indicated along its length (in this case an output of 200 of X). It resembles an indifference curve but differs from it in two important respects. First, it depends upon the *technical* conditions of production (the maximum output possible with the various combinations of inputs) and not in any way on a person's preferences. Secondly, *it is measured on a ratio scale* (so many cars per week, tonnes per month, litres per year etc.) and not – as with indifference curves – on an ordinal scale. (Now is a good time to remind yourself of the nature of these different kinds of measurement by turning back to chapter 5.) Because the production function (and hence isoquants) are technically determined, their use and application is far more mechanistic than was the case with the theory of behaviour.

In figure 9.3 the isoquant shows that, with the technology in use, 200 of X per week can be produced with 6 machine-hours per week and 1 labour-hour, *or* 3 machine-hours and 2 labour-hours, *or* 2 machine-hours and 3 labour-hours – or, of course, any other combination along the isoquant. Note two things. First, one is dealing with *rates* or *flows* of input and output (so much per day, per week etc.). Secondly, it is assumed that inputs and outputs can be finely divided. If one is dealing with stocks (e.g. so many workers, so many machines) then **indivisibilities** may arise (half a machine or worker is a silly concept), but with flows (half an hour of machine time or labour time) fine divisibility is possible because time can be finely divided.

Just as the slope of an indifference curve has a technical name (the marginal rate of substitution) so has the slope of an isoquant: it is the **marginal rate of technical substitution** (*MRTS*) (or, sometimes, the marginal rate of substitution in production). Thus, in terms of inputs of capital services K and labour L,

$$MRTS = \mathrm{d}K/\mathrm{d}L$$

SAQ 9.1

(a) Define a production function.

(b) Define an isoquant.

Case Study 9.1 Agricultural Isoquants

There have been many production function studies of agricultural processes. A famous worker in this empirical field is Earl Heady who has, among many other studies, calculated isoquants for maize production in North Carolina and Kansas (Heady and Tweeten, 1963).

The two isoquants in figure 9.4 show how fertilizer and land can be substituted to obtain two alternative rates of output of maize per acre, both of which are yields commonly obtainable for maize on land having a particular type of soil. Figure 9.4 tells you that a 42.4 bushel output rate can be obtained in North Carolina with, for example, 1.69 acres of land and no fertilizer, or 1.11 acres and 20 lb of fertilizer. With the latter combination, and a 42.4 bushel output, a pound of fertilizer substitutes for 0.0293 acres of land (0.0293 is the marginal rate of technical substitution at this point), so a ton of fertilizer nutrients spread similarly is estimated to substitute for 65.6 acres of land (2240 × 0.0293 = 65.6). With 60 pounds of fertilizer and 0.49 acres producing 42.4 bushels, the marginal rate of technical substitution is 0.0043 and a ton of fertilizer substitutes for 9.6 acres of land (2240 × 0.0043 = 9.6).

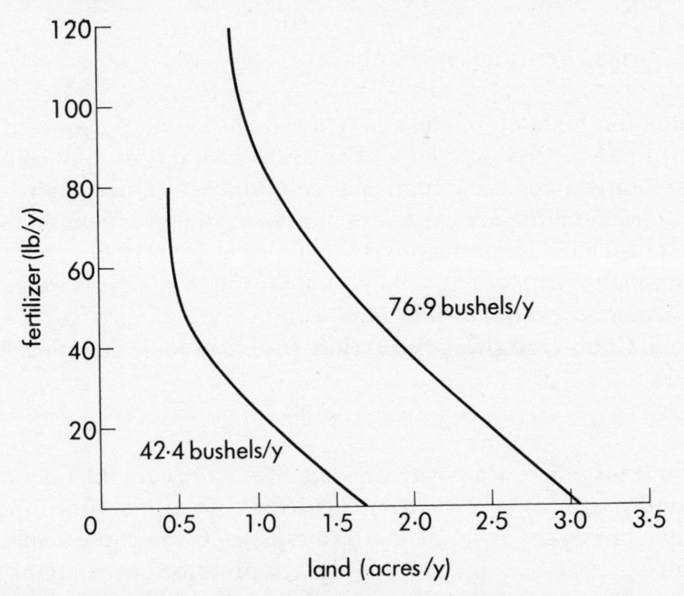

Figure 9.4 Isoquants for maize production in North Carolina with acres of land and pounds of fertilizer as variable inputs

Figure 9.5 shows how fertilizer substitutes for labour. Thus, for an output of 82.6 bushels, say either no fertilizer and 6.78 labour-hours or 40 lb of fertilizer and 5.93 labour-hours will suffice. At the latter ratio of inputs, a ton of fertilizer substitutes for 38 hours of labour, for the marginal rate of technical substitution is 0.017 (2240 × 0.017 = 38).

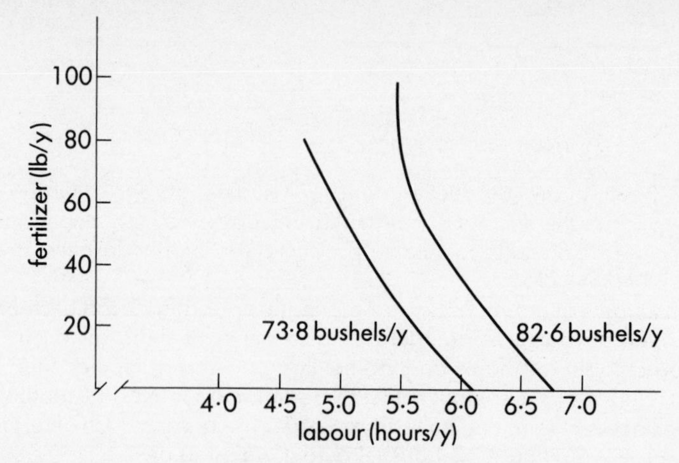

Figure 9.5 Isoquants for maize production in Kansas with labour and fertilizer as variable inputs

Earl O. Heady and Luther G. Tweeten (1963) *Resource Demand and Structure of the Agricultural Industry*, Iowa State University Press, Iowa, tables 5.2 and 5.3.

The Cobb-Douglas Production Function

A typical production function relates many inputs to the output (or outputs) rather than just two as so far considered. For this reason it is usually helpful to put the production function in mathematical symbols rather than to use geometry. A common mathematical representation of the production function is called the Cobb-Douglas production function. This can easily be used to handle many inputs (examples will follow), but for the present it is convenient to simplify by using an example with only two.

The two input **Cobb-Douglas production function** looks like this:

$$X = aA^{\alpha}B^{\beta}$$

where X is the output rate, a is a positive constant, A and B are the rates of two inputs and α and β are (as you will see) elasticities of output with respect to each input. Thus, if you set $a = 4$, $\alpha = 0.4$ and $\beta = 0.6$ you can calculate the various amounts of A and B that are needed to produce any amount of X. Figure 9.6 shows this for $X = 20$. You can see that $X = 20$ may be produced with $A = 8.00$ and $B = 3.66$, or $A = 7.00$ and $B = 4.00$, and so on.

SAQ 9.2

For this and several other SAQs in this chapter you will find it helpful to have a calculator to aid computation. In table 9.3, fill in the missing amounts of B either by estimating by eye from figure 9.6 or by calculation using $20 = 4A^{0.4}B^{0.6}$

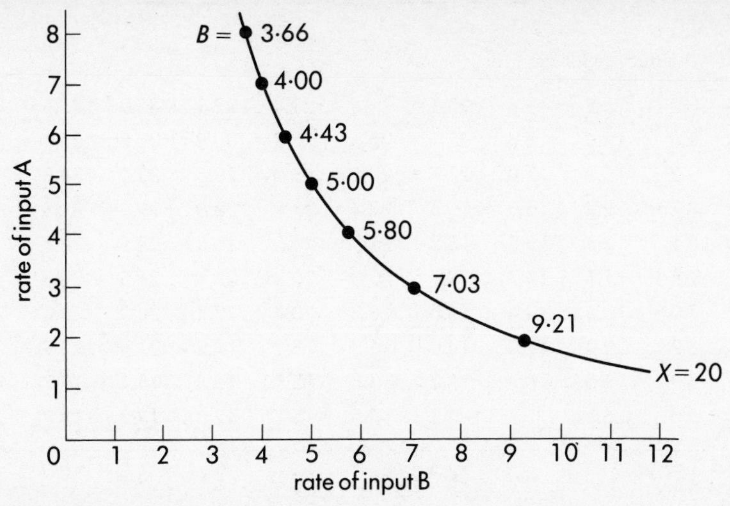

Figure 9.6 Graph of a Cobb-Douglas production function for $X = 20$

Table 9.3 Rates for SAQ 9.2

Output rate of X	*Input rate of A*	*Minimum input rate of B needed*
20	11.0	
20	9.5	
20	8.5	
20	5.1	
20	0.5	

You have just seen that an equation for the production function can be used to discover the *minimum* input rate of one input needed to produce a target output given the rate of use of other input or inputs. You ought to be able to see that it can also be used to calculate the *maximum* output rate that can be produced with various rates of inputs.

Returns to Scale and Returns to an Input

Two features of production functions that it is important to grasp are returns to scale and returns to an input.

Returns to scale describe what happens to the output rate when each input rate is increased by the same proportion. If output increases by a larger percentage than the increase in each input then there are *increasing* returns to scale; if it increases by a smaller percentage there are *diminishing* returns to scale; if it increases by the same proportion there are *constant* returns to scale.

Returns to an input describe what happens to output as only one input is varied, holding all others constant. Again, these returns may be increasing, diminishing or constant.

Table 9.4 Production function for $X = 4A^{0.4}B^{0.6}$

A per period										
10	10.0	15.2	19.4	23.1	26.4	29.4	32.3	35.0	37.5	40.0
9	9.6	14.6	18.6	22.1	25.3	28.2	30.9	33.5	36.0	38.3
8	9.2	13.9	17.8	21.1	24.1	26.9	29.5	32.0	34.3	36.6
7	8.7	12.9	16.5	19.6	22.4	24.9	28.0	29.6	31.8	34.7
6	8.2	12.4	15.8	18.8	21.5	24.0	26.3	28.5	30.6	32.6
5	7.6	11.5	14.7	17.5	20.0	22.3	24.4	26.5	28.4	30.3
4	7.0	10.6	13.4	16.0	18.3	20.4	22.4	24.2	26.0	27.7
3	6.2	9.4	12.0	14.2	16.3	18.2	19.9	21.6	22.9	24.7
2	5.3	8.0	10.2	12.2	13.8	15.5	17.0	18.4	19.7	21.0
1	4.0	6.1	7.7	9.2	10.5	11.7	12.8	13.9	14.9	15.9
0	1	2	3	4	5	6	7	8	9	10

B per period

Table 9.4 shows the production function for $X = 4A^{0.4}B^{0.6}$ for input rates of A and B of 1 to 10. (The data are presented so that you can, if you wish, imagine isoquants overlaid on the numbers.) This production function exhibits constant returns to scale: a doubling, trebling etc. of all inputs leads to a doubling, trebling etc. of output. If the coefficients α and β of the Cobb-Douglas production function sum to unity, there will always be constant returns to scale. If $\alpha + \beta > 1$ there will be increasing returns to scale (the proportional increase in output will be larger than the proportional increase in all inputs). If $\alpha + \beta < 1$ there will be diminishing returns to scale.

Table 9.5 has examples of production functions showing increasing and decreasing returns to scale. The first column shows how output behaves under this increasing returns to scale technology: when the input rates are all increased by 50 per cent from (2, 3) to (3, 4.5) the output rate rises from 16.3 to 29.9 or by 83 per cent. When input rates double from (2, 3) to (4, 6) or again from (4, 6) to (8, 12) the output rate rises by more than double. The second column shows a diminishing returns to scale technology: when input rates are all increased by 50 per cent (2, 3) to (3, 4.5) output rises from 16.1 to 21.9 or by

Table 9.5 Increasing and decreasing returns to scale

Inputs		*Outputs*	
A	*B*	$X = 4A^{0.6}B^{0.9}$	$X = 8A^{0.3}B^{0.45}$
2	3	16.3	16.1
3	4.5	29.9	21.9
4	6	46.1	27.2
8	12	130.4	45.7

only 36 per cent. Similarly, a doubling or trebling of input rates increases the output rate by less than double or treble.

SAQ 9.3

(a) For each of the following production functions, calculate output when $A = 5$ and $B = 7$:

1 $X = A^{0.9}B^{0.2}$

2 $X = 3A^{0.2}B^{0.7}$

3 $X = 7A^{0.4}B^{2.0}$

4 $X = 3A^{0.3}B^{0.7}$

(b) Identify the nature of the returns to scale for each of the foregoing production functions.

Case Study 9.2 Returns to Scale in British Industries

Alan Walters has helpfully reviewed (1963) a range of early statistical studies of Cobb-Douglas production functions (as well as some others you will meet in more advanced courses in economics). A sample of the results he summarizes is in table 9.6. (Walters is personal adviser to the UK Prime Minister Margaret Thatcher, and a well-known economist.)

Table 9.6 Returns to scale in various industries

		Coefficients on									
Country	*Industry*	*Labour*	*Capital*	*Raw Materials*	*Land*	*Livestock*	*Feeder cattle*	*Machinery and draft animals*	*Feed*	*Other*	*Sum of coefficients*
France	Gas	0.83	0.10								0.93
USA	Railways	0.89	0.12	0.28							1.29
UK	Coal	0.51	0.49								1.00
India	Jute	0.84	0.14		0.23	0.045	0.013	0.31			0.98
USA	Wheat	0.41									1.00
USA	Metals and machinery	0.71	0.26								0.97
Australia	Milk	0.23							0.13	0.62	0.98
USA	Cotton	0.45						0.13	0.29	0.033	0.90

In nearly all cases the studies found that the sum of the coefficients was about 1.00, indicating more or less constant returns to scale. Railways seem to be an exception and exhibit clearly increasing returns to scale. Note that for some industries the production function is $X = aA^{\alpha}B^{\beta}C^{\gamma}$ etc.

Alan Walters (1963) 'Production and cost functions: an econometric survey', *Econometrica*, **31** (1–2), 1–66.

Marginal Productivity

A constant returns to scale production function always has decreasing returns to each input. You can see this in table 9.4. For example, with A constant at, say, 6 you can see that the output rate increases as the rate of use of input B is increased – but at a decreasing rate. It is said that the marginal product of *B* falls as more is used. **Marginal product** is defined as the increased rate of output due to a unit increase in the utilization of *one* input with other inputs being held at a constant rate. The marginal product of *B* is 8.2 when there is one unit used rather than none, 4.2 (12.4 − 8.2) when there are two rather than one, 3.4 when there are three, 3.0 when there are four, and successively 2.7, 2.5, 2.3, 2.2, 2.1 and 2.0. Similarly, the marginal product of *A* falls as its rate of use increases for any *given* amount of *B*. You can also see that the marginal product of one input is not at all independent of the amount of the other. This is important in evaluating the argument one sometimes hears that inputs (especially human ones) *deserve* the value of their marginal products (the marginal product multiplied by the selling price of the output) as reflected in wages. For, even if wages do reflect the value of the marginal product (something to be discussed in chapter 17), it is somewhat strange to say that one deserves something that is not determined solely by one's own efforts.

SAQ 9.4

In table 9.7, input *B* is held constant at 3 units per period and *A* is varied as in the first column in the table. Output varies as in the second column. The price of *B* is £1 per unit per period and that of *A* £7. Complete the table by calculating the marginal product of *A* as its use increases by one unit per period, the average product of *A* and the total, average and marginal cost of output, assuming that no other costs are incurred than those of hiring inputs *A* and *B*.

Table 9.7 Data for SAQ 9.4

Rate of use of A	*Rate of output X*	*Marginal product of A, $\Delta X/\Delta A$*	*Average product of A (X/A)*	*Total cost TC*	*Average cost, TC/X*	*Marginal cost, $\Delta TC/\Delta X$*
1	5					
2	12					
3	20					
4	27					
5	32					
6	34					

Productive Efficiency

The information contained in the production function can be interpreted in either of two ways. It shows either the *maximum* rate of output attainable for given rates of inputs, or the *minimum* combinations of inputs necessary in order to realize a target rate of output. Remember always that you are dealing with *rates* – machine-hours not machines, acres of land per year not acres of land. The production function does not relate capital and labour to output, for capital and labour are *stocks* of machines, buildings, land, labour etc. that are counted up at a particular date. The production function relates the *flows of services* that these factors of production yield to the output rate.

The production function also assumes that the production process, whether in a commercial firm, a nationalized industry, a private household or a social service, is **technically efficient**: more inputs than are necessary to produce an output are not used, and less output than could be produced from given inputs is not produced. For example, in table 9.4, whereas it is *impossible* for the production process to produce more than 24 of X by using 6 of A and 6 of B, productive efficiency requires that less than 24 of X be *not* produced. If less than possible is produced, or more inputs than necessary are used, then the process in question is 'off' its isoquant and the production function can no longer tell us what will happen to output as inputs change.

SAQ 9.5

For the production function drawn in figure 9.7 (not a Cobb-Douglas constant returns to scale function):

(a) What is the marginal product of B when its use rises from 3 to 10 units when the rate of use of A is constant at 5?

(b) Is the marginal product of B increasing, decreasing, or constant as B increases to 3, 10, 15, 20 and 25 with A held at 5?

(c) In what area of the map is the marginal product of B negative?

(d) In what area of the map is the marginal product of A negative?

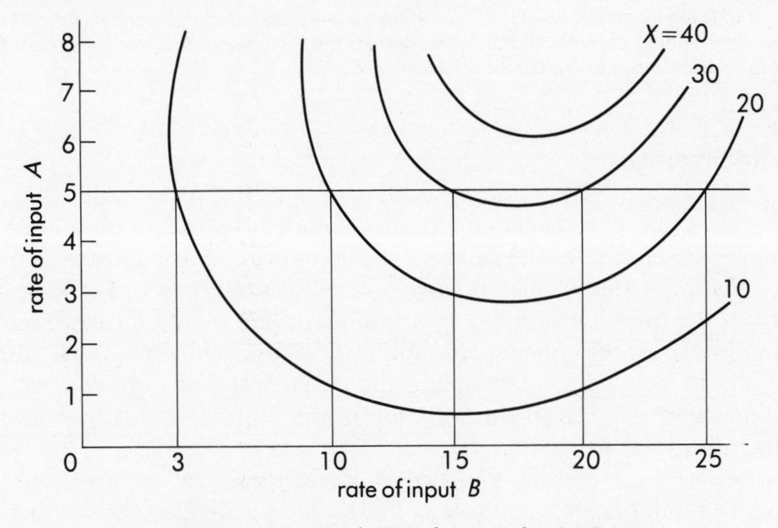

Figure 9.7 Production function for SAQ 9.5

Output Elasticities

The coefficients of the Cobb-Douglas production function (α, β etc.) can be usefully interpreted as measuring the responsiveness of output to changes in the rate of use of each input (the rate of use of others remaining constant). Thus, $\alpha = 0.4$ implies that output would increase by 0.4 of 1 per cent if input A

increased by 1 per cent. Another term for this is **elasticity of output** with respect to input:

$$\frac{dX}{dA}\frac{A}{X} = \alpha$$

or

$$\frac{dX}{dB}\frac{B}{X} = \beta$$

In table 9.4, suppose that use of both A and B is 6 units per period and that B increases to 7. This is a 16.7 per cent increase in the rate of use of B. Output rises from 24.0 to 26.3 or by 9.6 per cent, which is about 0.6 of the input increase. Alternatively, if the use of A rose to 7 and that of B remained at 6, output would rise from 24.0 to 24.9 or by nearly 4 per cent, which is something less than 0.4 of the increase in input (the numbers do not work out exactly because table 9.4 deals with finite changes, whereas the elasticity formulae just given are defined for limiting small changes in the inputs).

SAQ 9.6

Using the production function $X = 4A^{0.4}B^{0.6}$, suppose input A is increased by 1 per cent from 6 to 6.06 with input B remaining constant. What is the percentage increase in the rate of output? What relationship does this have to the coefficient on input A?

Cost-effectiveness

You have seen that one aspect of efficiency entails being on an isoquant – not using more inputs than are necessary to accomplish a particular outcome or, put the other way round, maximizing output for a given set of inputs. This leaves open the question of *where* on an isoquant one should locate. This is a question of **cost-effectiveness** – attaining the output chosen at least cost or, put the other way round, maximizing the output rate for a given cost. The further question, relating to the selection of the appropriate output level, is something discussed in chapter 12.

Cost-effectiveness requires knowledge of the prices of inputs. One can proceed in a similar fashion to the way budget lines were discussed in demand theory (now is a good time to refresh your memory by referring to chapter 6).

Suppose that there is a particular budget available for the production of an output X and, as before, that there are just two inputs, A and B, whose prices are P_A and P_B respectively. Assume that the prices of inputs are not affected by the amount of each purchased by the producer. The available budget is denoted by Y. Then the maximum amount of input A obtainable with the budget is Y/P_A and the maximum amount of B is correspondingly Y/P_B.

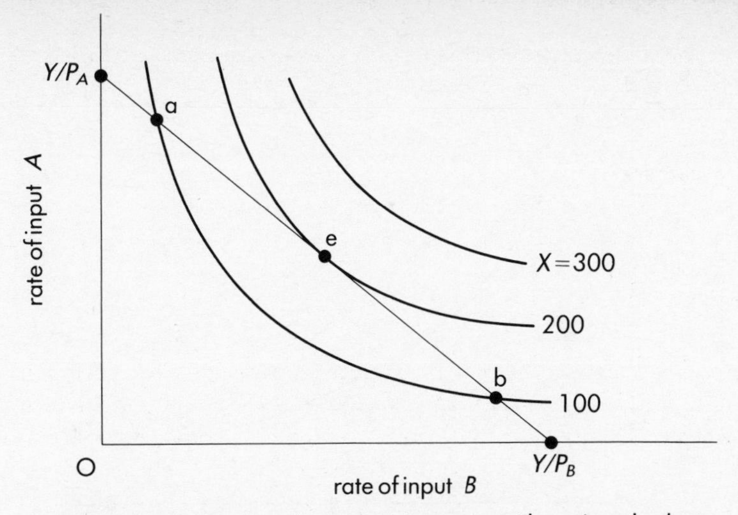

Figure 9.8 Attaining the highest isoquant with a given budget

In figure 9.8 these two points, Y/P_A and Y/P_B, are identified on the axes and the straight line connecting them shows the maximum rates of use of various combinations of A and B that are possible given the budget Y. This is exactly analogous to the budget line of demand theory, but in production theory the line is given the special name of **isocost line**. Cost-effectiveness requires that, for a given expenditure on A and B, output be maximized. This occurs when the highest isoquant is attained: in figure 9.8 this is at point e on isoquant $X = 200$. Isoquant $X = 100$ is, of course, attainable and, if points a or b were selected, would also exhaust the available budget. At these points, however, output is clearly not maximized. Isoquant $X = 300$ is not attainable given budget Y; hence $X = 200$ is the highest attainable. *Maximum output is where an isoquant is tangential to the isocost line.*

You could equally well look at the question from the other way round: what is the least cost way of attaining $X = 200$? In figure 9.9 there are three isocost lines corresponding to budgets Y_1, Y_2 and Y_3 in ascending order of size. They are necessarily parallel since the prices of A and B are the same: all that differs between them is the size of the budget. Output $X = 200$ could be produced with budget Y_3 by locating at point a or point b. Either would be efficient in the productive sense (for example, it is impossible to produce more X with the combination of A and B shown by point a). However, neither is cost-effective because, for a lower budget Y_2, the same output could also be produced. Again this involves producing at point e, where the chosen isoquant is tangential to an isocost line. Budget Y_1 is, of course, simply too small to permit $X = 200$ to be produced at the given prices of inputs A and B.

The general conclusion then is that *cost-effectiveness requires tangency between an isocost line and an isoquant.* Only then is output maximized for a given expenditure on inputs, or expenditure on inputs minimized for a given output.

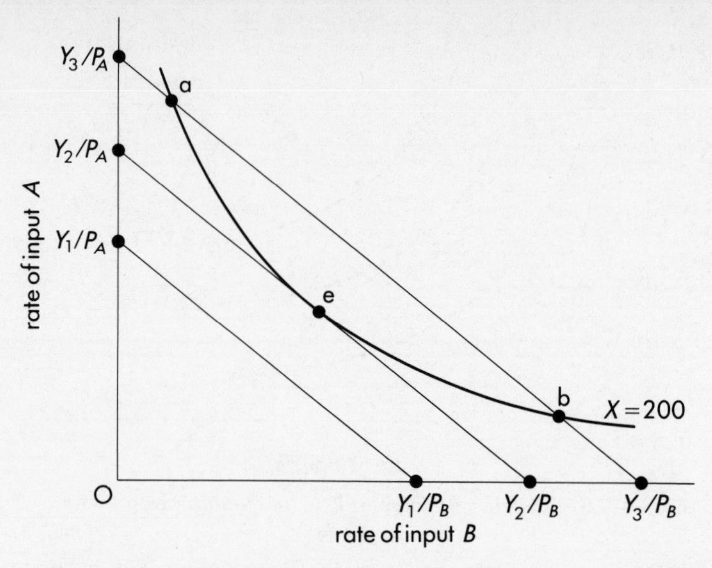

Figure 9.9 Attaining the lowest isocost line for a given output target

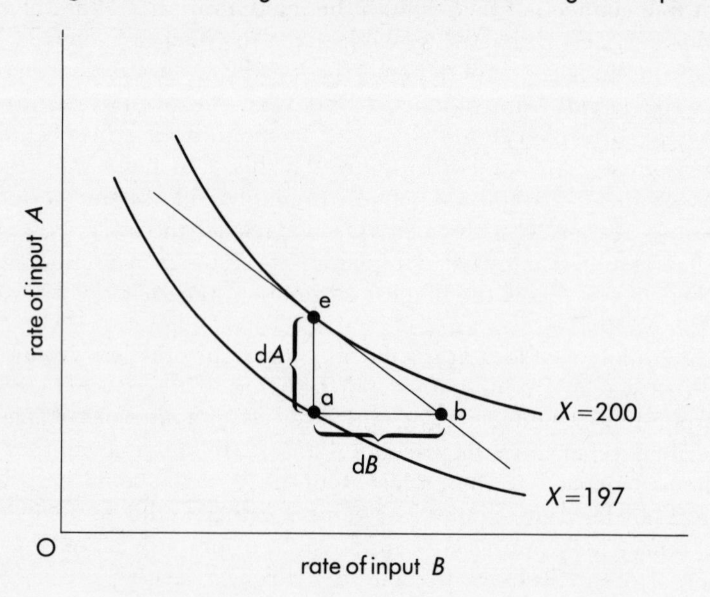

Figure 9.10 An isoquant and marginal products

Marginal Products and Cost-effectiveness

Now examine the isoquant in a little more detail. Figure 9.10 portrays a single isoquant, $X = 200$. At point e on this isoquant, its slope is given by the tangent $\mathrm{d}A/\mathrm{d}B$. Suppose that the marginal product of input A is 3 at point e and that the marginal product of B is 2. What does this mean? It means that, if the rate of use of A were reduced by one unit with that of B remaining the same, the output rate would fall by 3 of X. So, if the distance ea measures one unit of input A, the move from point e to point a must entail a move from isoquant $X = 200$ to isoquant $X = 197$. Now, to restore output to 200 by using more of input B, whose marginal product is 2, one would evidently need an additional 1.5 units of B. Consequently ab must correspond to 1.5 units of B just as ea corresponded to 1 unit of A. The ratio dA/dB is therefore 1/1.5 or 2/3, the inverse of the ratios of the marginal products of the two inputs. You may therefore say that the slope of an isoquant is equal to the inverse of the ratio of the marginal products. That is,

$$\frac{dA}{dB} = \frac{MP_B}{MP_A}$$

where MP stands for marginal product.

The absolute value of the slope of the isocost line, for the same resources as in the case of the budget line of demand theory, is P_B/P_A (check back to chapter 6 to make sure you understand why). Hence, you may say that cost-effectiveness requires the following condition to be met:

$$\frac{MP_B}{MP_A} = \frac{P_B}{P_A}$$

or

$$\frac{MP_A}{P_A} = \frac{MP_B}{P_B}$$

This says that cost-effectiveness (and hence efficiency) requires either that the *MRTS* be equal to the price ratio or that the ratio of the marginal product of each input to its price be the same for all inputs. This is true of all forms of production, whether in nationalized industries, private firms, profit or non-profit enterprises, social services or households.

Table 9.8 Annual percentage rates of growth of output (GDP) in 12 countries at constant prices

	1870–1913	*1922–9*	*1929–37*	*1951–73*
Belgium	2.0	3.4	0.1	4.1
Canada	3.8	6.2	−0.2	5.1
Denmark	3.2	2.6	1.9	3.9
France	1.6	4.4	−0.5	5.1
Germany	2.8	4.2	2.6	5.9
Italy	1.5	2.9	1.4	5.2
Japan	2.5	2.9	4.8	9.5
Netherlands	1.9	3.5	0.2	5.0
Norway	2.1	4.2	2.5	4.2
Sweden	2.8	5.0	2.2	3.8
UK	1.9	2.6	2.0	2.8
USA	4.1	3.3	−0.2	3.5

Case Study 9.3 Causes of Slow Growth in the UK

The growth of total output produced in the UK has been slower than in many other countries, as shown in table 9.8 (Stafford, 1981). Production theory tells one that the rate of growth of output is determined by the rate of growth of inputs, the efficiency with which they are used (cost-effectiveness) given prevailing technological know-how and, of course, the rate of change of technological knowhow.

Bernard Stafford (1981) has systematically investigated the various theories advanced for the relatively poor UK record over the past century (no new phenomenon this, apart from the 1930s: see table 9.8), and he came to the following conclusions:

(1) The immediate cause has been the slow expansion of the manufacturing sector. The non manufacturing sector (for example, services and the welfare state) has *not* expanded faster than elsewhere.

(2) The supply of available labour and capital equipment to manufacturing industry appears *not* to have held it back: in expansionary phases, industry seems always to have found the inputs it demanded.

(3) Productivity growth has been slow and seems to have been mostly due to a low rate of technological progress. The cause of this is partly the slow rate of growth itself in manufacturing industry (for example new machines are bought less frequently and so new technology is introduced more slowly), and partly the slow rate of introduction of new technology from other countries, mainly because the UK is already a technically advanced country.

(4) There is no evidence for the commonly held view that slow productivity growth is due to increasingly cost-ineffective use being made of manpower and machines.

(5) The main restriction on the expansion of overall output, especially in manufacturing, appears to have been the weakness of the demand for UK exports in world markets.

Bernard Stafford (1981) *The End of Economic Growth? Growth and Decline in the UK Since 1945*, Oxford, Martin Robertson.

SAQ 9.7

One often comes across statements like:

> The poor growth record of the British economy is attributable to relative inefficiency in the form of overmanning (more person-hours per machine) and underproduction (less output per machine) than in competitor countries.

Does this explain the UK's relatively poor growth rate?

Changes in Input Prices

In production theory, beware of jumping to conclusions that are based on misleading analogies with demand theory. One easy mistake to make is to suppose that the analysis of input price changes will be the same in production as in demand theory. To illustrate, suppose that a firm is efficiently producing output $X = 200$ at point e in figure 9.11. Then suppose that the price of input B falls so that the isocost line rotates from ab to ac. What can you say about the new situation? One thing is clear: if the firm chooses to keep the *same* rate of output, then it can do so at lower total cost by employing more B per period and less A, moving from point e to point e′ along the new, lower isocost line shown as a dashed line. Hence, you may infer that *if output remains the same* a fall in the price of one input will cause more of it to be used and less of the other, and that average cost will also fall.

However, why should output remain the same? As you will see later, decisions about output rates in (profit seeking) firms depend upon marginal costs of production and the prices at which output can be sold. It is possible (depending on the form of the production function) for either higher or lower output rates to be chosen. Hence one cannot unambiguously assert that changing input prices always necessarily have the same kind of effects as changing prices of consumer goods do on consumer behaviour. In production theory a change in input prices not only has the usual immediate effect on the slope of the isocost line but also may initiate a set of responses that generate further shifts in the isocost line as the preferred output rate changes. The

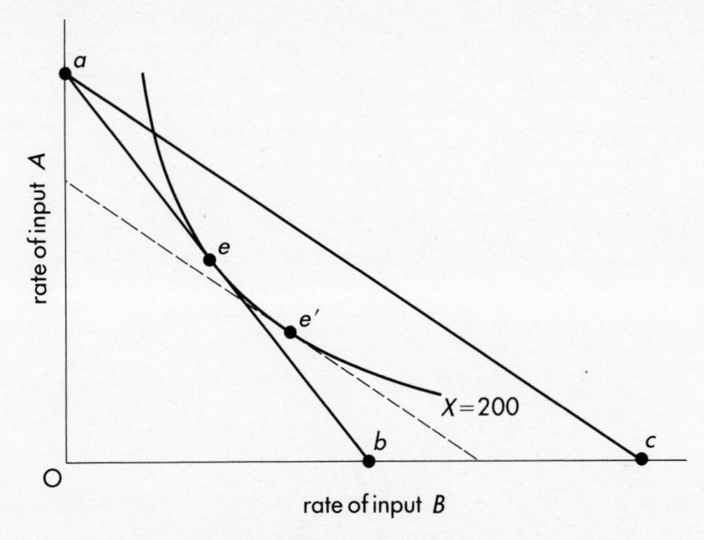

Figure 9.11 Effects of changes in an input price

analysis of these effects requires one to look in more detail at the question of what determines the chosen output rate.

SAQ 9.8

Comment on the following statements:

(a) If two inputs are capital and labour, the appropriate prices to use in a cost-effectiveness exercise are the purchase cost of machines and the hourly wage rate (gross of social insurance payments made by the firm) respectively.

(b) A production function shows the maximum amount of output that can be produced with varying quantities of inputs.

(c) If a production function shows increasing returns to scale, average cost per unit of output must fall as output rates increase.

What You Should Understand Now

The meaning of, and recent trends in, primary, secondary and tertiary production in the UK.
The definitions of a production function, inputs, intermediate outputs and final outputs.
The meaning of an isoquant and the marginal rate of technical substitution.
The Cobb-Douglas production function.
The distinction between returns to scale and returns to an input.
Total, average and marginal products.
Meanings of productive efficiency and cost-effectiveness.
Effects of input price changes on input ratios.

10

Cost and Cost Functions

Opportunity Cost

In everyday language, 'cost' usually means the money you pay to get something. In economics, however, the **cost**, or as it is often termed the **opportunity cost**, of any decision about the use of resources is the benefit forgone by not using resources in their most highly valued alternative use. This definition is adopted because of the central role that the analysis of efficiency plays in economics.

Consider what should be a familiar example from exchange theory. In figure 10.1 you see the demand curves of three people, labelled D_1, D_2 and D_3, for a resource A. S shows the stock of A available; it is distributed equally among the three individuals, so that each has s. The marginal value of A for individual 1 is MV_1, that for 2 is MV_2 and that for 3 is MV_3. You know that, in the absence of transaction costs, this is not an efficient distribution of A among the three. There are unexploited gains from trade: for example, 1 would be willing to

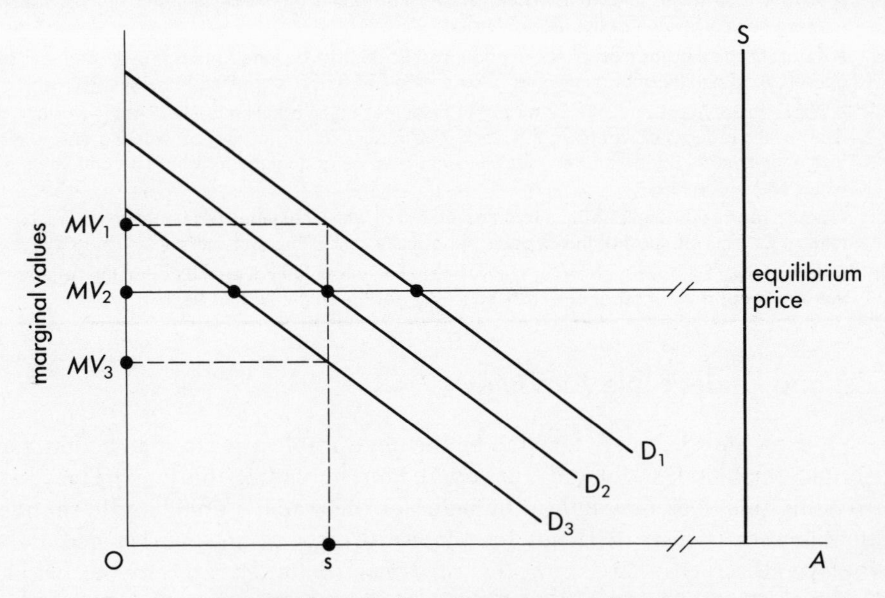

Figure 10.1 Exchange and opportunity cost

purchase A from either of the other two and 3 would be willing to sell to either of the other two. The efficient allocation is, as you know, where the MVs are all equal (shown by the dots on the demand curves).

Consider individual 3. A is least valuable (at the margin) when held by this individual. What is its opportunity cost? The value of a little more A for 1 and 2 is given by MV_1 and MV_2 respectively. Of these, MV_1 is the higher, so this is the (marginal) opportunity cost of 3 holding on to stock s. You would expect 1 to bid A away from 3 until the MVs (or marginal opportunity costs) are everywhere equal. But market prices may not reveal true opportunity costs. For example, 3 and 2 may not know of 1's existence. In that case, the marginal opportunity cost of A will appear to be MV_3 to 2, since that is what has to be paid to 3 in compensation for a small reduction in A. So 2 increases his or her A holding, 3's falls and 1's stays the same. The true opportunity cost of 2's expansion was, however, MV_1 – larger than MV_3 – and it is 1, not 2, who should have expanded on efficiency grounds.

Consequently what you have to pay may not truly represent opportunity cost. The circumstances under which markets reveal true opportunity costs are rather special and will be examined in chapter 19.

For the moment, note that the conventional usage of 'cost' can depart from the economic usage: prices paid for resources need not correspond to their opportunity cost.

SAQ 10.1

Which of the following is an opportunity cost of the resource in question and which not?

(a) An employer hires someone for £80 per week who would otherwise be unemployed (opportunity cost: £80).

(b) A school uses a hut it owns as a classroom that would otherwise be used as a toolshed (opportunity cost: value of hut as toolshed).

(c) A district hospital builds a hospital extension, cost £500,000, on land it already owns and uses as garden (total capital opportunity cost of extension £500,000, excluding running costs).

(d) A paper factory uses annually £2 million of resources but in addition freely deposits waste in a river, which reduces downstream fish stocks and raises costs to farmers of watering their cattle (opportunity costs £2 million per year plus annual value of damage to fish stocks and value of water cost to farmers).

(e) A new airport causes noise from aircraft as a result of which neighbouring house values fall by a total of £15 million (part of the airport's opportunity cost is thus £15 million).

(f) A student pays £2000 for one year's university tuition which just covers the cost of the resources she uses (opportunity cost of university education for the student is thus £2000).

Cost and Undesirable Attributes

Cost is sometimes wrongly taken to be the undesirable aspects of an action: for example, the blood, sweat and tears poured out in reading this book! The costs of reading this book may indeed by high, for the reader's time has alternative valuable uses (which need not be related directly to any market activity). Whatever these costs are, however, they most definitely are not the blood, sweat and tears.

Table 10.1 Advantages, disadvantages and opportunity cost

	Reading this book	*Taking the dog for a walk*	*Cooking dinner*
Advantages	20 utils	8 utils	15 utils
Disadvantages	18 utils	3 utils	11 utils
Net advantage	2 utils	5 utils	4 utils

Consider the example in table 10.1. It is about 6.00 p.m., and three effective choices confront you: read this book, take the dog for a walk or cook dinner. The pain, sweat etc. of reading this book is valued, say, at 18 utils (one is imagining that each activity can be rated on a ratio scale) which is far higher than the disutility of walking pooch (3 utils) or preparing dinner (11 utils). But this is not the opportunity cost of reading this book. To discover that one needs to know the advantages of the three options. As you can see, the *net* utilities from each are 2, 5 and 4 utils. So, if you read the book, you are actually forgoing a net utility gain of 5 utils (not 4, of course, since if you do not read this book you will take the dog out rather than cook). This is the highest alternative use value of your time (which is the resource being valued in this case). So you put the book down (being a utility maximizer) and take the dog out.

Note that here one is dealing explicitly with *subjective* opportunity cost. Ultimately, all opportunity costs relate back to utility and preferences, since these are the fundamental source of value. They are also affected by the distribution of income and wealth, since marginal values and marginal rates of transformation are affected by these. Sometimes these costs get revealed in market prices by what people are prepared to pay for things, or need to receive in compensation for parting with them. Markets are, however, but one (usually imperfect) way of revealing values and opportunity costs. So, although cost in economics is not blood, sweat and tears, neither is it necessarily what you pay in money for things. Blood, sweat and tears are, of course relevant; they help to determine the net value of any activity. However, it is the highest net value forsaken that is cost in economics – not only the highest use value forsaken by a particular individual, but also the use denied to whichever individual has the highest use value. To confuse cost with the *disadvantage* of an action would be as misleading as to identify it with the (gross) *advantage* of an alternative action. Both are mistakes to be avoided.

SAQ 10.2

In table 10.1, what is the opportunity cost of taking the dog for a walk?

How does this subjective notion of opportunity cost link up with costs revealed in the marketplace? Suppose there are just two of us, each owning a resource called land. Inside my head I have a whole set of opportunities for using that land, each having desirable and undesirable aspects, of which some are fairly confidently believed likely to happen and others less likely. Of these I select the use I prefer most (the most highly valued alternative rejected is the subjective opportunity cost). You have your plans and likewise select your most preferred option.

Now let the opportunity of our trading arise. Some of my plans may include using *your* land and some of yours may include using *mine*. If we trade, the minimum I must pay you has to compensate you for the best plan you had for the land I buy from you. Conversely, if you buy from me you must compensate me for forgoing my best plan for the land I sell. Thus trading reveals the opportunity cost of land. This cost is not, of course, in terms of either of our *rejected* plans (which are subjective and only in our heads). Rather it is in terms of the *highest* use the other person has for any traded land, which will in turn be higher in value than any other subjectively considered alternative in the mind of the person from whom resources were bid away or who failed to bid high enough for them in open competition.

Cost and Rent

> Shop prices in central London are high because the price of land is high.
> The price of land is high in central London because shop prices are high.

Which of these statements is correct? Are rents high because shoppers pull prices up, or are prices high because land owners push rents up?

Consider a major input like commercial land or the commercial buildings in a particular area. Their supply may be taken as fixed. In figure 10.2 this is shown as the fixed stock *S*. For simplicity assume that land and the buildings on it are rented together and owned by the same owner: there may be many owners but each landowner also owns the buildings on the land. There is also a demand for the land, indicated by the demand curve *D*. *R* is the equilibrium rent per unit of land. At a lower rent, demand exceeds the available supply and

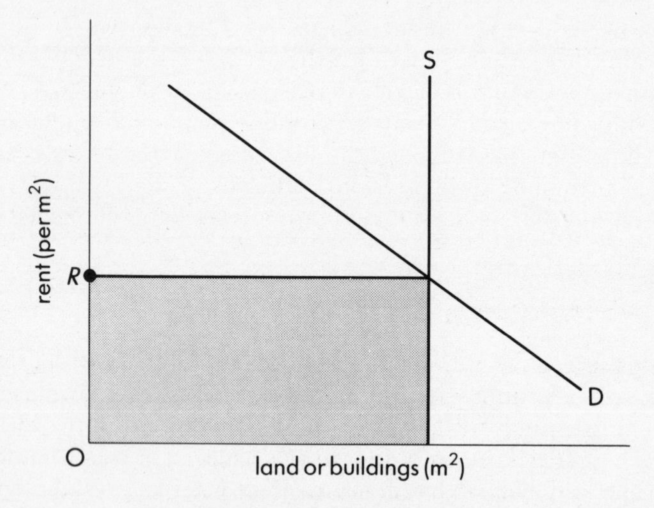

Figure 10.2 Rent as cost

competition among demanders will push rents up; at a higher rent, supply exceeds demand and competition among landowners will push rents down. The shaded area is the total rent payable to the landowners.

What determines the demand for the land? Clearly it is the demand for the goods that renters of land sell. If these goods suffer a fall in demand, shopkeepers and so on will place a lower value on the land and premises and demand will fall. Some may even go out of business altogether. If the demand for goods rises, shopkeepers place a higher value on land and premises and new traders will bid for existing properties, so demand rises. Consequently the answer to the puzzle that opened this section is that rents are high because demand, and hence prices, are high. The landlords simply have to seek out the highest bidder and let their land accordingly. They do not control the price of land, they merely get what the market will bear. The land does not have to be 'produced' (though it and the buildings will have to be maintained) so there is no reason to expect the rent to bear any relation to the expense of production or maintenance. The rent is purely demand determined: the costs of production are to all intents and purposes zero.

But as far as any single renter is concerned the land obviously has alternative uses: there are lots of other potential renters who are willing to pay a variety of prices for it. The successful renter, supposing the person letting to go for the highest bid, will be the one who can outbid all others. Since most landlords have a shrewd idea of what the potential of their property is, they know the kind of rent that will eliminate all but those placing the highest use value on the land. In this sense rent is an opportunity cost. In fulfilling the function of rationing the resource to the highest bidder, rent reveals the minimum required to bid it away from the next highest. And that, of course, is its opportunity cost.

Rent does not cause more or less to be supplied as it rises or falls, for the amount of the resource is fixed. Nor does rent reflect the cost of maintaining a property. It is demand determined. But rent does reveal the opportunity cost for any particular use.

Costs and Decisions

At any moment the cost of a resource is what you must pay to bid it away from its highest alternative use value. What that alternative value is will depend on lots of things, including the entirely subjective estimates of other people of its value to them – estimates that may, of course, prove to have been wrong!

Costs are not lying around simply to be counted up. They depend crucially on the type of choice one is considering. Take the apparently straightforward decision to purchase a car. It may 'cost' £10,000. But if its immediate resale value is, say, £9000 then the only real cost you have incurred is the difference between the two: £1000. That is the cost of the decision to purchase. Or one may be interested in the cost of purchasing and running the car for a year. In such a case the cost to you is the purchase price less what you expect to get for the car at the end of the year, plus tax and running expenses. Suppose you have already purchased the car. That expenditure is now in the past. It is a **sunk cost**. Whether you paid too much or too little is irrelevant for decisions you may take now. Sunk cost is not opportunity cost. Having purchased it, then, what is the cost of continuing possession and running for a year? It is the difference between its resale value now and its resale value in a year's time, plus tax and expected running costs. In all these examples it is assumed, of course, that the prices paid are adequate proxies for the resource's best alternative use values.

Sunk costs can be treacherous. One sometimes hears it argued that because so much has already been spent on a resource then that is itself a warrant for spending more. But the correct warrant must relate to the cost of *continuing* to use the resource in question: if that is less than the expected value of so doing then, and only then, is more spending warranted. Past expenditures are history. In economics bygones are bygones, of relevance only to the extent that past experiences may influence our expectations of the future.

SAQ 10.3

(a) A nationalized industry already owns a site with a warehouse (so expenditure on its purchase is a sunk cost). The operating costs of using the warehouse for storing some output are estimated, for the expected life of the building, to amount to £1 million. Supposing the operating costs to reflect accurately the opportunity cost of the resources used to run the place, the £1 million currently states the opportunity cost of the project. Right?

(b) 1 An airline purchases a used aircraft for £500,000. Since it is a used good and has moreover already been produced, the aircraft's true opportunity cost is really zero. Right?

2 Having purchased the aircraft for £500,000 and then discovered to its chagrin that it was worth only £250,000 on the open market, the company, knowing that to run the plane for 5 years (its expected life) will cost a further £2 million, concludes that with an expected revenue of £2.4 million it cannot cover costs. Was it right?

Cost Functions

You saw in chapter 9 that a production function shows the minimum inputs needed to produce various output rates. A cost function shows the minimum cost necessarily incurred at a variety of rates of output. Effectively, then, the decisions that one is implicitly concerned with relate to weekly, monthly, annual etc. rates of output. Assume for the moment that the prices paid for resources are true measures of their highest alternative uses (by other users) and that these prices do not change as lower or higher output rates are selected by decision makers. Implicitly one is also assuming that volume and rate of output move together, so that a 10 per cent increase in the rate (per year etc.) implies a 10 per cent increase in the total volume produced by a given date.

Table 10.2 is an illustrative cost function. The numbers in column 1 show various output rates X and those in column 2 show the associated minimum **total costs** C implied by the underlying production function and the prices of inputs. Column 3 shows **average cost** C/X, and column 4 shows the **marginal cost** $\Delta C/\Delta X$, the increased cost per unit increase in the output rate. For

Table 10.2 A cost function ($C = 90X - 15X^2 + X^3$)

1 *Output rate X*	2 *Total cost C*	3 *Average cost C/X*	4 *Marginal cost ΔC/ΔX*
0	0	0	0
1	76	76	76
2	128	64	52
3	162	54	34
4	184	46	22
5	200	40	16
6	216	36	16
7	238	34	22
8	272	34	34
9	324	36	52
10	400	40	76

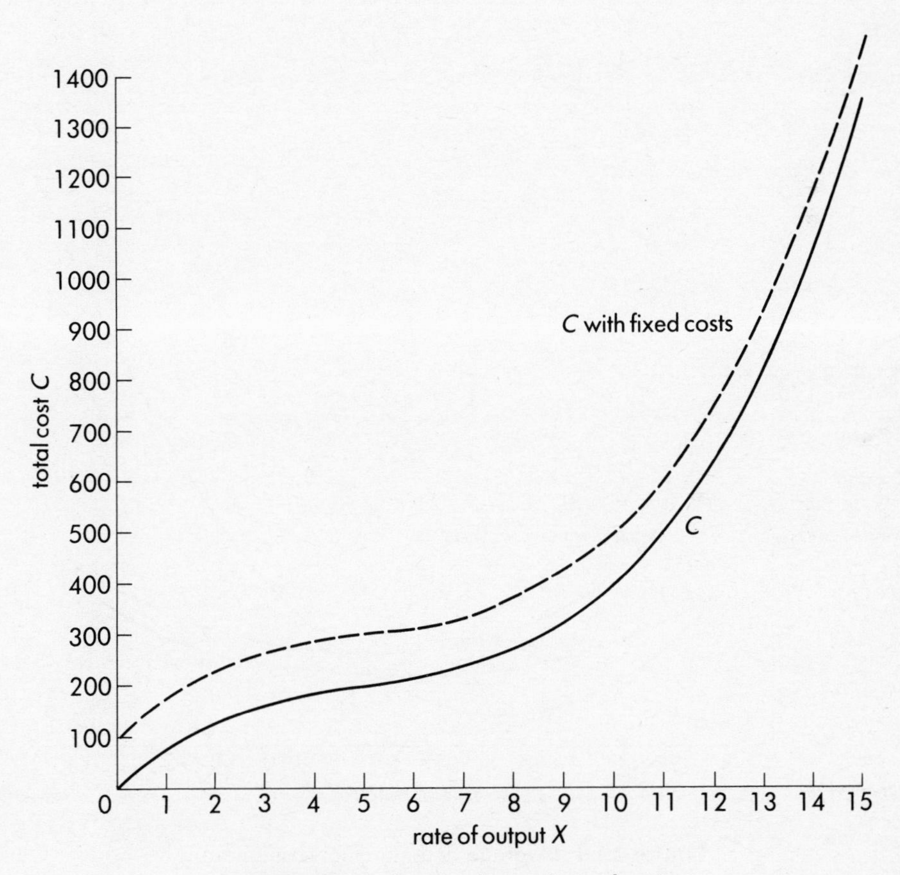

Figure 10.3 Graph of a total cost function

illustrative purposes marginal cost is calculated for discrete units of output rather than for very small changes.

In the example, note that there are no fixed (or overhead) costs; so if the output rate is zero, cost is zero. Figure 10.3 plots cost against the rate of output. For the moment ignore the dashed line and focus on the continuous line. As you can see from both the table and the figure, cost initially increases at a decreasing rate and then increases at an increasing rate. Since input prices are assumed constant, this reflects initially increasing returns (to either an input or to scale, depending on how many inputs are being varied) followed by decreasing returns around an output rate of 8.

This can be seen more clearly by looking at the graph of average marginal costs in figure 10.4. Here you can see that the average cost function is U shaped: initially average cost AC falls, revealing a minimum at an output rate around 7–8. This corresponds to that range of outputs where marginal cost MC is lower than average cost (hence the average must be falling). Thereafter the average cost rises, corresponding to output rates at which marginal exceeds average cost.

Note the shape of the marginal cost curve and its relationship with the

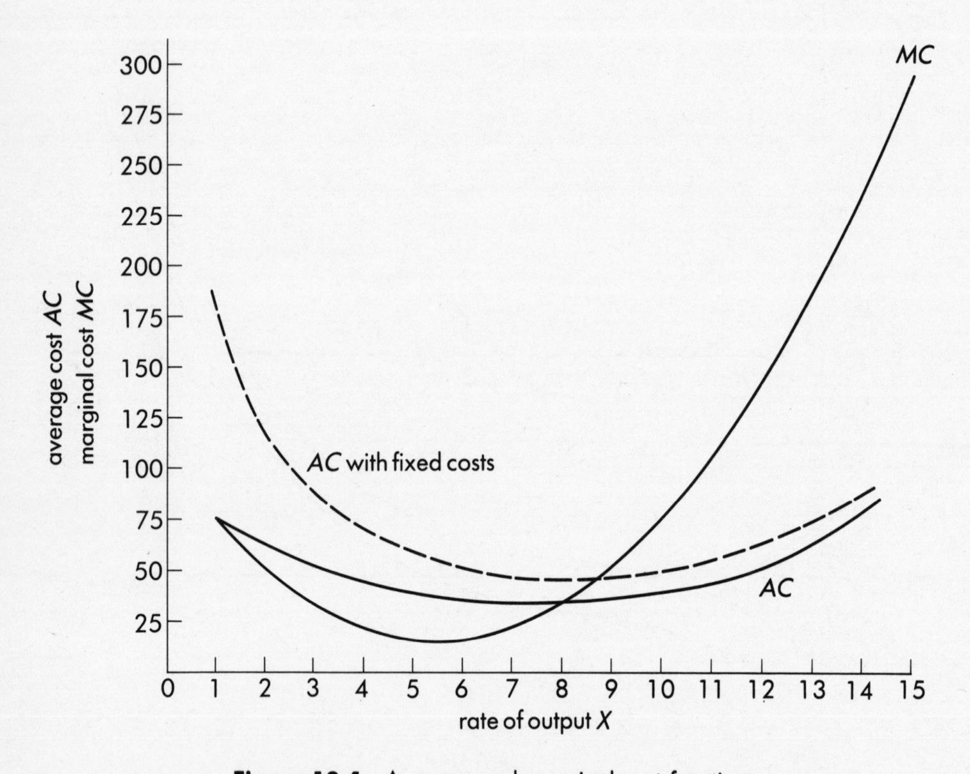

Figure 10.4 Average and marginal cost functions

Table 10.3 A cost function with fixed costs ($C = 100 + 90X - 15X^2 + X^3$)

1 *Output rate X*	2 *Total cost C*	3 *Average cost C/X*	4 *Marginal cost ΔC/ΔX*
0	100	∞	0
1	176	176.0	76
2	228	114.0	52
3	262	87.3	34
4	284	71.0	22
5	300	60.0	16
6	316	52.7	16
7	338	48.3	22
8	372	46.5	34
9	424	47.1	52
10	500	50.0	76

average cost curve. When average cost is falling, marginal cost lies beneath it. When average cost is rising, marginal cost lies above it. When average cost is at its minimum, it is equal to marginal cost.

The average cost curve shows the *lowest cost per unit* at which a given output rate can be produced. This follows from the assumption that the cost curve is drawn for an *efficient* production process. It is simply not possible for any organization to operate anywhere below its average cost function.

Suppose now that there are some **fixed costs** associated with this line of production (say the rent on land used). If these are set at £100 then the consequences, given the same **variable costs**, are shown in table 10.3. In column 2, total cost has everywhere been increased by £100 over that in table 10.4. Average cost rises by £100/X. These are shown as the dashed curves in figures 10.3 and 10.4. *Marginal cost is unaffected by the existence of fixed costs* because the latter are determined only by the decision to produce or not produce. They are not affected by the decision to produce at a faster or slower rate, which is what marginal cost measures.

The average cost curve is affected in the way shown. The impact on average cost becomes smaller at higher output rates because the fixed cost is being shared between ever increasing output rates. At infinitely high rates, the average cost curve with fixed costs and that without fixed costs merge together.

If input prices were to increase, the total average and marginal cost curves would all shift upwards. Conversely, if input prices were to fall, the curves would shift downwards. If technical innovations in the production process caused the production function to change, the cost curves would again shift – normally downwards.

SAQ 10.4

What is wrong in each of (a) – (d) of figures 10.5?

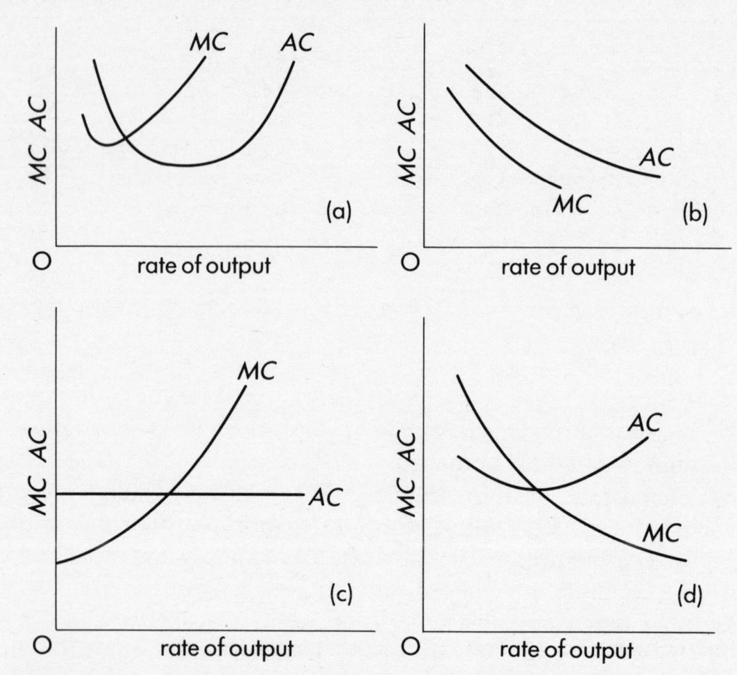

Figure 10.5 Marginal cost and average cost examples for SAQ 10.4

Case Study 10.1 Elusive Marginal Costs in Cancer Screening

Marginal costs can be both crucial and exceedingly elusive. The following example comes from a combining of economic and medical skills by Neuhauser and Lewicki (1976) and shows how easy it is not to perceive the size of *marginal* costs.

A guaiac is a chemical test for invisible (occult) blood in stools, and is widely used as a means of identifying the presence of cancer in the bowel sufficiently early for it to be operable. The test is not foolproof: sometimes cancer is present without the test detecting it, and rather frequently the test detects occult blood without there being any cancer. The first kind of error is called a false negative and the second a false positive. The number of false negatives (cancers missed) can be reduced by doing more than one test. In the USA around 1968 the average cost per cancer diagnosed if one test were done was $1175, and about six cancers would be missed out of 10,000 patients screened. If six tests were done the average cost was only about twice this ($2451) and the number of cancers missed fell to a very tiny fraction. Six guaiac tests were recommended to doctors as best practice. Unfortunately, the average cost was a very misleading number to use.

In table 10.4 you can see from column 1 that the marginal payoff to additional tests falls rapidly and that the marginal cost per additional test also falls (see column 5) despite the increasing number of false positives, each of which will have led to a follow-up with further tests (which are, of course, costly) to confirm the initial diagnosis but which will have proved negative.

Neuhauser and Lewicki chose as their output measure the numbers of cancers found, in order to compute the marginal costs of the output of the *diagnostic procedure* rather than the overall programme for identifying *and treating* cancer of the colon. By manipulating the information in table 10.4, table 10.5 can be derived.

Column 1 in table 10.5 (derived from column 1 of table 10.4) gives the marginal cancers found as the number of tests increases: if one rather than none is done, 65.946 are found; if two rather than one are done the number rises to 71.442, an increase of 5.496; and so on. Column 2 (derived from column 4 of table 10.4) shows the increase in total costs as the number of tests increases: when the number rises from one to two, costs rise from $77,511 to $107,690, a marginal change of $30,179, and so on. Column 3 shows the increase in costs per additional cancer found, i.e. the marginal cost per identified cancer: it is column 2 divided by column 1.

This calculation gives us the remarkable result that the marginal cost of the sixth stool guaiac is more than $47 million.

Table 10.4 Yield and cost of diagnosis in cancers of the colon for 10,000 patients screened using from one to six sequential stool guaiacs

Number of guaiacs	*1* *Number of cancers found (true positives)*	*2* *Number of cancers missed (false negatives)*	*3* *Number of false positives*	*4* *Total cost of diagnosis ($)*	*5* *Average cost per cancer found ($)*
1	65.946	5.995	309	77,511	1,175
2	71.442	0.4996	505	107,690	1,507
3	71.900	0.0416	630	130,199	1,811
4	71.938	0.0035	709	148,116	2,059
5	71.94172	0.0003	759	163,141	2,268
6	71.942	0.00003	791	176,331	2,451

Table 10.5 Marginal costs of sequential stool guaiacs

Numbers of guaiacs	*1* *Increase in cancers found*	*2* *Increase in total costs ($)*	*3* *Marginal cost per cancer found ($)*
1	65.946	77,511	1,175
2	5.496	30,179	5,491
3	0.458	22,509	49,146
4	0.038	17,917	471,500
5	0.00372	15,025	4,038,978
6	0.00028	13,190	47,107,143

D. Neuhauser and A. M. Lewicki (1976) 'National health insurance and the sixth stool guaiac', *Policy Analysis*, **2**(2), 179–96.

Fixed and Variable Inputs

Not all inputs are equally easy (cheap) to vary: there may be long term contracts made with some suppliers of inputs, with personnel, and so on that are costly to alter. Some economists go so far as to speak of fixed inputs or fixed factors of production. A classic example of such an input is held to be railway track: you can relatively easily vary the frequency of trains, but the track is

Table 10.6 A variable returns production function ($X = 10A^2B^2 - 0.1A^3B^3$)

rate of input A									
9	737	2,657	5,322	8,294	11,138	13,414	14,685	14,515	12,466
8	589	2,150	4,378	6,963	9,600	11,981	13,798	14,746	14,515
7	456	1,686	3,484	5,645	7,962	10,231	12,245	13,798	14,685
6	338	1,267	2,657	4,378	6,338	8,294	10,334	11,981	13,434
5	238	900	1,912	3,200	4,688	6,300	7,962	9,600	11,138
4	154	589	1,267	2,150	3,200	4,378	5,645	6,963	8,294
3	87	338	737	1,267	1,912	2,657	3,484	4,378	5,322
2	39	154	338	589	900	1,267	1,686	2,150	2,657
1	10	39	87	154	238	338	456	589	737
rate of input B	1	2	3	4	5	6	7	8	9

fixed. In fact, when the Great Western Railway's old broad gauge track was changed to the standard narrow gauge in 1892 the entire stretch of 213 miles from Exeter to Penzance was changed in one weekend. Moreover 177 miles of this had also to be altered from the longitudinal timbers to the modern cross sleepers! Of course it took an army of platelayers to do the job (4200 of them!) The point is that any factor or input *can* be varied in both the short and the long term. Inputs are not *technically* fixed. Rather they are fixed *by choice.* In general, the *sooner* and *faster* one seeks to vary any input, the more costly it is. It is consequently not very helpful to think in terms of absolutely fixed and absolutely variable inputs. What *is* helpful is to recognize that, depending on the underlying production function, if it is decided to vary some but not all inputs, the cost curve will look quite different from a decision to vary all, or more, or fewer of the inputs. This can be shown most easily by taking an example.

Table 10.6 shows a two input production function with *variable* returns to scale (not a Cobb-Douglas function). If it has been decided, for the particular purposes in hand, that input A is to be held at a fixed rate of 9, then the numbers in the cells of the row corresponding to $A = 9$ show how output will vary as input B is varied in rate from 1 to 9. Similarly, if A were chosen to be fixed at, say, 7, 5 or 3 per period, then the cells in the corresponding rows show how output will vary as B is varied.

This information can be plotted on a graph as in figure 10.6, where the outputs or total product produced as B varies are shown for $A = 3$, 5, 7 and 9. It is obvious that the productivity of one input depends on the amount of another. It may be enhanced by it. For example, when 6 units of A per period are used, for the range of outputs in table 10.6 and figure 10.6, you can see that the total product *rises* as more B is used. However, when 9 of B are used, total product *falls* as 9 rather than 8 of A are used.

It is more helpful still to look at the average and marginal contribution of the input to output. This is shown in table 10.7 and figure 10.7 for the case where $A = 9$. As with cost curves, if the marginal product is higher than the average, then the average will be rising. If the marginal product is less than the average,

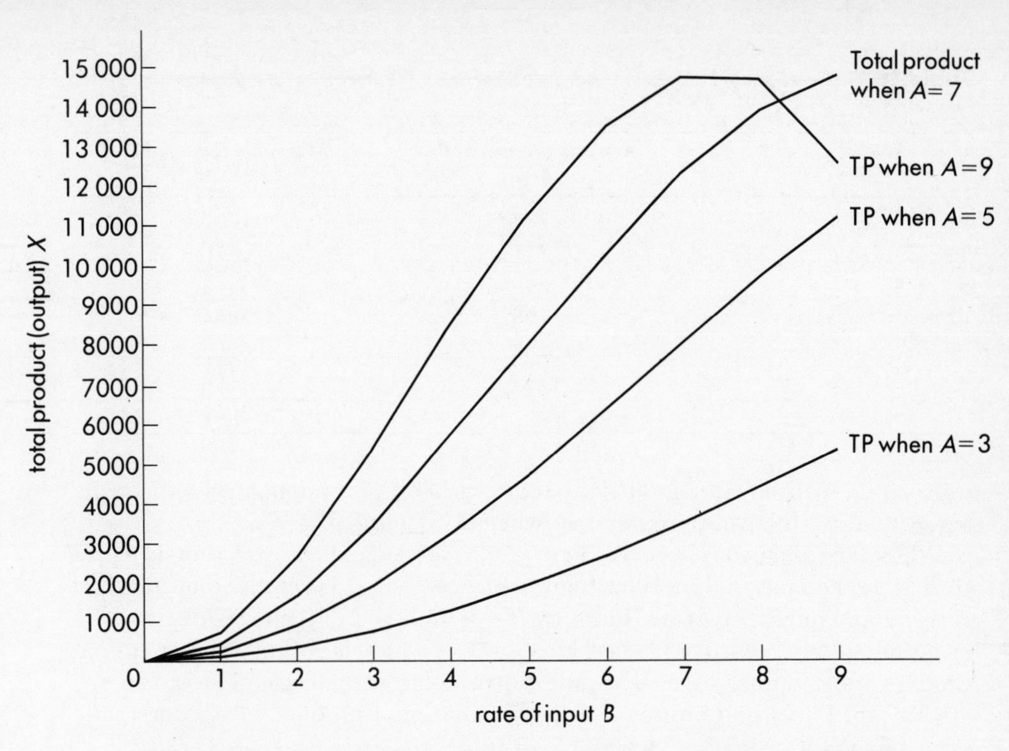

Figure 10.6 Total product curves (for function $X = 10A^XB^X - 0.1A^3B^3$)

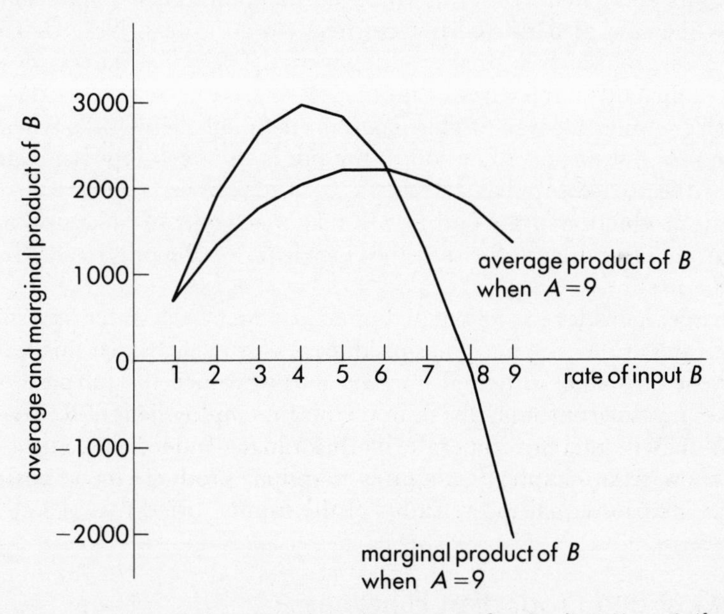

Figure 10.7 Average and marginal product curves for B when $A = 9$ (for function $X = 10A^2B^2 - 0.1A^3B^3$)

Table 10.7 Average and marginal products of one input (B), the other being fixed ($A = 9$) (for function $X = 10A^2B^2 - 0.1A^3B^3$)

Rate of use of B	*Average product of B, X/B*	*Marginal product of B, ΔX/ΔB*
1	737	737
2	1329	1920
3	1774	2665
4	2073	2972
5	2228	2844
6	2236	2276
7	2099	1271
8	1814	−170
9	1385	−2049

the average will be falling. They are equal when the average product is at its highest value (this is approximately when $A = 9$ and $B = 6$).

When the total product curve (figure 10.6) is rising at an increasing rate (up to $B = 4$) the marginal product (figure 10.7) is rising. When the total product is rising at a decreasing rate (between $B = 4$ and $B = 7$) the marginal product is falling but is positive. When the total product is falling, the marginal product must be negative, with additions to the rate of use of B (given the amount of A) causing output to fall. The marginal product is, of course, the slope of the total product curve.

It seems to be an empirical law that the marginal product of any input (other inputs being held constant) will eventually diminish. This is sometimes known as the **law of diminishing returns** (to an input). Note that the law does not assert that all marginal products always fall, only that they eventually will – at sufficiently high rates of input use. Were this not so, as the famous Nobel prize winner George Stigler has remarked, all the world's wheat could be grown in a flower pot! (The soil in the pot is the fixed input and the grain sown in it the varied input.)

Efficient production of the output will take place only in ranges of input use where marginal product is positive: that is, when $A = 9$ more than about 8 of B will not be used.

To see this, consider the following line of argument. Consider first the range of output rates where the marginal product of B is negative. In this range, the employment of further B actually *reduces* output. Since the purpose of using inputs is to produce outputs, this is an inefficient employment of B. No efficient organization will therefore operate in this range. Indeed efficiency, as you already know from chapter 9, requires marginal products to be positive (as well as their ratios equal to the ratios of the inputs' prices).

Linking Cost and Production Functions

You are now ready to make the link between production functions and cost functions. Suppose the cost of 9 units of input A is £100 and the unit price of B

Table 10.8 Production and cost functions ($X = 10A^2B^2 - 0.1A^3B^3$, $A = 9$)

1 Rate of use of B	*2* Variable cost of B (£)	*3* Fixed cost of A (£)	*4* Total cost (£)	*5* Output X	*6* Average variable cost (£)	*7* Average fixed cost (£)	*8* Average total cost (£)	*9* Marginal cost (£)
0	0	100	100	0	–	–	–	–
0.5	400	100	500	193	2.07	0.52	2.59	2.07
1.0	800	100	900	737	1.09	0.14	1.22	0.73
1.5	1200	100	1300	1,576	0.76	0.06	0.82	0.48
2.0	1600	100	1700	2,657	0.60	0.04	0.64	0.37
2.5	2000	100	2100	3,923	0.51	0.03	0.54	0.32
3.0	2400	100	2500	5,322	0.45	0.02	0.47	0.29
3.5	2800	100	2900	6,797	0.41	0.01	0.43	0.271
4.0	3200	100	3300	8,294	0.39	0.01	0.40	0.267
4.5	3600	100	3700	9,759	0.37	0.01	0.38	0.273
5.0	4000	100	4100	11,138	0.36	0.01	0.37	0.29
5.5	4400	100	4500	12,374	0.356	0.01	0.36	0.32
6.0	4800	100	4900	13,414	0.36	0.01	0.37	0.38
6.5	5200	100	5300	14,202	0.37	0.01	0.38	0.51
7.0	5600	100	5700	14,685	0.38	0.01	0.39	0.83
7.5	6000	100	6100	14,808	0.41	0.01	0.41	3.25

is £800. Table 10.8 extends the information previously given about the production function in table 10.6. Column 1 shows the rate of use of input *B*. Column 2 shows its cost – assuming that its price is £800 and that this reflects its highest value in other activities. Column 3 shows the fixed cost of nine *A*s at £100; it does not, of course, vary with output. Column 4 shows the total cost: variable plus fixed. Column 5 shows the highest output attainable with 9 of *A* and the various rates of *B*. The next column, 6, shows the average variable cost of output: total variable cost divided by output. Column 7 shows the average fixed cost, which approaches zero as output approaches infinity. When plotted on graph paper it is a simple rectangular hyperbola. Column 8 gives average total cost. Column 9 gives marginal cost: the cost per unit of increment in output. Thus, for example, as output rises from 14,685 to 14,808, the increase is 123. This is associated with an increase in cost of £400, so the marginal cost is £400/123 = £3.25.

Figure 10.8 plots the cost curves. Figure 10.8(a) shows the total cost curve *C* implied by the production function and the input prices. The curve begins at zero output with some positive cost, £100, which is the fixed cost. Just as the total product curve first rose at an increasing rate and then at a decreasing rate, so the total cost curve rises first at a *decreasing* rate and subsequently at an increasing rate. Figure 10.8(b) shows a U shaped average variable cost curve *AVC*, a similarly U shaped average total cost curve *ATC* and the marginal cost curve *MC*. The shapes are just as described earlier in this chapter, but this time the cost functions have been derived from an underlying production function.

Note that when average product is rising, average cost is falling and vice versa; and that when marginal product is rising, marginal cost is falling and

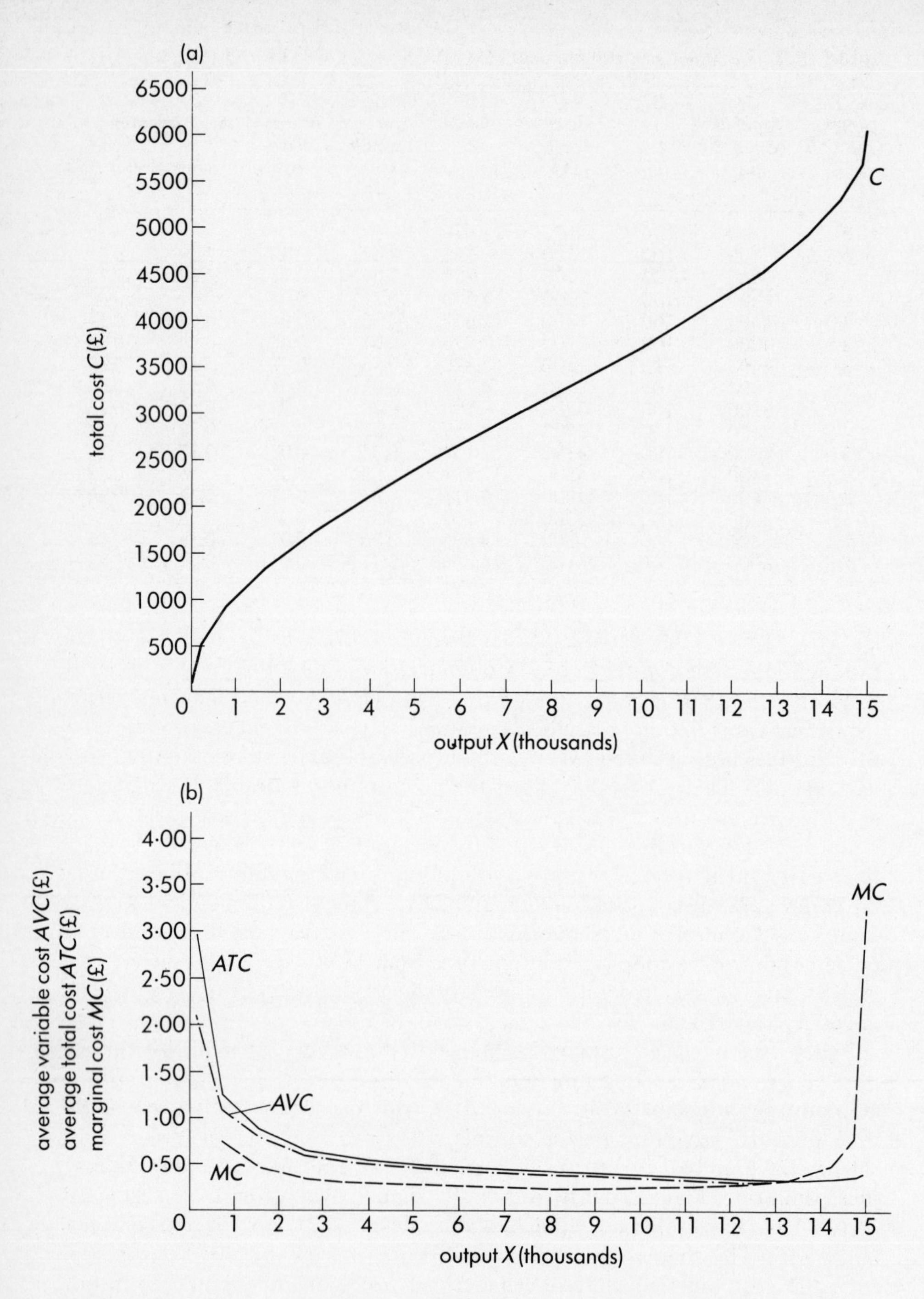

Figure 10.8 Total, average and marginal cost curves (for function $X = 10A^2B^2 - 0.1A^3B^3$)

vice versa. Note also that when average and marginal products are equal, so are average (variable) and marginal costs. In other words, cost curves are a kind of mirror image of product curves.

SAQ 10.5

Suppose an enterprise could produce increasing rates of output at a constant marginal cost but that there was also a fixed cost of production. Draw the average and marginal cost curves.

Case Study 10.2 Rising Marginal Cost in British Industry?

Table 10.9 contains a summary given by Alan Walters (1963) of a set of studies of industrial cost curves. There are lots of difficulties in estimating actual industrial cost functions; many firms have multiple products; the period over which costs are measured tends to be an accounting period (rather than a decision period as suggested by our theory); accountants assign values that are not good proxies of true opportunity costs; some studies have used businessmen's opinions about cost which can be entirely unreliable and are anyway likely to be contaminated by accounting information; the prices of inputs may change over time or between different locations; and so on.

A constant marginal cost has often been found but it remains a matter of controversy as to whether these findings are biased by sampling and other errors. Many economists (including Walters) believe that they are constant, at least in the short run, and that most marginal costs curves do eventually slope upwards.

Alan Walters (1963) 'Production and cost functions: an econometric survey', *Econometrica*, **31** (1–2) 1–66.

Table 10.9 Results of studies of industry demand curves

Date	*Industry*	*Type of result*
1933	Cement	Constant *MC*
1936	Furniture	Constant *MC*
1940	Steel	Constant *MC*
1941	Hosiery	Constant *MC*
1942	Shoe shops	U shaped *AC*
1947	Light plant	Increasing *MC*
1956	Retailing	L shaped *AC*
1959	Metal	Initial scale economies, then constant *AC*
1960	Multiple products	Constant *MC*

Short and Long Run Cost Curves

You have already seen that no input can ever really be regarded as technically fixed. What can make a difference to where an organization operates on its production function is the cost of varying inputs. Perhaps one could say that the only truly fixed input would occur where the cost of variation was infinite. Decisions about output rates are, however, often taken on the basis that some inputs will be varied and others not. It is this possibility that gives rise to the distinction between long and short runs.

Imagine a productive organization, say a business firm, engaged in a continuous production process, like producing motor cars, baked beans or plastic coat hangers. Suppose there is a drop in the demand for output. At current output rates the enterprise will begin to build up stocks. Before it decides on any reaction to this phenomenon it must take a view as to whether the drop in demand is going to persist or merely be temporary. If it takes the view that the drop is temporary, or decides to 'wait and see', it is likely slightly to alter its rate of use of those inputs that are the least costly to vary. It may perhaps use less energy by operating machinery more slowly or for shorter periods, perhaps cut back on workforce overtime, perhaps use fewer intermediate inputs, perhaps use less of temporarily hired-in services like cars, delivery vehicles etc. This can be characterized as a short run reaction.

If, on the other hand, the enterprise took the view that the drop in demand was permanent, its reaction might be quite different. It would be likely to scale down much of its activity right across the board, varying the inputs that were not varied (as well as those that were) in the case of a temporary drop. This is a long run reaction.

In reality there is a large variety of runs to be considered by any decision maker, and each will normally be associated with different costs. For simplicity, however, let us suppose there are only two runs to consider. The implications can be drawn out with the aid of figure 10.9, which shows a production function for a process using two inputs to produce one output. Suppose that the enterprise is initially at point e, producing efficiently its chosen output of 200 given the prices of the inputs shown by the slope of the isocost line tangential at point e.

A short run reaction to changes in output might be to keep A constant and vary B, so that if output fell to 100 the enterprise would move to point a, and if output rose to 250 it would move to point b. These are moves along the **short**

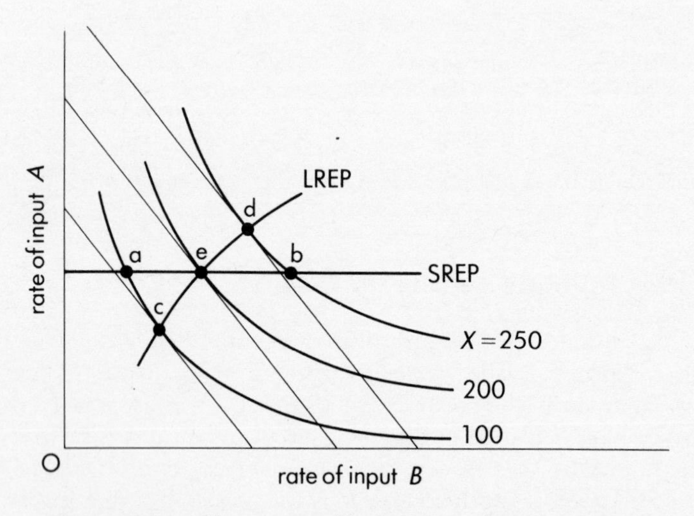

Figure 10.9 Short run and long run production reactions

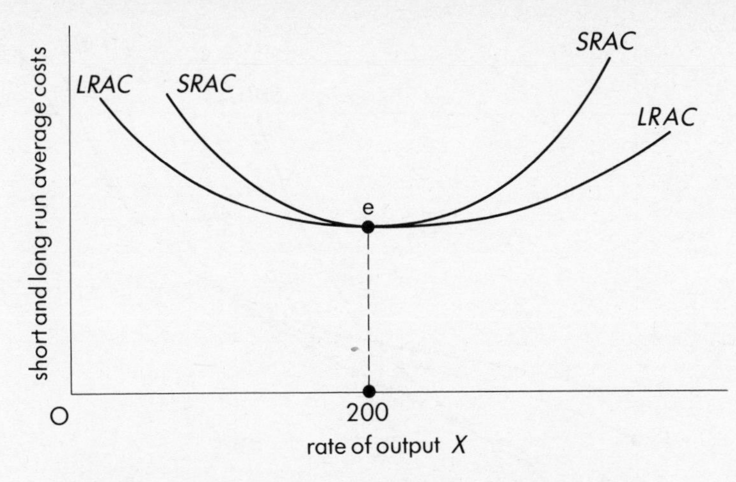

Figure 10.10 Short run and long run average costs

run expansion path (SREP). A long run reaction to changes in output would be to change both A and B to maintain the efficiency conditions, so that the enterprise moved to point c if output fell to 100 or point d if it rose to 250 along its **long run expansion path** (LREP). Now you can immediately see that, at point a, the cost to the enterprise will be higher than the cost at point c, for the isocost line through (not tangent to) point a must lie above the one tangent at point c. Thus locating at point a involves a higher cost of producing 100 units of output than locating at point c. Similarly the isocost line through point b must lie above that which is tangential at point d, so locating at point b is a costlier way of producing 250 than locating at point d. Therefore, short run reactions tend to result in higher average cost than long run reactions. The consequences for average cost curves are shown in figure 10.10, where point e is the initial point: short run moves from point e involve higher average costs (*SRAC*) than long run moves (*LRAC*).

Why then might an enterprise choose ever to make short term reactions? Because making changes is itself costly. There are **transaction costs**. For example, if A is labour and the management has an agreement with its labour force to employ so many people for so many hours at such a wage, then breach of the agreement may cause industrial action, legal damages, penal compensation to workers etc. These costs of change are not shown in the cost functions, which relate cost only to the costs represented by the alternative use values of the inputs or, as they are commonly termed, **costs of production**. Indeed, without transaction costs there would be no need to distinguish between the short and the long run: short and long run reactions differ *precisely because* it is costly to change input mixes and some inputs are costlier to alter than others.

There may none the less be *some* fixed *costs* (though not fixed *factors*) even in the long run as when, for example, a producer has to buy a franchise from a patent holder to manufacture a patented product.

Figure 10.11 shows a long run total cost *LRTC* curve. This passes through

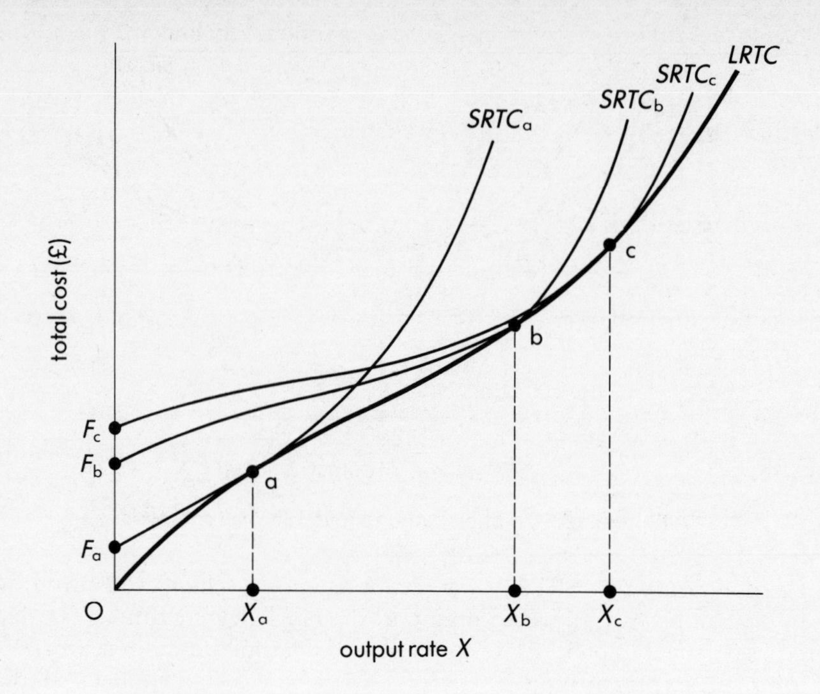

Figure 10.11 A family of short run total cost curves

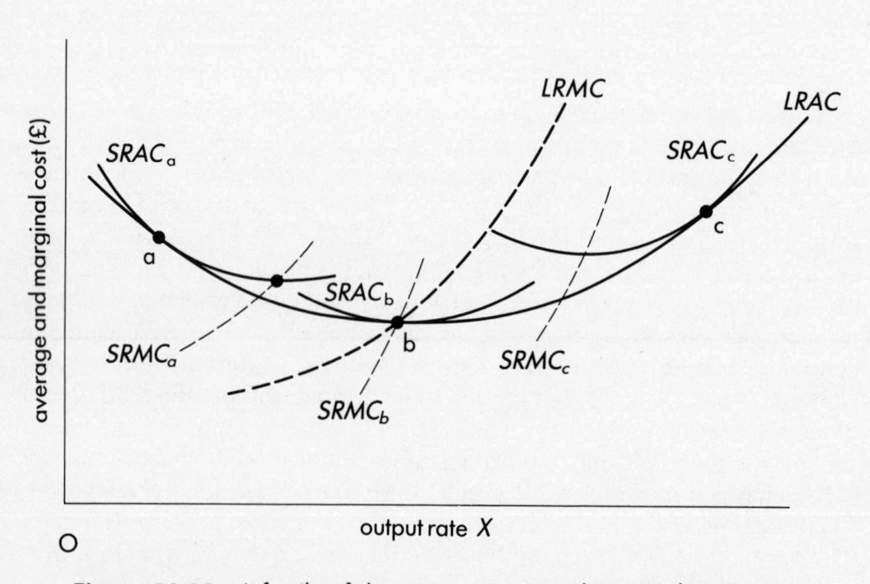

Figure 10.12 A family of short run average and marginal cost curves

the origin since it is supposed that the run is sufficiently long for no input to be treated as fixed. *LRTC* shows the lowest possible cost at which any output can be produced and is derived from a long run expansion path. Figure 10.11 also has three short run total cost *SRTC* curves, which show how total costs will behave if a short run alteration is made from either point a, point b or point c. Points a, b and c are at the lowest total costs of producing outputs X_a, X_b and X_c respectively. Short run movement from point a, for example, would take the enterprise along $SRTC_a$ which is everywhere (other than at point a) above *LRTC* and which at zero output entails a fixed cost of F_a. Note that the output rate that minimizes average cost is X_b, where a ray from the origin is tangential to *LRTC*.

From this *LRTC* curve and its associated family of *SRTC* curves (there are normally, of course, many more than just three, for there is an *SRTC* curve tangential to the *LRTC* at every point along the *LRTC* curve) you can derive average and marginal cost curves. This is done in figure 10.12 where, at point a, the $SRAC_a$ curve is tangential to the *LRAC* and the corresponding *SRMC* curve passes through the lowest point of $SRAC_a$. Similarly, the $SRAC_c$ curve is tangential to *LRAC* at point c and its $SRMC_c$ passes through its lowest point. At the lowest *LRAC* there is too an *SRAC* and its *SRMC* at point b is the same as *LRMC*. Note also that *LRMC* passes through *LRAC* at its lowest point. *SRMC*s are generally *less elastic* than *LRMC*.

SAQ 10.6

Which of the following are true and which false?

(a) *SRAC* is tangential to a *LRAC* at the lowest point of the *SRAC*.

(b) The distinction between short and long run output decisions arises only because there are transaction costs involved in changing input proportions.

(c) Long run marginal cost curves are more elastic than short run.

(d) Short run average total cost is never less than long run average total cost.

Case Study 10.3 Economies of Scale in British Industry

Estimating long run cost curves is even harder than estimating short run ones. It requires the accurate measurement of the opportunity cost of inputs that are fixed in the short run (and that did not affect marginal costs in that case), and an allowance for technical changes that may occur (or be expected to occur) in the long run but not in the short.

Pratten (1971) has examined the long run cost curves of many industries and has found widespread evidence of economies of scale (that is, declining *LRAC*). For example, in ethylene production, as plant sizes capable of producing 100,000, 200,000 and 300,000 tonnes are compared, average cost falls from £31.20 to £28.80 and £27.10 per tonne.

In the machine tool industry using batch production methods, as output per year rises from 5 to 10, 20, 50, 100 and 200, production costs per tool go from an index of 100 to 95, 91, 86, 83 and 81.

Results such as these have important consequences for industrial policy. Would more mergers reduce unit cost? Is there a danger of monopolistic practices? In the electronic capital goods industry, for example, the lowest estimated cost requires a scale such that only one firm would supply the entire British market.

They can also suggest scope for greater cost efficiency: many plants are a good deal too small to be at or near the lowest point on the *LRAC*. Thus, the minimum *AC* in oil refining is 10^7 tonnes output but the average actual plant output is 4×10^6 tonnes; in brewing the optimum is 1×10^6 barrels but the actual average 10^5; in cement plants the optimum is 2×10^6 tonnes but the actual average 0.3×10^6 tonnes.

C. F. Pratten (1971) *Economies of Scale in Manufacturing Industry*, University of Cambridge, Department of Applied Economics Occasional Paper 28, Cambridge, Cambridge University Press.

Constant Returns to Scale: Cobb-Douglas Product and Cost Curves

Because of the popularity of the constant returns Cobb-Douglas production function ($X = aA^{\alpha}B^{\beta}$, $\alpha + \beta = 1$) it is worth noting what it implies for product and cost curves. Because of the constant returns assumption, in the long run with all inputs variable the LREP is straight ray through the origin as shown in figure 10.13(a). The total product curve obtained as one input is increased, the rest staying constant, declines continuously but never turns down: total product increases as more input of *B* is added but the marginal product of *B* never becomes negative (see figure 10.13(b)).

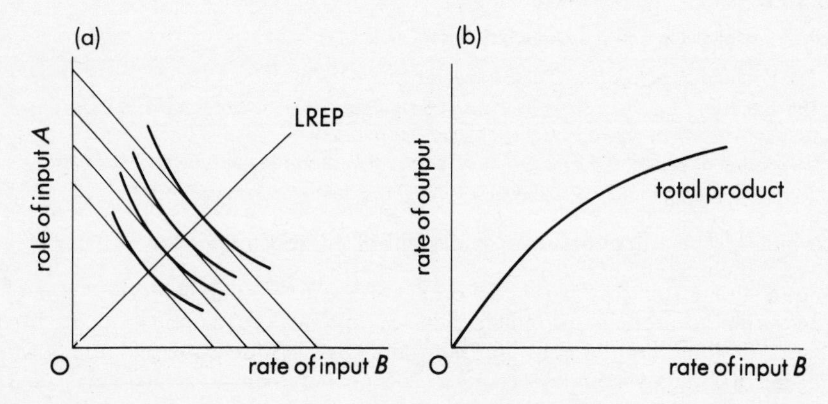

Figure 10.13 Long run expansion path and total product curve of a Cobb-Douglas production function

The implications for marginal and average product curves and marginal and average cost curves are shown in figure 10.14. Figure 10.14(a) shows the continuously falling marginal *MP* and average product *AP* curves, with the marginal lying below the average and neither becoming zero. Figure 10.14(b) shows a U shaped short run cost curve with *SRAC* falling from infinity and *SRMC* continuously increasing. *LRAC* and *LRMC* are constant and equal to one another. This assumes, however, that input prices are fixed. In general, *all* *LRAC* curves cannot be horizontal, for if *all* enterprises sought to increase

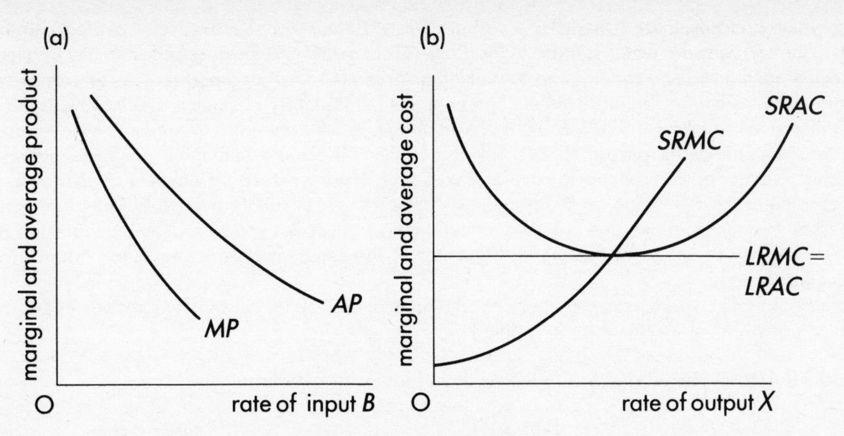

Figure 10.14 Marginal and average product and cost curves of a Cobb-Douglas production function

output as demand rose, and hired more inputs to do so, input prices would be bid up and costs would rise. This would reflect the generally rising value of the inputs in the economy everywhere else, and hence reflect correctly a rise in opportunity cost.

SAQ 10.7

This SAQ is unlike others you have done: answers will be given as you go along, and it is also very long. The purpose is to use a striking example to test your understanding of the meaning and importance of the idea of marginal cost. To get the most out of it, please follow the instructions you meet.

Suppose that in a community there are two illnesses prevalent that can be prevented by suitable procedures (say, early detection by a special check-up and treatment before symptoms develop, or by vaccination). These diseases are killers in at least some cases. The government has earmarked £1 million for the prevention programme. You are called on to advise on the way of spending the money that maximizes the reduction in deaths from the diseases. You have the benefit of some scientific medical evidence. This tells you that £1 million spent on preventing disease A will avert 49 expected premature deaths or, if spent on preventing disease B, will avert 101 expected deaths. How would you advise? (Answer before reading on.)

You probably (and rather reasonably) recommend spending £1 million on preventing disease B. Now, however, suppose that the available budget is only £500,000. The technical experts estimate that, if spent preventing disease A, 39 deaths would be averted or, if on B, 81 deaths would be averted. Which preventive programme would you now select? (Answer before reading on.)

You probably chose to prevent disease B again. Think back, however, to your original answer to the question of how to spend the £1 million budget. With the information you now have (but didn't have then), would you wish to revise your original advice? (Answer before reading on.)

Your original decision saved 101 lives at a cost of £1 million. With the new information, however, you know that you could avert 120 deaths. By spending half a million pounds on disease B, 81 deaths will be averted; an additional half million spent on B will avert only a further 20 deaths but, if spent on A, will avert a further 39 deaths. The highest pay-off to the marginal expenditure is therefore on A, yielding a total output of 120 (81 + 39).

This can be alternatively expressed in terms of the average and marginal costs of averting deaths. By spending the entire million on disease B, the average cost per averted death was £9901 (total cost of £1 million divided by total lives saved, 101) and the marginal cost was £25,000 (additional expenditure on B of £0.5 million divided by additional lives saved, 20).

You might be tempted to think (as many people all too often are) that the sensible *general* rule to apply would be to minimize the average cost per unit of output (in this case, deaths averted). Before reading further, consider whether this *is* a good rule (it is certainly one that is quite frequently applied).

That it is *not* a good rule can be seen by looking at table 10.10, which presents a more complete set of data than has hitherto been revealed. The numbers in the left hand column are varying levels of expenditure: for example, if £200,000 is spent on disease A, 19 deaths are expected to be averted at an average expenditure per death averted of £10,526. The same sum spent on B will avert 43 expected deaths. You can see that the average cost of each prevention programme is rising. If you are to spend the entire £1 million on B, the average expenditure per death averted is £9901, which is lower than the minimum average cost of averting deaths from A. But you already know that this is not the optimal way of spending the money ('optimal' in the sense of maximizing output for a given expenditure).

By examining table 10.10, can you figure out the optimal division of the expenditure between A and B? (Try to answer before proceeding further.)

Table 10.10 Expected deaths prevented at various levels of expenditure

	Disease A		*Disease B*	
Total cost (£)	*Expected deaths averted*	*Cost per death averted (£)*	*Expected deaths averted*	*Cost per death averted (£)*
100,000	10	10,000	26	3846
200,000	19	10,526	43	4651
300,000	27	11,111	58	5172
400,000	34	11,765	70	5714
500,000	39	12,821	81	6173
600,000	43	13,953	87	6897
700,000	46	15,217	92	7609
800,000	48	16,667	96	8333
900,000	49	18,367	99	9091
1,000,000	49	20,408	101	9901

You probably proceeded to find the answer by a trial and error method. The correct answer is to divide the money into £400,000 on A and £600,000 on B. In this way 121 deaths will be averted (34 from A and 87 from B). This is the maximum number possible out of the given budget of £1 million.

A simpler way of finding the correct answer is to calculate the marginal costs of a death averted in each programme and then to choose that combination of the two programmes that makes the marginal costs as nearly equal as possible. Marginal cost is given by

$$\text{marginal cost} = \frac{\text{change in total cost}}{\text{change in deaths averted}}$$

or (more generally) marginal cost is *change in cost divided by change in output*. The marginal costs are set out in table 10.11.

Table 10.11 shows that there are diminishing marginal returns to expenditure on both A and B. The £400,000/£600,000 mix brings the marginal costs as close as they can be to equality (£14,286 on A and £16,667 on B). If the money is divided £300,000/£700,000, the marginal costs would be £12,500 and £20,000 (further apart) and only 119 deaths would be averted (at an average cost of £8403). If the money is divided £500,000/£500,000, the marginal costs would be £20,000 and £9091 (again further apart than at the optimum) and only 120 deaths would be averted (at an average cost of £8333).

The efficient or optimal mix is therefore the ratio 4:6 in this case; to spend the money in any other way would involve unnecessary deaths. The optimal mix is the one with the lowest average cost (£8264) overall, but to determine the optimal mix you need to know the *marginal* costs. Averages and totals can be very misleading. Whenever there is more than one way of accomplishing something

Table 10.11 Marginal costs of preventing deaths from diseases A and B

	Disease A		*Disease B*	
Total cost (£)	*Deaths averted*	*Marginal cost per death averted (£)*	*Deaths averted*	*Marginal cost per death averted (£)*
100,000	10	10,000	26	3,846
200,000	19	11,111	43	5,882
300,000	27	12,500	58	6,667
400,000	34	14,286	70	8,333
500,000	39	20,000	81	9,091
600,000	43	25,000	87	16,667
700,000	46	33,333	92	20,000
800,000	48	50,000	96	25,000
900,000	49	100,000	99	33,333
1,000,000	49	∞	101	50,000

(there always is!), the efficient rule is to equalize marginal costs as far as possible. This is true of the cost-effectiveness case considered here – maximizing output for a given expenditure. It is also true of the converse case – minimizing expenditure for a given output. Of course, the budget has been taken as given. If you sought to determine what the budget *ought* to be, you would have to find a way of deciding whether additional deaths prevented were *worth* the additional expenditure.

SAQ 10.7 is reprinted from *Economic Review* (1, 1, (1983) pp. 21–3) with kind permission of Philip Allan.

What You Should Understand Now

The special meaning of cost in economics.
The relationships between total, average and marginal costs in the short and long runs.
The relationships between total, average and marginal products.
The links between production and cost functions.
The significance of marginal product and cost for decisions.
Some empirical material on cost functions.

11

Specialization and Comparative Advantage

Demand is not invariably revealed by consumers in markets; nor does production invariably take place within capitalist firms. This chapter contains an analysis of efficient production with more than one output in a world in which demand (desired output) is determined by central planners and production takes place in public enterprises. It later includes an analogous capitalist analysis.

Imagine yourself to be a senior Soviet economic planner, concerned with instructing a group of factories, with given output capacities, to produce goods X and Z. The USSR Central Statistical Administration has recently established the production potential for each factory. Each can produce either of the two outputs, given the production function for each and the available resources in each factory. Thus, factory 1 can produce a maximum output of either 4000 of X (point b) *or* 1000 of Z (point a), or any combination of X and Z along ab in figure 11.1, for example 2000 of X *and* 500 of Z, shown as point d. Other possible combinations of outputs include points c and e.

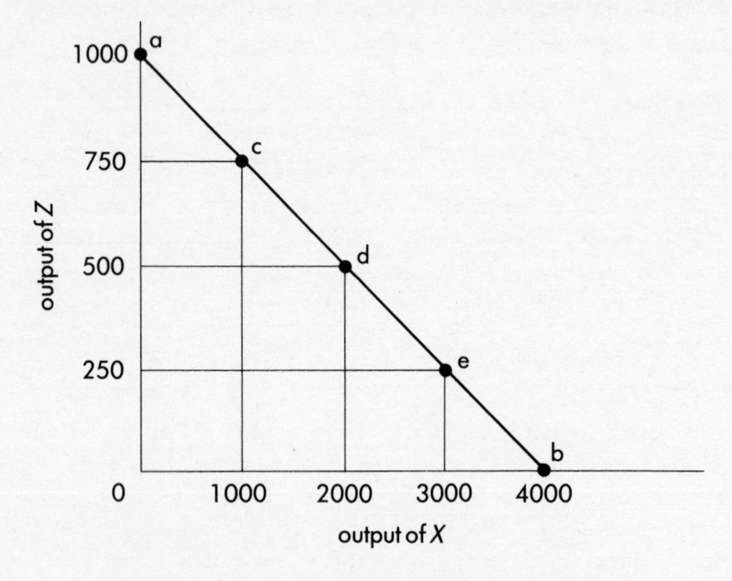

Figure 11.1 Production possibilities of factory 1

The line ab is termed the **production possibilities boundary** and is, in this case, a straight line. The factory is producing at maximum cost-effectiveness at any point along ab. Outputs to the right of ab are unattainable (see SAQ 1.4).

SAQ 11.1

For the enterprise shown in figure 11.1, the equation for the production possibilities boundary is $Z = 1000 - 0.25X$, as determined by the statisticians. Using this, fill the blanks in table 11.1.

Table 11.1 Production table for SAQ 11.1

Maximum output of Z	*when*	*Maximum output of X is*
–		0
750		–
600		–
–		2000
–		2500
250		–
0		–

There are five factories capable of making *X* and *Z* whose maximum outputs are shown in table 11.2. The planning problem is to *maximize the output of X and Z* subject to equal quantities of each being produced per day. This condition is equivalent to a statement of the relative demand for *X* and *Z* which is determined by planners.

Table 11.2 Production possibilities for X and Z in five factories

Factory	*Daily output*	
	X	Z
1	4,000	1,000
2	2,000	2,000
3	1,000	2,000
4	10,000	8,000
5	10,500	14,000

The solution to a problem such as this was developed by the Nobel prize winning soviet economist Leonid Kantorovich (born 1912). It is found by the use of a technique called **linear programming**, which Kantorovich invented and which is widely used both in planned economies and within firms in market economies.

One obvious solution would be simply to instruct each factory to produce *X* and *Z* in equal proportions. In that case, factory 1 would produce 800 each of *X* and *Z*, 2 would produce 1000 of each, 3 would produce 667 of each, 4 would produce 4444 of each and 5 would produce 6000 of each. Total output would be 12,911 each of *X* and *Z*. This policy, however, would not produce the maximum amount of *X* and *Z*, subject to equal amounts of each being produced overall. The reason for this is that this solution fails to take account of the different **marginal opportunity costs** in each factory. Before examining this statement in greater detail, however, see SAQ 11.2 to check that you understand how the outputs just given were calculated.

SAQ 11.2

The outputs in the preceding paragraph were calculated using the equations for each factory's production possibilities boundary and the constraint that $X = Z$ in each. These equations were:

factory 1	$Z = 1{,}000 - 0.25X$	, $X = Z$, therefore $X = Z =$	800
factory 2	$Z = 2{,}000 - X$	, $X = Z$, therefore $X = Z =$	1,000
factory 3	$Z = 2{,}000 - 2X$	, $X = Z$, therefore $X = Z =$	667
factory 4	$Z = 8{,}000 - 0.8X$	, $X = Z$, therefore $X = Z =$	4,444
factory 5	$Z = 14{,}000 - 1.33X$	, $X = Z$, therefore $X = Z =$	6,000
Total output		$X = Z =$	12,911

Thus, for factory 1, using $X = Z$, you have that $Z = 1000 - 0.25Z$, $1.25Z = 1000$, therefore $Z = 800$. What would be the output of each factory, and the total, if $Z - 2X$ was the constraint?

Opportunity Costs and Comparative Advantage

Look at the production possibility boundaries for all five factories in figure 11.2. Here you can see that factories 4 and 5 are (as table 11.2 indicates) very much larger than factories 1, 2 and 3. They each have an **absolute advantage** in both X and Z production over the three small factories. As you will see, however, they do not enjoy a **comparative advantage**.

Look at factory 1. If it is producing 4000 of X and is instructed to produce one unit of Z, it will have to produce 4 units less of X. Similarly if it is

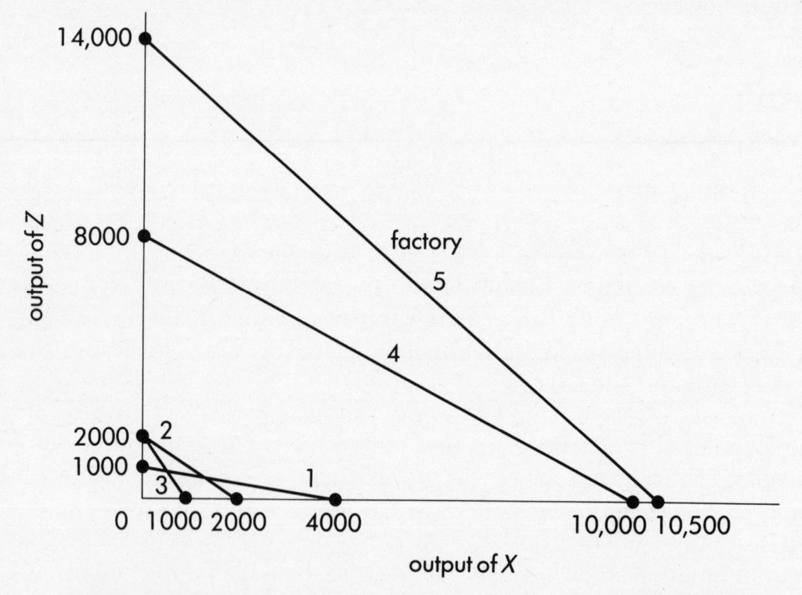

Figure 11.2 Production possibility boundaries for five factories

producing 2000 units of X and is told to produce a further unit of Z (501 rather than 500) it must forgo 4 units of X. The marginal opportunity cost of a unit of Z is therefore 4 units of X. Moreover, this marginal cost is constant. Alternatively, if it were to produce 1000 units of Z and was told to produce one unit of X, it would have to forgo a quarter of a unit of Z. Or if it were producing 500 units of Z and was told to produce a further unit of X (2001 rather 2000) it must forgo a quarter unit of Z. The marginal opportunity cost of X is therefore a quarter unit of Z. Marginal opportunity cost of X is thus described in terms of the minimum amount of Z necessarily sacrificed, and that of Z is the minimum amount of X necessarily sacrificed – always assuming that the factory is on its production possibility boundary, and the choice lies only between Z and X.

Now look at factory 5. You should be able to see that the marginal opportunity cost of Z in factory 5 is 0.75 of X and that of X is 1.33 of Z. Since the production possibility boundaries are straight lines for each factory, the average and marginal opportunity costs are the same in each (though different as between factories). Thus the easiest way of finding out the marginal opportunity cost of Z is to divide the maximum possible amount of X by the maximum possible amount of Z. Similarly, the marginal opportunity cost of Z is the maximum possible amount of Z divided by the maximum possible amount of X.

Opportunity cost, as you have seen before, is not a question of blood, sweat and tears. Neither in choosing between X and Z is it the value of materials, labour time and so on; it is the amount of output forgone by producing something else (or more of something else). If one knew the *value* of the forgone output then one would, of course, have a money measure of the opportunity cost. Here, however, one has the cost expressed in real terms: physical outputs forgone.

SAQ 11.3

What are the marginal opportunity costs of *X* and *Z* (in terms of *Z* and *X*) in each of the five factories?

The marginal opportunity costs of X and Z in each factory are set out in table 11.3, together with a column showing the **marginal rate of transformation** of X into Z, or $\Delta Z/\Delta X$, which is another name for the marginal cost of X in terms of Z. It is the slope of each factory's production possibility boundary.

Table 11.3 Marginal opportunity costs and marginal rates of transformation in five factories

Factory	*Maximum output of Z*	*Maximum output of X*	*Marginal opportunity cost of*		*Marginal rate of transformation*
			Z in terms of X	*X in terms of Z*	*(ΔZ/ΔX)*
1	1,000	4,000	4.00	0.25	0.25
2	2,000	2,000	1.00	1.00	1.00
3	2,000	1,000	0.50	2.00	2.00
4	8,000	10,000	1.25	0.80	0.80
5	14,000	10,500	0.75	1.33	1.33

For *efficient* production, the factory that should first begin to produce X is plainly the one having the lowest marginal cost in terms of Z forgone. Which is this? Certainly not factory 5 for, despite its absolute advantage in X production, it produces it at a relatively high marginal cost. Factory 1 is the most efficient producer of X in relative terms. An additional unit of X costs 0.25 of Z. It has a *comparative advantage* in X production. When factory 1 has reached the limit of its X output potential you then seek the next cheapest source of X output. This is factory 4, where an additional unit of X costs 0.80 of Z. Relative to factories 3, 4 and 5, it has a comparative advantage in X production. The order of comparative advantage in X production, as X output rises from zero, is therefore factories 1, 4, 2, 5 and finally 3.

Suppose you had started with only X production and asked which order to introduce the factories into Z production. The first would have been factory 3 – where an extra unit of Z costs only 0.5 of X. The others would have followed in order 5, 2, 4 and 1 – precisely the reverse of the previous order.

The Economy's Production Possibilities Boundary

The way in which the factories should specialize is shown in figure 11.3 which gives the economy's production possibility boundary for X and Z. If you begin by supposing that only Z is produced, total output will be 27,000 of Z. If you want some X to be produced, factory 1 has the lowest marginal cost in terms of forgone Z and so factory 1 is the first factory to be assigned the task of producing X. The *economy's* production possibility boundary over this range of Z and X output is therefore ab in figure 11.3. If more than 4000 of X is required, the next factory to come into X production is factory 4 and the economy's production possibility boundary is extended to bc. The next factory to produce X, if more than 14,000 of X is wanted, is factory 2, extending the boundary to cd. If more than 16,000 of X is required, factory 5 comes into production. Finally, if more than 26,500 of X is required, factory 3 produces the remainder up to the economy's capacity for X production. This is 27,500 at which Z production has fallen to zero. The economy's production possibility boundary is thus abcdef. It is concave to the origin, reflecting rising marginal costs of X in terms of Z and of Z in terms of X. (If each factory had a rising marginal cost then, of course, each straight segment of the boundary would also be concave to the origin. Moreover, with a large number of factories, the kinks in the boundary at points b, c, d etc. will tend to disappear.)

The economy's boundary tells you the maximum amount of X and Z producible when each factory specializes in production according to its comparative advantage (that is, according to who has the lowest marginal opportunity costs). Recall, now, that the problem was to produce equal amounts of X and Z at the highest rates of which the economy was capable. The line $Z = X$ in figure 11.3 shows all output rates such that $Z = X$. Where this ray from the origin intersects the boundary gives one the point at which

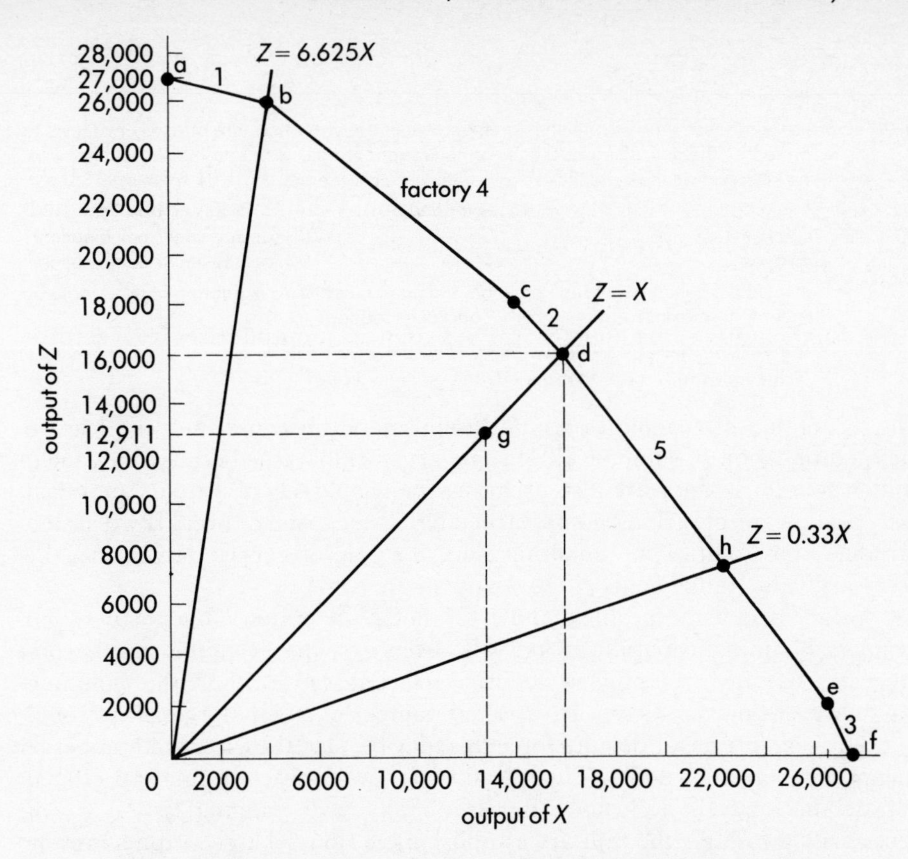

Figure 11.3 Economy's production possibility boundary for X and Z

both objectives are met: point d in figure 11.3. So you (the central planner) will assign factories 1, 4 and 2 to X production and factories 5 and 3 to Z production. The problem is thus solved.

The initial 'solution', requiring *each* factory to produce equal amounts of X and Z, was tantamount to operating at point g on the ray showing equal outputs of X and Z. Output there was only 12,911 of each, compared with 16,000 of each under the efficient solution where each produces according to its comparative advantage. In this case, specialization allows output to be much more than that when no factory is specialized.

If planned consumption did not require $Z = X$ but say, a ratio of 6.625 of Z for every X, then the appropriate ray would be that labelled $Z = 6.625\ X$ in figure 11.3 and the central planner would instruct only factory 1 to produce X, all the others making Z. Or if the desired ratio were 3 of X for every Z, then the appropriate ray would be that labelled $Z = 0.33\ X$, implying that production be at point h on the boundary, with factories 1, 4 and 2 producing only X, factory 3 producing only Z and factory 5 producing 6400 of X and 5467 of Z. Total output would be $X = 22{,}400$ and $Z = 7467$.

SAQ 11.4

(a) Why is the output of factory 5 at 6400 of X and 5467 of Z?

(b) You are a warehouse supervisor with two employees under you. There are basically two tasks to be performed by them: loading packages on to wagons for delivery, and making out invoices. After long observation the potential output of each employee per day is as follows:

	packages loaded	*invoices made up*
employee 1	500	200 (or any linear combination)
employee 2	200	100 (or any linear combination)

1. If you want 50 invoices made up, whom should you ask to do it, bearing in mind that you then want to maximize the number of packages loaded?
2. Which employee has a comparative advantage in invoicing?
3. Which employee has an absolute advantage in invoicing?

The techniques of economics are not useful merely because they can lead to the quantification of some or all of some key variables, or because they yield unique solutions. They are also useful – some would say of primary practical use – as a means of picking apart intractable issues so as to reveal key decision variables, possibilities for quantification, the role of expert judgement, the necessary value judgements (if any) and so on.

Consider a defence problem: how to allocate a military budget between strategic bombing capabilities and air defences. The economic framework suggests that it is helpful to identify relevant *outputs*. For the bombing capability this may be, say, the expected number of enemy targets that could be destroyed, for the air defence force this may be, say, the expected number of enemy bombers shot down. The selection of appropriate outputs is a crucial part of the analysis and, since it raises many wide ranging issues, is not necessarily a task for the military establishment alone. These outputs are the ultimate justification, if there is any, for having the military budget in question, and those who supply the budget clearly have interests in what they will get out of it.

A natural next step is to imagine that there are diminishing returns in each activity. If expenditure is fixed, then for each planned additional unit of defence output you must give up increasing units of attack capability. The marginal cost of one is rising in terms of the other. Hence one could draw up (and make quantitative estimates of) the production possibilities boundary, which will be concave to the origin, with the two outputs measured along each axis. In this, technical data about the production functions will come from the military experts and some detailed costings will have to be done.

One then has to select a point on the boundary (being *on* the boundary implies cost-effectiveness). At this point one may decide that political and other factors come into play with military and financial considerations taking a back seat. Thus, the 'solution' to a military problem is not to be determined, one would normally expect, solely by the military. Finally, one will have to decide whether the chosen output combination is *worth* its cost, or whether a larger or a smaller budget may be preferable. At various points in the solution, different skills and expertises are required, which the economic analysis has helped to identify.

Efficient Production without the Central Planner

Suppose that the central planner, who was armed with both the information and the effective power to order things and who determined what demand is to be, no longer exists. Suppose instead that there are five economies having the same output potentials as the five factories previously discussed, with each determining its own rates of output of X and Z. Suppose also that there are established international market prices for X and Z such that 5 of X exchanged for 6 of Z. Thus if Z cost £1 per unit, X would cost £1.20 per unit: for £6 you could buy either 5 of X or 6 of Z, or some combination of the two. However, all that matters for our purposes is the price ratio $P_X/P_Z = 1.20$.

Suppose that each country were initially self-sufficient in X and Z and that each had similar tastes, wishing to consume equal amounts of X and Z. In that case, under self-sufficiency in X and Z, country 1 would produce at 800 of X and Z, country 2 would produce at 1000 of each, country 3 at 667 of each, country 4 at 4444 of each and country 5 at 6000 of each.

The fully efficient outputs that result from specialization according to comparative advantage cannot in this situation arise from the activity of a central planner, for there is none. They can, however, arise if the countries are free to trade with one another at the going world price.

To add drama, let the outputs X and Z be produced using mainly skilled labour and raw materials that are very costly to transport. Country 1 is a small Third World country with low per caput incomes and little of either input. So are countries 2 and 3. Country 4 is large and industrialized but suffers from long standing industrial trouble with its labour force, which has both low productivity and, according to some at least, is overpaid. Country 5, though smaller than 4 in population, numbers of skilled workers and raw materials, is highly productive and so can actually produce more of *both* X and Z than country 4. Within the countries the reliance on central planning and market forces varies and does not matter for present purposes. What will be shown is that, despite all these differences in size, industrial structure and internal arrangements, the differences in relative marginal opportunity costs, or comparative advantages, imply that *each* can gain from trade. Consider now the position of country 1. It is initially in a position where it is both producing and consuming 800 of X and 800 of Z. At the world price ratio of 1.20, by specializing in X production it would produce 4000 of X, selling 1818 of X in exchange for 2182 of Z, such that production of X was 4000 and production of Z was 0, but consumption of X was 2182 (4000 production less 1818 exports) and consumption of Z was 2182 (imported). It would thereby increase its consumption of each commodity from 800 to 2182, i.e. by a factor of nearly 2.75.

This is shown in figure 11.4. Initially, country 1's production possibility boundary is shown by line ab and it is consuming 800 of X and 800 of Z at point d where the $Z = X$ line intersects the boundary. By specializing in X production it can move to the **consumption possibilities boundary** cb, producing $X = 4000$ and exchanging some for imported Z at the world price,

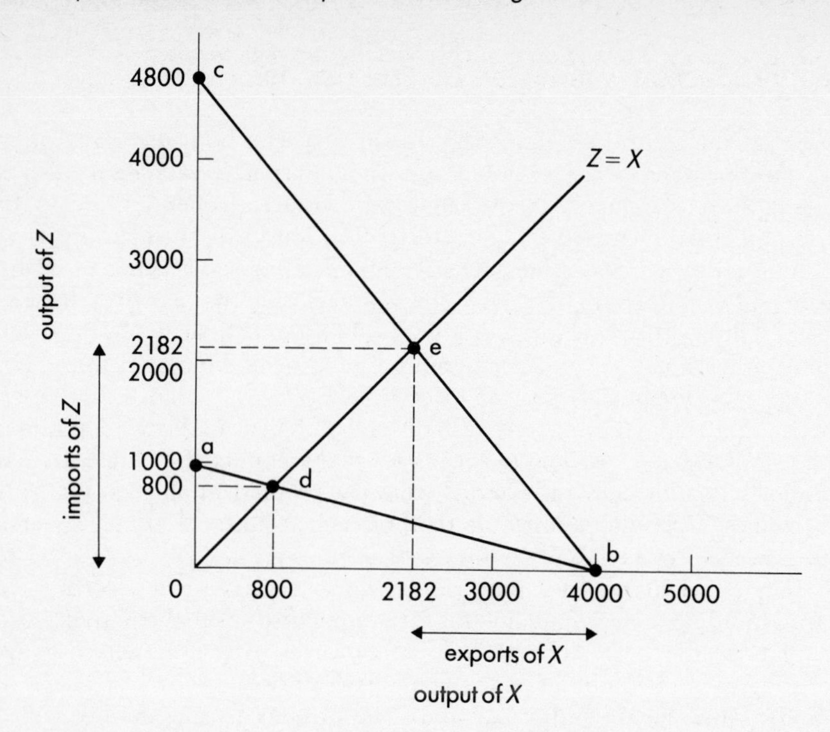

Figure 11.4 Gains from trade to country 1 from specialization and trade

enabling point e to be attained. Whereas the slope of ab is −0.25 (given by the marginal rate of transformation) the slope of cb is −1.20 (given by the international price ratio); it is the difference between these two that enables country 1 to gain from trade.

SAQ 11.5

What would country 1's production possibilities boundary look like if there were diminishing returns in the production of either *X* or *Z* or both?

Similarly country 4, by specializing in *X* production (in which it has a comparative advantage), could produce 10,000 of *X*. It could sell some at the world price in exchange for *Z* such that production of *X* was 10,000 and that of *Z* was zero, but consumption of each became 5454.5 instead of 4444.4. Of the 10,000 of *X* produced, 4545.5 would be exported in exchange for 5454.5 of *Z*.

Country 2, by specializing according to its comparative advantage, would produce 2000 of *X* and finish up consuming 1090.9 of both *X* and *Z*, exporting 909.1 of *X* in exchange for 1090.9 of *Z*.

Country 5 would do well to specialize in *Z* production at this world price ratio. It would produce 14,000 of *Z*, exporting 7836.4 of *Z* in exchange for 6363.6 of *X* and retaining 14,000 − 7636.4 = 6363.6 of *Z* for home consumption.

Likewise, country 3 would do best by specializing in Z, producing 2000 of Z, exporting 1090.9 of Z (keeping 909.1 of Z for home consumption) and importing 909.1 of *X* at the world price of *X*.

The diagram for a Z exporting country is shown using country 3's opportunities in figure 11.5. Its initial possibilities boundary is ab and it is located at c, producing and consuming 666.7 each of *X* and Z. By producing only Z and exporting some along the consumption possibilities boundary ad, it can select point e, at which it consumes 909.1 of each.

The final outcome of all this trading is shown in table 11.4. In the table you can see that specialization improves the consumption possibilities for each country, so that those countries with a marginal opportunity cost less than the world price produce the appropriate good. The total output of *X* and Z under (costless) trading is the same as under (costless) central planning and is also maximized. Given that the preferences in each country are for equal amounts of *X* and Z, this condition too is satisfied. World imports of each good are equal, of course, to world exports. The gains made by each country depend partly on their size in terms of output potential and partly on the extent to which their marginal costs are less than the world price. Thus country 1, though small, is very efficient at *X* production compared with the rest. It is

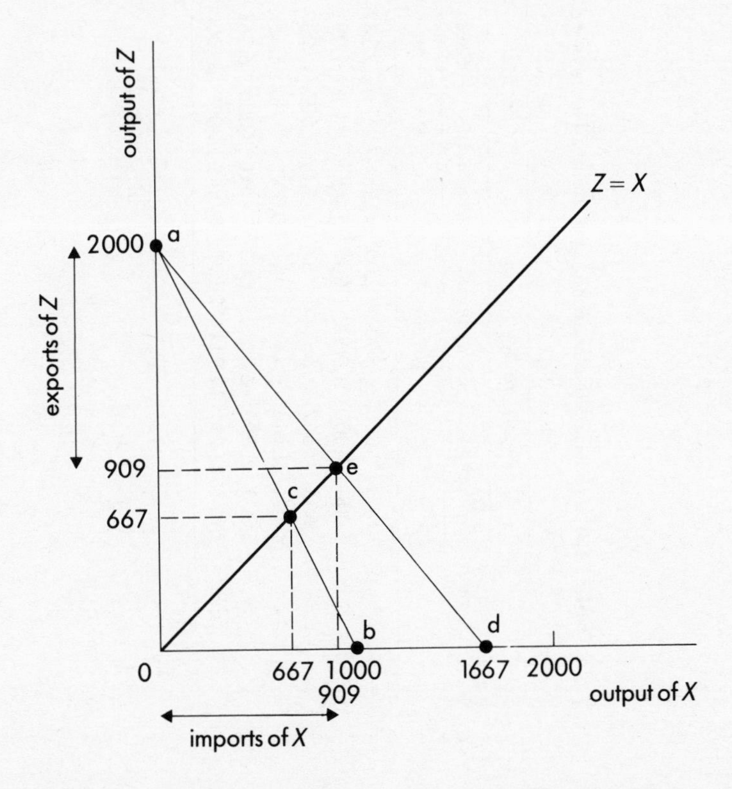

Figure 11.5 Gains from trade to country 3 from specialization and trade

Table 11.4 Production and consumption of *X* and *Z* before and after trade when equal amounts of *X* and *Z* are demanded in each country

Country	*Before trade*				*After trade*				*Trade*				*Increase in consumption*	
	Production		*Consumption*		*Production*		*Consumption*		*Imports*		*Exports*			
	X	*Z*	*X*	*Z*	*X*	*Z*	*X*	*Z*	*X*	*Z*	*X*	*Z*	*X*	*Z*
1	800	800	800	800	4,000	0	2,182	2,182	0	2182	1818	0	1382	1382
2	1,000	1,000	1,000	1,000	2,000	0	1,091	1,091	0	1091	909	0	91	91
3	667	667	667	667	0	2,000	909	909	909	0	0	1091	242	242
4	4,444	4,444	4,444	4,444	10,000	0	5,454	5,454	0	5454	4546	0	1010	1010
5	6,000	6,000	6,000	6,000	0	14,000	6,364	6,354	6364	0	0	7636	364	364
Total	12,911	12,911	12,911	12,911	16,000	16,000	16,000	16,000	7273	8727	7273	8727	3089	3089

more efficient at X production than, for example, country 5 is at Z production; so, despite being smaller than 5, it gains more.

Of course, if large countries like 4 could rig the world price to suit themselves they could reduce the gains to small countries and increase their own. Suppose, for example, that rich country 4 sought to put 'order' into the market, arranging for international agencies to control the trading and prices in X and Z with – of course – country 4 having the effective power in the controlling agency. Suppose, moreover, that the agency proceeded to outlaw the 'cheap and nasty' X output of country 1 (in order, of course, to 'protect' world consumers). Country 1 would be forced back into self-sufficiency (for if it could not sell its X it could purchase no Z) and would suffer a major reduction in living standards. With country 1's competition out of the way, country 4 might then be able to push up the price of X. It would thereby harm everyone else's living standards as well while increasing the value of its own exports, hence enabling it to purchase more Z (in this it may be supported by the other X producer, country 2). It would not want to push the price of X up so far that it became to big country 5's advantage to start producing it (higher than 1.33). However, it would gain if the price rose to, say, 1.32. It is always in the interests of some producers to seek to eliminate competition and capture control of regulatory authorities both national and international. The maintenance of open markets therefore requires constant vigilance and political activity. You will meet plenty of examples later of how it pays sellers to destroy competition.

History is not short of examples of exploitation. However, note that trade itself increases consumption possibilities for all. This result is similar to the 'invisible hand' theorem that you will meet in the next chapter: the individual pursuit of self-interest produces the same result as a consciously coordinated planning system but, with market trading, the 'hand' that coordinates is 'invisible'. Since it often puzzles people that apparently uncoordinated actions can (in this case, will) produce the same results as purposive control and planning, it would be worth while to check again though the reasoning that has led to such a remarkable result and satisfy yourself that you understand it.

Case Study 11.1 British Universities and Comparative Advantage

British universities have been in something of a state of crisis for some years, and from the late 1970s into the 1980s have been subject to severe financial pressure. At the time of writing the prospects for the future are not too rosy. The belief has grown up that British universities are inefficient in that more output (somehow measured) could be produced with the same real resources or that the same output could be produced with fewer resources. The universities in Britain are also being compelled to charge fees that are in excess of marginal cost and, in particular, to charge discriminatory rates against non-British, non-EEC students.

Table 11.5 (Marris, 1984) uses a simple index of productivity – degrees and diplomas awarded per teacher (the principal input) per year – to compare the UK's absolute advantage (if any) with ten other OECD countries. Quality differences, if any, are not allowed for. As you can see, in terms of absolute advantage, the UK ranks third after Canada and France. What, however, is more interesting are the data for comparative advantage. To get these you need to know the output per person per year in economic activity in general, i.e. net national product per person (the idea of net national product is discussed in chapter 24; for the moment just think of it as the money value of value added produced by the economy in a year). Taking the ratio of educational productivity to general productivity then gives an index of comparative advantage.

Table 11.5 Comparative advantage in university education (ten countries in the Organization for Economic Cooperation and Development, 1982)

	Graduations per staff	*Absolute advantage*	*Output per head*	*Comparative advantage*
Canada	3.25	114	151	75
Finland	1.63	57	128	45
France	3.09	109	131	83
Germany	0.77	27	136	20
Italy	1.82	64	87	74
Japan	2.22	78	124	63
Netherlands	0.77	27	113	24
Switzerland	1.50	53	160	33
UK	2.84	100	100	100
USA	2.51	88	166	53

As you can see, the UK's comparative advantage is greater than any other country's: the (average) opportunity cost of producing a graduate is lower than elsewhere, and by a substantial margin. Thus, not only are the UK universities relatively efficient in absolute terms but because the UK economy *in general* is less productive than the others (apart from Italy) the UK's *comparative* advantage in university education is greater than anywhere else in the table, even than Italy (for in Italy a fairly productive university sector is not sufficiently productive relative to the rest of its economic activity).

Under these circumstances, it seems strange that the myth has arisen that British universities are inefficient. They are clearly more efficient than most productive organizations in the UK, at least in their (primary) task of producing well-qualified graduates.

Robin Marris (1984) 'The great British university miracle', *Times Higher Education Supplement*, 6 April, 14–15, table 6.

SAQ 11.6

Two countries can produce as follows:

	annual output rate X	*or*	Z	
country 1	20,000		30,000	(or any linear combination)
country 2	10,000		20,000	(or any linear combination)

(a) Who has the lowest marginal cost of X production?

(b) Who has the lowest marginal cost of Z production?

(c) Suppose each wants to consume X and Z in equal amounts and that they can trade costlessly. Who will export what, how much and to whom?

(d) Suppose that country 3 can produce 4000 of X or 7000 of Z or any linear combination. Has country 3 a comparative advantage?

Case Study 11.2 Regional Specialization in Britain

As enterprises seek to take advantage of comparative advantages (or lower opportunity costs) one expects to see a concentration of production in particular locations rather than an even spread. This is quite unlike what one expects for consumption per head, which for similar incomes, prices and tastes will tend to be evenly spread.

Table 11.6 shows the ratio of employees by industry group in each region divided by the ratio of employees in that industry for all Britain. This statistic, if it is larger than 1.0, indicates relatively heavy specialization. Some industries are much more concentrated than others. For example, Greater London has next to no agriculture compared with East Anglia, which has nearly four times the national average. Mining and quarrying is particularly concentrated in the East Midlands, Yorkshire and Humberside, the North and Scotland. The advantages of these regions for the first two industry groups are largely related to the location of their basic industrial inputs, which are major determinants of costs. Similar considerations apply to the concentration of textiles in the East Midlands, Yorkshire and Humberside and the North West. Note that comparative advantage seems not to be particularly associated with location in several industries, notably distributive trades, though different *individuals* have comparative advantages in these, as in all activities, and so will specialize none the less.

If one focuses on the regions rather than the industry groups, it can be seen that London is relatively specialized in transport, financial and professional services and public administration. The South East is similar, with the addition of some manufacturing and distributive trades. London and the South East together have over 43 per cent of employees. East Anglia is heavily dominated by agriculture and by food, drink and tobacco. The South West is also mainly agricultural. The West Midlands mainly specializes in metal manufacturing. The East Midlands mainly specializes in mining and quarrying and in textiles. Yorkshire and Humberside mainly specializes in mining and quarrying, metal manufacture and textiles (both these regions also have more agriculture than average). The North West specializes heavily in coal and chemicals and in textiles. The North specializes in mining, coal and chemicals and metal manufacture. Wales specializes in mining and metal manufacture. Scotland specializes mainly in agriculture and mining.

If you re-examine table 11.6 you will see that there is scarcely any specialization in gas, transport and distributive trades. Can you think of any reason why this may be?

The main one is that comparative advantage can become dominated by factors like transport costs. These make specialization by region inefficient in the provision of local services like gas, electricity and water. In addition, comparative advantage may be offset by a demand for tailor made services (for example, financial or professional) which require easy contact between supplier and client. The same thing is seen internationally. Motor cars are produced in several countries, so that each gains scale economies from catering to particular preferences about types of car. Less differentiated products, as in mining and agriculture, tend to be more specialized. Also, in the international context, strategic defence considerations sometimes imply that a country

Table 11.6 Percentage of employees in each industry within a region divided by percentage of national employees in that industry (1982)

Industry group	*South East*	*Greater London*	*East Anglia*	*South West*	*West Midlands*	*East Midlands*	*Yorkshire and Humberside*	*North West*	*North*	*Wales*	*Scotland*	*% of total employees in this industry*
Agriculture, fisheries and food	0.7	0.0	3.9	2.2	1.1	1.6	1.1	0.5	0.8	1.8	1.6	1.4
Mining and quarrying	0.1	0.1	0.2	0.5	0.8	3.6	3.2	0.4	2.6	2.8	1.6	1.4
Food, drink and tobacco	0.7	0.7	2.0	1.2	0.9	1.3	1.6	1.4	0.9	0.7	1.4	2.8
Coal, petroleum and chemicals (manufacturing)	0.9	0.7	0.8	0.6	0.5	0.9	1.0	2.0	2.3	1.0	0.8	1.9
Metal manufacturing	0.3	0.3	0.2	0.3	3.1	1.4	2.4	0.6	1.9	3.2	1.0	1.3
Engineering	1.0	0.7	0.9	1.0	1.8	1.1	0.9	1.1	1.1	0.8	0.8	12.0
Textiles	0.4	0.5	0.6	0.7	0.6	3.6	2.0	1.7	1.0	0.8	1.2	2.6
Other manufacturing	1.1	1.0	1.2	0.9	1.3	1.0	0.9	1.1	0.9	0.8	0.7	5.5
Construction	0.9	0.9	1.1	1.1	0.9	0.9	1.0	0.9	1.2	1.2	1.4	4.8
Gas, electricity and water	0.9	0.8	1.0	1.2	1.0	1.0	1.2	1.0	1.1	1.4	0.9	1.5
Transport and communications	1.2	1.5	0.9	0.8	0.7	0.7	0.8	0.9	0.8	0.8	0.9	7.1
Distributive trades	1.1	1.0	1.0	1.0	0.9	0.9	1.0	1.0	0.9	0.8	1.0	12.9
Financial and professional services	1.1	1.2	1.0	1.0	0.8	0.8	0.9	0.9	0.9	0.9	1.0	37.1
Public administration and defence	1.1	1.2	0.7	1.0	0.9	0.7	0.8	0.9	1.0	1.2	1.0	7.5
% of total employees in this region	29.0	14.3	2.8	6.2	8.0	5.9	7.4	9.9	4.6	3.7	8.1	

Source: Employment Gazette, **91**(2), 1983, s17–s18, table 1.5

chooses less specialization, and hence trade dependence, than the full exploitation of comparative advantage would imply.

What You Should Understand Now

Cost-effective production with straight line individual production boundaries.

The production and consumption gains from specialization.

How planning and market trading can each encourage cost-effectiveness.

Some key concepts: production possibilities boundary, marginal cost, comparative and absolute advantage, marginal rate of transformation.

How economic principles can be used qualitatively to pick a problem apart.

Some empirical material relating to regional specialization in production in Britain and the measurement of the relative efficiency of public sector university education in Britain.

12

Business Firms, Profit Seeking and Price Taking

The analysis in chapters 9–11 has been quite generally applicable: for example, one can speak of production functions and cost curves in publicly owned industry, publicly run social services, private charities and private business. One can speak of factories, firms or countries having comparative advantages in various lines of production. The *incentives* that managers in businesses have, however, to be efficient in the way they run their affairs are often different, and there is argument about the kind of environment that is most conducive to productive efficiency. Despite this, however, the basic tools of analysis are essentially the same, as you have seen from some of the case studies drawn from different spheres of activity.

Firms, like families and governments, are collective organizations in which transactions within the group are not market transactions. Instead of using the price mechanism to signal the appropriate use of resources, other methods are used, like hierarchical command or consensus management.

Consider a family. This is a group of individuals, archetypically a mother, father and children, sometimes with other family dependants. There is specialization of function within each family, and also cooperation to use family labour time together with purchased inputs of goods and services to produce family outputs – meals, child rearing, an attractive home and so on. If a family is supposed to consist of utility maximizing individuals who are subject to constraints – the rules decided by family leaders for the conduct of affairs, the time available for in-family work and outside (market) work, the inherited wealth of the family and the pattern of wages that existed outside the family group – then insights can be obtained that make such a supposition less absurd than may at first appear. SAQ 12.1 offers an opportunity for you to test your imaginative and analytical skills.

SAQ 12.1

(a) Within the context of a utility maximizing family, what would you predict to be the effect of rising female wage rates for:

1. Care of elderly dependants?
2. The schooling and training of female children?
3. The use of labour saving domestic devices?
4. The pattern of work sharing in the home between adult males and adult females?

(b) 1 Can you think of any reasons why *love* should be such a common characteristic of family affairs?

2 Can you think of any economic implications of love for the sharing of family income?

Why Do Firms Exist?

Sir Dennis Robertson (1890–1963), the Cambridge economist, once described firms as 'islands of conscious power in this ocean of unconscious cooperation, like lumps of butter coagulating in a pail of buttermilk'. The 'ocean' is, of course, the market system with its price signals. Imagine a factory on line production in which one person receives television parts, fixes them to a chassis and passes the assembled parts to the next person, who affixes something else, and so on down the line. You could imagine each *buying* the bits from up the line and selling them on down the line at a price reflecting the extra work put in (*value added*, as it is termed: see chapter 9). Yet this is not done; the whole operation is instead conducted without any price mechanism. The end of the line for a particular process need not be a finished product ready for marketing. It may be what is called an *intermediate product* (see chapter 9) which *is* sold, to another firm, which then continues the process (and this firm too may not produce a *final product* for sale to consumers). Nor, evidently, need the beginning of the line be raw materials, for the firm in question may purchase an intermediate product or products as its 'raw' inputs.

So the question is, why are there these interruptions in market exchange? Why does a bureaucratic control mechanism replace the market control mechanism? Why, in other words, do business firms exist at all, rather than individuals directly trading with one another?

A part of the answer lies in the costs of using markets. As you will see in greater detail later, to make a deal with someone is not a costless affair: you may not trust the other either to deliver when you have paid, or to pay when you have delivered. You may have to take someone to court. It takes time to negotiate deals, time and other resources to invoice, check deliveries and so on. If these procedures can be avoided, costs fall, provided that they can be replaced with a more cost-effective procedure.

Another part of the answer lies in the notion of team work already met in the answer to SAQ 12.1. Team production is often less costly than separate production as each member of a team specializes in a particular part of a process (learns by doing) and time is saved as individuals do not have to switch from one activity to another. This process of specialization and team work can sometimes lead to the **alienation** of individuals from their work: a sociological term meaning the loss of involvement and sense of personal fulfilment that one would otherwise have in making something from start to finish and having personal control over one's style and speed of work. One can become a kind of cog in a machine. Important though this notion can be in the normative study of work, it is clear that the disadvantages of specialization are often not sufficient to compensate for its advantages: workers are not always willing to sacrifice the higher wages they can get in team production for the lower wages they would get in the less productive (and less alienating) traditional 'craft' methods of production.

Although specialization brings cost reducing advantages it is, however, subject to the problem that no one person's contribution to the end product that is sold can be easily identified. If they work as a team, it is the *team* that produces the output. This brings in the general management function, and it requires the monitoring of individual performances to identify slacking and a disciplinary system to stop slackers when they have been identified. A firm therefore combines two cost saving mechanisms and one cost increasing mechanism. By avoiding market transactions *inside* the firm it saves on market transactions costs. By taking advantage of specialization and team cooperation it gains a cost reducing method of production. By having an administrative structure to monitor performance, punish slackers and reward hard workers it raises costs but, as long as these costs are more than compensated by the cost-effectiveness gains, it pays to create a firm: a lump of butter in the sea of buttermilk.

In the firm, therefore, the owners either manage the overall enterprise or hire someone else to do so. This contractual relationship is then supplemented by contracts with other managerial and administrative staff who monitor, plan, hire and fire and so on. Any residual takings, after all contractual payments have been made, accrue to the owners as profit, which they can take out and spend as they like (after tax, if any) or plough back into the firm. The main monitoring job of owners in a capitalist system is to ensure as best they can that their senior managers maximize perceived opportunities for profit. With other systems, for example with public enterprise or in socialist firms, this monitoring role may be played either by the state or by a team of worker owners. Their incentive to pursue profit may be less if they do not actually have a legal title to any residual income of the firm. Sometimes they may deliberately, or be legally required to, pursue other objectives than profit as well.

Forms of Ownership of Enterprises

There are mainly five types of ownership of productive enterprise. In the public sector there are central and local government departments, nationalized industries and public corporations. In the private sector there are sole proprietorships, partnerships and joint stock companies.

Government Departments

Central and local government departments are responsible for such services as defence, law and order and public health (these are commonly governmentally run operations in all countries), and water, sewage, refuse collection and disposal, personal health services and education (the extent to which these are publicly or privately provided varies between countries). In the UK, for example, the National Health Service is run by a central government department (the Department of Health and Social Security) with its own Secretary of State. It has a strong decentralization of management to regions and, below the regions, to districts. Secondary education is run by local authorities, though their finance comes principally from central government taxes which are then paid to the local authorities.

Nationalized Industries

Nationalized industries (like coal) and public corporations (like the Post Office) produce goods and services for sale and often have their revenue supplemented by subsidies out of taxation and public borrowing. They also often borrow money on their own account. Although they are ultimately accountable through the appropriate minister to Parliament, they have their own managing boards and lower tier managerial structures.

Sole Proprietorships

Sole proprietorships are firms owned by an individual who is entirely responsible for all the firm does. Each proprietorship is thus owned by a self-employed businessman (or woman). Revenue comes mainly from sales, but they also borrow money from other individuals and institutions like banks. This is a common form of ownership for small businesses like local shops.

Partnerships

Partnerships are firms owned by two or more (not more than 20) joint owners, each of whom is personally responsible for the firm's debts and activity. Any profits are shared in agreed proportions. The liability of a partner is unlimited in that each partner is liable for the firm's debts up to the full amount of his or her private wealth (including house and furniture). This is a common form of ownership for businesses like solicitors, accountants and estate agents.

Joint Stock Companies

Joint stock companies or corporations arose in response to the limited powers of self-employed people and partners to raise finance. Their chief characteristic is that the owners have **limited liability** for the debts of the firm. Any owner is limited in liability up to the amount invested in the firm, and the owners are not responsible for the actions of the firm. In law the firm is itself a 'person' that can, for example, be sued or itself sue. With partnerships and self-employed firms, the individual owners can sue or be sued. The main point is, however, that limited liability enables investors to put money in risky enterprises without – if the worst happens – their whole wealth being put at risk. For example, if a firm is declared bankrupt its debts may simply be unpaid; the debtors have no claim on the personal wealth of the investors other than that portion which they have invested.

The great advantage of this form of organization is that the power to raise money to finance operations is greatly enhanced. If the company is *public* it can offer ownership shares like equities for sale to the general public. Most of the largest of these public companies are quoted on the Stock Exchange where their shares will be bought and sold. Public limited liability companies must have the initials PLC (public limited company) after their name. *Private* limited companies are not allowed to sell shares to the general public; ownership may, for example, be sold only to members of a particular family (such firms have Ltd after their names). In either case, liability is limited.

In addition to borrowing from banks, PLCs may offer *stocks* or *shares* (shares are also known as *equities*). If you buy, say, £1000 of equity in a firm then you receive certificates stating this. You become an owner of the firm with the right, first, to receive a *dividend* (a share of whatever profit the firm decides to distribute to shareholders in proportion to your share of the total equity) and, second, to vote at the annual general meeting (with votes in proportion again to your share in the total equity). If you disapprove of the firm's activity you can sell your shares. This will tend to reduce the value of shares and the value of the company (market value of its shares) falls.

In addition to issuing shares a company may raise finance by issuing stocks or *bonds* with a fixed rate of interest and a specific (redemption) date for repaying them at face value. Bonds are of two types: *secured* and *unsecured*. In Britain the term *debenture* is used to refer to secured bonds (in the USA it refers to unsecured bonds). For example a company owning and managing commercial office buildings might make a bond issue secured by a mortgage debenture on their buildings. In the event that the debenture holders were not paid their due interest or did not receive repayment of the principal on time, a trustee on behalf of the debenture holders could take over the ownership of the buildings and sell them to pay the debts due to the debenture holders and the expenses of the transactions. Provided the security is adequate there is very little risk attached to debentures. The riskiness of unsecured loan stock depends, however, on the standing and prospects of the company.

The interest payable on bonds is a charge against revenue in the profit and loss account before arriving at any profit. Dividends by contrast can be paid only out of profits, though retained past profits may be used if current profits are not available. The claims of bond holders on the firm's resources are therefore prior to those of equity holders if a firm goes bankrupt. On the other hand, if a firm does well, equity holders will get a share of profit but bond holders will receive only their contracted interest rate.

Although these are the main types of ownership pattern, there are others. *Charities*, for example, are not really owned by anyone but have trustees who are legally responsible for the conduct of the charity's affairs according to the law on charity. Among other things, this requires charities to have clearly specified objectives that are recognized as charitable in law and to devote all their net takings to these objectives. Another form of ownership arrangement is the *workers' cooperative*, widespread in Yugoslavia and in the form of kibbutzim in Israel; in this arrangement the workers are the owners. There are also special non-profit organizations like the *building societies* in Britain; their owners are the investors, but they are not entitled to receive any profits made in the course of trading.

Profit Maximization versus Utility Maximization

It will be assumed to start with that the objective of business in the private sector is to make profits. More strongly, assume that the businesses *maximize profits*. This seems to be in conflict with the general postulate of economics that all individuals are utility maximizers, and so you should pause to see whether there actually is any inconsistency. Utility maximization means that individuals desire more of *many* things. It has never been postulated that individuals maximize *income*. Profit maximizing, however, means that individuals (specifically, business managers) maximize *one* thing – profit, net revenue, or the differences between sales revenue and costs. Are business managers an exception, then, to the general utility maximizing rule? Or is economic theory schizophrenic? Neither is the case, as you will see.

Recall that the law of demand states that 'the greater the relative cost of an economic good, the lower the rate of purchase, acquisition and consumption' (chapter 3). Now suppose that a business manager has a utility function rather like anyone else's: it contains many things, of most of which the manager would like more, though the entities in the function and the weights put on them will vary according to individual taste. One of the entities in the utility function will be the profits or wealth of the firm. But there will also be other things, of which the important ones for our purposes are those that may conflict with the profitability of the firm. Thus a manager may prefer a large staff, giving him or her power and status, even though a large staff may contribute little to output at the margin (it may even have a negative marginal product) and so, since it adds to costs, may reduce potential profit. A manager may prefer attractive rather than efficient secretaries, or may enjoy entertainment on the firm's expense account that is extravagant but yields little in sales promotion or cost reduction. The manager may prefer a 'quiet life', letting opportunities for profit slip by in the interests of not altering established patterns of work or upsetting the staff.

The law of demand says that the lower is the cost of these non-profit oriented sources of utility, the more of them will be taken; and, of course, the higher the cost, the less of them will be taken. In order to identify the conditions under which profits will be the sole entity in the manager's utility function, one needs to identify the conditions under which these non-profit sources will be, so to speak, priced out of reach. There are two basic circumstances under which the cost of non-profit elements in the utility function become very high. One is when there is competition in the capital market; the other is when there is competition in the product market.

Competition in the Capital Market

Competition in the capital market (by which is meant competition for the *ownership* of firms) is strong when the firm's owners are free to buy and sell their ownership shares (or equity in the firm) and when it is cheap to do so. In these circumstances, if profitability falls, or other firms are more successful at making high profits, owners will either instruct managers to pull their socks up (under threat of being dismissed), or, which is usually much more convenient for owners, simply sell their ownership shares and buy elsewhere. As a result of the latter strategy, the market value of the firm in question falls as its share prices fall, it runs into difficulties in borrowing money to finance investment in plant and so on, goes into decline and, if nothing is done, eventually disappears through bankruptcy. Alternatively, as the firm's value falls, other potential owners may see an opportunity for profit; they may buy the new cheap shares in anticipation of making a gain so taking over the firm, dismissing the existing management team (or some of it) and replacing it with more profit oriented managers.

This assumes, of course, that owners of firms invest their wealth in shares so as to maximize their wealth, which seems not unreasonable whether they be private individuals or institutional investors (for example, pension funds).

It is sometimes said that, because the managers and owners in modern large businesses are typically no longer the same people, in contrast to the situation in the early days of the industrial revolution, the profit maximizing theory of the firm is no longer applicable. But this is not so. The so-called 'divorce' between ownership and control does not imply that firms will become general utility rather than profit maximizers, provided that owners can either directly control managers, or can divest themselves of shares, or both. As long as owners can do either or both of these things, managers will either have a strong incentive to maximize profit or will be replaced by other managers who do. In fact, the theory actually suggests that when ownership and management functions are combined in the owner manager one is more likely to observe utility rather than profit maximization.

One can never know whether profits in any firm actually *are* maximized. All one can predict is that competition in the capital market is highly conducive to profit seeking. It is then a theoretical simplification to go the whole way and assume – when these circumstances seem to apply – that managers actually maximize profit.

Case Study 12.1 Efficiency and Ownership Patterns

There are relatively few empirical studies that systematically compare the performance of firms in the same or similar types of business but with different ownership patterns. One, however, by Alfred Nicols (1967) compared the performance of US 'mutual associations', which among other things take people's savings and provide loans and insurance for housing, with joint stock savings and loans associations. In the former, rather like British building societies, the depositors or insurers are the 'owners' but there is no possibility that they can sell their ownership titles. In the latter, equity can be bought and sold by stockholders according to their inclination.

Nicols found in the mutuals higher reported costs per dollar of new loans, slower turnover of management, more nepotism and slower responsiveness of interest rates to changing market conditions, just as the theory predicts.

Alfred Nicols (1967) 'Stock versus mutual savings and loan associations: some evidence of differences in behavior', *American Economic Review*, **57**, 337–46.

Competition in the Product Market

The second basic circumstance that raises the costs to managers of *not* pursuing profit is when there is competition in the product market. If managers indulge in costly utility raising activities that do not contribute to profit, then costs and prices will tend to rise and firms will lose sales of their products to competitors and again tend to disappear; thus, once again, surviving managements will tend towards the profit maximizing model.

When there is competition in *both* the capital and the product market, the circumstances for profit seeking behaviour are ideal.

All this suggests that sole proprietorships, partnerships, publicly owned corporations, publicly owned schools and hospitals, charities and trusts, large private monopolies with sluggish shareholders, and private companies owned by families will tend, on average, away from complete profit maximizing. Sometimes these forms of ownership are selected precisely *because* it is desired by the owners, or society in general, to avoid the consequences of profit maximization, which may be felt undesirable on either private grounds (people, for example, who prefer a quiet life) or in the public interest (if it is felt, for example, that the meeting of suitably defined needs is more important than the meeting of market revealed demands). In such cases management has greater discretion in resource allocation and – especially in the charities and the public sector – one needs new guidelines, controls and punishment–reward systems to get them to fulfil what are perceived (by outsiders) to be the objective of the organization.

You should not, therefore, think either that profit maximization is necessarily always desirable or that modern capitalist firms necessarily have it as their sole aim. Nevertheless, there are many circumstances under which profit maximizing is a reasonable first approximation to the aim of the organization, and this is what will be assumed in this and the next few chapters.

SAQ 12.2

(a) Is profit maximization an *assumption* about the behaviour of managers in firms or an *implication* of some other theory?

(b) Outline the circumstances under which you would expect to see profit maximization by the managers of a firm.

(c) Suppose you wanted to make a gift to a charity for the benefit of stray dogs. Would you rather that this charity were for profit or not for profit? Explain. Is your answer different if you are wanting to pay for your own medical care when sick?

Price Takers

Suppose there is a sufficiently large number of firms in an industry such that, if any one of them were to withdraw its entire output from the market, the market price would be unaffected. Suppose also that the output of one firm is a very close substitute for that of any other (in the extreme, that the output of the entire industry is *homogeneous*). These two conditions describe the conditions of **price taking** by any individual firm.

Imagine that in figure 12.1 an industry is producing at the annual rate of X_I and, given a demand curve with a normal negative slope, that the price at which X sells is P_0. This is shown in figure 12.1(b). In figure 12.1(a) the individual firm produces a tiny fraction of the total output, shown by X_0. If X_0 were entirely withdrawn from the market, so that the individual firm produced nothing at all, industry output would fall by a tiny amount to $X_{I_I} - \Delta X_I$, where ΔX_I is equal to X_0. This would produce a barely discernible shift to the left along the industry demand curve, with price barely rising at all. Consequently the price at which the individual firm can sell its output is P_0 when its output is

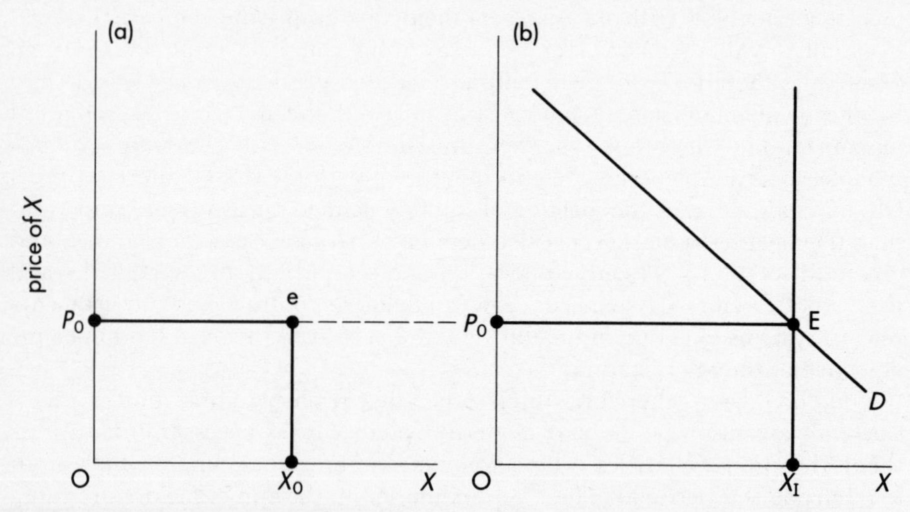

Figure 12.1 Consistency between negatively sloped industry demand curve and a perfectly elastic firm's demand curve. (a) A firm's output rate of X in hundreds per year. (b) The industry's output rate of X in millions per year.

X_0 and also P_0 (or only very marginally more than this) when its output is zero! From the perspective of the *individual* firm alone, price is not variable: it *takes* the market price as given. It is a *price taker.* The demand curve it operates by appears to be the flat line P_0e in figure 12.1(a). It is perfectly elastic, unlike the industry demand curve which is normally sloped.

SAQ 12.3

Suppose there are 1000 identical firms each producing an output of 1000 of *X* at a price of £10. The elasticity of demand for the industry is −1.0. What is the elasticity for an individual firm comparing output rates of zero and 1000 of *X*?

Case Study 12.2 Racial Discrimination in Employment

Suppose that blacks and whites are equally efficient as workers of various kinds. In a society in which employers were racially prejudiced but where all firms were profit maximizing price takers, firms could be expected to hire workers according to their efficiency as producers rather than their colour. There would be discrimination against blacks only if customers came into contact with employees and customers were racially prejudiced. If firms were not competitive profit maximizers, however, then employers would be more able cheaply to indulge *their own* prejudices, and you would expect blacks to be employed less frequently, or at lower wage rates, or both.

The southern states of the USA are known both for the predominance of whites as employers and for the racial prejudice of whites. Both features were more prominent in 1940 than they are today. Gary Becker (1957) has studied the relative numbers of blacks and whites employed in southern US industry according to occupation. As an index of competitiveness in the product market he used the share of industry output taken by the four largest firms. Industries with low concentration were classed as competitive industries, and those with a high concentration of output in the four largest firms were classed as not competitive. Although the dividing line between the two classes is arbitrary, competitive firms will be found mainly in low concentration industries. The theory implies that competitive firms will employ a higher ratio of blacks to whites than the others.

Table 12.1 Ratio of blacks to whites employed in competitive and other industries in the southern USA, 1940 (manufacturing industry only)

Occupation	*1* *Blacks/whites in competitive industries*	*2* *Blacks/whites in non-competitive industries*	*Ratio 2/1*
Professional and semi-professional	0.009	0.002	0.22
Officials and proprietors	0.008	0.001	0.13
Clerical and sales workers	0.024	0.009	0.38
Craftsmen	0.065	0.019	0.29
Operatives	0.136	0.122	0.90
Protective service workers	0.096	0.033	0.34
Other service workers	1.020	1.894	1.86
Labourers	1.046	0.579	0.56

Becker's results are shown in table 12.1. In each occupation (with one exception) you can see that the ratio of blacks to whites is higher under competition. The exception, 'other service workers', is interesting. This was the only occupation for which discrimination seems to be less in non-competitive industry. It is also the only occupation for which blacks outnumbered whites in absolute terms: in other words it is the occupation which most employers (competitive or not) will consider 'proper' for blacks. Here, then, one would expect non-competitive firms able to indulge their prejudices to have a *higher* proportion of blacks than competitive firms: and that was the case.

Gary S. Becker (1957), *The Economics of Discrimination*, Chicago and London, Chicago University Press, table 2.

Output Determination for a Firm in the Short Run

Given that the demand curve as it appears to a price taker is perfectly elastic, you can now use the analysis of cost functions to determine its profit maximizing output in the short run. In figure 12.2 the average total and variable cost curves (*ATC* and *AVC*) are drawn together with the marginal cost curve (*MC*) as the output rate is increased. Under price taking, output can be sold at a constant price regardless of the firm's output rate. This is drawn by the horizontal line from P_0, the industry price.

The firm does not have to choose its price; that is given. What it does have to choose is its output rate. Suppose that it is a profit maximizer: the output rate that it will select is X_0 in figure 12.2. Why is this? Consider an output rate lower than this, say X_1. At this rate of output an additional unit of output will

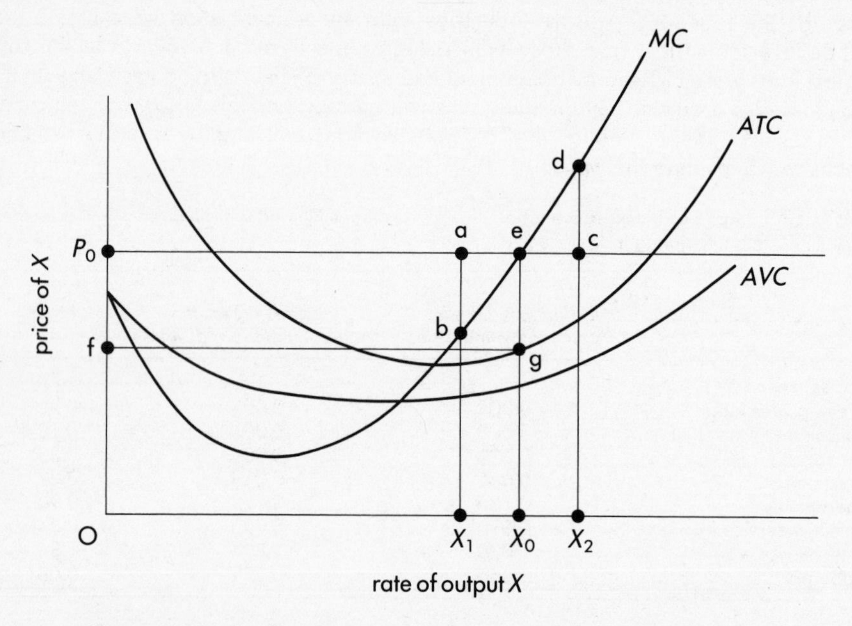

Figure 12.2 Profit maximizing under price taking in the short run

sell at X_1 a (= OP_0) and the additional (marginal) costs of producing it will be X_1b, as shown by the marginal cost curve. Producing the extra output will clearly *add* to profit since the extra (marginal) revenue is larger than the extra (marginal) cost. Hence a profit maximizing firm will *increase* output. Conversely, consider an output rate larger than X_0, say X_2. Here an additional unit of output will sell at X_2c (= OP_0) and the additional (marginal) cost of producing it is X_2d as shown by the marginal cost curve. Producing this extra output clearly *reduces* profit since the addition to cost is larger than the addition to revenue (marginal cost exceeds marginal revenue). Hence a profit maximizing firm will reduce output. Profit is maximized where $MC = P_0$, at point e.

SAQ 12.4

In figure 12.3, $P = MC$ at two points. At which output rate is profit maximized, X_1 or X_2?

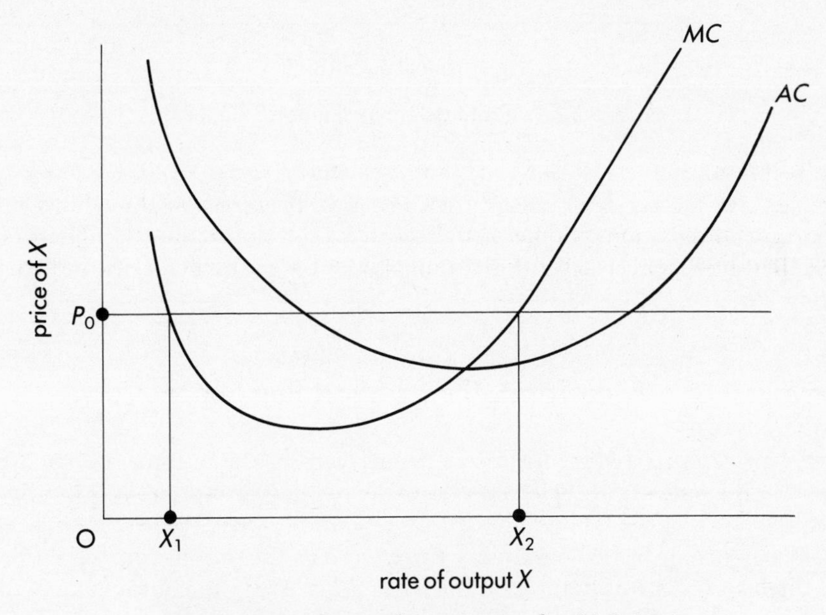

Figure 12.3 Output determination for SAQ 12.4

The average curves tell you what the size of profit will be. Since total revenue is price times quantity, this is shown by the rectangle OP_0eX_0 in figure 12.2. Total cost is average cost times quantity. This is shown by rectangle OfgX_0. The difference between them is profit: area fP_0eg.

SAQ 12.5

In figure 12.4, profit is measured by the rectangle aP_0bc. Can you identify another area that also measures profit, and explain why (assume zero fixed costs)?

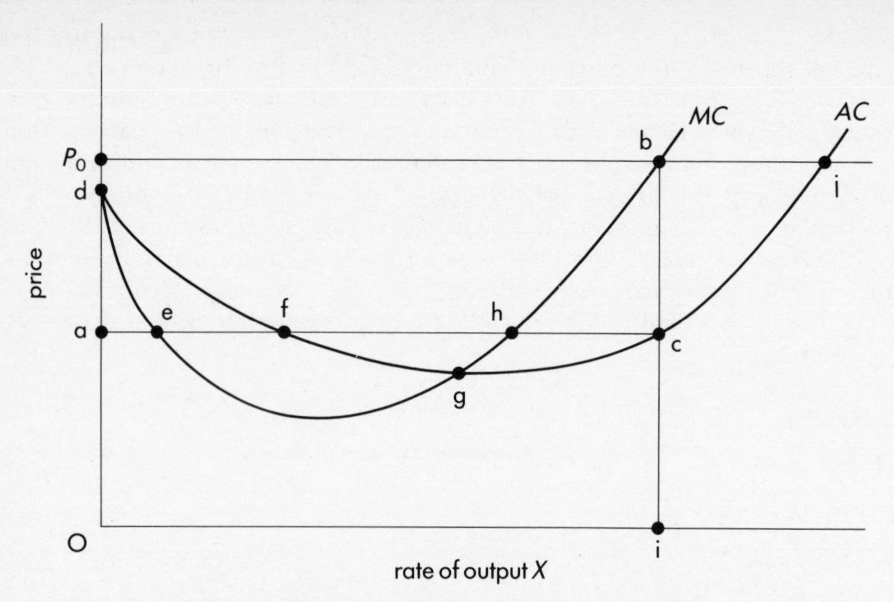

Figure 12.4 Profit determination for SAQ 12.5

The result you have just derived, that *a profit maximizing firm under price taking conditions will produce an output rate such that price equals marginal cost*, has many important implications. Some of these will be developed shortly. The first of them, however, concerns the derivation of the firm's (and hence the industry's) supply curve.

Derivation of a Price Taking Firm's Short Run Supply Curve

Since a price taker (who maximizes profit) will set the output rate such that $P = MC$, the output rate selected at a variety of industry prices is given by the marginal cost curve above the average variable cost curve. To see this, consider figure 12.5. If the industry price were P_0 the output rate would be X_0 and the firm will be at point a on the MC curve. At P_1, the output rate will be X_1 and the firm will be at point b on the MC curve. At P_2 output is X_2 and the firm is at point c on the MC curve and also at the lowest point on the ATC curve. At prices between P_2 and P_3 the firm will locate in the short run between points c and d, producing output rates between X_2 and X_3. It will not cover its total costs but will cover its variable costs. Hence, in the short run, it will continue in production even at prices less than P_2 so long as *some* contribution is made to fixed costs. Below P_3, however, variable costs will not be covered and the firm will shut down and cease production. Hence, the MC curve above the AVC curve (the boldly drawn section of the curve) is also the firm's supply curve, which indicates what output will be produced by the individual price taking firm at each industry price. Hence in figure 12.5 the MC curve (above AVC) is labelled $MC = S$.

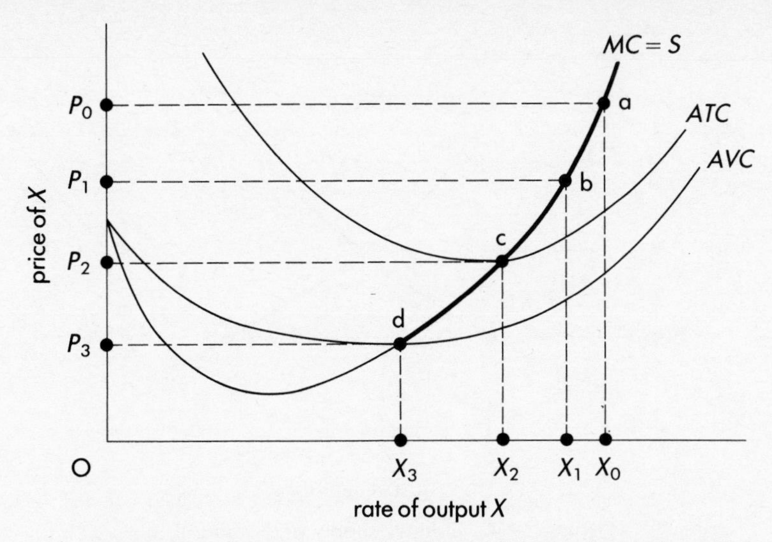

Figure 12.5 Supply curve of a price taking firm in the short run

If you can do that for one firm, you can, of course, do it for every firm. Adding up the rate of output of each firm at each price will give the industry supply curve. Thus, for the industry, $S = \Sigma MC$: the supply curve is the (horizontal) sum of all the marginal cost curves (above their *AVC*s). Figure 12.6 illustrates this for a two firm case. At P_0, firm 1 is just willing to produce some X (X_0^1), but firm 2 produces none (the price is well below its *AVC*). Total supply is hence X_0^1 in figure 12.6(c). At higher prices, firm 1 expands output hence the total supply rises to X_1^1. The total supply curve between A and B is the same as firm 1's supply curve between a and b. Above P_1, firm 2 enters production so that output rises immediately by X_0^2. (In this example firms are not willing to produce total outputs between X_1^1 and $X_1^1 + X_0^2$.) Beyond $X_1^1 + X_0^2$, total supply is the sum of the rate produced by *both* firms together. Under price taking conditions, of course, there are very many firms so that the total supply curve – the horizontal sum of all the many individual *MC* curves – will look

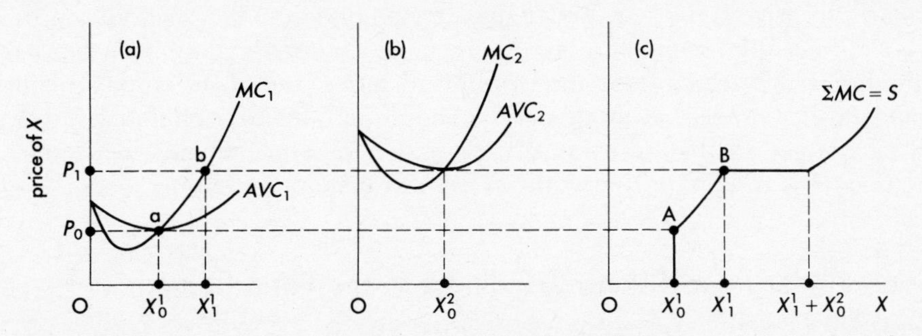

Figure 12.6 Derivation of total from individual supply curves. Output of (a) firm 1 (b) firm 2 (c) firms 1 and 2 together

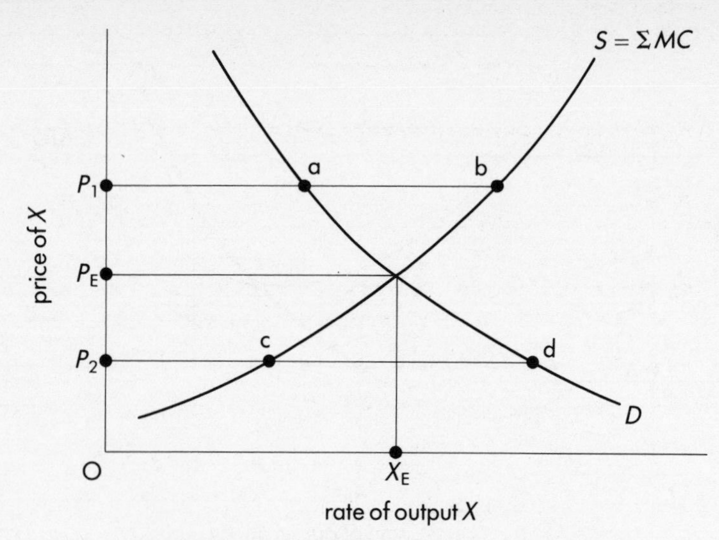

Figure 12.7 Industry supply and demand

like the S curve in figure 12.7. It slopes upwards because each MC curve above each AVC must also slope upwards.

In figure 12.7 the demand curve D is the demand for the output of the entire industry at a variety of prices. The supply curve shows the profit maximizing rates of output for all firms at a variety of prices. The equilibrium price and output rates are P_E and X_E. At prices higher than this, firms will increase output but find there is an excess supply. Thus at P_1, firms will produce P_1b, but consumers will purchase only P_1a. Quantity ab is the excess supply. Stocks of unsold goods will build up and competition among sellers will drive the prices downwards, so output plans will be revised downwards. At prices lower than P_E, consumers will demand more than profit maximizing firms are willing to supply. Thus, at P_2, firms will produce only P_2c but customers will want P_2d. Quantity cd is excess demand. Any stocks held by producers, retailers etc. will be run down and competition among buyers will push price upwards, so output plan will be revised upwards.

Although no *one* firm can on its own affect price, since each responds similarly to price signals and changing stock situations, they will all tend to revise output plans in the same direction. *Collectively* they affect price; individually they cannot. At the equilibrium price, each firm is maximizing profit and has no reason to change its chosen output rate. Similarly, at P_E, buyers can get all they want at that price. There is no impetus for change. The market is in equilibrium with zero excess demand or supply.

Supply under Price Taking Conditions in the Long Run

The long run differs from the short in two ways. First, as you saw in chapter 10, the longer the run the cheaper it is to vary more inputs, particularly those that may have been treated as fixed in the short run. Second, in response to changes in demand, technology and so on that are perceived by decision makers as being long run rather than temporary, new firms may enter or old ones exit. Any firm that in the short run is unable to cover its total cost will tend to exit, and any prospective new firm that believes that it will be able to cover its total cost will tend to enter.

For concreteness, take a situation where the least profitable existing firm in an industry is making profits over and above all costs – including the costs of capital equipment. Such a situation is depicted in figure 12.8(a). Further assume that any new entrants have higher average total costs than this firm (otherwise they would already be producing in the industry in question). Such a new entrant is depicted in figure 12.8(b). In the initial situation, the least profitable existing firm is making profits of aP_0bc at the going price, and is in long run equilibrium as far as adjustment of its own inputs to their cost-effective combination is concerned. As in the short run, and for the same reasons, long run equilibrium is given by $P = LRMC$. Given its cost structure, the new entrant in figure 12.8(b) expects to make long run profits of dP_0ef per period at the going price P_0.

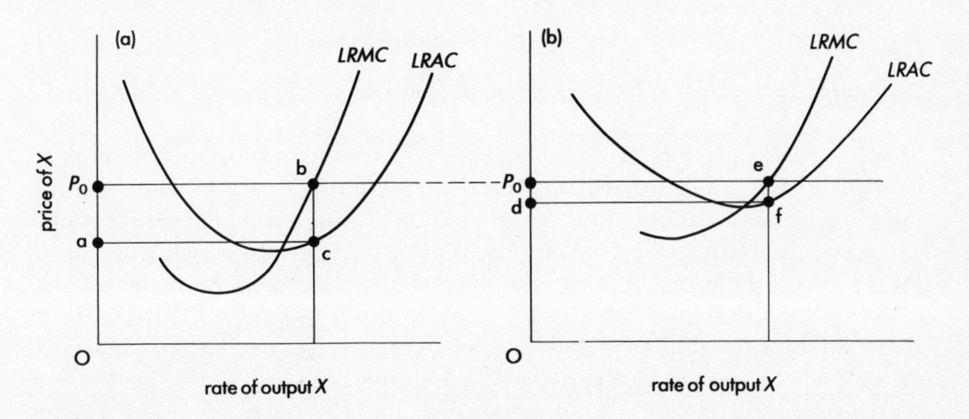

Figure 12.8 Incentive for new entrants to set up production (a) Existing firm (b) New entrant

However, as more new firms enter, their supply curves become added to those of the existing firms so that the *industry* long run supply curve shifts to the right, as in figure 12.9. As output rises, industry price must necessarily fall. New entrants, therefore, have the tricky problem of having to make some estimate of how prices are going to behave as the industry expands. For if any one of them sees an incentive to enter, so will others and it would be foolish of any one firm not to recognize the likely effect of others' decisions on its own.

Long run *industry* equilibrium exists when no firm has any long run incentive to enter or exit from the industry. Thus, after all output and price adjustments have been completed (including the entry and subsequent exit of new firms that made 'mistakes'), the position of the *marginal* firm will be that it just

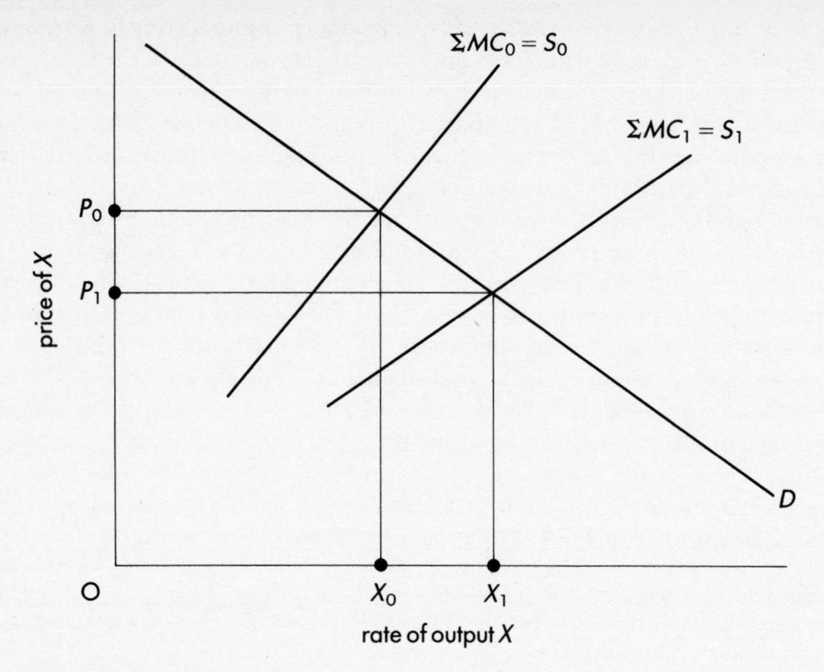

Figure 12.9 Shifts in the long run supply curve as new firms enter an industry

breaks even at the going price. Since there is no reason to suppose that all firms have identical long run cost structures, this will imply that there will be inframarginal firms (firms not at the margin of profitability) making positive profits and a marginal firm or firms making zero profits. This is shown in figure 12.10. Figure 12.10(c) shows the long run industry demand and supply curves that between them determine the long run equilibrium price P_E. Figure 12.10(a) shows an inframarginal firm making profits. Figure 12.10(b) shows a marginal firm for whom staying in the industry is just, but only just, worth while. Note that the equilibrium for the marginal firm has $P_E = LRMC = LRAC$: the

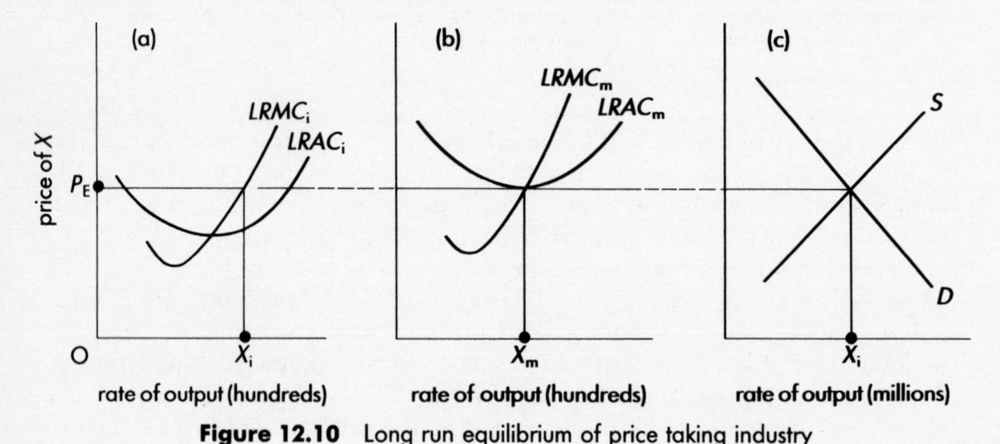

Figure 12.10 Long run equilibrium of price taking industry

LRAC is tangential to the perfectly elastic demand curve that the firm perceives.

In reality, owing to different factor prices in different regions, different productivities of land and labour in different places etc., the cost curves of firms producing the same product will vary. In the special case, however, of identical production functions and identical input prices, all firms will have the same *LRAC* and *LRMC* curves. In that case *all* firms will be marginal and their long run equilibria will *all* lie at the lowest point of the *LRAC* curve. All firms will appear as in figure 12.10(b).

SAQ 12.6

Would you expect to see price takers advertising their products? Why or why not?

Case Study 12.3 Coffee Destruction in Brazil 1931–4

Between 1931 and 1934 the Coffee Institute of Brazil discharged over two million tonnes of low grade coffee in an attempt to maintain prices and, hence, the incomes of the peasant growers. Why did they adapt such a flagrantly wasteful procedure? The answer (based on Benham 1960) can be seen with the aid of figure 12.11. After a succession of good harvests, stocks of coffee held by the Institute, representing the industry, had risen to *X*. Released on to the world market (world demand is indicated by the demand curve *D*) they would have fetched price *P* which was judged to be too low. Even releasing stocks over time would have made little difference; it was this policy that had led to the build-up of stocks, which were both costly to keep and subject to deterioration as time passed. The revenue maximizing price for the Institute was P_1, requiring the destruction of $X - X_1$ tonnes of coffee, and so the policy was

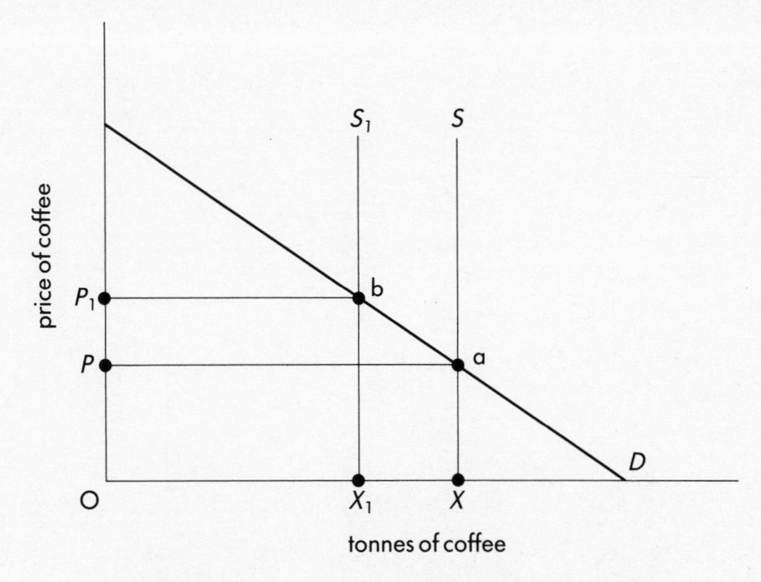

Figure 12.11 Why it paid Brazil to destroy coffee

(implicitly) to find a point on the industry demand curve where price elasticity was unity (namely point b).

It would have been even better (from the producers' point of view) to have got the peasant producers to reduce their plantings so as to avoid the costs of producing coffee that was subsequently destroyed. Unfortunately the peasants, all price takers, saw price P and adjusted output so that $MC = P$ and, hence, collectively produced OX. Had the Institute instead tried to give each producer a quota, so that each peasant produced an output reduced by the fraction $(X - X_1)/X$, the peasants would have each had an incentive to cheat by producing more since, for each of them, $MC < P$. This incentive would have been even stronger if the peasants had shrewdly perceived that the price was going to be even higher. The practical difficulties of enforcing a quota arrangement were simply too great, so crop destruction seemed the best solution to the dilemma.

F. Benham (1960) *Economics*, 6th edn, London, Pitman, pp. 308–9.

What You Should Understand Now

A rationale for the existence of firms: costs of using markets, advantages of team production.
Main types of ownership of firms.
Effects of competition in product and capital markets on managerial behaviour.
Consistency of profit and utility maximizing behaviour.
Meaning of price taking.
Marginal costs, supply curves and equilibrium of the firm and the industry under price taking conditions.

13

Implications of Price Taking Behaviour

In this chapter you will meet some of the main implications of price taking behaviour. These can be both normative and positive.

Price Taking Markets and Efficiency

Conditions of competition have been assumed so far such that all firms will be both technically efficient (will be on an isoquant) and cost-effective (will select the least cost combination of inputs on an isoquant). So far the idea of efficiency does not go beyond these two elements. Economists have tended to view price takers' markets with favour not only because they are highly conducive to such production efficiency but also because they are conducive to *overall* efficiency in the sense that *an optimal rate of output will also be achieved.*

Consider figure 13.1. The demand and supply curves there depict the long run, with a long run equilibrium price and output rate of P_E and X_E. At any output rate lower than X_E, the marginal value of output (as shown by the height of the demand curve, reading it *up*) is higher than the marginal

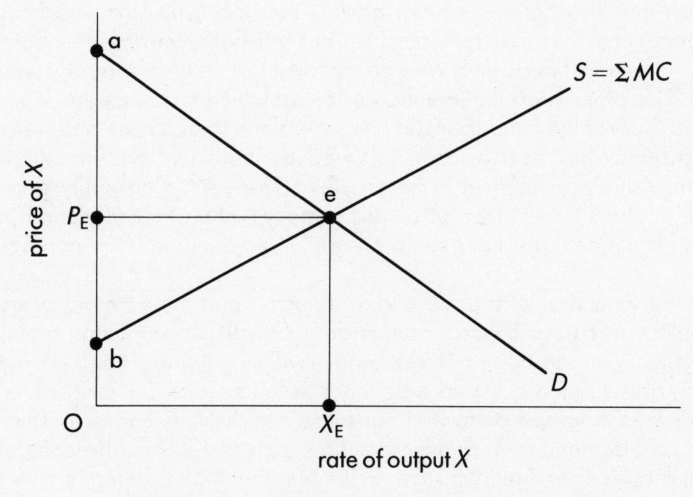

Figure 13.1 Efficiency of price takers' markets

opportunity cost of production as shown by the supply curve; hence there is a net benefit from *increasing* output. Conversely, at any output rate higher than X_E, the marginal opportunity cost is higher than the marginal value placed upon the output for which the cost has been incurred; hence there is a net benefit from *reducing* output.

The total value in use is given by OaeX_E: this is the value in use to all who consume X. The total cost of producing X_E is ObeX_E (recall the correct answer to SAQ 12.5). The difference between this total value in use and the opportunity cost is the **net social benefit** from X production. At X_E it is maximized. At X_E, $P = MC$, since, as you find in the last chapter, the supply curve of a price taking industry is the horizontal sum of all the firms' marginal cost curves. Optimal output is where $P = MC$.

The net social benefit can be divided into two portions. The first, with which you are already familiar, is consumers' surplus, equal to $P_E$ae in figure 13.1. The second is producers' surplus (the sum of all profits in the industry), which is equal to bP_Ee. The former is the excess of the maximum consumers would be willing to pay for X_E over what they actually do pay (value in exchange equal to OP_EeX_E). The latter is the excess of producers' receipts (again OP_EeX_E) over their opportunity costs.

Thus, if you find the idea of full efficiency attractive (maximizing the sum of consumers' and producers' surpluses) then you may well feel drawn (as have so many economists since Adam Smith) to the idea of competition as found in price takers' markets.

Case Study 13.1 Inefficiency and the Common Agricultural Policy (CAP)

The European Economic Community (EEC) seeks both to insulate its members' farmers from the instability of world prices and to ensure that farm incomes are high enough to keep even inefficient farmers in production. Thus, for example, no country should become politically endangered by relying 'too much' on overseas suppliers. To accomplish this they have used two basic weapons. One is a set of protective levies on agricultural imports from outside (but not between) the members, which enables suppliers to sell at or near an agreed target price that is usually well above world prices. The other is an 'intervention price' at which the European Agricultural Guidance and Guarantee Fund (EAGGF) will intervene to purchase and store unsold produce. The policy has been widely criticized as inefficient and inequitable. The essence of this criticism is shown in figure 13.2. (The CAP is in reality exceedingly complex. The analysis here rather heroically removes a lot of complications in order to expose the bare essentials. For example, supply and demand in the non-EEC world is ignored.)

The supply curve is that of a price taking industry, and the demand curve is EEC total demand for each agricultural commodity (cereals of particular kinds, sugar, butter, wine etc.). With an open market, output will be X_0 and price P_0. Consumers' surplus will be areas A + B + D and producers' surplus areas C + E. The intervention price is set at P_1, the lowest price that consumers in the EEC can pay. This has the effect of reducing demand to X_1 and increasing supply to X_2. The difference is bought up at the market prices and held in stock in the member states, being financed by the

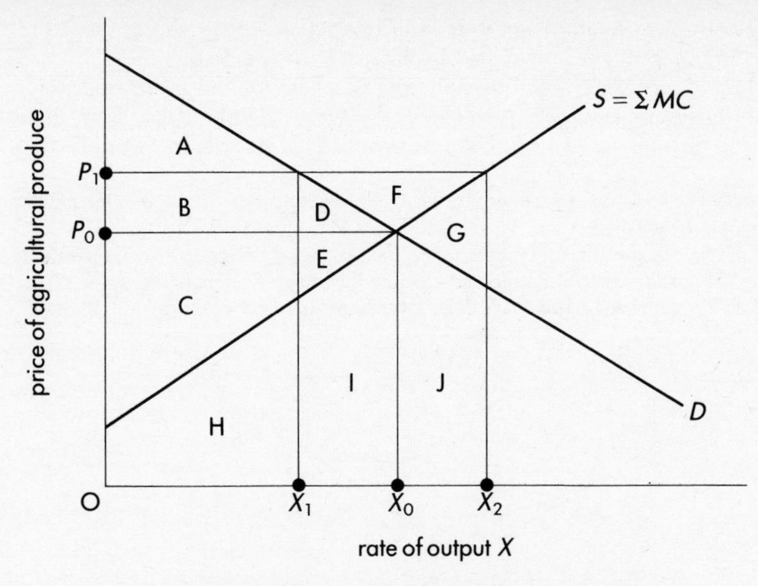

Figure 13.2 Gains and losses from the CAP

EAGGF. Under this system, consumers' surplus is A and producers' surplus is B + C + D + E + F.

The difference between an open market and the CAP is that consumers suffer a *welfare loss* of B + D and producers have a *welfare gain* (in addition to C + E) of the areas B + D lost by consumers and a further area F. Of total expenditure, B + C + H is paid for by consumers in their prices. The areas D + E + I + G + J are welfare losses felt by the Fund (ultimately taxpayers), ignoring storage costs and sales of the accumulated excess at the world price. So there is a net welfare loss (apart from sales of surplus stocks) of D + E + I + G + J (see answer to SAQ 13.1).

Table 13.1 Guarantee expenditure of EAGGF 1973–84 (millions of ECUs)

1973	*1974*	*1975*	*1976*	*1977*	*1978*	*1979*	*1980*	*1981*	*1982*	*1983*	*1984*
3928	3095	4522	5587	6830	8673	10,411	11,315	10,980	12,406	15,898	16,543

Note: from 1981 on there were ten rather than nine member states.
Source: Bulletin of the European Communities, 1983, annex II.

The accumulated stocks of produce have become notorious as the 'butter mountain', 'wine lake' and so on. The accumulating cost of intervention to the EAGGF is shown in table 13.1. The units of account in which the numbers of table 13.1 are presented have varied over the years, as has their given name. Since 1979 the unit has been termed the European Currency Unit (ECU). In 1980 one ECU was worth about 60 pence sterling at market rates. The so-called 'green pound', which is the rate set for CAP transactions, has recently tended to be a bit higher than this.

The foregoing analysis forms a basis for suggesting the general structure of support for farmers that would minimize the inefficiencies of the current CAP. Farmers could be guaranteed a net income of B + C + D + E + F by allowing competition at the world price P_0, which would yield them C + E; the remaining B + D + F could be simply transferred as a lump sum that would affect neither price nor marginal cost. One of the major political difficulties of this more efficient solution is that it would entail the high cost farmers who produce most of the output in the range $X_0 - X_2$ going out of business, particularly in Greece, Germany, Ireland and Italy, the last of which in 1980 had the lowest agricultural productivity per person employed.

J. Marsh (1983) 'The common agricultural policy', in R. Jenkins (ed.) *Britain and the EEC*, London and Basingstoke, Macmillan.
Bulletin of the European Communities (1983) *Adjustment of the CAP*, Supplement 4/83, Luxembourg, Office for Official Publications of the European Communities.
See also Ali El-Agraa (1984) 'The CAP: costs over benefits', *Economic Review*, **2**, 36–9.

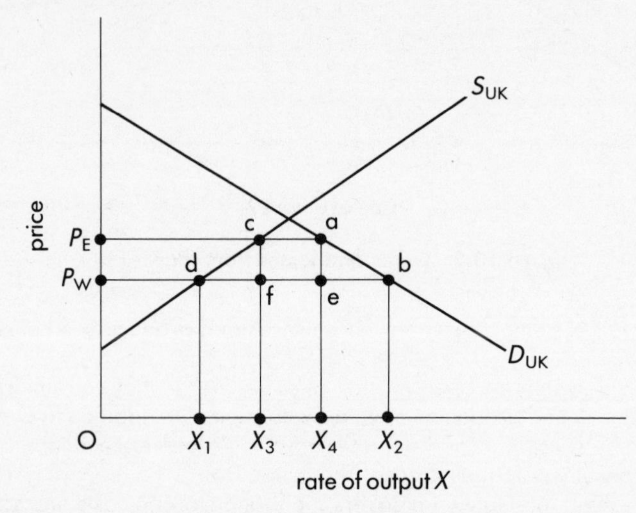

Figure 13.3 UK agricultural supply and demand curves for SAQ 13.1

SAQ 13.1

In figure 13.3, S_{UK} and D_{UK} are the UK supply and demand for agricultural output. P_W is the world price. Without intervention, this implies that the UK agricultural sector would supply X_1 to the domestic market and that $X_2 - X_1$ would be imported to meet UK demand. Assume that world supply is perfectly elastic at P_W.

(a) If the CAP set the price at P_E, with an external tariff of $P_E - P_W$, what is the net welfare loss that the CAP entails?

(b) If the CAP were organized differently so that farmers were guaranteed a price of P_E but consumers could purchase at the world price, with no external tariff, what would be the net welfare loss?

Pareto Efficiency

The idea of efficiency at which you have now arrived (technical efficiency plus cost-effectiveness plus ideal output rate) is commonly termed **Pareto efficiency** after the great economist (and sociologist) Vilfredo Pareto (1848–1923). It is another way of describing an *optimal* allocation of resources in and to production and between individuals. One of the major planks in the defence of capitalism is that *competitive* capitalism of the sort found in price takers' markets has this efficient quality.

Pareto efficiency exists when it is impossible to reallocate resources to make any one individual better off without making at least one other worse off. Thus, if a firm is not on an isoquant it would be possible to reduce at least one input and increase its use elsewhere, increasing other outputs without reducing output of the initial activity. Hence being off an isoquant is Pareto inefficient. If a firm is on an isoquant but not at tangency with the isocost line, it would be possible to reduce expenditure on producing that output (moving to tangency) and to increase expenditure on producing others without reducing output of the initial activity. Hence being off tangency between isoquant and isocost is Pareto inefficient. If a firm is on an isoquant and also at a tangency with an isocost line but not producing at the output rate for which $P = MC$, then it is also possible for some to gain without others losing. There are two cases. If price is more than the equilibrium price there will be excess supply and consumers of other goods will be able to compensate resource owners as resources are transferred from this use into more valued ones. If price is less than the equilibrium price there will be excess demand and consumers will be able to compensate resource owners as resources are withdrawn from other uses into this more valued one. In each case losers can be compensated by gainers to leave a net gain. Alternatively, if compensation is not paid, the value of the gains exceeds the value of the losses.

There are several important points to note about the notion of Pareto efficiency:

(a) It assumes that the relevant judges of benefit and opportunity cost are individuals in their capacity as consumers (who value outputs) and as resources (who have valued alternative uses for their labour time). Thus Pareto efficiency makes an *ethical* assumption – a value judgement – that each individual is the best judge of his or her own gains and losses, that is, of own 'welfare'.

(b) The Pareto efficient allocation is not *unique*. In particular, since total demand for each output (and, hence, opportunity cost) can be expected to vary with the distribution of income and wealth among individuals, for each distribution there will normally be a different Pareto efficient allocation of resources.

(c) Given the influence of income distribution just described, and given that individuals have different views about the acceptability of different degrees of equality and inequality, it follows that a Pareto efficient allocation may sometimes be less preferred in general than a Pareto inefficient allocation that had more acceptable distributional characteristics. One may, in other words, be prepared to trade off two 'ultimately' good things – efficiency and equity.

(d) None the less, if price takers' markets can be established, there is a choice between a variety of Pareto efficient allocations, each corresponding to a different income distribution. Thus, there will be a Pareto efficient allocation that corresponds to one's preferred income distribution, and this could be achieved via price takers' markets.

SAQ 13.2

The supply and demand curves for an industry of price taking firms are given by the following equations:

$$X_S = -20 + 2P$$
$$X_D = 220 - 4P$$

(a) What is the equilibrium price?
(b) What is the equilibrium rate of output and purchase?
(c) What is consumers' surplus?
(d) What is producers' surplus?

Suppose that the price takers organized themselves collectively and succeeded in restricting total output to 45.

(e) What is the maximum price they could get for X?
(f) What is the new consumers' surplus?
(g) What is the new producers' surplus?
(h) What is the difference between the sums of consumers' and producers' surpluses under the old and new arrangements?
(i) Which arrangement would benefit producers more?

The Invisible Hand Theorem

This theorem, which was first enunciated by Adam Smith in 1776 in *The Wealth of Nations*, goes as follows:

> But it is only for the sake of profit that any man employs a capital in the support of industry; and he will always, therefore, endeavour to employ it in the support of that industry of which the produce is likely to be of the greatest value, or to exchange for the greatest quantity either of money or of other goods. . . . As every individual, therefore, endeavours as much as he can . . . so to direct that industry . . . every individual necessarily labours to render the annual revenue of the Society as great as he can. He generally, indeed, neither intends to promote the public interest, nor knows how much he is promoting it. . . . He is in this, as in many other cases, led by an invisible hand to promote an end which was no part of his intentions. . . . I have never known much good done by those who affected to trade for the public good. It is an affectation, indeed, not very common among merchants, and very few words need to be employed in dissuading them from it.

What Smith offered was really two great insights, each of which continues to this day as an integral part of the economic way of thinking. One is that the economy is a *system* which, under circumstances that economists are far better able to be specific about today than was then possible, can be stable. Thus, despite the fact that innumerable decisions are taken by independent individuals in markets, one can say – for example, under price taking conditions – that there will be a single stable equilibrium price for each economic good that changes only if underlying determining factors change. These factors are on the one hand those that determine the position of the supply curve, and on the other those that determine the position of the demand curve. This insight involves no value judgement. But the second insight does.

The second insight is that the apparently unworthy pursuit of self-interest can produce an outcome whereby the interests of all are met. As you have seen, underlying this are at least two major value judgements: that the individual is always the best judge of his own welfare, and that the income distribution is fair. Given these, however, it is a quite remarkable result of the invisible hand theorem that welfare (the sum of consumers' and producers' surpluses) can be maximized without any overarching policy for society (for example, central economic planning) that explicitly sets out to achieve it. This aspect of the invisible hand theorem is the basic root of **economic liberalism** or economic libertarianism: the doctrine that individuals should, by and large, be left free to determine their own interests and transact with others whenever *mutually* agreeable terms can be arranged. The invisible hand cannot be relied upon to produce an income distribution that you may approve, but given that you can *redistribute* income in an appropriate fashion, you can, says the theorem, rely on the invisible hand to attain efficiency. As you may expect, this unambiguous message of the price taking model (which is the condition for the invisible hand theorem to work) becomes distinctly more blurred as the conditions for price takers' markets cease to apply. You will explore these in considerable depth later.

SAQ 13.3

This SAQ is about the *international* invisible hand! In figure 13.4 are shown the domestic demand and supply curves for an internationally traded good and the world demand and supply curves. Assume that the domestic supply and demand make a negligible contribution to world supply and demand. Thus the domestic economy is a price taker at world price P_0, supplying OX_0 of its demand by domestic production and meeting domestic demand of OX_1 by importing $X_1 - X_0$.

(a) If the world price is also the domestic price, what areas (such as D, E, H etc.) correspond to domestic consumers' surplus?

(b) What areas correspond to domestic producers' surplus?

Now assume a tariff is imposed that raises the domestic price to P_1 and makes the country 'self-sufficient' in X (imports falling to zero).

(c) What areas correspond to the new domestic consumers' surplus?

(d) What areas correspond to the new domestic producers' surplus?

(e) What areas represent a net social loss?

(f) Who gains what at whose expense?

(g) What other advantages and disadvantages are there of the tariff (protectionist) policy?

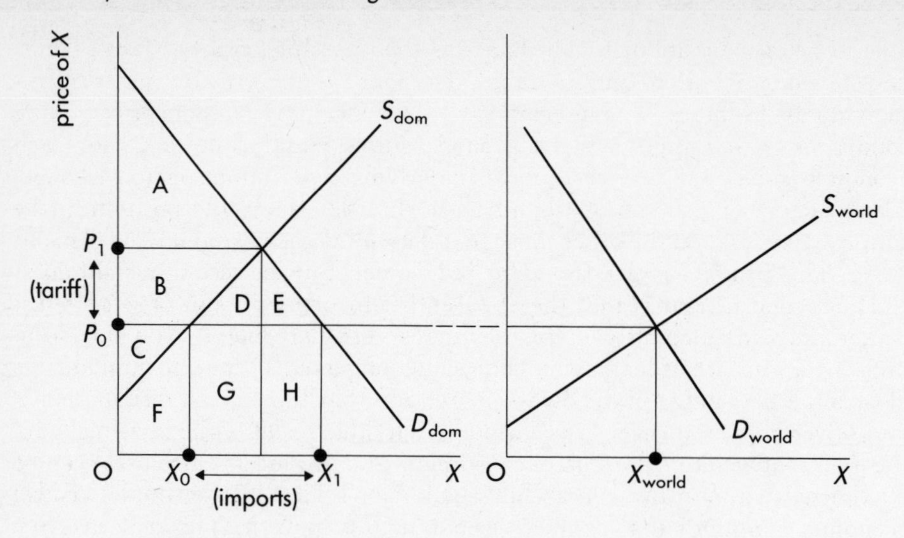

Figure 13.4 Demand and supply curves for SAQ 13.3

Effects of Taxes on Profits

A tax on pure profit will not, of course, affect a firm whose profit is zero, save in so far as it had an impact on the opportunity cost of its inputs (presumably lowering them as the profitability of forgone opportunities fell). But this effect will be ignored here; instead the focus will be on the direct effect of a profits tax on inframarginal price takers with positive profits.

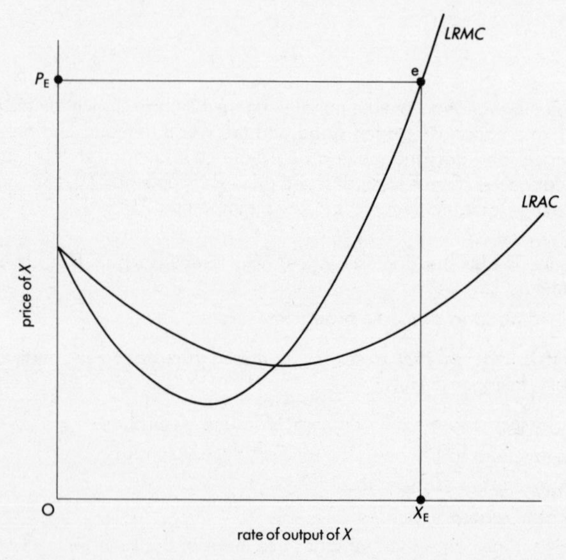

Figure 13.5 Output of an inframarginal price taker before a pure profit tax is imposed

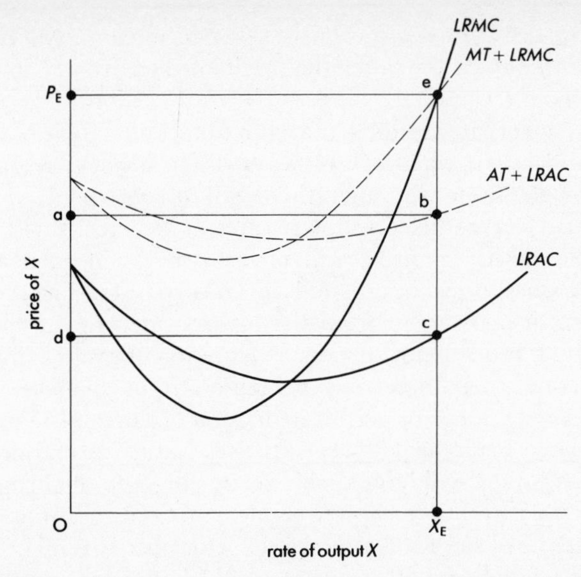

Figure 13.6 Effect of a pure profits tax on an inframarginal price taker

Figure 13.5 depicts an inframarginal price taking firm in long run equilibrium. Initially, it is in equilibrium at P_E and X_E (point e). Before proceeding further, ask yourself what effect you expect a 50 per cent profits tax to have on output and price. Do this now.

Since 50 per cent of every addition to profit will be taxed away, as far as the firm is concerned this will appear as an addition to its costs. Since the marginal profit at each rate of output is $P_E - LRMC$ (the extra revenue less the extra cost of each addition to the output rate), *LRMC* will rise by one half of this amount. This is shown in figure 13.6 by the dashed line labelled $MT + LRMC$ (marginal tax plus *LRMC*) drawn half way between the perfectly elastic demand curve and the *LRMC* curve. The profit maximizing firm will now set $MT + LRMC$ equal to price and, as you can see, this occurs at point e: the same equilibrium as before. Hence we infer that a tax on pure profits will *not* affect price or output! (Was that your expected answer?)

The common sense of this answer can be seen in two ways. On the one hand, at the profit maximizing output before the tax was imposed, marginal profit was zero (since $LRMC = P_E$). Hence a 50 per cent tax on a zero marginal profit is zero. Hence, at the margin, the *LRMC* is unaffected. On the other hand you can look at it in this way: if X_E was the output rate that previously maximized profit, and the firm is a profit maximizer, why should it change its output rate (and hence, if all firms have the same incentives and behave similarly, industry output)? To be sure, *after* tax it will have less profit than before, but it will still prefer to have 50 per cent of maximum profit than 50 per cent of some smaller profit!

Profits tax paid can be most easily seen by constructing an average tax plus *LRAC* curve. This is shown in figure 13.6 as $AT + LRAC$, which lies halfway between P_E and *LRAC*. Given this curve you can see that, whereas previously the firm had profits of d$P_E$ec, after the tax its profits are a$P_E$eb – exactly half the previous amount.

This perhaps surprising result – that a tax on profits does not affect output or price – should be qualified in two ways. First, if not *every* opportunity for profit is taxed in the same way, then there will be some tendency for activities that are not taxed, or are taxed at lower rates, to be substituted for those that are more highly taxed; so firms will tend to invest in such activities. For example, UK corporation tax falls only on incorporated firms, so one would predict a switch of investment from the incorporated to the unincorporated sector. Secondly, if the Inland Revenue's definition of profit is not the same as the theoretical one, then there may be some output changes. For example, suppose the Revenue does not permit deduction of some business expenses for tax purposes. Then in so far as these expenses feature in marginal costs (and are not overheads) they will have their effective price to the firm raised. If say £100 total expenses were not allowed against tax out of a total cost of £300, then with a revenue of say £500 and profits before tax of £500 – £300 = £200, instead of profits falling by 50 per cent to £100 after tax, profits will fall by 75 per cent. The firm will be taxed on £300 (£200 pure profit plus the £100 non-allowed expenses) with an after tax profit of £50. In the UK corporation tax excludes from taxable profits any *unrealized* rises or falls in the value of machines, plant etc., valuing such assets at their historical cost and hence – especially in inflationary times – exaggerating true profits through understating the true opportunity costs. This will cause the *LRMC* and *LRAC* curves to rise and output and profit to fall. If all firms react the same way then industry output will fall and price will rise.

Here, then, is an example of how 'common sense' expectations about the effect of a change (in this case the introduction of proportional profits tax) are shown, on more careful analysis, to be wrong. The 'common sense' general expectation that profits tax will raise prices and reduce outputs (or a rise or fall in such a tax rate will raise or lower prices and reduce or increase output) is actually to be predicted only in certain special circumstances (which you can now specify).

Effects of Excise Duties

Excise duties are a type of **indirect tax**. Indirect taxes are taxes on goods and services as distinct from those on capital, wealth, profits and income (**direct taxes**). The main indirect taxes in the UK are shown in table 13.2. Unit taxes, like excise duties, are a given amount on each unit of a product and, when imposed on sellers, have the effect of displacing the supply curve by the amount of the tax per unit. *Ad valorem* taxes are expressed as a percentage of the price, wholesale or retail, including or not including (as the case may be) excise. VAT is an *ad valorem* tax on the value added at each stage of production of manufacturing and distributive firms with a turnover of taxable goods in

Table 13.2 Main indirect taxes in the UK (1980–1)

Type	*Commodity*	*Rate of tax 1980–1*	*Estimated revenue 1980–1 (£ million)*	*Percentage of indirect tax revenue*
Physical units				
Duties	Tobacco	21% of retail price plus £13.42 per thousand (cigarettes only)	2,775	11.6
	Spirits	£11.87 per litre alcohol	1,270	5.3
	Beer	£13.05 per 100 litres at 1030° plus £0.435 per additional degree	1,130	4.7
	Wine	£81.42 per 100 litres not exceeding 15% alcohol + higher rates on heavier wines	363	1.5
	Petrol	£0.4546 per gallon	3,650	15.2
Ad valorem				
VAT	Most goods save food and some others	15%	12,450	51.9
Car tax	Motor cars	10% of wholesale price	575	2.4
Other			1,807	7.4
Total revenue			24,000	100.0

Source: C. V. Brown and P. Jackson (1982) *Public Sector Economics*, Oxford, Martin Robertson, table 17.1

excess of a certain amount. When a firm purchases goods from another it will be charged VAT by the supplier. When the firm sells its output to other firms or consumers it charges VAT to them. The firm is then liable to pay the difference between the VAT on inputs and the VAT on outputs (output tax minus input tax). Thus, if firm A produces a raw material supplied to firm B, which manufactures an intermediate good sold to firm C, which produces a final good sold to a distributor D, which sells in turn to a shop E, which sells in turn to the public F, the VAT is calculated as in table 13.3.

An excise duty imposes a tax at a fixed money amount per unit of volume. For example, at £15 per litre of alcohol, given that the alcohol content of a litre bottle of whisky is 40 per cent by volume, the duty per bottle is £6. Suppose now that whisky is initially selling at £3 per litre bottle without any duty imposed, and that duty is subsequently imposed at £6 per bottle; what do you predict will happen to price? Specifically, how much would you expect the price to rise? (Answer before reading on.)

Assume that output is produced under price taking conditions and that it is sufficiently homogeneous for you not to have to worry about the differences between brands. Figure 13.7 depicts the demand and supply curves for the product. Prior to the imposition of the duty, price and output are P_E and X_E respectively. The imposition of the duty as a fixed amount per unit sold means that the amount of the duty per unit has to be added to the supply price at each output, as shown by the supply curve S. Since the duty per unit does not vary with output, this means that the supply price plus duty is shown by the new

Table 13.3 Calculation of VAT

A	sells goods worth £100.00 to B + 15% VAT *£15.00* Total invoice £115.00	A's value added is £100 – £0 = £100. A pays output tax £15 minus input tax £0, i.e. £15, which is 15% of value added. *Customs and Excise receive* £15.00
B	sells goods worth £150.00 to C + 15% VAT *£22.50* Total invoice £172.50	B's value added is £150 – £100 = £50. B pays output tax £22.50 minus input tax £15, i.e. £7.50, which is £15% of value added. *Customs and Excise receive* £7.50
C	sells goods worth £250.00 to D + 15% VAT *£37.50* Total invoice £287.50	C's value added is £250 – £150 = £100. C pays output tax £37.50 minus input tax £22.50, i.e. £15, which is 15% of value added. *Customs and Excise receive* £15.00
D	sells goods worth £325.00 to E + 15% VAT *£48.75* Total invoice £373.75	D's value added is £325 – £250 = £75. D pays output tax £48.75 minus input tax £37.50, i.e. £11.25, which is 15% of value added. *Customs and Excise receive* £11.25
E	sells goods worth £390.00 to F + 15% VAT *£58.50* Total invoice £448.50	E's value added is £390 – £325 = £65. E pays output tax £58.50 minus input tax £48.75, i.e. £9.75, which is 15% of value added. *Customs and Excise receive* £9.75

Total value added = £100 + £50 + £100 + £75 + £65 = £390.
Total VAT paid = £15 + £7.50 + £15 + £11.25 + £9.75 = £58.50.
£58.50/£390 = 0.15

supply curve S', where the constant vertical difference between S' and S is the amount of the duty. The new equilibrium price is now P'_E, with corresponding output of X'_E. Price has risen – as you knew it would. But if you predicted that a

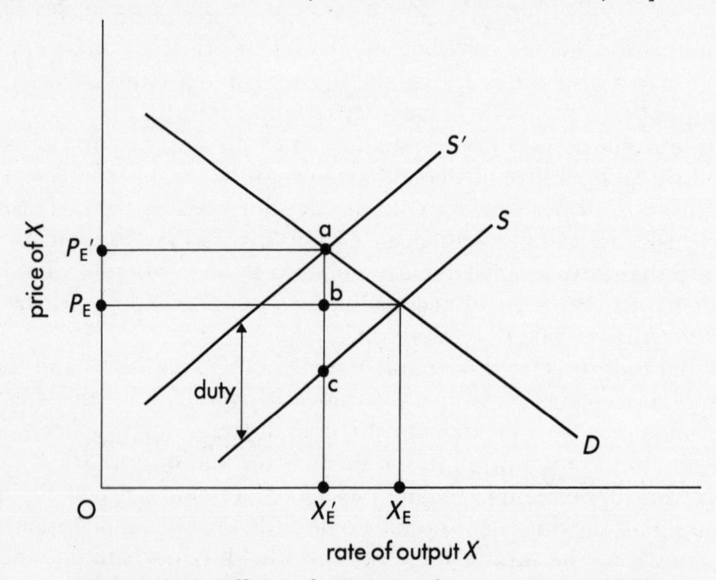

Figure 13.7 Effects of an excise duty on price and output

duty of £6 would raise price by £6 you can now see that that is, in general, a wrong answer. Price has risen by ab – less than the amount of the duty ac. The price to the consumer has risen by ab and that to the producer has fallen by bc. The sum of these equals the duty, but the **incidence** of the tax is not all on the consumer. In fact, in the case illustrated in figure 13.7 the incidence of the tax is heavier on the producer than the consumer.

As you can probably see, the incidence of the tax depends on the elasticities of demand and supply. You can make two general rules about the extreme outcomes of an excise duty. If industry demand is perfectly inelastic or industry supply is perfectly elastic, the incidence of the duty will fall entirely on the consumer; then (and only then!) will the price rise by the full amount of the excise (so again the 'common sense' approach is true only under rather special circumstances). If either industry demand is perfectly elastic or industry supply is perfectly inelastic, the incidence will fall entirely on the producer and price will not alter at all. More generally, other things equal, the more elastic is the demand the more the producer bears of the duty and, other things equal, the more elastic the supply the more the consumer bears the duty. (The analysis could be applied to *ad valorem* taxes, in which case the supply curve will not move parallel to itself but will shift in proportion to the supply price at each output rate).

SAQ 13.4

What is the difference for price, output rate and the incidence of the tax burden on producers and consumers between levying an excise tax on buyers and levying one on sellers?

Case Study 13.2 Indirect Tax Incidence

The analysis in the text is reliably applicable only in cases when a *particular* commodity becomes taxed (or the tax rate is changed) and when there are no marked effects elsewhere in the economy, for example on the demand and supply of inputs as a result of more or fewer being used in the production of the taxed good. When, as is more usual, the tax is on a very large set of goods or on a type of good that occupies a significant share of total output or expenditure, these second round effects have to be taken into account and the analysis complicated accordingly (an advanced topic in public finance). As a result, there are no good empirical studies that exactly fit the simple model developed in the text. There is, however, some incidental evidence. For example, Kay and King (1978) report that when a special discriminatory rate of VAT was imposed on television sets and some other electrical goods in 1975, their price rose and sales fell accordingly. The major incidence of the tax fell on consumers but some also fell on producers as profits and earnings in the industry fell.

There has been extensive work on the incidence of indirect taxes on people of different income levels. The usual (if extreme) assumption is that indirect taxes are fully shifted on to consumers. This leads to the conclusion that indirect taxation is rather regressive. Table 13.4 (Brown and Jackson, 1972) shows the average amount of indirect tax (excluding local authority rates) paid by each decile in the income distribution, the average original income (before tax and before transfer) and the tax as a percentage of the income. The first decile shows the income, tax etc. of lowest 10 per cent of income recipients, the second those of the next lowest 10 per cent etc.

As you can see, if one takes indirect tax paid as a percentage of original income, the percentage falls rapidly as income rises, for the rich spend a smaller share of their income on taxed commodities. If one takes tax as a percentage of income after various receipts (supplementary benefits etc.) then the percentage of income taken in tax still broadly falls, though less dramatically. In the second case the percentage paid in tax rises up to the third decile. This reflects the VAT zero rated status of food, expenditure on which occupies a large fraction of poor households' budgets. A tax whose amount rises as a percentage when income rises is called a **progressive tax**. One that stays constant is called a **proportional tax**. One that falls as a percentage is called a **regressive tax**. Hence, indirect taxes are regressive: the rich pay *more*, but pay a *smaller proportion* of income as indirect tax.

John Kay and Mervyn King (1978) *The British Tax System*, London, Oxford University Press.
C. V. Brown and P. Jackson (1982) *Public Sector Economics*, Oxford, Martin Robertson, table 17.3.

Table 13.4 Incidence of indirect taxes by income class, UK, 1979

1 *Decile*	*2* *Average original income (£ per year)*	*3* *Average income after direct cash benefits (£ per year)*	*4* *Indirect taxes paid per year (£)*	*4/2*	*4/3*
bottom	6	1,726	265	4416.7	15.4
2nd	270	1,903	336	124.4	17.7
3rd	1,394	2,828	533	38.2	18.8
4th	3,160	3,976	723	22.9	18.2
5th	4,378	4,906	901	20.6	18.4
6th	5,431	5,927	1024	18.9	17.3
7th	6,456	6,884	1153	17.9	16.7
8th	7,671	8,042	1357	17.7	16.9
9th	9,364	9,724	1557	16.6	16.0
top	14,038	14,418	2073	14.8	14.4

Changes in an Input Price

Suppose the price of an input falls. What effect do you predict this will have on price and rate of output? To figure this out you need to go back to production theory. Figure 13.8 shows a two input production process with the firm initially in long run equilibrium at point e where an isoquant and an isocost line A_1B_1 are tangential, with A_0 of A being used and B_0 of B. If B now falls in price, at the previous level of expenditure, the maximum amount of output producible is shown by the new tangency at point a on the new isocost line A_1B_2. However, to detect the effect on the cost curves it is easier to ask what happens to the cost of producing the initial output.

This is shown by the new isocost line A_3B_3 tangential to the original isoquant at point e′. Since this is a lower isocost line than A_1B_2, you know that total cost has fallen. What will have happened to marginal cost? To see this, the analysis gets a little tricky. At the original prices shown by A_1B_1, to have increased

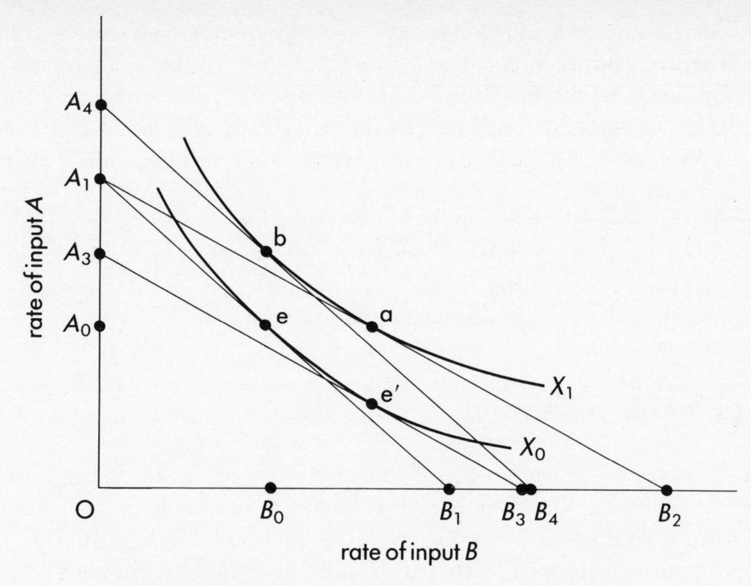

Figure 13.8 Effect of a fall in price of one input

output marginally from X_0 to X_1 would have needed a sufficient expenditure on A and B at their initial prices, as shown by the isocost line A_4B_4 (with a long run equilibrium at point b). In terms of input A, the marginal cost of this is measured by A_1A_4 or, in terms of B, by B_1B_4. (Remember that A_1 is the maximum amount of A that can be purchased at an expenditure shown by isocost line A_1B_1, and A_4 is the maximum A that can be purchased at an expenditure shown by isocost line A_4B_4. Hence A_1A_4 is the increase in the maximum purchaseable, or the increase in expenditure in terms of A, or the marginal cost in terms of A. Likewise you could tell the same story in terms of B.)

At the new price of B, by analogous reasoning, the isocost line shifts from A_3B_3 to A_1B_2, and the marginal cost in terms of A is A_3A_1. Now compare these two (long run) marginal costs, A_3A_1 and A_1A_4. You can see that they are *exactly the same* even though total cost is lower ($A_1 < A_4$ and $A_3 < A_1$). Hence marginal cost (in the long run with all inputs optimally varied) remains the same. Hence, under price taking, output and price remain the same! (Does this differ from what you predicted in answer to the question with which this section opened? It probably does, so recheck the argument to ensure that you grasp it.)

Economic analysis once again demonstrates the unreliability of 'common sense' (which may be common but is not always sensible!) What has happened here, to be fair, is that a special case has been rigged, in which input B is not a normal input whose demand rises, for given prices, as output rises. This you can see by noting that point a is vertically above point e′ and point b is vertically above point e. You can experiment yourself by showing that when B is a normal input in a Cobb-Douglas constant returns production function (with points a and b respectively to the right of points e′ and e) then the 'common sense' approach is correct: marginal cost will fall. Conversely, if *B* is an inferior input such that *less* is used as output rises with constant input prices, then marginal cost will rise as the price of *B* falls and output will also fall. If *B* falls in price for all firms in the price takers' industry, then the price of output will consequently rise.

In general, it seems fair to conclude from all these cases that careful analysis is preferable to 'common sense'. There are many other types of changes that one could consider, including the effects of other types of taxes. Some of them at least you should now be able to tackle for yourself.

Effect of a Rise in Demand

You can recover from the strain of the previous section by taking, as a final exercise in economic prediction, the effect of a rise in demand under price taking. Figure 13.9 has the essential analysis embodied in it. Initially, the firm is in equilibrium at point e_0, with price P_0 and output X_0. As demand rises from D_0 to D_1, the new equilibrium produced by this effect alone must be to the north east of point e_0 at a point such as e_1, entailing a *higher price and output rate.* For each firm, the perfectly elastic demand curve it confronts will rise by P_0P_1 and each will be producing where $P_1 = LRMC$, as will any new entrants.

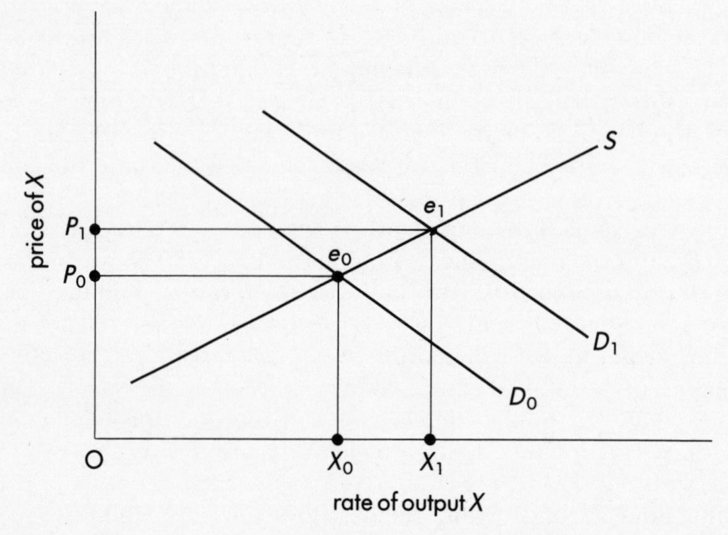

Figure 13.9 Effect of a rise in demand on price and output of a price taking industry

Equilibrium and Disequilibrium

The analysis so far has been conducted as though price and quantity adjusted to any change affecting them speedily, so that a short run equilibrium was instantaneously established. This is but a convenient fiction. A good deal of useful analysis can be done by *stylizing* the economy as though this were true. It is a quite common approach in economics to assume that the economy is in a short run equilibrium at any moment and that any exogenous changes, in the form of taxes, regulations, prices and quantities of foreign goods imported and so on lead to instantaneous short term readjustments. This method of analysis is called **comparative statics**: one compares, as it were, before-and-after equilibrium static states. In later chapters this book will discuss the consequences of taking a **dynamic approach**, which will naturally suggest itself to you as an alternative. This is a topic requiring more advanced analysis. But now you can explore the other alternative that will naturally suggest itself to you – that of **disequilibrium states**.

As has been noted before, one of the problems that any decision taker has to confront is the issue of whether any change is permanent or temporary. If, say, a price rise or fall is regarded as merely temporary, a manager may not alter prices (this is costly both to the manager and to customers, as they will respectively have to find means of distributing and obtaining the new price information) but rather allow stocks to rise or fall until a firmer view about what is happening is obtained. Thus, in figure 13.10, if demand rises to D_1 or falls to D_2, and price is left unchanged, there will be excess demand or supply

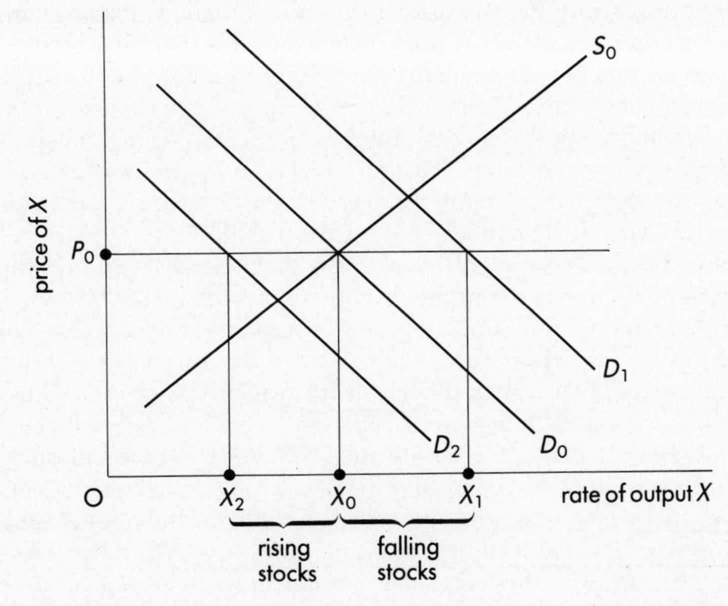

Figure 13.10 Quantity rather than price adjustment to changing demand

and stocks will fall or rise accordingly. Here you see *quantity* (*stock*) *adjustment* rather than price adjustment, together with a failure of equilibrium to be established, at least over the time it takes someone to make up their mind whether the change is temporary or permanent.

More generally, there are lots of reasons for supposing the *typical* state of the economy to be one of disequilibrium rather than equilibrium. Information about other prices and other goods (substitutes and complements), both for consumption and as inputs, is costly to acquire and, since the marginal value of *complete* information is bound to be far less than is the marginal cost of getting it, *perfect* information will never exist. Consequently *mistakes* about outputs, inputs and prices will be made – as it later turns out – and at any one time the same good may sell at more than one price.

SAQ 13.5

Would you expect to see the price of a homogeneous good sold at stalls 14 and 33 on York market to vary more than the average price of that good in York compared with Salisbury?

Information about the *future* is impossible to get: one must ultimately *guess*. No two people are likely to make the same guesses, and so they will respond to the same information that is currently available in different ways. Some may believe that demand will rise, others that it will fall: each will react accordingly, and differently. Moreover, the determinants of the supply and demand curves are always changing, so that even if price does play an equilibrating role, things may meanwhile have changed again. Thus equilibrium is, as it were, for ever coming into being without ever actually being attained.

Disequilibrium means, in general over the entire economy, that even in price takers' markets output will be *less* than the ideal or less than that predicted by equilibrium analysis. Excess demands and excess supplies, due to 'mistakes', sluggish adjustment, quantity rather than price adjustments and so on, will *not* simply cancel out, giving the general impression that on average the economy seems to be in equilibrium. Consider figure 13.11. At P_E, the market is cleared with zero excess demand or supply. If price is, however, higher than this at, say, P_1, only X_1 will be demanded – less than X_E. Similarly, if price is lower than P_E, only X_2 will be supplied – again less than X_E. Disequilibrium prices therefore confine the range of outputs to those indicated by the heavily drawn sections of the demand and supply curves – if producers adjust very quickly. More realistically, one expects stocks to rise when the price is greater than P_E, so that output rates fall less than the heavily drawn curve suggests. Thus, with disequilibrium, output will be lower and, on average, there will be fewer resources employed than in equilibrium. When, to these informational problems and constantly changing conditions of supply and demand, one adds the rigidities created by long run contracts with suppliers, labour etc. and legal controls on prices (floors or ceilings) and quantities (quotas), it becomes plain that for some purposes the emphasis on *disequilibrium* is going to be as important as, for other purposes, the emphasis on equilibrium.

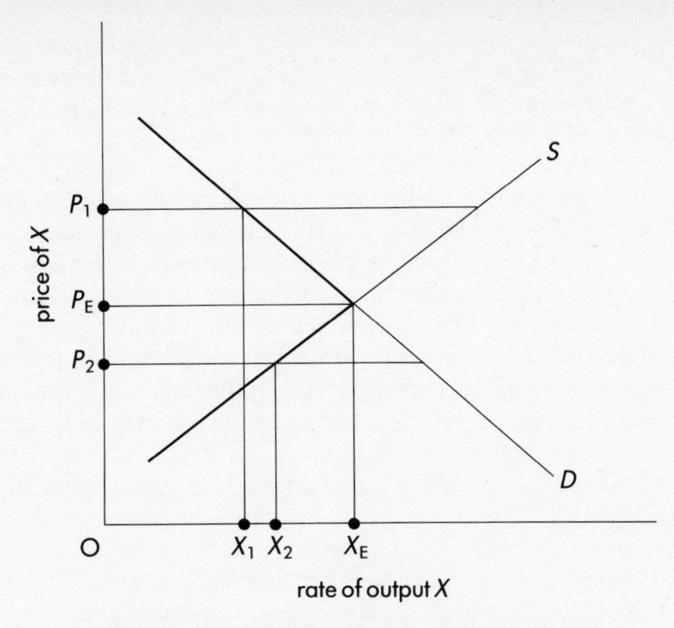

Figure 13.11 Disequilibrium implies lower output

You will have to use your judgement as to which approach is most appropriate for which type of problem. In much of the macroeconomics to be investigated later, it is assumed that microequilibrium is often not attained so that, even with price takers' markets, there may be inefficient outputs and unemployed inputs (even when extra inputs are offered for employment at going prices). These inputs will then earn no income, so that total demand is lower than it would otherwise be and the demand for highly income elastic goods in particular will be low. All markets are interdependent. A disequilibrium in any one must reduce incomes which will reduce demands in other markets. If they then go into disequilibrium, the process is reinforced. On the other hand, in many microeconomic analyses, it is judged that the assumption that the economy behaves 'as if' equilibria are attained is a reasonable enough approximation.

Predictions about the effect of changes in demand and supply on price become fuzzy under disequilibrium. Look again at figure 13.11. Suppose price is at P_1 and demand increases. What happens? In the short run probably all that will happen is that the price will be held and stocks of X run down. They will have been rising so long as output exceeded demand, but even if output had been cut back to X_1 there are still likely to be accumulated stocks that are costly to keep (and may also deteriorate in quality) and which can be used to meet the new demand. Thus increases in demand are met only eventually, after a period of falling stocks, by increased supply, with price remaining more or less the same.

The economic analysis of disequilibrium states is far less refined than the (easier) analysis of equilibrium states. A deeply ingrained tradition holds that disequilibrium is essentially transitory: that, as suggested earlier, equilibrium is always being approached. In this tradition it is natural to suppose that the greater the excess demand or supply at any price the greater the pressure on price to rise or fall; moreover, that the longer the time allowed for adjustment without any other disturbances in the equilibrium to which the economy is headed, the more complete the adjustment process is. According to this view, the longer the period available for adjustment, the closer one comes to equilibrium. This view has refutable implications as long as one can measure the size of excess demands and supplies and the rate of change of prices. But the longer is the period necessary to complete the adjustments, the greater is the probability that other factors will disturb the equilibrium to which one is headed. In any case, as Lord Keynes observed, in the long run we are all dead! So some long runs are extremely uninteresting! Consequently, when there are reasons to believe that adjustment is either slow or going to be subject to shocks that require its direction to be changed, the equilibrium approach becomes less useful.

To the extent that one thinks the opposite is true, the equilibrium approach is more useful. In particular, in Keynesian macroeconomic analysis, it has been widely held to be useful to consider that an economy with persisting extensively unemployed resources is best characterized, as a whole, as being in disequilibrium with quantities adjusting as demand changes (first stocks and, after a lag, production) rather than prices. On the other hand, for many microeconomic purposes, when one is investigating a particular firm or industry or consumer group, one may have sufficient specific information to be able to judge that the equilibrium approach is most appropriate. In either case, the relevant test in positive economics is an empirical one: the procedure one adopts should enable one to derive implications that can be tested in the actual economy and which, when tested, are more consistent with the theory one has used rather than some alternative.

What You Should Understand Now

Efficiency as technical efficiency, cost-effectiveness and ideal output.
Efficiency of price takers' markets.
Value judgements embodied in the notion of Pareto efficiency.
Non-uniqueness of Pareto optimum.
Invisible hand theorem.
Welfare effects of departures from efficiency.
Meaning of corporation and indirect taxation in the UK.
Effects of input, demand and tax changes on equilibrium prices and quantities.
Meaning of disequilibrium and its effects on output.

14

Production under Price Searching Conditions

So far it has been assumed that production takes place under price taking conditions. In practice many firms do not simply take the market price as given but have to select the price that is best from their own point of view. Imagine that you are the pricing manager of a large UK based pharmaceutical firm. Your laboratories have recently developed an entirely new product that provides both immunity from and a cure for a broad set of viral infections from AIDS to cold sores. Whereas the investment in research and development (R & D) has been immense, the actual manufacturing, packaging and distribution costs are trivial. The firm seeks to maximize its profit, and you are called upon to help determine the price at which the new drug is to be sold in the UK and various overseas markets. How shall you advise?

The main difference between your situation and that of the price taker is that the price as well as the output rate is something you must choose. Somehow, you must *search* out the right price for the firm. Hence the general name for firms in this kind of situation: **price searchers**.

One thing you might do is to look at the prices of a similar drug, set your price somewhat above it, and try that on the market. In some situations that might be a sensible policy. In this case, unfortunately, there is no truly relevant comparator. You might engage in some market research to find out the rates of prescribing that doctors are likely to adopt at a variety of prices. In that case, an appropriate conceptual experiment for the product managers in each market (UK, Germany, USA, Uganda etc.) would be to guess at a profit maximizing price and to ask themselves 'if price were to be reduced by x per cent, would the rate of prescribing be likely to rise by more or less than x per cent?' Indeed, even if you did no specific market research, this would be a useful way of getting your product managers to be explicit about their subjective judgements (based on hunch, flair, experience and so on) concerning the prices that each market would bear.

This mental experiment would be based upon the one factor that you *can* rely upon: that demand curves have a negative slope. Thus, in figure 14.1, if the price postulated on the basis of hunch were £23, the product manager in the market in question may predict sales of 5 million courses of treatment; if it were £15, 10 million; if it were £8, 15 million. Connecting such points as a, b, c etc. yields the expected demand curve (it need not, of course, be a straight line). This will give you information about the expected elasticity of demand.

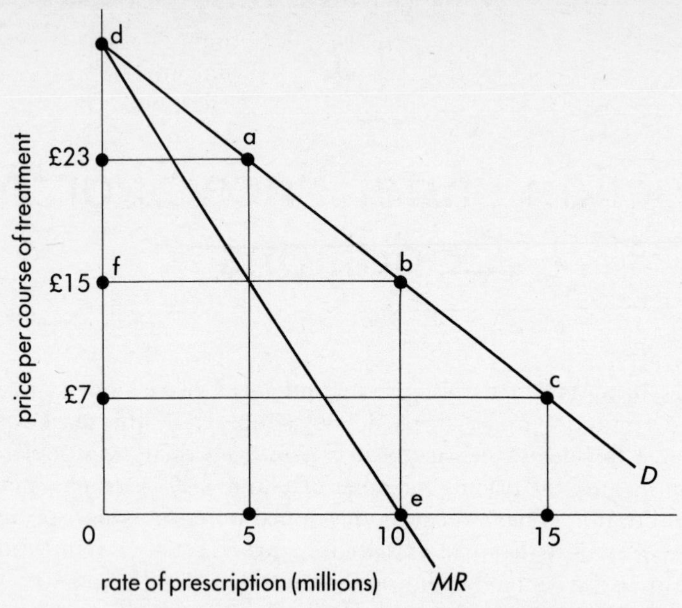

Figure 14.1 Searching for the ideal price

At point a, for example, price elasticity is relatively high, so a reduction in price yields a more than proportionate increase in prescriptions. Therefore total revenue must rise. Therefore *marginal* revenue (*MR*) is positive. (Now is a good time to refresh your understanding of marginal expenditure: see chapter 4.) If production costs are effectively zero (as has been supposed) this must be too high a price (assuming trust in the product manager's judgement about the demand curve) because a lower price will raise revenue at no additional expense. At a price of £8, price elasticity is relatively low, so a rise in price will cause prescriptions to fall *less* than proportionately. Therefore revenue will fall if price is lowered and prescriptions increased: marginal revenue must be negative. Clearly, the best price for the firm is £15 in this case, where elasticity is unitary and marginal revenue zero.

SAQ 14.1

(a) In figure 14.1, areas 0de and 0fbe are equal in area. Why is this?

(b) In the same figure, output rates higher than 10 million have a negative marginal revenue. Is total revenue higher or lower at higher rates than 10 million?

(c) Is total revenue higher or lower at lower output rates than 10 million?

(d) If total revenue is maximized at 10 million, what is the elasticity of demand at point b on the demand curve?

(e) What equation describes the demand curve in this figure?

You may find that the recommended ideal price in each market is different. That may raise difficulties. One product manager may say that the European Commission will not wear price differentials of more than 20 per cent in European markets. Another may say that the anti-trust legislation in a particular country is more likely to be invoked if price there exceeds price in the country of origin by more than 30 per cent. Such factors may constrain your freedom of choice; but it is always worth pressing enquiries as to whether the *beliefs* people hold about constraints are true beliefs, what the costs to the firm are likely to be if it is successfully prosecuted, what defences could be mounted, and so on.

Sometimes you may be in the fortunate position of having a home government that actively supports what it may none the less see as high prices, particularly if the product sells overseas and contributes to the value of exports. This may also be a factor in someone else's decision about where to locate production of the commodity.

Given the residual doubt you may have as to what the right price is *exactly*, it may be better to err on the high side on the grounds that it may be better subsequently to reduce price rather than have to raise it. On the other hand, despite the patent protection you undoubtedly have for a few years, a high price may encourage the entry of competitors with similar products that may reduce the demand for your own product, so you will have also to bear in mind the longer term cross elasticities of demand.

This illustrates the way in which a knowledge of rather basic economics can be used to pick apart an industrial pricing problem, and to identify the types of judgement that have to be made and where empirical evidence may be brought to bear to narrow down one's uncertainty.

The more common use of the theory in economics is, however, to *assume* that firms are successful at searching for the profit maximizing price (or at least that *surviving* managements are) in order to make predictions about their response to changes in input prices, taxes etc. and to provide accounts of the often puzzling phenomena that one encounters in the world of business.

One indicator of price searching is the degree to which industry output, employment or assets are concentrated in a few firms. Leslie Hannah and John Kay (1977: see table 14.1) examined the concentration of British industry in 1957–69. The share in assets held by the largest ten companies was one measure used, and this is reported in table 14.1 for a variety of industries. In only two industries, non-electrical engineering and building materials, did the concentration ratio fall. The fall in the first case was due to the poor performance of Vickers and the loss of its aircraft interests to BAC and its steel making through nationalization. In building materials, this period saw the growth of several previously small firms into prominence (especially Redland and Ready Mixed Concrete) so, although a single market leader (AP Cement) no longer existed by 1969, there were actually more large firms.

The most common cause of the general increase in concentration was merger – particularly spectacular in the brewing industry. One should be wary of drawing too strong an inference from these data about the extent of price searching in British industry, for they are very aggregated. The three largest firms in the food industry, for example, were Unilever, Rank Hovis McDougall, and Cadbury Schweppes: they not only produced relatively few products that were directly in competition with one another, but they also produced much through product diversification that was similarly produced

Table 14.1 Concentration in British Industry 1957–69

Industry	*Share of largest ten companies in industry assets (%)*	
	1957	*1969*
Food	62.1	80.5
Drink	40.8	45.4
Tobacco	100.0	100.0
Chemicals	80.6	86.4
Metal manufacture	58.7	74.3
Non-electrical engineering	39.0	32.1
Electrical engineering	60.4	81.2
Shipbuilding	80.3	93.3
Vehicles and aircraft	67.2	85.8
Other metal goods	67.2	77.1
Textiles	55.9	74.2
Building materials	71.2	65.0
Paper and publishing	63.6	78.1
Miscellaneous	58.3	65.5

Source: L. Hannah and J. Kay (1977) *Concentration in British Industry*, London and Basingstoke, Macmillan, table 6.2

by other firms. However, less aggregated studies have suggested that this aggregate trend towards greater concentration also exists elsewhere – especially where mergers were frequent. Note incidentally that even in a concentrated industry there may be some firms that are small enough to be considered as price takers.

Short Run Equilibrium of the Profit Maximizing Price Searcher

The main characteristic of a price searching firm is that, unlike the price taker, it can sell more under given demand conditions only by lowering price. This implies that the marginal revenue gained from additional sales is less than price. Figure 14.2 depicts a representative price searcher. The demand curve also shows the average revenue gained at each level of output. This should be clear when you realize that total revenue (TR) over a period is given by $TR = PX$, where P is the price of X and X is the rate of output of X. Average revenue is, of course, $TR/X = PX/X = P$.

SAQ 14.2

(a) For the demand curve $X = 60 - 3P$, fill in the blank spaces in the following table:

price	*quantity demanded*	*total revenue*	*marginal revenue*
20	—	—	—
15	—	—	—
10	—	—	—
5	—	—	—
0	—	—	—

(b) In figure 14.3, why must ab = bc?

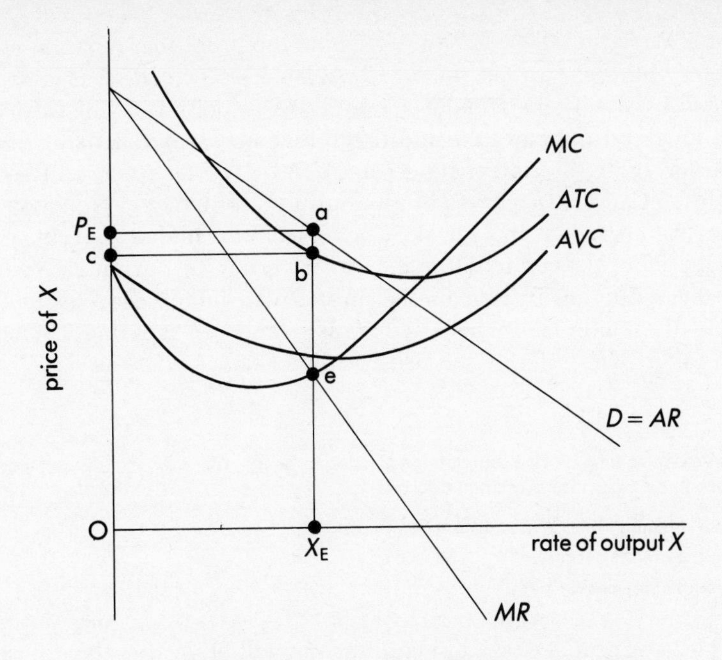

Figure 14.2 A representative price searcher

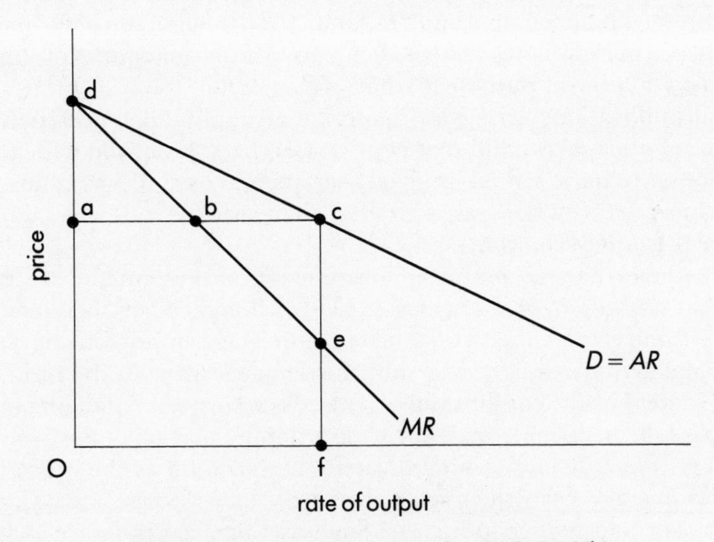

Figure 14.3 Revenue curves for SAQ 14.2(b)

If you now introduce the cost curves into figure 14.2 – average variable, average total and marginal – you can determine the profit maximizing output and price. This will be at an output rate for which $MC = MR$, that is P_E and X_E, determined by the intersection of MC and MR at point e. If the firm were to produce a lower output rate, the additional revenue from increasing output would be larger than the additional cost ($MR > MC$), as you can see by comparing the MC and MR curves at any output less than X_E. Hence profits will increase if output is increased. Conversely, at higher output rates, $MC > MR$; therefore the reduction in cost by lowering the output rate will be larger than the reduction in revenue, so profits will increase if output falls. Profit is evidently maximized where $MC = MR$ (and MC is rising). Whereas for the price taker $MR = P$, for the price searcher $MR < P$.

SAQ 14.3

The demand curve confronting a price searcher is estimated to be $X = 60 - 3P$. If (constant) marginal cost (assume zero fixed costs too) is estimated to be 10:

(a) What output maximizes the firm's profits?
(b) What price maximizes profits?
(c) What will profits per period be?

In figure 14.2 the profits earned in equilibrium will be $P_E$abc, the difference between total revenue and total cost. In the short run this need not be a positive amount, so long as variable costs are covered. Note that $MC = MR$ is a necessary implication of the profit maximizing firm. No matter how it selects the output that is ideal from its point of view (whether by copying other firms, doing market research, making inspired guesses or whatever), *if* it maximizes profits then it must necessarily have $MC = MR$. The theory does not *assume* that firms set about computing MC and MR (though some do make such estimates); it merely notes that if they successfully maximize profits then it follows, as a matter of pure logic, that $MC = MR$.

Several implications arise immediately that imply differences between the behaviour of price takers and that of price searchers. First, you will have noted that price searchers are more likely to incur costs of searching for the appropriate price (market research etc.) than price takers, who simply take whatever price they confront.

Second, note that, at the profit maximizing output rate, $P > MC$. This means that *at that price such firms would like to sell more*. They therefore have an incentive (unlike individual price takers) to engage in advertising and other promotional activity designed to shift the demand curve to the right.

Third, note that the equilibrium of a price searcher *may* entail an output rate that implies the firm being on a downward sloping portion of the average total cost curve. If one defines optimum capacity utilization as the utilization that minimizes average cost, then such firms may have 'excess' capacity: higher output rates could reduce unit costs. Such was the case in figure 14.2. Figure 14.4 illustrates a case where there is no excess capacity in this sense and the

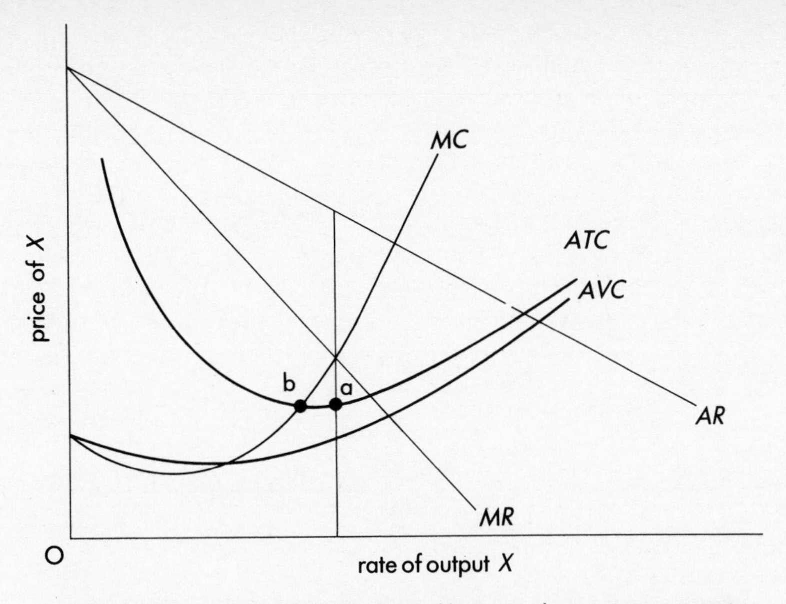

Figure 14.4 A price searcher's equilibrium without excess capacity

output rate is at point a, to the right (rather than the left) of the lowest point b of the average total cost curve. Consequently, price searchers may or may not produce an output that is fully cost-effective.

Monopolistic Competition

Where there are sufficiently large numbers of price searchers producing similar products with no barriers to entry into the industry, but not sufficient numbers to make a price taking market, a condition sometimes described as **monopolistic competition** prevails. This is one special type of price searching. It plainly pays price searchers to do their best to restrict entry (preferably in collusion with the government). However, if they are unsuccessful the presence of relatively high profits will encourage entry so that in the long run each producer's share of the market falls. The demand curve that each existing firm perceives thus shifts to the left. This process will continue until the relatively high profits are competed away and the marginal price searchers earn only the normal profit that would be received were each to invest its assets elsewhere in the economy in markets not protected by barriers to entry.

This is shown in figure 14.5. Initially a firm is in equilibrium with P_0 and X_0. In the long run entry of other firms shifts the firm's demand curve to the left until it is tangential to the long run average cost curve at point e (note that $MC = MR$ vertically below this point). At this point profits over and above the opportunity cost of profits elsewhere are zero.

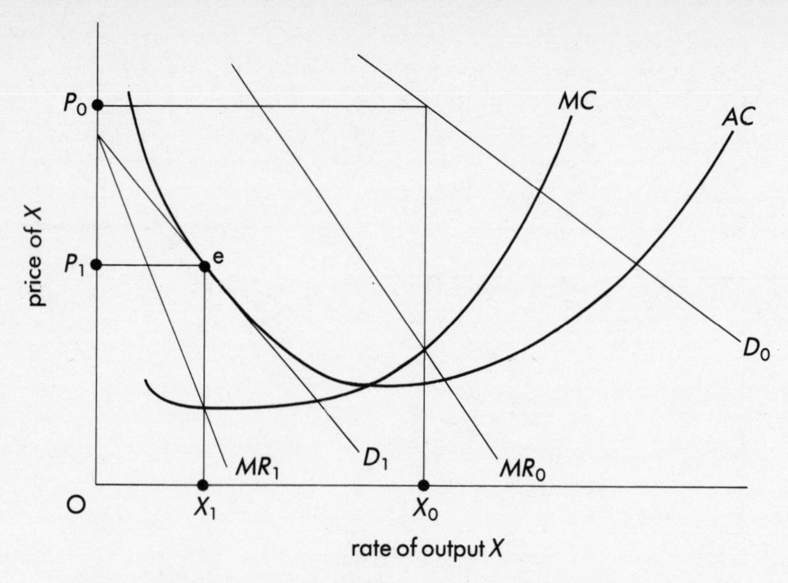

Figure 14.5 Long run equilibrium of a monopolistic competitor

The particular striking feature of this result is that the monopolistic competitor that earns only normal profits will unambiguously have excess capacity. If all firms have similar cost structures then they will all tend to have excess capacity, though the theory allows that inframarginal firms with lower cost curves may make both positive profits and use their capacity efficiently. The general result, however, which also implies that monopolistically competitive firms will tend to be smaller than price taking firms (each of which would, in terms of figure 14.5, produce in the long run at the output for which AC is lowest), is regarded by most economists as not much more than a theoretical curiosity. Most price searchers are *not* competing with large numbers of other producers – though there may be a large number of different products.

Other Implications of Price Searching Conditions

If marginal costs are positive – as they usually are, even if low – then a price searcher (any, not just a monopolistic competitor) will always produce at a point on the demand curve where elasticity is greater than unity. Remember that price elasticity is unitary when $MR = 0$. If $MC > 0$ then, since $MC = MR$ in equilibrium, it follows that $MR > 0$, so the output rate will be such that demand is elastic. Under price taking, elasticity of demand in equilibrium can be smaller than, larger than or equal to unity.

Since profits are higher under price searching than under price taking, all firms have an incentive to **differentiate** their products. The more that the styling, colour, image, technical specification and so on of a product can be differentiated from those of competitors (a process in which advertising can play an important role), the less the price elasticity and the greater the opportunity for larger profits. Product differentiation thus becomes a *purposeful* activity of price searchers, whereas price takers will not purposively differentiate their products (there are, of course, many different types of, say, potato but for each type there are so many producers that no single grower can affect price).

There is *no* supply curve under price searching. Under price taking, the MC curve *is* the supply curve. The price searcher, however, sets $MC = MR \neq P$. To discover the price searcher's supply at a variety of prices, *both* the demand and the marginal cost curves must be known, not just the marginal cost curve as under price taking. Consider figure 14.6. Imagine first that this portrays a price taking industry. If demand conditions are represented by D_1 then output and price are predicted to be X_1 and P_1. If demand changes to D_2, output and price are predicted to be X_2 and P_2. The firms all move along the ΣMC curve which, from chapter 12, is the industry supply curve S. Now suppose that the industry is monopolized by a single price searcher and that ΣMC represents its MC curve. When demand is D_1, output and price will be X_3 and P_3. When demand is D_2, output and price will be X_4 and P_4. Neither corresponds to a point on the MC curve, and a unique supply curve cannot be identified.

SAQ 14.4

What effect on short term profits, output and prices will the imposition on a price searcher of a 20 per cent tax on pure profits have?

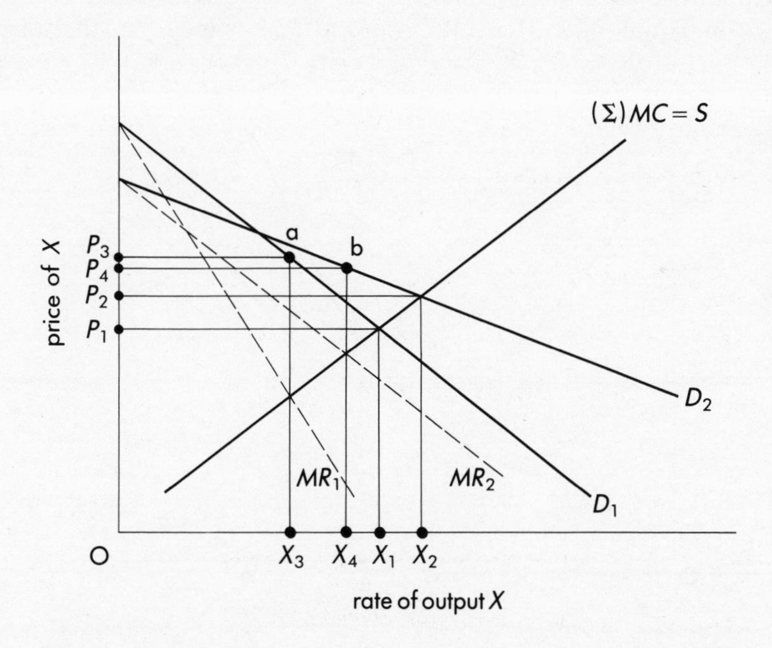

Figure 14.6 Absence of a unique supply curve under price searching

Long Run Equilibrium of a Monopolist

If there is but one price searcher the condition is termed **monopoly**. In this case, the monopoly firm is identical to the industry. For a monopoly to persist in the long run, there must be some barrier or barriers to the entry of other firms. These firms would otherwise see the advantage of the monopoly's short run profits and themselves set up in competition, thus making the industry resemble the price taking situation. Such barriers may take the form of legal licences (or franchises) to produce. This type of monopoly is thus effectively granted and enforced by government. At one time monopolies were granted in salt sales and playing card manufacture; in our own time, many of the professions require lengthy training before legal permission to practise is granted, and training schools are often regulated by government. Barriers may take the form of patents which grant the producer a *temporary* monopoly of the right to produce; barriers in the pharmaceutical industry are a good example of this. They may also take the form of scale economies: if one firm is able to reap scale economies, new and presumably smaller competitors would often be unable to achieve a sufficiently low average cost for them to be able to make positive profits.

The main difference between a monopolist in the short and the long run is therefore that it would be able to select its preferred point on the long run average cost curve, possibly gaining the advantage of scale economies, and in any event producing only when positive profits were attained (recall that in the short run a monopolist may sell at a price less than average total cost). This is shown in figure 14.7. Here $MR = LRMC$ at point e, so the long run

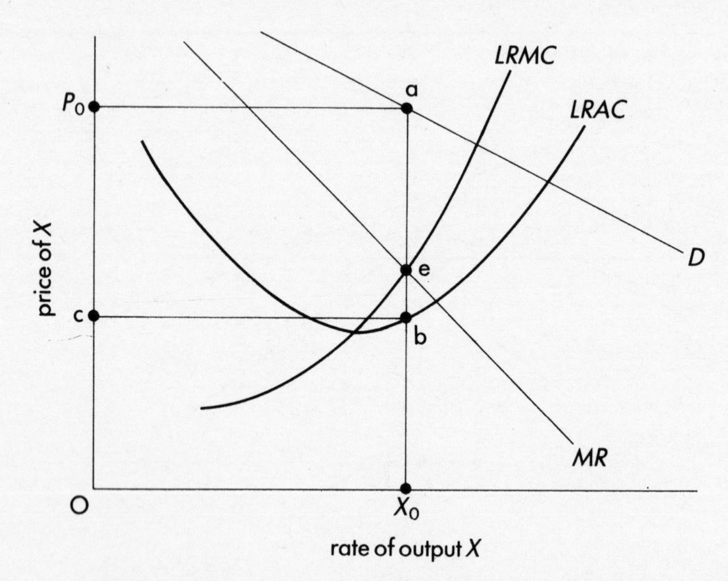

Figure 14.7 Long run equilibrium of a price searcher

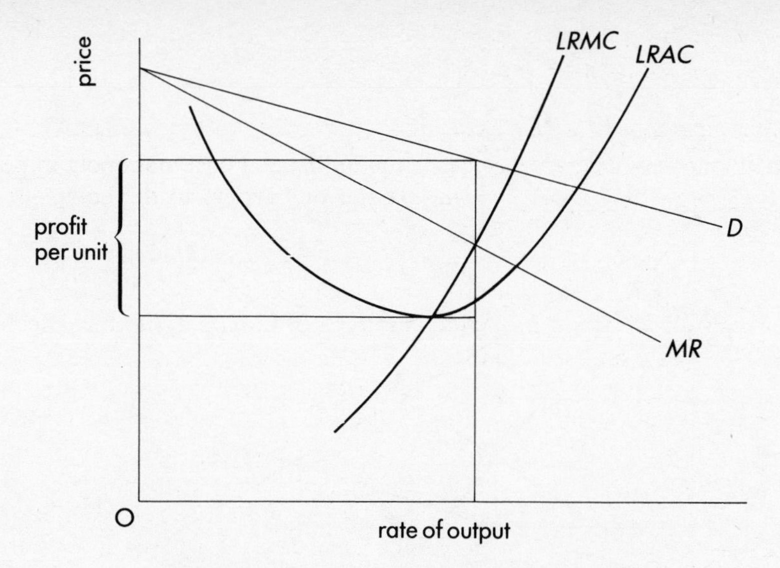

Figure 14.8 Monopoly diagram for SAQ 14.5

equilibrium has price at P_0 and the output rate at X_0, with profits per period equal to P_0abc.

SAQ 14.5

What is wrong with figure 14.8?

Efficiency Losses of Monopoly

The classic case against monopoly is based on the implication of a theory that it entails net losses of surplus. Consider figure 14.9. Initially imagine that this is a monopolized industry. For convenience assume no fixed costs. You can therefore say that at the equilibrium price and quantity, P_M and X_M, consumers' surplus is $P_M$ab and producer's surplus is $P_M$bcd (= $P_M$bef), giving a total surplus of abcd. Before going further, check your understanding of the calculation of consumers' and producer's surplus by doing SAQ 14.6.

SAQ 14.6

In figure 14.10:

(a) What areas correspond to consumers' surplus when price is P_0? (give your answer as, for example, C + D + H + K – F)
(b) What areas correspond to producer's surplus when price is P_o?
(c) What areas correspond to consumers' surplus when price is P_1?
(d) What areas correspond to producer's surplus when price is P_1?

Now suppose that the industry were, instead, composed of price takers. In that case, equilibrium price and quantity are P_P and X_P in figure 14.9. Consumers'

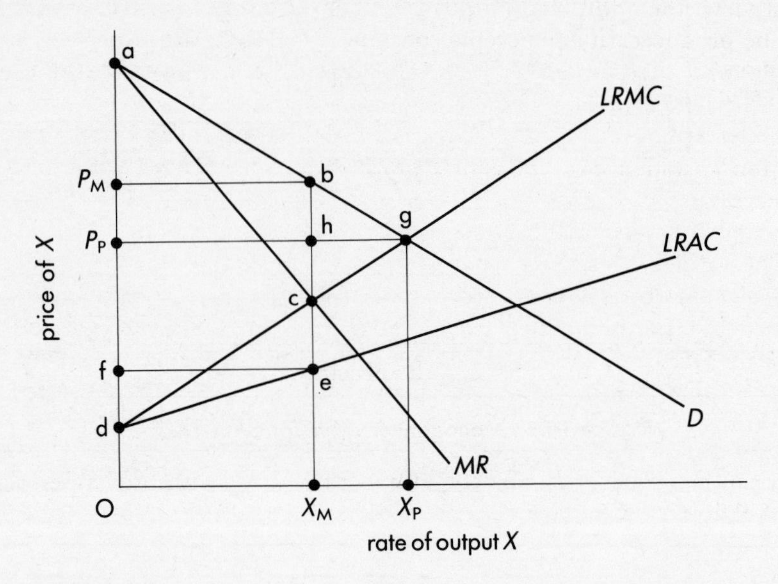

Figure 14.9 Comparison of efficiency of monopoly and price taking

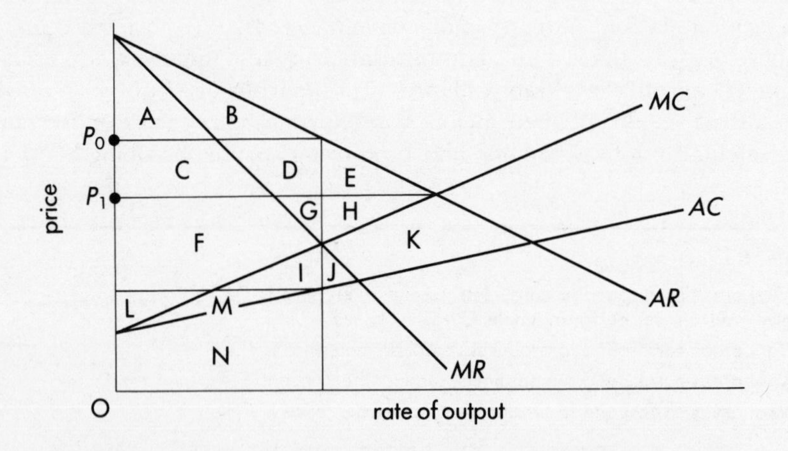

Figure 14.10 Consumers' and producer's surplus for SAQ 14.6

surplus is $P_P$ag and producer's surplus is $P_P$gd. The difference between the surpluses taken together in either situation is the area bgc: it represents the difference between the value in use of the output not produced by the monopolist ($X_M$bgX_P) and its cost of production ($X_M$cgX_P). From a 'social' point of view, the additional output is valued at more than its cost and so it should be produced (if one accepts consumers' value as the ultimate criterion of what ought to be produced). The monopolist will not produce it, however, since the loss of producer's surplus (hgc) is more than made up by the increase in profit by selling at a higher price ($P_M$bhP_P). Hence, consumers lose bgh *and* $P_M$bhP_P, and producers gain $P_M$bhP_P less hgc. There is a transfer of consumers' surplus of $P_M$bhP_P to producers. If you reckon that £1 is of equal worth whether received by producers or consumers, then the net efficiency loss is bgc. If, however, you take the view that £1 is more valuable in the hands of consumers than producers, then the net loss is larger than this, since the area $P_M$bhP_P is of less value to producers than to the consumers from whom it has been taken. On the other hand, if you make the opposite value judgement, that £1 is more valuable in the hands of producers, then the net loss is *less* than bgc, for the transfer of $P_M$bhP_P to producers will to some extent offset the loss of bgc.

Case Study 14.1 Consumers' Surplus Losses due to Monopoly in the USA 1924–8

Arnold Harberger (1954) has made calculations of the consumers' surplus losses from monopoly in the USA in the 1920s. He assumed (rather drastically!) that marginal costs were always constant and equal to average costs and that the elasticity of demand was constant. He then calculated the excess profit of each industry relative to the 'average' and was then able to derive in each case the consumers' surplus loss. Figure 14.11 shows the logic of this more plainly: the assumption about elasticity implies that the demand curve through point a is a

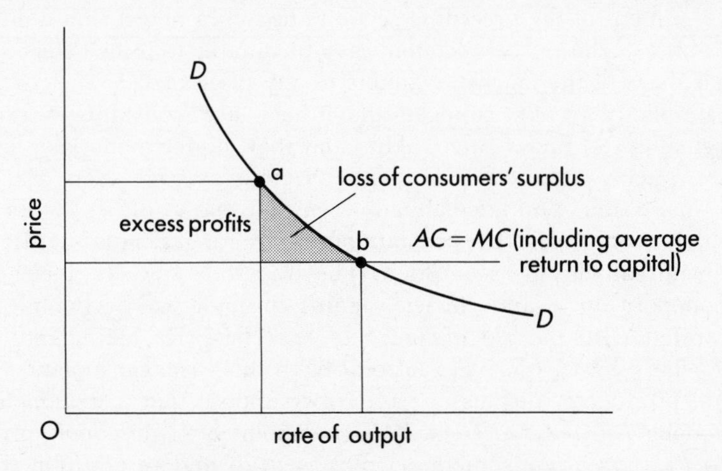

Figure 14.11 Harberger's geometry

rectangular hyperbola so that, given the estimate of AC with only a normal return on capital built into it, point b can be found. Then, assuming that ab is a straight line, the consumers' surplus can readily be computed.

Harberger's results for a selection of industries are given in table 14.2. His overall estimate of the losses of consumers' surplus due to $P > MC$ for any one year over this period was $59 million (in 1924 prices) or less than 0.1 per cent of US national income at that time. Harberger's pioneering study was rather crude, and later more sophisticated studies have tended to find that the efficiency losses from monopoly can be much larger (see, for example, Cowling and Mueller, 1978). See also case study 15.4.

Arnold Harberger (1954) 'Monopoly and resource allocation', *American Economic Review*, **64**(2) 77–87, table 1.
Keith Cowling and Dennis Mueller (1978) 'The social costs of monopoly', *Economic Journal*, **88**, 727–48.

Table 14.2 Consumers' surplus loss in USA 1924–8

Industry	*Loss ($ million)*
Bakery products	0.452
Cotton weaving	0.415
Weaving woollens	0.762
Newspapers	1.570
Petroleum refining	2.032
Castings and forgings	8.994
Electrical machinery	1.281
Railway equipment	1.148
Motor vehicles	3.878
Scientific instruments	1.163

Efficiency and Economies of Scale

To the argument of the preceding section one might object that a monopolist may be able to achieve scale economies not available to price takers in view of the small share of the market available to any price taker.

For simplicity's sake suppose that there are constant average costs (= marginal costs) under price taking and that, under monopoly, lower unit costs are quickly attained and, thereafter, that average costs are constant (= marginal costs). You have already seen that many studies have tended to suggest that average costs are constant over large ranges of output rates, so this is not so unrealistic an assumption. The trade-off between efficiency losses from monopoly *per se* and efficiency gains through scale economies can be demonstrated with the aid of figure 14.12. The price taking industry will produce where $\Sigma LRMC_P = P_P$, at point b. In this case, consumers' surplus is $P_P$ab and producers' surplus is zero. Now suppose that a monopolist could operate along $LRMC_M$. $MR = LRMC_M$ at point c, so monopoly price P_M is equal to P_P. Again, consumers' surplus is $P_P$ab and in addition there is a producer's surplus of $P_P$bcd. In this special case, output is the same (though note that efficiency would be even greater if the monopolist increased output

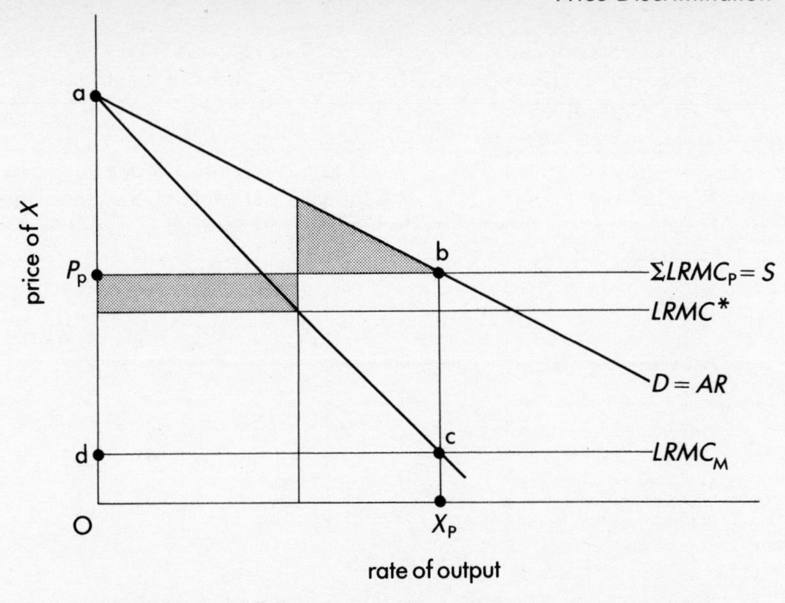

Figure 14.12 Possible efficiency gains from monopoly

beyond $X_M = X_P$). If lower $LRMC_M$s were attainable there would be net consumer gains from monopoly. However, *LRMC* does not need to be as low as this for there to be net gains to consumers and producers. If with economies of scale *LRMC* fell to *LRMC** in figure 14.12 the loss of consumers' surpluses (shaded triangle) would be just equal to the gain in producer's surplus (shaded rectangle). Any scale economies greater than this will cause the producer's gain to exceed consumers' losses. This defence of monopoly therefore hinges on the magnitude of the efficiency losses and the scale economies – something that can be determined only by empirical enquiry. It also ignores the redistribution of consumers' surplus to producers.

Price Discrimination

You have seen that, under both price taking and price searching, price depends in part on the costs of production. Price discrimination occurs when a good or service is sold at more than one price, unrelated to cost differences. It can take broadly two forms: charging different prices to an individual consumer, and charging different prices to different consumers.

You met the first type of price discrimination in chapter 8 (now is a good time to look back at that chapter). Suppose, for convenience, that all consumers have the same demand curves for a particular product and that the monopolist has a constant long run marginal cost curve. The situation for any one consumer can be represented by figure 14.13, where the demand curve *D* is the marginal valuation curve and *AV* is the average valuation or all-or-nothing demand curve. Initially, suppose the monopolist sells at P_0, determined by the

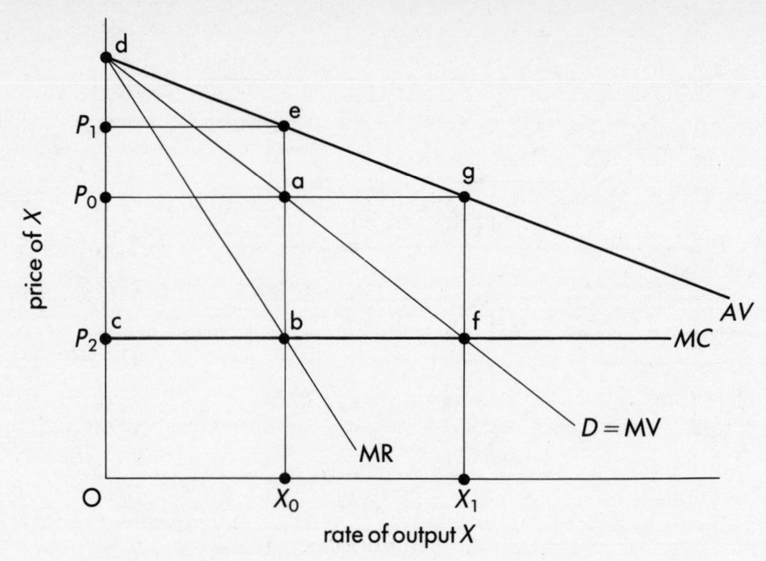

Figure 14.13 Charging more than one price to a consumer

maximum price attainable if X_0 is to be purchased, and X_0 is determined by $MC = MR$. In this case, the monopolist will get a profit of P_0abc, assuming no fixed costs (that is, $MC = AC$). The monopolist can plainly do better than this by adopting a price strategy exploiting the fact that, at P_0, consumers each have a consumer's surplus of P_0da, which is equal to the rectangle P_0P_1ea derived by using the all-or-nothing demand curve. Before exploring the possibilities, tackle SAQ 14.7.

SAQ 14.7

For the demand curve $X = 60 - 3P$, calculate:

(a) Consumer's surplus when price = 5.

(b) The maximum possible producer's surplus if marginal cost is constant at 10.

Consumer's surplus could be appropriated by the monopolist using any one of three strategies:

Strategy 1 Charge the consumer a price of Od (figure 14.13) for the first unit of consumption and then successively lower prices, as shown by the section da of the demand curve, until the marginal price is X_0a. In this case, profit will be P_0dabc = P_1ebc.

Strategy 2 Charge the consumer a lump sum per period for 'membership', or the right to buy X, for some amount of X less than X_0, and then permit as much consumption as is wanted by the consumer at a price of P_0. If the lump sum is set at P_0da = P_0P_1ea, then profit will again be P_0dabc = P_1ebc. Video cassette rental firms have used this technique. Telephones too are often charged as a rental plus price per call made.

Strategy 3 Charge the consumer a flat rate of P_1 for X_0 consumption in an all-or-nothing deal. Again profit will be P_1ebc = P_0dabc. Photocopiers are often rented on this basis: you get the machine for a low or nominal rate and are charged per copy made, which nicely measures your rate of use and correlates with your consumer's surplus.

Both strategies 1 and 2 involve a multiprice tariff to each consumer. The art for the monopolist is, of course, in making an estimate of the value of the consumer's surplus.

The monopolist, however, can do even better than any of these. At lower prices, consumer's surplus is higher. If, therefore, price is set at $P_2 = MC$ and X_1 output is produced the potential surplus to be exploited rises from P_0da to P_2df and potential profits rise from P_0dabc to P_2df – an increase measured by the area baf. Using the all-or-nothing demand curve, the potential profit rises from P_2P_1eb to P_2P_0gf. Thus the ideal strategy for the monopolist is to use any one of the three pricing strategies but with an output target of X_1 instead of X_0.

An interesting feature of this type of price discrimination is that it produces the same output and marginal valuation as is predicted under price taking and involves no efficiency loss. What is *does* imply is of course a net redistribution from consumers to producers: in the limit consumers will be only just on the point of buying X since their entire surplus of P_2df = P_2P_0gf will be transferred to producers. One's attitude to this may depend on whether one is a consumer of the product in question, whether one is an owner or shareholder in the firm selling X, whether one's pension funds are invested in it, or on more general ethical considerations about who should receive what share of the total potential gains from trade.

If now one were to relax the assumption that each consumer has the same demand curve, the monopolist using any of the strategies outlined would aim to charge different prices to each consumer according to the available consumer's surplus. This, of course, places tremendous informational demands on procedures. None the less, some have managed it, as is shown in case study 14.2.

Case Study 14.2 Full Line Forcing

Full line forcing, or *tie-in selling*, is a phenomenon that involves the 'forcing' on customers of a range of goods supplied by a seller without their having a choice of source of supply of products other than the one in which the seller has a monopoly. It has occurred quite frequently in the supply of machines and associated parts: photocopiers and paper, stapling machines and staples, can closing machines and tin cans, tabulating machines and cards. What is especially paradoxical – at least superficially – about full line forcing is that it pays the monopolist to sell the monopolized product at a price equal to marginal cost (that is, less than the monopoly price) and to sell the tied good, in which there may be no monopoly, at a price in excess of marginal cost.

In 1932 the United States filed an anti-trust suit against IBM and Remington Rand Inc., charging that they had unreasonably restrained and monopolized trade in

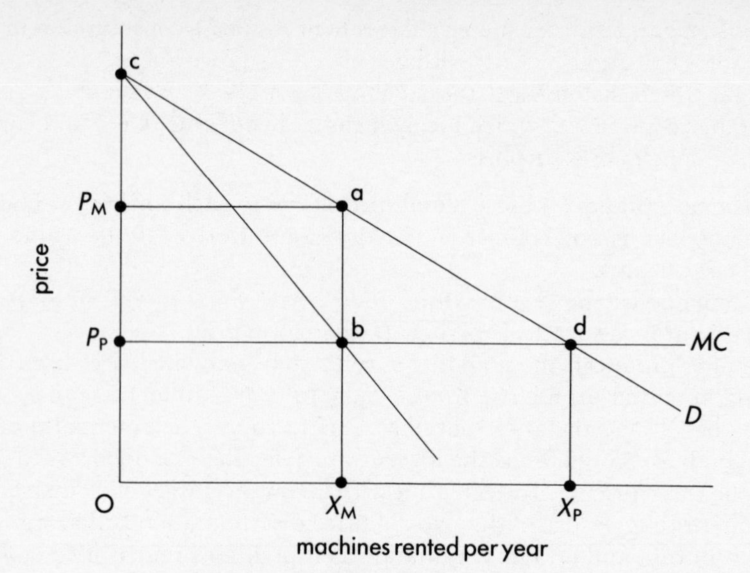

Figure 14.14 Full line forcing

tabulating machines (the precursors of modern computers) and tabulating cards by refusing to sell machines (leasing them only), fixing minimum rental prices for the machines and requiring customers to purchase their card requirements from the lessor. The agreements between the firms were cancelled prior to the trial and the provision involving the tie-in was judged illegal.

Suppose you were the monopolist. Why might such an arrangement have been to your advantage? Figure 14.14 has the appropriate analysis. If you were an unimaginative monopolist you might simply search for the monopoly price P_M and lease X_M machines per year. Your profit would be $P_M abP_P$ (assuming for convenience that $MC = AC =$ a constant). Since card production is not monopolized, these you would sell at a price equal to marginal cost and profits above a normal return would be zero (unless you were an unusually low cost producer).

But you can do better than this. Suppose you noted that the use of cards was a proxy for the value to a customer of having the machine: the larger the rate of use of cards, the larger the consumer's surplus on the machine itself. Why not tie in the leasing of the machine with the use of your cards (and *only* yours) and sell them above cost? The excess profit on the cards will correlate with the consumer's surplus $P_M ca$ and, if you can judge the mark-up right, will enable you to extract much of the consumer's surplus. Of course, you must punish those who use other people's cards. One way to do this would be to ban the *sale* of machines, leasing them exclusively, and then refusing to service any user's machine found to be jammed with 'inferior' cards.

But you can do even better still. Why be content with exploiting a consumer's surplus of only $P_M ca$ (plus your monopoly profit $P_M abP_P$)? Why not try to exploit the maximum consumer's surplus of $P_P cd$, which must be larger than the area $P_P cab$? Therefore charge the price taking price $P_P = MC$ and continue to sell cards above cost. You now, of course, have to enforce a minimum price on rentals. In this fashion you can approximately obtain the profits that a perfect price discriminator would get, but without having to know individual demand curves and without the costly business of charging different users different prices.

IBM has subsequently been ineptly charged with many monopolistic practices. Fisher, McGowan and Greenwood (1983) tell a fascinating story about the role of economists in anti-monopoly activity.

Franklin Fisher, John McGowan and Joel Greenwood (1983) *Fondled, Spindled, and Mutilated: Economic Analysis and US v. IBM*, Cambridge, Mass., MIT Press.

Not all price discrimination is designed to maximize profits. Electricity, telephone calls, railway journeys and airport landings and take-offs are charged according to the rate of demand at various times: popular times impose strain as the system reaches capacity and marginal costs rise rapidly. This is illustrated in figure 14.15. Here you can imagine demand centring around three basic levels: D_1, D_2 and D_3. In the case of telephone use, D_1 might correspond to demand between 18.00 and 08.00 hours and on weekends, D_2 might correspond to 08.00–09.00 and 12.00–18.00 Monday to Friday, and D_3 might correspond to 09.00–12.00 Monday to Friday. Rather than charge a single flat rate of P_2, which would cause a consumers' surplus loss of P_2abP_1 in periods of low demand and cause a massive excess demand (cd) and consequential loss of quality of service at peak times, prices are set at P_1, P_2 and P_3 such that P is kept as close to MC as possible. In principle, an infinity of different prices may be desirable. In practice, of course, to register, monitor

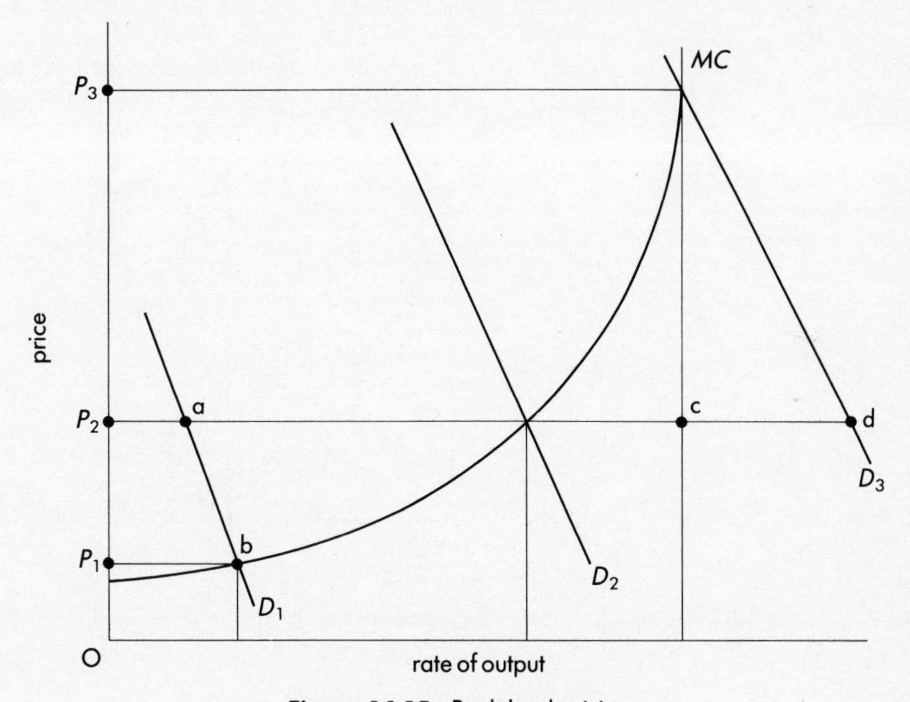

Figure 14.15 Peak load pricing

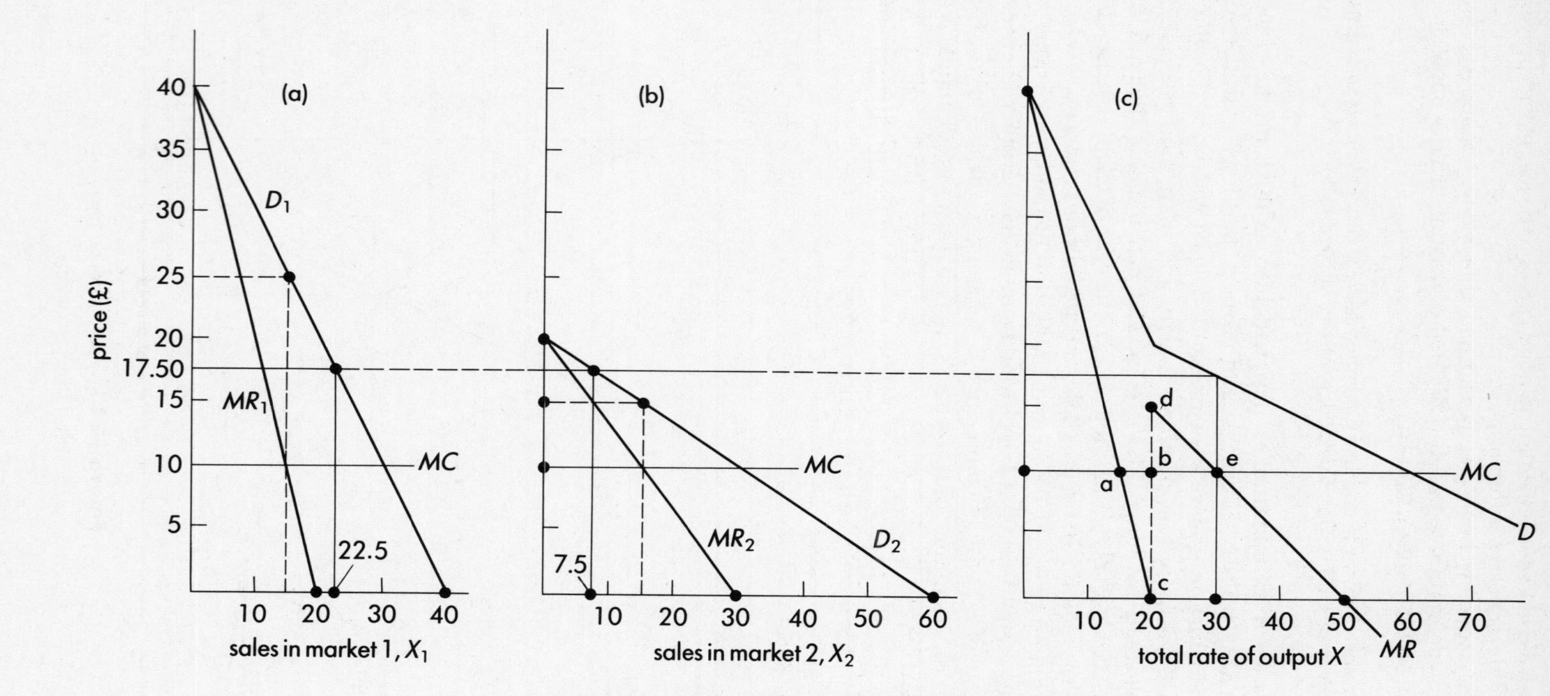

Figure 14.16 Price discrimination between markets

and bill customers under such a system is likely to be more costly than the value of the gains to be had therefrom.

Price Discrimination between Markets

A necessary condition for all price discrimination is that those who receive the good or service at a low price cannot resell to those having to pay a high price. In the case of personal services, like those of a doctor, the condition is readily met, and doctors in private practice have often charged lower prices to the poor (with high elasticities of demand) than to the rich (who have lower price elasticities). Such discrimination has often been justified on ethical grounds, possibly to detract attention from the increase in professional incomes that it makes possible. In other cases the seller (like IBM in case study 14.2) will have to use some other method.

Transport costs and other impediments to international trade may make the feasibility of charging different prices in different markets easier for the monopolist. Suppose, for example, that the demand curves in two markets are as shown in figure 14.16(a) and (b). The resultant market demand curve is shown in figure 14.16(c) and is, of course, the horizontal summation of D_1 and D_2. Assume that MC is constant. Suppose that the monopolist set a monopoly price by reference to the market demand and the associated MR curve. Note that this has a discontinuity at the output rate corresponding to the kink in the demand curve. To understand this you should now tackle SAQ 14.8.

SAQ 14.8

(a) The demand curves in figure 14.16 have the equations $X_1 = 40 - P$, $X_2 = 60 - 3P$. Given that $MR_1 = 40 - 2X_1$ and $MR_2 = 20 - (2/3)X_2$, you should be able to fill in the blanks in table 14.3.

(b) Why do barbers charge less for children's haircuts than adults', despite the fact that it is often harder to cut a wriggling child's hair than an adult's?

Table 14.3 Market demands for SAQ 14.8

	Price	*Demand in market 1*	*Demand in market 2*	*Total demand*	*MR in market 1*	*MR in market 2*	*Total MR*
40	—	—	—	—	—	—	—
35	—	—	—	—	—	—	—
30	—	—	—	—	—	—	—
25	—	—	—	—	—	—	—
20	—	—	—	—	—	—	—
15	—	—	—	—	—	—	—
10	—	—	—	—	—	—	—
5	—	—	—	—	—	—	—
0	—	—	—	—	—	—	—

In figure 14.16, by conventional monopoly pricing, price will be £17.50 and output 30; yielding the monopolist a revenue of £525 and a profit of £225.

At the price of £17.50, 22.5 units are sold in market 1 and 7.5 in market 2. By price discrimination the monopolist can do a great deal better than this. By setting $MC = MR$ in *each* market 15 would sell in market 1 at a price of £25 and 15 in market 2 at a price of £15. Total revenue is now £600 which, after deduction of costs of £300 leaves £300 profit. In this case – and whenever demand curves are linear – total output remains the same. By charging a higher price in the market with the less elastic demand at the conventional monopoly price and a lower price in the other, profits are increased.

Note that MC intersects MR at three points in figure 14.16(c). The first of these is a possible profit maximizing point for a monopolist charging a single price. So is the third. The 'intersection' at the discontinuity is not an equilibrium since a small increase in output will increase revenue by more than cost. Whether the first intersection is chosen rather than the third depends on whether the losses represented by triangle abc (costs in excess of revenue over output range ab) are larger or smaller than the gains represented by triangle bde (revenues in excess of costs over the output range be).

In international trade, such price discrimination is often termed **dumping** in the country with the lower import price.

What You Should Understand Now

The meaning of price searching and the price searcher's choice problem (output *and* price).
Difference between monopolistic competition and monopoly.
Relationship between elasticity of demand and marginal revenue.
Short and long run profit maximizing equilibria of monopolistic competitors and monopolists.
Differential implications of price taking and price searching: market research, advertising, excess capacity, product differentiation, absence of supply curve.
Barriers to entry and their effects.
Inefficiencies of monopoly and their measurement.
Price discrimination and the rationale of full line forcing.
Peak load pricing in nationalized industries.
Price discrimination between markets.

15

Oligopoly, Cartels and Price Stickiness

Oligopoly

The types of price searching conditions discussed so far have been two: *monopolistic competition*, in which high profits encourage long run entry into an industry, and *monopoly*, in which they do not. Although monopoly strictly implies only one seller of a good, in practice the monopoly model is often used by economists, even when there may be more than one firm in an industry, as long as they are price searchers and there are some effective barriers to entry.

For other purposes, however, it becomes important to pay specific attention to the case that lies between monopoly and monopolistic competition. The main reason for this is that when there are just a few firms in an industry there may be special firm-to-firm relationships that need investigation. For example, if there are just a few firms it may pay them to get together in order to avoid the monopolistic competition outcome and promote the monopoly outcome. Again, when there are just a few firms the price each can charge will depend upon not only the prices charged by others but how others are expected to respond to price changes.

The market condition that lies between monopolistic competition and monopoly is called **oligopoly**. It arises whenever there are few enough firms for them to have an interest in firm-to-firm relationships. This type of price searching behaviour is investigated in this chapter.

Cartels and Chiselling

A **cartel** is a group of independent firms which collude together so as to obtain the seller's advantages of monopoly. This is most likely to arise when the number of colluding producers is quite small – in other words, when there is oligopoly. Suppose that, without the cartel, each individual firm would act as a price taker. The industry long run equilibrium will then appear as shown in figure 15.1 with price and output rate set at P_P and X_P respectively. If the firms now collude to act as a monopoly, *joint* profits will be maximized at a price of P_C with output at X_C. An industry that wants to turn itself into a cartel must therefore find some way of sharing out the reduction in output ($X_P - X_C$) and of enforcing the agreed price. Sharing the market will usually be a matter of

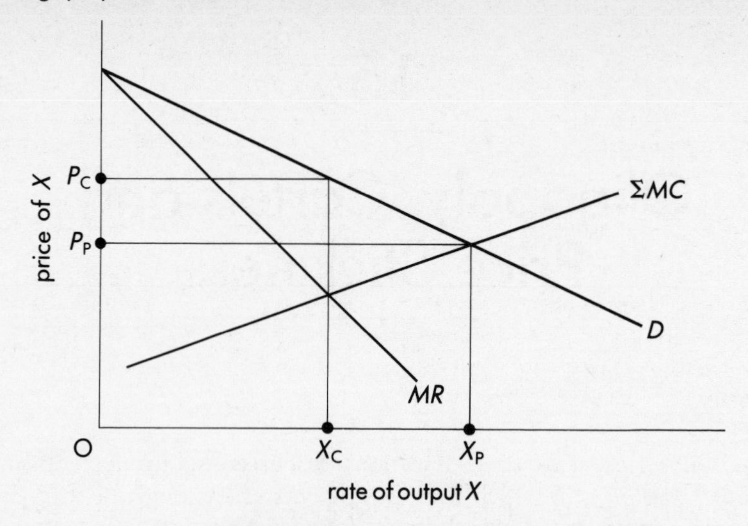

Figure 15.1 A cartel of firms

negotiating a formula upon which all can agree. For example, international airlines may agree that particular airlines will be assigned to particular routes, with each having a market share as close as possible to its pre-cartel market share.

Now consider the position of a representative firm in the cartel. As far as it is concerned it is a special kind of price taker: it must take the agreed price P_C. This will be higher than its marginal cost, as shown in figure 15.2, where X_C denotes the firm's agreed share of output. At that price the differential over marginal cost is ab, and if by fractionally reducing its price it can gain more trade (it plainly can, and a large amount too since the demand curve that it perceives is perfectly elastic) it will be able to increase its profits (by acb).

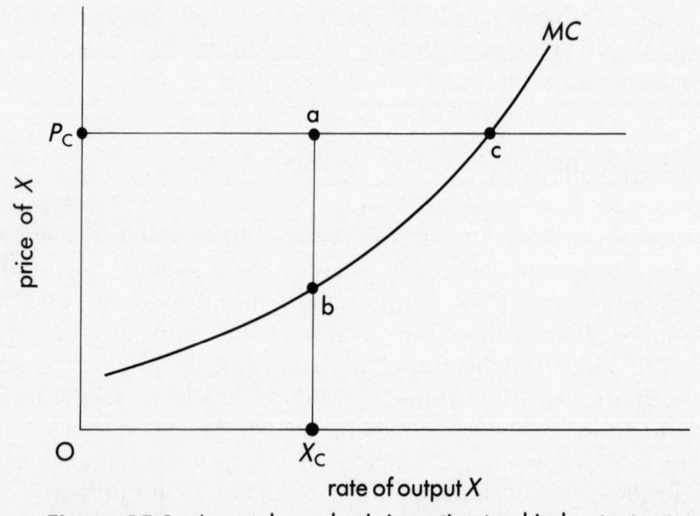

Figure 15.2 A cartel member's incentive to chisel output rate

Clearly *all* members face this incentive, and so there must be effective sanctions against **chiselling** the agreement away. From the firm's point of view the ideal would be governmentally enforced regulation of entry to the industry and of market shares and prices. If, however, the government takes a dim view of cartels, then the collusion and enforcement will have to be secret – and hence all the harder to secure. Typically, a cartel must regulate *all* aspects of the product that can be used to compete. For example, the International Air Transport Association (IATA), which regulates most international air routes, had to hold a plenary meeting in 1958 to define 'sandwich', and in 1966 many hours of debate preceded a decision to raise the charge made for in-flight film shows (which to the passengers was announced as 'owing to international regulations').

SAQ 15.1

The world demand curve facing oil producing countries for crude oil in barrels per year is estimated to be $X = 30 - 0.5P$. Let the (constant) marginal cost per barrel be 10.

(a) If oil producing countries act as price takers, what is consumers' surplus?

(b) If the oligopolistic oil producers form a cartel like the Organization of Petroleum Exporting Countries (OPEC), what is the maximum profit they can collectively earn by charging a normal monopoly price?

(c) Under the cartel, what is consumers' surplus?

Case Study 15.1 Resale Price Maintenance (RPM) and Oligopoly

Before the Resale Prices Act of 1964, manufacturers were free to set minimum prices to retailers. On the face of it that was puzzling behaviour. One would expect profit maximizing producers to sell their goods ex-factory at the profit maximizing price and then to be keen that wholesalers and retailers sell as many of the goods as possible – at the lowest price possible. Yet the practice was to stipulate a price to be neither exceeded nor cut, or to set a minimum price. (Some firms set a maximum price, a practice with which this discussion is not concerned.)

Clearly a degree of monopoly is necessary if a firm is to enforce RPM on retailers (for simplicity, ignore wholesaling and other intermediate distributors). Table 15.1 shows that the practice of RPM and the degree of monopoly are indeed related.

Table 15.1 RPM in Britain in 1938

Concentration (% employment in the three largest firms of the total employed in the production of the commodity)	*Percentage of commodities price maintained*	
	Insignificant or non-existent	*Significant (at least half of the commodity was price maintained)*
0–10	100.0	0.0
10–20	82.0	18.0
20–30	30.0	70.0
30–40	0.0	100.0
40–50	17.0	83.0
50–60	18.0	82.0
60–70	12.0	88.0
70–80	0.0	100.0
80–90	50.0	50.0
90–100	0.0	100.0

Source: Telser (1960)

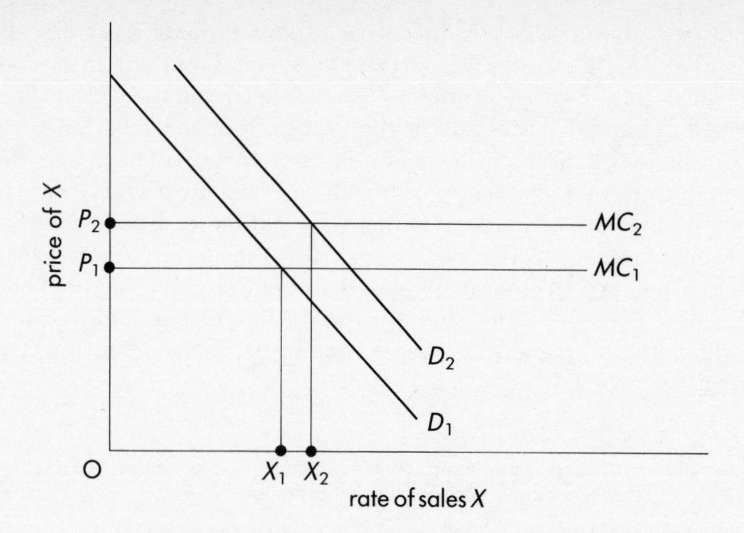

Figure 15.3 Effect of sales services on demand

There seem to be two basic reasons why it would pay a manufacturer to enforce RPM. The first relates to the effect that the provision of special services may have on demand, for example holding a large stock of books for customers to browse through (which is very costly) or providing personal demonstrations of high technology consumer durables (which is costly in shop staff time). Figure 15.3 shows a situation in which initially demand is D_1 and the shops can sell units of a good at a constant marginal cost MC_1 (wholesale price of the good plus selling costs). Sales are X_1. By supplying customer services, demand is shifted to D_2 and, allowing for the extra selling cost $(P_2 - P_1)$, it pays retailers to expand sales to X_2. Assume that retailers (unlike the manufacturer) operate in a price taking world. In this case the manufacturer benefits from the higher price P_2, because sales rise. But why should the manufacturer want to *enforce* the price P_2 via RPM? The short answer is to prevent shoppers from **free riding** (see chapter 19): that is, from taking the services at a shop offering them but then going round the corner to buy the product at P_1 from a (cheaper) retailer who does not. In that eventuality, the retailer providing services will lose much custom (possibly all of it), so that no one will provide such services and demand remains at D_1. This is an example of RPM that may benefit manufacturer, retailer and customer. In Britain, book prices are exempt from the general ban on RPM for this type of reason. In the case of other goods, it has generally been felt that sufficient alternative sources of shopper information would arise to fill the information gap – as has indeed been the case since the early 1960s.

A less attractive feature of RPM is that it can be a means of enforcing the pricing rules of a cartel of oligopolists. It will, of course, pay manufacturers to offer secret concessions to retailers and customers. To overcome this, RPM was often coupled with **exclusive dealing**. In this, each retailer sold only one brand of iron, television, radio etc., thus reducing the incentive for a manufacturer to cheat by offering any one retailer a specially favourable deal on one product relative to other lines carried by the retailer. For maximum effectiveness a further rule will tend to be observed requiring that a retailer may not drop one exclusive brand in favour of another. It was this aspect of RPM and its other attendant restrictions on retailers that accounted for its eventual illegality in Britain (with loopholes for exceptions who could prove their case).

Philip Andrews and Frank Friday (1960) *Fair Trade: Resale Price Maintenance Re-examined*, London, Macmillan.
Lester Telser (1960) 'Why should manufacturers want fair trade?' *Journal of Law and Economics*, **3**, 86–105, table 1.

Price and Output Depend on Others' Pricing and Output Decisions

Under oligopolistic conditions, as you have seen, producers have an incentive both to collude with other producers and, subsequently, to chisel the agreement to their own individual advantage. If oligopolists do not collude, they have the general problem that their decisions individually may make their competitors react in particular ways, which then destroys the assumptions originally made about pricing and output.

Take an extreme case of two competing firms producing an identical product. This special case of oligopoly is called **duopoly**. Suppose each firm has half the market and sets price such that $MC = MR$, earning profits above cost. Now each knows that by cutting its price a bit it could capture the entire market and put the other out of business. So each has an incentive to cut price. On the other hand, if *both* behave in such a fashion they will engage in a price war, the upshot of which can only be that each will end up in the price taker's position and, in the long run, earn no profits over cost.

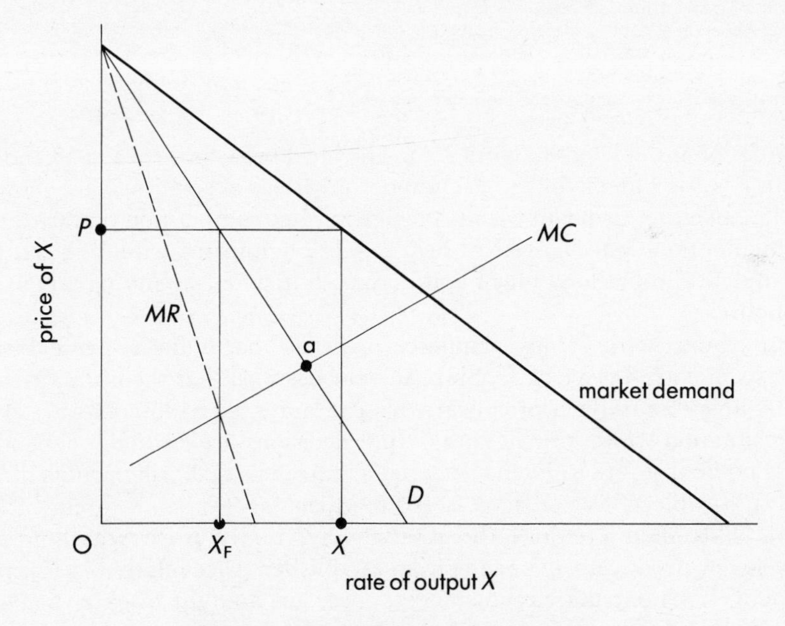

Figure 15.4 The duopolists' dilemma

In figure 15.4 the market demand is given by the boldly drawn demand curve. The demand curve for equal shares is given by D. Assuming cost curves to be the same in each firm, each will produce where $MC = MR$, setting a price P and producing X_F. Total output is $2X_F = X$. Profits of the two taken together are at a maximum (ignoring the possibility of price discrimination). A price war will serve only to bring each to point a. Both will lose profits. Therefore they also have a powerful incentive *not* to price cut. If the incentive not to cut dominates, then the situation for these two non-colluding firms turns out to be one in which they both make cartel-like profits but there is no conspiracy to restrain trade. Thus independent action can produce similar results to collusive action.

Take a rather more realistic case in which two firms share a market for the identical product each makes but in which each has a different cost structure. Each will therefore choose a different price; however, if a single price must exist in the market without them competing most of their profits away, they have to come to terms. Suppose that the market demand is given by $X = 100 - P$ and that demand confronting each firm is half of this: $X_F = 50 - 0.5P$. Suppose also that firm 1 has constant marginal (= average) costs of 10 and firm 2 has constant marginal (= average) costs of 30. Before proceeding further, tackle SAQ 15.2.

SAQ 15.2

With the information just given in the text, and assuming no fixed costs, calculate:

(a) Firm 1's preferred price, output and profit
(b) Firm 2's preferred price, output and profit
(c) Firm 1's profit if firm 2's price is charged
(d) Firm 2's profit if firm 1's price is charged
(e) Firm 1's profit if price is set at firm 2's marginal cost
(f) Firm 1's profit if it monopolizes the entire market.

The situation is depicted in figure 15.5. The ideal price for firm 1 is 55 and that for firm 2 is 65. The payoffs to each under a variety of strategies are shown in table 15.2. Neither firm will wish to engage in price competition that causes the extinction of the higher cost firm (firm 2): although firm 1 would benefit from the complete elimination of firm 2, it may wish to avoid becoming an outright monopolist.

Short of this, firm 2 may acquiesce in firm 1 becoming a **price leader**, setting its preferred price of 55. Since the low cost firm has the ultimate threat of being able to survive a price war, this is a quite likely outcome.

In a situation where pricing and output decisions are mutually dependent, there is no final solution. Even the cartel arrangement (sharing profits of 2025 equally) is subject, as you have seen, to chiselling (and the threat of legal action). This then provides the reason why, under price searching with relatively few producers, departing from established price relativities is fraught with danger. Under the circumstances, a certain amount of *price stickiness* is only to be expected.

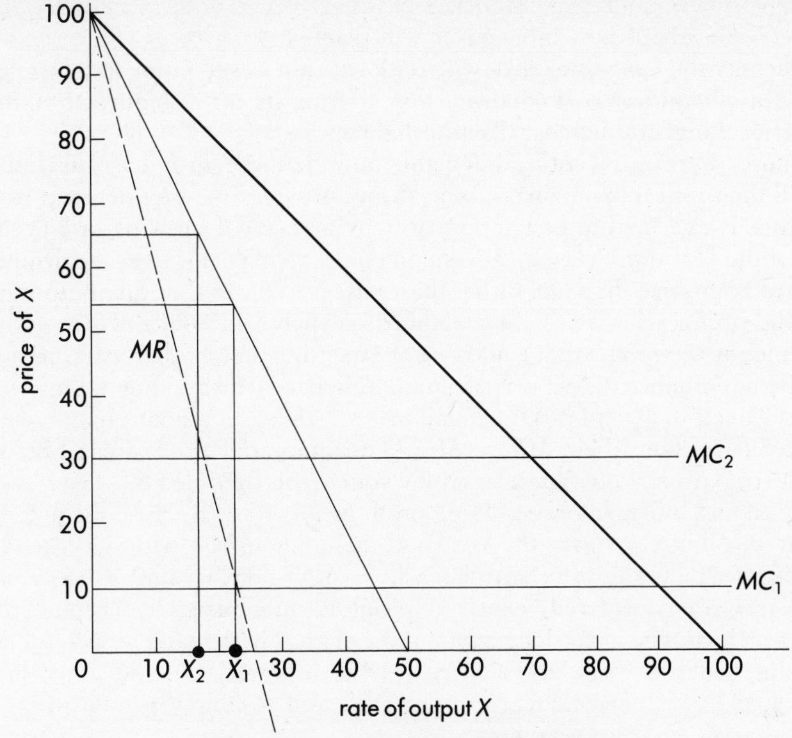

Figure 15.5 Duopolists' conflict over price

Table 15.2 Profits under alternative scenarios

	Firm 1's profits	*Firm 2's profits*	*Joint profits*
Each charges its own preferred price	1012.50	612.50	1625.00
Firm 1's price charged	1012.50	562.50	1575.00
Firm 2's price charged	962.50	612.50	1575.00
Price set at firm 2's *MC*	700.00	0.00	700.00
Firm 1 monopolizes industry	2025.00	0.00	2025.00

Disequilibrium and Sticky Prices

The discussion of disequilibrium in chapter 13 is particularly applicable to price searchers. Each producer has to decide not only whether changing cost or demand situations are permanent or temporary and so adjust output appropriately, but also whether to search out a new price. This is itself a costly process, tying up the most expensive of a company's managers in considerable meetings etc., involving market research and the like. There is also, once a price searcher thinks it has selected the profit maximizing price, the danger of reacting to new circumstances by setting a price worse than the first. There is also the cost of announcing new prices via advertising and so on. Finally, there is uncertainty about how other firms will react.

Consequently, an oligopolist will typically not react immediately to any change in demand or cost conditions by altering its price. Figure 15.6 shows the sort of thing that is most likely to happen.

Suppose that D_0 is current demand and that the firm has successfully selected the profit maximizing output X_0 and price P_0. Now let demand rise to D_1. If this is expected to be temporary – say a seasonal upswing or a cyclical boom of the sort that every businessman comes to expect – then the firm may decide to keep price the same rather than raise it to P_1. In that case output rises to X_1 and profits will rise by the area abcd – which is nice for the firm, though not as nice as the profits that could be got by setting $MR_1 = MC$. Alternatively, when demand falls to D_2, if price is maintained at P_0 rather than falling to P_2, output will fall to X_2 and profit will fall by eadf – a larger amount than it would fall if price were set where $MR_2 = MC$. (The alternative profit areas, obtained by adjusting price, you can draw in for yourself in figure 15.6).

Why should a firm choose to forgo profit in this way? Because the notion of cost in the figure *excludes* the costs of changing prices with its attendant hazards, of which any price searcher will want to take account. Clearly, if *all* the costs were considered, expected profit is maximized by keeping price constant. Of course, in the longer run, if the change in demand *persists*, the firm will adjust in the way suggested by earlier analysis. On the other hand, oligopolists have a specific fear of price wars and so may maintain prices for longer than other price searchers.

This theory has two main implications for oligopolistic industries. First, as demand changes, output rates will be adjusted faster than prices in the short run. Second, in the short term, as long as costs do not vary, price can be

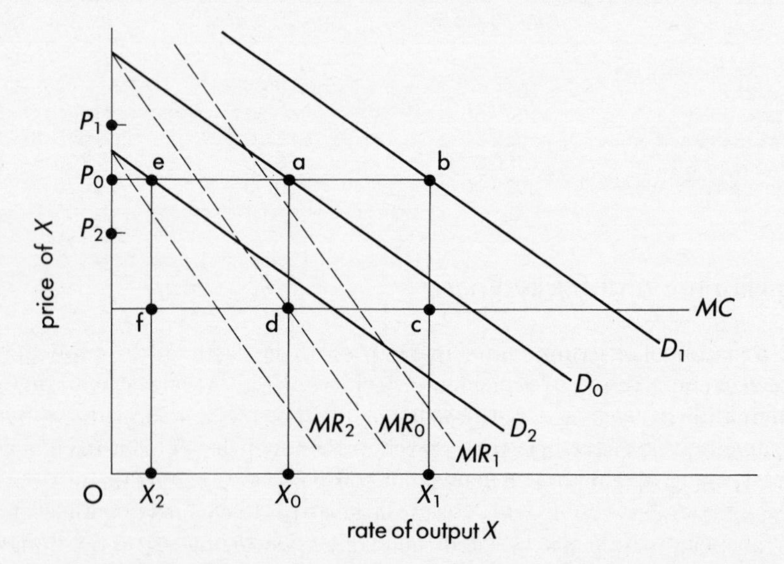

Figure 15.6 Sticky price under price searching and changing demand

interpreted as average cost plus a constant mark-up (of da in figure 15.6). Since the empirical evidence already surveyed suggests that cost curves are approximately flat up to the capacity of existing plant, the analysis of figure 15.6 suggests that businessmen may commonly use a mark-up rule of thumb in setting their prices in the short term, only changing the mark-up to make it equal to the difference between profit maximizing price and marginal cost when the change is perceived as long lasting.

Case study 15.2 reviews some evidence on these implications. The further implications of price stickiness for unemployment and macroeconomic policy are discussed in chapter 28.

Case Study 15.2 The Pricing of Manufactures

Barback (1964) has studied the pricing policies of manufacturing firms in lace finishing, raincoats, small wares and toys, nylon hosiery, glove fabrics, lace curtains and furnishings, and electrical equipment. Prices were generally set according to a conventional view about 'normal' prices for such goods or by adding on a margin to unit costs to produce a 'satisfactory' rate of profit.

In response to changes in costs and demand when each moved in the same direction, prices were generally adjusted so as to maintain the margin. If only one factor changed (cost or demand) output was very responsive to demand but price was not, so that profits moved along with output. There was resistance to cutting price if demand fell in the short term, partly to avoid alienating customers who held stocks bought at higher prices and partly because of alienating customers subsequently by raising price when demand picked up. There was resistance to raising prices when demand rose unless the rise in demand was both substantial and expected to be long lasting.

In the awkward situation when rising costs coincided with falling demand, again there was reluctance to cut price because of scepticism about its effect on demand. They chose instead a combination of lower output rates and putting a higher proportion of output into stocks. Of course, persistently falling demand means that prices must eventually give but, even in this very difficult situation for a firm, prices remained remarkably sticky and firms held on to customary margins for as long as possible. In the end they preferred to reduce margins and maintain prices rather than to reduce prices and keep margins, though lower, more closely at 'conventional' levels.

R. H. Barback (1964) *The Pricing of Manufactures*, London, Macmillan.

There is widespread disagreement among economists as to whether oligopolists' prices are less variable over the business cycle than price takers'. One reason for this disagreement is that the facts are extremely hard to assess empirically. One problem is that the easiest source of price information (price lists published by manufacturers) does not always correspond to the prices at which transactions actually take place (owing to discounts, trade-ins and the like). Another problem is that indexes of asset or employment concentration relate to firms in very broad product classes, whereas, as you have seen earlier, most large firms sell many products in many different product markets and

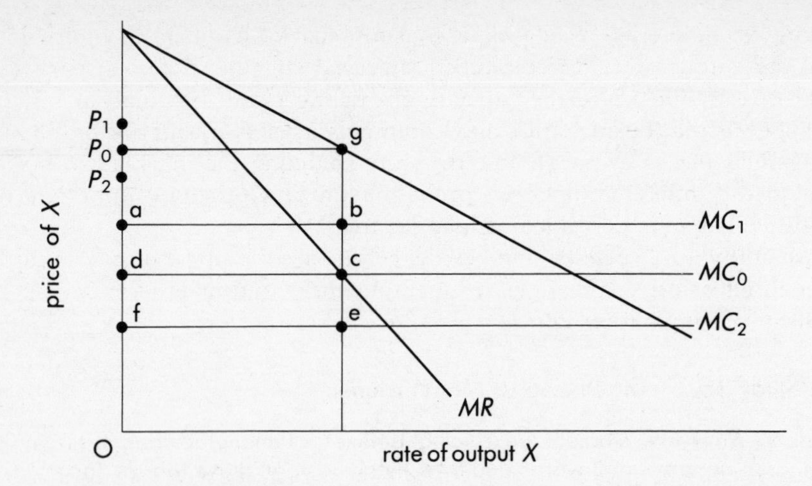

Figure 15.7 Sticky price under price searching and changing costs

their shares in particular markets are hard to identify. Another reason is that many economists take an ideological view: some are so drawn to the political attractions of competitive capitalism that their research is – consciously or (one hopes) subconsciously – influenced by the results they prefer to see, whereas for others the reverse is the case.

Prices may not be sticky only in their reaction to demand changes. They may also be sticky in response to changes in costs. Figure 15.7 shows the analysis for changes in costs (due, say, to changes in the prices of inputs). Instead of changing price from P_0 to P_1 or P_2 when MC shifts to MC_1 or MC_2, the firm may prefer to 'wait and see', holding price constant and taking a larger loss in profit of abcd or a smaller gain of dcef than the simple theory suggests is possible. In practice, however, costs are often determined by long run contracts with labour and other suppliers, and firms are often able to identify permanent changes in input prices rather quickly. This suggests that the response of prices to cost changes is likely to be faster than their response to demand changes and, indeed, the evidence does seem to support this view. Note also that, in figure 15.7, if the firm chooses to maintain its mark-up (cg) as costs change, price and output will vary by *more* than is suggested by previous theory, as well as yielding lower profits. Thus holding on to constant mark-ups as costs change manages to get the worst of all possible worlds for the firm – lower profits *and* price variability with its attendant costs and hazards.

Oligopolist's Kinked Demand Curve

The shape of the demand curve imagined by the decision maker in an oligopolistic firm depends upon expectations about other oligopolists' reactions to price changes. If an oligopolist believes that a price rise is not likely to be matched by rivals, the demand curve above the current price will be expected to be elastic. If the oligopolist also believes that a price reduction will be quickly followed by rivals, the demand curve below the current price will be expected to be inelastic. Many economists believe that these are the subjective expectations of a typical oligopolist. If so, the typical expected demand curve will be as in figure 15.8, where P_0 is the current price. As you can see, the demand curve abc is *kinked* at the prevailing price.

The marginal revenue curve for such a firm can be found by drawing an MR for each section of the demand curve. The appropriate MR for the section ab (produced) is ae (produced), and that for bc (produced to f) is fg (produced). The resultant MR curve for the kinked demand curve abc is aegh with, as you can see, a discontinuity at the rate of output corresponding to the kink. A profit maximum requires $MC = MR$. This occurs, with $MC = MC_0$, at output rate X_0 and price P_0. But note that if $MC = MC_1$, the *same* profit maximizing price and output are indicated. Indeed, cost could vary between point e and X_0 without affecting price or output. Hence an oligopolist who believes that the firm confronts a kinked demand curve is likely to vary price *and* output little as costs vary.

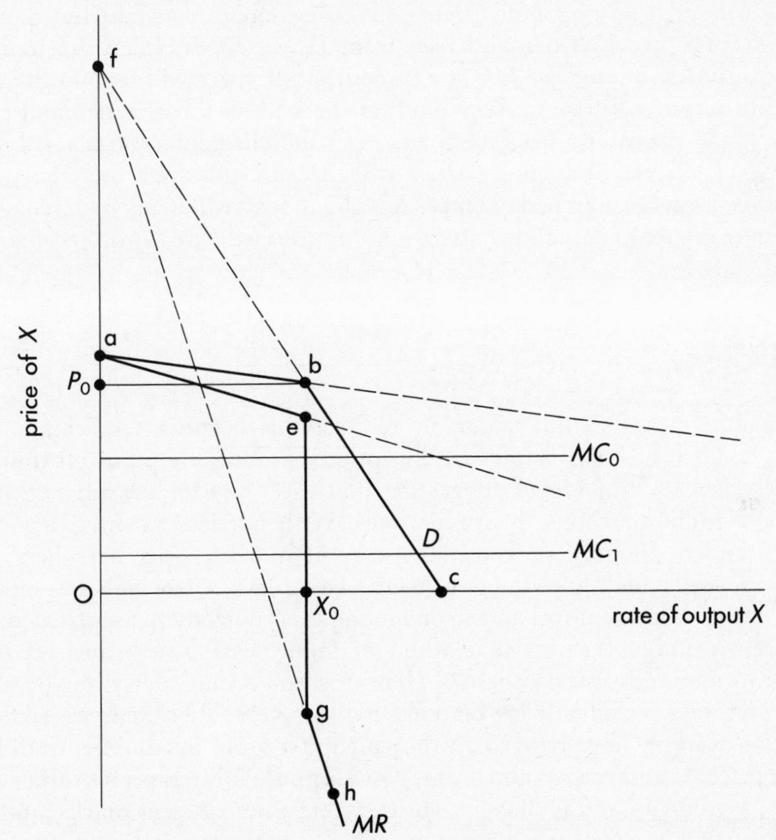

Figure 15.8 Kinked demand and price stickiness as costs change

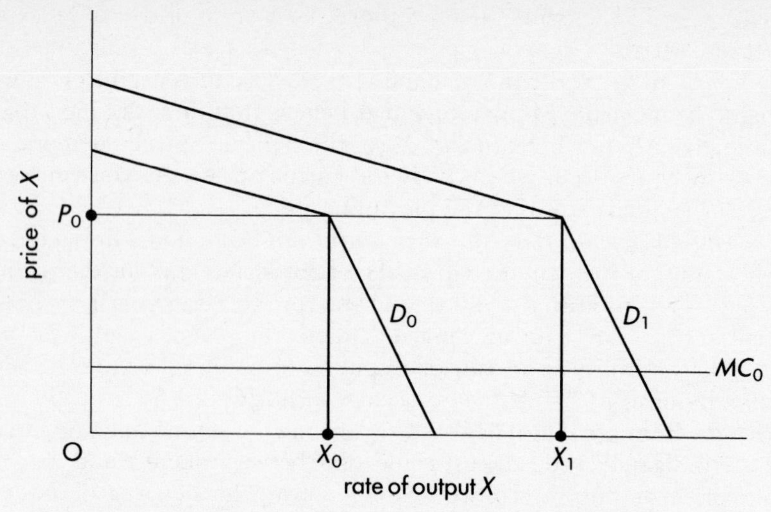

Figure 15.9 Kinked demand and price stickiness as demand changes

How will such an oligopolist behave if costs remain constant but demand changes? In figure 15.9 demand rises from D_0 to D_1. Provided that the *MC* curve continues to intersect *MR* at a discontinuity, price will remain the same at P_0 but output will rise to X_1. Note that the kink in the new demand curve occurs at the prevailing price because, even though demand has risen, each oligopolist believes that price rises will be not followed but that price reductions will be matched. Hence, an oligopolist will tend to have sticky prices in response to demand changes – but output will rise (or fall) as demand rises (or falls).

X-inefficiency

You have seen earlier that monopoly reduces the incentive for firms to seek profits. So far it has been supposed that price searchers are profit maximisers. Yet there is a lot of evidence suggesting that they may be less diligent in the pursuit of profit than this theory assumes. With barriers to entry, few competitors and a possibly slow reacting capital market, price searchers may include a 'quiet life', growth, patronage of the arts, a 'socially responsible' image, bureaucratic control and so on among their objectives, as well as profit.

There are many theories that admit of these possibilities (theories to be studied in more advanced courses). Here it is noted that such firms need not operate on their technically lowest marginal (or average) cost curves. In figure 15.10, for example, is portrayed a firm which, if a profit maximizer, would sell X_1 at a price P_1 and earn P_1abc profit. Now suppose it hired pretty rather than efficient secretaries and inefficient whites rather than efficient blacks, and ran unnecessarily large staffs with generous expense accounts – all of which add to managers' on-the-job sources of utility. The resultant observed *MC* curve will

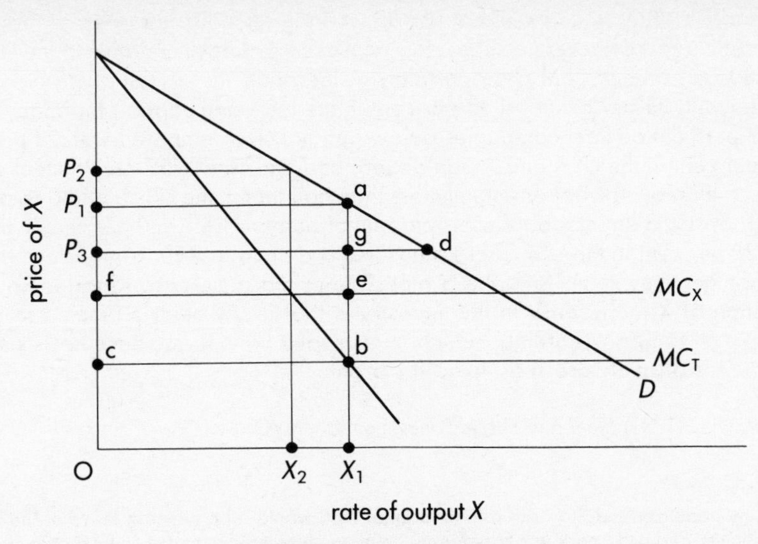

Figure 15.10 X-efficiency

be higher owing to this **X-inefficiency** – say MC_X rather than MC_T, the 'true' marginal cost curve. Suppose price is set according to a conventional mark-up on cost of ae. Price remains the same, but profit falls to P_1aef; the management receives its on-the-job utility at an opportunity cost to owners of febc forgone profit. Or if management sought to maximize profit *given* its inflated cost, output would fall to X_2 and the monopoly price would be yet higher at P_2. Or, again, management may gain utility by allowing an excess demand, enabling it to select the customers it felt best disposed towards. In such a case a mark-up of, say, bg on true costs, or eg on X-inefficient costs, would create an excess demand of gd at price P_3 and afford management the discretion it seeks.

Monitoring the efficiency of management's decisions is an important and difficult task for owners. It seems highly likely that there is some X-inefficiency in all businesses (some think this to be particularly true of publicly owned businesses), but perhaps most particularly under circumstances where the owners are also the management and hence have every reason (subject to competition in the product market) to pursue utility rather than maximizing profits.

SAQ 15.3

(a) Is public ownership preferable to private?
(b) Would you expect innovation to be greater under price taking or price searching?

Case Study 15.3 X-inefficiency in the Steel Industry

Charles Rowley (1971) has compared the performance of the British steel industry with the steel industries of other countries. Allegations of X-inefficiency in this industry have been made both by those who believe its nationalization in whole or part to be a promising solution and by those who think that greater privatization is desirable. The evidence does seem to suggest that the British industry does not operate along the lowest cost curves. Evidence includes: long run excess capacity relative to the US and Japan (80 per cent of capacity operating at less than the lowest cost output rate compared with 34 per cent and 38 per cent in the USA and Japan); too many small firms (53 per cent of steel companies below optimal size compared with 23 per cent and 24 per cent in the USA and Japan); overmanning (from 1955–66 UK steel output per person employed was consistently less than half that in the USA); and overpaying labour (from 1955 direct labour costs per unit of output rose by 60 per cent in the UK and by 36 per cent in the US). These measures are of course each imperfect, though taken together they seem to make a plausible prima facie case. Charles Rowley's explanation of X-inefficiency in this industry is that it has been subjected to heavy regulation of company earnings which encourages firms to increase costs as non-profit sources of utility are substituted for profit.

Charles Rowley (1971) *Steel and Public Policy*, London, McGraw-Hill.

SAQ 15.4

(a) In a monopolized industry with rising marginal cost, would it be better in terms of the sum of consumers' and producer's surpluses for the government to require that price be set equal to long run average cost? (Assume profit maximizing otherwise.)

(b) In a monopolized industry with falling average cost, compare the sum of consumers' and producer's surpluses under profit maximizing monopoly pricing, $P = AC$ and $P = MC$.

Case Study 15.4 Welfare Losses of Oligopoly

Under oligopoly – as indeed under monopoly – there is always the threat of the entry of new firms in response to higher than normal profits. One effect of this is that firms have an incentive to select a price lower than the ideal price that a cartel would choose. This price is called a **limit price**, and is set so as to balance the advantages of higher than usual profits against the risk of their long run erosion by entry of new firms. This implies that prices will be lower than short term profit considerations would imply, and also that these prices will be stickier in response to demand and cost changes for individual firms, since other factors like the probability of entry are also taken into account in the pricing decision.

Robert Masson and Joseph Shaanon (1984) have estimated firstly the welfare losses (triangles akin to that in figure 14.11) assuming linear demand curves, for oligopolistic industries at the actual limit prices charged, and secondly the potential welfare losses if monopoly (or cartel) prices were to be charged.

Table 15.3 shows some of their results. As you can see, the welfare losses with limit pricing are on average 2.9 per cent of the value of output, whereas they would have been 11.6 per cent under monopoly. Thus the 'social value', as the authors call it, of a combination of actual competition and potential competition (measured by the extent to which the limit price is less than the monopoly price) is $11.6 - 2.9 = 8.7$ per cent. To this should really be added any 'wasteful' advertising due to oligopoly, but even without this, the 2.9 per cent loss through limit pricing is much higher than Harberger's estimate described in case study 14.1. It is perhaps encouraging, however, that 2.9 per cent is closer to the zero per cent of price taking competition than the 11.6 per cent of pure monopoly.

Robert Masson and Joseph Shaanon (1984) 'Social costs of oligopoly', *Economic Journal*, **94**, (375), 520–35, table 3.

Table 15.3 Consumers' surplus losses of oligopoly (US industries 1950–66)

Industry	*Consumers' surplus loss with limit pricing (actual prices) as % value of output*	*Consumers' surplus loss at potential monopoly prices as % value of output*
Canned fruit	1.23	16.29
Bread	1.72	12.05
Biscuits	6.06	16.00
Chewing gum	10.03	13.67
Beer	0.91	15.14
Bottled soft drinks	0.60	17.62
Pharmaceuticals	7.66	19.07
Soap and detergents	1.62	17.97
Perfumes	3.13	29.53
Footwear	1.04	18.65
Flat glass	2.30	13.62
Cement	5.63	17.36
Metal cans	1.48	13.67
Radios and TVs	0.57	20.65
Motor cars	3.42	7.74
Weighted average of these and other industries	2.90	11.60

Oligopoly and Sticky Prices

From the analysis of this chapter you may conclude that there will tend to be sticky prices under oligopoly in response to both demand and cost changes if:

1. There is the risk that 'rocking the boat' may induce a price war.
2. There is a formal or informal cartel arrangement with negotiated prices or price leadership.
3. There is a practice of mark-up pricing (demand changes only).
4. There is uncertainty about the permanence of the demand or cost changes.
5. There is lack of pressure for cost-effectiveness and profit maximization (for example, X-inefficiency).
6. There is perceived to be a kinked demand curve.
7. There is limit pricing.

What You Should Understand Now

The meaning of oligopoly and duopoly.
Some reasons why cartels may be formed and some difficulties they have in holding together.
Economics of resale price maintenance (RPM).
Interdependencies between oligopolistic firms.
Reasons why firms may delay price responses to changes in demand and cost conditions.
Rationale of price leadership.
Some evidence on mark-up pricing by rule of thumb and the stickiness of prices.
Some evidence on the welfare losses of oligopoly under limit pricing.
Factors that make for price stickiness under oligopoly.

16

Interest and Capital

So far the choices considered have all related to rates of consumption, purchase, use, production and so on, without taking any account of the fact that the *dating* of each of these can also be an important decision variable. It may be necessary, for example, to decide whether to consume now or later or to invest or save now in anticipation of future gains, or to choose between two investment options one of which promises small but early profits and the other larger but later ones.

Intertemporal choices, as choices over different periods are termed in economics, can be analysed in much the same way as choices concerning a single period. Figure 16.1 embodies the essential analysis. The horizontal axis measures consumption or income this year (rate per year) and the vertical axis

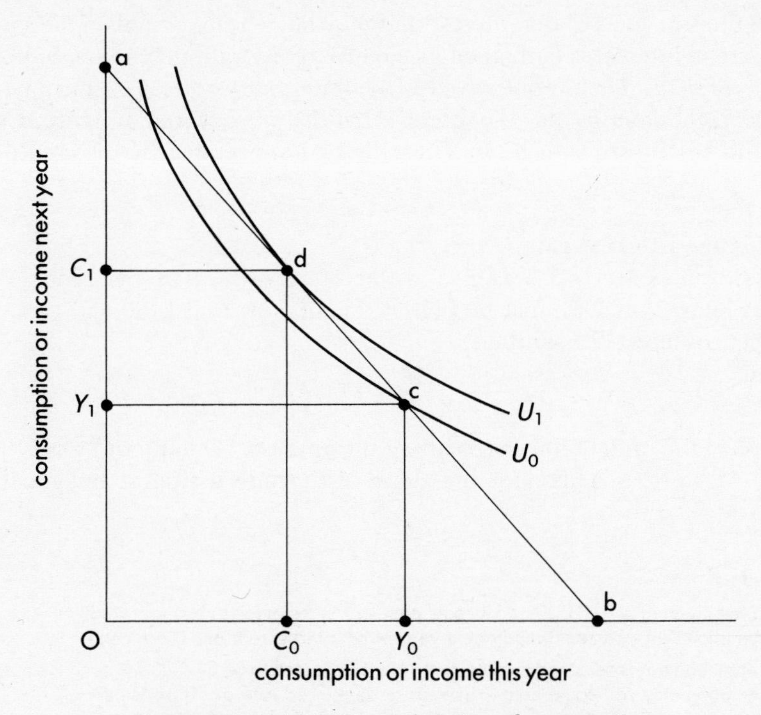

Figure 16.1 Intertemporal choice of consumption

measures consumption or income next year. The budget line ab shows the maximum rates of consumption that are possible for an individual in a two period world. Quantity Ob could be consumed in period 0, in which case none would be consumed in period 1; or OC_0 could be consumed in period 0, in which case OC_1 could be consumed in period 1, again nothing could be consumed in period 0, in which case Oa can be consumed in period 1.

Suppose the individual in figure 16.1 expected income in period 0 to be OY_0 and income in period 1 to be OY_1. This defines point c on the budget line, a point termed the *endowment position.* The individual could also expect to consume these amounts, neither saving nor borrowing between the two periods. However, it is rather unlikely that the expected flows of income will exactly correspond to a person's preferred flows of consumption and, indeed, they generally do not, as evidenced by the fact that individuals borrow and lend, save and invest.

Putting an intertemporal indifference map into the figure (now is good time to revise the indifference curve analysis of chapter 7) you will find that the highest indifference curve attainable is that labelled U_1, which is tangential to ab at point d. Point d is therefore the preferred *consumption* point, in contrast to the endowment point c (through which a *lower* indifference curve U_0 must necessarily pass). What does the figure say for the individual there depicted? In period 0 income is OY_0 but only OC_0 will be consumed. Hence $Y_0 - C_0$ will be saved (income less consumption). In period 1 income will be OY_1 but consumption will be OC_1. $C_1 - Y_1$ represents the forgone consumption of period 0 plus, of course, any interest that may have been earned on the savings.

The rate of interest is embodied in the intertemporal budget line. Suppose it were 10 per cent. Then if one saved £100 in period 0 one could consume £110 in period 1: the savings plus the interest. Let the present sum or **present value** be PV and the future sum be F. Then the two are related by the equation:

$$PV(1 + i) = F$$

where i is the **interest rate**.

So, if Ob in figure 16.1 is £100 and the interest rate is 10 per cent (or 0.1), then you know that Oa must be £110 – the amount that £100 will grow to at 10 per cent interest. In symbols,

$$\text{Ob}\ (1 + i) = \text{Oa}$$

The slope of the budget line is (recalling the analysis of chapter 6) Oa/Ob. But Oa/Ob = $(1 + i)$. Therefore the slope of the intertemporal budget line is $(1 + i)$.

SAQ 16.1

(a) If income this year is £10,000 and income next year is expected to be zero, what is the maximum consumption that you could enjoy next year at an interest rate of 10 per cent?

(b) If income this year is zero and income next year is expected to be £10,000, what is the maximum consumption that you could enjoy this year at an interest rate of 10 per cent?

The slope of an intertemporal indifference curve is similarly $(1 + r)$, where r is termed the **marginal rate of time preference**. It seems to be a part of human psychology that early consumption is preferred to later consumption: if one is to sacrifice £100 of current consumption one must receive *more* than £100 next period. Rate r must in general therefore be positive: individuals have positive time preference, preferring the 'here and now' to the 'there and later'. This seems to be true even ignoring the increased uncertainty about future consumption possibilities compared with present (for example, the possibility that the person to whom you lend your savings may default on the repayment).

In a utility maximizing (note *utility*, not wealth or income maximizing) equilibrium such as d in figure 16.1, the slope of the budget line and the indifference curve are the same. Hence $1 + i = 1 + r$. So the individual adjusts the rate of saving until the (subjective) rate of time preference r is equal to the (market) rate of interest i.

Multiple Periods

You have seen that $PV(1 + i) = F$. This is just saying that the amount PV invested at the interest rate i will grow in one period (say a year) to F. You could also ask what the future sum F is worth now. Rearranging the equation, it is evidently

$$PV = F \left(\frac{1}{1 + i}\right)$$

The conventional term for PV is present value. So you can say that the present value of a future sum F is F multiplied by a factor equal to $1/(1 + i)$. This factor is termed the **discount factor** D. So $D = 1/(1 + i)$. Given that $r = i$ in equilibrium and that individuals prefer the 'here and now', $r = i > 0$, so £100 in the future must be worth less than £100 now. In technical language the present value of £100 in the future is less than £100. For example, with $i = 0.1$ (10 per cent) £100 next year is worth £90.91. Alternatively, £90.91 invested now at 10 per cent will grow to £100 next year.

SAQ 16.2

(a) What would £100 grow to in one year if invested at 5 per cent, 10 per cent, or 15 per cent interest?

(b) What is £100 next year worth today at 5 per cent, 10 per cent or 15 per cent interest?

Note: for this and other SAQs you will find it handy to use a pocket calculator.

What would £100 invested at 10 per cent grow to in two years rather than one? After one year it will have grown to £110 and, reinvested at 10 per cent for a further year, it will grow to £121. In symbols, F_2 is given by

$$PV(1 + i)(1 + i) = F_2$$

or

$$PV(1 + i)^2 = F_2$$

Invested for three years, PV will grow to

$$PV(1 + i)^3 = F_3$$

and so on.

If instead of asking the question 'what will a sum grow to if invested at 10 per cent?' you ask 'what is the present value of a sum to be received at various future dates?', you get, for one period hence (as you have seen),

$$PV = F_1\left(\frac{1}{1 + i}\right)$$

or, for two periods hence,

$$PV = F_2\left(\frac{1}{(1 + i)^2}\right)$$

or, for three periods hence,

$$PV = F_3\left(\frac{1}{(1 + i)^3}\right)$$

and so on.

If you wish to know the present value of a *stream* of future sums accruing annually, you simply add up the successive present values for the sums at each date, namely

$$PV = \frac{F_1}{1 + i} + \frac{F_2}{(1 + i)^2} + \frac{F_3}{(1 + i)^3} + \frac{F_4}{(1 + i)^4} + \ldots + \frac{F_n}{(1 + i)^n}$$

or, if some accrues in the present period,

$$PV = F_0 + \frac{F_1}{1 + i} + \frac{F_2}{(1 + i)^2} + \frac{F_3}{(1 + i)^3} + \ldots + \frac{F_n}{(1 + i)^n}$$

SAQ 16.3

(a) A salesman offers to sell you a washing machine for £550 cash or £200 down plus two equal annual payments of £200. (1) At 10 per cent interest, which is the better deal for you? (2) At 8 per cent interest, which is the better deal for you?

(b) You invest £750 today in exchange for the promise to pay you (or your surviving dependants) £5047.50 in 20 years' time. What is the implied interest rate?

Note that in figure 16.1 Ob is a measure of **wealth**. It is equal to OC_0 (the amount of present consumption plus OC_1 $[1/(1 + i)] = C_0$b (the present value of next period's consumption). Evidently, $OC_0 + C_0$b = Ob. This measure Ob is the present value of consumption. It is also the present value of income, since it also equals income in this period (OY_0) plus the present value of next period's income: OY_1 $[1/(1 + i)] = Y_0$b, and clearly $OY_0 + Y_0$b = Ob. Ob is the market value (at the going rate of interest) of the present and future incomes an individual receives, and this is precisely the economic definition of wealth.

In the multiperiod version, assuming that over a lifetime an individual consumes all his or her wealth, you have the following. W is wealth, the present value (PV) of consumption C or income Y.

$$W = C_0 + \frac{C_1}{1 + i} + \frac{C_2}{(1 + i)^2} + \frac{C_3}{(1 + i)^3} + \ldots + \frac{C_n}{(1 + i)^n}$$

or

$$W = Y_0 + \frac{Y_1}{1 + i} + \frac{Y_2}{(1 + i)^2} + \frac{Y_3}{(1 + i)^3} + \ldots + \frac{Y_n}{(1 + i)^n}$$

A constant amount received each year is called an **annuity**. Suppose somebody left you £100 a year for the next five years. What is its present value at 2 per cent? Answer: £471.34. You get £100 next year (present value £98.04) plus £100 the following year (present value £96.12) plus £100 in year three (worth £94.23) plus £100 in year four (worth £92.38) plus £100 in year five (worth £90.57).

Suppose you could buy a bond that would pay you £50 a year for 25 years and the interest rate is 6 per cent. That is worth £639.17, so if you could buy it for less than this, you would gain.

SAQ 16.4

(a) You can borrow any amount up to £50,000 at 10 per cent from your bank. Your mother, however, offers to give you a house with a current market value of £40,000 in exchange for a payment of £80,000 in 15 years' time. Is it worth accepting you mother's offer?

(b) You expect a net income from work of £10,000 at the end of this year and the same amount each year until your retirement in 40 years' time. What is your wealth (sometimes termed the value of your **human capital**) at 5 per cent interest?

Some Useful Equations

The computation of present values and so on is made easier if you remember a few equations (and, of course, how they are arrived at). An equation showing how much £1 will grow to in n years if invested every year is

$$F = (1 + i)^n$$

The equation showing the present value of a single amount to be received in year n is

$$PV = \frac{1}{(1 + i)^n}$$

This is the discount factor for year n.

An equation showing the present value of an annuity of £1 receivable (or payable) for n years is

$$PV = \frac{(1 + i)^n - 1}{i\,(1 + i)^n}$$

To see how this formula is arrived at, consider an annuity A that is going to be received each year for n years. Its present value is

$$PV = \frac{A_1}{1 + i} + \frac{A_2}{(1 + i)^2} + \frac{A_3}{(1 + i)^3} + \ldots + \frac{A_n}{(1 + i)^n}$$

This can be simplified (since $A_1 = A_2, \ldots, A_n = A$) to

$$PV = A \left[\frac{1}{1 + i} + \frac{1}{(1 + i)^2} + \frac{1}{(1 + i)^3} + \ldots + \frac{1}{(1 + i)^n} \right]$$

Now multiply through by $(1 + i)$ to get

$$PV\,(1 + i) = A \left[1 + \frac{1}{1 + i} + \frac{1}{(1 + i)^2} + \frac{1}{(1 + i)^3} + \ldots + \frac{1}{(1 + i)^{n-1}} \right]$$

and subtract the original equation to get

$$PVi = A \left[1 - \frac{1}{(1 + i)^n} \right]$$

Manipulating this a bit, you will get

$$PVi = A \left[\frac{(1 + i)^n}{(1 + i)^n} - \frac{1}{(1 + i)^n} \right]$$

$$= A \left[\frac{(1 + i)^n - 1}{(1 + i)^n} \right]$$

and

$$PV = A \left[\frac{(1 + i)^n - 1}{i(1 + i)^n} \right]$$

For very long periods, as n approaches infinity, $1/i(1+i)^n$ approaches zero and $(1+i)^n / i((1+i)^n$ approaches $1/i$. Hence, an annuity for ever is worth

$$PV = A\left(\frac{1}{i}\right) = \frac{A}{i}$$

A consol is a bond issued by the British government that is a **perpetuity**. Suppose you thought of buying a 2.5 per cent consol with a face value of £100. If the rate of interest were 10 per cent, what price would just induce you to buy it? The consol will pay £2.50 per year for ever, so the present value at 10 per cent is easily calculated from the formula just given: £2.50/0.1 = £25. Thus a 2.5 per cent consol with a face value of £100 is worth not more than £25. If you could buy one for less than £25 you will earn a higher rate of interest than 10 per cent. For example, if the price of consols is £24, then the implicit interest rate is £2.50/£24 = 10.4 per cent.

SAQ 16.5

(a) You lend £50,000 today at 8 per cent and wish to receive equal annual payments beginning next year and running for seven years. What is the appropriate annual payment?

(b) You buy a house for £60,000 and borrow £45,000 from the building society at an interest rate of 10 per cent, repaying each year for 15 years (beginning next year) a sum that at the end of the period will have paid off the whole debt and interest. You find the £15,000 balance out of savings.

1 What is your annual payment to the building society?
2 After one year, what is your equity in the house?
3 After two years, what is your equity in the house?
4 After 15 years, what is your equity in the house, assuming its value still to be £60,000?

Irregular Flows

Suppose you own a small business and are considering the purchase of a machine costing £5000 now, lasting five years, with annual maintenance costs of £100. In the first period you expect to make £500, in the second £750, and £1000 a year thereafter. The labour costs associated with the use of the machine are £200 per year. Assuming there are no other costs, taxes, and so on, that inflation is zero, and that you could get 10 per cent if you invested your £5000 in the best alternative, is the machine worth buying?

It is helpful to set out the flows of cost and benefit systematically as in table 16.1. At the very beginning the only outlay is the £5000 on the machine. In year 1 total costs amount to £300 and there is a surplus of revenues over costs of £200. In year 2 the surplus is £450. And so on. To see whether this is a worthwhile investment you need to find the present value of these net gains. At 10 per cent the relevant discount factors are shown in the next row (using the formula $PV = 1/(1+i)^n$). When the net receipts are multiplied by the discount factors, the present values are obtained. When added up these give

$$-\text{£}5000 + \text{£}181.82 + \text{£}371.90 + \text{£}1089.41 + \text{£}1502.63 + \text{£}1676.49 = -\text{£}177.75$$

The present value of the revenues is thus less than the present value of costs by £177.75 and you would, in this case, be better off investing your £5000 at the 10 per cent you can get elsewhere, since it must earn less if invested in the machine.

Table 16.1 Hypothetical costs and benefits from an investment (£)

	Now	*Year 1*	*Year 2*	*Year 3*	*Year 4*	*Year 5*
Costs						
Capital cost	5000	—	—	—	—	—
Maintenance cost	0	100	100	100	100	100
Other costs	0	200	200	200	200	200
Total costs	5000	300	300	300	300	300
Revenues	0	500	750	1750	2500	3000
Net revenue	−5000	200	450	1450	2200	2700
Discount factors	0.0	0.9091	0.82645	0.751315	0.683015	0.620921
Present value	−5000	181.82	371.90	1089.41	1502.63	1676.49

Effects of Changes in the Interest Rate

The effect of changes in the interest rate can be demonstrated using the analysis with which this chapter opened. Suppose that an individual is initially in a two period consumption equilibrium at point e in figure 16.2, having chosen this intertemporal pattern of consumption given the endowment income flows shown by point a. This individual's wealth (present value of income) is denoted by W_0. Now suppose the rate of interest falls. This means that the budget line rotates anti-clockwise through point a. In period 0 an income Y_0 is expected and, instead of the present value of next period's income (Y_1) being Y_0W_0 it rises to Y_0W_0'. Hence wealth rises from W_0 to W_0'. At this interest rate the individual's wealth is too low for the original indifference curve to be attained. Thus, even though the monetary value of wealth has risen (because the present value of next year's income is now higher), there is a **wealth effect** analogous to the income effect of one period indifference curve theory that is, reducing utility. The level of wealth needed to maintain utility at the level U is evidently W_0'', which just enables tangency at point b on the original indifference curve.

Focusing only on the substitution effect of the interest rate change, the individual will move from point e to point b. Whereas originally saving was $Y_0 - C_0$, less must now be saved: the pure substitution effect of an interest rate fall must always reduce saving. But the wealth effect must now be allowed to operate, so that wealth falls from (notional) W_0'' to W_0'. In general one expects consumption to fall or rise as wealth falls or rises. Consequently one predicts a move from point b to a position to its left. If the final tangency is at a point like e′, then consumption will have risen from C_0 to C_0' out of income Y_0, so savings will have fallen in response to the fall in the interest rate. If the final tangency is at a point like e″, then consumption will have fallen from C_0 to C_0'' out of

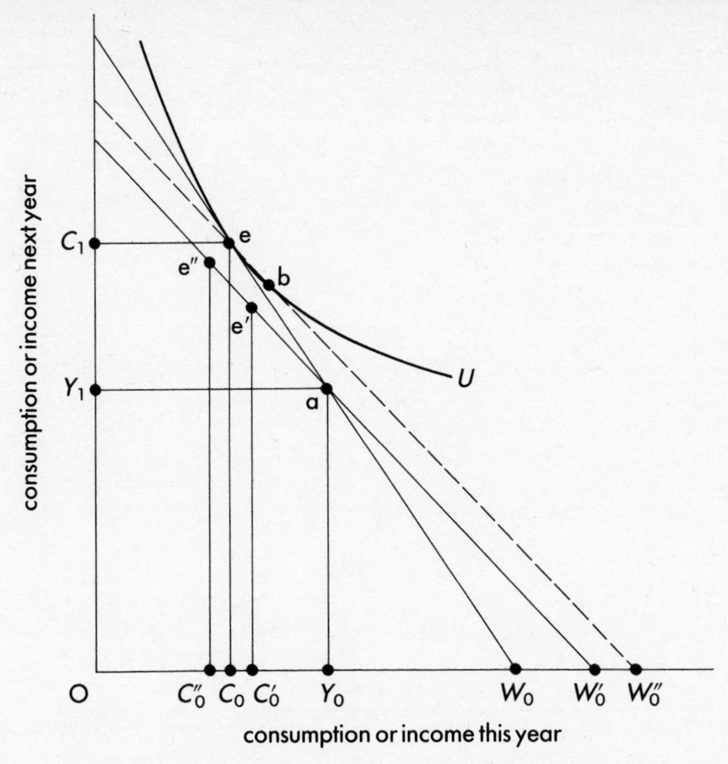

Figure 16.2 Effects of a change in the interest rate for a lender

income Y_0, so savings will have risen in response to the fall in the interest rate. Whether the tangency is at e″ or e′ depends of course on the shape of the indifference map below U. The pure substitution effect is always to cause savings to fall as the interest rate falls. The wealth effect (analogous to the income affect in one period analysis) will cause savings and consumption to rise and, depending on whether this effect is larger or smaller than the substitution effect, may cause consumption to rise overall (and hence savings to fall overall) or to fall (and hence savings to rise).

The case illustrated in figure 16.2 is that of an individual who consumes less in period 0 than period 0's income and more in period 1 than period 1's income. Such an individual may be described as a *lender*. The position of a *borrower*, who consumes more than income in period 0 and less in period 1, is shown in figure 16.3. Here endowment income is shown at point a, with wealth W_0. The preferred consumption pattern through time is shown by point e. The individual thus consumes C_0, but with an income of only Y_0 must borrow the difference. This, at the interest rate indicated by the slope of the budget line, means forgoing $Y_1 - C_1$ consumption next year. When the interest rate falls the budget line again rotates anti-clockwise through point a and a new wealth W_0' is established. The pure substitution effect is again from point e to point b, unambiguously causing consumption to increase as borrowing becomes

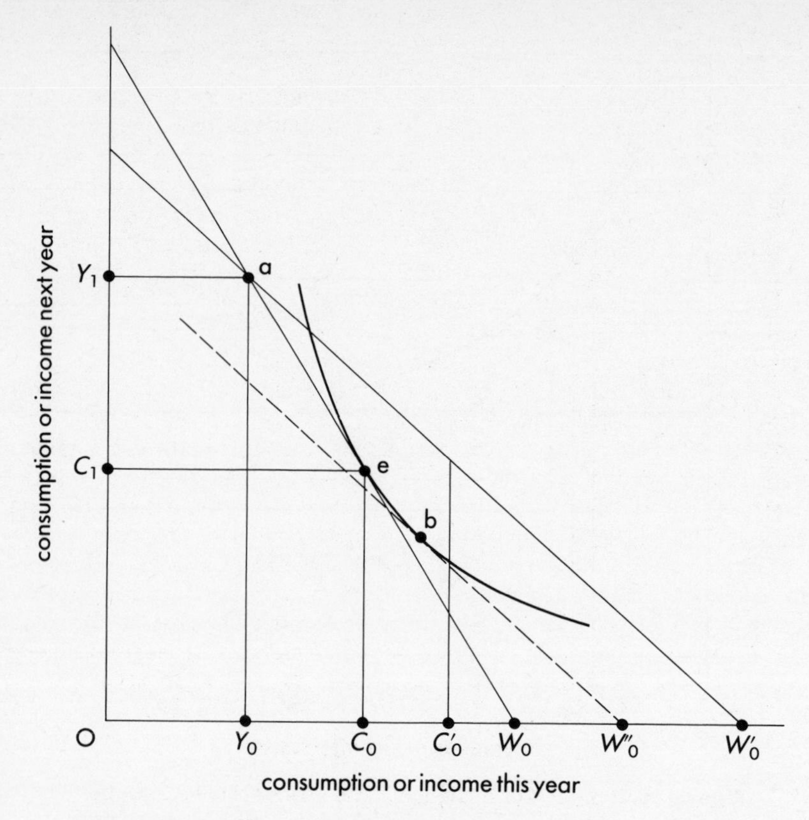

Figure 16.3 Effects of a change in the interest rate for a borrower

cheaper. Introducing the wealth effect causes wealth to rise from (notional) W_0'' to W_0' and, given that consumption increases with wealth, must mean that consumption rises even more to, say, C_0'. Hence borrowers unambiguously respond to a fall in interest rates by increasing borrowing and hence **dissaving** even more. Lenders, on the other hand, may save either more or less.

Case Study 16.1 Interest, Savings and Inflation in Britain 1964–81

Ordinary people in Britain save mainly via building societies and pension schemes. In the 1970s the rate of interest (net of income tax) on savings in building societies was not merely low, but in real terms negative. That is, after allowing for the fact that a future sum would buy less (even with interest) than its present value, the real interest rate was negative. Yet despite this, the share of savings in personal disposable income rose in the 1970s to historically high levels.

The data are shown in table 16.2. Column 2 gives the average rate offered by building societies, column 3 gives the inflation rate and column 4 the real rate of interest (column 2 minus column 3 – an approximation discussed in chapter 32). Column 5 shows the savings ratio (savings as a share of income).

Just as no reasonable person expects a physicist's expertise in gravity and aerodynamics to predict or explain the movement of a leaf through the air as it falls from a tree, so no one can reasonably expect every erratic nuance of economic life to receive a detailed account. The *general pattern* shown in table 16.2, however, puzzled many, including economists: why should savings *rise* (as they did, though in the table only savings as a percentage of disposable income are shown) when real interest rates are falling?

There seem to be two major candidates for an explanation. The first is that falling interest rates have increased wealth so that, as you saw in the text is possible, the positive substitution effect is compensated – in fact, over compensated – by the negative wealth effect. If this were true, then the pure substitution effect would have still been what theory says it is, with lower interest implying lower savings. The second is the effect of inflation in an economy where wage and salary contracts are made for long periods (say a year). According to this argument, let an individual be given a rise at the end of each year that just compensates for the increase in prices over that year. Prices will have been rising continuously, but wages jump suddenly at the year end (or whenever the contract is renegotiated). Consequently, in order to smooth out consumption, the individual will save more in the early part of the year and less in the later part than if (real) income had remained constant. Aggregating over many individuals, one would expect that the lower savings of some would offset the higher savings of others. But if inflation is *increasing*, then the extra savings of those who have recently had their awards will be larger than the reduction in savings of those whose most recent award was a year before. Hence aggregate savings rise if inflation is increasing. This seems consistent with the data in table 16.2, since in most years inflation and the savings ratio moved in the same direction.

George Bulkley (1981) 'Personal savings and anticipated inflation', *Economic Journal*, **91**(361), 124–35.

Table 16.2 Interest, inflation and savings in Britain 1964–81

1 *Year*	*2* *Building societies' average rate of interest (%)*	*3* *Rate of inflation (%)*	*4* *Real rate of interest (2–3) (%)*	*5* *Savings ratio (%)*
1964	3.5	3.2	0.3	8.2
1965	3.8	4.8	−1.0	8.5
1966	4.0	3.9	0.1	8.4
1967	4.2	2.4	1.8	8.4
1968	4.4	4.8	−0.4	7.9
1969	4.8	5.4	−0.6	8.2
1970	4.9	6.3	−1.4	8.9
1971	5.0	9.4	−4.4	8.5
1972	4.9	7.1	−2.2	10.5
1973	6.5	9.2	−2.7	11.7
1974	7.3	16.1	−8.8	14.1
1975	7.2	24.2	−17.0	15.3
1976	7.0	16.5	−9.5	14.6
1977	7.0	15.8	−8.8	10.8
1978	6.5	8.3	−1.8	12.8
1979	8.4	13.4	−5.0	14.4
1980	10.3	18.0	−7.7	15.6
1981	9.1	11.0	−2.8	13.4

Source: *Financial Statistics*, London, HMSO, various years

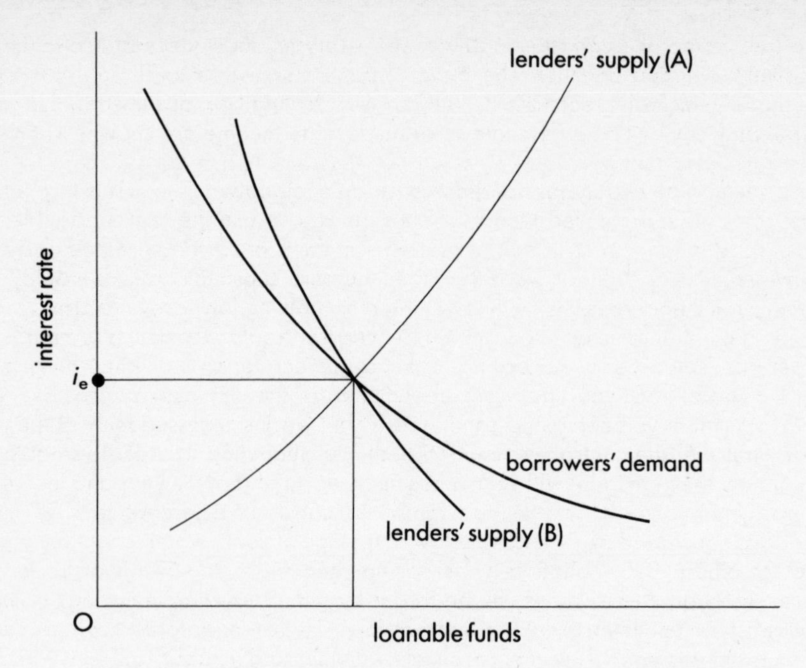

Figure 16.4 Exchange equilibrium of borrowers and lenders

Determination of the Interest Rate in a Pure Exchange Model

In a pure exchange model, in which endowment incomes in the two periods remain the same and individuals trade with one another according to who prefers to consume more now and who more later, the interest rate is determined by the intersection of the supply of savings to lend and the demand to borrow. This is illustrated in figure 16.4. The negatively sloped demand for funds to borrow shows that, as the rate of interest rises or falls, the demand for funds falls or rises in any period. Two possibilities are shown for the supply of funds. With curve A lenders increase lending (save more) as the interest rate rises. With curve B they reduce saving. (These are the two possibilities listed earlier for lenders.) As long as the supply curve intersects the demand curve from above there will always be excess supply of funds at an interest rate less than i_e, the equilibrium rate, forcing the rate up. Similarly, at higher rates there will be an excess supply, forcing the rate down. In equilibrium, supply equals demand: the amount lenders (savers) want to lend is the same as the amount borrowers (dissavers) want to borrow. If curve B intersected the demand curve from below the equilibrium would not be stable: excess demands would cause the interest rate to rise further and excess supplies would cause it to fall further. In practice, such does not seem to be the case, so the eventuality can be dismissed as merely a theoretical curiosity.

Note that one is focusing here on an equilibrium that is purely to do with *exchange*. It is the multiperiod analogue of the earlier analysis of one period trading of goods. It takes no account of production, specifically of **productive investment** – the sacrifice of current consumption not merely for more consumption later but for more *production* (and hence, ultimately still more consumption) later. This you will meet shortly.

The interest rate is a rather special kind of price. It has no £ before it. It is a pure number. It reflects the value of earlier availability of resources expressed as a percentage of the difference between a future sum and its present value. In percentage terms,

$$i = \frac{F - PV}{PV} 100$$

$1 + i$ is the intertemporal price ratio. It shows the amount of future consumption forgone per unit of present consumption.

SAQ 16.6

You live in a society in which the charging of interest is effectively prohibited.

(a) How could you tell by means of observed prices whether the rate of time preference had risen or fallen?

(b) What economic effects would you expect such a ban to have?

(c) Is it immoral to charge interest rates?

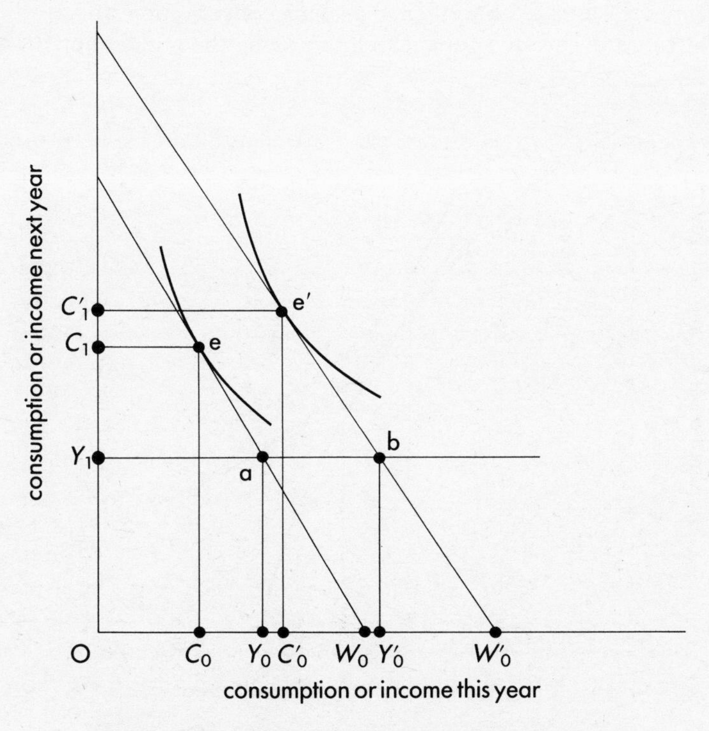

Figure 16.5 Effects of changes in current income

If an individual's current income rises, wealth rises too. This is shown in figure 16.5. Initially an individual is in equilibrium at point e, with an endowment at point a. If Y_0 rises to Y_0', the endowment point becomes b and wealth rises to W_0'. This will normally lead to an increase in consumption (say, to C_0'), and may or may not raise savings depending on whether $Y_0 - C_0$ (initial saving) is smaller or larger than $Y_0' - C_0'$ (subsequent savings). In the figure, savings do rise, hence enabling a higher level of consumption in the next period (C_1', rather than C_1).

Productive Investment

Suppose that individuals have the opportunity not merely to sacrifice current consumption at a rate of interest that enables them to enjoy higher consumption rates later, but also to engage in productive investments that cause output, and hence incomes and consumption, to be higher in the future. Further assume that such investments are subject to the law of diminishing returns so that, as more current consumption is forgone for the sake of say purchases of machines, land and other inputs, the output of goods in a future period rises but at a decreasing rate. The general picture will thus resemble that shown in figure 16.6, which shows an **intertemporal production possibilities boundary**. The individual can be imagined to start at an endowment point a, with incomes Y_0 and Y_1. Sacrificing present consumption and trading at the given interest rate, the individual can move along the budget line dW_0 and find

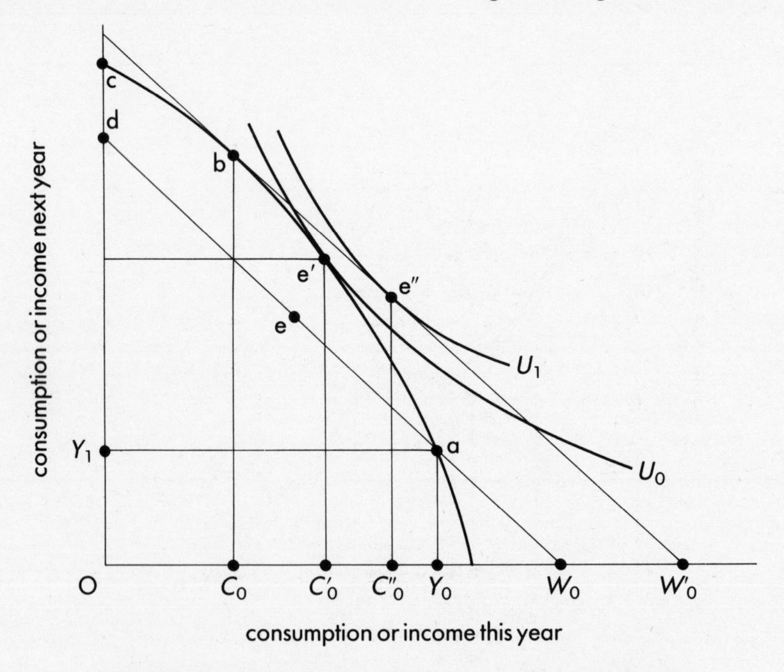

Figure 16.6 Intertemporal exchange with investment

a preferred point such as e. However, by engaging in *investment* – sacrificing current consumption *to increase production* – the individual can move along the boundary ae′bc. For example a farmer, instead of grinding wheat into flour to make bread to eat this year, can sacrifice some bread by planting more seed to produce more bread next year. In this way point e′ can be attained, enabling more consumption in both periods than point e. In fact the farmer (or any other producer) can do better than this. By producing at point b further consumption would be sacrificed ($C_0' - C_0$), taking the producer to C_0. Then, by borrowing at the market rate of interest, a move to point e″ could be made, so that actual consumption in the first period is C_0'' and utility is maximized on U_1 with wealth rising from W_0 to W_0'. The total investment is then $Y_0 - C_0$, of which $C_0'' - C_0$ is financed by borrowing and $Y_0 - C_0''$ by personal saving.

Of course, there must be other individuals willing to lend at the interest rate and, in equilibrium, the interest rate will settle where the demand and supply of funds for borrowing and lending are equal. Thus, in aggregate, the amount of desired borrowing has to equal the amount of desired lending – but this time it will also have been conditioned by the amount of profitable investment that individuals seek. Note also that total investment ($Y_0 - C_0$) equals total saving: $C_0'' - C_0$ provided by other people and $Y_0 - C_0''$ by this individual.

Note that the market rate of interest is, in equilibrium, equal both to the slope of the production possibilities boundary and to an indifference curve. Note also that the utility maximizing equilibrium is also the wealth maximizing equilibrium, with wealth equal to W_0' (a higher wealth is not feasible given the position of the production possibilities boundary). Thus, the investor can focus exclusively on the pursuit of wealth by locating points such as b and, provided that exchange can then proceed voluntarily, the utility maximizing point can then be attained. This is another aspect of the invisible hand theorem: the pursuit of wealth (coupled with the possibility of voluntary exchange) maximizes utility.

The tangency at point b has significance for the later analysis of the macroeconomics of investment in chapter 30 for, at point b, the rate of interest is equal to the **marginal productivity of investment** (MPI). Consider: at point b on the production possibilities boundary an extra sacrifice of current consumption will yield a marginal gain next year over and above this investment. This gain is called the marginal productivity of investment. So a one unit sacrifice this year produces that unit plus the gain (1 + MPI) next year. The slope of the boundary is therefore (1 + MPI)/1 = (1 + MPI). We know that the slope of the budget line is $(1 + i)$. Hence at point b, where the two slopes are equal, i = MPI. Investment will be pursued up to the point where its marginal productivity is equal to the rate of interest.

Case Study 16.2 The Rate of Return to Higher Education

Investment in human capital, of which education is one example, depends crucially on estimated *differentials* between what would be earned without the investment in additional schooling or training and what would be earned with it. In addition to the direct costs of the training (which may be borne only in part by the individual) must be added the forgone value of output (approximated by earnings) during the period of training (especially with full time education). It is also usual in this genre to distinguish between *private* returns (including education costs incurred only by the individual and deducting income tax from earnings) and *social* returns (including *all* education costs and not deducting income tax). Returns are the marginal productivities of investment from the two points of view.

Drawing on other studies and making his own estimates in order to achieve comparability, George Psacharopoulos (1973) has computed the rates of return to primary, secondary and higher education shown in table 16.3. Other studies have found, incidentally, that when greater disaggregation is undertaken the return to higher degrees in university is lower than that to first degrees and that the social return to higher education in economics is only 3.9 per cent compared with 7.5 per cent in accountancy (but only 1.4 per cent in both engineering and applied science). These averages across individuals, however, mask a considerable variation. Moreover, it is at least my own hope that you can see more than an earnings advantage from doing economics!

In the countries where primary education is compulsory it is difficult to derive some of the estimates since there are no people falling in the set that will earn an income with no primary education. It is typically found that the returns (both social and private) are higher in poor countries than in rich: diminishing returns imply, of course, that as one educates more people at a particular level, the rate of return will fall (mainly because competition forces down the future earnings of the better educated as their numbers increase).

Still, 12 per cent in 1966 was a good return on any investment for the average British citizen, and indicates that the big expansion of higher education in Britain following the Robbins Report in 1963 would create no difficulty for institutions in filling the places thus made available.

George Psacharopoulos (1973), *Returns to Education*, Amsterdam, Elsevier, table 4.1.

Table 16.3 Private rates of returns by educational level in ten countries

Country	*Year*	*Primary*	*Secondary*	*Higher*
Canada	1961	—	16.3	19.7
Ghana	1967	24.5	17.0	37.0
Great Britain	1966	—	6.2	12.0
India	1960	24.7	19.2	14.3
Israel	1958	27.0	6.9	8.0
Mexico	1963	32.0	23.0	29.0
New Zealand	1966	—	20.0	14.7
Norway	1966	—	7.4	7.7
Puerto Rico	1959	7100.0	23.4	27.9
USA	1959	155.1	19.5	13.6

Many Interest Rates

The analysis so far has treated the subject as though there were only one interest rate. In reality you know there to be many. There are several reasons for this. One is that lending and borrowing is itself a costly activity. Because of this it pays specialists to develop skills in particular fields that enable them to lower transaction costs. However, such costs can never be zero. Consequently, they have to be borne ultimately by customers. This is often done in such a way that original lenders will receive a lower interest rate than final borrowers will have to pay, the difference being used to cover the costs (and profits) of financial intermediaries.

Another all-pervading reason for varied rates is that lenders will want compensation from borrowers for the risks that arise from the possibility of default, bankruptcy and so on. Uncertainty causes interest rates to be higher than the 'pure' rate of time preference and the 'pure' marginal productivity of investment.

If the inflation rate is zero the *real* rate of interest that corresponds in equilibrium to the marginal rate of time preference and the marginal productivity of investment (ignoring transaction costs and uncertainty) corresponds to the money or *nominal* rate of interest. When there is inflation, nominal interest rates are higher than the real rate. If lenders are prepared to lend at say 5 per cent under zero inflation, they will require an additional premium roughly corresponding to the inflation rate if inflation is under way: otherwise they would be paid interest that in money terms next year will have a lower purchasing power than the same sum this year.

The effects of inflation on interest rates are not further pursued here but are discussed in some detail in chapter 32.

Investment Rules

Suppose there are two investment options that you are considering, each requiring an immediate outlay of £23. Option 1 yields net receipts of £5 per year for ten years (the first occurring at the end of the present period). Option 2 yields net receipts of £1 in the first year, £2 in the second, £3 in the third etc. up to ten years. Making whatever assumptions you like about interest rates, which seems to you the better investment?

There are two common rules for making investment decisions. The first is to select options that have a positive present value net of cost (the *net present value rule*) at the going interest rate. If you are a net lender of money it will be the lending rate that is the appropriate (opportunity cost) rate of interest to use; if you are a net borrower, it is the borrowing rate. The second decision rule is to select options that have an internal rate of return greater than the interest rate (the *internal rate of return rule*). The **internal rate of return** is defined as the rate of interest (or rate of discount) that makes net present value zero.

Look first at the *internal rate of return rule*. The internal rate of return for option 1 is about 17 per cent or 0.17. That for option 2 is about 14 per cent or

0.14. If you discount option 1 revenues at 17 per cent, the equation is

$$PV_1 = -23 + \frac{5}{1.17} + \frac{5}{1.37} + \frac{5}{1.60} + \frac{5}{1.87} + \frac{5}{2.19} + \frac{5}{2.57} + \frac{5}{3.00} + \frac{5}{3.51} + \frac{5}{4.11} + \frac{5}{4.81}$$

$$= -23 + 4.27 + 3.65 + 3.12 + 2.67 + 2.28 + 1.95 + 1.67 + 1.42 + 1.22 + 1.04$$

$$= +0.29$$

which is near enough to zero to make 0.17 the internal rate of return. Discounting the revenues of option 2 at 14 per cent gives

$$PV_2 = -23 + \frac{1}{1.14} + \frac{2}{1.30} + \frac{3}{1.48} + \frac{4}{1.69} + \frac{5}{1.93} + \frac{6}{2.19} + \frac{7}{2.50} + \frac{8}{2.85} + \frac{9}{3.25} + \frac{10}{3.71}$$

$$= -23 + 0.88 + 1.54 + 2.03 + 2.37 + 2.59 + 2.74 + 2.80 + 2.81 + 2.77 + 2.70$$

$$= +0.23$$

which is also near enough to zero to make 0.14 the internal rate of return for this option.

If, now, the relevant interest rate is 5 per cent, both options pass the internal rate of return rule since each has an internal rate of return higher than the interest rate. Moreover, if they are mutually exclusive options (e.g. build a school at *either* site A or site B, or build a house of brick *or* wood) then the preferred option will be option 1 since it has the higher internal rate of return.

The *present value rule* says adopt options with positive net present values when discounted at the appropriate rate of interest. If you do this for each option you get, for option 1,

$$PV_1 = -23 + \frac{5}{1.05} + \frac{5}{1.10} + \frac{5}{1.16} + \frac{5}{1.22} + \frac{5}{1.28} + \frac{5}{1.34} + \frac{5}{1.41} + \frac{5}{1.48} + \frac{5}{1.55} + \frac{5}{1.63}$$

$$= -23 + 4.76 + 4.55 + 4.31 + 4.10 + 3.91 + 3.73 + 3.55 + 3.38 + 3.23 + 3.07$$

$$= 15.59$$

and, for option 2,

$$PV_2 = -23 + \frac{1}{1.05} + \frac{2}{1.10} + \frac{3}{1.16} + \frac{4}{1.22} + \frac{5}{1.28} + \frac{6}{1.34} + \frac{7}{1.41} + \frac{8}{1.48} + \frac{9}{1.55} + \frac{10}{1.63}$$

$$= -23 + 0.95 + 1.82 + 2.59 + 3.28 + 3.91 + 4.48 + 4.96 + 5.41 + 5.81 + 6.13$$

$$= 16.34$$

Using the present value rule, then, both options are again recommended. However, if they are mutually exclusive, the present value rule says adopt option 2, in flat contradiction to the internal rate of return rule.

Which rule then should be generally adopted? In practice it will frequently not matter, for conflicts arise only with particular patterns of net benefits over time. The generally sound wealth maximizing principle is, however, to *use the present value rule* – since the net present value of receipts *is* wealth. In the case of mutually exclusive options, as well as in some other cases too, the internal rate of return rule blindly applied can give wrong answers to the investment question. This is true in the private sector, where profit may be the objective. It is also true in the public sector and in social services, where the net present value of benefits (embodying values that may not come from the marketplace) is an appropriate thing to maximize (or where the net present value of costs may be an appropriate thing to minimize, given alternative options with identical benefits).

Cost–Benefit Analysis and the Art of Investment Appraisal

Appraising investment options cannot be reduced to a mechanical activity performed simply by following a checklist of things to do. It is a creative, inspirational activity that depends crucially on imagining possible futures, identifying possible options and finding sensible ways of narrowing down their range to give a limited set of possibilities for more careful evaluation – without, in that process, eliminating one that may prove to be the 'best buy'. That is true of investment appraisal in the private sector, where the objective may be to maximize the present value of profits (the ultimate wealth that is embodied in an enterprise), and in the public sector, where the objective may frequently be hard to express in terms of financial outcomes, where benefit in particular is hard to pin down and where more than one agency may have responsibility for the activity in question. In cases where the benefits are hard to quantify, let alone value, it is often not possible as a practical matter to do more than a **cost-effectiveness** exercise. For example, the ultimate benefit of any investment in the National Health Service (NHS) is presumably an increase in the health of some individuals (or a prevention of its deterioration); however, this is notoriously hard to measure, let alone value in such a way as to enable the calculation of rates of return or net present values.

The remaining two case studies in this chapter look at a cost-effectiveness study in the NHS and a (positive) exercise in economic history. These are interspersed with some SAQs to enable you to get further practice in using the concepts introduced in this chapter.

Case Study 16.3 Cost-Effective Oxygen Supply

Fresh air for many of us is a free good: it costs nothing to acquire and we can have as much of it as we like. For smoggy city dwellers, deep sea divers and chronic bronchitics, however, fresh air is costly, requiring air conditioning or pollution control, compressors, or special oxygen supplies.

Chronic bronchitics can be supplied with oxygen at home in four basic ways: by large oxygen cylinders containing 3400 litres, by small cylinders containing 1360 litres, by regular refills of a liquid oxygen reservoir, or by the installation of an oxygen concentrator (an electrical machine which separates oxygen from other gases in the air). Each of these methods has different set-up and running costs. In particular, there are maintenance costs of the concentrators that have to be met irrespective of the number of bronchitics supplied, whereas with the other methods the set-up costs are, per person supplied, constant. These set-up costs can be made comparable with running costs by calculating the value of the annual annuity over the expected life of equipment whose present value is equal to the total set-up costs.

In this way, Karin Lowson and her colleagues (1981) were able to work out the cost-effective provision of oxygen to the homes of bronchitics, with the results shown in figure 16.7. This shows that two of the technologies are completely dominated by the others: whatever the number of bronchitics supplied, the cost per patient is higher with either cylinder. Of the remaining two technologies, if only about eight or nine bronchitics need to be supplied, the liquid oxygen method is cheaper. If more than that number are to be supplied, concentrators are cheaper. (The discontinuities in the concentrator cost curve are due to increases in workshop maintenance costs when more than 30 and more than 60 bronchitics are supplied.)

Since the benefits of these alternatives were judged to be the same, the conclusion is that the use of concentrators is a cost-effective method of supplying oxygen to bronchitics, thus making it unnecessary to compare and value benefits in detail for comparison with costs (as in **cost–benefit analysis**). Note that cost-effectiveness analysis can at best identify the least cost way of accomplishing something: it cannot determine whether the activity ought to be undertaken at all, or on what scale, for this requires information on benefits.

K. B. Lowson, M. F. Drummond and J. M. Bishop (1981) 'Costing new services: long-term domiciliary oxygen therapy', *Lancet*, **i**, May 23, 1146–9.

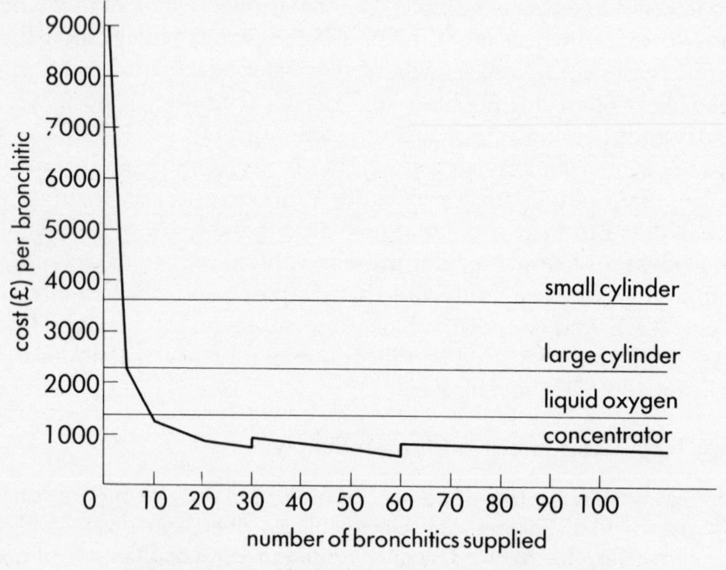

Figure 16.7 Alternative costs of oxygen supply

SAQ 16.7

(a) Your factory is worth £1 million. Its value suddenly falls to £500,000. This may have been due to a doubling in interest rates, or it may be caused by an IRA bomb. Either way your wealth in the factory is now only half a million pounds. Should you care which factor has caused your wealth loss?

(b) This question is designed to revise your understanding of the concept of wealth embodied in figure 16.1. Your income is £10,000 a year this year and next. Ignoring subsequent periods, at 10 per cent interest:

1. What is your wealth?
2. If you saved your entire income this year, what happens to your wealth this year?
3. If you saved your entire income this year, what will be your wealth next year?
4. If you consume your entire income this year, what is your wealth this year?
5. If you consume more than your income this year, what is your wealth this year?
6. If you consume £15,000 this year, what is your wealth next year?

Case Study 16.4 Slavery as Investment in the American South before the Civil War

Today when one talks of human capital we normally mean the value of the skills etc. embodied in free men. In slave societies, however, the analogy between human and physical capital is much closer – particularly when slaves (and children of slaves) can be bought and sold in organized markets just like other animal or non-animal capital goods.

A long tradition of economic history held, until about 1958, that negro slavery in the Southern States was not profitable and would have collapsed anyway, even without the Union's victory in the Civil War. It may, however, have been a rather romantic notion that slavery was commercially doomed as well as morally abhorrent. Alfred Conrad and John Meyer (1964) used capital theory of the sort outlined in this chapter to calculate both present values and internal rates of return to investment in slaves. They used estimates of the expectation of life of slaves (about the same as for whites in 1850), the cost of purchase of slaves , maintenance over their lives (food, clothing, medical care, taxes and supervision costs), the expectation of number of children born to a negro woman, the cost of childbearing of negro women and the costs of rearing child negroes, to set against the expected value of output per slave (allowing for absence of women during childbearing) including the future output of slave children and the sale of slave children.

The present value calculations were done for a period that, in the case of females, extended beyond their own lifetimes and incorporated the life up to age 18 of their youngest child (at which age it would normally be sold). The main yield on what was termed a 'prime yield wench' began to occur only after some 15 years after purchase of a mature (18 year old) slave. The internal rate of return on investment in a female slave of this type was about 8.1 per cent, which was slightly higher than the return on male slaves. In general, rates of return on investments at this time made between 6 and 8 per cent, and so it seems that slavery was *not* the unprofitable institution that some had claimed it be be. This is an important conclusion, not only for interpreting a possible claim made by historians, but also because it reminds one that it is romantic to suppose that institutions (like slavery) that may appal cannot have powerful economic survival characteristics.

Alfred Conrad and John Meyer (1964) *The Economics of Slavery and Other Studies in Econometric History*, Chicago, Aldine, chapter 3.

SAQ 16.8

(a) A sports star contracts with a sports club to play for its side in exchange for an agreed salary for the next five years. Subsequently the club sells its right to have the player to another club which also makes the player an acceptable offer as regards salary and bonuses. Is this slavery?

(b) A firm pays for a young employee to go to university on the understanding that, on graduation, the employee will work for at least three years for the firm on an agreed salary scale. Is that slavery?

(c) A film actor contracts with a motion picture company to appear in only its films for the next 20 years under agreed terms for each film in which the actor appears. Is that slavery?

(d) A young labourer indents with an employer to work for him for 30 years in exchange for pocket money, bed and board. Is that slavery?

What You Should Understand Now

The nature of intertemporal choice.
The meaning of interest.
The meaning of new terms: endowments, marginal rate of time preferences, discounting, present value, discount factor, annuity, internal rate of return, marginal productivity of investment or capital, perpetuity.
Calculation of present values and internal rates of return.
Effects on savings, wealth and consumption of changes in interest rates and income.
Determination of equilibrium interest rate in an exchange economy and with productive investment.
Reasons for multiple interest rates.
Present value and internal rate of return investment rules.
Why investment is an art rather than a science.
Some empirical material on recent savings behaviour in Britain, investment in education, investment in health care for chronic bronchitics, and the profitability of negro slavery in the American South before the Civil War.

17

The Demand for and Supply of Labour

The total population of the country can at any time be divided into three categories: those in work, those unemployed but seeking work, and the remainder. The last are classified as **economically inactive**; they include the young in full time education and of pre-school age, the elderly, those of independent means and not working or seeking work, and housewives. They are more numerous than those in the working population.

The working population includes all employees, all self-employed, the registered unemployed (including school leavers) and the armed forces. The employed labour force includes the self-employed, employees in employment and the armed forces.

Table 17.1 Employment and unemployment in the UK 1970–81

Year	*Population (000)*	*Economically inactive (000)*	*Working population (000)*	*Employed labour force (000)*	*Employees in employment (000)*	*Unemployed (including school leavers) (000)*
1970	55,522	30,214	25,308	24,753	22,479	555
1971	55,712	30,589	25,123	24,399	22,122	724
1972	55,869	30,674	25,195	24,391	22,121	804
1973	56,000	30,453	25,547	24,972	22,664	575
1974	56,011	30,410	25,601	25,059	22,789	542
1975	55,981	30,059	25,922	25,041	22,711	941
1976	55,959	29,828	26,131	24,809	22,524	1302
1977	55,919	29,678	26,241	24,837	22,606	1403
1978	55,902	29,530	26,372	24,984	22,762	1383
1979	55,946	29,300	26,646	25,356	23,139	1296
1980	56,010	29,141	26,869	25,284	22,950	1665
1981	56,020	29,239	26,781	24,297	21,845	2520
1982	56,067	29,236	26,831	23,959	21,446	2917
1983	—	—	26,856	23,765	21,182	3105

Sources: *Economic Trends*, 1983, Annual Supplement, table 99; *National Income Blue Book*, 1981 and 1983 editions, table 1.12; *Economic Trends*, August 1984, table 36

The amount of each of these in the UK is shown in table 17.1. Note that the population has been increasing slightly; the numbers of economically inactive have fallen slightly (remember that economically inactive does not mean unemployed); the working population has increased; and unemployment has increased most of all.

The distribution of employees in employment in Great Britain (i.e. the UK excluding Northern Ireland) is shown in table 17.2. Over the decade, only insurance etc. and miscellaneous services showed an increase, with professional and scientific services being about constant. Total manufacturing accounts for only a little over one quarter of employment.

Table 17.2 Employees in employment by industry in Great Britain (August 1983, seasonally adjusted)

	Number (000)	*% total*
Agriculture, forestry and fishing[a]	339	1.7
Mining and quarrying	307	1.5
Food, drink and tobacco	583	2.9
Coal and petroleum products	23	0.1
Chemicals and allied industries	367	1.8
Metal manufacture	256	1.3
Mechanical engineering	659	3.3
Instrument engineering	127	0.6
Electrical engineering	631	3.1
Shipbuilding and marine engineering	128	0.6
Vehicles	509	2.5
Metal goods	398	2.0
Textiles	287	1.4
Leather, leather goods and fur	28	0.1
Clothing and footwear	257	1.3
Bricks, pottery etc.	195	1.0
Timber, furniture etc.	206	1.0
Paper, printing and publishing	473	2.3
Other manufacturing	226	1.1
Construction	966	4.8
Gas, electricity and water	322	1.6
Transport and communication	1,328	6.6
Distributive trades	2,640	13.1
Insurance, banking etc.	1,325	6.6
Professional and scientific services	3,650	18.1
Miscellaneous services	2,450	12.1
Public administration and defence	1,495	7.4
Total manufacturing	5,355	26.5
Total	20,175	99.9

[a] June 1983
Source: *Employment Gazette*, 1983 **91**(10). table 1.2

There are very few employees in agriculture, forestry and fishing (under 2 per cent); however, in this sector there is quite a lot of self-employment. Probably a little under 3 per cent of all workers work in agriculture, forestry and fishing. In the middle of the last century about a quarter of the working population was in the agricultural sector, and this tremendous decline is perhaps the most significant long run trend; it is even used by some commentators as a rough index of the degree of development of an economy.

The service industries are, on the whole, increasing in terms of employment and this, rather than further declines in agriculture, is likely to be the basic trend for the foreseeable future.

Labour Demand

The demand for labour, like the demand for any input, is derived from its contribution to output. It is said to be a **derived demand**. It depends on the production function that relates labour as an input to output rates, upon the amount of other inputs, and upon the price at which output sells. Consider: if an employer who maximized profit thought that at the additional cost of £10,000 per year an additional worker would cause output to rise by 20,000 units a year, and each unit brought in 75p to the employer, then it would plainly pay the employer to hire the additional worker. Profits would be expected to rise by £5000, assuming that there were no other costs associated with employing the extra person.

The output that an additional input produces is called, as you know from chapter 9, the *marginal product* of the input. Since labour time is an input, one can speak of the **marginal product of labour time**.

You also know from chapter 9 that the marginal product of an input falls as more is used per period (the other inputs remaining constant). The same will be true of labour. If you were to graph the relationship between marginal product (increase in the output rate) and labour (measured in units of time: say labour-hours) you should expect to see a negatively sloped marginal product curve (*MP*) as in figure 17.1.

SAQ 17.1

In the production function $X = 5\,K^{0.6}L^{0.4}$, K is the annual flow of capital services (e.g. machine-hours per year) and L is the annual flow of labour time. For $K = 10$, use a pocket calculator to compute the marginal product of L when $L = 1, 2, 3, 4, 5$.

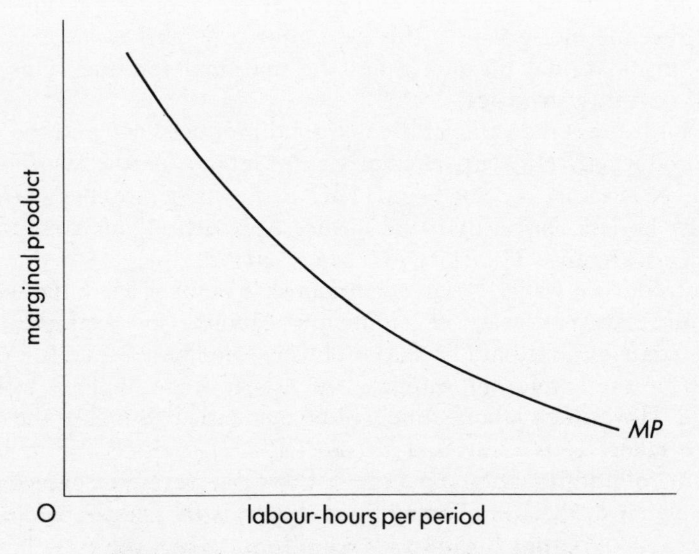

Figure 17.1 Marginal product curve of labour

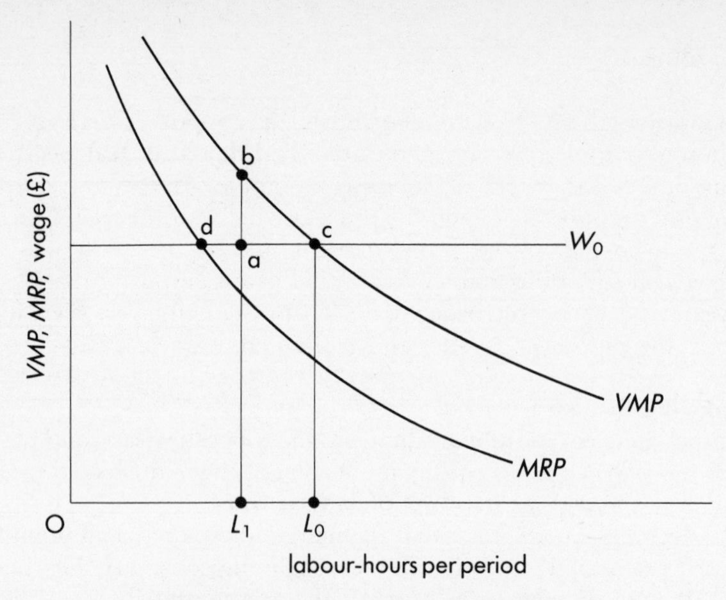

Figure 17.2 Demand curves for labour

The marginal product alone is, however, insufficient information to derive the demand for labour. The crucial extra bit of information needed is the **market value** of the extra output. If the employer is operating in a price takers' market, extra output sells at the price of the product. Hence the market value of the extra output is the marginal product times the price. Like most things in economics this has its own bit of jargon: it is called the **value of the marginal product**. If, on the other hand, the employer is operating in a price searcher's market, the additional value to the firm of extra output is given by the marginal revenue, not price. In this case, then, the market value of the extra output is the marginal product times the marginal revenue. This is called **marginal revenue product**.

Figure 17.2 shows the value of the marginal product *VMP* and the marginal revenue product *MRP* for a particular type of labour, on the assumption that the employer is either a price taker (*VMP*) or a price searcher (*MRP*). The latter must be less elastic than the former because, as you know, $MR < P$ under price searching. Therefore $MP\ MR < MP\ P$.

Now introduce a wage. From the employer's point of view the wage must include all marginal costs of employing labour (for example, national insurance contributions paid by the employer, contributory pension payments picked up by the employer). Suppose the hourly wage happens to be W_0 in figure 17.2. How much labour time will be demanded? Suppose the employer is a price taker. It is clear that to the left of L_0 where $W_0 = VMP$, the contribution of additional labour time to the value of output exceeds its cost. For example, at L_1 the cost of an additional hour is W_0 (shown by point a) but the extra value of output is shown by point b, so to hire the extra hour would add ab to profit. With price searching, at wage W_0, d is the profit maximizing point and is to the left of point c, the price taker's profit maximizing point. Profit maximizing implies, evidently, that whenever *VMP* or *MRP* is greater than the wage, employment will rise. By analogous reasoning, when *VMP* or *MRP* is less than the wage, employment will fall.

The profit maximizing employer thus must necessarily set *VMP* or *MRP* equal to the wage. Thus, if wages rose under price taking, a new point on *VMP* would be selected to the left of L_0. If wages fell, a new point on *VMP* would be selected to the right of L_0. A similar argument holds for price searching. Thus, *if the employer is a price taker, the demand curve for labour is the value of the marginal product curve; if the employer is a price searcher, the demand curve for labour is the marginal revenue product curve.*

Both *VMP* and *MRP* have a negative slope – *VMP* because the *MP* curve has a negative slope and price is constant, *MRP* because the *MP* curve has a negative slope and so has the *MR* curve. Hence, the demand for labour has a negative slope (assuming profit maximizing employers and all other inputs constant).

Industry Demand for Labour

When wages rise or fall they usually do so for *all* those firms employing labour of that type. Consequently all will change their rate of employment of labour, all will change their output and, hence, price of output must change. For the industry, therefore, even if it is a price taking industry, price must change as wages change. The *VMP* curve consequently shifts. Remember: the *VMP* curve is drawn on the assumption that price is constant – as it is with regard to any changes in output and employment made by the firm alone, but as it is *not* with regard to the same behaviour by *all* firms in the industry.

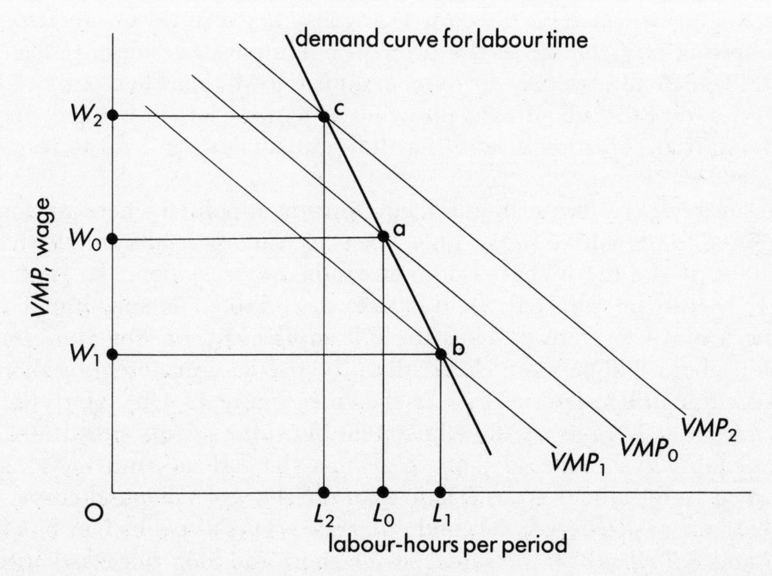

Figure 17.3 The demand for labour with industry price and output adjustments

In figure 17.3, imagine that a price taking firm is initially in profit maximizing equilibrium at point a, whose $VMP_0 = W_0$. Now let the wage fall to W_1. The firm starts to expand along VMP_0 but, as all firms do the same and industry output rises, the price of output falls, so *VMP* shifts to the left. $VMP_1 = MP\ P_1$, where $P_1 < P_0$. The new equilibrium is thus at point b where, once again, $VMP = W$ and the industry price has adjusted. Conversely, if the wage rises to W_2 from W_0 the firm will contract its employment to the left along VMP_0 but, as all firms do the same, industry output falls, output price rises and *VMP* shifts to, say, VMP_2 with a new equilibrium at point c.

The curve cab is the firm's demand curve for labour time allowing for industry adjustment. Note that, at any wage rate, it must be less elastic than the demand curve that ignores price effects. Note also that the more elastic the demand curve for the industry's output the less any output change will affect price and, hence, the more elastic the demand curve for labour.

SAQ 17.2

Under the same assumptions as in SAQ 17.1, and given that the industry demand for X is $X = 4500 - 30P$ and that there are 100 price taking firms in the industry all with identical production functions and each with $K = 10$, calculate the value of the marginal product curve when $P = 47$ and the demand curve for labour (maximum wage employers will pay) when $L = 1, 2, 3, 4, 5, 6$. (Use the MP_L data in the answer to SAQ 17.1.)

Other determinants of the wage elasticity of demand for labour include the variability of other inputs and the proportion that labour costs occupy in marginal costs. Consider other inputs first. The marginal product curve that underlies both *VMP* and *MRP* curves is defined to be the change in output induced by changing the rate of use of only the input in question: others are assumed constant. Recalling the analysis of efficient production, profit maximizing firms will seek to regain a tangency between isocost and isoquant lines following any change in the price of one input. The more time that is allowed for such adjustment, the more complete it will be. There are two basic possibilities: that the full adjustment will lead to more labour being demanded than the partial adjustment, and that full adjustment will lead to less being demanded.

In figure 17.4(a) a firm is in initial equilibrium at point a where an isoquant is tangential to the initial isocost line. The wage rate then falls and, with input A constant at A_0, the highest isoquant attainable is at point b. With time, however, A can be adjusted. In this case more labour is substituted for it, enabling a move to point c. Thus the full adjustment, or long run, demand curve for labour will be more elastic than the partial adjustment or short run demand curve. The opposite case is shown in figure 17.4(b). Here the firm moves from a′ to b′ in its partial adjustment but subsequently substitutes A for labour, enabling a move to point c′. Thus the full adjustment, long run demand curve for labour is *less* elastic than the short run demand curve. Only in the extreme case where the second tangency occurs at points b or b′ will the partial and full effects be the same, so the short and long run elasticities will also be the same.

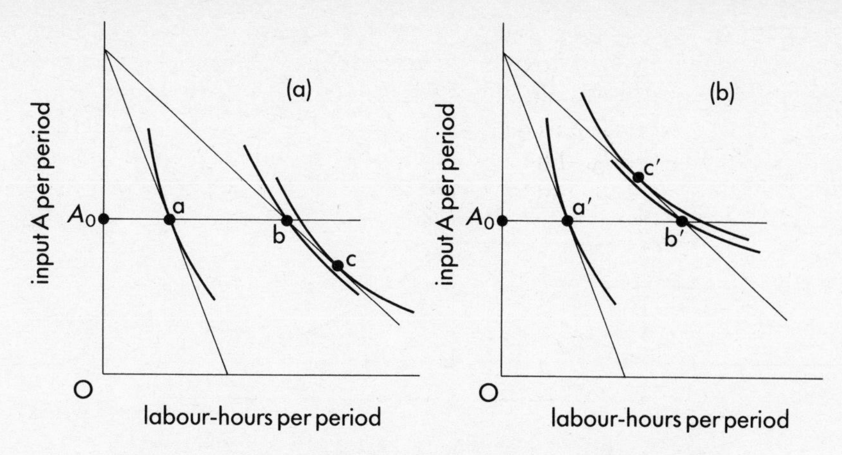

Figure 17.4 Full and partial adjustment to wage changes

SAQ 17.3

The more substitutable two inputs are in production, the greater the elasticity of demand for each of them. Right?

The proportion taken by labour costs in marginal costs is important for the elasticity of demand for labour because the change in output that a change in wage rates induces depends upon the impact of the wage rate change on marginal costs. If the wage component of marginal cost is small, then the impact of a rise in wages on marginal cost will be small. Hence, for any given elasticity in the demand for the output, there will be a small change in output and hence a small change in the amount of labour needed to produce it cost-effectively.

Supply of Labour

Some labour is monopolized by an individual, as is the case, for example, with a successful (living) composer and many sports and show business stars. In such cases, where high rewards for some are frequently found alongside low rewards for others in the same line of business, the payments received by the stars are usually well above what is necessary to induce them to do the work. The payments serve the function of allocating the stars' time among those who wish to use their services, but they do not affect the supply of labour. Earnings in excess of the minimum necessary to call forth the service are termed **rent** in economics. You can see that the rent of land discussed in chapter 10 fits this definition: with a fixed stock of land, its rent allocates it to the highest valued uses but does not increase the supply (though higher rents commonly induce the use of less productive land in agriculture, induce land reclamation and, of course, cause land uses to change.)

In general, any labour services that have an upward sloping supply curve

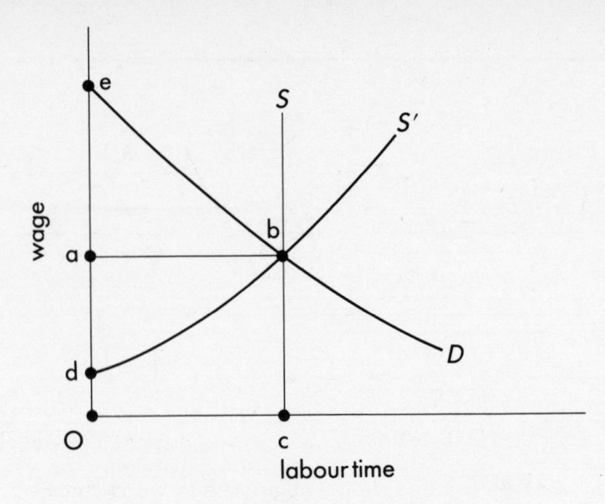

Figure 17.5 Supply curves for SAQ 17.4

earn economic rents – the difference between the sum paid to labour (as indeed any other input) and the *minimum* needed to induce the supply. This corresponds to the area above the supply curve and below the price per unit paid. (If you draw the diagram for yourself you will then see the analogy between economic rent and producer's surplus. The supply curve shows, of course, the minimum sum needed to compensate the supplier for each additional unit of labour supplied, whereas the price actually paid is the sum needed to compensate only for the last increment provided.)

SAQ 17.4

In figure 17.5, which area corresponds to economic rent if (a) *S* is the supply curve and (b) *S′* is the supply curve?

The total supply of labour is determined at the broadest level by the size of a country's population. Given the population, the supply of labour depends upon the size of the working population and the amount of hours each person supplies. Both of these are dependent in part on the wage rate.

The first of these points can be illustrated beginning with figure 17.6. This shows an individual's indifference map with earned income on the vertical axis and hours of work per period (say, per week) on the horizontal. Suppose that, at the margin at least, work is a 'bad' rather than a good and so the indifference curves will – in the range over which work is a 'bad' – have an upward slope rather than the downward slope taken as axiomatic in the case of economic goods. So the area concerned is to the south east of a *closed* indifference map of the sort discussed in chapter 7 (now is a good time to refer back to figure 7.6 and its associated discussion).

On to this indifference map can be projected an hourly wage rate as in figure 17.7. This is, of course, simply earned income divided by hours worked (e.g. Y_0/H_0) and is indicated by a ray like that labelled W_0. A higher wage is

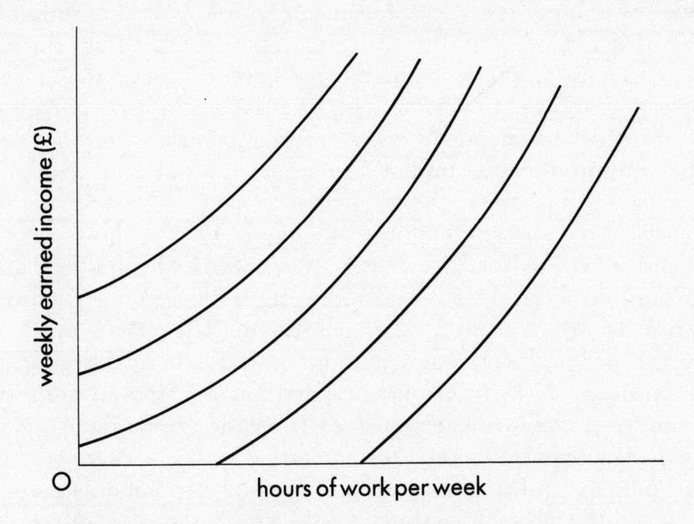

Figure 17.6 Indifference map for work and earned income

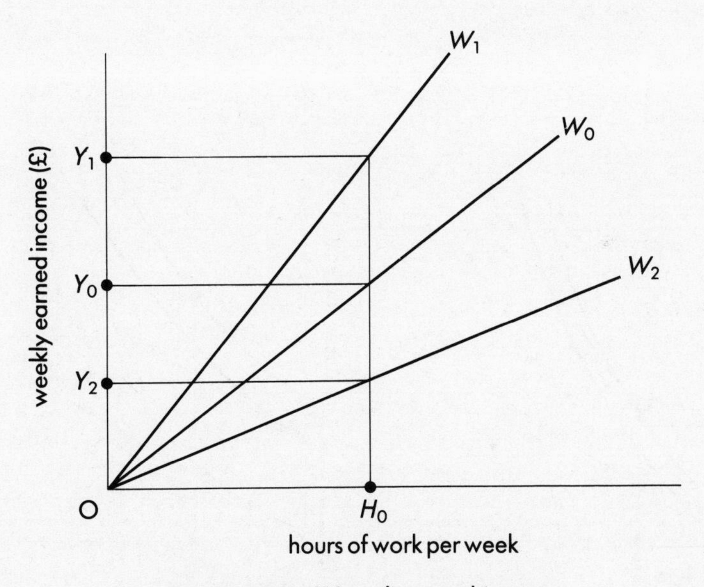

Figure 17.7 Wage lines and income

indicated by a steeper ray like W_1 (Y_1/H_0) and a lower wage by a flatter ray like W_2 (Y_2/H_0).

You should now be able to see that an individual will choose not to work either if the indifference curve through the origin is steeper than the wage line (for, in this case, the highest attainable indifference curve is the line going through the origin and the preferred point on it is at zero) or – in case you find implausible the idea of someone living on a zero income – when the presence of unearned income produces a similar corner solution but at a positive level of income.

These two cases are shown in figure 17.8. Figure 17.8(a) shows the result for zero work and zero income. At a wage rate of W_0 the highest attainable indifference curve is U_1 and this entails locating at the origin. If, however, the wage rate rose to W_1, tangency is at point a on U_2 and H_1 work is done: a higher wage has induced participation in the labour force or working population. In figure 17.8(b), Ob is unearned income (say an annuity left by Uncle George, or a cash transfer received from the government). Zero work then means that income is Ob and, at wage rate W_0, this is what will be chosen. If Ob can be made to fall to zero (say by cancelling entitlement) positive work may be done as the wage line shifts to W_0' and point a is selected on U_0. Another possibility, however, is that the individual will still choose a further solution on the vertical section Ob as unearned income is reduced: there is no necessary logic behind the hard hearted view that poverty encourages work. However, even if there is some unearned income (such as Ob), note that a higher wage will eventually induce some participation. For example, at W_1, H_1 hours are done and the individual has moved into the working population, locating at point c.

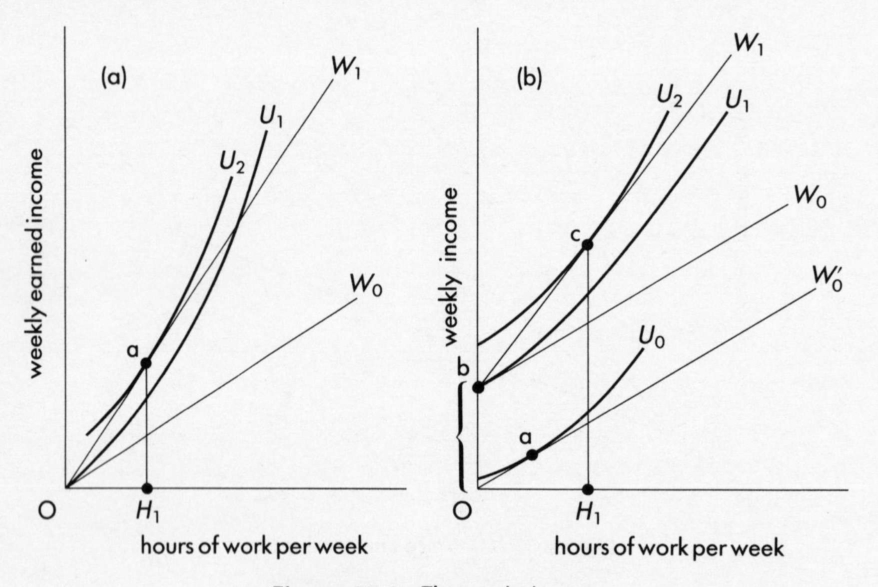

Figure 17.8 The work decision

You can conclude that lower unearned income may or may not encourage labour force participation, and that higher wages will encourage labour force participation.

Generally, of course, different individuals have different indifference maps and hence different thresholds of participation and non-participation. Thus, as wages rise, so participation can be expected gradually to increase, as people with higher thresholds find it to their advantage to participate.

The amount of work done is expected generally to rise as the wage rises but subsequently to fall. This is shown in figure 17.9. In figure 17.9(a) the chosen

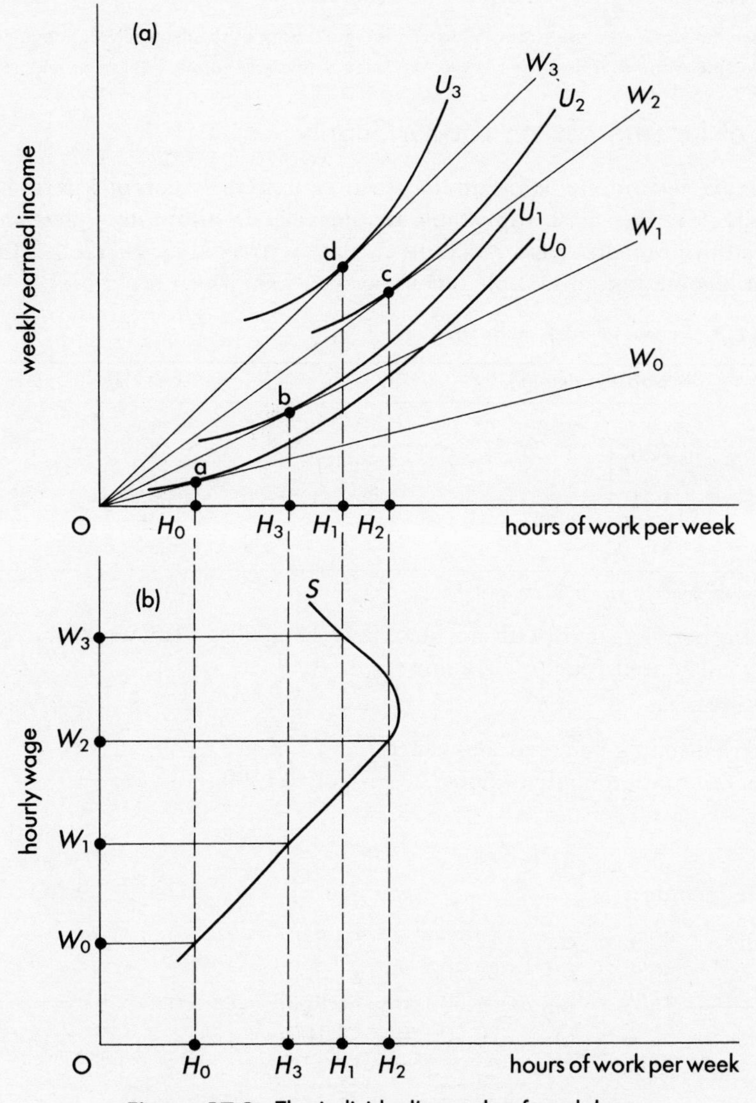

Figure 17.9 The individual's supply of work-hours

combination of income and work at a variety of wage rates is shown (points a, b, c and d). As the wage rate rises, work done initially rises but subsequently falls. This is portrayed in figure 17.9(b), which derives the individual's supply curve of labour hours at a variety of wages. With aggregation over all individuals to show how much all will supply (usually in a particular area and of a particular skill) at a range of wage rates, the total supply curve of labour in that particular market is produced, where the market is defined in terms of the type of labour being supplied rather than the type of product being produced.

SAQ 17.5

In figure 17.9:

(a) When the wage rate rises from W_0 to W_1, is the elasticity of supply positive or negative?
(b) When the wage rate rises from W_2 to W_3, is the elasticity of supply positive or negative?

Effect of Income Tax on Labour Supply

In practice, income tax computations can be extremely complex owing to the various rates that may apply and to the various allowances that may be deducted from income before taxable income is arrived at. In 1982–3 the UK rates of income tax on taxable income were as shown in table 17.3.

Table 17.3 Income tax rates in the UK 1982–3

Taxable income (£)	*Rate (%)*
0–12,800	30[a]
12,801–15,100	40
15,101–19,100	45
19,101–25,300	50
25,301–31,500	55
31,500–	60

[a] The so-called 'standard' rate is 30 per cent.

Thus a married man with an income of £30,000 a year would have a tax liability calculated roughly as follows:

Income					£30,000
less married man's personal allowance				£2445	
less superannuation contributions				£1500	
				£3945	£3,945
Taxable income					£26,055
Tax due:	30%	on	£12,800 =	£3,840	
	40%	on	£2,300 =	£ 920	
	45%	on	£4,000 =	£1,800	
	50%	on	£6,200 =	£3,100	
	55%	on	£ 755 =	£ 415	
Total			£26,055	£10,075	

Note that the *average* tax rate for this person is £10,075/£30,000 = 33.6 per cent, compared with a *marginal* tax rate of 55 per cent.

People often speak as though it were self-evident that the taxation of earned income must reduce the supply of work by individuals: that is, it must have a **disincentive** effect. This is often coupled with a belief that one lives in a relatively highly taxed society. Look first at what theory tells you before turning to the evidence in case studies 17.1 and 17.2.

In figure 17.10 an individual is initially in equilibrium at point a. Suppose this is a situation in which there is no income tax. Then let an income tax be introduced – suppose a proportional tax of 50 per cent. For any number of hours worked this means that take home pay falls by 50 per cent, so the net-of-tax wage line became $W_0 - T$. Where will the individual locate on this after tax line? The answer depends, of course on the indifference map. If the new tangency occurred at point b, H_0 hours would continue to be worked and the tax would have neither an incentive nor a disincentive effect on work done. If the individual chooses point c, H_1 hours will be worked and there will have been a disincentive effect. If the individual locates at point d, H_2 hours will be worked and there will have been an **incentive** effect. In principle, then, an income tax has no clear predictable effect on work done – contrary to popular supposition. The pure substitution effect works as a disincentive. For example, holding utility constant at the level U_0 means that the individual moves from point a to a point like e to its left, unambiguously implying less work. Leisure (including any non-market activity like DIY) has become relatively cheaper

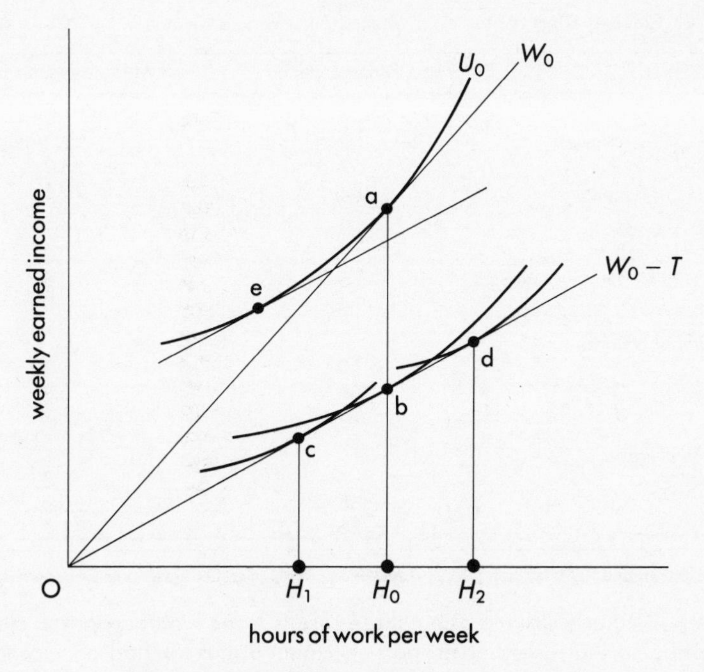

Figure 17.10 Effects of income tax on work

than it previously was, and hence one expects more of it to be substituted for the things earned income will buy. However, the fact that tax reduces take home pay provides people with an incentive to work harder to replace lost income and maintain living standards: but whether this effect moves them from point e to points like c to the left of point a, or points like d to the right of point a, is unclear.

Not everyone is free in the short run to vary their working hours: they may be contracted to work so many hours at a given (pre-tax) wage. Any change in hours will then have to wait until the next round of pay negotiations. This suggests that, at least in the short run, such people will tend to move from point a to point b – even if their preferred position is point c or point d. But in the longer run, when fuller adjustment can take place, the net effect of income taxation is ambiguous. There is no theoretical presumption. The issue is empirical. What the evidence says is discussed in case study 17.1.

Case Study 17.1 Evidence on Disincentive Effects of Income Tax

In various studies, Chuck Brown has investigated the workings of the British tax system. In one such study, with co-author Levin (1974), he interviewed 2000 weekly paid workers and included some questions as to whether income tax made them work more, less or the same amount of overtime. The results for those whose answers were judged 'plausible' (not inconsistent with other answers), of the 70 per cent who had discretion as to the amount of overtime worked (34 per cent of the sample), are shown in table 17.4.

Table 17.4 Claimed effects of tax on overtime hours worked by men

	Percentage	*Mean overtime hours*
All men		
Less	9	2.8
Neither	69	6.2
More	22	10.6
Single men		
Less	12	2.3
Neither	75	3.5
More	14	4.0
Married without children		
Less	10	3.1
Neither	68	5.9
More	23	11.2
Married with children		
Less	6	1.8
Neither	68	8.6
More	26	11.1

Source: C. V. Brown and P. M. Jackson (1982) *Public Sector Economics*, Oxford, Martin Robertson, table 14.9

What is particularly striking about these results is the high proportion claiming no effect. Note also that a higher proportion claimed that tax had an *incentive* effect than the reverse. The vast bulk of empirical investigations of disincentive effects of income taxation have found negligible effects either way.

C. V. Brown and E. Levin (1974) 'The effects of income taxation on overtime', *Economic Journal*, **84**, 833–48.

In order to show that the theoretical analysis is not limited to simple tax structures, suppose that there is no tax on annual income up to £1000, that the rate is 20 per cent on the next £4000 and 50 per cent on all income thereafter. In that case the tax due and after tax income will be that shown in table 17.5. Most income tax systems exempt low earners from tax so that even if the tax rate is proportional on whatever income is taxable, the average tax rate will be less than the marginal rate. In table 17.5, for example, at £3000, the marginal rate is 20 per cent, so 20p will be payable out of every additional pound earned, but the average rate (total tax divided by income) is only 13 per cent (check the arithmetic for yourself).

Table 17.5 Marginal, average and total tax at various income levels

Income (£)	*Marginal rate (%)*	*Income tax payable (£)*	*After tax income (£)*	*Average tax rate (%)*
0	0	0	0	0
500	0	0	500	0
1000	0	0	1000	0
1500	20	100	1400	7
2000	20	200	1800	10
2500	20	300	2200	12
3000	20	400	2600	13
3500	20	500	3000	14
4000	20	600	3400	15
4500	20	700	3800	16
5000	20	800	4200	16
5500	50	1050	4450	19
6000	50	1300	4700	22
6500	50	1550	4950	24
7000	50	1800	5200	26

If one pays a higher proportion of one's income in tax as one earns more, the tax structure is defined to be *progressive* as distinct from *proportionate* (constant proportion) or *regressive* (decreasing proportion) (see chapter 13). Even a constant rate can make the system progressive if there is tax exemption on low incomes, as is shown by the rising average tax rate in table 17.5. However, the basic analysis of incentives is not affected by the structure of the income tax system. For example, figure 17.11 shows the after tax wage line of an individual with an hourly wage of £3.57 and the tax structure of table 17.5. If the individual is initially at point a, after tax the move could be to points b, c or d, with the same ambiguous results as before.

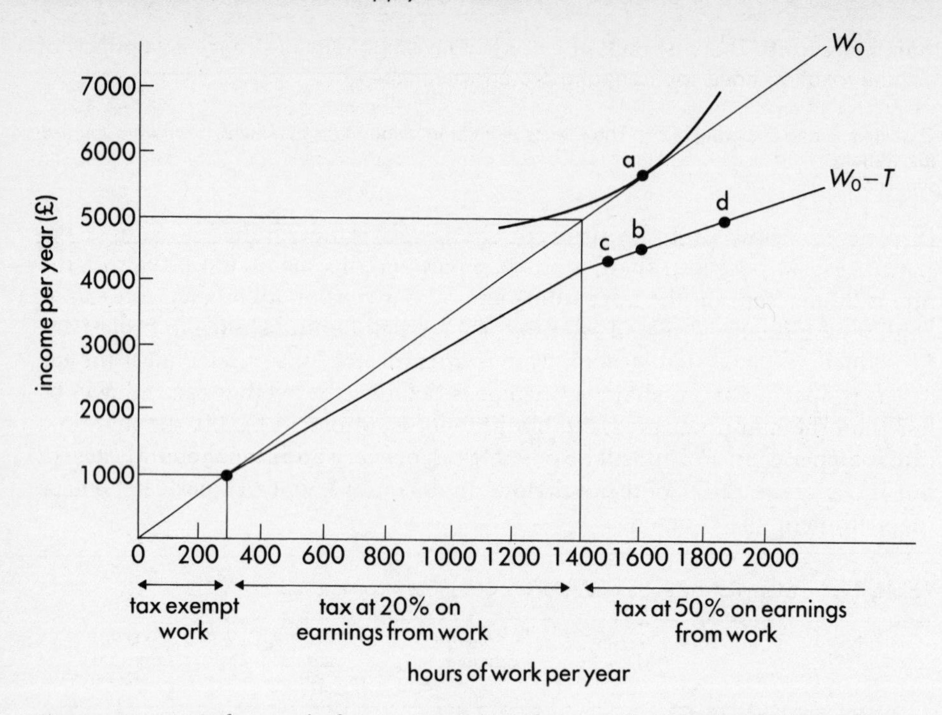

Figure 17.11 Before and after tax wage lines for an individual facing the tax rates of table 17.5

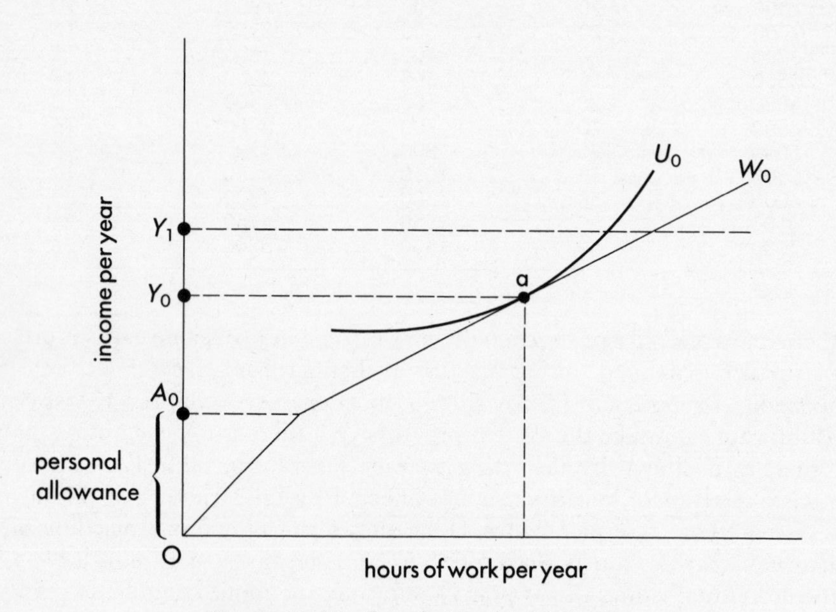

Figure 17.12 Tax choices for SAQ 17.6

SAQ 17.6

In figure 17.12, a representative individual is initially at point a. The Chancellor of the Exchequer wants to cut income taxes so as to leave the individual with Y_1 income instead of Y_0 (after tax). He has two basic choices: either to increase personal allowances, or to reduce the (single in this case) rate of tax. What are the pros and cons of each (especially as regards taxpayers' utility and work effort supplied)?

Case Study 17.2 International Comparison of Income Tax as a Percentage of GDP

The British – together with most other nations – are fond of imagining themselves among the more highly taxed of developed nations. Table 17.6 (Brown and Jackson, 1982) shows the share of gross domestic product (roughly equal to national income) taken by income tax and social security contributions in 22 member states of the Organization for Economic Cooperation and Development (OECD). Table 17.6 shows only *income* tax collections, but it is typically by these that people feel most hard pressed. In the years 1975 and 1979, the UK was below the OECD average and in all three below the EEC average.

Chuck Brown and Peter Jackson (1982) *Public Sector Economics*, Oxford, Martin Robertson.

Table 17.6 Income tax plus social security contributions in OECD countries, 1965, 1975 and 1979 as percentage of GDP at market prices.

Country	*1965*	*1975*	*1979*
Sweden	21.47	28.98	34.95
Netherlands	20.64	30.02	30.67
Belgium	16.21	26.20	28.98
Luxembourg	17.53	25.11	26.26
Norway	17.16	25.28	24.96
Germany	16.66	22.89	23.52
Denmark	14.08	22.99	22.86
France	15.65	19.84	22.74
Austria	15.66	19.08	22.26
Italy	12.29	17.69	20.01
USA	12.45	17.34	19.37
Finland	13.28	21.31	18.50
New Zealand	9.67	15.80	17.70
Switzerland	11.11	19.33	16.63
UK	13.93	20.08	16.56
Spain	6.27	12.15	15.98
Ireland	6.03	12.66	15.03
Canada	7.45	14.17	13.67
Australia	8.11	12.67	13.21
Greece	7.04	8.97	11.70
Portugal	3.62	7.76	6.95
Turkey	4.57	8.73	6.71

Overtime

The analysis so far can be easily extended to provide an explanation for why overtime rates of pay in excess of normal rates can be in the interests of both employers and employees.

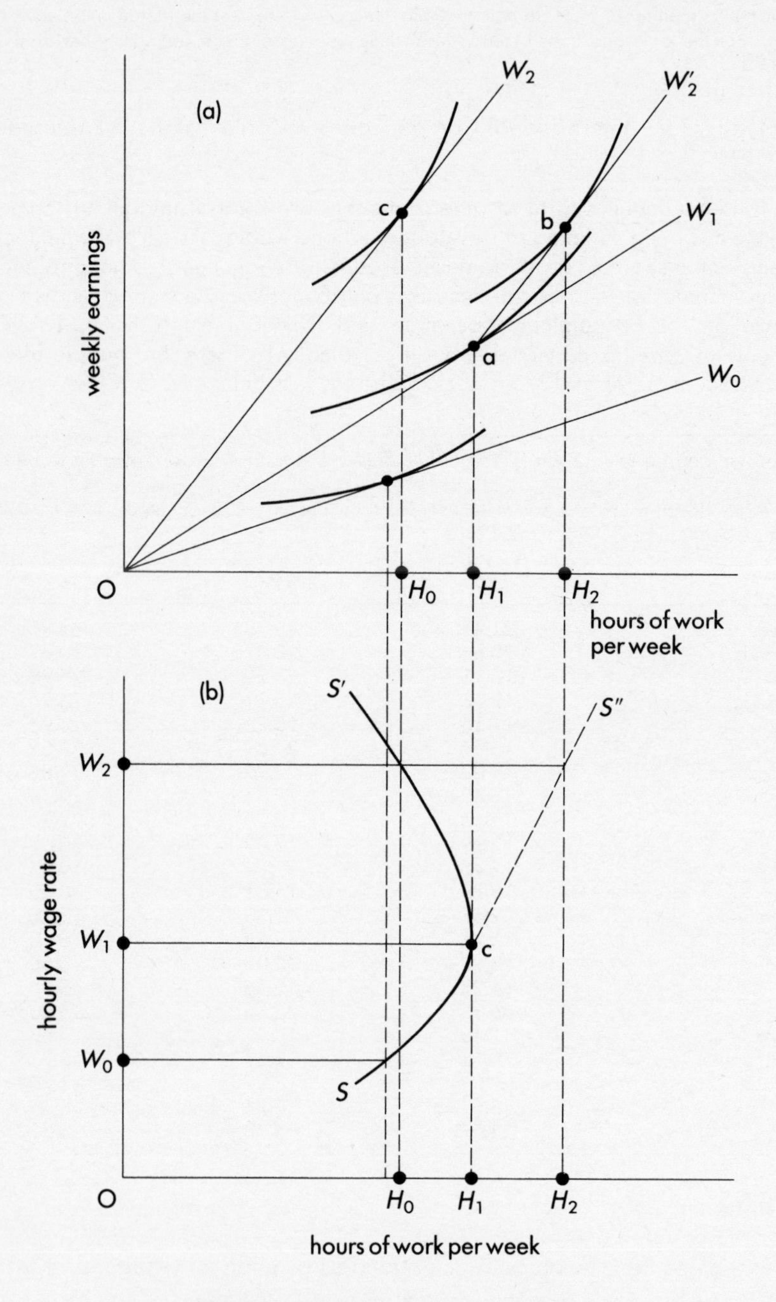

Figure 17.13 Economics of overtime

Suppose that the representative employee has a backward bending supply curve of labour time as illustrated by figure 17.9 and redrawn in figure 17.13. This implies that, at wage W_1, the employer can obtain more labour only by hiring additional workers. This the employer may prefer not to do because to do so requires a costly search, and possible additional contributions to social and other insurance or pension funds. In any case, additional labour may be required only on particular occasions when output peaks, or at weekends. In such cases the employer may find it cheaper to find a method of persuading the existing workforce to supply more labour time.

By offering a single hourly rate the highest number of hours obtainable from an employee is H_1 at wage W_1. By offering a deal that says work up to H_1 hours will be paid at wage W_1 but work beyond that will be paid at (say) W_2, the employee can move along the wage line W_2' from point a to a preferred point b at which H_2 hours will be supplied. OH_1 is normal time. H_1H_2 is overtime. The employer thereby gets the extra hours he wanted and the employee moves to a more preferred point (higher indifference curve). This is a special kind of price discrimination. Note that the employee would prefer a straight rate of W_2 for all work, enabling the attainment of point c. But in that case only H_0 hours would be supplied and this will not be acceptable to the employer. With overtime payments the supply curve is no longer ScS' but ScS'' in figure 17.13(b).

What You Should Understand Now

The pattern of employment in the UK.
The determinants of the demand for labour at firm and industry level with price taking and monopoly.
The meaning of economic rent.
Some determinants of labour force participation and the supply of labour.
Effects of unearned income on labour force participation.
Effects of income tax on supply of labour (theory and evidence).
An economic rationale of overtime.

18

Labour Market Imperfections, Wages and Unemployment

In this chapter some of the implications of the analysis of chapter 17 are further developed. There is particular emphasis on unemployment, but the full treatment of this topic must wait until chapter 28.

Minimum Wages and Involuntary Unemployment

Figure 18.1 brings together the demand (aggregated over all employees of a particular kind of labour – say bricklayers) and the supply (again aggregated over all labour of the relevant type). Assume (but only for the moment) that employers are all price takers and employees are not organized in trade unions. Demand equals supply at wage W_0. At wage rates higher than this, supply exceeds demand, tending to force wages down; at rates lower than W_0, demand from employers exceeds supply, tending to bid wages up. In equilibrium, there is neither excess demand nor excess supply and the wage also equals *VMP*. An increase in the demand for the product will cause its price to rise, *VMP* to shift to the right and the demand curve also to shift to the right. Thus the wage rate will be bid up and, provided that employees are on the upward sloping part of the curve, each will supply more hours. More workers will join the working population and, for those workers on the backward bending part of their individual supply curves, overtime rates will increase. For convenience, let W_0 represent the average rate (that is, including overtime). The supply curve combines the effects of increasing hours at normal rates, increasing hours at overtime rates, and new entrants to the labour force.

Now suppose that W_0 is judged to be an unfairly low wage. As a result, a minimum wage of W_1 is set above W_0 and employers are not permitted to hire labour at an hourly rate less than this. An excess supply of labour is created: workers will want to supply H_2 hours in total (a combination of people wanting to work more and some wanting to begin work) but employers will demand only H_1 hours. As they reduce employment and industry output contracts, the price of output will have risen so *VMP* will have shifted to VMP_1. Again, wage = *VMP* but there is now **involuntary unemployment** ($H_2 - H_1$) in the sense that, at the going wage, some workers are willing to supply labour time but are unable to. This has two components: the reduction in hours demanded ($H_0 - H_1$) and the increase in hours offered ($H_2 - H_0$). Some of it shows in inability to gain employment: explicit involuntary unemployment. Some of it will be

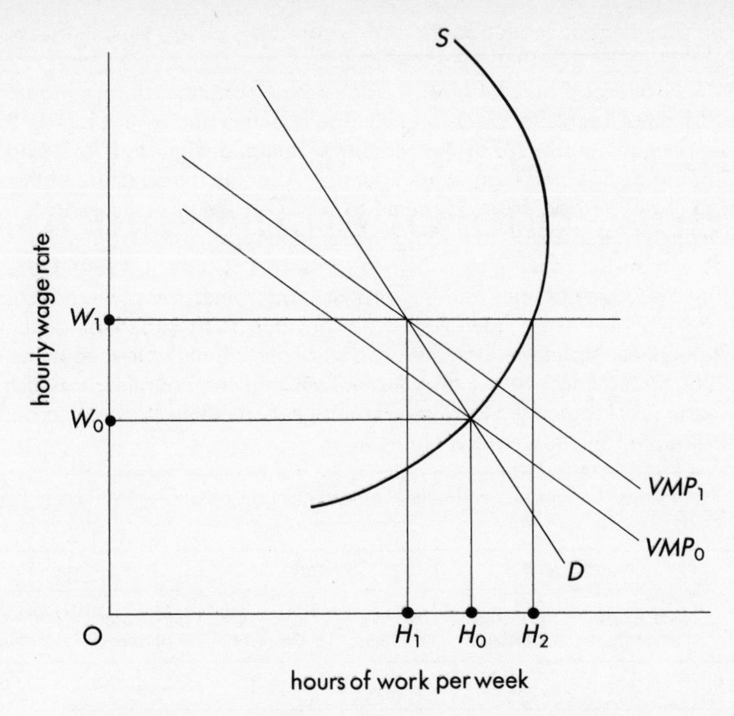

Figure 18.1 Equilibrium and minimum wages under price taking

hidden in that some workers will be unable to gain the *additional* employment they seek; this is disguised involuntary unemployment. Some workers will also withdraw from the labour force: this is another form of disguised involuntary unemployment since it will not show up in the published statistics of unemployed persons.

Note that at W_0 there is no involuntary unemployment. At that wage any workers wishing to work can work the hours they wish. Those who are not in employment are in *voluntary unemployment* (for example, searching for better jobs, preferring not to work at what they regard as disgracefully low wages). This analysis is not political. W_0 may be too low by some moral standard. The politics enters when it is considered that the best way to reduce poverty caused by low earnings is by introducing a minimum wage: is it better to have *more* employment at a low wage or less at a higher wage? Economics can point up the awkwardness of the dilemma but cannot resolve it.

There is evidence that minimum wages do have the effect of creating – or increasing – involuntary unemployment, as case study 18.1 shows.

Case Study 18.1 Minimum Wages in the US South: A Yankee Trick?

The USA has a long history of minimum wages in most occupations. In 1956 the national minimum wage was raised from 75 cents to $1.00 per hour. Theory predicts a fall in employment in the wage controlled occupations and, as a result, some increase in employment in occupations not wage controlled. These effects are obviously expected to be seen in low wage districts.

In January 1956 average normal hourly wage rates in manufacturing industry in Florida ranged from 79 cents to $1.21 in low wage counties and from $1.24 to $2.04 in high wage counties, with 24 of the counties being designated low and the remaining 23 being designated high wage counties. After the introduction of the new minimum wage, rates varied from 95 cents to $1.67 in the previously low wage counties and from $1.26 to $2.00 in the high wage counties (April 1956).

The changes in man-hours were as shown in table 18.1 (Colberg, 1960). Here you can see that the low wage counties had the largest – and rather speedy – reduction in employment. Part of this was, however, probably due to a seasonal decline in demand in all counties. None the less, the proportionate fall in the low counties was twice that in the high. Moreover, it also turned out that the counties in which the $1 minimum wage represented the largest percentage increase in wages also had the largest proportionate falls in employment.

Table 18.1 Percentage changes in man-hours of employment for production workers in Florida, January–April 1956

	Normal time		*Overtime*		*Total*	
	Low wage counties	*High wage counties*	*Low wage counties*	*High wage counties*	*Low wage counties*	*High wage counties*
Jan.–Apr. 1956	−13.8	−8.7	−39.0	−7.1	−15.2	−7.9

One occupation not 'protected' by minimum wages was private household work (house servants etc.). Yale Brozen (1962) has shown what one would expect for this group following successive increases in the minimum wage. After a rise from 40 to 75 cents in 1950, employment of private household workers rose from 3.07 per cent of employed persons to 3.23 per cent and unemployment among household workers grew from 5.2 to 5.6 per cent. After the rise from 75 cents to $1.00 in 1956, employment of these workers rose from 3.7 per cent of the employed workforce to 4.3 per cent and unemployment among them again grew. After a rise from $1.00 to $1.15 in 1961 the share of household workers in total employment rose from 3.4 per cent to 3.51 per cent (and the unemployment rate among these workers fell somewhat).

Small wonder that Marshall Colberg describes the national minimum wage as 'a device for waging regional economic warfare' by destroying one of the attributes of low cost labour regions that attracts industry to their areas, thus encouraging out-migration and generating unemployment – a Yankee trick played by the North on the South.

Marshall Colberg (1960) 'Minimum wage effects on Florida's economic development', *Journal of Law and Economics*, **3**, 106–17, table 3.
Yale Brozen (1962) 'Minimum wage rates and household workers', *Journal of Law and Economics*, **5**, 103–9.

SAQ 18.1

(a) Define involuntary unemployment.
(b) Define voluntary unemployment.

Trade Unions

Some workers are fortunate enough to be price searchers or even monopolists. John Le Carré, Elizabeth Taylor and Paul Samuelson have few close substitutes and can command huge rents. For the vast bulk of workers, however, this is not the case. These, just like price taking firms, have a strong incentive to create a monopoly of their labour. This has usually been done by forming trade unions whereby people in a particular trade or group of associated trades, or working for particularly large employers, join together to bargain collectively with employers. Since the number of people in this position is large, having substantial political clout in the democracies, their attempts to monopolize the supply of labour have usually successfully gained the sanction of governments.

The number of trade unions in the UK and their membership is shown in table 18.2. Although the number of unions has been falling since 1970 (with some exceptions), total membership rose until 1979. Since then it has fallen, mainly due to unemployment, with the greatest falls in non-service industries.

Table 18.2 Trade unions in the UK 1970–82 (numbers and membership)

Year	*Number of unions at end of year*	*Membership at end year (000s)*	*Percentage change in membership since previous year*
1970	543	11,187	+6.8
1971	525	11,135	−0.5
1972	507	11,359	+2.0
1973	519	11,456	+0.9
1974	507	11,764	+2.7
1975	501	12,193	+3.6
1975[a]	470	12,026	—
1976	473	12,386	+3.0
1977	481	12,846	+3.7
1978	462	13,112	+2.1
1979	456	13,289	+1.3
1980	438	12,947	−2.6
1981	414	12,106	−6.5
1982	401	11,445	−5.5

[a] Thirty-one organizations previously regarded as trade unions are excluded from 1975 onwards because they failed to satisfy the statutory definition of a trade union given in section 28 of the Trade Union and Labour Relations Act 1974.

Source: *Employment Gazette*, 1984, **92**(1), p. 18, table 2

Many unions are relatively small. Over half the 1982 total had fewer than 1000 members and together accounted for only 0.5 per cent of the total membership of all unions. At the other end of the scale there were 22 unions each with 100,000 or more members which together accounted for 80 per cent of the total membership. An analysis of the membership and the number of unions by size of union at the end of 1982 is given in table 18.3.

Table 18.3 Number of trade unions by size in 1982

Number of members	*Number of unions*
Under 100 members	78
100– 499	101
500– 999	46
1,000– 2,499	48
2,500– 4,999	37
5,000– 9,999	22
10,000– 14,999	3
15,000– 24,999	16
25,000– 49,999	15
50,000– 99,999	13
100,000–249,999	11
250,000 and more	11
Number of unions at end of year	401

Source: *Employment Gazette*, 1984, **92**(1), p. 18, table 1

The percentage of the working population in unions is shown in table 18.4 for 1970–82. As can be seen it tended to increase up to 1978, so membership was rising faster than the working population. A major reason for this was the increasing number of women both in the working population and as a share of unionized workers. Since 1979, however, the proportion unionized has been falling and in 1982 was lower than any proportion since 1970.

Table 18.4 Unionization of the working population

	Working population (000s)	*TU membership (000s)*	*TU members as % of working population*
1970	25,308	11,187	44.2
1971	25,123	11,135	44.3
1972	25,195	11,359	45.1
1973	25,547	11,456	44.8
1974	25,601	11,764	46.0
1975	25,849	12,026	46.5
1976	26,120	12,386	47.4
1977	26,276	12,846	48.9
1978	26,389	13,112	49.7
1979	26,781	13,289	49.6
1980	26,907	12,947	48.1
1981	26,803	12,106	45.2
1982	26,506	11,445	43.2

Source: *Employment Gazette*, 1984, **92**(1), table S1.1. See also table 18.2 in this book.

The ultimate strength of a trade union is the power to strike. A strike is not the same as a mass resignation or even a mass temporary resignation. A strike involves not merely the mass withdrawal of labour from an employer or employers, but also the effective prevention of the employer's ability to replace the withdrawn labour by hiring substitutes (blacklegs). Without this, of course, a strike would be no more than a mass resignation, which might be of considerable inconvenience to an employer but by no means as powerful a way of imposing costs on firms as the strike.

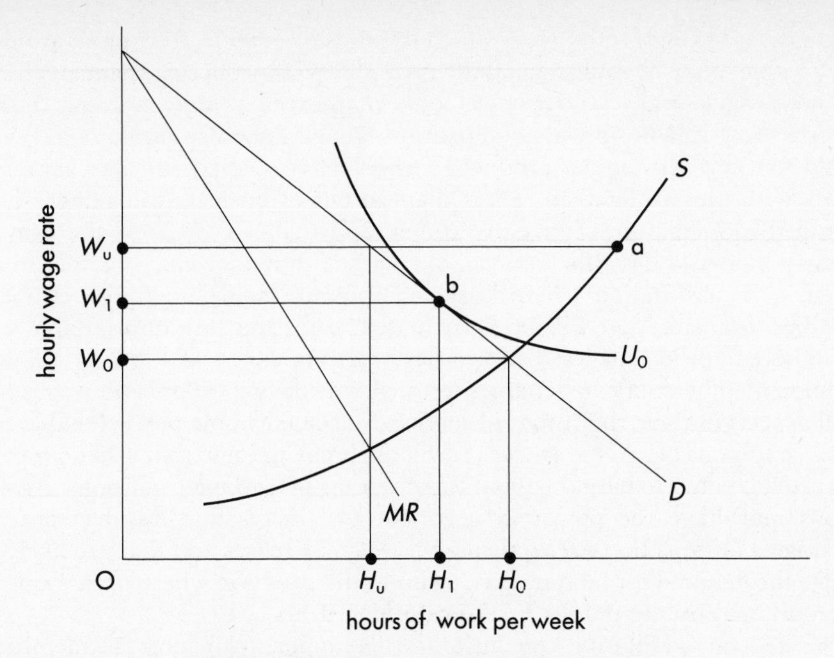

Figure 18.2 Some possible union objectives

Figure 18.2 shows a situation confronting a union. D is the demand curve for labour and S the supply curve. Under price taking conditions, $S = D$ and the equilibrium wage is W_0. Now suppose the labour force becomes unionized. As a seller of labour, the union has an MR curve analogous to that of a monopolist of an output. If the aim of the union is to maximize the collective earnings of workers for this firm (or in this industry) the best policy would be to search out wage W_u at which $MR = S$. The effective supply curve then becomes $W_u aS$: firms can have as much labour as they like at the wage W_u. Firms will not want, however, more than H_u, so there will be an excess supply at the union wage rate. If union membership is denied to the unemployed (or unemployed members have no voting rights) this may be a preferred policy for union leaders, for those thrown out of jobs as a result will have little weight in union decision making.

On the other hand, union leaders may seek also to increase membership: after all, this will increase their power and prestige. If so, they will react adversely to the unemployment that W_u may generate and, in seeking to gain more members, will have to trade higher wages off against higher membership. In terms of figure 18.2, they will trade wages off against hours: a wage lower than W_u (but higher than W_0) against hours more than H_u (but lower than H_0). Depending on union leaders' indifference maps, a point such as b may be selected, with W_1 and H_1 being the preferred wage rate and labour supply.

SAQ 18.2

In figure 18.2, is unemployment voluntary or involuntary at wage rates (a) W_u (b) W_1 (c) W_0?

If firms are making profits above the normal rate of return to capital, a union may be able to push employers off their *VMP* curves by offering them an all-or-nothing deal: so many labour hours to be guaranteed at a given wage. In this case the firm will be forced to substitute labour for other inputs and, even though output will not be produced cost-effectively, the firm may share its profits with union members rather than go out of business altogether. This will, in the longer run, reduce investment and reduce the size of the firm or industry; none the less, for appreciable periods the union may be able to do just this. In a situation where losses of firms are made up by government subsidies, this situation will be perpetuated; firms that are unprofitable will not only remain in business but will pay wages in excess of *VMP*.

Union members, of course, are interested not solely in hours and wages but in all aspects of their conditions of service. Since take home pay is taxable but many conditions of service are not, it will often pay unions (as it also does non-unionized labour) to bargain about these aspects of working conditions. Again, unions may have the power to negotiate cost increasing improvements in working conditions that are equivalent to wage increases and that are likely to reduce the demand for labour, save again in the situation where profits can be 'expropriated' by the unions in all-or-nothing deals.

The general qualitative conclusion is that unions can increase members' wages but only at some (long run or short run) cost in terms of job losses.

Monopsony

A case where unions may unambiguously raise both wages (or other on-the-job sources of benefit) *and also* employment occurs when there is a single major employer. This condition is known as **monopsony** and is illustrated in figure 18.3.

In this figure the labour supply curve is again denoted by *S*. If there is a single employer, that employer must pay higher wages if more labour hours are to be supplied. For example, if 2000 hours per week are obtained at an hourly rate of £3, 2001 hours may be obtained only at a higher wage rate – say £3.10. The total wage bill rises from £6000 (2000 × £3) to £6203.10 (2001 × £3.10). The marginal hour costs the employer not £3.10 but £203.10 (£6203.10 − £6000). Thus in this situation the marginal hourly wage exceeds the average as shown by the supply curve. In the figure, this is shown by *MW*, the **marginal wage** curve, which bears a similar relationship to *S* as *MC* does to *AC*.

SAQ 18.3

The supply curve of labour is given by the equation $L = -5 + W$, where L is hours of labour per employee per week and W is the wage rate. Compute (a) the wages that must be offered if hours supplied are to be 10, 20, 30 and 40 hours per week, (b) the marginal wage to a monopsonistic employer at these various hours.

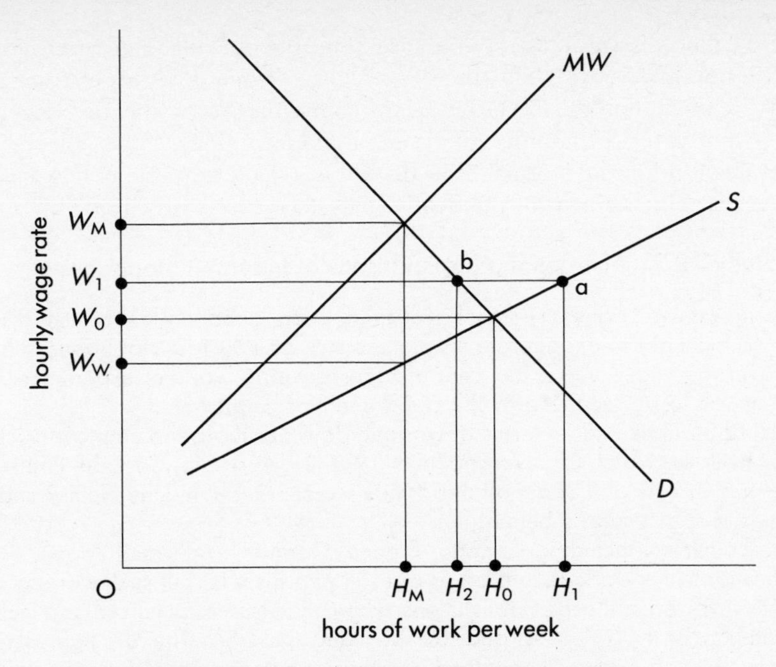

Figure 18.3 Monopsony in the labour market

Under monopsony, the employer will set *VMP* (or *MRP*) equal *not* to wage but to the increase in hourly wage costs, that is to *MW*. Hence marginal wage will equal W_M rather than W_0 and hours will be H_M rather than H_0. Workers will receive only wage W_W and will supply only H_M hours (which are all that are demanded given the marginal wage of W_M). Under these circumstances any wage negotiated by a union between W_W and W_M will not only raise wages but also increase hours (and employment) demanded. For example, if the union selects W_1, the supply curve of labour is W_1aS: the employer must pay at least W_1 to get any labour at all. If more than H_1 is demanded, the employer must pay more than the union rate and the marginal wage will jump immediately to a point on *MW* immediately above point a. In this case, as you can see, the firm will set *VMP* equal to its marginal wage costs (equal to W_1 up to H_1 hours) at point b, so that the wage rate rises from W_W to W_1 and hours rise from H_M to H_2. There is still excess supply of labour (and hence involuntary unemployment), measured by ba. If, however, the union selected any wage between W_W and W_0, wages would rise and so would hours (and employment); at no time would the supply of labour exceed the demand, and so there is no involuntary unemployment.

As you may imagine, there is considerable controversy over the effects that unions have on wages, profits and employment. This is partly because it is exceedingly difficult to sort out the impact of unions on these things as compared with, say, rises in import prices, increasing concentration of industry, changing participation rates in the labour force (especially by women), inflation and a host of other factors. But it is also due to economists' differing political views about the desirability of some features of trade union activity. Unfortunately, the latter seems sometimes to permeate (rather than merely motivate) economic analysis of trade unions. The alleged high frequency of industrial stoppages in Britain is a good example of how easy it is to exaggerate in the heat of political debate (see case study 18.2).

Case Study 18.2 International Comparisons of Industrial Stoppages

Strikes are news. British strikes have even been dubbed 'the British disease'. However, it is easy to exaggerate the significance of industrial stoppages in Britain. In an average year, only 2 per cent of manufacturing workers experience strikes large enough to be recorded by the Department of Employment.

Table 18.5 shows that, in terms of working days per thousand employees, the UK was far from the worst. On average, over 1972–81, Australia, Canada, Finland, the Irish Republic, Italy and Spain all performed worse. Germany, the Netherlands and Norway did spectacularly better.

Some countries, including Canada, France, Germany, Italy and Japan, exclude from their statistics workers laid off as a result of a dispute; but such workers (those indirectly involved at those establishments where the disputes occurred) are included, for example, in the UK, Australia, Sweden and the USA. The UK figures restrict coverage to those disputes concerned with terms and conditions of employment and associated 'sympathy' stoppages. Political stoppages are excluded not only in the UK but also in the USA and France, and in Italy prior to 1975, whereas such stoppages are included in several other countries.

C. T. B. Smith, Richard Clifton, Peter Makeham, S. W. Creigh and R. V. Burn (1978) *Strikes in Britain*, Department of Employment, Manpower Paper no. 15, London, HMSO.

Table 18.5 Industrial stoppages: working days lost per thousand employees in all industries and services, 1972–81

	1972	*1981*	*Average 1972–81*
United Kingdom	1081	197	531
Australia	433	814	674
Belgium	116	—	(208)
Canada	1041	899	944
Denmark	11	317	295
Finland	285	330	552
France	229	86	191
Germany	3	3	23
Irish Republic	285	—	(699)
Italy	1315	588	1217
Japan	149	14	99
Netherlands	3	6	19
New Zealand	112	238	272
Norway	9	17	48
Portugal	—	286	—
Spain	70	—	(949)
Sweden	3	54	138
United States	367	370	428

Source: *Employment Gazette*, 1983, **91**(3), table 1

On-the-Job Training

There are many sources of earnings differentials – natural aptitudes, trade unions, discrimination, handicaps and so on. Later sections will examine some of these. One important source, however, is acquired skill. You have already seen that individuals have an incentive to invest in themselves, thereby enhancing their **human capital**, if the net present value of future earnings with a skill exceeds the net present value of future earnings without that skill. If C denotes the cost of acquiring the skill and, for convenience, assuming that the differential earnings ΔE are constant over time and persist indefinitely, such investments will be pursued until

$$C = \frac{\Delta E}{i}$$

where i is an appropriate interest rate for the individual in question. Since people in lower social classes typically face higher borrowing rates than those in higher social classes (as witnessed, for example, by the more extensive use made of hire purchase arrangements than bank loans by people in lower social classes) one would expect to see less skill acquisition by members of lower social classes. And one does.

Such skill acquisition need not, of course, be formal schooling. Much training takes place on the job. In such cases it is useful to make a distinction between general and specific on-the-job training.

If a firm provides an opportunity for individuals to acquire skills that have value outside the firm, the other firms could compete such individuals away from the firm who trained them by offering them an appropriate wage. Such *general skills* will consequently usually be financed not by the firm but by the worker. In training (as, say, an apprentice) the worker accepts a lower wage – lower than actual productivity warrants. When training is complete a higher wage is received, reflecting the new productivity. Thus, the worker has paid the cost of the training and receives the return on it. With general skills, then, wages will be higher than for people not having these skills. In the case of *specific skills* that have no, or little, value outside the firm, the training firm faces no such competition and if it, rather than the worker, chooses to bear the costs of training, then it will later be able to recoup them by keeping wages lower than the value of the worker's contribution to output in the firm. Wage differentials between the more and the less (specifically) skilled will thus be small.

You can thus see that earnings differentials are predicted by human capital theory to arise mainly between the unskilled and those with general skills that have wide marketability.

Of course, this theory only explains a part of the inequality of earnings. For example, many professional groups have succeeded in establishing an occupational monopoly: entry to the profession is restricted, enabling higher returns to be sustained than the equation implies by virtue of keeping out many of the new entrants who would otherwise flock in. For other groups, non-pecuniary considerations may outweigh pecuniary ones (e.g. the priesthood).

SAQ 18.4

Suppose you are an employer who is considering providing on-the-job training for your employees that will enhance the value of their marginal productivities.

(a) Would you pay for it if the skills thus acquired were widely marketable to other firms who could compete your more highly productive labour away from you and hence deprive you of any return?

(b) Would you pay for it if the skills were very specific to your own firm? If so, how would you recoup the return on this investment?

(c) Can you see any case for government subsidies on industrial training?

Unequal Opportunities

Trade union practices can create unequal opportunities that may account for a greater inequality in earnings than the human capital theory alone would lead one to expect. Another major inequality in opportunities arises in access to the capital market. If employees are to bear the cost of skill acquisition, then they must somehow finance it. In a perfect capital market, the expected yield could be used as a pledge against loans, rather in the way that a building society lends to an owner occupier against the security of the house itself. Typically, however, society makes rules against this type of transaction in human capital: ownership of the present value of the skills is not permitted to be alienated from the possessor of the skills by, for example, long term indenture or by species of slave contracts. This has two consequences. First, loans made for acquisition of skills tend to be riskier, so that interest rates become relatively high, especially for those who have no other, non-human capital to borrow against. Secondly, it introduces inequalities between social classes, since they differ in the extent to which they own non-human capital that can be used either to secure loans for human investment or to be run down as human capital replaces non-human.

In addition to these and other market inequalities of opportunity, there are also differing opportunities because of people's differing abilities and aptitudes. More 'able' people, for example those with higher measured IQ or those whose social and personal upbringing has imbued them with values oriented towards high achievement, will tend to have a higher return to skill acquisition, are more likely to stay on at school after 16 and to be accepted into colleges of further education and universities, and so on. In any case, more able people are also simply more able; if two people have had equal training, it is not surprising if the more able of the two has higher earnings. Finally, some abilities are more valued than others. Independently of the training, intellectual skills, musical skills, persuasive skills, charm and so on all command different premiums in the marketplace.

Clearly the combination of training and ability is a powerful advantage. Many of the poor are those who have had little training and who possess few natural abilities of great value in the marketplace.

Discrimination

Not all disabilities are relevant to earnings; a one legged professor earns as much as two legged professors. But for those that are, the source of the low earnings lies either in the relatively low productivity of disabled workers, or in the relatively high cost of training them to productivity levels comparable with those of other employees and adapting the workplace in suitable ways, or both.

The most obvious indicator of discrimination against particular categories of worker, whether on grounds of disability, race or sex, is often thought to be the proportion of workers of that category in a particular occupation at a given wage relative to the proportion in the population as a whole. If the ratio is less than 1 it is often thought that there is prima facie evidence of discrimination. Consider workers whose labour time is perfectly substitutable. If employers are wealth maximizers, they will be perfectly indifferent as to which workers' labour time is used: whether, say, black or white. If, then, the proportion of blacks employed in a particular firm is smaller than the proportion in the total labour force having the relevant occupational skills, it must arise not from the employers' side but on the supply side of labour. In particular, it may arise because of differing supply elasticities. Imagine a labour force of equal numbers of black (B) and white (W) workers of equal skill. Wealth maximizing employers will (assuming away complications arising from union wage setting) employ each type up to the point at which the wage is equal to the value of additional output (the demand curve for labour time).

In figure 18.4 S_{B+W} indicates the combined supply of labour time from blacks and whites. Given the firm's demand D, an equilibrium wage W_0 is

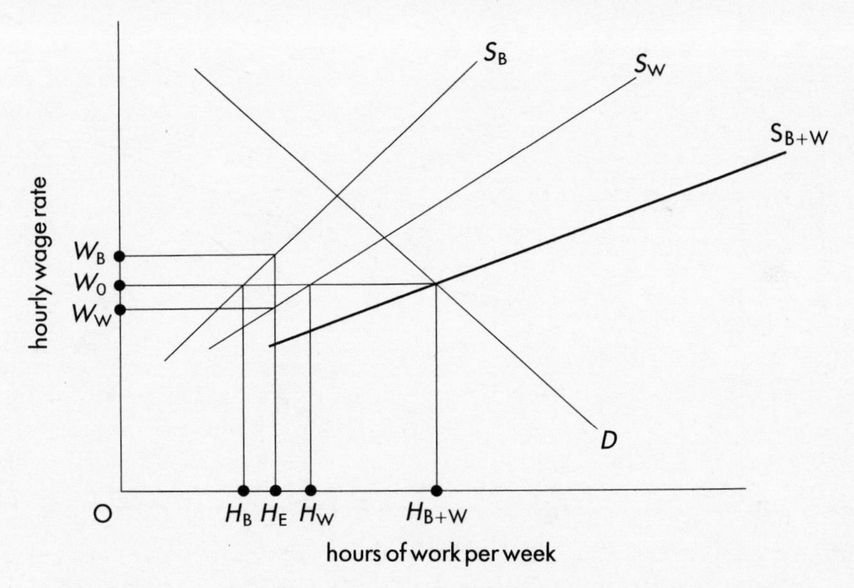

Figure 18.4 Wage discrimination with different labour supply elasticities

expected, under price taking in the labour market, to be established. This wage per hour will accrue to both types of labour. But if the supply elasticities differ, as they do in figure 18.4, then even though the numbers in the total population are (by assumption) equal, blacks will supply less labour time and will, as a group, take home a lower share OH_B/OH_{B+W} of the wages bill. As can indeed be seen in this example, for equal shares in employment to occur out of the same total (OH_E/OH_{B+W}), blacks' wages would have to rise to W_B and whites' to fall to W_W. In such a case, the blacks' share of wages would be larger than the whites'; there would be reverse discrimination, and a differential not sustainable under competition.

This example is not, of course, employment discrimination as it is commonly meant. It merely illustrates the danger of inferring too much from the 'obvious' indicator of relative employment rates of equally skilled workers from different social groups. More relevant are persisting wage differentials between equally skilled groups. This is stronger evidence both of discrimination and of the absence of wealth maximizing behaviour by employers.

It is assumed that if employers have different demands for equally productive workers, for example D_B and D_W in figure 18.5, that the supply characteristics of blacks' and whites' time are the same, and that they are equal in number ($S_B = S_W$). Then not only will fewer blacks be employed than their numbers in the workforce would lead one to expect, but also they will receive a lower wage. In figure 18.5, W_A is the (weighted) average wage received by all workers: the whites' rate of pay is higher than this and the

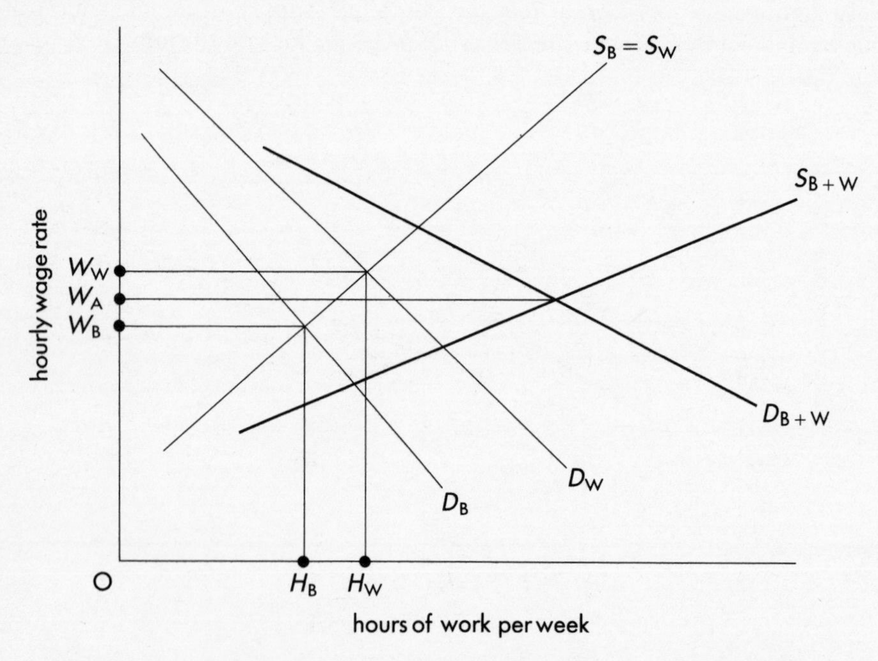

Figure 18.5 Wage discrimination without different labour supply elasticities

blacks' lower. The difference, $W_W - W_B$, is the monetary measure of the marginal disadvantage of employing an equally productive black worker to a (racially) prejudiced employer. Since this has nothing to do with relative marginal products you may infer that such employers are not pure wealth maximizers.

This analysis focuses on discrimination by employers. Other types include, in particular, discrimination by fellow employees (especially when unionized). The analysis of employer discrimination seems, however, consistent with much of the evidence. For example, you saw in case study 12.2 that there was relatively lower employment than expected of blacks in the Southern USA in price searching industries than in price taking: the price searcher's market insulates such employers from competition and hence reduces the costs of discrimination.

Case Study 18.3 Inequalities of Pay in the UK

It seems that relatively high pay is usually associated with grades of work requiring more education, experience, skill and responsibility. This is so not only for the UK but also for China and Cuba. Changes in differentials over time seem mainly to be determined by supply and demand factors. However, demand and supply seem to operate asymmetrically. The supply price of labour of a particular kind often forms a threshold rather than a ceiling: a fall in the supply of such persons will pull the rate up, and so will a rise in demand; an excess of qualified workers tends not to pull the rate down, nor does a contraction of demand. Sir Henry Phelps Brown, who has studied pay differentials in many countries and in different historical periods, and upon whose results these observations are based, attributes the asymmetry to the unwillingness of workers to offer themselves for employment at less than the going rate, the power of unions to resist cuts for those in employment, and the force of custom. In Southern England, one and the same differential between building craftsmen and labourers persisted for 500 years!

With economic development there seems to be a tendency for differentials to be reduced (possibly due to more extensive access to education), though the rankings do not change much. This is true in non-profit organizations like the civil service. It is generally true for the Registrar General's occupational classification of social class, as shown in table 18.6. It is also true broadly of relative wages in industry, as shown

Table 18.6 Average earnings of salaried white collar workers relative to average earnings of manual wage earners in Great Britain, 1913–60

	1913–14	*1922–4*	*1935–7*	*1955–6*	*1960*
Higher professional[a] (men)	373	357	409	256	250
Lower professional[b] (men)	176	197	179	109	121
Lower professional[c] (women)	101	131	123	79	86
Clerical[d] (men)	113	112	112	94	97
Clerical[e] (women)	51	65	58	57	61

[a] Barristers, solicitors, dentists, GPs, clergy, army officers, engineers, chemists, professors
[b] Qualified teachers, draughtsmen, veterinary inspectors, laboratory assistants
[c] Qualified teachers, nurses
[d] Civil service clerical officers, railway clerks, clerks in business, bank clerks
[e] Civil service clerical officers, shorthand typists, typists, clerical assistants, clerks in business and banks
Source: Phelps Brown (1977), table 3.6

Table 18.7 Weekly wages in five manual occupations in British industry as a percentage of the average of fitters and building craftsmen, 1793–1930

	1793	*1830*	*1880*	*1914*	*1930*
Compositor (printing)	206	138	116	105	145
Building crafts	101	100	104	96	105
Fitters in shipbuilding and engineering	99	100	96	104	95
Coalminer	—	—	75	100	86
Agricultural labourers	53	44	47	45	52

Source: Phelps Brown (1977), table 3.7

in table 18.7. The remarkably close agreement between fitters and building craftsmen for more than 100 years from the end of the eighteenth century down to 1914 is too sustained to be fortuitous. It broke down only in the inter-war years when the engineering industry was much more depressed than building. By 1970 the 1930 ranking of these two had been reversed, though with both industries expanding up to 1970 it is not clear why this should have been so. The compositors' story is probably due to the increasing plentifulness of literacy in the working population in the nineteenth century so that, despite an expanding printing industry, the differential based on a scarce basic skill could no longer be maintained.

Henry Phelps Brown (1977) *The Inequality of Pay*, Oxford, Oxford University Press.

Labour Market Disequilibrium and Involuntary Unemployment

A particular aspect of labour market disequilibrium that causes much social concern occurs when there is an excess supply of labour at the going set of wage rates, showing itself as involuntary unemployment. You have already seen some of the structural reasons why involuntary unemployment may occur. For example, union–employer negotiations may set a wage that is 'too' high to generate full employment, or there may be legislated minimum wages.

Another source of involuntary unemployment can occur, however, even when these structural forces are absent. As has been seen, both price taking and price searching producers may react sluggishly to changes in demand, owing to uncertainty about the permanence of change, limit pricing and so on, thus holding prices at their existing level and letting output rates (and stocks) take up the rises or falls in demand. There are good reasons why profit seeking firms may do this. On the other hand, firms that do not maximize profits even in the long run – pursuing, say, non-pecuniary sources of managerial satisfaction – or non-profit firms in the public sector evidently have no particular incentive to adjust prices promptly.

This **stickiness of output prices** which, with general inflation in the economy, will tend to be translated into a reluctance to change prices other than in line with the general inflationary trend, can have important effects on the labour market. Consider figure 18.6. Here a price taking industry is

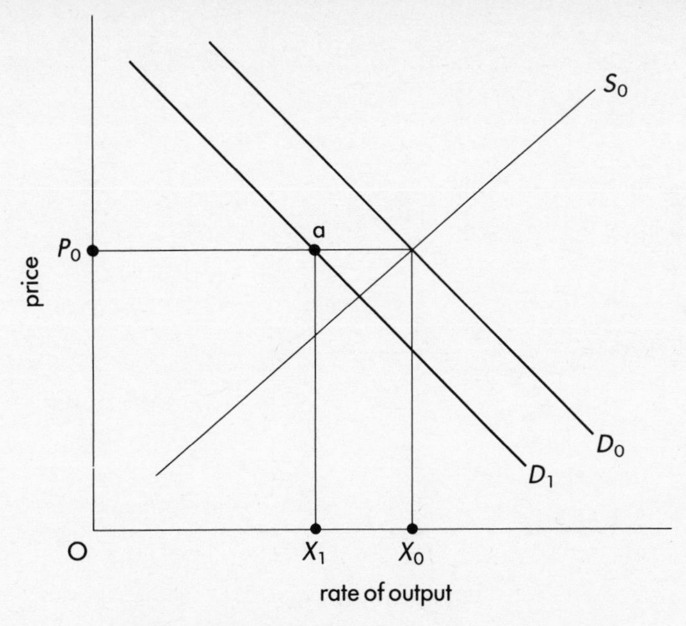

Figure 18.6 Price stickiness in the goods market

initially in equilibrium with demand at D_0, supply at S_0 and equilibrium prices P_0 and X_0. Now suppose that demand falls to D_1. Suppose that, at least in the short run, price is completely sticky. In that case, when demand falls output falls to X_1 and the goods market is in disequilibrium at point a. Ideally the industry members would like to produce X_0 but, instead, output is cut back (and/or stocks build up) with price remaining at P_0. If the demand fall is perceived, as time passes, to be permanent, the firms will tend to reduce prices and a new equilibrium may be established if nothing else happens to disturb demand and supply. In oligopolistic markets, however, one expects disequilibrium to persist longer owing to the inherent risks involved in changing prices. Similarly, non-profit firms are expected to react more slowly than price taking profit maximizers.

The impact of this sort of phenomenon on the labour market can be seen in figure 18.7. At any wage on the bold section of the supply curve there is no involuntary unemployment (though at wages lower than W_0 there is excess demand for labour), for all who want to supply hours of work at such wage rates can do so. Initially, suppose the labour market for a particular type of worker to be in equilibrium at W_0. There is therefore no involuntary unemployment. Also assume that no legal or monopolistic factors are creating involuntary unemployment.

What happens in the labour market when demand falls in the product market? Assume that product prices are sticky. In that case, when demand falls price remains the same. The marginal product curve will not move; nor, since price is the same, will the *VMP* or the *MRP* curve (whichever is applicable). Output *does* fall, however, and there will be a tendency for labour

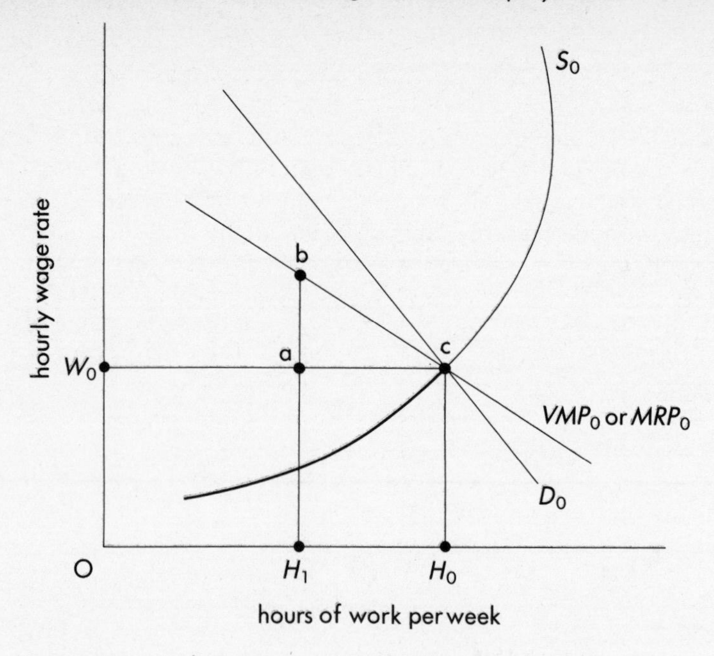

Figure 18.7 Deficient demand disequilibrium in the labour market

to be laid off. Hours fall to, say, H_1. At the given wage W_0, H_1 hours are now supplied: the labour market is in *disequilibrium* at point a, which is *off* both the demand and supply curves.

What will happen to wages? In a sense, W_0 is the 'right' wage: it is the wage at which demand equals supply. *VMP (or MRP)* will tend, however, to be higher than the wage. How much higher depends on whether the firm manages to lay off low or high productivity workers: the *smallest* rise in *VMP* (or *MRP*) is denoted by the distance ab.

SAQ 18.5

Why is ab in figure 18.7 the smallest rise in *VMP* or *MRP*?

However, although W_0 is the 'right' wage, there is an excess supply of hours $(H_0 - H_1)$ which is involuntary unemployment. This alone would tend to depress wages. However, *VMP* (or *MRP*) is higher than wage so employers would not be averse to *higher* wages. What will happen to the wage rate is ambiguous. Given agreements between unions and employers about wages, uncertainty about the duration of the fall in demand and so on, it is likely that wages too – at least in the short run – will be sticky. Indeed, this is true *even if product prices fell* and caused the *VMP* (*MRP*) and demand for labour to shift to the left.

Consequently price stickiness can lead to wage stickiness. Since changing wage rates in the short term is also costly (particularly if firms desire to *reduce* wages, which may mean abrogation of wage agreements with employees) this tends to reinforce the other causes of wage stickiness, and hence increase the amount of involuntary unemployment due to deficient demand (or lack of effective demand) for output.

As you will see in chapter 28, this type of unemployment, sometimes called Keynesian involuntary unemployment, is an important ingredient of Keynesian macroeconomics. Its removal is unlikely to be possible in the short run (which may be unacceptably long in terms of the hardship imposed on the working population) by the free operation of market forces and this, in turn, suggests that independent means of increasing demand need to be adopted – in practice, that the government becomes active in maintaining demand by suitable fiscal and monetary policies. These will be discussed extensively in later chapters.

This chapter ends with a historical case study showing an apparently curious system of paying wages in nineteenth century Britain. When you have read the opening paragraph, try to figure out an explanation of the truck system for yourself before reading on.

Case Study 18.4 The British Truck System in the Nineteenth Century

The *truck system* is the name given to various forms of tying consumption in with an employment contract. Up to the early nineteenth century a common form was the payment of wages in groceries or cloth or the product of the employee's employer. Sometimes it took the form of payment in part or whole by tickets redeemable for goods in a shop owned by the employer or in one owned by someone else who gave the employer a discount on employees' purchases. In the nineteenth century its main form was a requirement to purchase groceries at the employer's shop (where prices were higher than elsewhere) at risk of being reprimanded or sacked.

Why did it pay employers to engage in this practice? Any employer doing this, whether a competitor or a monopsonist, would have had to pay a wage higher than any not doing it in order to attract labour. Again, any employer doing this would have had to hire and fire people on grounds independent of their contribution to output. Several hypotheses have been advanced, of which the following seem to be the main ones:

(a) That it was an attempt by employers to get round minimum wages or union rates by offering a real wage less than the apparent money wage.

(b) That it was an attempt by employers to engage in monopsonistic wage discrimination: the larger a man's family the greater his immobility and also the greater his food purchases. By tying in food purchases, therefore, a lower effective wage was paid to those with a lower supply price of their labour time (recall IBM and its tied-in punch cards in case study 14.2).

(c) That it was due to a shortage of money (especially coins) and credit prior to the development of bank deposits.

(d) That it was an attempt by employers to ensure that wages were spent on food rather than alcohol and hence to reduce the then widespread problem of drunkenness.

In the handmade nail manufacturing business, where the truck system was common, the 'truck masters' were the smaller factors, derisively known as 'foggers'. They would issue iron to the domestic nailers each week and collect the handmade nails. The prices in their truck shops were about 25 per cent higher than general prices for staple foodstuffs. Standards of hygiene and quality were generally appalling. There can be little doubt that the main reason from the employers' point of view for using the truck system was to reduce piece rates below the standard rates (and standard nail prices) agreed by the major nail masters. The big firms were, of course, strongly against the practice which was a form of chiselling on their cartel. Employees found it of some advantage, partly because truck masters were more likely to have employment to offer than the major employers and partly because the truck shops offered credit against the weekly reckoning when nails would be brought in.

A similar credit system operated in colliery shops in South Wales and West Scotland, whereby an employee could obtain a chit stating his accrued earnings at some time before payday (called a 'tommy ticket') and purchase goods therewith at the shop. Pay periods were often long – perhaps a month – so the credit facility was useful to employees. Since drunkenness (and absenteeism) was common on the days immediately after payday, the system helped to militate against it. In the coalmining industry this was probably the main reason for its use by employers. Given the relative isolation of the collieries, the monopsonistic discrimination rationale also has plausibility in this trade.

George Hilton (1957), 'The British truck system in the nineteenth century', *Journal of Political Economy*, **65**(3), 237–56.

What You Should Understand Now

The effects of minimum wages (theory and evidence).
The distinction between voluntary and involuntary unemployment.
Degree of unionization and effects of unions in the UK.
Monopsony and the possibility of unions raising both wages and employment.
Investment in work skills.
On-the-job training: general and specific skills.
Reasons for pay differentials.
Labour market disequilibrium due to sticky prices, leading to sticky wages and involuntary unemployment.
Some theories of the truck system in nineteenth century Britain.

19

Efficiency and Property

In all societies, the institution of property rights is fundamental. Property has been implicit in all the analysis so far. Although in the discussion of exchange and production 'goods and services' were treated as the objects exchanged and produced, it would have been more accurate to have said that it is 'rights to use' goods and services that are exchanged and produced. The 'owner' of a resource is owner in the sense that that individual has the right (customary, legally enforceable, enforced by naked strength and so on) to select *some* of the uses to which that resource may be put. Some uses are denied by nature: you cannot, as owner of a wooden block, turn it into a gold bar. Some may be devised by man: you may not bat me over the head with it. Others, however, are usually permitted in liberal democracies; you may carve it, burn it and, in particular, you may sell it. That is, you may transfer the bundle of rights that inhere in that resource to someone else. By making better carvings than I can you may even be permitted to make me bankrupt which, if I am a professional woodcarver, is as bad for me as you burning my stock of wood – which you are *not* permitted to do! The reason is clear. The one kind of effect is permitted because it is conducive to the production of wealth; the other is not.

The rules that define the uses to which resources may be put and that govern the terms of their transfer from one person to another are called **property rights**. In developed societies these have become very sophisticated. You may, for example, 'own' a piece of land. Usually, however, this does not mean that you own the mineral rights that attach to valuable resources lying below 'your' land. Nor will you usually have the right to determine who flies over 'your' land. Sometimes you have the right to control soundwaves passing over 'your' land – but rarely radio waves. You will usually have rights about the access of light waves over 'your' land. Other people often own the right to hunt over 'your' land, especially in rural areas. Even the uses to which the surface of 'your' land may be put may be limited by law: you may be allowed to farm it, to dump rubbish on it, to play on it, but not to build on it.

In general, property rights

(a) Define the uses to which resources may be put
(b) Define the uses to which they may not be put
(c) Exclude others from using the resources without the owner's consent
(d) Define the terms under which the rights may be transferred to others.

It is a characteristic of most **private property** rights that they can be exchanged. For example, you may sell the right to farm land to someone else for a period (or for ever), the right to camp on it to others and the right to walk over it to yet others. It is also a characteristic of private property right *systems* that rights are necessarily limited. Your rights in your wooden stick excluded the right to bat me over the head because I (like you) have the private right not to have my head beaten in (at least, not involuntarily and sometimes not even voluntarily: in that case, my right is an example of a non-exchangeable right). Your right to light over your land (and the similar rights of your neighbours) implies that neither of you can erect high buildings on 'your' properties.

For exchange to work well, private property rights need to be defined and enforced. Both of these are costly processes involving statutes of Parliament, case law, and the activities of police and courts. Because they are costly, one sometimes finds that rights are not defined or enforced. Case study 19.1 provides an example of a case in which it was unclear who had what right and the law decided that the non-exchangeable right be assigned to one of the two parties.

Case Study 19.1 The Noisy Neighbour

Ronald Coase (1960) tells the following story in his classic article on social cost:

> A confectioner (in Wigmore Street) used two mortars and pestles in connection with his business (one had been in operation in the same position for more than 60 years and the other for more than 26 years). A doctor then came to occupy neighbouring premises (in Wimpole Street). The confectioner's machinery caused the doctor no harm until, eight years after he had first occupied the premises, he built a consulting room at the end of his garden right against the confectioner's kitchen. It was then found that the noise and vibration caused by the confectioner's machinery made it difficult for the doctor to use his new consulting room. 'In particular . . . the noise prevented him from examining his patients by auscultation (using a stethoscope) for diseases of the chest. He also found it impossible to engage with effect in any occupation which required thought and attention.' The doctor therefore brought a legal action to force the confectioner to stop using his machinery. The courts had little difficulty in granting the doctor the injunction he sought. 'Individual cases of hardship may occur in the strict carrying out of the principle upon which we found our judgement, but the negation of the principle would lead even more to individual hardship, and would at the same time produce a prejudicial effect upon the development of land for residential purposes.'

Coase thought that the court had made a decision inimical to efficiency because it denied the parties an opportunity to bargain, having first failed to assign to either one of them an exchangeable right.

Ronald Coase (1960) 'The problem of social cost', *Journal of Law and Economics*, **3**, 1–44.

SAQ 19.1

Suppose you live in a society in which stealing is rife, contracts are frequently not honoured, law enforcement is weak and, anyway, people are unclear about the rights they have in the goods they possess. Would you expect production and exchange to be more or less extensive than in a society in which these things were not so?

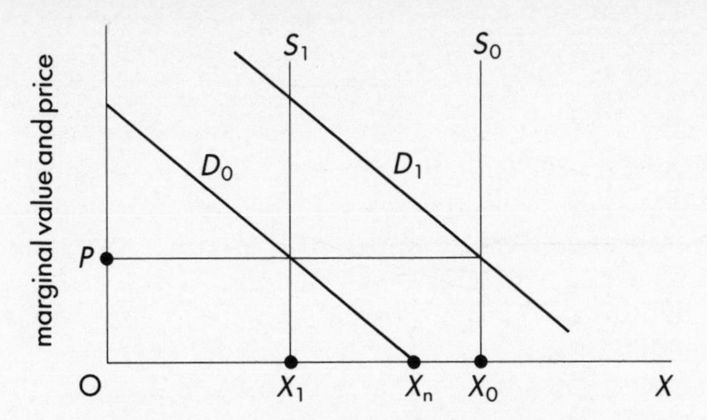

Figure 19.1 The value of exchange rights

Sometimes property rights are only partially assigned (with unfortunate consequences). For example, in the western USA, rights to live buffalo did not exist, only rights in buffalo meat and hides. Consequently, the buffalo population was wiped out when the white man went out West, for the buffalo (like the dodo) did not have the good fortune to be owned by anyone despite the undeniable fact that buffalo herds were valuable resources. Similarly property in Western forests did not attach to the timber stands, only to lumber, so those forests that were relatively cheap to fell were rapidly cleared. The plight of whales in our oceans is precisely analogous: property attaches not in the living animals, only in their carcasses. Even if property could be established in the whales while alive, the costs of enforcing the law (identifying abuse and punishing it) would be horrendous and are likely to be internationally acceptable only if the value (commercial *and* environmental) of the *living* whales were to be reckoned sufficiently high to warrant some form of institutionalized property rights.

Figure 19.1 show a demand curve D_0 for the right to use a resource (X) in specified ways. The current supply is S_0. There is sufficient of the resource to meet all demands – even of people who have a near zero marginal valuation. In such a circumstance it is hardly worth bothering to establish and enforce any property rights – at least as far as the exchangeability of X is concerned – and individuals simply take as much X as they want (X_n). If, however, X becomes relatively scarcer (S_0 moves to S_1) or its demand rises (D_0 moves to D_1) there is conflict over who shall acquire the rights to use X. Initial owners may then be assigned the rights and trading permitted (and its terms enforced) so that a price (P) becomes established in exchange. The costs of operating a property right system will be worth incurring if the sum of consumers' and producers' surpluses are larger with than without the property right system.

Some of the costs of using an exchange mechanism fall on the direct users. Suppose you are the owner of a resource (X) whose supply is shown in figure 19.2 as S_0. The demand curve is D_0. Now suppose that there are *transaction* costs. For example, if X is theatre seats, then there must be box office staff, ushers and so on to sell tickets and ensure that people sit only in seats of the

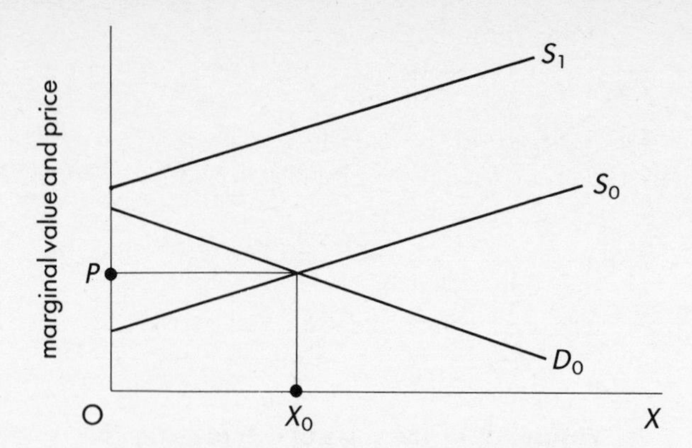

Figure 19.2 Pricing and transaction costs

type for which they have paid. Ignoring such costs you may infer that X_0 seats will be sold at a price P (or, with different classes of seats, there will be several such Xs each with its own demand, supply and price). If the effect of the transaction costs is, however, to raise S_0 to S_1, you simply will not provide the theatre show. Indeed, as labour costs have risen in many countries relative to other costs, one of the consequences has been that the variety of different types of seat (particularly in cinemas) has fallen: the advantages of having multiple prices were eroded by the transaction costs of having ushers and usherettes enforce the system of seating. The more costly the other components of the costs of putting a show on, the less significant enforcement costs of seating become and, hence, the more likely one is to see multiple prices (still usually common with the live professional theatre and concerts in contrast to the cinema, amateur theatre and amateur concerts).

SAQ 19.2

(a) Suppose you own a plot of valuable but vacant land in a town. It could be used for car parking, however, you reckon that the price that would maximize your revenue from its use would not cover the fixed cost of having someone to collect the parking fees, issue tickets etc. during the hours in which it would be used for parking. What will you do?

(b) Seats in churches are not usually allocated by price despite the fact that many churches have ushers to show worshippers to their pews. Why then do churches not charge for seats?

Where transaction costs are high relative to the value of the resource, one tends to find less resource allocation by market price. At one time, when road systems were poorly developed, it was possible to charge tolls. If you had a road on your land with only one entrance and exit, it might have paid you to charge for its use. As the number of entrances and exits rises, however, the transaction costs rise and charging becomes less likely. It becomes difficult (costly) to *exclude* people from its use. The sea is a kind of ultimate 'road' with infinite entrances and exits, and history seems to record charges being made for transit only in straits and narrows where 'ownership' was relatively cheap to enforce (hence 'the freedom of the seas'). Nations can relatively cheaply monitor and control the use of the sea as a resource (e.g. for fishing or mining its bottom) close to their shores. Originally, a three mile limit offshore was enforceable. Radar enabled its subsequent extension to 12 miles: as monitoring costs fell owing to technological advance, so the area of 'private' control increased. If oil is discovered 100 miles out it may become profitable to establish and enforce property rights that far away and to let or sell them to the highest bidder.

SAQ 19.3

Economic theory is applicable only in private property, capitalist economic systems. Is that right?

Pollution and Property

Environmental pollution covers a multitude of sins against society ranging from pouring out filth, poison and noise, through congestion of roads and cities, to the despoliation of natural beauty and wilderness and the depletion of fixed stocks of natural resources. One important clue to understanding the source of many such problems lies in the absence of property rights, or the non-enforcement of property rights. No one owns, or has an incentive to enforce their rights in, clean air, clean rivers and clean seas. These are among the most polluted goods available. The right to pass noise vibrations through the air-space surrounding other people and other people's property is not clearly owned by anyone. Beautiful views are usually not owned by anyone and are consequently frequently destroyed by advertisement hoardings. The right to use a particular road space is not owned by anyone, and the road is congested. The world's whales are not owned by anyone until they are killed, and they get killed off too quickly. Frequently the only way one can acquire ownership over many natural resources is to drill them or dig them out. Stocks tend to run down very fast.

Unfortunately, these problems tend to initiate an all-or-nothing response. Either let the pollution rip or ban it altogether. Either make sure people are compensated for all the harm done them or not at all. Very rarely is one concerned – or should one be concerned – with all or nothing. In short, policies and frameworks are needed within which individuals can act such that *optimal* (or *efficient*) rates of pollution occur. To prevent it altogether implies that the social benefits of no pollution at all exceed the opportunity costs of stopping it altogether and that there is no superior intermediate course, which is generally not the case. One probably could not anyway stop all pollution even by completely halting economic and population growth.

Private property has tended to evolve in Western society where it can be reasonably cheaply enforced. It rarely causes pollution or congestion problems. **Common property** frequently does, however, but before jumping to the (unwarranted) conclusion that common property rights ought to become invested in private individuals, pause to consider why common property exists. Usually there is simply no economical alternative. Although, for example, it is possible to imagine a world in which the right to pass sound waves, smells and light waves over private property could attach to the private ownership of the land (up to what height?), and it is possible to imagine these rights being bought and sold, it takes very little imagination to appreciate the enormous costliness of the procedure and of policing and enforcing the rights and contracts made about them.

SAQ 19.4

The dormitory towns of Smootham and Trendhill are linked by publicly owned roads to the industrial town of Claggbury (figure 19.3). These roads join at the Junction Hotel (see map). Between the Junction Hotel and Claggbury the road is very congested during the rush hours, when the traffic is almost entirely made up of commuters in motor cars. The other parts of the road network are not congested. There is also a railway between Claggbury and Trendhill. This railway, which carries only passenger trains, takes a large number of Trendhill residents to and from work in Claggbury. It is unprofitable and up to now has been subsidized by the national government.

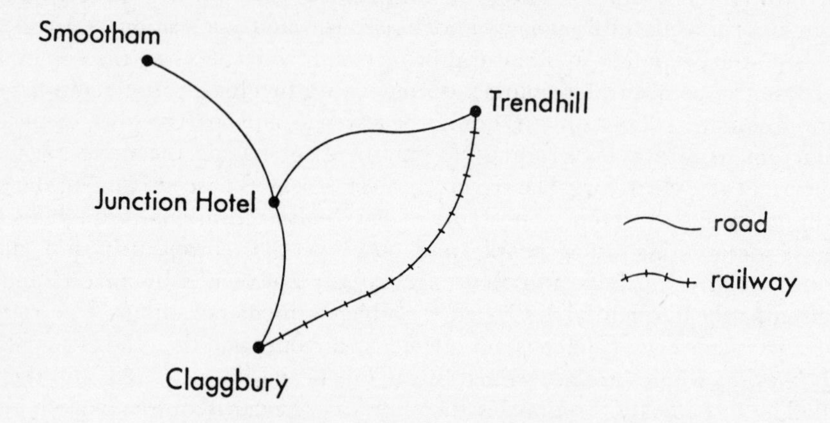

Figure 19.3 Transport routes for SAQ 19.4

The government has now refused to continue to subsidize the rail service and has told the Claggbury, Smootham and Trendhill District Council that the railway will be closed unless the District Council itself pays the subsidy out of rates levied on the people of the district. The District Council has asked local organizations to express their views as to whether or not the railway should be subsidized. The Smootham Motorists' Association (SMA) holds a meeting to discuss the issue. It is regarded as a foregone conclusion that the members will vote to recommend that the railway be allowed to close. Surprisingly, however, a prominent member, Mr Jones, has written a short paper arguing that it is in the interest of Smootham motorists that the railway be subsidized from the rates. Mr Jones, it should be added, has had the benefit of an introductory economics course and is well aware that there is a demand by SMA members for 'car journeys between Junction Hotel and Claggbury'. He also recognizes that the cost per journey rises as the more people travel on the road: it becomes more congested, average traffic speed falls, time costs, petrol consumption, brake and clutch wear etc. all rise. He also has dug out of his subconscious a useful concept known as 'SMA motorists' consumers' surplus'.

Write Mr Jones' paper.

Allocation of Rights and Wealth

Consider a homely example of dispute over a private right to pollute. A and B are neighbours and A enjoys using the power mower on Sunday afternoons, just when B likes to enjoy a snooze in a favourite chair underneath *The Sunday Times*. Should A have the right to mow noisily or should B have the right to snooze? If A has the right, losses are imposed on B; if B has the right, losses are imposed on A. Naturally enough, every dispute over rights implies that one or the other party will lose, depending on how the rights are assigned. It is possible to imagine a world in which, at some time, rights were simply put up for auction by the government and allocated to the highest bidder. In this way the rights would go to those who valued them most but they would also tend to go to the rich, and this method of assigning basic rights would generally be regarded as inequitable. One may be influenced by the economic consequences of different fundamental assignments in one's judgement, but basically that judgement must be a purely political one based upon concepts of justice and equity. In the example just given you may decide, since A would be the active imposer of costs on B while B would be merely a passive imposer of costs on A, that B ought to have the right. But whichever way you decide you will get little guidance from any social science.

Suppose now that the rights are not merely to be assigned but that they are also exchangeable. Whoever is awarded the rights now acquires wealth that can be valued in the marketplace; if A has the right, B can come along and offer to compensate A for shifting mowing time to Sunday morning. If B does not value Sunday afternoon peace enough to offer enough to persuade A, then it is efficient for the noise to continue – and it will. If B has the right, A can come along and offer B compensation for making the noise. If A offers enough B will accept, and again it will be efficient for the noise to continue – and it will. The differences between no rights assignment, non-exchangeable rights assignments and exchangeable rights is that only the last afford the opportunity of testing to discover whether the end result of any activity is socially preferred or not. Exchangeable rights enable each party to adjust in the light of the behaviour and preferences of the other, so that each moves to a preferred position (recall Coase's objection to the court's decision in case study 19.1).

The lesson to draw from this is that the exchangeability of rights is a necessary condition if the values placed upon different activities are to be revealed, even though unique efficient outcomes may not exist. Where feasible, therefore, exchangeable rights are more conducive to social welfare than non-exchangeable rights.

It is not always possible, however, to have exchangeable rights. Where very large numbers of people are involved jointly, exchangeability of rights in the way discussed is usually not possible. This is often the case with common property, in which governments often fail to enforce rights, and is also the case with valuable resources that no one owns at all. Take water pollution.

If private property and private exchange are not feasible or are not chosen on other grounds, there are broadly four other alternatives: regulation, subsidization, pricing and taxing. By *regulation*, a target level of pollution reduction is set according to some interpretation of the 'public interest', and all polluters would be monitored to ensure that they have complied with the regulation. By *subsidization*, either the government could set up a series of water purification plants of its own to ensure attainment of the target, or it could compensate individual polluters by subsidizing their efforts to process their own effluent. By *pricing*, the government would charge polluters for the right to pollute and adjust prices (probably on a sliding scale) until the desired reduction in pollution was attained. By *taxing*, the government would seek to select a tax on the polluter related to the rate of pollution such that it paid the polluter to reduce the effluent to the efficient level.

One's choice between these methods depends upon equity considerations in the implied rights assignments and upon the administrative and policing costs of each. In each case the government has to make a decision about the social value of clean water. But, most important, in each case there are social costs to be incurred in combating the pollution. With regulation, for example, an efficient policy would discriminate among the various polluters. Some of these would be major polluters and others minor; some would find it very much more costly to reduce pollution by x per cent than others; some would already be taking substantial voluntary measures to reduce their pollution. In practice this looks like implying a separate regulation for each polluter! The alternative would be not to discriminate, which would economize on administration but would be unfair and would also mean that pollution would not be reduced in the most efficient (least cost) way.

Externality

You can now make some formal links between the theory of exchange and production and the absence or attenuation of property rights. Suppose that theatre shows are produced under price taking conditions. The demand curve for theatre seats is the sum of all the individual demand curves. In figure 19.4 the equilibrium price is determined by the intersection of the market supply and demand curves (not shown). The figure also shows the demand curve or marginal valuation curve of one theatre goer A. This is labelled MV_A^A; the superscript A shows that it is A's *valuation* (a point of some significance as you will shortly see), and the subscript A shows that the *consumption* is also A's. You know from chapters 8 and 12 that A's efficient or optimal rate of consumption is X_0 per year. MV_A^A is an **internal valuation** (to A) of theatre going.

Now suppose that there exists an individual B who, in addition to caring how many visits B (himself) gets, also cares how much A gets. There is a sense, of course, in which everyone cares how much everyone else gets, for the more everyone else gets the less there is for oneself. This effect is, however, transmitted readily through the price mechanism and has helped to determine

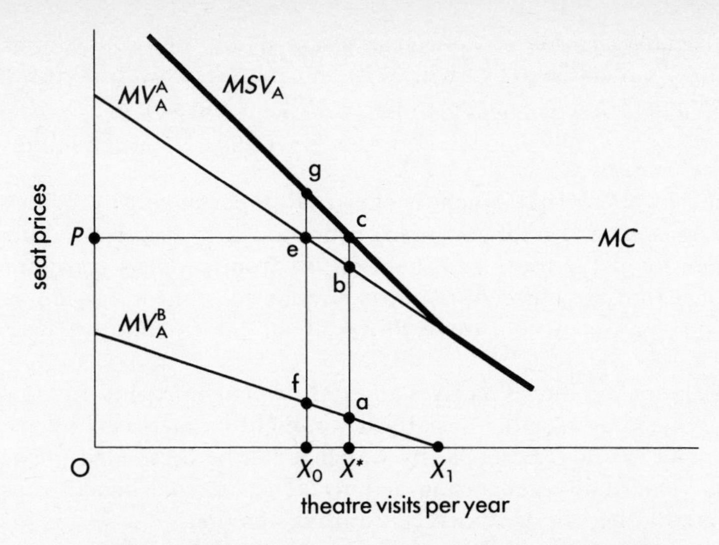

Figure 19.4 Individual and social marginal valuations

the competitive price. The kind of concern that B has is different from this: in B's opinion, A does not get enough culture; B has a preference about A's consumption. Theatrical shows consumed by A benefit, in other words, not only A but also B. Suppose that the marginal value placed by B on A's theatre visits (call it MV^B_A) falls in the usual way. It may look something like the MV^B_A curve in figure 19.4. Thus, when A is consuming X_0 A obtains a marginal (internal) benefit of X_0e and B obtains a marginal (external) benefit of X_0f.

If A were to make another visit (per year) A's additional benefit would be just slightly less than X_0e and B's would be just slightly less than X_0f, but together their additional benefit would be greater than the marginal cost of an additional theatre seat. Clearly, then, efficiency would be increased if A went more frequently to the theatre. In fact, with this externality, the efficient annual number of visits to the theatre by A is X^* rather than X_0, for at X^* the additional benefit to both A and B (**marginal social valuation**, or *MSV*) is just equal to the marginal cost of obtaining the additional benefit. With external benefits, therefore, the original rule for allocational efficiency must be modified.

Up to now, efficient consumption was where $MC = P$, or in the new notation:

$$MC = MV^A_A \ (= MV^B_B = MV^C_C \text{ etc.})$$

where internal or private marginal valuations only are considered. When this equation holds, there is no further scope for mutual gains from trade. Where there is an **external marginal valuation**, as here, the efficiency condition must be written as

$$MC = MV^A_A + MV^B_A \ (= MV^B_B \text{ etc.}) = MSV_A = MSV_B \text{ etc.}$$

Marginal social valuation of A's consumption should be equal to that of B's consumption (which is MV^B_B, with with no marginal externality, $MV^B_B = MSV_B$) and equal to marginal cost, where MSV_A is the sum of A's MV of own consumption (MV^A_A) and B's MV of A's consumption (MV^B_A). Note that MSV_A is the *vertical* sum of MV^A_A and MV^B_A.

This concept of external benefit is of crucial importance. It provides one of the major reasons why, for example, education and health are subsidized by the state, for if there are external benefits from people's consumption of these services that are ignored, too little may be consumed. For the moment, however, just pause to note three things about the (qualitative) result just obtained.

First, the mere fact that B receives an external benefit from A's actions is not sufficient in deciding whether social welfare might be increased by arranging some means (a subsidy, perhaps) by which A can be persuaded to engage in more of the externality generating activity. The external benefit must be a *marginal* external benefit at A's current rate of activity.

For example, if A's demand was such that he or she was already consuming X_1 theatre visits, then MV^B_A is zero and MV^A_A is therefore equal to MSV_A (see figure 19.4). Note also that even at the efficient rate of consumption, B derives a positive marginal external benefit (X*a) but this does not imply that A ought to get more. An efficiency-relevant marginal external benefit exists only where the sum of internal and external marginal values exceeds marginal cost. Today, when **externalities** have begun to become an incantation in popular journals and newspapers and where a divergence between social and internal benefits is held to warrant a whole range of government – or private – compensating actions, it is as well to emphasize that *the relevant divergence is between social benefits at the margin (i.e. the sum of internal and external marginal benefits at the margin) and marginal costs.*

Second, note that it is efficient for A to move from X_0 to X^* only if the externally affected parties (in this case there is only one: B) are willing to subsidize the additional consumption (whether they *actually* do is another matter). In figure 19.4 the minimum B will have to pay is ecb, the sum of the differences between A's MV of additional units and the price A will have to pay over the range X_0X^*, which B would be willing to pay since the *maximum* amount B is willing to pay is X_0faX^* = egcb. Recall that MV curves show the maximum willing to be paid for increments of a good or service. In the case of B, the maximum willingness to pay for additional consumption of X_0X^* is X_0faX^*. Since MSV_A is the sum (vertical) of MV^A_A and MV^B_A, ge = X_0f and bc = X*a. Therefore the area egcb also measures *B*'s maximum willingness to pay for *A*'s additional consumption.

Third, you may ask why, if B stands to benefit from helping A to go to the theatre more often, the 'invisible hand' has not already forced B to do so. If A and B can mutually benefit by a move from X_0 to X^*, why might it be necessary to get, say, the government to subsidize production? Why have A and B not already taken advantage of these potential gains? The answer is that sometimes they do. A great deal of charity has always existed without government

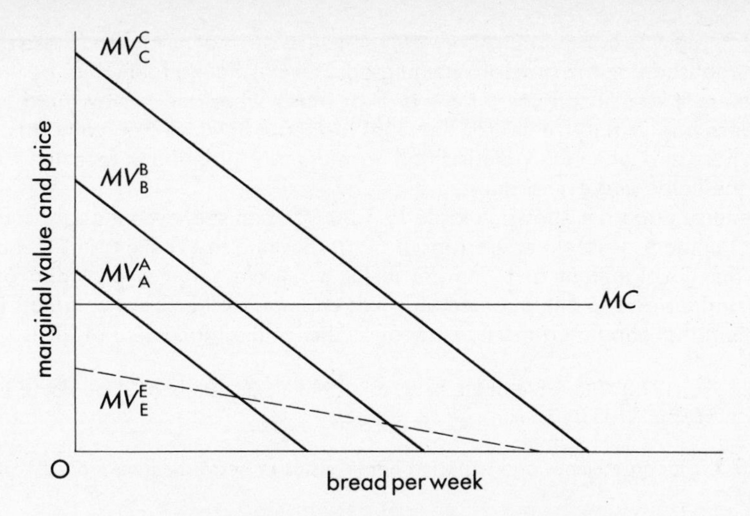

Figure 19.5 Bread demand for SAQ 19.5

intervention. But there are also good reasons why individuals may not have an incentive to reap the potential gains, and these arise especially when there is a large number of externally affected parties. As you will shortly see, they have a good deal to do with the excludability of others from benefit.

SAQ 19.5

In figure 19.5, MV_A^A is A's demand for bread, MV_B^B is B's demand for bread and MV_C^C is C's demand for bread. In addition, there is a standard external marginal value (MV_E^E), representing a 'general view' in society that each member derives some utility from the knowledge that others get bread to eat. *MC* is the marginal cost of bread production.

(a) Mark on the figure the amount of bread consumed per week by A, B and C, assuming that bread is sold at a price equal to marginal cost.
(b) Mark on the diagram the amount of bread that is optimal for each to consume.
(c) What pricing system for bread would achieve the optimal pattern of bread consumption?
(d) Suppose that underlying preferences for bread are the same for A, B and C and that the differences in demand arise because C's income is higher than B's is higher than A's. What is the relationship between income and the optimal pattern of price subsidy on bread consumption?

Case Study 19.2 The Orchard and the Bees

For many years economics texts relied on imaginary examples to help the analysis along. A famous example of this sort was given by the great Cambridge economist Arthur Pigou (1877–1959), who cited the case of apple orchards and bees as a good example of reciprocal external benefits. Apple growers provide nectar (though in fact apple blossom is a minor source of nectar) for beekeepers; however, since nectar is not marketed the benefit is not realized by orchard owners, so planting will be too little. Conversely, beekeepers provide a pollination service to apple growers but, since they are not paid for it, they take no account of the external benefit and too few hives will be established. The two self-interested parties are not guided by Adam Smith's invisible hand to the optimal amounts of apple and honey production. Some believe that government action is called for – subsidizing the production of each.

The example was a poor one, however, for it turns out that markets in these services do get established: in the state of Washington, Steven Cheung found that beekeepers and farmers trade. In places where and at times when the honey yield is high, beekeepers pay 'apiary rents' for the right to locate hives strategically among the crops. Where and when the yield is small, farmers pay 'pollination fees' to locate the hives in the fields and orchards.

The general pattern is shown in table 19.1. As you can see, even though there were sizeable numbers of beekeepers (about 60 at the time in Washington) this did not prevent the development of a market in the valuable services provided by beekeepers and farmers to one another. This was enabled by the use of contracts (verbal and written) that stipulated the time, location etc. of the placement of hives.

Steven Cheung (1973) 'The fable of the bees: an economic investigation', *Journal of Law and Economics*, **16**, pp. 11–33.

Table 19.1 Pricing schemes and expected honey yields of nectar-bearing crops (Washington, 1970–71)

Season	*Crop*	*Surplus honey expected (kg per hive)*	*Pollination fee per hive ($)*	*Apiary rent per hive ($) (usually paid in honey)*
Early spring	Almond	0	5–8	0
	Cherry	0	6–8	0
Late spring (main pollination season)	Apple and soft fruit	0	9–10	0
	Blueberry	18	5	0
	Cabbage	7	8	0
	Cherry	0	9–10	0
	Cranberry	2	9	0
Summer and early autumn (main honey season)	Alfalfa	27	0	0.13–0.60
	Alfalfa with pollination	11–16	3–5	0
	Fireweed	27	0	0.25–0.63
	Mint	32–34	0	0.15–0.65
	Pasture	27	0	0.15–0.65
	Red clover	27	0	0.65
	Red clover with pollination	16	3–6	0
	Sweet clover	27	0	0.20–0.25

Social and Internal Cost

Divergences between social and internal benefits have been discussed so far. It is a relatively easy matter to do the basic analysis of the case where there is a divergence between social and internal cost. Suppose that no one cares how often other people visit theatres. Return to a situation in which the optimum is where the horizontal sum of internal marginal valuations, rather than the vertical sum, equals marginal cost. The analysis thus begins again at X_0 consumption in figure 19.4.

Now suppose that, although all normal inputs are paid for in an entirely proper way, a theatre imposes **external costs** on the local community – noise in the evening, dubious characters in strange garb hanging around the stage door, and so on. The more shows that are put on, the greater is the nuisance. The theatre of course does not pay these as costs; it merely imposes them as adverse effects on the rest of the community. In figure 19.6 let MC_T represent the marginal internal costs paid for by the theatre and MC_E the external costs thrust upon the rest of society. Suppose, for convenience, that MC_T is constant and that MC_E rises as the number of productions increases: the marginal disutility of the nuisance rises as output rises. Thus, at output X_0, marginal value is X_0e but marginal costs are X_0e incurred internally by the theatre and eg incurred externally by the local residents – a total **marginal social cost** (MSC) of X_0g.

If the theatre reduced its output of shows by a small amount the sum of these marginal costs would fall, while marginal value would rise; a net social gain would take place. You will immediately recognize that the optimum will be at X^*, with fewer shows, where the marginal benefit to all consumers is just equal to the sum of internal and external marginal costs, i.e. marginal social costs. Thus, instead of

$$MV_A^A = MV_B^B = MC_T$$

which is the efficiency condition in the absence of any externality, the new efficiency condition is

$$MV_A^A = MV_B^B = MC_T + MC_E = MSC_T$$

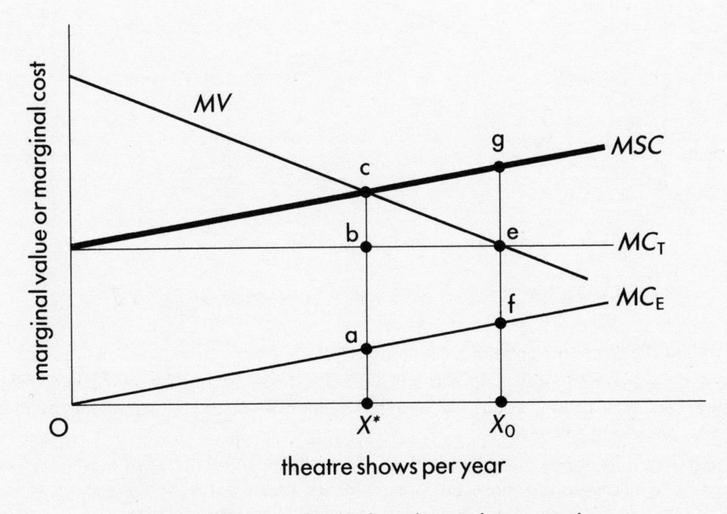

Figure 19.6 Individual and social marginal costs

the marginal valuation by each theatre-goer should be equal to the marginal social cost of a theatre production.

Once again, all the warnings concerning the interpretations of external benefits apply to external costs. Moreover, do not fall into the common trap of identifying external costs with social costs. Social costs (unless you exclude the theatre manager from society, which he or she will justly resent) are the sum of internal *and* external costs. To identify social with external costs is to ignore internal costs, which is as silly as ignoring external costs.

SAQ 19.6

In the answer to SAQ 19.4 Mr Jones mentioned the distinction between average and marginal costs. By how much would SMA members gain if a road pricing scheme could be introduced (costlessly) that set the *marginal* cost of road use equal to marginal value? (Assume the railway continues in existence and is subsidized by central government out of taxes, of which the share falling on SMA members is negligible.)

SAQ 19.7

You are a confectioner and I am a physician occupying neighbouring houses. In figure 19.7 the marginal benefit to you of making a racket with your machinery is shown as MV_C (you don't of course value the noise itself, but the output you produce which involves making a noise: MV_C is really measuring what you must be paid in compensation to make marginal reductions in noise). The marginal nuisance you impose on me is shown as MC_C. Currently you make noise N_0.

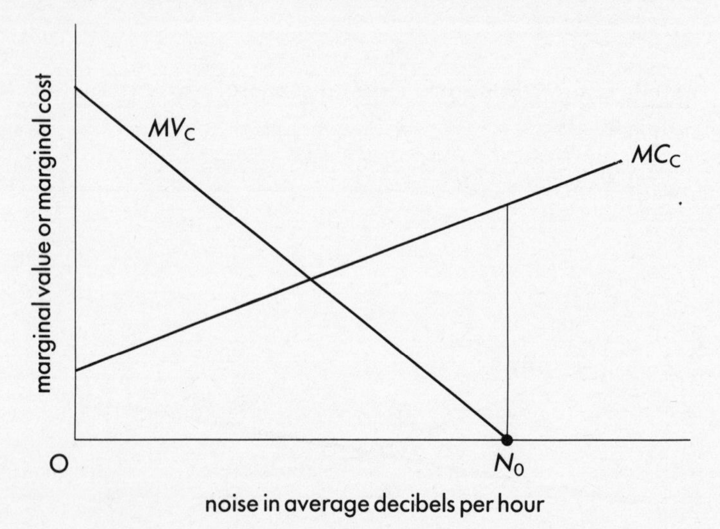

Figure 19.7 Cost and value curves for SAQ 19.7

(a) Mark on the diagram the optimal level of noise N^*.

(b) If you have the (exchangeable) right to make as much noise as you like, mark on the diagram the maximum I will pay you to reduce noise to the optimum level and the minimum you must receive for you to be willing to do so.

(c) If I have the right to peace and quiet and you currently make no noise, what is the maximum you will pay me to allow you to make the optimal noise, and what is the minimum I will accept?

(d) Does the efficient noise level depend on who has what right?

(e) Does the distribution of income depend on who has what right?

(f) I get an injunction that forces you to stop all noise. Who loses what?

Case Study 19.3 Noise and Airport Siting

One of the costs of having an airport on your doorstep is the noise from aircraft. It is possible to set about putting a money value on some of this cost by making estimates of the impact of noise on property values. Suppose, for example, that there are three areas near a proposed site. Those in area A enjoy peace and quiet currently and will still do so after the airport is built. Those in area B enjoy peace now but will be noisy later. Those in C are already as noisy as those in B will become. The housing mix in the three areas is identical.

Table 19.2 Impact of airport noise on house prices

Area	*Number of houses in the area*	*Average house price if airport not built (£)*	*Average price of house if airport built (£)*
A	15,000	35,000	39,000
B	12,000	35,000	30,000
C	5,000	30,000	30,000

Based on experience elsewhere, the house price differentials are as in table 19.2. Thus, if the airport is built, houses in B will depreciate by £5000 and those in A will appreciate by £4000, as peaceful housing becomes relatively scarce. Those in C are unaffected. An estimate of the value of the nuisance can be made by noting that 'noise' or 'peace and quiet' is tied in with the ownership or purchase of a house. Thus, before the airport is built, the 'price' of peace and quiet is £35,000 – £30,000 = £5000 (the average price differential between quiet and noisy areas as determined by what people are willing to pay in the marketplace.) After the airport is built, the 'price' of peace and quiet is £39,000 – £30,000 = £9000. This gives two points on a demand curve for 'peace and quiet' where the units are 'houses'. These are shown in figure 19.8 and the linear demand curve is extrapolated between them. Initially there are 27,000 units of 'peace and quiet' (15,000 + 12,000) available at price £5000. After the airport is built there are only 15,000 units at a price of £9000. Points a and b are the

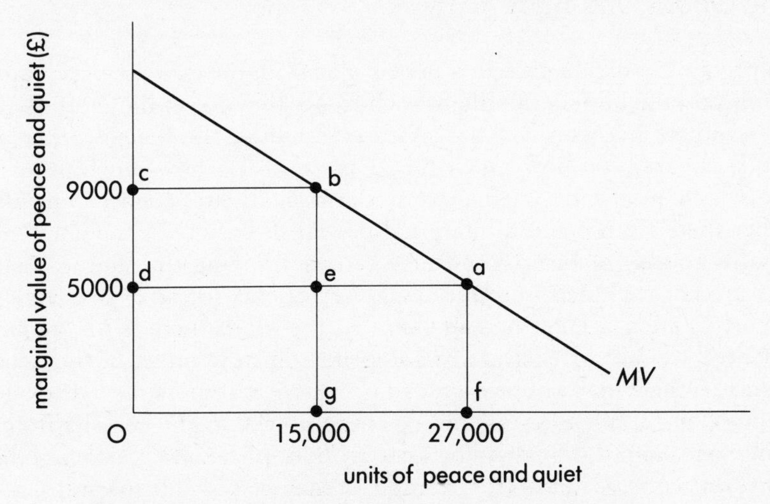

Figure 19.8 The implied demand for peace and quiet

two observed points on the demand curve. Area dcba measures the value of the loss of consumers' surplus from peace and quiet. Area dcbe measures the capital gain to owners with houses which still retain their peace. The area geaf represents the market value of the loss of peace and quiet to those in area B. The total loss imposed by the airport through noise is thus

$$\text{dcba} - \text{dcbe} + \text{geaf} = \text{gbaf}$$

Using the approximation that ba is a straight line, this can be calculated to be £84 million.

Table 19.3 Estimated noise costs of proposed third London airport (£ million 1962 prices)

	Cublington	*Foulness*	*Nuthampstead*	*Thurleigh*
Roskill Research Team's estimate	22.7	10.2	72.2	15.6
British Airports Authority's estimate	22.0	20.3	68.1	19.9

Source: Roskill Commission (1971) *Report of the Commisison on the Third London Airport*, London, HMSO, appendix 22, table 1

Using this basic rationale there were several attempts to estimate the noise costs of a proposed third London airport at four sites. These are shown in table 19.3. Some pretty heroic assumptions were needed to obtain these estimates to enable, for example, discrimination between airport noise effects and other effects (some of which would be beneficial, like proximity to destinations), estimates of noise on house prices, and the extent to which people would move in and move out. One of the great virtues of the Roskill Commission was its admirable clarity about concepts, analysis, assumptions and data sources. This enabled an unprecedentedly detailed public discussion– as a result of which no third airport has been built!

Alan Walters (1975) *Noise and Prices*, Oxford, Clarendon Press.

Public Goods and Bads

With private goods, the benefit a person gets from the exercise of private rights depends on how large a bundle of such rights they have: the more they have, the less others necessarily have. With externality, the benefit a person gets depends not only on how much they have but also how much other people have (which may either enhance or diminish their benefit) depending on whether there is an external marginal benefit or cost.

Public goods (or bads) are a new category having the characteristic that others are not excluded from receiving the benefits (or adverse effects). Thus the more of such a good or bad there is, the more there is for *everyone*, and the benefit (or harm) each derives depends on how much of the good is in existence. Others may not be excluded because it is impossible to exclude them from the benefit (for example, every street user at night benefits from street lighting: one cannot provide it for some without providing it also for others) or because one chooses not to (for example, it may be possible to control access to the street but one chooses not to). Some examples of public goods (though they are not all 'pure' public goods) include defence, national parks, immunization against communicable disease, fire engines and good ideas. Some examples of public bads are smog, poverty, criminals, asbestos dust and bad ideas. Many goods are a mixture of public and private.

With public goods, everyone need not have the same quantity of service as everyone else. To use the fire engine example, households nearest the fire station get more protection than those living some distance off. Moreover, even if they did receive the same quantity, they would not normally place the same value upon it because individuals' tastes differ. The case where everyone has an identically equal amount of a public good is usually termed a 'pure' public good case. But even in this case, whatever the quantity of a public good produced, individuals' marginal valuations will, as a rule, be different. One characteristic of publicness is thus that *marginal valuations cannot be brought into equality*. This in turn implies that one is not concerned with the efficient allocation of public goods *between* individuals once the goods are produced. Instead one is faced with the problem of how much of them to create. If A valued an additional unit of some public good at £5, B valued it at £10 and C at £15, then the total increase in benefit from providing the extra unit (in a three person world) would be £30. Clearly, if it cost less than £30 to create the extra unit, it ought to be provided. This gives the general rule for the efficient production of a public good. It is where the sum of all internal marginal values (marginal social value) is equal to marginal cost:

$$MSV = MV_A^A + MV_B^B + MV_C^C = MC$$

Efficient production is X^* in figure 19.9 where the sum of the marginal values (X^*a + X^*b + X^*c) is X^*e and is equal to marginal cost. In this case, note that no single person's marginal valuation is ever alone sufficient to warrant any

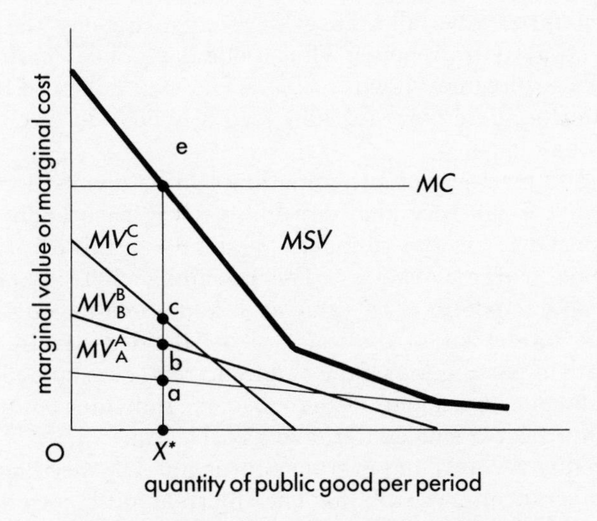

Figure 19.9 Efficient output of a public good

production at all because, for everyone, internal valuations are always less than cost at the margin. This situation is very commonly the case with public goods and bads: few people, if any, have sufficient wealth and value defence enough for it to be worth their while providing it for themselves individually. Even if they did, they would not provide as much as should be provided to maximize social welfare. Few people, again, have sufficient wealth or interest to make, by themselves, any significant dent in the poverty problem about whose reduction many non-poor may care and thus consider a reduction to be a public good. With public goods, individual action is seldom either desirable or desired by individuals themselves. Instead, they clearly have an incentive to act collectively to create public goods.

SAQ 19.8

The demand of two individuals (A and B) for a pure public good (X) are as follows:

(A) $X = 100 - 5P$
(B) $X = 50 - 10P$

(a) What equation gives the marginal social value (MSV) of the public good?
(b) If the marginal social cost is constant at 15, what is the optimal output of the public good?
(c) If the public good is sold at 15 per unit, how much will A and B each purchase?
(d) Draw your answers to (a) (b) and (c) on a diagram.
(e) In this two person case, is there any way in which private transactions may induce the optimal output rate of the public good?

In the practical world the existence of public goods and externalities affecting many people creates two closely related problems. The first is deciding how much to provide. The second is how to pay for it. The problems can be illustrated by a simple example. A small township of 500 persons contains an orphanage for 40 children. There is a general feeling in the village that it would be nice to provide the children with a touring holiday. Each day of the tour will cost £25 plus a progressive allowance for every extra day the driver and supervisors spend away from home. Thus a one day holiday costs £25, a two day holiday £55, a three day holiday £90, a four day holiday £130 etc. The problems for the community are (a) how long a holiday to give the children and (b) how to pay for it.

Suppose the 500 members of our community to be divided into two types of person. There are 200 very kindly people valuing each additional day of touring at a (constant) 15p (for simplicity, and only on this occasion, assume away diminishing marginal values). The remaining 300, although kindly, are less kindly and/or poorer; they value each additional day at 10p. Finally, assume that the total costs of the tour will be divided equally among the inhabitants. Note in passing that if the children are to get any holiday at all it has to be by the collective action of the villagers. Individual initiative is not enough even to provide a single afternoon's coach trip.

A village meeting is called and everyone turns up. The meeting has the job of deciding democratically what to do. The chairman of the meeting suggests that the children be given a day out in the coach at a cost of £25. That implies a per caput charge of 5p per villager and receives everyone's unanimous support (the more generous people each valuing it at 15p and the less generous at 10p). Obviously someone will suggest that the chairman's proposal is a bit on the mean side. Why not two days? Cost per person is 11p (marginal cost 6p); again everyone supports the idea. Similarly, everyone will support a three day holiday and consensus is obtained up to a six day holiday costing 45p each. One of the more generous villagers now proposes a seven day holiday, costing each member of the meeting an additional 11p, or 56p in all. Suddenly the happy unanimity with which everyone agreed that previous proposals were miserly disappears. This time the matter is actually put to a vote and 200 people approve the motion; 300 vote against. The meeting has decided that a six day holiday is what the children shall have.

Now assume instead that the village, as a whole, is more kindly than had been supposed before. Suppose now that 300 instead of 200 value additional days at 15p and that 200 instead of 300 value them at 10p. It can readily be foreseen that the meeting would, under these circumstances, vote for an eleven day holiday, for the 300 will outvote the 200 when a seven day holiday is proposed, but no one will vote for a holiday in excess of eleven days.

Compare these results with what theory says ought to be the length of the children's holiday. This is the length of holiday when the sum of all 500 marginal valuations is equal to the marginal cost of an additional day of touring. It will be eight days, when the sum of the marginal valuations (£60) is equal to the additional cost of the eighth day. (Alternatively it is nine days if 300 rather than 200 are relatively generous.) Collective action in general, and democracy in particular, seems to have failed to attain the ideal.

A general conclusion you reach is that majority decision rules tend, if people with strong feelings have a majority, to devote too many resources to producing public goods and, if they have a minority, to devote too few resources to such activities. There is a way out of this difficulty. Suppose a six day holiday had been decided. The less generous majority will not vote for any longer holiday unless the additional costs are borne entirely by the more generous minority or, alternatively, that the minority compensate the majority for the higher costs they will incur. It is quite conceivable that a scheme could be devised whereby each individual would agree to an eight day holiday, provided that the marginal cost to him or her never exceeded marginal benefit. In this way, a political consensus similar to the consensus of the 'perfect' market would dictate an eight day holiday. But it clearly requires a 'perfect' political mechanism – which is, unfortunately, just about as rare as the 'perfect' market – so that the relatively generous (or rich) compensate the relatively mean (or poor) for extending the holiday beyond the point that the latter prefer.

The main reason for this imperfection of the collective decision process, apart from the great costs sometimes incurred just in reaching any decision, is known as the **free rider problem**. Markets frequently fail to function efficiently because of this problem, and so do collective decision making organizations. The problem is this: although everyone stands to gain by getting together and acting collectively, each individual will gain even more, as each sees it, if each misleads everyone else about his or her true preferences. Thus, if one villager pretended not to care at all about the provision of a public good such as the children's trip, with a little luck the rest of the village may organize it and the one would – inescapably – benefit from it without having to contribute a penny. In short, as well as the children, that person gets a 'free ride' at the expense of everyone else. Obviously, if everyone tries to act as a free rider, nothing will get done at all. This is one reason why the contribution scales are often agreed in advance, so no one can be a free rider. The trouble is that this prevents the adjustments to the cost sharing agreement that are necessary for the ideal to be attained.

There are quite a large number of other methods devised to overcome the free rider problem. One is to 'fence off' the public good so that non-contributors can be excluded from enjoying it. This is possible with some public goods (such as light waves from cinema screens, theatres and television sets) but not others (such as lighthouses, or the benefits of defence and poverty eradication). Moreover, 'fencing off' in various ways can lead to inefficiency for, if an additional consumer can enjoy the (pure) public good at no additional cost of production, fencing off and charging admission will imply an *MSV* higher than marginal cost. Another technique is to tie in some private good benefit with subscription to public goods production. This is, in fact, a very common technique and can be seen in operation when people who support good (public) causes can be observed sporting badges letting the world know about their good deeds, or when subscribers to the National Trust (which lobbies on our collective behalf) get free admission to National Trust properties. Finally, and most important, members of the community may make a prior agreement that all will contribute to produce public goods. Acceptance of compulsory taxation is implicit in such an arrangement – a sort of social contract. In this case, the public good may be publicly provided by government (central or local) or at least publicly subsidized. But note that it is not a part of the *definition* of a public good that it be publicly provided or subsidized. Of course, none of these methods guarantees the efficient production of public goods. What should be emphasized is the great difficulty of ensuring an efficient rate of their production under any kind of institutional framework.

Public Goods and Public Expenditure

If one considers the mixture of goods and services produced by local and central government, or subsidized by it, or regulated by it, one comes across a fascinating mixture of public goods and bads, external costs and benefits, and private goods and bads. Most economists agree that national defence is an example of a public good. Similarly, the provision of law and order is largely public: all benefit (though some more and some less) from the *availability* of the legal enforcement of our rights, even though when I take specific legal actions the benefit is a private one to me.

At another extreme, the public sector produces private goods like coal, steel, electricity, gas, telephone calls and motor cars.

Much governmental activity seems also to exist to internalize externalities: people who care about others, for example, derive an externality from the health care, education, decent housing and so on received by others, and provided by the state at less than cost or provided privately and subsidized by the state. Each of these items in the 'welfare state' also confers substantial private benefits.

Major items of public expenditure in 1983 are shown in table 19.4. What proportion of the total of £121,513 million (which excludes the public corporations) would you say was on public goods? Probably most of items 1, 2, 3, 5, 7, 10, 11 and 12, or about 26 per cent in all. The remaining items doubtless have some element of publicness in them and may exist partly in response to externalities. If you apply the test question 'does the consumption of a service reduce the amount of it available for anyone else?', then what is fairly clearly true of research (some of which is recorded in items other than 7 and whose percentage share was actually 3.2 in 1983, hence raising the total from 26 per cent to about 30 per cent), and may be mainly true of (uncongested) roads, becomes much less clearly true of the social services.

Table 19.4 Total UK government expenditure on goods services and subsidies, 1983

	£ million	%
1 Military and civil defence	15,963	13.1
2 External relations	2,415	2.0
3 Roads and public lighting	3,147	2.6
4 Transport and communication	2,029	1.7
5 Employment services	2,917	2.4
6 Other industry and trade	3,087	2.5
7 Research	1,067	0.9
8 Agriculture, forestry, fishing and food	2,292	1.9
9 Housing and environmental services	11,581	9.5
10 Libraries, museums and arts	798	0.7
11 Police, prisons, parliament and law courts	4,867	4.0
12 Fire service	676	0.6
Social services:		
13 Education and school meals	16,147	13.3
14 National Health Service	16,016	13.2
15 Personal social services	3,028	2.5
16 Social security benefits	33,741	27.8
17 Finance and tax collection	1,810	1.5
18 Other services	−68	−0.1
	121,513	100.1

Source: UK National Accounts, 1984, table 9.4

Second Best

The idea of efficiency is very appealing. Indeed, it is a *moral* notion because inefficiency implies that with given overall resources less valued output is being produced than could be with some reallocation. Of course, one has different views about different outputs: an output of lives saved (recall SAQ 10.7) is viewed differently from an output of hamburgers. Nevertheless, and in every case, the notion of efficiency is a value laden notion: it is better (other things equal, especially perhaps the income distribution) to be efficient.

Competition and efficiency are invariably linked. But the one does not invariably imply the other. There are, for example, many good reasons why some outputs may be produced by the public sector without market competition. More generally, however, whenever there are distortions in one part of the economy that prevent the attainment of an efficiency condition like $MC = MV$, it does *not* generally follow that either competition or regulation to ensure $MC = MV$ elsewhere is the efficient thing to do. Since there always *are* distortions of that sort, the attraction of competitive, price taking markets must fade somewhat.

A first best allocation exists where $MV = MC$ everywhere (*and* MC is rising everywhere, *and* there are no externalities, *and* there are no public goods). When this condition is *not* met we have to seek a **second best** allocation.

This can be illustrated using again the example of traffic congestion. Suppose there are two routes from A to B. The first involves a bridge crossing. The second involves the use of a rather congested road and is the less direct route. The community's demand for the use of the bridge (MV_B) is shown in figure 19.10(a). The marginal cost is assumed constant (for convenience of exposition) and the first best rate of use is B_0 crossings for which a toll P_{B0} would be charged (assuming that the bridge owner does not act as a

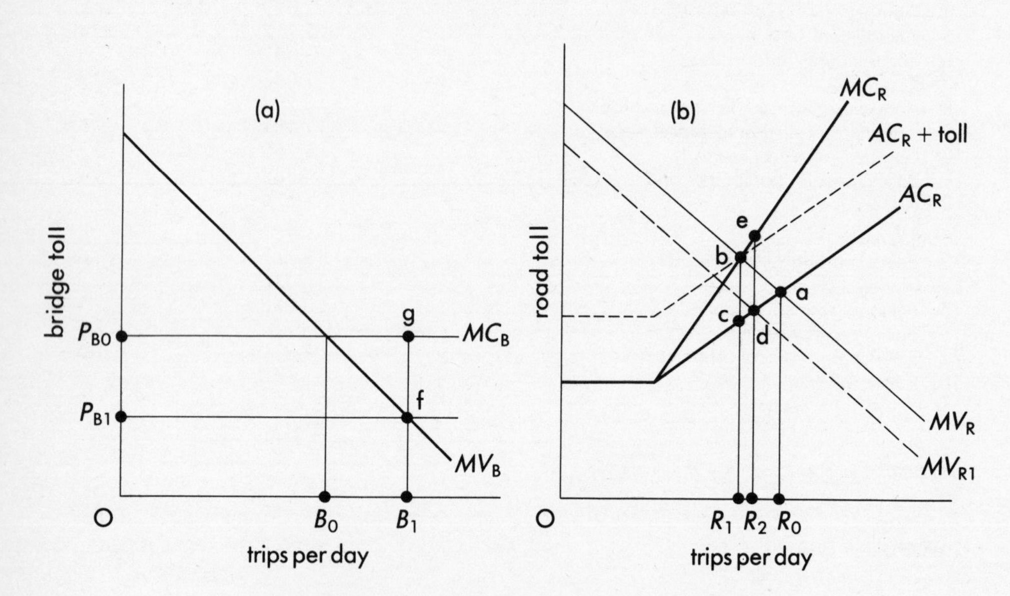

Figure 19.10 The second best (a) bridge (b) road

monopolist). The demand for road trips is MV_R in figure 19.10(b), given the toll P_{B0} for the bridge. The road's rate of use will be R_0 trips per day with each motorist confronting a user cost of R_0a. Note that $MC_R = AC_R$ up to a particular rate of use, whereupon congestion causes MC to diverge from AC. Now suppose that no toll can be charged for the use of the road (the ideal toll would, of course, be cb which would raise the AC_R by just sufficient to ensure that $MC_R = MV_R$). One reason may be that the transaction costs are far too large.

Does it follow that P_{B0} is the right toll for the bridge? Emphatically not, for a lower toll on the bridge would reduce the congestion on the road. Although the lower bridge toll would cause some welfare loss as MC_B exceeded MV_B, this can be more than compensated by the efficiency gains as traffic is diverted from the road to the bridge. The ideal (second best) pricing rule for the bridge is to charge a toll of P_{B1}, at which crossings will be B_1. This causes the demand for the road to fall to MV_{R1}, with a new equilibrium number of trips at R_2 (where $MV_{R1} = AC_R$). With this bridge toll, the marginal efficiency loss on the bridge (fg) is equal to the marginal efficiency loss on the road (de). As long as a small shift in traffic from road to bridge causes the inefficiency on the road to fall by more than the increase in inefficiency on the bridge, such shifts are efficient. But note that the marginal cost pricing rule no longer applies to the bridge. With a given distortion on the road it is no longer efficient to set $MV = MC$ on the bridge.

The reason why this rule is no longer efficient can be seen in terms of opportunity costs. The *apparent* opportunity costs to the bridge operator are shown in MC_B. But they are in fact *less* than this because using the bridge reduces external costs on the road – external costs which it was not efficient to remove by road pricing since the costs of operating such a system were (it was supposed) higher than the resulting efficiency gains.

It follows that in the real world (where distortions will always abound) there can be no *general* presumption that marginal cost pricing is the efficient, welfare maximizing, rule. Each case must be judged on its merits. In practice gaining more efficient resource allocations and rates of output must be done piecemeal.

Second best considerations were one reason why the UK government abandoned its original attempt (in 1967) to make nationalized industries operate a marginal cost pricing rule. Since for many public enterprises marginal costs were less than average (e.g. rural railway services) this meant that subsidies were needed – subsidies obtained by taxing other activities which necessarily caused MV to depart from MC. (They also tended to reduce incentives for cost minimization in nationalized industries.) There has now been a partial return to average cost pricing which, in the light of second best considerations, is not *necessarily* inefficient. There has also been a move to **cash limiting** public enterprise (including the National Health Service) and more efficiency auditing (including the possibility of **privatization**: contracting out some services to the private sector where this can be shown to reduce costs for a given quality of service).

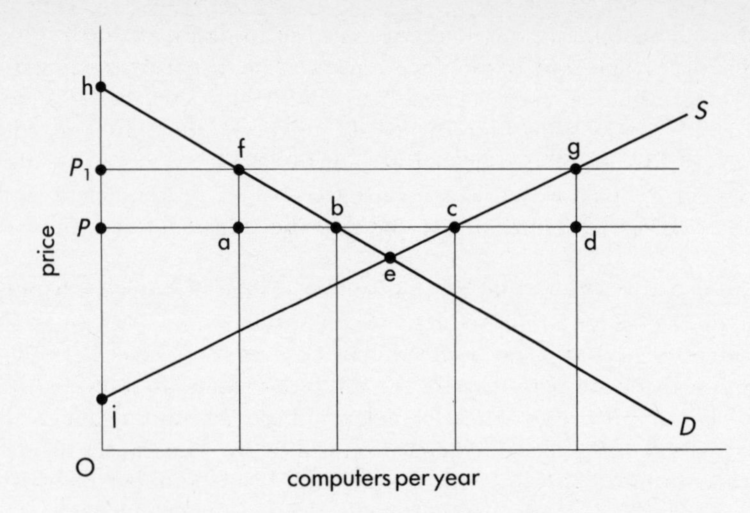

Figure 19.11 Computer demand and supply for SAQ 19.9

SAQ 19.9

D and S in figure 19.11 are the domestic demand and supply for computers. The world price is *P*. Answer in terms of the labelled points on the figure.

(a) With free trade, how many computers will be produced at home?
(b) With free trade, how many computers will be purchased at home?
(c) With free trade, how many computers will be imported and/or exported?
(d) With free trade, what is the sum of producers' and consumers' surpluses?

Now suppose the government becomes convinced that increased computer output generates valuable external effects and subsidizes the industry by PP_1 per computer exported (P_1 is now the price received by computer manufacturers for each computer *exported*).

(e) How many computers are now produced at home?
(f) How many computers are now purchased at home?
(g) How many computers are now imported and/or exported?
(h) What is the loss of consumers' and producers' surpluses?
(i) Can this be justified on first best or second best grounds?

What You Should Understand Now

The social role of property – private, common and public.
The significance of exchangeable and non-exchangeable property rights.
The effects of transaction costs on trading.
Sources of pollution and optimal pollution.
Consequences for behaviour and efficiency of marginal external costs and benefits (valuations).
Distinctions between internal, external and social costs and benefits.
Consequences for efficiency and income distribution of alternative rights assignments.
How to assess the size of external costs.
Consequences for behaviour and efficiency of public goods and bads.
Public expenditure on public and private goods.
The importance of second best resource allocation in the real world.

20

Uncertainty and Risk

Life is full of uncertainty. Risk is ever present. It is hard to think of any choices that do not involve it, from the selection of a marriage mate to the investment of one's wealth. So far, the analysis has been conducted on the implicit assumption that there is no risk in economic life. For many purposes, positive and normative, that is not too damaging an assumption. For example, one does not need to introduce the idea of risk in order to explain why demand curves have a negative slope. However, there are many phenomena that cannot be explained unless attention is paid to risk, because they are phenomena that crucially depend upon its existence: for example, why the average return on shares is larger than the average return on treasury bills. There are also some normative issues that inherently involve attitudes to risk: for example, how the government should value the reduction in risk of death from traffic accidents in investment decisions about road improvements.

Risk Aversion

Suppose you were offered the following choice: for £1 you can have a gamble with a 50–50 chance of gaining you £2 or nothing, or you can simply keep your £1. The usual presumption is that you would reject the gamble and keep your £1. The *mathematical expectation* of gain, if you take the gamble, is $(0.5 \times £2) + (0.5 \times £0) = £1$. In other words, in return for your £1 you have an expectation of receiving £1, but it is risky. As you will see in a moment, there is a good reason in general to expect people to be risk averse, that is, to reject all such gambles. However, if you did accept the gamble you would be described as either risk neutral or risk loving.

If you are **risk averse**, the element of risk reduces utility: the utility number assigned to the expected outcome of £1 is less than the utility number assigned to having the sure prospect of £1. If you are **risk neutral**, the utility numbers assigned to each will be the same and you are indifferent between the gamble and the sure prospect. If on the other hand you are a **risk lover**, the utility number attached to the risky prospect is higher than that attached to the sure prospect.

Case study 20.1 provides some general evidence from investment returns for the proposition that investors, like most other people, are risk averse.

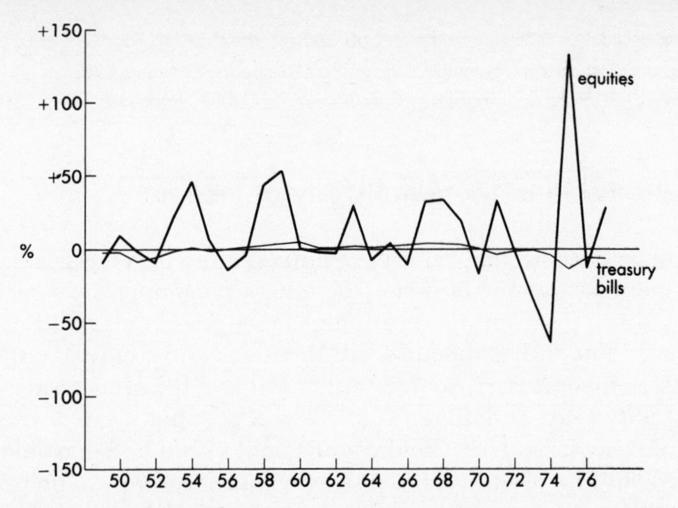

Figure 20.1 Variability of returns on equities and treasury bills 1949–1977

Case Study 20.1 Compensation for Risk Bearing

You can see the compensation required for risk taking in many ways – the premiums on wages for doing risky jobs, higher insurance premiums for high risk insured persons and so on. If one looks at the return on company shares (equities) compared with the very safe investments in the government's treasury bills, the difference in patterns over time is very striking. The return on shares is the sum of any *capital gains* made over the year (rise in the price of the share) and dividends paid, expressed as a percentage of the initial share price.

Figure 20.1 shows the variation in returns on equities and treasury bills for the period 1949–77. The average return on the safe investment was −0.9 per cent over the period. If you invested in bills the value of your wealth would have fallen very slightly in most years but, on the other hand, the risk of any major loss would have been smaller and you would have lost much more had you kept your wealth as money, thanks to inflation. Had you invested in equities, your average return would have been 10.6 per cent, but it would have been very variable. In the worst year (1974) your return would have been −63.5 per cent, whereas in the best year (1975) it would have been +132.9 per cent (of course, these are the averages over *many* shares. Had you invested in only a few the variation would, unless you were very successful, have been even greater). This average premium of 10.6 per cent is an indication of the compensation paid to investors who were prepared to take a greater risk.

Elroy Dimson and Richard Brealey (1978) 'The risk premium on UK equities', *Investment Analyst*, **52**, 14–18.

SAQ 20.1

In each of the following cases, the individual accepted or rejected as stated the gamble on the terms indicated. Was the individual in each case risk averse, risk neutral or a risk lover?

(a) Accepted a 0.5 chance of gaining £50 and a 0.5 chance of losing £50.

(b) Accepted a 0.25 chance of gaining £75 and a 0.75 chance of losing £25.

(c) Accepted a 0.33 chance of gaining £1000 and a 0.67 chance of losing £600.
(d) Rejected a 0.5 chance of gaining £100 and a 0.5 chance of losing £90.
(e) Rejected a 0.001 chance of gaining £50,000 and a 0.999 chance of losing £60.

Attitudes to Risk and Marginal Utility of Income

Suppose, since the marginal value or marginal utility of goods generally falls as you have more of any one of them (the others remaining the same), that the marginal utility of income (general purchasing power) also falls as you have more income. The utility function will then look something like the curve in figure 20.2: as income rises, so does utility but at a decreasing rate. Therefore marginal utility must be falling. You will now see that if this is the case then you must also be risk averse. (Before going on it would be a good idea to revise your understanding of utility measurement by re-reading chapter 5).

SAQ 20.2

Is the concept of utility embodied in figure 20.2 cardinal or ordinal?

Suppose your income is Y_0. The utility number assigned to this income according to figure 20.2 is $U(Y_0)$. If your income were to become Y_1, the utility number assigned must necessarily be higher, at $U(Y_1)$. If your income fell to Y_2 ($Y_1 - Y_0 = Y_0 - Y_2$) the utility number would be $U(Y_2)$, necessarily lower.

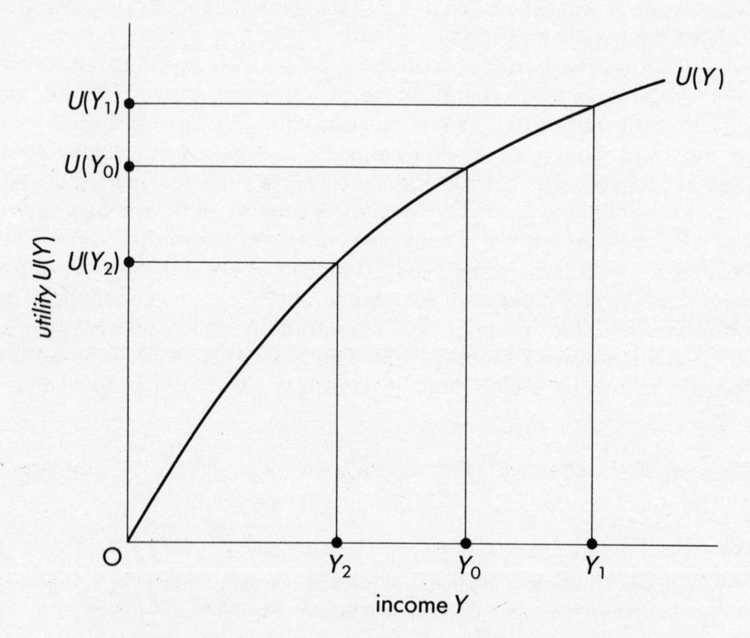

Figure 20.2 Diminishing marginal utility of income

However, it is not enough that the numbers simply be larger or smaller. For example, if $U(Y_0)$ were 10, we could not have that $U(Y_1) = 20$ *and* $U(Y_2) = 5$, for that would deny diminishing marginal utility. It would imply that utility rose by 5 as income rose from Y_2 to Y_0 and by 10 when income rose from Y_0 to Y_1 – *increasing* marginal utility. It is therefore clear that here one does not simply have *ordinal* utility (as was the case in revealed preference theory and indifference curve theory). The analysis here must assume that utility can be measured on an interval scale. A set of utility numbers like $U(Y_2) = 5$, $U(Y_0) = 10$ and $U(Y_1) = 13$ would do the trick.

Figure 20.2 can help you to see an important link between diminishing marginal utility of income and risk aversion. Suppose you have Y_0 (£10,000). You are now given a choice between having Y_0 for sure (suppose the utility number attached to this is 10) or a 50–50 chance of getting Y_2 (£7000) *or* Y_1 (£13,000). Suppose the utility numbers for these are $U(Y_2) = 5$ and $U(Y_1) = 13$. The choice is thus between having utility 10 or utility $(0.5 \times 5) + (0.5 \times 13) = 9$. Since you are a utility maximizer, you do not choose the risky option. You have rejected a gamble that has a mathematical expectation of giving you (0.5 × £7000) + (0.5 × £13,000) = £10,000 and have preferred the £10,000 for sure rather than the risky prospect of £10,000. In other words, diminishing marginal utility of income implies risk aversion. *Any* utility numbers you like to select will imply this – provided, of course, that they show diminishing marginal utility as income rises.

SAQ 20.3

(a) If the marginal utility from the last £10 of your income is 5 and the marginal utility of a further £10 would be 4, would you accept a 50–50 chance of gaining or losing £10?

(b) If everyone is always risk averse, why does anyone gamble at unfair odds at all?

(c) Draw a figure showing the utility of income function for a risk neutral person and for a risk lover.

Measuring the Quality of Life by Using the Standard Gamble

The 'quality of life' is one of those intangibles of which it can rightly be said that, in much hard headed policy analysis, the quantifiable tends to drive out the important. Utility theory can help here, however, by providing a means of measuring some aspects at least of these important but often unquantified elements.

Suppose that one wants to use information about sickness in various regions of the community, as recorded by the prevalence of various diseases, to build up an overall picture of the quality of health in the various regions (it is assumed that 'health' is a part of the quality of life). Obviously, it is unsatisfactory simply to add up all the cases of all diseases, for some are much more serious than others.

What one is after is the 'seriousness' (call it D for disutility) of various diseases as perceived by some appropriate persons. Doctors and nurses are in a better position than most to judge the personal and social consequences of illnesses. So use a sample of such people for an experiment. Offer each of them a list of diseases – A, B, C etc. – and ask them initially simply to rank them in order of disutility. Call perfect health Z. Then assign to any one disease a number such that it is larger than that for Z. Let Z's disutility number be 1. Assign disease B the disutility number 2. Now, in the initial ranking of disutility suppose that A was ranked worse than B. So the disutility of A, $D(\mathrm{A})$, is more than that of B, $D(\mathrm{B})$, and $D(\mathrm{B})$ is more than $D(\mathrm{Z})$. So you know that $D(\mathrm{B}) = 2$ and $D(\mathrm{Z}) = 1$. How can one assign a disutility number to disease A?

Offer one of the judges the following choice in the experiment. The judge can either contemplate an individual having disease B for sure, or the same individual having disease A (if they are unlucky) or perfect health Z if they are lucky. Whether they get A or Z will depend upon the judge drawing a ball blindly out of a jar containing 100 balls of which a known number are marked A and the rest Z. The question to ask the judge is now: is the individual better off with disease B or the gamble involving A or Z? If the judge says B or the gamble, adjust the number of balls with A on them and ask the same questions again but this time with altered probabilities of drawing A or Z. Keep doing this until the judge is indifferent between B for sure or the gamble between A and Z. When the judge is indifferent,

$$D(\mathrm{B}) = pD(\mathrm{A}) + (1 - p)\, D(\mathrm{Z})$$

where p is the probability of drawing a ball marked A and $1 - p$ is obviously the probability of drawing one marked Z. Suppose the judge became indifferent when $p = 0.4$ – that is, indifferent between a patient with B and one with a 40 per cent chance of having the worse disease A and a 60 per cent chance of perfect health. Recalling the initial disutility numbers, you how have

$$2 = 0.4\, D(\mathrm{A}) + (0.6 \times 1)$$

So $D(\mathrm{A}) = 3.5$. The value 3.5 is, of course, higher than the disutility number assigned to disease B.

Now repeat the experiment for all the other diseases so that each has its own disutility number. Also do it for each of the judges. If you know the number of people having each disease in the various regions, you simply weight them by, say, the average disutility index in order to get your quality of life (or health) index for each region. (The experiment may also produce the useful information that expert judges – say male compared with female – take *different* views about the seriousness of various diseases).

The interesting thing about this procedure (the **standard gamble**) is that, despite the seeming arbitrariness of the initial scoring of B and Z, the resultant scales are linear or interval scales (just like the sort of scales used to measure temperature; see chapter 5). Table 20.1 records in column 1 disutilities just calculated for A, B and Z. Had you selected $D(\text{B}) = 5$ and $D(\text{Z}) = 0$ (which are just as good as the initial numbers, as they preserve their rank order) the equation for indifference would have been

$$5 = 0.4\,D(\text{A}) + (0.6 \times 0)$$

So $D(\text{A}) = 12.5$. These disutilities are shown in column 2 of table 20.1.

Table 20.1 Measuring severity of disease

State	*1*	*2*
A	3.5	12.5
B	2.0	5.0
Z	1.0	0.0

Case Study 20.2 Two Applications of the Standard Gamble

The standard gamble method has been used by Alan Wolfson to measure the health status of populations in areas of Ontario, Canada. The average disutilities assigned by doctors to an illustrative set of diseases is shown in table 20.2 (Wolfson, 1974). Remember, the important thing about these numbers is not that the *ratios* mean anything (piles are not five times worse than flu). The measure is much more akin to that for temperature. The outcome of the exercise is a kind of 'health temperature' for each region.

Table 20.2 Severity weights of selected diseases

Disease	*Weight*
Leukaemia	0.7700
Tetanus	0.6996
Multiple sclerosis	0.4311
Cerebral haemorrhage	0.1366
Polio	0.1013
Hypertensive disease	0.0652
Peptic ulcer	0.0252
Osteoarthritis	0.0091
Cystitis	0.0064
Haemorrhoids	0.0024
Influenza	0.0005
Impetigo	0.0001

George Torrance (also in Canada) has used a similar method to get judges to assign disutilities to the various (carefully described in the experiment) qualities of life of kidney patients. These are shown in table 20.3 (Torrance, 1970) and provided decision makers with a 'quality temperature' of lifestyles of people having different types of treatment for their failing kidneys.

Table 20.3 Indexes of quality of life

	Kidney transplant	Home dialysis	Hospital dialysis
Average score of 11 judges	0.85	0.66	0.57

Alan Wolfson (1974) *A Health Index for Ontario*, unpublished, Ontario Statistical Centre, table 1. George Torrance (1970) *A Generalized Cost-Effectiveness Model for the Evaluation of Health Programmes*, Hamilton, McMaster University, Faculty of Business, appendix 1, exhibit 9.

Risk and Insurance

Because people are mostly risk averse, there is a demand for insurance. Insurance does *not* remove the riskiness from life in general. What it *does* do is to provide an opportunity for people who are risk averse to pay someone else to take the financial consequences of bad events occurring (for example, your house burning down or your being involved in a car accident). People who sell insurance are not necessarily risk *lovers*, but they are usually in a position to pool lots of risks so that on average the risk they take is much smaller than the risk any one individual faces.

Suppose, for example, that the risk that anyone's house will burn down in a particular year is p (some number between 0 and 1). Suppose the risk is the same for all houses, and let $p = 0.001$ (one in a thousand). Suppose that the average house costs £50,000 to replace if it burns down. Then the average risk in value terms that everyone confronts is 0.001 × £50,000 = £50. If average people are risk averse each will be prepared to pay *more* than £50 to avoid the risk. Now suppose that there are 10,000 risk averse house owners in a community who are willing to pay £55 each to avoid the risk. Suppose that an insurance company offers to insure your house for a *premium* of £55 so that, if it burns down, you will receive £50,000 (provided you have paid your premium of £55!). Since all householders are sufficiently risk averse to be willing to pay £55 (and some may be willing to pay more; those who are less risk averse will not, of course, insure and are not included among the 10,000) they will all insure.

What position does this leave the insurance company in? It collects 10,000 × £55 = £550,000 in premiums. In an average year 0.001 × 10,000 = 10 houses will burn down, so they will have to pay out 10 × £50,000 = £500,000, leaving £50,000 over for their administrative costs, compensation for bearing risk, and profit. If there is competition between insurers, the premium will be driven down to its lowest level, giving cost-effective administration, accurate estimation of risks and a profit rate just sufficient to deter resources in the insurance industry from moving into other sectors of the economy. If the insurance industry is monopolistic, premiums will of course be higher and monopoly profits will be earned, fewer people will insure (mildly risk averse householders will not bother) and the usual monopoly result – lower 'output' and higher 'price' – results. There may also be X-inefficiency.

The broad categories of insurance provided in the UK are indicated in table 20.4. The table is incomplete but shows the broad pattern. As you can see, premium income exceeded expenditure on claims substantially. For example, in life insurance, premium income was 1.73 times the amount of claims, so actuarially fair (see text following) insurance premiums seem not to be charged. The ratio of premiums to claims does, however, exaggerate the degree to which fair premiums are loaded by additional charges. This is because in any particular year some major events insured against may not occur (for example, major disasters) and the companies like to add to their reserves against such contingencies. Moreover, insurance is a growth industry, and current premiums have to pay for *future* claims. Thus, in 1973–4 assets held in general insurance were £3.2 billion and in life insurance £19.7 billion. In total, these assets produce income (£218 million for general insurance and £1.4 billion in life insurance) to supplement premium income. These assets are particularly important in life *assurance*, whereby at the end of the agreed period the sum assured will be paid (sometimes – according to the policy held – with a share of the accrued profits).

Table 20.4 Income from premiums and claims paid in the UK in 1974 (£ million)

Type of insurance	*Premium income*	*Expenditure on claims*
General		
Motor vehicle	938	586
Property (fire and theft)	868	428
Marine, aviation and transport	337	249
Pecuniary loss	186	98
Personal accident	73	36
Reinsurance	370	208
Total	2772	1605
Long term		
(mainly life insurance)	2662	1654
Total	5434	3259

Source: Dudley Jackson (1982) *Introduction to Economics: Theory and Data*, London and Basingstoke, Macmillan, tables 13.4 and 13.6

Premium Loading

Because insurance companies incur costs, make profits, pay taxes and require compensation for taking residual risks, the premium one pays is never **actuarially fair**. An actuarially fair premium is one that takes the actuary's calculation of what the risk (p) is and multiplies it by the amount of money for which one is insured. (An actuary is a professional specialist in working out the statistical probabilities of events occurring.) In the previous example the premium was £55, whereas the actuarially fair premium was 0.001 × £50,000 = £50. When there is a difference between the actuarially fair premium and the actual premium charged it is called **loading** the premium. The extent of

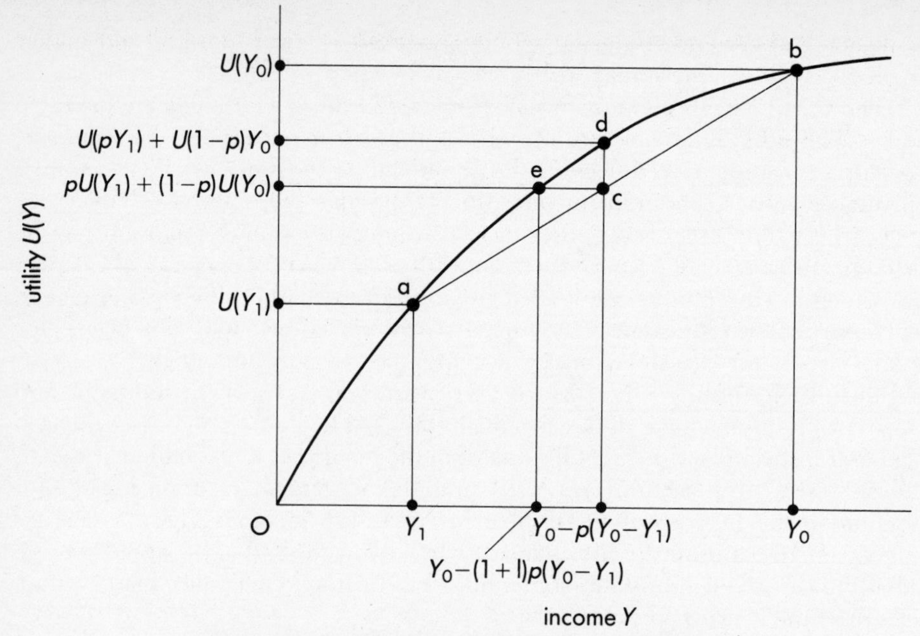

Figure 20.3 The limits of loading for an individual

loading is limited by the risk aversion of individuals. This can be seen by looking at figure 20.3.

Suppose your income is Y_0. Then your utility is $U(Y_0)$. Suppose that, if disaster struck, your net income would fall to Y_1 as a result of necessary expenditures incurred. Your utility of income in that case is $U(Y_1)$. The disaster might be, for example, a spell of serious illness requiring the payment of $Y_0 - Y_1$ in hospital charges. Let the probability of the event occurring be p. Therefore your expected (net) income is $Y_0 - p(Y_0 - Y_1)$ (income less the probability of losing $Y_0 - Y_1$), or alternatively it is $pY_1 + (1 - p)Y_0$ (a probability p of having Y_1 and the probability $1 - p$ of having Y_0). These are equivalent ways of saying the same thing.

SAQ 20.4

Prove that these two statements are equivalent.

The expected income $Y_0 - p(Y_0 - Y_1) = pY_1 + (1 - p)Y_0$ is marked on the bottom axis of figure 20.3. What is the utility of this? Call it the **expected utility** since one is seeking the expected utility of a risky outcome. Plainly it is the utility of Y_1 times the probability of getting it, plus the utility of Y_0 times the probability of getting it. That is, $pU(Y_1) + (1 - p)U(Y_0)$. This is marked on the vertical axis and is shown by the height of the point c.

SAQ 20.5

If $p = 0.5$, where is $Y_0 - p(Y_0 - Y_1) = pY_1 + (1 - p)Y_0$ on the horizontal axis, and where is point c along ab, in figure 20.3?

If you are not insured, your expected utility is $pU(Y_1) + (1 - p)U(Y_0)$, as you have just seen. Now suppose that you can insure the amount $Y_0 - Y_1$ for an actuarially fair premium. With a probability p, this premium must be $p(Y_0 - Y_1)$. If you pay this premium, your income will be $Y_0 - p(Y_0 - Y_1) = pY_1 + (1 - p)Y_0$. This has the same appearance as your expected income if you do not insure. But there is a crucial difference. If you pay the premium, you know *for sure* that your income is going to be $Y_0 - p(Y_0 - Y_1)$, even if you fall sick. The utility of this sure income is shown by $U(pY_1) + U(1 - p)(Y_0)$ on the vertical axis and is shown by the height of the point d. Clearly, since your utility function in figure 20.3 shows diminishing marginal utility (you are risk averse) point d lies above point c and you will choose to insure. Note in particular the subtle but important difference between $U(pY_1) + U(1 - p)(Y_0)$ and $pU(Y_1) + (1 - p)U(Y_0)$. The first of these is the utility of a sure level of income (Y_0 less the premium). The second is the expected utility of an unsure level of income (it may be either Y_0 or Y_1). For risk averse people, the utility of the sure prospect must be more than the utility of the risky prospect.

How far could an insurance company load its premium? The answer has to be up to that point at which the utility of the risky prospect (shown by point c) is equal to the utility of income net of the premium, which is shown by point e. If you take loading as a percentage mark-up l on the fair premium, then the maximum premium must be $(1 + l)p(Y_0 - Y_1)$. For example, if the premium were £50 and the maximum loading was 10 per cent, then the actual premium would be $1.1 \times £50 = £55$. The point $Y_0 - (1 + l)p(Y_0 - Y_1)$ is shown on the horizontal axis of figure 20.3: this is income less the loaded premium. With this l, the individual will be indifferent between insuring and not insuring, as utility is the same in each case. A loading factor just less than $1 + l$ will mean that you will still insure. But, of course, for any l greater than zero there will be some risk averse people who choose not to insure. The higher the l, the fewer who will insure. This has important policy implications because if there are economics of scale in insurance provision, amalgamation of insurance companies will enable a lower loading (as long, of course, as the industry is not thereby transformed into a price searchers' market).

Adverse Selection

A difficulty that arises with insurance in the market is called **adverse selection**. The example of health insurance is pursued here. Insurance companies will base their actuarial assessment of risk – the probability that an individual will fall sick and need a particular type of medical care – upon broad classes of experience across groups of the population (called **community rating**). Any individual who feels that the probability of their needing care is higher than that on which their insurer is assessing them will have an extra incentive to insure. Take a population of 100 people, 50 of whom on past history may be expected to pay £100 in medical fees, and 50 of whom may be expected to pay £300. The insurer offers premiums on the basis of the average risk so (ignoring the insurer's own operating costs) the fair premium will be set at £200, since £200 × 100 will just cover the expected pay-out of (£100 × 50) + (£300 × 50). This will seem an excessive premium to those expecting only £100 expenses, who will therefore not buy insurance unless they are quite extraordinarily averse to bearing the risk themselves. The insurer is left with the high risk cases insured at the risk calculated actuarially as low. In a pure market you therefore expect to see insurance agencies being forced away from community rating and having to tailor individual premiums more to individual risks.

Moral Hazard

Suppose you are insured against the financial consequences of a motor vehicle accident so that the insurance company will indemnify you for any damage or injury you cause or that happens to you. An important price has fallen from your point of view – the price of reckless driving. If you enjoy driving fast you will tend to drive faster; if you find being careful a chore, you will be less careful. What has happened is that the mere fact of being insured tends to increase the probability of adverse effects occurring.

If your life is insured, then part of the bad consequences of your early demise are removed – the part implying less wealth for your surviving family. Of course, life insurance does not compensate *you* for your early death and hardly *fully* compensates your surviving relatives either. None the less, you have a lesser incentive not to smoke, play dangerous games, eat rich food, drink lots and so on. Again you raise the probability of your earlier death. Likewise, if you are insured for medical expenses (or can get medical care free) you have a smaller incentive (not of course a zero incentive) to keep fit and healthy. The probability of needing care rises.

This is **moral hazard** – the tendency for the fact of being insured to raise the probability of the event against which you are insured actually occurring and a claim being made. It is a problem for insurance companies and gives rise to no claims bonuses (an incentive not to claim), to deductibles (you pay the first £x of any expense), coinsurance (you pay x per cent of any expense) and to preferential rates being offered to careful people (indicated sometimes by professional status), such as non-smokers, householders with burglar alarms and effective locks on their houses, and people who live in low risk areas.

SAQ 20.6

Figure 20.4 shows your demand as a car driver for car-miles per year at a (constant) marginal cost *MC* that includes the risk of incurring financial expense as a result of an accident. Assume that this risk rises the more you motor but that the marginal expected cost of an accident is constant. Show

(a) The effect of insurance against vehicle damage on *MC* and mileage
(b) The effect of your having to pay 30 per cent of any damage.

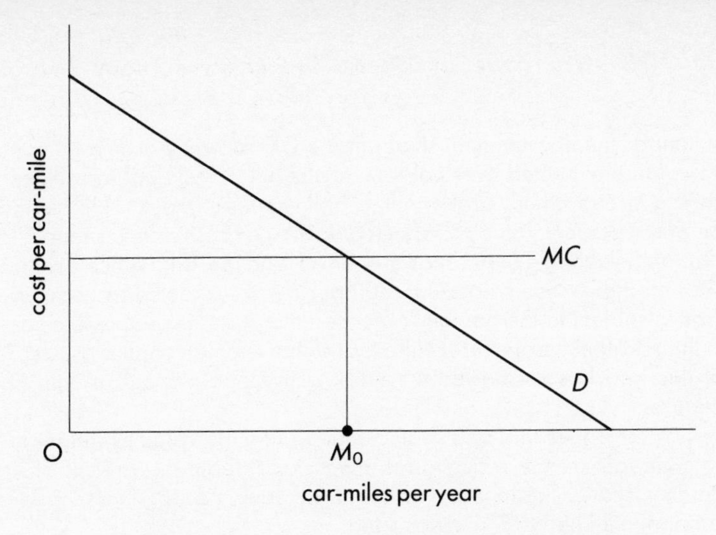

Figure 20.4 Car driver demand for SAQ 20.6

The Price of Safety

Risk averse people prefer safety. This is recognized by a host of public regulatory activity that ensures, for example, minimum quality in foods and medicines, and protection against dangerous machinery. In the UK, for example, moving parts of machines must be covered, tractors must have protective cabs to prevent drivers being crushed by tractors that roll over, and so on. The big question for public regulations of this type is how to determine the optimal amount of safety. Safety is a good. But making things safer is costly. In principle, optimal safety is where the value of a little more is equal to the cost of a little more. But there are lots of snags in identifying both benefits and costs. The benefit often has public goods characteristics (a safer car design can be of benefit to *all* road users including pedestrians). There are often externalities (people care about the risks to which others are exposed, especially vulnerable groups like children, the elderly and the poor). The probability changes that safety measures produce may be hard to measure. In any case 'safety' as such is not traded in markets. Sometimes it is *implicitly* traded (risky jobs pay higher wages than safe jobs) but to identify the risk premium in observed prices and wages is always hard because other aspects of any two things compared are also usually different and may also affect relative prices or wages.

Case study 20.3 describes a method used to assign a value to the reduction of risks of death through road safety investments by the government, and faces up to the horrendously difficult question of how the value of a life saved should be treated in cost–benefit analysis.

Case Study 20.3 The Value of Deaths Prevented in Road Improvement Programmes

The Department of the Environment (DoE) in the UK currently uses a human capital approach to valuing expected lives not lost as a result of installing crash barriers on roads, changing speed limits, straightening highways and so on. By this method a computation of the present value of expected earnings gross of tax is made, to which is added National Health Service costs averted and an allowance for 'pain and grief'. In 1983 the figure used was £119,300 per death expected to be averted.

This method is subject to the obvious objection that it treats people like cart horses – as though their 'value' were entirely like that of non-human capital assets. The DoE is aware of this and has supported the work of Michael Jones-Lee into finding a better procedure.

Jones-Lee (1976) argues that one should seek to find the value (willingness to pay) placed by individuals on the reduction in the risk of death as a result of any such improvement to discover the inherent value of life saving procedures, and then add on other components like NHS costs averted.

The essence of the analysis can be put as follows. An individual will have a particular utility, given his or her wealth, if death is not expected during a period, and another utility if it is expected. Essentially, each person has a utility of wealth curve $L(W)$ conditional on surviving through the period, and another (lower) utility of wealth curve $D(W)$ conditional on death during the period. These are charted for illustration in figure 20.5 where, at the level of wealth indicated by W_0, the marginal utility of wealth conditional upon life (slope of $L(W)$) is lower than the marginal utility of wealth conditional upon death (slope of $D(W)$), implying that this individual would take out fair life insurance.

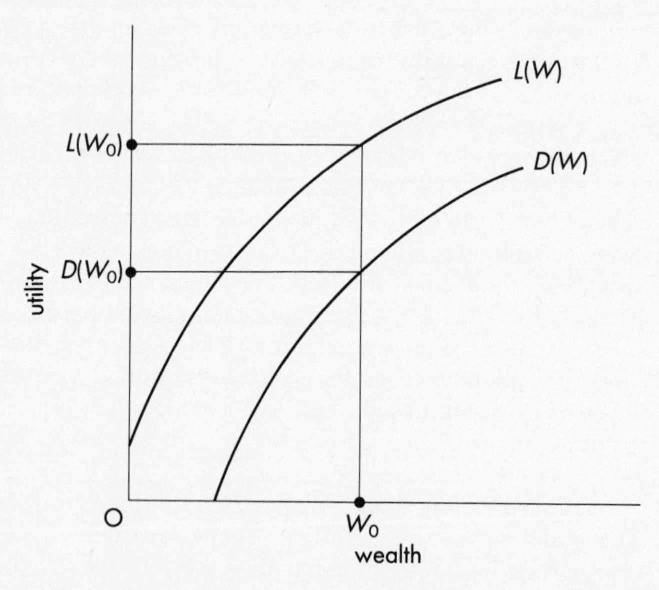

Figure 20.5 Marginal utility of wealth conditional upon earlier or later death

For an individual with wealth W_0 and a subjective probability p_0 of death occurring in the period, expected utility is given by

$$E(U) = (1 - p_0)L(W_0) + p_0 D(W_0)$$

It is now allowed that, at some cost, p_0 may be reduced to some lower value denoted by p_1. Given that marginal utility of wealth is always positive (both $L(W)$ and $D(W)$ slope upwards) and that the utility of wealth conditional on life is higher than when conditional on death ($L(W) > D(W)$ in the figure), then the individual will sacrifice some current wealth to reduce the probability.

In order to find the value placed by any individual on this reduction in risk, one seeks the maximum sum of money each will sacrifice (call it MV_r) for a marginal reduction in the risk of death. Call this small reduction $p_0 - p^*$. This *maximum* sacrifice will obviously leave the individual just indifferent between the new and the original situations, since the maximum paid will exhaust the whole benefit of reducing p from p_0 to p^*.

In a population of n individuals at risk, the social value of a marginal reduction in risk is the sum of all the individual marginal valuations (ΣMV_r): the risk reduction is a public good. The average marginal value across all n individuals is $\Sigma^n MV_r/n$. This, as it happens, is also the appropriate value of a (statistical or anonymous) life saved or death prevented, as may be seen by the following line of reasoning.

In a population of n individuals, suppose that the objective probability of death is p_0 as before. Suppose this corresponds to the death of a individuals. A proposal is made to improve road safety by reducing p_0 to p_1, corresponding to the expected deaths of b people, where b is less than a. Thus $p_0 = a/n$ and $p_1 = b/n$ and the change in the probability of death is s/n, where $s = (a - b)$ is the expected lives saved. The value of this reduction in probability is the marginal social value of risk reduction multiplied by the expected risk reduction, i.e. $\Sigma^n MV_r\ (s/n)$. This is expected to save s lives, so the value of a (statistical) life saved is $\Sigma MV_r\ (s/n)/s$, which is $\Sigma^n MV_r/n$.

In empirical work, Jones-Lee found values for a statistical life saved to be much larger than the current value used by the DoE, some of which were as high as £3 million. This suggests that the UK underinvests in road safety.

Michael Jones-Lee (1976) *The Value of Life: an Economic Analysis*, London, Martin Robertson.

Speculation

Each farmer with a harvest (a stock) of barley faces a problem: to hold or to sell. The more that is sold, the lower the price on the spot (the **spot price**). The less that is sold, the higher the spot price. The more that is used up now, the higher the future price of barley (until next harvest). The less that is used now, the lower the future price of barley.

A risky commercial judgement is clearly involved. Since holding a stock is costly in terms of interest that could have been had if the stock were sold and the proceeds invested, as well as in terms of insurance, warehousing and keeping the grain in good condition, the future price must be such as to compensate whoever holds the stock. It is hardly surprising that specialists in stockholding emerge (merchants) who gain scale economies from holding large stocks in suitable granaries. They are, however, taking a risk, for they cannot be *sure* at what price they will be able to sell their grain. They are necessarily **speculating** – taking a (more or less) calculated risk.

So the merchants buy from farmers at the spot price at harvest time. This means that the spot price at harvest must be higher than it would have been had farmers tried to sell all their stock to ultimate users, who do not want to hold vast stocks to see them through a whole year, or who would be willing to do so only if the price of grain were much lower. It also means that the future price of grain will be lower than it otherwise would have been, for, had the stock been immediately sold to more ultimate users who had made more beer, animal foodstuffs and so on, to reduce storage costs, then later in the year more of this output would have already been consumed; so the price of beer, foodstuffs and so on would have been higher and hence the (derived) demand for barley. Speculation thus tends to even out price fluctuations over time – price fluctuations not only in the raw materials but also in the products made from them. Consequently, one does not see very low prices of grain shortly after harvest time and very high prices just before. The price is relatively stable over the year, thanks to the speculative activity of merchants.

Futures Markets

How can manufacturers and other dealers protect themselves from fluctuating prices? Consider a brewer. If the brewer buys a large stock of barley at a particular price which then falls dramatically, competitors will get cheaper barley and be able to sell cheaper beer. The brewer is clearly at risk. One thing that could be done would be to buy only as much grain as is needed for, say, a month's production each month. This will be less risky but the brewer will still have to pay whatever spot price applied each month and so will not avoid all the risk. The brewer can do much better than this: he can make a **futures contract** with a merchant. According to this kind of deal, the brewer agrees to take delivery of the barley at some time in the future at a price to be paid then but agreed *now*. The **futures price** of seasonally produced goods will, of course, be higher than the spot price (to cover the merchant's costs) but this premium will be worth paying if the brewer is sufficiently risk averse. The brewer will thereby be **hedging** against the risk of a price rise, just as the merchant is hedging against a price fall. Since competition keeps the premium at a level just sufficient to compensate merchants' costs and give them a normal profit, this has to be cheaper than the brewer holding large stocks (for the merchant is by definition more cost-effective at this than the brewer) and it also avoids the risk inherent in buying small lots at whatever spot price applies.

The futures price will tend to be the market's best guess as to what the future *spot* price will be. Suppose, for example, that you believed that the future spot price is going to be higher than today's futures price of barley. It will pay you to buy futures now (the merchant holds the stock of course, not you). If 'the market' shares the same view the futures price rises. If you were right, then when the future date arrives at which the merchant has agreed to deliver the barley, the price you agreed to pay will be less than the spot value of the barley. So you sell your barley to someone else and tell the merchant to deliver it to them. You then settle with the merchant at the futures price you originally agreed. You do not need, of course, to be a brewer to do this, nor do you need to be a barley user at all! The more people who believe that the currently quoted futures price is too low, the higher the futures price rises. Whoever gets in first, of course, gets the best hedge against rising prices.

Once again, this type of speculation causes prices to converge over time rather than diverge – all within the bounds, of course, of what experience has taught traders of all kinds (farmers, merchants, manufacturers and any other futures trader) to expect.

Case Study 20.4 Commodity Markets and Futures Prices for Wheat, Barley and Potatoes

The largest futures market in the world is in Chicago. UK commodity markets also exist, however, and futures prices are quoted in the *Financial Times*. Table 20.5 shows futures prices for wheat, barley and potatoes – all seasonal crops whose prices, without traders being willing to store the goods and eke their delivery out over time, would be subject to extreme highs before harvest and extreme lows just after. Wheat and barley futures are normally quoted every second month. As you can see, futures prices are lowest at harvest time and highest just before – reflecting the costs of storage and so on.

Table 20.5 Futures prices (£s per tonne) for three products in May 1984

		Wheat	*Barley*	*Potatoes*
1984	May	124.85	120.25	280.00
	July	126.95	—	—
	September	107.30	106.70	—
	November	110.35	109.75	74.20
1985	January	113.30	112.85	—
	February	—	—	82.80
	March	116.05	115.50	—
	April	—	—	92.20
	May	—	—	105.10

Source: *Financial Times*, Thursday 24 May, 1984, p. 40 (British Commodity Markets Section)

SAQ 20.7

(a) What is the difference between a futures price and a future price?

(b) Does a speculator who buys futures avoid risk?

(c) For what types of product would you expect today's futures prices to fall with successive months, and for what type of product would you expect it to rise?

(d) An animal feed manufacturer buys 1000 tonnes of low grade wheat at £100 per tonne in March. He expects to sell the feed in two months' time. Suppose the price of wheat in the meantime falls to £98. How can the manufacturer hedge by selling 1000 tonnes of May wheat futures?

What You Should Understand Now

The meaning of risk aversion, risk neutrality and risk loving.
The relationship between the marginal utility of income or wealth and attitudes to risk.
Types of utility measurement under risky choices.
The role of compensation in risk bearing.
The sharing of risks via insurance and futures dealing.
Types of insurance in the UK.
How to derive experimentally revealed values for non-marketed entities.
The differences between actuarially fair and actuarially unfair premiums, and the role of loading.
The meaning and consequences of adverse selection.
The meaning and consequences of moral hazard.
The use of utility theory to derive the value of safety improvements and the valuation of human life not lost.
The role of speculation in determining spot and futures prices.

21

Income Distribution and Redistribution: Measurement and Ethics

The total income of a country can be classified according to the main types of income recipient (income from employment, self-employment, profits and rents). This is known as the **functional distribution** of income, and it has remained pretty constant over the years (income from employment being about 66 per cent of the total and from profits about 18 per cent). This chapter focuses on the *personal* distribution of income.

The *functional distribution of income* in the UK between earnings from employment, self-employment, profits and rents is shown in table 21.1. As you can see from the table, the shares have remained fairly stable over the 30 year period, with (pre-tax) income from employment taking about two thirds of total domestic income. Income from self-employment has tended to fall somewhat as a share, and rents have tended to increase.

Table 21.1 Functional distribution of income in the UK, 1952–82

Type of income	*1952*		*1962*		*1972*		*1982*	
	£ billion	*%*	*£ billion*	*%*	*£ billion*	*%*	*£ billion*	*%*
Employment	9.1	66.4	17.3	68.1	37.8	66.2	155.1	66.3
Self-employment	1.5	10.9	2.4	9.4	5.8	10.1	20.1	8.6
Company profits[a]	2.5	18.2	4.4	17.3	10.0	17.5	42.5	18.2
Rents	0.6	4.4	1.3	5.1	3.5	6.1	16.2	6.9
Total	13.7	99.9	25.4	99.9	57.1	99.9	233.9	100.0

[a] Includes surpluses of public sector enterprises.
Source: *National Income and Expenditure*, 1983 and 1974 sections

The **personal distribution** of income in the UK is routinely reported by the Central Statistical Office. Since this is based on income tax records it is likely to underestimate the incomes of the highest groups, owing to tax dodges (tax avoidance and – illegal – tax evasion). The distribution of wealth with and without the capital value of pension rights is shown in table 21.2 for 1971 and 1980. As you can see, the most wealthy tax units owned 31 per cent of marketable wealth in 1971 and 23 per cent in 1980. Both are high proportions, but the fall in the share of the richest is mostly due to inflation, with many capital assets like company shares (but not land and housing) not keeping up. More striking, perhaps, is that 97 per cent of marketable wealth in 1971 (94 per cent in 1980) was owned by 50 per cent of people. In other words, nearly all the nation's wealth is owned by 50 per cent of the (adult) population.

Table 21.2 Distribution of wealth in the UK, 1971 and 1980

Percentage of wealth owned by	*Marketable wealth*		*Marketable wealth plus pension rights*	
	1971	*1980*	*1971*	*1980*
Most wealthy 1% of adult tax units	31	23	21	12
Most wealthy 2% of adult tax units	39	30	27	16
Most wealthy 5% of adult tax units	52	43	37	25
Most wealthy 10% of adult tax units	65	58	49	35
Most wealthy 25% of adult tax units	86	81	70	59
Most wealthy 50% of adult tax units	97	94	87	81

Source: *Social Trends*, 1983, **13**, table 5.18

When pension rights are included, there is a much more marked trend towards equality, for the effects of inflation were combined with a growth of pension rights (occupational pension schemes often being inflation proofed).

Table 21.3 shows the distribution of personal gross income including cash benefits paid by the state in 1982. The income distribution is organized into 10 per cent bands (deciles) and these results are based on an annual survey (the Family Expenditure Survey) made by the government's Central Statistical Office. You can see clearly the extent to which those with lowest original income (mainly the retired) are dependent on state pensions. Note also that, after receipt of these benefits, the order of average income in the bottom two deciles is reversed. On average, original income was increased by 18 per cent as a result of government transfers, which are quite progressive. The impact of taxes and other benefits is discussed in case study 21.2.

Table 21.3 Distribution of personal income by household in the UK, 1982 (average per decile)

	Original income (£)	*Cash benefits (£)*	*Gross personal income (£)*
Highest 10%	21,260	471	21,731
2nd 10%	13,511	601	14,112
3rd 10%	10,950	637	11,587
4th 10%	9,122	726	9,848
5th 10%	7,511	807	8,318
6th 10%	5,874	966	6,840
7th 10%	3,819	1556	5,375
8th 10%	1,416	2377	3,793
9th 10%	288	2486	2,774
10th 10%	4	2855	2,889
Average	7,376	1352	8,728

Source: Central Statistical Office (1983) 'The effects of taxes and benefits on household income 1982', *Economic Trends*, November, 82–114.

There is no simple explanation of why the personal distribution is what it is, or why it changes. It evidently depends on the distribution of property rights and, in particular, the ownership and inheritance of marketable wealth which is, as you saw in table 21.2, extremely skewed in the UK. It also depends on the distribution of *human* capital – the skills and wealth of individuals with which they are naturally endowed and which they may have supplemented by appropriate human investments. It also depends on market opportunities, the extent and strength of the unionization of the workforce, the mobility of the workforce, and discrimination in the labour market. You saw in the discussion of productivity (chapter 9) that it also depends on the amount of other inputs that human inputs work with, since these affect marginal and average products. It also depends on chance and the willingness of individuals to take risks with their human and physical wealth: successful risk takers are (other things equal) better off than the unsuccessful and than those who take fewer risks.

Of the various interesting questions one can ask about the income (and wealth) distribution, there are perhaps three main ones. First, how does one *measure* the distribution and differences between distributions? Second, should the distribution be *changed*? Third, would changing it have damaging disincentive effects? In this chapter the concentration is on the first two of these. As was seen in chapter 17, theory is ambiguous about the third and the evidence seems to show little disincentive effect on work, at least for small changes in the tax system. Currently, those who have strong beliefs that major redistribution does or does not have big adverse effects on total output are really making large acts of faith.

But it is plain that the activity of the state does *affect* the income distribution.

Household Income Redistribution in the UK

The concept of **household** used by the UK Central Statistical Office is that used in its Family Expenditure Survey of about 7000 households: that is, persons living at the same address having meals together and with common housekeeping. Original income is household income in cash and kind before the deduction of those taxes and before the addition of those state benefits which are included in the analysis. It excludes all of the employers' social security contributions (treated as an indirect tax), all corporation tax and capital gains. Income in kind included consists primarily of an imputed value of income from housing for people in rent-free and owner occupied accommodation. The data for original income in are shown by decile in table 21.4.

The assumptions implicitly made about the incidence of taxes and benefits were rather extreme and were as follows: income tax was assumed to fall entirely upon the individual taxpayer; employers' social security contributions to fall entirely upon consumers; indirect taxes on final and intermediate goods were assumed to be passed on fully in higher prices (and thus to consumers).

Table 21.4 Average incomes, taxes and benefits, UK 1982 (£ per year)

	Lowest				*Details of original income*					*Highest*	
	1	*2*	*3*	*4*	*5*	*6*	*7*	*8*	*9*	*10*	*Average*
1 Household original income	4	288	1416	3819	5874	7511	9122	10,950	13,511	21,260	7376
Tax payments											
2 Direct taxes[a]	0	19	172	683	1245	1616	2031	2523	3070	5130	1649
3 Indirect taxes[b]	761	714	1068	1382	1599	1829	2064	2309	2623	3483	1783
4 Total tax payments	761	733	1240	2065	2844	3445	4095	4832	5693	8613	3432
Benefits											
5 In cash[c]	2885	2486	2377	1556	966	807	726	637	601	471	1352
6 In kind[d]	1265	1014	1105	1295	1330	1390	1395	1444	1444	1536	1323
7 Total benefits	4150	3500	3482	2851	2296	2197	2121	2081	2045	2007	2673
8 Fiscal residual (7–4)	3389	2767	2242	786	−548	−1248	−1974	−2751	−3648	−6606	−759
9 Final income after taxes and benefits (1 + 8)	3394	3055	3658	4605	5326	6263	7148	8199	9863	14,654	6613
10 Gross income (1 + 5)	2889	2774	3739	5375	6840	8318	9848	11,587	14,112	21,731	8728
11 Disposable income (10 − 2)	2889	2755	3621	4692	5595	6702	7817	9064	11,042	16,601	7079

[a] Taxes on income only. Corporation tax, taxes on wealth, gifts etc. excluded.
[b] Rates, import duties, VAT, employers' national insurance contributions etc.
[c] Includes age related, child related, income related and other direct cash benefits.
[d] Includes education, NHS, welfare foods, housing subsidies and other in kind benefits.
Source: Central Statistical Office (1983) 'The effects of taxes and benefits on household income 1982', *Economic Trends*, November, 82–114

On this basis the figures in row 4 of table 21.4 were derived, showing how the amount of tax paid rises with income.

On the benefit side, a far more restricted set of items of expenditure was included in the CSO study, namely family allowances, pensions and other cash benefits such as educational scholarships, and imputed values of state education services, the National Health Service and welfare foods, and indirect benefits such as housing subsidies. The cash benefits were what respondents stated the households received over a twelve month period. Educational benefits in kind were valued at cost according to the type of education being received and according to the number of persons receiving it in each household. Benefits from the National Health Service were also valued at cost to the health services and were allocated among households according to the average cost to the government of each type of service and to the estimated use made of each service by people of different age and sex. Benefits were then added up for the members of a household. School meals and other welfare foods were allocated according to the number of children and the cost was calculated net of household contributions. Housing subsidies (the difference between current expenditure by local authorities on housing and the rents paid by tenants) were estimated separately for each local authority dwelling in the sample.

The aggregate effect of these benefits is shown in row 7 of table 21.4 and reveals an inverse relation with original income. The net redistributive effect is presented in row 8, showing an apparently quite strong progressive element in the net redistribution.

If one compares original income (row 1) with final income (row 9), the poorest decile's average income rose from just £4 to £3394, and the richest decile's average income fell from £21,260 to £14,654. Disposable income (row 11) was less unequally distributed than originally, with the poorest decile receiving £2889 and the richest £16,601, but less equal than the distribution of final income.

Case Study 21.1 Income Distributions in Germany, UK and USA

Getting comparable international figures for income distributions is extremely difficult. This case study reports some (out of many) comparisons made by Malcolm Sawyer (1976). Table 21.5 shows the post-tax income distributions for the Federal Republic of Germany (1973), the UK (1973) and the USA (1972). As you can see, there is a general tendency for the share of the lower deciles to rise after taxation and public expenditure are taken account of, and for the share of the top deciles to fall.

Interesting questions to ask in making comparisons include: which society was the more (less) unequal? Is the post-tax distribution more (less) equal than the pre-tax distribution? You will be looking at the issues raised by such questions in the text. You might, however, like to make a tentative assessment of your own now, using the data in table 21.5.

Malcolm Sawyer (1976) 'Income distribution in OECD countries', *OECD Economic Outlook: Occasional Studies*, OECD, Paris, tables 3 and 4.

Table 21.5 Size distribution (per cent) of pre-tax and post-tax income in Germany, the UK and the USA, 1972–3

	Germany		*UK*		*USA*	
	Pre-tax	*Post-tax*	*Pre-tax*	*Post-tax*	*Pre-tax*	*Post-tax*
Top 10%	31.1	30.3	24.7	23.5	28.4	26.6
2nd 10%	15.7	15.8	15.6	15.2	16.4	16.3
3rd 10%	12.2	12.1	13.0	12.8	13.4	13.4
4th 10%	9.9	9.8	11.2	11.1	11.1	11.3
5th 10%	8.3	8.2	9.8	9.9	9.3	9.5
6th 10%	6.8	6.8	8.3	8.5	7.5	7.8
7th 10%	5.6	5.7	6.9	7.1	5.8	6.2
8th 10%	4.5	4.6	5.1	5.5	4.2	4.5
9th 10%	3.4	3.7	3.3	3.8	2.6	3.0
Bottom 10%	2.5	2.8	2.1	2.5	1.2	1.5

Measuring Income Distributions

Suppose one asked, with reference to the data in table 21.5, whether post-tax income is distributed more unequally in one country than another. After looking at the figures in closer detail you may conclude that, since in the UK the lower deciles always received a higher share than in the USA, and the higher deciles a lower share, post-tax income was more equally distributed in the UK than the USA. The judgement is harder to make in the comparison, say, between the UK and Germany, for in Germany the bottom three deciles and the top decile each received a higher share than in the UK, whereas the middle deciles received a higher share in the UK than in Germany.

This illustrates one difficulty in judging the extent of **inequality**: making a general statement, or inventing a summary statistic, about the extent of inequality may not be as obviously easy as one may at first suppose. A further difficulty – or set of difficulties – arises when one tries to quantify by precisely (or even approximately) how much more one distribution is unequal than another and how responsive one measure is compared with another when the distribution is changed in specified ways.

Table 21.6 Income distribution in six societies for SAQ 21.1

	Society A	*Society B*	*Society C*	*Society D*	*Society E*	*Society F*
	200	100	400	300	119	150
	200	100	40	100	119	130
	50	100	40	50	119	110
	50	100	40	50	119	90
	50	100	40	50	119	70
	50	100	40	50	5	50
Average income	100	100	100	100	100	100

SAQ 21.1

Table 21.6 gives the distributions of weekly incomes (in pounds sterling) in six societies A–F of six people whose average income is the same in each. How would you rank the six societies in terms of equality?

Lorenz Curves and the Gini Coefficient

Easily the most frequently used measure of inequality in income distribution studies is the Gini coefficient. This is most usefully explained using the Lorenz curve. If you rank households in the three countries in case study 21.1 by income from the lowest to the highest along the bottom axis of figure 21.1, and, along the vertical axis, measure the cumulative share of after tax income received by the households in question, a **Lorenz curve** is traced out. Zero per cent of the population has zero income and 100 per cent have 100 per cent, so the curve runs in a north easterly direction. If everyone has the same income, the curve will simply be the straight diagonal line, but if the lower households in the distribution have a proportionately lower share of total income, then the Lorenz curve will be below the diagonal. Figure 21.1 shows the diagonal (line of absolute equality) and Lorenz curves for the UK, USA and Germany based on the data of table 21.5.

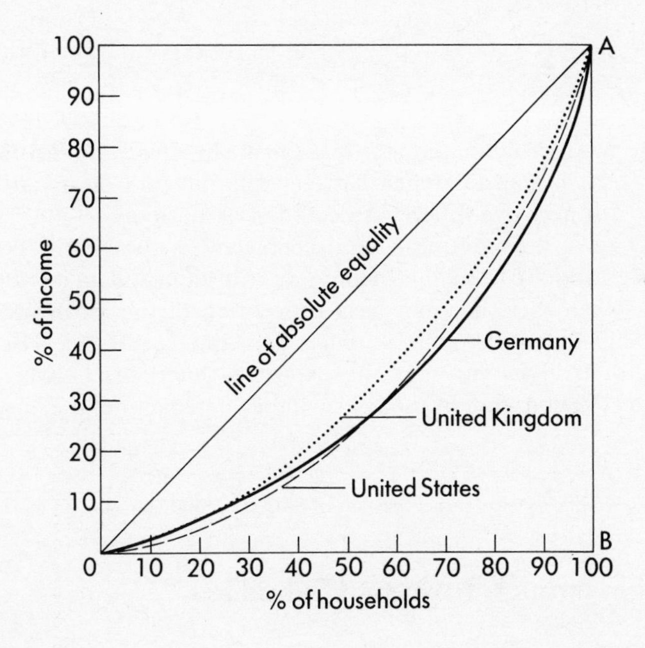

Figure 21.1 Lorenz curves in the UK, USA and Federal Republic of Germany

The Lorenz curves shows very clearly the problem noted, namely that whether one regards Germany as more or less unequal than the UK or the USA depends upon how one wishes to weight the shares going to the poorest and the richest. If the share of the poorest gets sufficiently high a weight, then Germany will be judged less unequal – despite the relatively high share of income going to the rich. Only if the Lorenz curves do not intersect can you conclude unambiguously that the distribution is more unequal in one country than another.

The **Gini coefficient** is the ratio of (1) the area between the line of absolute equality in figure 21.1 and a Lorenz curve to (2) the area of the triangle below the diagonal, shown as 0AB in the figure. The coefficient will take a value of zero when incomes are equally distributed (i.e. the Lorenz curve is coincident with the diagonal) and a value of one at the other extreme when the Lorenz curve has a ⌟ shape and all the income accrues to just one household. In the figure, the Gini coefficients were 0.318 in the UK, 0.381 in the USA and 0.383 in Germany: they are virtually the same in the USA and Germany despite the fact that the bottom 20 per cent of households in Germany had 6.5 per cent of all income compared with 4.5 per cent in the USA. The coefficients applicable in table 21.4 were 0.482 for original income, 0.362 for gross income, 0.332 for disposable income and 0.330 for final income indicating that, taken together, taxes and benefits tended to reduce inequality according to the Gini coefficient (cash benefits had the main impact; indirect taxes tended to increase inequality marginally).

The Gini formula is

$$G = \frac{1}{2n^2\mu} \sum_{i=1}^{n} \sum_{j=1}^{n} |y_i - y_j|$$

where n is the number of households, μ is the mean household income, and the modulus $|y_i - y_j|$ is the difference between the incomes of any two of the n households, with negative differences counted as positive.

A handy way of interpreting a Gini coefficient is that if one chooses two households at random from the income distribution and takes the absolute difference between their incomes as a proportion of the mean income, then on average this difference will be twice the Gini coefficient. For example, a coefficient of 0.38 means that the expected difference between any two randomly selected households' incomes will be 76 per cent of the mean income.

SAQ 21.2

Calculate the Gini coefficients for the six societies of SAQ 21.1 and comment on them.

Redistribution through Taxes and Subsidies

In modern societies, the redistribution of incomes is exceedingly complex. Flows from individuals into the budget of government can occur through income and wealth taxation, through indirect taxation, through the sale of government produced goods and services and through several other mechanisms. Similarly, the benefits provided by the government go to special pressure groups (e.g. farmers, intellectuals); to special interest groups in response either to externalities or to notions of fairness or both (the sick, the old); to everyone out of necessity in the case of mostly public goods (such as defence, and law and order). In short, resources are collected from and distributed to a motley collection of individuals. Moreover, the redistribution of resources, though mostly in money on the revenue side, takes the form of both money and of goods and services in kind on the expenditure side. Clearly the task of identifying the individuals who contribute and who receive, and the respective amounts contributed and received, is formidable.

Yet further difficulties relate to the concept as well as the measurement of the changes that occur in the economic position of individuals as a consequence of redistribution. One problem is that if one is to discover what redistribution has taken place, one needs to know what the distribution of incomes *would have been* if the redistribution that took place had not taken place. But this is by no means a simple task. One of the functions of government is to provide public goods and these certainly have redistributive impact. But the pre- and post-redistribution comparison is not as simple as imagining that currently publicly produced public goods were previously produced in the private sector. It may not be possible for them to be produced in the private sector, or not on the same scale. But if this is so, then redistribution cannot be considered to take place out of a constant total community income – redistribution cannot be considered apart from production. Moreover, even supposing this problem had been solved somehow and supposing also that a definition of 'income' to be used had been decided upon, one would still require a theory and measurement of the incidence of taxes and expenditures. For, as you know from earlier analysis, prices need not rise or fall by the amount of taxes: they depend on relative elasticities.

Finally, there remains the problem of defining the basic units of analysis – income and the unit receiving the income. The definition of *income* most commonly employed by economists is that it is **potential consumption** in the sense of the value of consumption that is possible in any period without reducing the value of wealth. This definition has the advantage of measuring the total potential increase in a person's wealth during the period (if nothing were consumed it would be the actual increase), or **economic power**. It has, however, the disadvantage of not corresponding to the Inland Revenue definition, which, for example, excludes unrealized capital gains.

As far as the *income unit* is concerned, the natural unit to take is that within which incomes are shared. The basic unit is naturally the **nuclear family** of adults and their children, but the question arises as to how far to include other household members such as married children, elderly persons or lodgers living with the nuclear family. If the fundamental concern in redistribution or poverty is with economic power, the choice would seem to depend upon the extent to which incomes were actually shared within households. If they were not shared very extensively, poverty among for example the elderly would be understated by using the household as the unit. In general the best definition seems to be the nuclear family. Intrahousehold transfers outside the nuclear family should therefore be treated as separate sources of income for those additional household members. In practice, however, one must often take households or tax units as the unit since that is the basis on which data are available.

In investigating empirically the redistributive effects of the government at the most general level, the effects of all government activities would be considered. For example, ideally one would include an assessment of the distribution (by family income class) of expenditure on defence, roads, agriculture, museums and art galleries. Alternatively, even though all these government activities have – and are sometimes intended to have – redistributive effects, one might take a narrower view and assess the redistributive effects of social policy. In that case, of course, one faces the problem of defining the activities that are held to constitute social policy.

SAQ 21.3

Outline some desirable properties of any summary measure of inequality.

The Uneasy Utilitarian Case for Equality

Two famous English economists have put one commonly heard argument succinctly. Arthur Pigou (whom you met in case study 19.2) wrote:

> It is evident that any transference of income from a relatively rich man to a relatively poor man of similar temperament, since it enables more intense wants to be satisfied at the expense of less intense wants, must increase the aggregate sum of satisfaction.

Hugh Dalton, who was reader in public finance at the London School of Economics and Chancellor of the Exchequer, wrote

> Put broadly, and in the language of common sense, the case against large inequalities of income is that the less urgent needs of the rich are satisfied while the more urgent needs of the poor are left unsatisfied. . . . This is merely an application of the economists' law of diminishing marginal utility.

SAQ 21.4

If (a) the aim is to maximize the total utility of society, (b) utility is measured on a cardinal scale, (c) everyone's marginal utility of income falls as their income rises, and (d) redistribution has no incentive or disincentive effects on work, saving, or risk taking, does it follow that an equal distribution of income fulfils the aim?

The arguments just quoted seem to have intuitive appeal, and you have just thought about them in tackling SAQ 21.4. Are the arguments sound? Consider

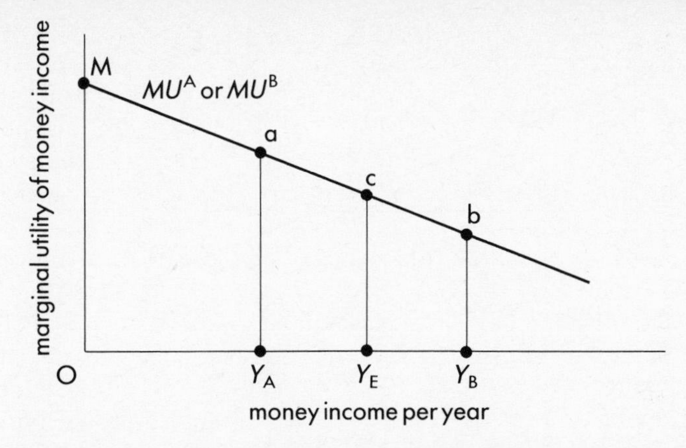

Figure 21.2 Utilitarian redistribution with identical preferences

figure 21.2. On the vertical axis is measured the marginal utility of money income. On the horizontal axis is the size of money income. The curve Macb shows how for two individuals, A and B, the marginal utility of money income falls as income increases. Now suppose that A has Y_A income and B has Y_B, i.e. B is the richer of the two. A's marginal utility is Y_Aa, which is higher than B's Y_Bb. The sum total of utility in this society of two individuals is OMaY_A plus OMbY_B. The utilitarian argument for redistribution would run thus: that by removing $Y_B Y_E$ income from B and giving it to A, B will lose less than A will gain, since B's marginal utility is lower than A's throughout this income range. With equal incomes of Y_E, each has the same marginal utility of money income and the sum total of utility in society is maximized, being equal to twice OMcY_E, which must be larger than OMaY_A plus OMbY_B. In fact, this is an argument for absolute *equality* of incomes.

In its strict form, the argument for absolute equality depends crucially upon an identity of tastes for money income among the population. But a weaker form will still hold even when tastes differ. In figure 21.3, for example, B (the rich person) has a marginal utility curve that is everywhere higher than A's. A possible reason for this is that great wealth has enabled B to appreciate delights such as cordon bleu cooking and opera, tastes that A has not had the opportunity to acquire.

According to this less radical utilitarianism, with different tastes, equality is not required in order to maximize the sum total of individual utilities. One still requires that the marginal utilities of each individual's income be the same, but this is now achieved with a transfer of $Y_B Y_B'$ $(=Y_A Y_A')$ from B to A; inequalities are reduced but not eliminated.

At this point you will doubtless be aware of a possible perversity in the argument: what if the marginal utility of income for the rich person (B) is higher rather than lower than that of the poor person? This seems to be a perfectly possible contingency. If the rich person were to say that more utility was to be had from the ability to buy an additional egg than the poor person,

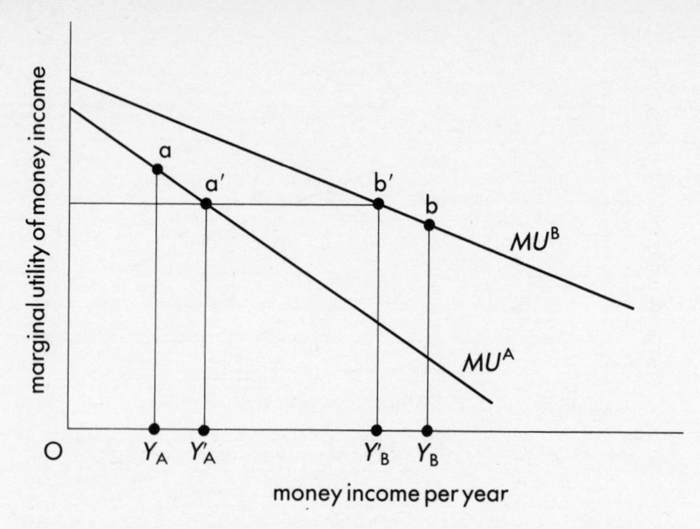

Figure 21.3 Utilitarian redistribution with differing preferences

who could gainsay it? But if this were the case, then income should be transferred from the poor person to the rich! You may find it odd to conceive that the rich could derive more utility from an additional unit than the poor. One reason for this may be that you are not really considering the subjective utilities of the two people, but are really bringing in your own values. One way of doing this is to ask: would I rather be the poor person with an additional unit or the rich person? If you answer 'the rich' then *your* utility would be higher and, on the usual assumptions, your marginal utility would be lower. But though this is an interesting way of making interpersonal comparisons (putting yourself in someone else's shoes) it is not the same as comparing the utilities of the rich and poor. The principal lesson from all this is that utilitarianism without identical preferences is by no means necessarily also egalitarian.

The utilitarian argument does not say that redistribution is itself desirable. It says that what is desirable is to maximize the sum total of utility in society (or the utility of an average citizen) and that redistribution is necessary to achieve this. Unfortunately for egalitarians, however, the type of redistribution that increases the total utility need not imply *complete* equality, as you have just seen. Moreover, it may even require increased *in*equality!

Look at figure 21.4. Initial incomes are Y_A and Y_B but A's marginal utility (Y_A) is lower than B's (Y_B). Thus, in this case there is an argument for transferring $Y_AY'_A$ from A and giving it to B ($Y_AY'_A = Y_BY'_B$) since $Y_B$bb′Y'_B is larger than Y'_Aa′aY_A. You can even have a case in which the utilitarian argument provides a case for making the rich poor and the poor rich, rather than just poorer and richer.

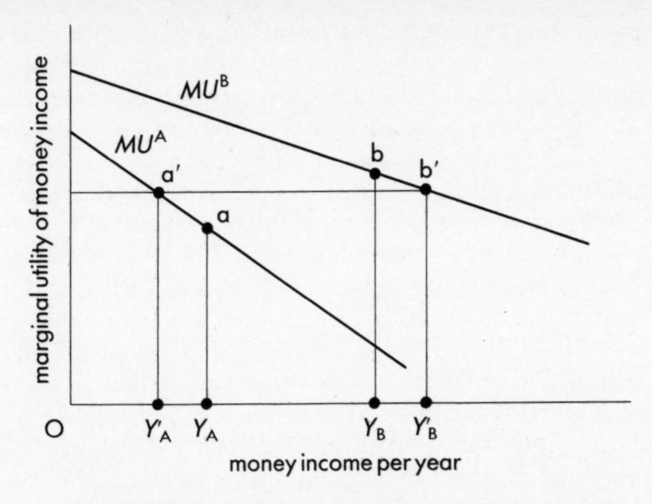

Figure 21.4 Utilitarian case for increasing inequality

SAQ 21.5

In figure 21.5, A is poor and B is rich. They each have the *MU* of income curves shown, so before redistribution A has an *MU* of Y_A and B has an *MU* of Y_B. Given a utilitarian objective to maximize the sum of utilities, what should the post-redistribution measures of Y_A and Y_B be, given a total income of T?

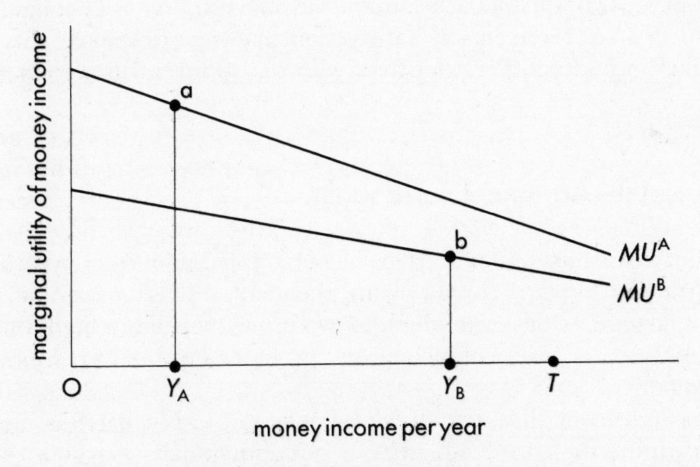

Figure 21.5 Incomes for SAQ 21.5

There are, of course, many objections to utilitarianism, both scientific and ethical. The chief of these is whether it is possible to make comparisons of the quantity of utility that different individuals receive at the margin. One difficulty lies in the use of the word 'utility' among earlier economists (and obviously they were speaking about *cardinal* utility as well). It was, for example, frequently identified with 'satisfaction'. But this raises problems of meaning; for, whereas it may make sense to talk about zero utility as an abstract idea, it clearly does not make a great deal of sense to talk about zero satisfaction. More fundamentally, however, what kind of sense does it make to say that one person has more utility (or satisfaction) than another? Clearly some meaning can be conveyed by such statements. It is not ridiculous to say that 'John is happier today than he was yesterday' or that 'John is happier than Fred', but it is very difficult to say how much more happy he is. It is also very difficult to be quite sure that in making such judgements one has not interpreted John's or Fred's behaviour quite mistakenly, and the relative happiness of two persons with different incomes is usually harder to observe than their relative happiness with their Christmas presents.

Since people's tastes do undoubtedly differ and therefore their marginal utilities of money income will differ (even if they have the same income) the absolute equality of incomes cannot be defended on these utilitarian grounds. Similarly, since utility is not an observable quantity and the relationship between it (or satisfaction) and a person's income is not at all clear, all one can say is that one thinks that John is more satisfied than Fred – and John need not be the richer man. Other than for the most extreme income differences, it also seems impossible to make the interpersonal comparisons of utility with anything like the degree of accuracy one would need to evolve even a qualitative redistribution policy, concerned simply with the *directions* of change. Nor have you any reason to suppose that satisfaction varies systematically for all people in society in the way such a basis for policy would require. Even if you allowed that one poor man received less satisfaction than one rich man, it would be unsurprising to find another poor man who was more satisfied than either of them.

An Uncertainty Argument for Equality

One famous economist, Abba Lerner, has attempted tc overcome these objections by putting forward the following theorem: if it is impossible, on any division of income, to discover which of two individuals has a higher marginal utility of income, the utility of income will probably be maximized by dividing income equally.

Lerner's argument, like the previous one, can easily be illustrated in a simple diagram. In figure 21.6, MU is one individual's marginal utility of income curve and MU' is the other's. The two individuals have, it is supposed, differing tastes and therefore different marginal utility of income curves. Empirically, however, one does not know where they lie relative to one another

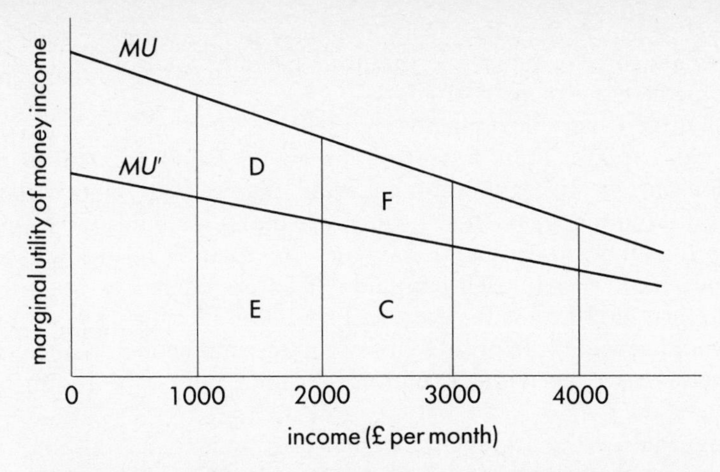

Figure 21.6 Utilitarian redistribution with uncertain preferences

and, in particular, one does not know whether *MU* belongs to A and *MU'* to B, or vice versa. What is assumed is that marginal utility falls and that their incomes can be measured.

Suppose that between them A and B have £4000, distributed such that A has £1000 and B £3000. Then by redistributing £1000 from B to A, each has a post-redistribution income of £2000 (assuming zero incentive or disincentive effects and zero transaction costs). If A's curve is *MU* and B's is *MU'*, then B will have lost area C of utility but A will have gained areas D + E. It follows from the diminishing marginal utility of income that E > C; therefore (D + E) > C and A's gain exceeds B's loss. But of course, A's curve may have been *MU'* and B's may have been *MU*. In this case, the redistribution will have cost B the areas (C + F) and A will gain only E. You know that E > C and that (D + E) > (F + C), but this is not enough to tell us whether E > (F + C). How then do you get out of the apparent impasse?

Lerner suggested that one is as likely to be incorrect in assigning *MU* curves to individuals as one is to be correct. There is thus a 50 per cent chance of gaining D + E but losing C and a 50 per cent chance of gaining E and losing C + F. From redistributing incomes equally there is therefore an expected gain in total utility of:

$$0.5\ [(D + E) - C + E - (C + F)]$$

What can you say about the sign of this term? The sign is important, because if it is positive you will have shown that equality leads to an increase in the probable sum total of utility. Comparing the terms in the round brackets, one can immediately see that (D + E) > (C + F), which follows simply from the negative slope of *MU* in figure 21.6. Therefore the latter subtracted from the former will leave a positive sum. It is also clear that C < E, which follows from the negative slope of *MU'*. Therefore the former subtracted from the latter will leave a positive sum. Since the sum of two positives is positive, and half of a positive sum is also positive, it follows inexorably that the whole term is positive. Therefore, to maximize the probable sum total of utilities requires that income be equally distributed.

Note that the Lerner theorem does not tell one whether, once the redistribution has taken place, there has been any actual utility gain to society as a whole, for one is still ignorant about the shapes and relative heights of marginal utility functions. All one can say is that if net gains were made they are larger than if net losses had been made. There can be no absolute certainty of gain but, as Lerner himself has said, 'If I were offered 11 cents for every head in return for 10 cents for every tail on 100 million tosses of an unbiased coin, I would consider the probability of gain certain enough'. Since all social policy decisions are taken under conditions of uncertainty, the argument seems fairly powerful.

Although the Lerner argument has many attractions, it is also not without disadvantages. First, it continues to assume, like utilitarianism, that utilities can simply be added up (even though it does not require us to observe them). Secondly, although it grants that the utility people receive is not statistically dependent upon their relative incomes, it still requires that the utilities of different people be commensurable. Third, it assumes that one is equally uncertain about a loss as one is about a gain. Each of these assumptions is somewhat metaphysical: you can test none of them, not even indirectly by their implications. Of the first it may be said to be highly improbable, for even if the utility received from X be known as well as that from Y, common experience suggests that the utility of X and Y together may be greater or smaller than the sums of their independent utilities. This is as true of an individual's personal view of different income distributions (for example, A may derive utility from the fact that B has more, or less, income than A) as it is of shoes and shoelaces.

None the less, this argument seems a lot better than the previous one. Some of its flaws can be eliminated by more sophisticated theorizing – but that is a matter for more advanced levels of economics.

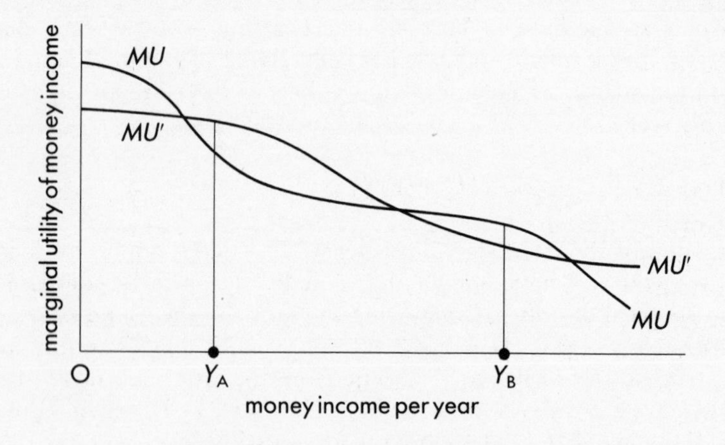

Figure 21.7 Incomes for SAQ 21.6

The arguments so far have related to **vertical redistribution** – that is, to redistribution from the rich to the poor. Another kind is **horizontal redistribution** – between persons or households with the same or similar incomes. The normative case for this type is developed in the next section.

SAQ 21.6

(a) Does the Lerner argument apply in the case of the two individuals shown in figure 21.7, where one has income Y_A and the other Y_B, but either may have *MU* or *MU'* (but not *both* having *MU* or *MU'*)?

(b) Would it be better, using the Lerner argument, to have only a partial move towards equality (ignoring disincentive effects and so on)?

Externality Arguments for Redistribution

Let individuals in society have *preferences* about income distribution, despite, or in addition to, the fact that they may also hold moral views about the justice of various distributions. Consequently, it seems not unreasonable to include within the choice set of each individual a set of choices to be made about transfers. In short, individuals derive utility from alleviating poverty or in assisting those families who have what they regard as special needs. Thus, both vertical and horizontal considerations can be brought under the same theoretical umbrella as allocational efficiency. One can describe an efficient redistribution policy. This approach to income distribution is based not on what utility A and B get from their respective incomes, but on what utility A gets from his or her own *and* B's income and what utility B gets from his or her own income *and* A's.

The argument can be illustrated in a diagram similar to the classical utilitarian diagrams, but crucially different in its interpretation. In figure 21.8, marginal utilities are shown on the vertical axis and the incomes of two individuals along the horizontal axis. MU^A_A is A's marginal utility of A's own income and MU^A_B is A's external marginal utility of B's income.

Suppose that A has £8000 income per year and B £2000. At the pre-distribution level of incomes A's marginal utility of own income (£8000) is ab. The *MU* placed by A on B's income is ac > ab. To increase own utility A will therefore transfer some income to B. In the diagram, A's utility is maximized when £2000 has been transferred. At this point the marginal utility from a pound's worth of income retained for own use equals the marginal utility (to A) of one pound increment in B's income. Thus, for social welfare to be maximized, the transfer ought to be made. Distributional efficiency obtains where, for A, $MU^A_A = MU^A_B$. The analysis gives explicit recognition to the fact that many people are (a) concerned about the welfare of others and (b) generous. If MU^A_B (A's marginal utility from B's income) was everywhere zero, A would be indifferent to B's welfare and therefore neither concerned nor generous. If it had positive values but lay below MU^A_A everywhere to the left of a, A would be concerned but not actually generous – not caring sufficiently to

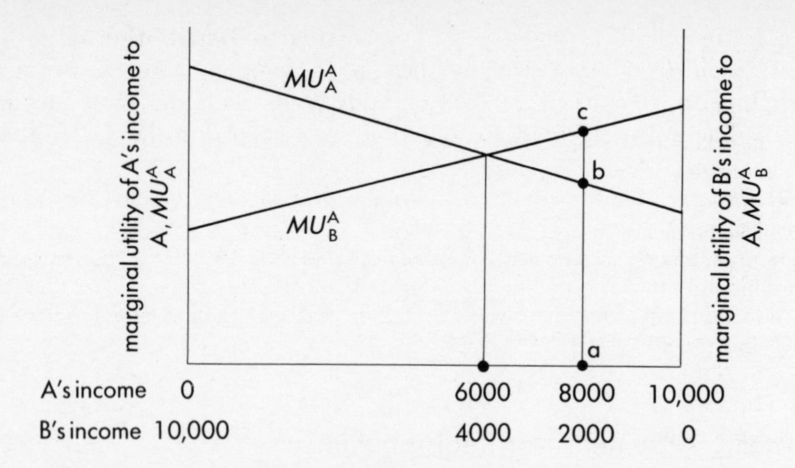

Figure 21.8 Efficient redistribution when there are preferences about income distributions

make the transfer. In both these cases a corner solution exists at which $MU^A_A > MU^A_B$ and it is inefficient to make the transfer.

Does the efficiency approach to income distribution imply that society ought to adopt a progressive, proportional or regressive tax structure (see chapter 13)? The conclusions worked out by Harold Hochman and James Rodgers, who pioneered this approach (see case study 21.2), are that the answer depends upon both the shape of the size distribution of income and the responsiveness of each person's 'demand' for transfers (to others) to changes in income differentials. If identical preferences are assumed at each level of income, with an income distribution that is skewed to the right (a higher proportion of families have incomes below the average income than above it), and with a responsiveness of the demand for transfers such that the size of the preferred transfer increases in proportion with the initial income differentials, the pattern of efficient redistribution is effected through progressive taxes on income. Even if the demand for transfers is independent of the size of the differentials, the tax structure, while somewhat complex, also ought to have marked progressive characteristics.

Thus an efficiency criterion can be used to assess even the goodness of income distributions. The test of a socially beneficial redistribution is that it should be voluntarily undertaken, taking voluntary behaviour to be behaviour that is not against the interest of the person or persons concerned. Usually, however, some judgement (but not a value judgement) will have to be exercised to decide the fact of voluntariness, and this is usually difficult with collective actions. (For example, there may be elements of coercion in order to overcome free riding rather than to force uncaring people to act as though they cared.) There will usually be a set of efficient redistributions and, moreover, the set will vary according to the initial distribution from which one starts.

Case Study 21.2 Efficient Redistribution in the USA

The externality theory of redistribution was pioneered by the US economists Harold Hochman and James Rodgers (1969). Using the assumption (they also tried others) that the elasticity of a person's demand for another's income depended on the income *difference* between them, and that this elasticity was unitary, they obtained the results shown in table 21.7.

Looking at the actual net receipts and tax contributions in the third column, you can see that the pattern is approximately progressive. The very poor ($800 families) seem to have fared badly. This is probably due to a combination of underestimates of true income (particularly for the rural poor, who may receive substantial amounts of income in kind) and of the fact that they have relatively little political clout. There is also an apparent aberration in the case of the $8750 families who actually received net transfers rather than, as one would expect, being net contributors.

Table 21.7 Personal income and net transfers/taxes in the USA, 1960, actual and 'efficient' ($)

Annual family income	*% of families*	*US actual net transfers*	*'Efficient' net transfers*
800	14	+441	+558
2,500	9	+1110	+338
3,500	9	+648	+288
4,500	11	−58	+188
6,250	28	−131	−13
8,750	15	+148	−239
15,500	14	−2046	−913

The computed efficient net transfers are shown in the final column. This shows a clearly progressive structure. The match between the actual and the 'efficient' is far from perfect (real world redistribution is, after all, bound to be affected by many other factors that are not to do with a desire for *vertical* redistribution). However, it is striking that, supposing preferences for redistribution to be as postulated by Hochman and Rodgers, a progressive tax and benefit structure emerges – not as the result of an ethical argument about equality, but as the result of a postulated 'caring' externality.

Harold Hochman and James Rodgers (1969) 'Pareto optimal redistribution', *American Economic Review*, **59**(4), 542–57, table 7.

You can also see that the externality argument can be used as a justification on efficiency grounds for engaging in *horizontal* redistribution. Suppose, for example, that another person's health (independently of their income or wealth) affected *your* utility. This is an external effect: the more healthy they are, the better off *you* are (as well, presumably, as they). In a private equilibrium that person (A) will set $MV^A_A = MC$ – supposing, say, health care, to be supplied in a price takers' market. But if you (B) value A's health because you are a caring person, then the efficient consumption of health care would be where $MV^A_A + MV^B_A = MC$: more health care should be consumed by A. If health care is provided in a price searchers' market, the shortfall between the actual and the efficient rate of A's consumption will be even larger. This leads to a case for the subsidization of health care (including prevention of ill health). By extension, the argument may also apply to education at various levels, industrial training, housing and, indeed, any set of attributes of individuals or their consumption patterns that affects others who care.

The argument is not, of course, only a *normative* one, stipulating the efficient or desirable distributions of health care, education and so on. It can also be used as a *positive* explanation for why we see so much redistribution in *kind* rather than cash: if such externalities exist, individuals have a behavioural incentive to do something about them. It seems rather likely that most individuals have views both about general income distribution (leading to vertical redistribution) and about specific distributions of important things, like health and education (leading to horizontal as well as vertical redistribution).

SAQ 21.7

It must be more efficient to make transfers in cash rather than kind, since the former enable the recipients to move to higher indifference curves than is possible with the latter. What do you think of that argument?

Redistribution and Justice

An efficient redistribution is not, of course, the same as a just or a fair one. To take an extreme example, the starting point may be one where one person owns all society's wealth and is, moreover, totally ungenerous. In this case, the initial distribution would be an efficient one, for no transfer could be made that would not harm this extraordinarily rich person. But it is not likely to be viewed as a just distribution – even by the extraordinarily rich person. That person may prefer to keep his or her own wealth rather than redistribute it, even though they regarded their own act in so doing as unjust. Efficient behaviour may therefore be unjust, and inefficient behaviour may be just, for efficiency depends upon preferences and justice is always defined by criteria external to preferences. Each aspect needs to be evaluated separately for an overall judgement to be reached. It seems sensible to describe the overall judgement as producing neither general efficiency nor justice, but consisting in some balance of both types of consideration – a balancing act social *scientists* cannot make. Note that, unless you equate efficiency with justice (which would be very odd) you do not need to get into the vexed question of what justice is in order to be able to say these things.

Redistribution can thus be justified that may actually harm some members of society, and such redistribution, though not warranted by the efficiency criterion, would be warranted on grounds of justice. (There are relevant criteria other than justice, such as whether the social structure is liberal, conducive to invention, or productive of variety.) Further redistribution may then be justified on the narrower interpretation of economic efficiency. Note, however, that the broader framework of justice in redistribution, like the narrower one of efficiency, does not imply or prescribe a uniquely just and efficient distribution of income. Nor does it imply any particular form of ownership of resources.

Any detailed discussion of justice or fairness in distributions would go too far into the terrain of political theory – fascinating though such a foray would be. Here it must suffice to observe that most economists tend to keep 'efficiency' and 'justice' as rather separate categories of (value) judgement. A particular arrangement may be efficient and just, inefficient and unjust, efficient and unjust or inefficient and just. Economics as such has little to offer as to how the various combinations can be compared. But one can insist on *explicitness*.

SAQ 21.8

Is equality the same as justice?

What You Should Understand Now

The functional and personal distribution of income in the UK.
Effects of the UK public sector on the post-tax and subsidy income distribution.
How to compare distributions using the Gini coefficient.
Limitations of the Gini measure.
The relationship between utilitarianism and the desirability of equality in the income distribution.
Implications of utilitarianism for inequality.
The Lerner argument for equality of incomes.
Externality arguments for redistribution in cash and kind.
Difference between vertical and horizontal redistribution.
Distributional externalities and the progressiveness of public sector taxes and subsidies.
The differences between efficient redistribution and just redistribution.

22

Government and the Economics of Politics

The value laden question of what government *ought to do* is the oldest political hot potato of all. There is a general consensus among most parties that the government, interpreted as the wielder of ultimate power in a society, ought to provide some basic public goods; in particular, that it should shoulder responsibility for the defence of a country against potential foreign attackers (and actual ones too, of course!) and also for any attacking. The general argument for this role is that the government can do this more efficiently than private organizations because there may be economies of scale in the production of military 'output', because the government has no incentive to use a profitability criterion of success or failure (which a private army is likely to do; mere profitability is not generally regarded as the appropriate test of military establishments), and because defence (or, come to that, attack) is a public good subject to the usual free rider problems of public good production.

There is also general consensus that the government should be responsible for the definition of property rights, their enforcement and the administration of justice. Again the essential argument is that the output of these services is a public good, may be subject to scale economies, and should be operated according to criteria that have little to do with profit.

Beyond these two roles, however, far less consensus exists. How far should the government engage in the production of private goods? Should the government *produce* goods and services at all or merely *finance* their efficient private production? Should there be a welfare state? Should the government monopolize the money supply? Should the government use its powerful fiscal leverage via taxes, subsidies and so on, to alter the distribution of income? Should it seek to alter the rates of output, inflation and employment via general policies of a fiscal or monetary type or by direct and specific interventions to affect aggregate investment, unemployment and so on? Much of the remainder of the book will be devoted to both the normative issues (what *should* the government do?) and the positive issues (what *can* it do, and *how* can it do it?).

Government is also, as a collection of people (politicians, civil servants, and so on), an object of behavioural study: what government does and the way it does it is a part of positive economics.

SAQ 22.1

'Government is bureaucracy and therefore wasteful'. What do you think about this assertion?

Government and Social Contract

One way of looking at government is to see it as a decision taking agency to which has been delegated particular responsibilities (or which has simply seized them). **Democratic government**, in particular, can usefully be seen as a kind of collective organization or club acting on behalf of its members. The delegation of collective decisions to a government over which citizens have some control is an extension of the general interest each has in getting goods (especially public ones) efficiently produced and it is, indeed, the appropriate agent when the affected community is the whole community under the jurisdiction of a government. There is a general presumption that collective interests of a village are most efficiently run by a local collectivity (e.g. the local church, the parish council, the British Legion). Collective interests of a whole country – such as law and order, the health and education of the nation – are plausibly most efficiently implemented by a national collectivity (that is, the central government). Clearly, depending on the nature and scope of the public good in question, there is a large variety of collective institutions that will be appropriate for different decisions.

There are lots of things wrong with markets as a means of producing and allocating goods. Sometimes these are dubbed **market failure** (uninternalized marginal externalities, suboptimal production of public goods, effects of monopoly and monopsony and so on) but do not commit the 'grass is greener' fallacy by supposing that government can necessarily order things better. Individuals in governments too face particular reward and punishment incentives and disincentives that may in practice make government activity no less subject to failure (when judged against some ideal) than markets. In practice one is always choosing between less than ideal alternatives: the problem of choosing a second best solution (see chapter 19) is ever present.

SAQ 22.2

'Private monopolies should be regulated by government'. Do you agree?

Government Behaviour and its Control

It is sometimes naïvely supposed that the individuals with executive and administrative functions in government are different from such individuals as, say, consumers or businessmen, and for some this is a sufficient reason for transferring decision making from one sector to another. This view cannot, however, be realistically sustained. Their behaviour may certainly be different, depending upon the function they perform, but economics asserts that their behaviour is different not because they are different *kinds* of people but because the *nature of the constraints* upon their behaviour is different. In particular, the costs of different choices will vary according to the constraints that govern those choices. The behaviour of persons working in a profit seeking business, a non-profit charity, a public utility, a government department or a local authority will differ not because they are essentially different kinds of people but because the constraints on their behaviour differ.

What are these constraints? At the broadest level they consist, as you have seen, of the range of **rights** owned by an individual in resources. They include not only the monetary wealth at one's disposal (whether one's own or someone else's) and one's time, but all other rights one possesses – rights to use, in specified ways, resources such as the air, rivers, office space, manpower, public parks and so on. Fortunately, it is not necessary to identify and measure the total constraint on behaviour for present purposes. It is sufficient to assume that there exists *some limit* to a person's rights (a realistic enough assumption). One can then investigate the consequence of changing the constraints (the rights structure) by using a fundamental implication of economic theory: the higher the personal cost of obtaining any entity or engaging in any activity, the less will be acquired or engaged in during any period.

Profit and Non-profit Motivation

A frequent difference between organizations in the public and private sectors is that usually (though not invariably) the former are not for profit and the latter (again not invariably) are for profit. Why is it that public ownership suppresses the profit motive so effectively? The answer lies in two key constraining elements to the rights of the owners: non-transferability of ownership and non-convertibility of revenues.

Non-transferability of Ownership

Transferability of ownership means that the *consequences* of ownership can be concentrated upon individuals. In a community of 1000 with ten separate organizations that are publicly owned but are never the less supposed to make profits, each individual has an 0.001 share in each organization. The consequences of each individual's actions to improve the profitability of any organization will be that each receives 0.001 of the additional profit with the other 0.999 going to the other 999 members of the community. Only if the others behave as one does in each organization will each receive the full benefit of his or her product.

By contrast, if ownership could be transferred, each person might have an 0.01 share of *one* organization (still with 'equal' distribution of rights) and the benefits of an individual's actions would depend more upon his or her *own* activity and less upon the activity of others. Divide each organization into 100 smaller organizations so that each can have sole ownership, and the cost–benefit consequences of each individual's activity will be entirely concentrated upon that individual. If the objective was, as assumed, to make profits, the ability to transfer and concentrate ownership will be more conducive to profit making. It only needs one person in the community who wants more wealth (and who will work for it) for it to be worth that person's while to buy other people's ownership shares and more effectively concentrate the rewards of his or her own activity away from others (also the consequences of mistakes), thereby relying less upon the wealth seeking motivation of others to get one's rewards and being less dependent upon their foolish choices. Moreover, since profit maximizing implies technical efficiency and cost-effectiveness in production, such firms are also likely to be efficient on the production side. In a more realistic world where individuals have different managerial capabilities, different technical knowledge, different attitudes to risk and so on, the transferability of ownership will tend to be even more productive of profits. Conversely, non-transferability, or public ownership, will be relatively more effective in emasculating the profit motive. This first argument thus shows why, even if publicly owned organizations are supposed to be every bit as profitable as privately owned organizations, they will tend in practice not to be so profitable, because the costs of not making profits are lower for each individual and the benefits of making more profits are less.

Even, however, if profits are not the objective, the cost–benefit consequences of decisions are less fully thrust upon owners, which means that they will have less incentive to control closely the behaviour of the management of publicly owned organizations. The absence of this incentive, or its weakening, means that other incentives are needed to replace those that are absent. In many areas of governmental activity profit seeking would have led to a neglect of some important social costs and benefits of the activities of an organization. Public ownership is one important method of emasculating the incentive to make profits. At the same time, if the incentive to operate in the social interest, more widely construed, is not also to be emasculated, and if technical efficiency and cost-effectiveness are to be maintained, additional constraints on the behaviour of management are required. There is a demand for such things, as public accountability, publicly available performance information and cost–benefit analysis are intended to provide precisely such decision making controls and aids.

Non-transferability of ownership, although not unique to public ownership, is its most important characteristic. Having thereby weakened the profit motive, it is a short step to prohibiting it effectively. This done, the second element constraining the rights of public decision makers comes to the fore: *non-convertibility*.

Non-convertibility of Revenues

Convertibility of ownership means that the firm's wealth can be converted into individual private wealth. Non-convertibility means that whatever revenues are brought into the organization through its activity cannot be converted by owners into personal wealth and is a constraint on owners of all non-profit organizations, whether publicly or privately owned. The inability of owners to take wealth out of the non-profit organization means that other owners, customers, patrons and suppliers of funds (whether subscribers or taxpayers) are protected against the – possibly self-seeking – behaviour of any individual owner. But this constraint on owners implies that they will tend to seek other ways of increasing their wealth at the expense of the organization. If they cannot do it by paying themselves agreed dividends or by selling their ownership, there exist other, less open methods. Owners who happened to be managers, for example, could pay themselves (and fellow managers) relatively high salaries; they could use luxury office accommodation; they could employ large staffs than are strictly necessary (X-inefficiency; see chapter 15).

Why should the non-profit form of organization be chosen in view of these potential dangers? The reason is that whatever profits the organization earns should be devoted *not* to the wealth of owners but to the well-being of those for whose benefit the non-profit organization has been formed. It is a guarantee to clients and (more important) to the suppliers of funds that the objectives of the organization will not be changed at an individual owner's discretion. Hospitals, for example, are almost universally non-profit organizations and in Britain they are mostly publicly owned as well. This guarantees that the costs and benefits of hospitals can be allocated in ways that are different from profit organizations. To be sure, the owners of a profit organization could devote their profits to charitable purposes *at their discretion*, but if the discretion of a few individuals is thought to be unreliable, the non-profit form of organization guarantees that the costs to manager owners of taking out profits are raised. Moreover, if the institutions in question are publicly owned by the whole community, the policies of these institutions can be designed to serve the wishes of agents interpreting the welfare of the whole community – for example, to internalize community externalities (see chapter 19).

Privately owned non-profit institutions tend to be formed to internalize externalities felt by the owners. Thus, free schools for certain types of children are or have been observed (for sons, sons of clergymen, daughters, Roman Catholic children, the very poor and so on). Similarly, charitable hospitals have been operated, serving particular areas, illnesses or classes of patient. More generally felt externalities, however, are more effectively internalized by *publicly owned* non-profit institutions that discriminate among their clients on a less narrow and specific basis. Nevertheless, they will still have to discriminate (hospitals and universities, for example, have substantial excess demands for their services from clients legally eligible to receive them). The cost–benefit consequences of ownership rights on management are not such as to guarantee that they will operate *automatically* in accordance with the objectives of the organization. Again, additional constraints will have to be supplied if they are to fulfil their functions properly (which patients should be assigned to hospital waiting lists, and how long, on average, should they have to wait? Which of the many qualified students should be admitted to university?

Equality and the Ownership of Rights

One major reason for public ownership is to reduce inequalities in the ownership of wealth (and, thence, political power and influence). Although public ownership does in one sense imply the equal ownership of property by citizens, the rights in that property are not the same as the rights they have in private property – for example, the right to transfer ownership. Moreover, equality in ownership rights does not necessarily require public ownership, for rights to various types of private property may be distributed in a variety of ways. The view held by some that 'property is theft (Pierre-Joseph Proudhon, 1809–1865) derives not from the nature of private property itself but from some historical time at which private rights were reassigned; perhaps some people had had their property rights expropriated in what they thought was an unjust way (the enclosure movement is one example, and the history of the British Empire provides endless examples). There may well indeed be theft in a literal sense, but this refers to the *allocation* of private rights, not to their *existence*.

A system of transferable private property rights implies that rights will tend to become distributed towards those who value them most or can increase their exchange value most. For example, the most able managers will tend to acquire more rights over wealth than the less able; people who enjoy taking risks will, if they take risks successfully, collect more wealth than people who dislike taking risks. Exchangeable private property enables individuals to specialize in the kind of wealth management in which they have a comparative advantage. Thus, private property systems require a more or less continuous redistribution of rights or wealth if egalitarian objectives are to be pursued, especially if the starting point is one in which there is already an unequal distribution of ownership rights. The need for this is absent with public ownership. Instead, one needs stringent controls over the stewards of publicly owned wealth and guidelines to indicate how best they might deploy publicly owned wealth in the social interest.

Much market failure results in the creation of harmful external effects simply because ownership rights have not been established in physical things. Remember, no one owns things; they own rights – if they have any at all – in *ways to use* things. One does not, for example, usually own the right to use one's property to destroy other people's property physically. In America, forests were often destroyed because no one had rights in living trees – only in lumber.

As you saw in chapter 19, it is not coincidence that many of the most serious threats to the environment, a major problem for public policy, take place in property that no one owns or that is common. One is assailed by noise because property rights in the use of the air for transmitting sound waves are not usually established. One is assailed by smells and ugly sights (or the removal of beautiful sights) for much the same reason. Rubbish and poisonous filth are poured out into commonly owned property, or non-owned property, at such a rate today that it is widely recognized that a social problem now exists.

One method of solving the problem would be for the government to take over specific ownership of such property and to use economic appraisal (for example cost–benefit analysis) to establish what the optimal rate of destruction of the environment should be by weighing the benefits of reduced environmental hazard against the costs in, say, lost production and lower money wealth. Many of the key variables required to make such an analysis more than merely an enumeration of points to consider – for example, the social value placed upon reduced noise from jet aircraft (recall case study 19.3) – are enormously hard to calculate, and the establishment of property rights where they do not exist and where external effects are the likely consequence is a method that can sometimes obviate the need for immensely complex, costly and possibly inconclusive cost–benefit calculations.

Cost–benefit Analysis

Case studies 10.1 (on the optimal number of guaiac tests), 16.3 (on oxygen supply), 19.3 (on airport noise), 20.2 (on seriousness of disease) and 20.3 (on the benefits of road improvements) were all examples of the kind of contribution economists can make to public sector economic appraisal.

Economic appraisals like cost–benefit analysis (CBA) and cost–effectiveness analysis (CEA) are essentially ways of presenting information. They do not, as such, impel governments or government departments to act in the social interest. The greater the degree of publicity associated with the techniques, however, the more embarrassing it is for governments, officials and politicians not to act in the potentially better ways suggested by the information. It is not, therefore, surprising that governments are reluctant to reveal all the information used as the basis of a decision or plan. But even if they did, the basis itself provides only a minor incentive for efficiency. Its proper use is far too heavily dependent at the moment upon the public-spiritedness of officials and politicians and upon the extent to which they believe that they can make a career, or prolong their political power, by advocating efficiency. Democracy is not so perfect that it forces them to be socially efficient or socially just. Although the economic techniques are a step in the right direction, one must not be over optimistic about the extent to which it is in the *private* interest of public decision takers to use them.

The case for a cost–benefit appraisal is essentially that it helps the systematic and explicit consideration of relevant issues, forces decision makers to state and defend their assumptions, value judgements and other kinds of judgement (for example about the size of costs and benefits), and provides some methods of organizing thinking and for quantification as aids to those who wish to make better decisions. It is not a substitute, however, for thought! A good CBA will: identify relevant options for consideration; enumerate all costs and benefits to various relevant social groups; quantify as many as can be sensibly quantified; *not* assume the unquantified is unimportant; use discounting where relevant to derive present values; use sensitivity analysis to test the response of net benefits to changes in assumptions; and look at the distributive impact of the options. (See also the discussion of investment rules in chapter 30.)

Some Economics of Politics

Why is majority voting so often adopted as a method of making decisions (not just in government)? What accounts for a variety of particular political phenomena like the convergence of political opinion in two-party systems, coalitions and apparent irreconcilable political differences (for example, in Northern Ireland)?

Why the Magic Majority?

Majority decision making is not used in the marketplace to determine what and how much you eat or play, your work and your wage. Nor is it used in the United Nations (UN) Security Council or the Commission of the European Communities (CEC). In each of these cases each decision maker has a *veto*. Whatever the music *I* think you should listen to, you can say 'no'. So can Britain's representatives in the organizations just mentioned. But in other areas, majority decision making is used: 50 per cent plus one of the voters can ensure that the issue goes one way or the other. Why 50 per cent? Why not, say, 10 or 90 per cent?

Suppose that individuals have to choose a method of choosing. This is sometimes called a question of choosing a **constitution**. Suppose that each individual wants to ensure that their own interests are protected. There is *only one* decision rule that ensures this fully: unanimity, consensus or the individual

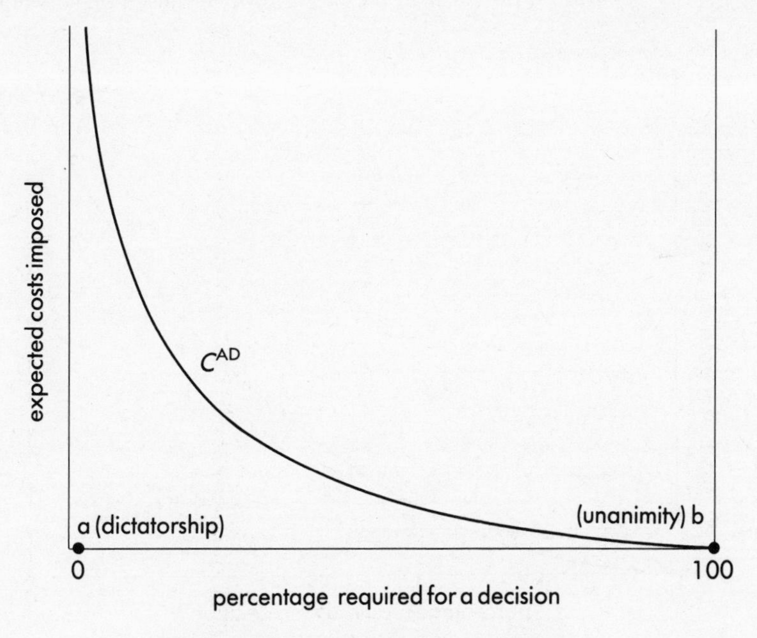

Figure 22.1 Costs of adverse decisions

member's veto (they are all the same). But a rational person need not choose this rule. Consider how the expected costs to an individual of an adverse decision behave as the required percentage for a decision increases. Clearly they fall, as shown in figure 22.1. At point a, representing just one person, we have **dictatorship**: whoever is dictator can decide what will be done. The costs to anyone other than the dictator are obviously very high indeed. At point b, 100 per cent agreement – **unanimity** – is required. Each has a veto. This is the libertarian ideal. There is no possibility of an adverse decision (AD) being imposed on you. Expected costs must be zero. The curve C^{AD} shows how expected costs of the various risks fall as the required percentage rises.

SAQ 22.3

What is the implied shape of the marginal cost curve for C^{AD} in figure 22.1?

The disadvantage of dictatorship is evident (unless you know that you are going to be dictator!). Unfortunately, there are also disadvantages to unanimity. To get unanimous support for any proposal will take a lot of persuasion, negotiation, placating, compensation and what is sometimes called log-rolling (I will support your proposal if you support mine). The larger the number of people whose agreement has to be obtained, the higher these costs become. The expected cost curve for negotiation (C^N) is therefore as in figure 22.2. It rises at an increasing rate and may become infinitely large as you come up against those who are implacably opposed to your favourite scheme, and is obviously zero if you are dictator and need persuade no one.

Suppose that a rational person will seek to minimize these two sets of costs of

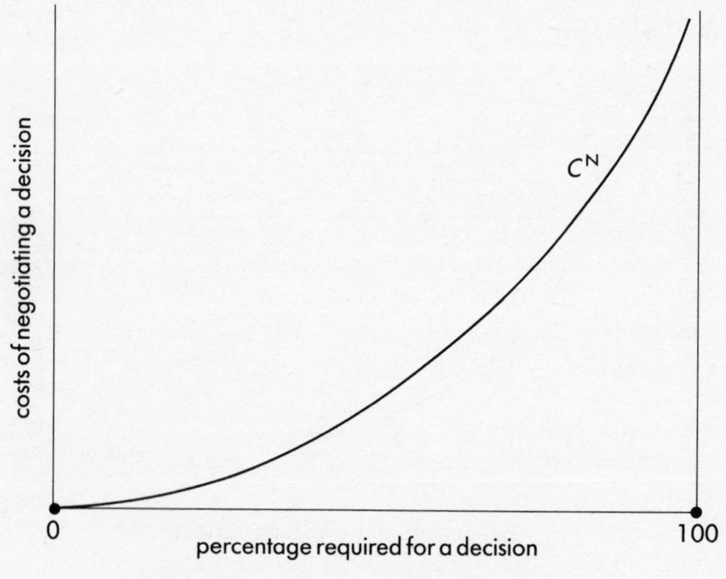

Figure 22.2 Costs of negotiating decisions

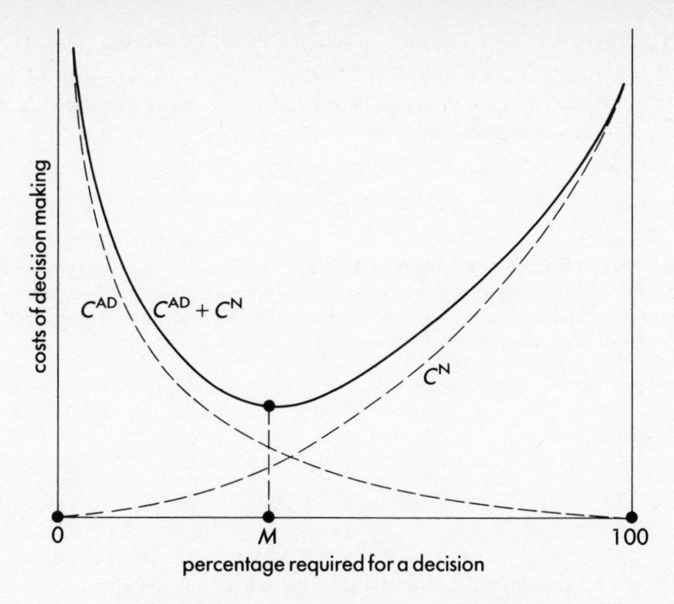

Figure 22.3 Determining the decision rule

collective decision making. The two curves are summed vertically in figure 22.3; where you can see that the resultant curve is U shaped, with the lowest point at M per cent. In this case you can see that the configuration implies a voting rule requiring *less* than a majority.

Of course, you do not know in detail what these curves look like, though their general shape is reasonably expected to be that postulated. But you can make some qualitative predictions:

(1) With issues that have no external impact on others (for example, what I shall have for breakfast) there will be zero pressure for collective decision making. Thus, whatever the pattern of C^{AD} and C^{N}, individuals will accept *dictatorship*. This is equivalent to individual sovereignty (consumer sovereignty and producer sovereignty) in decision making. (For example, I am dictator over what I shall have for breakfast.)

(2) The smaller is the group the lower are the negotiating costs, and therefore the more to the right is the lowest point on the $C^{AD} + C^{N}$ curve. In smaller groups, therefore, the higher the percentage that is expected to be required for any proposal to be adopted.

(3) The greater are the dangers of an imposed choice, the higher is the C^{AD} curve and the more to right is the lowest point on $C^{AD} + C^{N}$. Momentous decisions (for example, decisions about changing the constitution itself) are therefore predicted to require higher majorities than less momentous decisions.

(4) With small groups making momentous decisions, both effects reinforce one another and one expects to see decision rules that approach the unanimity rule or veto (as one does in the CEC and the UN Security Council).

The theory, alas, does not exactly predict when the simple majority rule will be adopted. It none the less gives some insight into the character of the rules that will be accepted under various circumstances, and provides a typology of factors that it seems reasonable to take into account in determining the desirability of individual and collective choice.

SAQ 22.4

There are five voters A, B, C, D and E and four policies W, X, Y and Z. The problem for the voters is to choose *one* of the four policies given the order of preferences of each in the following table (for example, voter A ranks policy X over Y, Y over Z, and Z over W). State the outcome under each of the decision rules (a)–(e) and comment on their desirability.

		voters				
		A	*B*	*C*	*D*	*E*
policies	W	4	4	3	2	2
	X	1	1	4	4	4
	Y	2	2	1	3	3
	Z	3	3	2	1	1

(a) The policy will be chosen that is ranked first by more than half the voters.
(b) The policy will be chosen that is ranked first by the largest number of voters.
(c) The policy will be chosen that beats all others in pairwise votes using majority rule.
(d) Each policy is given a score according to its order (first place gets score of 4, second a score of 3 etc.), and the policy will be chosen that receives the higher number of points.
(e) Each voter nominates their worst policy. The policy ranked lowest by a majority is then eliminated. Of the remaining three, that ranked lowest by a majority is then eliminated. Of the remaining two, that ranked lower by a majority is eliminated. The winning policy remains.

Voters and Vote Maximizers

Some economists have developed other theories of government behaviour and politics, not based on notions of social contract but on maximizing behaviour. In politics the first rule for a politician is to *survive*. Under representative democracy, in which some economists have suggested that politicians may be seen as trying to maximize their votes, politicians can set about this in two basic ways. First, they can *follow* public opinion and try to devise electoral packages that will command voting appeal. Second, they can *lead* public opinion by developing new policies that they think will win support, acting as political entrepreneurs. In either case, their behaviour can be stylized as vote maximizing (rather than utility or profit maximizing) since by failing to do so they will increase the probability of losing power (or failing to gain it). They must therefore respond to the political spectrum of public opinion.

Consider two distributions of political opinion in an electorate.

A single peaked normal distribution

Suppose political opinion is distributed along a spectrum of 'left' and 'right' as in figure 22.4. Such a distribution probably roughly reflects the current British pattern. The modal political position M is in the middle. This kind of distribution tends to produce a two-party system. Call the parties Lab and

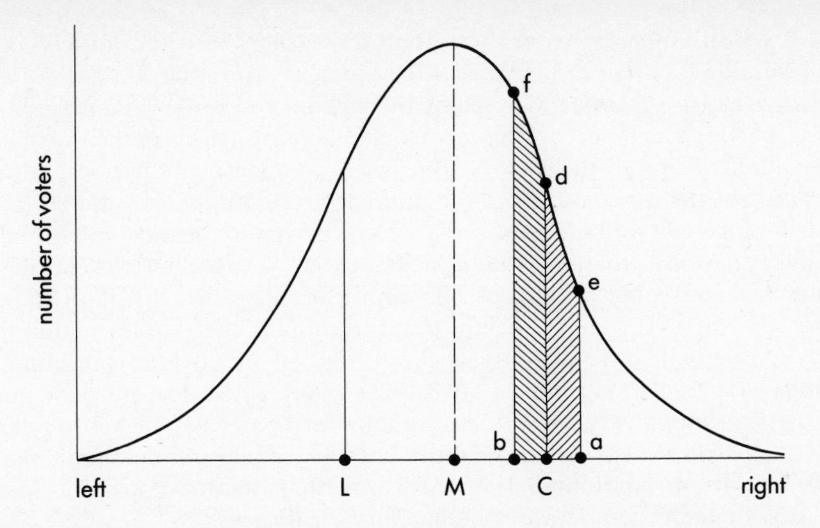

Figure 22.4 A single peaked normal distribution of voters along the political spectrum

Con with locations approximately shown as L and C. There is a tendency for the two parties to converge on the average position M, much to the irritation of those Lab members on the left of L and those Con members on the right of C. The reason for this is plain. Take the Cons. If their politicians sought to shift the flavour of their policies rightwards, say to a, this would be of appeal to the voters on the right of the party. However, these are fewer than those attracted by a move in the opposite direction to b, since the shaded area under de is smaller than that under fd. Vote maximizing Con politicians will therefore tend towards M. Thereby, their far right supporters will still support them (since they are still better off with Con than Lab) and they will appeal to the larger number of voters in the middle of the distribution. Similarly, Lab politicians will tend towards M from the other side: each will seek to play down policies of main attraction to the extremes, partly because the extremes will vote for them anyway and partly because there are relatively few people at the extremes.

In countries where the distribution of opinion is much flatter, you can expect to see more parties emerge, as in Italy. A result will often be that to secure an effective government, coalitions between two or more parties must be created.

If democratic politicians move towards the extremes, assuming the kind of distribution shown in bell-shaped figure 22.4, they run the grave risk of opening up the middle ground to new parties. What this risk is will depend largely on the method of election. The British 'first past the post' system tends to afford both the Labour and the Conservative parties partial immunity from this risk. In the 1970s and 1980s, most people have detected a rightward move of the Conservatives and a leftward move of the Labour party. The SDP and Liberal Alliance have succeeded in capturing a substantial share of the middle ground popular vote without, however, this having had much impact on their political power expressed in seats in parliament.

The **median voter theorem** states that, if all voters vote and if each votes for the candidate closest to the voter's most preferred position, candidates are driven towards the position favoured by the median voter (M). You may think that, as parties converge, abstention would increase ('why bother to vote? these politicians are all the same.'). But with a symmetrical distribution this will not affect the outcome, since the number of abstentions on the left and right will cancel out and the politicians are still driven to the median position.

In the real world, the issues upon which voters vote are both exceedingly complex and presented in bundles, the appeal of bits of which will of course vary for any voter. It pays politicians to try to simplify these issues so that the ordinary voter will have a pretty accurate idea of the style of the bundle. **Ideology** is a useful shorthand that enables many voters to vote quite confidently even though very few of them actually read party manifestos or follow detailed debates. It also makes the representation of political opinion along a simple Left–Right continuum less unrealistic than it may appear. It pays politicians therefore to adapt or manufacture ideologies.

Case Study 22.1 A Politico-economic Model of the UK

The Swiss economists Bruno Frey and Friedrich Schneider (1978) hypothesized that a vote maximizing government will use its influence on the economy to improve electoral popularity as its lead over the opposition falls (as witnessed by opinion polls) and, if its lead exceeds a particular critical level, it will see itself free to pursue ideological goals.

From 1959 to 1974 they found systematic links between principal economic goals and the electoral lead: a fall in the inflation rate by 1 per cent increased the government's lead by 0.6 per cent, a fall in unemployment by 1 per cent increased the lead by 6 per cent, and an increase in the growth range by 1 per cent increased the lead by 0.8 per cent. All governments over this period were found to expand the economy by raising public expenditure and reducing taxation when their leads were lower. Ideological goals were taken to relate to the share of public expenditure and taxation in national income. With 'safe' leads Conservative governments reduced both and Labour governments increased both, independently of the state of the economy.

Bruno Frey and Friedrich Schneider (1978) 'A politico-economic model of the UK', *Economic Journal*, **88**, 243–53.

SAQ 22.5

There are three selfish members of a society, A, B and C and two options up for committee consideration, Y and Z.

		committee members		
		A	B	C
options	Y	−90	−10	+100
	Z	−10	+20	−10

These options relate to income redistribution. Under option Y, A loses £90 and B £10, and C gains £100. Under Z, A and C each lose £10 and B gains £20. These are summarized in the table. Which will be chosen under majority voting – Y, or Z, or both, or neither?

A bimodal distribution

Suppose the distribution of popular political opinion is as shown by the unbroken line in figure 22.5. Here the median is again shown as M, but the distribution has two *modes* or peaks (it is *bimodal*) and there are roughly equal numbers of people at each mode, and hardly anyone at the median position M. Again politicians have an incentive to move towards the median position. Suppose there were two parties with political positions at points a and b. The party at point a would gain votes by moving to position M, drawing away voters who were previously closer to point b than to point a. Conversely, it pays the party at point b to move to M. However, if moves towards M alienated supporters to the left of point a or the right of point b ('the party is betraying its principles') in sufficient numbers for them to abstain from voting, then there will be a tendency for the parties to locate somewhere between the two modes and the median. This will be the more so if the distribution is not symmetrical about each mode. Suppose, for example, that there were fairly large numbers of extremists as well as relatively few people at the median, as shown by the dotted curve in figure 22.5. In this case, the risk of alienation becomes much greater and political parties (as in Northern Ireland) will tend to have dramatically different policies.

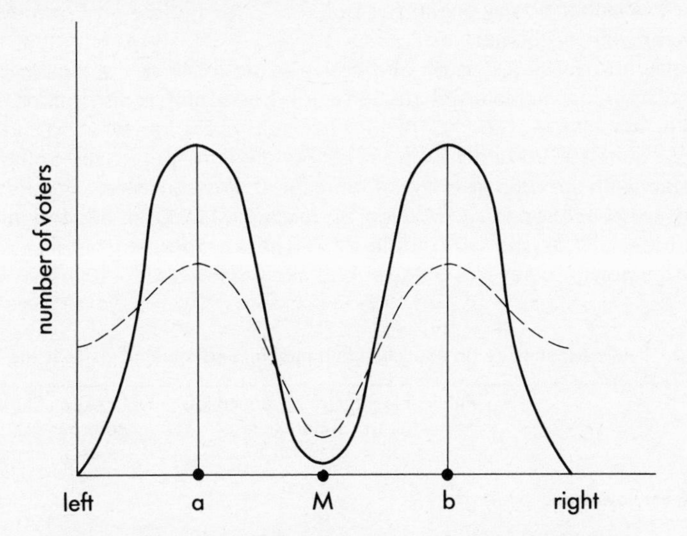

Figure 22.5 A bimodal distribution of political opinion

SAQ 22.6

There are three voters (A, B and C) and three policies (X, Y and Z) which are ranked by each voter as shown in the table. X, Y and Z are different (increasing) rates of output of a public good. Under majority decision making, which rate of output of the public good will be chosen?

		voters		
		A	*B*	*C*
policies	X	1	3	2
	Y	2	1	3
	Z	3	2	1

Case Study 22.2 Democracy and Income Redistribution

One positive economics argument, due to Anthony Downs (a pioneer of the vote maximizing theory), is that income redistribution will go from the rich to the poor since the bottom n per cent of the income distribution ($n > 50$) could take money, via vote maximizing governments, from the top $100 - n$ per cent. The trouble with this argument is evidently that the *top n* per cent (again $n > 50$) could equally gang up in a coalition to immiserize the bottom $100 - n$ per cent. A way out has been developed by Gordon Tullock (1973). He emphasized again the importance of the *median* voter. For example, if 51 votes out of 100 people are needed for a decision then the middle two people can decide which coalition will win. If they join the rich 49 and vote a government into power that will redistribute from the *poor* to the rich, then they could exact some share of the spoils of this redistribution. If they join the poor 49 and vote in a government that will redistribute from the *rich*, they could share in the spoils from taxing the top 49 in the income distribution.

How will the median voters choose? They will choose to join the *poor* 49, for there are more spoils to be had from taxing the rich than the poor. Since, however, they will do this only if they stand to gain (unlike the caring people discussed in chapter 21, the voters here are nothing if not selfish!), then although the rich will be taxed, the benefits will not just go to the poor *but will also be shared by the middle groups.* Moreover, if the poor are rather poorly organized politically, the middle groups may be able to do extremely well for themselves.

This is offered by Tullock as an alternative explanation to the Hochman–Rodgers theory that there is an external demand for horizontal redistribution which was discussed in case study 21.2. In particular it is held to explain why the middle income groups gain quite substantially from redistribution in the public sector (however, it is not consistent with the data in row 8 of table 24.4). It *is* consistent with the patterns of subsidy by socio-economic class found by Julian Le Grand in education and health services in the UK, as shown in table 22.1. There appear to be similar effects in housing, transport and several other public expenditures.

Table 22.1 Public expenditure on education and the National Health Service in the UK, 1972–3

	Public expenditure on education (all types) per client as % of mean [a]	Public expenditure on health care per sick person as % of mean
Professional, employers and managers	128	120
Intermediate and junior non-manual	121	114
Skilled manual	81	97
Semi- and unskilled manual	84	85

[a] Excludes private education; this biases the numbers for the higher groups downwards, since privately educated children are included in the denominator.
Source: Julian Le Grand (1982) *The Strategy of Equality*, London, Allen and Unwin, tables 3.1 and 4.1.

Gordon Tullock (1973) 'The charity of the uncharitable', in A. A. Alchian *et al.* (1973) *The Economics of Charity*, London, Institute of Economic Affairs.
Anthony Downs (1957) *An Economic Theory of Democracy*, New York, Harper.

The theory of public choice, which explores the kind of issues discussed in this chapter and which has revolutionized political theory, is one of the fastest growing specialist areas of economics. The present chapter can, alas, do little more than whet the appetite. The field is also rather short on well-worked expirical tests of the various theories that are being developed apace.

SAQ 22.7

Since voting is costly for any one individual and his or her vote will have a negligible impact on the result of any election, the rational individual will never vote. Is that right?

What You Should Understand Now

How to discuss the role and behaviour of government from normative and positive viewpoints.
Reasons why rational individuals may choose to delegate decision making to collective agencies like government.
Reasons why government agencies are less likely to pursue profit.
Reasons why the pursuit of profit may sometimes be undesirable.
Relationships between equality and types of property right (public and private).
Majority decision making versus dictatorship and unanimity.
Vote maximizing politicians and their response to the distribution of political opinion in the electorate.

23

National Income, National Welfare and Standards of Living

The previous chapters have been taking you on to increasingly aggregated levels of decision making. The rest of the book is going to focus on such aggregates: aggregate income, the general price level, employment and unemployment, the balance of trade between countries and so on. **Macroeconomics** is the study of the behaviour of these national aggregates, as distinct from **microeconomics**, which is the study of the behaviour of individual units and smaller aggregates.

One of the most important aggregates with which macroeconomics is concerned is the total rate of output or income of a country. There are some fine distinctions to be made about the definition of aggregate income, and the next chapter will distinguish between national income, gross (and net) national product, gross domestic product and so on. For the moment just think of national output as the value added produced in a country in a year or, since this output generates the income used to buy it, as national income. The empirical data in this chapter will refer variously to gross national product (*GNP*), gross domestic product (*GDP*), national income, and so on, reflecting the sources drawn on. But for the moment no distinction will be made between these various definitions.

One of the reasons for having measures of national output and income is to see what an economy has 'earned' over an accounting period. It does not matter whether one takes the value of output produced or the value of incomes received. As you will see in chapter 24, the figures work out the same. Few people are uninterested in such a statistic or how it changes over time, how it relates to other interesting statistics like those for unemployment and inflation, how it compares with similar statistics for other countries, whether there exists the possibility of getting it to grow faster, and so on.

Underlying all these considerations, however, is the basic feeling that national income is somehow related to the **welfare** of a community. If the national income per head rises the rise is judged to be a 'good thing'. If it falls, the fall is judged 'bad'. The measure of national income is so comprehensive – it is the most comprehensive summary quantitative indicator of aggregate welfare that we have – that it has acquired a unique importance. Even governments' performances are judged in large part by the electorate in terms of what happens to *GDP* during their term of office (recall case study 22.1).

One of the important factors influencing one's judgement about whether a nation's welfare is improving is the *distribution* of income (and wealth) between households, generations, classes, regions, and so on. Since within country distributional issues were discussed extensively in chapter 21, they will not be further dealt with here, important though they are.

International per caput *GDP* Comparisons

Table 23.1 gives *GDP* per head in US dollars for a selection of rich and poor countries. Of these, Brunei is the richest, with a per caput *GDP* of $21,147, and Bangladesh the poorest, with a per caput *GDP* of $145. On the face of it, comparing these two extremes, it appears that the average resident in Brunei is 146 times better off than the average resident in Bangladesh. As you will see later, however, there are good reasons to suppose that such comparisons both overstate the degree of poverty of the poor countries and the difference between the rich and the poor. This is not, of course, to say that the differences are not, none the less, something about which every caring person should be concerned.

Table 23.1 Per caput *GDP* in US dollars, 1980 (selected countries)

Argentina	5,666
Australia	10,210
Bangladesh	145
Belgium	12,080
Brunei	21,147
Canada	10,585
Denmark	12,964
France	12,137
Germany (Fed. Rep.)	13,304
Greece	4,181
Haiti	283
Hong Kong	4,264
India	241
Ireland	5,243
Israel	5,431
Italy	6,907
Japan	8,873
Kenya	426
Mexico	2,591
Netherlands	11,855
New Zealand	7,578
Sweden	14,882
Syria	1,437
Tanzania	266
Thailand	709
UK	9,351
USA	11,416
Zimbabwe	747

Source: Yearbook of National Accounts Statistics 1981, vol. II, table 1

SAQ 23.1

(a) Calculate the ratio of UK *GDP* per caput to that for the USA, Federal Republic of Germany, France, Thailand, Hong Kong and Tanzania.

(b) What inferences would you make from these ratios?

The Nation as an Individual

Abstracting from distributional matters inside a country, assume that the welfare of a community can be represented as though it were the welfare of a representative or average member of that community. Make the now familiar further normative assumption that welfare can be identified with a utility index, so that if a representative or average individual moves to a higher indifference curve you can say that the individual has more welfare. If the focus is on *changes* in *GDP*, the natural question then to ask is: under what circumstances can one infer from national income data that the representative individual has moved on to a higher indifference curve?

Over time, the production possibilities of a country usually rise owing to technological development, growth of available inputs for production and a variety of other factors. Hence both the quantities and the relative prices of goods and services change.

Now consider a representative individual at a particular time. In figure 23.1(a) there is an individual in equilibrium where an indifference curve is tangential to the production possibility boundary. For simplicity, the boundary is assumed to be a straight line indicating constant marginal costs of producing goods Z and X. In equilibrium price is equal to marginal cost in both Z and X production and there are price taking conditions. At time t_0, in figure 23.1(a) the individual is at e_0 on indifference curve U_0. Assume no taxes, subsidies or any other distortions of the price mechanism. The price of a unit of X_0 is P_{X0}, and so on.

What is the national income in this situation? At t_0 it is

$$Y_0 = P_{X0}X_0 + P_{Z0}Z_0$$

This is measured in figure 23.1(a) by the distance OY_0 in units of Z consumption. Why is this a measure of national income? Simply because *any* point on a budget line represents a constant expenditure by the individual. Thus the expenditure when at e_0 must be the same as that had the individual chosen point Y_0. At e_0 expenditure is $P_{X0}X_0 + P_{Z0}Z_0$. At Y_0, however, the individual has only good Z, so you can measure the expenditure on the bundle $X_0 + Z_0$ by the equivalent amount of Z purchasable out of income, given its price. This is income divided by the price of Z, i.e. Y/P_{Z0}. Thus, although the amount of *welfare* is not the same at Y_0 and e_0, the amount of *expenditure* is the same and it is indicated by the point where the budget line touches the Z axis. This has the great pictorial advantage of enabling you to see changes in

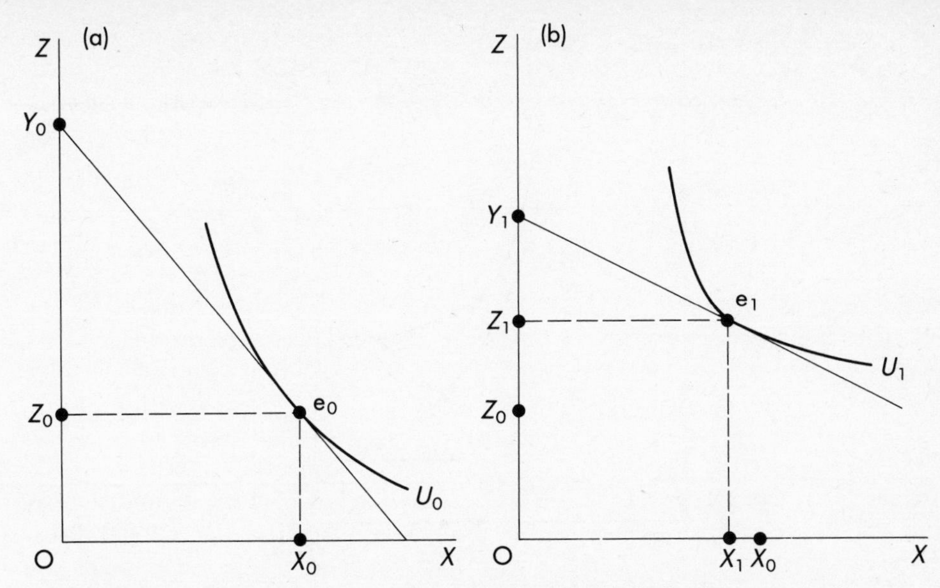

Figure 23.1 Welfare changes of a representative individual with economic change. (a) time t_0 (b) time t_1

national income as moves of points like Y_0 up and down the Z axis: real *GDP* is effectively being measured in terms of one real final output.

SAQ 23.2

A simple national economy's annual final outputs and prices are as in the following table:

	Q	*P*
food	500	£1.50
clothing	300	£2.00
recreation	200	£1.00

What is the national income of the economy?

Now consider a later time t_1, when economic change has taken place. Figure 23.1(b) shows the new budget line, with a new preferred consumption bundle $Z_1 + X_1$ indicated by the equilibrium point e_1. Quantities have changed. The economy is producing more Z but less X. In this case, the price of X has also fallen relative to Z. As you can see, less X is, however, chosen despite the relative price change, and one may suppose that this is because X is an inferior good. The new indicator of *GDP* is OY_1. This is *smaller* than OY_0. So *GDP* has *fallen*. But the individual is now on indifference curve U_1, which is *higher* than U_0. So welfare has *risen*.

You are now confronted with a dilemma: the *GDP* measure is giving a false indication of what has happened to welfare. This has nothing to do with any increase in market imperfections, adverse redistributional effects, changes in basic tastes or any other complicating feature of the real world that one may

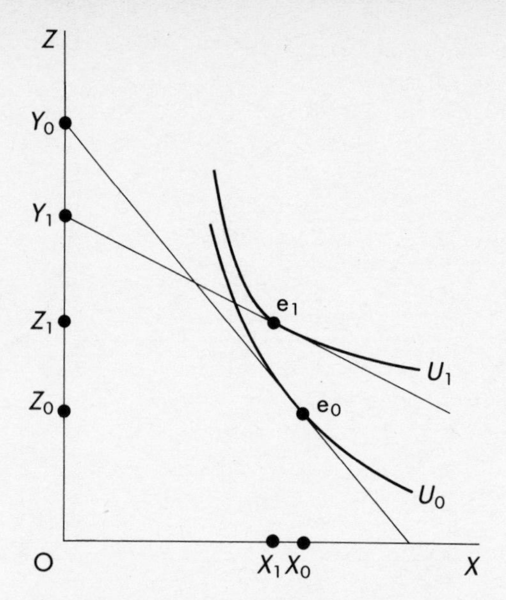

Figure 23.2 Standard of living comparisons

have in practice to consider. Even under the 'purest' circumstances, when price signals are doing their proper job and the 'invisible hand' is operating as in a marketeer's dream, *GDP* is simply misleading.

This can be seen very clearly by putting (a) and (b) of figure 23.1 together. This is done in figure 23.2. Here you can see that Y_1 is lower than Y_0 but that e_1 is on a higher indifference curve. Although in practice one cannot actually observe indifference curves (at least, not without a tremendous amount of research of the type reported in case study 7.1), note that this is not the point. The point is that there is nothing logically to prevent the *possibility* of the *GDP* indicator moving in the opposite direction from the 'true' indicator of welfare. Hence you can conclude: an increase in *GDP* may correspond to a fall in welfare and a fall in *GDP* may correspond to an increase in welfare. Of course, the movement of *GDP* and welfare can also be in the same direction. SAQ 23.3 gives some practice at working through such a case.

SAQ 23.3

In a simple economy you are given the following two sets of data:

time 0				*time 1*			
quantity		*price*		*quantity*		*price*	
Z	*X*	*Z*	*X*	*Z*	*X*	*Z*	*X*
3	2	2	2	1.5	5	2	3

(a) Calculate national income in each period.

(b) What is the ratio of income in t_1 to income in t_0?

(c) Draw a diagram with the two budget lines and mark on them the two consumption bundles $a(t_0)$ and $b(t_1)$.

(d) Has welfare increased in t_1 compared with t_0?

The problem just encountered arises because of changes over time in prices and quantities. *The change in the quantities constitutes the real change in income.* If *all* quantities increased over time, then welfare would have increased unambiguously (given no changes in other things like political freedom and the income distribution). But in the example of figure 23.2 the two budget lines intersect, and it is this that is giving rise to the difficulty.

One way of escaping from the dilemma (to believe or not to believe in what *GDP* data seem to be saying) is to take constant price comparisons. What level of income at t_1 would have enabled the representative individual to have the same bundle of Z and X associated with e_1 *but at the prices of time* t_0? The answer is shown in figure 23.3. The level of income (in terms of Z) is OY_1^L, which is an income that gives a budget line parallel to the Y_0 budget line but passing through e_1. (Actually, since at e_1 the individual's indifference curve is tangential to the Y_1 budget line, the opportunity to move on to the Y_1^L budget line must entail higher welfare; SAQ 23.5 explores this. However, for the moment assume that the welfare levels at e_1 and at a point on the Y_1^L budget line a bit to its left are the same.)

SAQ 23.4

Calculate Y_1^L for the data in SAQ 23.3

What is Y_1^L in terms of prices and quantities? The answer is

$$Y_1^L = P_{Z0}\, Z_1 + P_{X0}\, X_1$$

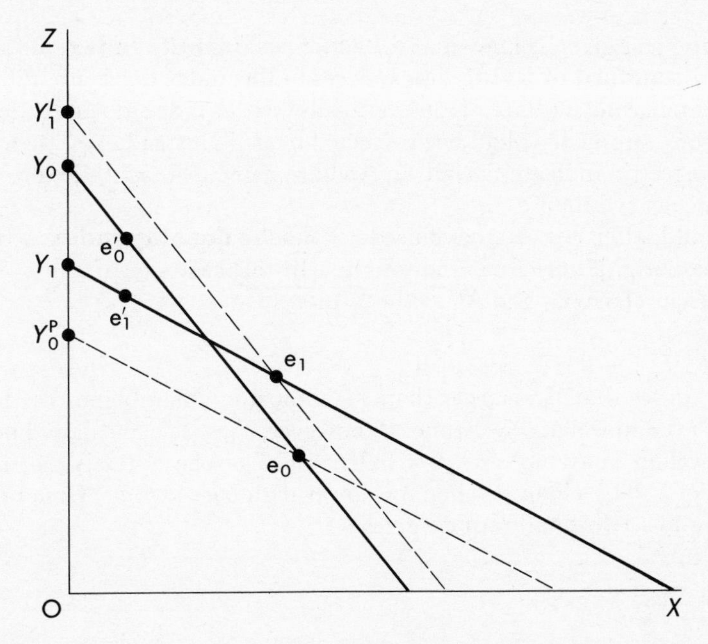

Figure 23.3 Comparison of Laspeyres and Paasche indexes of the standard of living

i.e. the quantities consumed at time t_1 valued at the original base prices at t_0. Now you can see that Y_1^L is unambiguously larger than Y_0 and seems to indicate that an increase in welfare has taken place. However, you cannot conclude that an increase in welfare has taken place when

$$\frac{Y_1^L}{Y_0} = \frac{P_{Z0} Z_1 + P_{X0} X_1}{P_{Z0} Z_0 + P_{X0} X_0} > 1$$

or, using Σ to indicate aggregation over as many goods and services as there are in national income,

$$\frac{\Sigma P_0 Q_1}{\Sigma P_0 Q_0} > 1$$

because it is perfectly possible (as you should be able to see for yourself) for e_0 to be either a higher or a lower indifference curve than that associated with Y_1^L at e_1.

For example, since all you know is the total expenditure corresponding to Y_0, the representative individual may have been at e_0' rather than e_0 and, whereas e_0 must be on a lower indifference curve than e_1, e_0' may be either a lower or a higher indifference curve than e_1. So $Y_1^L/Y_0 > 1$ may arise when welfare has either risen *or* fallen. In a comparison of this sort, it is only when the Y_1^L budget line lies entirely *inside* the Y_0 budget line that one can predict an unambiguous change in welfare: it must have fallen. Only, then, when $Y_1^L/Y_0 < 1$ can one unambiguously say that welfare moves in the same direction as the real income measure.

The ratio just given is known as a **Laspeyres quantity index**, a (base price weighted) **standard of living** index. Rises in this index do *not* unambiguously indicate increasing welfare. However, falls in the index do indicate falls in welfare: for example if e_1' had been selected *inside* Y_0 instead of e_1, then $Y_1^L < Y_0$ would correctly indicate a fall in welfare, since e_1' *must* lie on a lower indifference curve than e_0.

You could, alternatively, have used a **Paasche quantity index**, with *current* rather than original prices as the weights. In this case, the amount of income needed to purchase Z_0 and X_0 at the t_1 prices is

$$Y_0^P = P_{Z1} Z_0 + P_{X1} X_0$$

and you can see that Y_1 is larger than Y_0^P, indicating unambiguously that there has been a rise in welfare over time. If, however, $Y_1 < Y_0^P$, you should be able to see that welfare may have risen *or* fallen: the Paasche index is an unreliable indicator of welfare changes when it is lower than base income. Generalizing to more than just two final outputs gives

$$\frac{Y_1}{Y_0^P} = \frac{\Sigma P_1 Q_1}{\Sigma P_1 Q_0} > 1$$

as the case when the direction of welfare change is correctly given.

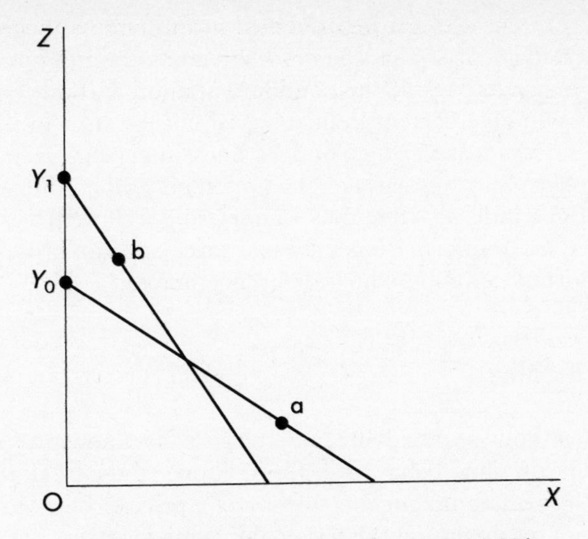

Figure 23.4 Budget lines for SAQ 23.5(d)

SAQ 23.5

(a) Calculate Y_0^P for the data in SAQ 23.3.

(b) Calculate the Laspeyres index of the standard of living in t_1 relative to t_0.

(c) Calculate the Paasche index of the standard of living in t_2 relative to t_0.

(d) In figure 23.4, point a is the initial position and point b is the subsequent position. Has welfare increased in the move from a to b?

(e) Draw budget lines on figure 23.4 corresponding to Y_1^L and Y_0^P. What do these suggest has happened to welfare?

(f) In figure 23.5 an initial budget line corresponding to Y_0 and one corresponding to Y_1^L are drawn. If the individual were actually given income Y_1^L, would he or she remain at point e_1?

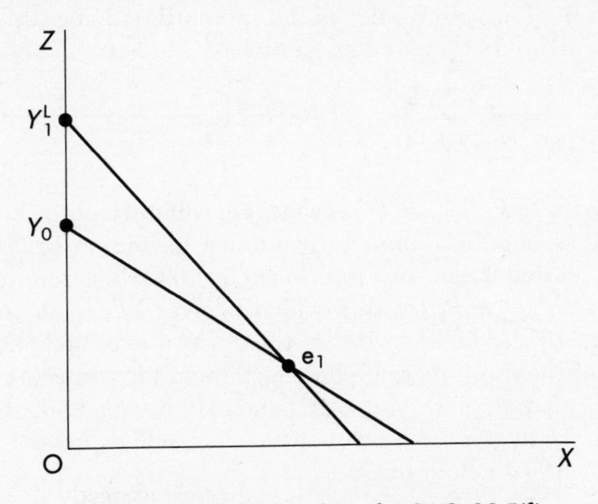

Figure 23.5 Budget lines for SAQ 23.5(f)

Provided that the process of growth represents an increase in the economy's ability to produce *all* goods so that the production possibilities boundary at one date lies wholly inside or outside the boundary at another, both Laspeyres and Paasche indexes will give correct indications of falls or rises in welfare. They will also do so in *some* cases when budget lines intersect, as in figure 23.3. In general, Laspeyres indexes can be relied upon only when they signal falling welfare and Paasche indexes when they signal rising welfare. In all other cases you need to have more information than just price and quantity information: for example, information about the indifference maps.

UK National Income

Table 23.2 shows how national income (technically known as net national product at factor cost) has behaved in the UK over the period 1973–83. The first column shows national income in current prices. The second column shows the result of recalculating the national income for every year (save 1980) in 1980 prices. In earlier National Income *Blue Books*, you will find constant price time series of national income (as well as *GNP*, *GDP* etc.) in 1948, 1954, 1958, 1963, 1970 and 1975 prices.

The method used by the UK national income accountants is a base weighted (Laspeyres) system such that

$$\frac{\Sigma P_b\, Q_t}{\Sigma P_b\, Q_b} \times 100 = \text{index}$$

where b is the base year (1980) and t is the year in question. What is fairly readily observable is $\Sigma P_t\, Q_t / \Sigma P_b\, Q_b$, which is simply the ratio of two years' national income in current prices. This is shown in colum 2 of table 23.2. For example, at current prices, national income was double in 1980 what it was in 1975. To obtain the Laspeyres index of the standard of living, this ratio has to be divided by a (Paasche) *price* index so that

$$\frac{\Sigma P_t\, Q_t}{\Sigma P_b\, Q_b} \Bigg/ \frac{\Sigma P_t\, Q_t}{\Sigma P_b\, Q_t} = \frac{\Sigma P_b\, Q_t}{\Sigma P_b\, Q_b}$$

This **price deflator**, $\Sigma P_t\, Q_t / \Sigma P_b\, Q_t$, is shown in column 3 of the table. Thus, to get real national income in column 4 the number in column 1 must be divided by the index in column 3 and then multiplied by 100. Since column 1 is $\Sigma P_t\, Q_t$ and column 3 is $\Sigma P_t\, Q_t / \Sigma P_b\, Q_t$, this evidently gives $\Sigma P_b\, Q_t$ in column 4. For example, in 1974 (67.9 / 40.9) × 100 = 166.0. (You may find small rounding errors in some of these numbers if you check them for yourself.)

Given the population data you can then readily calculate the per caput national income shown in column 6, which is itself expressed as an index number (1980 = 100) in column 7.

Table 23.2 National income in current and constant prices and per caput, UK 1973–83.

	1 National income at current prices (£ billion)	2 Index	3 Price deflator	4 National income at constant (1980) prices (£ billion)	5 Population (million)	6 National income (real) per caput (£ thousand)	7 Index
1973	59.2	34.7	35.0	169.0	56.2	3.01	99.3
1974	67.9	39.8	40.9	166.0	56.2	2.95	97.4
1975	84.8	49.7	52.3	162.2	56.2	2.89	95.4
1976	101.0	59.2	59.7	169.1	56.2	3.01	99.3
1977	112.3	65.8	66.8	168.0	56.2	2.99	98.7
1978	129.4	75.8	74.7	173.2	56.2	3.08	101.7
1979	148.3	86.9	84.1	176.4	56.2	3.14	103.6
1980	170.6	100.0	100.0	170.6	56.3	3.03	100.0
1981	186.9	109.6	110.5	169.2	56.3	3.01	99.3
1982	202.5	118.7	118.3	171.2	56.3	3.04	100.3
1983	222.9	130.7	125.4	177.8	56.3	3.16	104.3

Source: UK National Accounts, 1984 edition, tables 1.1, 1.5, 1.17

As you can see, real income per head has not shown much growth over this period. It seems doubtful whether welfare rose either, though it unambiguously fell in 1981 (using 1980 prices), since the 1981 to 1980 comparison is a Laspeyres comparison.

Although in the absence of crossing budget lines both Laspeyres and Paasche tell the same *qualitative* story, they do not tell the same *quantitative* story. Which should one choose? It depends on the question one really wants to address. If, for example, one wants to know whether we, with standards to which we have become accustomed, are better off today than we would have been had we been alive when our grandparents were our age, then it is natural to compare the consumption bundles now and then using *our* price weights (Paasche approach). On the other hand, if one wished to know whether previous generations would have been better off with the consumption bundle of today rather than the one they actually had, it would be natural to compare the two bundles using *their* price weights.

A similar problem arises in comparing *international* per caput national income levels: should one use the prices in one's own country or the prices in the other to weight the different consumption bundles? Again the answer depends on the purpose of the exercise. If one asks whether *we* would be better off with the consumption we have or with *their* consumption, then *our* prices are the appropriate weights, for these are money measures of the marginal value we place on the consumption items we currently consume. If, on the other hand, one asks whether *they* would be better off with the consumption they actually have or with *our* consumption, then *their* prices are, for the same reason, the appropriate weights. (This will not, however, help much if two countries have no common outputs, in which case the basis for comparison is lost.)

Choice between Paasche and Laspeyres may also be based on their propaganda value. You may have already spotted the fact that the effect on measured growth rates of *GDP* of choosing Laspeyres or Paasche is closely tied up with income elasticities. In figures 23.1 and 23.3 you saw that rising income caused an increase in the demand for Z and a fall in the demand for X, so X was an inferior good. In general, the rate of growth of real *GDP* will be higher when the relative price of income elastic goods is high, and these receive a larger weight in the index.

Consider table 23.3. Here you can see that the income elastic good Z is relatively cheaper at time t_0 than at t_1 (at t_0 it is half the price of X, at t_1 it has the same price). If you now compute the two standards of living indexes you get:

$$\text{Laspeyres} \quad \frac{\Sigma P_0 Q_1}{\Sigma P_0 Q_0} = \frac{80 + 120}{20 + 160} = 1.11$$

$$\text{Paasche} \quad \frac{\Sigma P_1 Q_1}{\Sigma P_1 Q_0} = \frac{64 + 48}{16 + 64} = 1.40$$

Using original prices (Laspeyres) you clearly get a lower rate of increase in real national income (11 per cent) than using time t_1 prices (40 per cent). Why? Because using the original weights means that the income elastic good is receiving a lower relative weight (10/20) than using the later weights implies (8/8). Here then is a good way of 'fiddling' growth rates of real income! Conversely, of course, if income elastic goods tend to have *falling* relative prices over time, the Laspeyres index will show a faster growth rate than the Paasche. In practice, the fastest growing products generally show a fall in relative price. The chief recent exception to this is oil, whose rise in use in the last 15 years has been accompanied by a very large rise in its relative price.

Table 23.3 Raw data for calculating an index of standards of living

Time 0				*Time 1*			
Quantity		*Price*		*Quantity*		*Price*	
Z	*X*	*Z*	*X*	*Z*	*X*	*Z*	*X*
2	8	10	20	8	6	8	8

SAQ 23.6

(a) Using the data in table 23.3, calculate the ratio of national income in t_1 to that in t_0.

(b) Did national income rise or fall between t_0 and t_1?

Similar propaganda purposes can be served by careful choice of weights in international comparisons of real income. The ratio of the per caput income of a rich country to that of a poor country will be larger using the poor country's prices if income elastic goods (so-called luxuries) are relatively cheap in the rich country. They usually are. Case study 23.1 discusses some problems in comparing welfare in a historical context.

Case Study 23.1 Standards of Living of Glasgow Handloom Weavers, 1810–31

Over long periods, judgements about standards of living are made complex by the possibility of taste changes, introduction of new commodities, changes in non-priced aspects of life and so on. In historical studies these difficulties are intensified by patchy and unreliable data, requiring carefully researched sources that can at best overcome only some of these problems.

Gourvish (1972) has made a study of Glaswegian handloom weavers in the early nineteenth century. In 1815–16 the consumption pattern of such a family (man, wife and two children) was estimated to be as in table 23.4. Thus, out of a total weekly income of about 9.5 shillings (12 old pence per shilling), about 71 per cent went on food, 42 per cent on cereal foods, 25 per cent on rent, lighting and fuel and 12 per cent on rent alone.

Table 23.4 Handloom weaver's weekly expenditure in 1815–16

Item	*Quantity Q*	*Price P (pence)*	*Expenditure PQ*
Oatmeal	12 lb	2.25	27.00
Potatoes	40 lb	0.31	12.50
Bread	4.5 lb	1.83	8.25
Buttermilk	6 qts	0.50	3.00
Salt herrings	2 lb	3.75	7.50
Salt king fish	2 lb	3.00	6.00
Irish butter	0.5 lb	16.38	8.19
Salt	0.5 lb	2.50	1.25
Tea	0.5 ozs	5.00	2.50
Sugar	0.5 lb	10.50	5.25
Candles	0.5 lb	11.50	5.50
Soap	0.5 lb	9.00	4.50
Coal	1.2 cwt	7.25	8.70
Rent	2 rooms	13.85	13.85
Total			113.99

Using these data as the base year, Gourvish computed a Laspeyres *price* index of the *cost* of living for the years 1810–31, as shown in table 23.5 column 2. He also calculated an index of money income (column 3). He then divided the latter by the former to give an index of real wages. This is the Paasche *quantity* index of the *standard* of living.

A Laspeyres price index (or index of the **cost of living**) measures the change in prices over a period using the consumption bundle of the original period as weights. That is:

$$\frac{\Sigma P_1 Q_0}{\Sigma P_0 Q_0} = \frac{\text{original consumption valued at (say) 1818 prices}}{\text{original consumption valued at (say) 1815–16 prices}}$$

Table 23.5 Cost of living indexes for Glaswegian handloom weavers 1810–31 (1815–16 = 100)

1 Year	2 *Price index (× 100) (Laspeyres index of cost of living)*	3 *Index of weekly money wages*	4 *Index of real wages (3/2) (Paasche index of the standard of living)*
1810	100.9	134.5	133.3
1811	101.8	103.4	101.6
1812	113.2	117.2	103.5
1813	117.5	134.5	114.5
1814	106.1	134.5	126.8
1815	98.2	134.5	137.0
1816	101.8	65.5	64.3
1817	110.5	65.5	59.3
1818	102.6	91.4	89.1
1819	86.8	56.9	65.6
1822	81.6	56.9	69.7
1831	76.3	75.9	99.5

He also computed an index of wages, which is defined (assuming, as is in this case reasonable, that all income is spent) as

$$\frac{\Sigma P_1 Q_1}{\Sigma P_0 Q_0} = \frac{\text{income in 1818}}{\text{income in 1815–16}}$$

In dividing one by the other, you get

$$\frac{\Sigma P_1 Q_1}{\Sigma P_0 Q_0} \bigg/ \frac{\Sigma P_1 Q_0}{\Sigma P_0 Q_0} = \frac{\Sigma P_1 Q_1}{\Sigma P_1 Q_0}$$

which, as you know, is the Paasche quantity index of the standard of living.

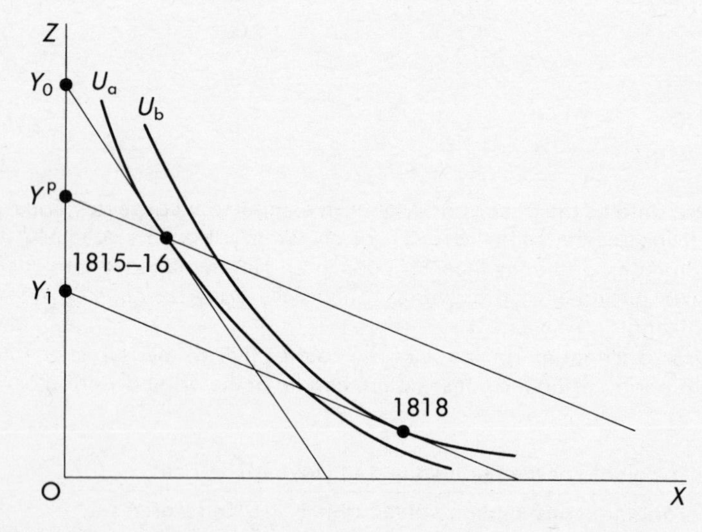

Figure 23.6 Ambiguity of a falling Paasche index of the standard of living

Now, if the Paasche standard of living index rises the individual must be unambiguously better off in terms of utility (that is, must be on a higher indifference curve even though you cannot actually observe indifference curves). If, however, it falls you cannot say in general whether the individual is better or worse off. Figure 23.6 shows a case in which the Paasche index of the standard of living falls but the true standard of living rises. Initially an individual is at the point marked 1815–16 with an income indicated by point Y_0 on the vertical axis (measured in terms of Z). Subsequently money income falls (say from 100 to 91.4) and prices change to produce the new budget line labelled Y_1 and a new preferred consumption bundle at the point 1818. If you revalue the original bundle at the new prices by passing a line through the 1815–16 point parallel to the Y_1 line you get the point Y^P which is an indicator of $\Sigma P_1 Q_0$. This is plainly less than Y_0 so, as in table 23.5, you have

$$\frac{Y^P}{Y_0} = \frac{\Sigma P_1 Q_0}{\Sigma P_0 Q_0} < 1$$

The Paasche index tells you that the standard of living has fallen. But actually 1818 is on a higher indifference curve than 1815–16, so the *true* standard of living has *risen.* Of course, the indifference map could have been such that U_b lay below U_a, in which case the reverse would have been true. The point is that you cannot tell for cases in which the Paasche index falls.

Hence, in column 4 of table 23.5, when the index number exceeds 100 you can infer that the Glasgwegian handloom weavers were better off than in 1815–16. But when it is lower, you cannot say. It is commonly believed by economic historians that living standards rose for most workers in this period. They *appear* to have fallen for the weavers, but really one cannot say.

T. R. Gourvish (1972) 'The cost of living in Glasgow in the early nineteenth century', *Economic History Review*, **25**, 65–80.

International Comparisons and Purchasing Power Parity

Suppose one wanted to compare the standard of living in Thailand and the UK. The national accounts will tell you that the national income in Thailand ($\Sigma P_{iT} Q_{iT}$) and the UK ($\Sigma P_{iU} Q_{iU}$), where each i denotes a final good or service, and the other subscripts denote Thailand (T) or the UK (U). Each of these aggregations is expressed in terms of the local currency: baht in the case of Thailand and sterling in the case of the UK. The standard way of comparing the two countries in terms of a common currency is to use the foreign exchange rate. Thus, if there were 58 baht to the pound, by dividing the Thai national income by 58 you would get a comparison in terms of pounds sterling and the Thai national income would be $\Sigma P_{iT} Q_{iT} \times 1/E$, where E is the baht–sterling exchange rate. The ratio of the national incomes expressed in sterling would be

$$E \frac{\Sigma P_{iU} Q_{iU}}{\Sigma P_{iT} Q_{iT}}$$

Is this a sensible way of using the exchange rate between two countries? The answer depends on the applicability of the theory of **purchasing power**

parity (PPP). This theory says that, in equilibrium, an exchange rate will be equal to the ratio of the purchasing powers of the two currencies. Suppose there is *just one* good in each country called 'rice'. In the UK it costs £1 per kilogram and in Thailand it costs 58 baht per kilogram. Assuming no transport costs, the exchange rate must be £1 = 58 baht, according to the PPP theory since, if it were say £1 = 100 baht, it would pay Thai residents to export rice. For each kilogram of rice exported they would get £1 which they could trade in at the exchange rate for 100 baht – 42 baht more than they would get at home for a kilogram of rice. This type of trading, that takes advantage of different prices of the same good in different places, is called **arbitrage**. Similarly, UK residents could get Thai rice cheaper than UK rice: a kilogram would cost them 58 baht or, in terms of sterling, only 58 pence – much less than the £1 that domestic rice costs. Consequently, the supply of sterling rises and so does the demand for baht, leading to a fall in the sterling exchange rate until £1 = 58 baht. (The theory of exchange rate determination is discussed in more detail in chapter 29.) Hence

$$\frac{\text{price of rice in UK (£1)}}{\text{price of rice of Thailand (58 baht)}} = \frac{1}{58} = E$$

where E is the exchange rate.

If the PPP theory is true, then it will also apply to bundles of final goods and services weighted by prices. You can therefore also write

$$\frac{\Sigma P_{i\mathrm{T}}\, Q_{i\mathrm{U}}}{\Sigma P_{i\mathrm{U}}\, Q_{i\mathrm{U}}} = E$$

and

$$\frac{\Sigma P_{i\mathrm{T}}\, Q_{i\mathrm{T}}}{\Sigma P_{i\mathrm{U}}\, Q_{i\mathrm{T}}} = E$$

when you want to make the kind of comparison discussed before.

Now something interesting emerges. Multiply both of these ratios by the ratio of the national incomes measured in local currencies ($\Sigma P_{i\mathrm{U}}Q_{i\mathrm{U}}/\Sigma P_{i\mathrm{T}}Q_{i\mathrm{T}}$) to get

$$\frac{\Sigma P_{i\mathrm{T}}Q_{i\mathrm{U}}}{\Sigma P_{i\mathrm{U}}Q_{i\mathrm{U}}}\ \frac{\Sigma P_{i\mathrm{U}}Q_{i\mathrm{U}}}{\Sigma P_{i\mathrm{T}}Q_{i\mathrm{T}}} = E\,\frac{\Sigma P_{i\mathrm{U}}Q_{i\mathrm{U}}}{\Sigma P_{i\mathrm{T}}Q_{i\mathrm{T}}} = \frac{\Sigma P_{i\mathrm{T}}Q_{i\mathrm{T}}}{\Sigma P_{i\mathrm{U}}Q_{i\mathrm{T}}}\ \frac{\Sigma P_{i\mathrm{U}}Q_{i\mathrm{U}}}{\Sigma P_{i\mathrm{T}}Q_{i\mathrm{T}}}$$

and cancel to get

$$\frac{\Sigma P_{i\mathrm{T}}Q_{i\mathrm{U}}}{\Sigma P_{i\mathrm{T}}Q_{i\mathrm{T}}} = E\,\frac{\Sigma P_{i\mathrm{U}}Q_{i\mathrm{U}}}{\Sigma P_{i\mathrm{T}}Q_{i\mathrm{T}}} = \frac{\Sigma P_{i\mathrm{U}}Q_{i\mathrm{U}}}{\Sigma P_{i\mathrm{U}}Q_{i\mathrm{T}}}$$

Can you see what this is telling you? If PPP is true, it says that the ratio of final outputs in each country will be the same whether it is valued in Thai or in UK currency. It is also saying (look at the term in the middle) that the simple ratio (per caput if you like) of the national incomes multiplied by the exchange rate will give the appropriate comparison. So international comparison can, after all, be made quite easily – as long as PPP is true. If PPP is true, relative prices of all goods would be the same in each country, so it does not matter whose prices are used.

Unfortunately, PPP seems not to be true because of transport costs, taxes, the presence of goods not traded internationally, fixed exchange rates and a host of other factors. In fact, the prices in poor countries seem *systematically lower* relative to those in the rich countries than the exchange rate usually suggests. Hence

$$\frac{\Sigma P_{i\mathrm{T}} Q_{i\mathrm{U}}}{\Sigma P_{i\mathrm{U}} Q_{i\mathrm{U}}} > E$$

and

$$\frac{\Sigma P_{i\mathrm{T}} Q_{i\mathrm{T}}}{\Sigma P_{i\mathrm{U}} Q_{i\mathrm{T}}} < E$$

Therefore

$$\frac{\Sigma P_{i\mathrm{T}} Q_{i\mathrm{U}}}{\Sigma P_{i\mathrm{T}} Q_{i\mathrm{T}}} > E \, \frac{\Sigma P_{i\mathrm{U}} Q_{i\mathrm{U}}}{\Sigma P_{i\mathrm{T}} Q_{i\mathrm{T}}} > \frac{\Sigma P_{i\mathrm{U}} Q_{i\mathrm{U}}}{\Sigma P_{i\mathrm{U}} Q_{i\mathrm{T}}}$$

Thus, in comparisons between rich and poor countries, the use of the exchange rate in practice means that the true relative standard of living in the poor country (Thailand in the example) valued at its marginal valuations (price weights) is understated, whereas that for the rich country is overstated. An example of the possible extent of such distortions is given in case study 23.2.

SAQ 23.7

Given

$$\Sigma P_{i\mathrm{T}} Q_{i\mathrm{U}} / \Sigma P_{i\mathrm{U}} Q_{i\mathrm{U}} > E > \Sigma P_{i\mathrm{T}} Q_{i\mathrm{T}} / \Sigma P_{i\mathrm{U}} Q_{i\mathrm{T}}$$

derive the inequalities immediately preceding in the text.

Case Study 23.2 International Comparisons of Living Standards

Dan Usher has compared the UK's and Thailand's national income per head. Table 23.6 (Usher, 1968) contains the details. In column 1 you can see the Thai national income per caput by category of expenditure expressed in sterling at the average 1963 rate between sterling and baht (1:58). This is calculated by, for example, taking

Table 23.6 National income per head in Thailand and the UK, 1963 (£)

	1	2	3	4	5	6	7	8
	P_TQ_T	P_UQ_U	P_TQ_U	P_UQ_T	$\frac{P_UQ_U}{P_TQ_T}$	$\frac{P_UQ_U}{P_UQ_T}$	$\frac{P_TQ_U}{P_TQ_T}$	Ratio of UK prices to Thai prices
Consumption	28.37	375.49	165.22	144.60	13.23	2.60	5.82	3.40
Food	13.62	99.39	37.57	55.24	7.30	1.80	2.76	3.27
Alcohol, tobacco and soft drinks	1.89	49.11	29.47	22.44	25.98	2.19	15.59	3.87
Clothing	2.07	31.93	7.32	9.02	15.42	3.54	3.54	4.36
Housing (rent and fuel)	2.92	54.70	5.84	27.35	18.73	2.00	2.00	9.37
Transport and communication	3.07	17.05	10.43	6.66	4.50	2.56	3.40	1.84
Automobiles	0.52	23.59	24.52	0.53	45.33	44.51	47.15	0.99
Other durables	0.65	22.37	22.37	0.65	34.41	34.42	34.42	1.00
Miscellaneous	0.72	14.68	4.89	2.16	20.38	6.30	6.79	3.00
Domestic services	0.10	1.60	0.22	0.75	15.39	2.13	2.20	7.26
Recreation	0.92	19.00	6.33	2.76	20.65	6.88	6.88	3.00
Health	1.11	16.22	6.87	2.14	14.61	7.58	6.19	2.13
Education	0.75	16.52	1.28	9.71	22.02	1.70	1.71	12.95
Finance and expenditure abroad	0.14	10.54	10.54	0.14	75.29	75.29	75.29	1.00
Legal and religious services	0.15	1.94	0.11	5.42	13.13	0.36	0.73	25.25
Public administration	1.52	25.56	2.96	13.10	16.82	1.95	1.95	8.63
Net capital formation	4.40	46.74	46.74	4.40	10.62	10.62	10.62	1.00
Total (weighted)	34.55	450.97	217.10	162.47	13.05	2.78	6.28	3.12

Thai expenditure on food, dividing it by 58 and dividing again by the Thai population. This gives the figure £28.37 in 1963. The second column is the UK national income per caput. The third column is UK national income per caput valued at Thai prices and then converted into pounds by dividing by 58. The fourth column is Thai income per caput valued at UK prices. The fifth column is the ratio of UK income per caput to Thai income per caput (the latter expressed in pounds, that is Thai income in baht divided by 58). This is the standard kind of comparison that is usually made. By looking at the bottom of the column you can see that the average UK resident seem to be 13.05 times better off than the average Thai. The sixth column shows the ratio of the UK to the Thai income per caput when valued at UK prices. Looking at the bottom of the column, which shows the weighted average, you can see that using UK weights, the average UK resident was only 2.78 times better off. The seventh column shows the ratio of the UK to the Thai income per caput when valued at Thai prices. At the bottom of the column, this shows that the average UK resident was 6.28 times better off than the average Thai.

Thus, the average income of a Thai is £34.55 and that of a UK resident £450.97. But the value of purchases at UK prices of the Thai resident is £162.47 (column 4), giving a ratio of 2.78 (column 6). Thus, from the UK resident's point of view he or she is only 2.78 times as well off as the Thai: this is how much more it would cost to buy the Thai bundle of goods in the UK. The value of purchases of a UK resident at Thai prices is £217.10 (column 3) compared with a Thai income of £34.55, giving a ratio of 6.28 (column 7). Thus, from the Thai point of view, the UK resident is 6.28 times as well off as the Thai. This is how much more it costs to buy the UK bundle of goods in Thailand.

Column 8 shows some estimated price ratios (in sterling) for each country. If the PPP theorem were true, these should all be equal to 1.00, since the Thai prices are all divided by 58, the then exchange rate. The disparity is especially noticeable in those items like legal and educational services that are not traded internationally. On average you can see that UK prices were 3.12 times higher than Thai prices. This is one reason why the simple comparison (column 6) exaggerates poverty in Thailand. For example, if the bottom line ratio in column 5 (13.05) is divided by this price ratio, you get a ratio of 4.18, roughly halfway between the two ratios in columns 6 and 7. Looking at this another way, if Thai per caput income of £34.55 is multiplied by 3.12 to allow for higher UK prices, you get a figure of £107.80 and the UK per caput income (£450.97) is only 4.18 times larger than this.

Whatever adjustments you make, it is quite clear that the real per caput national income in Thailand was a much higher fraction of UK income than simple comparisons suggest. Poverty is, of course, a serious world problem – there is scarcely one more serious. But serious problems deserve serious analysis. Uncritical exaggeration is not the soundest foundation for policy advocacy.

Dan Usher (1968), *The Price Mechanism and the Meaning of National Income Statistics*, Clarendon Press, Oxford, 1968, table 10.

Goods that Appear and Disappear

It has been assumed that goods and services are present in both periods or in both countries. But this is not always so. Yams are hardly available in the UK, and microwave ovens are scarcely found in Namibia. Magic lanterns are hard to come by in the UK today, and home movies were unknown to our Victorian forebears. In such cases one cannot perform the types of calculation discussed. In practice one has to find reasonably close substitutes to compare – an exercise that involves judgements, and ultimately value judgements at that. For example, one might consider a magic lantern to be a reasonable substitute for a home video recorder, yams for bread, and microwave ovens for other cookers.

But there is a host of other difficulties.

Omitted Final Outputs

Although, as you will see, the national accounts (at least in developed countries) do make imputations for some outputs (for example, the services of owner occupiers' housing) many goods that are not traded in markets are omitted. The value of the services of household members to one another is one major category of omission. The value of leisure is another. If a society prefers to reduce produced output and increase its leisure time (increased output of, say, hobby activities) then conventional national income falls, whereas, if the increase in leisure were really preferred, welfare must have risen in the sense that individuals are on higher indifference curves. The list can be readily extended: improved health, literacy, appreciation of the arts, life expectation, increased sharing of public goods whose output does not increase, and so on must be readily conceded to be important parts of welfare. But they do not feature in national income as conventionally measured.

Does it matter? Again it all depends on the uses to which the national accounting data are to be put. If one wants to calculate the necessary tax rate increases to generate government revenue to finance increased public expenditure, or to compute the effect of those expenditure and tax rises on employment, unemployment and inflation, then perhaps it does not matter much. But if one wants to use national income as an indicator of society's changing *welfare* then it plainly does matter. These considerations do not make measured national income *valueless* as a welfare indicator. But they do suggest that it needs *supplementation* by other indicators. National income is *an* indicator; it is not *the* indicator.

The omissions therefore teach one to be cautious and to try to figure out what kinds of supplementary information would be most useful. At any point in time, measured national income is at best only a *part* of true welfare (which may be larger *or* smaller). If changes in omitted final outputs are small relative to changes in measured income, then the changes are more useful as measures of trends. But, of course, to find out if they *are* small one needs to measure the changes in the omitted factors.

Do not assume that omissions necessarily give a *depressed* image of change or of differentials in the standard of living. In poor countries, where omissions are more substantial than in the rich partly because less of the economy is monetized and partly because fewer resources are put into data collection and processing, there is a real danger of exaggerating poverty owing to this factor, apart from the others discussed.

Included Intermediate Outputs

Is public expenditure on 'law and order' (£4867 million in the UK in 1983; see table 19.4) really a final output? Is it not an expenditure on intermediate services that enable other final outputs to be produced in a market economy? Is expenditure on military defence (£15,963 million in 1983) really a final output? Is it not expenditure on an intermediate set of services to produce – what? shall we say 'protection from attack'? Does the fact that real spending on defence in the UK rose by 7.8 per cent between 1970 and 1980 mean that the residents had 7.8 per cent more 'protection from attack' in 1980 compared with 1970?

The list can easily be prolonged. Is not food an intermediate good used to produce the final product 'survival'? Or clothing an intermediate good producing 'warmth'? Or transport an intermediate good necessary in the production of whatever one produces by being 'there' rather than 'here'?

This is treacherous territory and you will ultimately be forced to face up to the value judgemental problem of stating what the final outputs 'really' are that ought to count in making comparative statements about welfare. One thing, however, is clear: adverse externalities adversely affect welfare and cause measured national income to exceed true national income. If all else remains the same but crime increases and expenditure on law and order is increased in response, people are unambiguously *worse off* (if crime is a 'bad') for two reasons: less expenditure is available for true final outputs *and* there is more crime (though hopefully less than if spending on law and order had not increased). If it is a colder winter than usual and people spend more on clothing, they cannot (other things being the same) be *better off* (and they may still be colder than last year). Yet in both cases the national income data will say that people are better off, because output of these things will have increased and the expenditure on these outputs will have been received by someone as income. If the extra spending comes out of past savings, no one will have spent any less on other outputs. Even if it comes entirely from expenditure switching, falling welfare will be accompanied by constant output.

Such considerations again lead naturally to the need for developing supplementary indicators, often called **social indicators**, to complement whatever final outputs are judged fit to remain in the national income statistics.

You have already seen how indices of relevant 'qualities of life' can be computed for specific purposes (recall for example the aspects of health discussed in case study 5.1 on the measurement of handicap, case study 5.2 on social deprivation and case study 20.2 on the severity of sickness). You have also studied the conceptual issues that such measures raise: some of them ethical, some scientific and some practical. Social indicators, particularly in international comparisons, are invariably less detailed than these. The amount of detail needed depends, of course, on the purposes for which indices and indicators are going to be used. Case study 23.3 reviews some recent developments in international comparisons of the 'quality of life'.

Table 23.7 Some OECD social indicators (1960–72) for various member states

Country	*Transport accidents per 10,000 population*	*Dwellings with two or more persons per room (%)*	*Formal educational experience in age group 25–34 (years)*	*Female life expectancy at birth (years)*	*Maternal mortality per 10,000 live births*	*Median literacy score of children aged 14 (%)*
Australia	32.30	1.30	—	—	1.75	—
Canada	29.60	1.00	11.00	76.70	2.08	—
Denmark	27.80	4.90	10.20	76.30	1.68	—
Finland	27.70	27.60	—	—	1.48	64.2
France	23.50	10.60	10.10	77.10	2.49	—
Germany (FR)	28.30	2.50	9.40	74.20	5.42	—
Greece	12.90	37.80	8.00	—	2.27	—
Ireland	17.00	8.50	9.80	73.40	3.18	—
Italy	24.00	20.70	7.90	75.20	6.05	64.0
Japan	22.90	15.00	11.10	76.30	5.78	—
Netherlands	25.20	4.30	9.70	76.90	2.34	65.0
New Zealand	23.80	1.60	—	—	2.39	—
Sweden	19.40	2.50	9.60	—	1.02	65.0
Switzerland	24.40	1.20	—	—	2.92	—
England & Wales	14.70	0.70	11.00	75.30	1.94	61.6
USA	29.90	1.40	12.00	—	—	66.6

Case Study 23.3 Social Indicators

There seems (alas!) little government interest in supporting the development of internationally consistent social indicators to complement conventional national income statistics. The Organization for Economic Co-operation and Development (OECD) began a comprehensive programme of social indicators in 1971 in which there was broad consensus among the member states about 'common concerns'. These were divided into 'fundamental concerns' and 'sub-concerns' (the terms are irritatingly unimaginative, as is nearly always the case with international initiatives of this sort). The fundamental concerns included things like

A health
   A1 probability of a healthy life through all stages of the life cycle
   A2 impact of health impairment on individuals
F physical environment
   F1 housing conditions
   F2 population exposure to harmful and/or unpleasant pollutants

and a host of others. Sub-concerns included things like

A2a quality of health care in terms of reducing pain and restoring functional capabilities
F1c accessibility to neighbourhood shops, services and workplaces.

Unfortunately, the detailed (and costly) development of this framework has never been completed in a systematic fashion in the member states. Had it been done, it would have doubtless caused embarrassment to governments as invidious comparisons became possible. Some of the data that were available for (some) OECD states on a roughly (but not always perfectly) comparable basis are shown in table 23.7.

In the UK the most comprehensive regular set of data is to be found in *Social Trends*, published annually with commentaries on data, nearly all of which are produced by government departments. Its organization is in chapters dealing with population, households and families, education, employment, income and wealth, resources and expenditure, health and personal social services, housing, transport communications and the environment, leisure, participation in trade unions, churches and other organizations, law enforcement, and social groups including ethnic minorities.

It is a rich source of information but is, alas, neither set out nor intended as a systematic complement to the 'hard' data of national income and, although a richly textured picture of the UK can be had by trawling through it, there is a tremendous amount of work that yet remains to be done if a more comprehensive picture of welfare in the UK is to be systematically painted.

OECD (1976) *Measuring Social Well-Being*, Paris, OECD, tables I, II, V, VI, VII, XVI, XIX.
Central Statistical Office, *Social Trends*, London, HMSO.

Omitted Costs

Some ecologists have dubbed *GNP* 'gross national pollution'. Here you must again tread with care. Take a concrete example to show the danger of *overestimating* the consequences for welfare of omitted costs such as pollution – a danger that it is all too easy for environmentalists to fall foul of.

Suppose a factory produces £1000 of final output but pours out smoke that imposes an external cost of £100 on others even after they have spent £400 on (partial) protection from smoke by installing air conditioning. Measured national income will be £1400 (the value of the factory's final output plus the £400 output of air conditioning services) all of which must be received by people as income. *True* national income will be £900: the value of marketed output (the factory's output of £1000 plus the £400 of the air conditioners' industry) less the residual pollution cost (£100) less the £400 intermediate **defensive expenditure** on air conditioning. The omitted costs plus the intermediate expenditure cause measured national income to overstate true welfare by a large amount (1.56 times true income) because measured income consists of all marketed output (or the incomes earned therefrom) and ignores environmental damage.

Now suppose *either* that local residents have to be compensated for the harm the factory does them *or* that the government imposes an optimal tax on smoke production (or regulates emissions of smoke to their optimal level). (Now is a good time to check back to chapter 19 and refresh your understanding of the idea of optimal externality.) Suppose that these mechanisms are equally effective in promoting the optimal level of smoke emission but all involve an (optimal) reduction in output so that the factory's value of output falls from £1000 to £950. Suppose in this situation that there is still £50 of smoke damage but that to reduce this further would cause an even greater reduction in the factory's value of output and, moreover, that households no longer deem it necessary to install air conditioning. (Imagine, for convenience, that existing air conditioners collapse into uselessness after one year.)

What is national income now? Measured national income is £950 (the only output is now that produced by the factory). 'True' national income is also £950, for the cost of the smoke is now correctly accounted for by the managers of the factory: the residual £50 damage is a cost of production of exactly the same kind as the other costs incurred by the firm. It should not be deducted from the value of output (or income) any more than the 'damage' done to leisure by paid work needs to be deducted. It is now a species of, as it were, intermediate activity necessary if the optimal output is to be produced. To ban *all* smoke would be to reduce national income below £950 for, if £950 were the optimal output, then the saving of £50 of smoke damage would be offset by a larger fall in the value of output. Indeed, because it was assumed that pollution fell to its optimal level, true national income must have risen: as it has in the example, from £900 to £950. With *optimal* externality, however, true national income also equals measured national income. Note that *measured* national income falls from £1400 to £950, whereas *true* national income rises from £900 to £950 after optimal emission control.

The mere *presence* of external costs such as those imposed by smoke pollution is not a sufficient ground for saying that welfare is being understated by measured national income. The understating happens only when there are *uncompensated* external costs or higher than optimal levels of pollution. The problem is not to eliminate these costs entirely. Nor should one deduct *all* externalities from measured national income, but only uncompensated ones: in the original situation these were the sum of defensive expenditures and residual smoke.

Once again, care and caution rather than extremism are the order of the day. Should the time arrive when a set of social indicators has been developed to complement the national income data, uncompensated external costs should have their place in such accounts.

Omitted Non-economic Elements

The borderline between the 'economic' and the 'non-economic' is hard to discuss fruitfully. As you saw in chapter 1, it may be defined either by convention or by the logical limits of the applicability of economic analysis. As a (descriptive) matter of fact, however, it is obviously the case that there are countless features of life that ought to be considered as part of welfare but that are not produced (at least in any obvious sense) by economic activity: the love and security of family life, the attraction of living in a caring community, freedom from oppression, freedom for self-expression – the list is potentially endless.

Although such factors are indisputably part of welfare (arguably its greater part), it seems doubtful whether any formal system of accounting either could or should attempt to measure them (even ordinally). It is all too easy, however, to predjudice these sources of welfare by an obsession with the more materialistic components of welfare, particularly when they are not measured at all: the quantifiable drives out the important.

When all that can be fruitfully understood by economic analysis has been understood, one can go no further as an economist. The politician and moralist in one must take over completely.

What You Should Understand Now

Some empirical material on international national income per caput.
How to represent the nation as an individual in indifference curve analysis.
How to construct and interpret Laspeyres and Paasche indexes of the standard of living.
Difference between indexes of the cost of living and the standard of living.
How to interpret international national income data and make suitable adjustments.
The implications of the purchasing power parity theory, both when it holds and when it does not, for international comparisons.
How to evaluate claims that national income both includes and excludes too much.
The social indicators approach to dealing with some of the deficiencies of national income as an indicator of national welfare.

24

National Income Accounting

The most fundamental of all the macroeconomic aggregates is, as you have seen, the value of output of goods and services produced per year. This chapter explores the idea of national income in more detail. Chapter 23 asserted that national output is equal to the total income of the community. This can be seen from considering what is known as the circular flow.

The Circular Flow

The notions of aggregate output and income can most readily be introduced by looking at the flow of goods and services (and the reciprocal flows of money) between two sectors: households and firms. This is shown in figure 24.1. In this figure you can see that households supply inputs to the firms in the form of labour, land, capital equipment etc. and that firms supply produced goods and services to the households as consumers. The top part of the loop shows the flow of inputs and the bottom part the flow of outputs.

The households ultimately own all the firms as well as the inputs. These are all *real* flows – so many hours of labour, so many hours of machine time etc. per year on the input side, and so many units of produced goods and services per year on the output side.

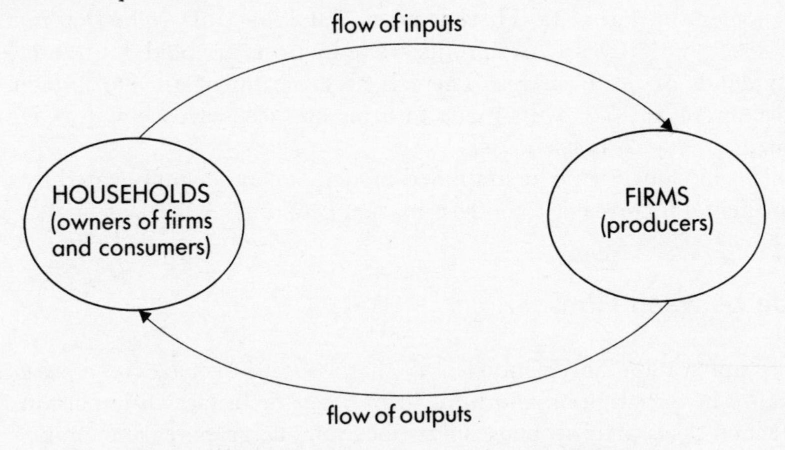

Figure 24.1 The circular flow of inputs and outputs

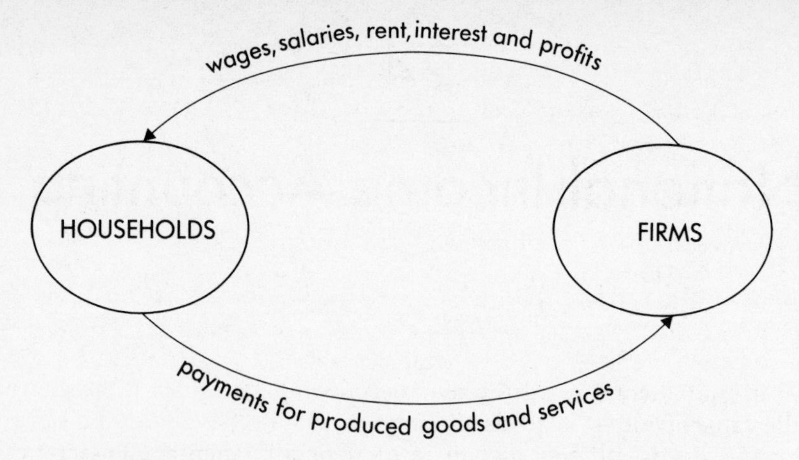

Figure 24.2 The circular flow of payments for inputs and outputs

Corresponding to these real flows are monetary payments. In exchange for the services of labour, capital and so on, firms pay labour wages and salaries, landowners (including owners of buildings) rents, and owners of firms (suppliers of financial capital) interest and profits. These monetary flows, since they are rewards or compensations to the owners of inputs, are in the opposite direction to the real flows in the upper loop. In exchange for the receipt of produced goods and services, households pay firms prices. Again these monetary flows are in the opposite direction to the real flows in the lower loop. Both sets of monetary flows are shown in figure 24.2.

It is these monetary flows that enable the national income accountants to calculate total income or the national product (= output). *Total income* is the sum of all payments in the upper loop of the circular flow in figure 24.2, and *national product* is the market value of all goods and services sold, shown in the lower loop.

In this simple circular flow model there is no saving: all income in a given year is spent in that year. There is no stockholding: all production in a given year is sold in that year. Any profits made by firms are paid out to households as dividends or profit shares. There is no government and no foreign trade. Hence, aggregate payments made to firms are necessarily equal to aggregate payments made to households.

This is obviously an oversimplified model. It can be complicated by adding the principal features of a modern market economy.

Trade between Firms

One simplification not mentioned is that households have been assumed to specialize in consumption and firms in production. In fact an important part of production takes place in households (for example, groceries are combined with household labour to produce the output 'meals'). This sort of production (which is very extensive, especially in subsistence economies) is typically not matched by flows of monetary payments and is typically excluded altogether from the measures of national income and output. You have already seen some of the problems this creates in using national income statistics in chapter 23.

SAQ 24.1

Make a list of as many items of non-marketed household production as you can think of.

Within the firms sector, however, are many transactions that do have corresponding monetary flows, as firms buy and sell products to one another, for it is only final *output* that is sold to households and it is obvious that a good deal of trade in *intermediate outputs* goes on between firms (see chapter 9).

Suppose firm A supplies firm B with glass that A has manufactured using inputs from the household sector (including raw materials owned by the household sector). Firm B now uses the glass together with further inputs from the household sector to produce a final output, mirrors, that is sold to the household sector. A difficulty clearly arises: if you add the value of the output of firm A to that of firm B you would be counting some inputs *twice*. If A sells glass to B and B sells mirrors to households, the value of the glass is already included in the selling price of B's mirrors.

Take a longer chain of inter-firm specialized production and trading. Farmers produce barley that is sold to merchants who provide a service by grading and bulk storing the grain. Merchants sell barley to brewers (as well as to animal feed manufacturers and so on). The brewers use barley to brew beer which they sell to publicans. Publicans stock beer and provide services to customers by selling beer. The final output is beer (along this chain; it may be, say, beef along a chain through feed manufacturers) whose market value is given by sales to final customers. But if one added up the value of the barley to be used in beer production that was sold to merchants and the value of barley sold by merchants to brewers, and the value of brewers' beer sales to publicans, and the value of publicans' beer sales to the public, one would arrive at a market value of barley or beer that greatly exceeded its actual value.

This is known as the problem of double counting (or, more generally, **multiple counting**). In order to calculate national product *each good or service should be counted once and only once.* This is a fundamental rule of national income accounting. With successive stages of production taking place in separate firms, the value of output *added* at each stage of production is the measure of that firm's contribution to national product. Were this not so, national output would rise and fall according as firms were more or less *vertically integrated* (that is, less or more separately specialized in successive stages of the process by which a final output is produced). This contribution of each firm is called *value added* (recall case study 13.2 on VAT) for rather obvious reasons. The value of intermediate goods and services is *not* included in national product, only the *value of final goods and services or (which must be the same thing) the sum of values added.*

To see equivalence of the sum of values added and the value of output, consider table 24.1. Here you can see that multiple counting would produce a false estimate (£730) of the contribution to the value of national product by these four firms. This is the total value of sales, not product. The value added at each stage is shown in the second column and adds up to £250. This is equal to the value of final output sold by firm D.

Table 24.1 Avoiding multiple counting by using value added

	Selling price (£)	*Value added (£)*
Firm A produces a raw material sold to firm B for	100	100
Firm B produced an intermediate product sold to firm C for	180	80
Firm C produces an intermediate product sold to firm D for	200	20
Firm D produces an final product sold to households for	250	50
Total value of sales	730	
Total value added		250

This must be so, as you can see from considering that value added is the difference between a firm's sales (S) and the sales to it. Hence:

$$\text{value added} = S_A + (S_B - S_A) + (S_C - S_B) + (S_D - S_C)$$

Since S_A (sales of firm A) appears twice (once positive and once negative) and so do S_B and S_C, all these cancel out to leave you with

$$\text{value added} = S_D = \text{final output}$$

SAQ 24.2

Complete the missing values in table 24.2.

Table 24.2 Value added for SAQ 24.2

	Selling price (£)	*Value added (£)*
Firm A produces a raw material sold to firm B for	50	—
Firm B produces an intermediate product sold to firm C for	—	100
Firm C produces an intermediate product sold to firm D for	—	70
Firm D produces an intermediate product sold to firm E for	250	—
Firm E produces a final product sold to households for	300	—
Total value of sales	—	
Total value added		—

National product can therefore be measured on the *expenditure* side (that is, expenditure on marketed goods and services) *either* as the value of final output *or* as the value added by all firms. Since you have already seen that it can also be measured by the sum of payments to the suppliers of inputs, there are three theoretical ways to measure national product or national income: the *income method* (adding up all incomes generated by production in a year), the *final output method*, and the *value added method*. Each will give the same answer (provided that the data are accurately collected).

The value added approach is really exactly equivalent to the income method of calculating national output, as can be seen from table 24.3. In this table you can see the total value of sales (£730) broken down into the value of sales to firms (£480) and value added (£250). Since value added is what a firm has to distribute to suppliers of inputs (including profits to owners) and there is nothing else that can be done with it, it must necessarily be the same as the sum of all payments of wages, salaries, rents, interest and profit – that is, income.

Table 24.3 Equivalence of value added and income methods of calculating national product

	Firm A	*Firm B*	*Firm C*	*Firm D*	*All firms*
Payment to other firms	0	100	180	200	480 (value of sales to firms)
Payments to suppliers of inputs (wages, rent, interest, profits)	100	80	20	50	250 (value added)
Value of firm's output	100	180	200	250	730 (total value of sales)

Categories of Final Output by the Expenditure Method

Because the underlying *determinants* of different elements in final output are hypothesized to vary according to their type, the accounting conventions break total output down into the following main categories:

Household consumption (C)
Government expenditure on final goods and services (G)
Investment expenditure (I)
Net exports ($X-M$)

Introducing these is the next step in national income accounting.

Consumption (C)

This is total expenditure on *final* outputs by households. It is the largest component of national product and includes in practice durable goods like television sets and cars, non-durable goods like food and clothing, and personal services like accountancy services, private education, and hair-dressing. It *excludes* household expenditure on the purchase of houses which are counted as an investment expenditure. The dividing line between durable consumer goods and investment goods is rather arbitrary. *Any* good that yields services over a period is strictly speaking an investment good – it involves the sacrifice of some present consumption for the sake of future consumption. Pure consumption goods are either those that can exist only at one moment (like the services of your hairdresser) or those that are destroyed the moment they are consumed (like food). The divisions conventionally adopted by national income accountants are made for reasons of practicability and correspond only roughly to the theoretical definitions of consumption and investment goods.

Consumption does not include purchases of second hand goods that were produced in earlier accounting periods or that have already been accounted for in this period. Such purchases represent a *transfer* of ownership rather than new final output (though the *services* of those who trade in such goods are services produced in this accounting period and *are* included).

Government Expenditure (G)

All government expenditure on goods and services is conventionally assumed by national income accountants to be *final* consumption, even though some of it is clearly in the nature of an intermediate good (for example, expenditure on roads). This category of final output potentially embraces a tremendous diversity of outputs – from defence, through law and order, to the output of steel and motor cars. The output of public corporations and other trading bodies like the BBC, the British Steel Corporation, the Post Office and even the Bank of England are excluded from G (their final outputs are included under C).

Although all these outputs are 'public' outputs in the *descriptive* sense that they are produced in the publicly owned sector of the economy, they are in practice a mixture of public and private goods in the economic sense discussed in chapter 19. Most are supplied free or at less than cost. In Britain, the principal components of G are defence, health and education, as you saw in table 19.4.

Transfer payments are excluded since such payments neither create net incomes (other than for the bureaucrats employed to make them) nor produce output. Transfers include things like public pensions and unemployment benefits. Essentially, such transfers merely reshuffle income from one group in society to another. This is not to say, of course, that these transfer activities are without value to members of society. In so far as they can be interpreted as *internalizing externalities*, transfers clearly are a source of utility. Ultimately, one could view production as *any* procedure that increased utility but, since this would embrace a range of activity whose final value is exeedingly hard to measure, such activity is excluded. Clearly this has implications for the use of national product as an indicator of a nation's welfare, as you have seen in chapter 23.

The value of G is taken as expenditure by government at both central and local levels (the two together are conventionally termed *general government*). Although these goods and services are all ultimately consumed by households they are treated as though the government itself were some kind of 'collective consumer'. The convention is to value them at the expenditure laid out by the government in supplying health services, defence, education and so on.

Investment (I)

Total or gross investment (GI) falls into several categories. You have already met housing investment in the discussion of consumption. That is one important form of investment. A second type is investment in capital goods – purchases of plant and equipment either to replace existing capacity that wears out or to increase capacity. This is termed **fixed capital formation**. A third type is investment in stocks (or inventories) that are held by firms, shops and so on to cover unexpected variations in demand or supply and to economize on storage and delivery costs.

Investment of all three types includes only *new* output produced in the accounting period. For example, if a firm purchases a second-hand machine, that is not included (it will have been included in a previous period's investment). The asset is merely having its ownership transferred and so it is just like a government transfer. Since stocks can be inherited in one accounting period from the previous one, it is *changes* in stocks that represent investment here (which may be negative if the stocks at the end of the accounting period are smaller than at the beginning: this is *disinvestment* in stocks).

Gross Investment in the UK, 1983

The total amounts invested in the UK in 1983 were as shown in table 24.4. As you can see, investment in housing was a significant fraction of the total (22 per cent) and there was some investment too in stocks.

Table 24.4 Gross investment in the UK, 1983 (£ million)

Gross domestic fixed capital formation excluding housing in:		
private sector	27,519	
general government	3,302	
public corporations	7,791	
	38,612	38,612
Gross domestic fixed capital formation in housing in:		
private sector	8,592	
general government	2,129	
public corporations	226	
	10,947	10,947
Value of physical increases in stocks		267
Gross domestic fixed capital formation (including stocks)		49,826

Source: UK National Accounts, 1984, tables 10.1 and 12.2

Fixed capital formation is obviously something of an intermediate good. Fixed capital is usually produced and bought by firms and not sold as final output to households. What *is* sold to households is the output produced *using* capital goods whose value will be included in the value of final sales. Is it not, then, inconsistent with the rule that *each good should be counted once and only once* to include investment as a component of final output? It certainly would be if investment goods as such were simply added in with the other components. But that is not quite what is done in national income accounting.

Remember that investment goods last for a long time. If a firm buys a machine it may expect it to last several years. In the first year, the machine is used, together with other inputs, to produce, let us suppose, a final output.

What you need to know, then, is how much of the machine's value is to be attributed to production in that first year. This is termed **capital consumption**, for it suggests (not very reasonably) that some of the machine is 'used up', as it were, in the first year. Another term for the same thing is **depreciation**. Each year (including the first) *some* of the machine will depreciate (wear and tear etc.) until at the end of its useful life it will be discarded.

This depreciation is the (conceptual) measure of that part of investment that is 'used up' in an accounting period, and it is therefore this that must be deducted if double counting is to be avoided. If you start with *gross investment* (total value of investment goods produced in a year) and deduct depreciation, you are left with *net investment*. This is the amount of investment goods produced in a year that is *not* 'used up' and which is therefore a proper addition to national product in that year. Over its entire life, a machine or any other item of capital will have been fully depreciated. Thus, when it comes to the scrap heap, the average intermediate contribution in each year will have been fully deducted from average gross investment and, on average, no double counting will have taken place ('on average' because estimates of depreciation are necessarily rather arbitrary and in any one year may not be quite right). In the long run, however, the average amount will be right. The accounting convention is to take gross investment and divide it by the assumed years of life on average of each capital item. A given capital stock is thus assumed to depreciate by a constant amount each year.

The important thing to remember is that the investment component of national product has to be *net* investment, not gross investment, if double counting is to be avoided. You may be interested in gross investment for other reasons, however. For example, employment in the investment goods industries will be a function of gross rather than net investment. If all the machines produced suddenly depreciated fully owing to a remarkable invention that made them all valueless, net investment would fall to zero but the employment generated by their manufacture would have been determined partly by the rate of output of the machines, which is gross investment.

Table 24.5 UK capital consumption by sector, 1983 (£ million)

Housing		
Private sector	3,794	
General government	1,346	
Public corporations	116	
	5,256	5,256
Other fixed capital		
Private sector	21,623	
General government	2,367	
Public corporations	7,244	
	31,234	31,234
Total		36,490

Source: UK National Accounts, 1984, table 11.5

Table 24.5 shows the amount of capital consumption in various industries in the UK in 1983. The (replacement) value of the capital stock of houses in the UK in 1983 was £304,100 million (*UK National Accounts (Blue Book)*, 1984, table 11.7) which, with an average depreciation per year of £5256 million (table 11.5 in the *Blue Book*) implies that the average life of a dwelling is 58 years at current rates of depreciation. The value of all other capital stock was £523,300 million, so the capital value of housing represents a bit more than one third of the total: it is a tremendously important national asset. With average annual depreciation of £31,234 million, the average life of all other assets is about 26 years.

Investment in the national accounts does not include the purchase of bonds, bills, or shares in firms. Once again, although these titles to ownership (*financial* investments) are often bought and sold, they constitute *transfers* of title and are not themselves a part of final output, or come to that even of intermediate output. If a firm, however, issues *new* equity and uses the proceeds of its sales to buy *new* plant and equipment, then the purchase of that plant and equipment will (net of depreciation) count as a part of investment.

Note that investment in stocks or inventories may include investment in intermediate as well as final goods. Any increase or decrease in stocks of intermediate goods adds to or subtracts from national product, for intermediate goods not used in production are a part of final output (even though not sold to households) or value added; they are, at least in this accounting period, the end of the production chain. Thus, it is still true that every item of production is included once and only once in the calculation of national product. Although this means that *most* intermediate goods are *not* included, those that are not used up in production during the accounting period, but are added to stocks are quite properly included as final output or value added.

The sum of consumption, government expenditure on final goods and services and gross investment is called *total domestic expenditure* (*TDE*).

Net Exports (X – M)

Some output (both goods and services) produced in the accounting period may be sold abroad. Such exports (X) are included in national product (though they are obviously not a part of national consumption). Similarly, goods and services supplied within the UK to foreign nationals (e.g. tourist services or the financial services of the City of London) are exports (tourist expenditures have to be estimated by a sample survey).

Imports (M) from abroad are expenditures by domestic residents but they are not a part of national product (they are part of other countries' national products). They must therefore be deducted from the expenditures by households, firms and governments since otherwise C, I and G would be inflated. The difference between X and M is called *net exports*.

When a country has positive net exports ($X > M$ by value), its residents will be adding to their stocks of foreign financial assets like foreign currencies, foreign bonds and shares and foreign real assets like factories. Conversely, when net exports are negative ($X < M$), its residents will be reducing their stock of ownership of foreign assets. Hence, net exports add to or detract from what is also termed *net investment abroad.* This will be explored in more detail in chapters to come dealing with balance of payments and the role of money in the macroeconomy.

Total domestic expenditure plus exports is known as *total final expenditure* (*TFE*). This is the total gross expenditure by residents and foreigners on domestically produced output and imports. Total final expenditure less imports is known as *gross domestic product at market prices* (GDP_M). This is the total gross expenditure by residents and foreigners on domestically produced output.

The key difinitions derived so far can be summarized:

$TDE = C + GI + G$
(total domestic expenditure is the sum of consumers' expenditure, gross investment and government final expenditure)

$TFE = TDE + X = C + GI + G + X$
(total final expenditure is the sum of total domestic expenditure and exports)

$GDP_M = TFE - M = C + GI + G + (X - M)$
(gross domestic product at market prices is total final expenditure net of the import content in C, GI, G and X)

Table 24.6 shows the values for *TDE*, *TFE* and GDP_M in 1963, 1973 and 1983 at current prices (prices in the year in question). As you can see, the share of consumption expenditure in GDP_M has fallen (from about 66 per cent to about 60 per cent). Gross investment in 1973 was higher than in 1963, but in 1983 was similar to 1963. The share of government expenditure increased over these 20 years from 17 per cent to 22 per cent. Note that when *TDE* exceeds GDP_M, *M* exceeds *X*, and vice versa.

The spectacular rise in all the monetary numbers over the 20 year period (especially the period 1973–83) is, of course, mainly due to inflation.

Table 24.6 *TDE, TFE* and GDP_M in 1963, 1973 and 1983 at current prices (£ million)

	1963	GDP_M %	*1973*	GDP_M %	*1983*	GDP_M %
C	20,319	66.4	46,004	62.2	182,427	60.5
G	5,139	16.8	13,429	18.1	65,859	21.9
GI	5,305	17.3	16,364	22.1	49,826	16.5
TDE	30,763	100.5	75,797	102.4	298,112	98.9
X	5,877	19.2	17,233	23.3	79,768	26.5
TFE	36,640	119.7	93,030	125.7	377,880	125.4
M	−6,027	19.7	−19,033	25.7	−76,582	25.4
GDP_M	30,613	100.0	73,997	100.0	301,298	100.0

Source: *UK National Accounts*, 1984, table 1.2

Some Further Refinements

The discussion of the calculation of national product is now almost complete. There remain a few technicalities outstanding which, once you have grasped them, will enable you to read the published national income accounts with reasonable ease.

Gross National Product and Gross Domestic Product

So far the facts that households in the UK own income producing property overseas and that foreigners similarly own property in the UK have not been considered. If you want to know the total income or output generated by the property of UK residents *wherever it may be*, you should add in income from real property abroad and subtract income going to foreigners from real property they own here. The difference between UK income from property owned abroad and foreign income from property owned in the UK is called *net property income from broad* (*NPI*). If this is added to gross domestic product at market prices you get *gross national product at market prices* (GNP_M). In summary form:

$$GNP_M = GDP_M + NPI$$

The difference made by *NPI* is the difference between the value of output produced by the residents of the country at home and abroad (GNP_M) and the value of output produced within the domestic territory of the country (GDP_M), no matter who owns that output. In some countries (for example, Middle Eastern oil producing states, where a large part of the capital stock is owned by foreigners) the difference between GDP_M and GNP_M may be substantial.

Which concept (GNP_M or GDP_M) one uses depends on the focus of interest. If one is interested in the total income accruing to residents, GNP_M is the natural focus. If one is interested in, say, the domestic employment creation that production makes possible, then GDP_M is the natural focus.

Market Prices and Factor Cost

Government has so far been treated as an innocent contributor to the public good: there are no taxes in the picture at all. If the government levies taxes that affect prices, it becomes useful to distinguish between gross national product at market prices and *gross national product at factor cost* (GNP_{FC}). The former is a measure of gross final output at the prices actually paid in the marketplace (except in the case of *G*, where output is assumed to be 'sold' at average cost) and hence includes the effects of indirect taxation like VAT. Similarly, government pays subsidies to agriculture, housing, transport and so on that have the effect of reducing market prices below what they would otherwise have been.

Since indirect taxes and transfers do not *directly* affect real output of goods and services (though changes in rates and levels of taxes will obviously affect the value of output) it is useful to net them out. Moreover, you have already seen that transfers are merely reshufflings of purchasing power. Indirect taxes (direct taxes too, for that matter) can be seen in the same light: firms collect indirect taxes from consumers and the firms' owners (depending on the tax incidence) and then pay the proceeds to the government. Abstracting (as the convention is) from the incentive or disincentive effects this may have on consumers and producers, real output is the same. Firms just act rather like tax collectors.

If you *subtract* all indirect taxes and *add* all subsidies to *GNP* at market prices you get *GNP* at factor cost. Thus

$$GNP_{FC} = GNP_{M} - T + S$$

where T are indirect taxes and S are subsidies. The expression $(-T + S)$ is termed **factor cost adjustment**. In the UK T is much larger than S, and so GNP_{FC} is always less than GNP_{M}. Likewise, making the factor cost adjustment to GDP_{M} gives you *GDP* at factor cost:

$$GDP_{FC} = GDP_{M} - T + S$$

Gross and Net National Product

As you saw in the discussion of investment, not to deduct depreciation of capital goods would be to double count. If depreciation (D) is deducted from GNP_{FC} or GDP_{FC} you get *net national product at factor cost* (NNP_{FC}) or *net domestic product at factor cost* (NDP_{FC}):

$$NNP_{FC} = GNP_{FC} - D$$

and

$$NDP_{FC} = GDP_{FC} - D$$

Net national product at factor cost is what is generally called *national income*; it shows the income accruing to UK residents, after allowing for depreciation, in an accounting period. In view of the accounting arithmetic just gone through, you can now see why national income was left ill defined in chapter 23!

Looking at National Income Explicitly from the Income Side

GDP at factor cost is the sum of income E from employment and self-employment, profits π (including interest and dividends) and rent R. Hence

$$GDP_{FC} = E + \pi + R$$

If you now add net property income from abroad you would (as you should now know) get gross *national* product at factor cost, and if you further deduct depreciation, you get net national product at factor cost, or national income:

$$NNP_{FC} = E + \pi + R + NPI - D.$$

In rent is included an imputation for the rent of owner occupied houses. Suppose all owner occupiers suddenly sold homes and rented them back from the new owners. If rents were not imputed, GDP_{FC} would suddenly (and substantially) rise. Yet no *real* change would have taken place. To avoid this artificiality, owner occupiers are envisaged to rent their homes from themselves so that the real income they derive from their residence is properly included in the national income statistics.

SAQ 24.3

An economy is represented in the following table:

income (£ million)		*expenditure* (£ million)	
employment	400	consumers' expenditure	400
profit	70	net investment in houses	50
rent	30	net investment in stocks	30
		depreciation	20

(a) What is this economy's gross national product at factor cost?
(b) What is this economy's net national product at factor cost?
(c) What is this economy's national income?

Table 24.7 gathers together all the accounting definitions.

Table 24.7 National income accounting identities

Expenditure method	
$TDE = C + GI + G$	
$TFE = TDE + X$	$= C + GI + G + X$
$GDP_M = TFE - M$	$= C + GI + G + (X{-}M)$
$GNP_M = GDP_M + NPI$	$= C + GI + G + (X{-}M) + NPI$
$GDP_{FC} = GDP_M - (T - S)$	$= C + GI + G + (X{-}M) - (T{-}S)$
$GNP_{FC} = GNP_M - (T - S)$	$= C + GI + G + (X{-}M) + NPI - (T{-}S)$
$NNP_{FC} = GNP_{FC} - D$	$= C + I + G + (X{-}M) + NPI - (T{-}S)$
	$(I = GI - D)$
Income method	
$GDP_{FC} = E + \pi + R$	
$GNP_{FC} = GDP_{FC} + NPI$	$= E + \pi + R + NPI$
$NNP_{FC} = GNP_{FC} - D$	$= E + \pi + R + NPI - D$

Hence

$$C + I + G + (X{-}M) + NPI - (T{-}S) = E + \pi + R + NPI - D$$

or

national expenditure = national income

Glossary of Terms

C	consumers' expenditure at market prices
D	depreciation or capital consumption
E	income from employment and self-employment (including employers' national insurance contributions)
G	current expenditure by general government on final goods and services
GDP_{FC}	gross domestic product at factor cost
GDP_{M}	gross domestic product at market prices
GNP_{FC}	gross national product at factor cost
GNP_{M}	gross national product at market prices
GI	gross investment in housing, fixed capital goods and changes in stocks
I	net investment in housing, fixed capital goods and changes in stocks
M	imports of goods and services: overseas purchases by UK residents (including government)
NDP_{FC}	net domestic product at factor cost
NNP_{FC}	net national product at factor cost
NPI	net property income from abroad
π	gross profits of domestic companies and financial institutions including trading surpluses of public corporations and government enterprises and including interest payments and dividends (other profits are in NPI)
R	rent of land and buildings net of maintenance costs and including imputed income of owner occupiers from their dwellings
S	subsidies by general government
T	taxes on expenditure: indirect taxes including local authority rates
TDE	total domestic expenditure at market prices
TFE	total final expenditure at market prices
X	exports of goods and services

Table 24.8 shows the values for GDP_{M}, GDP_{FC}, GNP_{FC} and NNP_{FC} for the years 1963, 1973 and 1983. The equivalent figures for national income at constant (1980) prices in 1963, 1973 and 1983 are £123,882, £168,978 and £177,777. Thus, although in current prices national income rose nearly nine times, in *real* terms it rose just under one and a half times.

Table 24.8 National income aggregates in the UK in 1963, 1973 and 1983

	1963	*1973*	*1983*
GDP_{M}	30,613	73,997	301,298
Factor cost adjustment ($T-S$)	−3,458	−8,687	−43,809
GDP_{FC}	27,155	65,310	257,489
Net property income from abroad	398	1,257	1,948
GNP_{FC}	27,553	66,567	259,437
Depreciation	−2,518	−7,365	−36,490
NNP_{FC} (national income)	25,035	59,202	222,947

Source: UK National Accounts, 1984, table 1.2

Looking at it using the income approach, the values for the same years are set out in table 24.9. Note that there is a discrepancy in GDP between the income method and the expenditure method. Since the expenditure method is generally regarded as the more reliable, the income method estimate is reconciled to the expenditure based method: this is the residual error shown in table 24.9. This error, in well-developed statistical systems like that in the UK, is usually very small. In 1973, for example, the income based estimate was only very slightly more than one per cent more than the expenditure based estimate. The difference (positive or negative) is usually much less than that (as it was in 1963 and 1983).

Table 24.9 Gross domestic product by category of income 1963, 1973 and 1983 in current prices (£ million)

	1963	*1973*	*1983*
Income from employment and self-employment	20,776	51,517	193,195
Profits etc. (net of stock appreciation)	4,874	9,770	46,756
Rent	1,320	4,137	17,424
Imputed charge for non-trading capital consumption	202	589	2,456
GDP_{FC} (income based)	27,172	66,013	259,831
Residual error	−17	−703	−2,342
GDP_{FC} (expenditure based)	27,155	65,310	257,489

Source: UK National Accounts, 1984, table 1.3

SAQ 24.4

Get hold of a copy of the 1984 *Blue Book* (*UK National Accounts*) and find:

(a) Consumers' expenditure at current prices in 1981
(b) Gross investment at market prices in 1981
(c) *TDE* at market prices in 1981
(d) Net exports at market prices in 1981
(e) Factor cost adjustment in 1981
(f) Income from employment in 1982
(g) Total personal income in 1982
(h) Personal disposable (after tax etc.) income in 1983
(i) Gross fixed domestic capital formation in the construction industry in 1983 (i.e. excluding investment in stocks)
(j) Depreciation in the transport industry in 1983
(k) Total subsidies in 1983
(l) Total government expenditure in 1983
(m) Total government expenditure on final goods and services in 1983.

What You Should Understand Now

The basic circular flow of national output and income.
How to avoid multiple counting by allowing for inter-firm trading and depreciation.
The logical equivalence of the income, expenditure and value added methods of calculating national output.
The difference between *GDP* and *GNP*.
The difference between aggregates at market values and factor cost.
The derivation of national income.
How to use the main tables in the *Blue Book*.

25

Introduction to Macroeconomics

With the background of chapters 23 and 24 you are now poised to tackle the central questions that generally go under the name *macroeconomics*: the determination of the level of national income, and its links with employment, unemployment, investment, inflation and the effects that the government can have on them through monetary policy (controlling the supply of money to the economy and affecting interest rates) and fiscal policy (taxation and public expenditure).

The way in which the following chapters develop these themes is sequential. Several chapters explore **Keynesian** macroeconomic theory (so called after John Maynard Keynes, 1883–1946, the great Cambridge economist), showing how it develops from the microeconomic theory of previous chapters and applying it to real world phenomena. This will be sequential: the Keynesian theory of how various sectors of the economy interact is built up bit by bit. The full *model* will then be summarized, together with its policy implications. Finally, there is an examination of some of the controversies that currently exist between Keynesians and **monetarists** (the latter are so called because of their belief that too fast a growth in the supply of money is the invariable cause of inflation and monetary control its only effective cure). The Keynesian theory developed here will not be quite as Lord Keynes himself developed it but as it has developed since the Second World War.

Unfortunately not all economists agree on what Keynesian economics really is. These differences need not bother you at this stage. The important thing to get hold of is the general kind of model (which is called Keynesian in this book) that has dominated official and academic thinking about macroeconomic policy for the last 40 years and whose use as the framework for policy thinking has had an immense impact on the economic history of the post-war period in the Western world.

Two threads in the microeconomic part of this book will particularly help you to understand the Keynesian approach to the principal aggregates (national income, employment and unemployment, the price level and inflation) and to the appropriate role of government. The first of these is the idea that prices and wages are often *sticky* when there is uncertainty, when relatively few markets can be categorized as price takers' markets, and when contracts (especially employment contracts) last for long periods. This implies that output will often respond more rapidly than prices and wages to changes in demand. So Keynesian analysis emphasizes, at least in the first instance, the link between demand and *output* (and hence employment) rather than demand and *prices*.

The second thread, not unrelated to the first, is the idea of *disequilibrium* (see chapter 13), particularly in labour markets, which can lead to what was in earlier chapters called involuntary unemployment. In addition, it is useful to recall that when Keynes wrote his great book *The General Theory of Employment, Interest and Money* in 1936, *the* great economic problem was unemployment; this is still one of the great economic problems confronting us today. Because of this, and because then (but not today) inflation was not a great worry, Keynesian theory begins by assuming stable prices. Of course, that assumption will have to be abandoned later on. In the sequencing of the analysis, however, it is easier to assume that economic conditions are such that there is zero inflation. You will shortly see what kind of conditions they are.

In summary, then, the Keynesian analysis is based upon the notion that, owing to price and wage stickiness and the existence of disequilibria in the economy, the whole economy can come to be in a kind of pseudo-equilibrium in which there is unused capacity of capital and labour, which can cause great distress and political unrest, and from which there is no automatic tendency for the economy to move. Moreover the economy will tend to have severe ups and downs in economic activity (called the **business cycle**). Both of these problems can be substantially relieved by appropriate government fiscal action – as had indeed been apparent from the Fascist German rearmament programme of 1933–7 which eliminated most of Germany's earlier massive unemployment.

This immediately gave rise to a major political controversy, which is today as strong as if not stronger than ever before. If Keynesian policies required active fiscal intervention through public expenditure and public investment (which they did), this increased involvement of the government in economic affairs represented a threat to economic freedom, a threat to the use of markets in resource allocation and a threat to the private property basis of a so-called 'capitalist' economy – all anathema to economic liberals and libertarians. As you will see, in an important sense, the modern prominence of the monetarists, whose intellectual leader is Milton Friedman (born 1912), is in part due to a continuing research effort by libertarians to undermine the basis of Keynesian theory. It is no coincidence that monetarists and libertarians are often the same people, though there are important variations in opinion among them. Libertarianism and monetarism are not the same thing, as you will see, but often the same people espouse both. Although both are characteristics of 'right wing' economists, it should not need saying that they are not characteristics of Fascists. The modern economic 'right' is above all anti-collectivist and pro-individualist. It has many powerful arguments in its support. So, of course, have modern Keynesians and modern socialists (not by any means always the same people: most British post-war Conservative governments up to Mrs Thatcher's were thoroughly Keynesian).

So a third thread to be aware of consists of the *political issues* that surround the theories to be developed in the next chapters. That should add spice to the purely scientific parts of the analysis. But there is also the danger that it may cause you to prejudge what are really scientific issues of positive economics. I shall try to be fair to all parties. So should you if you are to come to terms with the genuine scientific issues that are at stake in modern macroeconomics. Try at least to suspend political judgement until you reach the end of the book.

SAQ 25.1

In the light of the foregoing, do you think that it is possible to have a positive macroeconomic theory to inform policy discussion?

The Questions of Macroeconomics

There are five principal questions addressed in macroeconomics. First, what determines the level and growth of national income or output? Following from this are other questions like: what can public policy do to raise national income, and what harm may such policies do? Second, what determines the level of unemployment or the percentage of the labour force that is unemployed? Related to this fundamental question is one about the determinants of the number of people in employment and the number seeking employment. Following from this is a set of questions about what public policy can do to reduce unemployment and what harmful side effects may result. Third, what determines the structure of interest rates in an economy and changes in it? What policies may be adopted to affect interest rates and what desirable and undesirable consequences follow? Fourth, what determines the balance of payments: the balance of transactions between a country and the rest of the world? Related to this is the question: what determines the exchange rate? Again there are secondary questions relating to the effect of public policies and their desirable and undesirable consequences. Fifth, but not least, what determines the price level and the rate at which it rises or falls (inflation and disinflation)? Secondary questions concern the harm that inflation does, policies to control it and their desirable and undesirable consequences.

Note that, in each case, the *first* question asked is 'what determines . . .?' The first task is therefore to understand why things are the way they are. As with microeconomics, this requires you to invent theories and build models that can be applied retrospectively to provide explanatory accounts of what happened in the past (macroeconomic history) and to predict what in the future will happen if . . . (public spending falls, rises etc.). The theories to be developed are theories of the behaviour of **aggregates** like the price level, national income and unemployment, rather than the theories of individual agents (producers, consumers etc.) used hitherto. But there are important links between micro and macroeconomics: one obviously wants a macroeconomic theory that is not inconsistent with the implications of microeconomic theory. The remainder of this chapter does two things: it reviews the course of British macroeconomic

Table 25.1 Some major aggregate measures since 1901

Year	*GDP (£ million)*	*RPI (% p.a.)*	*Unemployment (%)*	*Growth rate of GDP (%)*	*Consumers' expenditure (£ million)*	*Gross domestic capital formation (£ million)*
1901	2,010	0.4	3.3	3.9	1,669	207
1902	2,018	0.1	4.0	0.4	1,678	217
1903	2,018	0.2	4.7	0.0	1,685	222
1904	2,031	−0.1	6.0	0.6	1,709	210
1905	2,065	0.3	5.0	1.7	1,719	202
1906	2,111	0.0	3.6	2.2	1,749	194
1907	2,115	1.3	3.7	0.2	1,772	162
1908	2,041	0.3	7.8	−3.5	1,766	142
1909	2,108	0.6	7.7	3.3	1,774	146
1910	2,181	0.8	4.7	3.5	1,803	148
1911	2,232	0.1	3.0	2.3	1,857	141
1912	2,225	3.0	3.3	−0.3	1,869	138
1913	2,341	−0.4	2.1	5.2	1,937	157
1914	4,626	−0.3	3.3	0.8	3,560	274
1915	5,091	12.6	1.1	10.1	3,637	182
1916	5,084	18.0	0.4	−0.1	3,335	130
1917	5,109	25.3	0.6	0.5	3,074	144
1918	5,018	22.0	0.8	−1.8	3,045	143
1919	4,580	10.1	3.4	−8.7	3,485	172
1920	4,273	15.4	2.0	−6.7	3,493	295
1921	3,857	−8.6	11.3	−5.8	3,143	326
1922	3,992	−14.0	9.8	3.5	3,254	300
1923	4,115	−6.0	8.1	3.1	3,349	308
1924	4,238	−0.8	7.2	3.0	3,428	359
1925	4,449	0.4	7.9	5.0	3,508	410
1926	4,243	−0.7	8.8	−4.6	3,496	397
1927	4,539	−2.4	6.8	7.0	3,631	442
1928	4,617	0.2	7.5	1.7	3,690	438
1929	4,726	−0.9	7.3	2.4	3,765	461
1930	4,720	−2.8	11.2	−0.1	3,822	463
1931	4,480	−4.3	15.1	−5.1	3,863	454
1932	4,493	−2.6	15.6	0.3	3,839	396
1933	4,544	−2.1	14.1	1.1	3,937	409
1934	4,851	−0.1	11.9	6.8	4,051	498
1935	5,033	0.7	11.0	3.8	4,163	518
1936	5,190	0.7	9.4	3.1	4,285	565
1937	5,411	3.4	7.8	4.3	4,357	584
1938	5,572	1.5	9.3	3.0	4,392	592
1939	5,790	6.4	5.8	3.9	4,416	530
1940	6,625	16.6	3.3	14.4	3,999	460
1941	7,024	10.8	1.2	6.0	3,837	370
1942	7,094	7.2	0.5	1.0	3,796	320
1943	7,225	3.3	0.4	1.8	3,751	220
1944	6,898	2.7	0.4	−4.5	3,864	170
1945	6,471	2.9	0.5	−6.2	4,108	190
1946	6,433	3.1	1.9	−0.6	4,533	480
1947	6,278	7.1	1.4	−2.4	4,675	560

Table 25.1 Some major aggregate measures since 1901 *(Continued)*

Year	*GDP (£ million)*	*RPI (% p.a.)*	*Unemployment (%)*	*Growth rate of GDP (%)*	*Consumers' expenditure (£ million)*	*Gross domestic capital formation (£ million)*
1948	102,388	6.2	1.3	2.6	65,689	12,291
1949	105,525	3.0	1.2	3.1	66,738	13,422
1950	109,378	2.9	1.3	3.7	68,519	14,185
1951	111,834	9.0	1.1	3.6	67,621	14,301
1952	113,047	9.4	1.6	0.0	67,647	14,451
1953	118,079	3.1	1.5	4.6	70,593	16,089
1954	122,779	1.7	1.2	3.7	73,513	17,481
1955	126,975	4.6	1.0	3.6	76,620	18,493
1956	129,065	5.0	1.1	2.0	77,299	19,354
1957	131,589	3.6	1.3	1.9	78,908	20,405
1958	131,924	3.2	1.9	−0.5	80,809	20,595
1959	137,203	0.6	1.9	3.3	84,300	22,184
1960	143,564	1.1	1.5	4.6	87,541	24,180
1961	148,328	3.3	1.4	3.7	89,491	26,541
1962	149,899	4.2	1.9	0.9	91,508	26,723
1963	156,208	2.0	2.1	4.2	95,719	27,095
1964	164,380	3.2	1.5	5.3	98,636	31,581
1965	168,142	4.8	1.3	2.6	100,124	33,095
1966	171,384	3.9	1.5	2.0	101,907	33,907
1967	176,181	2.4	2.3	2.8	104,360	36,902
1968	183,574	4.8	2.5	4.5	107,273	39,191
1969	185,981	5.4	2.4	1.6	107,880	38,932
1970	190,158	6.3	2.6	2.0	110,777	39,925
1971	195,272	9.4	3.4	2.5	114,211	40,700
1972	199,836	7.3	3.7	1.4	121,204	40,594
1973	215,599	9.1	2.6	8.1	127,436	43,535
1974	213,332	16.0	2.6	−0.8	125,630	41,734
1975	211,827	24.2	3.9	−0.5	124,748	41,808
1976	220,050	16.5	5.2	3.9	125,175	42,434
1977	222,215	15.9	5.6	1.1	124,564	41,323
1978	230,290	8.3	5.5	3.0	131,373	42,938
1979	235,221	13.4	5.1	1.9	137,256	43,925
1980	230,197	18.0	6.4	−1.9	136,789	41,628
1981	227,555	11.9	10.0	−0.9	136,714	38,075
1982	231,895	8.6	11.7	1.4	138,135	40,645
1983	239,626	4.6	12.3	3.4	144,008	42,348

Notes

1 *GDP:* this is at market prices. For 1901–13 it is at 1900 prices, for 1914–47 it is at 1938 prices, and for 1948 on it is at 1980 prices.
Sources: 1901–47, Charles Feinstein (1972) *National Income, Expenditure and Output of the UK 1855–1965*, Cambridge, Cambridge University Press, table 5. Data from 1921 on exclude Southern Ireland in all series.
2 *RPI:* for 1901–47 this is the index for consumers' goods and services in Feinstein (1972), table 61. From 1948 to 1983 the source is *Economic Trends Annual Supplement*, 1983 and *Economic Trends*, September 1984, p. 42.
3 Unemployment (excluding school leavers): for 1901–65 the source is Feinstein (1972), table 57. For 1966–83 it is *Economic Trends Annual Supplement*, 1985.
4 Consumers' expenditure: for 1901–47, Feinstein (1972), table 5. For 1948 on, *Economic Trends Annual Supplement*, 1985, table 13.
5 Gross domestic capital formation: as for consumers' expenditure.
6 Growth rate: this is for *GDP* at factor cost after 1948.

history in the twentieth century, and introduces the new concepts of aggregate supply and demand. The first of these is dealt with in the next section.

SAQ 25.2

What are the five main aggregates that are studied in macroeconomics?

Historical Aggregates

Table 25.1 summarizes some major trends, and is a table to which reference will frequently be made in subsequent chapters. You should note that there are some discontinuities in it. For example, the UK prior to 1921 included Southern Ireland. Also the financial data have been expressed in constant prices: for the period up to 1913 they are in 1900 prices; for 1914–47 they are in 1938 prices; and for 1948 on they are in 1980 prices. The techniques used to eliminate inflation so that one can focus on *real* changes are discussed in chapter 32. Now study the table and see if there is anything in particular that strikes you. (Do this now.)

One thing you may have noticed is that in wartime the price index (*RPI*: see later) rises, indicating inflation, and the unemployment rate falls. As you will see later, this is something to expect when the economy approaches its maximum output capacity. Consumers' expenditure and investment (gross fixed capital formation) also tend to fall.

You may have explored the possibility of relationships between some of the data. One particularly striking relationship exists (as you will see in chapter 26) between consumption and *GDP*.

You may find it helpful to exclude the wartime data and consider four periods: 1901–13, 1922–38, 1948–69 and 1970–83. Figure 25.1 summarizes the information about inflation (percentage change in the retail prices index), unemployment and growth.

1901–13

The period running from the opening of the century to the beginning of the First World War was characterized by a stable price level (relative to other periods). Since 1949 this is measured by the retail prices index (*RPI*) (see chapter 32). This is one index of the general level of prices in the economy (you will meet another important one later in the book) and is currently based on a representative sample (currently some 150,000) of the goods and services including housing purchased by UK households. For most years in this period there was an almost negligible change in the price level. The average over the period was an inflation rate of 0.4 per cent. The relative stability of prices can easily be seen from figure 25.1, where $\dot{P}$ (read as *P* dot) shows the smallest range of any of the four periods. Unemployment was fairly high, though it was not far from the average for 1901–82, and was not as variable as in other periods. The growth rate of gross domestic product was on average very low at 1.4 per cent per year and it swung up and down quite substantially, with a

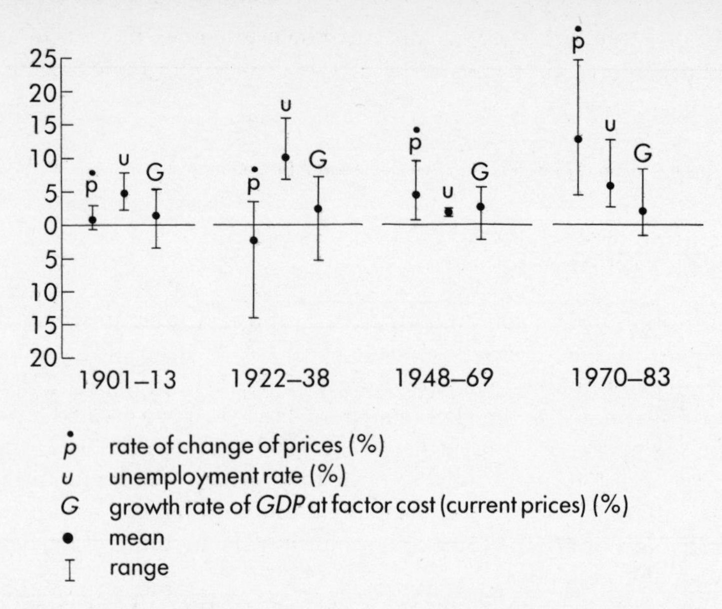

Figure 25.1 Means and ranges of three economic aggregates 1901–82.

particularly bad year in 1908. It does not have much of a relationship with the price level, however, and there seems to have been sufficient spare capacity in the economy for the output rate to have risen and fallen without affecting overall prices. Surprisingly, however, the negative relationship you might expect between growth and unemployment is not very strong, though with these early data the inaccuracies may mean that too much should not be made of this apparent anomaly.

1922–38

The next period runs from four years after the end of the First World War to the outbreak of the Second World War. Although the average growth rate was 2.3 per cent per year, it swung about enormously and was accompanied by the century's worst unemployment record (reaching a peak of 15.6 per cent in 1932) and a very unstable price level with an average of −1.8 per cent. The worst drop in prices occurred in 1922. In the first of these twentieth century periods of peace the price level was more stable than either unemployment or growth. In the second period, however, all were far more variable. Even in the depths of the great depression, when output fell by 5.1 per cent and unemployment rose to over 15 per cent, the price level fell by only about 4 per cent. For nearly all years in this period, growth above the period's average was associated with unemployment below the average and the exceptions all have rising growth associated with falling unemployment rates. In this period it also seems that a falling price level was associated with rising unemployment and vice versa.

1948–69

The third period runs from the resumption of peacetime activity after the Second World War (in which inflation rose and unemployment fell dramatically) to the advent of Edward Heath's highly expansionary government in 1970. In this period there is steady inflation, averaging 4.1 per cent per year (about the average for 1901–82) but with a couple of high years in the early 1950s. Unemployment was very low, averaging only 1.6 per cent and having a very small variation. The growth rate was well above average for 1901–82, at 2.7 per cent per year, though in the 1960s many people felt dissatisfied with the growth rate in comparison with that experienced by some other developed countries. Again, in general, growth above the period's average was associated with unemployment below it, though even the highest unemployment rate was lower than had normally previously occurred in peacetime. As in the previous period, a rising or falling price level was usually associated with a falling or rising unemployment rate. In general this post-war period showed better average attainment of these three main macroeconomic aggregates and also greater stability in each of them. A difference between the second two periods and the first period was that the price level was less stable than either growth or unemployment.

1970–83

The 1970s were a remarkable decade by any standards. The price level rose by an average of 12.1 per cent per year and was highly unstable. Unemployment was both higher on average and less stable than in 1948–69 – in fact it behaved in a similar way to unemployment between the wars. Growth was very erratic and below the average for 1901–82. Lower than average growth, or falling growth, was accompanied by rising unemployment – indeed, unemployment tended to rise steadily throughout the period. In the early part of this period there was still some tendency for a rising price level to be associated with a falling unemployment rate, but by 1975–6 inflation was associated with fairly steadily increasing unemployment. Falling or rising inflation (i.e. a falling or rising *rate of change* of the price level rather than a falling or rising price *level*) was from 1975 on usually associated with a falling or rising unemployment rate. The first years of the 1980s were noted for one of the highest rates of inflation (18.0 per cent) in the twentieth century and the largest unemployment rate (12.3 per cent) since the 1930s.

Aggregate Supply and Demand

You are already familiar with the idea that higher prices normally induce higher output rates and lower consumption rates. As mentioned earlier, however, an initial assumption is going to be that, at the aggregate level, prices are constant and that aggregate supply of goods and services responds positively to the aggregate demand for goods and services without any increase

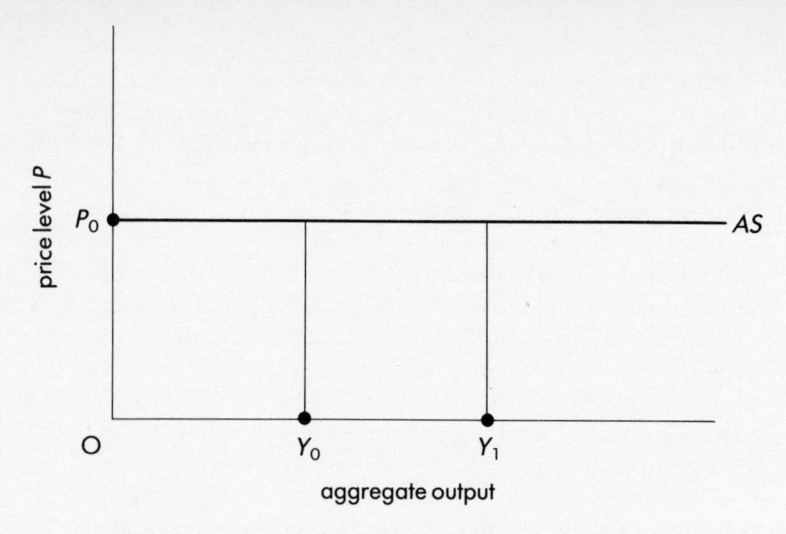

Figure 25.2 A perfectly elastic aggregate supply curve

in average prices. Some prices may rise and some fall, but on average, even when demand is on average rising, prices are constant owing to unemployed inputs, wage and price stickiness, constant marginal costs, falling marginal costs offsetting rising marginal costs, absence of profit maximizing motivation and so on.

Recall that, in microeconomic theory, with monopoly or oligopoly there is no supply curve of the firm. The aggregate supply curve does not depend upon the existence or otherwise of microeconomic supply curves. It simply shows how output responds to changes in demand and, under the assumptions made, is perfectly elastic with respect to the price level, as shown in figure 25.2. In this figure, the aggregate supply AS curve shows that output can be at either Y_0 or Y_1 without any effect on the general price level which is, it is supposed, constant at P_0 and measured by an index like the retail prices index.

SAQ 25.3

(a) Draw a diagram showing the equilibrium of a profit maximizing industry of price taking firms under constant costs. Allow the demand for the industry's output to increase at all prices (imagine this is a 'growth' industry producing an income elastic product). What happens to price?

(b) Draw a diagram showing the equilibrium of a profit maximizing price searcher under constant costs. Allow the demand for the firm's output to increase at all prices. What happens to price?

(c) You are the owner of a firm producing a prestige product whose prestige derives from the fact that there is a waiting list of customers. You are content to make a constant mark-up on your product. Suppose demand rises but average costs remain the same. Will you raise price?

The Aggregate Supply Curve

Evidently a perfectly horizontal AS curve at *all* output levels is unrealistic. Beyond a particular level of output, involuntary unemployment of labour will be very low (qualified workers who are willing to work at the going wage will increasingly be able to find work), and unused machine capacity and so on will have become utilized. The bitter fact of resource scarcity will begin to bite; producers will start to bid up input prices and will require higher prices if they are to produce more, cover costs, maximize profits and survive in a world of increasing scarcity.

The *AS* curve therefore begins to acquire a positive slope. In the longer run the slope will depend upon factors like the rate of growth of the working population relative to the rate of growth of output: the faster is the former, the less wages are likely to rise in order to ration out the available labour supply. But in the short term, over say a year or two, the stock of inputs available to the whole economy (including capital) is pretty well fixed and increased demand will need to be rationed out, leading to a tendency for input (and output) prices to rise. Some sectors will reach their full capacity sooner than others and need substantial heavy investment in plant, machinery and buildings. They will no longer be able to draw on a pool of suitably skilled but unemployed workers, having instead to train new workers – which is costly and takes time.

In the shortish run, then, prices tend to rise. In figure 25.3, up to output Y_0, prices are constant. At outputs beyond Y_0, however, prices will rise. Some industries with an oligopolistic structure may have dominant firms that act as price leaders. Their prices will be the first to rise. Others will follow. Limit prices will be gradually adjusted upwards. In other industries, as the rise in demand is perceived as permanent rather than just transitory, prices will also

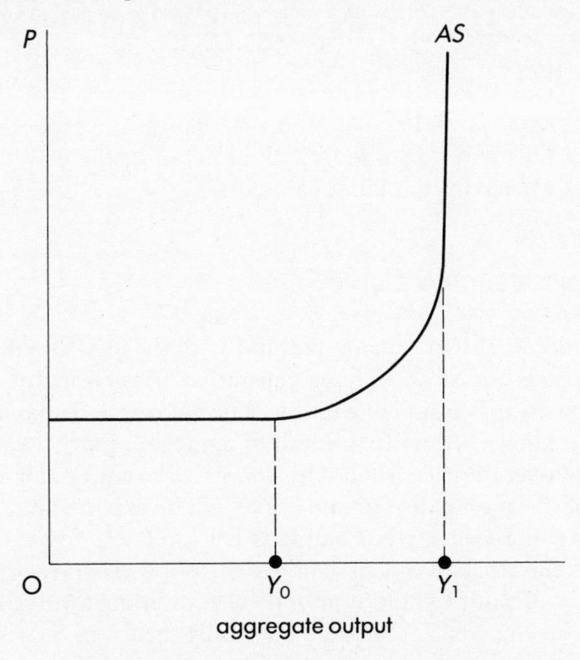

Figure 25.3 A rising aggregate supply curve

rise. New firms will be created to exploit new profit opportunities. New wage contracts will be made to retain existing workers and encourage new ones into industry.

SAQ 25.4

(a) Redo SAQ 25.3 (a), but this time with a rising marginal cost curve.
(b) Redo SAQ 25.3 (b), but this time with a rising marginal cost curve.

At Y_1, however, the economy is at its capacity. There are no unemployed resources of any kind. Further expansion is possible only in the long run vía investment in human and non-human capital and through natural growth in the labour force. The world economy tends to move in unison, so there will be limited opportunity to import further resources and in any case there are substantial natural and manmade barriers to the migration of labour and other inputs.

At Y_1 the economy is at **capacity employment**. In the long term, of course, population growth, discoveries of new raw material sources, new inventions and technological progress will enable the economy to grow, but in the short term, with these things given, output capacity has been reached. If demand rises, prices will rise in the same proportion, and the prices of inputs will similarly rise. All that happens is that the given outputs and inputs get revalued in terms of money.

SAQ 25.5

Does the perfectly inelastic section of the aggregate supply curve imply that all firms have perfectly inelastic marginal cost curves?

Much of what is to follow is concerned with the factors that determine the shape of the aggregate supply curve and where on it the economy happens to lie at any time. This will lead one to look in detail at the way the market for inputs behaves (especially the labour market).

The Aggregate Demand Curve

From microeconomic theory you are familiar with the idea that demand curves for individual goods and services have a negative price elasticity – the demand curves slope downwards from left to right. The aggregate demand curve shows the relationship between the rate of desired aggregate purchases of goods and services and the overall price level. This too has a negative slope. The precise determinants of the aggregate demand curve will be explored in detail later on. For the moment, the gist of what happens is as follows.

Suppose that the stock of money held by the public is given and that at any time the public will want to hold *some* of its wealth in the form of money rather than trade it all for goods. If the price level falls then it is clear that, with the amount of money that they hold, the public can buy more than hitherto. You know also from microeconomics that when any relative price falls more will be bought. Suppose that when the price level falls, all prices fall by the same proportion. There is no change in *relative* prices, so there will be no change in the demand for any particular good or service. Right? No, alas, it is wrong. And the reason why it is wrong is easy to miss but crucially important never to forget: one very important commodity, money itself, has not been considered. Even if a falling (or rising) price level keeps the relativities between all goods and services constant, the relative price of money itself is *not* constant. (Of course, the relativities between goods and services never do really remain constant and so there will be some substitution of purchases between them. It is helpful to abstract from these phenomena to look at something more crucial for aggregate demand *as a whole*.)

Suppose, then, that the price level falls. This implies that a pound of money will now buy more. *A pound has become relatively expensive to hold as money rather than to exchange for goods*. The demand for money, therefore, will fall and the demand for all other goods and services will in aggregate rise. Exactly the opposite holds true for a rise in the price level. With a given stock of money available, a rise in the price level means that goods and services become relatively more expensive than money, or money becomes relatively cheap. Therefore money is substituted for goods and aggregate demand falls.

The aggregate demand (*AD*) curve is shown in figure 25.4.

One of the tricky features of this analysis is that it deals with the relationship between a *stock* (the amount of money held by the public) and a *flow* (desired purchases of goods and services per period). The distinction between stocks and flows, and how they interact, is important in macroeconomics and will be met several times in what is to come. Note also that interest rates have not

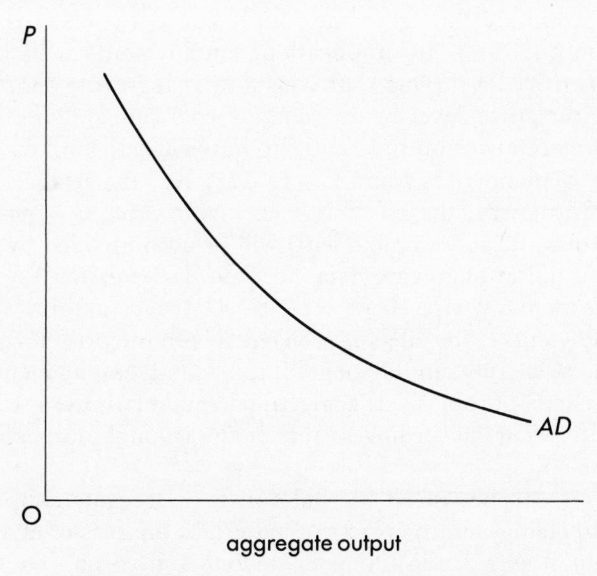

Figure 25.4 The aggregate demand curve

been mentioned. Many people naturally think of 'dear money' as money that can be borrowed only at high interest rates, and 'cheap money' as the contrary case. Interest rates do, indeed, play an important role in the determination of aggregate demand and will be investigated in detail later. For the moment, however, the main point to be made in this section has been established: the aggregate demand curves slope downwards for the same reason as do micro-economic demand curves. At lower price levels goods are cheap *relative to holding money* and at higher price levels goods are dear *relative to holding money*.

SAQ 25.6

Suppose the stock of money in the community is fixed and the economy is producing all it can given available resources. Suppose also that the amount of money that people hold on average in a period is a fixed percentage of money income, and the price level doubles. Since the money earned by producers of goods and services all becomes *someone's* income, money incomes will also double. But they can't, because the available stock of money is fixed. With a fixed total stock of money, total expenditure is also fixed. But the price level has doubled.

(a) What happens to the amount of output demanded?
(b) What does the aggregate demand curve look like if the money stock is fixed and the demand for money is a fixed percentage of money income?
(c) What is the elasticity of aggregate demand with respect to the price level?

Interaction of Aggregate Supply and Demand

You can now put the aggregate demand and supply curves together to see how they interact in this fundamental macroeconomic model of the economy. This is done in figure 25.5. Here you see three pairs of aggregate demand curves and one aggregate supply curve. If aggregate demand rises from AD_1 to AD_1^* over the first section of the aggregate supply curve, the effect is seen entirely in terms of output (and, by implication, employment), which will rise in proportion, the price level remaining constant. If aggregate demand falls from AD_1^* to AD_1, the price level again remains constant and the effect is seen entirely in terms of lower output (and, by implication, employment).

If aggregate demand rises from AD_2 to AD_2^* over the second section of the aggregate supply curve, the effect is seen in the price level *and* the rate of output: rising output (and employment) will be accompanied by inflation and vice versa for a fall in aggregate demand from AD_2^* to AD_2.

If aggregate demand rises from AD_3 to AD_3^* over a third section of the aggregate supply curve, the effect is seen entirely in the price level, which rises in proportion, with full employment output (and employment) remaining constant at capacity output Y_C. If aggregate demand falls from AD_3^* to AD_3 the precise opposite occurs according to this model (though not, as you will later see, in practice).

Similar effects can be traced for shifts in the aggregate supply curve that are due, say, to changes in the prices of materials, imports or changes in legislated minimum wages, trade union behaviour and so on. These will all be investigated later in the book.

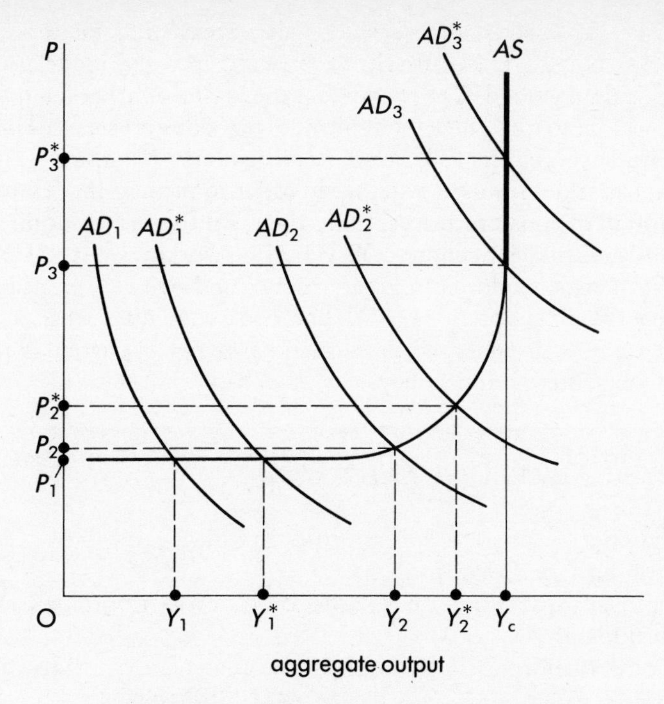

Figure 25.5 Aggregate supply and demand

You will see from the aggregate supply and demand model that the response of the price level, output and employment to changes in aggregate demand depends very much on the slope (and stability) of the aggregate supply curve. These issues will be explored in depth later on. The next few chapters, however, are going to assume that changes in aggregate demand do not affect the price level at all. This is very much in the spirit of early Keynesian analysis developed, as you have seen, in the period of high unemployment before the Second World War. The Keynesian view also dominated post-war macroeconomic policy in Britain and elsewhere until the late 1960s. The Keynesian approach, then, rests on the assumption that output and employment react much more than prices to changes in aggregate demand and that the economy is on the flat part of the aggregate supply curve, to the left of Y_2 in figure 25.5. It will be recalled from earlier in this chapter that the period before the First World War seems to fit this assumption best. In the other periods the price level was more volatile than unemployment and growth though, save for the inter-war period, it seems to have been more volatile upwards than downwards (the mean is lower than the midpoint of the range).

When one comes to consider inflation, however, the assumption that the *AS* curve is perfectly elastic will no longer do. It will then be dropped in order to tackle the problems of explaining phenomena and devising acceptable policies in an inflationary economy. Prior to that the idea will be developed that, with a constant price level, demand is mainly determined by income, and a model of the market for goods and services will be explored on this assumption (chapter 26). The government will be brought into the model (chapter 27). The model is then extended to encompass the labour market (chapter 28). The next stage will be to introduce foreign trade in goods and services (chapter 29); then investment (chapter 30); and finally money (chapter 31). All these components are then brought together in order to present the full model under the assumption of constant prices. Only then will that assumption be dropped as inflation is discussed (chapters 32, 33). The workings of the UK monetary system will then be explored in greater detail and overseas transactions more fully incorporated (chapters 34, 35). The book concludes with an analysis of 'where we are now' in macroeconomics and a review of current controversy in macroeconomic theory and policy.

What You Should Understand Now

Why political interest in macroeconomic problems does not preclude their positive analysis.
The five main questions addressed by macroeconomics (and some related questions).
The broad pattern of UK macroeconomic history in the twentieth century.
Three possible shapes of (or sections of) the aggregate supply curve and their underlying determinants.
Why the aggregate demand curve has a negative slope.
The provisional assumption, to underlie the next few chapters, of a constant price level.

26

The Basic Keynesian Macroeconomic Model

Expenditure Identities

You saw in chapter 24 that national income must, by definition, be equal to all aggregated expenditures. This follows from the simple arithmetic that tells you that what one person spends in the form of expenditure, another receives in the form of income. Suppose that aggregate expenditure is divided into two basic types, consumption and investment, the distinction being based on the theory (which has yet to be developed) that the determinants of one are rather different from the determinants of the other. Investment includes expenditures on plant, machinery, new housing and the building up (or running down) of stocks of goods (running stocks down is, of course, *dis*investment). You can now write the simple identity:

$$E_A \equiv C_A + I_A$$

which simply says that actual consumption expenditure C_A plus actual investment expenditure I_A is equal by definition ($\equiv$: identity sign) to actual aggregate expenditure E_A.

The income received by individuals may be taxed. What is left over can be spent on consumption or saved. For the moment assume no government and so no taxes. So you can also write that

$$Y \equiv C_A + S_A$$

which simply says that actual consumption and actual savings S_A will add up to money income Y (since there is nothing else one can do with one's income). You know that actual aggregate expenditure must be equal to national income, or

$$E_A \equiv Y$$

Therefore you can say that

$$Y \equiv C_A + I_A$$

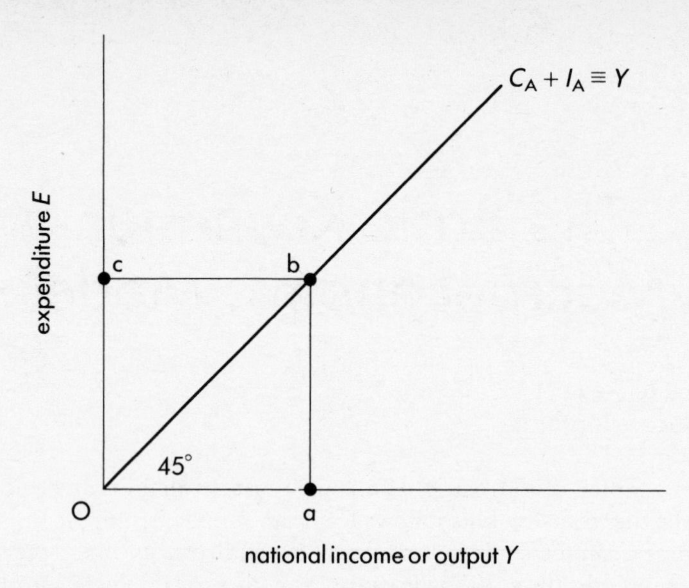

Figure 26.1 Identity between actual expenditure and actual income

This relationship can be put on a diagram that looks very trivial but that has an important role to play in the development of the Keynesian model (figure 26.1). The 45° line simply joins all those values for aggregate expenditure that are equal to national income, so ab = bc = Oa = Oc.

Now the actual expenditures made may or may not be those that people really intended or planned to make. Assume that decision makers would never in aggregate plan to do the impossible (for example spend more than their incomes plus past savings), and suppose that the sum of *planned* consumption C_P and *planned* saving S_P will be equal to whatever income they have over a period. Write this as

$$Y = C_P + S_P$$

Assuming that planned consumption (and hence planned savings) are always actually carried out, you have

$$C_P = C_A \text{ and } S_P = S_A$$

Even if planned consumption is larger than money income, provided that people plan for negative saving (drawing on past savings), they can actually realize their plans.

However, there is no particular reason why actual investment should be equal to planned investment. For example, if the level of consumer demand happens to be higher than shops expected, they may run down their stocks faster than expected, so in addition to their planned investments in stocks they may have unplanned disinvestments in stocks. The same thing goes in reverse:

if demand is lower than sellers expected, their stocks will increase faster than planned and there will be unplanned investment in stocks. Consequently, actual investment equals planned investment I_P plus unplanned investment I_U:

$$I_A \equiv I_P + I_U$$

Aggregate planned expenditure E_P is the sum of planned consumption and planned investment:

$$E_P \equiv C_P + I_P$$

and actual aggregate expenditure E_A is given by

$$E_A \equiv C_P + I_A \equiv C_P + I_P + I_U$$

(remember the assumption that $C_P = C_A$).

Consumption and Investment Functions

So far the analysis has dealt with *definitions* which must be true; Hence the continual use of the identity sign ($\equiv$) save for when $=$ was used to indicate an *assumed* equality. Now ask what determines planned consumption (and, by implication, planned saving) and planned investment. This is where the model building really starts. Begin by assuming that consumption expenditure is a rising function of income and that investment expenditure has a zero income elasticity (it depends on other things like the rate of interest and profit expectations that are not yet in the model but will be brought in later).

Specifically, assume that planned consumption and income are related linearly by an equation such as

$$C_P = C_0 + cY$$

You will recall from earlier chapters that this is a simple linear equation. C_0 is a constant showing the amount of planned consumption when (hypothetically) aggregate income is zero. c shows the increase in planned consumption that each additional unit of income will induce; c is termed the **marginal propensity to consume**. The equation for C_P also has a technical name: it is a **consumption function**. Do not take the linear relationship as realistic for all (especially very low) levels of income. The linear relationship is merely a reasonable approximation over the range of incomes commonly observed.

SAQ 26.1

Given the data in table 26.1:

Table 26.1 Data for SAQ 26.1

Y	C	ΔC	$\Delta C/\Delta Y$	C/Y
0	50			
10	58			
20	66			
30	74			
40	82			
50	90			
60	98			
70	106			
80	114			
90	122			
100	130			

(a) Fill in the remainder of the table. Note that Y is income, C is consumption (C is change in consumption, (C/(Y is the ratio of the change in consumption to the change in income (which is another way of describing the marginal propensity to consume), and C/Y is the ratio of consumption to income (termed the **average propensity to consume**).

(b) The first two columns are related by an equation of the form $C = C_0 + cY$. What are the values for C_0 and c?
Hint: C_0 is consumption that is independent of income, i.e. consumption even when income is zero. c is the marginal propensity to consume, or $\Delta C/\Delta Y$.

(c) What is the general relationship between the average and the marginal propensity to consume?

Since planned investment is independent of income, you can write:

$$I_P = I_0$$

where I_0 remains the same regardless of changes in national income. I_0 is planned investment when income is zero.

Note that identity signs are no longer being used. Instead equals signs (=) are used to indicate that these are *behavioural functions* or *equations*, not identities. They are telling you how plans change in response to changes in an independent variable, income.

You can plot these planned expenditure functions on a diagram in much the same way as the 45° line identity was plotted. This is done in figure 26.2. In this figure, the investment function is simply a straight horizontal line set at a height of I_0 and the consumption function is the rising straight line with intercept on the expenditure axis of C_0 and a slope ($\Delta C/\Delta Y$) equal to the marginal propensity to consume. The E_P line is the vertical sum of the two functions and indicates total planned expenditure at each level of income. Its intercept is $C_0 + I_0$ and its slope is the same as that of the consumption function.

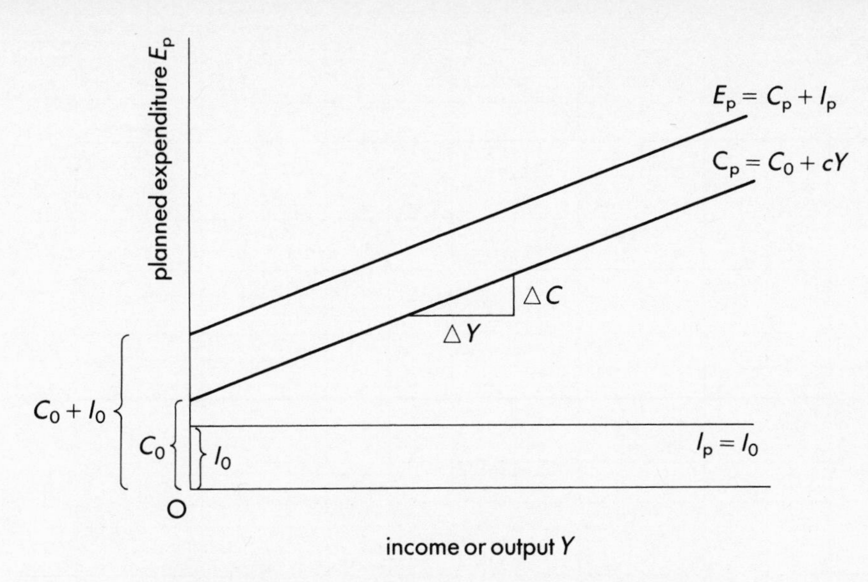

Figure 26.2 Aggregate planned expenditure functions

Case Study 26.1 A Consumption Function in the UK, 1900–13

You saw how consumption, investment and *GDP* behaved in the first of the four periods considered in chapter 25. Investment is taken as excluding stocks, since this includes unplanned investment which may be expected anyway to bear no simple relationship to *GDP*. However, even planned investment in fixed capital was exceedingly erratic over the period and, whatever did determine it, it did not appear to have been current *GDP*.

Consumption, by contrast, was systematically related to *GDP* and is quite well approximated by the linear consumption function:

$$C = 181 + 0.75Y$$

This is, of course, an oversimplification. For one thing, consumption (as you will see later) is more closely related to *disposable* income (income after direct taxes) than total income. For another, consumption is also a function of other things, for example, the previous period's consumption (reflecting the possibility that people's consumption is partly habitual) and wealth. None the less, this will do at least as a first approximation and indicates that the theory is not wildly at odds with the facts.

SAQ 26.2

(a) On figure 26.3, plot investment and consumption using the data for 1900–13 in table 25.1.

(b) Which seems to be related to *GDP*?

(c) Draw a straight line through the consumption points that best seems to 'fit' the data and judge its intercept C_0 and slope c. (If you have learned how to calculate a regression equation in statistics you will be able to make an accurate judgement.)

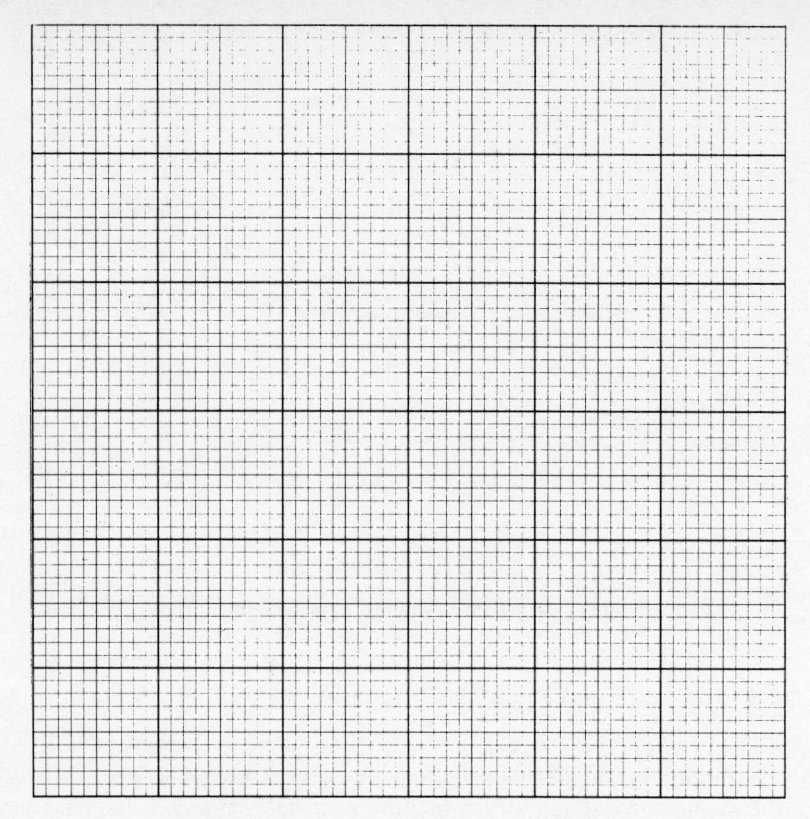

Figure 26.3 Graph paper for SAQ 26.2

Macroeconomic Equilibrium

If you put figures 26.1 and 26.2 together you obtain a figure popularly known as the 'Keynesian cross' (though Keynes himself never actually drew it). This is shown in figure 26.4.

Suppose that national income were Y_1. Planned (and actual) consumption will be Y_1a. Planned investment will be Y_1b (= ad). Planned aggregate expenditure will be these two added togehter: Y_1d. Actual investment will be ad − fd; ad is planned investment and, to meet the level of consumption and investment, there will be an unplanned running down of stocks of consumption and investment goods to the value of fd. The output of the economy is Y_1f (= OY_1) and the difference between this and planned expenditure (Y_1d) is fd, which is met out of stocks.

If planned expenditure were equal to income, the economy would be at point f. Planned expenditure is larger than this, however. Signals will be passed back to profit maximizing producers to produce more to replace depleted stocks at a faster rate than expected and perhaps to meet revised expectations about the level of planned expenditure, and output – and incomes

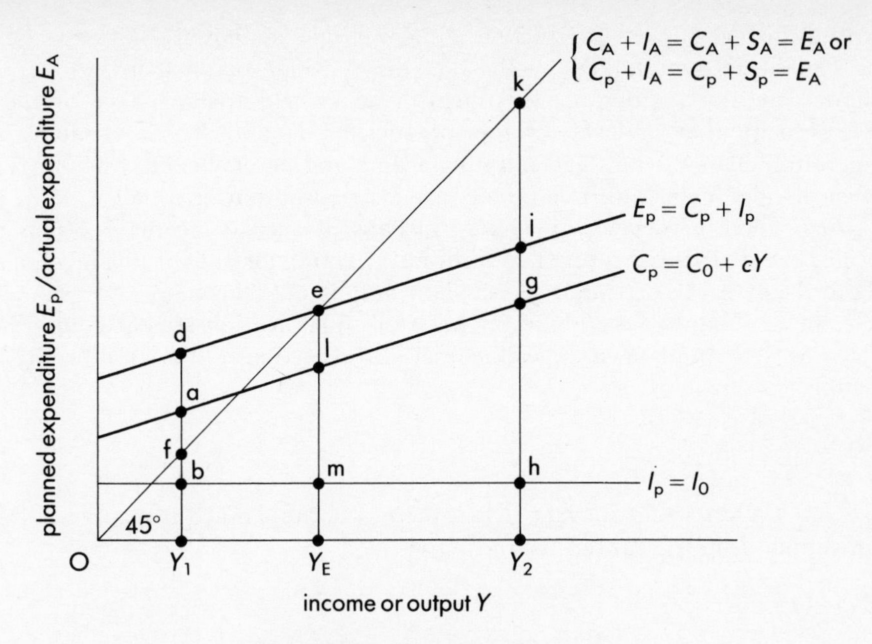

Figure 26.4 The Keynesian cross

– will grow so the economy moves from Y_1 in the direction of Y_E. This is possible because of the assumed existence of unused reserves of machines, labour and so on, with planned expenditure larger than actual income. Under these circumstances output (and employment) rises (with prices constant). You will note that the slope of the consumption function appears to be much smaller than it was found to be in case study 26.2. This is so as to present the figure clearly.

Now suppose instead that national income were Y_2. Planned (and actual) consumption will be Y_2g. Planned investment will be Y_2h (= gj). Planned aggregate expenditure will be these two added together: Y_2j. Actual investment will be gj + jk. gj is planned and jk is unplanned investment in stocks of produced goods (that generated income Y_2) that cannot be sold because of deficient planned expenditure. Accumulating stocks are signals to profit maximizing producers to reduce their rates of output, so output – and incomes – will fall and the economy will contract towards Y_E.

Y_E is obviously a rather special level of income and will be investigated presently. Before doing so, first check the way in which the working of the model related to the accounting identities discussed earlier.

Look at Y_1. Recall the identity:

$$E_A \equiv C_P + I_P + I_U$$

At Y_1, $C_P = Y_1$a, $I_p =$ ad and $I_U =$ fd. The last is a negative amount, and adding them together, you get the distance Y_f (Y_1a + ad − fd). Thus actual expenditure on current production equals output, as it must. The accounting equality is maintained by the fact that positive planned investment is counteracted by a strong disinvestment in stocks held at shops, factories etc.

It is plain that at levels of income such as Y_1 and Y_2 the economy is generating changes that lead output, income and employment either to rise when planned expenditure is larger than current output or to fall when it is smaller. These tendencies for change are absent only at income Y_E. This is termed the **equilibrium level of national income**, for only at this income is planned aggregate expenditure equal to output (and income) and planned investment equal to actual investment. At Y_E, planned investment Y_Em = le. There is zero unplanned investment or disinvestment. The equilibrium is written

$$Y = C_P + I_P$$

or, since $C_P = C_A$ and $I_P = I_A$ (when there is no unplanned investment) you can simply drop the subscripts and write

$$Y = C + I$$

Read this as: equilibrium exists when output equals planned expenditure (*on final goods and services*: in this case including only consumption and investment goods). Now tackle SAQ 26.3, which will introduce you to an important new concept: the *reduced form* of the Keynesian model.

SAQ 26.3

The *equilibrium* of a simple economy is given by

$$Y = C + I$$

In addition, there are two behavioural functions:

$$C = C_0 + cY \text{ and } I = I_0$$

This is the simple version of the Keynesian model.
An easy algebraic way of computing the equilibrium level of national income is to substitute the behavioural equations into the equilibrium condition:

$$Y = C_0 + cY + I_0$$

With some rearrangements of this equation, you will get:

$$Y - cY = C_0 + I_0$$
$$Y(1-c) = C_0 + I_0$$
$$Y = (C_0 + I_0)\frac{1}{1-c}$$

The last equation is known as the **reduced form** of the simple Keynesian model. Given the variables C_0, I_0 and c, which are determined outside the model and just taken as given, it can be used to compute equilibrium *GDP*.

(a) Given $C = 10 + 0.6Y$ and $I = 15$, calculate equilibrium Y using the reduced form.
(b) If I rises to 20, what happens to Y?
(c) If I falls to 5, what happens to Y?

Case Study 26.2 Rival Theories of the Consumption Function

As in many other spheres of economic theory, there are rival hypotheses about the behaviour of consumption. If you pursue your economics you will come across several such theories later and will have to use your judgement in discriminating between them – as you did about the macroeconomic theory of demand. This case study briefly describes three theories other than that given in the text.

The *relative income hypothesis* was developed by James Duesenberry (1952), and hypothesizes that current consumption is determined by one's position in the income distribution and by past income. It reflects on the one hand a 'keeping up with the Joneses' effect and, on the other, a 'customary' or 'habitual' effect.

The *permanent income hypothesis* was developed by Milton Friedman (1957) and hypothesizes that current consumption is a function of *permanent income*. Permanent annual income is similar to the annual annuity whose present value is equal to the sum of a person's physical and human capital. Although actual income may depart from this owing to transitory elements, this theory asserts that such transitory income will not affect consumption in the long run (see answer to SAQ 26.2).

The *life cycle hypothesis* is due to Franco Modigliani (summarized in his 1975 paper) and asserts that consumption depends upon where one is in the life cycle. Young adults will tend to consume more out of income as they raise their families, whereas the middle aged will consume a smaller fraction of their (usually higher) incomes and retired people will consume a high fraction of their (usually lower) incomes. So the age distribution becomes an important determinant of consumption.

James Duesenberry (1952) *Income, Savings and the Theory of Consumer Behavior*, Cambridge, Mass, Harvard University Press.
Milton Friedman (1957) *A Theory of the Consumption Function*, Princeton, Princeton University Press.
Franco Modigliani (1975) 'The life cycle hypothesis of saving twenty-five years on', in Michael Parkin and A. R. Nobay (eds) *Contemporary Issues in Economics*, Manchester, Manchester University Press, 2–36.

The equilibrium at Y_E is a central ingredient of Keynesian analysis. It has two important insights to offer into the way the economy works and, by implication, for policy:

(1) There is no reason for the economy to settle at an equilibrium, from which there is no automatic tendency to move generated within the economy itself, and at which there is also no involuntary employment. Since, as you saw earlier, the flat section of the aggregate supply curve is particularly applicable under stable prices and not very low unemployment such as obtained in the early years of the twentieth century, the Keynesian analysis is especially applicable then. It suggests that the economy may get 'stuck' at a less than full employment level of income and it will remain there unless aggregate expenditure can somehow be increased. This will not, however, happen automatically. The door was opened for an active

role for government to raise aggregate expenditure to levels higher than private decisions determine – for example, by transferring income from individuals with a low to those with a high propensity to consume (essentially from richer to poorer), or by raising government expenditure (in the simple model from zero to a positive amount).

(2) Independent shifts in the expenditure functions (particularly in the investment function, though in principle also in the consumption function) will have a magnified impact on output, incomes and employment. This is a source of instability in the economy unless means can be found to introduce more stable components into the aggregate expenditure function – for example, by shifting investment decisions from the private sector more into the public sector. You can see the political implications of each of these inferences from the model.

Stability in the Economy and the Multiplier

A magnified effect of changes in autonomous entrepreneurial decisions about investment on national income and employment can easily be seen from the Keynesian cross. Suppose the economy is initially in a less than full employment equilibrium at Y_E in figure 26.5. Suppose planned investment increases by ΔI_0 so that the planned expenditure function rises from E_P to E'_P. A new equilibrium will be established at Y'_E (which may still fall short of the full employment level). The change in investment ΔI_0 has created a change in

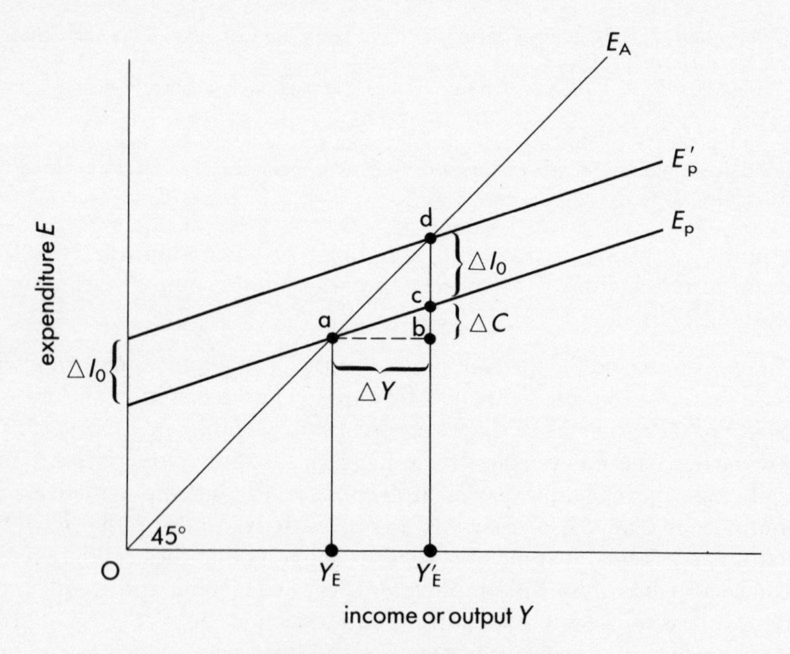

Figure 26.5 The multiplier

income ΔY that is *larger*: $\Delta Y/\Delta I_0 > 1$. This ratio, $\Delta Y/\Delta I_0$ (the change in income divided by the change in investment that caused it) is termed the **multiplier**. It bears a close relationship to the marginal propensity to consume (c or $\Delta C/\Delta Y$).

Look again at figure 26.5. The distance ab (equal to ΔY) is the same as bd because the slope of the 45° line is +1.0. Therefore bd also equals ΔY. bd can be divided into the distance cd (ΔI_0, the autonomous change in investment) and the distance bc ((C, the change in consumption induced by the higher income). So:

$$\Delta Y = \Delta I_0 + \Delta C$$

Divide both sides of this equation by ΔY to get

$$1 = \frac{\Delta I_0}{\Delta Y} + \frac{\Delta C}{\Delta Y}$$

Rearrange to get

$$1 - \frac{\Delta C}{\Delta Y} = \frac{\Delta I_0}{\Delta Y}$$

Now note that $\Delta C/\Delta Y$ is c, the marginal propensity to consume. You can therefore write:

$$1 - c = \frac{\Delta I_0}{\Delta Y}$$

or, turning it all upside down:

$$\frac{\Delta Y}{\Delta I_0} = \frac{1}{1-c}$$

The multiplier is thus the reciprocal of unity minus the marginal propensity to consume. Since $c < 1$ it follows that the multiplier must be greater than unity. *So a rise or fall in investment of a given magnitude will create a multiplied effect on output and income.*

SAQ 26.4

The reduced form of the simple Keynesian model is

$$Y = (C_0 + I_0)\frac{1}{1-c}$$

From this, changes in the autonomous components of planned expenditure (C_0 and I_0) imply

$$(\Delta Y = (\Delta C_0 + \Delta I_0) \frac{1}{1 - c}$$

So, for a change in planned investment alone,

$$\Delta Y = \Delta I_0 \frac{1}{1-c}$$

Dividing both sides by ΔI_0,

$$\frac{\Delta Y}{\Delta I_0} = \frac{1}{1-c}$$

which is the same result for the multiplier that was obtained geometrically in the text.

(a) Using the reduced form, calculate the multiplier for the following economies:
$I = 10$, $C = 5 + 0.5Y$
$I = 15$, $C = 10 + 0.8Y$
$I = 5$, $C = 15 + 0.6Y$

(b) Which economy is the potentially least stable, and which the most?

The political implications of the Keynesian analysis are thus clear: a capitalist economy may get stuck at less than full employment and will also tend to be unstable. The remedy is clear (or so it seems): there must be more public expenditure (or lower taxation) and more stable (public) investment and other expenditures – or even counterbalancing adjustments of the public element to offset the vagaries of the private. More socialism, then, seemed to be the answer. Of course, the question remains whether the government itself may operate a destabilizing policy, for example by getting its timing wrong. Moreover, increased public borrowing and taxation may also have disadvantageous effects. Of these, more anon.

SAQ 26.5

Given the consumption function

$$C = C_0 + cY$$

and the equation that says that income must be either consumed or saved, i.e.

$$Y \equiv C + S$$

(a) What is the general form of the savings function?

(b) (Do not tackle this part until you are clear about the answer to (a).) Given $C = 10 + 0.8Y$, what is the level of savings at the following levels of national income: $Y = 10, 50, 100$?

Equilibrium in Terms of Injections and Withdrawals to and from the Circular Flow

It is often useful to look at national income determination in terms of savings and investment instead of aggregate expenditure and aggregate output. Since

$$S \equiv Y - C$$

(that is, planned savings are income less planned consumption) you can, instead of using the equilibrium condition

$$Y = C + I$$

rearrange it to make

$$Y - C = I$$

and then substitute the identity to get

$$S = I$$

as an alternative way of stating the equilibrium condition. The algebra of these two alternative ways of finding the equilibrium is set out below:

Aggregate expenditure and output approach

Behavioural equations:

$C = C_0 + cY$ (consumption function)
$I = I_0$ (investment function)

Equilibrium condition:

$$Y = C + I$$

Reduced form:

$$Y = (C_0 + I_0)\ \frac{1}{1-c}$$

Injections and withdrawals approach

Behavioural equations:

$S = S_0 + sY$ (savings function)
$I = I_0$ (investment function)

Equilibrium condition:

$$I = S$$

Reduced form:

$$Y = (-\ S_0 + I_0)\ \frac{1}{s}$$

You are familiar with the aggregate expenditure and output approach. The injections and withdrawals approach proceeds in exactly the same way. $S = S_0 + sY$ is the saving function, where S_0 is the intercept and s is the marginal propensity to save. You have already derived the relation between the savings and consumption functions in SAQ 26.5. The investment function is as before. The equilibrium condition requires that injections into the circular flow of income (like investment) be equal to withdrawals from it (like savings) – hence the term for the approach. The reduced form is similar to that for the aggregate expenditure approach since $S_0 = -\ C_0$ and $s = 1-c$. The multiplier is therefore the same as the reciprocal of the marginal propensity to save.

This can be shown on a Keynesian cross diagram as in figure 26.6. To see this recall the consumption function $C = C_0 + cY$ and the savings function $S = S_0 + sY$. Since $Y \equiv C + S$, you can write $Y \equiv C_0 + cY + S_0 + sY$. Since $-\ C_0 = S_0$, this implies that $Y \equiv cY + sY$ so, dividing through by Y gives $1 \equiv c + s$, or $1 - c \equiv s$.

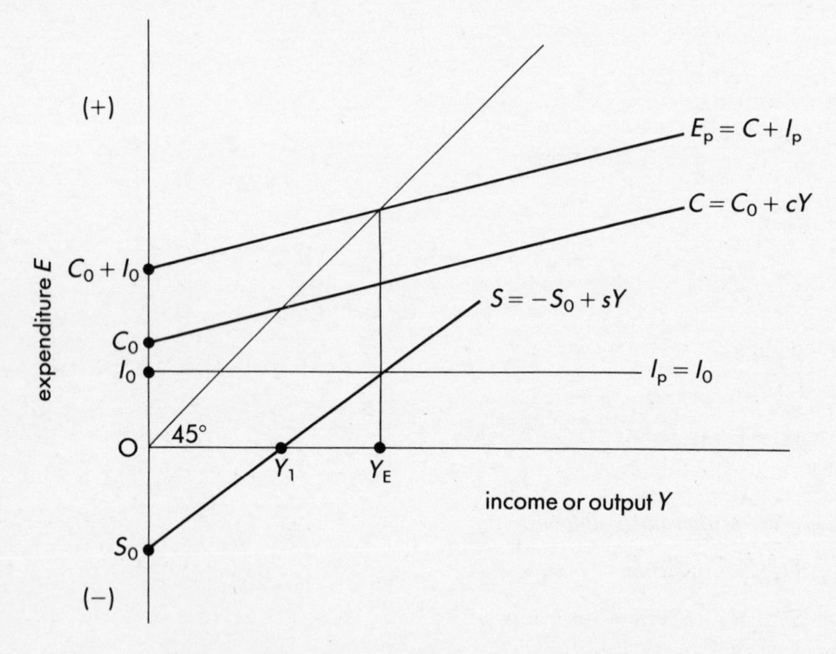

Figure 26.6 The consumption and savings functions

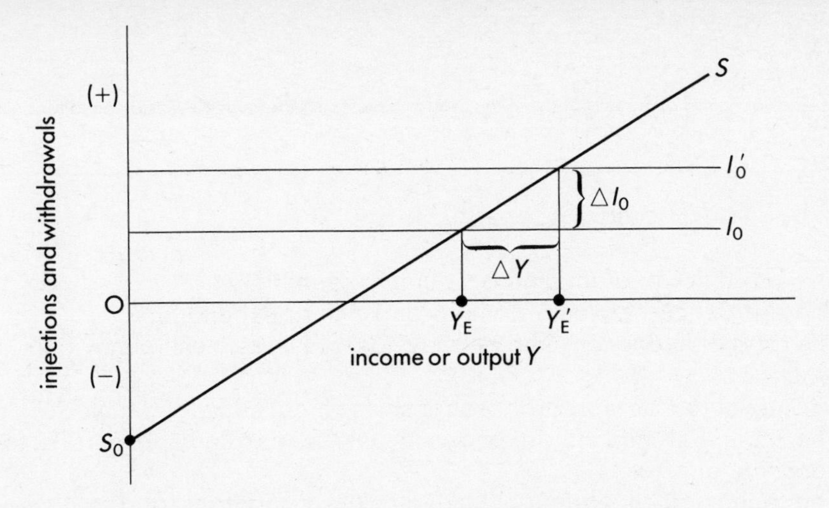

Figure 26.7 Injections and withdrawals equilbrium

SAQ 26.6

From the behavioural equations for savings and investment, and the equilibrium condition $I = S$, derive the reduced form using the injections and withdrawals approach.

Figure 26.7 shows the effect of a shift in the investment function. An increase in investment from I_0 to I'_0 raises equilibrium income from Y_E to Y'_E. As before, ΔY is larger than ΔI_0 because of the multiplier. Note that the slope of the savings function is $\Delta S/\Delta Y$ – the marginal propensity to save s. This slope, as can be seen from figure 26.7, is equal to $\Delta I_0/\Delta Y$. Therefore, in a move from one equilibrium to another,

$$\frac{\Delta I_0}{\Delta Y} = s$$

or

$$\frac{\Delta Y}{\Delta I_0} = \frac{1}{s}$$

This only goes to show what you know already: that the multiplier ($\Delta Y/\Delta I_0$) is the reciprocal of the marginal propensity to save ($1/s$), or $1/(1-c)$.

SAQ 26.7

Given $S = -23 + 0.3Y$ and $I = 10$, use the injections and withdrawals approach to calculate:

(a) Equilibrium income
(b) The multiplier
(c) The change in income if investment falls by 5, rises by 5, rises by 10.

SAQ 26.8

Three kinds of notion of 'equality' have been used in developing the basic Keynesian equations. What are they, and how do they differ from one another?

What You Should Understand Now

The basic national income accounting identities.
The difference between planned and actual expenditures.
The form of linear consumption, savings and investment (behavioural) functions.
The definition of marginal propensities to consume and save.
The multiplier and its dependence on the marginal propensity to consume or save.
The behavioural equations, equilibrium conditions and reduced forms of the two versions of the basic Keynesian model (aggregate expenditure and output, injections and withdrawals).
The construction and interpretation of the Keynesian cross.
The reasons why an economy may be unstable and may also get 'stuck' at a less than full employment equilibrium national income.

27

The Keynesian Model with Government

You are familiar with the inherent controversy about the political implications of the Keynesian model. The positive economics of the Keynesian model does not, of course, contain any political or social value judgements. The politics come in when to the purely scientific content of the model one adds value judgements of the sort: 'It is a good thing for the government to use its taxing and spending power to raise the equilibrium level of national income, reduce involuntary unemployment and level out the ups and downs of the economy.' The model itself predicts that these things *can* be done. It does not say that they *ought* to be done. That requires additional assumptions – and they are clearly value judgements. One aspect of the value judgements involved obviously (and not very controversially) identifies higher income, lower unemployment and greater stability as inherently good things. Another (much more controversial) asserts that these good things are still desirable even if it means (which it does not *necessarily* mean) 'bigger' government with its associated threat to individual freedom (a matter of concern particularly to liberals and libertarians). On the political left a relevant value judgement is that such macroeconomic policies may shore up a still essentially capitalist society and postpone a socialist revolution so that, even though the objectives are themselves desirable, there are other longer term desirable objectives with which they conflict.

There is also controversy about *means*. For example, the so-called **supply side economists** might accept the desirability of the macroeconomic objectives just described but argue that there are other ways of raising incomes and lowering unemployment – for example, by attacking monopoly in production and the restrictive practices of trade unions, reducing income tax rates to liberate the entrepreneurial spirit and so on. These other means, so the argument goes, conflict less with libertarian principles and are therefore preferable. You have already read some potential 'supply side' effects of this sort (recall case studies 14.1 on the losses from monopoly, 15.4 on the losses from oligopoly and 17.1 on the disincentive effects of taxes). There is doubt, however, as to the extent of the gains that can be realistically expected, particularly in the short term, from such policies. Moreover, they may also clash with other moral objectives: some restrictive practices may reduce incomes in total but also enhance job protection (at least for those in jobs) and preserve traditional ways of life. These cannot be dismissed out of hand as unworthy objects because large numbers of people clearly regard them as very desirable. You must therefore reach a judgement by balancing the various pros and cons. This has to be done at two levels. One is political, involving value judgements about what you think makes for a good society. The other is scientific and concerns the effectiveness of various policies in affecting the main aggregates in which one is interested.

This chapter focuses on the scientific task of introducing public expenditure and taxation into the model in order to show their impact on income (or output) and employment. In recent times, public expenditure on goods and services has averaged about 28 per cent of *GDP*.

Table 27.1 Public expenditure and *GDP* in the UK, 1960–83 (£ in current prices)

	1 GDP *at factor cost*	*2* *General government expenditure on final goods and services*	*3*	*4*	*5* *Current grants in subsidies (including debt interest)*	*6* *4/1 (%)*	*7* *5/1 (%)*
		Final consumption	*Gross fixed capital formation*	*Total*			
1960	22,822	4,224	860	5,084	3,263	22.3	14.3
1970	43,836	8,991	2431	11,422	8,212	26.1	18.7
1980	196,642	48,387	5742	54,129	46,201	27.5	23.5
1981	215,328	54,677	4612	59,289	54,407	27.5	25.3
1982	233,996	59,871	4713	64,584	60,805	27.6	26.0
1983	256,780	65,635	5816	71,451	66,194	27.8	25.8

Sources: 1950–70: *Economic Trends*, Annual Supplement, 1984, tables 8, 48 and 162
1980–83: *Economic Trends*, August 1984, tables 14 and 56

Table 27.1 shows how the aggregates have moved over this period. You will be immediately struck by the enormous rise in the size of each of the aggregates. This is mainly due, of course, to inflation. If one were primarily interested in the growth of public spending it would be necessary to use a price index to *deflate* these data and represent them in constant prices (say the prices of 1980). For the purposes of seeing the importance of public expenditure in total expenditure, however, you do not have to do this. Instead, you can look at the shares of public expenditure in the total. These are shown in columns 6 and 7, and will be the same whether the original data were in current prices (as here) or in constant prices, as long as the relative prices of goods and services purchased by government stay the same.

The main items in (general) government expenditure on final goods and services (table 27.1 omits public corporations' spending) are defence, the National Health Service and education. Note that general government expenditure on fixed capital formation has been falling as a share of public expenditure – from about 17 per cent in 1960 to about 8 per cent in 1983. In recent times this is mainly because the government has used this item as a way of reducing public expenditure as a whole (and it means either that the government will have *not* undertaken some investments that microeconomic principles would suggest to have been desirable because of countervailing macroeconomic principles, or that previously fixed capital formation was too large in terms of microeconomic principles so that micro and macro considerations may not conflict).

Particularly striking is the way that government expenditure on final goods and services in *GDP* (column 6) has risen from about 22 per cent in 1960 to nearly 28 per cent in 1983. Even more dramatic is the rising share of transfers (including social security payments to the unemployed), shown in column 7.

Pressure on government to control public expenditure has evidently been felt mainly in capital expenditure by the government. Given the basic structure of the welfare state, expenditure there is in large part determined by demographic factors such as the number of children of school age and the number of persons needing health care, whereas personal subsidies like social security are in total determined largely by the numbers out of work. Transfers and public consumption expenditure are far harder to reduce politically than government investment spending – whose consequences come to be felt only later.

Table 27.2 shows the pattern of taxation that has developed in the UK in the period 1960–83. The types of tax are divided broadly into two – those that are directly related to earned income, profits and wealth, and those that are imposed on other kinds of activity, like the sales of a good, termed indirect taxes (see chapter 13). The main direct tax is the personal income tax. This is usually deducted by employers under the Pay As You Earn system (PAYE). National Insurance contributions are also usually deducted by employers. This column includes the National Insurance surcharge introduced in 1977. It also includes the petroleum revenue tax, which is a tax on profits (in addition to corporation tax) on oil obtained under licence in the UK and UK waters; it has, since its introduction in 1978, become a major revenue source for the government. Corporation tax is a tax on company profits.

Table 27.2 Direct and indirect taxation in the UK, 1960–83 (£ million at current prices)

	Direct taxes including local authority rates and National Insurance contributions	*Indirect taxes*	*Total*	*Indirect as % direct*	*Total as % GDP*
1960	3,732	2,620	6,352	70.2	27.8
1970	12,574	6,636	19,210	52.8	43.8
1980	53,033	27,914	80,947	52.6	41.1
1981	62,270	31,677	93,947	50.9	43.6
1982	70,569	35,016	105,585	49.6	45.1
1983	76,228	37,409	113,637	49.1	44.3

Sources: UK National Accounts, 1984, tables 7.2 and 8.1; *National Income and Expenditure,* 1970

The main indirect taxes are excise duties and VAT. Excise duties are levied on the quantity of the commodity in question, not its value, and apply to beer, spirits, wines, tobacco and hydrocarbon oils. Purchase tax (a tax on the *value* of a commodity when sold) was replaced in 1973 by value added tax. Other indirect taxes include such taxes as betting and gaming tax, and motor vehicle duties.

Note that the share of indirect taxes in total taxation has been falling since 1960, whereas taxation has risen as a share of *GDP* since 1960 and has been recently averaging about 43 per cent. As you saw in case study 17.2, Britain is not particularly heavily taxed in comparison with other developed countries but has tended to become increasingly taxed.

Table 27.3 gives a breakdown of the main items of expenditure and receipts of central and local government in 1983 (with transfers between the two netted

Table 27.3 Expenditure and receipts of general government in the UK, 1983 (£ billion)

Expenditure			
Current			
Current expenditure on final goods and services			
Military defence	15.7		
National Health Service	15.4		
Education	11.8		
Other	20.8		
Total	63.7	63.7	
Subsidies		6.1	
Current grants		41.5	
Debt interest		14.7	
Capital consumption		2.1	
Total current expenditure		128.1	128.1
Capital			
Gross domestic capital formation (including increase in value of stocks)		5.8	
Grants and transfers		3.6	
Total capital expenditure		9.4	9.4
Total expenditure			137.5
Receipts			
Taxes			
Income	43.1		
Expenditure	49.9		
National Insurance	20.6		
Capital	1.5		
Total	115.1		115.1
Property income			11.9
Balancing item			0.2
Total receipts before borrowing			127.2
Financial deficit			10.3
Other adjustments			1.7
General government borrowing requirement			12.0
Total receipts after borrowing			137.5

Source: UK National Accounts, 1984, tables 9.1, 9.4 and 13.13

out). On the expenditure side, current expenditure on goods and services is broken down by the principal areas of spending. 'Others' includes final expenditure on roads, police, prisons, parliament and the law courts, personal social services and a miscellany of small items like public parks and museums. The main subsidies are on local authority housing and nationalized transport undertakings. Grants include those to the personal sector (like National Insurance benefits, supplementary benefits and child benefits) as well as net contributions made to the European Economic Community (EEC) and foreign aid. Debt interest is that paid by central and local governments on past borrowing. Together these give a total current expenditure of £128.1 billion. Government investment, the value of changes in stocks and capital grants (for example regional development grants and grants to universities and colleges) bring the total to £137.5 billion.

On the receipts side, the main tax items have already been discussed, though the classification in table 27.3 differs from that in table 27.2 in that taxes on income and expenditure in table 27.3 are not quite the same categories as the direct and indirect taxes discussed in connection with table 27.2. Also, in this table, local authority rates are included in expenditure taxes.

Property income includes the trading surplus of government undertakings (harbours, passenger transport etc.) that are not public corporations. It also includes the rents from local authority housing and interest on loans made to public corporations.

The balancing item is a residual category that rectifies any omission or errors elsewhere in the accounts. The financial deficit shows the difference between total receipts before borrowing (and other adjustments) and total expenditure. The 'other adjustments' include things like accrued taxes from previous years. This leaves the borrowing requirement for general government. The general government borrowing requirement shows the shortfall of all receipts by central and local government with respect to all expenditure. It is the ultimate **budget deficit** of central and local government.

The accounts here omit public corporations like the nationalized industries, the Bank of England, the Post Office and the British Broadcasting Corporation. The borrowing requirement shown in the table does, however, include borrowing by the central government that is used to make loans to local government and public corporations. They also, however, borrow on their own accounts. In 1983, as it happens, the public corporations' own debts were reduced, so it turned out that they made a contribution of £0.5 billion to the overall **public sector borrowing requirement** (PSBR) which therefore, after allowing for this, stood at £11.5 billion.

Fiscal Policy in the Keynesian Model

The discussion now returns to the Keynesian model introduced in chapter 26.

Suppose the economy has got 'stuck' at an equilibrium level of *GDP* with less than full employment. At one time, people were exhorted to increase their

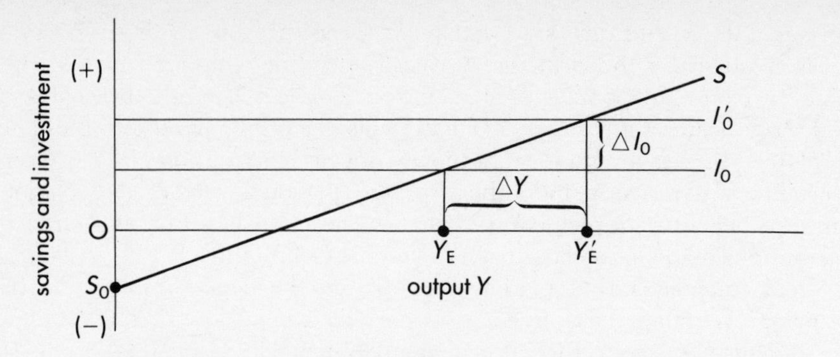

Figure 27.1 The multiplier effect of a change in investment

average propensity to save, thereby (or so it was hoped) forcing down interest rates and encouraging new investment. Such exhortations were often accompanied by attempts to drive down wages, hence encouraging employers to move down their demand curves for labour and reduce unemployment. For the moment set aside any effects in the labour market (these will be discussed in chapter 28) and focus on the effects of a change in the savings ratio.

Begin by recalling the effect in the Keynesian model of a rise in investment expenditures. In figure 27.1 the investment function shifts in response, say, to falling interest rates from I_0 to I_0'. Via the multiplier, this causes equilibrium income to rise from Y_E to Y_E'. Using the injections and withdrawals approach you have (see chapter 26):

Behavioural equations:

$$S = S_0 + sY \text{ (savings function)}$$

$$I = I_0 \qquad \text{(investment function)}$$

Equilibrium condition:

$$I = S$$

Reduced form:

$$Y = (-S_0 + I_0)\frac{1}{s}$$

Effect of a change in investment:

$$\Delta Y = \Delta I_0 / s$$

Therefore, given the value of the marginal propensity to save (or its reciprocal, the multiplier), the effect on income can be computed.

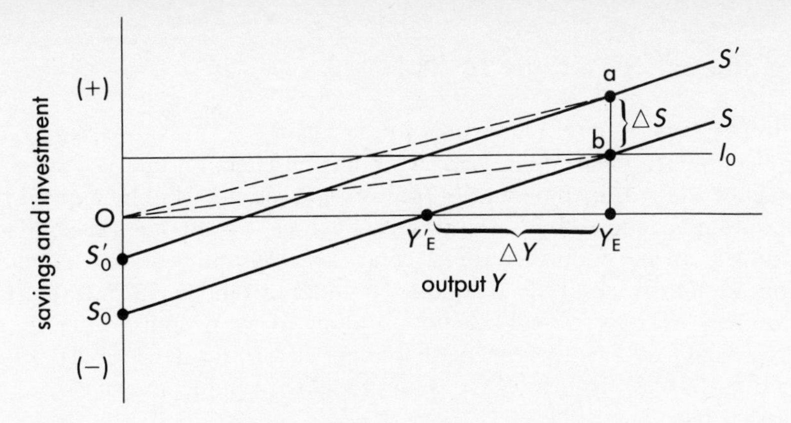

Figure 27.2 The paradox of thrift

Now assume that the investment function remains where it was (at I_0) and look at the effect of a shift in the savings function. This is shown in figure 27.2.

Initially the economy is in less than full employment equilibrium at Y_E, and the savings function is S. If the savings function shifts to S' (in this case it moves parallel to itself with S_0 rising to S_0' up the vertical axis) then the planned saving at Y_E rises from Y_Eb to Y_Ea and the savings ratio rises from Y_Eb / OY_E to Y_Ea / OY_E, as shown by the dashed lines from the origin. This causes aggregate expenditure to fall and the old equilibrium is no longer attainable: a new, *lower*, level of income is attained at Y_E'. In this case the multiplier is working through the change in S, and the fall in income is equal to the change in S, multiplied by the reciprocal of the marginal propensity to save (that is, the multiplier), i.e. $\Delta Y = \Delta S/s$.

Here there are two forces working in contrary directions – the rise in investment tending to cause *GDP* to expand, and the fall in savings causing it to contract. The latter effect is sometimes called the **paradox of thrift** to remind one that what may be virtuous for an individual may not be so for a nation. The net outcome evidently depends on which effect is the larger. One thing seems clear: if investment is constant, successful exhortations to raise the propensity to save will *reduce* output (and hence unemployment).

Closer attention to the behaviour of private investment will be given later (chapter 30). Here it is noted that few economists believe that the effect of an increase in savings or interest rates, and the consequential effect of interest rates on private investment, is sufficient to overcome the depressing effect of reduced saving on the economy.

The Keynesian way out is to seek the solution through fiscal policy, either by increasing public expenditure or by using tax policy to promote an increase in private expenditure.

Public Expenditure and the Multiplier

Focus, to begin with, on public expenditure. Assume that taxation is zero and that any (implicit) government borrowing has no effect on interest rates, the price level or the real income and output of the economy. Public expenditure on final output is denoted by G and this is, of course, a component of aggregate expenditure – an injection into the circular flow. Assuming that G is neither behaviourally nor structurally related to national income or output, that is, it is determined by government (an assumption to be dropped later in this chapter in SAQ 27.7 with respect to public sector transfers to the private sector), then $G = G_0$ and the Keynesian model with public expenditure (and no taxation) becomes:

Aggregate expenditure and output approach

Behavioural equations:

$$C = C_0 + cY \quad \text{(consumption function)}$$
$$I = I_0 \quad \text{(investment function)}$$
$$G = G_0 \quad \text{(government expenditure function)}$$

Equilibrium condition:

$$Y = C + I + G$$

Reduced form:

$$Y = (C_0 + I_0 + G_0)\frac{1}{1 - c}$$

Injections and withdrawals approach

Behavioural equations:

$$S = S_0 + sY \quad \text{(savings function)}$$
$$I = I_0 \quad \text{(investment function)}$$
$$G = G_0 \quad \text{(government expenditure function)}$$

Equilibrium condition:

$$I + G = S$$

Reduced form:

$$Y = (-S_0 + I_0 + G_0)\frac{1}{s}$$

SAQ 27.1

Suppose that $S = -10 + 0.2Y$, $I = 10$ and $G = 15$.

(a) What is the value of the multiplier?
(b) What is the size of equilibrium income?
(c) If government expenditure falls to 10, what happens to national income?

You can easily see that an increase in G will generate an increase in Y. Again, on the savings side, the amount of the change in Y, will be equal to the change in G times the multiplier: in symbols, $\Delta Y = \Delta G_0/s$.

This is shown in diagrammatic form in figure 27.3, but for the aggregate expenditure and output approach (compare with figure 26.4). You can see that ΔG_0 is performing in the same way as ΔI_0 did in the earlier analysis. Again the multiplier is the reciprocal of the marginal propensity to save. Thus, with a marginal propensity to consume of 0.6, the multiplier will be 2.5 and a change in G_0 of £100 billion will bring about an eventual increase in Y of £250 billion. Changes in fiscal spending thus affect national income in much the same way as changes in other components of aggregate demand. The big difference is that government expenditure is more directly controllable by the authorities; thus it can be used to compensate for deficiencies in aggregate demand when the economy has got 'stuck' at a less than full employment equilibrium and has no automatic mechanism that will generate a move towards full employment. Moreover, to the extent that private investment is volatile and tends to cause an amplified fluctuation in incomes and employment, higher public expendi-

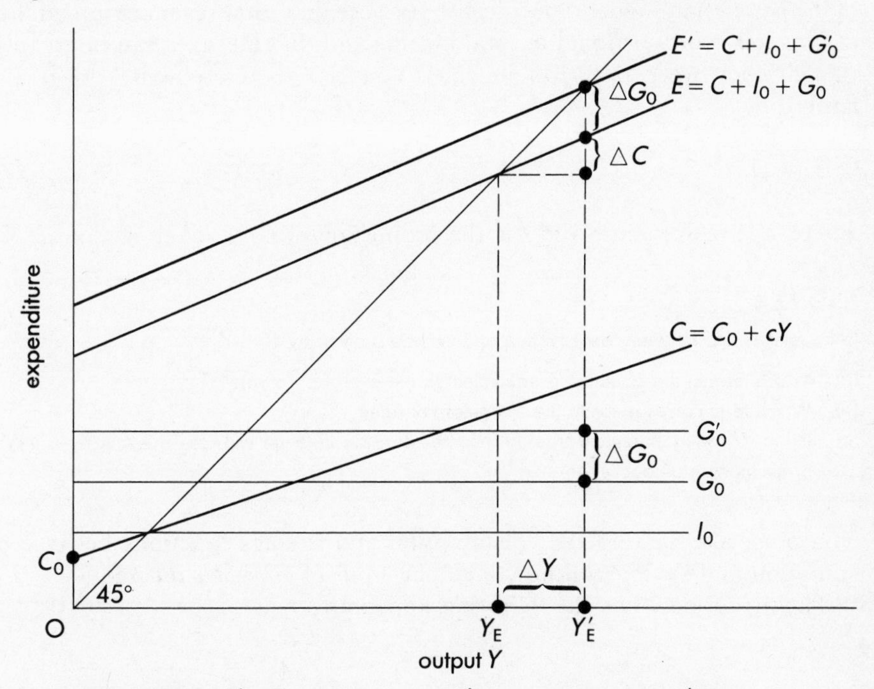

Figure 27.3 The Keynesian cross with government expenditure

ture can reduce the instability of a capitalist economy (either by being relatively stable or by being used to compensate for changes in investment, provided that the authorites can detect changes in investment and act quickly enough).

SAQ 27.2

If the economy is on the flat part of the aggregate supply curve and is suffering from heavy unemployment, would an increase in public expenditure

(a) Increase income by more than the increase in public spending?
(b) Reduce unemployment?

Taxation and the Multiplier

So far, public expenditure has been conjured out of thin air. Effectively, it has been supposed that the government can simply print or borrow money and spend it without any effects on the economy other than those described. More realistically one should consider how public expenditure is financed. This chapter on fiscal policy focuses on taxation as the means by which public spending is financed.

The actual tax structure will be simplified very drastically – but even this simplification will have dramatic consequences for the appearance of workings of the Keynesian model. Specifically, suppose that total revenue from all forms of taxation is proportional to total income and that all taxes can be treated as though they were taxes on income. You can therefore write down a **tax function**

$$T = tY$$

where T is tax revenue and t is the proportion of *GDP* taken in taxes.

SAQ 27.3

If the relationship between tax revenue and income is given by $T = tY$:

(a) Which term in the equation is equivalent to the average tax rate?
(b) Which term corresponds to the marginal tax rate?
(c) Is the following statement true: 'if income rises, tax revenue will also rise, but by a less than proportionate amount'?

You must also modify the consumption and savings functions because consumption and saving will now take place out of *disposable* income $(Y - T)$.

The model now has the following appearance:

Aggregate expenditure and output approach

Behavioural equations:

$$
\begin{aligned}
&C = C_0 + c(Y - T) && \text{(consumption function)}\\
&T = tY && \text{(tax function)}\\
&I = I_0 && \text{(investment function)}\\
&G = G_0 && \text{(government expenditure function)}
\end{aligned}
$$

Equilibrium condition:

$$Y = C + I + G$$

Reduced form:

$$Y = (C_0 + I_0 + G_0)\frac{1}{1 - c\,(1 - t)}$$

Injections and withdrawals approach

Behavioural equations:

$$
\begin{aligned}
&S = S_0 + s(Y - T) && \text{(savings function)}\\
&T = tY && \text{(tax function)}\\
&I = I_0 && \text{(investment function)}\\
&G = G_0 && \text{(government expenditure function)}
\end{aligned}
$$

Equilibrium condition:

$$I + G = S + T$$

Reduced form:

$$Y = (-S_0 + I_0 + G_0)\,\frac{1}{1 - (1 - s)\,(1 - t)}$$

SAQ 27.4

Derive each of the reduced forms just given by substituting the behavioural equations into the equilibrium conditions.

As before, the ratio on the right hand side of the reduced form is the multiplier. the multiplier with taxation proportional to income must necessarily be smaller than the multiplier when there is no taxation. For example, for the aggregate expenditure and output approach, with $c = 0.6$ and no taxation, the multiplier is 2.5. For an economy with $c = 0.6$ and $t = 0.33$, the multiplier becomes 1.67. Taxation thus reduces the potential impact of public expenditure on equilibrium income and employment. But it also reduces the inherent instability of the economy since any unstable element in aggregate expenditure, whether it be investment, consumption or public expenditure itself, will be less magnified in its impact on output and employment. Taxation that is related positively to income can therefore be described as a **built-in stabilizer**.

As before, the model can be used to compute equilibrium national income. It can also be used to compute the public sector surplus or deficit, that is, the difference (positive or negative) between taxation and public expenditure. Consider the following numerical example:

$$C = 10 + 0.8\,(Y - T)$$
$$T = 0.25Y$$
$$I = 15$$
$$G = 30$$

You can easily verify that, in this model, the value of the multiplier is 2.5. By using the reduced form again, the equilibrium level of income works out at 137.5. By using the tax equation, you can calculate taxation to be 34.375 so, with public expenditure at 30, the government was running a surplus of 4.375. Alternatively, with $G = 50$, the multiplier remains at 2.5, equilibrium income is 187.5, taxation amounts to 46.875 and the government is running a deficit of 3.125.

Note that in the foregoing numerical example, the change in public expenditure from 30 to 50 was 20, which generated an increase in national income from 135.5 to 187.5: a difference in income of 50. This income difference is – as you should expect – equal to the change in public expenditure times the multiplier (20×2.5).

SAQ 27.5

Let $C = 15 + 0.6(Y - T)$, $T = 0.2Y$, $I = 10$ and $G = 20$.

(a) What is the numerical value of the multiplier?
(b) What is the equilibrium level of income?
(c) Do taxes exceed public expenditure?

Changes in taxation can be (and are) used as instruments of macroeconomic policy as well as changes in public expenditure. To illustrate, suppose that the economy is as described before:

$$C = 10 + 0.8(Y - T)$$
$$T = 0.25Y$$
$$I = 15$$
$$G = 30.$$

Equilibrium income is, as you have seen, 137.5. Suppose now that, instead of increasing public expenditure, the government wants to increase income to 187.5 by changing taxes. What tax rate (t) will produce a target equilibrium income of 187.5? The reduced form will give the answer:

$$187.5 = (10 + 15 + 30)\frac{1}{1 - 0.8\,(1 - t)}$$

$$187.5 = 55\,\frac{1}{0.2 + 0.8t}$$

Multiplying both sides by $(0.2 + 0.8t)$ gives

$$187.5\,(0.2 + 0.8t) = 55$$
$$37.5 + 150t = 55$$
$$150t = 17.5$$
$$t = 0.1167$$

With a tax rate of 0.1167, the multiplier is 3.409 and the equilibrium level of income is 187.5. The same target level of income can be accomplished either by an increase in public expenditure from 30 to 50 or by a reduction in the tax rate from 0.25 to 0.1167. You should bear in mind, of course, the assumptions of constant prices, interest rates and wages. It is also implicitly assumed that changes in public expenditure and taxation have no effect on the supply of labour, business investment and so on. Such complications will have to be considered before you have reached a reasonably full understanding of the macroeconomy. For the moment, then, remember that one is really only manipulating *some* of the building blocks of macroeconomic theory: the model is becoming slightly less unrealistic, but there is still some way to go.

The Keynesian Cross with Public Expenditure and Taxation

As the Keynesian model is made more complex, the Keynesian cross is going to become too difficult a diagram to handle. Before, however, you say farewell to it, see how it looks when government expenditure and taxation are introduced. The introduction of public spending brings no special problems. Since it is assumed to be invariant with respect to national income, government expenditure appears simply as an additional horizontal line on the diagram, rather like investment. This too, of course, must be added to aggregate expenditure. This has already been seen in figure 27.3.

The effect of taxation in the diagram is subtler: it causes the consumption function to *rotate* around its intercept at C_0. Its slope is no longer c, the marginal propensity to consume, but $c(1-t)$: this is the marginal propensity to consume less that part of consumption that the extra taxes make impossible. c is the marginal propensity to consume out of *disposable* income, not total income. Figure 27.4 shows two consumption functions. Each has an intercept (C_0) of 10, but one has a slope of 0.8 and the other has a slope of 0.6 (i.e. assuming a proportional tax rate of 0.25).

The implications of introducing the government sector into the Keynesian cross diagram are shown in figure 27.5. Aggregate planned expenditure is now the sum of the consumption, investment and government expenditure functions ($C + I_0 + G_0$) and its slope is $c(1 - t)$. Initial equilibrium is at Y_E. If government expenditure rises by ΔG_0 to G_0', national income or output rises by ΔY to Y_E'. As you saw in chapter 26, this increase can be divided into two components: the change directly brought about by ΔG_0, and the change in consumption brought about by the increase in (now after tax) income ΔC. Because, on the 45° line, output equals expenditure, you can write

$$\Delta Y = \Delta G_0 + \Delta C$$

Dividing through by ΔY, you get

$$1 = \frac{\Delta G_0}{\Delta Y} + \frac{\Delta C}{\Delta Y}$$

You know that the consumption function is

$$C = C_0 + c\,(1 - t)\,Y$$

and therefore

$$\Delta C = c\,(1 - t)\,\Delta Y$$

So, dividing through by ΔY,

$$\frac{\Delta C}{\Delta Y} = c\,(1 - t)$$

which is, of course, the marginal propensity to consume cut of pre-tax national income. If you now substitute this term into the equation $1 = (\Delta G_0/\Delta Y) + (\Delta C/\Delta Y)$, you get

$$1 = \frac{\Delta G_0}{\Delta Y} + c\,(1 - t)$$

$$1 - c\,(1 - t) = \frac{\Delta G_0}{\Delta Y}$$

$$\frac{1}{1 - c\,(1 - t)} = \frac{\Delta Y}{\Delta G_0}$$

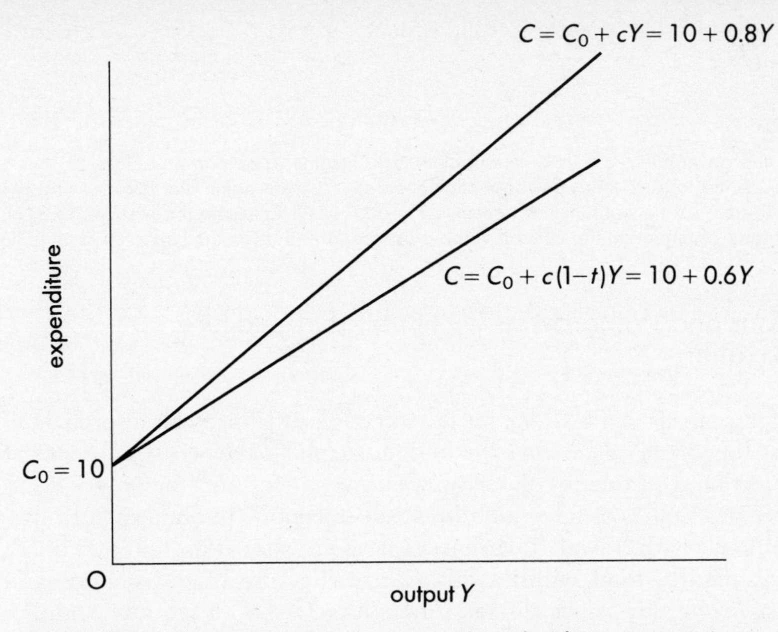

Figure 27.4 The consumption function with and without a rax on income

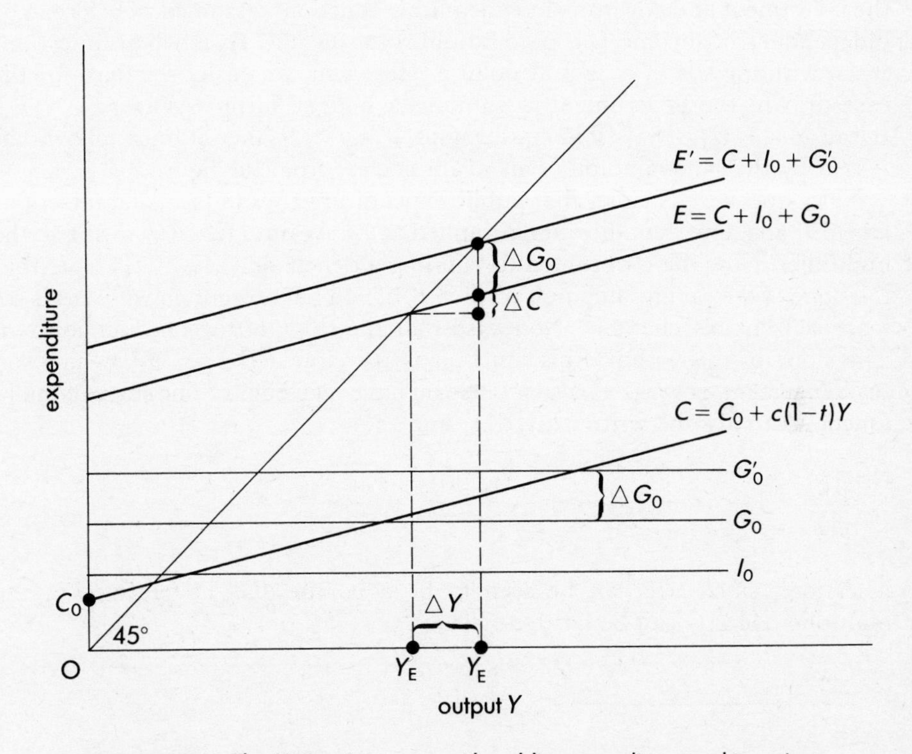

Figure 27.5 The Keynesian cross with public expenditure and taxation

Thus the multiplier effect of public expenditure with a given tax rate is as you found before.

SAQ 27.6

Suppose the government allows a certain amount of income to be earned before any tax rate is applied. Call the total of these personal allowances A_0. Assume again that tax is in proportion to *taxable* income, so the tax function becomes $T = t(Y - A)$. Calculate the reduced form and the multiplier, and comment on the effect that the presence of A_0 has on the impact of fiscal policy.

Injections and Withdrawals with Public Expenditure and Taxation

A similar analysis can be done for the injections/withdrawals approach, which also has the virtue of showing the budget surplus or deficit. In chapter 26 the only injection into the circular flow was investment and the only withdrawal was savings. You now have an additional injection (public expenditure) and an additional withdrawal (taxation). These are shown in figure 27.6.

In this figure, total withdrawals W are the sum of the savings and tax functions. Note that, since the tax function is $T = tY$ (forget the complication introduced in SAQ 27.6), it is a ray from the origin (showing that at a (notional) zero income there is zero taxation). Total injections J are the sum of the investment and government expenditure functions, assumed as before to be independent of income (I_0, G_0). Equilibrium income Y_E is where injections equal withdrawals ($J = W$) at point e. Here you can easily see that, for the case drawn, the government is running a budget surplus, since $T_E > G_0$. Because $I_0 + G_0 = S + T$ in equilibrium, if $T_E > G_0$ then it must follow that $I_0 > S$ by the same amount. This again is clear from the figure.

Now suppose, as before, that public expenditure rises to G_0'. Total injections rise to J' and a new equilibrium is implied at Y_E'. Again $\Delta Y > \Delta G_0$ owing to the multiplier. Now the government is running a deficit since $G_0' > T_E'$. Note that the slope of the savings function is $s(1 - t)$ (if you have forgotten why this is so, look back in this chapter). Note also that the slope of the tax function is t. The slope of the withdrawals function is therefore $s(1 - t) + t$ which, on rearrangement, is $1 - (1 - s)(1 - t)$ as you have seen before. The slope of the W function can also be written $\Delta W/\Delta Y$, and so

$$\frac{\Delta W}{\Delta Y} = 1 - (1 - s)(1 - t)$$

Therefore, since ΔW can be seen to be equal to ΔG_0 in figure 27.6, the multiplier $\Delta Y/\Delta G$ can be written

$$\frac{\Delta Y}{\Delta G} = \frac{1}{1 - (1 - s)(1 - t)}$$

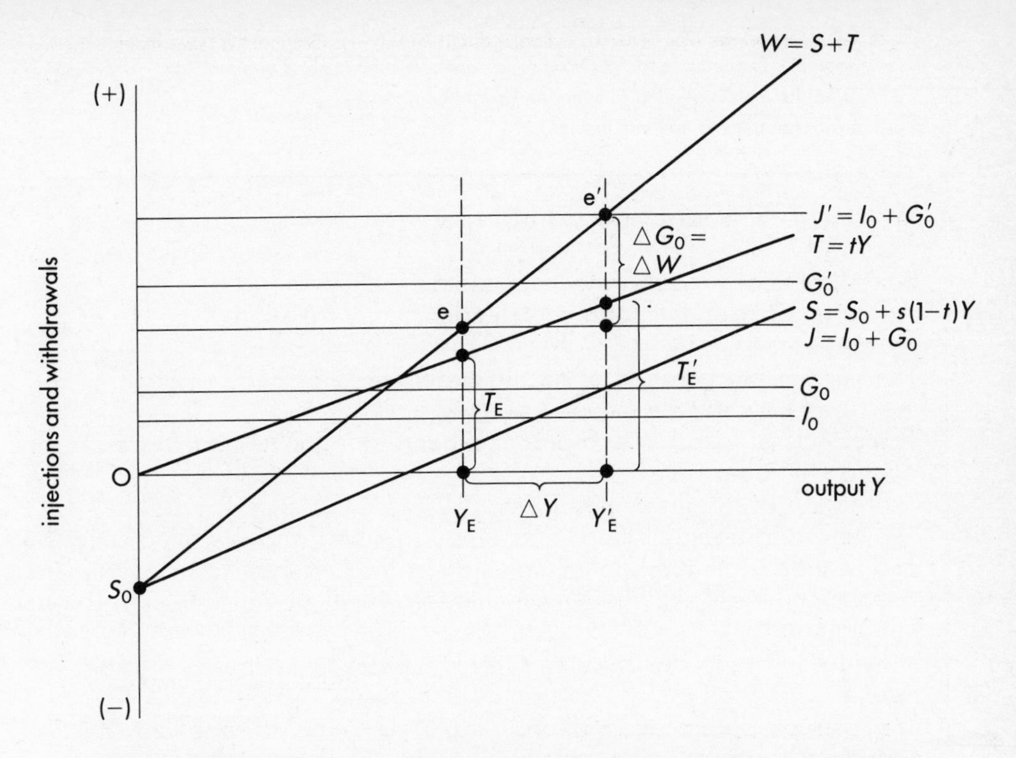

Figure 27.6 Injections and withdrawals with public expenditure and taxation

Since $c = 1 - s$, you thus derive exactly the same result as for the aggregate expenditure and output approach in the Keynesian cross.

As has been said before, these diagrams can easily become cumbersome (you may think they have already become more cumbersome than helpful!) and they will not be used in more complex analysis, for which algebra is more convenient. None the less it is important to recognize that both the *algebraic* and the *geometric*, and the *aggregate expenditure and output* and the *injections and withdrawals* approaches, give essentially the same results.

SAQ 27.7

(a) You have seen that taxation, by reducing the size of the multiplier, can reduce the instability of the economy (provided, of course, that tax policy itself is not manipulated so as to generate unwanted fluctuations). Taxes are, as you have seen, automatic stabilizers. So are subsidies. Suppose for example, that unemployment varies inversely with the level of national income and that there is a social programme that provides benefits to the unemployed at a fixed rate per person. Call this benefit in total U, and suppose that it is not taxed and is related to national income in the simplest possible way: $U = U_o - uY$. With the tax function $T = tY$, compute the reduced form and the multiplier, and comment on the effect this complication has on the impact of fiscal policy.

(b) Consider the following economy: $C = 10 + 0.75(Y - T)$, $T = 0.333Y$, $I = 10$, and $G = 40$.

1 Compute the equilibrium level of income and the budget surplus or deficit.

Check your answer to (b1) before proceeding further. Now suppose that the government wants to raise public expenditure to 50 *and also to continue to balance its budget.*

2 What tax rate is needed to keep the budget balanced?

3 What happens to national income?

What You Should Understand Now

Some political issues of macroeconomic policy.
The principal trends in public expenditure and taxation in the UK in recent years.
The current composition of public expenditure by general government and how it is financed.
The effects of taxation and public expenditure (including transfers) on the multiplier.
The notion of a built-in stabilizer.
The aggregate expenditure and output method and the injections and withdrawals method of calculating the reduced form of the Keynesian model with a government sector, and their diagrammatic equivalents.
How to compute the budget surplus or deficit in the Keynesian model.
The use of public expenditure and/or taxation to stabilize the economy or adjust to a target equilibrium *GDP*.

28

The Keynesian Model and the Labour Market

This chapter explores in greater detail the phenomenon of involuntary unemployment, its precise meaning and its causes. Before reading on, it would be worth while for you to review chapter 18, particularly the analysis there of how unemployment can arise through specific market imperfections. This will both serve to remind you of the basic analysis underlying the demand for and supply of labour and provide the starting point for the further developments to be found in this chapter. A major point of this chapter is to show that involuntary unemployment can occur even if the 'villains' of chapter 18 (minimum wages, monopolies and so on) are *absent*.

The total population of a country can at any time be divided into three categories – those who are in work, those who are unemployed but are seeking work, and the remainder who are officially described as economically inactive (see chapter 17). The last group includes the young in full time education and of pre-school age, the elderly, those of independent means, and housewives. The exclusion of housewives parallels the exclusion of the value of housewives' work from the national income statistics.

Unemployment (see table 25.1) is usually measured as a percentage or ratio, where the numerator is persons claiming benefit and available for work, and the denominator is the economically active population (usually excluding those in the armed forces, school leavers and the self-employed). The data for the numbers unemployed tend to underestimate the actual number unemployed, since not everyone claims; without the underestimate, the unemployment ratio would be about 0.5% greater. This distortion does, however, probably not affect *trends* or *changes* in the unemployment rate too much. The denominator can, however, lead to problems if individuals switch from being economically active to economically inactive rather than register as unemployed. This is likely particularly to be the case with a rising proportion of women in the labour force, who may move from employment into housewifely work and not be counted as unemployed. When this happens there is said to be a change in the **participation rate**.

The civilian labour force has shown a steady growth over the whole of this century. However, the trend of unemployment has been quite unstable, as you saw in chapter 25, with particularly high rates in the 1920s, even higher rates in the 1930s (the Great Depression), unprecedentedly low rates in the 1950s and sharply rising rates towards the end of the 1970s, and into the 1980s.

Types of Unemployment

The total number of unemployed people as officially measured is, as you have seen, the difference between those with jobs and the civilian labour force. Although at any date there is a given *stock* of claiming unemployed persons, there are many more who enter and leave the stock over a year. There is a *flow* of people becoming unemployed – school leavers who are unable to find a job, people who are re-entering the labour force who previously were not in it or who dropped out, people who have been fired, people who have been made redundant and people who have voluntarily quit. There is also a flow *out* of the stock of unemployed – people who withdraw from the labour force (perhaps because they have given up hope of getting a job), people who reach retirement age while unemployed, people who die and, of course, people who find jobs.

Descriptive Classification

There are many ways in which one may wish to see the unemployment data disaggregated. For example, one may be interested in student or school leaver unemployment (data on each are available in the UK Department of Employment's *Employment Gazette*).

Table 28.1 UK unemployment by sex and duration, July 1984 (per cent of all unemployed)

	Up to 2 weeks	*2–4 weeks*	*4–8 weeks*	*8–13 weeks*	*13–26 weeks*	*26–52 weeks*	*Over 52 weeks*
Male	6.1	4.4	6.4	6.6	13.0	19.1	44.4
Female	8.7	5.9	8.0	8.5	16.1	23.3	29.4
Male and female	6.9	4.8	6.9	7.2	13.9	20.4	39.8

Source: Employment Gazette, 1984, **92**(8), table 2.8

Table 28.1 shows unemployment by sex and duration in July 1984. As you can see, female unemployment rates are higher than male for all durations save those over a year. The lower female percentage for those who have been unemployed for longer than a year is mainly due to long term unemployed females dropping out of the labour force. Note the very high proportion of people who have been unemployed for more than a year – nearly 45 per cent of all unemployed men and nearly 40 per cent of all unemployed.

Duration of unemployment is also associated with age. Table 28.2 brings out the striking fact that the proportion of short term unemployment falls the older the age group of workers, and the proportion of long term unemployment rises the older the age group.

Descriptive data of this sort are invaluable in assessing some of the social consequences of unemployment and can provide some pointers about the kind of financial support different groups may need, retraining possibilities, and so on.

Table 28.2 UK unemployment (both sexes) by age and duration, July 1984 (per cent of unemployment in each age group)

Age	*Up to 26 weeks*	*26–52 weeks*	*Over 52 weeks*
Under 25	48.7	21.9	29.3
25–54	35.6	18.8	45.6
55 and over	28.1	21.8	50.1

Source: Employment Gazette, 1984, **92**(8), table 2.5

Another important descriptive way of categorizing unemployment is by region. Table 28.3 shows the regional pattern of unemployment in the UK in July 1984. It also shows the number of vacancies notified to Jobcentres. In 1984 the worst hit region was Northern Ireland, followed by the North, the North West, Wales, the West Midlands and Scotland. The Department of Employment reckons that about one third of all vacancies are notified to Jobcentres. As you can see, however, even if vacancies were tripled, in no region were the estimated vacancies anything like sufficient to meet the unemployment.

Table 28.3 Unemployment and vacancies by region July 1984

Region	*Unemployed persons (000)*	*Per cent*	*Vacancies (000)*
South East	735.9	9.5	64.5
East Anglia	74.0	9.7	5.6
South West	183.9	10.9	15.3
West Midlands	341.3	15.0	12.4
East Midlands	190.6	11.9	8.3
Yorkshire and Humberside	287.2	14.0	10.5
North West	434.5	15.7	16.6
North	227.8	17.9	8.9
Wales	162.7	15.6	8.0
Scotland	336.5	14.9	15.7
Great Britain	2978.9	12.7	165.8
Northern Ireland	121.6	21.0	1.8
UK	3100.5	12.9	167.6

Source: Employment Gazette, 1984, **92**(8), 1984, tables 2.3 and 3.2

Analytical Classification

Another way of classifying unemployment is more analytical and relates to the causes of the unemployment. The main categories here are frictional and structural unemployment.

Frictional unemployment is, as its name implies, unemployment due to the frictions in a dynamic economy: as demand and supply patterns change over time, some workers are unable to find another job before their old one disappears. In the short spell between jobs they are frictionally unemployed. This is also sometimes called **search unemployment**. It exists when there are simultaneously both workers seeking jobs and suitable unfilled vacancies.

Workers 'shop around' for the best wages and conditions of service. The better and the more information provided by Jobcentres and the like, the shorter this spell is likely to be.

Structural unemployment exists when there is major structural change in the job market, with the result that the skill mix demanded in a particular location does not match the skill availability, or when a major industry goes into decline (like textiles in the UK) and no other major employers exist in the local area. This is one of the major reasons for the differing rates of unemployment in various regions. With structural unemployment workers have to retrain or move home to areas where there is greater demand for their skills, or new employment has to be brought into their locality. Structural unemployment thus tends to last longer for each person than frictional and to require more substantial remedies on the part of the individual, potential employers, or the government (possibly justifying selective industrial subsidies on second best grounds; see chapter 19).

Behavioural Classification

A third way of classifying unemployment is behavioural. The distinction between voluntary and involuntary unemployment is of this kind (see chapter 18). If workers are *on* their supply curve and there is an excess demand for labour, there is **voluntary unemployment**. If they are *off* their supply curve and supply exceeds demand, there is **involuntary unemployment**. In the former case all who wish to work at the going wage do so; in the latter some who wish to cannot. Involuntary unemployment is the product of disequilibrium in the labour market. This is shown in figure 28.1. Given the supply and demand curves shown, if the disequilibrium wage is W_0 there is an excess demand of $N_1 - N_0$ and any unemployment is voluntary (more workers than N_0 do not want to work at wage W_0). If the disequilibrium wage is W_1 there is involuntary unemployment of $N_1 - N_0$ (only N_0 workers get jobs when N_1 want them at that wage). At any wage less than W_E, unemployment is defined to be voluntary. This does not mean, of course, that such unemployment may not be a major social problem: after all, wages may be so miserably low that workers prefer poverty without work to poverty with work.

You will probably have noted that, in contrast to the demand and supply analysis of chapter 17, figure 28.1 portrays demand and supply of *workers* or *jobs* (rather than hours) for the *whole* labour market (rather than one particular market). The links between the micro analysis of chapter 18 and the macro of this will shortly be investigated.

Related to the notion of voluntary unemployment is the idea of *natural* unemployment. At the equilibrium wage W_E, as many workers want jobs as there are jobs available (N_E). But even in this case there will be some unemployment. There will, for example, be frictional or search unemployment. Natural unemployment is therefore the voluntary unemployment that exists when the labour market is in equilibrium. The unemployment rate when the labour market is in equilibrium is called the **natural rate of unemploy-**

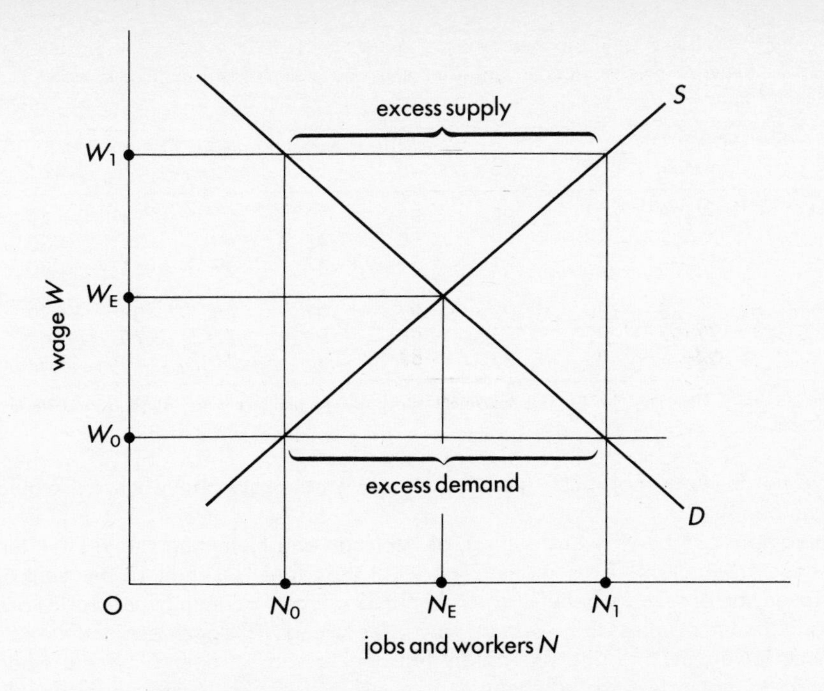

Figure 28.1 Voluntary and involuntary unemployment

ment. This is also what shall be taken behaviourally to correspond to **full employment**.

SAQ 28.1

Define search, frictional, structural, voluntary, involuntary and natural unemployment.

Case Study 28.1 Is One Better Off on the Dole?

Tony Atkinson and John Flemming (1978) have challenged the popular notion that current levels of benefit to the unemployed prevent their incomes from falling much below normal earnings, and that 'being better off on the dole encourages scrounging' (in posher language, high benefits increase voluntary unemployment).

The popular notion was often illustrated by the hypothetical example of a married couple with two children (say aged 4 and 6) where the man earns £55 a week (1977 data). The net income after income tax, National Insurance contributions, child benefit and working expenses of £2 a week would have been £45.55. If the man lost his job, the family would still have received child benefit, would have had £30.30 flat rate National Insurance benefit and (after two waiting weeks) earnings related supplement (ERS) of £8.50. Including child benefit, the family's net income would have been £41.30 or 91 per cent of that in work. After a month of unemployment, the family would also in the short term receive refunds of income tax previously paid under PAYE. After adding other benefits like free school meals, rent rebates and so on, the **replacement ratio** (RR) (the ratio of net income out of and in work) rises to 101 per cent, suggesting that this 'typical' family is better off on the dole. Economic protection for the unemployed is complete (more than complete!) and there is a massive

Table 28.4 Replacement ratios (percentages), earnings and unemployment duration for two family types, November 1977

	Duration (weeks)	*Weekly gross earnings in work (£)* 25	35	45	55	65	75	85
Single person	3–28	107	97	83	70	61	54	49
	29–52	88	72	59	48	40	34	30
	53–	87	71	59	47	39	34	30
Couple and two children (ages 4 and 6)	3–28	120	102	97	101	95	88	79
	29–52	95	86	88	84	77	70	62
	53–	95	86	87	83	77	70	62

A. B. Atkinson and J. Flemming (1978), 'Unemployment, social security and incentives', *Midland Bank Review*, Autumn, 6–16.

incentive not to work that must raise the unemployment rate above what it would otherwise be.

This example can be very misleading, as Atkinson and Flemming show. First, the family described is not representative: in fact, it describes less than 13 per cent of unemployed social security beneficiaries. About 52 per cent of male beneficiaries are *single* and for these, unless they were on very low earnings (£25 per week) the RR was very much lower. Second, the RR rapidly fell after a year of unemployment when entitlement to flat rate and ERS benefits was exhausted and the family had only supplementary benefits. The proportion of unemployed people who had been unemployed for more than a year was, in early 1978, 22.5 per cent. This percentage was rising and continues to rise. Third, the example assumes that all benefits to which a family is entitled are claimed; yet many do not claim the more obscure benefits (e.g. free school meals) or even supplementary benefit, and fewer than half received even the basic National Insurance benefit (because they had exhausted entitlement or did not qualify for other reasons).

Table 28.4 (Atkinson and Flemming, 1978) shows the replacement ratios for a single person and a couple with two children aged 4 and 6 at various in-work earnings and for various periods of unemployment, assuming that there is entitlement to all benefits and that all are claimed. Generally speaking, the more dependants (wife and children) a man has, the lower his gross wage, the shorter his duration of unemployment, the higher the RR.

The Demand and Supply of Workers

A set of conditions is to be specified under which one would expect unemployment to be impossible, namely when labour markets are competitive: there is no monopsony, and no labour is monopolized.

In order to conduct the analysis in terms of jobs rather than hours of work, some modifications will have to be made to the microeconomic analysis of chapter 18. Suppose that for each job there is a specified number of hours per week and that firms, instead of hiring labour by the hour, hire it by the worker – one worker one job. The demand curve for labour is shown in figure 28.2. The demand curve is found by taking the marginal physical product *per worker*,

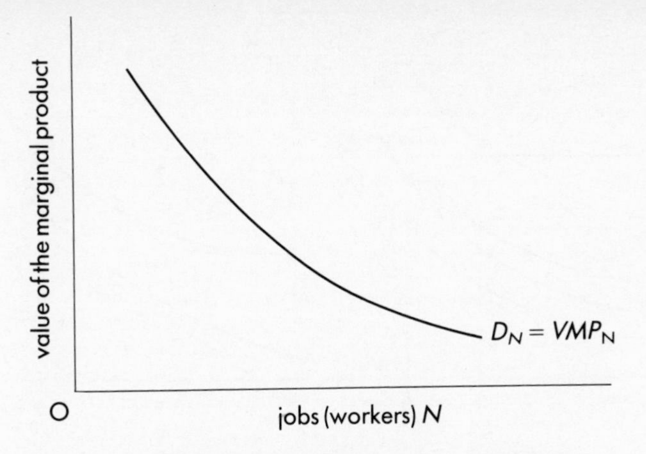

Figure 28.2 The demand for workers

rather than per hour, and multiplying that by the price per unit of the product. The demand curve is therefore the *value of the marginal product of workers*, and it has a negative slope for the same reasons as the *VMP of labour hours* had in chapter 17.

When all employers' demands are added (horizontally of course) you obtain the market demand curve for labour in the economy. More realistically, one might want to identify market demand curves for specific skills, types of worker and so on. For simplicity, however, assume that workers are homogeneous as to skill and productivity (though not as to their preferences); that is, each worker is a perfect substitute for any other from each employer's point of view. This – admittedly unrealistic – assumption does not affect the conclusions but it makes life a lot simpler at the analytical level.

SAQ 28.2

(a) Define the value of the marginal product.

(b) What is the difference between the value of the marginal product of labour time and that of a worker?

The supply of workers is determined by similar considerations to the supply of labour time. Figure 28.3 portrays the indifference maps of two individuals, A and B. The point u is the amount of income an individual will receive net of any tax if no work is done, (income from assets owned by the worker, social security benefit, and so on). This yields each individual the utility number associated with indifference curves U_0^A and U_0^B. Now suppose the wage rate is W_0. Individual A would prefer to work h^A hours since this entails a higher indifference curve U_2^A than that for no work U_0^A. However, he or she may not be able to get quite the match of wage and hours that is most preferred. The offer may be, say, for h_1^A hours at W_0. This requires A to locate either at point u (no work) or at point b. Since point b is on U_1^A, higher than U_0^A, the individual will choose to work. However, there are many employers offering various

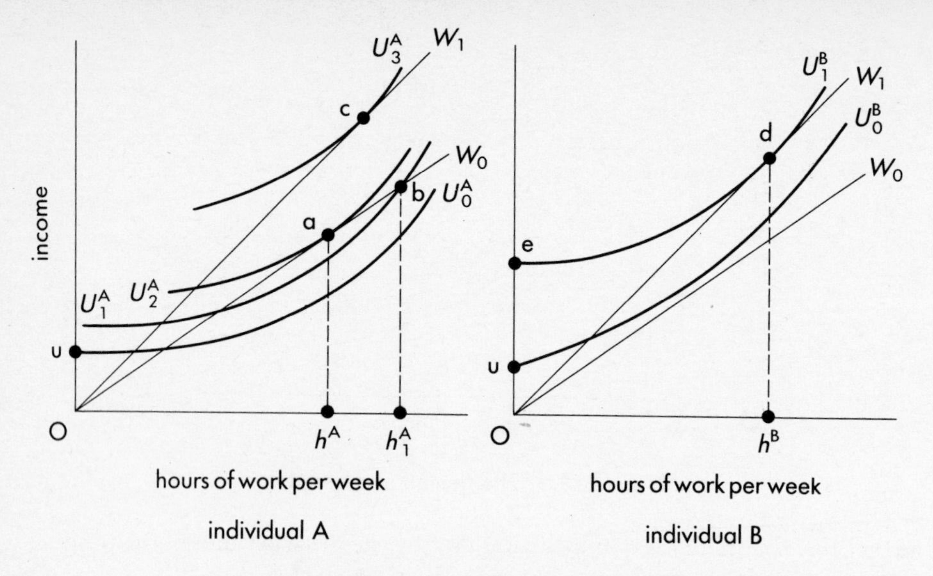

Figure 28.3 To work or not to work?

combinations of wages and hours (not to mention other fringe benefits etc. not considered here) so it is quite likely that each individual will be able to approximate to his or her most preferred point on any wage ray from the origin and work, say, h^A hours.

Now consider individual B. B's preferences differ from A's and, since B's indifference curve U_0^B through point u everywhere lies above the available wage W_0, B will at that wage prefer not to work. At a higher wage W_1, however, B will prefer to work and will locate at point d on the W_1 ray, on a higher indifference curve than that through point u, supplying h^B hours.

Thus, if individuals choose to remain at u, they are voluntarily unemployed (so far there is no involuntary unemployment). Given that preferences for income and leisure differ, you can easily see that the higher the wage the more workers will participate in the labour force. Hence the supply curve of workers slopes upwards, just like the supply curve of labour hours. Putting the demand and supply curves together, as in figure 28.4, a competitive market will tend towards an equilibrium wage of W_E and an equilibrium level of employment N_E. At any wage less thn W_E, employers' demands will exceed supply and wages will tend to be raised towards W_E. At any wage above W_E, supply will exceed demand and wages will tend to fall towards W_E.

SAQ 28.3

(a) What are the effects of a decrease in rates of social security benefit in figure 28.3?

(b) At what rate of unemployment pay would B cease to offer work even at wage W_1?

Full Employment

As you have seen, full employment exists when all workers who offer their services at a particular wage gain employment. In figure 28.4 *full employment therefore exists at wage W_E and all wages less than that.* Full employment, in other words, exists all along the heavily drawn section of the supply curve of workers, for at all the wages along that section of the supply curve the workers who offer their services will find jobs.

At W_E demand equals supply and there is full employment and neither excess demand nor excess supply of labour. At W_1 there is still full employment, but demand exceeds supply so there is an excess demand for labour measured by ab. At W_2 there is an excess supply of labour and there is *involuntary unemployment* equal to cd. Under competition, however, this involuntary unemployment is a temporary phenomenon since there will be pressure on wages to fall until W_E is established, with full employment and no involuntary unemployment. Remember, of course, that at any wage there may – and usually will – be voluntary unemployment, particularly of the frictional or search type.

Since the analysis seems to suggest that involuntary unemployment occurs whenever $W > W_E$, a natural focal question to ask is why wages are too high. The list of potential villains is, of course, long – trade union restrictive practices, irrational workers, overpaying public sector employers and so on.

A natural policy prescription would be to try to depress wages, either by operating directly on money wages, or by trying to remove the market 'imperfections' that are believed to be the cause of the too high wages, or by increasing the price level so that *real* wages fall. At this stage in the book a fixed

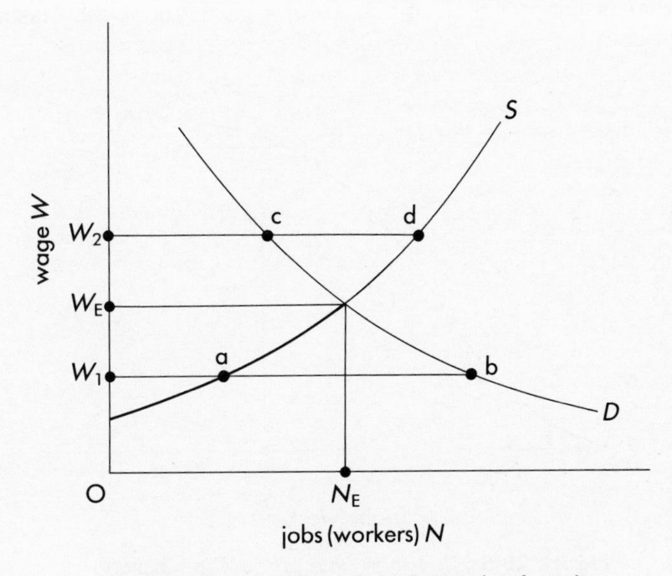

Figure 28.4 Equilibrium in the market for jobs

price level is still assumed, and this assumption is continued. The crucial insight that Keynes offered was that one may have involuntary unemployment *even without* any of the market 'imperfections' usually complained of, so that, although it is *possible* for unions and so on to cause involuntary unemployment, there is an even more fundamental reason why a market economy can settle in an equilibrium where there is involuntary unemployment. You are now at a point where the centrepiece of Keynesian employment theory can be revealed.

SAQ 28.4

What percentage of the labour force unemployed corresponds to full employment?

Keynesian Involuntary Unemployment

You are familiar with the idea of a production function from chapter 9 (now is a good time to refresh your memory if you think it is necessary). At this stage a new but related idea is introduced: the **aggregate production function**. This shows, given an economy's capital stock, how output varies according to the number of workers employed. It is really no more than an aggregation of the individual production functions of firms. Since capital stock is assumed constant, it is obvious that one is considering the fairly short run.

Figure 28.5 shows that the aggregate production function $Y = f(N)$ has the usual shape – a set of output rates showing increasing returns to labour, followed by another showing decreasing returns to labour. At output Y_0, labour N_0 is employed; at output Y_1, labour N_1 is employed. Remember, labour is measured in terms of workers or jobs rather than hours of work.

The analysis of the aggregate production function follows much the same pattern as that of chapter 9, so if you are not clear about the reasons for its

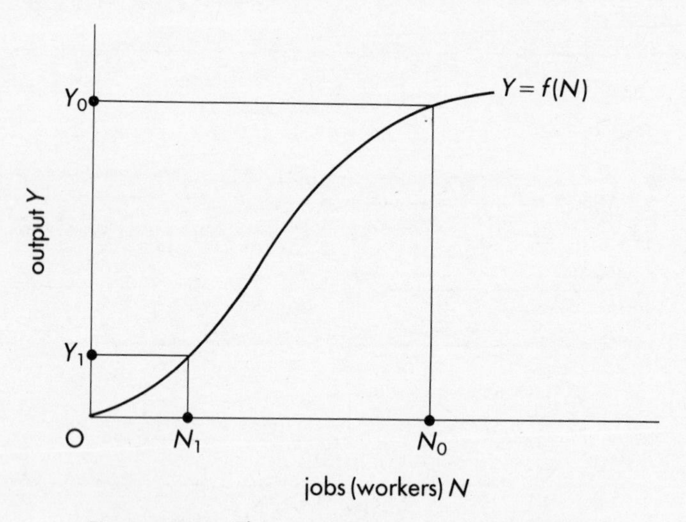

Figure 28.5 The aggregate production function

shape, or how it is derived from the technical characteristics of production processes, you should check back to that chapter.

The analysis of this chapter can now be combined with that of the Keynesian cross (chapters 26, 27) in order to demonstrate the source of Keynesian involuntary unemployment. Figure 28.6 appears complex but is really no more than three familiar figures placed in a particular relationship to one another. Figure 28.6(a) is the familiar Keynesian cross with an aggregate expenditure line drawn in. Begin by assuming that aggregate planned expenditure is $E = C + I + G$. The starting point is equilibrium with *GCP* at Y_E.

Figure 28.6(b) shows the aggregate production function. If the economy is producing Y_E output, then the aggregate production function tells you that N_E labour must be employed (point a). The scale of the vertical axis is the same as that of the horizontal axis of figure 28.6(a).

Figure 28.6(c) shows the labour market. If this is in equilibrium too, and employment is N_E, as determined by the equilibrium in the market for final goods and services and by the aggregate production function, then the equilibrium wage must be W_E.

So far so good. The economy is in full equilibrium. There is no involuntary unemployment. Everyone who wants work at wage W_E can get it and employers want neither more nor fewer workers than they have. Planned expenditures are just sufficient to exhaust the available output. Given the available capital stock, no one wants more work than they have and no more output can be produced and sold than is produced and sold. The system is efficient. There is no waste of resources.

Now suppose there is a fall in aggregate planned expenditure from E to E' owing to a change in any one or all of its components. Via the multiplier, output will contract by more than the fall in aggregate expenditure: in this case to Y'_E by the amount ΔY. At Y'_E, the production function says that only N'_E workers will be employed and employment falls by ΔN. At point b on the aggregate production function, firms are selling all the output they produce, just as they were when they were at point a, but they are no longer producing all they would like to produce at the going wage W_E.

Consider figure 28.6(c). Prices have not changed; nor has the production function. Therefore the marginal physical product curve is as before, and the value of the marginal product curve remains as before. Nor has the labour supply curve changed: nothing has happened to alter workers' preferences. So the demand and supply of labour both remain unchanged. Suppose the equilibrium wage stays the same. But at W_E only N'_E workers are being hired. The labour market has been forced *out of equilibrium* to the point c and there is involuntary unemployment (even without the usual villains). W_E is the 'right' wage rate in the sense that it is the wage that is consistent with equilibrium in the labour market, but ΔN workers who are willing to work at wage W_E cannot find employment. The unemployed workers are very likely those with the lowest values of their marginal products, though they are not necessarily those with the highest supply prices, as shown by the section de of the supply curve.

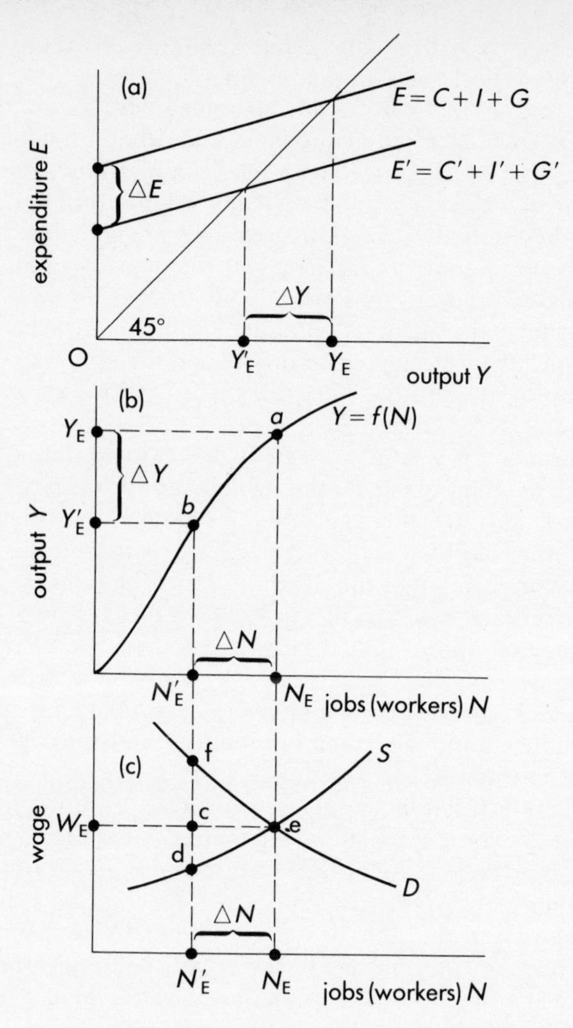

Figure 28.6 Keynesian involuntary unemployment

There is no excess of output, for firms are still selling all they produce. But at W_E they would like to produce more. They cannot because there is no **effective demand** for more. With employment at N'_E, the wage is only W_E but the value of output produced by a marginal worker is N'_Ef. Firms have excess capacity (unemployed capital stock) and there is also an excess supply of labour (involuntary unemployment). There is no automatic mechanism for bringing the labour market into equilibrium and thereby restoring full employment. There is no effective demand for the extra output that profit seeking firms wish to produce, and so there is no effective demand for the work the involuntarily unemployed would like to supply. Of course, the wage rate may change as time passes. But the market does not signal the direction in which it will move. As the demand and supply for labour change, as they well might as tastes and technology alter (even without unions flexing their industrial muscles), no one will know what the full employment wage actually is. The goods market can stay in equilibrium, with the labour market staying out of equilibrium and producing involuntary unemployment.

What has gone wrong? The problem is *not*, as was once thought, that wages are too high. Even at the full employment equilibrium wage W_E, the problem exists. The problem *is* that supply and demand curves of labour have not moved. *And they have not moved because the price mechanism has failed to do its job of equilibrating supply and demand in the labour market.*

The unemployed workers have a supply of labour and also a demand for output. But their demands cannot be made effective until they receive the wages to make it effective. Firms will not hire the labour until they see the effective demand. Keynesian involuntary unemployment is a Catch 22. The relevant information is not being transmitted by market prices. If prices could fall, then full employment equilibrium could be re-established, for if prices fell, the value of the marginal produce curve would shift downwards since the marginal physical products would all be multiplied by lower prices. The supply of labour curve would shift to the right, since a given money wage would be worth more in real terms. Consequently W_E, the money wage, would fall, enabling full employment to be re-established. But that does not happen because the economy is located along the section of the aggregate supply curve at which the price level is constant. The economy is 'stuck' at less than full employment.

Firms are evidently adjusting quantities produced and employed faster than they are adjusting prices. Why might this be? Consider the matter from the point of view of a firm. The first signals firms receive about a fall in aggregate expenditure is that their stocks begin to increase as their customers require less to meet anticipated demands. But this may only be a temporary matter. After all, firms' stocks rise and fall all the time. It is generally not good sales policy to vary prices continuously with the ups and downs of stocks, especially if demand changes are thought to be temporary. As stocks mount, therefore, most firms will cut back on output rather than lower prices, to allow sufficient time to elapse to enable them to diagnose a general and permanent fall in demand rather than a temporary hiccup. Oligopolistic firms in particular are, as you have seen, likely to be reluctant to alter their prices in the short term owing to uncertainty about the reactions of other firms and concern about the effects of altering limit prices on entry, and because some wait for price leaders to show the way.

The Keynesian way out, of course, is for the government to increase aggregate expenditure by changing C, I or G. The relationship between aggregate expenditure and employment is given by the production function. Its slope determines $\Delta N/\Delta Y$. Thus, if the government knows, say, the public expenditure multiplier $\Delta Y/\Delta G$, then the effect of public expenditure on employment can be calculated.

This demonstration of the possibility of an equilibrium in the market for final goods and services, combined with disequilibrium in the labour market owing to a failure of effective demand, was one of Keynes's central contributions.

SAQ 28.5

For the following economy, estimate the effect of a 10 per cent decrease in public expenditure, all else the same, on employment N. All values are in thousands of millions ($\times 10^9$)

$C = 10 + 0.8(Y - T)$	(consumption function)
$T = 0.3Y$	(tax function)
$I = 10$	(investment function)
$G = 30$	(government expenditure function)
$N = 0.000125Y$	(production function)

Case Study 28.2 Causes of the Rising Male Unemployment in Britain in the 1970s

In a very careful study of the problem, Stephen Nickell (1982) has examined the determinants of equilibrium unemployment in Britain. Using sophisticated econometric methods he attempted to account for a rise in male unemployment (females were excluded because of unsatisfactory data on female unemployment) from 3.13 per cent in 1969 to 6.90 per cent in 1977. Equilibrium unemployment was defined to exist when the inflow into unemployment equals the outflow into employment. The rise of 3.77 percentage points was broken down into six main and one residual category, as shown in table 28.5. Over 60 per cent of the rise could be attributed to these six factors.

Table 28.5 Contributions to the rise in male unemployment in Britain, 1969–77

	Percentage points
Decline in the proportion working in production industries	1.40
Rise in real wage relative to value added	0.35
Decline in the replacement ratio (RR)	−0.27
Increase in unfair dismissal cases	−0.97
Decline in unemployment benefit disqualifications	0.57
Decline in direct demand	1.28
Unexplained trends (plus other minor factors)	1.41
Total	3.77

The most important was the decline in employment in non-service production industries, showing that 1.40 per cent unemployment could on average over the period be attributed to this effect. It is a structural unemployment effect; declines in some industries were not compensated by growth in others, and there was a deficit in local demand for the relevant skills. The second was the decline in direct demand (partly due to a fall in world trade), showing that 1.28 per cent of unemployment could be attributed to this Keynesian deficiency of aggregate expenditure. Third was the decline in the pressure exerted by the employment service on men to obtain jobs; the service took a more lenient attitude to the entitlement to unemployment benefit of men who declined jobs (0.57 per cent). Next came the rise in real wage relative to value added, which (possibly through trade union pressure) caused employers to move along their labour demand curves to the left (0.35 per cent).

Offsetting these effects were the fall in the replacement ratio over 1969–77, which (though its effect can, as you have seen, be easily exaggerated) reduced unemployment by an estimated 0.27 per cent, and the increase in unfair dismissal cases, which increased the costs to employers of firing workers.

Stephen Nickell (1982) 'The determinants of equilibrium unemployment in Britain', *Economic Journal*, **92**, 555–75, table 4.

What You Should Understand Now

The principal features of unemployment in Britain recently.
The various types of unemployment.
The cause of Keynesian involuntary unemployment.
The impact of replacement ratios and other determinants of contemporary unemployment.
The meaning of full employment.
The role of the aggregate production function in the Keynesian model.
The reasons why the labour market may find itself in a disequilibrium from which the economy produces no automatic tendency to move into equilibrium.

29

The Keynesian Model with Foreign Trade

So far only a *closed economy* – that is, one without any foreign trade – has been considered. The UK, however, together with her major trading partners, is an *open economy* and, like her partners, is becoming more open. In the case of the UK, whereas imports of food and raw materials (other than oil) have been a fairly constant proportion of *GDP* (about 7 per cent), imports of oil (by value) rose sharply in the early 1970s but the rate of growth then fell off with North Sea production. Imports of manufacturers have shown a steady rise over the last ten years and are now about 14 per cent of *GDP*. Imports are rising fastest from EEC trading partners and, until very recently, the oil producing countries.

Exports have been rising too. The main UK item is manufactures – about 13 per cent of *GDP* – which have risen strongly over the past 15 years. Exports have risen most strongly to the EEC countries. The recent pattern of UK visible trade (goods but not services) is described in table 29.1.

Table 29.1 UK trade by commodity group as a percentage of total trade

	1971	*1981*	*1982*	*1983*
Exports				
Food beverages and tobacco	6	7	7	7
Basic materials	3	3	2	3
Mineral fuels and lubricants	3	19	20	22
Semi-manufactured goods	33	26	25	26
Finished manufactured goods	52	43	42	40
Other	3	3	3	3
Imports				
Food, beverages and tobacco	22	13	12	12
Basic materials	12	7	6	7
Mineral fuels and lubricants	11	15	14	11
Semi-manufactured goods	26	24	24	26
Finished manufactured goods	27	39	41	43
Other	2	2	2	2

Note: percentages may not sum to 100 owing to rounding.
Source: UK Balance of Payments, 1982 and 1984, table 2.3.

In 1971 UK exports were, in total, about 22 per cent of *GDP* and total imports were about 21 per cent. In 1983 exports were about 27 per cent of *GDP* and imports 25 per cent. Within this overall increase in the openness of the UK economy there were changes in both the composition of exports and imports and in their destinations and origins. Table 29.1 shows the pattern of visible trade classified into six broad commodity groups.

The most immediately striking thing about table 29.1 is that, whereas UK exports were far more specialized than UK imports, so that there was specialization in production (as the theory of comparative advantage predicts) but not in consumption (as the theory of demand assumes), subsequently production specialization seems to have fallen a great deal. British exports none the less remain heavily specialized in semi-manufactures and finished manufactures. However, the UK also imports a substantial amount of these goods too. Indeed, whereas the proportion of these in visible exports fell from 85 per cent to 66 per cent over 1971–83, the proportion in imports rose from 53 per cent to 69 per cent.

A major reason for this relative change has been the place that mineral fuels and lubricants have increasingly taken in exports, rising from only 3 per cent in 1971 to 22 per cent in 1983, which necessarily reduced the share of manufactures.

The bulk of UK trade is thus in manufactures, indicating that UK trade is mainly concentrated with other industrialized countries. This is brought out in table 29.2, where the share of UK exports going to the rest of the developed world rose from 72 per cent in 1971 to 77 per cent in 1983 (there is a dip in the middle at the height of the oil boom) and the share of UK imports from the rest of the developed world rose from 76 per cent to 83 per cent. In 1971 the UK's principal trading partners were in the EEC (taken as the 1980 nine member states for the whole of this period) as they were in 1983, only more so, with their share in UK exports rising from 28 per cent to 44 per cent and their share of imports rising from 31 per cent to 47 per cent. This rising share has been at the expense chiefly of the USA and the commonwealth developed countries.

Table 29.2 Destinations and origins of UK exports and imports (percentage of total trade)

	1971	*1981*	*1982*	*1983*
Exports				
European Community	28	41	41	44
Other Western Europe	16	13	12	13
North America	16	14	15	15
Other developed countries	12	6	6	5
Oil exporting countries	6	12	12	10
Rest of world	22	15	14	13
Imports				
European Community	31	44	46	47
Other Western Europe	17	15	15	16
North America	18	14	14	13
Other developed countries	10	7	7	7
Oil exporting countries	9	7	6	4
Rest of world	16	13	12	12

Note: percentages may not sum to 100 owing to rounding.
Source: UK Balance of Payments, 1982 and 1984, table 2.4.

Fitting Imports and Exports into the Keynesian Model

The two principal determinants of imports and exports are incomes at home (for imports) and abroad (for exports) and the prices at which goods trade on the international market, which depend upon the foreign exchange rate.

Aggregate expenditure in an open economy is the sum of consumption, investment and government expenditure (these are often referred to as **domestic absorption**) together with net foreign demand – exports minus imports. From the point of view of the home economy, exports are determined by overseas incomes and, although these may be affected in a roundabout way by domestic imports from abroad, it is convenient to assume that foreign *GDP*s are unaffected by changes in *GDP* at home. Exports will therefore be taken as given. Imports will be taken as a positive function of *GDP*, like consumption, but not of disposable income since the government sector, among others, also demands imports, as does investment. The modification required to the Keynesian model can be set out directly in each of the two approaches (compare with chapters 26 and 27):

Aggregate expenditure and output approach

Behavioural equations:

$C = C_0 + c(Y - T)$	(consumption function)
$T = tY$	(tax function)
$I = I_0$	(investment function)
$G = G_0$	(government expenditure function)
$X = X_0$	(export function)
$M = M_0 + mY$	(import function)

Equilibrium condition:

$$Y = C + I + G + X - M$$

Reduced form:

$$Y = (C_o + I_0 + G_0 + X_0 - M_o)\frac{1}{1 - c\,(1 - t) + m}$$

Injections and withdrawals approach

Behavioural equations:

$S = S_0 + s(Y-T)$	(savings function)
$T = tY$	(tax function)
$I = I_0$	(investment function)
$G = G_0$	(government expenditure function)
$X = X_0$	(export function)
$M = M_0 + mY$	(import function)

Equilibrium condition:

$$I + G + X = S + T + M$$

Reduced form:

$$Y = (-S_0 + I_0 + G_0 + X_0 - M_0)\frac{1}{1 - (1 - s)(1 - t) + m}$$

Exports are an additional injection into the circular flow and imports are a withdrawal. In the expenditure and output approach net exports are $X - M$, whereas in the injections and withdrawals approach each appears on its appropriate side of the equilibrium condition.

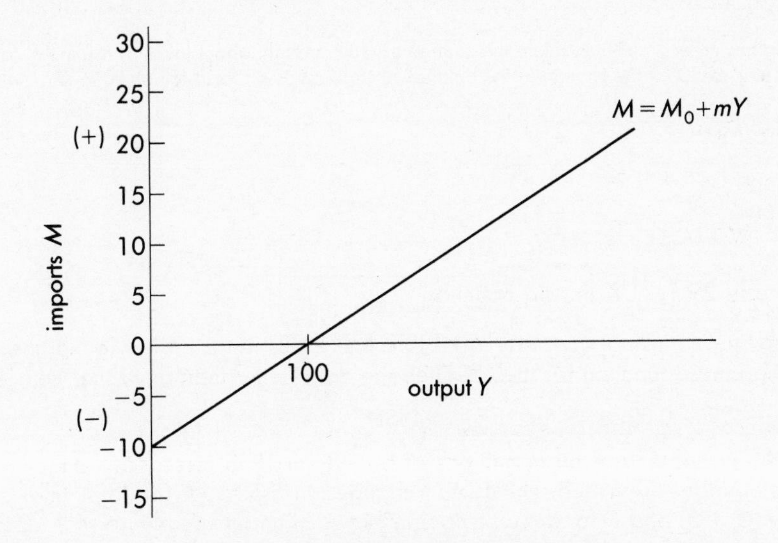

Figure 29.1 Import function for SAQ 29.1

SAQ 29.1

Consider figure 29.1.

(a) What is the value of M_0? (Do not take M_0 as a literally observable point: it just happens to be the intercept on the imports axis that is implied by a straight line approximation to the relationship between M and Y over observable ranges. Negative M is plainly impossible!).

(b) What is the value of m?

(c) What is M when $Y = 0$?

(d) What is M when $Y = 100$?

(e) What is M when $Y = 300$?

SAQ 29.2

Derive the reduced forms that include the import and export functions from the structural equations and equilibrium conditions.

The effect of adding a positive term to the denominator of the multiplier is obviously to reduce its size. This term, m, is the marginal propensity to import. In the absence of foreign trade and with $c = 0.8$ and $t = 0.25$, the multiplier would be 2.5. With a marginal propensity to import of say 0.33, the multiplier falls to 1.37. As you have seen before, the larger the size of the leakages, or the more of them there are, the smaller the multiplier. Thus, the more the government taxes out of incremental income and the greater the propensity to import out of incremental income, the smaller the amplifying effects of any shock that hits the economy – the greater its stability. Since the 1930s, the size of the multiplier in the UK may therefore be expected to have fallen quite substantially since both t and m have increased and the economy will have become less prone to extremes of variation in *GDP*.

SAQ 29.3

For the following economy, calculate the change in *GDP* brought about (a) by a rise in M_0 to zero (b) a fall in X to 20 (c) the change in the balance of trade $(X - M)$ for a fall of 10 in G:

$$C = 10 + 0.8(Y - T)$$
$$T = 0.25Y$$
$$I = 10$$
$$G = 30$$
$$X = 30$$
$$M = -10 + 0.33Y$$

Case Study 29.1 UK Import Function

Michael Surrey, using quarterly data for the 1950s and 1960s, found that the following import function for the UK fitted the data better than any other he tried:

$$M = -429 + 0.322\Delta S + 0.218F + 0.455D$$

where the variables are all in millions of pounds at 1963 prices. M stands for the value of imports in a quarter, ΔS for changes in stocks, F for total final sales $(C + I + G + X)$ and D for the discrepancy between final expenditure $(F + \Delta S)$ and *GDP* (mostly unrecorded stockbuilding). Since stockbuilding is a tiny proportion of *GDP*, the main interest focuses on F, indicating a marginal propensity to import of about 0.22.

This, of course, is very aggregated. The marginal propensity to import by different sectors of the economy can vary widely. For example, the average import content of consumers' expenditure was about 17 per cent, of public expenditure (on current account) 9 per cent, of investment 14 per cent and of exports 23 per cent. In practice, the high import content of exports is an important feature that must be allowed for in policies designed to affect the balance of payments. The exposition in this chapter does not, however, incorporate this effect directly.

M. J. C. Surrey (1971) *The Analysis and Forecasting of the British Economy*, Cambridge, Cambridge University Press, chapter 4.

SAQ 29.4

Suppose the economy is in the original situation described in SAQ 29.3.

(a) What happens to the balance of trade $(X - M)$ if, over a period, the *GDP* of the economy grows by 10 per cent and the rest of the world's *GDP* grows, leading to a rise in exports of 20 per cent?

(b) What happens to the balance of trade if, over a period, the *GDP* of the economy grows by 10 per cent but (for whatever reason) exports remain the same?

The Balance of Payments

The UK balance of payments in 1983 is set out in table 29.3. The balance of payments, as its name implies, is a record of payments to and from any particular country. Any transaction giving rise to the purchase of foreign currency, for example to enable the purchase of an import, is recorded as a debit item; any transaction giving rise to a sale of foreign currency (or overseas purchase of domestic currency), for example to enable the overseas purchase of the home country's exports, is recorded as a credit item. Thus, if a British importer purchases a German machine this counts as a debit: the German exporter will require to be paid in Deutschmarks, which the British importer must purchase in exchange for sterling. Conversely, if a German importer purchases a British machine, this counts as a credit: the British firm will require to be paid in sterling, which the German exporter must purchase in exchange for Deutschmarks.

Table 29.3 UK balance of payments, 1983 (£ million)

	Exports		*Imports*		*Balance*
Current account					
1 Goods (visibles)	60,625		61,341		−716
2 Services (invisibles)	19,143		15,241		3902
3 Total trade		79,768		76,582	3186
4 Interest, profits and dividends	12,473		10,525		1948
5 Transfers	3,359		5,577		−2218
6 Total current account		95,600		92,684	2916
Capital account					
7 Investment and other capital transactions					−3648
8 Balancing item					−84
9 Balance for official financing (6 + 7 + 8)					816
Official financing					
10 Net transactions with overseas monetary authorities					−36
11 Foreign currency borrowing (net)					249
12 Official reserves (drawings on are +)					603
13 Total					816

Source: UK Balance of Payments, 1984, table 1.3.

The balance of payments account is divided into three main sections: current, capital and official financing. Taking **current account** first, you can see that in 1983 the UK exported £60,625 million and imported £61,341 million of goods, leaving a (deficit) *balance of visible trade* of −£716 million. The second line of the table shows the amount of exports and imports of services, or invisibles, leaving a *balance of invisible trade* of £3902 million. These invisible services consisted mainly of transport services like shipping and civil aviation, travel and tourist services (if a German takes a holiday in Britain, this counts as a British invisible export), and financial and other services by the City of

London. The sum of visibles and invisibles gives total exports and imports and the difference between them is the **balance of trade**. This was £3186 million in 1983.

The balance of trade is a part of what is termed the *current account balance*. The remainder consists first of property incomes in the shape of interest, profit and dividends received by UK residents on their investments in the rest of the world and paid to residents of the rest of the world on their investments in the UK. These are all calculated net of taxes: UK receipts are taken net of any taxes paid overseas since these are not received by UK residents, and UK payments are also taken net of UK taxes since the tax revenue remains in the UK. The second part of the remainder consists of transfers made by private people and the government. Part of the government transfers are receipts and payments from and to EEC institutions. In the case of credits they include receipts from the EEC Agricultural Guidance and Guarantee Fund and the Regional Development Fund. In the case of debits they include the EEC's share of UK VAT (about half the total transfers), agricultural levies and customs duties paid to the EEC. Economic and military aid also feature in this category. Private transfers include gifts sent or received, transfers of a charitable type and pensions from the UK to overseas beneficiaries or from abroad to beneficiaries in the UK.

In 1983 the net effect of all these current account transactions was positive, giving a surplus on current account of £2916 million.

The **capital account** refers not to *physical* but to *financial* capital – the issue or repayment of debts. For example, if Germans purchase shares in a British company this counts as an *import* of capital, as it would if Germans bought a factory in the UK. The main item here is investment and other capital transactions. These relate to changes in holdings of foreign assets and liabilities of the UK. The main items are overseas investment in the UK, for example purchases of shares in UK companies and of British government stock, together with similar investments made abroad by UK residents. The main reason why in 1983 net capital transactions were negative is that UK private investment overseas far exceeded private overseas investment in the UK (£10,560 million compared with £4750 million).

The balancing item is there to compensate for statistical errors and omissions that are due, for example, to the under-recording of exports and reliance on survey data for elements like tourist expenditures. It is also affected by the fact that transfers of goods and services may take place – and usually do – at a different date from the payment therefor. Thus, if the value of exports is reckoned at one time, but payment received only in the following year, the value of exports will seem larger than has actually been paid for.

The balance of these three items on the capital account is what remains for **official financing**. What this means can be illustrated by looking at the situation in 1983. In that year there was a surplus on current account – the value of all exports was larger than that of all imports by £2916 million (though there was a deficit on the *visible* balance of trade). Foreigners were buying more in total from the UK than were UK residents from them. To do this, overseas purchasers of our exports needed more sterling than the UK needed foreign currencies. One way for them to obtain the extra was for UK residents to lend sterling or buy foreign assets. To buy foreign assets UK residents would have to sell sterling and buy the appropriate foreign currency. In 1983, however, investors were buying overseas capital more than overseas residents were buying in the UK, leading to a net demand for other currencies rather than a net supply of sterling. This difference (£3648 million) needs then to be subtracted from the current account surplus, leaving −£816 million to be found elsewhere (after adjusting for the balancing item.) This balance of sterling that was supplied to finance the shortfall came from the Bank of England and the Treasury and is called official financing. It is met partly by public sector borrowing of foreign currencies and partly by running down the UK official **reserves** of gold and foreign currencies. In 1983 these fell by £603 million despite the current account surplus and mainly because of the relative attractions of overseas compared with the UK investment (reflected in higher interest rates abroad than in the UK). Overall, therefore, there was a balance of payments deficit (before official financing).

In total the balance of payments will *always* balance for, if everything is properly measured on current and capital account, any remaining balance must be met through official financing. To take a homely example, suppose in a given year you received a net income of £10,000 from the sale of your labour and your total expenditure was £15,000. You financed part of your excess expenditure of £5000 by borrowing £4000. Where did the remaining £1000 come from? You must have run down your holdings of cash since, as you spent £15,000, you must have had £15,000 to spend. The running down of your holding by £1000 is analogous to a change in the UK's reserves. Conversely, were your total expenditure only £9000 out of a net income of £10,000, then your cash asset holdings must have increased by £1000, analogous to a rise in reserves.

Balance of payments *problems* arise when, for example, there is a persistent excess of imports over exports, the exchange rate is not free to alter, and private investment transactions fail to provide a sufficient supply of foreign currencies to meet the persistent deficit. Official borrowing would have to increase indefinitely and the reserves of gold and foreign exchange would come under heavy pressure. Sterling interest rates will rise together with the increase in borrowing, leading to reductions in aggregate expenditure, and the government itself is likely to reduce its public expenditure in order to reduce incomes and hence the demand for imports. If the economy is at full employment or less than full employment, unemployment may be one price paid for a persistent current account deficit. There may be pressure to restrict imports directly through quotas or tariffs, which is one way of exporting unemployment to one's trading partners.

The reverse problem exists when there is a persistent surplus on current account. The full analysis of these problems must wait, however, until money has been explicitly introduced into the macroeconomy.

Exchange Rates

Suppose there are two trading partners, the US and the UK. Their currencies are dollars and pounds sterling respectively. These currencies are traded in a highly competitive market, so that the rate at which one trades for the other is everywhere the same through instantaneous (for example, telegraphic) arbitrage.

The exchange rate is defined as the relative price of the two currencies. Thus, if a dollar sells for 50p, a pound sells for two dollars and the exchange rate is either 0.5 (the price of dollars in terms of pounds) or 2.0 (the price of pounds in terms of dollars). In the UK the convention is to express the exchange rate as the amount of foreign currency obtainable per pound. In January 1985, for example, the exchange rate of sterling for dollars was 1.06, having fallen fairly steadily from an average 1970 rate of 2.394. Normally banks have a buying and selling rate for foreign currencies, with the margin between representing their reward for providing the middleman services. (This spread of rates is ignored in the analysis here.) Recall that sterling is demanded by US residents to enable them to purchase British exports. Dollars are demanded by UK residents to enable them to purchase US exports. Sterling is *supplied* by UK residents when they purchase dollars, and dollars are *supplied* by US citizens when they purchase sterling. The exchange rate is thus determined by supply and demand. It will be plain that in looking at the supply and demand for dollars one is also implicitly looking at the demand and supply of sterling.

Although the analysis of this chapter treats the exchange rate as being between sterling and only one other currency (the US dollar), there are in reality as many exchange rates as there are other currencies. Table 29.4 shows the rates for a selection of major currencies in 1983. There is, however, a technique for arriving at a single sterling exchange rate known as the **effective exchange rate**. This is a weighted average of the pound sterling in terms of the currencies of Britain's major trading partners, where the weights used are based on the share of the UK's total trade with each country. In UK official publications this is calculated as an index – the *sterling exchange rate index*, or *sterling index* for short. For example, the USA has a weight of about one quarter

Table 29.4 Sterling exchange rates, 1983

Country	*Average sterling exchange rate over 1983*
US dollar	1.516
Japanese yen	359.9
Swiss franc	3.182
French franc	11.55
Italian lira	2302.0
German mark	3.870

Source: Economic Trends, July 1984, table 50

so that a 1 per cent depreciation of the US dollar has the same effect on the balance of UK trade as a 0.25 per cent appreciation of sterling against all currencies. In general the exchange rate of sterling against the US dollar follows the same pattern as that against the weighted set of currencies. Table 29.5 shows how indices of the dollar exchange rate and the effective exchange rate have varied over 1970–83. The dollar rate, although following the same general pattern as the effective rate, is less stable. The substantial slide in 1982 and 1983, which continued into early 1985, was largely due to relatively high interest rates in the USA (also relative to many other countries) which encouraged an outflow of investment and a large supply of sterling in order to purchase dollars.

Table 29.5 Variations in the dollar and effective exchange rates, 1970–83 (1975 = 100)

	US dollar	*Sterling index*
1970	108	128
1971	110	127
1972	113	123
1973	110	112
1974	105	108
1975	100	100
1976	81	86
1977	79	81
1978	86	81
1979	96	87
1980	105	96
1981	91	95
1982	79	91
1983	68	83

Source: Economic Trends, July 1984, table 50

SAQ 29.5

Using the data in table 29.4:

(a) What was the value of sterling in terms of dollars?
(b) What was the value of a dollar in terms of sterling?
(c) What was the value of a dollar in terms of yen?
(d) What was the value of a mark in terms of lire?

Demand for and Supply of Sterling

Sterling is demanded by US residents because these holders of dollars want to purchase UK exports and to invest in the UK. The latter motive will be a function of profit expectations. The former, which is focused on here, will depend on the demand for UK exports. Sterling is supplied by UK residents as they exchange it to purchase dollars to finance the import of US goods.

Figure 29.2 shows the demand and supply of sterling as a function of its dollar price. The demand curve has a negative slope: as the exchange rate *depreciates* (falls) the demand for sterling rises, as UK exports become cheaper

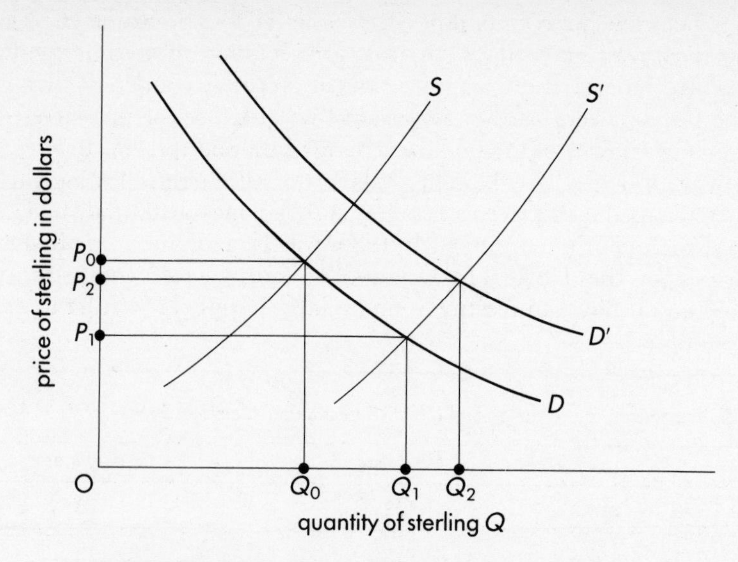

Figure 29.2 Demand for and supply of sterling

to US residents and they wish to purchase more of them, or UK investments become cheaper for US residents and they wish to make more investments. The supply curve of sterling slopes upwards. This means that as the exchange rate *appreciates* (rises), UK residents will supply more. Why is this? Remember that a rise in the dollar price of sterling is the same thing as a fall in the sterling price of dollars. Thus, if the exchange rate rises from 2.0 to 3.0 in terms of dollars, then it falls from 0.5 to 0.333 in terms of sterling. Hence, an appreciation of sterling means that US exports become cheaper to UK residents. They therefore demand more of them and, *if this demand is relatively elastic*, the demand for dollars will rise. More sterling will therefore be necessarily supplied.

SAQ 29.6

What does the supply curve of sterling look like if the UK demand for US exports is relatively *inelastic*?

Flexible Exchange Rates

If sterling is *undervalued* – lying below P_0 in figure 29.2 – the demand for sterling will exceed the supply. US residents will be wanting to purchase UK exports but will be short of the sterling they need to do so, for at that rate of exchange UK residents are not wanting enough US exports to supply the sterling US residents need. The price of sterling will therefore be bid upwards, the quantity demanded will fall, and the quantity supplied will increase (as UK importers increase their demand for US exports and supply more pounds in exchange for the dollars they need). Conversely, if sterling is *overvalued* – lying above P_0 in figure 29.2 – then what in the other case was true for US residents is true for UK residents, so the price of sterling will be bid down and the exchange rate will depreciate.

This analysis emphasizes the importance of trade flows in the determination of exchange rates. Relative price levels and interest rates, and changes in them, are important too, and these are discussed in later chapters. For the moment the focus is on the effects of changing demands for imports and exports on the exchange rate.

Suppose the exchange rate is free to find its equilibrium level. Suppose the price of an important import were to rise as did, for example, oil in the early 1970s. Assuming that the UK demand for oil is relatively inelastic then more overseas currency will be needed to finance the imported oil, leading to a rise in the UK supply of sterling (to purchase the necessary dollars) and a shift of the supply curve in figure 29.2 to S', a depreciation of sterling to P_1 and an increase in the supply of sterling to Q_1. Subsequently, oil becomes domestically produced and exported leading to a rise in overseas demand for sterling to D' and an appreciation of sterling to P_2 (also accompanied by a shift back – not shown in figure 29.2 – of the S curve as less oil is imported by the UK).

Fixed Exchange Rates

Between the end of the Second World War and 1972 the sterling exchange rate, like that of most other major currencies, was not permitted to find its own level in the way just described. The rate did not float but was *fixed* or *pegged* at a particular rate to the dollar and the Bank of England entered the foreign exchange market and bought or sold foreign currencies so as to keep the rate close to the agreed **par value**.

In a situation where there was a balance of payments deficit on current and capital account, the demand for sterling would have been less than its supply at the fixed exchange rate. This led to pressure on sterling to depreciate. The Bank of England entered the market and bought sterling (sold dollars) to make up for the deficient demand for sterling. This required the UK to have sufficient holdings of reserves and also led, under conditions of persistent balance of payments deficits, to the use of other direct controls on the demand for other currencies (for example, limits on the amounts UK tourists travelling abroad could take). With persistent drains on reserves, it would eventually have become impossible to maintain the par value and a **devaluation** would have become necessary, moving the exchange rate towards equilibrium. Incidentally, currency speculators would then be offered an effectively free gift for, by obtaining dollars (etc.) during a period in which a devaluation looked increasingly inevitable, the sterling value of those dollars would immediately jump upon devaluation. Such speculation, of course, increased the pressure on sterling.

Under floating exchange rates, any systematic attempt to hoard dollars in anticipation of a sterling depreciation tends to be self-defeating as the exchange rate will depreciate immediately as a result of the increased speculative demand for dollars. With a purely floating exchange rate there is no need for official financing of the balance of payments: a current account surplus will be exactly matched by a capital account deficit and vice versa, with the exchange rate adjusting so that the supply of and demand for sterling are equal. With a fixed rate, however, this cannot happen and official financing takes up the difference: reserves will fall if there is an overall deficit and rise if there is an overall surplus. Currently the UK operates a 'dirty' float, with some official financing. Had sterling not depreciated over the period since 1980 you may therefore infer that the amount of official financing would have been very much larger – probably large enough to have required a formal devaluation.

Table 29.6 Oil and the sterling exchange rate

	Balance of trade in oil (£ million)	*% of current account balance*	*Exchange rate ($/£)*
1973	−941	95.9	2.45
1974	−3357	102.6	2.34
1975	−3057	201.0	2.22
1976	−3947	451.1	1.80
1977	−2771	12,595.5	1.74
1978	−1984	−194.9	1.92
1979	−731	85.7	2.12
1980	+273	9.5	2.33

Source: Balance of Payments (Pink Book), 1982, tables 1.1, 9.1 and 13.1

Case Study 29.2 The Oil Crisis and the Exchange Rate

In crude terms, what has just been said in the text seems to accord with UK experience in the 1970s. Table 29.6 shows the balance of trade in oil (exports less imports), the percentage of the current account deficit or surplus that this occupied and the exchange rate (annual average) of the dollar against sterling. The early 1970s showed an increasing trade deficit in oil that constituted a sharply increasing percentage of the current balance overall. The exchange rate depreciated substantially throughout these years, as is predicted by the theory. It appreciated in 1978 despite a continuing heavy deficit in oil, but this was the first year in this series when there was an overall current account surplus. Thereafter the oil deficit fell dramatically (exports almost doubled) until by 1980 the UK had a trade surplus in oil and the exchange rate had risen for the third year in succession.

Fixed versus Floating Exchange Rates

The arguments – which have at times been heated – between economists who prefer fixed and those who prefer floating exchange rates essentially hinge on the issue of whether or not a fixed rate imposes a useful discipline on economic planners. There are other issues too, of course, such as whether a floating rate is going to be stable enough to enable international traders to make reliable contracts with one another. This partly depends on the elasticities (discussed in SAQ 29.6) and partly on theories about how speculators react to fixed (but periodically revised) rates on the one hand and to floating rates on the other. Experience, indeed, seems to suggest that floating rates are not inherently wildly fluctuating. The 'discipline' argument is, however, still alive.

Those in favour of a fixed rate argue that the balance of payments constraint compels governments to forgo profligate domestic expansionary policies, as an economy that expands too fast will cause the balance of payments to go into deficit as imports grow. This will force the government into contractionary policies as well as automatically inducing a domestic contraction through monetary mechanisms (see later chapters). This argument can be illustrated in practice by the quite deflationary policies of the British Labour government from 1964 to the 1967 devaluation, which went very much against the grain of a party committed to extensive programmes of public expenditure.

Those in favour of floating rates argue that even if, on the average, the chosen par value is more or less right, rigging a price ratio in such a fashion almost inevitably brings in a whole train of further restrictions, quotas, subsidies and so on to control imports and exports of various kinds. These controls become more vexatious the further away the par value is from equilibrium and they cause losses of wealth (as specialization according to comparative advantage is diminished), possible retaliation from trading partners, losses of consumers' and producers' surpluses and losses of individual freedom. As for discipline, they propose an alternative constraint – control of the money supply (of which more anon).

Case Study 29.3 The 1967 UK Devaluation

From 1949 onwards, sterling was fixed in relation to the dollar (which was in turn fixed in value in terms of gold) at the rate of 2.80 (give or take a bit). By the 1960s this rate became increasingly difficult to maintain. In 1961 there was a large balance for official financing, and again in 1963 and following years there were large deficits on current and capital account to be met by official financing as shown in table 29.7.

Table 29.7 The balance of payments, exchange rate and official reserves, 1960–70

	Balance for official financing (£ million)	*Dollar exchange rate (annual average)*	*Reserves ($ million)*
1960	−293	2.808	3231
1961	339	2.802	3318
1962	−192	2.808	2806
1963	58	2.800	2658
1964	695	2.793	2315
1965	353	2.796	3004
1966	591	2.793	3100
1967	671	2.828	2694
1968	1410	2.394	2421
1969	−687	2.390	2528
1970	−1420	2.396	2827

Sources: Balance of Payments (Pink Book), 1982, table 1.1; *Economic Trends*, Annual Supplement, 1981, table 142

Reserves were falling and devaluation became inevitable. This took place in November 1967, with a new rate pegged at 2.40 (give or take a bit). The balance of payments began to improve as soon as transactors were able to adjust to the new exchange rate. In 1969 and 1970 there were surpluses on current and capital accounts taken together, and reserves began to rise again. The devaluation was helped by domestic policies to restrain aggregate expenditure, so that the demand for imports fell as the growth of *GDP* fell.

What You Should Understand Now

The principal features of UK commodity trade.
The Keynesian model with imports and exports: the difference their introduction makes to the reduced form and multiplier.
The main features of the UK's balance of payments.
The meaning of foreign exchange rates.
The determination of foreign exchange rates in terms of the demand and supply of a currency.
The impact of the oil crisis on the sterling exchange rate.
Some consequences of fixed or floating exchange rates.

30

The Keynesian Model and Investment

In the model so far, investment has been determined *exogenously*, that is by factors that are not (as yet) included in the model. Investment is not readily and powerfully related to *GDP*, as was observed earlier.

The determinants of investment can be usefully divided into two broad types: those that seem to have predictable consequences in economic models, and those that seem not to. The main predictable determinants are interest rates and *changes* in income. The main unpredictable determinants are the expectations of businessmen – what Keynes called their 'animal spirits' – that may make them more or less optimistic about the future and hence affect their investment plans. Economics has as yet to develop a satisfactory theory of business expectations. Indeed, it is at the heart of the entrepreneurial function for people to gamble on the future according to their own judgements about what will pay off and what will not, and if economists were able to model their expectations well, particularly if they were able to identify correct (as it turned out) expectations, then economists would all be rich – which they are not!

What economists do, therefore, is something less ambitious. The first part of the chapter will look at the effects that interest rates have on investment. The second part will look at the impact of *changes* in income on investment, particularly in the context of the business cycle.

Interest and Investment

Although later analysis will not treat interest rates as entirely exogenously determined, for the present it is assumed that they are given. For simplicity's sake, assume that there is just one rate and ignore the fact that, in the real world, risk and uncertainty, transaction costs and a variety of other factors mean that there is a host of different interest rates (for example, borrowers judged to be riskier than others by lenders will normally have to pay a higher rate of interest to compensate lenders for the perceived higher risk of default). The analysis of this host of interest rates is a topic in advanced economic analysis.

Consider, then, a manager contemplating an investment. Suppose the interest rate is 10 per cent and continue to assume (as has been done so far) that the price level is constant. The investment can be financed in two basic

Table 30.1 Present value of investment plan

Expenditure	*Now*	*End Year 1*	*Year 2*	*Year 3*	*Year 4*	*Year 5*	*Year 6*	*Year 7*
1 Plant	1000	0	0	0	0	0	0	0
2 Labour etc.	0	100	100	100	100	100	100	100
Receipts								
3 Sales	0	0	100	250	500	750	1000	1250
4 Scrap value of plant at end	0	0	0	0	0	0	0	100
5 Net receipts	−1000	−100	0	150	400	650	900	1250
6 Discount factor ($i = 0.1$)	1	$\frac{1}{1+i} = 0.909$	$\frac{1}{(1+i)^2} = 0.826$	$\frac{1}{(1+i)^3} = 0.751$	$\frac{1}{(1+i)^4} = 0.683$	$\frac{1}{(1+i)^5} = 0.621$	$\frac{1}{(1+i)^6} = 0.564$	$\frac{1}{(1+i)^7} = 0.513$
7 Present value of net receipts	−1000	−91	0	113	273	404	508	641
Net present value of investment: £848								

Table 30.2 Debt and debt repayments on a loan of £1000 over seven years with interest 10 per cent (£)

	Now	*End year 1*	*End year 2*	*End year 3*	*End year 4*	*End year 5*	*End year 6*	*End year 7*
Debt	£1000	1100	984.05	856.51	716.22	561.89	392.13	205.406
Repayments		205.406	205.406	205.406	205.406	205.406	205.406	205.406
Net debt	£1000	894.59	778.64	651.11	510.81	356.49	186.73	0.00

ways. The money could be borrowed to purchase the plant, equipment and so on. In this case the firm will have to pay 10 per cent on its borrowing. Alternatively, it could finance the investment out of retained profits – that is, profits not distributed to shareholders. Again the cost is 10 per cent since the firm could have lent the retained profits at 10 per cent or, alternatively, it could have distributed the profits to its owners who themselves could lend them out at 10 per cent. In other words, 10 per cent is the *opportunity cost* of obtaining finance for investment. Never make the gross error of supposing that *internal* funding of investment expenditure is interest free!

To be concrete, suppose that the plan is to invest in plant costing £1000 now, and to repay the £1000 and the interest on any outstanding amount of debt at the end of each year for a period of seven years (the expected life of the plant). Whether the investment is worth while will evidently depend on the firm's expectations of other costs in the future and its expected receipts. Suppose the expectation is that labour costs will be a constant £100 per year payable at the end of the year (assume all receipts and payments occur at the end of each year to keep the arithmetic simple).

These expectations are set out in rows 1 and 2 of table 30.1. Expectations of sales are set out in row 3 and the expected scrap value of the plant at the end of its expected life is in row 4. You now have sufficient information in table 30.1 to determine whether the proposed investment is worth while. Note that the table does not include interest charges as an expenditure. That is for a very good reason, as you will see shortly.

A positive flow of net receipts occurs only during year 3. In that year a profit of £150 will be made. However, you know from chapter 16 that a profit of £150 in three years' time is not at all worth the same as a profit of £150 now. Recall: if you had £150 now and invested it at 10 per cent, after three years it would have grown to a much larger amount. £150 today is therefore worth *more* than £150 in three years' time or, putting it the other way around, £150 in three years' time is worth less than £150 today. Now is a good time to refresh your memory of discounting by rereading chapter 16.

SAQ 30.1

(a) What will £150 invested now at 10 per cent interest grow to be in three years?
(b) What is £150 in three years worth now if the interest rate is 10 per cent?

To calculate the desirability of the investment you need to calculate the present value of net receipts over the entire lifetime of the plant. Net receipts in each year are recorded in row 5 of table 30.1. These are the sums of the items in rows 1, 2, 3 and 4. Below that, in row 6, is the appropriate discount factor at 10 per cent interest. Applying the discount factor for each year to the receipts of each year gives the present value of net receipts for each year, shown in row 7. These, when added together, give the net present value of the investment plan: £848. It is positive, so the investment seems worth while. The prudent decision maker would not stop here, however. He or she would be wise to subject this result to **sensitivity analysis**, in order to see what changes in the assumptions about, say, sales and labour costs, had an important impact on

Table 30.3 Present value of cash flow (interest rate 10 per cent)

	Now	*End year 1*	*End year 2*	*End year 3*	*End year 4*	*End year 5*	*End year 6*	*End year 7*
Payments								
Purchase of equipment	1000	—	—	—	—	—	—	—
Labour	—	100	100	100	100	100	100	100
Capital repayments and interest	—	205.406	205.406	205.406	205.406	205.406	205.406	205.406
Total	1000	305.406	305.406	305.406	305.406	305.406	305.406	305.406
Receipts								
Sales	—	—	100	250	500	750	1000	1250
Borrowing	1000	—	—	—	—	—	—	—
Scrap value	—	—	—	—	—	—	—	100
Total	1000	—	100	250	500	750	1000	1350
Net receipts	—	−305.406	−205.406	−55.406	194.594	444.594	694.594	1044.594
Present value of net receipts by year	—	−277.64	−169.76	−41.63	132.91	276.06	392.80	536.04

Net present value = £848

the calculated net present value: a project that is very sensitive may not be such a good idea after all. It is also good practice to test the **robustness** of the analysis. This refers to the flexibility of the investment in the event that things turn out differently from what is expected. Thus, if the plant can be cheaply adapted to alternative uses (say, to produce a modified product in the light of market experience) then the investment decision will be more robust than if it is very specific. In addition, if the decision maker has limited investment funds (which often happens under the budgetary arrangements adopted in many private and public organizations), it is important to look at alternative investments that may have higher net present values (and be less sensitive and more robust).

The process of discounting future net receipts automatically takes account of debt charges and repayments, which is why they do not feature in table 30.1. To show this, consider table 30.2. Here suppose that the initial borrowing of £1000 at 10 per cent is to be repaid with interest in seven equal annual instalments of £205.406 (in practice, £205.41). This firm begins with a debt of £1000. At the end of year 1 the debt has risen to £1100 (with the interest on the initial debt). The sum of £205.406 is repaid, leaving a net debt of £894.59 (allowing for rounding off to the nearest penny). The beginning of year 2 sees an inherited debt of £894.59 (rounded) that rises to £984.05 after addition of interest over the second year. Of this, £205.406 is paid off at the end of the year, leaving £778.64 after the repayment. In the final year (year 7) the inherited debt is £186.73 which, together with the interest over year 7 is just paid off by the final instalment of £205.406. The present value of the seven repayments of £205.406 is exactly £1000. The present value of net receipts *excluding* the £1000 purchase price of the plant is £1848. Repaying the debt therefore leaves the firm with a present value of £848, which is what you had before.

This method of looking at debt and its repayment (whether payments are actually paid on a debt actually incurred, or notionally paid on a debt notionally incurred as when the firm lends, so to speak, to itself) is exactly analagous to the mortgage repayments most home owners pay on the debt they incur to buy their houses. An annual equivalent charge is calculated whose present value equals the debt and which incorporates both an interest component and a repayment of the capital sum.

The same story can be seen by using a complete account of all cash flows, as in table 30.3. By working through this table, you can again see that the net present value of all cash flows is £848.

As seen in chapter 16, the *net present value rule* is the most reliable indicator of the profitability of an investment project. There is, none the less, an *internal rate of return* on this investment. This, you should recall, is the rate of discount that equates the present value of receipts and expenditure, or that makes the net present value zero. You will also recall that if the net present value is positive, the internal rate of return will be greater than the interest rate.

SAQ 30.2

Is the internal rate of return of the project shown in table 30.2 larger or smaller than 20 per cent?

Marginal Efficiency of Capital

The internal rate of return was termed by Keynes the **marginal efficiency of capital** (*MEC*). Suppose all firms rank all the capital projects they can in terms of their marginal efficiencies. With general (eventual) diminishing returns one expects that the most profitable capital projects will have been undertaken and, indeed, that all projects showing a marginal efficiency of capital greater than the rate of interest will have been undertaken. This is shown in figure 30.1. Here the heroic leap has been made of representing the entire capital stock of the economy on the horizontal axis ranked in order of each unit's marginal efficiency. Since firms will tend to invest and thereby increase the capital stock wherever *MEC* or the internal rate of return (*IRR*) is greater than the interest rate, with an interest rate of i_0 the capital stock will be K_0. One is implicitly assuming here that the rate of return includes some allowance for the uncertainty about whether or not estimated costs and revenues will actually accrue. Since the *MEC* curve has a negative slope, a lower interest rate will induce a higher preferred capital stock and vice versa. Thus, if the economy is in equilibrium with $i = i_0$ the capital stock will be K_0, since all capital projects with an *MEC* higher than i_0 will have been undertaken. Let i_0 fall to a new equilibrium level i_1. The desired capital stock rises to K_1 and investment will take place over and above any made to replace worn out stock until K_1 is attained.

A fall in the rate of interest therefore induces a *permanent* increase in the planned capital stock and a *temporary* increase in the flow of net investment

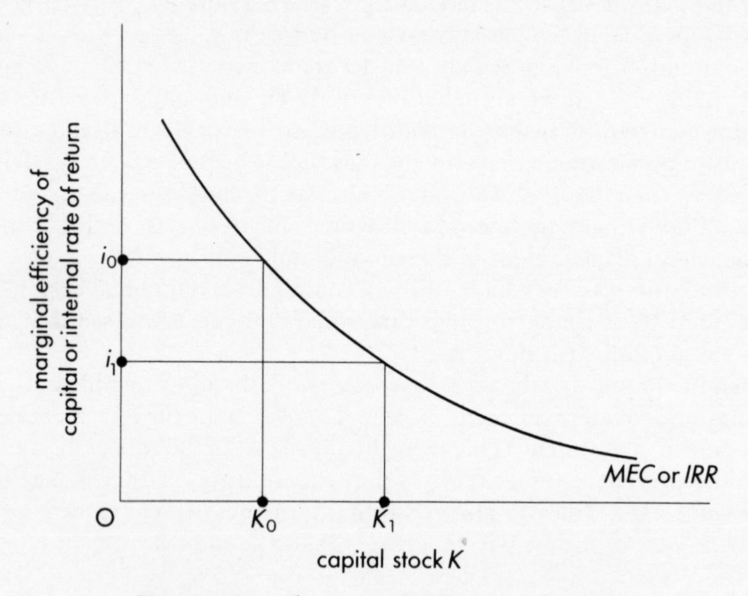

Figure 30.1 The marginal efficiency of capital

until the planned capital stock is attained. This will, of course, take time, depending on the costs of adjustment and the speed at which it is profitable for capital goods industries to produce the new capital goods. Eventually net investment will cease and only replacement investment will take place in full equilibrium. Such an equilibrium is, however, unlikely ever to be attained because the factors that ultimately determine the *MEC* and the interest rate are always changing, as are expectations.

Note that there is no *permanent* relationship between net investment and the rate of interest. The permanent relationship is between the interest rate and the planned capital *stock*. Investment is a *flow*. It is transitory – a means of adjusting to a preferred capital stock. If everything is constant, net investment is zero. Net investment occurs only when something changes, for example interest rates. Hence, a fall in interest rates induces net investment, and a rise induces net disinvestment (not replacing obsolete equipment, buildings and so on). The amount of investment that will eventually bring the capital stock up to its desired level in figure 30.1 is, of course, K_0K_1. But this may take several years (or at least several quarters). In the short run what one expects to see is that a fall in the rate of interest will be accompanied (with a lag in time) by a rise in (net) investment and a rise in the rate of interest by a fall in (net) investment.

SAQ 30.3

(a) 1 Consider two communities that are identical except that one has a higher rate of time preference than the other. Each has experienced long periods of interest rate stability, but one at a higher rate and the other at a low rate. Which community will have the higher rate of net investment?

2 What is net investment?

(b) Suppose that the short term relationship between investment and the rate of interest is given by

$$I = 40 - 200i$$

where I is total investment and i is the interest rate expressed in decimals (0.01, 0.02 etc). In an economy where the multiplier is 1.60 and changes in interest rates do not affect anything else (e.g. consumption or capital inflows and outflows in the balance of payments), what will be the impact on *GDP* of a fall in the interest rate from 0.15 to 0.10?

Case Study 30.1 Lags in Investment

Nobay (1970) has studied the lags that existed in the engineering industry around 1965. This industry produces capital goods and the demand of its customers is, of course, an investment demand. The lags can be divided into two kinds: the time in quarters (of a year) it took for the engineering industry to produce the goods ordered, and additional queuing time due to the fact that the industry could not immediately set in hand all the production demanded. The estimates are shown in table 30.4 (Nobay, 1970).

Within each category there was, of course, considerable variation in delivery lag after ordering, but the average lags reported in table 30.4 illustrate the importance of the lapse of time between the decision to invest and the actual expenditure. In only one case (small tools and gauges) was the production time slower than the queuing time, and here the overall waiting time was only about four and a half months. Some

Table 30.4 Waiting for engineering equipment in the UK, 1965 (in quarters)

Type of capital equiment	*Queuing time*	*Production time*	*Total time*
Metal working and welding	2.11	1.23	3.34
Engineers' small tools and gauges	0.70	0.75	1.45
Industrial engines	8.50	0.74	9.24
Textile machinery	2.25	1.10	3.35
Mechanical handling equipment	3.27	1.00	4.27
Pumps and industrial valves	2.54	1.15	3.69
Food and drink machinery	2.44	1.00	3.44
Packing machinery	2.03	1.26	3.29
Steel and non-ferrous rolling mills	4.16	0.71	4.87
Others except electricals	1.86	1.19	3.05
Shell boilers and boilerhouse plant	5.78	0.84	6.62
Chemical plant	3.17	1.83	5.00
Iron and steel and non-ferrous (excluding rolling units)	2.27	0.83	3.10
Other industrial plant and fabricated steel works	3.61	1.04	4.65
Other electrical machinery	3.55	0.90	4.45
Electronic capital equipment	2.22	0.48	2.70
Weighted average	2.96	1.00	3.96

parts of the industry were evidently very heavily pressed: for example, industrial engines took only an average of a bit longer than two months to manufacture, but the overall waiting time was well over two years.

A. R. Nobay (1970), 'Forecasting manufacturing investment – some preliminary results', *National Institute Economic Review*, no. 52, 58–66, table 1.

GDP and Investment

Just as changes in the interest rate cause investment to be positive or negative, so *changes in income* can cause it to be positive or negative. In this case, however, the theoretical relationship is expected to be positive: a rise in income causes investment and a fall in income causes disinvestment (other things equal). The relationship between changes in interest rates and investment was of course inverse, a *fall* in the interest rate inducing investment and vice versa.

For simplicity, begin by assuming that the long run planned capital stock is proportional to income. This ratio of capital stock to *GDP*, K/Y, is called the **capital–output ratio**. If now you consider an economy in equilibrium, so that the actual capital stock is equal to the planned capital stock and net investment is zero, an increase in aggregate expenditure will cause a short run increase in incomes via the multiplier and, since the capital–output ratio will have fallen below the preferred ratio, firms will seek to increase their employment not only of labour but also of capital. Net investment will therefore take place in response to the change in income. This will induce a further increase in income and output via the multiplier until – provided no

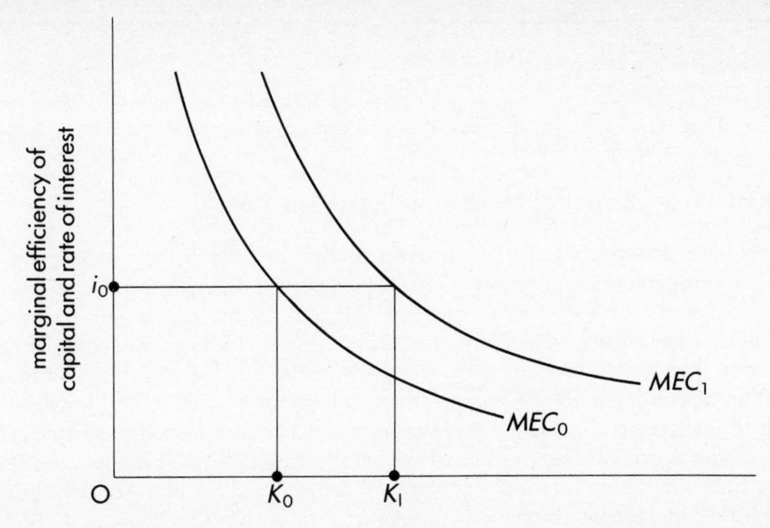

Figure 30.2 Effect of an increase in aggregate expenditure on the marginal efficiency of capital

further exogenous changes occur – the planned capital stock is attained, the preferred capital–output ratio reached, and net investment again falls to zero.

The change in income is impinging on the marginal efficiency of capital. As aggregate expenditure rises, firms find they can sell more even at the same price. This increases the flow of expected receipts (provided the aggregate expenditure rise is not believed to be very temporary) and hence increases the present value of profits. At each rate of interest, the *MEC* curve shifts to the right, from MEC_0 to MEC_1 in figure 30.2, so that previously unprofitable capital projects now become profitable at a constant rate of interest. The planned capital stock rises to K_1 from K_0 in figure 30.2 and, over time, investment in the amount K_0K_1 will have been undertaken.

In the short term, it will appear that income and investment are positively related. In the longer run, however, the effect of a rise in income on investment will peter out as the desired capital–output ratio is approached.

In the short run, therefore, investment will be negatively related to the rate of interest and positively related to changes in *GDP*. It seems that a theory that makes investment a function of income *and* interest rates (as well as animal spirits) may better explain the cause of investment in the economy over time than any simple unicausal theory.

SAQ 30.4

Consider the structural form of the following economy:

$C = C_0 + c(Y - T$
$T = tY$
$I = I_0 - ai + bY$
$G = G_0$
$X = X_0$
$M = M_0 + mY$

The interest rate is i, replacement investment is I_0, and a and b are constants.

(a) What is the reduced form?

(b) What is the multiplier?

(c) Let $c = 0.8$, $t = 0.3$, $b = 0.1$, $m = 0.3$, $a = 200$ and $i = 0.10$.
What is the change in *GDP* if i falls to 0.05?

Case Study 30.2 Empirical Models of Investment

Estimating investment functions has proved far more difficult than estimating consumption or import functions, and the results that different people have come up with vary a good deal. The main reason for the difficulty is that investment plans in the private sector are largely determined, as you have seen, by *expected* rates of return, and no one has yet come up with a satisfactory way of second-guessing the imagination of entrepreneurs. Another difficulty lies in the complicated lags between deciding to invest and getting the investment goods on line (recall case study 30.1).

In the UK there are several models of the whole economy (the Treasury model, the National Institute of Social and Economic Research model, the London Business School model, the Cambridge Growth Project model, the City University Business School model, and the Liverpool University Research Group in Macroeconomics model) which are used to forecast the future course of the economy. They differ significantly in size, detail and underlying theory. But each has to model investment.

In the Treasury model (which has 700 equations and 1000 variables) there are separate equations for public investment, private investment in housing and land, private non-manufacturing and private manufacturing investment. Part of the private manufacturing investment function (where the variables are measured in natural logarithms) looks like this:

$$I = 0.530 + I_{-4} + 0.520\ (Y - Y_{-4}) + 0.946\ (Y_{-5} - Y_{-9}) + \ldots - 0.142(i_{-6} - i_{-7}) + 0.00159\ CBI_{-6}$$

The data are quarterly and the subscripts indicate the quarter in question (for example, Y_{-5} is the value of *GDP* in the private manufacturing sector, Y, five quarters ago). Thus you can see that this model postulates that investment in the current quarter depends upon investment a year ago, the annual change in *GDP* in this sector and a lagged change in *GDP*. It also depends on changes in interest rates i eighteen months previously, and the *CBI* variable similarly lagged. *CBI* is the percentage of manufacturers answering 'yes' to the Confederation of British Industry's question 'Is plant capacity likely to limit output?', and is an attempt to get at entrepreneurial expectations at the time when they were shaping investment plans.

Details of the Treasury model can be found in HM Treasury (1982) and a discussion of the various UK models in Wallis (1984). See also Holden *et al.* (1982).

HM Treasury (1982) *Macroeconomic Model Technical Manual 1982*, London, HM Treasury.
Ken Wallis (1984) *Models of the UK Economy: A Review by the ESRC Macroeconomic Modelling Bureau*, Oxford, Oxford University Press.
K. Holden, D. A. Peel and J. L. Thompson (1982) *Modelling the UK Economy: An Introduction*, Oxford, Martin Robertson.

SAQ 30.5

(a) 'Since it is changes in interest rates and income that are hypothesized to affect net investment, if these are constant net investment will be zero'. Right?

(b) 'Capital is a stock and investment is a flow'. Right?

The Accelerator

Suppose that the capital–output ratio in the furniture industry is one lathe for every 500 chairs made per year. The industry has 50 lathes in use for chair manufacture. These each last for 10 years and past investments in lathes are such that each year 5 lathes are replaced. Total sales of chairs are evidently 50 machines × 500 chairs = 25,000 chairs per year, assuming that firms are operating at full capacity. In table 30.5 the industry in year 1 has an output of 25,000 chairs with a desired capital stock of 50 lathes. Five lathes wear out and are replaced. Net investment in lathes is zero, replacement investment is 5 and gross investment is therefore also 5. The same pattern exists in year 2. In year 3 demand rises to 30,000 chairs per year. Expecting this to be a permanent increase in demand, the desired capital stock rises to 60 lathes. The 5 lathes that wear out are replaced so there is new (net) investment of 10 lathes and gross investment of 15. Next year a further rise in demand occurs – to 40,000 chairs per year. Desired capital stock is now 80. Net investment rises to 20 and gross investment to 25 machines. The boom continues next year with demand rising to 60,000 chairs per year, desired capital stock to 120, net investment to 40 and gross investment to 45. The boom has now peaked. Next year demand is the same. Desired capital stock is the same. Five machines wear out and are replaced. There is no net investment in capacity since demand has not changed and, in this case, where capital adjustment can take place quickly, investment is an *immediate* function of the change in demand. Gross investment is therefore only 5. Then in year 7 demand starts to fall – to 58,000 chairs per year. Desired capital stock falls to 116. Five machines wear out but only one is replaced. Net investment is −4. Gross investment is 1 lathe. Demand remains the same in subsequent years and, to begin with, gross investment returns to 5 and stays there, with net investment remaining zero.

In year 13, 15 lathes wear out – the 15 that were purchased in year 3. In that year, even though output is the same and net investment zero, gross investment rises to 15. The next year, the 25 lathes bought in year 4 wear out. Gross investment rises to 25. The following year, the 45 lathes bought in year 5 wear out. Gross investment rises to 45. In year 16, only 5 lathes wear out and gross investment falls to 5; and so on.

Here you see that *gross* investment reflects *past* investment decisions as well as changes in expenditure. A relatively small percentage change in output can generate a relatively large percentage change in net investment and, moreover, these effects can be felt at later stages of an industry's history.

What is true of the industry is also true of the economy. Although the working life of machines and plant will vary from firm to firm and industry to industry, a *general* increase in aggregate expenditure will tend to generate an accelerated change in net investment. Hence the term **accelerator**. In its simplest form, the accelerator theory says that net investment (I_n) is the (physical) desired capital output ratio multiplied by the change in output:

$$I_n = \frac{K}{Y} \Delta Y$$

Table 30.5 Investment over time in the chair industry

1 *Year*	2 *Chair output*	3 *Change in chair output*	4 *Desired capital stock of lathes*	5 *Depreciation*	6 *Replacement*	7 *Net investment in new lathes*	8 *Gross investment in lathes*
1	25,000	0	50	5	5	0	5
2	25,000	0	50	5	5	0	5
3	30,000	5,000	60	5	5	10	15
4	40,000	10,000	80	5	5	20	25
5	60,000	20,000	120	5	5	40	45
6	60,000	0	120	5	5	0	5
7	58,000	−2,000	116	5	1	−4	1
8	58,000	0	116	5	5	0	5
9	58,000	0	116	5	5	0	5
10	58,000	0	116	5	5	0	5
11	58,000	0	116	5	5	0	5
12	58,000	0	116	5	5	0	15
13	58,000	0	116	15	15	0	25
14	58,000	0	116	25	25	0	45
15	58,000	0	116	45	45	0	45
16	58,000	0	116	5	5	0	5

In the example in table 30.5, K/Y was 50/25,000, which produces the numbers in columns 3 and 7. K/Y is the **accelerator coefficient**. If this capital–output ratio is not constant then it will be necessary to modify the coefficient so as to reflect the *additional* capital required to produce the extra output. It then becomes $\Delta K/\Delta Y$, termed the **incremental capital–output ratio** (ICOR). Normally the capital–output, or incremental capital–output, ratio is expressed in monetary terms rather than the physical terms used in the example and, since *in any one year* expenditure on capital will usually exceed the value of output it produces, the accelerator coefficient will be larger than unity. Hence the (lagged) effect of a change in output has an accelerated effect on net investment.

On an economy scale, the resultant changes in gross investment will have multiplier effects on income that will feed back on the demand for output, thus setting up a series of cyclical fluctuations in investment and output, income and employment.

Case Study 30.3 Multiplier–Accelerator Interaction in the UK Treasury's Model

The UK Treasury model, with that of several other economic groups, is designed to forecast what will happen to the economy as outside factors change, and in response to government policy. H. P. Evans and C. J. Riley (1975) have made some simulations of the predicted response of the main aggregates to various changes. In the simulations reported in the following, the exogenous change was a sustained increase in government current expenditure of £100 million per quarter (about 3 per cent of government current expenditure per quarter) in 1972. The simulation then tracks out the effects of this permanent increase in expenditure assuming no other exogenous factor varies.

These effects are shown in table 30.6. The immediate impact is large on *GDP*, and this sets off the multiplier and accelerator in the model. Stocks are initially run down and output rises, generating higher personal incomes and, hence, consumption. Initially this is accomplished by increased working hours and overtime. Subsequently employment increases (unemployment falls). Income continues to grow via the multiplier, to a peak increase of £133.8 million in 1974's fourth quarter. The increase in the *GDP* generates a higher desired capital stock and an accelerator effect on private investment and stock building. These reach a peak in 1973 and then fall off eventually to zero as *GDP* levels out and the desired capital stock and level of stocks are obtained. Consumption continues to grow, however, through 1975 and so does employment owing to the long lags in response to earlier changes in incomes and output. There is little effect on imports initially since public expenditure itself has a small import content – but as *GDP* rises so do imports, after a lag.

The impact of various policies on unemployment was examined using a model, with the results reported in table 30.7 (Evans and Riley, 1975). Although there are reasons for supposing that the effect on unemployment of public expenditure on goods and services is somewhat underestimated (owing to the relative labour intensity of public production, which is not allowed for in the model), the impact of the net increase in National Insurance payments is both strong and fast acting. Purchase tax reductions (purchase tax was the indirect tax replaced by VAT in 1973) have a small initial

Table 30.6 Quarterly differences in various aggregates simulated in response to a sustained increase in public expenditure on goods and services in 1972

Quarter		*GDP (£ million)*	*Consumers' expenditure (£ million)*	*Public expenditure in goods and services (£ million)*	*Fixed investment (£ million)*	*Investment in stocks (£ million)*	*Imports (£ million)*	*Unemployment (%)*
1972	1	95.3	8.3	100.0	0.0	−3.9	5.2	−0.06
	2	109.1	12.4	100.0	3.7	10.5	12.8	−0.11
	3	111.9	16.2	100.0	5.9	11.9	16.6	−0.16
	4	118.0	20.9	100.0	7.9	13.7	18.2	−0.20
1973	1	123.1	25.6	100.0	9.7	13.9	19.0	−0.23
	2	122.4	29.7	100.0	10.3	7.7	17.8	−0.26
	3	128.4	34.2	100.0	10.0	9.1	16.7	−0.28
	4	130.0	37.8	100.0	9.3	7.5	16.2	−0.30
1974	1	131.1	41.0	100.0	7.9	5.9	15.0	−0.32
	2	132.8	44.1	100.0	6.9	5.4	14.6	−0.34
	3	133.7	46.7	100.0	6.2	4.5	14.5	−0.36
	4	133.8	48.8	100.0	5.2	3.5	14.5	−0.38
1975	1	133.7	50.9	100.0	4.1	2.5	14.4	−0.39
	2	133.6	52.7	100.0	3.0	1.7	14.4	−0.41
	3	133.5	54.5	100.0	2.0	1.0	14.4	−0.42
	4	133.4	56.0	100.0	1.4	0.4	14.2	−0.43

Table 30.7 Impact of various policy changes on unemployment percentages simulated by the Treasury model of the UK

Quarters	*Increase in public expenditure on goods and services by £100 million*	*Increase in National Insurance benefits and contributions to produce £100 million increase of expenditure in this item*	*Reduction in purchase tax rates to produce £100 million reduction in tax revenue*	*Reduction in income tax via raising personal allowances by £100 million*
1972, 4th	−0.20	−0.50	−0.16	−0.12
1973, 4th	−0.30	−0.62	−0.29	−0.24
1974, 4th	−0.35	−0.62	−0.37	−0.32
1975, 4th	−0.43	−0.61	−0.45	−0.38

impact, but after three years have an effect that is about the same as the increase in public expenditure on goods and services.

H. P. Evans and C. J. Riley (1975) 'Simulations with the Treasury model', in C. A. Renton (ed.) *Modelling the Economy*, Heinemann, London, pp. 213–36, table 3.8.

SAQ 30.6

Consider the following closed economy:

$$C = C_0 + c\,(Y - T)$$
$$T = tY$$
$$I = I_0 + \alpha \Delta Y$$
$$G = G_0$$

where I_0 is (constant) replacement investment, α is the accelerator coefficient, ΔY is the change in income over the previous period, and all the other terms have their familiar meaning (see chapters 26, 27). Let $C_0 = 10$, $c = 0.75$, $t = 0.333$, $I_0 = 5$ (except when desired net investment is less than -5, when gross investment is zero), $\alpha = 1.5$ and $G_0 = 10$. The economy has been in a stationary state for some time, with net investment zero and $I = I_0 = 5$.

In table 30.8 fill in the initial equilibrium values for the economy, then trace out the consequences of a sustained rise in G_0 to 15 in each period from period 1 on, assuming that equilibrium is attained in each period (and remembering to set $I = 0$ whenever desired net investment is less than -5).

Table 30.8 Equilibrium values for economy of SAQ 30.6

Period	*C*	*I*	*G*	*Y*	*ΔY*
0	—	—	10	—	0
1	—	—	15	—	—
2	—	—	—	—	—
3	—	—	—	—	—
4	—	—	—	—	—
5	—	—	—	—	—
6	—	—	—	—	—
7	—	—	—	—	—
8	—	—	—	—	—
9	—	—	—	—	—
10	—	—	—	—	—
11	—	—	—	—	—
12	—	—	—	—	—

The Complexity of the Economy

One often hears complaints from the lay public that economics has not attained the capability of prediction that exists in the natural sciences. This problem, however, lies less in economics itself than in the sheer complexity of the world around us. Of the four main macroeconomic models of the UK economy in the 1970s, the simplest was that of the National Institute of Social and Economic Research, which contained but 11 behavioural equations. The Treasury's model then had 49, Southampton University's had 52 and the London Business School's 68. Of necessity these can but summarize broad relationships, and getting the most *efficient* summaries takes a good deal of patient exploration. The record of prediction of these models is, of course, mixed. One reason is that some of the underlying theories have still not been fully tested. Thus it is still possible to say even today that we do not know the impact of changes in interest rates on investment in the UK, so it is possible for economists to take quite different views about the relative effectiveness of fiscal policy and interest rate policy. Another difficulty lies in the inadequacy, or non-existence, of many of the data needed to test macro theories. Yet another problem is that predictions are bedevilled by changes in government policies; and so on.

An Introduction to Growth Theory

Despite much theoretical research, fully validated theories of the determinants of economic growth still elude us. The theory of economic growth is a subject mainly for advanced study in economics, and so this final section provides only an introduction.

It is quite easy to see that, if government expenditure in a closed economy remains constant, then investment increases both the capacity of the economy to produce (given a desired capital–output ratio) and, via the multiplier, also increases incomes and hence aggregate planned expenditure. If you suppose that an economy remains in continuous (full employment) equilibrium, then you know that planned savings equal planned investment. Now the question arises: will an increase in investment generate a sufficient increase in planned aggregate expenditure for the additional capacity to be used fully?

In simple closed economy you know that the equilibrium in the injections and withdrawals approach is where

$$S = I$$

and that, if equilibrium is to be retained,

$$\Delta S = \Delta I$$

Any change in investment induces a change in income via the multiplier:

$$\Delta Y = \frac{1}{s} \Delta I,$$

where s is the marginal propensity to save.

For equilibrium to be maintained this ΔY must correspond to the change in output generated by the investment. Take a simple form of the investment function:

$$I = \alpha \Delta Y$$

where α is the accelerator or K/Y. For greater generality you can as well write $\alpha = \Delta K/\Delta Y$. So

$$I = \frac{\Delta K}{\Delta Y} \Delta Y$$

In other words, (net) investment is equal to the change in the capital stock (as you already know).

If you rearrange this, you get

$$\Delta Y = \frac{I}{\Delta K/\Delta Y}$$

which is the additional output produced by investment. For equilibrium to be maintained, this must equal the change in aggregate income produced by the change in investment, so

$$\frac{I}{\Delta K/\Delta Y} = \frac{1}{s} \Delta I$$

or

$$\frac{\Delta I}{I} = \frac{s}{\Delta K/\Delta Y}$$

This implies that the proportionate growth of investment must be equal to the ratio of the marginal propensity to save divided by ICOR (the incremental capital–output ratio) if the economy is to remain in equilibrium.

Suppose now that investment grows at less than this rate, so that

$$\frac{\Delta I}{I} < \frac{s}{\Delta K/\Delta Y}$$

In such a case (dividing though by s and multiplying through by I)

$$\frac{1}{s}\,\Delta I < \frac{I}{\Delta K/\Delta Y}$$

so that the income generated by the change in investment (on the left hand side) is less than the addition to output (on the right hand side). Producers perceiving this are likely to take a depressed view of the future and reduce investment still further, thereby exacerbating the problem and leading to a cumulative slump in economic activity.

In the reverse case, with investment growing at a faster rate than is necessary for equilibrium, the addition to income will be greater than the addition to output. Producers will tend to increase investment still further, thereby leading to a cumulative boom (and a rise, incidentally, in imports to fill the gap between planned expenditure and output).

It thus appears that the economy, left to its own devices, can also be dynamically unstable: economic growth is likely to be characterized by **dynamic instability** as well, as we have seen before, by static instability. Growth positively takes off cumulatively or negatively collapses cumulatively. Steady economic growth therefore requires a knife-edged balance that can only happen by chance or by appropriate government intervention to affect either investment or aggregate planned expenditure.

And there the snags begin, because the combination of needing to know the nature of any actual imbalance, the mechanisms of investment and the lags in the system, and of being able to intervene at the appropriate moments, are horrendous informational requirements.

This analysis was pioneered by Evesey Domar and Sir Roy Harrod. A common distinction arising from this theory is that between the **natural growth rate** from the investment equation:

$$\frac{\Delta Y}{Y} = \frac{I}{\Delta K/\Delta Y}\,\frac{1}{Y}$$

and the **warranted growth rate** from the multiplier equation:

$$\frac{\Delta Y}{Y} = \frac{1}{s}\,\Delta I\,\frac{1}{Y}$$

When the warranted rate exceeds the natural rate, as has often been asserted to be the case in the UK, the actual growth rate must be less than warranted rate at full employment, which sets a limit on the rate at which the economy actually can grow. The dismal prospect then arises of a deepening recession.

A fuller analysis would have to take explicit account of changes in the working population over time, the productivity of capital, the differences between the manufacturing and other sectors of the economy, foreign trade effects and other complications. But these considerations, alas, will have to await your second and third years of study.

Case Study 30.4 Growth and Investment Internationally Compared

One of the best recent surveys of economic growth theory and its testing has been made by Bernard Stafford (recall case study 9.3). He calculated the growth rate (annual) comparisons given in table 9.8. The periods in table 9.8 were selected so that they roughly speaking began and ended with equal achievement of productive potential in the economies in question. What has been of major concern since the 1950s in the UK has been its relatively poor growth performance relative to other developed countries. (The measurement of productive potential is discussed in greater detail in chapter 33).

Stafford, in reviewing the evidence, found that investment rates *per se* were not highly correlated with growth rates, which seemed more strongly associated with the producivity of investment, the share of manufacturing output in total output, the growth of employment in manufacturing (which is regarded as a **key sector** in economic growth), the speed with which new technologies are embodied in new investments, and the extent to which exports are focused on high quality income elastic goods rather than on low quality income inelastic goods.

He concludes with the judgement that there is little evidence in support of the Conservative government's belief that the control of inflation and the removal of obstacles to efficiency and competition will be sufficient to generate a spontaneous and sustained increase in the growth rate. Rather what is needed is a steadily sustained increase in investment in the manufacturing sector, especially in those parts of it that produce or could produce goods with a high income elasticity in world markets.

Bernard Stafford (1981), *The End of Economic Growth? Growth and Decline in the UK since 1945*, Oxford, Martin Robertson.

What You Should Understand Now

The relationship between net investment and the rate of interest.
The calculation of present value and internal rate of return in an investment project.
The meaning of the marginal efficiency of capital.
The difference between actual and planned capital stock.
The nature of lags in investment decisions.
Some empirical evidence on investment functions.
The accelerator.
The interaction of the multiplier and the accelerator to generate cycles in economic activity.
The relationship between investment and economic growth.

31

The Keynesian Model and Money

Why Money?

The analysis of exchange and production, or demand and supply, proceeds without the explicit use of money in the familiar form, for example, of notes and coin. The reason for this is straightforward. All the analysis sought to do could be accomplished by looking at exchange *ratios* – marginal rates of substitution, relative marginal costs and so on. Even when you have dealt (especially in SAQs) with money prices, rather than relative prices, the prices were implicitly relative: a fall in price from £10 to £5 meant a halving of the price of one thing relative to another. Even if, as is sometimes convenient, one assumes that other prices are constant, an absolute fall or rise in one price is still a relative fall or rise, and it was the *relative* change that mattered, particularly in explaining and predicting behaviour. You were not concerned so much with the quantity actually consumed or produced in any period as in how it *changed* in response to (relative) price changes. Even in the calculation of consumers' and purchasers' surpluses, all one needs is some *index* of relative prices; money itself (for example, pounds sterling or dollars) was never a crucial feature even though (because one is so familiar with a sterling index of relative value) money was talked about.

SAQ 31.1

(a) If the price of *X* rises from £5 to £10 and other prices are the same, what happens to the relative price of *X*?

(b) If the price of *X* stays the same and other prices double, what happens to the relative price of *X*?

(c) If the price of *X* rises from £5 to £10 and the price of *Z* falls from £20 to £15, what happens to the relative price of *X*?

(d) In (c), what happens to the relative price of *Z*?

(e) If the price of *X* rises from £5 to £10 and the price of *Z* rises from £20 to £30, what happens to the relative price of *X*?

(f) If the relative price of *X* falls and *X* has a positive income elasticity, what happens to the demand for *X*?

(g) If the relative price of *X* rises, what happens to the opportunity cost of using *X* in production?

What, then, is the economic rationale for money? What *is* money?

To answer these fundamental questions, imagine a world in which there is no money, and speculate about how trade would occur. Your world consists of a variety of people having different collections of (rights to use) goods and abilities to produce goods, with different preferences about what they want to consume. In particular, not everyone is equally expert about the characteristics of the goods – either about those they own or those that others own which they may like.

Suppose I own a car and so do you. Suppose I suggested that we should swap. I know more about my car (probably) than you do and you know more about yours than I. The trouble is that I cannot be sure, even if in principle I would rather have your car than mine, that I would not be getting a clapped out old hulk. Likewise you, even if in principle you prefer my car to yours, cannot be sure about the quality of mine relative to the quality of yours.

But if we wanted to trade, what could we do? One thing would be to call in an expert to assess the respective qualities. We may then find it worth while to swap. Unfortunately, the expert (say, a garage mechanic) would need compensation, so we would both incur costs of authenticating our cars' qualities even when our trading is only a speculative possibility. The introduction of a middleman may reduce transaction costs, particularly if (as is likely) the middleman we choose is a specialist whom we both trust more than we can trust one another. But it will not reduce the information costs to nothing. Whether we sell our cars to the middleman who then sells them back to us, or we swap our cars directly having used the specialist's information, we also have the problem of how to pay the specialist. If we paid him in other goods, we again have the problem of how the *expert* is to know their quality and so on; the expert may be an expert in cars, but not in *all* goods. So we shall need yet *another* expert to evaluate the other goods! And that expert needs paying too!

Barter, or swapping, is bedevilled by this problem of risk arising from imperfect knowledge about the quality of goods. Trade will evidently be aided if one could think of some good for which the costs of identifying its characteristics are (a) *low* and (b) low for *everyone*. If such a good existed I could sell my car to you in exchange for this good (we need to identify only the qualities of my car, not both its and those of this other good) or you could sell yours to me in exchange for that good. Or we could pay the expert in terms of that good.

With more complicated deals – for example, A has a car and wants wheat, B has barley and wants a car, C has cutlery and wants barley, D has wheat and wants cutlery – it is obvious that the presence of a fifth good, whose dependability was known and known to all, would greatly facilitate trade. If such a good existed it would pay A, B, C and D to hold it in a stock so as to be able to offer it in exchange for whatever each wanted and to acquire it in exchange for whatever each wanted to sell. This **medium of exchange** would *not* be chosen because it was something that everyone happened to have some of; it would be something that everyone chose to have because of the low cost of identifying its qualities.

The medium of exchange would have to be something that did not deteriorate over time (milk would not do very well), or its quality would vary and the costs of identifying its quality would accordingly be the greater. It would have to be something whose quality was cheaply guaranteed by specialist experts or that was generally known to be fixed by, say, nature. If such a commodity were to be found and used as a medium of exchange, it could be used as **money**.

SAQ 31.2

(a) A good is chosen as a medium of exchange partly because it is a good that most traders hold. Right?

(b) Some people argue that a medium of exchange arises in order to avoid the so-called **double coincidence of wants**. For example, if I have wheat and want a book, with barter I need to find someone who has a book and wants wheat. What do you think of this rationale?

The nature and form of money has varied over the course of human history. In some primitive societies it was (and is) sea shells. In prisoner of war camps it has been cigarettes. Precious metals have a long history of acting as money. As time passed, gold's usefulness as a medium of exchange was enhanced by governments guaranteeing its purity, often putting the ruler's portrait in pieces of it as a guarantee and later milling edges of coins so that they could not be clipped and the money's value thus debased.

Paper money emerged as a result of a particular form of middleman specialization. People found it cheap to hold their gold and silver with goldsmiths who had large and secure safes. They received receipts certifying their deposits with the goldsmiths. Rather than reclaim gold on production of their receipt in order to make purchases, with the recipients of the gold then going back to the goldsmiths with more deposits for which they in turn received receipts, people perceived that the receipts, especially if denominated in handy amounts of gold, could themselves be traded for goods. Thus the trustworthy goldsmiths developed into what eventually became banks. In Britain, paper notes issued by the Bank of England could originally be exchanged for gold. For many years, however, the note issue has been **fiduciary**: issued on trust and used so long as individuals are willing to hold it for the purposes of exchange.

In modern times other forms of money have also emerged. Bank deposits are one such. Banks hold notes and coins in their vaults (*vault cash*, as it is termed) but never enough to meet everyone's demand for money. Instead people write cheques on their accounts; for many purposes this is much cheaper than incurring costs by going along to the bank to collect the notes and coins they are entitled to receive if they so wish (so-called *shoe-leather costs*), and is also much safer by leaving one less likely to be robbed. It also reduces the risk of losing one's notes and coins accidentally.

SAQ 31.3

Which is the money: the cheque you write, or the bank deposit you draw on in writing the cheque?

Although the forms of money vary between societies and through time, the basic rationale is the same: it is that medium of exchange that is least costly to check as to quality, and with a quality that is widely known in society. Baht are the currency in Thailand and are universally accepted there, try buying bread for baht in Britain, however! One still needs expert middlemen – banks – to hold baht and sterling, who know their relative qualities and who are trusted so as to be able to exchange the one type of money for the other.

Although the medium of exchange function is the prime rationale underlying money's existence, it also serves other functions. Almost any good that is durable can serve as a *store of value*: you can pile it up and use it as and when convenient for trading. Money, however, is a particularly good store of value because of its unchanging quality. Coins hardly deteriorate at all, but when they do you can always trade them in for equivalent new (or newer) ones. The same applies to faster deteriorating paper notes. Chequing accounts do not vary in the quality of their moneyness at all provided that the banks at which they are held are properly insured or are guaranteed by the government not to go bankrupt. All forms of money are, however, subject to the hazard of inflation. If someone finds a new supply of shells or of gold, or the government mints lots of coins or prints notes, or the banks start establishing new chequing accounts, the supply of the medium of exchange will rise, people will trade more, and the prices of goods will normally tend to rise so that purchasing power of a unit of money falls. This is one way in which inflation can arise. It clearly detracts from the usefulness of money as a store of value: if the prices of all goods double then your stock of money is half as valuable in terms of what it will buy. If you are uncertain about what your future stock of money will be and about future inflation, you may prefer to store more of your wealth in the form of *real* goods rather than money.

Once a commonly accepted medium of exchange has become adopted, it can also be used as a *unit of account*. Decision makers can be given *budgets* denominated in money which tells them how many resources they can buy over a period. Some may be earmarked for particular purposes (so much for wages, so much for advertising, and so on). Senior planners and managers can also thereby check on what has been happening in their particular organizations (households, firms, charities, public sector agencies and so on).

Similarly, money can be used as a *standard of deferred payment*. If I sell you wheat futures we agree a price now in money terms which you will pay later when I deliver your wheat to you. If I lend you money, we contract that you pay me back, with interest, at some future date. In both cases we may want to make allowances for inflation (as you will see later) but in both cases the transactions are in terms of money – money paid and/or received in the future.

The use of money as a store of value, unit of account and standard of deferred payment are supplementary uses of money that follow from its use as a medium of exchange. One could use other goods for each of these purposes (and to varying extents one does). For example, all could be done by using cigarettes, even if cigarettes were not used as a medium of exchange. So I could store my wealth in the form of cigarettes. I could set you a budget defined in cigarettes per year (which you will then have to trade for money to buy your inputs). I could lend you cigarettes and demand repayment in five years' time in cigarettes. But it is often much less costly to use the medium of exchange for these purposes. And that is what is done.

Chapter 34 contains a description of the various official definitions of money that are currently in use in the UK. You may like to look ahead to that now. For the moment, however, all you need have in mind as modern money is notes and coin together with chequing accounts held at banks.

The Demand for Money

The demand for money is the demand to hold a *stock*. What the determinants of this demand are can be seen by considering the possible ways in which one's wealth can be held. One could, of course, hold *all* one's stock of wealth in the form of a stock of money. This would admittedly be rather absurd when you consider the opportunity cost involved. For example, since some of one's wealth is one's human capital, it would mean selling one's human capital to someone else for money – effectively selling oneself into (voluntary) slavery.

One would also have to sell one's *physical* capital in exchange for money, for example one's house, land and car. Again one would incur opportunity costs, forgoing the stream of services yielded by these items of physical capital.

One would go without consumer goods and services, instead holding on to one's stock of money like Scrooge. Again, the opportunity cost is clear: one forgoes the utility streams represented by consumption.

One could go without investments in bonds, equities and so on. Again, in so doing one would forgo the stream of future income that such investments would yield.

It is therefore clear that holding a stock of money is not costless. It is but one way of holding one's wealth. Typically, people choose to hold their wealth in a fairly complex *portfolio* of assets: some in human capital, some in physical capital, some in financial assets and, of course, *some* in money. The word **portfolio** is used as an extension of the literal notion of portfolio as a collection of papers kept in a case. Some *will* be held in the form of money because holding money, although having opportunity costs, also has benefits. In particular, if one is going to consume goods and services, it reduces the costs of exchange, as you have just seen. Moreover, when individuals receive their money incomes from work or from investment, the receipt of money does not coincide precisely with their pattern of spending. For example, on payday, the stock of money one holds is usually at a maximum. Suppose one is paid monthly. Then this stock of money has to cover one's planned expenditure over the rest of the month, falling to a minimum just before the next pay packet or pay cheque is received. Consequently, one's monthly stock of money rises and falls over the month as money receipts and money transactions are not coincidental in time. The *average* amount held over a period (say a month) is what is referred to as the stock of money. It is held either in the bank or in one's purse or pocket as currency.

One determinant of the demand for money is therefore going to be one's total wealth – partly because one will expect that as wealth rises the demand for *all* types of asset will increase, and partly because wealth and income are associated and higher wealth or income implies higher consumption, so there will be a higher demand for money to finance the higher level of transactions.

The Keynesian tradition has been to emphasize the relationship between the demand for money and current income, rather than wealth or an annuity whose present value was equal to wealth (termed **permanent income**, see case study 26.2). This simplification will be used here. It is termed the **transactions demand** for money. Assume that the aggregate relationship is a simple proportional one:

$$L = kY$$

where L is the demand for money, Y is national income and k is the propensity to hold money for transactions purposes. The factor k depends on the degree of coincidence between receipt of incomes and expenditures: the longer, for example, the periods between receipt of your wage or salary, the higher your average k. It is assumed that this feature of the economy does not change significantly in the short term, and it is therefore excluded from subsequent analysis.

Case Study 31.1 Individual Demand for a Stock of Money

The Culyers' demand for a stock of money in the form of current account holdings at the bank and in currency are shown for the month of June in a recent year in figure 31.1. The month began with a stock of £1635 held in the bank and £100 in currency. The stock of currency was replenished each Thursday or Friday and run down during the week, with the largest run down taking place through Saturday shopping. Replenishing the stock of currency depleted the current account by a corresponding amount, but this was in several cases partially offset by payings in of odd cheques.

As can be seen, the money stock held as currency is run down to near zero over a weekly cycle and the money stock held in the current account runs down to near zero over a monthly cycle. The average stock held as cash was £40 and the average stock held as current account was £667 – the relatively large size of the latter representing the convenience of using cheques for making payments. The Culyers' average demand for money in July was thus £707. The 'sawtooth' pattern of the monthly and weekly balances is fairly typical and the convention is to regard the demand for money as the *average* stock held over a period.

The other main determinant of the demand for the stock of money is the rate of interest. The higher the rate of interest, the more attractive it becomes to hold one's wealth in the form of investments for money itself yields no interest or, in some bank accounts, only low interest.

You may therefore expand the demand for money equation so that it looks like:

$$L = kY - li$$

where i is the rate of interest. The parameter l is a simple proportionate (negative) relation between the interest rate and the demand for money: it is

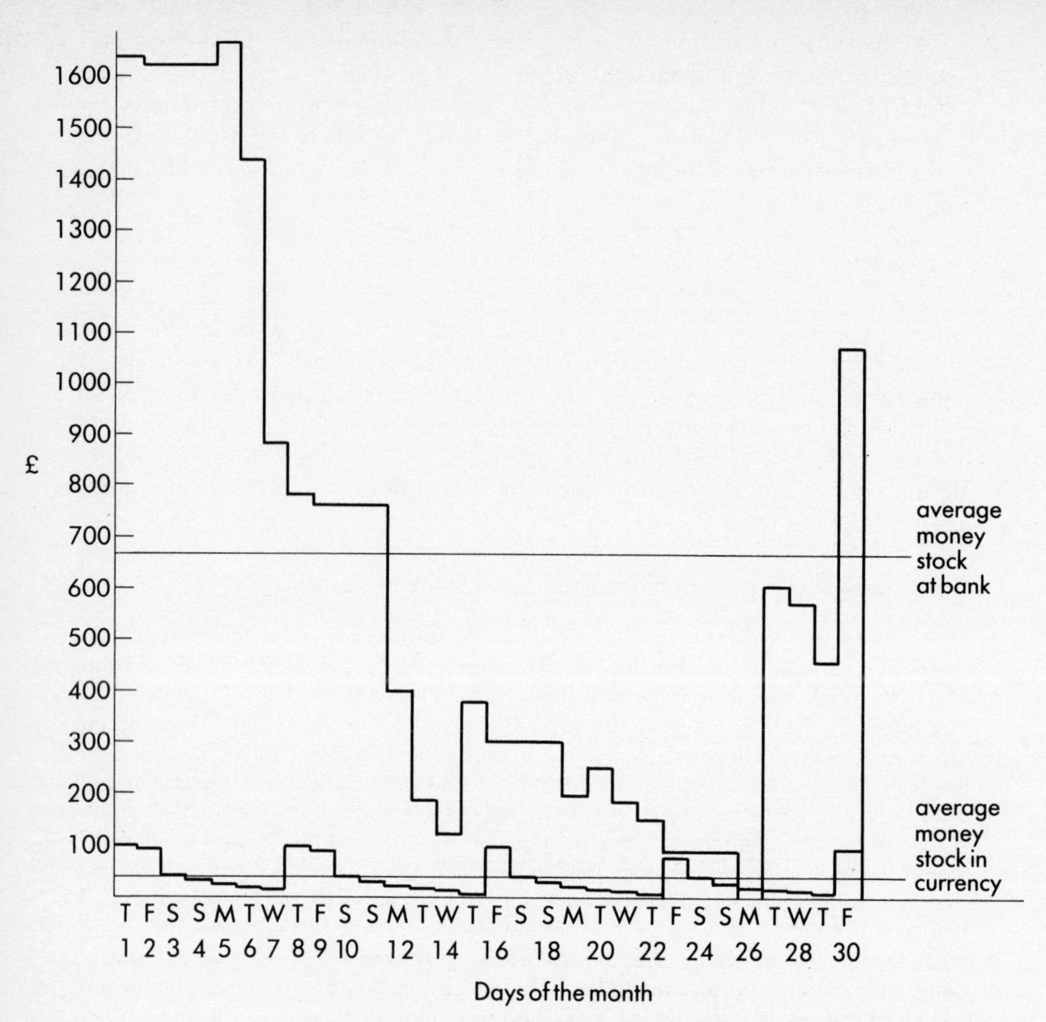

Figure 31.1 The Culyers' stock of money

the responsiveness in absolute terms of the demand for money to changes in the interest rate ($l = \Delta L/\Delta i$).

SAQ 31.4

(a) Let the relationship between the demand for the stock of money and income be

$$L = 0.14Y$$

1 If $Y = £200$, what is the demand for money?

2 If Y increases by 5 per cent, what is the percentage increase in L?

(b) If $k = 0.1$ and $l = 1.0$:

1 What is the demand for money when $Y = £250$ and $i = 0$, 1.0, 2.0, 3.0, 4.0 and 5.0 per cent?

2 What is the demand for money when $Y = £300$ and $i = 0$, 1.0, 2.0, 3.0, 4.0 and 5.0 per cent?

Precautionary Demand for Money

The Keynesian tradition usually supposes that, in addition to the transactions demand, there is a **precautionary demand**. The precautionary demand arises since money can be used as a buffer stock to iron out *unexpected* changes either in receipts or expenditures when money may be needed at rather short notice – perhaps too short to convert other parts of one's wealth into money. Moreover, holding money for precautionary purposes avoids one incurring the transaction costs of converting other forms of wealth into money. For some assets these costs can be very high (think of the costs of selling a house) and even for financial assets there are costs of brokerage, the cost of the time it takes to determine which assets to dispose of, to consult with financial advisers and pay their fees etc., some of which may be important costs to firms and other institutions as well as to individuals. The precautionary demand is therefore going to vary positively with the level of income (the higher the level of transactions, the more the unexpected events that are likely to occur) and negatively with the interest rate (the lower the interest rate, the less costly it is to allow for the unexpected).

Demand for Money and Interest Rates

A further link between interest rates and the demand for money exists also because money is a relatively riskless form in which wealth can be held. The variety of forms chosen by an individual to hold assets is called, as you have seen, a *portfolio*. Assume that the total amount of wealth to be held in the form of financial assets is given and that the simplest type of portfolio of financial assets contains just two: bonds and money. The advantage of bonds is that they earn interest, unlike money (or, since sometimes sight deposits do earn interest, the advantage of bonds is that they can earn *higher* interest). The disadvantage of bonds is that they are riskier ways of hoarding wealth than money (they are subject to capital gains and losses) and they are less **liquid**: they are costly to convert into money. Since most transactions involve exchanging cash for goods or services, other assets, like bonds, need to be converted into cash in order to make transactions. This is costly. There are costs of instructing one's financial advisers – personal visits, telephone calls, and so on. There are brokerage fees to be paid. Hence, bonds are less liquid than money (though a good deal more liquid than, say, a house, which can be very costly to convert into money).

None the less, because bonds earn interest, this will to a degree compensate both for their riskiness and their illiquidity. Normally, an individual will require a higher interest rate to compensate for higher risks since risk is assumed to be a 'bad' and individuals are assumed to be risk averse (which arises, as you have seen, from a declining marginal utility of income).

What will determine the amounts of the financial asset portfolio that will be held in cash and bonds respectively? The demand for bonds depends, it may be supposed, on the expected return on wealth held in the form of bonds and the risks of capital gains or losses. The risk can be measured by the dispersion of capital gains or losses that are possible. Expected capital gains may be zero, but *actually* they may be either positive (a capital gain if the price of bonds rises) or negative (a capital loss if the price of bonds falls).

Suppose you buy a bond for £100 that promises to pay you £10 a year. If, after a year, you sell your bond for £100 you will have made neither a capital gain nor a capital loss. You will have received £10 yield on your investment. If, at the end of the year, the price of bonds has risen to £110, you will get your £10 *plus* the £10 more that the bond is worth: interest of 10 per cent *plus* a 10 per cent capital gain. If, alternatively, the price of bonds falls to £90, you will get your £10 *less* the £10 capital loss: interest of 10 per cent *less* a 10 per cent capital loss. (Note that if you purchase another bond at the new price of £90 the £10 annual annuity it pays is now equivalent to £10/£90 = 11 per cent interest.)

Let the expected rate of return on bonds be i, the rate of interest, but allow that there may be capital gains or losses. Two thirds of the actual gains or losses will fall within one standard deviation on either side of an average zero capital gain or loss if gains or losses are normally distributed. The standard deviation is one measure of dispersion. The bigger the standard deviation, the riskier bonds are to hold. Also, the more bonds you hold as a share of your financial assets the riskier your portfolio. Thus, if you hold 99 per cent of your financial assets as money and 1 per cent as bonds, your overall risk is small; but if you hold 99 per cent as bonds and only 1 per cent as money, your risk is high.

In figure 31.2 the vertical axis above zero shows the average return Bi on money invested in bonds, where B is the amount invested in bonds. The horizontal axis shows the riskiness $B\sigma$ of bond holdings, where σ is the standard deviation of capital gains/losses. The line OC_0 shows how the investor, by increasing his bond holdings, can increase his overall returns (Bi) but only at the cost of increased risk ($B\sigma$), and the slope of OC_0 is i/σ. In this diagram there is also an individual's indifference map showing preferences for returns and risk: the curves are upward sloping to capture the idea that higher risk (a 'bad') must be compensated by a higher return if the individual is to remain indifferent.

Consider an individual at point a. To get an increase in return from Bi_0 to Bi_1, the indifference curve U_0 tells you that a maximum acceptable degree of additional risk is up to level $B\sigma_3$. But according to OC_0 the individual need only incur additional risk up to $B\sigma_1$. As it happens, this would take the individual to point b where the highest attainable indifference curve U_1 is reached at a familiar tangency. Utility maximizing investors will always select points such as b where the amount of risk one is *willing* to bear is (just) equal to the amount one *has* to bear to gain the chosen return.

In the lower part of figure 31.2 the level of bond holding associated with each level of risk (and return) is shown by the line OB. For example, given OC_0, the chosen position is point b, corresponding to return Bi_1, risk $B\sigma_1$ and bond holdings B_1. The level of bond holdings corresponding to point a is by

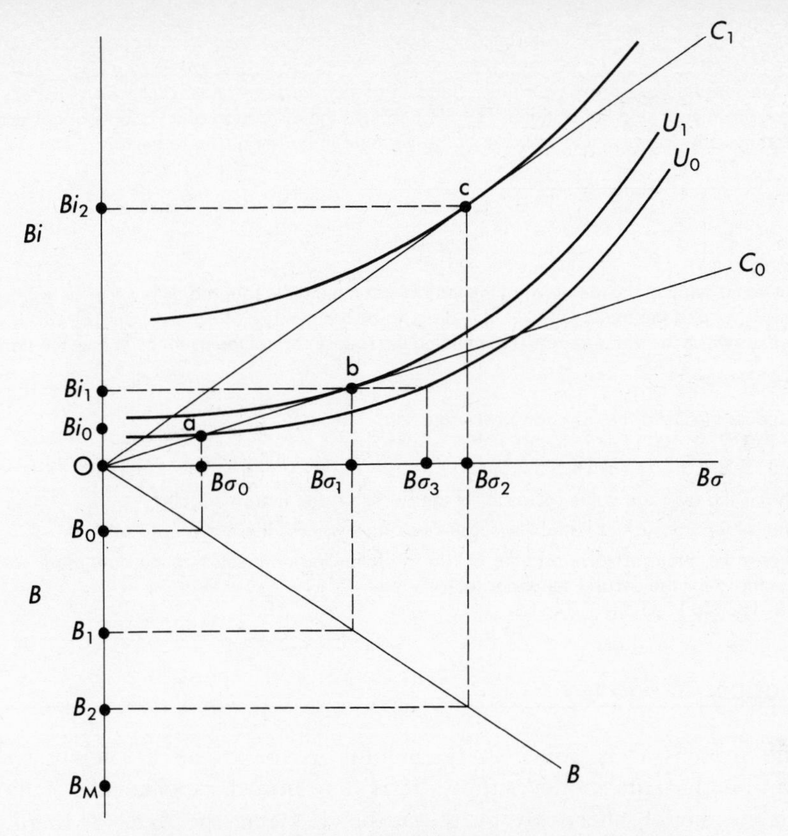

Figure 31.2 The trade-off between risk and return

similar reasoning B_0. The maximum is B_M, corresponding to a portfolio in which no money at all is held. The amount of money held at point b is thus $B_M - B_1$, given the assumption that the total amount of wealth to be held in financial assets has been already decided (and is equal in value, of course, to B_M).

Now, if the interest rate rises, a higher return is possible at every level of risk. The OC line thus rotates – anticlockwise for a rise in interest rates, and clockwise for a fall. Suppose when the interest rate rises OC_0 rotates to OC_1. The new tangency with an indifference curve is at point c, indicating (a) a higher return to the investor, (b) a higher risk, (c) a rise in desired bond holdings B_2 and hence (d) a fall in desired money holdings. In this case, therefore, a rise in the interest rate causes a *fall* in the amount of money demanded. The general presumption is that the substitution effect dominates the income effect, so that tangency at point c is to the *right* of point b when interest rates rise (now is a good time to revise your understanding of income and substitution effects by turning back to chapter 6).

As you can see, the theory predicts that the demand for money will be inversely related to the interest rate.

SAQ 31.5

This SAQ is designed to refresh your understanding of *standard deviations* (*SD*) which you will have learned about in your study of statistics. The *SD* measures the dispersion of a variable about its mean value, and its units are the same as those of the variable in question. The formula is

$$SD = \sqrt{\left[\frac{1}{n} \sum_{1}^{n} (X_i - \bar{X})^2\right]}$$

This involves calculating the mean ($\bar{X}$) of the variable; summing the squared differences between each observation (X_i) and the mean ($\sum_{1}^{n}(X_i - \bar{X})^2$); dividing by the number of observations (n), which yields a number known as the *variance*; and then finding the square root of the variance to give the standard deviation.

(a) Compute the *SD* of the following two data sets:
1, 3, 7, 9, 10, 11, 12, 17, 29
6, 7, 8, 10, 11, 13, 14, 15, 15

(b) What is the average value for each set, and which is the more variable?

(c) What other measure of variability suggests itself to you for these two data sets?

(d) What is the average value and the *SD* for the following data set? Are the data more variable than those for the second set under (a)?
6, 8, 10, 10, 11, 12, 13, 14, 15

The Supply of Money

For the present it is going to be helpful to make the heroically simple assumption that the money supply M is determined exogenously – that is, outside the model, effectively by the authorities (i.e. the Bank of England). You will see later that this assumption cannot be sustained for an economy with a fixed exchange rate engaging in international trade. Nor is it by any means as simple as you may imagine for the Bank of England to control the supply of money, even in the absence of international transactions. The important thing to emphasize is that, provisionally, it is assumed that the supply of money is affected neither by the rate of interest nor by the level of income. So you can write

$$M = M_0$$

signifying that the supply of money is exogenous and set at the level M_0. Note that the same symbol is used for the money supply as was previously used for imports. The context should make clear which is the appropriate interpretation of M.

Figure 31.3 shows the aggregate demand and supply of money, with money stock measured along the horizontal axis and the interest rate on the vertical axis. The demand for money L has a negative slope, since you have seen that it varies inversely with the interest rate. Since the demand for money also varies with the level of GDP, this demand curve is defined for a specified level of GDP, Y_0, with a given supply of money set at M_0.

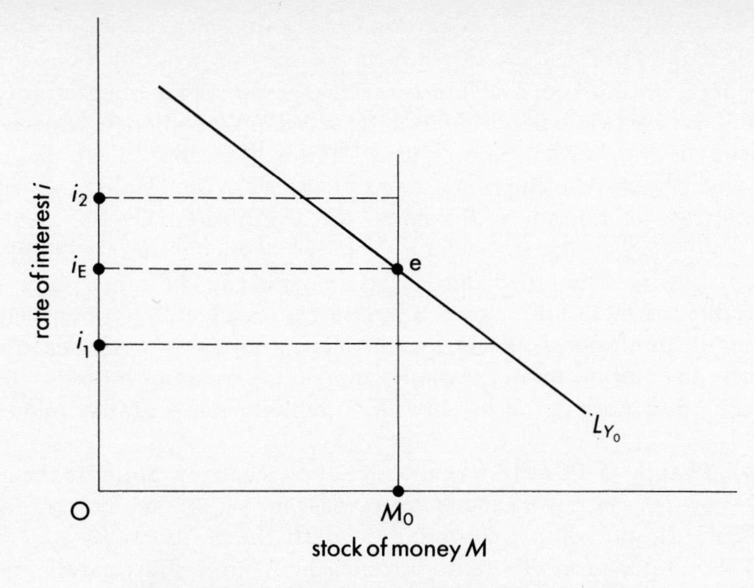

Figure 31.3 The demand and supply of money

SAQ 31.6

Given

$L = kY - li$	(demand for money function)
$M = M_0$	(supply of money function)
$M = L$	(equilibrium condition)

(a) What expression defines the equilibrium level of the interest rate?

(b) With $k = 0.13$, $l = 1.2$, $M_0 = 25$ and $Y = 300$, what is the equilibrium interest rate?

Suppose the rate of interest were at i_1. At this rate the demand for money exceeds the supply available. Individuals in the economy will therefore be forced to revise their portfolios of assets, selling those that are interest bearing in exchange for money. However, *not everyone* can do this because the stock of money available is fixed. The attempt to do so can only drive down the price of other assets so that their proportionate yields rise, which is equivalent to an increase in the rate of interest. Recall the relationship between the price of a very long lived asset, its annual income, and the annual interest rate (chapter 16):

$$PV = \frac{A}{i}$$

Let A (the annual income from the asset) be fixed (it may vary, of course, but not due to any of the changes here considered). Now suppose that individuals, firms etc. want to sell assets so that PV (their present value, which is also their market price) falls. If PV falls and A is fixed, the only thing that can give is i: it must rise.

As i rises, so the excess demand for money is reduced. As long as there is any excess demand there will be downward pressure on PV and hence upward pressure on i, until an equilibrium is reached in the money market at $i = i_E$.

The opposite occurs when there is an excess supply of money, say when $i = i_2$. Individuals want to hold less than M_0 and will attempt to run down their money stocks by purchasing other assets whose PVs rise, leading to a fall in i. Again the rate of interest is driven to the equilibrium level i_E. At i_E the available stock M_0 is just that which people in aggregate want to hold.

Now, it has been assumed that L has remained in the same place all the time, despite the fact that changes in interest rates affect investment which in turn, via the multiplier, affects income. The rationale for this is that the adjustment to equilibrium in the money market is very quick indeed – so quick in fact that, given M_0 and a level of GDP, equilibrium is always maintained with $M = L$.

But what happens if GDP or the money supply changes? Suppose the level of GDP rises owing, say, to an exogenous increase in investment. This means that L will shift. In the simple formulation, with the transactions part of the demand for money proportional to income, the L curve shifts parallel to itself to a position such as L_{Y_1} in figure 31.4. The interest rate rises from i_E to i'_E. This generates a fall in investment and a consequential fall in the level of GDP. In turn this leads to a fall in the demand for money: L shifts downwards. The rate of interest falls, leading to an increase in investment etc. The final situation is shown where L has settled at a new equilibrium level L_{Y_E}. The net effect of these adjustments is that GDP is higher and the rate of interest is also higher than initially, at i''_E.

SAQ 31.7

In figure 31.4, why is the final equilibrium Y_E higher than Y_0 but lower than Y_1?

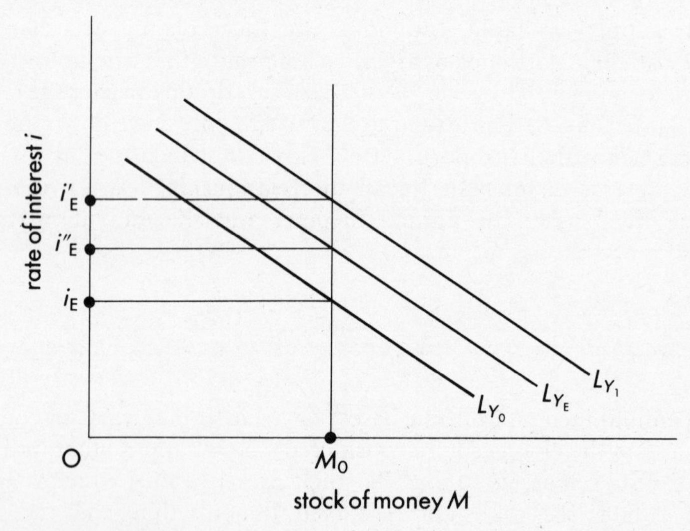

Figure 31.4 Effect on the interest rate of an exogenous rise in investment

From your answer to SAQ 31.7, you can see that the final equilibrium level of income will be less than that implied by any multiplier analysis that ignores the monetary implications of changes in aggregate demand. This is termed **crowding out**. Suppose that public expenditure is raised in order to increase economic activity. Some of the effect will be crowded out by the consequential rise in interest rates as the demand for money rises, hence reducing the multiplier. An exception occurs if the demand for money is perfectly elastic. These circumstances, termed by Keynes the **liquidity trap**, imply that the L curve is horizontal. If the interest rate is above the equilibrium rate then *no money at all* will be held; if it is below, then the *only* asset held will be money. Under these improbable circumstances, money demand is not affected at all by the level of income and the interest rate will not alter. Consequently the multiplier analysis of previous chapters will work in the way there described, and there will be no crowding out.

A similar result occurs if investment is completely interest inelastic. In that case, even if the interest rate changes, there will be no feedback effects on the markets for goods and services and again the multiplier analysis of earlier chapters will not be affected by monetary factors and there will be no crowding out.

Although these two extremes are unlikely to occur in practice, they do bring out the important point that the *more* elastic the demand for money and the *less* elastic the response of investment to changes in interest rates, the more closely the economy would resemble the model of earlier chapters. Conversely, the *less* elastic the demand for money and the *more* elastic the response of investment to changes in interest rates, the greater the impact of the monetary sector on the markets for goods and services and hence, of course, employment.

Effects of Changes in the Money Supply

What happens if the supply of money increases? Suppose the economy is initially in equilibrium at i_E, with $M = M_0$ and with $Y = Y_E$ as in figure 31.5. The money supply is increased by the authorities such that it rises by ΔM_0 to M_0'. A new equilibrium is established where $L_{YE} = M_0'$ and the rate of interest has fallen to i_E'. This generates an increase in investment, a further increase in GDP via the multiplier, a shift in the demand curve for money and a partial rise in the interest rate. This leads to a fall in investment, and so on. Eventually, the process works itself out so that a new equilibrium level of GDP is established, Y_E', higher than previously, with a lower rate of interest than previously prevailed, i_E'' compared with i_E, and a higher demand for money $L_{Y_E'}$. A fall in the supply of money has the opposite effect.

Again, the impact of monetary policy operating on the supply of money depends on the interest elasticity of the demand for money and on the elasticity of investment with respect to interest. If either of the two extreme cases mentioned prevails, then monetary policy will at most affect only interest rates and have no impact on GDP or employment.

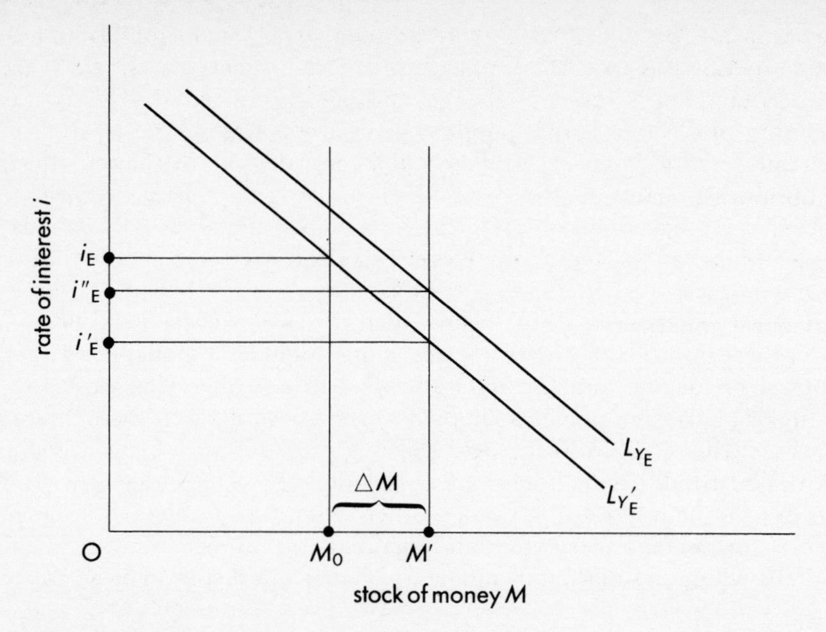

Figure 31.5 Effect on the interest rate of an increase in the supply of money

The Algebra of the Full Keynesian Model

Everything that has gone before can now be summarized in a set of behavioural equations and equilibrium conditions. To avoid needless complexity the foreign trade sector is omitted – the impact of changing interest rates on the balance of payments and the effects of international payments on the money supply have yet to be examined. Some of the more detailed refinements that any model used to plan the economy would have to include (for example, the inclusion of a social security benefit function) are also omitted.

With these simplifications, the model (in the aggregate expenditure and output approach) can be summarized in nine equations: four that describe behaviour in the markets for goods and services, together with an equilibrium condition (chapters 26, 27, 30); two that describe the behaviour of the money market (and also, implicitly, the market for other assets), together with an equilibrium condition (this chapter); and a final equation that relates employment and *GDP* via the production function (chapter 28):

Behavioural equations:

Market for goods and services

$C = C_0 + c(Y - T)$ (consumption function) (1)

$T = tY$ (tax function) (2)

$I = I_0 - ai + \alpha \Delta Y$ (investment function with accelerator) (3)

$G = G_0$ (government expenditure function) (4)

Equilibrium condition:

$Y = C + I + G$ (5)

Money market
Behavioural equations:

$L = kY - li$ (demand for money function) (6)

$M = M_0$ (supply of money function) (7)

Equilibrium condition:

$M = L$ (8)

Labour market
Behavioural equation:

$N = nY$ (employment or production function) (9)

Equilibrium in the entire economy exists when there is equilibrium in both the goods market and the money market (though not necessarily full employment equilibrium in the labour market). To find equilibrium in the money market, equations (6) and (7) are substituted into the equilibrium condition (8), which is then solved for i:

$$M_0 = kY - li$$
$$li = kY - M_0$$
$$i = (kY - M_0)/l \qquad (10)$$

This equilibrium expression for i can then be substituted into the investment function (3) to give

$$I = I_0 - a(kY - M_0)/l + \alpha\Delta Y$$

This can then be substituted into the equilibrium condition for the goods market to give

$$Y = C_0 + c(1 - t)Y + I_0 - akY/l + aM_0/l + \alpha\Delta Y + G_0$$

which in turn yields the reduced form for the whole model:

$$Y = (C_0 + I_0 + G_0 + aM_0/l + \alpha\Delta Y)\frac{1}{1 - c(1 - t) + ak/l} \qquad (11)$$

From this, and using the employment function (9), the equilibrium level of employment can be found.

SAQ 31.8

(a) Derive the reduced form of the Keynesian model in (11) from the equations (1) – (9).

(b) Given $c = 0.8$, $t = 0.25$, $a = 75$, $k = 0.05$ and $l = 8.0$, what is the value of the multiplier?

What is the meaning of this grand summary of the Keynesian model, all contained in equation (11)? It can be summarized in a series of points:

(1) Look at the term for the multiplier. This has ak/l added to the denominator. What do you know of the sign of this term? If a, k and l are all positive, the ratio ak/l will be positive. If you are adding a positive term to the denominator, the value of the multiplier must fall. This is what you found in the earlier diagrammatic analysis; a change in a component of aggregate expenditure will have a smaller impact on *GDP* (and employment) when account is taken of the money market. The economy becomes less inherently unstable – and the impact of fiscal policy is lessened.

(2) The impact of fiscal policy depends on the value of the coefficients l and a. Taking l first: if the demand for money is very elastic with respect to the rate of interest (when it is extremely elastic, this is the liquidity trap), then l is very large. ak/l is consequently very small, and the multiplier is effectively as it was before the impact of the money market was considered. If the demand for money is very interest inelastic then l is very small, ak/l becomes very large and the multiplier becomes very small, so fiscal policy becomes ineffective.

(3) Consider the implications of different values of a for the effectiveness of fiscal policy. If investment is very insensitive to changes in interest rates then a will be very small. In this case ak/l will be very small so the multiplier will be again effectively as it was before the impact of the money market was considered. If investment is interest elastic, on the other hand, then ak/l becomes very large and the multiplier becomes very small, so fiscal policy becomes ineffective.

(4) The impact of monetary policy also depends on the value of the coefficients l and a. It is easy to see that the occasions when fiscal policy is least effective are also those when monetary policy is most effective, and vice versa. Take l first. If the demand for money is very elastic with respect to interest rates then l is very large and ak/l becomes very small, so monetary policy becomes ineffective (the liquidity trap). If the demand for money is very inelastic with respect to interest rates then l becomes very small and, even though the multiplier falls to below unity, the size of ak/l is sufficiently large to have an impact on *GDP* (and employment).

(5) If the interest elasticity of investment is very low, then a is very low and ak/l relatively small also. A change in the money supply will have little effect on *GDP* (and employment). On the other hand, if a is large, when investment is highly responsive to interest rate changes, then even though the multiplier has a low value, ak/l is large also and monetary policy will have an effective impact on *GDP* (and employment).

(6) Finally, note the impact of k. If the demand for money is highly elastic with respect to changes in income, then k is large and the multiplier correspondingly smaller: *both* fiscal and monetary policy become less effective. On the other hand, if k is small, then *both* fiscal and monetary policy become more effective.

These results are summarized in table 31.1 to make them more memorable.

Table 31.1 Effectiveness of fiscal and monetary policy

		Fiscal policy	*Monetary policy*
Value of l (responsiveness of demand for money to interest rates)	high	large	small
	low	small	large
Value of a (responsiveness of investment to interest rates)	high	small	large
	low	large	small
Value of k (responsiveness of demand for money to income)	high	small	small
	low	large	large

Empirical Evidence on Effectiveness

In recent years there has been extensive research into the size of the crucial coefficients of the macroeconomic model. Previously much of the debate between those who favoured monetary policy and those who favoured fiscal policy (whose participants, incidentally, usually divided on a political spectrum too, with those favouring fiscal policy tending to the left and those favouring monetary policy tending to the right, since it minimizes the role of the public sector) was conducted on a highly judgemental basis. For example, the responsiveness of investment to changes in interest rates was often discussed in terms of businessmen's answers to questionnaires eliciting what they thought their responsiveness would be.

Most empirical work departs from the rather simple linear specification used here for the macroeconomic model. You will recall (see chapter 4) that the elasticity of demand, for example, varies along a straight line demand curve. Most empirical studies of the demand for money, however, use a *constant* elasticity specification of this type:

$$L = AY^{\alpha}i^{\beta}$$

where α and β are the elasticities of the demand for money with respect to income and the interest rate, and A is a constant.

To summarize the empirical results very briefly: although there is some variation in the conclusions, most evidence seems to point to an interest elasticity of about -0.5 and (though with less certainty) an income elasticity of about $+0.6$. However, as in the case of the response of investment to interest rate changes, the evidence suggests that there are complex lags in the system.

The general conclusion, then, is that the evidence does not support any *extreme* view about the responsiveness of the demand for money to income

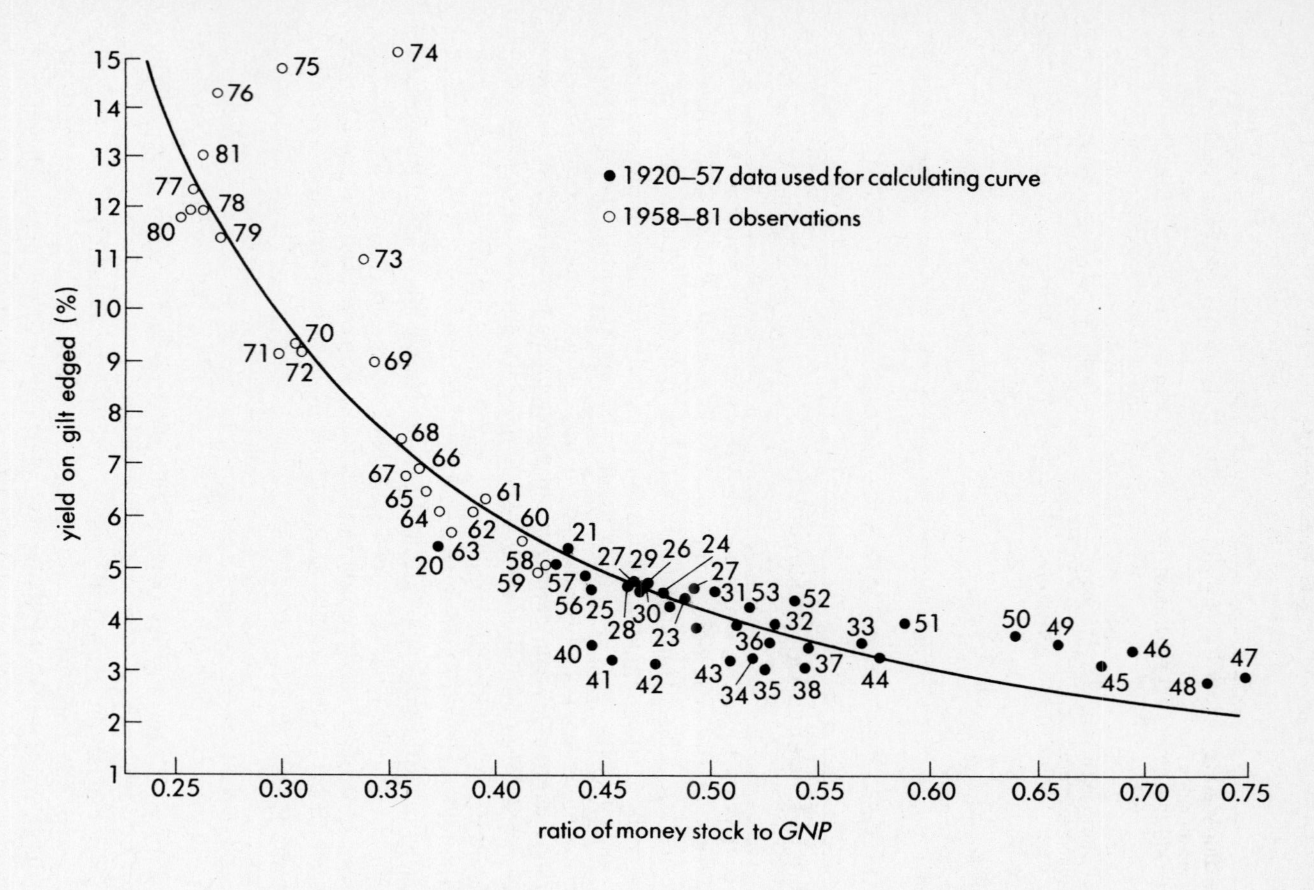

Figure 31.6 Interest rates and the demand for money, 1920–81

changes and interest rate changes. Nor, as you saw in chapter 30, does it support any extreme view about the responsiveness of investment to changes in interest rates. *Both* fiscal and monetary policy *can* be effective.

Case Study 31.2 How Interest Elastic is the Demand for Money?

Nearly all the empirical studies of the demand for money have found that it varies inversely with the rate of interest; the exceptions have suffered from defects in data or in statistical method. These studies have been surveyed by David Laidler (1977) who concluded: 'Of all the issues in monetary economics, this is the one that appears to have been settled most decisively.' Moreover, at low interest rates there is little evidence of the liquidity trap – though there has been some evidence to suggest that a liquidity trap may have existed in the 1940s in the UK and USA. Accordingly, Laidler cautiously concluded: 'The conclusion to which we subscribe, that the liquidity-trap hypothesis is of no empirical significance, must rest on an uncomfortable degree of personal judgement.'

The long run stability of the demand for money (as a ratio to *GNP*) has recently been rather dramatically illustrated by Artis and Lewis (1984), and their diagram is here reproduced as figure 31.6. As you can see, the curve fits the data for 1920–57 rather well, and also predicts subsequent data (apart from 1973–6) quite accurately. This suggests that, in the long run, if you know the interest rate and the *GNP* you can use the following equation to predict M:

$$\log \frac{M}{Y} = 4.718 - 0.584 \log i$$

If you look at the scatter for the 1930s and 1940s you can also see why the belief in the liquidity trap arose in those decades. It seems that in the period 1973–6 the private sector was 'off' its demand curve. This may have been due to the major changes in monetary policy that took place at that time, as some controls on banks' lending were removed and a flexible exchange rate was introduced.

Empirical work on short term demand indicates, however, that it is quite unstable, so monetary policy is inappropriate for short term policy purposes.

David Laidler (1977), *The Demand for Money: Theories and Evidence*, Dun-Donnelly, New York
M. J. Artis and M. K. Lewis (1984) 'How unstable is the demand for money in the UK?', *Economica*, **51**, 473–6.

The *income* elasticity of the demand for money is by no means as settled as the *interest* elasticity of the demand for money, and there is considerable controversy concerning the appropriate definition of income (e.g. current income versus permanent income) and the nature of the lags that exist in the relationship. The ratio of *GDP* to the money stock has been rising in the UK since the early 1960s, and in 1980 was about 7.4. Since Y/L (often termed the **income velocity of circulation** because it represents the rate of circulation of money relative to the output bought with it) is the reciprocal of k, it is plain that k has been falling, largely owing to inflation which – as you will see – is a strong incentive to hold as small a stock of money as possible.

Several studies indicate an income elasticity between 0.39 and 1.32. Any plausible value is likely to be sufficiently low at least to eliminate the pessimistic conclusion that *neither* monetary *nor* fiscal policy can have any effect on the economy. On the other hand, it does not seem that the short term demand for money as a fraction of the rate of interest is very stable, since it also depends (though how much one cannot be sure) on the level of income.

What You Should Understand Now

The reasons why a medium of exchange comes into existence and the other consequential functions of money: store of value, unit of account and standard of deferred payments.
The dependency of the demand for a stock of money on wealth (human and physical) or income, the rate of interest and the timing of receipts and payments.
Equilibrium in the money market.
Effects on the interest rate of changes in income and the money supply.
How to incorporate the money market into the full Keynesian model.
The conditions under which *GDP* and employment will be more and less responsive to fiscal and monetary policy.
Some empirical material on the elasticity of the demand for money with respect to interest rates and income.

32

Inflation

If one price rises relative to another this is not necessarily an inflation, for it is simply a change in a ratio; if one price has risen relative to another then in addition, of course, the other has fallen relative to the first. Inflation is *rising prices*. When the *general* price level rises, there is inflation. This may be because the price of one important good has risen relative to others, or because a few prices have risen, or because all are rising relative to what they previously were. The important thing about inflation, however, is that it is characterized by a rise in the *average* price of everything in terms of money relative to a previous period. Some money prices may actually *fall* in an inflation but, if the average of all prices rises, then one still has inflation. Inflation results in a higher price level compared with a previous lower one. It is a process that takes place through time. Consequently it is usual to express inflation as a rate (usually a percentage rate) per period (usually a year).

Some economists like to make a distinction between a continuously rising price level and a once-and-for-all rise in the price level, reserving the term inflation only for the former. The difficulty with this distinction, which is popular with the monetarists, is that, since inflation can by definition take place only through time, and no one believes that the term inflation should be reserved for price levels that rise everlastingly, the distinction depends on an arbitrary definition of the period over which rising prices are experienced. So nothing will be made of this distinction here.

The indicator of inflation used earlier in this book was the retail prices index (*RPI*). (Now is a good time to refresh your memory about UK inflation in this century by turning back to chapter 25.)

SAQ 32.1

Define inflation.

Measuring the Level of Prices

There are several measures of inflation in use in the UK. Some of them are designed to measure changes in the prices of a particular set of goods and services (e.g. the wholesale prices index) and others the prices of goods and services consumed by particular sets of people in the community (e.g. the pensioners' price index). This chapter focuses on the two most important *general* measures of the price levels: the retail prices index and the *GDP* deflator.

The Retail Prices Index

The *RPI* is an index of the prices paid by consumers for a bundle of some 350 goods (with, in 1984–5, the 1975 price level taken as being equal to 100). The price information (some 150,000 prices) is recorded each month by the Department of Employment in a representative selection of retail outlets or by other appropriate means. (For example, newspaper prices are the same everywhere and so are collected centrally.) Prices include indirect taxes on goods and services. The goods and services selected are based on another survey – which you have already met – called the Family Expenditure Survey, which yields information on the patterns of spending of different types of family. The *RPI* excludes spending by pensioners (about 10 per cent of householders) and the 3 to 4 per cent highest income householders.

SAQ 32.2

Consider the following price index for a two person pensioner household iun the UK (data from *Economic Trends*, October, 1984, table 42):

1973	1974	1975	1976	1977	1978	1979	1980	1981	1982	1983
68.7	79.8	100.0	118.8	138.7	149.8	167.6	194.6	217.2	236.8	247.6

(a) How much did prices rise for this group between 1975 and 1976?
(b) How much did prices rise between 1982 and 1983?
(c) Was the average rate of inflation higher from 1973 to 1978 or from 1978 to 1983?

Case Study 32.1 Weights Used in the Retail Prices Index

The proportions of income spent by the average household (excluding pensioners and the high income groups) on different commodities form the weights used in the *RPI*. The 350 items are categorized into 11 major groups. The proportions of net income spent on each group by the average family in 1984 are shown in table 32.1. These weights are varied each year in January according as the proportion of expenditure revealed by the Family Expenditure Survey varies, and are then applied to the proportionate changes in prices.

The procedure mentioned in case study 32.1 can be illustrated for a two good case. Let there be just two goods X and Z, the consumption of which is X_0, Z_0 in the first period (say January) and X_1, Z_1 in the second (say December). Corresponding prices are P_{X0}, P_{X1}, P_{Z0} and P_{Z1}. The January weights for X are thus

$$\frac{P_{X0}X_0}{P_{X0}X_0 + P_{Z0}Z_0} = W_X$$

Table 32.1 1984 weights used in the *RPI*

Consumption category	*Weight (per cent of expenditure)*
Food	20.1
Alcoholic drink	7.5
Tobacco	3.6
Housing	14.9
Fuel and light	6.5
Durable household goods	6.9
Clothing and footwear	7.0
Transport and vehicles	15.8
Miscellaneous goods	7.6
Services	6.5
Meals bought and consumed outside the home	3.6
	100.0

Source: Department of Employment Gazette, September 1984, table 6.4

and for Z

$$\frac{P_{Z0}Z_0}{P_{X0}X_0 + P_{Z0}Z_0} = W_Z$$

since these are the proportions of expenditure going on each commodity. The change in the *RPI* is the change in each price weighted by these ratios added together:

$$\Delta RPI = \frac{\Delta P_X}{P_{X0}} W_X + \frac{\Delta P_Z}{P_{Z0}} W_Z$$

Thus, if the prices and quantities are as in table 32.2,

Table 32.2 Sample components of the *RPI*

	P_X	X	P_Z	Z
January	5	10	4	7
December	7	—	3	—

$$\Delta RPI = \left(\frac{2}{5} \times \frac{50}{78}\right) - \left(\frac{1}{4} \times \frac{28}{78}\right) = 0.167$$

With the index arbitrarily set at 100 in January, by December it has risen to 116.7, or by nearly 17 per cent. (Note the minus sign for negative ΔP_Z.)

Now, with some gentle manipulation, which it is best to take in easy stages, an interesting transformation occurs.

$$\Delta RPI = \frac{\Delta P_X}{P_{X0}} \frac{P_{X0}X_0}{P_{X0}X_0 + P_{Z0}Z_0} + \frac{\Delta P_Z}{P_{Z0}} \frac{P_{Z0}Z_0}{P_{X0}X_0 + P_{Z0}Z_0}$$

$$= \frac{P_{X1} - P_{X0}}{P_{X0}} \frac{P_{X0}X_0}{P_{X0}X_0 + P_{Z0}Z_0} + \frac{P_{Z1} - P_{Z0}}{P_{Z0}} \frac{P_{Z0}Z_0}{P_{X0}X_0 + P_{Z0}Z_0}$$

$$= \frac{(P_{X1} - P_{X0})X_0}{P_{X0}X_0 + P_{Z0}Z_0} + \frac{(P_{Z1} - P_{Z0})Z_0}{P_{X0}X_0 + P_{Z0}Z_0}$$

$$= \frac{P_{X1}X_0 - P_{X0}X_0 + P_{Z1}Z_0 - P_{Z0}Z_0}{P_{X0}X_0 + P_{Z0}Z_0}$$

$$= \frac{P_{X1}X_0 + P_{Z1}Z_0}{P_{X0}X_0 + P_{Z0}Z_0} - \frac{P_{X0}X_0 + P_{Z0}Z_0}{P_{X0}X_0 + P_{Z0}Z_0}$$

$$= \frac{P_{X1}X_0 + P_{Z1}Z_0}{P_{X0}X_0 + P_{Z0}Z_0} - 1$$

$$1 + \Delta RPI = \frac{P_{X1}X_0 + P_{Z1}Z_0}{P_{X0}X_0 + P_{Z0}Z_0}$$

The ratio on the right should look familiar. It is a base quantity weighted Laspeyres *price* index or cost of living index. Inserting the numbers of table 32.1 gives the same result as before: $1 + \Delta RPI = 91/78 = 1.167$ or, with the base year set at 100 in January, the *RPI* in December becomes 116.7.

The general form of the *RPI* at any time *t* can be written as

$$RPI_t = \frac{\Sigma P_t Q_0}{\Sigma P_0 Q_0}$$

which is exactly the same as the alternative formulation

$$\Delta RPI = \sum_i \Delta P_i \frac{P_i Q_i}{\Sigma_i P_i Q_i}$$

Where the *i*th commodity and its price are denoted by Q_i and P_i.

Note that in this numerical example, although there was inflation over the period, one money price actually fell. Inflation does not mean that *all* prices necessarily rise; only that the *weighted average* of prices rises or, as it is commonly termed, the *price level* rises.

SAQ 32.3

You purchase two goods only, *X* and *Z*. In January you purchased 12 of *X* and 7 of *Z* at prices of £6 and £7. In December their prices had risen to £7 and £10. What was the increase in your personal retail prices index?

The *RPI* since 1948 has behaved as recorded in table 32.3 (the percentage inflation rates are the same as in table 25.1).

Table 32.3 Retail prices index and inflation in the UK, 1948–83 (1975 = 100)

	Index	*Annual inflation rate (%)*		*Index*	*Annual inflation rate (%)*		*Index*	*Annual inflation rate (%)*
1948	23.1	6.2	1961	37.7	3.3	1974	80.5	16.0
1949	23.8	3.0	1962	39.3	4.2	1975	100.0	24.2
1950	24.5	2.9	1963	40.1	2.0	1976	116.5	16.5
1951	26.7	9.0	1964	41.4	3.2	1977	135.0	15.9
1952	29.2	9.4	1965	43.4	4.8	1978	146.2	8.3
1953	30.1	3.1	1966	45.1	3.9	1979	165.8	13.4
1954	30.6	1.7	1967	46.2	2.4	1980	195.6	18.0
1955	32.0	4.6	1968	48.4	4.8	1981	218.9	11.9
1956	33.6	5.0	1969	51.0	5.4	1982	237.7	8.6
1957	34.8	3.6	1970	54.2	6.3	1983	248.6	4.6
1958	35.9	3.2	1971	59.3	9.4			
1959	36.1	0.6	1972	63.6	7.3			
1960	36.5	1.1	1973	69.4	9.1			

Sources: Economic Trends, Annual Supplement, 1983, p. 114; *Economic Trends*, September 1984, p. 42

Note that the method of construction of the *RPI* involves changing the weights periodically. Thus it is not *strictly* legitimate to compare the 1948 and 1983 levels and infer that the price level has risen over tenfold, since the bundles of goods at each date are not the same. Moreover, other technical changes have been made from time to time to the *RPI*. None the less the table brings out the dramatic size of the post-war inflation in Britain.

You can be less squeamish about making year to year comparisons, since the weights change little on an annual basis (and not at all on a monthly basis within the year). You can see that the big increases in the price level got going around 1971 with a 9.4 per cent increase, followed by high annual inflation rates through to 1980, after which there was a steady fall in the rate to 4.6 per cent in 1983.

Reverting to the more hazardous long term comparisons you find that the price level doubled form 1948 to 1967, doubled again by mid 1974, doubled again by 1979 and between 1979 and 1983 rose by 50 per cent. Thus, until 1981, inflation was accelerating in the UK.

The *GDP* Deflator

The *GDP* deflator differs from the *RPI* in two major ways. First, it is much broader in its coverage than the *RPI* because it includes all final goods and services produced in the UK rather than a sample of mostly *consumption* goods only. Second, its weights are *current* quantitites rather than base quantities. The *GDP* deflator is thus measured by

$$GDP \text{ deflator } = \frac{\Sigma P_t Q_t}{\Sigma P_0 Q_t}$$

and is a Paasche *price* index (again recall chapter 23). It is most conveniently obtained by taking the ratio of *current GDP* at market prices ($\Sigma P_t Q_t$) to *constant price GDP* at market prices ($\Sigma P_0 Q_t$) and multipliying by 100 so that the base year (currently 1980) has an index of 100. There is a similar *GDP* deflator for *GDP* at factor cost that is known as the 'implied index of total home costs' in official national income statistics. Table 32.4 shows how the UK *GDP* deflator has behaved since the Second World War.

Table 32.4 *GDP* deflator 1948–83 (1980 = 100)

	Index	*Annual inflation rate (%)*		*Index*	*Annual inflation rate (%)*		*Index*	*Annual inflation rate (%)*
1948	11.6	—	1961	18.5	2.8	1974	39.4	14.5
1949	11.9	2.6	1962	19.2	3.8	1975	50.2	27.4
1950	11.9	0.0	1963	19.6	2.1	1976	57.6	14.7
1951	13.0	9.2	1964	20.3	3.6	1977	65.6	13.9
1952	14.0	7.7	1965	21.4	5.4	1978	72.9	11.1
1953	14.5	3.6	1966	22.3	4.2	1979	83.5	14.5
1954	14.7	1.4	1967	23.0	3.1	1980	100.0	19.8
1955	15.2	3.4	1968	23.9	3.9	1981	111.8	11.8
1956	16.2	6.6	1969	25.2	5.4	1982	119.6	7.0
1957	16.8	3.7	1970	27.1	7.5	1983	125.7	5.1
1958	17.5	4.2	1971	29.6	9.2			
1959	17.7	1.1	1972	32.1	8.4			
1960	18.0	1.7	1973	34.4	7.2			

Sources: Economic Trends, Annual Supplement, 1983, p. 4; *Economic Trends*, September 1984, p. 6

The pattern can be seen to be very similar to that shown by the *RPI* over this period: a more than tenfold rise in prices between 1948 and 1983 and an accelerating rate of inflation after the late 1960s.

SAQ 32.4

Using the data of table 32.4;

(a) If *GDP* in current prices was £57.3 billion in 1971, what was it in constant prices, with 1980 = 100?

(b) If *GDP* in 1980 prices was £226.7 billion in 1978, what was it in 1978 prices?

World Inflation

Table 32.5 shows the *GDP* (market prices) deflators computed by the Statistical Office of the United Nations for a set of countries. The 18 selected countries exhibit widely different inflationary experiences. The Federal Republic of Germany had the most stable price level over this period. The highest inflation rates occurred in the developing world – though the data for poorer countries, which often lack the necessary resources to compile *GDP* accurately, are not to be too heavily relied upon (note, for example, Zambia's erratic performance). By the end of 1980, when the data set runs out, Argentina held the record with an annual inflation rate of over 200 per cent! At that rate the value of money halves every six months! The overall record holder seems to be Chile, however, whose price level rose from 0.2 to 2178.6 (1975 = 100) over the decade and which suffered a desperate *hyperinflation* in the mid 1970s.

Table 32.5 Annual inflation rates (per cent) in selected countries 1971–80 (*GDP* deflators)

	1971	*1972*	*1973*	*1974*	*1975*	*1976*	*1977*	*1978*	*1979*	*1980*
Argentina	37.1	63.5	64.3	29.1	300.3	422.1	259.5	257.4	250.7	201.1
Australia	6.6	9.2	14.7	18.4	15.3	11.0	7.7	8.1	10.8	9.9
Canada	3.2	5.0	9.2	15.5	10.7	9.4	7.2	6.5	10.6	10.7
Chile	50.0	133.0	314.3	689.7	336.7	250.7	103.7	56.5	44.4	35.0
Denmark	7.8	9.0	10.5	12.7	12.9	8.7	8.8	10.3	7.7	8.4
France	5.8	6.2	7.9	11.0	13.5	9.8	9.0	9.5	10.1	11.6
Germany (FRG)	7.7	5.6	6.6	6.8	6.7	3.3	3.8	3.8	3.7	4.8
Ghana	4.8	15.4	17.9	24.5	26.5	28.1	67.2	73.3	—	—
India	5.1	11.2	18.9	18.0	−3.0	6.4	3.9	1.8	14.4	11.2
Ireland	10.5	13.6	15.2	6.1	22.2	20.2	12.3	10.5	12.4	14.1
Israel	14.3	16.4	21.7	35.5	35.9	31.0	41.0	54.6	77.9	126.8
Italy	7.3	6.3	11.5	18.5	17.5	18.0	19.1	13.9	15.7	20.4
Japan	5.2	5.2	11.9	20.7	7.8	6.5	5.6	4.6	2.5	3.0
Netherlands	8.6	9.4	8.4	9.2	11.2	8.9	6.3	5.2	4.2	5.2
South Africa	4.7	11.0	19.0	14.6	9.8	11.0	11.4	12.0	14.7	20.9
Sweden	7.7	7.1	7.1	8.5	14.8	11.6	10.7	10.0	7.4	12.0
UK	9.2	8.3	7.0	15.0	26.9	14.7	14.0	10.9	15.1	18.9
USA	5.2	4.3	5.6	8.8	9.1	5.7	6.0	7.5	8.7	9.4
Zambia	−6.8	3.8	19.1	11.5	−14.2	13.4	9.4	10.8	29.1	11.5

Note that the UK data do not accurately correspond to those in table 32.4, which are more recent.
Source: Yearbook of National Accounts Statistics 1981, vol. II, table 9A

Anticipated and Unanticipated Inflations

It is useful to distinguish between anticipated and unanticipated inflations both because the social consequences of each are different and because of their different behavioural implications – implications that, as you will see in later chapters, have immense consequences for the way macroeconomic policy is conducted. When people have experienced an inflation rate of, say 1 to 4 per cent per year for some time, as in the later 1950s and early 1960s in the UK, it seems reasonable to suppose that they expect inflation within that band of rates in the future. If, then, the rate suddenly jumps outside that band as it did in 1969 to 5.4 per cent, and to 6.3 per cent and 9.4 per cent in the following years (*RPI* changes), it will take time for people to adjust their expectations. The sudden jump is not likely to have been anticipated by most.

The main effect of unanticipated inflations is that they change the wealth distribution. Those who hold money or who have lent money to others at fixed interest rates lose. Those who hold their wealth in other forms, for example in physical and human capital, keep their wealth constant. Debtors whose debt is contracted at fixed interest rates gain and lenders under the same terms lose.

To illustrate the first kind of effect, consider two individuals, A and B, each having £50,000 of wealth. A is the owner of a £49,000 house and holds £1000 in cash and in a bank current account; B holds £49,000 in cash and a bank current account and has a £1000 print by Henry Moore. Suppose an unanticipated inflation of 10 per cent occurs over the year in all goods and services. At the end of the year, A's house has increased in vlaue to £53,900 which, together with the £1000 cash, gives A a wealth of £54,900. B, by contrast, has £49,000 cash still and a Henry Moore worth £1100 – a total of £50,100 in wealth. In money terms both appear wealthier but A much more so. In fact, of course, B is actually much poorer since the purchasing power of the cash has fallen by 9 per cent; so B's real wealth is actually only £45,545 in terms of the original price level, whereas A has lost only the reduced purchasing power of the £1000 and so has wealth of £49,909.

Of course, had B anticipated the inflation it is unlikely that he or she would have held wealth in the form of money, investing it instead in real rather than money assets and hence avoiding the consequences of the inflation.

People sometimes make long term contracts in monetary (or *nominal*) terms. Many elderly people, for example, who made their wills 20 or more years ago made specific cash provisions therein that have not been revised and that imply, on death, that intended beneficiaries will inherit far less in real terms than the deceased person intended. Some people's retirement pensions are cast in nominal terms and are not subject to renegotiation – they can lose very heavily from inflation that they (or their spouses) failed to anticipate. State pensions and benefits likewise, unless they are raised in line with inflation, lose real value as the price level rises.

SAQ 32.5

(a) You are a pensioner who in 1975 began receiving a fixed nominal (money terms) pension of £5000 per year. Using the *RPI* of table 32.3, what, if its purchasing power in 1975 was £5000, was its purchasing power in 1979, 1981 and 1983?

(b) During an inflation, would you expect the share value of firms with a high proportion of monetary liabilities (like debentures and outstanding accounts) in total assets to rise or fall relative to a firm with a low proportion of monetary liabilities? Answer, then look at case study 32.2.

Case Study 32.2 Inflation and the Value of Firms

Armen Alchian and Reuben Kessel (1959) have explored the idea that firms tend to benefit from inflation, and found that *it is true for firms that are net monetary debtors*, as the preceding analysis would suggest. The value of firms quoted on American stock exchanges was taken as being the price of their shares multiplied by the number of shares. Over a period the increase in value was measured as the increase in share price per dollar invested in the firm in a base year.

Assets of the firms examined were divided into two kinds: monetary and real.

A monetary asset is one whose value is independent of changes in the price level (e.g. money, accounts receivable, bonds and prepaid taxes). A monetary liability is similarly defined as one that is independent of changes in the price level (e.g. accounts payable, mortgages, bonds and preferred stock). A net monetary debtor was a firm whose monetary liabilities exceeded its monetary assets; conversely for a monetary creditor. The ratio of net monetary debts or assets to the total value of the firm was the indicator of the size of net monetary liabilities or assets relative to total value.

The performance of groups of firms was then compared during periods of inflation and deflation, with the results shown in table 32.6 (Alchian and Kessel, 1959). In every case, as the table shows, the net monetary debtors did better under inflation and worse under deflation than the net monetary creditors.

Table 32.6 Performance of US firms during inflation and deflation

	Market value at end of period per dollar invested at beginning ($)	
	Net monetary debtors	*Net monetary creditors*
Inflations		
New York stock exchange 1915–20	2.7	1.6
New York stock exchange 1940–52	5.9	4.5
American stock exchange 1940–52	11.3	8.0
Steel industry 1940–52	6.9	6.7
Chemical industry 1940–52	7.2	4.5
Textile industry 1940–52	16.3	9.7
Department stores 1940–52	9.0	4.1
Deflations		
New York stock exchange 1921–2	1.5	1.8
New York stock exchange 1928–33	0.5	1.1

Alchian and Kessel also found that between 1915 and 1952 the percentage of firms that were net monetary debtors fell dramatically: almost all firms were net monetary debtors in 1915, which may account for the common view that firms *in general* gain from inflation. However, by 1952 the proportion in each category had fallen to about 50 per cent, so this general presumption was no longer valid. It has occasionally also been speculated that firms gain in inflation because increases in money wages lag behind increases in prices, thereby enhancing profits (at the expense of wage earners). No evidence was found for this – the only factor that correlated with increases in the value of firms was their net monetary debtor status.

Armen Alchian and Reuben Kessel (1959) 'Redistribution of wealth through inflation', *Science*, **130**, 535–9, table 1.

Inflation and Interest Rates

Suppose you lend £1000 to someone at 4 per cent interest for a year, neither of you expecting inflation. Your debtor will pay you £1040 next year. Now suppose that, contrary to your expectations, inflation occurs at 3 per cent per year. What happens? In effect you receive only about 1 per cent interest in terms of the prices initially prevailing. If you were just willing to forgo current consumption at 4 per cent in the original period, then you will plainly lose from the exchange – and your debtor will, of course, gain, since the £1040 payable to you in the second year will be worth only £1040 × 100/103 = £1009.71. Thus you only receive £9.71 in *real* terms for your loan of £1000 instead of £40, which is 0.971 per cent rather than 4.0 per cent (this is why I wrote 'about' 1 per cent three sentences earlier).

Now suppose that you both *expect* inflation to be 3 per cent over the next year. What is the interest rate that you will be able to negotiate, assuming that 4 per cent continues, in real terms, to be the one at which you agree to exchange? The answer is 7.12 per cent. Next year you will receive £1071.2, whose value in constant purchasing power is £1071.2 × 100/103 = £1040.

The distinction that is important to recognize here is that between **nominal interest rates**, or monetary interest rates, and **real interest rates**. The former have two components: the basic real rate of interest, reflecting time preference, and a second component to allow for expected falling purchasing power. If inflations are correctly anticipated by everyone, then the nominal rate will become higher than the real rate, for lenders will not lend unless they are compensated for the devalued money in which they will be repaid. But if inflation is not sufficiently anticipated, the nominal rate will be lower than this, and creditors will lose. The relationship between the nominal rate of interest i_n, the real rate i_r and the percentage rate of change of prices $\dot{P}$ is as follows when inflation is correctly anticipated:

$$i_n = (1 + i_r)(1 + \dot{P}) - 1$$

Thus if the real rate is, as before, 0.04, and the expected inflation rate is 0.03, then $i_n = 0.0712$, which is what you had before.

This formula is arrived at in the following way. (Now is a good time to remind yourself of the discounting procedure of chapter 16.) You were originally, with no inflation, prepared to lend £1000 at 4 per cent in order to receive a future sum (F) of £1040. The amount £1040 next year had a present value (PV) of £1000. Thus

$$PV = \frac{F}{1 + i_r}$$

where i_r is the real rate of interest reflecting the real compensation you required to make the loan. With expected inflation of $\dot{P}$ present you want to charge a nominal interest rate i_n such that the present value of the future sum adjusted for inflation also has a present value of £1000, namely

$$PV = \frac{F(1 + \dot{P})}{1 + i_n}$$

To compute i_n, the simplest thing is simply to set these two *PV* equations equal to one another. After all, the *PV* in each case has to be £1000. Thus

$$\frac{F}{1 + i_r} = \frac{F(1 + \dot{P})}{1 + i_n}$$

Multiplying through by $(1 + i_r)$ and $(1 + i_n)$ yields

$$F(1 + i_n) = F\,(1 + \dot{P})\,(1 + i_r)$$

Dividing by F yields

$$1 + i_n = (1 + \dot{P})\,(1 + i_r)$$

$$i_n = (1 + \dot{P})\,(1 + i_r) - 1$$

It is quite common to use a rule of thumb that says the nominal rate is the real rate of interest plus the inflation rate ($i_n = i_r + \dot{P}$). For low real rates and low rates of inflation, this gives a close approximation to the correct calculation. For example, with a real interest rate of 0.04 and inflation at 0.03, the sum of this, 0.07, is only 0.0012 smaller than the nominal rate correctly calculated.

Table 32.7 Short term interest rates in the UK, 1960–83 (per cent)

	Inflation rate (GDP *deflator)*	*Treasury bill yield*
1960	1.7	4.4
1961	2.8	5.5
1962	3.8	3.8
1963	2.1	3.8
1964	3.6	6.7
1965	5.4	5.6
1966	4.2	6.6
1967	3.1	7.6
1968	3.9	6.9
1969	5.4	7.8
1970	7.5	6.9
1971	9.2	4.5
1972	8.4	8.5
1973	7.2	12.8
1974	14.5	11.3
1975	27.4	10.9
1976	14.7	14.0
1977	13.9	6.4
1978	11.1	11.9
1979	14.5	16.5
1980	19.8	13.6
1981	11.8	15.4
1982	7.0	10.0
1983	5.1	9.0

Sources: Economic Trends, Annual Supplement, 1981, table 194; *Economic Trends*, September 1984, table 66, table 32.4 in this book

However, with a real interest rate of, say, 10 per cent and high inflation at 50 per cent, the sum, 0.60 is 5 percentage points smaller than the nominal rate correctly calculated: 0.65. As you can see, with positive changes in the price level, the rule of thumb procedure makes too small an allowance for inflation.

One implication of the foregoing is that, provided the underlying real rate of interest is constant, and that the inflation is correctly anticipated, nominal interest rate will vary together with inflation.

Table 32.7 shows how short term interest rates (Treasury bill yields) and inflation (*GDP* deflator) have moved in the UK from 1960 to 1983. As you can see from this table there have been years when the short term nominal interest rate has actually been *less* than the rate of inflation (1970, 1971, 1974, 1975, 1976, 1977 and 1980); more years would doubtless have to be added if one took the interest rate net of tax paid on income from investments. Since no one believes that the real rate of time preference was *negative*, the explanation must lie elsewhere. It lies partly in the fact that government policy has been directed to keeping interest rates artificially low; even though in the late 1970s they were at record levels, in a free market they would certainly have been higher. The other main part of the explanation lies in the fact that inflation is imperfectly anticipated. Notice that the inflation rate fluctuates more than the interest rate.

Inflation and the Exchange Rate

Suppose that inflation in the UK is 10 per cent and inflation in the USA is zero. UK exports therefore rise in price by 10 per cent and US demand falls. Given that the US elasticity of demand for UK exports is relatively elastic, US demand for sterling also falls. US imports will now appear relatively cheap to UK residents compared with UK goods. The demand for imports will therefore rise and the supply of sterling will also rise. A leftward shift in the demand curve for sterling coupled with a rightwards shift in the supply curve means that the sterling exchange rate must fall.

If inflation in the US is at the same rate as inflation in the UK, then there will be no impact on the exchange rate. If inflation in the US is faster than in the UK, then sterling will appreciate.

In general, then, if the price level in one country rises relatively faster than those in other countries, its exchange rate will depreciate; if it rises more slowly or falls relative to other countries, its exchange rate will appreciate. Relatively high inflation causes the exchange rate to depreciate. Do not fall into the trap of supposing that falling exchange rates always cause inflation. Although it is possible for this to happen, it is more likely for a falling exchange rate to be a consequence rather than a cause of inflation.

SAQ 32.6

Draw a demand and supply figure for sterling showing the effect on the exchange rate when UK inflation is less than that in trading partner countries.

Real and Nominal Variables in General

Economics assumes that individuals make their choices in terms of *real* variables. They may, of course, make mistakes owing to imperfect information about things that are relevant to a choice. Moreover, the future is uncertain and any choices that affect the future or depend upon future factors are of necessity conjectural or expectational. Some important issues relating in particular to expectations about inflation will be discussed later. Economics does not, however, assume that people suffer from what is sometimes called **money illusion** – that is, the inability to tell the difference between a 5 per cent interest rate when inflation is zero and at 5 per cent, or a £100 weekly wage this year and £100 next year when the price level is expected to be between 5 and 10 per cent higher. Up to this chapter one has not had to face up to the consequences of making a distinction between real and nominal values. From now on, however, you must do just that.

To prepare the way, consider the simplified picture of a competitive labour market used so far in the Keynesian model. Figure 32.1(a) shows that one has

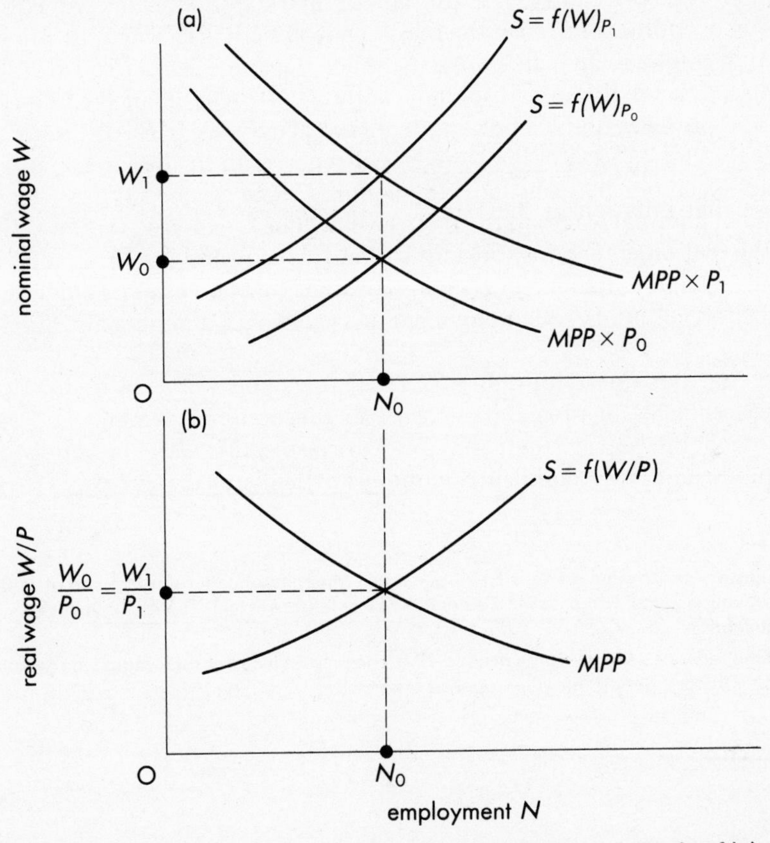

Figure 32.1 Nominal and real wages and the demand and supply of labour

so far measured employment as a function of the *nominal* wage. This did not matter so long as the price level was assumed constant for, with a constant price level, a 10 per cent change in nominal wages is the same thing as a 10 per cent change in real wages. The demand for labour is the physical product of a marginal worker (*MPP*) multiplied by the constant price level P_0. The supply of labour is a function of the nominal wage, given that $P = P_0$.

What happens in this figure if the price level rises to, say, P_1? The demand for labour evidently shifts rightwards to $MPP \times P_1$. The supply curve shifts leftwards to $S = f(W)_{P1}$. If the price level rose by x per cent, a new nominal wage is established x per cent higher than the previous one at W_1. In *real* terms, nothing has happened: the real wage and the level of employment (N_0) are the same. There has been no productivity growth (*MPP* is as before) and nothing has happened to affect workers' preferences. The only change in the nominal wage is therefore that necessary to keep it the same in real terms.

It is often more convenient to replace the nominal variables with real ones. You can then measure the *real* wage on the vertical axis (figure 32.1(b)). The real product of a marginal worker (*MPP*) is the demand curve. You can also show labour supply as a function of the real wage (W/P), or nominal wage divided by the price index. If the labour market (assumed competitive as before) is in equilibrium, then the real wage will be W_0/P_0 when the price level is P_0 and employment will be N_0. Now let the price level rise to P_1. What happens in the diagram? Absolutely nothing! *MPP* is unaffected since it is defined in physical units. The supply of labour may, as W/P falls, move down the supply curve, but nominal wages will be bid up in the face of an excess demand for labour by firms until the nominal wage reached W_1. At this point the ratio of nominal wages to the price level will be restored at $W_1/P_1 = W_0/P_0$. Thus the real wage remains constant (or returns to its old level after a period of adjustment) and employment remains constant (or returns to its old level after a period of voluntary unemployment if real wages temporarily dip below W_0/P_0).

Note that both parts of figure 32.1 tell the same story. In figure 32.1(a), however, changes in prices cause *shifts* in the nominal demand and supply curves. In figure 32.1(b) there may be short term shifts *along* the supply curve, but equilibrium is re-established without any shifts of the curves.

SAQ 32.7

(a) Suppose your nominal wage is £120 per week when the price level is indexed at 100. Next year, your nominal wage is still £120 and the price level rises to 110. What is your real wage in that year?

(b) For the series of nominal wages in table 32.8, compute an index of real wages with real wage = 100 in the first period using the supplied price index.

Table 32.8 Computation of index of real wages for SAQ 32.7(b)

Period	*Nominal wage*	*Price index*	*Index of real wages*
1	£90	100	—
2	£100	111	—
3	£110	122	—
4	£110	130	—
5	£130	150	—
6	£140	160	—
7	£160	165	—

What You Should Understand Now

The meaning of inflation.
The *RPI* and *GDP* deflator measures of inflation and their construction.
The recent UK history of inflation.
The differences between anticipated and unanticipated inflation and their consequences for different kinds of asset portfolios and creditor–debtor relations.
The relationship between inflation and interest rates, nominal and real interest rates.
The relationship between inflation and exchange rates.
The distinction between real and nominal values, and how they are linked by an index of prices.
Alternative (real or nominal wage) versions of demand and supply in the labour market.

33

Inflation and Unemployment

In post-war Britain up to the mid 1960s unemployment was quite low and the rate of inflation was low as well. In the mid 1960s, however, something dramatic seems to have happened. *Both* inflation *and* unemployment began to rise. Moreover, a long standing inverse relationship between unemployment

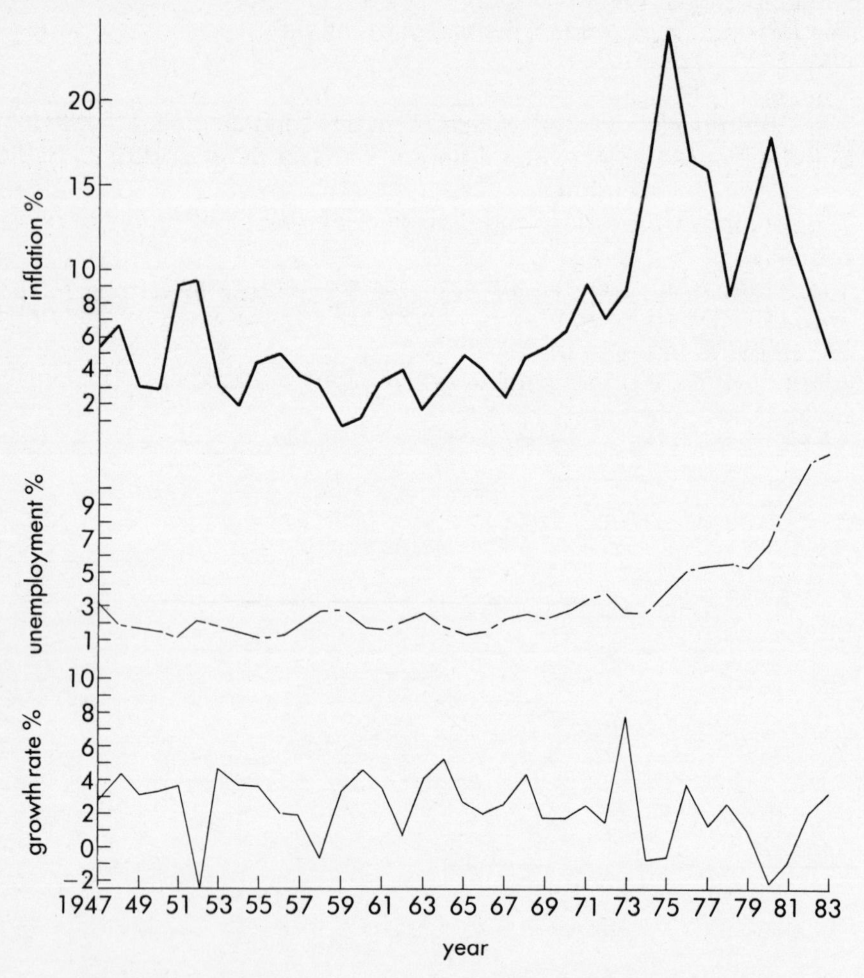

Figure 33.1 Inflation, unemployment and growth in the UK 1947–83

and inflation seemed to break down. By the later 1970s both were at unprecedently high levels. In the 1960s and 1970s policy makers were faced with the problem of **stagflation** – inflation coupled with low growth. In the later 1970s and early 1980s the major problems were very high rates of inflation and unemployment.

The post-war trends in inflation, unemployment and growth are shown in figure 33.1. The graph for unemployment shows a periodic cycle since 1947, reaching highs that correspond to slumps in aggregate output in 1947, 1952, 1959, 1963, 1972, 1977 and 1981 or, roughly speaking, at intervals of four years. In 1983 unemployment was at a record for the period and still rising. Growth rates slumped in 1952, 1958, 1962, 1966, 1970, 1974 and 1980 and tend to lead to rises in unemployment. The peaks in the inflation rate occurred in 1952, 1956, 1962, 1965, 1971, 1975 and 1980 and seem not to bear much relation to unemployment (though up to the mid 1960s inflation and unemployment seem to have moved in opposite directions) or growth (save after 1973 when inflation and growth seem to have moved in opposite directions).

Effects of Aggregate Demand Changes in the Price Level

Although for long periods in British history the price level was very stable and inflation close to zero, the post-war period was characterized up to the late 1960s by mild inflation (averaging roughly 3 per cent). According to the

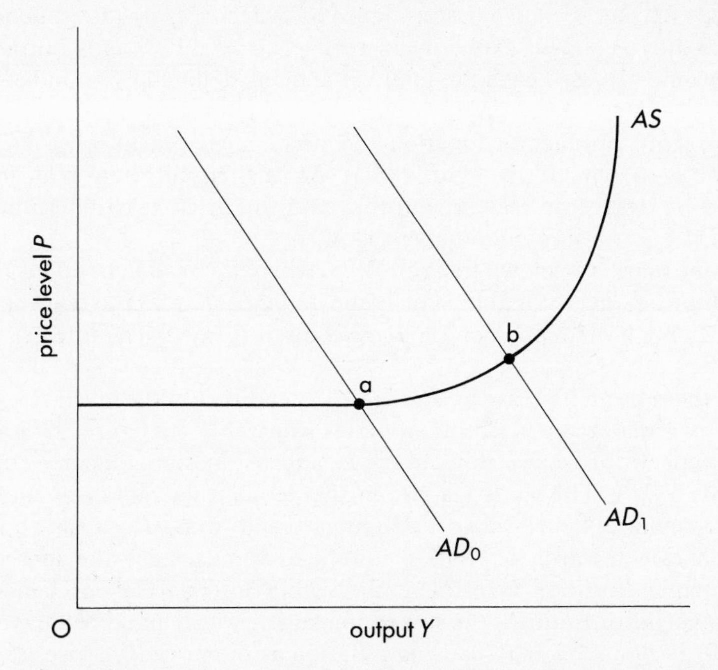

Figure 33.2 A rise in aggregate demand, with aggregate supply given

aggregate demand and supply analysis of chapter 25, which must be re-introduced now that inflation is explicitly to be brought into the macro model, it looks as though the economy was operating on an upward sloping *AS* curve. Unemployment was low and so the economy was operating near to capacity. Consequently, if aggregate demand were to rise, this would be reflected in *both* rising prices *and* increasing output rather than, as hitherto supposed in the model, in output alone.

Figure 33.2 is like the *AS* and *AD* figure 25.5. As aggregate demand rises from AD_0 to AD_1 the equilibrium price level and output rate both rise from point a to point b. Suppose this shift in *AD* occurred via an increase in the money supply.

SAQ 33.1

Why will a rise in the money supply cause the aggregate demand curve to shift to the right?

The Keynesian Model with a Variable Price Level

Now introduce the aggregate demand and supply curves more fully into the Keynesian model. A hint as to how this is done will have already been given in SAQ 33.1. Just as in the case of the labour market in chapter 32, the goods market and the money market need to be analysed in terms of real variables that reflect a changing price level when the economy can no longer be taken to be on a horizontal aggregate supply curve.

The goods market is shown first in figure 33.3. Here, aggregate expenditure in figure 33.3(a) is shown explicitly in real terms (E_0/P_0), as is output and national income (Y_0/P_0), each nominal value being deflated by an index of the price level.

The aggregate production function too now shows real income *Y/P* as a function of employment in figure 33.4. At the equilibrium real income determined by aggregate real expenditure and the price level determined by *AS* and AD_0, equilibrium employment is N_0.

The money market is shown in figure 33.5, where the real demand for money at the equilibrium level of real income is shown by L_0/P_0 and the real supply of money is M_0/P_0; both depend on the *nominal* interest rate *i*. The interest rate is initially i_0.

Now let there be an increase in aggregate expenditure at the given price level while the nominal money supply remains constant. In figure 33.3(a) the aggregate expenditure curve shifts to E_1/P_0 and real national income starts to rise towards Y_1/P_0. This causes a rise in the demand for money at the given price level shown, in figure 33.5, as a rightward shift to L_1/P_0 causing a rise in the interest rate towards i_1. This counters to some extent the increase in aggregate expenditure as investment and other interest elastic elements of aggregate expenditure fall. At the same time, aggregate demand will have risen to, say, AD_1 in figure 33.3(b), causing inflation as the price level rises towards

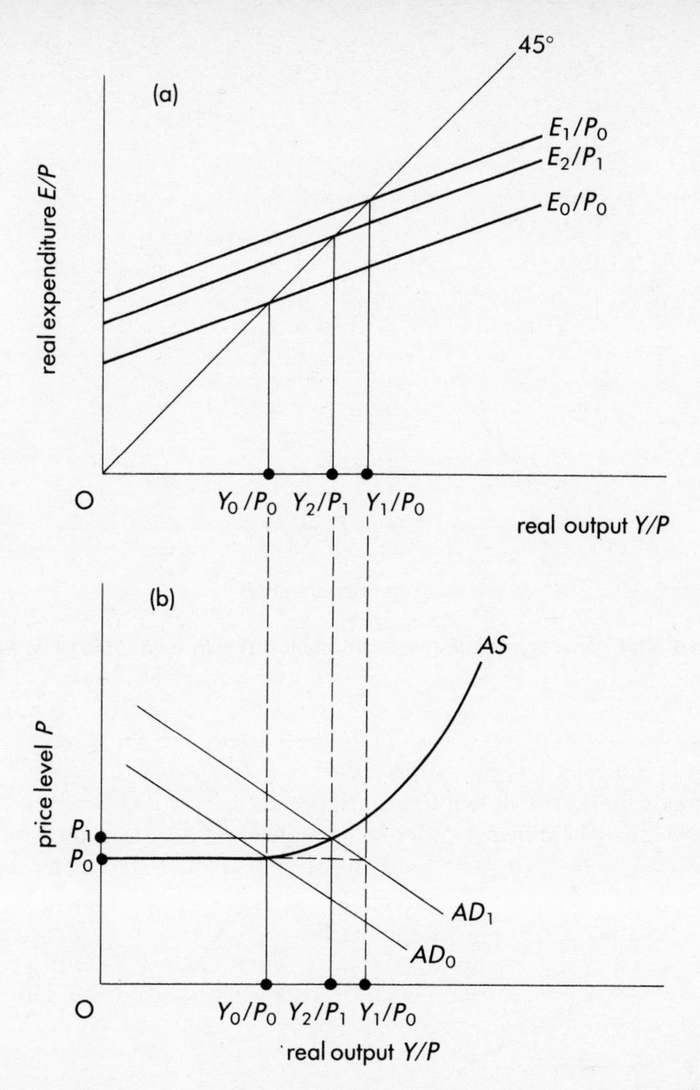

Figure 33.3 Aggregate expenditure and output, and aggregate demand and supply with a variable price level

the new equilibrium price level P_1. But the rising price level causes the demand for money to rise so as to maintain the real demand for money. Hence the new demand for nominal money balances L_2 rises in the same proportion as the price level; $L_2/P_1 = L_1/P_0$. The rise in the price level will also have caused the real money supply to fall to, say, M_0/P_1 and a new equilibrium interest rate at, say, i_4. The upshot is a new equilibrium level of real income Y_2/P_1 determined by the eventual interest rate, the eventual level of aggregate expenditure and the eventual price level. This level of real income is higher than before (provided that there is some involuntary unemployment and the economy is on

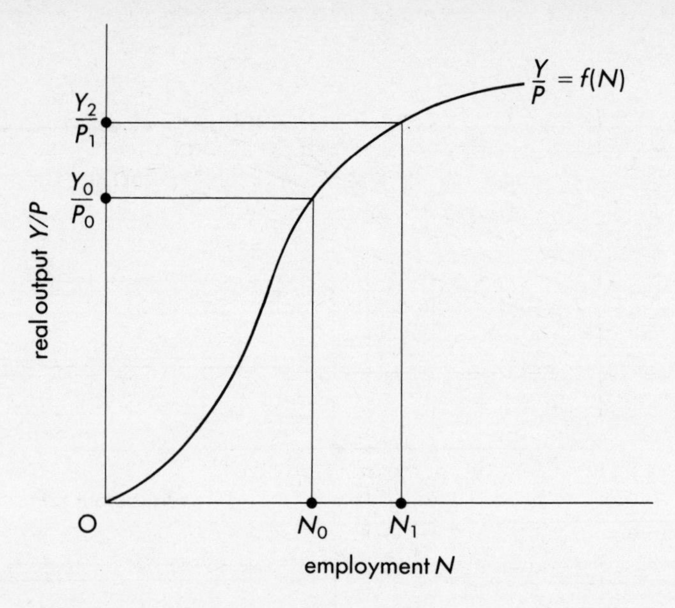

Figure 33.4 The aggregate production function with a variable price level

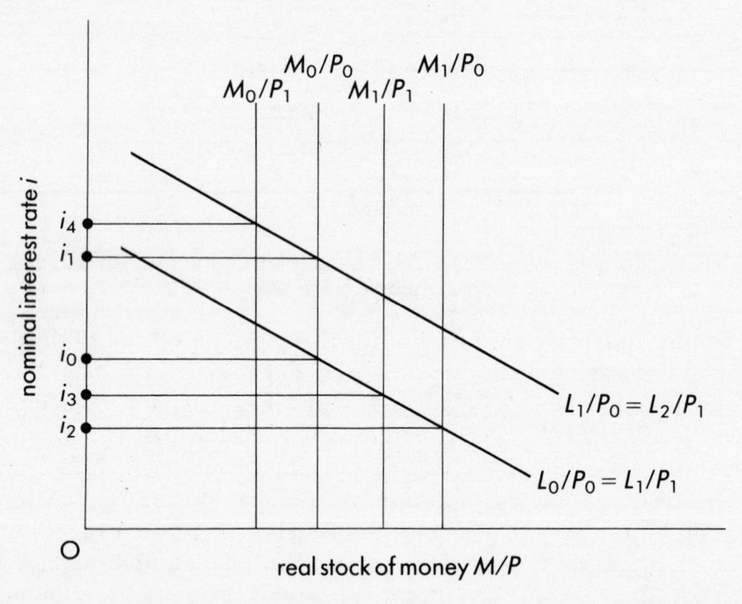

Figure 33.5 Supply and demand for the money stock with a variable price level

an upward sloping aggregate supply curve) and, in figure 33.4, generates a higher level of employment N_1.

Alternatively, let there be an increase in the nominal supply of money by the government. M rises so that M/P shifts to the right from M_0/P_0 at the current price level to M_1/P_0. This causes the interest rate to fall and investment to rise. With larger money balances people will also probably increase other elements of planned expenditure. So for both reasons the aggregate expenditure curve shifts to, say, E_1/P_0 in figure 33.3(a). This causes the aggregate demand curve to shift to the right at the existing price level. A new equilibrium in the goods and money market (though not necessarily in the labour market) is eventually established where the aggregate demand curve has shifted to AD_1, the price level will have risen to P_1, and real aggregate expenditure has shifted to E_2/P_1. The real money supply will have fallen somewhat to M_1/P_1, with the nominal interest rate at i_3, lower than before, and the demand for nominal money balances L will have risen to offset the rise in the price level, so that $L_0/P_0 = L_1/P_1$. Again, employment will have risen to N_1. In the new equilibrium any inflation generated by the increase in M will have worked itself out so that the nominal interest rate equals the real interest rate: there will be a new, higher, price level but no inflation.

This seems very complicated, but is really no more than the Keynesian model of chapter 31 with the assumption of a constant price level dropped. In the original model nominal and real values were the same since inflation was assumed away. The only new features added here are the determination of the price level by aggregate demand and supply and then the feeding back of changes in the price level into the rest of the model (with further feedback on aggregate demand). To check your understanding of the way the aggregate demand curve behaves, be sure to tackle SAQ 33.2.

SAQ 33.2

What determines the position of the aggregate demand curve?

Asymmetries in Responses

The aggregate demand and supply addition to the model suggests that output, employment and the price level will rise and fall together and that the price level and unemployment will vary *inversely*. As it happens, the price level has not risen and fallen as the theory suggests. Up to the late 1960s, unemployment and *inflation*, rather than the *price level*, varied inversely. Moreover, the analysis so far identifies inflation as a *transitory* phenomenon that is eliminated once the price level has risen and a new equilibrium established. Britain together with other countries, however, has had *continuing* inflation, so further modifications evidently need to be made to the analysis.

In the course of this chapter, two major modifications will be made. The first of these is to recognize that the short run pricing decisions of firms, particularly in oligopolistic industries, are such that they are more likely to respond to rising demand by raising prices than they are to falling demand by lowering prices. This arises for reasons already discussed, for example asymmetries in contracts with suppliers of inputs: it is easier to negotiate an increase in nominal wages than it is to alter an existing agreement with the labour force so as to *reduce* nominal wages. Consequently, when permanent demand increases are perceived and price and output both adjusted upwards, the demand for labour (and other inputs) will usually rise (unless they are *inferior* inputs) and their wages (and prices) will be bid up. However, when a permanent *fall* in demand is perceived (let alone a fall about whose permanence people are unsure) reductions in wages cannot be quickly negotiated and, moreover, the suppliers of labour and other inputs may take a less sure view that demand for the final output really has fallen and, hence, resist falling nominal wages.

The asymmetry is also reinforced by another factor emphasized by the Keynesian Nobel prize winner James Tobin, born 1918. Suppose that in the utility function of workers there are not only the goods and services that income can buy (ignoring for present purposes all the other entities that are sources of utility) but also status at work as revealed in *real wage differentials*. Thus workers (and unions) will be concerned not only to raise real wages and improve conditions of service, but also (as you saw in case study 18.3) to maintain the real differentials between grades and skills that may have become established over the years. In that case, workers will resist piecemeal reductions in money wages (with a given price level) in the face of falling demand for two reasons. First, some parts of the economy will have demand falling faster than others (in some sectors it may even be rising) so that the pressure for a reduction in money wages in the same skills and same localities will vary from market to market, hence increasing differentials. Second, since wage agreements occur at different times, there will be *transitional* differentials even if all demand curves for labour are shifting proportionately. On the other hand, a fall in real wages produced by a rise in the price level does not alter any existing differential and so, in the face of inflation, any reduction in real wages that operates on the denominator in the real wage W/P will be less resisted. Accordingly, when demand falls, wage reductions are resisted and firms' costs are maintained at higher levels than they would be were wages to fall and the appropriate substitutions in the production process made. Hence when aggregate demand falls, the price level does not fall as much as the previous simple labour market model suggests is likely.

SAQ 33.3

(a) Your money (nominal) wage is £100 a week. In a year's time your wage is still £100 but the price level has risen by 10 per cent. What has happened to your real wage?

(b) Your wage is £150 and your rival's is £100. What happens to the real and proportionate differential if the price level rises by 10 per cent?

(c) Would you prefer a fall in your money wage (your rival's staying the same) from £150 to £136.36 with the price level the same, or a fall in your real wage from £150 to £136.36 with money wage staying the same but the price level rising by 10 per cent?

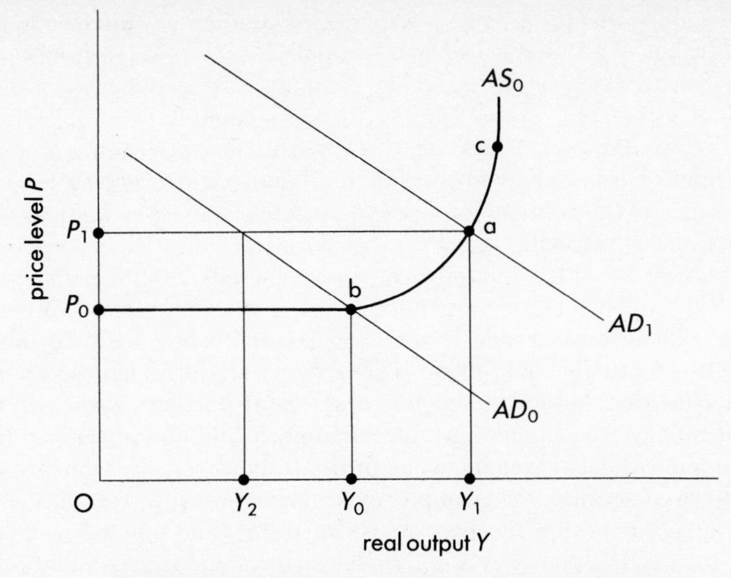

Figure 33.6 Asymmetrical changes in the price level

These asymmetries impart an asymmetry in AS and AD theory; if aggregate demand rises in the upward sloping section of the aggregate supply curve, prices will eventually rise. This causes the aggregate supply curve to shift *upwards* so that there is relative resistance to reduce prices were aggregate demand to fall again. This is illustrated in figure 33.6. Initially suppose that $AD_0 = AS_0$ with output at Y_0 and the price level at P_0. (Take Y as *real* income, the price deflator is suppressed.) When aggregate demand rises to AD_1, if this is perceived as a permanent increase in demand, firms will raise prices and the price level rises to P_1. A return of aggregate demand to AD_0 will not, however, cause a symmetrical fall in prices and output. At its most extreme, the aggregate supply curve will become P_1ac instead of P_0bac and the fall in AD will produce a large drop in output (to Y_2) with the price level roughly constant at P_1. It is undoubtedly an exaggeration to suppose that the aggregate supply curve is *perfectly* flat to the left of point a and, as has been seen, the historical record shows periods of falling as well as rising price levels. None the less, this **ratchet effect** seems to capture a real characteristic of the way the economy behaves, and it is certainly an asymmetry that many Keynesians believe to be an important fact of macroeconomic life. (Note that the price deflator has been dropped from the figure and that Y now represents *real* income.)

Persistent Inflation

So far you have seen that inflation is essentially a *transitory* phenomenon: if aggregate demand rises, inflation is an *equilibrating* reaction that ceases once the new equilibrium price level is established at the new intersection of AS and AD. If, however, there is a persistent policy of, say, tax cutting or public expenditure increases, then aggregate demand will keep rising, as will the equilibrium price level, hence leading to persistent inflation – providing, of course, that the responsiveness of the demand for money to interest rate changes, and of investment to interest rate changes, are not so low, or the responsiveness of the demand for money to income changes so high, as to make these fiscal measures ineffective.

Another way in which inflation can be perpetuated is through monetary policy. With a fixed supply of money and a once-and-for-all increase in aggregate expenditure, a new price level is established because monetary adjustments eventually choke off any excess demand: the higher the price level, the greater the demand for money for transactions purposes and, with a fixed supply of money, the higher the rate of interest and the lower the interest elastic components of aggregate expenditure. If, however, the money supply is allowed to rise (because, for example, government seeks to restrain the rise in interest rates) then this mechanism is frustrated and the price level will continue to rise. If the money supply rises at the same rate as inflation there will be no rise in real interest rates. The effect of an increase in the money supply is thus to increase aggregate demand – a process that can continue for as long as monetary policy **validates** the inflation.

This is shown in figure 33.7. Initially the economy has output Y_0 and a price level P_0. An increase in aggregate demand to AD_1 produces an excess demand at that price level of $Y_2 - Y_0$. The price level, once this excess demand is

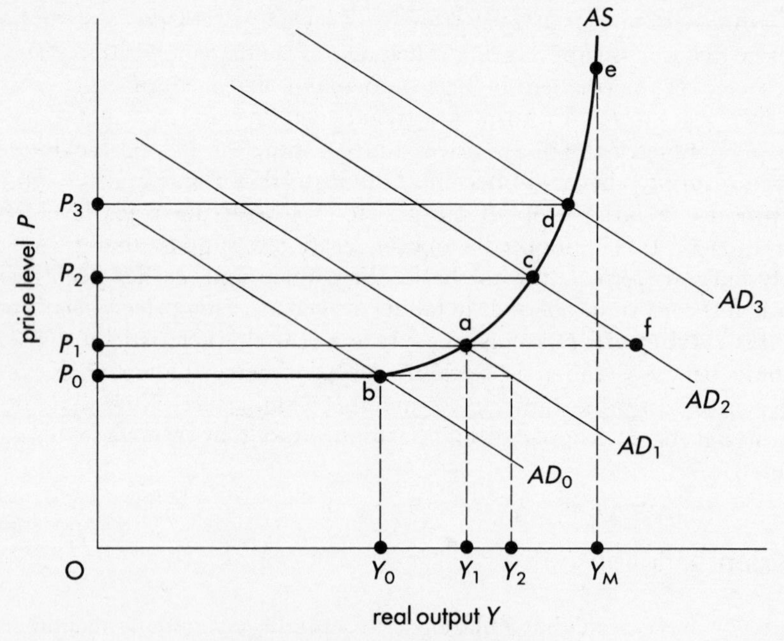

Figure 33.7 Validated inflation

perceived as permanent, begins to rise and inflation is under way. If the nominal money supply is constant, a new price level will be established at P_1 with output having risen to Y_1 (and a new, higher, set of interest rates). Inflation will have done its equilibrating work and, once output Y_1 and the price level P_1 are reached, will cease. If, however, the inflation is validated by a rise in the nominal money supply, this causes aggregate demand to rise to, say, AD_2. In this case, when the price level reaches P_1 there will *still* be excess demand (of af in figure 33.7), so the price level will continue to rise. Continued validation through monetary expansion will mean further rises in aggregate demand (to AD_3 etc.) and the price level continues to rise (to P_2 etc). Inflation is now persistent: it cannot perform its equilibrating function because it is being continuously frustrated by monetary expansion.

The level of national income that is consistent with zero inflation becomes higher as aggregate demand moves through an upward sloping *AS* curve. When aggregate demand was at AD_0, national income was Y_0 and inflation was zero. When aggregate demand was raised to AD_1 and the new price level P_1 was established, the level of national income consistent with zero inflation was Y_1. Call the maximum potential output of the economy Y_M. This is reached when it is not possible for the economy in the short term to produce any more output at all (there will evidently be full employment in the labour market in the absence of any labour market imperfections). The *AS* curve has become vertical. In the long run, of course, as innovation, growth in the working population and so on occur, the *AS* curve shifts to the right. However, the focus here is on the short run and the analysis abstracts from long term growth in the economy.

Recalling the (extreme) ratchet effect of inflation on the *AS* curve, what is

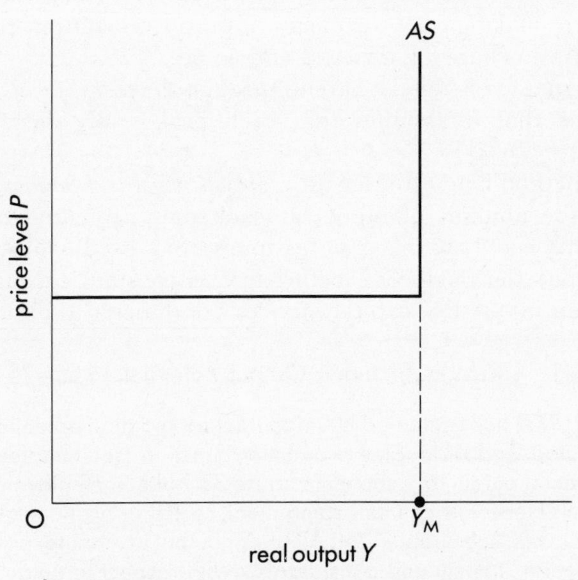

Figure 33.8 The kinked aggregate supply curve

effectively happening in the upward sloping part of the *AS* curve is that, as the price level rises, the effective *AS* curve shifts *upwards*, from P_0be to P_1ae to P_2ce to P_3de and so on. In this range, output, employment and prices all move in the same direction. When the point e is reached and the *AS* curve has become vertical, however, no further increase in output and employment is possible. The aggregate supply curve thus becomes the mirror image of an L shape. If aggregate demand falls, the short term asymmetry relationships imply that prices will not fall, and changes are reflected in output; if aggregate demand rises, the changes are reflected in prices and output remains the same. The aggregate supply curve now looks as in figure 33.8. A less extreme version of the ratchet effect will, of course, produce a less extreme kink. The implications for continuing inflation if it becomes validated by monetary policy, however, remain the same.

Actual and Potential Output

The **potential output** of an economy is hard to define and even harder to measure, as is the associated idea of an **output gap** – the difference between potential and actual output. The concept of potential output means the output that the economy would (not necessarily *ought to*) produce if the labour force is fully employed and the only unemployment is voluntary or structural.

There are three basic ways in which economists have set about trying to estimate potential output. None is perfect. Each involves judgements (for example about how much unemployment is structural). The first method is by *surveying employers* and asking them about their preferred or full capacity output rates. This method is unsatisfactory because it is never clear what assumptions respondents are making about capacity, input prices, output prices, speed of output response to changing demand and so on.

The second method is to take a trend through the *peaks of output*. A snag with this method is that it assumes that each peak really does represent *full* potential.

The third method is to estimate an *aggregate production function* so that, given estimates of the amount of inputs at each date, potential output can be estimated. This too has snags: it assumes that production processes are efficient (or that the degree of inefficiency is constant through time), and reliable data on inputs like capital services are difficult to obtain.

Case Study 33.1 UK Manufacturing Output Potential 1955–75

Jacques Artus (1977) has estimated UK manufacturing output potential over 1955–75 using an estimated Cobb–Douglas production function (see chapter 9). His results, together with actual output, are shown in figure 33.9 (the unemployment rate is taken from table 30.1). Here you can see some clear cycles in economic activity (the so-called *business cycle*; see chapter 25). Although output in manufacturing grew in real terms in every year, it fluctuated considerably with respect to output potential, with slumps in 1958, 1962, 1967, 1970 and 1974–5, and booms in 1955, 1960, 1965, 1969

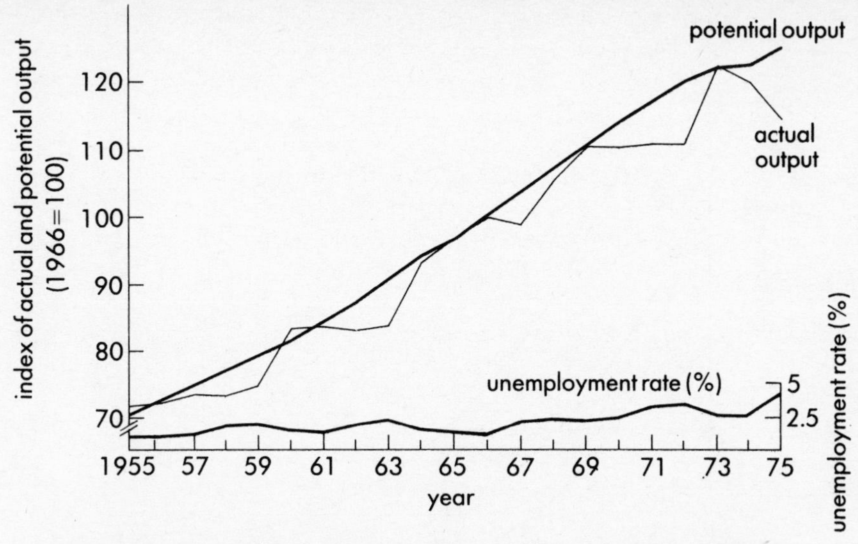

Figure 33.9 Actual and potential output in UK manufacturing 1955–75

and 1973. In three of these boom years actual output exceeded potential – frictional unemployment was uncharacteristically low in these booms. The overall pattern of unemployment also shows the same cyclical pattern: when actual output is below potential, unemployment is high; when actual output is above or near potential, unemployment is low. Employment tends to move pro-cyclically with output, and unemployment to move counter-cyclically.

Jacques Artus (1977) 'Measures of potential output in manufacturing for eight industrial countries 1955–75', *IMF Staff Papers*, **24**(1), 1–35, table 10.

The Phillips Curve

What does this analysis imply for the relationship between inflation and unemployment? As long as the equilibrium level of output is less than the potential output Y_M, increases in aggregate demand cause transitory inflation (if the inflation is not validated by monetary policy) and raise output and employment, hence reducing unemployment. Decreases in aggregate demand reduce output and employment and hence increase unemployment, but with a (more or less) constant price level.

If you now suppose that the greater the increase in aggregate demand the faster the rate of inflation but the smaller the increase in output and employment, as is suggested by the rising section of the aggregate supply curve, then the relationship you should expect to see between inflation and the unemployment rate is shown by the curve in figure 33.10. This is known as the Phillips curve (see later), where $\dot{P}$ represents the rate of change of prices over time, or inflation.

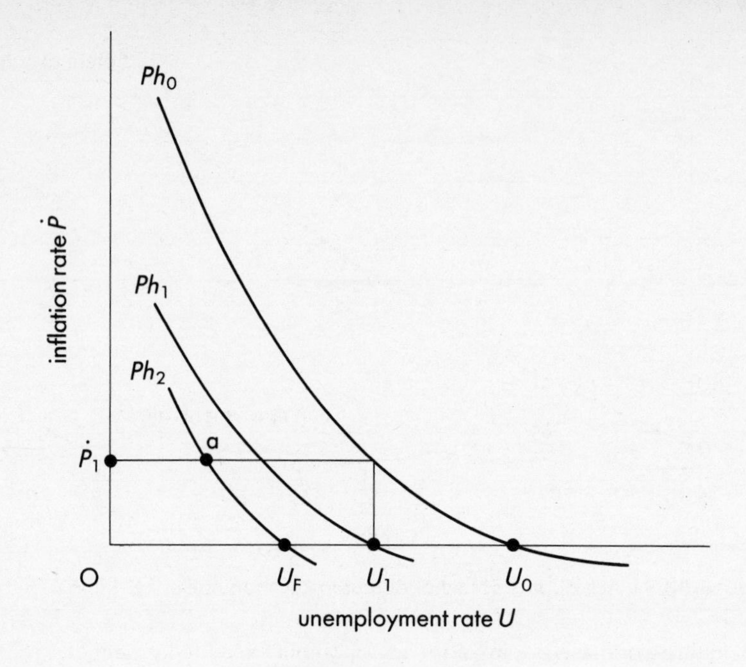

Figure 33.10 The Phillips curve

At the unemployment rate denoted by U_0, there is zero inflation. This can be reduced at the price of some inflation by raising aggregate demand. For example, if it is sought to reduce unemployment to U_1, this can be done if the inflation rate $\dot{P}_1$ is accepted. There seems to be a trade-off between inflation and unemployment. However, this is only a short term phenomenon. As soon as the excess demand has been eliminated, inflation will stop and there will be a new price level, a new *AS* curve with the (roughly) horizontal section higher than before, and a new level of unemployment consistent with zero inflation at U_1. So the Phillips curve has shifted from Ph_0 to Ph_1. If the aggregate supply curve remains constant and demand management by the government seeks ever lower levels of unemployment, *AD* will be continuously shifted to the right and the Phillips curve to the left until a rate of unemployment U_F is reached that corresponds to full employment *and* maximum output potential Y_M, on Phillips curve Ph_3. Note that there may be zero involuntary unemployment at unemployment rates *higher* than this and hence full employment if, at the going wages, all who wish to work do so. U_F is an unemployment rate such that there is no involuntary unemployment *and* output is at its maximum.

If, over time, the *AS* curve shifts to the right as potential output rises, then increasing aggregate demand may not reach the vertical section of the *AS* curve. In this case as, say, the labour force increases, the reduction of involuntary unemployment may require continuing increases in aggregate demand, associated with inflation that does *not* tend to zero as a unique equilibrium price level is attained, for the equilibrium price level will be rising continuously. In this case the Phillips curve remains relatively stable and there is a long run trade-off between inflation and unemployment. To keep unemployment below its natural rate will, in other words, require *continuous* inflation. The natural rate is thus, in the context of a model with a variable price level, not only that rate at which the labour market is in equilibrium, but in addition is a rate of unemployment associated with zero, or at least non-accelerating inflation. In the short term, however, once the Phillips curve corresponding to Ph_2 in figure 33.10 has been reached, the economy can move only temporarily below U_F. Suppose the economy is initially in full equilibrium in all markets (including the labour market) with zero inflation. The government now increases the nominal money supply. Interest rates fall leading to an increase in aggregate planned expenditure and aggregate demand at the existing price level. Since the economy is at capacity output, the aggregate supply curve is vertical. The excess demand for final goods and services may initiate a temporary increase in output and abnormally low level of frictional unemployment. However, this is only temporary, for sooner or later nominal wages will be bid up and the price level will rise. As the price level rises, the *real* money supply falls (*nominal* money supply remaining constant) so interest rates rise causing a fall in aggregate planned expenditure and aggregate demand. As long as the excess aggregate demand over aggregate supply persists, the price level continues to rise, the real money supply falls and interest rates rise. The process ends when the inflation ceases, a new equilibrium price level is established and the unemployment level returns to its original level. In terms of figure 33.10, the government initially sought to move from U_F to point a. So long as monetary policy did not validate the inflation, however, the economy eventually returned down Ph_2 to point U_F.

The New Zealand economist Bill Phillips (1914–75) has the credit for making the remarkable discovery about the relationship between changing wage rates and unemployment which has become enshrined in the jargon as the **Phillips curve**. Phillips seemed to have found a rather stable relationship between the rate of change of money wages $\dot{W}$ and the rate of unemployment. For the period 1861–1913 this is shown in figure 33.11. By looking ahead to figure 33.13 you can see that points in the 1950s and up to the mid 1960s were fairly close to this curve.

For a while the Phillips curve was a phenomenon without an explanation. One was provided in 1960 by Richard Lipsey. He argued that when the demand for labour rises this leads to a temporary excess demand at the going money wage rates. This causes money wages to rise: the greater the excess demand as a proportion of current supply, the faster the rate of change of money wages and, as the proportionate excess demand rises the rate of unemployment falls. This fall is less than proportionate, so that as the proportionate excess demand approaches infinity, the unemployment rate reaches a limit that is higher than zero, but less than the natural rate. This yields the shape of the relationship between $\dot{W}$ and unemployment rates found by Phillips.

Phillips had concluded that, for plausible assumptions about growth of labour productivity, an unemployment rate of around 2.5 per cent would be

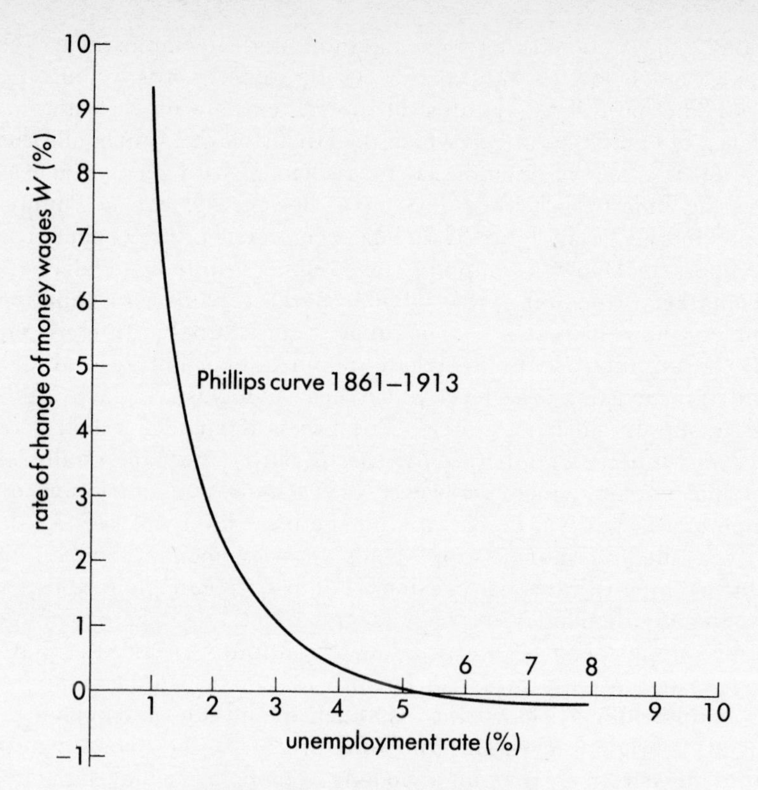

Figure 33.11 The Phillips curve

consistent with zero inflation, and unemployment of around 5.5 per cent would be consistent with stable money wages. Such a rate of unemployment at zero price inflation, which includes normal frictional unemployment, is, as has been seen, the natural rate of unemployment. On the other hand, the relation seemed also to imply that if a permanent state of excess demand could be maintained in labour markets, unemployment could be permanently reduced below 2.5 per cent but only at the price of some inflation.

The link between the *wage Phillips curve* that relates unemployment and the rate of change of *money wages* and the *price Phillips curve* that relates unemployment and the rate of change of *prices* (inflation) is shown in figure 33.12, where $\dot{P}$ is the rate of change of prices. Here it is assumed that price changes depend on wage and productivity changes: with a given rate of productivity growth, the inflation rate will be less than the rate of increase in money wages at a given rate of unemployment.

SAQ 33.4

Why is the Phillips curve concave from above at unemployment rates below the natural rate?

The stability of the price Phillips curve was shattered from the mid 1960s. Figure 33.13 shows the Phillips curve for 1861–1913 and points for the decade

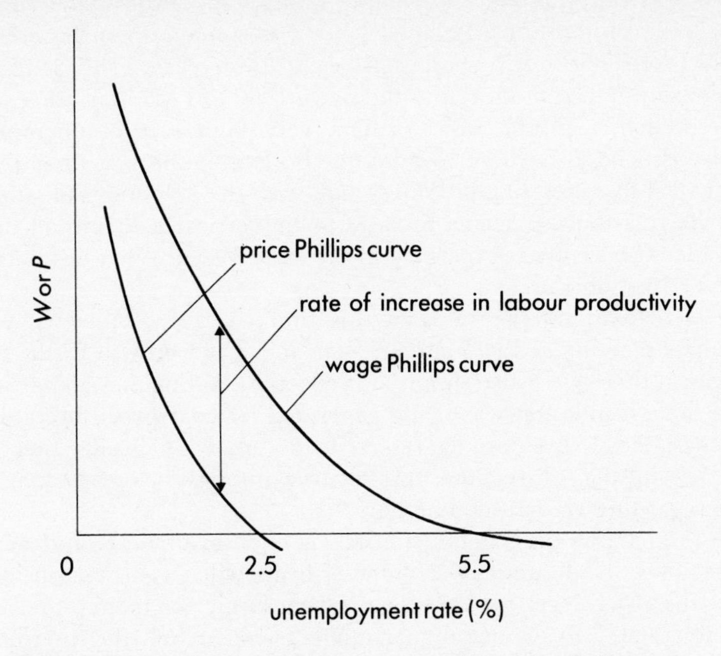

Figure 33.12 The wage Phillips curve and the price Phillips curve

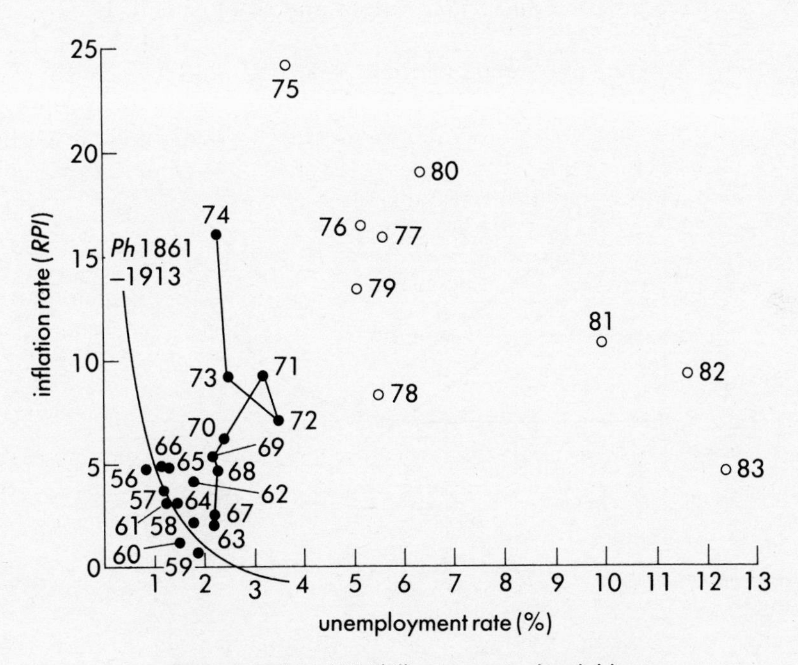

Figure 33.13 UK Phillips curve in the doldrums

preceding 1966. From 1967 to 1974 the somewhat erratic pattern indicated took place: the Phillips curve seemed to have become more or less vertical or was subject to quick shifts as inflation began to increase. From 1975 to 1979 the relationship had shifted well to the right, 1980 to 1983 indicate a shadowy curve even further to the right, with a very high rate of unemployment notionally associated with zero inflation. Both inflation *and* unemployment rose from 1967–8, 1969–70 and 1970–1 and, with the exceptions of 1971–2 and 1972–3, the relationship seems broadly to be vertical rather than negative, with a trade-off possibly re-emerging in the early 1980s. What has been called *stagflation* arrived on the scene.

There were demand pressures at this time, notably connected with the inflationary financing of the Vietnam War and rapid growth in the German economy. But there were also supply side effects operating and, in particular, it seems as though inflation was being generated by **cost-push** forces, particularly (some believe) by more aggressive trade unions. Consider first what in principle a shifting aggregate supply curve implies before looking at the evidence regarding trade union activity.

Figure 33.14 shows the economy initially in equilibrium at P_0 and Y_0. If costs rise due to, say, trade union pushfulness, firms will pass these on in higher prices so the price level rises. With a given supply of money and a rising demand for money to finance higher monetary spending, the interest rate is driven up and interest elastic components of real aggregate expenditure fall; so output falls to a new level where the new AS curve AS_1 intersects the (same) AD curve. Output falls to Y_1, unemployment rises, and the price level rises to P_1. Now you have inflation and *falling* output and employment. If AD is also

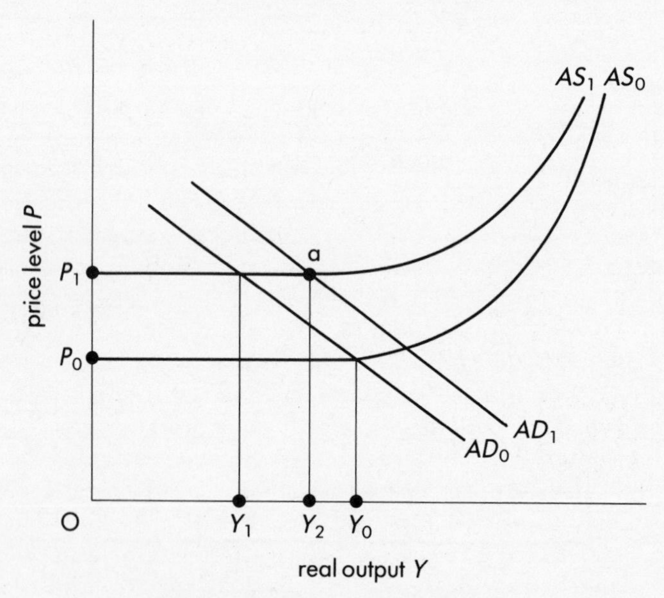

Figure 33.14 Cost-push inflation

rising at the same time, the effect on output will be dampened. For example, if AD rises to AD_1, a new equilibrium is established at point a, and output falls only to Y_2 for the same inflationary experience. This is stagflation: inflation coupled with low growth and inflation.

Trade union membership declined from 1952 to 1963 with only three years of slight increases. From 1967 to 1970 it grew very fast and thereafter, as you saw in chapter 18, grew fairly steadily up to 1979. This seems to indicate a growing strength of the trade unions during the 1970s. However, these trends do not correlate well with trends in unemployment.

Some economists have taken trade union membership as an indicator of pushfulness, but early findings around 1964, that the rate of increase in money wages and unionization were associated, have been largely discredited. There is some evidence of an association between strike activity and inflation, though the story is by no means clear.

One of the difficulties in testing the trade union pushfulness hypothesis is that it is hard to separate it from **demand-pull** factors: perhaps unions were pushing against open doors! For example, if aspirations for higher real wages are increased in inflationary times, unless one has a clear specification of what determines aspirations (which one does not have) the implications of this type of supply shock, other supply shocks (e.g. the oil price rise) and demand shocks are difficult to disentangle. There are other difficulties too. For example, existing studies have used strikes regardless of cause rather than strikes in support of wage claims. And there have to be doubts about the adequacy of strikes as a measure of pushfulness (compared, say, with degree of unionization, days work lost through strikes, length of strikes etc.)

By 1973, particularly after the supply side shock induced by the very large increase in oil prices, the inflation rate rose to 9.1 per cent. Under Chancellor of the Exchequer Barber, there was also a substantial expansion of the money supply. The inflation has sometimes been largely blamed on him; this is probably a harsh judgement, for in 1971–2 actual output was well below potential and there was plenty of scope to increase output by raising aggregate demand without there necessarily being much impact on the price level. The oil price rise, however, imparted a massive shift to the AS curve and by 1974 and 1975 had worked itself through the economy to produce all time inflation records (16.0 per cent and 24.2 per cent) and a negative growth in *GDP* for the first two years in succession since the Great Depression.

Although there were subsequent increases in nominal oil prices, the early real increase could be seen (at least in retrospect) as essentially a one off event. The model predicts that, once its effects had worked through, and provided that the inflation was not validated by monetary policies that caused aggregate demand to *continue* to rise, the price level would have eventually stabilized at the new level P_1 in figure 33.14 and the inflation rate fallen to zero. Again, inflation is a transitory, equilibrating phenomenon. There is a permanent reduction in real income of either $Y_0 - Y_1$ or $Y_0 - Y_2$ depending on domestic policies to promote demand led growth. This is effectively a transfer of income from the domestic economy to the OPEC countries, which could be compensated for over time by increasing aggregate expenditure (either directly by fiscal policy or indirectly by monetary policy). Moreover, the model tells you that this can be done without further validating the supply induced inflation, as long as aggregate demand is not expanded so far or so fast as to bring it on to the rising section of the *AS* curve (to the right of point a in figure 33.14). This was the essence of the Barber policy, for which he and the Heath government were so maligned.

Although requiring a nice judgement, the policy response to both demand and supply induced inflation in the model so far is relatively straightforward. One must now, however, introduce a further complication. This is the second major modification of the two referred to earlier, and it relates to the effect that expectations about inflation by firms and workers can have on the actual progress of inflation.

SAQ 33.5

In the face of the sustained oil price rises in the 1970s, should the government have adopted an expansionary or a contractionary macroeconomic policy?

Inflationary Expectations

An important distinction was made in chapter 32 between anticipated and unanticipated inflations. So far in this chapter it has been implicitly assumed that inflation is unanticipated. Anticipated inflation, like monetary validation of unanticipated inflation, can also cause inflation to persist and even, given the right circumstances, to accelerate. Since the UK along with most other countries has a long history of inflation, it seems implausible to suppose that each year's experiences of rising prices comes as a surprise to everyone. On the contrary, it is natural for them to seek to *anticipate* what they have come to expect in their negotiations about prices and wages. For example, a trade union, expecting inflation to be at 5 per cent in the coming year, would rationally seek to incorporate this, or at least half of it, in its current wage negotiations for the wages to be paid next year. Thus for the first six months of next year each will be paid 'too much', in the second six months 'too little' but, over the year as a whole, the real wage will be just about 'right'. If employers share these expectations they have no reason not to grant the higher money wages. There is no particular pushfulness on the part of unions.

How may such expectations be formed? There are several models. No one, of course, can know the future. But it may be natural to extrapolate the past. Most people are probably content to predict the rising of the sun next morning on no more than their experience that it has rarely failed to rise on past mornings! Take a simple version of extrapolative expectations used by Milton Friedman, the leading monetarist economist, who first introduced the idea of expected inflation into macroeconomics. Let us suppose that the inflation rate expected next year is that experienced this year.

Now suppose that initially there is no inflation. Next year, therefore, people expect inflation to be zero. Suppose also that the government increases aggregate demand to reduce unemployment below the natural rate even if this means that it (the government) knows that according to the Phillips curve inflation will become positive. Employees and employers settle wages for next year on the assumption that inflation will, however, be zero.

Suppose there is some involuntary unemployment and that therefore in at least some labour markets both employers and workers are off their supply and demand curves at the going real wage rate. As aggregate expenditure rises, output and employment rise. In labour markets that are in equilibrium, money wages rise. There may be some tendency for this to happen also in labour markets that are in disequilibrium. As firms' costs rise these increases are passed on in the form of higher prices, which restores the original *real* wage but at a higher level of employment and output. In markets that were in disequilibrium and whose nominal wages have stayed the same, the real wage will have fallen and there may be some successful attempts by workers to restore their original real wage by negotiated increases in the money wage.

So far, expectations of inflation have played no role because workers and employers have engaged in – at best – a 'catching up' excercise.

The process is shown in figure 35.15. In figure 33.15(a) the demand and supply of labour are shown as dependent on the money wage rate in a labour market initially in equilibrium. As demand rises from D_0 to D_1 new wage deals are concluded so that the excess demand for labour (ab) is choked off. Money wages rise from W_0 to W_1 and employment rises from N_0 to N_1. However, as the price level rises the real wage falls, so workers are (in expecting last year's inflation rate of zero) deceived into supplying more labour at the same *real* wage. In figure 33.15(b) the real demand and supply are shown as dependent on the real wage. As money wages rise the whole supply curve moves to the right and N_1 labour is supplied at the real wage W_1/P_0, which is less than $W_0/P_0 = W_1/P_1$.

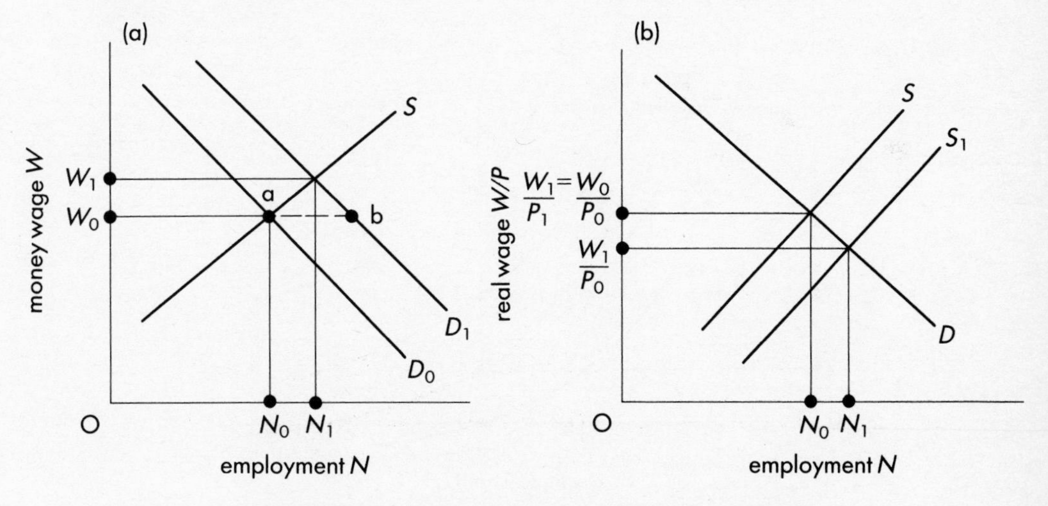

Figure 33.15 Price expectations in the labour market

Expectations of inflation are therefore revised upwards. In figure 33.15(b) the supply curve *shifts back* until it occupies its previous position and employment returns to its initial level. The reduction in unemployment is thus short lived. The Phillips curve has shifted. This is shown in figure 33.16. Here the initial Phillips curve was Ph_1, intersecting the horizontal axis at the natural rate of unemployment U_0, which was the point at which the story began. The government then attempted a trade-off of more inflation for less unemployment by selecting point a with an inflation rate of 2 per cent and an unemployment rate of U_1. Once this became recognized by workers, however, the real wage was bid up to its previous level and the original level of employment and unemployment re-established at U_0. The upshot is that there is inflation of 2 per cent (the anticipated rate now equals the actual rate) *and* unemployment at the original level, with a new Phillips curve passing through point b. If the government persists in seeking level U_1, then a higher inflation rate must be induced at point c on the new Phillips curve Ph_2. For the same reasons as before, the original level of unemployment U_0 will be re-established as workers come to anticipate 5 per cent inflation and the Phillips curve shifts again to Ph_3.

Three dramatic implications seem to follow and have been much emphasized by Milton Friedman. The first is that unemployment can be reduced below its natural rate of U_0 only at the price, not merely of some inflation, but of *accelerating* inflation. This arises from the shape of Phillips curves as the distance between points on the curve above U_1 increases for successive curves. The second is that the long run Phillips curve is a *vertical line* at the natural rate of unemployment. The political implication is enormous; the inflation rate must become infinite (unless a social revolution intervenes) if unemployment is to be kept below the natural rate! Third, it implies that, after a period of very

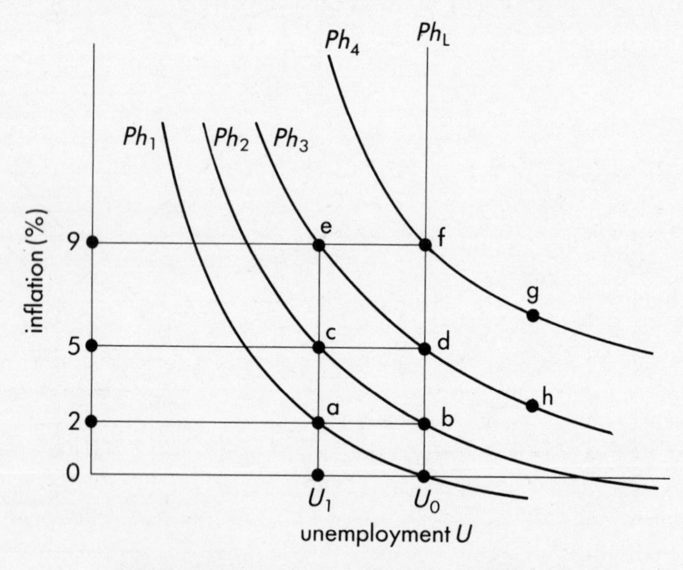

Figure 33.16 A vertical long run Phillips curve?

fast inflation, the level of unemployment associated with zero inflation will be very high indeed. The question whether this is really so or whether there *is* none the less some possibility of reducing unemployment without bringing about accelerating inflation through continuous demand expansion is one that divides Britain's Thatcher government from all its predecessors and that also divides economists.

Suppose the economy is at point f on figure 33.16. The government wants to reduce inflation from 9 per cent to, say, 5 per cent. Appropriate policies are set in train – say, a reduction in the rate of growth of the money supply. The economy moves along the short run Phillips curve from f to, say, g. Inflation falls somewhat and unemployment rises. If workers can be persuaded that the government is going to stick to its monetary targets then the hope is that inflationary expectations will be revised downwards so that at the current unemployment rate a shift to Ph_3 takes place and the economy moves from g to h and subsequently back to d, where the natural unemployment is re-established and inflation is reduced to the target 5 per cent level. That is the *hope*. The trouble is that it seems that the dampening of inflationary expectations involves both a large rise in unemployment above the natural rate and a long adjustment period. And that is where the political acceptability of this essentially Thatcher/Reagan style policy becomes a crucial issue.

Involuntary Unemployment and the Phillips Curve

The analysis so far has neglected those sectors of the economy where there may be involuntary unemployment. In the upward sloping section of the aggregate supply curve, some sectors of the economy are at full employment whereas others have both employers and employees off their demand and supply curves. Recognition of the latter markets modifies the extreme results of Friedman's analysis.

As aggregate demand rose in the previous analysis, employment in the equilibrium markets fell to its original level as real wages were re-established. However, this will not be the case in the disequilibrium markets. There, real wages may rise or fall as effective demand rises (money wages are expected to rise somewhat as workers seek to restore wages differentials). But employment will rise and hence unemployment fall. Thus, in depressed areas of the economy, one expects to see employment permanently rising as aggregate demand rises, with consequential reductions in unemployment, but money wages rising (if at all) less fast than in the more prosperous regions. This increase in employment and output is what enables the aggregate supply curve to take a positive slope. In figure 33.17, as effective demand rises, employment rises from N_0 towards N_1. This implies in turn that, even though the *equilibrium* labour markets in the end see no increase in employment (or output), some permanent reduction in unemployment *can* be obtained. In particular it implies that the Phillips curve will not shift as far to the right as is implied in figure 33.17 and that the long run Phillips curve will be less inelastic than

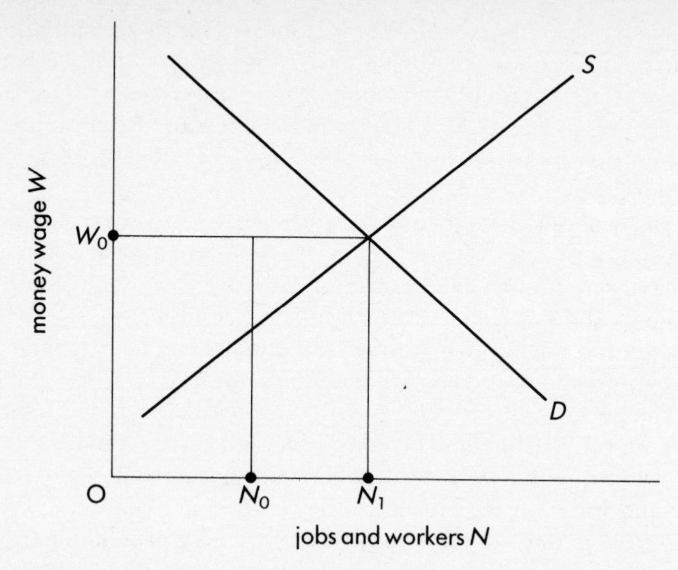

Figure 33.17 Effective demand expansion in a disequilibrium labour market

suggested by Friedman. It will be less elastic than the short run Phillips curve suggests, and may take the shape of figure 33.18. Here, if the government aims for unemployment level U_0 inflation again rises to 2 per cent, but there is a permanent fall in involuntary unemployment to U_2 as the short run Phillips curve shift to Ph_2. The long run Phillips curve then has the shape indicated by the bold curve and, in the figure, the unemployment rate U_1 is attainable at 5 per cent inflation where the long and the short run Phillips curves intersect. However, the snag with this is that the more ambitious the government is in selecting unemployment rates lower than U_0, the more successful successive expansions of demand are going to be at bringing disequilibrium markets into equilibrium. If the long run Phillips curve becomes vertical *to the right* of the target unemployment rate, then again only *accelerating* inflation will do the trick. In this case, with all labour markets in equilibrium, you get the Friedman result: a vertical Phillips curve and no permanent trade-off between unemployment and inflation, with attempts to reduce unemployment below the natural rate being possible only via accelerating inflation.

More Sophisticated Expectations

According to the analysis so far, the inflation rate is made up of two components; expected inflation $\dot{P}_e$ equal to last period's inflation, and demand induced inflation $\dot{P}_d$. Letting $\dot{P}_t$ denote the inflation rate in time t, you have

$$\dot{P}_t = \dot{P}_d + \dot{P}_e$$

or, with $\dot{P}_e = \dot{P}_{t-1}$,

$$\dot{P}_t = \dot{P}_\mathrm{d} + \dot{P}_{t-1}$$

This is a very simple formulation. An alternative would be to suppose that expected inflation is some weighted average of past inflation or that only some fraction α of last year's inflation is expected to happen next year. People have **adaptive expectations** – expectations that adapt to past experience. Suppose, for example, that inflation next year is expected to be half of this year's rate. Then the equation becomes

$$\dot{P}_t = \dot{P}_d + \alpha\dot{P}_{t-1}$$

or

$$\dot{P}_t = \dot{P}_\mathrm{d} + 0.5\dot{P}_{t-1}$$

Now, even in equilibrium labour markets, the rise in money wages required to compensate workers for expected inflation will be only half the actual inflation rate of last year. As a result of demand induced inflation, therefore, real wages will fall and employers will hire more workers. Hence employment in *both* equilibrium and disequilibrium markets will rise and the long run Phillips curve will be more elastic than the curve in figure 33.18.

The issues at stake here are by no means fully resolved. The modelling and

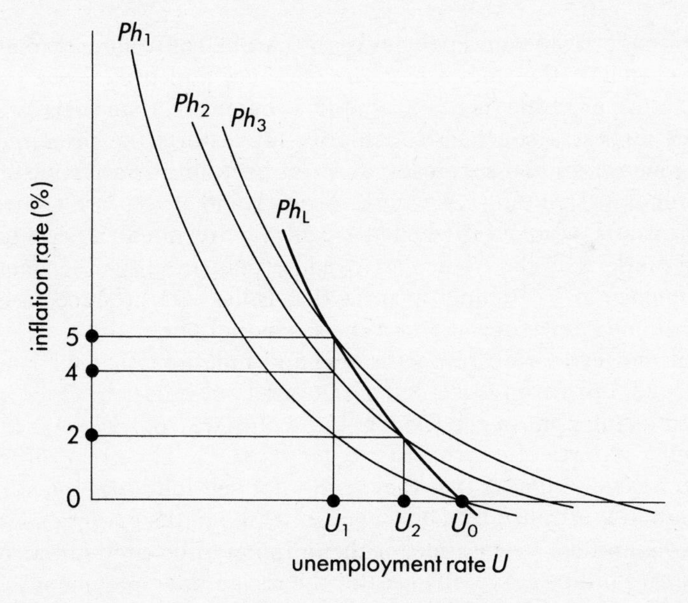

Figure 33.18 The long run Phillips curve with falls in involuntary unemployment

testing of theories about how expectations are formed is difficult and still in its infancy. You will have to exercise your own judgement in deciding whether the output gap and the presence of disequilibrium labour markets are sufficient in any period to warrant the conclusion that a trade-off between unemployment and inflation is possible and whether it is large or small.

A major contemporary issue concerns whether people have **rational expectations** – expectations that are formed on the basis of knowing the 'true' model of the economy. This analysis forms a major part of the more advanced analysis of inflationary processes.

There have been several studies that have sought to find empirical values for α. Several UK studies around 1960 found α to lie between 0.46 and 0.85. A 1980 study estimated it to be 0.30. A 1969 study found $\alpha = 0.8$. One study has found $\alpha = 1.0$. There is, of course, much argument as to whether inflationary expectations really are formed on the basis of past experience. Some other formulations suggest that the presumption that $\alpha = 1$ is consistent with the evidence. The empirical problems of sorting out the effect of expectations from all the other demand side and supply side possibilities are horrendous. A useful survey by David Laidler and Michael Parkin (*Economic Journal*, 1975, **85**, 741–97) found that 'about half of the recent studies that have used this expectations hypothesis have generated a coefficient α significantly different from unity.' Evidently, the more expected inflation depends upon past inflation, the longer it will take to eradicate it from the economy.

Incomes Policies

The claim made for incomes policies is *not* that, by controlling through various more direct means the rate of increase of wages and prices, one can control inflation. It is generally agreed among economists that merely *suppressing* inflation is at best a short term palliative. It distorts the price mechanism, producing shortages and surpluses, and can be administratively complex and socially unfair (depending on whose incomes and prices are controlled and how rigorously). Moreover, when the controls are lifted, as eventually they must be if markets are not to be destroyed permanently, every economic agent is free to engage in a catching-up spree that is likely to produce an intensified short inflationary burst instead of a more gradual one.

It is not, however, with respect to demand inflations that incomes policies are advocated, but with respect to *expectations* about inflation. Once inflation is established as inherent in the economy, the only way of *reducing* it (as distinct from slowing its rate of increase) is to get $\dot{P}_e < \dot{P}_t$. The great difficulty with inflationary expectations is that they tend to be self-fulfilling. Even if $\dot{P}_e$ is last year's inflation multiplied by some factor < 1 (0.5 in the earlier examples) and if $\dot{P}_d = 0$, it can take a long time for the inflation to be eliminated. The flatter the short run Phillips curve, the greater the rise in unemployment in the short run as inflation is reduced. This will tend to moderate the political will to use demand management (whether via monetary or fiscal policy) to reduce inflation quickly (though it seems not to have inhibited the Thatcher government). As soon as inflation starts to fall, however, then expected inflation will also fall and will proceed to fall to zero as long as demand inflation is not injected into the economy. This was, of course, the long term strategy of the Thatcher government.

Incomes policies are seen as speeding up the process of adjusting expectations downwards and must be used in conjunction with deflationary monetary and fiscal policies. Despite the short run market distortions that may be induced, if wage and price increases can be controlled at rates lower than they would otherwise have been, and these lower rates become embodied in lower inflationary expectations, then – to the extent that expectations are based on past inflationary experiences – the costs of temporary inefficiencies of one sort may be more than compensated by lower unemployment and a faster rate of reduction in inflation than a policy relying solely on fiscal and monetary restraint. This is clearly an issue on which the Thatcher government judged the temporary costs to be greater than the long term benefits.

Incomes policies may take the form of direct controls or freezes on wages, salaries, prices and profits, or of taxes on increases in any of these above a norm. They can be assisted by reductions in indirect tax rates; the 1979 VAT increase in the UK was unfortunately extremely counter-productive in its probable effect on expectations in a year in which the inflation rate according to the *RPI* was already rising.

SAQ 33.6

Make a judgement about the current gap between actual and potential output at present (plotting recent cycles in actual output and extending a trend through the peaks is probably the easiest way for you to do this). Look at current trends in the price level. From these form a view about the slope of the aggregate supply curve. Check this against the current unemployment rate and its recent trend. In the light of what you know about recent economic events, make a judgement about the appropriateness of current government fiscal and monetary policy.

What You Should Understand Now

How to introduce real variables explicitly into the Keynesian model.
Effects of changes in real and nominal variables.
The relationship between inflation and unemployment in the UK before and after the mid 1960s.
Inflation as an equilibrating device.
Asymmetric short term response of the price level to rises and falls in aggregate demand.
Transitory inflation and validated (continuing) inflation.
The meaning and measurement of potential output.
Short run trade-offs between inflation and unemployment.
Rationale of the Phillips curve.
Inverse relationship between inflation and output with supply shocks.
The breakdown of the Phillips curve in the mid 1960s.
Impact of anticipated inflation on the Phillips curve.
Effects of holding unemployment below the natural rate.
Role of nominal and real interest rates in the macro model.
Role of incomes policies in reducing inflationary expectations.

34

Money, Banking and Financial Intermediaries

Monetary policy has been discussed so far as though the definition of money were quite unambiguous and as though the supply of money were perfectly under the control of the authorities. Unfortunately, each is very far from being the case. To see why, it is necessary to consider the main features of the money market, its key institutions, and the ways that the Bank of England – the UK's central bank – has sought to discharge its duties.

Financial Institutions in the UK

Clearing Banks

The types of financial institutions in the UK are bewilderingly varied. First of all are the banks themselves – the London clearing banks (Barclays, Lloyds, the Midland and the National Westminster are the 'big four'). They are called clearing banks because they are members of the London Clearing House. Rather than each bank transferring money from itself to another when a cheque drawn on it is paid into the other (and vice versa) at the end of a day's trading, all the cheques drawn against bank A in favour of bank B are totted up and set against those drawn against B in favour of A. With the cheques thus cleared in a jointly operated clearing house (a computerized operation, of course) only the net difference need be transferred from the one bank to the other. This is done by drawing on the accounts that the commercial banks hold with their bank – the Bank of England. In addition, there are other banks like the Scottish banks (who have their own clearing arrangements), overseas banks, merchant banks and other deposit taking institutions.

The public can hold two types of account with a bank: sight deposits (including current accounts) and time deposits (deposit accounts). Most sight deposits earn no interest (though about a third of them do) and may even be charged for in exchange for services like the provision of standing orders and credit transfers. The latter are an arrangement by which many employers arrange with their own bank to pay salaries directly into the accounts held by employees in other banks. Current account deposits can be withdrawn on demand by the depositor either by using a cash card or by writing a cheque.

Cheques are also used, of course, as a means of making transactions with third parties. Deposit accounts earn interest and technically require seven days' notice of withdrawal. Cheques are not drawn on deposit accounts. However, in practice money can easily be transferred from time deposits to sight deposits without penalty and so time deposits are scarcely distinguishable from sight deposits in their use as a means of payment. The banks are in business for profit. Like an individual asset holder they hold portfolios of assets, financial and real (like their buildings) and seek, by taking deposits and providing customer services, by borrowing and lending, to increase their owners' wealth.

Building Societies

Another important type of deposit taking institution in the UK is the building society. Building societies have a variety of deposit accounts, earning various rates of interest according to, for example, the terms under which withdrawals can be made. They use their deposits principally to lend to borrowers for house purchases and improvements. Cheques can even be drawn on some building societies' accounts, and most societies will make standing order payments for their depositors. The ease with which depositors can withdraw cash (often via a cashpoint facility like those offered by banks), or arrange a transfer into their current accounts at a bank, makes these deposits scarcely distinguishable from bank deposit accounts in their use as a means of payment. Building societies are, however, non-profit organizations, so their reserves are not owned by shareholders in the same sense that banks' net assets are the property of their shareholders.

Banks and building societies are the main short term deposit taking financial institutions used by the general public in the UK. There is considerable blurring today between the functions of banks as conventionally understood and other financial intermediaries like the building societies.

Insurance Companies

Insurance companies are an important class of financial institution. These charge premiums to their customers in return for paying out particular sums of money if a particular event occurs. For example, motor vehicle insurance is an arrangement whereby in exchange for a premium the insurance company will agree to pay claims that others may have against a driver, replace or repair damaged vehicles, and so on. With life assurance, premiums are paid in return for payment of an agreed sum (or a minimum sum plus profits) if the insured person should die or at an agreed date in the future if the insured person is still alive. Most insurance agencies are non-profit. They compute premiums on the basis of overhead costs and the probability of the insured event occurring and then invest the monies they receive to achieve a balanced portfolio of assets, some financial and some real (for example, farm land), to meet their obligations as and when they arise.

Pension Funds

Pension funds, operated as a separate activity by insurance companies or by large companies for their own employees, provide ways in which people in occupational pension schemes can provide for their retirement. They make, together with their employers, regular monthly payments into the fund of their employer, in return for benefits to be received by the member of the scheme on retirement or, in the event of early death, by the surviving spouse. As is also the case with life assurance, the funds received are usually invested in UK company securities, and pension funds are therefore important owners of companies' equity.

Discount Houses

Other specialized financial agencies include discount houses, accepting houses and investment banks, finance houses, investment and unit trusts and property unit trusts. Discount houses make their profits by borrowing money mainly from the banks *at call* (that is money that can be immediately reclaimed by the lender) at low interest rates and lending it to other institutions, including the government, by buying bills of exchange that have been accepted by merchant banks (see later), local authority bills and Treasury bills, which carry a rather higher interest rate and have only a short time before they mature (usually not more than six months). These short term bills take the form of a promise by the borrower (an importer, say, or the government, central or local) to pay a sum of money in, say, three months. Suppose the borrower promises to pay £10,000 in three months' time. The discount house buys that promissory note for, say, £9500; the bill or note has then become *discounted.* So the borrower receives £9500 in return for a promise to pay £10,000 when the bill matures, equivalent to an interest payment of £500 or an interest rate of £500/£9500 = 5.3 per cent over three months. There is said to be a *discount rate* of 5 per cent over three months (the percentage by which the face value of the bill is discounted); this is inevitably smaller than the implied interest rate, for the discount rate is the discount as a percentage of the face value and the interest rate is the discount as a percentage of the *discounted* face value. In the example just given, the interest rate was 5.3 per cent compared with the discount rate of 5 per cent. The discount rate is thus expressed as a percentage of the amount to be repaid and the interest rate as a percentage of the amount borrowed.

Discount houses are in a somewhat exposed position for, if a situation arose in which many banks started to call in their money at call, the houses might not have sufficient cash or highly liquid assets to meet the demand. In such a case they can always go to the Bank of England and borrow money at a quite high interest rate. This has variously been called the *bank rate* or the *minimum lending rate*, and is now usually called the **intervention rate**. But if they do so, they will make a loss on such transactions. They are therefore specialists in judging an appropriate portfolio of maturing assets to hold as well as judging appropriate discount rates and rates on money at call. Discount houses also engage in a lot of ordinary lending.

Accepting Houses (Merchant Banks)

Accepting houses (merchant banks) grew up as specialists in judging the riskiness or creditworthiness of traders. Suppose you are a manufacturer wanting to export some goods to an overseas importer. You will not be paid until the goods arrive at their destination and have been checked by your customer. This can take weeks or months. If you want the cash sooner than this you draw up a **bill of exchange** stating that the importer will pay you a certain sum in, say, three months' time. The importer certifies that he will so pay. You can now sell that bill to who ever will buy it and they, in turn, become entitled to receive the importer's money. But, of course, what anyone will pay you for your bill will depend upon what they know about the reliability of the transactors. If a potential buyer knew nothing about their trustworthiness, he would pay you relatively little for the bill, thus discounting it heavily. Suppose the bill promised to pay £13,524. Supposing you thought that there was only a 50–50 chance that the importer would actually pay up. The *maximum* you would pay would be only £6762 so, on grounds of risk *alone*, you would apply a 50 per cent discount rate. If you were risk averse you would not, of course, be willing to pay as much as this.

The accepting houses *accept* such bills, based on their specialized knowledge of importers and exporters world wide, by either accepting the bill and discounting it at an appropriate rate themselves or by guaranteeing it so that a discount house will buy it, thus providing an exporter with ready cash and enabling him in turn to extend credit to his customers. Thus, even if the importer defaulted, the owner of the bill would receive his or her money on the bill's maturity, enabling it to be discounted by a discount house at a riskless rate of discount.

The merchant banks today also engage in regular banking business and are usually specialists in investment advice services for the clients. Similarly, clearing banks today will also do some of the traditional merchant bankers' business.

Finance Houses

Finance houses specialize in borrowing money and accepting deposits from large scale lenders like banks and commercial firms and then lending it to customers for the specific purchase of goods. They are profit seeking firms. These houses, however, specialize in consumer durables, especially motor cars, rather than in dwellings. They also own and lease cars and equipment to firms and lend to firms for the purchase of equipment. 'Hire purchase' or 'consumer credit' is the name of their game. They also often act as financial advisers to pension funds, rich investors and so on.

Trusts

Unit, investment and property trusts specialize in various kinds of portfolio management for their clients. Clients lend them money which is then invested and the clients receive their returns by taking advantage of the more diversified portfolios and greater economies of scale in transactions than are usually possible, particularly for the small investor. Property trusts, however, specialize in real property investments and their clients are large investors like pension funds and large charities.

As you can see, all these various financial intermediaries specialize in various aspects of the provision of services to clients: some specialize in assessing particular forms of risk, some in particular types of property. Some cater for particular types of borrower and lender. Over the years they have developed comparative advantages in their various activities that reduce the costs of making financial transactions, and have developed various kinds of financial instruments like bills and other securities, with different lives to maturity, having different risk attributes, and catering for different kinds of demand for credit and liquidity. In recent times, however, as you can see, there has been an increasing overlap in the functions of financial intermediaries. This has probably been due to the reduced regulation of the institutions in the money market. It seems unlikely that the current interlocking pattern is a long term equilibrium, for the more liberal climate of today permits the more accurate identification of true comparative advantages. Where the final pattern of division of labour in financial services finally will lie is, however, anyone's guess.

Banks and Money

Banks provide two obvious types of monetary service. One is the provision of **legal tender** – coins and paper notes which a depositor can obtain by drawing on a sight deposit or current account. This is cash. The second type, usually used for transactions involving larger sums than in cases when cash is used, is to enable the writing of a cheque drawn on one's current account. So the most basic notion of a stock of money is simply the sum of cash and current accounts (sight, or demand deposits).

The most basic function of banks is to provide cash and deposits for the public. The sum of the cash and current account deposits held by the public comprises a widely used definition of the money supply and is termed M_1 or narrow money. These are *assets* of the non-bank public and form a part of its non-human capital or wealth. For the banks, current account deposits are *liabilities* since the sums of money deposited belong to the non-bank public, while cash held by the banks is an asset for the banks just as cash held by the public is an asset for the public.

Table 34.1 shows the principal assets and liabilities of the clearing banks in 1984.

Table 34.1 Balance sheet of clearing banks in UK at 15 February 1984 (£ billion)

Assets		*Liabilities*	
Sterling		Sterling	
Notes and coin	1.73	Sight deposits	32.43
Deposits at the Bank of England	0.58	Time deposits	57.38
Market loans and bills	20.68		
Advances	63.97		
Investments	8.46		
Lending in foreign currencies	30.70	Other currency deposits	29.14
Miscellaneous	10.98	Miscellaneous	18.15
Total	137.10	Total	137.10

Source: Bank of England Quarterly Bulletin, March 1984, table 3.2

The main cash assets are notes, coins and the banks' own deposits at the Bank of England (these are all liabilities of the Bank of England; the relationships between assets and liabilities of the whole financial system is discussed in the next chapter). The next item, market loans and bills, shows the banks' short term lending to other financial intermediaries, local authorities, and their holdings of Treasury and other bills of exchange. Advances, the most important set of assets, are loans made mostly to private individuals or companies but also some to the public sector and to overseas customers. Investments are longer term financial assets the banks hold. These are mainly government bonds and company securities. Foreign currency lending includes all lending in foreign currencies to other financial intermediaries, the private sector and overseas. Total assets were £137.10 billion in early 1984. Real assets such as buildings and computers are excluded from this balance sheet.

The main liabilities are deposits – sight deposits (or current accounts) and time deposits. Other currency deposits are deposits in foreign currencies. Notice that the ratio of cash (notes and coin plus banks' deposits at the Bank of England) to total assets is 2.31:137.10 = 0.017. So less than 2 per cent of assets are held in cash form (which earns no interest for the commercial banks).

The commercial banks hold a rather small fraction of the total amount of note and coin in circulation: usually about 10 per cent. The rest is held by the public.

As you have just seen, the overwhelming bulk of the banks' liabilities are in current and deposit accounts, whereas only a small fraction of their assets are held in the form of cash. Since banks are in business to make profits, it is scarcely surprising that they hold as few as possible of the assets in their portfolio in the form of cash since it earns no interest. That they hold so little in relation to current account deposits is possible because, over any period, the public is content to hold its money assets in the form of deposits rather than cash.

Suppose that a bank decides to make someone a loan. Suppose it grants a customer an overdraft facility. As soon as the customer draws on this facility, new money is created for, in writing out a cheque to pay for whatever is purchased, the bank has enabled a deposit to be created in someone else's name either held with itself or at another bank: A gets the overdraft, pays B, and B pays the cheque into an account. A's bank, in making the advance or overdraft, created an asset (the debt of the borrower to itself) and a liability of the same amount (the obligation to pay out). A obtained an asset (whatever A bought with the money) and a liability (the obligation to pay the bank back). B obtained one asset (the deposit now in B's account) in exchange for another (the goods now transferred to A). B's bank (which may or may not be the same as A's) obtained a liability exactly equal to the initial liability created when the overdraft was used and also an asset, which is its own deposit with the Bank of England into which it pays the cheque drawn on A's account. As far as the banking sector, therefore, is concerned, the creation of the new asset (the loan) has created an equal liability (the increase in current account deposits). Since this type of liability of banks is money, the banking system, by creating loans, has created money.

Although banks can create money in this way, they cannot do so without limit. It pays them to make loans only if they receive interest therefrom and, at any rate of interest, there is a limit on the demand for loans. More loans can be made only at lower and hence less profitable interest rates. This does suggest, however, that if the demand for loans rises, interest rates will also tend to rise and that banks will make more loans, hence increasing the money supply.

Banks usually need to keep some reserves to meet the public's demand for cash. Suppose, rather mechanically, that this is a fixed proportion of sight deposits. Let C_p stand for cash held by the non-bank public and D_p for deposits (sight and deposit accounts) held by the non-bank public. The money stock M is then given by

$$M \equiv C_p + D_p$$

The equation is a *definition*, not a behavioural equation or an equilibrium condition. Note that, given the ease with which deposit accounts can be converted into current accounts, the definition lumps the two together in D_p.

The relationship between D_p and C_p obviously depends on the non-bank public's preferences for holding money in the form of cash or bank deposits. Assume for the moment that there is a stable proportion of its money that the public wants to hold as cash, and write

$$p = \frac{C_p}{D_p} \text{ or } C_p = pD_p$$

where p is the non-bank public's preferred ratio. Unlike the previous equation, this is a postulated *behavioural* relationship. p will depend in part on the rate of interest available on deposit accounts: as it rises the opportunity cost of holding cash rises and vice versa, so p will fall or rise as the interest rate rises or falls. For the moment, however, abstract from this factor determining the mix of monetary assets held by the public and take p as given. Since p shows the ratio of cash to deposits (including newly created deposits) that the public wants to hold, it is sometimes called the **cash drain**.

The money held by the banks consists of the cash they hold in their vaults and their accounts with the Bank of England. These are held mainly so that banks can make transactions with one another via the cheque clearing process. Term the cash held by banks C_b and their deposits with the Bank of England D_b. So the cash reserves R of the banks are given by

$$R = C_b + D_b$$

Since commercial banks are profit maximizing institutions they have an incentive to use the deposits they receive from the public to purchase interest yielding assets including loans and advances to businesses and households. The higher the rate of interest obtainable, the lower the amount of non-interest bearing cash and deposits with the Bank of England they will wish to hold. On the other hand, they will always want to hold *some* money in order to meet the public's demand for cash and to make inter-bank transactions. Generally, the larger the size of the non-bank public's deposits with the banks, the larger one expects the banks' preferred money holdings to be. Thus R will vary *directly* with D_p and *inversely* with the rate of interest. Again, however, abstract for the moment from the effects of interest rate changes and simply write

$$C_b + D_b = bD_p$$

or

$$R = bD_p$$
$$b = R/D_p$$

where b is the banks' preferred ratio of money holdings to deposits. Again, these equations are behavioural.

You now have terms for p and b, and if you add them together you get

$$p + b = \frac{C_p + R}{D_p}$$

From this equation you get that

$$D_p = (C_p + R)\,\frac{1}{p + b}$$

Now recall that $M \equiv C_p + D_p$ and that $C_p = pD_p$, so that

$$M = pD_p + D_p = (1 + p)D_p$$

Now, using the equation for D_p just given, you get

$$M = (1 + p)\,(C_p + R)\,\frac{1}{p + b}$$

or, expanding R,

$$M = (C_p + C_b + D_b)\,\frac{1 + p}{p + b}$$

Letting the sum of all the bracketed terms be H, you could also write

$$M = H\,\frac{1 + p}{p + b} \text{ or } M\,\frac{p + b}{1 + p} = H \text{ or } \Delta M = \frac{p + b}{1 + p}\,\Delta H$$

H, which is the sum of the bracketed items, is called **high powered money** (or sometimes the *monetary base*). You can see why it is called high powered: the money supply is some multiple of it, namely $(1 + p)/(p + b)$, which is the limit, at given interest rates, to which banks can increase the supply of money for any change in H if b and p are given. The ratio $(1 + p)/(p + b)$ also has a special name – the **bank multiplier** (sometimes also called the *money* or *credit multiplier*). You can also see why the monetary base is so called, for it is the base on which the supply of money is built.

Definitions of Money

There are several definitions of money in use in the UK. These arise partly because of the different functions of money (for example, as a medium of exchange and as a store of value), partly because not all money is in practice regularly traded for goods and services and hence not all is related very directly to transactions in the goods market, and partly because there is no precise dividing line between liquid assets that makes those on one side of the line obviously money and those on the other side obviously not.

The various definitions in official use are set out as follows.

Narrow Money Aggregates

Notes and coin

Notes and coin held by the public are the narrowest definition of money. This definition focuses exclusively on money produced by the government.

M_0

This is commonly referred to as the *wide monetary base*. It includes notes and coin held by the public (about 91 per cent), notes and coin held by the banks or *till money* (about 8 per cent), and banks' deposits at the Bank of England, known as *bankers' balances* (about 1 per cent), which are used for clearing and other purposes. This corresponds to what has been called high powered money.

$NIBM_1$

This is also known as *retail M_1*. It consists of notes and coin together with non-interest bearing (NIB) sight deposits (i.e. current accounts). This definition is closely related to the use of money for transactions – money as a medium of exchange. As you would expect, this is relatively responsive to changes in interest rates; as rates rise it pays people to move deposits into interest bearing accounts.

M_1

This is often just called *narrow money* (though there are *five* narrow money definitions!). It consists of M_0, $NIBM_1$ and all interest bearing sight deposits – that is, deposits that can be transferred or withdrawn on demand. Most of these are held by companies as 'overnight' balances which are more likely to be used to buy gilt edged securities and other financial investments than to buy goods and services. Like $NIBM_1$ it includes government produced and bank produced money. M_1 is also responsive to interest rate changes. A 1 percentage point rise in interest rates generates a fall in M_1 of about 3 per cent.

M_2

This definition arose as an attempt to find a comprehensive measure of money used for transactions purposes. It includes notes and coin and all retail sterling deposits with UK banks except the overnight balances that are included in M_1. The deposits in banks that are in practice included as a way of excluding overnight balances are those less than £100,000, which are commonly referred to as *retail deposits*. It also includes building society deposits that are withdrawable within one month, and ordinary National Savings accounts. The idea of getting a measure closer to the transactions motive implies that this measure will be more sensitive to *GDP* changes. The inclusion of interest bearing deposits also makes it less sensitive to changes in interest rates. It is thus a wider measure than M_1 by its inclusion of building societies and National Savings, but at the same time narrower by its exclusion of overnight balances. M_2 is probably a better indicator of the transactions demand for money than M_1, but it is a relatively new measure whose empirical properties remain to be investigated.

These narrow definitions imply different sizes of the money stock. In October 1983, for example, notes and coin amounted to £11.5 billion, M_0 was £12.8

billion, $NIBM_1$ was £30.8 billion, M_1 was £42.0 billion and M_2 was £112.4 billion. Notes and coin and M_0 tend to move closely together. They have not moved very closely with M_1, however (especially in the 1970s). $NIBM_1$ and M_1 have diverged considerably with a rise in the interest bearing elements of M_1. $NIBM_1$ and M_1 have the greatest responsiveness to interest rate changes and notes and coin and M_0 the least. The ratio of *GDP* to M_0 has risen faster than any other ratio mainly because firms are increasingly paying employees by credit transfer rather than in cash.

Broad Money Aggregates

£M_3

Sterling M_3 comprises notes and coin plus *all* sterling deposits (sight and time) held by both the private and the public sector.

M_3

This is sterling M_3 plus all deposits in UK banks held by the private and public sectors in currencies other than sterling. It thus allows for the fairly close substitution between interest bearing and non-interest bearing deposits as well as the close substitution between sterling and other currencies.

PSL_1

Private sector liquidity is measured by PSL_1 as M_1 plus private sector time deposits (sterling), together with short term (original maturity less than one year) financial investments like Treasury bills.

PSL_2

This is a variant of PSL_1 that adds in short term private sector deposits in building societies and National Savings.

The use of these *institutionally* defined measures of money can only approximate to the definitions that theory suggests. The effects that changes in any of them may have on, say, interest rates or aggregate planned expenditure is an empirical matter. One of the difficulties in any institutionally based definition of money is that the nature of the monetary services offered by financial institutions is changing all the time (building societies offering chequing facilities is a good recent example). Consequently, the official definitions need to be changed, or new ones added, in response to changes in the marketplace.

In September 1983 the amount of notes and coins held by the non-bank public was £11,659 million and the sum of sight and time deposits was £86,878 million. p was therefore about 0.13. At that time the banks' cash holdings were £1689 million and deposits at the Bank of England were £465 million, so their total reserves were £2154 million and b was about 0.02. With these ratios, therefore, the bank multiplier was about 7.5 (1.13/0.15).

SAQ 34.1

(a) If $p = 0.15$ and $b = 0.05$, what is the value of the bank multiplier?
(b) If p rises to 0.20, does the bank multiplier rise or fall?
(c) If b rises to 0.08 ($p = 0.15$), does the bank multiplier rise or fall?
(d) Which affects the bank multiplier more, a 10 per cent rise in p or a 10 per cent rise in b?

Are b and p constant, as the mechanical argument assumes? What determines their size?

Consider first p – the proportion of the non-bank public's monetary wealth held as cash. This one expects, as has been seen, to vary with the rate of interest; the higher the rate on deposit accounts, the smaller the amount held as cash. There are outside influences on p as well. For example, the development of cashpoint cards makes cash easier (less costly) to obtain and hence can be expected to reduce the demand for cash to be held on one's person. The development of credit cards (whose numbers more than doubled from 1976 to 1981) has a similar effect. Since liabilities of the public to pay credit card debts are discharged via cheques, more transactions are conducted without cash, using the card instead, with debts being settled by cheques drawn on current accounts; so as the demand for cash falls, the demand for money in the form of deposits rises. But with such outside factors constant, one expects p to fall as interest rates rise. This causes the bank multiplier to rise as interest rates rise. In terms of the previous example, if p fell to 0.1, the bank multiplier will rise to $1.1/0.12 = 9.2$. A fall in the cash drain consequently increases the bank multiplier and an increase reduces it.

Consider b – the proportion of bank assets held as cash (the reserve ratio). As you have seen, it is prudent for banks to keep cash reserves to meet the cash demand of the public and avoid crises of confidence. The cost, however, is the forgone interest. If the rate of interest at which banks can borrow rises, then the cost of the risk of being short of cash rises, for if banks do not get cash from the public they must do so elsewhere, usually by selling short term assets like Treasury bills. The higher the interest rate, the higher the cost of having to trade bills for cash, and so the prudent level of reserves will tend to rise: b increases. Conversely, if the interest rate banks can get on loans rises then the opportunity cost of holding cash rises relative to holding more loans in their portfolios of assets, so b tends to fall. A fall in b tends to increase the bank multiplier. For example, in terms of the previous computation, if b falls to 0.01 the bank multiplier increases to $1.13/0.14 = 8.1$. Conversely, a rise in b reduces the bank multiplier.

Thus, according to the initial simple model,

$$M = H\frac{1 + p}{p + b}$$

or, if for convenience one terms the bank multiplier h,

$$M = hH \text{ or } H = \frac{1}{h} M$$

Since H depends on the preferences of banks and the public, it is a *demand* notion. To make this clear, write H^D to indicate that the amount of high powered money demanded is dependent on b and p. Call H^S the amount of high powered money supplied by the authorities. Then, in equilibrium,

$$H^S = H^D$$

which says that the amount of high powered money demanded will adjust until it is equal to the amount of the money base supplied. If supply exceeds demand the excess will be partly spent on goods and services and on the purchase of bonds and other investments. Hence in equilibrium

$$H^S = M \frac{1}{h}$$

or

$$M = hH^S$$

This suggests that, if the monetary authorities can control the amount of high powered money they supply, H^S, they can also control the supply of money M.

It thus seems that, since the amount of notes and coin available is controlled by the authorities, and assuming that commercial banks' deposits at the bank of England are a stable part of the monetary base, the authorities have effective control over the money supply via the notes and coins component of high powered money: printing and minting money and putting it into circulation increases the money supply by a knowable and stable relationship.

As it happens, however, there is immense controversy over the ability of the authorities to control the money supply in the way the foregoing analysis suggests, and this is one of the issues that divides most monetarists from Keynesians. Just as Keynesians take a sceptical view of the impact of money supply changes on aggregate investment and, hence, income and employment (preferring active fiscal policies), so they also take a sceptical view of the ability of the authorities to control the money supply anyway. Monetarists take the opposite view.

The issues are ultimately empirical ones to which there is no final answer as yet. But they can be picked apart so as to enable one both to take an intelligent view of what the issues are essentially about and also to see the kind of research that may eventually produce the answers that will settle the controversy.

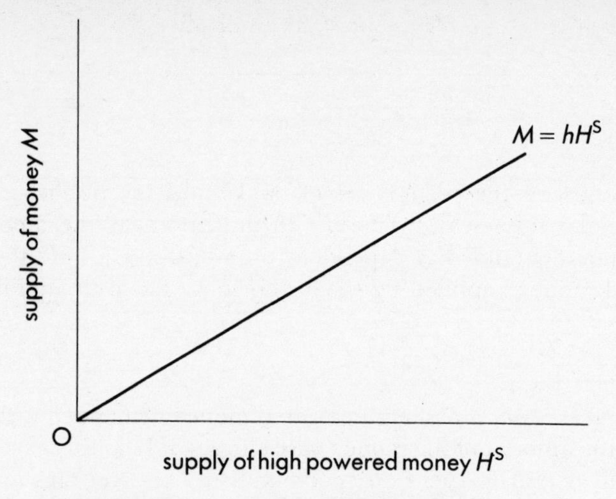

Figure 34.1 Money supply as a function of H^S

Begin by representing the model so far in diagrammatic form. Figure 34.1 shows the supply of money as a function of the supply of high powered money. In this figure, the line $M = hH^S$ is straight. In other words, h is assumed to be constant along it since p and b are also assumed constant.

If you plot the money supply against the interest rate, you get a graph like that in figure 34.2. In these circumstances, the money supply does not vary with the interest rate (assuming that p and b do not), but it will vary according to the supply of high powered money.

In figure 34.2 M_0 corresponds to money supply when $H^S = H_0^S$, and M_1 is money supply when $H^S = H_1^S$ (larger than H_0^S). The demand for money is also drawn in the figure and labelled L. This is assumed (as in chapter 31 onwards) to be negatively related to the rate of interest, and is the standard version already met of the determination of the interest rate. Note that here the interest rate is determining the *total demand* for money but *not* its division into different kinds of money – the division between cash and deposits held by banks and the non-bank public.

SAQ 34.2

(a) Given $h = 7.5$, by how much will M rise if H rises by £10?

(b) If H rises by £1, with $h = 7.5$, by how much will i fall if the equation for the demand for money is $L = kY - li$, where $k = 0.13$, $l = 1.2$, Y is constant at 300, the initial money supply is 25, and i is denominated in percentage points (for example 5.0 per cent)?

Effects of Interest Rates on the Supply of Money

Now relax the assumptions that p and b do not depend on the rate of interest. The reasonable expectation is evidently that higher interest rates make cash and non-interest bearing deposits less attractive than interest bearing deposits.

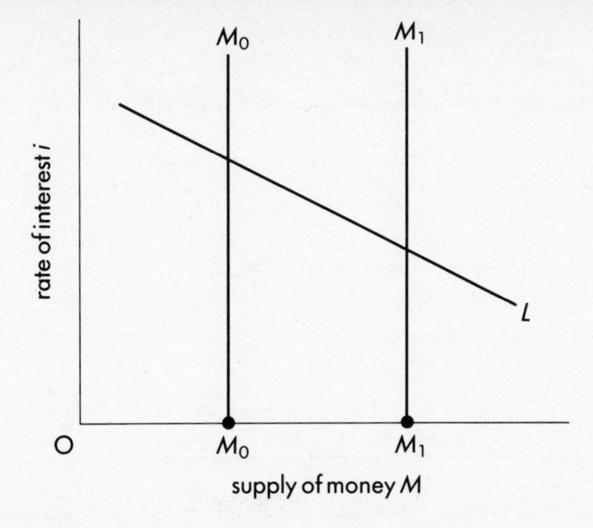

Figure 34.2 The supply of money when it has zero interest elasticity

Therefore as interest rates rise you should expect p to *fall* as C_p falls and D_p (or at least deposit accounts with banks) rises. You should also expect to see b fall as R is reduced (both banks' cash in vaults and their non-interest bearing deposits with the Bank of England). As you have seen, a fall in p and b increases the bank multiplier, so a rise in interest rates increases h. This means in turn that the money supply is directly related to the interest rate: as interest rates rise, so does the money supply. Figure 34.2 needs therefore to be changed so as to appear as in figure 34.3. In this figure, you can see that there is a given positively sloped money supply curve for each level of high powered money supplied. M_0 corresponds to H_0^S and M_1 to H_1^S.

The money multiplier is thus not a fixed number but varies with the rate of interest. Provided that the interest rate dependence is stable and does not jump around, there is still the possibility of control by the authorities over the money supply by controlling high powered money. In addition, however, it looks as though there is another way of controlling the money supply – through interest rate policy.

The way that *monetary base control* can be envisaged as working can be illustrated as in figure 34.4. If the economy is initially in equilibrium with the interest rate at i_0, H at H_0^S, M at M_0 and *GDP* at Y_0, an increase in H^S to H_1^S shifts the supply of money function causing a fall in the rate of interest to i_1. This generates an increase in investment and, via the multiplier, an increase in equilibrium *GDP* and a shift in the demand for money until a new equilibrium level of income Y_1, interest rate i_2, money demand L_1 and money supply M_2 is established. There may also be a direct effect on the demand for goods and services. Hence, an increase in the monetary base still increases the money supply, lowers the rate of interest, and increases *GDP* (assuming, of course, that the economy is not on the vertical section of the aggregate supply curve).

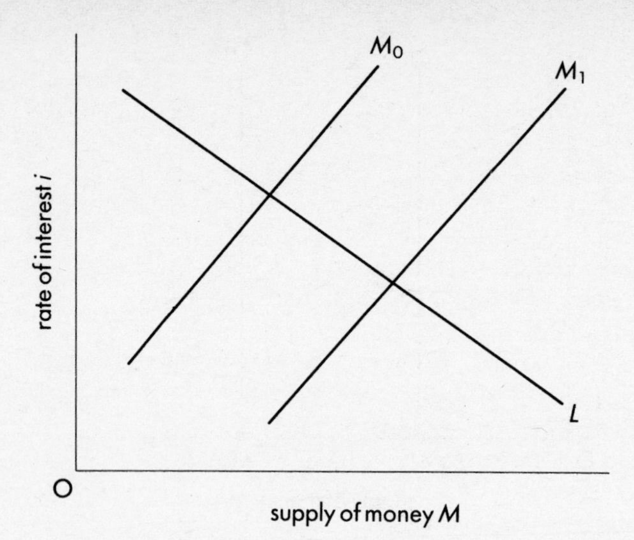

Figure 34.3 The supply of money depends on the interest rate

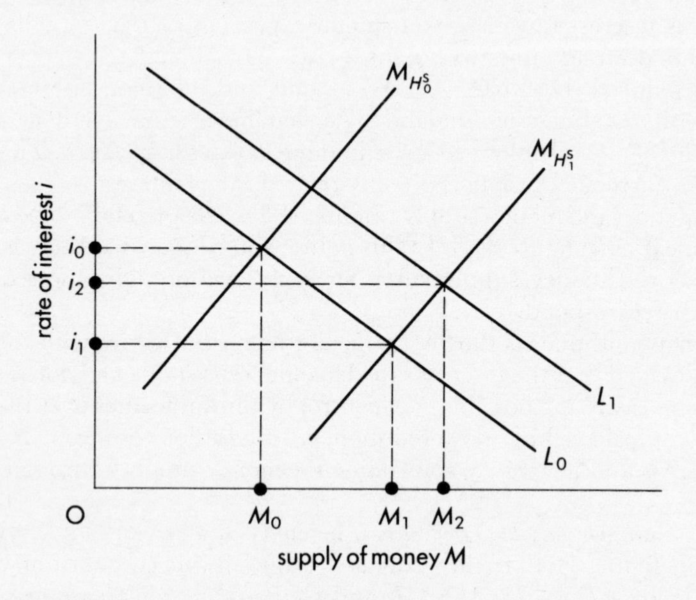

Figure 34.4 Effects of changes in the monetary base on the supply of money and the interest rate

SAQ 34.4

(a) Let the supply curve of money be $M = -20 + 2i$ and the demand curve be $L = 39 - 1.2i$. What is the equilibrium rate of interest?

(a) Suppose the supply curve shifts to the right such that $M = -10 + 2i$. Ignoring any feedback effects via investment, *GDP* etc., what is the new equilibrium interest rate?

An Extreme Monetarist View

Monetarists in particular emphasize that there is a direct connection between the demand for money and the demand for goods and services that does not operate only via interest rates. Thus an excess supply of money is brought into equilibrium not only by purchases of bonds, which pushes their prices up and hence the rate of interest down, but also by purchases of goods and services. Moreover, since monetarists customarily assume also that the aggregate supply curve is vertical, this leads directly (as well as indirectly via interest rate changes) to a rising price level. Hence, control of high powered money is seen by them as the crucial element in controlling inflation.

This can be summarized in the **quantity theory** of the demand for money. On this view the nominal demand for money depends upon (a) the size of real national income multiplied by the price level and (b) the size of the desired **velocity of circulation** of money. The idea of desired velocity expresses the notion that people will have a preference for how much 'work' each unit of money is to do. For example, if interest rates are high, then the opportunity cost of holding money rises and, to finance the same level of transaction, a small money stock will be preferred that 'turns over' faster than before. Let V stand for the average number of times that it is desired that a unit of money turns over in the various transactions that produce *GDP*. Then the simplest version of the monetarist theory is

$$L = \frac{1}{V}(\Sigma PX)$$

where a determinant of V is the interest rate and ΣPX is nominal *GDP*. Thus, if i rises, desired velocity V rises and therefore $1/V$ falls; so the demand for money falls. In equilibrium, supply equals demand; therefore

$$M = L$$

and

$$M = \frac{1}{V}(\Sigma PX)$$

Rearranging this, you get

$$MV = \Sigma PX$$

which says that, in equilibrium, the money supply, multiplied by the desired velocity, equals nominal income. In equilibrium, moreover, desired velocity will equal actual velocity (otherwise people would be changing V). Here you can see that the impact of changes in H^S depends not only on the stability of the bank multiplier that relates H^S and M but also on the stability of the velocity of circulation. Actual velocity is given in equilibrium by

$$V = \frac{\Sigma PX}{M}$$

and, if the money market can be taken as adjusting fast enough so as to be in equilibrium at any time, then the ratio of nominal income Y to the money supply M can be directly measured from published data. Case study 34.1 discusses the evidence for this. If real income is at its limit, and the economy is on the vertical part of the aggregate supply curve, then increases in the money supply generate a rise in prices only: the X remain the same but the P all rise. Extreme monetarists take the view that changes in the money supply have an effect only on the price level and leave *real* variables unchanged.

The stability of the desired velocity is important. If it *is* stable (or if its relationship with the interest rate and other determinants is known) then the impact of monetary policy on prices and output can be predicted, provided the bank multiplier is also stable. If it is not stable, then monetary policy has unpredictable effects. Case study 31.2 suggested that the ratio of M to GDP was, in the long run, stably related to interest rates. The short run stability of V seems, however, far less.

Case Study 34.1 Velocity of circulation in the UK, 1977–83

The velocity of circulation in the UK has recently behaved as shown in table 34.2.

Table 34.2 Velocity of circulation in quarter years

		M_1	£M_3	M_3
1977	(4)	7.03	3.56	3.27
1978	(1)	6.92	3.52	3.24
	(2)	7.02	3.52	3.18
	(3)	6.93	3.51	3.21
	(4)	6.97	3.56	3.25
1979	(1)	6.87	3.51	3.22
	(2)	7.14	3.65	3.34
	(3)	7.45	3.78	3.48
	(4)	7.49	3.78	3.45
1980	(1)	7.87	3.80	3.49
	(2)	8.09	3.82	3.46
	(3)	8.11	3.65	3.35
	(4)	8.22	3.61	3.33
1981	(1)	8.28	3.61	3.27
	(2)	7.94	3.50	3.11
	(3)	8.00	3.46	3.03
	(4)	8.21	3.46	3.00
1982	(1)	7.63	3.13	2.81
	(2)	7.82	3.15	2.80
	(3)	7.65	3.14	2.78
	(4)	7.61	3.16	2.79
1983	(1)	7.60	3.17	2.77
	(2)	7.25	3.04	2.66
	(3)	7.32	3.07	2.69

Source: Financial Statistics, March 1984, table 11.1

The official method of calculation is to take *GNP* at current market prices (seasonally adjusted) for each quarter, multiply it by 4 to obtain an annual rate (thus enabling computation for recent quarters before annual data are all in), and then divide by the monthly average stock of money (seasonally adjusted) held over the three months of the relevant quarter. *GNP* does not, of course, include *all* the transactions for which money is demanded, and both this number and the derivation in the text have to assume that the ratio of all monetary transactions to those featuring in *GNP* is constant, there being no data on *all* transactions. Moreover, *GNP* includes some imputations (e.g. owner occupiers' imputed income from housing) that correspond to no money transaction.

Ideally, of course, one would like data on *desired* rather than actual velocity. If individuals are, however, able to adjust their desired money stock quickly (as monetarists tend to assume) then actual V will not be far from desired V. According to the data of table 34.2 the largest positive quarterly variation on the previous quarter was, in column 1, +5.1 per cent and the largest negative one was −6.7 per cent; the overall range was 6.87–8.28. These differ by 20.5 per cent. For the second column, the largest positive quarterly variation was +4.0 and the largest negative one −4.1 per cent; the overall range was of 3.04–3.82. These differ by 25.7 per cent. Similar variations for the third column were +4.2 and −6.0 per cent, with a range of 2.66–3.49. These differ by 31.2 per cent.

For what it is worth, this evidence does not support any view that short term velocity is very stable. This is one reason why monetarists argue that monetary policy should should not be used as a means of short term regulation of the economy (a proposition with which most Keynesians would agree).

An Extreme Keynesian View

All the theories discussed so far assume that the money supply, even though its impact may be imperfectly predictable, is none the less determined by the authorities and not 'inside' the model; that is, it is taken as exogenous rather than endogenous. An entirely different view, associated particularly with Nicholas Kaldor, is that the money supply is endogenous; that is, that the authorities operate in such a fashion as to adjust the money supply so that the actual stock held at any time is determined only by demand.

This is particularly likely to be the case if the authorities have interest rates rather than the money supply as their targets. Thus, in figure 34.5, if it is desired to hold interest rates at level i_0 then, given the demand, they must supply M_0. Or if the target interest rate were i_{q1}, then they must supply M_1. The money supply is thus perfectly elastic at each target rate of interest. A monetarist retort might well be, of course, that the government *can* act in such a fashion as to make the money supply endogenous, but that it does not follow that M is *necessarily* and always endogenous. As you will see later, the authorities can raise interest rates by raising the rate at which the Bank of England will lend money to the discount houses (its intervention rate), and then making this *effective* by selling bonds which causes their prices to fall and interest rates to rise.

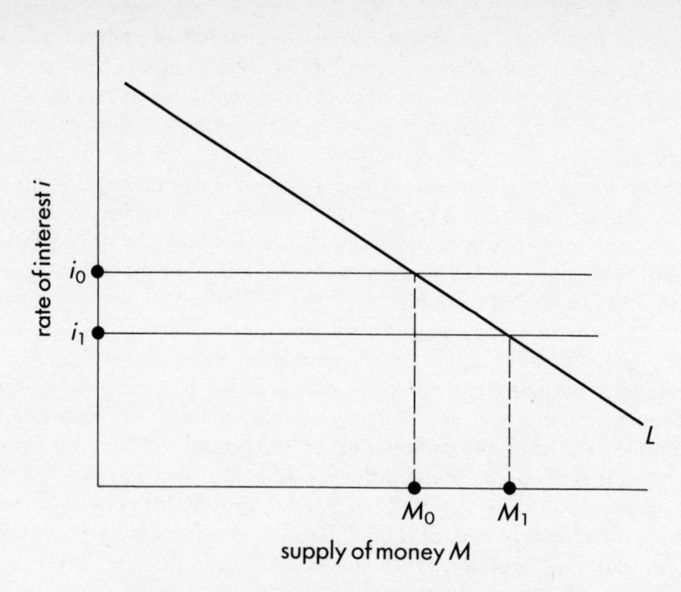

Figure 34.5 Endogenous money supply

Moreover, the monetarists' direct link between the demand for money and the demand for goods is denied strenuously: the availability of *credit* may affect consumption but not money *per se*. Hence credit control is important rather than money control, and this should be done either by operating on the price of credit (interest rates) or by rationing it (hire purchase controls, ceilings on bank lending and so on).

SAQ 34.4

Given that the demand for money equation is

$$L = 39 - 1.2i$$

(a) If the authorities have a target rate of interest of 15 per cent what must the supply of money be?
(b) If the bank multiplier is 5.75, what is the supply of high powered money?
(c) If the target rate of interest becomes 10 per cent, what must the new money supply be?
(d) What is the interest elasticity of the demand for money at $i = 15$ per cent?
(e) What is the interest elasticity of the demand for money at $i = 10$ per cent?
(f) What is the interest elasticity of the supply of money?

Both the extreme monetarist and the extreme Keynesian views raise important issues. The evidence, however, suggests that such extremism is not warranted (the evidence is often only subjective, unambiguous empirical evidence is still hard to come by, and what empirical evidence exists is hotly contested). It seems likely that the supply of money can have important impacts on both the price level and real output (though predicting the division of this impact is no exact science), and also that control of the money supply is not as easy as the model developed so far suggests. But this issue, together with the relationship between the money supply, the public sector borrowing requirement and the balance of payments, needs more careful exploration to see the sources of the difficulties. It is this that the next chapter addresses.

SAQ 34.5

Which definition of the money supply do you think would be most appropriate for the government to focus on and try to control if:

(a) The authorities can control cash, and the ratio of cash to all assets is constant?

(b) The authorities peg interest rates, and hence the price of bills, so that bills become a close substitute for cash?

(c) p and b in the bank multiplier were constant?

What You Should Understand Now

The main types of financial intermediary in the UK and what they do.
The ways in which commercial banks can create deposit money.
The definitions of the money supply and high powered money.
The bank multiplier and how it depends on p and b.
The effects of interest rates on the demand and supply of money.
The monetarists' quantity theory of the demand for money and the relationship between the money supply and the price level.
The consequences of an endogenously determined money supply.

35

Public Sector Borrowing, the Overseas Sector and Macroeconomic Policy

The previous chapter looked at the banking sector of the economy without, however, the government and the central bank playing any explicit role in what was going on. In this chapter the analysis is extended to make good that omission and to extend the analysis so as to take account of overseas monetary transactions. A major concern will be government borrowing.

Government marketable debt is often called **gilt edged** because of both the literal reason that it used to have a gilt edge and the practical characteristic of the near zero probability of the government defaulting. Consequently, it is a relatively risk free way of holding one's wealth (particularly if one invests in index linked securities that are inflation proofed). The main categories of government marketable debt are the following. Treasury bills are government IOUs that promise to pay a certain amount in three months' time. They are issued in multiples of £5000. Then there is a variety of other types of borrowing taking the form of stocks due to mature in 1–5 years' time, 5–15 years' time and more than 15 years' time. The perpetuities called *consols* are no longer issued. All these bills and bonds have it in common that they can be sold to other people by the initial purchaser; hence their description as 'marketable'.

Non-marketable government debt includes certificates of tax deposit, which companies may buy in anticipation of tax liabilities and then subsequently pay in lieu of money. The other main category is National Savings Certificates and National Savings Bank deposits. None of these is marketable, but each can be redeemed for cash.

Table 35.1 Central government net debt issues in 1982–3 (£ million)

Marketable debt	
Treasury bills	195
Stocks	5140
Non-marketable debt	
National Savings	3028
Certificates of tax deposit	1035
Other debt (excluding notes and coin)	−104

Source: Bank of England Quarterly Bulletin, March 1984, table 7

In 1982–3 the amounts borrowed by the (central) government under each of these heads was as shown in table 35.1.

Financial Balance Sheets and Flows of Funds

If one divided the economy into five major sectors – the non-bank private sector (households and firms), the commercial banks, the Bank of England, general government (plus public corporations) and the overseas sector – and then examined the structure of their financial assets and liabilities, it would appear in stylized form as in table 35.2.

The balance sheet of the non-bank private sector excludes household lending to firms since this cancels out within the sector (the households' assets are equal to the firms' liabilities). Aside from this, its financial assets are those itemized – currency holdings, deposits with commercial banks, lending to government (that is, non-bank private sector ownership of government

Table 35.2 Financial assets and liabilities of the five main sectors of the economy

Assets		*Liabilities*	
Non-bank private sector (households and firms)			
Cash holdings (notes and coin)	C_p	Bank lending to the private sector	*BLP*
Deposits (sight and time)	D_p	Foreign lending to the private sector	*FLP*
Private lending to government	*PLG*		
Private lending to foreigners	*PLF*		
Commercial banks			
Cash (vault cash)	C_b	Deposits by the private sector	D_p
Bankers' deposits at the Bank of England	D_b	Deposits by the government	D_g
Bank lending to the government	*BLG*	Deposits by foreigners	D_f
Bank lending to the private sector	*BLP*		
Bank lending to foreigners	*BLF*		
Bank of England			
Bank of England lending to government	*BELG*	Public deposits	*PD*
Bank of England lending to foreigners	*BELF*	Bankers' deposits	D_b
		Cash in circulation with the non-bank private sector	C_p
		Cash held in the commercial banking sector	C_b
		Cash held by foreigners	C_f
Government			
Deposits with banks	D_g	Bank of England lending to government	*BELG*
Public deposits at the Bank of England	*PD*	Bank lending to government	*BLG*
		Private sector lending to government	*PLG*
		Foreign lending to government	*FLG*
Foreign sector			
Foreign lending to government	*FLG*	Bank lending to foreigners	*BLF*
Foreign lending to private sector	*FLP*	Private sector lending to foreigners	*PLF*
Foreigners' cash holdings	C_f	Bank of England lending to foreigners	*BELF*
Foreigners' deposits	D_f		

securities and national savings) and lending to foreigners (ownership of foreign private and government securities). Its main liabilities are debts to the banks and to foreigners. The non-bank private sector is a net financial creditor; its financial assets exceed its liabilities to other sectors (largely due to the presence in the sector of insurance and pension funds).

The commercial banks' assets are cash in their vaults, deposits at the Bank of England, ownership of government securities, loans and advances (overdrafts) to the private sector, and ownership of foreign securities. Their financial liabilities are mainly deposits held by the public, the government and foreigners. Again, internal assets and liabilities cancel out. Unlike the non-bank private sector, the banks' financial balance sheets balance out so that they are neither net financial creditors nor net debtors (assuming equality between non-deposit liabilities and real assets). The banks can always get as many notes as they wish from the Bank of England by drawing on their balances with the Bank, and the bankers' balances can be replenished by the Bank by its buying bills from the banks. This is an automatic procedure known as **money market assistance**. It enables the banks to supply as many notes to customers as they wish, and in practice means that the government has no direct control over M_0.

The Bank of England's assets include government securities that it has purchased from the government but not sold to commercial banks or the rest of the private sector, and its holdings of foreign securities and of foreign currencies (foreign exchange reserves). Its liabilities include all notes in circulation with commercial banks, the rest of the private sector and foreigners, since these are promises to pay even though they can be redeemed only in exchange for notes and coin, bankers' deposits and public deposits (which are the main accounts held by the government in the Bank). Like the banks, the Bank of England is neither net financial creditor nor a net debtor. In table 35.2, the government appears as a net debtor, but the table excludes a major asset: the power to tax, of which more anon. The foreign sector can be either a net financial debtor or net creditor.

The Bank of England

The central bank in the UK is the Bank of England. It has two main functions: a banking function in which it acts as banker primarily to the government and to the commercial banks, and an issue function in which it issues notes (coin minting and issue is a function of the Royal Mint, which is a separate government department).

As banker to the government, the Bank operates four main accounts for its most important customer. The first is the *consolidated fund* (CF), which is a bit like anyone's ordinary sight deposit account with a commercial bank. Into this account the government pays all its receipts other than proceeds of the sales of government debt and National Insurance contributions. Out of it go all payments other than loans and interest payments and National Insurance benefits. The government is not allowed to go into the red in the CF.

What, then, happens if receipts are less than outgoings? This is where the second main account comes in. This is called the *national loans fund* (NLF), into which go all proceeds from the sale of government debt, and out of which payments are made for interest on government debt, loans made and debt repurchased. When the CF looks like going into the red, transfers are made from the NLF which may then have to be made good by the sale of new government debt. Any of this new debt not sold is held by the Bank and sold *on tap* in the future.

Under its issue function, the Bank of England issues banknotes, which it does by the purchase of government debt or the debt of the private sector or local authorities. There is no limit to the amount of notes that it can issue, provided that it holds sufficient assets to balance these liabilities. The liabilities of the Issue Department are rather special. Although any holder can take a note (which is an asset to the holder and a liability of the government) to the Bank and ask for it to be repurchased, all the holder can get in return is a further banknote. Thus the Bank cannot go bankrupt!

The third main account held for the government is the *National Insurance fund*, into which all receipts from National Insurance contributions go, and outgoings are paid, with any discrepancy being made up by transfers from other accounts.

The fourth main account is called the *exchange equalization account* (EEA), which holds the country's official reserves. If a UK resident needs, say, Deutschmarks to import a German machine or to buy securities in Germany, he will, via his or her bank, obtain them from the EEA in exchange for sterling which the EEA then pays into the NLF. (This assumes the importer does not already hold an adequate stock of Deutschmarks.) Alternatively, if a UK resident acquires marks, these are usually paid into the EEA (via the resident's bank) in return for sterling which the EEA obtains by drawing from the NLF.

Table 35.3 Balance sheet of the Bank of England, February 1984 (£ billion)

Assets		*Liabilities*	
Issue Department			
Government securities	1.7	Notes in circulation	11.4
Other securities	9.7		
	11.4		11.4
Banking Department			
Government securities	0.4	Public deposits	0.7
Advances	0.6	Bankers' deposits	0.8
Other assets (premises etc.)	1.9	Reserves	1.4
	2.9		2.9

Source: Bank of England Quarterly Bulletin, March 1984, table 1

The first three of these main accounts add up to what are called *public deposits*. These, together with the commercial banks' deposits and the notes in circulation, make up the main liabilities of the Bank of England. The main assets held against these liabilities are government, local government, private sector and overseas securities.

The main assets and liabilities of the Bank of England in February 1984 are shown in table 35.3.

The Bank of England is also a **lender of last resort** (not, as one examinee once quaintly put it, the last resort of Lent!). This means that the Bank of England guarantees to supply sufficient cash on loan to the banks when they need it (for example, if a run on the banks threatened, as has happened in the past when there were rumours that a bank might be going bankrupt). This facility means that no one need fear that any bank will ever be unable to convert a deposit into notes on demand. As a result, the need for the Bank to implement this role is unknown in modern times. But the price the Bank exacts for this 'insurance policy' is that the banks must behave prudently, and this gives the Bank of England tremendous powers over the ways in which the commercial banks do their business.

Consolidating Balance Sheets

It is going to be rather useful to set the balance sheets out in the form of identities and to *consolidate* (that is, add together) the balance sheets of various sectors. If one writes out the Bank of England's balance sheet as an identity one gets the following:

$$BELG + BELF \equiv PD + D_b + C_p + C_b + C_f \qquad (1)$$

with the assets on the left hand side and the liabilities on the right. Since *changes* in assets and liabilities are going to be the main focus, and changes in assets must equal changes in liabilities, one can also write:

$$\Delta BELG + \Delta BELF \equiv \Delta PD + \Delta D_b + \Delta C_p + \Delta C_b + \Delta C_f \qquad (2)$$

Since the commercial banks' balance sheet also balances, one can similarly write for this sector:

$$\Delta C_b + \Delta D_b + \Delta BLG + \Delta BLP + \Delta BLF \equiv \Delta D_p + \Delta D_g + \Delta D_f \qquad (3)$$

You have already seen that the balance sheet of the government sector does not balance because of the omission of an implicit asset: the power to tax. Any shortfall of government revenues relative to its outgoings has to be met by borrowing: the *public sector borrowing requirement* (*PSBR*) (see chapter 27). This can be written:

$$PSBR \equiv T - Tr - G - DI \qquad (4)$$

where T are tax revenues, Tr are net transfers, G is public expenditure on final goods and services and DI is debt interest payments on outstanding government debt (the **national debt**).

In terms of changes in assets and liabilities, the *PSBR* must be accompanied by appropriate changes in the government's balance sheet, so that

$$\Delta D_g + \Delta PD + PSBR \equiv \Delta BELG + \Delta BLG + \Delta PLG + \Delta FLG \tag{5}$$

what is the link between the *PSBR* and the money supply? This can be derived by consolidating the Bank of England's, the commercial banks' and the government's balance sheet changes (identities (2), (3) and (5)) to give the following cumbersome identity:

$$\begin{aligned} &\Delta C_b + \Delta D_b + \Delta BLG + \Delta BCP + \Delta BLF + \Delta BELG + \Delta BELF + \Delta D_g \\ &+ \Delta PD + PSBR \\ &\equiv \Delta D_p + \Delta D_g + \Delta D_f + \Delta PD + \Delta D_b + \Delta C_p + \Delta C_b + \Delta C_f + \Delta BELG \\ &+ \Delta BLG + \Delta PLG + \Delta FLG \end{aligned} \tag{6}$$

Fortunately, lots of these terms cancel on consolidation and, eliminating these, you get

$$\begin{aligned} &\Delta BLP + \Delta BLF + \Delta BELF + PSBR \equiv \Delta D_p + \Delta D_f + \Delta C_p + \Delta C_f + \Delta PLG \\ &+ \Delta FLG \end{aligned} \tag{7}$$

and, rearranging identity (7):

$$\begin{aligned} &PSBR \equiv \Delta C_p + \Delta D_p + \Delta PLG - \Delta BLP - (\Delta BELF - \Delta FLG - \Delta C_f + \Delta BLF \\ &- \Delta D_f) \end{aligned} \tag{8}$$

SAQ 35.1

Show in systematic stages how identity (8) can be derived from identities (2), (3) and (5).

The terms $\Delta C_p + \Delta D_p$ in identity (8) are changes in the £M_3 money supply excluding government deposits with the commercial banks, and the terms in brackets in (8) are all associated with foreign transactions, collectively termed the overseas impact (OI). Replacing the bracketed terms with OI gives

$$PSBR \equiv (\Delta M - \Delta D_g) + PLG - \Delta BLP - \Delta OI \tag{9}$$

This shows plainly that, for given levels of government bank deposits, non-bank private lending to government, bank lending to the private sector and overseas external financing, *PSBR* must be financed by a change in the money supply.

Financing the Public Sector Borrowing Requirement

The *PSBR* can be financed in several ways. You can see the possibilities on the liabilities side of the government and Bank of England balance sheets in table 35.2. One way is to sell more government debt in an **open market operation** (mostly long term gilts) and National Savings to the non-bank private sector (ΔPLG). Thus the reduction in the money holdings of the non-bank private sector is exactly equal to the money injected into the economy by the excess of public spending over receipts, and therefore it has a zero effect on the money supply. It will tend of course to raise interest rates but it is not inflationary via any impact on the money supply.

A second way is to borrow from overseas (ΔFLG). Since this does not mop up money from the private sector, to run a *PSBR* financed in this way must increase the money supply.

A third way is to increase the supply of cash to the public (C_{p}, implicitly including coins as well as notes), for example by paying public employees more, which directly raises the money supply.

A fourth is to borrow from the commercial banks mainly by selling Treasury bills (ΔBLG). Again, this does not mop up the extra money put into circulation by public spending, so the money supply (and interest rates) tend to rise using this method. The government can also borrow from the banks indirectly via what is called *residual finance*. For example, the government pays a salary cheque to an employee who pays it into a bank. The money supply immediately rises. The bank now has a cheque which is a debt of the government, so the government has indirectly borrowed from the bank. The bank may later pay the cheque into its bankers' deposits at the Bank of England and later buy government securities. Whatever it does, it simply trades one form of government liability for another. The bank is thus lending to the government.

These are the main options, and only one has no effect on the money supply when taken in conjunction with public spending – selling public sector debt to the non-bank public. The other liability items are of no use: *PD* cancels out since it is a liability of the Bank but an asset of the government. Likewise *BELG*. The others are either too trivial or not directly available to public sector manipulation.

You can therefore write

$$PSBR \equiv \Delta PLG + \Delta FLG + \Delta C_{\mathrm{p}} + \Delta BLG \tag{10}$$

The financing of the *PSBR* by these methods in recent years is shown in case study 35.1.

Case Study 35.1 Financing the *PSBR*, 1979–83

Table 35.4 shows how the *PSBR* has been financed in the five most recent years for which data are available. As you can see, the *PSBR* rose sharply in 1983 after three years in which it had fallen. Foreign lending to the government has shown a steady increase. Non-bank purchases of public debt (*PLG*) fell until 1982 but rose sharply in 1983 and, hence, offset the effect that the higher *PSBR* would have had on the money supply by mopping up almost as much money as the *PSBR* was, in net terms, putting into the economy. In fact, the money supply (£M_3) rose in that year by only a little more than its average increase in the previous four years (£9.6 billion compared with £8.7 billion) and certainly by much less than the fact of a more than doubled *PSBR* would have suggested.

Table 35.4 The *PSBR* and its financing, 1979–83 (£ billion)

	PSBR	ΔPLG	ΔFLG	ΔC_p	ΔBLG
1979	12.64	10.94	−0.62	0.78	1.54
1980	12.17	9.03	0.03	0.74	2.37
1981	10.73	8.71	1.18	0.59	0.25
1982	5.45	5.82	1.43	0.47	−2.27
1983	11.68	11.46	1.59	0.70	−2.07

Source: Financial Statistics, March 1984, table 2.6

Table 35.5 shows the annual increase in £M_3 as a percentage of the first quarter's money stock and the percentage of the *PSBR* financed by non-bank purchases of public debt. As you can see, the growth of the money supply has been fastest when the least reliance has been placed on sales of public debt to the non-bank public and slowest when the most reliance has been placed on this method of financing *PSBR*.

Table 35.5 Percentage growth of £M_3 and ratio *PLG:PSBR*, 1979–83

	$\Delta £M_3$ (%)	$\Delta PLG/PSBR$ (%)
1979	12.8	86.6
1980	18.9	74.2
1981	13.7	81.2
1982	9.3	106.8
1983	10.0	98.1

Source: Financial Statistics, March 1984, tables 11.1 and 2.6

The Government's Budget Constraint

By looking at the consolidated balance sheets for the public sector (government and Bank of England) one can identify the government's **budget constraint**. Consolidating identities (2) and (5) you have:

$$\Delta BELG + \Delta BELF + \Delta D_g + \Delta PD + PSBR \equiv \Delta PD + \Delta D_b + \Delta C_p + \Delta C_b + \Delta C_f + \Delta BELG + \Delta BLG + \Delta PLG + \Delta FLG \tag{11}$$

from which comes:

$$PSBR \equiv (\Delta C_p + \Delta C_b + \Delta D_b) + \Delta BLG + \Delta PLG - \Delta D_g - (\Delta BELF - \Delta FLG - \Delta C_f) \tag{12}$$

SAQ 35.2

Show in systematic stages how identity (12) is derived.

Identity (12) is the government's budget constraint. It says that *PSBR* can ultimately be financed either by creating high powered money ($\Delta C_p + \Delta C_b + \Delta D_b$), or it might be financed by running down net foreign assets ($\Delta BELF - \Delta FLG - \Delta C_f$), or by running down (trivial possibilities here) government deposits with banks (ΔD_g), or by increasing borrowing from either the banks (ΔBLG) or the non-bank public (ΔPLG). Note that public deposits of the Bank of England (*PD*) are not in the government's budget constraint. If the government sells Treasury bills to the banks (ΔBLG) or other debt to the non-bank public (ΔPLG) this will show up in public deposits automatically as transfers are made into the national loans fund. To include *PD* in the constraint would involve double counting, which is why *PD* cancels out in identity (11).

The public sector does, of course, own other (non-financial) assets like buildings which could also be sold. Although this method can be used, and it does mop up money injected by public spending, it is expensive in terms of transaction costs (that is, valuing and selling publicly owned buildings and enterprises). It would normally be determined by decisions related either to real investment possibilities of the sort discussed in chapter 30 or to questions of principle concerning political preferences for and against public ownership and privatization.

In the long run, public sector deficits cannot be met by disposing of existing assets of the government, whether financial or real. They must be met by increasing either high powered money, or debt, or both. Debt cannot be increased indefinitely for interest on it must be paid and that must involve either a rise in taxes or an increase in high powered money.

In the long run, then, debt interest and repayment can be met only out of taxation or out of increased supply of high powered money. Setting out the *permanent* budget constraint, you have

$$G + Tr + DI - T \equiv \Delta B + \Delta H^S \qquad (13)$$

where ΔB is the change in borrowing and ΔH^S is, of course, $\Delta C_p + \Delta C_b + \Delta D_b$. The present value of debt interest must be equal to the present value of increased taxation to pay it off. Since the present value of debt interest is the same as the value of bonds sold, $DI = \Delta B$ on average, then

$$G + Tr - T \equiv \Delta H^S \qquad (14)$$

where T now excludes allowance for debt interest payments. Since H^S and the money supply are connected by the bank multiplier h, a budget deficit must in the end be met by monetary expansion.

SAQ 35.3

Since maturing government debt is usually replaced by the issue of new government debt, it makes sense to think of a unit of government debt as a 'consol' or a perpetuity according to which, in exchange for a sum of money *P*, the government promises to pay an annual sum or annuity *A* for ever.

(a) What equation links *P*, *A* and the interest rate?

(b) If the government has to pay out *A* each year, how much on average must it take in taxation each year to meet this obligation?

(c) What is the present value of this infinite stream of tax receipts?

(d) What is the relationship between the sum of money the government gets from the sale of the consol and the present value of the annuity payments?

(e) Suppose the goverment issued a bond that would mature in two years' time, paying its holder £100, and that yielded £5 at the end of each year. What is its *P* if the interest rate is 10 per cent?

(f) What is the present value of taxes needed to pay *A* and redeem the bond at maturity?

(g) If the government issued a new perpetuity each time it had to pay interest on a £100 consol rather than raise taxes, what will its debt be after five years at 10 per cent interest?

(h) What would be its annual interest obligation in the fifth year?

Case Study 35.2 The National Debt

In essence, the national debt is what the government (via the national loans fund) owes people (mainly British) or institutions through its borrowing over the years. Some of it is very old: the Treasury still pays interest on sums raised by King Charles I. The national debt was only initiated in any large way, however, to finance foreign wars under William III, and the foundation of the Bank of England in 1694 was essentially to raise £1.2 million from private subscribers and purchase the necessary foreign currency to finance British armies overseas. Until recently, the national debt was mainly incurred so as to finance major wars.

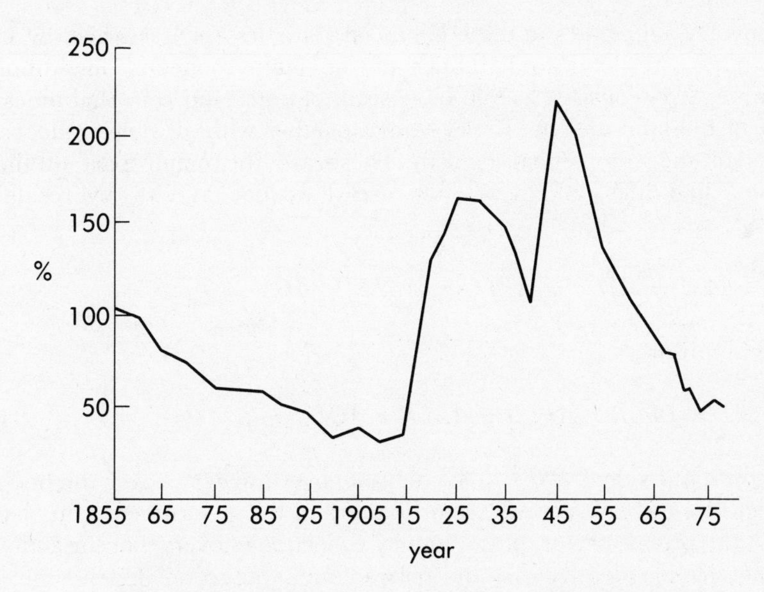

Figure 35.1 Ratio of national debt to *GDP*, 1855–1980

Victorians were worried about the national debt and tried to reduce it, with some success, by running budget surpluses. For many years, public expenditure was split about 50:50 between defence spending and paying interest on (servicing) the national debt. In the nineteenth century the debt never rose above £840 million and by 1914 had been reduced by £650 million. The next two world wars increased it dramatically: in 1921 it had risen to £7.8 billion and by 1947 to £25.6 billion. By 1970 it was about £33 billion and by 1980 it was about £110 billion. Since all these sums are nominal values of outstanding debt, they have been much affected by inflation, especially in very recent times.

A more realistic picture can be had from figure 35.1, which shows the ratio of nominal national debt to nominal *GDP* since 1855. This dramatically brings out the impact of the two world wars and shows that size of the debt as a proportion of *GDP* has been falling and has now pretty well 'bottomed out'.

Figure 35.1 Ratio of national debt to *GDP*, 1855–1980

Nearly one sixth of the national debt is held by official bodies such as the Bank of England: this is debt of one part of the public sector to another. Of the rest, about 24 per cent is held by individuals and private trusts, 38 per cent by insurance companies and pension funds, 7 per cent by banks and the rest by other financial institutions like building societies and unit trusts.

HM Treasury (1982) 'The "national debt" and public sector debt', *Economic Progress Report*, no. 147.

Counterparts to the Money Supply

Most monetary aggregates in the UK official statistics are assets held by UK citizens that correspond to liabilities of the main monetary institutions. For example, £M_3 consists, as you have seen, of notes and coin (liabilities of the Bank of England and the Royal Mint) together with all sterling deposits (liabilities of the commercial banks). These are the major part of these institutions' liabilities, and it is often useful to look at £M_3 by recalling identity (9):

$$PSBR \equiv (\Delta M - \Delta D_g) + \Delta PLG - \Delta BLP - \Delta OI$$

and rewriting it as

$$\Delta M - \Delta D_g \equiv PSBR - \Delta PLG + \Delta BLP + \Delta OI \qquad (15)$$

on the right hand side is *PSBR* (new debt of government to cover the budget deficit) net of non-bank private sector lending to the government, plus bank lending to the private sector, plus a motley collection of overseas transactions. Expanding *OI* (see identity (8)) and rearranging, you get

$$\Delta M - \Delta D_g \equiv (PSBR - \Delta PLG + \Delta BLP + \Delta BLF) + (\Delta BELF - \Delta D_f - \Delta FLG - \Delta C_f) \qquad (16)$$

The first bracketed terms are called *domestic counterparts* to changes in the money stock, and the second are called *external and foreign currency counterparts*. The domestic counterparts are basically measures of credit generated in the domestic economy, and the external and foreign currency counterparts reflect the balance of payments of the private sector on current and capital account. For example, the effect of a current account deficit will be to reduce £M_3: residents will need to obtain more foreign exchange than exports are generating to pay overseas suppliers, so they either run down their bank deposits by buying foreign exchange from the exchange equalization account or they pay the foreigners in sterling cash (so C_f rises) or by sterling cheque (so D_f rises). In any of these cases, M must fall.

Table 35.6 shows the counterparts for 1979–83. In practice, bank lending to foreigners (ΔBLF) is matched by foreigners' deposits with UK banks (ΔD_f), and so this is omitted from the table. Changes in non-deposit liabilities have become substantial in recent years, and consist of other capital liabilities of banks, net of other non-financial investments, as well as residual errors required for the monetary sector's balance sheet to balance. Since ΔD_g is insignificant, this too has been dropped from the table. Column 4 is 1 − 2 + 3, and column 7 is 4 + 5 + 6.

Table 35.6 Counterparts to changes in £M_3, 1979–83 (£ billion)

	1 PSBR	*2* ΔPLG	*3* ΔBLP	*4* Total domestic counterparts	*5* External and foreign currency counterparts	*6* Change in non-deposit liabilities	*7* Δ£M₃
1979	12.64	10.95	8.59	10.28	−3.11	−0.57	6.60
1980	12.17	9.43	10.02	12.76	−0.44	−1.39	10.93
1981	10.73	11.27	11.40	10.86	0.26	−1.74	9.38
1982	5.45	10.54	17.56	12.47	−2.32	−2.16	7.99
1983	11.68	10.73	12.85	13.80	−0.52	−3.70	9.58

Source: Financial Statistics, March 1984, table 11.3

The main advantage of this presentation is that the domestic counterparts effectively show the pressure from domestic sources on the money supply. The International Monetary Fund was very keen on this feature when it was lending the UK government money in the face of persistent balance of payments deficits (and fixed exchange rates) and was anxious to see domestic 'discipline' over the money supply. Hence the emphasis on what was termed *domestic credit expansion*. But, of course, different arrangements of the accounting identities would illuminate other aspects that may be of policy relevance. This is now particularly likely given that the UK is no longer formally committed to supporting a fixed exchange rate.

SAQ 35.4

Suppose the Bank of England sells government debt to a private individual who pays for it by writing out a cheque drawn on a sight deposit.

(a) What happens to the balance sheet of the buyer's bank?
(b) What happens to the balance sheet of the Bank of England?

(c) What happens to the money supply?

Suppose the Bank of England sells government debt to a commercial bank which pays for it by drawing a cheque on its account at the Bank of England.

(d) What happens to the balance sheet of the commercial bank?
(e) What happens to the balance sheet of the Bank of England?
(f) What happens to the money supply?

Fixed and Flexible Exchange Rates and Monetary Policy

Suppose the exchange rate is fixed. Suppose also that there is a balance of payments deficit after a situation in which it was previously zero. This means that the UK is buying more goods, services and investments abroad than it is selling, and there will be downward pressure on the sterling exchange rate since the supply of sterling exceeds its demand. To maintain the fixed rate, the Bank of England must buy sterling and sell foreign exchange, thus running down the reserves. This must be balanced by a fall in liabilities. The fall in liabilities occurs naturally as sterling accounts and cash are exchanged for the foreign currency. Consequently the money supply falls. Conversely, if there is a balance of payments surplus, there is a corresponding rise in sterling liabilities of the Bank of England, so the money supply rises.

With a fixed exchange rate, then, the money supply is largely out of the control of the authorities. They could, of course, operate on the assets side by buying bonds to restore balance. Thus, if the Bank bought bonds via an open market operation to compensate for the fall in reserves, then it could maintain the money supply as long as its purchases equalled its sales of foreign currency. The open market purchases would increase the money supply and exactly compensate for the fall induced by the purchases by the public of the foreign exchange it needed to buy the imports (or make overseas investments). This sort of operation is called **sterilizing** the monetary impact of the balance of payments. For a balance of payments surplus, the sterilizing operation would require sales of bonds via an open market operation.

Fixed exchange rates do, however, make control of the domestic money supply much harder. Persistent bond sales, for example, to meet persistent balance of payments deficits and sterilize the domestic money supply, will drive up the long term burden of public debt interest payments and hence add to the *PSBR*; thus this is not a policy any government would want to see pursued over the long term. In the end, devaluation will be preferred or, of course, more flexible exchange rates, so that the rate can find its own level with relatively little effect on reserves since the balance of payments will be near to zero (depending on how 'dirty' the floating of the exchange rate is) and relatively little on the money supply.

Moreover, there are direct interest rate effects. With a fixed exchange rate, if for domestic purposes the authorities want to increase the money supply, then they may engage in open market purchases of bonds. The rate of interest domestically tends to fall. However, as this happens, overseas investments become relatively more attractive, so foreign currencies are demanded to make overseas purchases of financial assets: the increase in money gets syphoned off into overseas markets, and is not cut off by a fall in the exchange rate that makes overseas assets more expensive in terms of sterling. Or if there is a balance of payments deficit, then as the authorities seek to sterilize the effects on the money supply by buying bonds and hence increasing the money supply, interest rates are driven down as the price of bonds rises; so more funds are invested abroad, intensifying the balance of payments deficit.

As a broad approximation, therefore, you can say that the government can control the money supply *or* the exchange rate but not, in the long run, both.

SAQ 35.5

Why can the government control the exchange rate *or* the money supply, but not both simultaneously?

Fixed and Flexible Exchange Rates and Fiscal Policy

You have just seen that monetary policy is relatively limited in an open economy with a fixed exchange rate. If the authorities want, say, to raise the level of activity by increasing the money supply, there will be a short term effect that reduces interest rates at home; however, this leads to a capital outflow that will continue until interest rates have returned to world levels. Fiscal policy, by contrast, is *more* effective in an open economy with a fixed exchange rate. An increase in public expenditure to raise the level of activity will, as you saw in chapter 31, cause some crowding out as interest rates rise. However, you can now see that, with a fixed exchange rate, international capital movements will over the longer run prevent the domestic interest rate from rising as much as it would in a closed economy; so crowding out is reduced, and the multiplier is larger as a result.

Under flexible exchange rates monetary policy is more effective than under fixed exchange rates. In this situation, an increase in the money supply reduces interest rates, leading to a capital outflow and a consequential fall in the exchange rate. Fiscal policy, by contrast, is *less* effective under flexible exchange rates because an expansionary fiscal policy raises planned expenditure, the demand for money and interest rates, which are no longer forced to remain at or near world levels; so there is a greater degree of crowding out as rising interest rates choke off the interest elastic components of aggregate planned expenenditure.

With fixed exchange rates, interest rates will remain more or less at the world level and fiscal policy is less subject to crowding out. With flexible exchange rates, monetary policy can determine domestic interest rates, but fiscal expansion causes interest rates to rise with consequential greater crowding out effects.

Some Methods of Controlling Bank Lending

The supply of credit by commercial banks to the non-bank private sector (*BLP*) is, as you have seen, a domestic counterpart to £M_3 (identity (16)). How might the government set about trying to influence *BLP*? One way would be to get interest rates to rises. The non-bank private sector's demand for bank loans thus falls and new loans are not made, so the rate of deposit creation falls and, as old overdrafts are not renewed, deposits fall and therefore M falls. This evidently requires the Bank of England to be ready to vary its intervention rate and/or to buy and sell bonds to the banking sector: selling bonds tends to reduce their price and hence raise the rate of interest. Another way is through a variety of direct controls, for example, limiting the number of loans banks may make (putting a ceiling on permissible loans) or making regulations about lending to particular types of client (say, only, 70 per cent of the finance a private person wants to purchase a car will be supplied by the bank).

The use of the intervention rate *alone* is not of much use. As you will recall, this is the rate, determined from day to day, at which the Bank will lend money to the discount houses. Recall that the commercial banks lend money at call and short notice to the discount houses. When banks want cash, they can call in such money from the discount houses who, since they borrow 'short' (from the banks) and lend 'long', need to obtain money quickly. Thus the Bank of England as lender of last resort will provide, but at a rate that is uncertain in advance and which may be penal.

The general idea is that a high (and uncertain) intervention rate would induce discount houses to raise their interest rates and thus generate an increase in interest rates throughout the economy. In former times, the bank rate was announced in advance with considerable ceremony so that discount houses could judge the rates they would offer on money and call lent them by the banks. The bank rate was made effective by being used in conjunction with open market operations. If the government wanted to contract the money supply, you have seen that this can be accomplished by the Bank of England selling government bonds. This has the effect of contracting the amount of high powered money and setting in train a multiplied contraction of deposits as the banks seek to restore their desired reserve ratios. If they rectified the ratio by calling in cash from the discount houses, this would then lead to rising interest rates generally as the discount houses were forced 'into the Bank'; so the multiple expansion of deposits diminished, but interest rates rose (so p and b tended to fall, expanding the bank multiplier). In this way the Bank was able directly to affect interest rates (at least in the short term and within limits set by the international pattern of interest rates), the demand for loans and, ultimately, the public's demand for money.

There are snags with all of these methods. People who are frustrated from getting the loans they want will look elsewhere and, if someone can see a way round the regulations, there is profit to be had in so doing; so financial 'black markets' can arise in response to direct controls. Interest rate variations have their disadvantages. They make investment planning harder as business people have to guess the future course of interest rates in making their investment plans over time; this particularly affects investment in long lived assets like buildings, and hence creates more uncertainty and instability in the construction industry, and hence reduces employment and raises its variability in a major employment sector.

Attention thus becomes focused on the *PSBR* itself. If financing it is so problematic, perhaps the best thing is to reduce it. This can be done either by raising taxes (not the politicians' dream solution) or by reducing public expenditure on final goods and services and on transfers. It is not surprising, therefore, that controlling public expenditure has become a hallmark of recent macroeconomic policy. Note that the underlying rationale is twofold: (a) financing the *PSBR* via domestic credit expansion has unpleasant side effects; (b) other things equal, a higher *PSBR* raises the money supply which, in an economy on the upward sloping part of the aggregate supply curve (let alone in the vertical section), intensifies inflationary pressure. Even selling debt to the private sector to finance a *PSBR*, though it may not increase the money supply directly, will drive interest rates up and reduce private sector investment, hence damaging future growth. So the government has somehow to choose between these various undesirable consequences of public expenditure and weigh them against the desirable consequences of the public expenditure itself. Monetarists, of course, are politically antipathetic towards public expenditure anyway and, since they assume a vertical aggregate supply curve and hence see monetary expansion as the chief cause of inflation, they argue strongly for lower public expenditure (as well as lower taxation) and for planned, steady, increases in the money supply so as to match a rising demand for it as real incomes rise. For Keynesians, the dilemma is tough.

Required Reserves

A favourite recommendation of monetarists is that the authorities should control the money supply by instituting *required reserve ratios*. A required reserve ratio is a minimum ratio of reserves to deposits (b) that the Bank of England requires – obviously in excess of that which the banks would choose for themselves based on profit considerations in the management of their portfolios of assets. Thus, if the Bank of England wants to reduce the money supply, it could raise the required reserve ratio. Suppose, for example, that initially $p = 0.2$ and $b = 0.04$. By raising b to, say, 0.06, the bank multiplier falls from 5.0 to 4.62, bank deposit creation is reduced and hence, for any given level of high powered money, so is the money supply.

The effect of requiring the banks to maintain a higher b than they would prefer is shown in figure 35.2. If initially $b = b_0$, then $h = h_0$ and the supply of money associated with a given supply of high powered money is M_0. An increase in b for a given level of H^S rotates the curve clockwise by reducing h from h_0 to h_1 and reduces the money supply as shown.

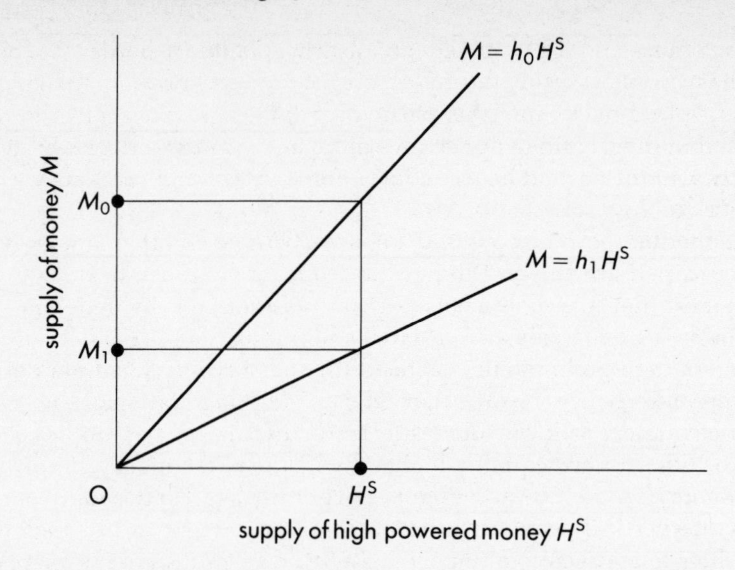

Figure 35.2 Supply of money as required reserves are changed

The authorities cannot simultaneously have a policy about interest rates *and* another about the money supply. For example, if under interest rate policy the Bank sought to maintain interest rates, it would have to stand ready to buy or sell Treasury bills and other (usually short term) government securities so as to keep the desired rates, with whatever consequences for the money supply that would follow any open market operations. Alternatively, if it sought to control the money supply via open market operations or controlling reserve ratios, then the interest rate would turn out to be whatever followed on from that policy.

On that most economists agree. But they hardly agree about (a) whether monetary policy should be addressed primarily to interest rate levels or the size of the money stock, or (b) which method of controlling the stock is most effective.

SAQ 35.6

Why can the government control the money supply *or* interest rates but not both simultaneously?

The arguments about interest rates versus money stock targets are partly concerned with stability. If it is desired to keep interest rates relatively stable (at either high or low, or gradually rising or falling, levels) then, given that the link between the money supply and interest rates is complex and subject to the impact of other variables, it may be better to monitor interest rates and adopt appropriate strategies to keep them at the rates preferred. As you have seen, the money supply then becomes endogenous. If stability of the money supply is preferred (or a stable growth of it) then policy should be addressed to that, accepting whatever variability may result in interest rates as other factors intervene.

As to methods of controlling the money stock, the direct method of required reserves has obvious logical attractions. In practice, however, it has never been systematically adopted in Britain.

In the UK the commercial banks have at times been required to hold particular ratios of reserves to assets, but these have never been manipulated so as to control the money supply in the way the model suggests could be done. One reason for this was that the various ratios that have at times been required were sometimes less than those the commercial banks selected on commercial grounds anyway. Another reason was fear that either this procedure or direct controls of the monetary base itself might lead to unacceptable fluctuations in interest rates (politicians in the UK have always had an eye to the electoral unpopularity of high and fluctuating mortgage interest rates in particular, and the effect of interest rate variation on the building industry has already been mentioned).

Yet another reason has been that the imposition of effective reserve ratios would lead to a relative penalization of the commercial banks compared with other financial institutions who, if not controlled in the same way as the commercial banks, would tend to supply substitute forms of money. For example, suppose b were raised leading to a reduction in the supply of currency and deposits. What might a firm do that wanted a loan but was unable to obtain it by, say, borrowing from a commercial bank because the government was requiring the banks to reduce their loans and advances relative to their money reserves? It would, of course, look elsewhere to, say, an overseas bank, or some other financial institution, or make some direct deal with another firm that had funds to lend. These alternative sources of liquidity may not themselves be money, but in so far as they lead to the eventual creation of deposits somewhere in somebody's bank, they effectively increase the supply of money and in any case enable firms to purchase the goods and services they want and thereby raise aggregate planned expenditure. Alternatively, the firm's own bank may do a deal in foreign currency in an overseas bank, or arrange the loan through one of its own overseas branches. In order to make their monetary policy effective it is therefore clear that the monetary authorities would be forced to extend controls to foreign transactions and other financial intermediaries. Problems of monitoring and enforcement would become increasingly difficult as the ingenuity of those seeking ways of avoiding controls was pitted against that of the authorities seeking to maintain them. And with controls would, of course, come increasing inefficiency and complaints of unfairness as some institutions became more penalized than others, some individuals more discriminated against than others, and some better at evasion than others.

The Bank of England has, however, tried other forms of control. For example, it has required commercial banks to discriminate between borrowers (so, for example, that the private citizen might be able to borrow only a small portion of the amount demanded to purchase a private car, whereas a car hire firm would be able to borrow a larger portion). It has placed ceilings on the amount of loans the banks may make. It has required banks to hold special deposits at the Bank of England. All were subject to the kinds of difficulty noted above regarding evasion, unfairness and inefficiency.

SAQ 35.7

Suppose you were a banker and the government said that you could not make profitable loans to your customers above a fixed amount. What would you do?

Perhaps the most fundamental reason why the Bank of England has never placed any reliance on reserve ratio manipulation (or monetary base control) as a weapon of monetary policy is its belief that the short term money multiplier is in any case not stable. The stability of the money multiplier depends on the stability of the demand for money to be held in various forms: if it is unstable, then so is the money multiplier, which would make the relationship between the high powered money supplied and the total supply of money also unstable. As you saw earlier, in the short term the multiplier is rather unstable. Most economists agree that in the long term it is more stable, or at least that changes and trends can be predicted. Monetary fine tuning does not, however, seem to be on.

Although the Bank of England takes the view that the money multiplier is unstable, it is still a controversial empirical issue as to how far this is so in the long run. Case study 35.3 discusses some of the ways in which the Bank of England has tried to operate monetary policy in recent times.

Case Study 35.3 Some Bank of England Attempts to Control the Money Supply

The Bank of England has, as you have seen, never operated a reserve asset ratio system. It has, however, required banks at various times to make special deposits at the Bank of England and to hold particular ratios of assets and liabilities. The rationale has, however, always been to influence interest rates rather than the money supply. *Special deposits* were introduced in 1960 in order to reduce the impact of open market operations on interest rates. The banks were required to hold these deposits with the Bank of England (and received interest on them), but they did not count as part of the then required ratio of liquid to total assets. This meant that the banks had to hold 30 per cent of their assets in liquid form, that is, in the shape of cash in tills, deposits at the Bank of England, money lent at call to the discount market, and a selection of other short term assets like Treasury bills. What this was intended to do was to enable the authorities to sell long term government debt (bonds) rather than Treasury bills, whose sale has a sharper impact on interest rates. By selling bonds (not in the 30 per cent ratio) to banks, the banks were supposed to be less free to run down their holdings of short term assets (in the ratio) and hence would have to curtail advances. In practice, however, as the banks accumulated bond holdings they tended to sell these rather than reduce profitable advances to their customers. Who bought them? Mainly the Bank of England, which always sought to even out its repurchase of debt before its full maturity so as to avoid, through appropriate 'debt management', massive dislocations of the market as entire bond issues reached maturity. Moreover, it bought them at the prevailing market price.

With the introduction into this system of special deposits in 1960, the authorities tried to have a direct impact on the banks' portfolios. As you have seen, special deposits did not count as a part of the 30 per cent liquidity ratio. Hence to keep the ratio intact it was hoped that direct pressure would be put on the banks, whenever there was a call for special deposits, to reduce their advances. But again the banks were able to avoid the desired effect by selling maturing bonds rather than reducing advances.

Subsequently, the reserve assets ratio was reduced to 12.5 per cent and other variations made. But throughout the period, banks (and other financial intermediaries) have been able to sidestep the authorities' attempts to control the availability of credit and the money supply. This is well illustrated by the ceiling on IBELs.

In 1973 the authorities introduced a ceiling on the banks' interest bearing deposits of the public in an attempt to control the money supply. Known as a limit on **IBEL**s (*interest bearing eligible liabilities* of the banks), for breaking which the banks had to lodge *supplementary special deposits* (the so-called 'corset') at the Bank of England on which they received no interest, you can see how they were to work. Banks turned deposits away, or suffered lower differentials on interest rates paid and received as the rates on deposits were reduced so as to reduce the demand to hold money in this form. Short term government debt therefore became more attractive to the public, and by the sale of Treasury bills the government was able to reduce the money supply. However, because the government maintained the IBELs limits for some time, it paid people to find ways around them by creating dodges of the kind one expects to see when price ceilings and quotas are imposed anywhere.

One short term obvious dodge was that banks which were up against their limits could pass the custom on to subsidiaries that they owned which were not against it. Another was to switch from time deposits to sight deposits and not make bank charges on them (equivalent to offering interest on them). Another became known as the *bill leak*. Instead of making a customer a loan, the banks would accept a bill of exchange, so its seller acquired cash or an entry in a sight account and the banks could then sell the discounted bill and a make a profit too. The bill's seller has obtained the funds needed and the bill's buyer acquires an investment which is a pretty close substitute for a time deposit. Yet another ruse was to use overseas banks not subject to the controls – made easier in a system that places few restrictions on international currency exchanges. When IBELs ceilings were finally removed in 1980, the money supply rose by 5 per cent in one month. This was a rough measure of the extent to which the 'black market' operations were coming back into the official statistics, and illustrates another argument against such controls: they distort the statistics on which monetary policy has to be based.

More recently the 12.5 reserve asset ratio has been abolished (though special deposits can still be called for) and policy is less concerned with interest rate stability. The focus now is much more on sales of government debt to the non-bank public and much less on controlling bank lending, together with the introduction of new kinds of government debt (e.g. index linked bonds) that would be attractive to the public. Thus the reliance is now much more on open market sales with whatever bank multiplier effects arise from the chosen ratios that profit seeking banks select. The Bank is also more ready to use *ad hoc* (and unpredictably high) interest rates when acting as lender of last resort, hence encouraging banks to hold larger reserves. With the introduction of target rates of growth for each of the money supply measures and the introduction of the new M_2 measure of money (see chapter 34), which is a definition close to that preferred by many monetarists, it could be that the next major shift in the authorities' attempts to control the money supply will be, at long last, the explicit use of required reserves.

David Gowland (1982) *Controlling the Money Supply*, London, Croom Helm (especially chapter 8).

Money, Inflation and the Exchange rate

If inflation in country A is higher than in the rest of the world, country A's currency will depreciate relative to the rest: its exchange rate will depreciate. Under a system of perfectly flexible exchange rates, one therefore would expect that

$$\dot{P}_W - \dot{P}_A = \dot{E}$$

where $\dot{P}_W$ is the percentage rate of change of prices in the rest of the world, $\dot{P}_A$ is the rate of change of prices in the country and $\dot{E}$ is the rate of change of the exchange rate. For example, suppose a machine costs £5000 in the UK. At an exchange rate of \$2 = £1, the dollar price of the machine (ignoring transport costs etc.) will be \$10,000. Now suppose that all prices in the USA are stable, but that in the UK prices are rising at 10 per cent per year. Next year the machine's price will be £5500. But sterling will have depreciated by 10 per cent, so that \$2 now buys 10 per cent more pounds: the exchange rate is now \$2 = £1.10. The dollar price of the machine is thus £5500 × (2/1.1) = \$10,000. It has remained the same. The *purchasing power parity theorem* states that exchange rates adjust so as to hold the relative price levels constant when measured in either currency (recall chapter 23). Here it is assumed that the PPP theorem works perfectly even though, as you saw in chapter 23, in practice it does not.

Suppose that the exchange rate is fixed. In that case $\dot{E} = 0$, so $\dot{P}_A = \dot{P}_W$. For a small country like Britain, which has an unimportant impact on world inflation, this means that the UK inflation rate is determined by the world inflation rate. This is consistent with the argument that domestic control of the money supply is lost under a fixed exchange rate regime (assuming full employment and a vertical aggregate supply curve). Hence, control over the domestic inflation rate is also lost.

With a flexible exchange rate system, however, greater control over the domestic money supply brings the possibility of greater control over the domestic inflation rate. Thus, if the authorities reduce the rate of growth of M and hence the rate of inflation (supposing, of course, a vertical aggregate supply curve) then, for a given inflation rate in the rest of the world, the exchange rate will appreciate. Thus, the authorities can choose to control the exchange rate, in which case inflation will be set at the world rate of inflation (or at least tend towards it in a less strict version of the PPP theorem), or they can control the domestic rate of inflation, in which case the exchange rate will be set by world demand and supply. They cannot, however, set *both* the exchange rate *and* the inflation rate.

If inflation in the rest of the world is 10 per cent and inflation in the UK is 5 per cent, it follows from the purchasing power parity theorem that the exchange rate of sterling will be rising. This will continue for as long as the inflationary differential continues. Raising the domestic rate of inflation will reduce the differential. Reducing it will increase the differential. Thus, appropriate fiscal or monetary policies affect not only the exchange rate but also, via their impact on the rate of inflation, the rate of change of the exchange rate as well.

In practice, policy changes operate with lags. Suppose the economy is experiencing inflation at full employment, the economy is on a vertical aggregate supply curve and there is a flexible exchange rate. A reduction in the money supply – supposing this to be controllable by the authorities – raises domestic interest rates. This leads to an inflow of capital and a rise in the exchange rate to maintain equilibrium in the balance of payments. The rise in interest rates reduces planned expenditure and aggregate demand, leading to a fall in inflation – but only after a lag during which producers and workers have come to revise their expectations downwards and overcome the rigidities in the system. As inflation falls, the rate of growth of the real money supply *rises* and interest rates fall towards world levels. The exchange rate eventually settles at a new level higher than initially but lower than the amount to which it rose when the monetary contraction was first initiated. Thus, in the short term, monetary policy is more powerful in its impact than in the longer term. In the short term, monetary contraction causes a larger rise in the exchange rate than in the longer term, and likewise a larger rise in domestic interest rates. Both cause reductions in aggregate demand that are larger in the short run than the long.

Monetary Discipline

Under fixed exchange rates, as you have seen, the money supply is largely out of the control of the authorities. With flexible rates the authorities can exercise *some* control, provided that they can keep ahead of those who can profit from the development of new forms of money. A snag, however, lies in the willingness of governments to exercise the self-restraint that floating rates make necessary. Another snag is, of course, that governments may seriously misjudge the extent of capacity utilization and the slope of the aggregate supply curve and hence, if they are keen on 'sound money', may exercise altogether too much restraint and exacerbate slumps and unemployment – as it would seem the Thatcher government has done.

Many economists – and most monetarists – doubt the ability of governments to handle discretion appropriately, especially in regard to monetary policy.

This has led some extreme Keynesians to argue for the full endogeneity of the money supply, with monetary policy focusing on interest rate targets. It has led many monetarists to argue for money supply *rules*, like having the long term growth of the money supply set equal to the long term real growth rate of the economy. But unless such rules can be embodied in a 'monetary constitution', the monetarists are really requiring governments to forgo discretion – not a very politically appealing request.

A form of discipline adopted by members of the EEC, though not by the UK, was the creation of the European Monetary System (EMS). In this the member states fix exchange rates relative to one another (with some flexibility on either side of parity) while allowing the rates as a set to float against non-EMS currencies. Within this agreement there are periodic devaluations and revaluations. This system has the advantages of imposing some monetary restraint and of providing some of the benefits of floating exchange rates.

The point has, however, now been reached at which settled opinions based on well-tested theories cease to exist. Future research and practical experience must provide the answers. As always, political preferences – both those of politicians and those of economists – often obtrude. The next and final chapter looks at some of the political disagreements that characterize the economics profession at the moment. Although your politics should not determine the kind of positive economic theory you believe to be best founded, they will, of course, affect your appreciation of normative issues, both those theoretical and those that permeate attitudes to economic and social policy and policy making.

What You Should Understand Now

The functions of the Bank of England.
How to manipulate the balance sheets of the main sectors to show links between the money supply, *PSBR*, bank lending to the private sector, and government borrowing.
The government's budget constraint.
Relationship between the money supply and the balance of payments.
Monetary and fiscal policy and their effectiveness under fixed and flexible exchange rates.
Some problems in controlling the money supply in Britain.
Some issues in choosing between interest rates and money supply as policy targets.
Purchasing power parity and its implications for monetary control.
Some pros and cons of monetary discipline and monetary discretion.

36

Controversy, Politics, Economics and Economists

Now, at the end of the book, is a good time to reflect on the status of economics as a social science and economists as social scientists. How scientific *is* economics? Are economists *really* just apologists for capitalism, socialism or any other system? One often hears assertions to the effect that social science cannot be morally neutral, is value laden, is necessarily evaluative. Economists often write to the newspapers giving opinions on highly political issues. Moreover, they frequently disagree with one another on political and analytical issues (recall case study 1.2).

Science and Values in Economics

Let us begin by exploring the value issue in greater depth. My own position – to be clear about it from the start – is that economics is *not* necessarily laden with value judgements but that, none the less each of the following assertions is true:

(1) The questions selected by economists for investigation are often (and perhaps even invariably) selected on value grounds (out of a sense of political commitment, out of moral commitment or outrage, because one is paid to investigate them, and so on).

(2) Economists sometimes carelessly inject value judgements into allegedly value-free utterances.

(3) Some economic concepts and constructs (for example, the idea of efficiency or an index of poverty) are necessarily value laden.

(4) Individuals' behaviour and perceptions are in part determined by their values (for example, their indifference maps).

(5) The identification of 'good' or 'bad' scientific theories requires value judgements about what is 'good' science (for example, a theory *ought to have* empirically refutable implications if it is to be labelled 'scientific'; or a theory that is logically more elegant is 'better' than one that is clumsy or long winded; or a testable theory that has frequently been tested and not falsified is better than a rival that has not).

(6) Purely factual statements, which may be true or false, often cause people to have emotional reactions (for example, the real value of unemploy-

ment benefit always rises faster under Conservative governments than under Labour).

(7) Evaluative appraisals of alternative options (in, for example, macro-economic policy, financing schemes for higher education, investment in road safety) necessarily involve value judgements.

(8) Economic models may be biased by implicit and unrecognized value judgements (for example, that the value of females' time is lower than that of males' – after all, women are not supposed to 'work', are they?).

(9) The constraints that limit people's discretion for action, or raise the costs of particular actions, are themselves partly determined by values (for example, property right laws, rules of decent behaviour, even income itself).

(10) Scientific results can be used for moral or immoral purposes (for example, the behavioural proposition that, other things equal, heavier criminal penalties deter crime, may be used to justify capital punishment which to many is morally abhorrent).

All the foregoing statements are true. But none implies that *all* the judgements that need to be made are *value* judgements (one may have to exercise a judgement about whether the recorded unemployment percentage is more likely to be an underestimate of the true percentage than an overestimate of it, or whether Charles Feinstein's estimates of *GDP* between 1855 and 1914 are reliable, or what single figure for the elasticity of demand for imports best summarizes a range found in empirical studies). Moreover, not all economic analyses contain any value judgement at all (for example, the proposition that the elasticity of demand of an individual for a particular good depends in part on the relative sizes of the income and substitution effects has no value content whatever).

What is crucially important is, of course, to keep the value issues distinct from the scientific ones. In social science, especially *applied* social science, there is nearly always some ultimate link to be made between the purely scientific and political, policy and ethical concerns. The reason why the two must be kept distinct is that the criteria used to judge them are different. When economists are being prescriptive, saying what ought to be done and offering advice to firms, governments or the public at large, they should be clear about those elements of their assertions that are scientific (factually descriptive or based upon theories in which one has well-founded empirical confidence); they should be clear about the reliability of these scientific results; they should be clear about those elements of their assertions that are ethical; they should be clear about how these various strands interact; and they should be clear about the kinds of assumption (scientific and ethical) that form the basis of the assertions. After all, one may accept the scientific content and dissent from the ethical, or dissent from the scientific content while accepting the ethical, or dissent from both, or assent to both. This becomes possible only when economists are clear about what they are doing, and clarity depends upon making distinctions of the sort just made, not upon denying that they can be made. It is true that science *can* be used to compromise and confuse ethical issues. But it is also true that ethics can be used to compromise and confuse scientific issues. Both are important. Both need clear discussion. There is, moreover, a danger that the great prestige that our society attaches to science (especially the natural and medical sciences) attaches to the non-scientific pronouncements of scientists, who may be singularly ill equipped to make moral or political judgements.

So do not fall into the trap of thinking that economics is not scientific, or cannot be free of social value judgements. It is and can be. But because it is so often used in conjunction with value judgements about society, and also because economists (like everyone else) are not always as careful as they should be in identifying what is scientific and what value laden, be sure always to scrutinize what you hear and read and, in your own talking and writing, try to distinguish between value assumptions and pronouncements and scientific ones. You could do worse than to scrutinize this book for cases in which I have fudged such issues or been careless about injecting judgements of various kinds, including value judgements.

Economic Controversy

It is rather crude, but none the less useful, to distinguish three principal areas in which economists disagree. These are disagreement about the logical or philosophical truth of economic theories, disagreement about the empirical validity of theories or about the relevant facts in a particular issue, and disagreement about the ethical or political desirability of proposals.

Theoretical Controversies

In early chapters, substantial space was devoted to rival theories of demand. The issues involved were primarily theoretical, concerned with logical consistency, simplicity, generality and such like. Now is a good time to review your understanding of such issues. But you have also touched on dozens of other theoretical disagreements. What theory best explains the truck system? What theory best explains aggregate consumption patterns? It is reasonable to use the assumption of other things equal (*all* other things, or only some)? When is it reasonable to assume price taking or oligopoly in the manufacturing sector? It is sensible to assume in one's model building that markets generally and quickly clear so that there is neither excess demand nor supply? Are moves towards equilibrium facilitated chiefly by price or quantity adjustments? When is it reasonable to assume the absence of risk and uncertainty? It is reasonable to assume a perfectly inelastic aggregate supply curve?

All these (and lots more) are the subject of theoretical controversy, sometimes in the context of a specific problem (for example, shall we model the tomato industry as price taking or price searching?) and sometimes in the context of a whole system of theorizing about the economy (shall we assume that markets always adjust instantly to equilibrium, or do so only after adjustments that may take many years?). You will have to exercise your judgement in the light of the purposes in hand, your experience and your knowledge.

Factual Controversies

Evidence is never conclusive. The fact (if it *is* a fact!) that a particular theory has never been refuted by evidence does not imply that it will *never* be refuted. Many common *qualitative* predictions (such as that demand curves slope down from left to right) are still disbelieved by some economists or, at least, not believed in by some as generally reliable predictions to the extent that they are by others. *Quantitative* predictions (for example, a statement that the income elasticity of the demand for money is + 0.6) are inherently more controversial because they are more precise: there is a degree of precision to be argued about as well as the qualitative sign (+ or −).

The cultivation of a judgement about the facts is aided by the study of history, statistics and by a knowledge of the methods by which factual information is derived and the reliability of its various possible sources. The necessity for the use of one's judgement is inescapable. The judgement required is not to do with *values*. It is to do with assessing the reliability of asserted facts.

Political Controversies

Politics are not merely a source of controversy. They are also a spur to invention and, as we have seen in chapter 22, an object of study. As a *source of controversy*, political value judgements and party political loyalties condition and flavour a good deal of economic writing. The most obvious division between economists on political grounds is that between the libertarian individualists and the socialists. It is important to recognize a distinction between the use of the theory of individual behaviour (for example utility maximizing theory) in both positive and normative economics and the use of individualism as a political principle. *Both* the pro-market libertarians and the anti-market collectivists (not to mention most of us between) often use the assumption of utility maximizing individuals in positive economics and the notion of Pareto efficiency in normative economics. But what divides the pro-marketeers and the anti-marketeers is their view of the beneficial effects of markets in the promotion of efficiency and the relative lack of concern among the pro-marketeers for distributional effects. The basic reason for this is that the pro-marketeers place a very high moral premium on the freedom of the individual from government interference and take a dismal view of the possibility of government action improving anyone's welfare other than that of special and dominant interest groups. The role of government, according to them, should be limited to the assignment and enforcement of (preferably private) property rights and the subsidy (preferably not the public provision) of public goods. The anti-marketeers tend to take a dismal view of the efficiency of markets, see all-pervading external effects and public goods, want the government to improve (according to *their* lights) income and wealth distributions and to stabilize the economy at high levels of employment. For them, individual freedom may be a good thing but it is far from being the *only* good thing and can anyway, so they claim, be enhanced by government action.

Political differences also act as a *spur to invention.* If someone produces a theory whose implications are not consistent with one's own political beliefs, or some evidence that is uncomfortable, the political motive provides a spur for criticism and further theoretical and empirical work that supplements the motivation provided by purely theoretical or empirical curiosity. This does not mean that any such work is politically tainted. It is, however, a characteristic of modern progress in economics that it is interactive, even competitive, and accounts for the fact that the most common form of academic research communication is through journals rather than definitive works appearing in the shape of books. Books tend to be consolidating things that draw together theoretical and empirical work that has preceded them, usually in journal articles. The 'pursuit of truth' is a collective endeavour.

Political issues and political phenomena are also the *object of much economic study*. There are normative political issues (for example, what income redistribution should there be?) which have been usefully studied by economists. There are empirical political issues (for example, what income redistribution actually takes place?). There is also the study of political behaviour (for example, the vote maximizing theory of politicians' behaviour) and there is the study of techniques to aid political decision making (for example, cost–benefit analysis or the standard gamble for revealing preferences over alternatives). There is also, of course, an immense range of theoretical and empirical work in microeconomics and macroeconomics that is designed to inform government about the way the economy works so that the possibilities, limits and consequences of alternative policies can be assessed.

Libertarian and Socialist Attitudes

Both libertarian and socialist economists share the same basic analytical framework. This enables economists of such different political opinions as Abba Lerner and Milton Friedman to talk the same technical language, and testifies to the power of economics as a tool for use by *many* rather than by those of only a *particular* political viewpoint. Things are never as simple as a straightforward dichotomy of attitudes would suggest. None the less, some idea of the principal differences between the broad schools of economic thought can be had by considering the following checklist. It is unlikely that there is *any* libertarian or socialist who subscribes to *every* attitude attributed, for the checklist deliberately polarizes matters. Moreover, evidence does cause people to modify their views, so stylizations of the sort that follow eventually become too strained and new battle lines are drawn up. There does tend to be a rough parallel between libertarian and monetarist, and between socialist and Keynesian views. It is, however, very rough and the identification of monetarism and Keynesianism with these two schools should not be overdone.

(1) Libertarians tend to be in favour of open market allocation of nearly everything and believe, by and large, that government intervention (a) reduces efficiency (b) serves special interest groups (especially industrial and labour power concentrations) (c) reduces freedom (from interference, oppression, arbitrariness and so on) (d) serves no systematic cause of justice in income and wealth distribution. Socialists tend to believe that government policy can (a) usually improve efficiency (b) control vested interests (c) enhance freedom (from poverty, unemployment, racial and sexual discrimination) (d) promote more equitable access to basic goods (health care, education, housing and so on) and a more equal distribution of income and wealth, where equality is often taken to be synonymous with justice. This difference relates to underlying political predispositions and general empirical experiences of how government works.

(2) Related to the above tendencies is the tendency of libertarians to think that tax reductions will increase entrepreneurial and work incentives, whereas socialists tend to be sceptical on both theoretical and empirical grounds.

(3) Libertarians tend to be suspicious of public ownership as a means of promoting either equity or efficiency. Socialists often take the desirability of public ownership as axiomatically good on both counts.

(4) Libertarians tend to believe that markets clear by price adjustments, so that unemployment (for example) is either voluntary (search unemployment) or created by misguided government policies (minimum wages or sanctioned labour monopolies, for example). Socialists tend to believe that markets do not always clear (especially labour markets), that much unemployment is involuntary, and that many industries are oligopolistic with sticky prices and quantities that adjust more quickly than prices.

(5) Libertarians are sceptical about the possibility (or practicability) of fine tuning the economy, and believe that governments should run balanced budgets and that monetary policy should be orientated to the long run and operated according to a rule like 'set the growth rate of the money stock equal to the growth rate of productivity'. Socialists think that fine tuning is possible via fiscal policy and that monetary policy is unpredictable in its consequences (and is anyway relatively ineffective).

(6) Libertarians tend to believe that the interest and income elasticities of the demand for money are not so unstable and the interest elasticity of investment so low as to render monetary policy in the long run ineffective. They also believe that changing the money supply can affect aggregate demand

for final goods and services directly rather than only indirectly via interest rates and investment. Socialists tend to the opposite view.

(7) Libertarians believe that public expenditure crowds out a roughly equal amount of private expenditure, reducing the effectiveness of fiscal policy. Socialists believe that this is not the case.

(8) Libertarians tend to believe that the aggregate supply curve is vertical so that inflation results from monetary and fiscal expansion. Socialists believe that the aggregate supply curve is often flatter than this, so that expansionary policies can increase output and wealth and reduce unemployment with relatively smaller effects on the price level.

(9) Libertarians believe that the stock of money would be controllable if only the authorities adopted a minimum reserve asset ratio system. Socialists are highly sceptical.

(10) Libertarians believe that inflation is always and everywhere due to monetary mismanagement and therefore requires monetary control. Socialists see other (supply stock) causes of inflation and, hence, other cures (for example, prices and incomes policies, import quotas).

(11) Libertarians believe that there is no permanent trade-off between inflation and unemployment. Socialists believe that some reduction in unemployment can usually be had at the price of a higher inflation rate.

Most of these issues are, at least in principle, resolvable by careful empirical research. But this does not apply, of course, to the *fundamental* differences in political values. Extremists on both sides have an unfortunate tendency, however, to elevate matters that are ultimately empirical to the status of articles of faith (for example, libertarians the universal beneficence of markets and socialists the universal beneficence of public ownership of the means of production).

Discipline, Imagination and Judgement

Keynes once wrote that economics was a *way of thinking*. The principal characteristics of the compleat economist are three, and it is these that form the typical way in which economists organize their thinking: imagination, theoretical discipline, and judgement about the evidence.

For the beginner, the strains imposed by the discipline are severe and you have doubtless often failed to perceive much scope for the exercise of your imagination and judgement. Although in this book the SAQs and the case studies provide some opportunities for both of these, it is undoubtedly the case that all three talents can be fully exercised only in the context of a problem that you have to research for yourself, once you have mastered the basic tools of analysis.

The exercise of *imagination* becomes crucial when you first come to think about a problem of choice. For *whom* is it a problem? From whose perspective might you set about elucidating the issues involved? What are the objectives? Are they all equally important? What alternative means exist to solve the problem? Can one divest oneself of inherited prejudice, beliefs about what is possible and so on, in order to brainstorm imaginatively about possible objectives and alternative means? How can one select a few of the possible alternative means for more detailed investigation?

It is typically at this stage of thinking that the possibility of innovation either becomes apparent or is definitively buried for good, and this is as true of a macroeconomic problem like 'what can be done about unemployment?' as it is of an industrial problem like 'what price should I charge for this newly developed produce?' or a social policy problem like 'how shall we care for the elderly?' Whether the problem comes to you from outside in your role as adviser or consultant, or is one of your own devising, the early phases of turning a rather vaguely specified issue into a more precise one, identifying the possible courses of action, and so on, are crucial. The economist's distinctions between ends and means, objectives and constraints, normative and positive, input and output, costs and benefits, marginal and total, real and nominal, behavioural equations and identities, equilibrium and disequilibrium, and so on, are useful *general* sorting devices that help one to pick the problem apart in an imaginative and constructive fashion. At the same time it is also usually helpful to think in terms of consequences. By what measures are the outcomes of a choice to be represented? How are they to be monitored? How flexible is policy if, as nearly always happens, circumstances change?

The *discipline* comes to the fore when one goes on to develop models, predict behaviour, measure elasticities, measure inputs and outputs, estimate production functions, take account of side effects and feedbacks, measure opportunity costs, assess benefits and so on. Here one has the whole corpus of economic theory on which to draw or, if necessary, adapt and extend, and empirical results that may be taken for granted or may need to be newly discovered in the particular context in which you are working.

When tackling a problem for the first time it is nearly always a mistake to *begin* by looking up all the known facts about an issue or reading up all the past things theorists have had to say about it. This immediately *tramlines* one's thinking so that it becomes wellnigh impossible to escape from *other people's* thoughts and the facts that *other people* have thought worth collecting. It is much better (but much more challenging!) initially to speculate for oneself, discuss with one's 'clients' in the way outlined, and even to sketch out the lines along which relevant theory that one thinks will be needed might go and the type of information one thinks will be relevant. One is *then* in an excellent position to engage in literature searches, talks with other experts and so on, in the course of which it is just possible that the realization will dawn on you that you are actually coming up with something new!

Finally, *judgement*. The theory – other people's or your own – will never be perfect. What is possible will never be ideal. The relevant facts will never be sure and some may be impossible to find out. You have to use your judgement.

Is your analysis and are your results good enough for the purposes in hand? Have the matters omitted been omitted for good reasons? Would their inclusion affect your conclusions? How sensitive are your answers to changes in some of your assumptions or to variations in some of your results?

Some people seem determined to make the perfect become the enemy of the merely good. In economics that is a prescription for total helplessness, for what economists have to offer is a means of picking difficult issues apart into more manageable components, identifying things that can be quantified, quantifying some of them (such as elasticities or the size of some important quantities like costs, inflation rates, balance of payments effects and so on), separating issues that may be resolvable by evidence from those that cannot be, exploring value judgements in detail and so on. Very often, the *process* of asking such questions and thinking about them is every bit as valuable – and may be more valuable – than any solution that may be identified. This is what is meant when economists stress, as like Keynes they invariably do, the importance of seeing economics as a *mode of thinking*.

I hope that, at the end of this book, you now feel able to approach issues in the spirit of the economist's mode of thinking and have begun to cultivate your judgement, whether you incline to the libertarian or the socialist end of the political spectrum. To help you on the way, case study 36.1 contains two quotations relating to the importance of economics, one from Keynes and one from Marshall, that I have found an inspiration – as I hope you will.

Case Study 36.1 Keynes and Marshall on Economics

If the ideas are correct . . . it would be a mistake, I predict, to dispute their potency over a period of time. At the present moment people are unusually expectant of a more fundamental diagnosis; more particularly ready to receive it; eager to try it out, if it should be even plausible. But apart from this contemporary mood, the ideas of economists and political philosophers, both when they are right and when they are wrong, are more powerful than is commonly understood. Indeed the world is ruled by little else. Practical men, who believe themselves to be quite exempt from any intellectual influences, are usually the slaves of some defunct economist. Madmen in authority, who hear voices in the air, are distilling their frenzy for some academic scribbler of a few years back. I am sure that the power of vested interests is vastly exaggerated compared with the gradual encroachment of ideas. Not, indeed, immediately, but after a certain interval; for in the field of economic and political philosophy there are not many who are influenced by new theories after they are twenty-five or thirty years of age, so that the ideas which civil servants and politicians and even agitators apply to current events are not likely to be the newest. But, soon or late, it is ideas, not vested interests, which are dangerous for good or evil.

Enthusiasm for the idea in faith, in hope, and in charity is the best of human possessions; and the world owes very much to those who have been thrown off their balance by it. But, on the other hand, a responsible student of social problems must accept mankind as he finds them; and must base his estimates on that which is practicable. He must nourish the ideal in his heart; but his actions, his conversation, and even his thought must be occupied mainly with the actual: he must resist every temptation to make a short cut to the ideal. For indeed a traveller in a difficult country, who makes for his ultimate goal by a straight course, is likely to waste his time and strength and perhaps to meet disaster.

The first quotation is by John Maynard Keynes in:

J. M. Keynes (1936) *The General Theory of Employment, Interest and Money*, Macmillan, pp. 383–4.

The second is from Alfred Marshall in:

A. C. Pigou (1956) 'In memoriam: Alfred Marshall', in A. C. Pigou (ed.) *Memorials of Alfred Marshall*, Kelley and Millwan, pp. 83–4.

Answers to Self-assessment Questions

Chapter 1

1.1 To illustrate: the discipline of economics might, when applied to the topic of advertising, tackle the question 'what effects does advertising have in promoting monopoly?'; to balance of payments, ask 'what effects on employment and production do floating exchange rates have?'; to business taxes, ask 'what effect on profits, output, prices and employment will a corporation tax have?'; to education, ask 'why should the government subsidize secondary schooling?'; to equality, ask 'do income taxes on the one hand and social security benefits on the other create work disincentives?'; to housing, ask 'do owner occupiers or municipal housing tenants receive the greater subsidy?'; to illness, ask 'should health services be free of charge to patients?'; to inflation, ask 'is monetary restraint the key to controlling inflation?'; to majority voting, ask 'why is majority voting itself so often chosen as a way of making choices?'; to the truck system, ask 'why were wages paid in kind rather than cash?'.

1.2 The answer is (a). It is probably a bit early for you to have tackled this (unless you have previously done some economics). It is not (b) because lots of people study the economy (e.g. investment analysts and politicians) who are not economists. It is not (c) because some economists study only topics that are not in 'the economy'.

1.3 (a) Positive but untrue (b) positive but hard to test (c) positive but untrue (d) positive but untrue (e) positive and usually true (f) positive but untrue (you could, for example, give them free comprehensive health insurance) (g) positive and answerable (h) positive but hard to test (i) positive (many did think just that even if you disagree with the opinion they held) (j) neither positive nor normative: it is an *analytical* statement having the characteristic that Mary makes what are known as *transitive* choices (k) neither positive nor normative: it is an analytical statement showing Peter's choices to be what is called *intransitive*.

1.4 (a) 52.5 tonnes (b) 120 tonnes (c) 70 tonnes, (d) tonnes: 40, 45; 30, 35; 70, 35; 60, 55; 50, 50

(e) A *or* C. Each of these has more of both crops than B; but as A has more wheat and C more potatoes, the theory so far gives you no basis for predicting choice between them. D and E, of course, are unattainable.

(f) C. Since E will be chosen rather than A by the first postulate, and C is chosen rather than E by the factual statement, C will be chosen rather than A by the second postulate. D and E remain actually unobtainable.

(g) You need it to establish the logical link between A and C via E. The first postulate alone does not permit you to compare A and C in terms of predicting choice.

(h) You may have misspecified the technological constraint; you may have made an erroneous first or second postulate; you may have made an erroneous statement about the choice between E and C; you may be erroneously observing what you think is the actual choice.

Chapter 2

2.1 The graph is as in figure A2.1. (a) $Z = 10$ (= 180/18) (b) $X = 8$ (= 180/22.50) (c) £45 (d) $X = 2$ (= 45/22.50) (e) $Z = 2.5$ (f) £180, i.e. £90 on each – which exhausts your income. (g) All points showing a constant total expenditure on X and Z will lie on a straight line. The constraint here is £180 = $P_X X + P_Z Z$. If you let Y stand for income, this becomes $Y = P_X X + P_Z Z$ which is the general (**linear**) equation for a *budget line*, as lines such as ab are usually called. (h) $X = 12$ (i) $X = 8.4$ (j) $X = 6$, $Z = 5$ (k) $X = 4$, $Z = 5$ (l) to the right, indicating more X consumption.

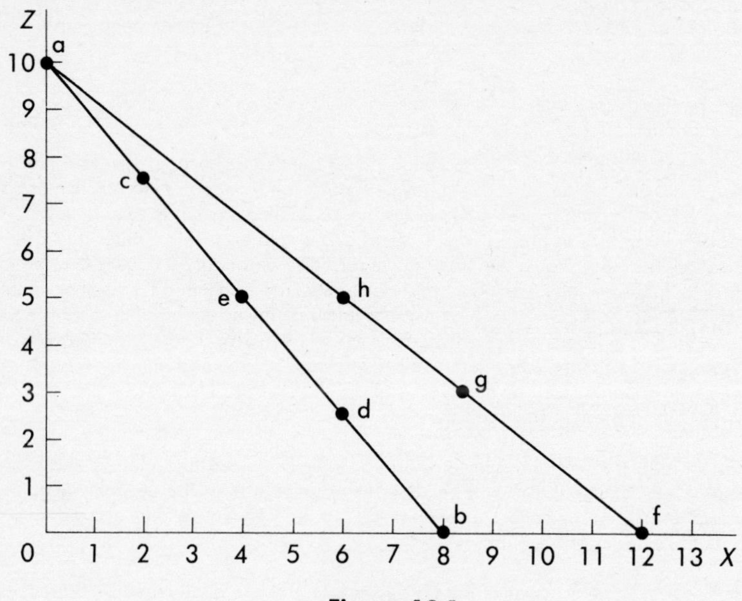

Figure A2.1

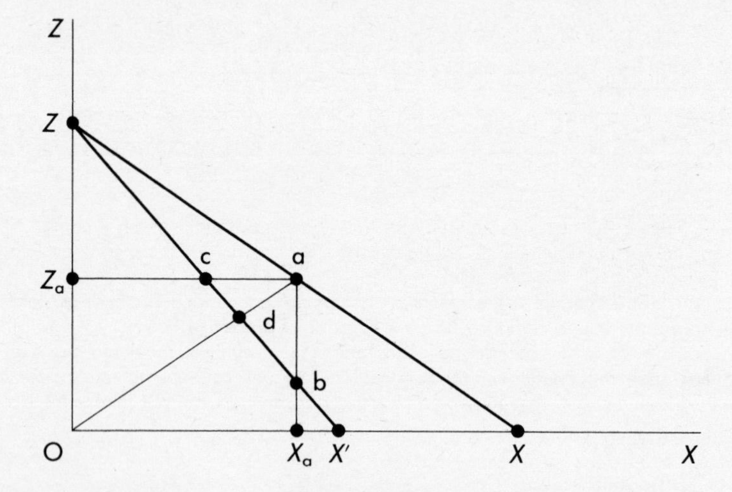

Figure A2.2

2.2 My argument for saying that extreme conservatism is irrational (or at least implausible) goes like this. Consider figure A2.2 like figure 2.1. Suppose the average individual is at point a (people being distributed along the initial *budget line* – remember this jargon word from SAQ 2.1 – $Z'X'$. Now let the price of X rise so that the new budget line becomes $Z'X''$. Initially the average person consumes OX_a and OZ_a. After the price rise this combination is impossible; a point must be chosen somewhere on $Z'X''$ which is possible with the given income and the new prices. The conservative may move to point b – being 'conservative' about X consumption but radical about Z (whose consumption will fall by the amount measured by ab). Or the individual may be conservative about Z, moving to point c. This seems strangely arbitrary and combines extreme conservatism about one form of consumption with extreme radicalness about the other. 'Proportionate conservatism' would involve each person moving on to $Z'X''$ by proportionate reductions in X and Z – on average moving from point a to point d along the ray Oa. But who behaves by doing this kind of arithmetic?

2.3 (a) Even if a person believes in the higher risks faced as a result of smoking, there is nothing in economics to say that person is irrational, since good health is not postulated to be the *only* thing in life rational people may choose.
(b) B is not irrational since there are no presumptions either that people always tell the truth or that they never change their minds.
(c) D is not irrational since there is no presumption that selfishness is more rational than self-sacrifice.
(d) E may or may not be irrational, but as it happens it is not assumed in economics that individuals make detailed calculations of this sort – or any other!
(e) Members of neither society are necessarily irrational with respect to *their* objectives.

2.4 (a) G did not violate any postulate since no postulate asserts that an economic good is characterized by a desire to use it *for oneself* (G may have collected cigarettes for smoking friends). Was I irrational to stop offering mine?
(b) Fresh air *is* a free good to those living where it is abundant. But it is not to many city dwellers, or to deep sea divers (see case study 16.3 for a rather different case).
(c) The trouble with this statement is that all the postulates relate to choices of *individuals*, whereas the department in question is a *group*. Most groups have systems of reaching a collective decision but, at root, only individuals choose (or are overridden), whether they choose rules about how to make group decisions or participate in the group's decision making procedure. (Chapter 22 discusses ways in which groups reach decisions.)
(d) As put, this statement violates postulate 3 in that it suggests that the need for health care is absolute. It also contains a *non sequitur* since, even if you decided that people ought not to be deterred by prices for care, making it free of charge is not the only way of doing it; they could, for example, be given insurance free of charge. But even if services, or insurance, were free of charge, one could never, *ever*, provide enough care for it to be a free good in the technical sense.
(e) This proposition violates postulate 3 which *specifically denies* generalized hierarchies of wants of this kind. The question is how much of some of these shall be sacrificed to obtain more of the others, and how much private consumption shall be sacrificed for more public expenditure, and *not* that one should completely satisfy one's desire for one thing before beginning to get some of another.
(f) Again, this denies substitutability. The evidence is that everyone chooses. Of course, rich people have more in total, otherwise they wouldn't be rich. But even those whose choices are tightly constrained by their limited personal resources choose.

Chapter 3

3.1 These puzzling phenomena are, in fact, all implications of the law of demand and were first shown to be such by Armen Alchian and William Allen in *University Economics: Elements of Inquiry* (London, Prentice/Hall International, 1974, pp. 70–1), the answers are in each case due to differences in the *relative* prices of the goods in question.

(a) Good quality wine in France has a higher price than *vin ordinaire*. Let good quality wine cost, say, £3 and *vin ordinaire* £1. The relative price of good wine is therefore 3:1. A bottle of wine shipped to England costs the same in transport regardless of the quality of its contents. Let this transportation and handling cost be £1 per bottle. In England, then, the prices become £4 and £2 and the relative price of good wine is 2:1. Good French bottled wine is cheaper relative to *vin ordinaire* in England than in France; therefore *relatively* more of it is predicted to be purchased than in France.

(b) Assume that any individual, when offered a choice between a crate of small wrinkled apples and a crate having the same weight of large juicy ones, will choose the large juicy ones. Since Indiana apple eaters have to pay the cost of transporting and handling apples (the same per crate regardless of the quality of contents) the *relative* price of a crate of good quality apples is lower.

(c) The cost of sending a letter has risen relative to the cost of writing it.

(d) Childless couples do not have to pay baby sitting charges. Since these are the same regardless of whether one goes to the theatre or the cinema, the *relative* cost of the more expensive theatre trip is lower for couples with children.

3.2 None is an exception:

(a) If the price of apples today is lower than that expected next week, the law of demand leads one to expect *more* to be purchased today.

(b) Expensive goods are bought more often by the rich than by others, but they still have negative slopes; if they did not, the makers of mink stoles and Rolls Royces would be able to raise their prices without limit!

(c) Drug addicts have their 'taste' for the drug continuously intensified, causing an individual's demand to rise through time; however, at any particular time, the addict's rate of consumption will rise or fall as price falls or rises.

(d) I might, in fact, take another holiday a year, or still only one but a longer one, or stay in a better quality hotel, or . . . .

3.3 (a) Price of Scotch. This causes a move *along* a demand curve; any of the others might cause a *shift* of the curve.

(b) The first four are normal, the second three are inferior.

(c) The substitutes are fish and meat, cabbage and broccoli, theatre shows and television shows. The rest are complements.

3.4 (a) 150 kg, 300 kg, 750 kg, 1200 kg

(b) £2100 (£7 × 300 kg), £2700, £1200. Note how total expenditure rises as price falls, then stabilizes and then falls as price falls still further.

(c) £2400, £5400, £6000. To see this, note that the amount someone in the community is prepared to pay for just one kilogram per week is £9, very slightly less for another kilogram, and so on until the price that the community will pay for 300 rather than 299 kg is £7. The sum of these values for the 300 kg is £2400. It is equal to the area under the demand curve up to a rate of consumption of 300 kg, which can easily be calculated by adding the amount *actually* spent (the market value) at that price (£7 × 300 kg = £2100), shown by the rectangle in figure 3.4, to the value of the triangle above it (£2 × 300/2 = £300). Total willingness to pay is a topic addressed in greater depth later on so, if you have not quite grasped it in this SAQ, do not worry.

(d) 300 kg. The community has to pay £200 for the privilege but, on the assumption that this reduction in disposable income is so distributed among members of the community that their demands for sheep meat are not affected in any significant way, they will continue to purchase the amount indicated by the group demand curve.

(e) £2300. Note that this is less than the £2400 value placed on the meat. Had the licence fee exceeded £300, then no meat would have been bought.

Chapter 4

4.1 (a) (4/−1) (9/14) = −2.57; and similarly, −1.27, −0.67, −0.32, −0.09
(b) (4/1) (0/50) = 0.00; and similarly, −0.19, −0.47, −0.92, −1.78

4.2 (a) 5, 14, 48, 95
(b) −10 (9/10) = −9.0; and similarly, −19.0, −1.22.

4.3 (a) 0, £500, £375
(b) £100, £100, £100. This curve has a constant elasticity of demand that is equal to −1.00 at every price.
(c) Wrong in general: it depends on the elasticity.

4.4 If carefully done, the elasticity will be equal to −2.00, which is the power to which P_X is raised in the equation that generates this curve.

4.5 (a) −10, 0, 10, 30, 190. The −10 is a 'theoretical' result since negative consumption is not possible – unless you interpret the Engel curve to show the demand for a *stock* of X as income rises, in which case negative numbers may be taken to represent *disinvestment* in stocks. The point is that a linear Engel curve has meaning only over a relevant range of Y.
(b) +60, +2.0, +1.05

4.6 (a)

$$Y = P_X X + P_Z Z$$

says that income Y is equal to expenditure on good X (the amount of X purchased multiplied by its price) plus expenditure on good Z. Similarly:

$$\Delta Y = P_X \Delta X + P_Z \Delta Z$$

which says that a change in income must be equal to the change in expenditure on X and Z. Now divide through by ΔY to get

$$\frac{\Delta Y}{\Delta Y} = \frac{P_X \Delta X}{\Delta Y} + \frac{P_Z \Delta Z}{\Delta Y} = 1$$

Now multiply the first term in the middle by (X/X) (Y/Y) (which is obviously equal to unity) and the second term in the middle by (Z/Z) (Y/Y) (which is again obviously equal to unity) to get

$$\left(\frac{P_X \Delta X}{\Delta Y}\right)\left(\frac{X}{X}\frac{Y}{Y}\right) + \left(\frac{P_Z \Delta Z}{\Delta Y}\right)\left(\frac{Z}{Z}\frac{Y}{Y}\right) = 1$$

and rearrange each term to get

$$\left(\frac{P_X X}{Y}\right)\left(\frac{\Delta X}{\Delta Y}\frac{Y}{X}\right) + \left(\frac{P_Z Z}{Y}\right)\left(\frac{\Delta Z}{\Delta Y}\frac{Y}{Z}\right) = 1$$

What does this mean? The second and fourth bracketed terms are, of course, the income elasticities for X and Z respectively. The first bracketed term is expenditure on X divided by income, or the fraction of income spent on X. The third bracketed term is likewise the fraction of income spent on Z. Hence the sum of income elasticities weighted by the fraction each good occupies in total expenditure must equal unity.

(b) +2.80. Let R_C and R_S be the proportions of income spent on consumption and saving respectively, and ε_C and ε_S represent the income elasticities of consumption and saving. Then you have $R_C\varepsilon_C + R_S\varepsilon_S = 1$, whence $(0.9)\ (0.8) + (0.1)\ (\varepsilon_S) = 1.0$.

4.7 That they were perfect substitutes for one another; as far as an individual's choices are concerned he or she may as well have one as the other.

Chapter 5

5.1 Only (a) is correct. Utility can be, but is not necessarily to be, identified with 'satisfaction' (whatever that is) or 'happiness' or 'usefulness'. As table 5.1 makes clear, any numbers (positive *or* negative) that preserve the order correctly will do as utility numbers.

5.2 (a) (1) falling (2) falling (3) falling

(b) 28 utils, assuming that the initial utility numbers were assigned in such a fashion that they can be added up. Note also that these are *my* utils – not the elderly person's, even though that person doubtless has preferences which could be represented by a set of numbers as mine can (not likely to reflect quite the same preferences, however). Don't make the mistake of supposing that utility implies selfishness: both saints who love their fellow men and misanthropes who hate them have preferences about *other people's* consumption and characteristics, not just their own.

5.3 (a) Because doubling or adding a constant to a scale preserves any falling, rising or constant marginal utility in the original.

(b) True.

(c) They are equally good *ordinal* measures but they are not equally good *cardinal* measures.

(d) True. The equation linking them is D = 0.5B + 1. Also note that D = A + 1; D = 0.5E.

(e) False. The statement is as silly as saying that 1 kg of wheat is 0.001 times as heavy as 1000 g of wheat.

(f) True only for scale C and, moreover, only if scale C is to be interpreted as a ratio scale rather than, for example, simply an indicator of rank order.

(g) False. Cardinal utility does not necessarily imply that there is no diminishing marginal utility, though it does imply that the utility number, say 135, has twice the utility of 67.5, and not just 'more'.

5.4 (a) 0.2. Since $P_X MU_Y = MU_X$ and $P_X = 50$, $MU_X = 10$, only $MU_Y = 0.2$ per penny ensures equality.

(b) Nothing, as long as *all* utility numbers are doubled. Just as it matters little if one weighs in kilograms or grams, pounds or ounces.

(c) Rises from 10 to 20 utils, as it must to keep $MU/P = 0.2$.

(d) +0.5.

(e) Use the elasticity formula $\eta = (dX/dP)\ (P/X) = 1.5$. You need to find dX, given that $dP = -5$, $P = 50$ and $X = 2$. This yields $dX = 0.3$. Therefore after the price fall, $X = 2 + 0.3 = 2.3$. Expenditure is now 2.3 kg × £0.45 = £1.035. Dropping the halfpenny, expenditure rises to £1.03 from £1.00.

(f) If expenditure of £1 initially represents 1 per cent of income, then £1.03 is 1.03 per cent of income (which has not, of course, changed) and the percentage of income left over to spend on other things falls from 99 per cent to 98.97 per cent, or by 3p.

5.5 (a) Consumption falls from 20 kg to 15 kg per week and expenditure rises from £20 to £22.50. Income left over for other purchases falls from £80 to £77.50 – a fall from 80 per cent to

77.5 per cent in income available for other purchases. If anything, this will increase the marginal utility of income MU_Y, which will reinforce the effect of the rising price on the demand for food (recall that the individual always keeps $P_X MU_Y = MU_X$).

(b) Let Y stand for money income. Then you have:

$$Y = P_X X + P_Z Z = (£5 \times 20) + (£2 \times 50) = £200$$

At the new P_X, the cost of the original bundle of X and Z is $(£2.50 \times 20) + (£2 \times 50) = £150$. The reduction in money income required is therefore £50.

Chapter 6

6.1 Four triples are intransitive:

B_1 **P** B_3 and B_3 **P** B_4 but B_4 **P** B_1
B_1 **P** B_3 and B_3 **P** B_5 but B_5 **P** B_1
B_2 **P** B_3 and B_3 **P** B_4 but B_4 **P** B_2
B_2 **P** B_3 and B_3 **P** B_5 but B_5 **P** B_2

6.2 (a) $X = 10$ (b) $Z = 5$ (c) $X = 20$ and $Z = 10$ (d) -0.5

6.3 (a) £100 (b) £10
(c) Nothing: it remains where it is. Let the proportionate increase in prices and money income be a. Then multiplying the relevant terms in the equation for the budget line,

$$Z = \frac{Y}{P_Z} - \frac{P_X}{P_Z} X$$

by a yields

$$Z = \frac{aY}{aP_Z} - \frac{aP_X}{aP_Z} X$$

which, when the a are cancelled, leaves the original equation.

6.4 (a) In figure A6.1 the budget line $G = 10 - 0.5M$ is the original budget line found by substituting the given values in the equation

$$G = \frac{Y}{P_G} - \frac{P_M}{P_G} M$$

(b) This is the budget line labelled $G = 15 - 0.5M$.

(c) This is the budget line labelled $G = 15 - 1.0M$.

(d) One cannot tell without knowing the initial point chosen on the original budget line. For example, if B_1 were initially chosen, the new budget line ($G = 15 - 1.0M$) enables you to move to a position on the new budget line that was not previously available – such as B_2. In this case you will be better off. If, on the other hand, you were originally at B_3, this is no longer available to you. If you move to B_4 then you will be worse off since B_4 was previously available when you chose B_3. If you move to B_2 you may be either better or worse off, since B_2 was not previously available.

(e) The intersection point can be found either by inspection of the (carefully drawn) diagram or by setting the two budget line equations equal to one another, namely

$$G = 15 - 1.0M = 10 - 0.5M$$

and solving for M. This gives $M = 10$ and $G = 5$, and is labelled point B_5. B_5 has been revealed to be preferred to all points along the original budget line like B_1 and B_3. Hence, *if you change consumption at all*, it will be to that section of the new budget line ($G = 15 - 1.0M$) to the left of B_5 and you will be better off (e.g. at B_2). If you do not change, but continue to consume B_5, then you are not in real terms worse off. In general, therefore, the combined price and income change cannot have made you worse off and may have made you better off – if your most preferred point was initially B_5 when your income was only £100.

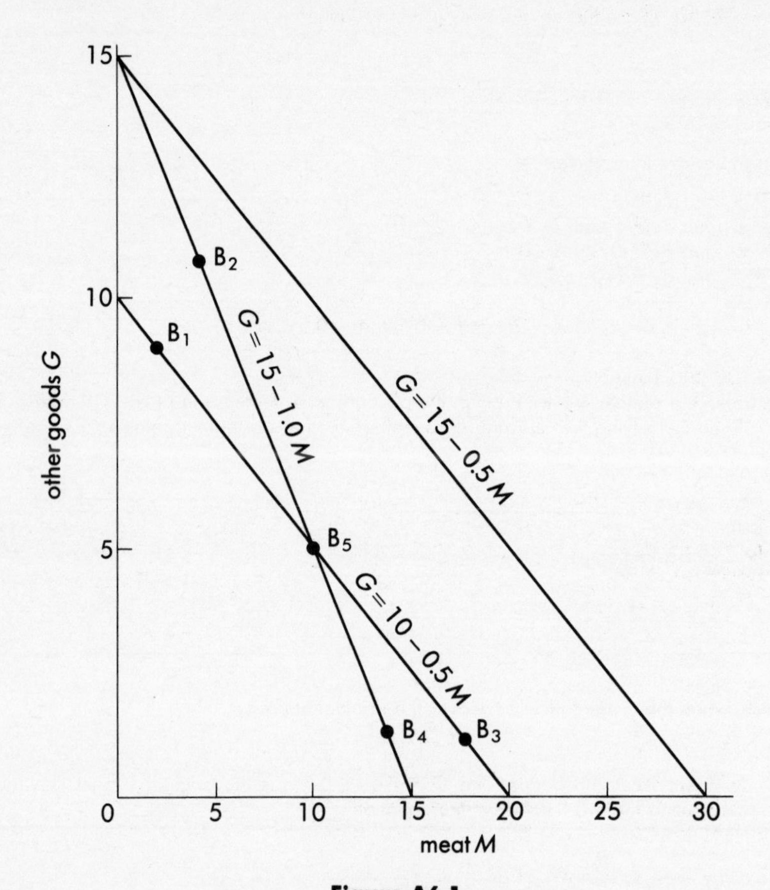

Figure A6.1

6.5 (a) Any save the set 5: this assigns the same number to B_2 and B_3, indicating they are equal in rank. (You are indifferent between B_2 and B_3.) But they are not, since B_3 **P** B_2. Revealed preference theory does not permit any ties (or indifference) in a set of ranked choices. It uses *strong* rather than *weak orderings.*

(b) Ordinal.

(c) Yes, B_3 **P** B_1. In a comparison of B_1 and B_2, B_2 **P** B_1, since B_2 is chosen when B_1 is available along the second budget line. When budget line 3 applies, B_3 **P** B_2. Therefore, by transitivity, B_3 **P** B_1.

6.6 (a) £100 (b) £90 (c) Rise

(d) Relative price of Z rose (or that of X fell)

(e) Can't tell, even though your income has risen. The two situations can be represented in figure

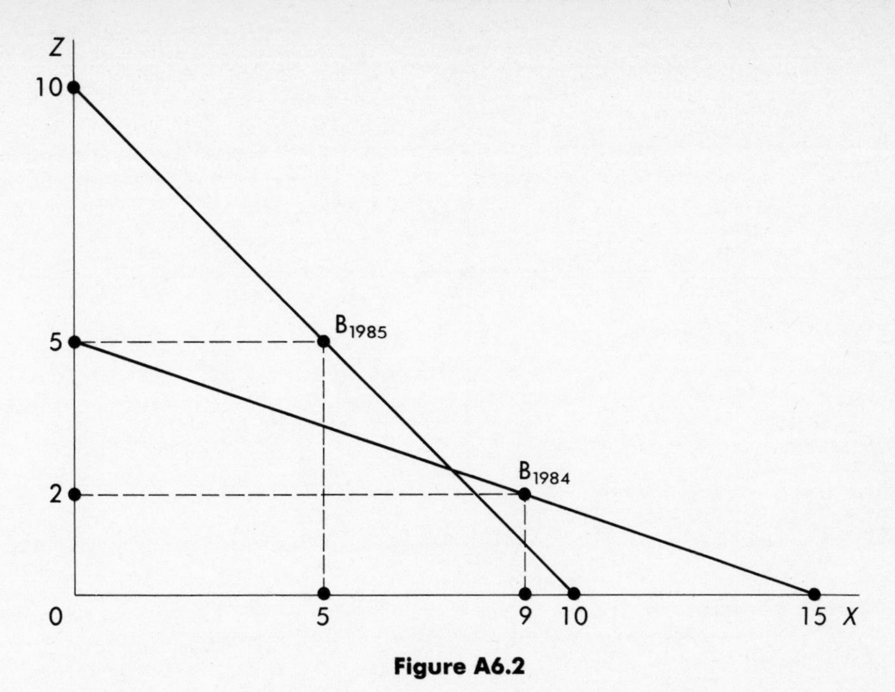

Figure A6.2

A6.2, where B_{1984} and B_{1985} are the bundles consumed in each year and the two budget lines are as drawn. At the income and prices of 1985, B_{1985} was chosen but B_{1984} was not available (at 1985 prices, 2 of *Z* and 9 of *X* could not be afforded out of 1985 income). Conversely, however, in 1984 B_{1985} was not available (at 1984 prices 5 of *Z* and 5 of *X* could not be afforded out of 1984 income). So neither bundle has been revealed preferred to the other.

Chapter 7

7.1 (a) 6 (b) 3 (all bundles between which one is indifferent must have the same utility number) (c) B_1 **P** B_3 (d) B_1 **I** B_3 (e) B_1 **P** B_3 (f) B_1 **P** B_3 (g) B_1 **P** B_3 (h) B_1 **P** B_3 (i) B_1 **P** B_3 (j) B_1 **I** B_3

7.2 (a) B_1 **I** B_2; B_1 **P** B_7; B_2 **P** B_5; B_5 **P** B_6

(b) $U(B_6) = 10$; $U(B_2) = 200$

(c) $U(B_3)$ must be less than 200, so it cannot be 205. $U(B_5)$ could be 199, as ordinal utility requires only that it exceed 10 and be less than 200.

7.3 (a) Consider point a in figure A7.1. The horizontal and vertical lines through it define four areas of space: in region I all combinations are preferred to point a (since there is more of at least one good and no less of the other). In region III all points are inferior to point a. If an indifference curve exists at all, therefore, it must pass through regions IV and II – and thence slope down from left to right.

(b) Convexity. (Plot the three bundles on a graph and see for yourself.)

7.4 (a) Because the indifference curve on which they lie (which happens to be the same one) has a lower utility number than that at point a: these points are less preferred.

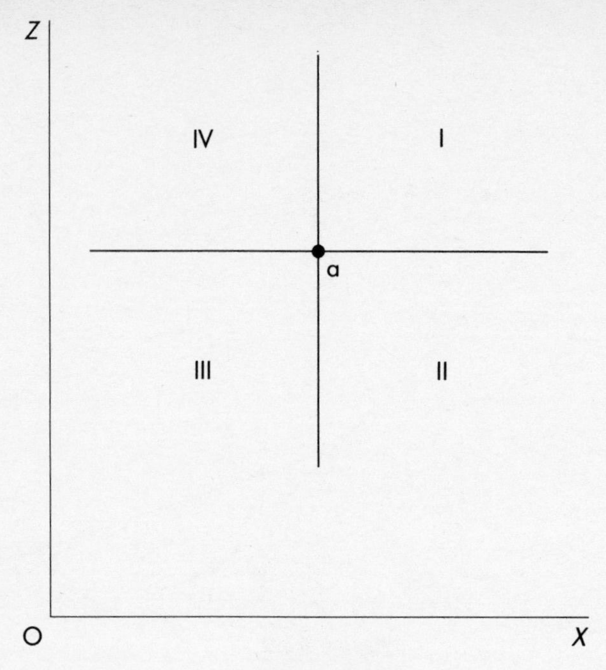

Figure A7.1

(b) In Marshall's theory you had $P_X/P_Z = MU_X/MU_Z$ (recall chapter 5). In Hicks's you have $P_X/P_Z = \mathrm{d}Z/\mathrm{d}X$. Since along an indifference curve $MU_X\mathrm{d}X = MU_Z\mathrm{d}Z$, it follows that the ratio of $\mathrm{d}Z$ and $\mathrm{d}X$ is an observable representation of the ratio of the marginal utilities of X and Z but without using any of the strong assumptions made by Marshall.

7.5 (a) Because they have backward bending (not merely upward sloping) sections.
(b) No.
(c) Yes.
(d) Yes.
(e) No.
(f) No.

7.6 (a) See figure A7.2. The initial position is point a. An inferior good must have point b to the left of point c.
(b) True for normal goods, false for inferior goods.

7.7 (a) Z is a good and X is a bad.
(b) Z and X are partially substitutable goods.
(c) Z is a bad and X a good.
(d) Both Z and X are bads.
(e) X is a good; Z is a non-good.
(f) Z is a good; X is a non-good.
(g) Z and X are complements: increases in *both* are required if utility is to increase (e.g. shoes and shoelaces).
(h) Z and X are *perfect* substitutes; there is no diminishing rate of substitution of one for the other.

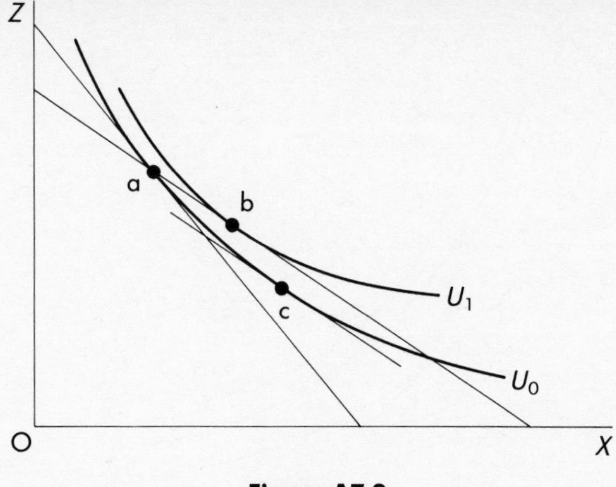

Figure A7.2

Chapter 8

8.1 Essay answer. Some of the criteria that I would use to evaluate the merits of rival theories would be:

(a) does any one make assumptions that are more often violated in reality than others?

(b) is any one less economical in its use of assumptions?

(c) does any one have other implications for what will be observed (other than the specific phenomenon it explains) that are violated by the evidence?

(d) does any one of them contain internal logical contradictions?

(e) is any one of them inconsistent with other theories that have been found to be empirically reliable?

(f) does any one of them have a less rich set of empirically valid implications than the others?

Any theory that scores a 'Yes' on each of these is plainly a worse theory (on my criteria). The problem of judgement is plainly toughest when theories get different mixes of 'No' and 'Yes' answers. You may well, of course, have produced other criteria than these, but the ones suggested seem to me to be the main ones most scientists would want to use. They amount to some value judgements about what makes for a *good theory*.

8.2 (a) Initially the individual is at point a on figure A8.1. If income rises from Y_0 to Y_1 the new tangency for an income elastic good must be a point such as b *to the right* of a point a on a higher indifference curve (U_2 rather than U_0). The question asks what happens to the *MV* of X_0 consumption. This is shown by the slope of U_1 at point c: the *MRS* at point c shows the maximum amount of *Z* the individual will sacrifice for a little more of *X*. The slope of U_1 at point c is steeper than that of U_0 at point a, so the maximum amount that will be sacrificed has risen: *MV* has therefore risen.

(b) *MV* falls.

(c) *MV* remains the same if the individual is free to take as much *X* as is wished at the going price.

8.3 (a) £20 (b) £10 (c) £200 (d) £300 (e) £100

8.4 (a) Value in use: 20, 38, 54, 68, 80, 90, 98, 104, 108, 110
All-or-nothing value: 20, 19, 18, 17, 16, 15, 14, 13, 12, 11

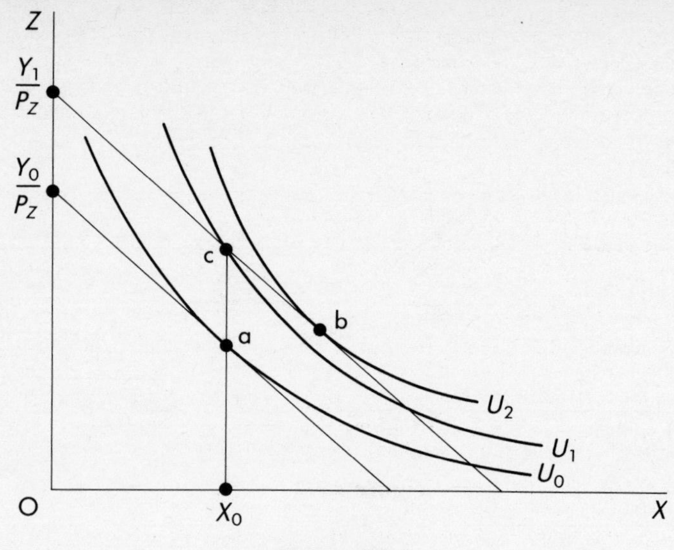

Figure A8.1

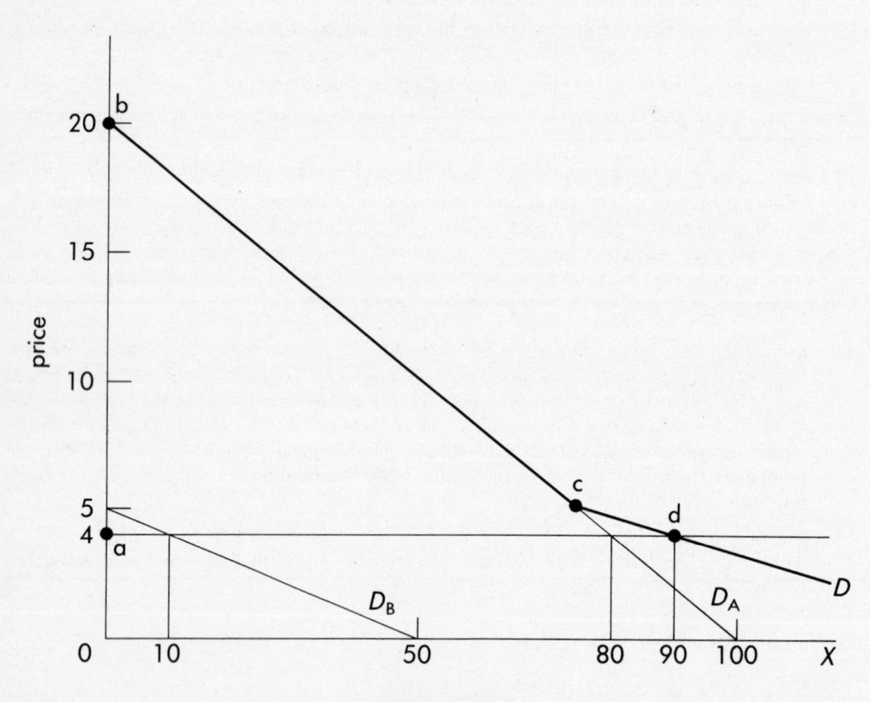

Figure A8.2

(b) They are equal in area. One measure of value in use is area ObaX_1 (the area under the demand curve). Another measure is OP_2hX_1 (the maximum that could be got by a monopolist selling on an all-or-nothing basis). The two areas have area OP_2iaX_1 in common, leaving the two triangles P_2bi and iha which must therefore be equal in area.

(c) 1 38
2 38
3 None: the membership fee exceeds the consumer's surplus at £1 a cassette.
4 The first offer leaves you with a consumer's surplus of £361 − £25 = £336. The second gives a consumer's surplus of £324. You therefore join the club with the membership fee. (You probably figured out for yourself that the demand curve is given by the equation $X = 40 - 2P$).

8.5 (a) 1 The diagram, compressed, is as given in figure A8.2, where the heavy line is the combined demand of A and B (you can show it in three panels, one for A, one for B, and one for A plus B, if you like).
2 A's consumer's surplus is £640, B's is £5.
3 The total surplus is £645, which is also the area abcd.

(b) 1 4,999,000 litres
2 5,000,000 litres
3 None, as long as the charge is not greater than any one consumer's surplus.
4 If heating costs vary directly with hot water consumed, cold water taps are more likely to be left running.

8.6 (a) Because only at P_E does the demand of the two individuals exactly equal the available stock.

(b) 1 In equilibrium, $X_A + X_B = 80$. Substituting the demand equations into this equilibrium condition, you have

$$\begin{aligned}(100 - 5P) + (50 - 2P) &= 80\\ 150 - 7p &= 80\\ 7P &= 70\\ P &= 10\end{aligned}$$

2 A has 50, B has 30.
3 A's value in use is £640 before trade and £750 after; B's value in use is £600 before trade and £525 after. For trade voluntarily to occur, B must be compensated by A by at least £75 (which is clearly possible since A gains £110). Before exchange the combined consumers' surpluses amounted to £1240 and, after exchange, they amounted to £1275: the difference is excess value in use over and above the minimum required to compensate B.
4 If you think it a good thing for value in use to be maximized, and if no one is adversely affected by the exchange, and if you are not concerned that exchange may increase inequality of X consumption while reducing the inequality of other types of consumption through the compensation one must pay the other, then you may conclude that exchange is a 'good thing'.
5 Since tastes and incomes usually differ, voluntary exchange is unlikely to promote equality of consumption of the good or service exchanged.

8.7 (a) 1 They would both pass through the vertical axis at P rather than at P_B and P_A.
2 They would also both pass through P on the vertical axis.
3 Each would pass through P on the vertical axis.
4 Exactly where they were previously located.

(b) Setting $X_B^T = X_A^T$ and solving for P, you have

$$\begin{aligned}50 - 2P &= 20 + 4P\\ 6P &= 30\\ P &= 5\end{aligned}$$

8.8 (a) Yes.

(b) Since willingness to pay is dependent, among other things, on ability to pay, the rich have in general a higher value in use for goods than the poor. In a costlessly operating market, however, anyone who engages in some consumption of X (rich or poor) will adjust to the *same marginal value* of X.

(c) If by an efficient allocation one means an allocation that it is not possible to depart from without imposing some *uncompensated* losses of value in use (this is a definition of efficiency that implies that the exchange equilibria discussed in this chapter are efficient) then it is quite possible to judge an efficient allocation to be an 'unfair' one. It may be unfair because, for example, one does not 'deserve' to be where one is, or because fairness is identified with equality, or because the process of getting to an efficient allocation may have been unfair, and so on.

Chapter 9

9.1 (a) A production function shows the maximum *rate* of output that can be obtained from various combinations of *rates* of inputs. The emphasis on *rate* means that the production function relates to so much output or input per hour, day, week, year etc. It is to be distinguished, particularly on the input side, from *stocks* of inputs. Thus, on 31 December 1985 a person may own a stock of X machines valued at £Y. The production function, however, counts as an input the number of machine-hours per week or machine-weeks per year etc.

(b) An isoquant is a line connecting *equal* maximum output rates attainable from various combinations of input rates.

9.2 2.96, 3.26, 3.51, 4.93, 23.21

9.3 (a) 1 6.3 2 16.2 3 653.0 4 19.0

(b) 1 Increasing 2 decreasing 3 increasing 4 constant

9.4

A	X	MP_A	TC	AC	MC
1	5	5	10	2.0	2.0
2	12	7	17	1.4	1.0
3	20	8	24	1.2	0.9
4	27	7	31	1.1	1.0
5	32	5	38	1.2	1.4
6	34	2	45	1.3	3.5

Don't forget to add in the cost of B to the cost calculations! Note that in this case, MP_B rises and then falls, that the average cost of output falls and then rises, as does marginal cost too.

9.5 (a) 1.43 (the increase in output, 10 of X, is divided by the increase in input, 7 of B).

(b) An increase from zero to 3 of B raises output by 10, so the marginal product is, on average, 3.33 in this range. An increase in B from 3 to 10 raises output a further 10, so marginal product in this range is on average 1.43 – lower than before. An increase in B from 10 to 15 raises output by 10, so marginal productivity is on average 2 (now rising). An increase in B from 15 to 20 leaves output the same, so marginal product is zero on average. An increase in B from 20 to 25 reduces output by 10, so marginal product is negative and on average equal to -2.0 in this range.

(c) The area to the right of the horizontal part of the isoquant map.

(d) The area above the vertical part of the isoquant map.

9.6 Output rate rises by 0.4 per cent, which is what the elasticity coefficient says will happen.

9.7 Poor *growth* must be explained in terms of *increasing* overmanning and underproduction, not their absolute levels. One rarely hears the argument that the UK suffers from a *faster* rate of increase in overmanning and underproduction than other countries. Of course, it is possible that absolutely high overmanning and underproduction may reduce entrepreneurship and technical innovation. However, these mechanisms are rarely spelled out. In actual fact there is no empirical evidence for relatively high rates of increase of overmanning and underproduction in the UK. So slow growth in the UK must be explained in some other way.

9.8 (a) Wrong! This statement muddles up stocks and flows. The appropriate price of capital is not the purchase price (or the replacement cost, or the interest charges) of machines, buildings or land. It is the *price per unit per period*, for example what a firm or productive institution would have to pay per hour to rent an item of capital or, if it already owned the item, the price per hour it could get if it rented it out to the highest bidder.

(b) Nearly right! The definition should be stated in terms of quantities per period to be completely correct.

(c) Right, as long as input prices remain constant. Fewer inputs per unit of output can, however, mean that average cost will rise if, as more inputs are used, their prices rise more than enough to offset the increasing returns to scale.

Chapter 10

10.1 (a) No valuable alternative uses are lost other than the value of the hired person's leisure time which, though likely to be positive, is unlikely to be worth £80. Opporunity cost is probably less than £80.

(b) Correct.

(c) Wrong. The cost should include the value of the land as garden – or any higher alternative use that may be perceived.

(d) Correct. The fish and water costs are genuine opportunity costs, commonly referred to as 'external' costs since they are not borne by the firm via market prices or taxation, and thus recognized as costs.

(e) Correct. The value of the services yielded by housing has fallen by £15 million.

(f) Wrong. The cost should include the forgone earnings that the student would have obtained as an estimate of the output he/she would have produced. Do *not* include board and lodging, as these (or roughly the same) expenditures would have been incurred anyway and so are not an opportunity cost of going to university.

10.2 Opportunity cost is 4 utils (cooking dinner is the highest valued alternative action).

10.3 (a) Although it is true that the expenditure on the site is a sunk cost, the site will still have valuable alternative uses. The most highly valued of these should be included as a cost (minimally its current market value).

(b) 1 Wrong. The opportunity cost is what the airline had to pay to bid the aircraft away from whomever valued it most highly of the unsuccessful bidders (including its previous owner). £0.5 million may well be a reasonable estimate of this.

2 No, it was talking economic (and commercial) nonsense. The £0.4 million it can get by operating the plane is more than the £0.25 million it would get by selling it.

10.4 (a) *MC* does not pass through the lowest point of *AC*.

(b) Nothing.

(c) *AC* cannot be constant if total cost is rising at an increasing rate (which is what the *MC* curve says).

(d) *MC* should pass through *AC*'s lowest point when it is rising, not falling.

10.5 The curves are as in figure A10.1. The marginal cost curve is perfectly elastic and the average cost descends from infinity to equal marginal cost at infinitely high rates of output.

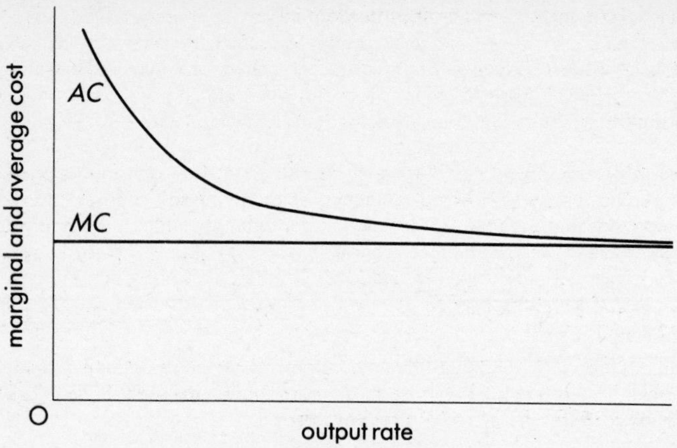

Figure A10.1

10.6 (a) False. Look carefully at figure 10.12.
(b) True.
(c) True.
(d) True. They are the *same* at tangency but *SRAC* exceeds *LRAC* at all other output rates.

10.7 Answers given as SAQ proceeds.

Chapter 11

11.1

Z	X
1000	0
750	1000
600	1600
500	2000
375	2500
250	3000
0	4000

11.2

factory 1	$Z = 1{,}000 - 0.25X$,	$2X = Z$, $X =$ 444.5,	$Z =$ 889.0
factory 2	$Z = 2{,}000 - X$	$2X = Z$, $X =$ 666.5,	$Z =$ 1,333.0
factory 3	$Z = 2{,}000 - 2X$,	$2X = Z$, $X =$ 500.0,	$Z =$ 1,000.0
factory 4	$Z = 8{,}000 - 0.8X$	$2X = Z$, $X =$ 2,857.0,	$Z =$ 5,714.0
factory 5	$Z = 14{,}000 - 1.33X$,	$2X = Z$, $X =$ 4,200.0,	$Z =$ 8,400.0
Total output		$X =$ 8,668.0,	$Z =$ 17,336.0

11.3 See table 11.3.

11.4 (a) The desired total output ratio is 3 of X for every Z. Factories 1, 4 and 2 between them produce 16,500 of X; factory 3 produces 2000 of Z. Given that factory 5 has outputs X_5 and Z_5, and that, overall, there are to be 3 of X for every Z, then

$$16{,}000 + X_5 = 3\,(2000 + Z_5) \qquad (1)$$

Factory 5's production possibilities are given by

$$Z_5 = 14{,}000 - 1.33X_5 \tag{2}$$

Using equation (1) you get

$$X_5 - 3Z_5 = -10{,}000 \tag{3}$$

and using equation (2)

$$4X_5 + 3Z_5 = 42{,}000 \tag{4}$$

Adding equations (3) and (4) you get $5X_5 = 32{,}000$ and hence $X_5 = 6400$. Multiplying equation (3) by 4 and subtracting from equation (4), you get $Z_5 = 5467$.

(b) 1 If employee 2 does the invoicing, 2 will be able to spend some time loading 100 packages which, with employee 1's loading, makes a total of 600 packages loaded. If employee 1 does the invoicing, 1 will be able to load 375 packages which, with employee 2's loading, makes a total of only 575 packages. Employee 2 should invoice.

2 Employee 2.

3 Employee 1: 1 is, in absolute terms, better at *both* loading and invoicing.

Note that the efficient allocation of jobs hinges on who has the *comparative* advantage, that is, the lowest marginal opportunity cost. Each has a comparative advantage: 1 in loading, 2 in invoicing.

11.5 Since increasing (say) X output would involve increasing amounts of inputs per unit produced, increasing amounts of inputs would have to be withdrawn from Z production for each additional unit of X rather than, as is assumed, a constant amount. Hence the boundary will bend down as more X is produced, and it will be concave to the origin.

11.6 (a) Country 1. An X costs 1.5 of Z in forgone output, whereas for country 2 it costs 2.0 of Z.

(b) Country 2. One unit of Z costs 0.5 of X in forgone output, whereas for country 1 it costs 0.67 of X.

(c) Country 1 will specialize in X production, producing only X with a total output of 20,000. Country 2 will specialize in Z, producing 20,000. Without trade, 1 would produce and consume 12,000 of each and 2 would produce and consume 6667 of each. Thus, by specializing, total output rises from 18,667 of each to 20,000 of each. If these are the only traders they will have to agree a price for X and Z, but there are many price ratios that lie between their respective marginal rates of transformation, at which both will gain.

(d) Country 3 has a comparative advantage in X compared with country 2 and in Z compared with country 1.

Chapter 12

12.1 (a) 1 The opportunity cost of caring for the elderly at home would rise as the earnings opportunities of women rise. The amount of family care devoted to the elderly (and all dependants) would tend to fall. The demand for external help would rise, as would the demand for institutional care for the elderly in publicly and privately provided 'homes for the elderly'.

2 Rise. As future employment opportunities for females increased it would pay families to equip their children – female as well as male – to take advantage of a more open job market.

3 Rise as the opportunity cost of female time rises: capital services (automatic washing machines, dish washers etc.) tend to be substituted for labour time. Video recorders would become more valued as the flexibility of female TV viewing time at home

decreased. These effects are all *independent* of any increase in family income which may further enhance their demand.

4 Adult males would take a greater share as the *relative* costs of their time fell in home based activity.

(b) 1 There are almost certainly strong bio-evolutionary reasons for the existence of loving relationships. There are also, however, some economic ones. Family production is *team* production even though each member may specialize in particular tasks according to comparative advantage (productivity at various tasks inside and outside the home). With team production there is always a problem of ensuring that each does his or her appointed share and does so as efficiently as possible. In business firms, this requires the performance of team members to be monitored by supervisors, charge hands, and so on (whose performance likewise needs monitoring) and rewards or penalties as appropriate to be devised. In the family, love can substitute for these costly procedures. If each cares about the welfare of the others, each has a reduced incentive to shirk, to dispose of family wealth selfishly outside the family and so on. Thus the efficiency of family production of the things that matter to the family rises. Thus, love, no matter how desirable for its own sake, serves a useful economic function.

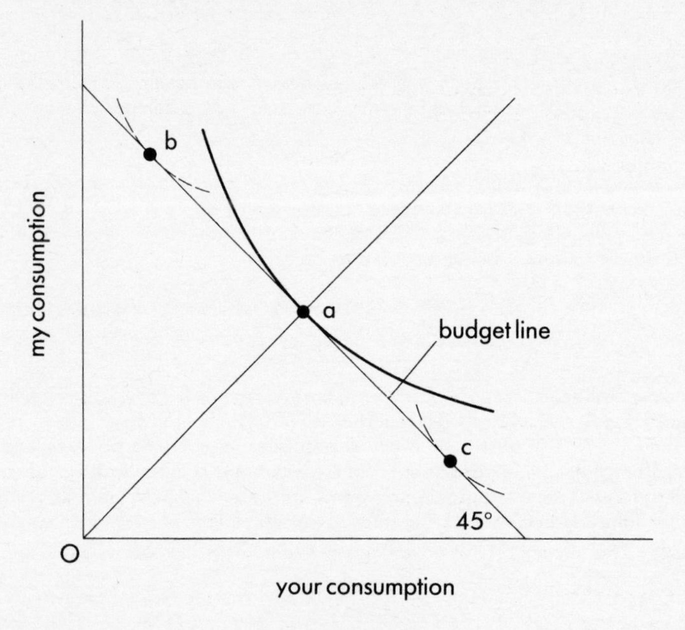

Figure A12.1

2 If I love you, your consumption and other aspects of your life affect me. I prefer you to be better off. Put in economic jargon, my utility is higher if you have more leisure, income, meals out and so on. Thus, even if I am formally entitled to the family income I will want to share it with you. In figure A12.1 the budget line shows the family income. The vertical axis measures my consumption and the horizontal axis measures yours. If I care as much for you as I do for myself, one of my indifference curves will be tangential to the budget line at the halfway point a. If you have the same love for me as I for you, all is well.

Suppose we each love ourself rather more than the other. Then I will have a tangency at somewhere like point b and you at point c and, despite our love, there will be conflict over who gets how much. If you love me more than I you, we may share a tangency at b and we will agree a division between us. Alternatively if I love you more than you me, we may agree on point c, where both of us may have a common tangency. We may also locate at points like b and c if one has an agreed greater need for income than the other (say one is disabled). Note the problem of 'too much' love; if I want to locate at point c and you at point b we may quarrel about how we share our income – just (though the character of the argument will be different) as when I preferred point b and you point c. You can amuse yourself by now hypothesizing the existence of 'hate' so that one person's utility is a *decreasing* function of another's well-being!

12.2 (a) Sometimes it is taken as axiomatic – particularly by Marxist economists, but sometimes also by neoclassical economists who use the kind of analysis in this book. As presented, however, in the preceding pages, profit maximizing is a tendency produced by the environment in which managers operate.

(b) Broadly, when there is competition for the ownership of firms and when there is competition in the market for the firms' outputs.

(c) The difficulty with charitable activity of this sort is that, after you are dead and stray dogs are still around, neither you (being dead) nor they (being mere dogs) are in a position to enforce your wishes. Nor, in the event that the problem of stray dogs has been licked by that time, is it clear what should become of your gift. For these, and other reasons the conditions that control those who administer charitable trusts are tightly specified by law and monitored by a special agency called the Charity Commissioners. A trust that was profit seeking would have a difficult conflict of interest between its owners (who would want to maximize their wealth) and your wishes (which may mean, say, maximizing the number of dogs taken into an acceptable type of care), and few would trust such an outfit with their gifts.

12.3 Using the formula

$$\frac{dX_I}{dP}\,\frac{P}{X_I} = -1.0$$

the rise in market price can be computed if one firm withdrew all its output such that $dX_I = -1000$, $P = £10$, $X_I = 1{,}000{,}000$ and dP remains to be determined. This gives;

$$\frac{-1000}{dP}\;\frac{£10}{1{,}000{,}000} = -1.0$$

so that $dP = 1$ penny. Thus price will rise by 1 penny if a firm withdraws all its output. The elasticity of demand facing the firm, given by the formula $(dX_F/dP)\,(P/X_F)$, is -1000.0. The individual firm confronts an elasticity of demand 1000 times larger than that of the industry demand.

12.4 X_2. At X_1, profit is *minimized* (and is negative, as you can see from the position of the *AC* curve above X_1). $P = MC$ is not a sufficient condition for profit maximizing. *MC must also be rising.*

12.5 Area *P*bhged. Note that there are no fixed costs, so *AC* is not infinite at zero output. Total cost is therefore the sum of the cost of producing one unit rather than none, plus that of two rather than one, three rather than two etc. It is the sum of all marginal costs: area Odeghbci. Since total revenue is OP_0bi, profit is the difference between these, namely *P*bhged.

12.6 No. Price takers can sell all they want at the going price and so have no incentive, as profit maximizers, to try to sell more. It is a basic implication of price taking theory that no advertising will be observed. Price takers would have an incentive only if *collectively* they believed that entry to the industry were costly and collectively they could act together. If they then formed an industry association to promote the industry product, this would (if successful) shift the industry demand to the right, raise price and (if a suitable rate of advertising were selected) increase each firm's profits over and above its share of the advertising expenses. Hence *individual* price takers will not advertise, but the price takers' industry *as a whole* may do so if – but only if – entry to the industry is difficult for new firms.

Chapter 13

13.1 (a) At P_E consumption falls from X_2 to X_4, so the *loss* of consumers' surplus is $P_E\text{ab}P_W$. Domestic production increases, however, from X_1 to X_3, so there is *gain* of producers' surplus of $P_E\text{cd}P_W$. Imports fall from $X_2 - X_1$ to $X_4 - X_3$, but on these there is the income from the tariff, which amounts to caef. The *net* loss is therefore

$$P_E\text{cd}P_W + \text{caef} - P_E\text{ab}P_W = \text{aeb} + \text{cfd}$$

which is therefore the relevant measure of welfare loss.

(b) If farmers were guaranteed price P_E, they would purchase X_3. The subsidy, or 'deficiency payment' as it was termed under the British system of agricultural support prior to membership of the EEC, would be $P_E\text{cf}P_W$ and the producers' surplus gain would be $P_E\text{cd}P_W$. Consumers would purchase X_2 (of which $X_2 - X_3$ would be imported) at price P_W and would suffer no welfare loss. Therefore the net loss of the deficiency payments scheme is

$$P_E\text{cf}P_W - P_E\text{cd}P_W = \text{cfd}$$

This method of support thus avoids the welfare loss of aeb. In 1978 the value of aeb has been estimated to be £88.85 million (see the article by El-Agraa, 1984, referred to in case study 13.1).

The rationale, in case study 13.1, for claiming that the net loss of CAP relative to the open market was D + E + I + G + J, goes as follows. In the open market situation, net welfare was the sum of consumers' and producers' surpluses: A + B + C + D + E. With CAP, consumers/taxpayers got value in use A + B + C + H less total expenditure B + C + H + D + E + I + F + G + J. In net welfare terms they therefore had A − D − E − I − F − G − J. With CAP farmers got B + C + H + D + E + I + F + G + J less costs of H + I + G + J. In net welfare terms they therefore had B + C + D + E + F. Letting a pound count equally whoever receives or pays it, the net benefit for all under CAP is therefore A + B + C − I − G − J. The difference in net welfare between the two situations is thus A + B + C + D + D + E − (A + B + C − I − G − J) = D + E + I + G + J. This is the sum of the costs of producing unconsumed products (I + J + G) plus lost consumers' and producers' surpluses (D + E).

13.2 (a) Equilibrium is where $X_D = X_S$, namely

$$220 - 4P = -20 + 2P$$

Rearranging this gives

$$240 = 6P$$
$$40 = P$$

So the equilibrium price is 40.

(b) Substituting $P = 40$ into *either* the demand or the supply curve gives the same answer in equilibrium, namely $X = 60$.

(c) Figure A13.1 shows the supply and demand curves according to the equations given.

The easiest way to draw these is to find two points on each curve (say where $X = 0$ and $X = 60$) and then draw an extended straight line between them. Consumers' surplus is therefore

$$[(55 - 40) \times 60] / 2 = 450.$$

(d) By the same procedure as in (c), producers' surplus is $[(40 - 10) \times 60] / 2 = 900$.

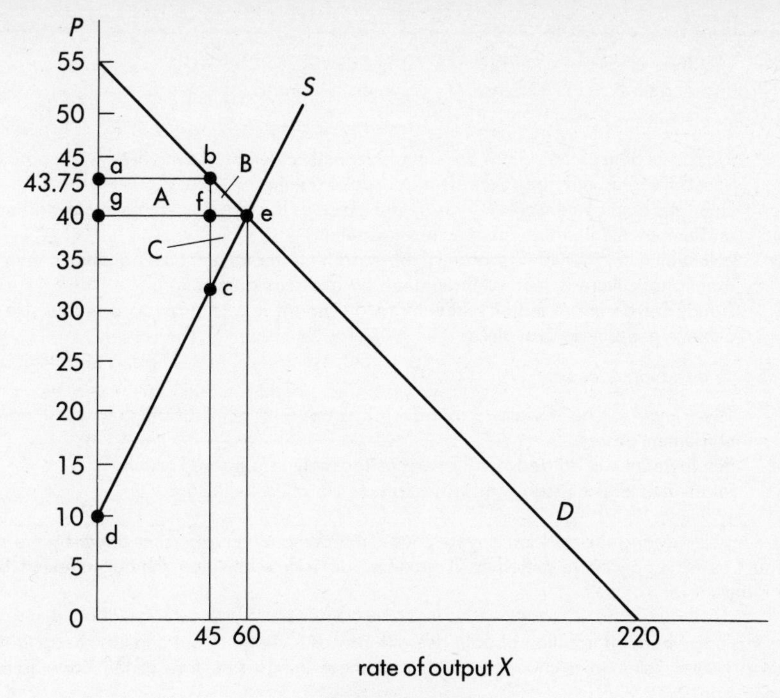

Figure A13.1

(e) Putting $X = 45$ into the demand equation gives $P = 43.75$.

(f) Consumers' surplus is now

$$[(55 - 43.75) \times 45] / 2 = 253.125$$

(g) Producers' surplus is now the area marked abcd in figure A13.1 (assuming no fixed costs). Dividing this into a rectangle and a triangle for ease of calculation, you get

$$[(43.75 - 32.5) \times 45] + [(32.5 - 10) \times 45] / 2 = 1012.5.$$

So the net gain to the producers is 112.5.
(Note that point c is found by putting $X = 45$ into the supply equation to give $P = 32.5$.)

(h) Producers gain area abcd less fec, which you now know to leave them 112.5 better off. Consumers lose area abeg, which is worth $450 - 253.125 = 196.875$. If one counted a pound gained or lost by a producer as equal to a pound gained or lost by a consumer, one can say that, since consumers lose the areas marked A and B and producers lose C but gain A, the net loss to society is B + C. This amounts to $112.5 - 196.875 = -84.375$, which is a deadweight efficiency loss. You can check this by calculating the area bec (= B + C). Triangle bef $= [3.75 \times 15] / 2 = 28.125$ and triangle fec $= [7.5 \times 15] / 2 = 56.25$. Then $28.125 + 56.25 = 84.375$.

(i) The restricted output. In fact, an output rate of 45 is the one that maximizes producers' surplus in this example, given that only one price can be charged.

13.3 (a) Consumers' surplus is A + B + D + E.

(b) Producers' surplus is C.

(c) Consumers' surplus is A.

(d) Producers' surplus is B + C.

(e) D + E (these are lost by consumers but not gained by producers).

(f) Producers gain B at the expense of consumers, who also lose D + E.

(g) Some advantages are:

Producers gain (if their gains are sufficiently highly weighted compared with consumers' losses, then this may be taken as a net social gain)
Domestic employment creation as output expands (if there is unemployment, and output and employment in this industry move together)
Self-sufficiency (may be important if the importer is dependent on a potential enemy or if a national culture is seen as threatened by overseas domination)
X may be an infant industry needing protection if it is to grow to a viable size and achieve economies of scale.

Some disadvantages are:

There may still be a welfare loss even if producers' gains are higher weighted than consumers' losses
Employment will be destroyed overseas (possibly in a poorer country)
Infant industries blessed with protection all too often fail to grow up.

13.4 None at all. Levying the duty on buyers causes the demand curve to shift down by the same amount as the supply curve shifted up. It makes no difference on whom the duty is levied. Draw the diagram for yourself.

13.5 Less in York, where information about price differences is cheap to get and it is cheap to move from a dearer seller to a cheaper. Neither of these things is so true of the York–Salisbury comparison.

Chapter 14

14.1 (a) Ode is the sum of all marginal revenues which must be equal to total revenue. Ofbe is average revenue times output, which is also equal to total revenue.

(b) Lower. Additions to output reduce total revenue.

(c) Lower. Additions to output raise total revenue, so the total must be less than at 10 million output.

(d) Unity. A unitary elasticity means that a small change in price will leave total revenue constant.

(e) $X = 19.375 - 0.625P$

14.2 (a)

price	*quantity demanded*	*total revenue*	*marginal revenue*
20	0	0	20
15	15	225	10
10	30	300	0
5	45	225	−10
0	60	0	−20

Note: with $X = 60 - 3P$, $MR = 20 - (2/3)X$. This gives the figures for *MR* in the table. Using the approximation $MR = \Delta TR/\Delta X$ gives *MR*s of 15, 5, −5 and −15.

(b) *MR* always bisects a horizontal line between the vertical axis and the demand curve when the demand curve is a straight line. This is a useful rule to remember when you are drawing your own figures. The proof is simple: triangles dba and bce are similar: the angles at points a and c are right angles and the opposite angles on either side of point b are also equal. Total revenue can be measured *either* as price times quantity (area Oacf) or as the sum of all marginal revenues (area Odef). Therefore these two areas are equal. Therefore triangles dba and bce are equal in area. Since they are also similar, they are equal in all respects. Therefore ab = bc (and da = ce, and db = be).

14.3 (a) Profit maximization occurs when $MC = MR$. Noting that total revenue $TR = PX$, you have:

$$X = 60 - 3P$$

Hence

$$P = 20 - \tfrac{1}{3}X$$

Hence

$$PX = 20X - \tfrac{1}{3}X^2$$

Hence (recalling simple differentiation)

$$MR = 20 - \tfrac{2}{3}X$$

Hence, setting $MC = MR$,

$$10 = 20 - \tfrac{2}{3}X$$

Thus

$$X = 15.$$

(b) $15 = 60 - 3P$ yields $P = 15$.

(c) With no fixed costs, $AC = MC$, so total costs are $10 \times 15 = 150$. Total revenue is $15 \times 15 = 225$. Profit $= 225 - 150 = 75$.

14.4 Profits fall, price and output remain the same. Since, in equilibrium, marginal profit is zero, marginal profits tax is also zero. Therefore marginal cost is unchanged and so are price and output.

14.5 The average cost is incorrectly specified by the lower horizontal line.

14.6 (a) A + B

(b) C + D + L + F + G (since profit or producer's surplus is the difference between total revenue and the sum of marginal costs) *or* C + D + F + G + I (since profit is also the difference between total revenue and average cost times quantity). Note that L = I in area.

(c) A + B + C + D + E

(d) L + F + G + H

14.7 (a) When $X = 0$, $P = 20$. When $P = 5$, $X = 45$. Consumers' surplus is therefore $0.5\,[(20 - 5)45] = 337.5$.

(b) The maximum possible is found by setting price (*not MR*) equal to marginal cost. Output at this rate is thus given by $10 = 20 - (1/3)X$, i.e. $X = 30$. At this output, price ($= MC$) is 10, so consumers' surplus is $0.5\,[(20 - 10)\,30] = 150$. This, by suitable exploitation, could be appropriated by the producer.

14.8 (a)

Price	Demand in market 1	Demand in market 2	Total demand	*MR* in market 1	*MR* in market 2	Total *MR*
40	0	0	0	40	0	40
35	5	0	5	30	0	30
30	10	0	10	20	0	20
25	15	0	15	10	0	10
20	20	0	20	0	20	(0)(15)
15	25	15	40	−10	10	5
10	30	30	60	−20	0	−5
5	35	45	80	−30	−10	−15
0	40	60	100	−40	−20	−25

Note that total demand is given by $X_1 + X_2$. At prices between 40 and 20, $X_2 = 0$, so the total demand curve's equation is the same as that in market 1, that is $X = 40 - P$. Therefore *MR* in the market as a whole is the same as in market 1. At prices lower than 20, however, there are sales in *both* markets, and the demand curve has the equation (from $X_1 + X_2$): $X = 40 - P + 60 - 3P = 100 - 4P$. The total demand curve therefore 'kinks' at price 20 and its slope changes. The marginal revenue curve for a demand curve $X = 100 - 4P$ is (recalling simple differentiation and using $P = 25 - (1/4)X$ to give $TR = PX = 25X - (1/4)X^2$) $MR = 25 - (1/2)X$. This can then be used to calculate *MR* in the remainder of the column. When total demand is almost 20, the marginal revenue is 0; when it is just above 20 it is 15. This discontinuity in the *MR* curve occurs at the rate of consumption where the demand curve kinks.

(b) The demand for children's haircuts is more elastic than that for adults' haircuts because parental amateur haircutting is a close substitute for professional haircutting.

Chapter 15

15.1 (a) Under price taking $P = MR = MC$. Therefore $P = 10$ and $10 = 60 - 2X$, so $X = 25$. When $X = 0$, $P = 60$. Therefore consumers' surplus is 0.5 [(60 − 10)25] = 625.

(b) Price will be set such that $MC = MR$, i.e. $10 = 60 - 4X$. From this, $X = 12.5$ and $P = 35$. Profits are $TR - TC = (35 \times 12.5) - (10 \times 12.5) = 312.5$.

(c) Consumers' surplus at $P = 35$ is 0.5 [(60 − 35) 12.5] = 156.25.

15.2 (a) The demand curve perceived by each firm is $X_F = 50 - 0.5P$. Therefore $P = 100 - 2X_F$. Total revenue for firm 1 is therefore $TR_1 = P_1X_1 = 100X_1 - 2X_1^2$ and marginal revenue is $MR_1 = 100 - 4X_1$. Setting this equal to *MC*, you get $10 = 100 - 4X_1$. Thus $X_1 = 22.50$, $P_1 = 55.00$, $TR_1 = 1237.50$, $TC_1 = 225.00$, $\text{profit}_1 = 1012.50$.

(b) $30 = 100 - 4X_2$ gives
$X_2 = 17.50$, $P_2 = 65$, $TR_2 = 1137.50$, $TC_2 = 525.00$, $\text{profit}_2 = 612.50$.

(c)
$TR_1 = 1137.50$ (65 × 17.50)
$TC_1 = 175.00$ (10 × 17.50)

$\text{profit}_1 = 962.50$

(d)
$TR_2 = 1237.50$ (55 × 22.50)
$TC_2 = 675.00$ (30 × 22.50)

$\text{profit}_2 = 562.50$

(e) If $P_2 = 30$, $X_1 = 35.00$. Hence $TR_1 = 1050.00$, $TC_1 = 350.00$, so $\text{profit}_1 = 700.00$.

(f) Given market demand $X = 100 - P$, you have $P = 100 - X$. Total revenue is $PX = 100X - X^2$. Marginal revenue is $MR = 100 - 2X$. Setting this equal to 10 you get $10 = 100 - 2X$. Thus (where $X_1 = X$) $X = 45.00$, $P = 55$, $TR = 2475.00$, $TC = 450.00$, profit $= 2025.00$. (Alternatively, the answer is twice the profit in case (a).)

15.3 (a) There is no uniquely correct answer to this SAQ. It depends in part on the purposes sought. Public ownership can be an effective means of suppressing the profit motive if that is desired, and it does so by changing the nature of competition in the capital market. Under public ownership the ownership of 'shares' in an enterprise is not transferable and so one cannot signal one's disapproval of company policy by selling one's stock. Under public ownership, moreover, revenues brought into the firm cannot be converted by owners into *personal* wealth by, say, voting themselves higher dividends. The same, incidentally, is also true of charities where 'trustees' replace 'owners'. Hence subscribers, taxpayers, buyers can be more sure that income received by the enterprise will be used to promote the activity of the enterprise. However, this does not stop the government adjusting the rules of the game so as to try to get the level of funding for any publicly owned industry that it prefers (subject to cost and demand conditions), nor does it stop managers of such enterprises seeking to enhance their personal interests in other ways. Consequently, additional constraints, rules of behaviour and accountability and so on are invariably needed in public sector enterprises and charities.

'Equality' is not very relevant in an answer to this question since, although there is in one sense an equal 'share' for everyone in a publicly owned industry, this is not of the same value as a share in privately owned industry. The latter can be sold and, in any case, it is possible to have equal share ownership of private industry by appropriate regulation.

It is sometimes argued that publicly owned industries are better able to achieve scale economies. Against this it can be argued that the market test of profitability is the best guarantee that largeness really does correspond to the achievement of scale economies (if they exist).

It is also sometimes argued that the sheer scale of some government enterprises is too large for the private sector to fund. Against this, there is absolutely no evidence that joint stock financing cannot fund large enterprises – that are *efficient*.

The key really seems to be the suppression or at least modification of the profit motive, which is held to be desirable in particular cases (e.g. the Bank of England, the National Health Service).

(b) All profit seeking firms have an incentive both to develop cost reducing technologies and to develop new products that are expected to be profitable. Under price taking, however, with no barriers to entry, any profits made by innovation will tend to be eroded in the long run as competitors copy innovators. Under monopoly, with patent protection and other barriers to others copying one's innovations, the profits will persist longer and hence constitute a more powerful incentive. A further advantage for monopolists or price searchers is that since they can always sell products above average cost in the long run, they can also better recoup the overhead costs of innovation, research and development which do not feature in marginal costs. Consequently, unless the efficiency losses from monopoly pricing are believed to be very large, it may from a long run perspective be better to put up with some degree of monopoly for the sake of the cost reductions and the new products it tends to generate.

15.4 (a) Figure A15.1 shows the situation. Under monopoly, the sum of surpluses is abcd. Under regulation with $P = AC$ it is aed − efg. The latter triangle is the excess of cost over value in use of producing beyond the point where $P = MC$. The answer therefore depends on the relative sizes of areas bec (which is a net gain from increased output at the lower price) and efg. If efg $>$ bec, regulation reduces total surplus; if efg $<$ bec, it increases it.

Note that if price can always be set at average cost, the firm has no incentive to keep AC as low as possible; this encourages X-inefficiency and discourages innovation.

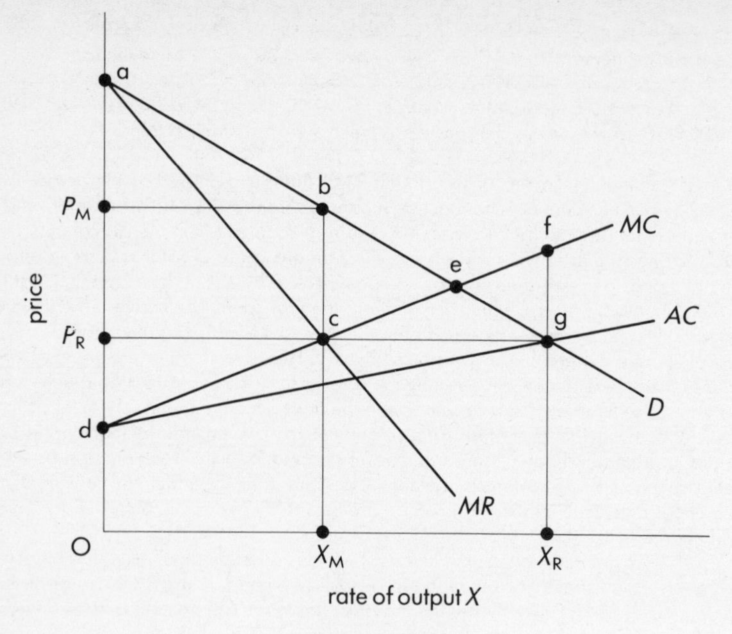

Figure A15.1

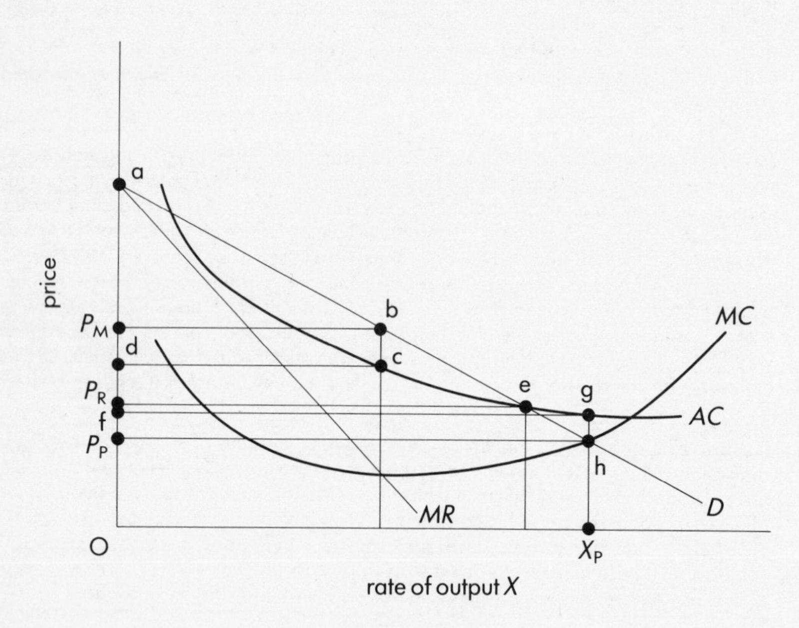

Figure A15.2

(b) Figure A15.2 shows the situation. Under monopoly, total surplus is the area abcd (consumers' surplus abP_M + producer's surplus $P_M$bcd). Under regulation, with $P = AC$, the total surplus is $P_R$ae (producer's surplus being zero). Under the efficient rule $P = MC$, total surplus is $P_P$ah (consumers' surplus) minus $P_P$fgh (negative producer's surplus). The latter must yield the largest surplus since any output rate that is lower than X_P entails $P > MC$ and hence surplus must rise if X rises. However, note that at X_P – the 'ideal' output – the firm must make a financial loss. For this reason, such firms have an incentive to engage in price discrimination. Alternatively, such 'natural monopolies' are sometimes nationalized or else remain private with a public subsidy. Each of the latter policies, like the rule 'set $P = AC$', will tend to encourage X-inefficiency and discourage innovation. Price discrimination can enable the firm to attain the ideal output, make a profit and retain incentives to innovate and eliminate X-inefficiency.

Chapter 16

16.1 (a) £11,000. If you saved all of this year's income of £10,000 at 10 per cent, next year you would have your £10,000 plus £1000 interest: $PV(1+i) = F$; £10,000 (1+0.1) = £11,000.

(b) £9091. If you borrowed £9091 you could consume that this year and then pay back £9091 plus £909 interest out of next year's income of £10,000: £9091 (1+0.1) = £10,000.

16.2 (a) £105, £110, £115.

(b) £95.24 (discount factor is 1/1.05 = 0.9524)
£90.91 (discount factor is 1/1.1 = 0.9091)
£86.96 (discount factor is 1/1.15 = 0.8696)

16.3 (a) 1 The credit deal. The present value of £200 + £200 next year plus £200 the year after that is £200 + (£200 × 0.9091) + (£200 × 0.8264) = £547.10.

2 The cash deal. The present value of the credit deal is £200 + (£200 × 0.9259) + (£200 × 0.8573) = £556.65.

(b) 10 per cent. £750 invested now at 10 per cent will grow by a factor of 6.7275 to £5045.63 in 20 years. 6.7275 = 1.10^{20} which you should be able to calculate on your pocket calculator – laboriously if you multiply 1.10 by itself 20 times, easily if you have an x^y button on your machine.

16.4 (a) The present value of £80,000 at 10 per cent is only £19,151, which is much less than the value of the house. The relevant discount factor is $1/1.1^{15}$ (or 1.1^{-15}), which equals 0.23939. Your mother has made you a highly favourable offer. The most favourable deal you get from the bank would be one in which you paid only the interest on an indefinite debt (much more generous than in practice you could get). You would thus pay £4000 a year indefinitely. Over a 15 year period the present value of £4000 paid out each year is (£4000 × 0.909) + (£4000 × 0.826) + ... = £30,440. This is already well in excess of the present value of the cost to you of your mother's offer.

(b) The present value of £10,000 for the next 40 years at 5 per cent is £10,000 × 17.15909 = £171,591. Your human capital is, if you are an average sort of student, the most valuable item in your capital stock (even if you are the outright owner of a house that has no debt on it). (Note: $17.15909 = (1.05^{40} - 1) / [0.05(1.05)^{40}]$.)

16.5 (a) £50,000/5.2064 = £9,603.56. Note that £5.2064 is the amount to which £1 will grow in seven years at 8 per cent interest. The present value of £9,603.56 received at the end of each of seven years at 8 per cent interest is £50,000.

(b) 1 £45,000/7.6061 = £5,916.30.

2 After one year you have paid £5,916.30. The interest on the loan was £4,500, so you have paid off £5,916.30 − £4,500 = £1,416.30 of the debt. Your equity (ownership of the capital value of the house) is therefore £15,000 + £1,416.30 = £16,416.30.

3 After two years you have paid 2 × £5,916.30 = £11,832.60. The interest on year one was £4,500. The interest on year two was 10 per cent of the outstanding debt (£45,000 − £1,416.30 = £43,583.70) which is £4,358.37. So the total interest paid is £8,858.37. This is less than the amount you have paid by £11,832.60 − £8,858.37 = £2,974.23. Your equity has therefore become £15,000 + £2,974.23 = £17,974.23.

4 £60,000.

16.6 (a) By looking at changes in the relative prices of short and long lived products or changes in the pattern of investment decisions in favour of or away from investments with different patterns of future costs and benefits. Thus, if individuals are free to buy and sell goods with different lives and the price of long lived goods rises relative to short lived ones that are otherwise the same in all other characteristics, then you may infer that the rate of time preference has fallen, corresponding to a fall in the (implicit) interest rate.

(b) An increased use of intertemporal barter (A promises to pay B goods instead of money in future periods in exchange for B making earlier consumption possible for A)
The use of rents, fees and other disguised forms of interest payments and receipts
An excess demand for funds to borrow
Black markets in debts (with relatively higher illegal interest rates than would otherwise prevail in order to compensate lenders for the risk of being prosecuted and punished for breaking the law)
Lower rates of saving.

(c) At one time it was regarded as immoral for Christians to charge interest rates but not immoral for them to pay interest rates to Jews. The morality of this, or any general ban on interest charges, is obscure.

16.7 (a) Yes. The rise in interest rates will cause all your other forms of wealth to fall in value too; the bomb has damaged only your factory. Can you see why a doubling of interest rates may cause a halving of the value of your factory? The value of your factory is the present value of expected future profits. Suppose profits are constant each year and the factory's life is effectively infinite. Then its value in present value terms is $PV_0 = \pi/i$, where π is the annual profit. If i rises to $2i$, $PV_1 = \pi/2i$, so $PV_1 = 0.5\ PV_0$. You may also care because the effect of the bomb is irreversible – but interest rates may fall later.

(b) 1 £19,091 (rounded from £19,090.91)

2 Stays at £19,091; your consumption point moves along your intertemporal budget line but your wealth now remains the same.

3 £21,000: you will have next year's £10,000 plus this year's £10,000 plus the interest of £1000.

4 £19,091

5 £19,091

6 £4500: next year's income less the repayment of the £5000 you borrowed and the interest you will have on it: £10,000 − £5500 = £4500.

16.8 Each of these transactions involves a sharing of a person's human capital with an employer. None involves the outright expropriation of a free person's right not to sell human wealth to another should that person prefer not to, so none is slavery in this sense. To the extent, however, that employers are very much more powerful negotiators than employees, or that one fears that employees may make ill-advised long term contracts of this sort, one may wish to outlaw or limit such contracts – even though individuals would voluntarily engage with employers in the absence of such bans or limitations. Such issues tend to divide mere liberals from thoroughgoing libertarians!

Chapter 17

17.1 If $X = 5K^{0.6}L^{0.4}$, the marginal product of L is given by $MP_L = 2K^{0.6}L^{-0.6}$. This is the appropriate Nmeasure to use (i.e. the first order partial derivative of X with respect to L) if L is finely divisible. Alternatively you could compute X for each rate of use of L and take $\Delta X/\Delta L$ as your measure of the marginal product if L comes in single units. In the following table, both methods are shown.

L	MP_L	X	$\Delta X/\Delta L$
1	7.96	19.91	19.91
2	5.25	26.27	6.36
3	4.12	30.89	4.62
4	3.47	34.66	3.77
5	3.03	37.89	3.23
6	2.72	40.76	2.87

17.2

L	MP_L	Industry X	P	Maximum wage (PMP_L)	VMP_L (P=47)
1	7.96	1991	83.6	665.5	374.1
2	5.25	2627	62.4	327.6	246.8
3	4.12	3089	47.0	193.6	193.6
4	3.47	3466	34.5	119.7	163.1
5	3.03	3789	23.7	71.8	142.4
6	2.72	4076	14.1	38.4	127.8

Note that, as in figure 17.3, the wage employers are willing to pay, as shown by the demand curve (PMP_L) is higher than the VMP_L with $P = 47$ when $L < 3$, and lower when $L > 3$.

17.3 Wrong. The statement is true if *output* is constant but, if output rises as more of an input is demanded when its price falls, the move from one isoquant to another may generate 'output' effects analogous to the income effects of consumer theory that make the full adjustment demand curve *less* elastic than partial adjustment demand curve – even though the two inputs are close substitutes in the sense of having rather shallow isoquants. The elasticity depends not only on the slope of the isoquant but also on how demand for an input changes as one moves from one isoquant to another.

17.4 (a) Oabc (b) abd

17.5 (a) Positive (b) negative

17.6 Suppose that the supply of hours falls if income rises but the wage rate is constant. In that case, an increase in allowances from A_0 to A_1 (see figure A17.1) produces the new wage line W_0' with a kink at point c rather than point b and a new equilibrium at point d, where less work is done. The tax rate change that produces the same post-tax income gives wage line W_1 (with allowances still at A_0) which produces the new equilibrium at point e. In this case more work is done. Whether or not, in the general case, more or less work is done with a fall in the tax rate, one can generally conclude that a tax rate fall will have a *smaller* disincentive (or a larger incentive) effect on work than an increase in allowances that leaves the individual in the same after tax position. Note that the analysis abstracts from the possibly important effects that the policy may have for output, wage rates and hence income when these wider effects are taken into account. The taxpayer is, of course, on a higher indifference curve with the increase in allowances, and so will prefer this method of reducing tax.

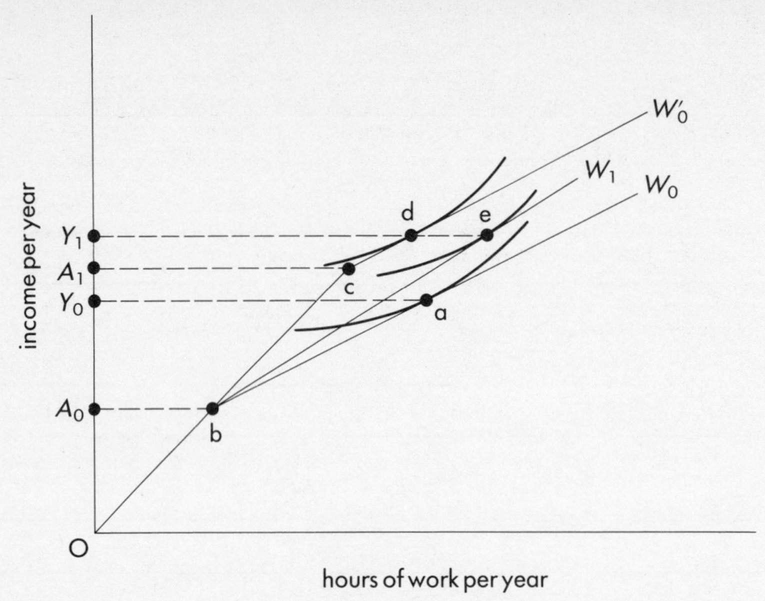

Figure A17.1

Chapter 18

18.1 (a) Involuntary employment exists when, at going wage rates, qualified workers want to supply more hours but are unable to, or want to be employed but are unable to find a job.

(b) Voluntary unemployment exists when at going wage rates workers choose not to supply further hours or choose not to be employed.

When workers are on their supply curves unemployment is voluntary. When they are off the supply curve (as in figure 18.1 at wage rate W_1) there is involuntary unemployment. Note that if wage were set at *less than* W_0, there would be an excess demand for labour and only voluntary unemployment.

18.2 (a) Involuntary (b) involuntary (c) voluntary.

18.3 (a)

hours:	10	20	30	40
wage:	15	25	35	45

(b)

hours:	10	20	30	40
marginal wage:	25	45	65	85

The figures in (b) are obtained by using the appropriate marginal equation, $MW = 2L + 5$. If you calculate the total wage bill at each level of hours and then, from this, the marginal wage (Δ wage bill / ΔL), the MW you will have calculated should be: 15, 35, 55, 75.

18.4 The analysis of this issue was developed by Gary Becker in his pioneering book *Human Capital* (London, Columbia University Press, 1964; second edition 1975) in which he introduced the distinction between *general* and *specific training*.

(a) You view costs of providing the general training in terms of lost productive current time and the direct training costs. If you cannot recoup these costs through an acceptable rate of return by paying such labour a subsequent wage *less than VMP* because such wages will cause the trained labour to be competed away, you will not provide it. Instead employees will pay for it by, say, working at an apprentice's rate, reflecting net *VMP* at the time, and then later at the craftsman's rate, reflecting *VMP* then.

(b) In this specific training case, by no longer having the more skilled labour traded away (since the skills are valueless elsewhere) you may be willing to pay for it, paying labour a wage equal to or more than *VMP* during training and less than *VMP* subsequently. Such is arguably the case in the university industry in the UK, which effectively acts as a single employer as far as salary negotiation is concerned.

(c) If there is a case, it does not arise from the 'poaching' problem in the general skills case, for there should be no 'underinvestment' in skills due to this factor, despite the commonly heard case that this *is* an argument for subsidy. There may be a case for it on grounds of the financial hardship imposed on trainees: either a moral case based on considerations of 'fair' wages, or an efficiency case based on the inability of workers to borrow against future expected high earnings to finance their training period, which *can* cause underinvestment in skills.

18.5 Because it assumes that only labour hours in the range bc will be forgone by the employer. If hours (and workers) to the left of point b on *VMP* or *MRP* are forgone (because it is hard to identify *precisely* who is least productive at the margin) then there may be hours retained with a *VMP* (*MRP*) smaller than ab.

Chapter 19

19.1 Less.

19.2 (a) Either let people park on it for nothing or, if this has undesired effects from your point of view (you may feel that there are already too many cars allowed into the town centre) you could allow no one to park there. (If you have to fence it off, however, the costs of this may exceed the value to you of fewer cars in the centre, so you will again let anyone park at will.) The message is, of course, that to operate a price mechanism is itself costly and the market gains may not be worth incurred transaction costs. (Note the assumption that marginal cost is zero.)

(b) Churches are not profit seeking institutions and most prefer to see their buildings as full as possible at services; hence positive prices are not used. However, there have been times when pews could be 'purchased' by benefactors who donated sufficiently large sums, and these arrangements gave such people the right to the exclusive use of their pews. You might think that churches would be even fuller if worshippers were *paid* to attend (a negative price per pew)! Can you think of any reasons why this practice is never observed?

19.3 Wrong. Production and exchange are often facilitated by private property arrangements (though by no means always). Economic theory, however, is no less applicable in the absence of prices and private property. Demand curves still have a negative slope, though the 'price' upon which the rate of consumption depends may be paid in terms of time spent waiting, time devoted to befriending those with the authority to allocate resources, or may take the form of baksheesh, bribes and black market prices. Likewise, behaviour generally will still conform to the axioms of economics and production will still be subject to the nature and constraints of production possibilities, though the form in which opportunity costs are revealed to decision takers may be different.

19.4 A report on his paper follows. Mr Jones draws figure A19.1. *MV* is the sum of all SMA members' marginal valuations for trips from Smootham to Claggbury via Junction Hotel. APC_0 is the average private cost curve confronting members while the railway is in operation. SMA members select the number of trips that makes $MV =$ price ($= APC_0$), that is, X_0 trips. Were the railway to close, the road between Junction Hotel and Claggbury would become clogged by the increased traffic from Trendhill, so the *APC* curve for SMA members shifts to APC_1 and Mr Jones argues correctly that trips demanded will fall to, say, X_1. The consumers' surplus loss to

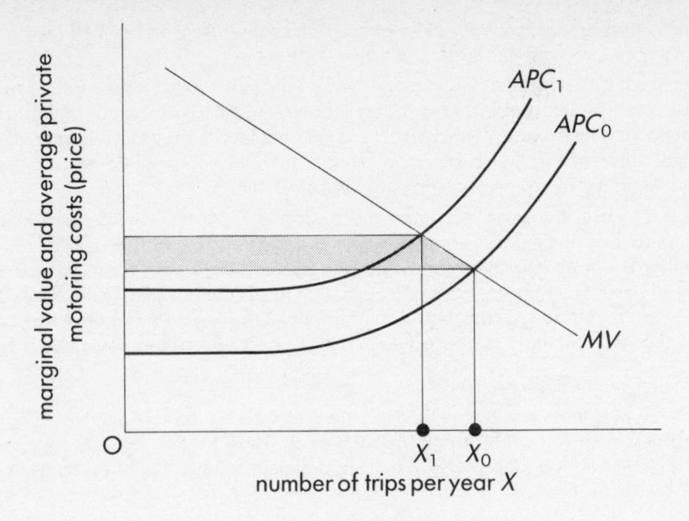

Figure A19.1

SMA members is the shaded area in the figure (Jones patiently explains in response to a query that the motorists take account of only the average rather than the marginal cost per trip and that, because of this, the road is already used more than is optimal).

Jones has prepared estimates of this shaded area as well as an estimate of SMA members' share of the higher rates needed to keep the railway open, and finds that the latter is a good deal smaller than the former. He has even varied his assumptions according to what seem to him to be reasonable guesstimates of *APC*, demand elasticity, and SMA members' share, and the increase in the rates burden is consistently less than the consumers' surplus loss.

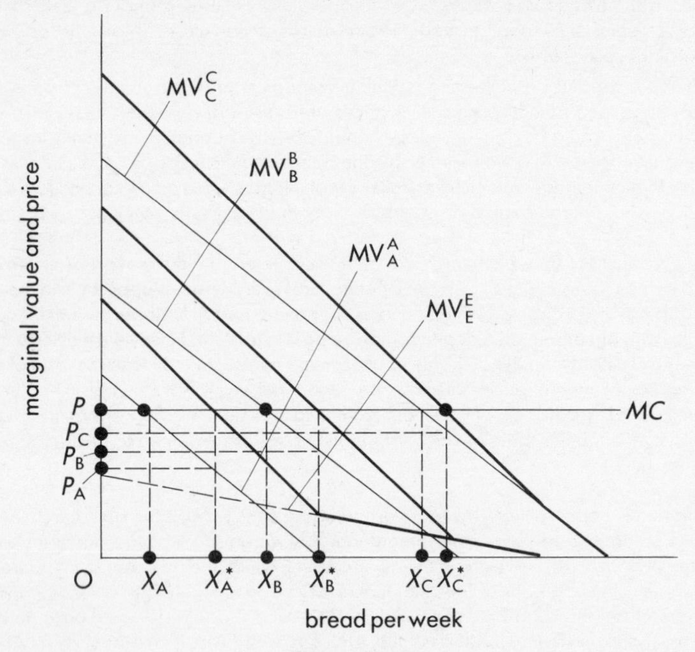

Figure A19.2

19.5 Figure A19.2 shows the results.

(a) X_A, X_B and X_C, determined by the intersection of MC (= price) and each demand curve.

(b) These are determined by the vertical sum of the internal marginal values and the external, that is $MV^A_A + MV_E$, $MV^B_B + MV_E$ and $MV^C_C + MV_E$. This gives the MSV curves shown in bold and the optimal points are where the MC curves intersect MSV_A, MSV_B and MSV_C, yielding optimal consumption rates X^*_A, X^*_B and X^*_C.

(c) To get A, B and C to consume at the optimal rates the (marginal) price to A must be P_A, that to B P_B and that to C P_C, for at these prices (and only these) will they choose the optimal consumption.

(d) The optimal per unit subsidies, that is $P - P_A$, $P - P_B$ and $P - P_C$, are inversely related to income. In popular parlance, this is equivalent to saying that bread subsidies should be *selective* and related to 'need' (namely, inversely related to income). However, in practice it may be difficult to discriminate in this way: it will be costly to identify the various degrees of 'need' and to prevent those who get bread at a relatively low price from reselling to those who get it at a higher price. Note that this difficulty is absent in the case of services like education and health where selective subsidies, say in the form of vouchers, have often been suggested, or where institutions can be established that cater explicitly for particular groups (e.g. state schools for 'the poor' and private schools for 'the rich').

19.6 Initially, APC_O equals MV when X_O trips are made (figure A19.3). The marginal cost curve (MPC_O) shows the increase in the costs of making a trip as each additional journey is made. Thus, at X_O trips, the average cost to each SMA member is X_Oa. However, the cost imposed by an additional car making the journey is X_Ob. This cost is imposed on *all* road users and not just the marginal user, who sees a cost of X_Oa. Since, however, the additional cost is X_Ob and the marginal value of the additional journey only X_Oa, there is too much congestion on the road. The optimal usage is X_1, where APC_O is only X_1d but marginal cost (X_1c) equals marginal value. Since each motorist at this rate of use sees a cost of only X_1d, the appropriate road user charge is dc, which forces each motorist to see the true MPC. The welfare gain is area cba – the elimination of the excess of cost over benefit. Note that at traffic flows lower than X_M, there is no divergence between average and marginal cost: at flows at or less than this, additional cars impose no costs on the rest of the traffic on the road.

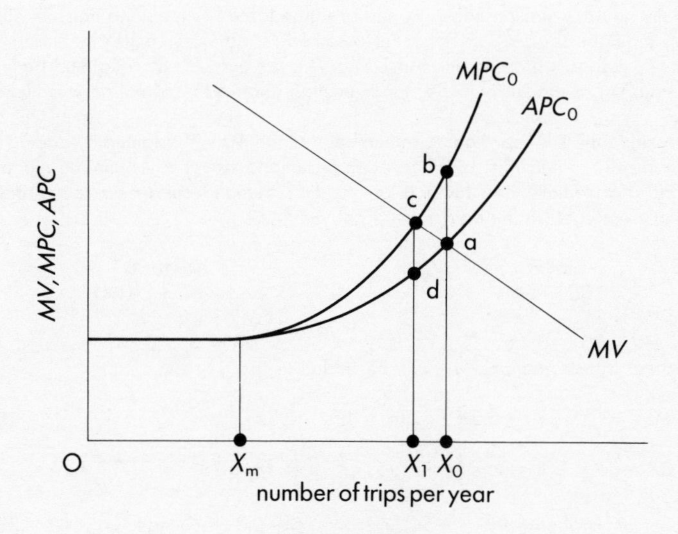

Figure A19.3

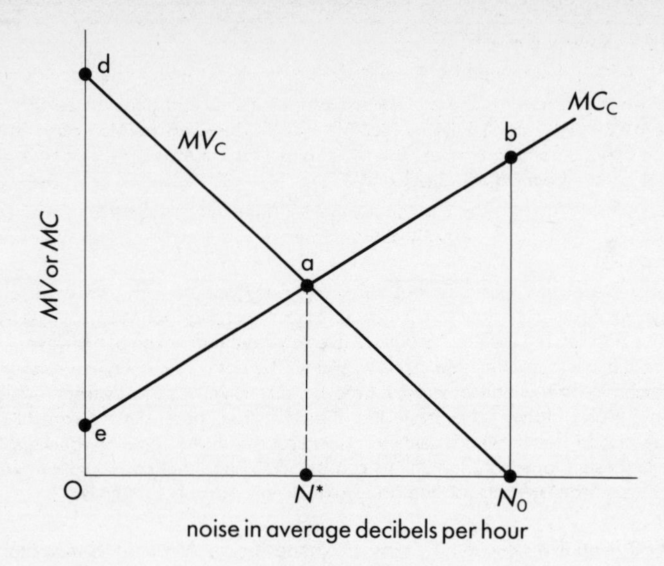

Figure A19.4

19.7 (a) See figure A19.4. N^* is the noise level at the intersection of MC_C and MV_C.

(b) The maximum I will pay you is the total cost imposed on me above the optimal rate, that is, N^*abN_0. The minimum you must receive is the value of the noise to you, that is, N^*aN_0.

(c) The maximum you will pay is the value to you of the N^* noise, that is, $OdaN^*$. The minimum I will accept is the value of the optimal nuisance to me, that is, $OeaN^*$.

(d) Not in this case. Whoever has the right, there is an incentive for each party to reach the optimal level N^*, which is the same under either assignment of rights.

(e) Yes. If *I* have the right, I am richer and could, at a maximum, get $OdaN^*$ from you. If *you* have the right, you are richer and could, at a maximum, get N^*abN_0. Property is, of course, wealth.

(f) If initially you are making noise N_0 and are then forced to make no noise at all, you lose OdN_0 and I gain $OebN_0$, leaving a net loss of eda $-$ abN_0. If, on the other hand, you make noise N^*, you gain $OdaN^*$ and I lose $BeaN^*$ a net gain of eda. eda must be larger than eda $-$ abN_0, so the social loss of the injunction relative to optimal noise pollution is eda.

19.8 (a) In answering this it is important to remember that the *MSV* is obtained by adding individual *MV*s vertically rather then, as when adding demand curves to obtain the market or total demand, horizontally: the focus is on reading demand curves *up* rather than *across*. Substitute *MV* for *P* in the equations to get:

for A	for B
$X = 100 - 5MV$	$X = 50 - 10MV$
$5MV = 100 - X$	$10MV = 50 - X$
$MV = 20 - 0.2X$	$MV = 5 - 0.1X$

With these transformations *MV*s can be added to get

$$MSV = 20 + 5 - 0.2X - 0.1X = 25 - 0.3X$$

$MSV = 25 - 0.3X$ (for $X \leqslant 50$) is the equation you are after. For $50 \leqslant X \leqslant 100$ it is $20 - 0.2X$, that is, A's *MV* only.

(b) The optimum is where $MSV = MSC$, i.e. $15 = 25 - 0.3X$. Solving this gives $X = 33.3$, which is the optimal output.

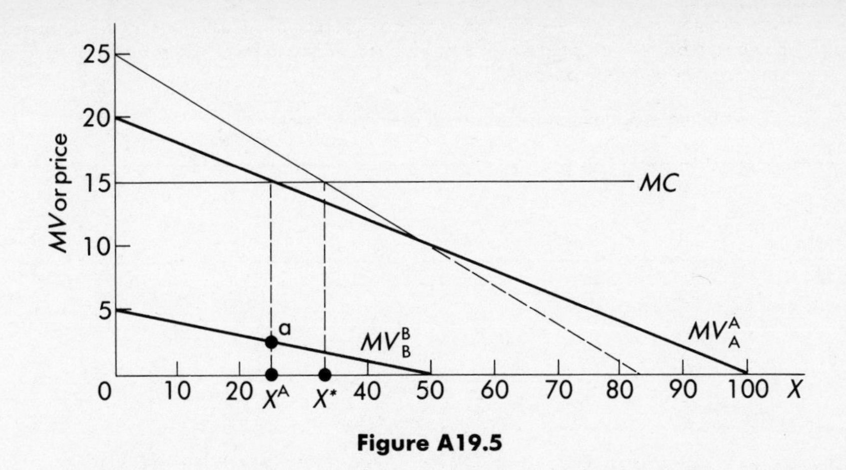

Figure A19.5

(c) A will set $P = MV$, so $15 = 20 - 0.2X$ implies that A will purchase 25 units of the public good. At $P = 15$, B will purchase none at all since even at the smallest output of X B's MV is never more than 5. In this situation, then, only 25 units will be produced, which is clearly less than the optimal amount.

(d) See figure A19.5.

(e) Yes. Consider a situation in which only A is buying the public good. In the figure A19.5, A buys X^A. But B places a marginal value of X^Aa on this amount. A could be induced to buy more of the public good if B compensated A for the difference between the cost of A and A's marginal valuation. The amount A needs to be compensated for additional purchases of X is the difference between MV_A^A and MC, shown as S^A in figure A19.6. This is equal to B's marginal value of X at X^*, the optimal output, and at all outputs less than that, the amount A needs in compensation is less than what B is willing to pay. Hence by bargaining they could get to the optimum. Alternatively, if B is to pay for the extra public good, B must be compensated for the difference between MC and MV_B^B. This is shown by S^B. This is equal to

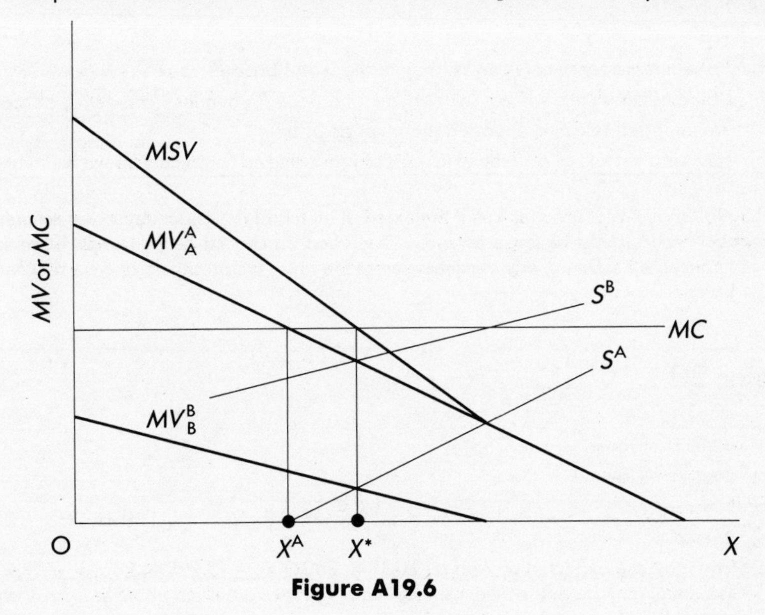

Figure A19.6

A's marginal value at X^*, the optimal output, and at all outputs less than that the amount that B needs to be compensated is less than what A is willing to pay. Hence, by bargaining they could again get to the optimum.

The optimal amount can therefore be defined as either

$$MSV = MV_A^A + MV_B^B = MSC$$

or as

$$S^A = MV_B^B$$

or as

$$S^B = MV_A^A$$

which, since

$$S^A = MSC - MV_A^A$$

and

$$S^B = MSC - MV_B^B$$

amount to exactly the same optimum condition. However, this is likely to be a solution only when there are few people. When many individuals enjoy the benefits of public goods (or suffer public bads), individual deals are likely to be too costly to negotiate and other solutions, like having politicians interpret *MSV* and *MSC* and then determining the preferred output, may become more desirable.

19.9 (a) *Pc*
(b) *Pb*
(c) bc exported
(d) *P*hb + j*Pc*
(e) P_1g
(f) *Pb* (domestic consumers can still buy at the world price *P*).
(g) Domestic producers will not sell at home at a price *P* when they can get P_1 abroad. So P_b are imported and P_1g exported (net exports of bd).
(h) There is a net loss of cgd: the extra cost of producing cd computers above their value (given by *P*).
(i) Not on first best grounds but, if the external effects of the expanded domestic industry are reckoned at least as large as cgd, it is justified on second best grounds. If the subsidy is financed by taxation, any efficiency losses the taxes create should also be reckoned in the balance.

Chapter 20

20.1 (a) Neutral or lover.
(b) Neutral or lover.
(c) Lover.
(d) Averse.
(e) Can't say: the expected pay-off is (0.001 × £50,000) − (0.999 × £60) = −£9.94, so the individual may be risk averse, risk neutral or risk loving but *did not love the risk enough* to accept these adds.

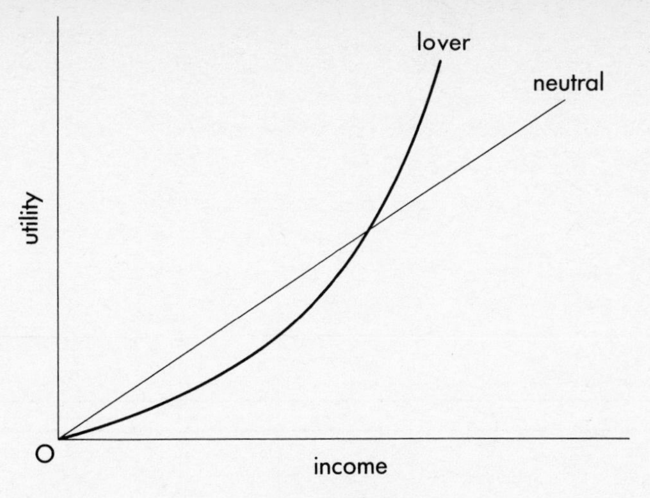

Figure A20.1

20.2 Cardinal. Since it contains a proposition about marginal utility (namely that it falls as income rises) it must be assuming that utility is at least being measured on an interval scale, if not a ratio scale.

20.3 (a) No, your expected utility gain is -1. Because you have a diminishing marginal utility of income you are therefore risk averse.

(b) Some have suggested that the utility of income function may have a small concave section (viewed from above) that explains willingness to risk small stakes offering a small chance of a high pay-off. Sometimes you engage in such gambles in order to support 'good causes' that are being funded by raffles, tombolas and the like.

(c) See figure A20.1.

20.4 $Y_0 - p(Y_0 - Y_1) = Y_0 - pY_0 + pY_1 = pY_1 + (1-p)Y_0$

20.5 Exactly half way between Y_1 and Y_0 and between a and b.

20.6 (a) When one is insured, the *MC* shifts from MC_0 to MC_1 in figure A20.2. The premium does not affect *marginal* motoring cost and is excluded from MC_1 which is less than MC_0 by the amount of the financial risk per mile no longer borne by you (ab). This amount is, however, borne by the insurance company. If it computed the expected claims payouts on the basis of M_0 miles, it would expect to pay out acdb in claims. However, as you now increase mileage per year to M_1, the true expected pay out is aefb, for which its initial premium may be insufficient.

(b) By introducing a copayment of gb (gb/ab = 0.30) your *MC* becomes MC_2, mileage becomes M_2 and the expected claims payout falls to ahig.

20.7 (a) A futures price is a price agreed now for future settlement. A future price is the spot price that will exist in the future.

(b) No. The future spot price may be lower than the futures price.

(c) With seasonally produced goods like barley the futures price will normally be expected to rise with each successive month up to harvest so as to cover storage costs and so on. Particularly with goods that are less seasonal, like wool, futures prices quoted today may fall in successive months if current holders of stocks want to hedge against possible falls in the spot prices that may come about in the future. Thus if current stock holders expect production to rise faster than demand and spot prices are expected to fall, current futures prices may also show a decline month by month for, as long as they can sell stock at a

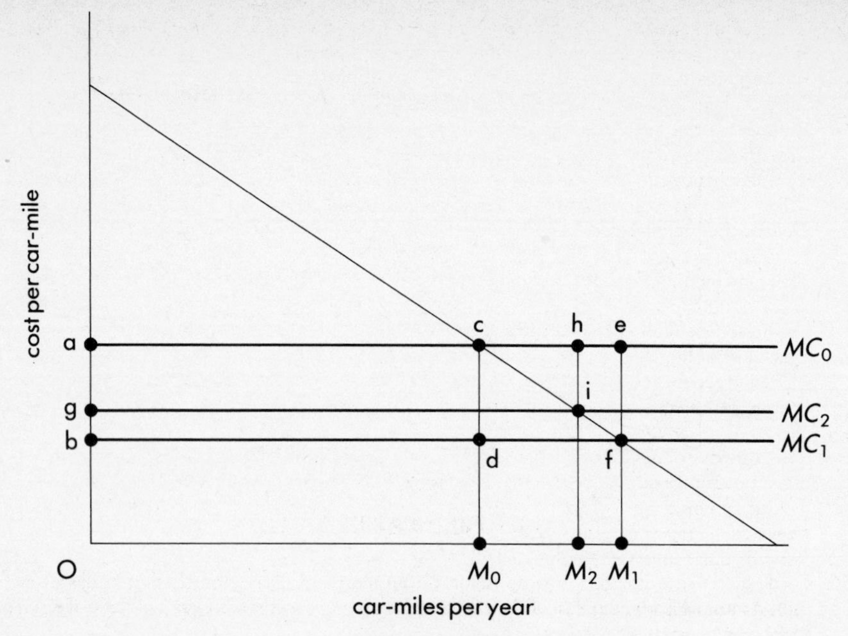

Figure A20.2

futures price higher than the expected spot price, they will do better (provided of course that they are right!) than simply holding their stock and selling at a future spot price lower than the futures price they can negotiate today. The pattern of futures prices quoted today is thus an indicator of what the market generally expects to be happening to future spot prices. If you hold equity in firms producing goods whose futures prices show monthly falls, it could be that you should revise your portfolio of assets, unless you want to 'second guess' the market.

(d) Suppose the manufacturer made a futures contract to supply wheat in May at £100. In May he can then buy at £98 and make a profit of £2 × 1000 = £2000. If the fall in value of the manufacturer's wheat by £2000 means that the market value of the animal feed manufactured with the wheat initially purchased also falls by £2000, then the manufacturer will have been exactly compensated for this loss. Normally, of course, the hedge may slightly under- or overcompensate, unless the manufacturer has guessed the effect on the processed product's price dead right. What, however, he does *not* have to do is to guess the future spot price dead right. The futures price agreed may not be £100 but if the futures price he can get falls by the same amount as the spot price (£2) he can still hedge successfully: it is the difference between the futures and the future spot price that enables one to hedge. If the price of wheat does *not* fall after all, then he will not make a profit on the futures deal but then there will be no loss on the feed either. If the price of wheat rises, then the loss on the futures deal will be compensated by a rise in the value of the animal feed.

Chapter 21

21.1 Society B is clearly more equal than the others. In comparing C and E, however, it rather depends whether one lays emphasis on the few outlying rich or poor. In comparing most of them it rather depends on the extent to which one weights incomes that are further from the mean relative to those that are close to it. Society F seems very unequal – but is it as unequal as A, C, D or E?

21.2 $G^A = 0.33$, $G^B = 0.00$, $G^C = 0.50$, $G^D = 0.39$, $G^E = 0.16$, $G^F = 0.19$. If you had difficulty calculating these numbers, here is one way to do it.

Consider society C. The difference between the income of individual 1 and 2 is 360. This is added to the difference between the incomes of person 2 and person 1 (360 again, ignoring the negative sign). This is added to the differences between 1 and 3, 1 and 4, 1 and 5, 1 and 6 (and 3 and 1, 4 and 1, 5 and 1, 6 and 1) to give a sum of differences of 3600 since all other differences are zero. The expression $1/2n^2\mu$ is the same for all the distributions, since n and μ are the same, and this works out to be 1/7200. G^C = 3600/7200 = 0.50. (Note that a completely unequal distribution with the same mean – 600,0,0,0,0,0 – will not in fact have G = 1.00. The Gini coefficient for a completely unequal distribution approaches 1.00 only as n approaches infinity.) The Gini coefficients rank the five societies in the following order of increasing inequality: G^B, G^E, G^F, G^A, G^D and G^C. Note that in society F no two people have the same income, so that it is very unequal in that sense. The Gini measure, however, places it as more equal than society A and less equal than society E. G^E and G^C differ so much because the Gini coefficient stresses the absolute differences in income between people, and 400–40 is much larger than 119–5. However, if one placed an emphasis on *relative* differences, E is likely to be judged more unequal than C since 119/5 is much larger than 400/40. Hence, if you are a 'relativities' emphasizer, do not trust Gini coefficients!

21.3 One obvious one is that, if income is transferred from a relatively rich to a relatively poor person, the measure should indicate a fall in equality. Another is that a measure should incorporate the feelings people have about the relative weights to be attached to incomes further from the average. Another is that it should reflect any feeling about the significance of absolute or relative differentials in income.

21.4 No. As you will see, one also needs the assumption that everyone's marginal utility of income is the same at each income level.

21.5 See figure A21.1. Y_BY_A income should be taken from B and given to A, so A will have Y_B income and B will have Y_B! At this division of the total (T) $MU^A = MU^B$ ($Y_Bc = Y_Ad$) which is required for maximum utility in this society of two people. In a society of more than two, the condition is $MU^A = MU^B = \dots$. Note that the equilibrium MU is given by the intersection of the total income line vertically above T and the (horizontal) sum of the MU curves labelled Z at point e.

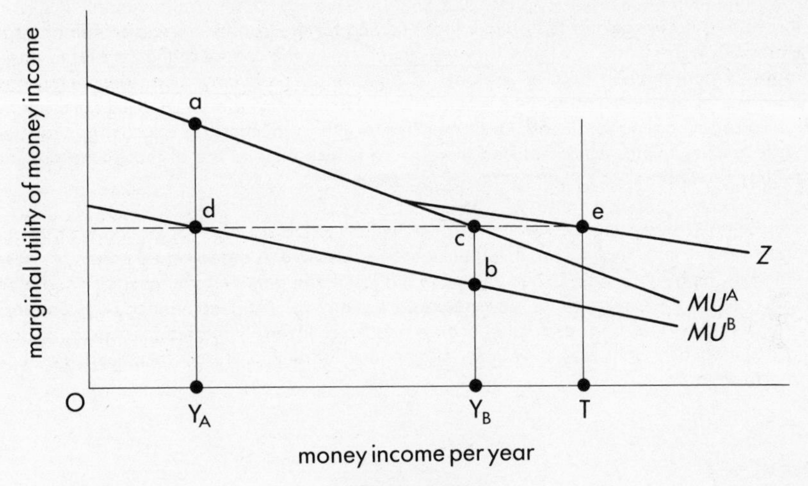

Figure A21.1

21.6 (a) Yes, it applies as long as the MU curves have negative slopes, whether or not they intersect and no matter how many times they intersect. If B has MU and A has MU' (figure A21.2), then the move to equality at E means that A gains C+D and B loses G+H+F. If B has MU' and A has MU, then A gains C and B loses H+F+I. The expected total utility gain is therefore

0.5 [C+D+C−G−H−F−H−F−I]

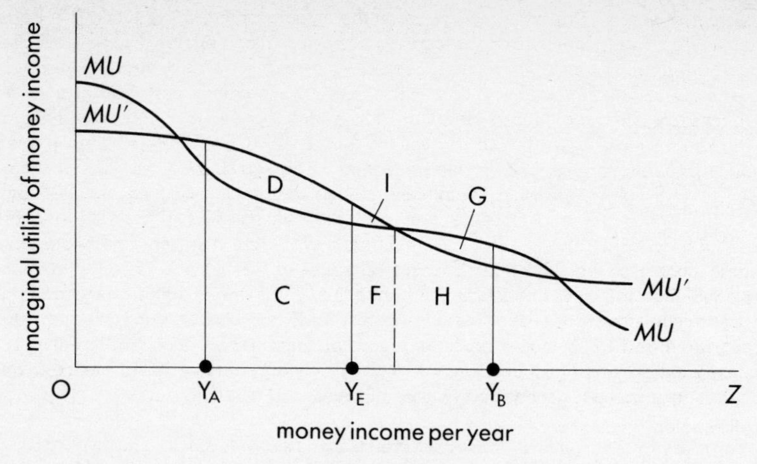

Figure A21.2

Regrouping these terms,

0.5 [(C+D) +C − (F+I+H) − (F+H+G)]

Now, (C+D) must be larger than (F+I+H), so these two net out as positive, since $Y_A Y_E = Y_E Y_B$ and *MU′* slopes downwards. Likewise, C must be larger than (F+H+G), so these two net out as positive. The total is therefore positive, as it was in the non-intersecting case.

(b) No. There will always be further expected gains to be made by all moves towards equality until equality is reached. The greatest expected gains accrue, of course, from the first redistributions from rich to poor.

21.7 It considers only a part of the issue. If those paying for the transfer do so because of a specific externality experienced by them, they will gain by tying the receipt of the transfer to particular forms of consumption (e.g. education). To give simply cash may mean their intentions are thwarted. In these circumstances, it is more efficient to make transfers in kind (e.g. provide free or subsidized schooling) or in cash tied to specific uses (e.g. vouchers for education), provided the welfare of recipients is not reduced thereby. To ignore the welfare of those who provide the subsidy is as partial as to ignore that of recipients.

21.8 Clearly not. Depending on your concept of what is just, a society may be more or less equal. Some people think that it is just if you get what you deserve. A desert based notion of justice will normally imply inequality. Others think that it is just if you get what you need. If needs vary, so will income and consumption. Nevertheless, for many people, income inequality and injustice are often associated: for example because needs are inversely related to income, or because (gross) inequality of income may imply an unequal distribution of political influence and power in a society.

Chapter 22

22.1 All organizations have bureaucracies, including firms, charities, universities and, of course, governments. Whether they are wasteful depends upon their goals (whether you think the goals are worth while or not) and the extent to which the bureaucracy in question is efficient in attaining these goals. I shall not treat the government explicitly as a bureaucracy in this chapter.

22.2 It is hard to tell. Regulation *may* make things worse. Public ownership is certainly no sure way to efficiency. Neither regulation nor public ownership is any sure and certain road either to equity or to efficiency. For one thing, regulatory authorities are often dominated by 'experts' from the regulated industry!

22.3 It falls as the percentage required to take a decision rises.

22.4 (a) No policy meets this *majority rule* condition!
(b) This rule (sometimes called *plurality*) produces a tie between X and Z, since each is ranked first by two voters.
(c) This rule was first proposed by the Marquis de Condorcet in 1785, after whom it is named (the *Condorcet rule*). Y is the winner, since it beats W, X and Z in pairwise majority votes.
(d) This rule is known as the *Borda count*, after Jean-Charles de Borda in 1781. W scores 10, X 11, Y 14 and Z 15, so Z is chosen.
(e) This is called *exhaustive voting*. In the first round, X is eliminated since three voters place it last. In the next round W is eliminated, since three voters place it last. In the final round Z is eliminated, since 3 people prefer Y. So Y is chosen.

The rules pick (a) none (b) X *or* Z (c) Y (d) Z and (e) Y. A problem with majority voting is (as here) that there may be no winner because no policy has a majority for it. Plurality will usually produce a winner (though not in this case) but the winner may not be all that attractive; for example, Y seems quite popular compared with X. The Condorcet rule does not always produce a winner. It also suffers from the fact that it decisively rejects an option like X which 2/5 of the votes rank first, yet in no pairwise comparison will X win. The Borda count selects the option that on average is preferred (which in principle could be nobody's favourite). The exhaustive vote, like the Condorcet rule and the Borda count, eliminates extreme policies. None of them takes account of *strength* of preferences in the rankings (unlike market systems which enable one to 'vote' with one's money – though the vote is, of course, 'contaminated' by the amount of money one has).

22.5 A and B will not vote for Y since they both lose. A and C will not vote for Z since they would both lose. So both Y and Z will be defeated. However, C wants Y and B wants Z. Suppose they agree to 'do a deal': B will vote for Y if C votes for Z. In that case, both options are agreed. B gains £10 net and C gains £90 net. Poor old A loses £100. This type of *vote trading* is called *log-rolling* and is quite common in legislatures, committees and so on, whereby individuals, parties or whatever form temporary coalitions against others.

22.6 No option is ranked first by more than one person, so try the Condorcet rule. In a comparison of X and Y, X wins so X **S** Y where **S** means 'socially preferred'. In a comparison of Y and Z, Y wins so Y **S** Z. You thus have that X **S** Y **S** Z. Therefore X **S** Z by transitivity. However, in a comparison

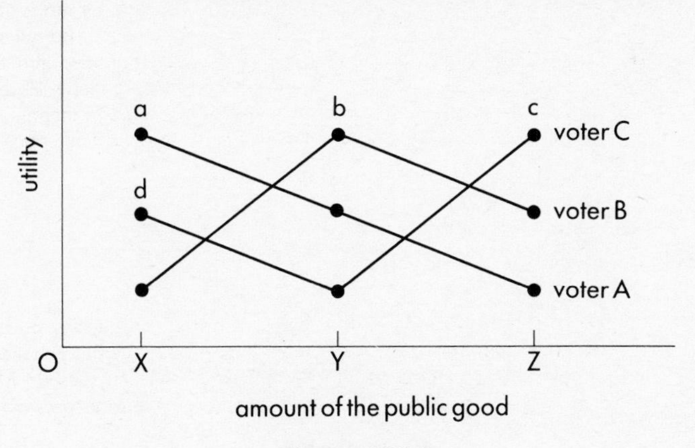

Figure A22.1

of Z and X, Z wins so Z **S** X. Therefore Z **S** X **S** Z! This is the possibility met previously (chapter 6) of intransitivity in public choice. It is sometimes known as the *paradox of voting.* It arises when voters' preferences are not *single peaked.* Plot the utility of each voter according to the amount of the public good as in figure A22.1. Voter A's utility curve has a peak at a: so does voter B's at b. But voter C has two peaks, at c and d. Kenneth Arrow (born 1921) is a Nobel prize winning economist who demonstrated that it is *impossible* to devise a public choice making rule that is transitive, non-dictatorial and that satisfies a number of other reasonable (and desirable) properties.

22.7 It is certainly puzzling to figure out why any selfish individual should ever vote in an election involving large numbers of voters. Gordon Tullock (born 1922), who is a famous public choice theorist, never votes, on precisely these grounds. Quite large numbers of people probably also abstain on these grounds – but why not *all*? Economics does not yet have the answer. The best answer I can give is that most feel a sense of *duty* to vote that derives from an awareness that if everyone acted entirely selfishly, our democratic procedures would simply collapse. There is also the feeling of solidarity that participation in elections brings: one derives the (selfish) feeling of belonging to the group that votes the same way.

Chapter 23

23.1 (a) 0.82, 0.70, 0.77, 13.19, 2.19, 35.15.

(b) On the face of it, for example, the UK average resident had only about 80 per cent the standard of the average US resident, but 35 times that of the average Tanzanian resident.

23.2 The sum (Σ) of all i (three in this case) prices times quantities $\Sigma P_i Q_i$ = £750 + £600 + £200 = £1550.

23.3 (a) $\Sigma P_0 Q_0 = 6 + 4 = 10$, $\Sigma P_1 Q_1 = 3 + 15 = 18$

(b) $\Sigma P_1 Q_1 / \Sigma P_0 Q_0 = 18/10 = 1.8$

(c) See figure A23.1.

(d) Yes. If indifference curves are tangential at each of points a and b, there is no way point b can be on the same or a lower curve than point a without the two curves crossing.

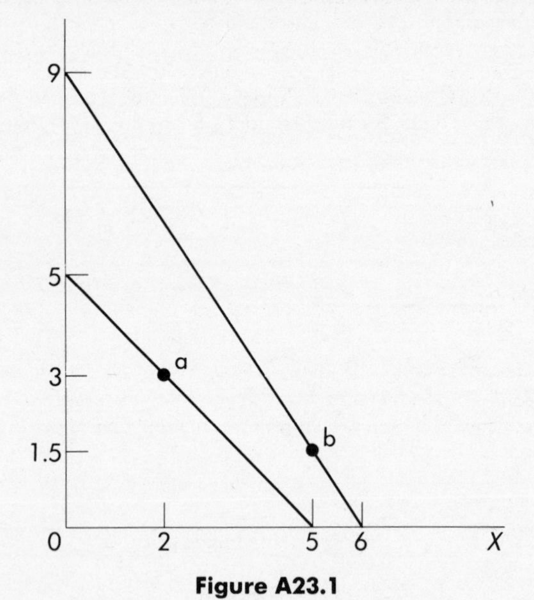

Figure A23.1

23.4 Y_1^L is the income that (just) enables the individual to purchase the t_1 bundle at the t_0 prices. It is, therefore, $(2 \times 5) + (2 \times 1.5) = 13$. In symbols it is $\Sigma P_0 Q_1$.

23.5 (a) Y_0^P is the income that (just) enables the individual to purchase the t_0 bundle at t_1 prices: $\Sigma P_1 Q_0$. It is therefore $(2 \times 3) + (3 \times 2) = 12$.

(b) $\Sigma P_0 Q_1 / \Sigma P_0 Q_0 = 13/10 = 1.3$

(c) $\Sigma P_1 Q_1 / \Sigma P_1 Q_0 = 18/12 = 1.5$

(d) Not possible to say. The indifference curve tangential at point a may lie above or below that which is tangential at point b without the two crossing. In terms of revealed preference theory, when point a was chosen, point b was not available (it lay outside the set of consumption possibilities). Likewise, when point b was chosen, point a was no longer available, so neither has been revealed as preferred to the other.

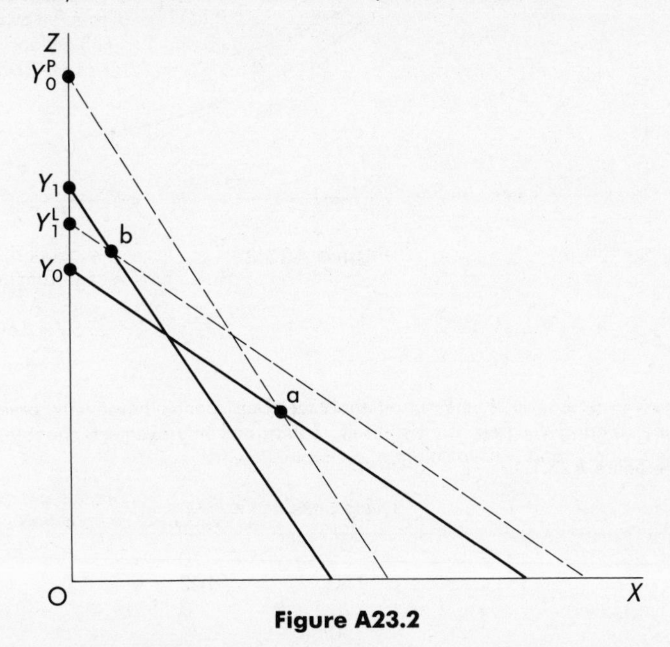

Figure A23.2

(e) See figure A23.2. The Laspeyres index (Y_1^L/Y_0) suggests that welfare has risen; the Paasche index (Y_1/Y_0^P) suggests that it has fallen.

(f) No. The individual will move to a point such as e_2 on figure A23.3 where a higher indifference curve is necessarily attainable (U_2 compared with U_1). This suggests that Y_1^L is really associated with a higher level of welfare than Y_0, rather than the same level. An ideal (adjusted) Y_1^{LA} would be as shown by the dashed line that is tangential to U_1, so Y_1^{LA} is associated with the same welfare as Y_0, but in practice this needs knowledge of the indifference maps of individuals. Y_1^L is, then, taken as an approximation to Y_1^{LA}.

23.6 (a) $\Sigma P_1 Q_1 / \Sigma P_0 Q_0 = (64 + 48) / (20 + 160) = 112/180 = 0.62$

(b) It fell according to the raw data. It rose in the sense that at either the original prices or at the later prices the value of output rose. What happened, of course, was that money prices of both goods fell over the period, hence causing the money value of national income to fall.

23.7 Multiply the inequalities in the question by $\Sigma P_{iU} Q_{iU} / \Sigma P_{iT} Q_{iT}$ to get

$$\frac{\Sigma P_{iT} Q_{iU}}{\Sigma P_{iU} Q_{iU}} \frac{\Sigma P_{iU} Q_{iU}}{\Sigma P_{iT} Q_{iT}} > E \frac{\Sigma P_{iU} Q_{iU}}{\Sigma P_{iT} Q_{iT}} > \frac{\Sigma P_{iT} Q_{iT}}{\Sigma P_{iU} Q_{iT}} \frac{\Sigma P_{iU} Q_{iU}}{\Sigma P_{iT} Q_{iT}}$$

Cancelling $\Sigma P_{iU} Q_{iU}$ and $\Sigma P_{iT} Q_{iT}$ gives the inequalities in the text.

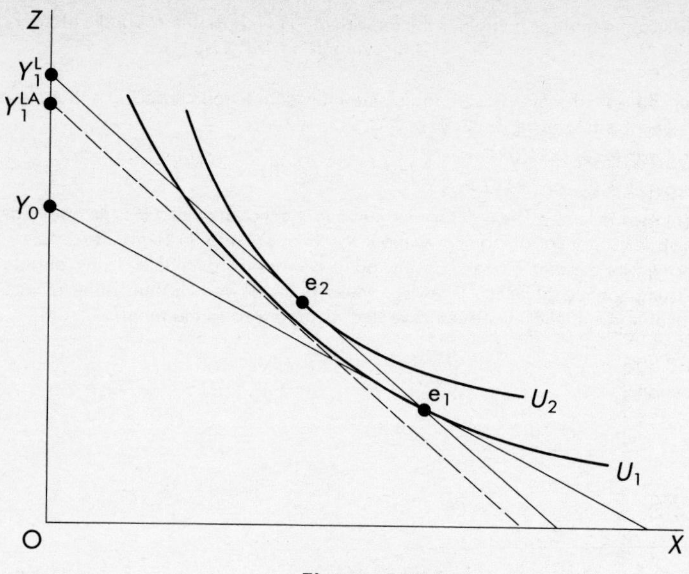

Figure A23.3

Chapter 24

24.1 Some obvious ones include time of household members spent in housework, preparing meals, gardening, rearing children, do-it-yourself repairs and improvements, hobbies, caring for dependent elderly and sick, voluntary and charitable work.

24.2

	selling price (£)	*value added* (£)
	50	50
	150	100
	220	70
	250	30
	300	50
total value of sales	970	
total value added		300

If you got stuck, you may have forgotten that final sales (£300) equal total value added which enables you immediately to put the value added total in. Remember also that A's value added is equal to its sales to B. Thereafter it should be plain sailing.

24.3 (a) *GNP* (there are no taxes or subsidies, so you need make no distinction between *GDP* at market prices and at factor cost) is the sum of all output gross of depreciation, namely £400 + £50 + £30 + £20 = £500. It is the same as *GDP* as there is no net property income from abroad.

(b) £480 (*GNP* less depreciation).

(c) £480 (the sum of all incomes less depreciation).

24.4 All figures in millions. Tables are those in the *Blue Book*.

(a) £152,125

(b) £41,794 – £3148 = £38,646

(c) £246,093
(d) £68,042 – £59,932 = £8110
(e) £36,183
All of (a) – (e) are easily got from table 1.2.
(f) £158,183 (table 1.3)
(g) £240,868 (table 1.7)
(h) £204,684 (notice the large size of National Insurance contributions relative to income taxes)
(i) £531 (table 10.6)
(j) £2717 (table 11.1)
(k) £6056 (table 1.2)
(l) £138,306 (table 9.4; notice that the figure asked for was total expenditure, not just expenditure on goods and services, which excludes transfers in particular)
(m) £65,859 (table 1.2)

Chapter 25

25.1 Yes, just as it is possible to have positive microeconomic analysis of politically and ethically controversial issues (recall chapter 22). In *all* economics, political motives often drive particular individuals to pursue particular lines of research (e.g. to refute results that they find politically unattractive) but, whatever side one is on, it is still possible to do *positive* analysis and empirical research. The danger lies in *muddling* fact and fiction, description and prescription, ethics and science.

25.2 National income; employment and unemployment; the rate of interest; the balance of payments (together with the exchange rate); and the price level (and inflation rate).

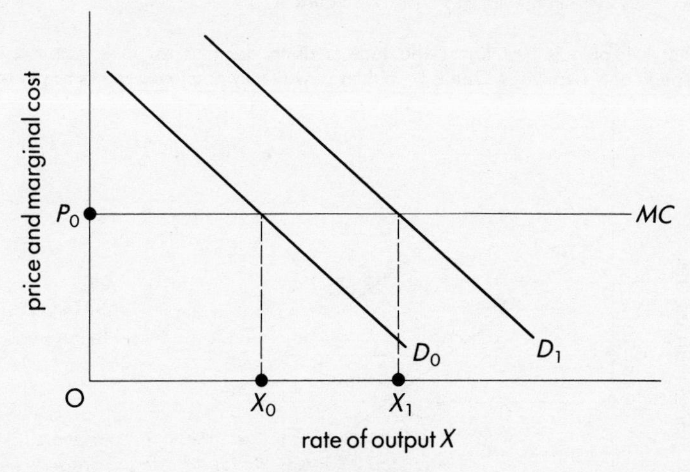

Figure A25.1

25.3 (a) Price remains the same: see figure A25.1.

(b) Price will stay the same in a limiting case when the elasticity of demand is the same at each price on the new curve as on the old: see figure A25.2. If the demand curve shifts out parallel to itself price will rise; if it shifts so that elasticity falls at each price then price will fall. Note that the elasticity of demand is the same at point a as at point b in the figure.

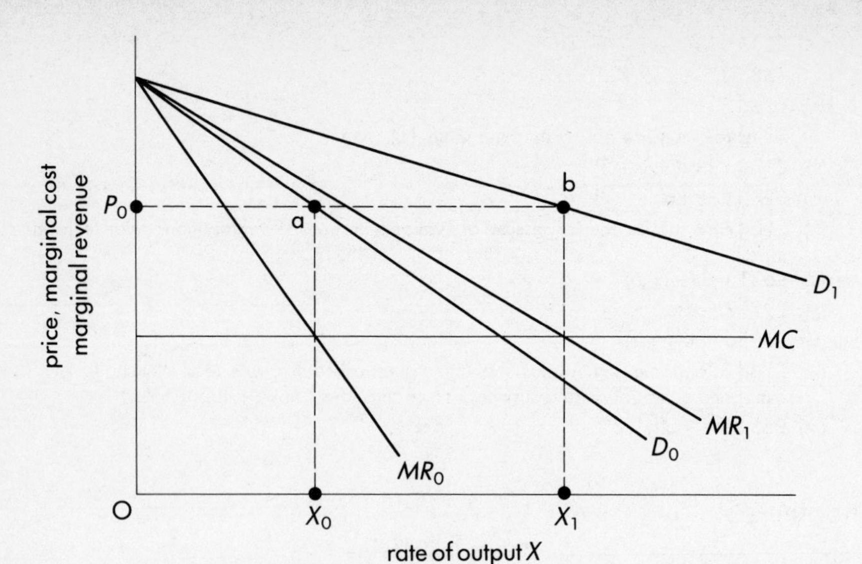

Figure A25.2

(c) Keep it constant – you will get lots of utility from the increase in the waiting list. Even better, you can expand output and hire more labour, hence getting yourself a good name in the press, and still have a higher waiting list than before while maintaining your profit margin on each unit purchased.

25.4 (a) Price rises: see figure A25.3.

(b) Price rises even in the limiting case: see figure A25.4.

25.5 No. What it implies is that firms who face a rising demand for their output can increase production in only two ways. One is by bidding away fully employed inputs from elsewhere, so

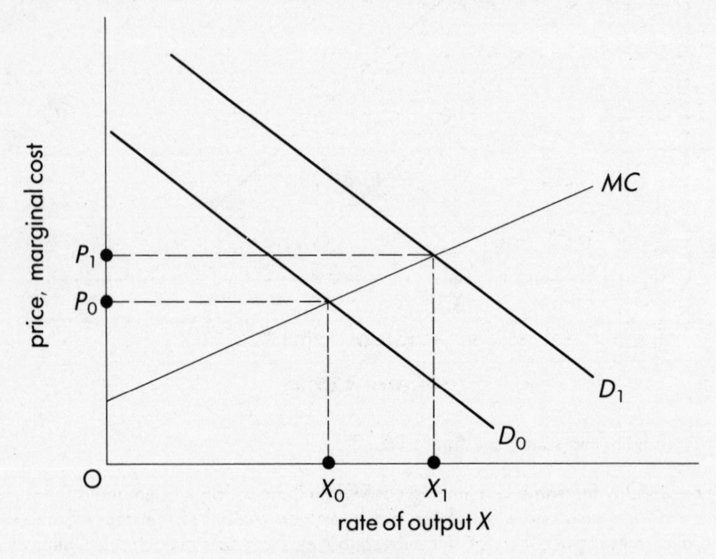

Figure A25.3

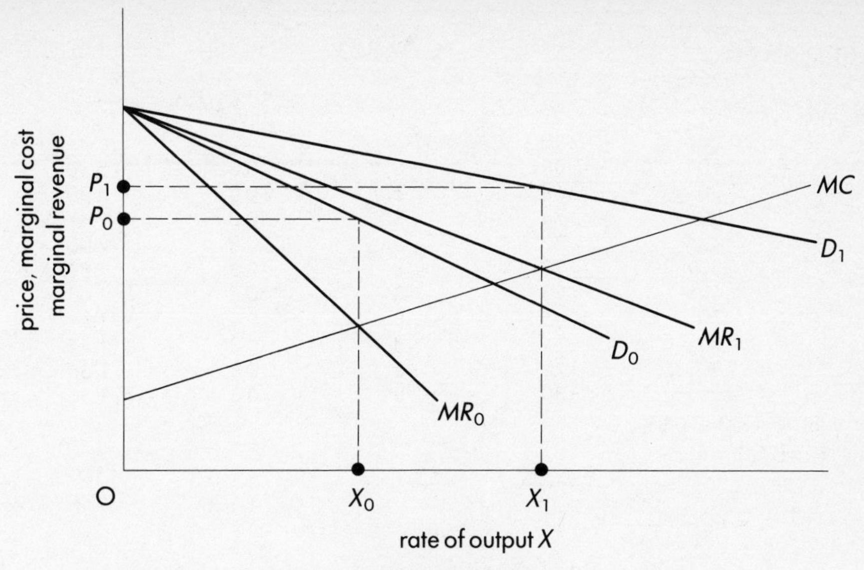

Figure A25.4

that as output prices rise, so do input prices (this has nothing necessarily to do with greedy trade unions pushing up wages regardless of the value of output, for it will happen independently of the existence of trade unions.) The other is by making output reductions elsewhere in the economy, so the increase in output of some firms is offset by a decrease in output elsewhere. Prices elsewhere will rise if demand does not fall. If demand for some other products does fall then so will their prices, but the overall price level must rise since there has been an increase in aggregate expenditure with little or no increase in aggregate output.

25.6 (a) The demand for output falls by half.
(b) If the aggregate demand curve (see figure A25.5) is a rectangular hyperbola (output times the price level is everywhere constant).
(c) −1.0

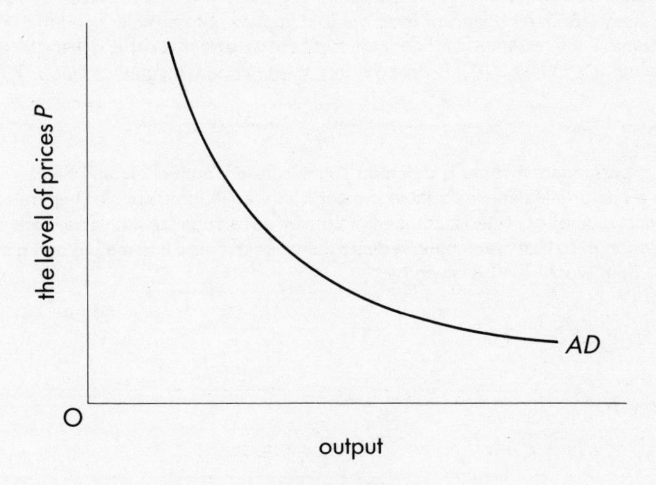

Figure A25.5

Chapter 26

26.1 (a)

Y	C	ΔC	$\Delta C/\Delta Y$	C/Y
0	50	—	—	∞
10	58	8	0.8	5.80
20	66	8	0.8	3.30
30	74	8	0.8	2.47
40	82	8	0.8	2.05
50	90	8	0.8	1.80
60	98	8	0.8	1.63
70	106	8	0.8	1.51
80	114	8	0.8	1.42
90	122	8	0.8	1.36
100	130	8	0.8	1.30

(b) $C = 50 + 0.8Y$

(c) $C = C_0 + cY$

or

$$C = C_0 + \frac{\Delta C}{\Delta Y} Y$$

$$\frac{C}{Y} = \frac{C_0}{Y} + \frac{\Delta C}{\Delta Y}$$

Thus, at each finite level of income Y, the marginal propensity to consume is less than the average. (You should be able to see why the word 'finite' is in this sentence.)

26.2 (b) Consumption.

(c) $C_0 = 2981$, $c = 0.588$

You should note that the consumption function you have drawn is a *short run consumption function.* Most of the analysis of macroeconomics in this book is short run, covering periods of one to 10 years. Over very long periods, economists have found that consumption is a pretty stable proportion of (disposable) income so that the *long run* average = marginal propensity to consume, in contrast with a *falling* short term average and constant short term marginal propensity. An interesting theory, consistent with utility theory, that accounts for the difference in short and long run consumption functions is due to Milton Friedman (cited in case study 26.2). As a kind of footnote (but you do not normally need this in introductory economics) the essence of Friedman's **permanent income theory** is as follows. Consumption at time t (C_t) is proportional to permanent income at time t (Yp_t)

$$C_t = kYp_t$$

where permanent income is defined as that *constant* annual income whose present value over a person's lifetime is equal to the person's wealth (physical plus human capital) or the present value of expected incomes. For convenience, suppose that individuals expect to live long enough so that discounting reduces the value of future income beyond a certain age to zero. Then wealth (W) is given by

$$W = \frac{Yp}{i}$$

and

$$Yp = iW$$

where i is the interest rate (recall discounting in chapter 16).

Unfortunately, future income is not known, and so wealth and permanent income are not known. To make a testable theory, therefore, Friedman suggested that, for the economy as a whole, permanent income can be taken as a weighted average of current and past actual incomes (Y_t), where the t subscript denotes the year in question, on the grounds that future income expectations may, on average, be based on past experience. Thus,

$$Yp_t = qY_t + q(1-q)Y_{t-1} + q(1-q)^2Y_{t-2} + \ldots + q(1-q)^nY_{t-n}$$

where the weights q lie between 0 and 1 and if, for example, $q = 0.50$, the weights would be 0.25, 0.125, 0.063 and so on. If you look at this equation carefully, you see that it can be written as

$$Yp_t = q_tY_t + (1-q)\ [qY_{t-1} + q(1-q)Y_{t-2} + \ldots + q(1-q)^{n-1}Y_{t-n}].$$

This way of looking at the equation reveals something important, for the terms in the square brackets are, by analogy with the first equation for Yp_t, the equation for permanent income *in the previous year,* Yp_{t-1} except that it misses out the last term, $q(1-q)^nY_{t-n-1}$, in the previous year's equation (check this for yourself). This is small enough to ignore (with $q = 0.5$ and $n = 10$, the term is equal to 0.0005) so

$$Yp_t = qY_t + (1-q)Yp_{t-1}.$$

Friedman's consumption function can then be written as

$$C_t = kqY_t + k(1-q)\ Yp_{t-1}.$$

In this equation, $k(1-q)Yp_{t-1}$ is independent of current income Y_t and is equivalent to C_0 in the short run consumption function. kq is, of course, the (short run) marginal propensity to consume out of current income, corresponding to c in the short run consumption function. Thus, in the long run $C_t = kYp_t$, and consumption over long periods of time (say 100 years) will tend to be proportional to average incomes. But in the short run, $C_t = C_0 + cY_t$, and consumption behaves as described in the text.

26.3 (a) $Y = (10 + 15)\ \dfrac{1}{1 - 0.6} = 62.5$

(b) Y rises by 12.5 to 75.0.

(c) Y falls by 12.5 to 37.5.

26.4 (a) 2.0, 5.0, 2.5. Note that the information about I_0 and C_0 is irrelevant in calculating the multiplier, which depends only on the value of the marginal propensity to consume (0.5, 0.8 and 0.6 in the question).

(b) The second economy has the largest multiplier and is therefore going to have a less stable *GDP* if investment rises or falls by a given amount in each economy. Note that the higher the marginal propensity to consume, the higher the multiplier.

26.5 (a) If $Y \equiv C + S$, then

$$\begin{aligned} S &\equiv Y - C \\ &= Y - C_0 - cY \\ &= -C_0 + (1-c)Y \end{aligned}$$

Thus, the intercept of the savings function is $-C_0$, and its slope, the marginal propensity *to save,* is $1 - c$. Alternatively, you could write the savings function as $S = S_0 + sY$, where S_0 is the (negative) savings that would take place at a (hypothetical) income that was zero, and s is the marginal propensity to save.

(b) -8.0, 0.0, 10.0

26.6 Behavioural equations:

$S = S_0 + sY$ (savings function)
$I = I_0$ (investment function)

Equilibrium condition:

$I = S$

Substituting the behavioural equations into the equilibrium condition, you get

$$I_0 = S_0 + sY$$
$$sY = I_0 - S_0$$

$$Y = (I_0 - S_0)\ \frac{1}{s}$$

26.7 (a) 110 (b) 3.33 (c) $-5 \times 3.33 = -16.67$; $+ 5 \times 3.33 = + 16.67$; $+ 10 \times 3.33 = + 33.33$.

26.8 The first notion was that of *identity* for entities that were defined to be equal to one another (e.g. actual total expenditure equals actual consumption expenditure plus actual investment expenditure, or investment expenditure equals planned plus unplanned investment expenditure).
The second was that of a *functional behavioural relation* (e.g. consumption is related to income by a relationship such as $C = C_0 + cY$). It is an empirical matter whether the form of this equation and the value of its parameters are correct predictors of consumption.
The third notion was that of *equilibrium* (e.g. $S = I$). This notion of equality is simply a condition under which there is no tendency for anything to change.
It is important not to get these three notions muddled up.

Chapter 27

27.1 (a) 5.0 (b) 175 (c) falls by 25 to 150.

27.2 (a) Yes
(b) Yes, assuming that more people are employed when output rises.

27.3 (a) The average tax rate is T/Y. Given $T = tY$ then $T/Y = t$, so t is the average tax rate.
(b) The marginal tax rate is the increase in tax as a ratio of the increase in income that generated it: $\Delta T/\Delta Y$. Given $T = tY$, you have, for a change in income, $\Delta T = t\Delta Y$, so $\Delta T/\Delta Y = t$. t is also the marginal tax rate. (Further question: can you see that the marginal and average tax rates would *not* be equal if the tax function were written $T = T_0 + tY$?)
(c) False. Tax revenue rises by the *same proportion* if $T = tY$.

27.4 *Aggregate income and expenditure approach*

$$Y = C_0 + c(Y - tY) + I_0 + G_0$$
$$Y = C_0 + cY - ctY) + I_0 + G_0$$
$$Y - cY + ctY = C_0 + I_0 + G_0$$
$$Y(I - c + ct) = C_0 + I_0 + G_0$$
$$Y[I - c(I-t)] = C_0 + I_0 + G_0$$
$$Y = (C_0 + I_0 + G_0)\ \frac{1}{I-c(I-t)}$$

Injections and withdrawals approach

$$I_0 + G_0 = S + s(Y - tY) + tY$$
$$I_0 + G_0 = S_0 + sY - stY + tY$$
$$I_0 + G_0 - S_0 = sY - stY + tY$$
$$I_0 + G_0 - S_0 = Y(s - st + t)$$
$$I_0 + G_0 - S_0 = Y[1 - (1-s)(1-t)]$$
$$Y = (I_0 + G_0 - S_0)\ \frac{1}{1-(1-s)(1-t)}$$

Note that since $S_0 = C_0$ and $c = 1-s$, these two reduced forms amount to the same thing.

27.5 (a) 1.92. Note that the multiplier is *not* equal to $1/(1-c) = 1.67$.
(b) 86.5
(c) $T = tY = 0.2 \times 86.5 = 17.3$. Since $G = 20$, the government is spending 2.7 more than it gets in taxes; it is running a budget deficit.

27.6 The structural form of the model now looks like:

Behavioural equations:

$C = C_0 + c(Y-T)$	(consumption function)
$T = t(Y-A_0)$	(tax function)
$I = I_0$	(investment function)
$G = G_0$	(government expenditure function)

Equilibrium condition:

$Y = C + I + G$

The reduced form is derived thus:

$$Y = C_0 + c[Y - t(Y - A_o)] + I_0 + G_0$$
$$Y = C_0 + c(1-t)Y + ctA_0 + I_0 + G_0$$
$$Y - c(l-t)Y = C_0 + ctA_0 + I_0 + G_0$$
$$Y[l - c(l-t)] = C_0 + ctA_0 + I_0 + G_0$$
$$Y = (C_0 + ctA_0 + I_0 + G_0)\ \frac{1}{l-c(l-t)}$$

From this you can see that the multiplier is unchanged at $1/[l-c(l-t)]$, but any effect on income and output by changing personal tax allowances (A_0) will have a smaller effect than by changing G_0. The reason is clear: if the government increased A_0, the only part of A_0 that affects consumption is that part no longer taxed: $t\Delta A_0$. Moreover, only that part of disposable income that is consumed enters aggregate expenditure, so the net addition to aggregate expenditure is $ct\Delta A_0$.

27.7 (a) The structural equations now look like:

Behavioural equations:

$C = C_0 + c(Y-T+U)$	(consumption function – note that U is part of disposable income)
$T = tY$	(tax function)
$I = I_0$	(investment function)
$G = G_0$	(government expenditure function on final goods and services)
$U = U_0 - uY$	(unemployment benefit function)

Equilibrium condition:

$$Y = C + I + G$$

The reduced form is calculated thus:

$$\begin{aligned}
Y &= C_0 + c(Y-T+U) + I_0 + G_0 \\
Y &= C_0 + c(Y-tY+U_0-uY) + I_0 + G_0 \\
Y &= C_0 + cY - ctY - cuY + cU_0 + I_0 + G_0 \\
Y - cY + ctY + cuY &= C_0 + cU_0 + I_0 + G_0 \\
Y(1 - c + ct + cu) &= C_0 + cU_0 + I_0 + G_0 \\
Y[1 - c(1-t-u)] &= C_0 + cU_0 + I_0 + G_0 \\
Y &= (C_0 + cU_0 + I_0 + G_0)\frac{1}{1-c(1-t-u)}
\end{aligned}$$

The multiplier is now smaller than before. For example, with $t = 0.25$ and $c = 0.8$ the multiplier was previously $1/[1-c(1-t)] = 2.5$; with unemployment benefit the multiplier is $1/[1-c(1-t-u)]$, and with $t = 0.25$, $c = 0.8$ and $u = 0.05$ it becomes 2.27. Without any taxation at all, the multiplier would have been $1/[1-c] = 5.0$. Thus, both taxation and social security are stabilizing features of an economy. They also, of course, reduce the impact that changes in public expenditure will have on the economy.

(b) 1 $Y = 120$, $G = T = 40$. The budget is balanced.

2 $t = 0.385$. Calculate this as follows:

$$C = 10 + 0.75\,(Y-T)$$
$$T = tY = 50 \text{ (set equal to } G)$$
$$I = 10$$
$$G = 50$$
$$Y = 10 + 0.75\,(Y-50) + 10 + 50$$
$$Y = 130$$
$$T = tY$$

Therefore

$$50 = t130$$

Therefore

$$t = 0.385$$

3 Rises to 130. Note that it rises by exactly the increase in public expenditure. You have just discovered the so-called **balanced budget multiplier theorem**, which states that a balanced increase in public spending and taxation will increase *GDP* by just that amount: the balanced budget multiplier is equal to unity. As it happens the important thing about this theorem is that it does not apply only to a budget that is always balanced, but also holds if the budget surplus or deficit is held constant: again, output changes by the amount of the balanced *change* in G and T. Invent a numerical example for yourself, this time holding $G-T$ constant.

Chapter 28

28.1 Search unemployment is unemployment of those who are searching and have not yet received job offers, or who receive job offers but decline them in expectation of finding better offers.

Frictional unemployment is that associated with normal turnover of employed staff.

Structural unemployment is unemployment attributable to structural change in the economy, particularly drastic changes that have heavy impact in a particular locality.

Voluntary unemployment is unemployment of those who have or could have received job offers.

Involuntary unemployment is unemployment of those who seek work but can get none at going wage rates.

Natural unemployment is the frictional and search unemployment associated with equilibrium in the labour market.

28.2 (a) Marginal physical product times price of product.

(b) The *VMP* of *labour time* is the change in the value of output for a marginal increase or decrease in labour time. The *VMP* of a *worker* is the change in the value of output for a marginal increase or decrease in the number of workers.

28.3 (a) No effect on A. If it falls enough, B will seek employment even at wage W_0.

(b) Shown by the point in B's diagram where U_1^B cuts the vertical axis (point e).

28.4 For many years it was held to lie between 1.5 and 2.5 per cent. Improved social benefits for the unemployed probably imply that it is higher than this today. The main difficulty in establishing the full employment unemployment rate (the natural rate) is in identifying the number of voluntarily unemployed. If, for example, they amounted to 4 per cent of the labour force, then 4 per cent would be the full employment unemployment rate. Monetarists tend to the view that the overwhelming bulk of unemployment (even when historically high) is voluntary. Keynesians do not.

28.5 The multiplier is 2.273, generating a fall in *GDP* of 6.819×10^9 and, via the production function, a fall in employment of 852,000.

Chapter 29

29.1 (a) −10 (b) 0.10 (c) −10 (though such extreme values will not of course be observed in practice) (d) 0 (e) 20

29.2 With the expenditure and output approach, substituting the behavioural functions into the equilibrium condition gives

$$Y = C_0 + c(1-t)Y + I_0 + G_0 + X_0 - M_0 - mY$$

$$Y - c(1-t)Y + mY = C_0 + I_0 + G_0 + X_0 - M_0$$

$$Y[1 - c(1-t) + m] = C_0 + I_0 + G_0 + X_0 - M_0$$

$$Y = (C_0 + I_0 + G_0 + X_0 - M_0)\,\frac{1}{1-c(1-t)+m}$$

With the injections and withdrawals approach:

$$I_0 + G_0 + X_0 = S_0 + s(1-t)Y + tY + M_0 + mY$$

$$I_0 + G_0 + X_0 - S_0 - M_0 = s(1-t)Y + tY + mY$$

$$Y[s(1-t) + t + m] = I_0 + G_0 + X_0 - S_0 - M_0$$

$$Y = (I_0 + G_0 + X_0 - S_0 - M_0)\,\frac{1}{1-(1-s)(1-t)+m}$$

29.3 (a) −13.7 (i.e. −10 times the multiplier of 1.37)

(b) −13.7

(c) The fall in income is 13.7, so the fall in imports ($\Delta M = M\Delta Y$) is $0.33 \times 13.7 = 4.521$. The balance of trade rises by 4.521.

29.4 (a) Exports increase by 6, imports increase by 4.07. So the trade deficit falls by 1.93 – provided of course that no price changes take place and all demands can be met.

(b) Imports increase by 4.07. Since exports remain the same, domestic growth makes the balance of trade move further into deficit. If this persists, and there are no compensating flows into the economy from overseas (e.g. foreign loans), the economy's reserves of foreign exchange will fall (since overseas suppliers will have to be paid in their own currencies), leading eventually to a depreciation of the exchange rate – a devaluation of the (assumed) fixed exchange rate. Of this more anon.

29.5 (a) 1.516 (b) 0.66 (c) 237.4 (d) 594.8

29.6 If the UK demand for US exports is relatively inelastic then, as the sterling exchange rate appreciates, or the sterling price of US exports falls, although more US exports will be demanded, total expenditure in terms of sterling falls. A higher sterling exchange rate is therefore associated with a *lower* supply of sterling and the supply curve has a *negative* slope. Whether this causes a problem depends on the relative positions of the demand and supply curves. If, at an exchange rate below the intersection of the supply and demand curves, the amount of sterling supplied is greater than the amount demanded, then market forces will cause sterling to depreciate rather than appreciate towards the equilibrium. If, above the equilibrium, demand exceeds supply, then the exchange rate will appreciate instead of depreciating towards the equilibrium. With this kind of perversity, movements of exchange rates will *intensify* rather than ameliorate balance of payments difficulties and, since any movement away from equilibrium tends to widen the gap between demand and supply, there is a case for institutional pegging of the rate at a predetermined level. Although this is a *conceivable* case, it does not appear to be a case that *actually* occurs.

Chapter 30

30.1 (a) £199.65 (b) £112.70. You can get these answers by solving the following equations:

For (a) $X = £150\,(1 + 0.1)^3$

For (b) $X = £150\ \dfrac{1}{(1 + 0.1)^3}$

30.2 Larger, as may be seen by applying the discount factors for a 20 per cent interest rate. This leaves a net present value of £108.

30.3 (a) 1 Neither. They will each have zero net investment, since each will have adjusted to its preferred capital stock. The community with the lower interest rate will, however, have a larger capital stock.

2 Net investment is a change in the capital stock. When net investment is zero, the only investment going on will be (replacement) investment to keep the capital stock intact. Gross investment (gross fixed capital formation) is the sum of net investment and replacement investment.

(b) *GDP* rises by 16 (*I* rises by 10).

30.4 (a) $Y = (C_0 + I_0 - ai + G_0 + X_0 - M_0)\ \dfrac{1}{1 - c(1-t) - b + m}$

(b) $1/[1 - c\,(1-t) - b + m]$

(c) + 15.625

30.5 (a) Right – apart from animal spirits! (b) Right!

30.6

Period	C	I	G	Y	ΔY
0	35	5	10	50	0
1	40	5	15	60	10
2	55	20	15	90	30
3	85	50	15	150	60
4	130	95	15	240	90
5	175	140	15	330	90
6	175	140	15	330	0
7	40	5	15	60	−270
8	35	0	15	50	−10
9	35	0	15	50	0
10	40	5	15	60	10
11	55	20	15	90	30
12	85	50	15	150	60

Note that the cycle in *GDP* and components of aggregate expenditure takes nine periods, by which time the economy has returned to its position in period 1 and then the cycle starts off again. Note also that the desired disinvestment in period 8 of 270 × 1.5 is shown in the investment column as zero; replacement investment falls to zero but that is all.

The cycle in this example is, of course, an extreme one. Other patterns (including those less violent and also those explosive) can be got by taking different values for the accelerator and the multiplier (which, incidentally, is 2.0 in this case) and by assuming more realistically that consumption is a function of recent disposable income rather than current.

Chapter 31

31.1 (a) doubles (b) halves (c) rises from 0.25 to 0.35 (d) falls from 4.0 to 1.5 (e) rises from 0.25 (5/20) to 0.67 (10/15) (f) rises (g) rises.

31.2 (a) Wrong. A medium of exchange becomes widely held because its qualities are cheaply knowable and knowable by most traders. The sentence in the question gets it the wrong way round. Most people own used clothes, but they are hardly likely to be used as a medium of exchange!

(b) Not a lot! Any good that both I and anyone else want could serve as a medium of exchange under this rationale. For example, most people want and have bread. So I could sell my wheat for bread and then the bread for a book (not necessarily trading with just one person). The requirement of a double coincidence of wants is thereby circumvented, but bread may not become a medium of exchange, any more than any other commonly held good.

31.3 The amount written on the cheque *in the deposit* is the money. It is the deposit ownership that is traded for goods. The cheque is an instruction to one bank to transfer a stated sum from one account to another. When notes were backed by gold, it was the legal titles to gold that were traded; the notes were evidence of ownership of titles to gold and were directly tradable as money. Cheques, then, are instructions to change the ownership of deposits, and it is the deposits that are the money.

31.4 (a) 1 28 2 5 per cent

(b)

i (%)	*demand for money when* 1 $Y = 250$	2 $Y = 300$
0.0	25	30
1.0	24	29
2.0	23	28
3.0	22	27
4.0	21	26
5.0	20	25

Note that the change in income simply shifts the demand for money as a function of the rate of interest by a constant equal to the change in income times k.

31.5 (a) 7.79 and 3.27 respectively. Thus, in the case of the first set of data, two thirds of the numbers are expected to lie between the mean, 11.0 and + or − 7.79, that is between 3.21 and 18.79, which they do. In the case of the second, less variable data, about two thirds of the numbers are expected to lie between 7.73 and 14.27 which, again, they (roughly) do. Note that the mean of each set is the same: 11.0.

(b) 11.0; the first set is more variable as measured by the *SD*.

(c) The *range* of the first set is 1–29 compared with that of the second, 6–15.

(d) Again the mean is 11.0. Note that the range is also the same as that for the second set of data. The *SD* for this set is, however, 2.71, indicating slightly less variability or lower dispersion about the mean than in the second set. Note that the *SD*, by using the *squares* of the differences between the mean and each actual value, gives a high weight to values that are far from the mean, so outlying values increase the measure of dispersion more than values that are near the average.

31.6 (a) $i = \dfrac{kY - M_0}{l}$

(b) $i = 11.7$ per cent

31.7 The shift of the L curve to L_{Y1} was due to the multiplier effect ignoring any feedback from the money market. Allowing for the money market feedback means that the resulting rise in the interest rate both reduces the demand for money (a movement *along* the L curve) and, via a reduction in investment, causes investment and income to be lower. Income is none the less higher than initially because the rise in interest rate does not choke off *all* the increased investment.

31.8 (a) Given that

$$i = \frac{kY - M_0}{l}$$

and that

$$I = I_0 - ai + \alpha \Delta Y$$

the equilibrium condition for income becomes

$$Y = C_0 + c(1 - t)Y + I_0 - \frac{akY}{l} + \frac{aM_0}{l} + \alpha \Delta Y + G_0$$

$$Y - c(1 - t)Y + \frac{akY}{l} = C_0 + I_0 + G_0 + \frac{aM_0}{l} + \alpha \Delta Y$$

$$Y[1 - c(1 - t) + ak/l] = C_0 + I_0 + G_0 + aM_0/l + \alpha\Delta Y$$

$$Y = (C_0 + I_0 + G_0 + aM_0/l + \alpha\Delta Y)\ \frac{1}{1 - c(1 - t) + ak/l}$$

(b) 1.151

Chapter 32

32.1 Inflation is rising prices or, more precisely, a rising average price level.

32.2 (a) 18.8 per cent

(b) 4.6 per cent. Do not confuse the number of points the index rises each year with the percentage increase in prices. Between 1982 and 1983 the index rose by 10.8 points; this is 4.6 per cent of the index number for 1982 (236.8).

(c) Over 1973–8 the index rose by 81.1 points or by 118 per cent. Between 1978 and 1983 it rose by 97.8 points or by 65.3 per cent. For this group, therefore, the average rate of inflation was higher in the first than in the second half of the period.

32.3 $$\frac{(7 \times 12) + (10 \times 7)}{(6 \times 12) + (7 \times 7)} = \frac{154}{121} = 1.27$$

The increase is from 100 to 127, taking January = 100. The percentage increase is 27 per cent.

32.4 (a) £193.6 billion (100.0/29.6 × £57.3 billion)

(b) £165.3 billion (0.729 × £226.7 billion)

32.5 (a) £3016, £2284, £2011. Its value more than halved between 1975 and 1983.

(b) Rise. In an inflation debtors with debt expressed in terms of money and at fixed interest will gain relative to creditors. See case study 32.2.

32.6 See figure A32.1. Demand for sterling rises and its supply falls, leading to an appreciation in the exchange rate.

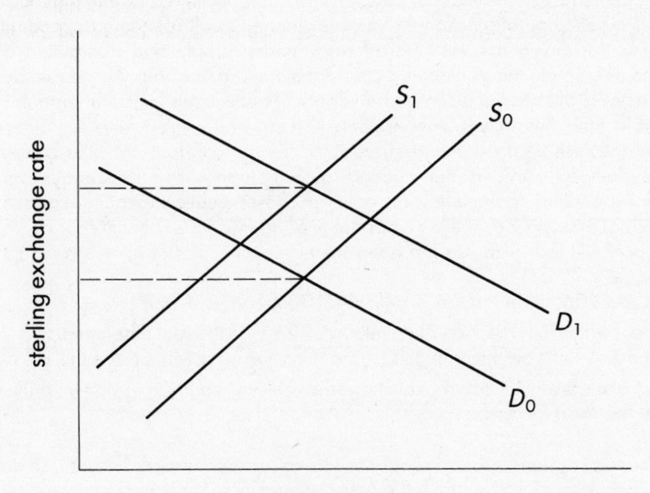

Figure A32.1

32.7 (a) £109.09

(b) The simplest procedure is simply to divide the nominal wage by the price index to derive the values in the W/P column in the following table and then, setting the real wage in period 1 equal to 100, compute the remainder as $[(W/P)/90] \times 100$.

period	*W/P*	*Index of real wages*
1	90.0	100.0
2	90.1	100.1
3	90.2	100.2
4	84.6	94.0
5	86.7	96.3
6	87.5	97.2
7	97.0	107.8

Note that in interpreting figures like 32.1, there may be lags in adjustment. For example, if the price of a firm's product rises, the $MPP \times P$ curve moves outwards: a rise in the demand for labour at the current wage. If workers do not immediately perceive this, there will be an increase in employment and a rise in the money wage rate. After a while, however, they will perceive the rise in the price level and realize that the rise in money wages was not the *real* rise initially perceived. Hence the supply of labour at the given money wage will shift to the left until the equilibrium real wage is again attained. In this sort of situation you can thus get *temporary* increases in employment due to asymmetrical perceptions of price changes by employers and employees.

Chapter 33

33.1 The mechanism is that the increase in the money supply causes interest rates to fall. This increases aggregate expenditure for all components that are interest elastic (like investment) so that, at a given price level, aggregate demand rises. However, the economy cannot produce the additional output to meet the new demand at given prices, so the multiplier effect on output is dampened, and prices begin to rise until the new equilibrium at point b in figure 33.2 is established. As an alternative to an increase in the money supply, public expenditure may have risen, or the demand for exports, with similar effects.

33.2 Aggregate demand should never, of course, be confused with aggregate planned expenditure. The latter is a behavioural function that makes planned (real) spending dependent on planned (real) income (assuming a given interest rate, money supply and distribution of income, to mention the three main things assumed constant along the function). Aggregate demand shows *equilibrium* levels of national income at a variety of price levels. Since, at different equilibria of output and income, investment, consumption, savings, and interest rates are different, all these vary along the aggregate demand curve and are *not* constant. What *is* constant along an aggregate demand curve is the nominal money supply and exogenous components of aggregate expenditure (particularly, for policy purposes, public expenditure and taxation). So if any of the money supply or these components of aggregate expenditure vary, the aggregate demand curve will shift – as has just been seen.

33.3 (a) Fallen to £90.91. Real wage is W/P = £100 / 1.10 = £90.91.

(b) Your real wage falls to £136.36, rival's to £90.91, so the real differential falls to £45.45. As a percentage of your income, this is one third, just as it was before the inflation.

(c) If you care about the differential between you and your rival you will dislike the second option less than the first.

33.4 Because the relationship between proportionate excess demand for labour and unemployment is concave from above. This in turn is the case because increasing amounts of excess demand for labour are required for equal reductions in unemployment; in the limit, excess demand must be infinite if unemployment is to fall to zero.

33.5 The impact of a vertical shift in aggregate supply due to, say, rising import prices, is to cause inflation until the new higher price level is established and to reduce real income and output. Keynesian analysis suggests that an appropriate response is *expansionary*: effectively to validate a supply induced inflation in order to maintain real output and prevent unemployment from rising. Monetarists tend to disagree with this prescription since they hold that the aggregate supply curve is much steeper and hence the depressing effect of the supply side shock on output and employment much less than the Keynesian analysis suggests. One's answer therefore depends both on the shape of the shifting *AS* curve and on the priority placed on maintaining employment levels. Monetarists, unlike Keynesians, tend to the view that involuntary unemployment due to insufficient effective demand is trivial and that most unemployment is either voluntary (e.g. job search) or structural. In other words, they hold that (aside from structural transitions as some industries decline) the labour market quickly adjusts to maintain zero involuntary unemployment at competitively determined money (and real) wage rates.

33.6 Most Keynesians argue that in the 1980s there was a substantial output gap and that labour markets were quite severely out of equilibrium with substantial involuntary unemloyment, so that expansionary monetary and fiscal policies would not have been inflationary and would have reduced unemployment – particularly if combined with measures like incomes policies to prevent expectations of inflation from rising. In addition, policies to combat *structural* unemployment in declining industries would be needed. Some monetarists take the view that labour markets clear immediately, with workers and employers having symmetrical knowledge about current price movements and expectations of future inflation, so all unemployment is voluntary and employment is fixed at the intersection of the real demand and supply of labour. In this case the current unemployment rate is the natural rate and the aggregate supply curve is vertical, since increased aggregate demand cannot be met by increased output produced by more workers in employment, so Keynesian policies can only raise the price level. (See the Answer to SAQ 32.7.) Unemployment can be reduced only by policies designed to have an effect on the *real* factors affecting it, like social security payments (reduce them in real terms), trade union restrictive practices (eliminate them) and minimum wages (eliminate them). Others argue, less extremely, that there is a short run gain to be had, in terms of reduced unemployment, through increasing aggregate demand and moving up a short run Phillips curve, even though the long run Phillips curve is vertical at the natural rate of unemployment. Again, however, only attacks on the *real* determinants of the natural rate will reduce it in the long run. You must make up your own mind about who is (or was) right – or mostly right!

In 1980 the Thatcher Government set out what has become known as the *Medium Term Financial Strategy* (MTFS) and has stuck consistently to it since that time. It is essentially a commitment to stick to announced lower public sector borrowing and progressively lower growth rate targets for the money supply, both to influence directly the rate of inflation and to encourage the *expectation* that current monetary policy will not cause future inflation. As you know, the inflation rate fell from about 18 per cent to around 5 per cent over 1980–5. What you have to decide is (a) whether the MTFS was a cost-effective strategy – that is, whether other policies (e.g. Keynesian ones) may have been equally (or nearly) as effective in reducing inflation but have involved fewer disadvantages in terms of unemployment, low growth, bankruptcies, industrial unrest, etc. (b) in the light of the judgement you have just made, the priority to be placed on the various macroeconomic goals (*at the margin*) relative to marginal reductions in inflation, which may be in short, medium or long run conflict. Mrs Thatcher repeatedly emphasized that there was no alternative to the MTFS as practised by her government. There plainly *were* alternatives: but would they be (a) cost-effective and (b) politically desirable (according to *your* lights)?

Chapter 34

34.1 (a) 5.75 (b) falls (to 4.8) (c) falls (to 5.00) (d) A 10 per cent rise in p causes the bank multiplier to fall from 5.75 to 5.42. A 10 per cent rise in b causes the bank multiplier to fall to 5.61.

34.2 (a) £75 (b) i falls by 6.3 percentage points from 11.7 to 5.4 per cent

34.3 (a) i = 18.4 per cent (b) i = 15.3 per cent

34.4 (a) Since $M = L$ in equilibrium, then $M = 39 - 1.2\,(15) = 21$.
(b) 3.65
(c) 27
(d) The elasticity formula is

$$\frac{\Delta L}{\Delta i}\,\frac{i}{L} = -0.86$$

when i = 15 per cent (and L = 21).
(e) −0.44
(f) Zero. The interest elasticity of the supply of money is $(\Delta M/\Delta i)\,(i/M)$; since Δi is maintained at zero, the elasticity is infinity. What happens is that the supply of money has to be whatever will keep the interest rate constant, so the money supply is endogenous and is determined jointly by the target interest rate and the demand for money. Some extreme Keynesians argue that the supply of money is determined *solely* by demand. The logic of the situation demonstrates clearly, however, that it is *jointly* determined by the government's target rate of interest *and* the demand for money.

34.5 (a) M_0 (b) PSL (c) M_0

Chapter 35

35.1 There are three identities:

$$\Delta BELG + \Delta BELF \equiv \Delta PD + \Delta D_b + \Delta C_p + \Delta C_b + \Delta C_f$$
$$\Delta C_b + \Delta D_b + \Delta BLG + \Delta BLP + \Delta BLF \equiv \Delta D_p + \Delta D_g + \Delta D_f$$
$$\Delta D_g + \Delta PD + \text{PSBR} \equiv \Delta BELG + \Delta BLG + \Delta PLG + \Delta FLG$$

(Check table 35.2 to ensure that you know what is going on here.)
Adding these three gives:

$$\Delta BELG + \Delta BELF + + \Delta C_b + \Delta D_b + \Delta BLG + \Delta BLP + \Delta BLF + \Delta D_g + \Delta PD + \text{PSBR} \equiv \Delta PD + \Delta D_b + \Delta C_p + \Delta C_b + \Delta C_f + \Delta D_p + \Delta D_g + \Delta D_f + \Delta BELG + \Delta BLG + \Delta PLG + \Delta FLG$$

$\Delta BELG$, ΔC_b, ΔD_b, ΔBLG, ΔD_g and ΔPD all cancel out in consolidation to give

$$\Delta BELF + \Delta BLP + \Delta BLF + PSBR \equiv \Delta C_p + \Delta C_f + \Delta D_p + \Delta D_f + \Delta PLG + \Delta FLG$$

This is the same as identity (7) and, on rearrangement, gives identity (8).

35.2 Identities (2) and (5) are:

$$\Delta BELG + \Delta BELF \equiv \Delta PD + \Delta D_b + \Delta C_p + \Delta C_b + \Delta C_f$$
$$\Delta D_g + \Delta PD + PSBR \equiv \Delta BELG + \Delta BLG + \Delta PLG + \Delta FLG$$

Adding these together gives:

$$\Delta BELG + \Delta BELF + \Delta D_g + \Delta PD + PSBR$$
$$\equiv \Delta PD + \Delta D_b + \Delta C_p + \Delta C_b + \Delta C_f + \Delta BELG + \Delta BLG + \Delta PLG + \Delta FLG$$

$\Delta BELG$ and ΔPD cancel out in consolidation to give:

$$\Delta BELF + D_g + PSBR \equiv \Delta D_b + \Delta C_p + \Delta C_b + \Delta C_f + \Delta BLG + \Delta PLG + \Delta FLG$$

which, on rearrangement, is identity (12).

35.3 (a) $P = A/i$, where i is the interest rate.
(b) It must raise A each year in taxes.
(c) $T = A/i$, where T is the present value of taxes.
(d) They are the same.

(e) $$P = \frac{A}{1+i} + \frac{A}{(1+i)^2} + \frac{R}{(1+i)^2}$$

where R is the redemption value. In the question $i = 0.10$, $A = £5$ and $R = £100$. Hence

$$P = \frac{£5}{1.10} + \frac{£5}{1.21} + \frac{£100}{1.21} = £91.32$$

(f) £91.32

(g)

year	starting debt	interest due	closing debt
0	£100	0	£100
1	£100	£10	£110
2	£110	£11	£121
3	£121	£12.10	£133.10
4	£133.10	£13.31	£146.41
5	£146.41	£14.64	£161.05

The answer is £161.05.

(h) £14.64. Note that the interest burden rises at the same rate as the interest rate.

35.4 (a) The purchaser has exchanged one asset (a deposit with the bank) for another (the government security). Since the deposit at the bank falls when the cheque is cleared, the bank's liabilities fall. There is a direct impact on the money supply by the same amount. The Bank of England has now acquired a claim on the commercial bank which will be met by the bank drawing down its account at the Bank of England, so the bank's assets (its account at the Bank) fall by the same amount as its liabilities have fallen. With the disturbance to its desired asset ratio, the bank may reduce advances and set in motion further rounds of contractions, reducing the money supply further.
(b) It has lost an asset (the government security it just sold) and also lost a liability (the reduction in the bank's deposits at the Bank).
(c) Reduced.
(d) It gains one asset (the government security) and loses another (its deposits at the Bank of England).
(e) It loses one asset (the government security) and a liability of the same amount (the bank's deposits at the Bank of England).
(f) Nothing. However, there may be second round effects as the reduction in its deposits with the Bank will tend to set in motion a multiple contraction of deposits as advances are

reduced. Note that open market sales or purchases to the banking sector affect neither the net indebtedness of the government to the banks nor, directly, the money supply.

35.5 Suppose there is a deficit on current account. There will be pressure on the sterling exchange rate to fall. To counter this the government buys sterling and supplies foreign exchange out of the EEA. The sterling purchases necessarily reduce the money supply. If, to counter this, the Bank of England engages in 'sterilization' operations by buying bonds, interest rates will tend to fall, encouraging investment overseas and further demands for foreign currency as private lending to foreigners (*PLF*) rises, so the exchange rate tends to fall again, requiring further loss of reserves, sterilization operations etc. With a floating exchange rate the government can, however, control the money supply. Imposing exchange controls can help but brings in its train a host of problems associated with ceilings, quotas and non-price rationing effects.

35.6 Because to control interest rates the government must sell bills to or buy them from the non-bank private sector. Selling to or buying from banks has less impact because, as seen before, this merely rearranges interest bearing assets/liabilities. In so doing, to achieve a target interest rate structure, the money supply will become whatever it becomes directly as a result of the sales or purchases together with any subsequent bank multiplier effects.

35.7 There are lots of possibilities. One is that you could buy a finance company that did not count as a 'bank' and direct your customers to your new subsidiary. Another is that you could arrange (for a fee of course) to put your clients in touch with someone with funds to lend. You could arrange (for a fee) for the loan to be made in foreign currency in a bank operating overseas (perhaps guaranteeing it on behalf of your client) and then making a further gain on the conversion of the foreign currency into sterling. The possibilities are really limited only by your imagination – and your contacts. There is nothing particularly mysterious about banking – once you see it as just another way that people seek to make money!

Index